A CENTURY OF CANADIAN CINEMA

Gerald Pratley's Feature Film Guide

1900 to the Present

Editor: Amy Harkness
Cover and Design by: Andrea Gutsche
National Library of Canada Cataloguing in Publication
Front Cover: Courtesy of the Toronto Film Reference Library: (Left) *Bye Bye Blues* (1989) (Center) *Jésus de Montréal* (1989) (Right) *Goin' Down the Road* (1970)
Back cover: *Strange Brew* (1983)

Pratley, Gerald
        A century of Canadian cinema : Gerald Pratley's feature film guide, 1900 to the present.

Includes index.
ISBN 1-894073-21-5

        1. Motion pictures--Canada--History. 2. Motion pictures--Canada--Reviews. I. Title.

PN1993.5.C3P687 2003   791.43'0971
C2003-904725-3

A CENTURY OF CANADIAN CINEMA

Gerald Pratley's
Feature Film Guide

1900 to the Present

To my daughters Orize, Denise and Jocelyn
and their families for their love and support
during a time of need.

In Memory of Roger Manvell
1909-1987

ACKNOWLEDGMENTS

I am deeply grateful to the friends and associates who have given me unfailing support, advice and encouragement in bringing this guide to completion. They include Ralph Ellis, Paul Gratton, James (Jim) Murphy, Kevin Tierney and Jan Uhde. And to my colleagues who have also followed this path: John Robert Columbo, Ian Easterbrook, Robert Gutteridge, Piers Handling, Peter Harcourt, Peter Morris, Ronald Paquet, John Turner and Strat & Dreck. And thank you to those who were always only a phone call away or available in their offices: Abby Anderson, Alison Bennie, Lisa Brown, Michael Cosentino, Robert and Violet Crone, Lisa-Marie Dooring, Lisa Fisher, Caron Feldman, Joanne Foster, Anne Frank, Karen Gaulin, Julia Hitchcock and Vodeck Fedorowicz, Helicia Glucksman, Hugh Jemmott, Janice Lee, Michele Melody, Tamara Mackeighan, Betty Palick, Anne Marie La Pointe, Yvonne Ng, Danielle St. Amant, Robert Sherrin, Risa Shuman, David McCaughna, Deborah Tiffin and the late and lamented Patricia Thompson. And remembering Richard Winnington, Josh Billings, Leslie Halliwell, Maurice Speed and, with affection and admiration, Dilys Powell. And, too, the indispensable Toronto Film Reference Library, with its dependable director Sylvia Frank and ever helpful staff: Eve Goldin, Robin MacDonald, Rosanne Pavicic, Theresa Rowat, Hubert Toh and the many others over the years. And to Louise Goldberg and her staff at the CBC Reference Library, and Lee Ramsay at the Toronto Reference Library. Thanks to the three indexers: Ginny Chow, Alex Bushell and Richard Partington; and the last-minute typists: Sue Lebrecht, Diane Waldock, Katherine Slavin and Michelle Hayles. Also, Geoff King for adding the accents. Charles Harlton for his work consolidating the index. With very special thanks to Peter Cowie. To my publisher, Lynx Images, eternal gratitude—Andrea Gutsche, Russell Floren, Barbara Chisholm, and Amy Harkness—for believing in this project and carrying it out, where five other companies did not. In the writing and publishing of this book, no funding came from either government or private agencies. All films listed here that were produced after 1974 are registered Canadian with the Federal agency CAVCO (Canadian Audio Visual Certification Office).

INTRODUCTION

This guide and index does not include, with a few notable exceptions, documentary, experimental, collage, underground, compilation, music and dance, or animated films. Those listed are dramas, fiction, comedy or true stories, written for the screen and portrayed by actors, made for showings in cinemas or on television, all of which have been made by the talented and not so talented, whose names as directors, writers, performers, cinematographers, editors, composers etc., have come to be recognized as being accomplished or otherwise. Producers, companies and distributors, again with a few notable exceptions, are not listed, there being so many of them! Most of the films with French titles made in Québec and spoken in French were in many cases also shown with English subtitles or dubbed. The vast majority of the films are in colour, with some black and white (b/w) exceptions. Official co-productions are noted. These are spoken mainly in the languages of the countries involved and subtitled in French or English. Films marked as being (a Canadian-American film) means American films made by Canadian producers; or those passed off as being American, while calling themselves Canadian; or those in one guise or the other preferring to hide their Canadian identity. There are several other variations—such as a (a U.S.-Canada film), in which an American company has played a major part. Has-been Hollywood players usually thrive in these pictures. Note that there are no official U.S.-Canada co-productions. Hollywood doesn't need a government agency to make its films abroad with foreign producers. American films shot on location in Canada to take advantage of our low dollar and misplaced subsidies are not included here. There are, however, films made jointly by Canadian-American companies and properly known as commercial co-productions, and these are included. The objectionable practice of putting stars after a film's title is not used here. The "syn-com" (meaning synopsis with comment) provides an indication of the value of the film. Due to limited space, individual contributions by technicians and artists behind the cameras are not named. If a film as a whole is spoken well of, then it follows that performances, etc., are of a high standard. Finally, all the films listed here have been shown, somewhere over the years, in cinemas, on television, at film festivals in Canada and around the world—in the Canadian Film Awards, the Genie showings, in rep houses, at film societies, special programmes

and other avenues of motion picture exhibition. For award listings, readers are referred to the Film Canada Yearbook (1952–2002). This guide-index is not intended to be an academic critical analysis of the motion pictures listed, but a treasury, if you will, of what Canada has done in the world of cinematic achievement since dark and light figures first moved on white screens. Every effort has been made to get the spellings of names correct. Any corrections and missing films please email cinema@lynximages.com.
—Gerald Pratley

d: director
s: writer

Note:
The fact that this compilation includes feature films, not series, made for television will possibly cause dismay among critics and film lovers who cannot rid themselves of the belief that all television movies are of little value, labeling them "film of the week" "tv fodder," "disease of the week," miniseries. Others look down on them simply because of the medium in which they are shown. The following incident might help to put this mistaken approach into perspective. The famous director, King Vidor once came to the Ontario Film Theatre in Toronto to attend a retrospective of his films. During the discussion period that followed, a member of the audience asked him what he thought about "those movies being made for tv." Wasn't it a fall from grace for the filmmaker? Should we even think of them as being films? Vidor, with his humorous look, said gently, "Well, let me paraphrase myself, and a well known writer, and say 'a film is a film is a film.' Your question should be 'is a film in particular brilliant, poor or indifferently made?' The director worthy of the calling is working in a studio or on location exactly as he would if his film was intended to go into the movie houses. We have fought commercial interruptions and lost. But one day there will be channels without commercials." And time has proved him right. Vidor was warmly applauded by the audience. Today it is possible to see movies from the past and the present, together with those made for the new TV systems, without interruptions.

A.K.A. Albert Walker (2002) (120mins) d: Harry Hook s: Philip Palmer : John Gordon-Sinclair, Alan Scarfe, Sarah Manninen. A tangled tale here with shades of a real life counterpart. The film makes its way clearly, with tension and muted drama, about a man found dead in the nets of a fishing trawler, and who is discovered to have a girlfriend, with the two of them having assumed other identities. This almost Agatha Christie–like mystery story is neatly told with excitement and conviction.

Ababouinée (1994) (100mins) d&s: André Forcier : Sarah-Jeanne Salvy, François Cluzet, Michel Côté, Céline Bonnier, Donald Pilon. A tit-for-tat love story about a mother who seduces her daughter's lover, much to the father's despair. Then the daughter, now a writer, falls for a literary celebrity who is stolen from her by her younger sister. Forcier overdoes it this time.

Abducted (1985) (87mins) d&s: Boon Collins : Dan Haggerty, Roberta Weiss A mad mountain man abducts a beautiful hiker in the Rocky Mountains. The scenery is dramatic, the plot snowed in.

Absence, The (*L'absence*) (1976) (90mins) d&s: Brigitte Sauriol : Frédérique Collin, Monique Mercure, Jean Gascon, Guy Thauvette, Jocelyn Bérubé. A poignant study of emotions as a daughter responds to her dying father, who deserted her twenty years earlier. One of her friends tries to help her come to terms with a new life developing around her.

Absent One, The (1997) (95mins) d&s: Céline Baril : Roland Kadar, Roland Bréard, Anna Maria Giannotti, Gabor Zsigovics, Edward Ziernicki, Vratislav Hadrava, Shinji Hashigucki, Istvan Lakatos, Rozsika Lakatos. Roland, now an adult, goes back to where his father drowned himself in the Danube. On his trip, which takes him to Budapest, Warsaw, Rome, Prague and Tokyo, he searches for family and friends and the reasons behind his father's suicide. A travelogue looking for the truth. This is a quietly told and perceptive study of loss and longing.

Accident at Memorial Stadium, The (1983) (104mins) d: Donald Brittain s: William Gough : Fiona Reid, Terence Kelly, Frank Perry, Michael Hogan, Anne Anglin. Brittain, Canada's distinguished documentary director, produces a drama with a clear documentary cloak about a story of people who died when the roof of a hockey arena collapsed. One mother is guilt stricken over being with her lover when her son was killed. Other characters are affected in different ways. Low budget for the CBC but well done, based on actual incidents.

Accidental Truths: *see* Red Eyes

Act of the Heart (1970) (103mins) d&s: Paul Almond : Geneviève Bujold, Donald Sutherland, Monique Leyrac, Bill Mitchell, Suzanne Langlois, Sharon Acker, Ratch Wallace, Jean Duceppe, Gilles Vigneault, Eric House, Jean Dalmain, Claude Jutra, François Tassé. Paul Almond has long been recognized as one of Canada's individualistic filmmakers with the courage to express himself without regard for standard forms of fashion. Here he has followed *Isabel* by taking up the subject of religious fervour, which literally burns up his heroine, a young girl who wants to touch God. She falls in love with a priest, who is forced to leave the church. Neither finds happiness. Beautifully made and acted, it is not always convincing and leaves most audiences emotionally unaffected. (See *Isabel* and *Journey*)

Acts of Love Series (Love) (Series) (1980) (105mins) Six short films linked together to make one complete film. Beautifully written and acted and, for the most part, affecting, witty and sensible. Filmed in Toronto by producer René Perlmutter.
1: **Love From the Market Place**: d&s: Mai Zetterling : Gordon Thomson, Maureen Fitzgerald
2: **The Black Cat in the Black Mouse Socks**: d: Mai Zetterling s: Joni Mitchell : Joni Mitchell, Winston Rekert, Dixie Seatle, Robert Dermer, Margaret Dragu
3: **For Life**: d&s: Nancy Dowd : Nicholas Campbell, Toni Kalem
4: **Love on Your Birthday**: d: Annette Cohen s: Gael Greene : Marilyn Lightstone, Moses Znaimer, Linda Rennhofer
5: **Julia**: d: Mai Zetterling s: Edna O'Brien : Janet-Laine Green, Lawrence Dane, Elizabeth Shepherd
6: **Parting**: d&s: Liv Ullmann : Charles Joliffe, Rita Tuckett.

Ada (1981) (65mins) d&s: Claude Jutra (from Margaret Gibson's short story) : Janet Amos, Anne Anglin, Jayne Eastwood, Sabina Maydelle, Kay Hawtrey, Kate Reid. A searing, perceptive and understanding representation of life in a women's mental institution. Unforgettable. This is Jutra's first English-language film. (See: *For the Record*)

Adjuster, The (1991) (102mins) d&s: Atom Egoyan : Elias Koteas, Arsinée Khanjian, Maury Chaykin, Gabrielle Rose, Jennifer Dale, David Hemblen, Don McKellar. More of the same from the director of *Speaking Parts*, this time with extra servings of kinky behaviour. A cold, dreary, hermetic film about voyeurism (perhaps), with a silly censorship sequence, communicating to very few.

Adolescence of P-I, The (Hide and Seek) (1983) (65mins) d: René Bonnière s: Barrie Wexler : Robert Martin, Ingrid Veninger, David Patrick, John Friesen, Robert Haley, Alan Scarfe, Leslie Carlson, John Blackwood. One of the very first films about artificial intelligence, dealing quietly but disturbingly with a computer program going seriously wrong at a nuclear power station. The computer has the ability to think for itself and the power to make moral decisions. Frightening.

Adolescente sucré d'amour, L' (*Gazi el banat*) (The Sweet Teenager Love) (Suspended Life: The Charming Story of the Adolescent Sugar Love) (1985) (102mins) (a Canada-France-Lebanon co-production) d: Jocelyn Saab s: Gérard Brach : Jacques Weber, Hala Bassam, Juliet Berto, Youssef Housni, Denise Filiatrault, Claude Préfontaine. In her first fiction film, Saab, a young Lebanese director, gives a finely wrought story of her country, giving rise to hopes for survival after its terrible civil war. The whole contains keen perspectives that make this a valid and forthright drama.

Adolescents, Les: see **That Tender Age, The Adolescents**

Adramelech: see **King of Fire**

Adrift (1993) (90mins) d: Christian Dugay s: Graham Flashner, Edward Gernon, Terry Gerretsen : Kenneth Welsh, Kate Jackson, Bruce Greenwood, Kelly Rowan. A dead steal from Australia's *Dead Calm*, all washed up with nowhere to go!

Adventure for Two, An (À nous deux) (1979) (112mins) (a Canada-France co-production) d&s: Claude Lelouch : Catherine Deneuve, Jacques Dutronc, Jacques Villeret, Émile Genest, Paul Préboist, Monique Melinand. A man and a woman who have committed numerous robberies in Paris elude the police, flee to Montréal and then proceed to New York for further adventures before being apprehended. Disappointing.

Adventure for Two, An: see **Nous deux, À**

Adventures in the Great North: see **Aventures du grand nord, Les (series)**

Adventures of a Very Special Agent, The: see **Aventures d'un agent très spécial, Les**

Adventures of Faustus Bidgood, The (1986) (110mins) d&s: Michael and Andy Jones : Andy Jones, Greg Malone, Mary Walsh, Jane Dingle, Maisie Rillie, Robert Joy. From Newfoundland, this movie was ten years in the filming, with long waits in between stops to find more money. Newfoundlanders have a boisterous comedy tradition unlike that of any other province, and their friendly wit and high good humour don't always rub off on all audiences—nor will this outrageous film. Bidgood is a dreamer and a minor functionary in the department of education. A meek man who suffers the torments of his detractors, he escapes from reality and imagines he is president of an independent Newfoundland. Of course, he carries his dreams into real life with resulting confusion for all concerned. The political jokes and jibes are all directed at contemporary elected representatives. A brave and bold attack on the establishment, and other things!

Adventures of Ti-ken, The (1961) (65mins) d&s: Roger Laliberté : Jean-Guy St-Gelais, Jacques Riopelle, Gaston Gilbert, Léon Caron, Francis Bouchard. Children's movies made in Québec between 1958 and 1964 took a turn toward the dark and unpleasant with this scary mystery. (A companion picture to *Ti-ken in Moscow*.)

Affair with a Killer (1967) (100mins) (a Canada-U.K. film) d&s: Maxine Samuels : Stephen Joyce, Austin Willis. A tense drama defining the task of police officers on the St. Lawrence Seaway who spend most of their time collaborating with their U.S. opposite numbers on tracking down the peddlers of drugs controlled by a vicious group of thugs and profiteers. (Made for the then popular tv series *Seaway*.)

Affaire Coffin, L': see **Coffin Affair, The**

After the Harvest (Wild Geese) (2000) (120mins) d: Jeremy Podeswa s: Suzette Couture (based on the highly acclaimed 1920's novel *Wild Geese*, by Martha Ostenso) : David Lereaney, Alberta Watson, Sam Shepard, Liane Balaban, Jonathan Eliot, Nadia Litz, Shawn Mathieson. Set against the sweeping landscape of the Canadian prairies in the early 1920s, this astonishing story concerns a wealthy farmer who keeps his wife and children in abject poverty, forcing them to work like slaves in the wheat fields from dawn to dusk. Running throughout this story is a strong vein of morality in which the power of love attempts to overcome human cruelty. An extraordinary piece of work from Podeswa. (See: *Signature series*)

Agaguk (Shadow of the Wolf) (1993) (112mins) (a Canada-France co-production) d: Jacques Dorfman s: Rudy Wurlitzer, Evan Jones, David Milhand (from the novel by Yves Thériault) : Toshiro Mifune, Donald Sutherland, Jennifer Tilley, Lou Diamond Phillips, Bernard-Pierre Donnadieu. Agaguk, the son of Kroomak, the chief of an Inuit tribe, leaves his people, only to return to find his village in a bitter conflict between a hunter and a white trader, resulting in the death of the latter, with Agaguk disappearing into the tundra. An affecting remembrance of life in the Arctic.

Age de braise, L': see **When I Will Be Gone**

Age of Innocence: see **Ragtime Summer**

Agency (1980) (94mins) (a Canadian-American film) d: George Kaczender s: Noel Hynd (from the novel by Paul Gottlieb) : Robert Mitchum, Lee Majors, Valerie Perrine, Alexandra Stewart, George Touliatos, Saul Rubinek, Gary Reineke, Hugh Webster, Donald Davis, Eric Donkin, Walter Massey, Henry Gamer. A good idea gone dark: a crook transmits secret industrial information subliminally within television commercials. The result is neither astonishing nor of any importance; it crashed, as they say. A huge cast, a huge investment, a huge amount of work, done for no good reason other than to profit financially through the Capital Cost Allowance Act.

Agent of Influence (2002) (120 mins) d: Michel Poulette s: Ian and E Riley Adams (From Ian Adams novel of the same title) : Christopher Plummer, Maria Orsini, Ted Whittall, Shaun Johnston, Kurtis Sandheim. In 1964, at the request of the CIA, the RCMP interrogated John Watkins, Canada's ambassador to the USSR, because they were certain he was a Soviet agent. Watkins died of heart failure. This dramatic chapter in our political past relationship with the US has been fictionised to such an extent that it loses much of its credibility in spite of Plummer's understanding portrayal of John Watkins.

Agnes of God (1985) (98mins) d: Norman Jewison s: John Pielmeier (from his play of the same name) : Jane Fonda, Anne Bancroft, Meg Tilly, Winston Rekert, Gratien Gélinas, Gabriel Arcand, Guy Hoffman. Heavy religious-crime drama concerning the murder of a young nun thought to be pregnant. A court psychiatrist finds no cause for this, and audiences are left to decide for themselves. Mostly for true believers. This is one of Jewison's notable American films, but shot almost entirely in Canada.

Ah! Si mon moine voulait: see **Oh, If Only My Monk Would Want**

Ainsi soient-ils: see **Day Without Evidence, A**

Air Bud (1997) (98mins) (a U.S.-Canada film) d: Charles Martin Smith s: Kevin DiCicco, Paul Tamasy : Michael Trier, Kevin Zegers, Wendy Makkena, Eric Christmas. A young boy finds that a stray dog he takes under his care is a highly talented pooch amazingly adept at playing basketball. A funny and delightful Disney family film. This picture was so successful it resulted in two sequels, with the popular dog playing football and then soccer. Followed by: **Air Bud: Golden Receiver** (1998) (80mins) d: Richard Martin s: Kevin DiCicco, Paul Tamasy : Tom Conway, Dick Martin, Kevin Zegers, Cynthia Stevenson. **Air Bud: World Pup** (2000) (83mins) d: Bill Bannerman s: Kevin DiCicco, Paul Tamasy : Kevin Zegers, Dale Midkiff, David Glyn-Jones, Caitin Wachs.

Air Bud: Seventh Inning Fetch (2002) (93mins) d: Robert Vince s: Anne and Robert Vince : Jay Brazeau, Jeffrey Ballard. From the family that gave us *Jack the Chimp*, this sequel to *Air Bud: World Pup* brings us the boy and his pooch who, having succeeded in playing basketball, football and soccer, now turn their attention to winning on the baseball diamond. More of the same, and audiences who liked the previous films will probably enjoy this chapter, too.

Airborne (1998) (105mins) (a-Can-U-UK-film) d: Julian Grant s: Tony Johnston & Grant : Steve Guttenberg, Colm Feore, Sean Bean, Kim Coates, Philip Akin, Torri Higginson, David Fraser. A covert espionage team goes to work for a government, to steal biochemical weapons from a terrorist organization. Notable for an extraordinary and spectacular attempt by an agent to stand on the roof of a speeding car and get himself into a fast moving airplane hurtling down a run-way about to take off. Impossible in real life of course, but here he seems to pull it off. The rest is the usual, ordinary, minor Bond stuff.

Airport In (1996) (81mins) d&s: Erik Whittaker : George Majoros, Geoff Naylor, Scott Tate, Bill Evans. For most audiences, it will be a quick airport out from this creaking and laboured comedy set during a podiatry conference in Winnipeg during a rowdy hockey series. Murder and the RCMP are dragged in, and the entire enterprise looks like some tattered old work left behind at an airport.

Ala: see **Best Bad Thing, The**

Albertine, en cinq temps (Albertine in Five Times) (1999) (90mins) d: André Melançon, Martine Beaulne s: Michel Tremblay : Monique Mercure, Andrée Lachapelle, Sophie Clément, Élise Guilbeault, Macha Limonchik, Guylaine Tremblay. Albertine, one of Tremblay's most important characters, moves into her final home, a residence for seniors. Here she is visited by ghosts from the past. An enchanting, and perceptive film.

Alégria (1998) (92mins) d: Franco Dragone s: Rudy Barichello : René Balinet, Frank Langella, Julie Cox, Clipper Miano, Mako, Heathcote Williams. Franco Dragone has been associated with Québec's renowned Cirque du Soleil since 1985, and has directed eight of the Cirque's nine stage productions. This film was inspired by the 1994 stage presentation of the same name. A street mime decides to end his life, but not before he meets two people— one a street urchin, the other a beautiful singer— who make his life worth living again. This is not a record as such of the stage performance but an adaptation for the screen, with all the charm, colour and humour of the original.

Alexander Bell: The Sound and the Silence (1991) (186mins) (a Canada-U.K. co-production) d: John Kent Harrison s: Tony Foster, William Schmidt, John Kent Harrison : John Bache, Elizabeth Quinn, Vanessa Vaughan, Ian Bannen, Brenda Fricker. This splendid and fascinating biography of the life and career of the Scottish-Canadian-American inventor of the telephone and the time in which he lived is intelligent and finely detailed.

Alias Will James (1988) (83mins) d&s: Jacques Godbout : Michael Benard, Carole David, Daniel David, Tan Tyson. An absorbing drama-doc, a biography with life teeming through it, recalling the extraordinary career of Ernest Dufault, a French-Canadian who, dreamed of becoming a cowboy. In pursuit of his desire he left Quebec in 1911 and went out to the American West and did what he had dreamed of – became a cowboy. Changing his name to Will James, he also became a writer of several novels, but no less a Canadian. He died in 1942. *Shootout* (1971) with Gregory Peck was based on one of his books. This NFB film is an intelligent human history. He wrote his own biography: *The Lone Cowboy: My Life Story* (1930).

Alice's Odyssey: see **Odyssee d'Alice Tremblay, L'**

Alien Thunder (Dan Candy's Law) (1973) (92mins) d: Claude Fournier s: George Malko, W.O. Mitchell : Donald Sutherland, Gordon Tootoosis, Chief Dan George, Kevin McCarthy, Jean Duceppe, Jack Creley, Francine Racette. Based on a true story in which a Cree kills a North West Mounted Police sergeant. The killer is hunted for two years; the end brings tragedy for all those involved. An unusual, quiet and engrossing frontier story and far from the conventional American Western. Fournier does well as director and cinematographer. This picture marked the beginning of Sutherland's long career in film.

Aline et Michel **(Aline)** (1992) (90mins) d&s: Carole Laganière : Philippe Volter, Véronie Quinn Chasle, Dominique Leduc, Rodrigue Proteau. Aline is away at the beach when she is kidnapped by her father. She feels sorry for him and knows he loves her. They go away together but the father meets a questionable woman who becomes his lover. Then an ex-boyfriend turns up. He needs her love, too. All told, a pretty desperate film. Aline comes to realize that her father is really a tired, fickle and fragile man. When it comes to depicting the range of human relations and emotional responses, most Québec filmmakers cannot be surpassed.

Alisée (1991) (90mins) d&s: André Blanchard : Elsa Zylberstein, Jacques Godin, André Montmorency, Denise Filiatrault, Roger Joubert. A small but poignant drama about a young woman from France who comes to Québec to find her long-lost father, and of the men who become part of her life.

All About Women (*À propos de la femme***)** (1969) (85mins) d: Claude Pierson s: Huguette Boisvert : Marie-Christine Auréfil, Marlène Alexandre, Astrid Frank, Jean Perrin, Robert Piquet. All about sex and sleaze turning around a man and his erotic fantasies about the women surrounding him.

All in Good Taste (1983) (84mins) d: Anthony Kramreither s: Rick Green, Anthony Kramreither : Jonathan Welsh, Jack Creley, Harvey Atkin, James B. Douglas, Jo-Anne Kirwan, Linda Rennhofer. A filmmaker in an Ontario town has written a serious dramatic script that the producers turn into a pornographic movie to make more money. A funny film, made even more so by the fact that Kramreither, a colourful, cheerful and likeable producer, was noted for his "serious" documentaries about world affairs in which he always found a way to bring in nudity one way or the other, such as *Mondo Nude, Mondo Strip* and *Some Do It for Money*.

All the Days of My Life (1982) (95mins) d: Edward Thomason s: Jeanine Locke : Norma Tenault. When an elderly woman decides she must move to a seniors' home, she is discouraged by what seems to be a dismal, crowded residence. But once she settles in, she finds support, understanding and friendship from other residents. A film filled with an appreciation for life.

All the Fine Lines (Full Disclosure) (1999) (96mins) d: John Bradshaw s: Tony Johnston : Virginia Madsen, Penelope Ann Miller, Rachel Ticotin, Christopher Plummer, Fred Ward, Roberta Maxwell, Kim Coates, Nicholas Campbell. A reporter hard up for a story gets into trouble with the FBI and a radical Palestinian group. A huge cast with not much to do in this timely but slow-moving thriller.

Allées de la terre, Les: see **Paths of the World, The**

Alley Cat, The (*Le matou***)** (1985) (135mins) d&s: Jean Beaudin : Serge Dupire, Jean Carmet, Monique Spaziani. Based on the popular novel by Québec writer Yves Beauchemin, this is an involved and difficult tale about a young man and his wife. They run a restaurant with an outspoken French chef and find their lives intermingled with a young boy who runs the streets and loves only his cat. There is also a mysterious stranger called Ratablavasky, who seems to have demonic powers. There are moments of strength and insight, laughter and tears, but good performances and fine photography are not enough to keep this rambling adaptation from slipping into a state of lethargy.

Alligator Shoes (1981) (98mins) d&s: Clay Borris : Gary Borris, Ronalda Jones, Clay Borris, Rose Maltais-Borris, Len Perry. A clever first film by short-film maker Clay Borris concerning two beer-swilling Acadian brothers in Toronto and the death of their young aunt. These working-class worries are lively and promising but somewhat out of control.

Almost America (*Come l'America***)** (2001) (140mins) (a Canada-Italy film) d: Andrea and Antonio Frazzi s: Stefano Rulli, Sandro Petraglia : Sabrina Ferilli, Massimo Ghini, Henry Czerny, Tony Nardi, Dominic Zamprogna, Byron Chief Moon, Giola Spaziani. This is a rare and valuable work, a chronicle of the immigrant experience, made by those who have lived it. Here the Italians, a family among the thousands who came to Canada after WWII. This one in particular, goes to Edmonton where a wife and mother expects to be re-united with her husband and son's father, but instead suffers a disappointment. From then on, we watch the daily events unfold, the small triumphs, the pleasures of the newcomers as they adjust to living among the other Italian families, and on finding themselves becoming a part of Canadian life. This is not a documentary, but contains the truth of life nevertheless. Poignant, but never synthetic, sadness followed by happiness and laughter, beautifully acted and skillfully made with a fine eye for details, all done by Italian filmmakers working in Alberta. This is an unforgettable film.

Almost Grown (1987) (120mins) d: David Chase s: Lawrence Konner, David Chase : Timothy Daly, Eve Gordon. Inept and silly business about a married couple in Toronto adjusting to the changes the 1980s have wrought on their marriage and family. Too bad!

Alter Ego: see **Dead Ringers**

Alone or With Others: see *Seul ou avec d'autres*

Amanita pestilens (1963) (78mins) d: René Bonnière s: David Walker : Jacques Labrecque, Huguette Oligny, Geneviève Bujold, Blake James, Ronald France, J.-Léo Gagnon, Denise Bombardier. A charming comedy-satire showing how a suburban family in Montréal almost destroys itself in the attempt to achieve materialistic perfection in life. Among the metaphors are the mushrooms that spoil the look of the lawn. Originally titled *Ville jolie,* this is Geneviève Bujold's first film, the first to be directed by René Bonnière and the first feature to be produced by F.R. (Budge) Crawley. He followed this the next year with the now classic *The Luck of Ginger Coffey* (see under this title).

Amateur, The (1981) (111mins) (a Canadian-American film) d: Charles Jarrott s: Robert Littel, Diana Maddox : John Savage, Christopher Plummer, Marthe Keller, Arthur Hill, Nicholas Campbell, Jan Rubes, Jacques Godin, Tedde Moore, Irena Mayeska, John Kerr, Graham Jarvis. A miscast and misdirected production set in Europe in which a CIA computer expert hunts down terrorists who murdered his girlfriend in Munich. A complicated and ridiculous spy thriller wasting its cast.

Ambush At Iroquois Pass (1979) (90mins) d: Ralph Thomas s: Barry Pearson : R.H. Thomson, Kenneth Pogue, Sonja Smits, Frank Moore, Diana Barrington, Michael Hogan, Lesleh Donaldson, Geraint Wyn Davies, Miles Potter, Stephen Markle. Set during the War of 1812, this is a poignant historical drama about a family of Loyalists with mixed emotions over the invasion by the Americans. This film brings to life one of the most important chapters in our neglected movie history. The characters are alive and convincing in their ambiguities and doubts, played in a triumph of ensemble acting. Thomson was great even this early in his career.

American Beer (1996) (82mins) d: Grant Harvey s: Harvey, Brent and Jordan Kawchuk : Jordan Kawchuk, Jason Thompson, Scott Urquart, Adam Leigh. Four Canadian youths are driving through the barren Alberta flatlands when their car breaks down. In searching for another car, these somewhat tiresome types discover aspects of their characters of which they had been unaware. Much related to and influenced by American pop culture. This is a weak beer going flat pretty quick.

American Boyfriends (1989) (89mins) d&s: Sandy Wilson : Margaret Langrick, Liisa Repo-Martell, Delia Brett, Michelle Bardeaux, John Wildman. This is the disappointing sequel to the delightful, autobiographical *My American Cousin,* in which Sandy goes to her cousin's wedding in the U.S. and seeks further adventures in California. Some bright and pleasing moments, however.

American Christmas Carol, An (1979) (120mins) (a Canada-U.S. co-production) d: Eric Till s: Jerome Coopersmith (based on the book by Charles Dickens) : Henry Winkler, David Wayne, Chris Wiggins, R.H. Thomson, Kenneth Pogue, Gerard Parkes, Susan Hogan, Linda Goranson, Cec Linder, James B. Douglas, Ruth Springford. The title tells all, the lovely familiar story picked up once again and placed in the United States, snow courtesy of

Guelph and Elora, Ontario. Fairly faithful, directed knowingly and gently, it is properly Dickensian, with a spirited cast.

American Film Theatre Series (Play of the Week): In the late 1960's, Ely Landeau and his wife, Edie, who owned NYC's tv channel 13, before PBS came on the scene, produced a highly regarded series called *Play of the Week*. It consisted of filmed plays, mostly contemporary, fourteen in all, with great actors and directors of film and theatre, just one example, Katherine Hepburn, Lindsay Anderson and Ralph Richardson, who like Ely Landau, have passed on. In 1970, after much discussion and planning, everyone involved in producing these filmed plays thought it worth trying to have them shown in cinemas. They started at the Lincoln Center, were highly successful, and soon, movie houses throughout the US asked to show them. They were artistically and financially viable. People in many small towns never saw Broadway plays now they could on film. The one important difference in their exhibition, in a move to bring back audiences who had abandoned cinema for tv, was they were presented like plays, two evenings a week with subscriptions to the entire series, or booking ahead for certain evenings with a numbered seat of the patron's choosing. It was, it could be said, the theatre playing cinema. They were shown in Toronto at the Capital cinema, and the Canadian in charge was Stan Helleur, who had left the *Toronto Telegram* as film reviewer when Clyde Gilmour came from Vancouver. The full story of this enterprise, which brought about a significant change in the pattern of filmmaking and exhibition, is fascinating. Note: The AFT films are now available in a boxed set on DVD and VHS. See under their respective titles:

1: **Butley**
2: **Galileo**
3: **In Celebration**
4: **Jacques Brel Is Alive and Well and Living in Paris**
5: **Luther**
6: **Maids, The** (a US-Can-UK-film)

American Night, An: see *Nuit en Amérique, Une*

American Psycho (2000) (97mins) (a Canadian-American film) d: Mary Harron s: Guinevere Turner, Mary Harron (based on the novel by Bret Easton Ellis) : Christian Bale, Willem Dafoe, Jared Leto, Reese Witherspoon, Samantha Mathis, Chloe Sevigny, Guinevere Turner, Cara Seymour, Josh Lucas, Justin Theroux. An abomination of a book becomes an abomination of a film. A homicidal maniac lives in luxury with a well-paid job at an investment firm, ruthlessly killing men and women alike. Unbelievable and gruesomely hideous, depraved, shallow and immoral. This film has been widely acclaimed as a satirical and hilarious takeoff of consumerism and materialism. When did bloody murder become a subject to be satirized? The acting, writing and direction are out of control throughout.

Amie d'enfance, Une: see **Childhood Friend, A**

Amityville Curse, The (1990) (91mins) d: Tom Berry s: Michael Kruger, Rose Norvell (based on the book by Hans Holzer) : Kim Coates, Dawna Wightman, Helen Hughes, David Stein, Anthony Dean, Casandra Gava, Jan Rubes. Yet another chapter in the tired *Amityville* series about haunted houses. The spirits are missing here, on the screen and behind the camera.

Amour blessé, L': see **Confidences of the Night**

Amour comme le nôtre, Un: see **French Love**

Amoureuses, Les **(Women in Love)** (1993) (90mins) d&s: Johanne Prégent : Louise Portal, Kenneth Welsh, Lea Marie Cantin, Tony Nardi. Two women, friends about to become forty, are involved in troubling love affairs. Relationships are not what they were; original passions have cooled and love and friendship take on new meaning. Québec's women filmmakers are very good at relating these subjective, emotional experiences, and this sensitive discourse is no exception.

Amoureux fou (Madly in Love) (1991) (100mins) d: Robert Ménard s: Claire Wojas : Rémy Girard, Nathalie Gascon, Jean Rochefort, Danielle Proulx, Jessica Barker. A forty-year-old man meets a former lover and finds himself overwhelmed by feelings of love for her. Both are married, and their partners cannot understand what has happened. There follows a painful struggle of possessiveness and jealousy, and then self-destruction when they are all unable to come to terms with this fire of passion. Anyone who has gone through this torment will be touched by its truth and despair.

Anatomy of a Horror: see **Deadline**

Anchor Zone (1994) (90mins) d: Andrée Pelletier s: T.H. Hatte : Henry Czerny, Nicole Stoffman, Mark Critch, Pheilm Martin, Michael Luke. In 2010, the world is in chaos and, in a small seaport town in Newfoundland, the economy has collapsed. A company called Wondercorp is training the town's youth to stem the decline, but actually wants to take control of them. A young woman who is part of the group suddenly learns that her dead father is alive, and she leaves to search for him. Her journey is a nightmare of decadence and decay with her father lost in mystery. A searing sci-fi social-study allegory.

And I Love You Dearly (La maîtresse) (1973) (111mins) d: Anton Van de Water s: Gemma Barra, Anton Van de Water : Karina Tonisso, Jean Coutu, Pierre Dufresne, Robert Rivard, Pierre Lalonde, Len Watt, Rita Lafontaine. A touching and tender tale about a young woman searching for the right man to love.

And Miles to Go (1985) (90mins) d&s: Gordon Pinsent : Gordon Pinsent. A teacher who has been dismissed from an exclusive school for boys moves to northern Ontario and opens a mobile school on the railway to bring education to families living where schools do not exist. Our extraordinarily talented and gifted actor-writer Gordon Pinsent makes a compelling drama of this true story.

And Then You Die (1987) (115mins) d: Francis Mankiewicz s: Wayne Grigsby : Kenneth Welsh, R.H. Thomson. A fast-moving, taut and absorbing thriller about biker gangs in Montréal, mafia mobs and overlords, and a detective doggedly on the trail of an Irish-Canadian cocaine dealer. Great work from all concerned. Penetrating social realism.

And When the CWAC's Go Marching On (*Du poil aux pattes***)** (1985) (120mins) d: Daniel Roussel s: Maryse Pelletier : Michelle Allen, Anne Bryan, Hélène Mercier, Lucie Routhier. This text was adapted for the screen in a realization by Daniel Roussel, *Théâtre d'Aujourd'hui*, March 4, 1982 and was translated into English by Louise Ringuet. In 1942, four women from different surroundings enrolled in the Canadian Women's Army Corps, each with her own assets, dreams and ambitions. The laughter and tears alternate during the intensive five-week training course that will make them interdependent in their isolated base. World War II is raging overseas, and they must leave for service in London. A marvelous portrait about one of the vital sides of our armed forces during the times of grave danger.

André Mathieu, Musicien (1994) (80mins) d&s: Jean-Claude Labrecque : Jean-Alexandre Sarrazin, Jean Simon. A beautiful portrait comprised of personal recollections and archival film of the life and career of composer-musician André Mathieu, who wrote music for both the concert hall and the cinema. He was exceptionally talented, but died at the age of 39, abandoned and forgotten. This document gives him a life again, made by the distinguished cinematographer Jean-Claude Labrecque.

Ange de goudron, L' **(Tar Angel)** (2001) (90mins) d&s: Denis Chouinard : Zinedine Soualem, Hiam Abbas, Catherine Trudeau, Rabah Ait Ouyahia. An important and deeply moving film centering around an Algerian family in Montréal, three years after the final steps towards Canadian citizenship. The father becomes afraid it will be denied them because his son has been engaged in political protests and is involved with a group of terrorists. He need not have worried; Canada is known around the world as a home for everyone from tinkers to terrorists. The final gripping sequences in the snowbound north country where the father with, his son's girlfriend searches for him on their snowmobiles are dense with atmosphere and remarkably photographed and acted. An affecting portrait of life in Québec, directed with great skill and imagination. The title comes from the father's occupation as a roof repairman. Easily the best film of its year.

Ange et la femme, L': see **Angel and the Woman, The**

Ange gardien, L' **(The Guardian Angel)** (1978) (98mins) d&s: Jacques Fournier : Francis Lemaire, Margaret Trudeau, Joanne Côté, André Falcon,

Jacqueline Jefford. A wealthy Montréal industrialist married to a ravishing young lady hires a private detective to watch her while she's on holiday on the French Riviera. Of course, the detective falls in love with her. A colourful romantic comedy in which Margaret Trudeau acquits herself well. This was her second film. She'd previously performed in *Kings and Desperate Men*.

Ange noir, L' (The Black Angel) (Nelligan) (1991) (100mins) d: Robert Favreau s: Aude Nantais, Jean-Joseph Tremblay, Robert Favreau : Marc St-Pierre, Lorraine Pintal, Luc Morissette, Gabriel Arcand, Dominique Leduc, David La Haye. Émile Nelligan, who published his first poem at the age of 17, is held in high regard by many Québécois. A dark, brooding and passionate man, his short and difficult life is well dramatized here. Two other films were made about him during the same year: *Nelligan*, the opera by André Gagnon and Michel Tremblay (d: Bernard Picard) and *Nelligan: The Making of an Opera* (d: Richard Bocking).

Angel and the Woman, The (*L'ange et la femme*) (1977) (87mins) d&s: Gilles Carle : Carole Laure, Lewis Furey, J.-Léo Gagnon, Pierre Girard, Jean Comtois. A heavy-handed piece of erotic and violent supernatural symbolism about an angel who takes possession of the body of a murdered woman.

Angel in a Cage (1998) (92mins) d&s: Mary Jane Gomes : Tony Nardi, Maurina Gomes, Damon D'Oliveira, Michael Cherrie, Christopher Pinheiro. A moody and part-biographical portrait of struggle, deception, despair and loneliness in the life of a family working towards a better future in a winery in 1930s Trinidad. Photographed against the tropical beauty of the Caribbean.

Angel in a Cage (The Woman in the Cage) (*La bête de fiore*) (1993) (70mins) d&s: Isabelle Hayeur : Linda Roy, David La Haye, Catherine Senart, Nicolas Paré, Catherine Lachance, Vincent Houdet. A young woman in Montréal shares her apartment with her lover, but when he is away she lives in a large cage. This behaviour is apparently the result of being haunted by memories of what happened in Leningrad during World War II. Sensitively treated but hard to care about her.

Angel Life (*Vie d'ange*) (1979) (84mins) d: Pierre Harel s: Paule Baillargeon, Pierre Harel : Pierre Harel, Paule Baillargeon, Jean-Guy Moreau, Louise Portal, Priscilla Lapointe. In this piece of tripe, the writer and director meet at a party, retire to an apartment, have sex and cannot come apart. Nevertheless, they fall in love. A waste of time.

Angel Square (Angel Street) (1990) (104mins) d: Anne Wheeler s: James DeFelice, Anne Wheeler : Jeremy Radick, Ned Beatty. Set in Winnipeg at Christmas of 1945, this comedy-drama with animated sequences is a charming and sensitive tale of a young boy chasing down the attacker of his best friend's father. Somewhat in the tradition of *Hue and Cry* and *Emil and the Detectives*.

Angel Street: see **Angel Square**

Angela: see **Pleasure Palace**

Angela (1978) (100mins) (a Canada-U.S. co-production) d: Boris Sagal s: Charles Israel : Sophia Loren, John Huston, Steve Railsback, John Vernon, Michelle Rossignol, Luce Guilbeault. A clumsy, confusing and slow story about a love affair between a woman and a young man—who turns out to be her son! Good cast wasted in a troubled production.

Angelo, Fredo and Roméo (1996) (88mins) d: Pierre Plante s: François Camirand : Benoît Brière, Martin Drainville, Luc Guérin, Macha Limonchik, Amulette Garneau. Fredo inherits a fortune from an old uncle and finds himself with a transport company. His friends Angelo and Roméo persuade him to put his money into making movies. This makes for a comedy with too few laughs as it attempts to parody the process of making movies. This film received bad publicity when it opened at Québec City's Lido cinema, where the owner wrote "rotten" on the advertising posters to discourage people from buying tickets. "It's a film you can't make head or tail of," he said at the time.

Angry Man, An: see **Jigsaw**

Anne of Green Gables (1985) (197mins) d&s: Kevin Sullivan (based on the classic children's books by Lucy Maud Montgomery) : Megan Follows, Colleen Dewhurst, Patricia Hamilton, Marilyn Lightstone, Charmion King, Rosemary Ratcliffe, Jackie Burroughs, Jonathan Crombie and many others. Anne, a young orphan, arrives at the Prince Edward Island home of the family, a sister and brother, who have adopted her. This was the beginning of a delightfully human and lovely tv series telling the story of Anne, who is played to perfection, especially in her older years, by Megan Follows. The knowing cast of actors, the well-written scripts, expert photography and highly convincing settings and sets capture the passing years with a rewarding authenticity. Attitudes and manners of each generation are skillfully expressed, and the trench warfare of World War I is strikingly recreated. The whole is given a never fading appeal by Megan Follows. (see series: *Anne of Green Gables: The Continuing Story*)

Anne of Green Gables: The Continuing Story (Series) (1985-1999) (220mins) d: Stefan Scaini s: Kevin Sullivan (adapted from the books of Lucy Maud Montgomery) : Megan Follows, Jonathan Crombie, Cameron Daddo. The tv series *Anne of Green Gables*, which ran from 1985 to 1999 and is based on Montgomery's much loved and widely read stories, proved to be the most popular programs the CBC has ever presented. A multi-award-winning series, it found huge audiences when shown abroad, particularly in Japan. This conclusion, so well set and detailed during World War I, sees Anne going to the battlefields in Europe looking for the man she loves. Far from being overly sentimental or cloying, it becomes a moving and captivating depiction of family life in Canada at that time, and will long be remembered. The series includes:

1: **Anne of Green Gables: A New Home**
2: *Anne of Green Gables: A Bend in the Road*
3: **Anne of Avonlea**
4: **Anne of Green Gables: The Sequel**
5: *Anne of Green Gables: The Final Years*, all produced by Kevin Sullivan. All faithful, charming and true to life adaptations. Principal players are Megan Follows, Colleen Dewhurst, Patricia Hamilton, Marilyn Lightstone, Charmion King, Rosemary Radcliffe, Richard Farnsworth, Frank Converse, Schuyler Grant.

Anne Trister (1986) (105mins) (a Canada-Switzerland co-production) d&s: Léa Pool : Albane Guilhe, Louise Marleau, Guy Thauvette, Hughes Quester, Lucie Laurier. Pool's second film is the story of a Swiss girl who leaves her fiancé to find herself as an artist in Montréal. Her search for meaning and happiness becomes psychologically impossible as events unfold in this slow, coldly related narrative.

Années de rêve, Les: see **Years of Dreams and Revolt**

Années Lumières or Années Terribles: see **French Revolution, The**

Années, Les **(The Years)** (1997) (107mins) d: Jacquelin Bouchard s: Cindy Lou Johnson (from her play of the same title) : Markita Boles, Louise Bombardier, Normand Canac Marquis, Vincent Gratton. The story unfolds over a 16-year period, beginning with a young woman being attacked on her wedding day. The life that follows is one of small family moments and traumas, with moving, comic and surprising events from long-forgotten times. A delicate work with memorable results.

Anomaly (*Anomie***)** (1973) (69mins) d&s: Claude Castravelli : Jane Poulin, Mary Perez, Gordon Lewis, Paula Dickan. Filmed at McGill University in Montréal, this effective and tightly told drama concerns a kidnapped student and her roommates' search for her. This film provides a look into a future that has sadly come to pass.

Another Country: A North of 60 Mystery (2003) (92mins) d: Gary Harvey s: Peter Lauteman, Andrew Wreggitt : Tina Keeper, Dakota House, Ron White, Hugh Thompson. A businessman visiting Calgary is arrested on a trumped up murder charge. Being an Indian he finds himself up against prejudice and scorn. A female RCMP corporal investigates the charges, but while doing so the accused man flees to Lynx River, far from the city. The officer must now decide whether to arrest him or fail in her duty by letting him go. An interesting portrayal of opposite characters caught up in an unsettling dilemma. (This is a long-version episode in the popular tv series.)

Another Day (2001) (120mins) (a U.S.-Canada film) d: Jeffrey Reiner s: Helen Frost, Donald MacLeod : Shannen Doherty, Max Martini, Julian McMahon. This is a fascinating and unusual story about a woman whose happy life suddenly takes a turn towards the supernatural. Her life and the lives of those close to her turn nightmarish. There is a gripping tension and creation of fear in this film that is cleverly sustained and frightening about forces we never think will enter our lives.

Another Man: see *Autre homme, Un*

Another Planet (2000) (90mins) d&s: Christene Brown : Daniel Lévesque, Tiemoko Simaga, Mathieu Dutan, Kevin White, Sandy Daley, Monique MacDonald, Panchetta Barnett, Marcia Brown. A young black woman has immigrated to Canada from the West Indies and seems to find life in Canada is failing to satisfy her spiritual and emotional needs. She goes to work on a farm in Québec with a cheerful young family but yearns to travel to Africa, certain that there she will find strength from traditional and ancient customs and beliefs. Much talk, little to think about, and illustrated with images of proud Africans in flowing clothes.

Another Smith for Paradise (1972) (102mins) d&s: Tom Shandel : Henry Ramer, Frances Hyland, Otto Lowry, Harry Sanders, Pia Shandel, Linda Sorensen, Wayne Robson. A dismal tale of big-business blunders, an unfaithful wife and other assorted agonies. Set in Vancouver.

Another Woman (1994) (120mins) d: Alan Smythe s: Jim Henshaw, Lee Langley, Lyle Slack (based on the novel by Margot Doltan) : Justine Bateman, Peter Outerbridge, James Purcell, Kenneth Welsh. After a brutal attack leaves a woman without her memory, her husband declares that she is a new woman. She finds out just what he means while trying to recover her lost memory. The picture that emerges is one of a bitter and depressed woman who has apparently alienated everyone, including her husband. He has already filed for divorce. This new woman she has become, though, convinces him to stop. As she rebuilds her life, thry fall in love again. An interesting change to the "other woman" scenario, and entirely credible. (See: *Harlequin* series)

Anthrax (2001) (90mins) d: Rick Stevenson s: David Schultz : Cameron Daddo, David Keith, Joanna Cassidy, Ed Begley Jr., Jan Rubes, William David, Allison Hossack. In a small Alberta ranching community, the cattle begin to die from anthrax poisoning. The ranchers blame an agricultural research centre and begin a protest movement. An elderly rancher dies from an anthrax infection, and finally a newspaper reporter arrives to investigate. When the confusion of these developments is at its highest, someone finally notices that the reporter has disappeared with any number of vials of the substance. This is a highly unusual, gripping, tense and deadly thriller with a purpose, also, unknowingly when made how topical it would be.

Anything For Love (1992) (91mins) d: Michael Keusch s: Raul Fernandez : Nicole Eggert, Corey Haim, Cameron Bancroft. Another piece of cheap entertainment at the expense of today's college students, which would have us believe that they are only interested in driving fast, getting drunk, swearing and being rude, fighting, and chasing girls for sex. Here, Haim disguises himself as a girl to avoid a bully, which is not in itself worth the price of admission, but it does lead to a genuinely funny but slow conclusion when his parents find out and are bewildered as to whether he is a cross-dresser or gay. Alanis Morissette is in here somewhere.

Apartment Hunting (1999) (90mins) d&s: William Robertson : Andrew Tarbet, Kari Matchett, Valerie Jeanneret, Arnold Pinnock, Tracy Wright. A journalist living with his wife in Toronto's Kensington Market area finds that life has become fraught with anxieties and setbacks. His marriage is failing, he cannot find a publisher for his book, and he cannot find a new apartment. Then he begins to talk to a woman from Québec about an article he is writing on telephone dating; he falls deeply in love with her. Whom should he choose to live with? The new woman or his wife? A genuinely romantic and frank depiction of heartache, passion and longing.

Appalachian Child, The: see *Enfant des appalaches, L'*

Apparition, The (The Unexpected Phantom*)*** (1972) (119mins) d: Roger Cardinal s: Pierre Labelle, René Angélil : Pierre Labelle, Katerine Mousseau, René Angélil, Jean Coutu, Guy L'Écuyer, Céline Lomez. A parody on religious fanaticism and those who profit from it. This almost tabo subject opens up issues not to be found in the Bible. Kindly done without being cutting.

Apple, the Stem and the Seeds, The (*La pomme, la queue et les pépins***)** (1974) (88mins) d: Claude Fournier s: Marie-José Raymond, Claude Fournier : Donald Lautrec, Han Masson, Roméo Pérusse, Janine Sutto, Réal Béland, Thérèse Morange, Jean Lapointe, Danielle Ouimet, Louise Turcot, Denis Drouin. An amusing sex comedy about a busy playboy politician in Montréal who suddenly finds he is impotent after he gets married. His wife takes him around looking for a cure, with varying results. Never distasteful, always good natured.

Apprentice, The (*Fleur bleue***)** (1971) (81mins) d: Larry Kent s: Edward Stewart : Steve Fiset, Céline Bernier, Susan Sarandon, Jean-Pierre Cartier, Paul Berval, Gerard Parkes, Carole Laure, Nana de Varennes, Dorothy Davis, Patrick Coulon, Howard Ryshpan. The story of a Montréal youth whose apprenticeship in life is doomed to failure. There are some heavy-handed references to franco-anglo animosities, but what could have been a funny, vital,

revealing and ultimately tragic story of Québec society is rendered superficial and unconvincing.

Apprenticeship of Duddy Kravitz, The (1974) (120mins) d: Ted Kotcheff s: Mordecai Richler (based on his novel) (adaptation by Lionel Chetwynd) : Richard Dreyfuss, Micheline Lanctôt, Jack Warden, Randy Quaid, Joseph Wiseman, Denholm Elliott, Henry Ramer, Joe Silver, Zvee Scooler, Robert Goodier, Barrie Baldaro. Mordecai Richler's popular novel about a determined Jewish lad in Montréal during the 1940s comes to the screen with most of its humanity, pathos and good humour intact. The use of five American actors in the lead roles tends to give the Montréal setting the flavour of New York's lower east side. A profitable picture given good reviews, the film gave rise to exaggerated claims about Canadian cinema becoming famous at last! After its successful run, producer John Kemeny left Montréal for Los Angeles, where he spent the remainder of his career.

Après-ski : see **Sex in the Snow**

April One (1994) (91mins) d&s: Murray Battle : Stephen Shellen, Janet Sears, David Strathairn. This film is set in Ottawa and based on a true story from 1986, when a former convict took the Bahamian High Commissioner hostage in an attempt to get his lover out of jail. This remarkable film deals with a subject seldom, if ever, touched on in Canadian films. It offers a revealing, behind-the-scenes look at the Ottawa police force and federal politicians. Fascinating, often exciting drama, even if it doesn't always seem to ring true.

Ararat (2002) (126mins) d&s: Atom Egoyan : David Alpay, Charles Aznavour, Eric Rogosian, Brent Carver, Marie-Josee Croze, Bruce Greenwood, Arsinée Khanjian, Elias Koteas, Christopher Plummer, Simon Abkarian. Too many narrative strains, a confusion of characters, places, names and events, encumbered by a film being made within a film, make this actual film hard to take. Flashbacks and various points of view confuse this depiction of what the Turks did to the Armenian community of Van under siege in 1915. Originally chosen by Cannes to be in competition but withdrawn under protests from the Turkish government. In any case, Egoyan is not cut out for films of this scope.

Archangel (1990) (90mins) d: Guy Maddin s: Maddin & George Toles : Kyle McCulloch, Kathy Marykuca, Ari Cohen, Sarah Neville, Michael Gottli. This is "more of the same" from the creator of *Tales from the Gimli Hospital*, a surreal comedy-tragedy of the Great War set in the Russian Arctic, sometimes clever, mostly confusing, often pointlessm in which a Canadian officer goies on a mission to help the White Russians.

Armen and Bullik (1993) (95mins) d: Alan Cooke s: John Goldsmith, Raffy Shart : Roch Voisine, Mike Conners, Maruschka Detmers. An American police man and his nephew come to Canada to search for a lost treasure of the Templar Knights. Why? To give pop star Voisine a chance to sing!

Around the Pink House: see *Autour de la maison*

Arrache-coeur, L': see **Heartbreak**

Arrow, The (1997) (180mins) d: Donald McBrearty s: Keith Ross Leckie : Dan Aykroyd, Sara Botsford, Ron White, Aidan Devine, Michael Ironside, Michael Moriarty, Christopher Plumme. Many Canadians are familiar with the story of the Arrow, the most advanced fighter plane of its time (the 1950s), and how Prime Minister John Diefenbaker stopped production on it due to the enormous cost involved. This film depicts the plane as an engineering accomplishment, but some plot details involve politics and power struggles. It was a difficult film to make, and the result is not always accurate, though compelling and exciting with excellent flying scenes. Dan Aykroyd gives his best-ever performance as Crawford Gordon, president of A.V. Roe, the company that built the plane.

Art of Murder, The (1999) (94mins) d: Ruben Preuss s: Sean Smith, Anthony Stark : Michael Moriarty, Joanna Pacula. A philandering couple is lured into a murder but find it a complicated manoeuver they do not understand. There is no art to this feeble thriller.

Art of War, The (2000) (117mins) d: Christian Duguay s: Wayne Beach, Simon Davis Barry (based on a story by Beach) : Wesley Snipes, Anne Archer, Maury Chaykin, Donald Sutherland, Cary-Hiroyuki Tagawa, Marie Matiko, Michael Biehn, James Hong, Liliana Komorowska. A topical thriller about an American agent who becomes caught up in a dangerous political game based on the successful outcome of an agreement on trade relations between China and the U.S. The Chinese ambassador is killed, terrorists strike, and destruction and havoc are everywhere in a series of fast and never-ending shots and explosions photographed with much colour and glitter. Chaykin is good as the world-weary detective, and Sutherland enjoys being the head of the UN. The setting is New York City, but the filming was done in Montréal.

Art of Woo, The (2001) (95mins) d&s: Helen Lee : Sook-Yin-Lee, Adam Beach, Kelly Harms, Joel Keller, Alberta Watson, John Gilbert, Siu Ta. A light character study about several 20- and 30-somethings living in a rundown apartment building in Toronto. The coil tightens when their lives converge in unexpected ways. Funny moments but the overall effect is breezy. And who is Woo?

Arthur Rimbaud: L'homme aux semelles de vent (1995) (150mins) (a Canada-France co-production) d: Marc Rivière s: Jean-Louis Benoît : Laurent Malet, Jacques Bonnaffe, Florence Pernel, Franck Lapersonne, Yan Epstein, Samuel Labarthe, Thierry Frémont. An impressive document recalling the last ten years of the life of Arthur Rimbaud, the great fig-

ure of French literature, after he had stopped writing poetry and went to Africa to seek his fortune, travelling through Morocco, Ethiopia, and into Yemen. He became a man determined to forget his poetry and his art. He is powerfully portrayed by Laurent Malet.

Artichoke (1978) (90mins) d: Stanley Olson s: Joanna Glass (based on her play of the same title) : Patricia Collins, Frank Adamson, David Gardner, Robert Christie, Tami Tucker. It's always rewarding to see on screen actors who are better known for their stage performances. Here, a group of well-regarded actors (who are working in Manitoba) brings life to this tangled tale of friendship, love and betrayal in a moving and very honest Canadian style.

Artificial Lies (*Le manipulateur***)** (2000) (93mins) d: Rodney Gibbons s: David Wiechorek : Jack Wagner, Daphne Zuniga, Stewart Bick, Claudia Ferri, Maxim Toy. A psychiatrist is found murdered, and the police investigating the crime discover that one of his patients was his lover. The lover finds herself a suspect, and the inevitable complications follow in this rather tame thriller.

Ascent, The (1994) (96mins) d: Donald Shebib s: David Wiltse : Vincent Spano, Joe Valadez, Ben Cross, Jon Freeman, Tony Lo Biano, Rico Vanden Hurek, Rachel Ward, Kenneth Mason, Mark Ingall, Nigel Kynaston, John De Veillers. Set in a POW camp on a dusty plain near Mt. Kenya in British East Africa during World War II, this suspense drama is about Italian soldiers who try to best their British captors by climbing the mountain and raising the Italian flag. They may have lost the war, but in this they would be the victors. Based on a true story, this is a gripping, often funny and splendidly acted and made film.

Assassin jouait du trombone, L': see **Keep an Eye on the Trombone**

Assistant, The (1996) (105mins) (a Canadian-American film) d&s: Daniel Petrie (from the novel by Bernard Malamud) : Gil Bellows, Armin Mueller-Stahl, Joan Plowright, Kate Greenhouse. A young drifter during the Great Depression robs a grocery store owned by an elderly Jew. The thief, wracked with guilt over what he has done, persuades the shopkeeper to let him work without pay and to give him the chance to make amends. A beautifully told tale of remorse and redemption. Knowingly directed by Petrie with a splendid cast.

At the Autumn of Life (The Human Misery) (*À l'automne de la vie***) (***La misère humaine***)** (1987) (105mins) d&s: Yvan Chouinard : Blaise Gagnon, Sylvia Potvin. Travelling around Rimouski, Baie-Comeau and other scenic places in Québec, a young traveller is stranded in a village when his motorcycle is stolen. He meets a young waitress in the cafe and falls in love with her. It is autumn. They decide to stay in the village, but life is anything but smooth for them. A slight but charming romance.

At the End of the Day: The Sue Rodriguez Story (1998) (120mins) d: Sheldon Larry s: Linda Svendsen : Wendy Crewson, Al Waxman, Carl Marotte, Patrick Galligan. From the time she was diagnosed with amyotrophic lateral sclerosis (ALS), Susan Rodriguez struggled to fight for her life. The disease brought with it complete paralysis and constant pain. She then fought for the right to die by euthanasia, which is forbidden under Canada's Criminal Code. Her wishes were refused by the courts. "Who owns my life?" she asked. Her fight became one of the most public debates in Canada's history. This film faithfully and honestly relates her tragedy with a deeply moving performance by Wendy Crewson as Susan Rodriguez.

At the Midnight Hour (1995) (120mins) d: Charles Jarrott s: Joseph Wiesenfeld (from the novel by Alicia Scott) : Patsy Kensit, Keegan MacIntosh, Cynthia Dale, Lindsay Merrithew. A well-told contemporary murder mystery and romance about a widowed scientist, his estranged son and the nanny who brings new meaning into their lives. But the nanny soon finds her own life threatened when she becomes aware of how the late wife had died. (See: *Harlequin* series)

Atanarjuat: The Fast Runner (*L'homme nu*) (2000) (120mins) d: Zacharias Kunuk, Paul Apak Angilirq s: Inuit elders, Paul Apak Angilirq : Natar Ungalaaq, Peter Arnatiaq, Sylvia Ivalu, Lucy Tulugarjuk, Paul Qulitalika. Kunuk has adapted the ancient legend of an evil shaman and the long-standing rivalry between two families. Atanarhuat following an attempt on his life escapes into the Arctic wilderness, but returns to confront the evil that threatens his community. The intrigue which this brings about gives us an authentic inside portrait of Inuit life. There has never been anything like this on film before. (note: described by the National Film Board (NFB) as the world's first Inuit produced and directed feature film) (Highly regarded at the Cannes F.F.).

Atlantic City, U.S.A (1980) (104mins) (a Canada-France co-production of an American film set in the United States) d: Louis Malle s: John Guare : Burt Lancaster, Susan Sarandon, Kate Reid, Michel Piccoli, Hollis McLaren, Robert Joy, Al Waxman, Robert Goulet, Sean Sullivan, Louisdel Grande, Eleanor Beecroft, Sean McCann, Cec Linder. This character study of gamblers, losers and the down-and-out is notable for Burt Lancaster's fine performance as a flashy small-time crook who realizes his game is over. Excellent cameos by supporting Canadian players. On its release in Canada, this hybrid was highly praised by Canadian critics as being a distinguished Canadian film.

Attache ta tuque (2003) (98mins) d: Denis Boivin s: Boivin & Anastasia Bourlakova : Wally Cheezo, Ioulia Volka, Brenda Papatie, Marianne Cheezo, Jean-Louis Fontaine. Largely filmed in the Anishnabe Innu and Wendate communities of Quebec, we meet a young Native man who leaves home to visit his girlfriend. On the way he meets a young Russian woman and decides to accompany her instead on her journey. Not very nice of him, but there you are, unknown scenery, pleasant with the ethnic touch!

Au clair de la lune: see **Moonshine**

Au fil de l'eau (**By the Riverside**) (2002) (90mins) (a Canada-France co-production) d&s: Jeannine Gagné : Gabriel Gascon, Margot Campbell, Frédérique Collin, Claude Laroche, Guy Thauvette, Paul Ahmarani, Michelle Rossignol. Four men and three women find themselves in a strange place, which could be a forest. It's a hard fantasy life, and as if what ails them isn't enough, they are haunted by memories of love and childhood. All something of a nightmare, actually, but strangely affecting, with all manner of meanings.

Au pays de Zom: see **In the Land of Zom**

Au plus pres du paradis: see **Nearest to Heaven**

Au revoir, à Lundi: see **Goodbye, See You Monday**

Au rythme de mon coeur: see **To the Rhythm of My Heart**

August 32nd on Earth (*Un 32 août sur terre*) (1998) (88mins) d&s: Denis Villeneuve : Pascale Bussières, Alexis Martin, Richard Hamilton, Paule Baillargeon. This is a wafer-thin drama about a self-centered young woman who cannot pull herself together after being in an auto accident. She calls a male friend and suggests they have a baby together. He agrees on condition that the sexual act be consummated in the desert. And so they go to Utah. This plot line and the film itself are so ridiculous as to be laughable. But no one laughs in this dreary concoction. Fine photography marks this self-indulgent work as being quite clearly all style and no substance.

August and July (1973) (92mins) d: Murray Markowitz s: Francesca Krushen : Sharon Smith, Alexa De Wiel. Two young women, close and affectionate friends, spend a tranquil summer holiday at a remote Ontario farm. A film of delicacy and charm, pleasing to watch. Later, all-knowing critics declared it to be the first Canadian film about a lesbian relationship. This analysis is open to interpretation, however.

Aujourd'hui ou jamais: see **Today or Never**

Aurora Borealis (*Une aurore boréale*) (1981) (90mins) d: René Lucot s: Jean-Claude Deret (based on the novel of the same title by Jacques Folch-Ribas) : Charlotte Laurier, Marcel Leboeuf. A lovely story delicately told about a Métis living on the banks of the St. Lawrence River. His world changes when he meets a young orphan girl from the city. She teaches him to read, and he introduces her to the world of nature. When summer ends, she returns to the city and he is left asking himself whether they will ever see each other again.

Aurore et crepuscule: see **Cosmos**

Autobiography of an Amateur Filmmaker, The (L'autobiographe amateur) (1999) (116mins) d&s: Claude Fortin : Claude Fortin, Brigitte Lacasse, Madeleine Bélair, Pierre Goupil, Gaspard Fortin, Mireille Charron. A cineaste wins a prize for his first film, and this encourages him to record his life story with family and friends. A great mistake. With this slow, heavy-going, flimsy piece, Fortin holds the doubtful distinction of having made one of the most boring, self-indulgent and never-ending movies in the annals of Québec film.

Automne sauvage, L' (The Savage Autumn) (1992) (102mins) (French, English, Japanese and Attikamek versions) d: Gabriel Pelletier s: Robert Girardi, Gabriel Pelletier : Serge Dupire, Anne Létourneau, Raymond Bouchard, Raoul Trujillo, Marie-Josée Gauthier, Leslie Yéo. The small community of Indian Heart has seen years of conflict and hostility between native and European settlers. The film shows how logging and land claims issues have become tangled up in family relations, friendships and the secrets of some with regard to a murder. Very well done, neither sensational nor over-dramatized, with particularly well-drawn characters.

Autour de la maison rose (Around the Pink House) (1999) (92mins) (a Canada-France-Lebanon co-production) d&s: Joana Hadjithomas, Khalil Joreige : Mireilla Safa, Joseph Bou Nassar, Hanane Abboud, Asma Andraos. Lebanon's civil war is over, and Beirut is trying to clean up the damage by pulling down bombed buildings. One such building is a pink mansion that served as a place of refuge during the war. Land developers want to destroy the house, but various families fight to save it for historic and sentimental reasons. This is a new view of a universal social issue and an interesting look at Lebanon.

Autre bord du fleuve, L': see **Dollar, The**

Autre homme, Un (Another Man) (1991) (85mins) d: Charles Binamé s: Marcel Beaulieu : Denis Bouchard, Dorothée Berryman, Gilbert Cantois, Louise Marleau, Louise Latraverse, Gildor Roy. A satirical yet penetrating look into the human condition as seen through the life of a long-time parliamentarian who, after suffering an airplane crash, must pull himself out of depression and make peace with himself. An absorbing lesson in dignity and humanity.

Autumn Born (1979) (74mins) d: Lloyd Simandl s: Shannon Lee : Dorothy Stratten, Ihor Procak, Dory Jackson, Giselle Faedette. A family business in Manitoba runs into difficulties when a wealthy orphan decides to take control once she becomes 18. Average and strained.

Avalanche Alley (2001) (92mins) (a U.S.-Canada film) d: Paul Ziller s: Elizabeth Sanchez and Paul Ziller : Ed Marinaro, Nick Mancuso, Kirsten Robek, Wolf Larson. A small ski resort and lodge (could be Jasper or Banff) is in nothing but trouble—both financially and in terms of the personal relationships among the guests. And now an avalanche could bury the lot of them. One disaster after another, with the film itself being a disaster in spite of having the worthy Roger Corman listed as the executive producer.

Avec des amis: see **With Friends Like These**

Aventures d'un agent très spécial, Les (The Adventures of a Very Special Agent) (1985) (68mins) d&s: Roger Normandin : Roger Normandin, Serge Linch, Denis Lavoie, Jean-Guy Fortin. A private detective becomes involved in a startling series of misadventures while investigating break-ins at cottages in the Mauricie region of Québec. Too brief and inconsequential to arouse much interest.

Aventures d'une jeune veuve, Les (1974) (94mins) d: Roger Fournier s: Fournier and André Dubois : Dominique Michel, Claude Michaud, Jacques Bilodeau, J.-Léo Gagnon, Amulette Garneau, Denis Drouin. A likeable comedy set in rural Québec and woven around family and friendly relations.

Aventures du grand nord, Les (Adventures in the Great North) (Tales of the Wild) (1995) (a Canada-France co-production) This production consists of six made-for-tv feature films that run approximately 95 minutes each. Filmed in northern Canada, with snow, sleighs, wolf dogs and the mountains serving as backdrops for stories about heroes and villains, passionate love affairs, murder, betrayal and life-threatening adventures. The whole series is a rewarding enterprise.See Under resepective titles: *Warrior Spirit, Legends of the North, The Other Side of the Law, Blood of the Hunter, Kazan* and *Barée*.

Aventuriers du timbre perdu, Les: see **Tommy Tricker and the Stamp Traveller**

Avoir 16 ans: see **To Be Sixteen**

Awakening, The (1995) (120mins) d: George Bloomfield s: Maria Nation (from the novel by Patricia Coughlin) : Cynthia Geary, David Beecroft, Sheila McCarthy, Maurice Godin. A single and sensible young woman takes in boarders at her family home to help with the mortgage payments. She rents out a room to a man who, unbeknownst to her, is an international criminal on the run from a bounty hunter. She agrees to help him, leading to emotional upsets when the two become attracted to each other. Effectively done, with genuine characters. (See: *Harlequin* series)

Awakening, The (L'amour humain) (1970) (91mins) d: Denis Héroux s: Roger Fournier : Louise Marleau, Jacques Riberolles, Ovila Légaré, Germaine Giroux, Charlotte Boisjoli, Suzanne Valéry. A nun and a priest fall in love. They leave their respective orders, get married and learn to enjoy sex without guilt. Quite touching at times.

Babel (1999) (96mins) (a Canada-France co-production) d: Gerard Pullicino s: Vincent Lambert, Gerard Pullicino : Mitchell David Rothpan, Maria De Medeiros, Michel Jonasz, Tcheky Karyo, Bronwen

Booth. A strange family film about television programs and children known as "babels" who find help from a 10-year-old. Too much television can do things like this to viewers.

Baby John Doe, The: see **Kidnapping of Baby John Doe, The**

Baby on Board (1992) (90mins) (a U.S.-Canada film) d: Francis Schaeffer s: James Shavick : Judge Reinhold, Alex and Holly Stapley, Carol Kane, Geza Kovacs. A woman kills her husband's murderer, leaves her baby with a cab driver, and goes on the run from the gangsters they were mixed up with. A tiresome violent slapstick of errors. Run for the nearest exit. Set and filmed in NYC.

Babyface (1998) (112mins) d: Jack Blum s: Sharon Corder, Jack Blum : Lenore Zann, Elisabeth Rosen, Shawn Doyle, James Gallanders, Sharon Corder. Comparisons to *Lolita* can hardly be avoided while watching this film about a sexy 13-year-old girl who falls in love with her mother's boyfriend. While *Babyface* doesn't attempt to be another go at Nabakov or Kubrick, it has strong appeal and is deeply affecting in its depiction of suburban "ordinariness." There is also enough sadness and drama in the violent relationships shown to make it frequently and disturbingly real. These characters have lost control of their lives. The performances have depth and understanding.

Babylone (Halfway House) (1991) (95mins) (a Canada-Belgium co-production) d: Manu Bonnariage s: Luc Jabon, Manu Bonnariage : Frédéric Deban, Charlotte Laurier, Marie Tifo, Pierre Curzi. A low-life melodrama that is striking in its depiction of a drunken man, a husband and father, who gambles away the trailer that houses his family. When the man is accidentally killed by his wife, one of two sons takes the blame for his death and serves time in a halfway house known as Babylon. Further complications involve a second son. Filmed in Québec.

Bach and Broccoli (*Bach et bottine*) (1986) (95mins) d: André Melançon s: Bernadette Renaud, André Melançon : Mahee Paiement, Raymond Legault, Harry Marciano, France Arbour, Andrée Pelletier. This is the story of Fanny, an 11-year-old orphan, and a tame skunk named Broccoli who is the only thing she has kept from her past. When Fanny is forced to live with her uncle, a middle-aged bachelor whose only passion in life is the music of Bach, she brings chaos and ultimately love to his organized but lonely life. A clever study of an adult-child relationship. (See: *Tales for All* series)

Back Stab (1990) (90mins) (a U.S.-Canada film) d: James Kaufman s: Paul Koval : James Brolin, Dorothée Berryman, Meg Foster, June Chadwick, Robert Morcelli, Brett Halsey. This complicated and predictable thriller opens with familiar crowded party drinking scenes, followed by humping back-seat car sex. The man in question, an architect, after a night with the woman, wakes to find her gone, with his boss in the bed, stabbed to death. He's arrested, and the plot then follows a broken trail, going through the courts and finally arriving at a flat and simplistic conclusion after involving several suspects, mostly women. The backgrounds, courts, police and characters are all American.

Back to Beulah (1974) (60mins) d&s: Eric Till (based on the play by W.O. Mitchell) : Jayne Eastwood, Norma Renault, Martha Henry, Tony van Bridge. Here, a young boy comes of age and develops a wider appreciation of the world around him. Beautifully portrayed by the director and his cast. This led to Mitchell's famous novel *Who Has Seen the Wind?*

Back to God's Country (1919) (72mins) d: David Hartford s: Nell Shipman, James Oliver Curwood (based on his short story "Wapi the Walrus") : Nell Shipman, Ralph Laidlaw, Wheeler Oakman, Charles Arling, Wellington Playter. A straight-to-the-heart melodrama about a young girl living in the forest. Her father is murdered, she is assaulted, and everywhere she goes up into the snowy reaches of the far north, she runs into the villain. This story of love and adventure in the North with a dog called *Wapi* is an important film from the early days of Canadian cinema, and Nell Shipman made a name for herself when it was almost unheard of for women to act in and produce films. She and her producer husband Ernest Shipman were the two most prolific and popular personalities during the silent period of Canadian film. The scene when she is washing under a waterfall and appears to be nude was quite risqué for its time. In the NFB documentary *Dreamland,* Donald Brittain provides a hilarious commentary on the story. (Remade in Hollywood with Rock Hudson by director Joseph Pevney, 1953.)

Back to God's Country (1953) (78mins) d: Joseph Pevney s: Tom Reed : Rock Hudson, Steve Cochran, Marcia Henderson. A sea captain and his wife are stranded in the Canadian wilderness thanks to a jealous villain. Hollywood's version of Curwood's story, complete with dog!

Backlash: see *Ménace, La*

Backroads (Bear Walker) (2000) (82mins) d&s: Shirley Cheechoo : Renae Morriseau, Sheila Tousey, Shirley and Greta Cheechoo, Max Martini. *Backroads* go nowhere in this first film by Native Canadian Shirley Cheechoo. A muddled and strident piece of folk-tale mysticism set in the Canadian north during the 1970s, the movie deals with the lives of four sisters. Murder and rape seem to be their lot in life. It's hard for the viewer to accept much of what is shown because of the way it's presented. Filmed on Manitoulin Island.

Bad Faith (Cold Blooded) (1999) (99mins) d: Randy Bradshaw s: Ian Adams (from his novel) : Tony Nardi, Gloria Reuben, Michael Moriarty, Patti LuPone, Kenneth Welsh, John Kapelos. A serial killer escapes from the police when an overzealous newspaper reporter releases confidential information about the crime. Not much to become involved with here.

Bad Money (1999) (95mins) d: John Hazlett s: Blake Brooker : Graham Greene, Karen Sillas, Stephen Spender, Alisen Down, Joe Turvey, Tamsin Kelsey. Four individuals and their families go to all lengths to keep up with their materialistic lifestyles. Described by its director as "a lively, satirical look at contemporary life," the film cuts very close to home.

Baker County, U.S.A.: see **Chatwill's Verdict**

Ballerina and the Blues, The (1987) (76mins) d: Glenn Bydwell s: Tannis Kobrin, Julian Roffman : Tamara Chaplin, Rex Smith, Jean-Pierre Matte, Dennis O'Conner. A young ballerina opens a dance school after a leg injury ends her stage career. A blues musician living in her apartment building distracts and annoys her with his constant playing. But music brings the two together in a romantic relationship. Light and easy to go with. (See: *Shades of Love* series)

Balls Up (1998) (94mins) d: Alan Erlich s: Richard Nielson : Albert Schultz, Brent Carver, Torri Higginson, Angelo Mosca. A good cast wasted in a trifle of nonsense going on within a scheme to beat the lottery. Hijinks all the way with no winners at the end.

Bananas From Sunny Québec (1993) (93mins) d: Peter Pearson s: Terence Heffernan : Marc Marut, Mathieu Kermoyan, Jessica Barker. A cheerful family film about children, set in 1956, where dreams and reality mix in a fantasy of adventure and make-believe.

Bar Salon (1974) (84mins) d: André Forcier s: Jacques Marcotte, André Forcier : Guy L'Écuyer, Jacques Marcotte, Madeleine Chartrand, Lucille Blair, Gélinas Fortin, Michèle Dion, André Forcier. An extraordinary low-budget film about the owner of a small pub in an impoverished area of Montréal, his customers, and their respective failings and bleak futures. Mostly a hopeless lot, they are observed with a stark realism and a love for the lower depths of cinema expressionism.

Barbaloune (2002) (118mins) d&s: Jean Gagné and Serge Gagné : Patrick Robert, Kathia Cambron, Benoît Ranger, Valentine Cambron, Jocelyn Bérubé. Made by the brothers Gagné, known by some audiences for their underground films, this one tries to tell a baffling tale about a young cineaste trying to be involved in making a film about an explorer lost at the North Pole. This is the kind of undertaking that will be a masterpiece to some and a major headache to others.

Barbara James (2001) (80mins) d: Winston Washington Moxan s: Gerry Atwell, Storma McDonald and Moxan : Storma McDonald, Ross MacMillan, Ron Dini, Mariette Kiroual, Valentina Wilson, Miako Watson. Barbara James is a pregnant woman in Winnipeg who attempts to come to terms with a life that has been nothing but mistakes,

miscalculations, misinterpretations and sheer misery. Storma McDonald portrays this sad existence realistically, and for the most part, the film is human and affecting.

Barbarian Invasions, The (*Invasions Barbares, Les***)** (2003) (113mins) (a Canada-France co-production) d&s: Denys Arcand : Remy Girard, Stephane Rousseau, Dorothee Berryman, Marie-Josee Croze, Dominique Michel, Louise Portal, Marina Hands, Johanne Marie Temblay, Yves Jacques, Pierre Curzi. The genius that is Arcand has given us one of the truly great films of our time. It would be possible to write pages describing and determining the elements of this study of characters hovering between life and death while making everything seem so humourous and honestly funny. If this is a sequel, in this case to *The Decline and Fall of the American Empire* made 17 years ago, then there has never been as brilliant as one like this before, capturing and portraying these later years of the characters we met in the original film, most played by the original actors, who cannot be faulted. It is nostalgic, bittersweet, and satirical yet wise about love and life, vice and virtue, politics and pretentiousness. It is all Arcand, with his humour, charm and clear-minded intellectual expressionism. And behind it all, we can imagine his serious creativity, mixed with his spontaneous laughter and sense of enjoyment. If we were to mention just one humourous strain, it's the barbs at the expense of Canada's mismanaged health service. Thanks for unforgettable work of cinema.

Battle of St. Denis... Yesterday, Today, The (*St-Denis dans le temps***)** (1969) (85mins) d&s: Marcel Carrière : Marie-Claire Nolan, Gilles Philippe Delorme, Donovan Carter, Jackson Quirk. A Québec couple visits St. Denis street in Montréal on the anniversary of the battle of Saint Denis that took place during the 1837 Rebellion. They are disturbed to see that many of the street's historical references to St. Denis have been allowed to deteriorate. But the St. Denis theatre remains. As the cinema where many Québec-made films had their premieres, it holds a special place in the hearts of Montréal moviegoers, and in Quebec's film history.

Battle Queen 2020 (Millennium Queen 2000) (2000) (92mins) (a Canada-U.S. film) d: Daniel D'Or s: William Bostjancic, Michael Druxman, Caron Nightingale : Julie Strain, Jeff Wincott, William Baker, Brian Frank, Celia Hart. In 2020, a sensual headmistress entertains a group of powerful men while trying to bridge the gap between those who are rich and those who are poor. There are lots of scantily dressed girls around. All very peculiar.

Bay Boy, The (1984) (100mins) (a Canada-France co-production) d&s: Daniel Petrie : Liv Ullmann, Kiefer Sutherland, Mathieu Carrière, Peter Donat, Alan Scarfe, Jane McKinnon, Isabelle Mejias, Thomas Peacocke, Leah Pinsent, Peter Spence,

Chris Wiggins, Stéphane Audran. The director returned from Los Angeles to write and direct this recollection of his boyhood in Nova Scotia. The principal event concerns his witnessing a murder. It is beautifully made, intelligently told and charmingly acted by the young players. But, at times, predictable and remote. This is Leah (daughter of Gordon) Pinsent's first film.

Bay of Love and Sorrows, The (2002) (97mins) d: Tim Southam s: Southam and David Adams Richards (based on his novel) : Peter Outerbridge, Jonathan Scarfe, Joanne Kelly, Christopher Jacot, Elaine Cassidy, Zachary Bennett, Torquil Campbell. David Adams Richards has written several humane and successful stories and screenplays, but this is not one of them. Set in the countryside of Miramichi River, New Brunswick, and the town of Newcastle, it tells a confused, tangled tale of a farming family whose raving-mad members destroy themselves. Hard to believe and even harder to watch.

Bayo (1985) (100mins) d&s: Mort Ransen : Ed McNamara, Patricia Phillips, Stephen McGrath, Hugh Webster. Based on Chipman Hall's novel *Lightly,* this film presents a view of Canada not seen since Gordon Pinsent's *The Rowdyman*. The setting is Newfoundland, and the story concerns a young boy, his relationship with his seagoing grandfather and his conflict with his divorced mother, who wants to pursue a more exciting life in Toronto. Quietly told with a spirited cast, but slow and limp in developing its points. A likeable tale about kindly people.

Bean Pole Man, The (*Homme perché***)** (1996) (67mins) d&s: Stefan Pleszczyhski : Marcel Sabourin, France Arbour, Lise Roy, François Papineau, Brigitte Paquette. Here, the veteran Québec actor Marcel Sabourin, whom one thinks of as having been in almost every Québec film ever made, plays the role of a man who decides to spend the last days of his life in a tree near his farm in the Eastern Townships south of Montréal. There, he plans to contemplate the mystery of the natural world around him. This lovely little film works as a bittersweet fable, a morality tale and an often whimsical comedy. The cast might well have been raised in the country surroundings.

Bear Island (1979) (118mins) (a Canada-U.K. co-production) d: Donald Sharp s: David Butler, Murray Smith, Donald Sharp (based on the novel by Alistair McLean) : Donald Sutherland, Vanessa Redgrave, Richard Widmark, Christopher Lee, Barbara Parkins, Lloyd Bridges, Lawrence Dane, Patricia Collins, August Schellenberg, Bruce Greenwood. A splendid novel about intrigue, murder and missing bullion becomes a disappointing film. But it's hard to fault the directing, acting or the splendid photography. It's simply that the whole becomes too hard to bear!

Bear Walker: see **Backroads**

Bear With Me (2000) (96mins) d: Paul Ziller s: Lewis Chesler, Paul Ziller : Kaitlyn Burke, Michael Ontkean, Helen Shaver, Kimberley Warnat, Gordon Tootoosis, Eric Johnson, Alan Thicke, Kristian Ayre. A sequel of sorts to *Ms. Bear,* this film places us back in the wilderness of British Columbia with a family of nature lovers and Masha the bear, who was saved from poachers in the previous film and has since grown very big. This good-looking adventure in nature makes ideal family entertainment and presents a serious argument for the protection of animals and their habitat.

Beat (1976) (64mins) d&s: André Blanchard : Bertrand Gagnon, Nicole Scant, Dominique Ayotte, Daniel Laurendeau. A minor teen musical lining a creaky and limp comedy-drama about the diversity of opinions among individuals who also have a lot in common. Set in the mining town of Rouyn-Noranda in northeastern Québec.

Beauté de Pandore, La: see **Beauty of Pandora, The**

Beauté des femmes, La: see **Beauty of Women, The**

Beautiful Dreamers (1990) (107mins) d&s: John Kent Harrison : Rip Torn, Colm Feore, Wendel Meldrum, Sheila McCarthy, Colin Fox. The 19TH-century American writer Walt Whitman made a short visit to London, Ontario, in 1880 to stay with Dr. Maurice Bucke and discuss sex and mental illness. This, Harrison's first feature, is a picture postcard pastiche that is not always true to historical fact, but the performances are pleasing.

Beautiful Facade, A (*La belle apparence***)** (1979) (93mins) d&s: Denyse Benoît : Anouk Simard, Françoise Berd, Michel Gagnon, Anne-Marie Ducharme. A woman visiting a convict in a Montréal prison finds herself becoming psychologically affected by her visits. The situation worsens when he is released, they meet again, and fall in love. A troublesome issue as seen from a woman's point of view. Intelligently done.

Beautiful Sundays (*Les beaux dimanches***)** (1974) (93mins) d: Richard Martin s: Marcel Dubé (based on his play) : Jean Duceppe, Louise Portal, Denise Filiatrault, Yvon Dufour, Luce Guilbeault, Andrée Lachapelle, Yves Létourneau, Gérard Poirier, Robert Maltais, Catherine Bégin. On the morning after holding a party for neighbours and friends, a husband and wife talk about the emptiness of their life. This leaves the audience with more than enough to reflect on, including their own lives. A nicely observed and knowing look at life.

Beauty of Pandora, The (*La beauté de Pandore***)** (2000) (92mins) d: Charles Binamé s: Suzanne Jacob, Charles Binamé : Jean-François Casabonne, Gary Boudreault, Pascale Bussières, Annick Bergeron, Maude Guérin. An overcharged, overplayed, high-gloss melodrama about a woman who sleeps with a married man and then tells him that she has HIV. The sex scenes leave nothing out. The agonizing accusations that follow, along with the declarations of love, become absurd. At the end, the woman catches a bus and travels to Arizona. Upon arriving in the desert, she walks toward the distant horizon and into the film's final fade—never, one hopes, to be seen again. The fast and furious location shooting of Montréal on rainy days is the film's only asset. The screenwriter should also have known that there is only one Pandora in cinema: Louise Brooks. And how she would have laughed at this atrocity.

Beauty of Women, The (La beauté des femmes) (1994) (83mins) d: Robert Ménard s: Claire Wojas : Monique Spaziani, Marc Béland, Jean-Louis Roux, Dorothée Berryman, Louise Latraverse. Three beautiful women have much in common; they are all in their 30s, own a clothing boutique and dream of commercial success in the design industry. But, of course, there are career problems and the sadness of loves lost. Slender material but easy to take.

Beaux dimanches, Les: see **Beautiful Sundays**

Beaux souvenirs, Les: see **Happy Memories**

Because Why (Parce que Pourquoi) (1993) (110mins) d&s: Arto Paragamian : Michael Riley, Martine Rochon, Doru Bandol, Heather Mathieson, John Dunn-Hill, Victor Knight. An eccentric and unconventional ramble about an urban tragic-funny Everyman who decides to end five years of wanderings and find some stability in life. He takes over a friend's apartment in Montréal, only to be thrown in with a collection of unlikely, eccentric and unpredictable characters. This is a repetitious, self-indulgent and depressing exercise in innocence and confusion.

Beckett on Film series: see **Happy Day, and Krapp's Last Tape**

Becoming Laura (1982) (90mins) d: Martin Lavut s: Rob Forsyth : Jennifer Jewison, Deborah Kipp, Neil Dainard, Sherry Hoffman and the Sharks. Combining documentary of street kids with drama using professional actors, this chapter of contemporary life brings up the problems of adolescent depression and crisis through the experience of a troubled teenage daughter and the responses of worried parents. (See: *For the Record*)

Bed, The: see **Lit, Le**

Bedroom Eyes (1984) (89mins) d: William Fruet s: Michael Alan Eddy : Kenneth Gilman, Dayle Haddon, Christine Cattell, James B. Douglas, Roy Wordsworth. While on his nightly jog, a successful Toronto stockbroker catches glimpses of sexual activity in the homes he passes. One night, he witnesses a murder; very soon, the killer is after him. A nifty murder-melodrama, if not always believable.

Beefcake (1999) (90mins) d&s: Thom Fitzgerald : Daniel MacIvor, Jonathan Torens, Joshua Peace, Carroll Godsman, Jack Griffen Mazeika, Joe Dallesandro, Jack LaLanne. Looking somewhat like a faded 1950s scrapbook, this docu-drama tries to recreate the heyday of the American muscle magazine *Physique Pictorial* and its editor, Bob Mizer (well played by Daniel MacIvor), who brought male models into the world of advertising through more than 500,000 photographs. Financed largely by the U.K.'s Film Four, *Beefcake* evokes interest in recalling a time when homosexuality was a crime and censorship was draconian. However, the healthy young men capering about in their "posing pouches" seem to have distracted the director from keeping track of his narrative. The Hollywood settings, mocked up in Halifax, Nova Scotia, studios do look like the pastel tourist postcards of the time.

Before the Time Comes (Le temps de l'avant) (1975) (88mins) d: Anne-Claire Poirier s: Louise Carré, Marthe Blackburn, Anne-Claire Poirier : Luce Guilbeault, Paule Baillargeon, Pierre Gobeil, J.-Léo Gagnon, Marisol Sarrazin, Nicolas Dufresne. This was the first film from Québec (or any other part of Canada) to deal with the subject of abortion. Here, a 40-year-old pregnant woman thinks seriously of having an abortion. Her husband won't hear of it. Not only does he want this child, but also a great many more. Anne-Claire Poirier has blazed many trails since in her concern to show, on film, issues important to women.

Beijing: see **Bullet to Beijing (Len Deighton's Bullet to Beijing)**

Being at Home With Claude (1992) (85mins) d&s: Jean Beaudin (from a story by René-Daniel Dubois) : Roy Dupuis, Jacques Godin, Jean-François Pichette, Gaston Lepage. A police inspector is interrogating a young homosexual, trying to understand why he has murdered his lover. Apart from some dramatic black and white photography of Montréal by night, this film takes place in the panelled study of a home. Slightly static and dry, and perhaps better suited to the stage, this film is of interest because it was one of the first Canadian films to deal openly with the subject of homosexuality. Roy Dupuis became a star in Québec due to his appearance here, although many observers thought it an odd film for Beaudin to make. At the same time this film was being shot, Beaudin completed 20 episodes of the immensely popular tv Québec family series *Les Filles de Caleb*, which were broadcast on Radio-Canada, the CBC's French-language network, and translated for the CBC's English-language network as *Caleb's Daughters*.

Believe (2000) (96mins) d: Robert Tinnell s: Richard Goudreau, Roc Lafortune (from Tinnell's story) : Elisha Cuthbert, Ben Gazzara, Andrea Martin, Jan Rubes, Stephanie Morgenstern. A tired thriller about a teenager living with his grandfather in Maine and discovering a ghost haunting the property. This should have been laid to rest before making its appearance.

Belle apparence, La: see **Beautiful Facade, A**

Belle étoile, La: see **Lucky Star, The**

Bells: see **Murder by Phone**

Bernie and the Gang (*Ti-mine Bernie pis la gang*) (1977) (124mins) : d: Marcel Carrière s: Jean P. Morrin : Marcel Sabourin, Jean Lapointe, Rita Lafontaine, J.-Léo Gagnon, Guy L'Écuyer, Anne-Marie Ducharme, Ginette Morin. A funny family comedy, lightly written and acted, about get-rich-quick fantasies and wonderful winters in Florida. It may be inferred that this is the secret dream of the Québécois!

Best Bad Thing, The (1997) (92mins) (a Canada-Japan co-production) d: Peter Rowe s: David Preston (based on *Ala*, a book by Yoshiko Uchida) : George Takei, Kirin Kiki, Robert Ito, Lana McKissack, Bryan Matsurra. This lovely, pastoral and gentle film based on the popular children's story depicts the struggle of a Japanese-American farm family trying to exist in rural California during the Great Depression. We see much of their life through the eyes of a young girl. This familiar situation is given new meaning and depth of understanding about a society different from our own in many ways.

Best Damn Fiddler From Calabogie to Kaladar, The (1968) (50mins) (b/w) d: Peter Pearson s: Joan Finnegan : Chris Wiggins, Kate Reid, Margot Kidder. (The 21st annual (reorganized) Canadian Film Awards competition was very successful in that it drew 110 entries and brought nationwide recognition to this beautiful, sensitively made 50-minute NFB dramatized documentary that had earlier been pushed aside and ignored by CBC-tv). *The Best Damn Fiddler From Calabogie to Kaladar* (two small communities in the Ottawa Valley) depicts a rural family struggling with poverty. Yet, it is not a dismal picture. It is infused with a love of life, of children and of freedom within society, no matter how unfavourable the socio-economic terms. (*Fiddler* won seven major awards, including best actor for Chris Wiggins. The international jury—comprised of Peter Watkins (U.K.), Elmer Bernstein and Delmer Daves (U.S.), and Joan Fox and Marc Gervais (Canada)—unanimously described it as "the best damn film" from anywhere. Kate Reid played the mother, and Margot Kidder made her first, and delightfully sexy, screen appearance. This was Peter Pearson's first film, and, until the awards were announced, he had been unable to find further work. The film was used as a brilliant example of what our filmmakers could do if they had the opportunities and the material to replace the run-of-the-mill American films that dominate our theatres and television—the kind of inexpensive creativity private broadcasters continue to say they cannot afford.

Best of Both Worlds (1983) (88mins) d: Douglas Williams s: Sugith Varughese : Sugith Varughese, Gaye Burgess, Malika Mendez. This is a slight but serious first work from Varughese about an East Indian immigrant who plans to marry a mail-order bride. But, after taking her generous dowry, he deserts her for his Canadian lady friend—not an uncommon practice. Tightly done and genuinely affecting.

Best Revenge (Misdeal) (1981) (96mins) (a Canadian-American film) d: John Trent s: David Rothberg (from his story) : John Heard, Levon Helm, Alberta Watson, John Rhys-Davies, Moses Znaimer, Michael Ironside, Sean Sullivan, August Schellenberg. This is a fast-moving action-adventure about two men involved in a scheme to obtain hashish and make a fortune. However, it becomes far-fetched and gets lost in its Spanish setting.

Bête de foire, La: see **Angel in a Cage**

Bethune (1977) (88mins) d: Eric Till s: Thomas Rickman : Donald Sutherland, Kate Nelligan, David Gardner, James Hong. An absorbing story and fine acting make this CBC biography of Bethune a living chronicle of the successes and triumphs he brought about by sheer willpower and courage. Next, the Chinese made a film tribute to him, *Baiquien Dafu (Dr. Norman Bethune)* (1964) (90mins) : Gerry Tannenbaum (an American actor living in China playing Bethune). Then came the big picture. **Bethune:** *The Making of a Hero* (1990) (120mins) (a Canada-China-France co-production) d: Phillip Borsos s: Ted Allan (from his book) : Donald Sutherland, Helen Mirren, Helen Shaver, Colm Feore, James Pax, Ronald Pickup, Guo Da, Harrison Liu, Anouk Aimée. The life of Norman Bethune was the subject of two books: one by Roderick Stewart, the other by Ted Allan and Sydney Gordon. Otto Preminger tried for many years to bring Stewart's book to the screen, but Canadian financing for it never materialized. Ted Allan's book was to have been made into a film by John Kemeny and Ted Kotcheff, but nothing came of it until 1990, when this movie was produced in China. It had a $30-million budget and was one of the most expensive Canadian films ever made until that time, but the production was poorly managed. There were disagreements between writers, producers, actors and the director. The result was a patchwork of a picture in episodic parts, covering everything from Bethune's love life to his work during the Spanish Civil War. Donald Sutherland plays Bethune without revealing much about his beliefs and his inner passions. The late Phillip Borsos, ever the gentleman, was patient to the bitter end and never joined in the mud-slinging and finger-pointing to blame others for this botched effort. For the documentary see: **Bethune** (1965) (60mins) (b/w) d&s: Donald Brittain. This superior documentary-drama by one of Canada's most distinguished filmmakers was the first of four films devoted to Norman Bethune, the well-known Canadian doctor, scholar and philosopher. Much of Bethune's dramatic and controversial life shown here comes from films and photography. He is rightly seen as a hero in his native Canada, but it is in China that his legend, strengthened by his premature death, lives on. There, he is called the White One in respectful remembrance of the unceasing care he gave to Mao Tse-tung's soldiers during the Chinese civil war of the 1930s and '40s. Bethune pioneered the practice of taking blood to the front lines to treat soldiers rather than waiting for them to be brought to medics working behind the line of fire. For its sheer power of detail and narrative control, this biographical film ranks with the work of Erwin Leiser and Paul Rotha.

Betrayed (2003) (90mins) d: Anne Wheeler s: Wheeler & Jeremy Hole : Kari Matchett, Michael Hogan, Janet Wright, Raoul Trujillo. Three years after tainted water killed seven people, with hundreds more still suffering from E coli in an Ontario town, Walkerton, we have this film which is based every so slightly on this tragedy which came about through the incompetence of two brothers who worked at the filtration and treatment plant. But the CBC, part-producer of this film, out of fear of being sued, was not looking for a documentary. Instead we have a drama of a different kind, in which a recently divorced young mother returns to here hometown in Saskatchewan where her father works as the municipal water manager, and becomes a nurses' aid. The stress on the town's people is there, but that's it. The message? This could happen anywhere around the world. But audiences will say to themselves 'yes, this is Walkerton', and so the film cleverly brings it to the screen after all.

Better Than Chocolate (1999) (98mins) d: Anne Wheeler s: Sharon McGowan : Wendy Crewson, Karen Dwyer, Christina Cox, Ann-Marie MacDonald, Peter Outerbridge, Marya Delver, Kevin Mundy, Tonny Nappo, Jay Brazeau, Beatrice Zellinger. Lesbian love in Vancouver is the theme of this comedy that is partly based on the real-life difficulties of the Little Sisters bookshop in its struggles with Canadian customs over importing books about homosexual life. Well made and acted, this film would have been far more enjoyable had the usually reliable Anne Wheeler left the sexual activities of the protagonists to the imagination and spent more time satirizing the censors.

Betty Fisher and Other Stories (*Betty Fisher et autres histoires*) (2001) (102mins) (a Canada-France co-production) d&s: Claude Miller (based on *The Tree of Hands* by Ruth Rendell) : Sandrine Kiberlain, Nicole Garcia, Mathilde Seigner, Luck Mervil, Édouard Baer. Set in Paris, this marvellous and unusual film is difficult to describe because it involves many stories and characters and goes in many directions. It is a delightful web of separate narratives that become a cleverly directed collection of drama, comedy, romance and more. At the centre of the movie is Betty, a writer who has found fame with her work, but the plot revolves around the kidnapping of a young boy. This is not a children's film but very much a psychological statement for adults.

Very original—nothing quite like this had previously been done on the screen.

Betty Fisher et autres histories: see **Betty Fisher and Other Stories**

Between "tu" and "you": see *Entre tu et vous*

Between Friends (Get Back) (1973) (91mins) d: Donald Shebib s: Claude Harz : Michael Parks, Bonnie Bedelia, Chuck Shamata, Henry Beckman, Hugh Webster, August Schellenberg, Joanna Noyes, Michael Kirby. After becoming good friends in California, two young men meet again in Toronto and decide to steal the payroll of a mining company in Sudbury, Ontario. The scheme fails. A story as bleak as the winter snows and as desperate as the characters themselves, this is a poignant, understanding, and extremely honest film that further enhanced the reputation of Donald Shebib (*Goin' Down the Road*) as Canada's best English-language filmmaker. The moral of the movie is clearly stated: there is no easy way out of life's difficulties, whether they are emotional or physical, unless the individual is prepared to face them with confidence and determination.

Between Friends: see **Nobody Makes Me Cry**

Between Strangers (2002) (97mins) (an Italy-Canada co-production) d&s: Edoardo Ponti : Sophia Loren, Mira Sorvino, Deborah Kara Unger, Pete Postlethwaite, Klaus Maria Brandauer, Gerard Depardieu, Malcolm McDowell, Wendy Crewson. A great cast completely wasted in a complicated clichéd melodrama involving undeveloped characters in various stages of misery and remorse. Set and filmed in Toronto, with an Italian background.

Between Sweet and Salt Water (Drifting Downstream) (*Entre la mer et l'eau douce*) (1967) (85mins) (b/w) d: Michel Brault s: Denys Arcand, Marcel Dubé, Gérald Godin, Claude Jutra, Michel Brault. : Denise Bombardier, Geneviève Bujold, Robert Charlebois, Claude Gauthier, Paul Gauthier, Gérald Godin, Pauline Julien, Louise Latraverse, Suzanne Valéry. Michel Brault, who worked for the NFB and is an exponent of *cinéma-direct,* made *Entre la mer* his first feature in fictional and dramatized form. It has strong factual, political and documentary overtones. It is also a moving, if somewhat depressing, story (filmed in drab locations) of a lonely young man who leaves his home and his dull life in Québec's North Shore region to try his luck in Montréal. There, he gets a succession of jobs and falls in love with Geneviève, a pretty waitress working in a rundown café. Unexpectedly, he finds a career as a singer-songwriter—music by Claude Gauthier—and becomes attracted to another woman. Although he achieves success, he loses the waitresss, who was the only person to ever mean anything to him. He remains as lonely and unfulfilled as in his previous life.

Between the Moon and Montevideo (2000) (111mins) d&s: Attila Bertalan : Pascale Bussières, Attila Bertalan, Gérald Gagnon, Kena Molina.

Filmed on a scrap heap of rusting metal parts in crumbling Havana (passing for Montevideo), this is a picture of never-ending brutality and violence. It has a confused plot line, is shallow and repellent, and full of mostly nasty, vicious and ugly men who do nothing but fight, swear and use women for sex. Although a young boy adds a touch of innocence to this evil, the viewer remains unmoved by most of these characters and cannot respond to them. It strains belief to learn that several granting agencies, including Telefilm Canada, put up money to make this non-Canadian trash.

Between Two Loves: see **Where Two Roads Cross**

Beaux souvenirs, Les: see **Happy Memories**

Beyond Forty see *Quarantaine, La*

Beyond Suspicion (1993) (102mins) d: Paul Ziller s: Simon Abbott : Jack Scalia, Francesco Ferrucci, Stephanie Kramer, Roger Cross, Howard Dell. The murder of a policeman is witnessed by a journalist who begins a relationship with the dead man's friend, whom she discovers is not as free from suspicion as he first seemed. A tightly told little thriller with a romantic touch.

Big Bear (1988) (240mins) d: Gil Cardinal s: Gil Cardinal, Rudy Wiebe (based on Wiebe's novel *The Temptation of Big Bear*) : Gordon Tootoosis, Tantoo Cardinal, Michael Greyeyes, Iain Maclean, Ian Black, Gordon Sonmor, Mel Melymick and others. Set in 1875 against the hilly, green Qu'Appelle Valley in Saskatchewan, Big Bear and the Cree refuse to acknowledge British-Canadian ownership of the land. Armed resistance flares up leading to confrontation, imprisonment and deaths. Seen from the natives' point of view.

Big Day, The (*Le grand day*) (1988) (98mins) d: Jean-Yves Laforce s: Michel Tremblay : Charlotte Laurier, Michel Poirier, Louisette Dussault. A wonderful and human comedy about parents who are so determined to give their children a memorable wedding that it becomes a frustrating experience for everyone.

Big Meat Eater (1982) (81mins) d: Chris Windsor s: Phil Savath, Laurence Keane : George Dawson, Andrew Gillies, Clarence "Big" Miller, Stephen Dimopoulos, Georgina Hegedos. On a modest budget of $150,000, young filmmakers joined forces at Simon Fraser University in Vancouver to make this musical-comedy-horror-farce. One of the few comedy films made in Canada at the time, it strengthens the category considerably. It is so artless that it becomes entertaining, and the only mystery to the plot is in trying to find it. What little plot there is becomes further diffused by some delightful songs. The film is about a mad butcher and his equally mad friends, who become involved in some of the most awful capers ever found in B-movies!

Big Rock, the Big Man, The (*Le Grand Rock*) (1969) (73mins) d&s: Raymond Garceau : Francine Racette, Guy Thauvette, Pat Gagnon, Jacques Bilodeau, Ian Ireland, Ernest Guimond. A young trapper in northern Québec is very much his own man. He drinks and jokes with friends, meets a pretty young girl and marries her. But their marriage soon breaks down, and in attempting to get closer to her, he unknowingly becomes involved with criminal elements and his life becomes dark and lonely. Who is to blame? The film's often troubling answers reflect rural society as it was for many Québécois.

Big Sabotage, The (*Le grand sabordage*) (1973) (85min) (a Canada-France co-production) d: Alain Perisson s: Thierry Joly, Alain Viguier, Alain Perisson : Luce Guilbeault, Jean Dansereau, Bernard Gosselin, André Mélançon. A sensitive and charming portrait of two children and their life in the city.

Big Slice, The (1991) (85mins) d&s: John Bradshaw : Casey Siemaszko, Heather Locklear, Leslie Hope. In their desperation to become well known, two struggling writers devise a foolproof plan to bring them success. It doesn't work, of course; nor does this film.

Biker Wars: see **Last Chapter**

Bilan (2003) (72mins) d: Lorraine Pintal s: Gilles Desjardins (a film of the important play by Macel Dube) : Vincent Bilodeau, Ginette Morin, Maxime Gaudette, Henri Chasse. This is a rare and fascinating film of the kind we seldom, if ever, see among our motion pictures, a polished, sophisticated story about a wealthy and powerful Quebec business man who enters politics and becomes involved in conflict and intrigue, loses his family and his self-respect. Beautifully set, dressed and played out.

Billion Dollar Brain: see **Bullet to Beijing**

Bingo (1974) (112mins) d&s: Jean-Claude Lord : Réjean Guenette, Anne-Marie Provencher, Claude Michaud, Alexandra Stewart, Gilles Pelletier, Manda Parent, Janine Fluet, Jean Duceppe. The most important film of 1974, this is a disturbing, dramatic fiction with documentary overtones set in Montréal during the October crisis of 1970. Two young students are unwittingly involved in the *Front de Libération du Québec*, and their lives are destroyed by politics and big business. Under its deceptively lighthearted title, which refers to an aunt's mania for the game, *Bingo* brings out the ugliest aspects of French-Canadian nationalism. The film shifts its focus to terrorism, and the guilty go free while the innocent suffer. As right-wing factions plot to seize power, the tragedy of a society torn by indecision and despair reveals itself. Jean-Claude Lord never again made a film with such power and sense of purpose. (First shown outside Montreal at the Stratford Film Festival)

Bingo Robbers, The (2000) (85mins) d&s: Lois Brown, Barry Newhook : Barry Newhook, Lois Brown, Phil Dinn, Janis Spence, Sheila Redmond, Bryan Hennessey, Jody Richardson, Roger Maunder, Andy Jones, Ron Hynes. A loathsome couple, man and woman, having sex and swearing, with whom few would want to spend five minutes, pass time in St. John's committing armed robberies and arguing over who they are and what they are doing with their lives. Filmed in the digital mode. Not that it helps.

Birds of Prey (1985) (90mins) d: Jorge Montesi s: Peter Haynes : Jorge Montesi, Joseph Patrick, Linda Elder, Maurice Brand, Jennifer Keene, Mike Douglas. An aimless, pointless and dull story of a detective who thinks his friend has committed a murder until he finds out who really did it.

Bitter Ash, The (1963) (80mins) (b/w) d&s: Larry Kent : Alan Scarfe, Lynn Stewart, Philip Brown, Douglas Reid, Diane Griffith. This is a drama about a shiftless, talentless playwright who lives off the money his pregnant wife earns as a waitress. After a party, a sex-hungry woman friend pays him to go to bed with her. His wife then goes to bed with a young printer after a chance meeting. The wife ends up hating both men. This was Larry Kent's first film and made while he was at the University of British Columbia. At a time of much censorship of motion pictures, his film was banned everywhere, and so he arranged private showings to cover the film's $5,000 budget—a large sum at the time. The talented Kent played an important part in the new film movement slowly springing up in English Canada. In his early black and white films, he conveyed a down-to-earth realism, dramatic tension and sexual eroticism, which came as an unexpected force on screens that were then so empty of Canadian films.

Bitter Ash, The: see **Facade**

Black Angel, The: see **Ange noir, L'**

Black Cat in the Black Mouse Socks, The: see **Acts of Love** Series

Black Christmas (Silent Night, Evil Nights) (Stranger in the House) (1974) (98mins) (a Canadian-American film) d: Bob Clark s: Roy Moore : Olivia Hussey, Keir Dullea, Margot Kidder, Andrea Martin, Marian Waldman, Art Hindle, Lynne Griffin, James Edmond, Doug McGrath, John Saxon, Pamela Barney. A nasty, abysmal horror film about an unspeakable "something" that terrorizes a college for girls during the Christmas season. But, it made a lot of money.

Black List (Liste noire) (1995) (86mins) d: Jean-Marc Vallée s: Sylvain Guy : Michel Côté, Geneviève Brouillette, Sylvie Bourque, Raymond Cloutier, André Champagne, Louis-Georges Girard. A silly, sensational and nasty film about a prostitute blackmailing her clients: the judges, lawyers and politicians who represent the establishment of Québec and stop at nothing to take revenge on her and protect their position. A black mark for Québec cinema. It is the first Québec (French-language) film to be remade in English with U.S. actors set in the US) and was called The List. See also Caboose, The.

Black Mirror (Haute surveillance) (1981) (87mins) (a Canada-France co-production) d: Pierre Alain Jolivet s: Pierre Alain Jolivet, Jean-Claude Carrière, Arthur Samuels (from Jean Genet's play Haute surveillance) : Louise Marleau, Lenore Zann, Françoise Dorner, Alberta Watson, Carolyn Maxwell. A ludicrous, stylized and tiresome study of women in prison.

Black Robe (1991) (101mins) (a Canada-Australia co-production) d: Bruce Beresford s: Brian Moore (from his novel of the same title) : Lothaire Bluteau, Aden Young, August Schellenberg, Sandrine Holt, Tantoo Cardinal. Set in the hostile wilderness of 17TH-century New France (Québec), this compelling study of an ambitious young Jesuit driven by religious fervour to "save the souls of the savages" is intimate and introspective, yet epic and inspiring in its concept and realization. The cold, bleak, awe-inspiring wilderness is strikingly caught. A great film in every respect.

Black Swan (2002) (90mins) d: Wendy Ord s: Matt John Evans, Christopher Bruce, Wendy Ord : Melanie Doane, Michael Riley, Ted Dykstra, Matt John Evans, Hannah Clayton, Sammy Jay Osborne, Pam Lutz. A pity that this film, set against the beauty of the Bay of Fundy, in a small town that holds an annual Black Swan Festival, turns out to be anything but beautiful. A murder is thought to have taken place. The characters who inhabit this space are so ugly, in speech and behaviour, that one quickly tires of them. Two children provide some relief, Melanie Doane sings, the black swan is understandably missing.

Blackheart (1997) (92mins) d: Dominic Shiach s: Brad and Brock Simpson : Richard Grieco, Christopher Plummer, Fiona Loewi, Maria Conchita Alonso, Jack Duffy, Lisa Ryder, William MacDonald. Two unscrupulous men meet a beautiful heiress and scheme to make her part of their lives. A good cast cannot do much with this. Predictable and routine.

Blackout (Blackout in New York) (1978) (92mins) (a Canadian-American film) d: Eddy Matalon s: John C.W. Saxton, Jean-Jacques Tarbes : Jim Mitchum, Robert Carradine, Belinda Montgomery, June Allyson, Jean-Pierre Aumont, Ray Milland, Terry Haigh, Don Granbery, Victor Tyler. A silly pseudo-American disaster film: the power fails in New York and the city is terrorized by violent criminals. Rubbish.

Blacktop (2000) (99mins) d: T.J. Scott s: Kevin Lund, T.J. Scott : Lochlyn Munro, Kristin Davis, Meatloaf, Victoria Pratt, Blu Mankuma. Violent, mediocre and silly business about a boyfriend who goes after his angry girlfriend when she accepts a ride from a disreputable truck driver, who turns out to be a murderer. Overlong, but a well-staged finale with the speeding truck going over the cliff into the river, in B.C.

Blades of Courage: see **Skate**

Blanche and the Night (*Blanche et la nuit*) (1989) (85mins) d: Johanne Prégent s: Yvon Rivard, Johanne Prégent : Jean L'Italien, Léa Marie Cantin, René Gagnon, France Castel. A man stops the woman he loves from committing suicide and then goes to great pains to reawaken her interest in life. This troubles him, and he becomes dependent on her. Slight but serious stuff.

Blessed Stranger: After Flight 111 (2001) (120mins) d: David Wellington s: Michael Amo : Kate Nelligan, Hugh Thompson. Swissair Flight 111 crashed off the coast of Nova Scotia in 1998 with the loss of all 229 people aboard. The profound impact the accident had on the people of Peggy's Cove is seen through the relationship that develops between an American businesswoman who has travelled to the scene of the tragedy, desperately hoping that her daughter is not among the dead, and a fisherman, who goes out in his boat to help where possible. A sombre portrait of the tragedy. (See: *Signature* series)

Bleue, la magnifique: see **Magnificent Blue, The**

Blind Faith (1982) (65mins) d: John Trent s: Ian Sutherland : Allan Royal, Heath Lamberts, Rosemary Dunsmore. What is the appeal of tv's salvation hucksters to vast and profitable audiences? This report reveals the power of television as a medium that can be manipulated. The matter is given a human dimension through the pain of a middle-class housewife neglected by her husband. He has become part of a powerfully persuasive fundamentalist group that has learned all the tricks of the game of faith. (See: *For the Record*)

Blind Terror (2000) (94mins) d: Giles Walker s: Douglas Soesbe : Natassja Kinski, Maxim Roy, Stewart Bick, Gordon Pinsent, Victoria Snow, Jack Langedijk. A divorced husband tells his new wife that he suspects his first wife is mentally deranged and capable of violent behaviour. Wife no. 2 suspects wife no. 1 of having caused strange deaths. Is there a psychiatrist in the house? Confused but reasonably suspenseful.

Blind Trust: see **Intimate Power**

Blindside (1986) (103mins) (a Canadian-American film) d: Paul Lynch s: Richard Beattie : Harvey Keitel, Lori Hallier, Michael Rudder, Marc Strange, Lolita Davidovich. A bleak, minor movie in which a former surveillance expert from the U.S. buys a Canadian hotel, spies on his guests and becomes involved in a murder plot. Doesn't hold up.

Blizzard, The (*Rafales*) (1990) (87mins) d: André Melançon s: Denis Bouchard, Marcel Leboeuf, André Melançon : Marcel Leboeuf, Rémy Girard, Denis Bouchard, Monique Spaziani, Guy Thauvette, Claude Blanchard. This was easily one of the best Québec films of the year. It is Christmas Eve and three men stage a hold-up in a shopping mall in Montréal. By accident, Santa Claus is shot. One man drives away in a raging blizzard but is followed by a radio announcer who has seen the robbery. What transpires is a thoughtful, suspenseful and perceptive study of human relations. An entirely engrossing film full of atmosphere and conviction.

Blood and Donuts (1995) (90mins) d: Holly Dale s: Andrew Rai Berzins : Gordon Currie, Justin Louis, Helene Clarkson, Fiona Reid, Frank Moore, Hadley Kay, Winston Carroll, David Cronenberg. The distinguished documentary filmmaker Holly Dale turns to fiction in her first dramatic feature but cannot do much with this bloodless script about a vampire who, when awakened after a century of sleep by a golf ball, finds himself at a loss in the present day. So will the audience as this dark comedy limps from one banality to the next.

Blood and Guts (1978) (93mins) d: Paul Lynch s: Joseph McBride, William Gray, John Hunter : William Smith, Micheline Lanctôt, Henry Beckman, Ken James. A violent melodrama, which may or may not be set in Canada, about wrestling and a young hopeful who takes up the sport. The only surprising part of the picture is that we find the talented Micheline Lanctôt playing in it.

Blood Clan (1991) (87mins) d: Charles Wilkinson s: Glynis Whiting : Gordon Pinsent, Michelle Little, Robert Wisden. Another entry in the horror class, this one concerning a Scottish family living in a remote Alberta prairie community haunted by killings from its ancestral past. Not much of a haunt.

Blood of Others, The (*Le sang des autres*) (1984) (130mins) (a Canada-France co-production) d: Claude Chabrol s: Brian Moore (from the novel of the same title by Simone de Beauvoir) : Jodie Foster, Michael Ontkean, Sam Neill, Stéphane Audran, Lambert Wilson, Alexandra Stewart, Monique Mercure, John Vernon, Kate Reid, Micheline Presle, Jean-Pierre Aumont. Another brilliant film from Chabrol. Set in German-occupied Paris during World War II, a woman is torn between her love for a French youth working for the Resistance movement and a German administrator who is deeply in love with her. A masterly portrait of a doomed love. (Not to be confused with *By the Blood of Others*.)

Blood of the Hunter (*Sang du chasseur, Le*) (**Lone Eagle**) (1995) (93mins) : Gabriel Arcand, Michael Biehn, Alexandra Vandernoot, François-Éric Gendron, Edward Meeks. Through ice and snow, a mysterious hooded killer is stalking a beautiful woman. When he tricks his way into her isolated log cabin, the suspense is tightly maintained. (see *Aventures du grand nord, Les*)

Blood Relatives (*Les liens de sang*) (1978) (101mins) (a Canada-France co-production) d: Claude Chabrol s: Claude Chabrol, Sydney Banks (from *Blood Relatives* by Ed McBain) : Donald Sutherland, Stéphane Audran, Micheline Lanctôt, Aude Landry, Lisa Langlois, Donald Pleasance,

David Hemmings, Walter Massey. As far as Canadian horror films go, this is far better than most. Claude Chabrol brings a keen mind to this depiction of a secret and incestuous relationship. He is supported by an interesting cast of players. In lesser hands, this would have been most unpleasant.

Bloody Brood, The (1959) (70mins) (b/w) d: Julian Roffman s: Elwood Ullman (from the story by Anne Howard Bailey) : Jack Betts, Barbara Lord, Peter Falk, Robert Christie, Kenneth Wickes, Ronald Hartman, William Brydon, Ronald Taylor, Michael Zenon, Sammy Sales, Card Starkman, Rolf Carston, Ann Collins. A laughable yet cynical tale of romance, love and murder among young people of the beat generation. One controversial scene shows Falk feeding a young boy a hamburger laced with broken glass. Filmed in and around Toronto in 16 days, this was the first of three B-movies made by Meridian Films, backed by N.A. Taylor, the cinema owner and film distributor.

Blue Butterfly, The (*Papillon bleu, Le***)** (2003) (96mins) d: Lea Pool s: Peter McCormack : William Hurt, Pascale Bussieres, Marc Donato. Lea Pool, this time around, tells us 'a true story' about a ten-year-old boy, terminally ill with cancer, whose last wish is to catch the Blue Morpho butterfly, found only in South America. His mother convinces a famous entomologist to take the boy in his wheelchair to the rainforest, where they are deep in the majesty and mystery of the jungle. This experience, Ms, Pool, is telling us, makes it possible for man and boy to emerge from this protective chrysalis. Well, I never!

Blue City Slammers (1987) (90mins) d: Peter Shatalow s: Layne Coleman (based on his play) : Mary Ellen Mahoney, Eric Keenleyside, Tracy Cunningham. In Blyth, Ontario, the women's softball championship is won by the local team, the Blue City Slammers, to cheers all around. A good-natured little sports film of interest probably only to the fans.

Blue Man, The (1985) (81mins) (a Canada-U.S. co-production) d: George Mihalka s: Robert Geoffrion : Karen Black, Winston Rekert, Patty Talbot, Andrew Bednarski, Tom Rack, Joanne Côté. Far-fetched bit of nonsense about a man who learns the secret of astral travel from a drug addict. He takes a trip, gets involved in some gruesome murders and finds a detective is on his trail. Tiresome.

Blue Winter (*L'hiver bleu***)** (1980) (81mins) d&s: André Blanchard : Christiane Lévesque, Nicole Scant, Lise Pichette, Alice Pomerleau, Michel Chénier. A fresh and pleasing portrait of two young women and their discovery of what it means to be an adult as they live through a long, cold winter of unemployment in the mining town of Abitibi.

***Bob Million: Le jackpot de la planète* (Bob Million and His World Jackpot)** (1997) (90mins) (a Canada-France co-production) d&s: Michael Perrotta : Bernadette Lafont, Yves Jacques, Madeleine Barbulée, Roger Van Hool, Erick Desmarestz. An exuberant and scattered comedy in which tv personality Bob Million takes his world lottery to Paris only to find that the winner, an elderly lady, has passed on. The grieving family has only two hours to qualify. Lots of fun at the expense of tv game shows and their ever happy hosts.

Bob's Garage (2001) (90mins) d&s: Harper Quantrill : Kenneth McGregor, Adrian Churchill, David MacKay, Richard Sutton, Aurora McLoughlin, Bruce Nagy, Scott Clarke. A comedy in which an old and messy garage serves as a metaphor for a world falling into decay as a result of crime, poverty and despair. Here, an off-duty policeman and four friends find a sense of community and purpose as they sit around a table playing poker. One day, someone gets shot and their world goes crazy. To save their friend, they fall back to primitive means and operate on him with tools from the garage. A bleak attempt at showing how some individuals try to survive.

Body and Soul (*Corps et âme***)** (1971) (94mins) (b/w) d: Michel Audy s: Jean-Louis Longtin, Michel Audy : Jacques Pothier, Pierre Héroux, Danièle Panneton, Jean Sauvageau, Jeannine Lebel. When a car accident kills the best friend of a talented pianist, he suffers a mental collapse. A revealing and multi-faceted look into Québec society.

***Boîte à soleil, La* (The Box of the Sun)** (1988) (73mins) d&s: Jean-Pierre Lefebvre : Simon Esterez, Barbara Easto, Joseph Champagne, Arsinée Khanjian. This personal film finds the director in a different mood once again, this time with a film of images and music depicting a melancholy world redeemed by innocence. Part children's fable, part polemic, experimental and whimsical, it reveals a beautiful imagination at work.

Bollywood/Hollywood (2002) (110mins) d&s: Deepa Mehta : Rahul Khanna, Lisa Ray, Moushumi Chatterji, Dina Pathak, Kulbushan Kharbanda, Ranjit Chowdhry, Jessica Pare. After her unsuccessful attempt two years ago to film *Water,* the third film after *Fire* and *Earth,* her trilogy, the Canadian-Indian filmmaker Deepa Mehta tells us that she looked for a change with a story that would make her laugh. The result is *Bollywood/Hollywood,* which she describes as a "madcap love song to both East and West." Combined here are comedy, romance, family drama, songs and dances, and satire with subversive touches, linking characters from Mumbai, London, New York and Toronto. (For those not familiar with the term Bollywood, the following may help. As Hollywood is to filmmaking in North America, Bombay (now known to some as Mumbai) is to Indian film production. Thus, the term Bollywood has been used to describe Indian cinema. Bollywood has a lengthy history going back to 1913, when the first silent movie was screened. Output is massive; each year, there are approximately 500 feature films released in India, more than half of which are in Hindi, the language of Bollywood cinema.

Language, however, is a small barrier. Like Hollywood, many contemporary Bollywood films follow conventions developed through timeless film classics.) (This term, need it be said, doesn't apply to the cinema of the great Satyajt Ray, who made his films in Bengal.)

Bombardier (1992) (156mins) d: François Labonté s: Jacques Savoie : Gilbert Sicotte, Marcel Leboeuf, Sylvie-Catherine Beaudoin, Denis Bernard, Dorothée Berryman. An impressive biography about the life of Joseph-Armand Bombardier, the man who gave us the snowmobile and other moving and flying objects. Skilfully played by Gilbert Sicotte, with fascinating natural and industrial Québec backgrounds.

Bonheur d'occasion: see **Tin Flute, The**

Bonjour, monsieur Gauguin **(Good Day, Mr. Gauguin)** (1989) (80mins) d: Jean-Claude Labrecque s: Jacques Savoie : Lothaire Bluteau, Gérard Poirier. A computer expert takes on a job to cut off a security system protecting a Gauguin exhibition. He is assisted by a blind musician who is convinced that his music alone can do the trick. As a mainly two-character study there is not much to get excited about.

Bonjour, Timothy (1995) (95mins) (a Canada-New Zealand co-production) d: Wayne Tourell s: David Preston (based on a story by David Parry) : Dean O'Gorman, Sylvia Rands, Sydney Jackson, Sabine Karsenti, Milan Borich, Angela Bloomfield, Richard Vette. Michèle, an exchange student from Montréal studying at a high school in Auckland, becomes involved with a student whose passion is football. A small, pleasant, and funny family film providing an engaging look at life in New Zealand. Even the bully gets his comeuppance.

Bons débarras, Les: see **Good Riddance**

Book of Eve (*Histoires d'Eve*) (2002) (98mins) (a Canada-U.K. co-production) d: Claude Fournier s: Terri Hawkes, Claude Fournier (based on the novel by Constance Beresford-Howe) : Claire Bloom, Daniel Lavoie, Susannah York, Julian Glover, Angele Coutu, Marie-Jo Therio, Fanny Lacroix. A 65-year-old housewife living in West Mount, Montréal, receives her first pension cheque one fine morning. This indication of the coming of old age prompts her to walk away from her husband, home and the life she has known for so many years. So begins her difficult task of survival. And how very welcome are the appearances of Claire Bloom and Susannah York, and also Julian Glover, in this likeable, honest portrait.

Bookfair Murders, The (1999) (120mins) (a Canada-Germany co-production) d: Wolfgang Panzer s: Herman Stuck (based on the book by Anna Porter) : Saul Rubinek, Samantha Bond, Linda Kash, Bernd Michael Lade, Geneviève Bujold, Eli Wallach. Set against the annual international book fair in Frankfurt, a furor breaks out when the author of one of the most anticipated novels is found murdered. It turns out that the book seems to implicate

a prominent German family in acquiring stolen works of art. A crowded event brings about a somewhat confusing storyline. (See: *Mystery* series)

Boomerang (2002) (93mins) (a Canada-Yugoslavia co-production) d: Dragan Marinkovic s: Svetislav Basara : Lazar Ristovski, Paulina Manov, Nebojsa Glogovac, Dragan Jovanovic, Petar Bozovic. Life in Belgrade after the fall of Milosevic. The Boomerang is a café that serves as a haunt for many young people who see themselves made losers by the war. Into their lives come drink, drugs, the Mafia, and all things down and depressing. Will life ever be normal? asks this film, cast in the documentary tradition and revealing much of the truth of the life of the characters it depicts. Canada doesn't enter the picture. We put up much of the money.

Boost: see **Cosmos**

Boozecan (1995) (97mins) d: Nicholas Campbell s: Luciano Diana : Justin Welsh, Jan Rubes, Leslie Hope, Eugene Lipinski. A boozecan is a slang term for an illegal after-hours drinking club. Here come the strippers, bikers, dealers and, on the other side, the lawyers, doctors, politicians and sports and show business people. Pasqua is an Italian Canadian trying to run a string of boozecans, but he is doomed to failure. Quite frankly, Nicholas Campbell, one of our most talented actors, is better in front of the cameras than in directing beer-stained material such as this.

Border Line: see *Frontieres*

Borderline Normal (2000) (95mins) (a Canada-U.S. film) d: Jeff Beesley s: Larry Mollin : Robin Dunne, Corbin Bernsen, Caterina Scorsone, Michael Ironside, Stephanie Zimbalist, Eugene Lipinski. An American teenager's parents have divorced. Their troubled son must make up his mind and decide whether he will return to Detroit with his father and brother or stay here with his mother. Nicely done with feeling and understanding.

Bordertown Café (1991) (100mins) d: Norma Bailey s: Kelly Rebar : Susan Hogan, Janet Wright, Gordon Michael Woolvett, Sean McCann, Nicholas Campbell. A first film comedy-drama about a family-run café located on the Manitoba-U.S. border. It's all cheerfully domestic, yet very real, colourful and likeable. A bit on the long side, but it doesn't drag.

Born for Hell (*Né pour l'enfer*) (1976) (92mins) (a Canada-France-German-Italy co-production) d: Denis Héroux s: Geza von Radvanyi : Mathieu Carrière, Deborah Berger, Christine Boisson, Myriam Boyer, Leonora Fani, Ely Gagliani, Carole Laure, Eva Mattes, Andrée Pelletier. It took four countries to produce this cheap pseudo-thriller about a psycho killer and his women.

Borrower, The (1985) (96mins) d&s: Peter McCubbin : Jeff Holec, Jan Taylor. A bank teller has been embezzling money to pay his gambling debts. After a final theft, he discovers he's become a participant in a widespread conspiracy. Is anyone watching?

Bottle, The: see *Bouteille, La*

Boulevard (1994) (96mins) d: Penelope Buitenhuis s: Rae Dawn Chong : Rae Dawn Chong, Kari Wuhrer, Joel Bissonnette, Lou Diamond Phillips. A cast of sketchy characters on Toronto's Yonge Street: a young woman in trouble, an innocent prostitute, the knowing pack, the vicious pimp, a foul-mouthed detective. A sleazy box office brew descending into a frightening pit of sex, blood and violence.

Bounty Hunters (1996) (98mins) (a U.S.-Canada film) d: George Erschbamer s: Jeffrey Barmash, George Erschbamer : Michael Dudikoff, Peter LaCroix, Lisa Howard, Freddy Andreiuci. A film of appalling violence in a contrived story about an American 'bounty hunter' trying to trap a convicted car thief. It's not this simple of course; if they remain in their seats, an audience must endure a blood bath between explosions, kicking, punching, pounding and beatings, and bodies being thrown from cars.

Bouteille, La (The Bottle) (2000) (103mins) d: Alain DesRochers s: Benoît Guichard, Alain DesRochers : Réal Bossé, Jean Lapointe, François Papineau, Louis Champagne, Stéphane Crête, Pascale Bussières, Hélène Loiselle, Sylvie Moreau. A classic case of much ado about very little. Réal on his motorcycle and François in his Ferrari, two old friends drive into the country to dig up a piece of paper they buried 15 years earlier and on which they had written the goals they wanted to achieve in life. But the old man who owns the land wants money. The search now becomes a quagmire of symbolism about youth, dreams, differences and convictions. As if this were not enough, even the local villagers become involved in this thin social comedy turned sour.

Bowling for Columbine (2002) (123mins) (a U.S.-Canada film) d&s: Michael Moore. Twelve students and one teacher died in the massacre at Columbine High School in Littleton, Colorado, on April 20, 1999, thus prompting Michael Moore to make this film about the accessibility of guns in the U.S. With many interviews, he covers a lot of ground in his trademark baseball cap, from Manhattan to Toronto, and brings in every conceivable point of view and argument about the ownership of guns and the resulting tragedies. A powerful work, both revealing and frightening, about society at its worst in politics and business. Listed here for the record, this documentary was the first to be accepted in competition at Cannes in 50 years.

Box of the Sun, The: see *Boîte à soleil, La*

Boy in Blue, The (1986) (99mins) (a Canadian-American film) d: Charles Jarrott s: Douglas Bowie : Nicholas Cage, Christopher Plummer, Cynthia Dale, David Naughton, Sean Sullivan, Melody Anderson, James B. Douglas, Walter Massey, Austin Willis, Ted Dykstra. An American actor plays the 19TH-century Canadian rowing champion Ned Hanlan in this uneven biography, which washes along on a tide of tedium.

Boy Meets Girl (1998) (97mins) d&s: Jerry Ciccoritti : Sean Astin, Emily Hampshire, Kate Nelligan, Joseph Mantegna, Kevin McDonald. Set in Toronto's Little Italy neighbourhood, this is a rickety concoction. A supposedly romantic tale complete with songs and music about a jaded writer and a waitress, it drags in every lovestruck cliché and becomes a painful pastiche of supposedly lovable Fellini-esque characters who are sadly lacking in genuine *amore*.

Boy Next Door, The (1984) (65mins) d&s: John Hunter : Chapelle Jaffe, Kate Reid, Michael Hogan, Charles Templeton, Christopher Owens. A woman with a successful career in real estate has been raising her 19-year-old son, and now he has turned bitter and hostile, with little regard for his mother and what she has done for him. A keenly observant drama. (See: *For the Record*)

Boys, Les (The Boys) (1997) (107mins) d: Louis Saia s: Christian Fournier (based on an original idea by Richard Goudreau) : Marc Messier, Rémy Girard, Patrick Huard, Serge Thériault, Michel Barrette, Paul Houde, Luc Guérin, Yvan Ponton, Roc Lafortune. This boisterous comedy about an incompetent hockey team is funny, good humoured and fast moving. It is full of working-class language and behaviour, and sharp satirical comments on politicians and other public figures. Québec audiences loved it so much that it became the highest-grossing Québec film in history, generating enough revenue in the province to pay for itself several times over. Québec critics are not kind to these low-brow, homegrown pictures on the grounds that they project a poor picture of the Québécois. This doesn't seem to worry moviegoers in the slightest.

Boys II, Les (The Boys II) (1998) (120mins) d: Louis Saia s: René Brisebois, François Camirand, Louis Saia (based on an idea by Richard Goudreau) : same cast as in *Les Boys* More of the same and still hugely successful. Combined, the two films have made over $10 million in Québec alone. When the videos were first released, they sold over 11,000 copies each, making them the best-selling videos in the history of French-language film in Canada.

Boys III, Les (The Boys III) (2001) (120mins) d: Louis Saia s: Louis Saia (from the original story by Richard Goudreau) : Marc Messier, Patrick Huard, Rémy Girard, Serge Thériault, Paul Houde, Luc Guérin, Yvan Ponton and the rest of the Boys. Two years ago, the Boys went to play in France. Now they are home, and the hockey season is about to begin. However, the team is but a shadow of its former self. Pride in and loyalty to the team has disappeared. In spite of this, we get a good dose of humour and a sense that the friendship between the boys will help them overcome their problems and become winners once more. The box office returns certainly make this film a winner, as were its predecessors.

Boys' Club, The (1996) (91mins) d: John Fawcett s: Peter Wellington : Christopher Penn, Dominic Zamprogna, Devon Sawa, Stuart Stone, Jarred Blancard, Nicholas Campbell. A silly and immoral film about three boys who have built a clubhouse in the woods. One day, they find a wounded man in their cabin, who threatens them with a gun. The stranger claims to be a policeman shot by another policeman, and the boys take pity on him, captivated by his stories. The youngsters become suspicious of the man but, in their young minds, he remains something of a hero. None of the other characters, including the boys' parents, attempt to show them how mistaken they are in their beliefs. A very pale shadow of the much earlier British film *Whistle Down the Wind*.

Boys of St. Vincent, The (1992) (210mins) d: John D. Smith s: Desmond Walsh, Samuel Grana : Henry Czerny, Brian Dooley, Sebastian Spence, Philip Dinn, Gregory Thomey, Michael Wade. In 1988, the public was shocked to read of the widespread sexual abuse of children, mostly young boys, that had been taking place in Roman Catholic orphanages since the end of the Second World War. Beginning with Mt. Cashel in Newfoundland, and spreading to other institutions across the country, the cruelty of the priests came to light when former residents, now adult men, came forward to lay criminal charges. Priests were arrested, tried and sent to prison. This film is not a re-enactment of any actual case but is inspired by events in Newfoundland. Powerful and compelling, disturbing and psychologically sound, there is nothing deliberately sensational about this film. It cleverly relates the struggle to uncover the truth and show the causes and motivation behind the behaviour. Henry Czerny's remarkable, unforgettable performance as a priest was much praised and brought him wide public attention. Sadly, our half-baked producers failed to take advantage of his great talent after his appearance here, relegating him to minor films.

Brain, The (1988) (91mins) d: Edward Hunt s: Barry Pearson : Tom Breznahan, Cyndy Preston, David Gale .A silly film about a tv psychiatrist who grows a human brain three times its normal size. Still brainless!

Brain Candy: see **Kids in the Hall: Brain Candy**

Breach of Faith: A Family of Cops II (1996) (95mins) (a Canadian-American film) d: David Greene s: Joel Blasberg : Charles Bronson, Barbara Williams, Angela Featherstone, Diane Ladd, Sebastian Spence, David Hemblen, David Ferry. A police inspector, his two sons (who are also in the police force), and his two daughters join together to find out who shot a Russian priest to death during a confessional. Above average.

Breach of Trust: see **Crash**

Bread Pudding: see *Pudding chômeur*

Breaking All the Rules (1985) (98mins) (a Canada-U.S. co-production) d: James Orr s: Edith Rey, Rafal Zielinski (based on their story *Breaking All the Rules*) : Carl Marotte, Thor Bishopric, Carolyn Dunn, Rachel Hayward, Walter Massey, Judith Gault. Four youngsters get up to tricks at an amusement park and unwittingly become part of a jewel robbery. Lively performances fail to make this more than a tedious watch.

Breaking Point (1976) (92mins) (a Canadian-American film) d: Bob Clark s: Stanley Mann : Bo Svenson, Robert Culp, Belinda Montgomery, Stephen Young, John Colicos, Linda Sorensen, Jeffrey Lynas, Ken James. A family marked by the mob for murder in Philadelphia finds a new identity in Toronto—not that this helps the picture to be anything more than standard fare.

Breakthrough, The: see **Lifeforce Experiment**

Brethren (1976) (91mins) (b/w) d&s: Dennis Zahoruk : Tom Hauff, Kenneth Welsh, Richard Fitzpatrick, Sandra Scott, Larry Reynolds, Candace O'Connor, Maury Chaykin, David Hughes, Alison MacLeod. A remarkable first feature about three brothers who return to a small Ontario town to attend the funeral of their father. The various family stresses and resentments that come to light are treated and developed with considerable wit and ironic observation, with no lack of feeling or understanding of the emotional aspect involved. A small gem for its time.

British Quota Era Films: The following films mark the busy period between 1933 and 1940, when production flourished in Vancouver. Companies from Hollywood (Columbia, Paramount) made so-called Canadian films to take advantage of British quota laws that encouraged filmmaking in Britian and the Commonwealth. When shown in the U.K., these movies became known as "quota quickies"; they were quickly and cheaply made with Hollywood casts, producers, writers and directors, and found few audiences. Leon Barsha and Kenneth Bishop made most of them. British Quota Era titles:

1: **Across the Border** (1937)
2: **Convicted** (1938)
3: **Crimson Paradise, The** (1933)
4: **Death Goes North** (1937)
5: **From Nine to Nine** (1936)
6: **King's Plate, The** (1935)
7: **Lucky Corrigan** (1936)
8: **Lucky Fugitives** (1935)
9: **Manhattan Shakedown** (1937)
10: **Murder Is News** (1937)
11: **Secret Patrol** (1936)
12: **Secrets of Chinatown** (1934)
13: **Stampede** (1936)
14: **Tugboat Princess** (1936)
15: **Undercover** (1935)
16: **Vengeance** (1936)

17: **Wildcat Trooper** (1935)

18: **Woman Against the World** (1937)—and as a special note **Special Inspector (Across the Border)** (1937), with Rita Hayworth, whose Hollywood career really began as production of the "quota quickies" ceased. There are scenes from many of these pictures at the end of the NFB documentary *Has Anyone Here Seen Canada?*, the second part of *Dreamland*.

Broken Dishes: see *Pots casses, Les*

Broken Lullaby (1994) (120mins) d: Michael Kennedy s: Guy Mullally, Jim Henshaw (from the novel by Laurel Pace) : Melvin Harris, Robert Stewart, Oliver Tobias, Jennifer Dale. A genealogist crosses Europe to search for information about her aunt's mysterious past. At the same time, she is searching for the family of a friend from whom she was separated seventy years ago; there aren't many clues to go by. Her travels, however, provide fascinating backdrops touched with surprising developments. (See: *Harlequin* series)

Brood, The (1979) (90mins) d&s: David Cronenberg : Oliver Reed, Samantha Eggar, Art Hindle, Cindy Hinds, Nuala Fitzgerald, Susan Hogan, Henry Beckman, Nicholas Campbell, Larry Solway, Michael Magee, Robert Silverman. Another of this director's dismaying horror films. In this one, Samantha Eggar eats her afterbirth while grandparents and teachers are beaten to death.

Brooklyn State of Mind, A (1997) (87mins) (a Canadian-American film) d: Frank Rainone s: Frederick Stoppel, Frank Rainone : Vincent Spano, Maria Grazia Cucinotta, Danny Aiello, Ricky Vetrino, Abe Vigoda, Tony Danza, Morgana King. With Montréal passing for Brooklyn, we meet a mixed group of Italians who all seem to be involved in corruption, crime and the mafia in some way or the other, with not much to light their way.

Brother André (Le frère André) (1987) (87mins) d: Jean-Claude Labrecque s: Guy Dufresne : Marc Legault, Sylvie Ferlatte. A religious film dealing with the fears and emotions of a 61-year-old Catholic brother who is afraid the college board will take him from his beloved Saint Joseph's Oratory and send him into exile in New Brunswick. In conversation with his teenage niece, we learn of the man's dreams, ambitions and insecurities.

Brothers by Choice (1985) (60mins) d&s: William Fruet : Yannick Bisson, Charley Higgins. Two brothers, one of whom is adopted, grow up in the British Columbia interior. One day, the adopted boy runs away to Vancouver. His brother finds him and persuades him to return home. A minor work from Fruet, but well intentioned and sympathetic in its understanding and depiction of family relationships.

Brown Bread Sandwiches (1990) (92mins) d&s: Carlo Liconti : Tony Nardi, Lina Sastri, Daniel DeSanto, Kim Cattrall, Giancarlo Giannini. A simple, noisy and tedious comedy-drama of immigrant Italian family life in Toronto in which Giancarlo Giannini sits around with nothing to do.

Brûlés, Les: see **Promised Land, The**

Bubbles Galore (1996) (93mins) d&s: Cynthia Roberts : Nina Hartley, Tracy Wright, Daniel MacIvor, Annie Sprinkle, Shauny Sexton, Sky Gilbert, Andrew Scorer. A year after this film was made and released, it raised a public outcry concerning the wisdom of putting public money into "indecent material" such as this. No one need have worried about this silly work in which several nude ladies try to make a porn picture. It's all very boring, seldom real and hard to make out in both visual and narrative terms. The outrage died and the bubbles blew away.

Bulldozer (1974) (93mins) d: Pierre Harel s: Claudine Monfette, Pierre Harel : Claudine Monfette, Donald Pilon, André St-Denis, Pauline Julien, Raymond Lévesque, Pierre Curzi. The world as a rubbish dump containing nothing but garbage to be cleared away by the bulldozer. Add this film to the pile.

Bullet to Beijing (Len Deighton's *Bullet to Beijing*) (1995) (122mins) (a Canada-Russia-U.K. co-production) d: George Mihalka s: Peter Welbeck (based on Deighton's *Beijing*) : Michael Caine, Jason Connery, Mia Sara, Michael Sarrazin, Michael Gambon, Burt Kwouk, Sue Lloyd, Patrick Allen. In 1965, Canadian director Sidney Furie, who had left Canada for England, found success and recognition with *The Ipcress File*. It made a star of Michael Caine in the role of Harry Palmer, a Cockney crook turned secret agent who is always wearing an overcoat. *Ipcress* was followed by two other Deighton successes: *Funeral in Berlin* and *Billion Dollar Brain*. But when Caine became Alfie, Harry Palmer disappeared from the screen until this film. Now, much older, wiser and slower, he is back at MI5 on a mission to St. Petersburg, where he gets involved in a chain of events involving biological weapons. The story never goes to extremes. It's exciting, believable and atmospheric. Caine is great, and so are the other players, including Sue Lloyd (who was also in *Ipcress*). References to James Bond, other spies and political issues add to the fun, as does a trip on the fabled Trans-Siberian Express.

Bulletproof Heart: see **Killer**

Bullies (1986) (96mins) d: Paul Lynch s: John Sheppard : Jonathan Crombie, Janet-Laine Green, William Nunn, Stephen Hunter, Dehl Berti, Becky Cullen, Olivia D'Abo, William Croft. Another bloody awful film from producer Peter Simpson in which a family, recently moved to a small B.C. town is set upon by a group of sadistic thugs who murder, rape, beat and terrorize. Trash piled on trash.

Burial Society, The (2002) (110mins) d&s: Nicholas Racz : Rob LaBelle, Jan Rubes, Allan Rich, Bill Meilen, David Paymer, Seymour Cassel. The three kindly old men who form the local Chevrah Kadisha, the Jewish burial society that prepares bodies for interment, are taken in by a likeable visitor to their town who offers to work for them. They become friends, but the visitor has his own set of plans, involving the theft of millions and the staging of what will look like his own death. A tense plot with an unusual background filled with intrigue and twists.

Buried on Sunday (1993) (90mins) d: Paul Donovan s: William Fleming, Paul Donovan : Paul Gross, Maury Chaykin, Denise Virieux, Louis del Grande, Tommy Sexton. This film was produced in the Maritimes and, in its political orientation, is a close cousin to Newfoundland's *Secret Nation*. Using comedy similar to that in *Passport to Pimlico* and *The Russians Are Coming, the Russians Are Coming,* it expresses some blunt, outspoken opinions about the federal government's mishandling of the Atlantic fisheries and the overfishing crisis that has put thousands of people out of work. With the assistance of a Russian submarine, the island of Solomon Grundy decides to leave Canada, in protest over the lack of economic prosperity. But fine speeches are not enough to keep this well-intentioned film afloat, and it sinks all too soon into heavy-handed humour.

Burn: The Robert Wraight Story (2003) (92mins) d: Stefan Scaini s: Shelley Eriksen, Sean O'Byrne : Jonathan Scarfe, Alan Scarfe, Kristen Booth. This is a well-told documentary-shaped film telling about events carried, far and wide by the media, which happened to the family who moved to Alberta to make a new start and became sick as a result of petroleum in the air caused by the industry. Wraight meets Wiebo Ludwig, whom he thought was an ally, but turned out not to be. A timely and provocative film about an environmental tragedy.

Burning Season, The (1993) (103mins) d&s: Harvey Crossland : Akesh Gill, Ayub Khan Din, Om Puri, Habib Tanvir, Uttara Boakar, Pankaj Kapoo. A complicated mix of anarchy, tradition, love and passion involving an Indian woman living in an arranged marriage in the Vancouver home of her wealthy in-laws. Her life changes when she falls in love with a teacher and returns to India with him. Once back in Canada, she tries to find a way to live that suits her lifestyle rather than the rules imposed on her by her former life. A disturbing depiction of rigidly held beliefs and practices. Sensitively played out against impressive location photography. (not to be confused with John Frankenheimer's *The Burning Season* 1994.)

Burning, The (1981) (91mins) (a Canada-U.S.-Hong Kong co-production) d: Tony Maylam s: Peter Lawrence, Bob Weinstein : Brian Matthews, Leah Ayres, Brian Backer, Larry Joshua, Lou David, Holly Hunter. A miserable and bloody Canadian rip-off of *Friday the 13th*. Holly Hunter's first film and one she would rather forget.

Burnt Eden (1997) (83mins) d&s: Eugene Garcia : Romano Orzari, Marisa Malone, Ivaylo Founev,

Larry Cohen, Lane Middleton. The dismal story of a young man whose life is one long trail of disasters, lies and bouts of begging, drinking and drug taking. He finally discards everything, including his friends, and leaves to meet his death—or so it seems. By the time the end rolls around, it's hard to feel sympathy or understanding for this man.

Bush Pilot (1946) (63mins) (b/w) d: Sterling Campbell s: W. Scott Darling : Jack La Rue, Austin Willis, Rochelle Hudson, Frank Perry, Joe Carr, Florence Kennedy, Robert Christie, Gordon Burwash, Nancy Graham. A romantic melodrama set on Lake Muskoka in Ontario about the rivalry between two brothers, both airmen, for the same girl. Simplistic and slight, it nevertheless conveys a quaint, fresh charm in its depiction of an earlier time. This was the first film produced in Ontario after the World War II.

Bust a Move (1993) (90mins) d&s: Julian Grant : Francine Paul, Michael Bederman, Jacen Braithwaite, Venetia Marie. A frantic low-budget picture urban drama about four young Toronto friends who want to get out of their troubled immigrant neighbourhood—Jane-Finch—and get on with their lives. But drugs, booze, sex and violence leave them more confused than ever. An appealing and honest attempt at portraying teenage troubles in an uncertain world. Grant was an early independent filmmaker who shot this film on a shoestring budget, meaning no government funding.

Busted Up (1986) (90mins) d: Conrad Palmisano s: Damian Lee : Paul Coufos, Stan Shaw, Tony Rosato, Irene Cara, Damian Lee, Claude Rae. Slight script about a boxer who owns a gym in Toronto and must cope with a developer who plans to take over the club. Then, the boxer's former girlfriend returns to claim the daughter she left with him six years earlier. A few bright moments in an otherwise complicated chronicle.

Buster's Bedroom (1991) (90mins) d: Rebecca Horn s: Martin Mosebach, Rebecca Horn : Donald Sutherland, Geraldine Chaplin, Valentina Cortese, Amanda Ooms, Ari Snyder, Taylor Mead, David Warrilow. A film student and admirer of the late, great Buster Keaton goes to see the house in the California desert where the actor once lived. Much to her surprise and shock, she finds it has become a sanatorium with a strange collection of patients presided over by a mad doctor. Although not without laughs, loves and lively performances, one cannot help but wonder what Buster would have made of this film. Interesting performances from a cast one would one not have expected to be here.

Butler's Night Off, The (1948) (57mins) (b/w) d: Roger Racine s: Anton Van der Walter, Stanley Mann (based on story by Silvio Narizzano) : Paul Colbert, Peter Sturgess, Eric Workman, Mary Lou Hennessy, Charles Rittenhouse, William Shatner, Maurice Gauvin, Robin Pratt, Michael Oliver, Leroy

Fallana, Henry Ramer, Willard Sage. A disappointing comedy-drama about a butler who becomes romantically involved with a flirtatious woman during his off-duty hours. William Shatner, playing the small role of a crook, later found fame as a Shakespearean actor and as Captain Kirk in the long-running television series *Star Trek*. (An early post-war Canadian film.)

Butley (1974) (127mins) d: Harold Pinter, play by Simon Gray : Alan Bates, Jessica Tandy, Michael Byrne, Georgia Hale, Susan Engel, Richard O'Callaghan. Allan Bates re-creates his stage triumph as a troubled teacher in this outrageous comedy. (see: *American Film Theatre Series*)

Butterbox Babies (1995) (89mins) d: Donald McBrearty s: Raymond Storey (adapted from the book by Bette Cahill) : Susan Clark, Peter MacNeill, Catherine Fitch, Michael Riley, Shannon Lawson, Nicholas Campbell, Corinne Conley, Cedric Smith, Dan MacDonald, Colin Fox. Based on a true story about a couple who ran a maternity home in East Chester, Nova Scotia, during the 1930s. The home provided a loving residence for unwed mothers, whom society viewed as immoral women. However, the couple was found to be illegally trafficking in the babies. This is a compelling well-made drama with a memorable performance by Susan Clark as the woman at the centre of the scandal.

Buying Time (1988) (104mins) d&s: Richard and Mitchell Gabourie : Jeff Schultz, Leslie Toth, Dean Stockwell, Laura Cruickshank. A thick-ear melodrama in which two young drug dealers work undercover for the police. Fast, loud, furious and hard to believe.

By Design (1981) (91mins) d: Claude Jutra s: Jutra, Joe Wiesenfeld, David Eames : Saul Rubinek, Sarah Botsford, Patty Duke Astin, Clare Coulter, Sonia Zimmer, Ralph Benmergui, Jan Muszynski. Two wealthy lesbian dress designers decide to have a baby and inveigle a young photographer to be the father. Tedious, superficial and unpleasant. Vancouver is passed off as an unnamed American city. Most of us expected better from Jutra.

By Reason of Insanity (1982) (65mins) d: Donald Shebib s: David McLaren : Patricia Collins, John Wildeman, Michael Kirby, Barbara Williams, John Neville, Neil Munro, Hrant Alianak, Sheila Moore, Richard Blackburn. A young, strong and wretched youth is brought to trial for killing a man. He is defended on grounds of insanity. So, in come the lawyers, psychiatrists, family members of the victim and others to take part in a legal circus that might well allow the prisoner to leave as a free man. Hard hitting and controversial, we see how red tape, the possibility of financial gain, and a twisting of the principle of justice for all becomes ridiculously complex and as twisted as the alleged killer. (See: *For the Record*)

By the Blood of Others (*Par le sang des autres*) (1974) (95mins) (a Canada-France co-production) d: Marc Simenon s: Jean Max : Bernard Blier,

Denise Filiatrault, Jacques Godin, Daniel Pilon, Mylène Demongeot. Marc Simenon is the son of the famous mystery novelist, and in this, his first film as director, he tells a gripping story about a deranged man holding two women hostage in an abandoned farmhouse. But he goes deeper, giving us a study of moral responsibility and a detailed look at life in a small French town. (Not to be confused with Chabrol's *The Blood of Others*.)

By the Riverside: see *Au fil de l'eau*

Bye Bye Blues (1989) (117mins) d&s: Anne Wheeler : Rebecca Jenkins, Luke Reilly, Michael Ontkean, Robyn Stevan, Kate Reid, Sheila Moore, Wayne Robson. *Bye Bye Blues* is Wheeler's third and best film,which continues to be one of her finest. Like the promising *Loyalties* and *Cowboys Don't Cry,* it is set in western Canada and conveys a marvellous, graphic sense of people and place. The story takes place during World War II. When Daisy Cooper's husband, a doctor with the British army, is transferred from India to Singapore, she returns to her parents' home on the Alberta prairie with her two young children. There, she learns that Singapore has fallen to the Japanese, and her husband has been captured as a prisoner of war. She must find a way to earn a living, and her gift for music prompts her to play and sing for a local band. Soon, she is away from her family on tour, where she meets a trombone player who falls in love with her. With no word from her husband as to his fate in prison, Daisy has her own war to contend with over her mixed emotions and sense of loyalty to her husband. Dismissed by several critics as being "another conventional film," *Bye Bye Blues* is much more than that. Its narrative is straightforward and consistently fills ordinary things with life and meaning. It is strikingly photographed by Vic Sarin and captures the sense of wartime Canada and has a lively, jazz background. The characters are perfectly played. Rebecca Jenkins (herself a singer and musician) as Daisy conveys a sense of decency and goodness without being prim, dull or bland.

Bye Bye Red Riding Hood (*Bye bye, chaperon rouge*) (1989) (94mins) (a Canada-Hungary co-production) d: Marta Meszaros s: Eva Pataki, Marta Meszaros : Fanny Lauzier, Pamela Collyer, Margit Makay, Jan Nowicki. A modern re-telling of the childhood classic about Fanny, who lives in the forest with her meteorologist mother. One day, on the way to visit her grandmother and great-grandmother on the other side of the forest, Fanny has three encounters that will change her life forever. First, she runs into an apparently kind and gentle wolf. A mysterious and marvellous tale. (See: *Tales for All* series)

Bye bye, chaperon rouge: see **Bye Bye Red Riding Hood**

C'est ben beau l'amour: see **It's a Wonderful Love**
C'est jeune et ça sait tout!: see **There's Nothing Wrong With Being Good to Yourself**

C'est pas la faute à Jacques Cartier: see **It's Not Jacques Cartier's Fault**

C'est pas parce qu'on est petit qu'on peut pas être grand!: see **Great Land of Small, The**

C'était le 12 du 12 et Chili avait les Blues: see **Chili's Blues**

C't à ton tour, Laura Cadieux: see **It's Your Turn, Laura Cadieux**

Ça peut pas être l'hiver, on n'a même pas eu d'été: see **It Can't Be Winter, We Haven't Had Summer Yet**

Cabaret neiges noires (1997) (85mins) d: Raymond St-Jean s: Dominic Champagne : Suzanne Lemoine, Didier Lucien, Norman Helms, Jean Petitclerc, Julie Castonguay. This is a musical show comprising a mix of cabaret acts in burlesque, song and dance. A dingy business with characters living a tragicomedy life. Destiny has a lot to do with this, and the whole makes an unusual trip into the musical macabre. Satisfying and, at times, sharply satirical.

Caboose (1996) (92mins) d: Richard Roy s: Odile Poliquin, Michel Michaud, Richard Roy : Gildor Roy, Céline Bonnier, Bernard-Pierre Donnadieu, James Hyndman. Described as Québec's third police thriller after *Black List* and *Mistaken Identity* (neither of which is anything to be proud of), this dark and desperate film is about a policeman who has gone bad. And bad it is wading through Montréal with its violence, murder, sex, drugs, hookers and street gangs. Not a responsible social study but a repellent piece of sensationalism.

Cadillac Girls (1993) (105mins) d: Nicholas Kendall s: Peter Behrens : Jennifer Dale, Gregory Harrison, Mia Kirshner, Adam Beach, Anna Cameron. Part American, part Canadian, this is a tangled and wildly uneven tale of reconciliation between a mother and daughter. Their family complications are more likely to put audiences to sleep than to entertain them.

Café Olé (2000) (92mins) (a Canada-Mexico co-production) d: Richard Roy s: Emil Sher : Andrew Tarbet, Laia Marull, Dino Tavarone, Stephanie Morganstern, Dorothée Berryman. Trying hard to be a romantic comedy but more concerned with sex and splash, this is the story of a shy man in Montréal. He is kind and considerate to women but seldom goes beyond friendship until he meets a lively Chilean dancer and begins to warm up to wine, women and dancing. Sentiment surrounded by slop with drama suffering accordingly.

Café Romeo (1992) (93mins) d: Rex Bromfield s: Frank Procopio : Catherine Mary Stewart, Jonathan Crombie, Michael Ironside, Joseph Campanella. A mild semi-drama set mainly in a café where several youngsters gather to talk interminably with the attractive waitress. They are supposed to be of Italian origin but remain unconvincing. Their conversation is poorly accented and of no interest whatsoever. Leave this café after a quick coffee.

Cain (1965) (90mins) d: Pierre Patry s: Jacques Proulx (from the novel *Les Marcheurs de la Nuit* by Réal Giguère) : Yves Létourneau, Réal Giguère, Ginette Letondal, Rose Rey-Duzil, Gaétane Létourneau, Gabbi Sylvain, Yvon Dufour. A group of individuals in Montréal—friends and enemies, lovers and lost souls—are caught up in unexpected murder and violence. This is a fast-moving and well-acted mystery, the sociological aspects of which give the events a deeper context. Pierre Patry played an important part in laying the foundations of the new Québec cinema with Coopératio Inc., a determined group of actors and writers striving to produce films, even for minimal financial returns. This picture was one of their first.

Caleb's Daughters: see **Being at Home With Claude**

Calendar (1993) (75mins) d&s: Atom Egoyan : Atom Egoyan, Arsinée Khanjian, Ashot Adamiam. A Canadian photographer (Egoyan) travels with his wife to Armenia to take pictures of historic churches for use as a calendar. A local driver—a woman—takes them to see the sights. The photographer realizes he is becoming estranged from his wife due to a growing attraction to their guide. Back home, he invites a number of women for dinner while attempting to discover the reason his relationship has failed. Funny, sad and simple, a departure for Egoyan. But boredom soon sets in.

Camera Thief, The (*Le voleur de caméra*) (1993) (106mins) d&s: Claude Fortin : Claude Fortin, Madeleine Bélair, Jacinthe Marceau, Johanne Goulet, Régis Boivin. An imaginative and original film questioning the nature of filmmaking and those who control the rapidly developing world of media communications. The director plays an aspiring videographer who learns his craft, makes a film and turns the tables on the system. Set against a lively Montréal background, the events include a witty working-class version of Denys Arcand's *The Decline of the American Empire*.

Cameron of the Royal Mounted (1921) (60mins-silent) (b/w) d: Henry MacRae s: Faith Green, Ralph Conner (from his book *Corporal Cameron of the North West Mounted Police*) : Gaston Glass, Irving Cummings, Vivienne Osborne, Frank Lanning. A popular film with audiences, it transported them from Winnipeg to the far reaches of Manitoba to participate in the adventures of this brave Mountie. Fast moving, set against great locations.

Camilla (1994) (95mins) (a Canada-U.K. co-production) d: Deepa Mehta s: Paul Quarrington (based on an original story by Ali Jennings) : Jessica Tandy, Bridget Fonda, Elias Koteas, Maury Chaykin, Graham Greene, Hume Cronyn. This film would have been a waste of time were it not for a beautiful performance by Jessica Tandy, in her final film appearance. She plays an elderly lady who likes her sherry, talks about her past as a concert musician and is somewhat out of this world. With characters springing up here and there and with everyone, it seems, driving from Toronto to the U.S. and back again for no good reason, the narrative wallows in confusion.

Canada's Sweetheart: The Saga of Hal C. Banks (1985) (115mins) d&s: Donald Brittain : Maury Chaykin, R.H. Thomson, Gary Reineke, Sean McCann, Colin Fox, Chuck Shamata, Jason Dean, Peter Boretski, Jonathan Welsh, Marie-Hélène Fontaine. This is a dismaying story that began in the late 1940s. The federal government invited an American gangster, Hal C. Banks, to Canada so he could smash the Canadian Seamen's Union, which was allegedly influenced by communist activists. Banks was successful in his endeavour, and he went on to control the seamen in a tyrannical, violent and murderous 13-year reign that amounted to a dictatorship over operations at the Montréal docks. This was Donald Brittain's finest film and deals with a subject about which he felt strongly. Chaykin is excellent as Banks, and a small army of our finest actors brings this disgraceful episode in our history to life.

Canadians, The (1961) (85mins) d&s: Burt Kennedy : Robert Ryan, John Dehner, Torin Thatcher, John Sutton, Teresa Stratas. History made palatable as our Mounties, portrayed by mostly British actors, pacify warring natives. Teresa Stratas, having left the Met behind, sings! This is Twentieth Century Fox's view of us. Listed for archival records. (Filmed in Western Canada, Kennedy's first film as director.) (see: Hollywood Productions)

Candy Mountain (1987) (91mins) (a Canada-France-Switzerland co-production) d: Robert Frank, Rudy Wurlitzer s: Rudy Wurlitzer : Kevin O'Conner, Harris Yulin, Tom Waits, Bulle Ogier, Roberts Blossom, Leon Redbone, Dr. John, Joe Strummer, David Johanson, Buster Poindexter. When certain Canadian critics and academics heard that New York documentary filmmaker Robert Frank was planning to make a film in Canada, their response was sheer ecstasy. The result is an uneven record of a former rock musician and his trip through the U.S. and Canada in search of a legendary guitar maker named Yulin, whom he finds on Cape Breton Island. The film is an interesting attempt to combine photography and music, but in the end it succumbs to dullness and tedium.

Cannibal Girls (1973) (83mins) d: Ivan Reitman s: Robert Sandler : Andrea Martin, Eugene Levy, Earl Pomerantz, Joan Fox, Randall Carpenter, Bonnie Neilson. Women who eat men: a horror in every sense. Andrea Martin and Eugene Levy went on to better things. Ivan Reitman went to Hollywood.

Canvas, artiste et voleur **(Canvas)** (1993) (94mins) d&s: Alain Zaloum : Gary Busey, Vittorio Rossi, John Rhys-Davies, Cary Lawrence. A tight little crime piece about misdeeds in an art gallery, with thefts, cover-ups, bribery, drugs and death.

Canvas: see *Canvas, artiste et voleur*

Cap Tourmente **(Cape Torment)** (1993) (110mins) d&s: Michel Langlois : Roy Dupuis, Élise Guilbault, Gilbert Sicotte, Andrée Lachapelle, Macha Limonchik. A house on the banks of the St. Lawrence River is home to a closely knit family whose members are very much in love but tearing each other apart over their fears of the future— which becomes imperilled with the arrival of an old friend who discovers what has gone wrong. Often tense and well told, but heavy going in spite of a good cast.

Cape Torment: see *Cap Tourmente*

Capital Cost Allowance Films (Tax-Shelter Era): during the period between 1974 and 1982 allowed investors in movies to deduct 100 percent of their investment. This complicated scheme, prompted by Telefilm and its chairman, Michael McCabe, saw the production of mostly pseudo Canadian films with Hollywood has-beens, in which the producers took their money up-front and worried not at all whether the films were genuinely Canadian, or even made money. Very few were, the rest passed Canada off as "somewhere else", meaning the US. The scheme became known as the "doctor, dentist, lawyer" movies. A sad joke. It no longer exists.

Captains Courageous (1996) (92mins) (a Canadian-American film) d: Michael Anderson s: John McGreevy : Kenny Vadas, Robert Urich, Kaj-Erik Eriksen. A pleasant and agreeable contemporary version of Rudyard Kipling's widely read novel about a rich orphan who learns the value of hard work and true friendship. Well acted and well made under the always reliable Michael Anderson. This is the third time around for the classic story.

Captive Heart: The James Mink Story (1996) (120mins) (a Canadian-American film) d: Bruce Pittman s: Bryon White, Brian Bird, John Wierick : Louis Gossett Jr., Kate Nelligan, Ruby Dee, Peter Outerbridge, Winston Rekert, Rachel Crawford, Eric Peterson. Canada stands in for Virginia in this intelligent and well-acted drama. The story begins in 1852. James Mink is a wealthy hotelier in Toronto. His daughter marries a white man who takes her to the southern U.S. where, among other atrocities, he sells her into slavery. Mink arranges for her to return to Canada via the historic Underground Railroad. Much of this is familiar, but it is never sensational.

Capture of Karna Small, The (1987) (77mins) d&s: Sidney Bailey : Veronica Stocker, Andrew Johnston, Margarita Stocker. Karna Small is a young prostitute from a middle-class family who is forced by her parents and social workers into a rehab program. The pressure of conflicting advice from the many experts drives her away, although she is determined to work out her future for herself. A realistic little social drama.

Careful (1992) (95mins) d: Guy Maddin s: Maddin & George Toles : Gosia Dubrowolska, Kyle McCulloch, Jackie Burroughs, Paul Cox. Maddin continues his eccentric course with this novelty supposedly set in the Alps. The citizens of a town live in fear of avalanches. Quaint characters juxtaposed with cardboard backgrounds provide a funny send-up of fairy tales and are photographed in what looks like an early colour process. Has an inappropriately scratchy soundtrack. Twenty minutes would have been enough.

Caressed: see **Sweet Substitute**

Caretaker's Lodge, The: see *Conciergerie, La*

Cargo (1990) (90mins) d: François Girard s: Michel Langlois, François Girard : Michel Dumont, Geneviève Rioux, Guy Thauvette. This was Girard's first feature. He later received acclaim for *Le dortoir, Thirty-two Short Films About Glenn Gould* and *The Red Violin*. Here, a woman, her father and her lover embark on a sailboat for what becomes an eerie and surreal experience on a freighter to nowhere. Stylish but obscure.

Caribe (1988) (86mins) d: Michael Kennedy s: Paul Donovan : Kara Glover, John Scott, Stephen McHattie, John Savage, Sam Malkin, Maury Chaykin. In the jungles of Belize, a double-crossed arms smuggler tries to survive a lethal game of chase and kill. All routine and ramshackle.

Carnival in Free Fall (*Carnaval en chute libre*) (1966) (79mins) (b/w) d&s: Guy Bouchard : Nicole Blackburn, Normand Truchon, Guy Tremblay, Margot Roberts. Set in Chicoutimi at carnival time, we meet Nicole, Lili and Claudie, their husbands and former lovers. All are present for a *tournée des grands ducs,* a tour of bars, restaurants and clubs with striptease, songs and dancing. Everyone tries to come to terms with those they love or do not love, but happiness eludes them all. The cast is likeable and play well, and obviously Chicoutimi is the place to be at carnival time.

Caro Papa: see **Dear Father**

Carpenter, The (1987) (87mins) d: David Wellington s: Douglas Taylor : Wings Hauser, Lynne Adams, Pierre Lenoir. Wellington's first feature is the story of a young woman who has suffered a nervous breakdown, her unfaithful husband, and the spirit of the carpenter who partly built their house but whose violent death prevented him from finishing the job. Nothing quite works the way it was intended. Competent.

Carry on Sergeant (1927–1928) (117mins) (silent) d&s: Bruce Bairnsfather : Nancy Ann Hargreaves, Louise Cardi, Jimmy Savo, Nils Welch, Hugh Buckler. This was one of Canada's most spectacular attempts to make its name in the cinema. The attempt failed because this movie began production in 1927, when 'talkies' were still thought to be a fad, and finished in 1928, when the public acceptance of sound in cinema rendered silent films obsolete. *Carry on Sergeant* was a World War I drama about Canadian soldiers in France. This was a subject that had never been previously filmed. W.F. Clarke of London (England) organized British Empire Films of Canada and a subsidiary company, Canadian International Pictures, to make the film. Thirty-five shareholders invested $500,000 and the Trenton, Ontario, studios were leased from the Ontario government Motion Picture Bureau for five years. Bruce Bairnsfather, the famous British cartoonist of the day, was hired as screenwriter and director. For more than a year, Trenton became the little Hollywood of pioneer George Brownridge's dreams. Newspapers announced that, once again, "Trenton was the centre of the motion picture industry of Canada" and that the film would "assist the trade of the country by showing Canada in its true light rather than in the popular concept of a land of ice and snow." To ensure Bairnsfather directed competently—it was his first and only film—a technical crew was brought in from Hollywood. A Paris street and an authentic-looking French village were built and stood for 15 years. The western front was recreated and troops marched, clashed and died in big battle scenes impressively staged. The details and the cast were perfect. The $500,000 budget was a huge sum at the time and spent before the film was completed. Bairnsfather reportedly used his own money to finish it. But the excitement and anticipation of the first weeks of filming turned to gloom and despair by the end. Cinemas were installing audio equipment but *Carry on Sergeant* had no sound. Nevertheless, a big première was arranged at the Regent Theatre in Toronto and it almost succeeded in creating a genuine Canadian motion picture event. A huge banner across Adelaide Street read, 'Canada's First Mammoth Motion Picture'. Technicians created sound effects backstage and Ernest Dainty conducted his own score. Initially, audiences were large enough to make the showings profitable but backstage quarrels between the producers and theatre owners over rental charges brought the engagement to an early end. The film was withdrawn from distribution by its discouraged producers. The money invested was totally lost. The film passed into the custody of the Ontario government. With the coming of the Depression, Premier Mitchell Hepburn closed the Trenton studios and disbanded the Motion Picture Bureau. The prints of *Carry on Sergeant* would have probably been lost had it not been for Gordon Sparling, the film's assistant director and a future director of the short subjects in the *Canadian Cameo* series. He rescued a copy of the movie and stored it in his office at Associated Screen News, a company formed in 1932 to make short subjects and industrial films. In 1954, ASN donated the copy to the newly formed Canadian Film Archives.

Carver's Gate (1996) (97mins) d&s: Sheldon Inkol : Michael Paré, Tata Maria Manuel, Kevin Stapleton. Once again, the future holds nothing for us but misery, murder and other deadly misfortunes—leading to our own extinction. Until then, we will play a virtual reality game called DreamLife, followed by AfterLife. All rather boring, actually, in spite of its visual horrors.

Casa con vista al mar, Una: see **House With a View of the Sea, A**

Casablancais, Les (The Casablancans) (1998) (90mins) (a Canada-France-Morocco co-production) d&s: Abdelkader Lagtaa : Karina Aktouf, Salah Eddine Benmoussa, Aziz Saadallah, Khadija Assad, Amine Kably. Forget Rick's Café. Time really has gone by, and this is the new face of Morocco! A three-part story about repression, the misuse of power, and the social effects of religious fundamentalism. A brave film, original and engrossing, that might never have been made without Canadian financing.

Case of Libel, A (1985) (90 mins) (a Canada-US film) d: Eric Till s: Henry Denker (from his play) : Gordon Pinsent, Daniel Travanti, Edward Asner, Lawrence Dane. The first part of US lawyer Louis Nizer's fascinating biography, *My Life in Court* is brought cleverly and dramatically to the screen detailing the famous Westbrook Pegler-Quentin Reynold's libel case in which Peglar attempted to smear Reynold's reputation. A good day at court.

Case of the Whitechapel Vampire, The (2001) (120mins) d: Rodney Gibbons s: Joe Wiesenfeld (from the book by Sir Arthur Conan Doyle) : Matthew Frewer, Kenneth Welsh, R.H. Thomson, Shawn Lawrence, Neville Edwards, Cary Lawrence, Michel Perron, Joel Miller, Tom Rack. We are back on Baker Street in 1892 London, not far from the slums of Whitechapel, where Jack the Ripper went on his killing spree only two years earlier. Now, a brother from the Hermitage of St. Justinian is found dead with bite marks on his neck. Although vampires have never been seen around here, the monks are convinced this is what killed him and turn to Sherlock to solve this terrible murder. Holmes, logical as always, sets out to prove that a human hand was responsible, not that of a vampire. This short series about the world's most famous detective, keeps the high standard of previous Holmes portrayals with Frewer and Welsh, the casts, scripts and direction, living up to what aficionados expect. (See: *Sherlock Holmes* series)

Case of the Witch Who Wasn't, The (*Pas de répit pour Mélanie*) (1990) (92mins) d: Jean Beaudry s: Stella Goulet and Jean Beaudry : Marie-Stéfane Gaudry, Kesnamelly Neff, Vincent Bolduc, Madeleine Langlois. Another winning entry in this series; it tells of the efforts of two young girls on holiday in Québec who go to the aid of an eccentric old lady when she is robbed. She lives alone and is thought to be a wicked witch. A finely made film relating quiet and pertinent observations about race relations, friendship and the love of animals. (See: *Tales for All* series)

Castle of Cards, The (*Le château de cartes*) (1980) (91mins) d: François Labonté s: Marthe Boisvert : Kim Yaroshevskaya, Denis Bouchard, Marcel Sabourin, Gilbert Sicotte, Paul Dion. A likeable children's film about eccentric characters in a castle of cards and their misadventures with pseudo-scientific equipment. In the spirit of Radio-Canada's broadcasts for children, in which Kim Yaroshevskaya was a long-time personality.

Cat in the Bag, The (*Le chat dans le sac*) (1964) (74mins) (b/w) d&s: Gilles Groulx : Barbara Ulrich, Claude Godbout, Manon Blain, Jean-Paul Bernier, Véronique Vilbert, André Leblanc. An "improvised documentary" set in the early 1960s in the world of theatre and journalism in Montréal. It concerns a young couple—she is an anglo and Jewish, he is a francophone Québécois—on the verge of separating. Generally considered the first film to mark Québec's "new" cinema.

Cathy's Curse (1977) (91mins) (a Canada-France co-production) d: Eddy Matalon s: Alain Sens-Cazenave : Alan Scarfe, Beverley Murray, Randi Allen, Roy Witham, Mary Morter. Another B-picture horror. An eight-year-old girl is possessed by the spirit of her aunt, who died in a car accident and activates strange forces from beyond the grave. Enough to send audiences to theirs!

Catsplay: (1977) (90mins) d: Stephen Katz s: Timothy Findley (adapted from the play by Istvan Orkeny) : Helen Burns, Angela Fusco, Doris Petrie, Moya Fenwick, Frances Hyland, Jan Rubes. An exploration of the passions and pains of old age as seen through the relationship between two sisters separated by the Iron Curtain. One finds affection in the attention given her by an absent-minded opera singer. Delicate, sensitive, beautifully acted and brought to the screen as a satisfying whole.

Cauchemar: see **Nightmare, The**

Celebrations, The (1979) (86mins) d&s: Yves Simoneau (a filmed version of the play by Michel Garneau) : Léo Munger, Normand Lévesque, J.-Yves Dussault. An early work by Simoneau about a children's psychologist and a university professor and their dreams, obsessions, jealousies and fears. The film tends to strengthen the suspicion that both professions attract strange individuals.

Celui qui voit les heures: see **One Who Sees the Hours, The**

Cementhead (1979) (65mins) d: Ralph Thomas s: Roy MacGregor, Ralph Thomas : Tom Butler, Martin Short, Kenneth James, Kate Lynch, Kenneth Welsh, Eric Nesterenko. The issue examined here concerns the ethics of professional hockey. A remarkable visual statement of the sport and the price a player must pay to become a winner. (See: *For the Record*)

Century Hotel (2001) (96mins) d: David Weaver s: Bridget Newson, David Weaver : Lindy Booth, Eugene Lipinski, Noam Jenkins, Colm Feore, Earl Pastko, Sandrine Holt, Joel Bissonnette, David Hewlett, Tom McCamus, Mia Kirshner. A series of seven intricately written and interwoven stories.

Beginning with the Century Hotel's opening night in 1921, we meet the first of many patrons and hear their tales of love, betrayal, passion and tragedy. There are a few scenes in which the room seems to be overbooked, but we are still left with a sense of wonder. Not quite *Grand Hotel*.

Cerro Torra: see **Scream of Stone**

Certain Fury (1985) (87mins) (a Canadian-American film) d: Stephen Gyllenhaal s: Michael Jacobs : Tatum O'Neal, Irene Cara, Nicholas Campbell, Peter Fonda, Moses Gunn. An unbelievably poor film about two women on the run. Audiences are advised to do the same: from the box office.

Certain Practices (1979) (65mins) d: Martin Lavut s: Ian Sutherland : Richard Monette, Alan Scarfe, Susan Hogan, David Gardner, Hugh Webster, Michael Tate, Philip Akin. A bitter conflict of ethics erupts between two doctors, when a young resident discovers his hospital's chief neurosurgeon is experimenting on patients with an untried surgical technique. Doubted at the time, but true today. (See: *For the Record*)

Chain Dance (Common Bonds) (1991) (110mins) (a Canadian-American film) d: Allan Goldstein s: Michael Ironside, Alan Aylward : Michael Ironside, Brad Dourif, Rae Dawn Chong, Bruce Glover. A social worker puts two prisoners, one of whom is disabled, in a rehabilitation program. After several disagreeable incidents, they reach a better understanding of each other. Violent, ugly and unpleasant. One assumes this is taking place in Canada, but there is nothing to show for it. Just as well, perhaps.

Chained Heat II (1993) (95mins) d: Lloyd Simandl s: Chris Hype : Brigitte Nielsen, Paul Koslo, Kimberley Kates, Kari Whitman, Jana Svandova. A lurid melodrama set in a privately run women's prison known as the "recreational facility" in post-communist Prague. A lot goes on here, and not all of it occurs behind bars. Everything is awful and embarrassing. Produced in Vancouver (with no connection to the original U.S.-German film of the same title starring John Vernon).

Challengers, The (1990) (120mins) d: Eric Till s: Ralph Endersby : Gema Zamprogna, Eric Christmas, Gwynyth Walsh, Steven Endrade. A pertinent, unaffected and likeable children's film about love of family and friends. It concerns an 11-year-old girl who joins a boys-only rock band in a small Manitoba town.

Chambre blanche, La: see **House of Light, The**

Champagne for Two (1987) (74mins) d: Lewis Furey s: Amelia Hass, Julian Roffman : Nicholas Campbell, Kirsten Bishop, Carol Ann Francis, Terry Haig. Two strangers meet and fall in love, but their career interests and other differences almost pull them apart. It holds an audience's interest and has an unexpected twist. (See: *Shades of Love series*)

***Championne, La*:** see **Reach for the Sky**

Change of Heart (1984) (65mins) d: Anne Wheeler s: Sharon Riis : Joy Coghill, Kenneth James, Paul Wood, Ian Tracey, John Thompson-Allen, David Sivertsen, Susan Stackhouse, Patricia Hamilton. A beautifully played and modulated emotional experience seen through the eyes of a middle-aged farmer's wife living in northern Alberta. After years of anguish and misunderstanding, she leaves her husband and struggles to rediscover her self-esteem. (See: *For the Record*)

Change of Heart (1993) (96mins) d: Donald Shebib s: Terence Heffernan : Sarah Campbell, Jeremy Ratchford, Heath Lamberts, Barbara Hamilton, Lenore Zann. After spending many years working in television, Shebib made a welcome return to cinema screens with this charming family film. An eight-year-old girl whose mother has died searches for her father during the Christmas season. She meets eccentric characters along the way. A good-humoured tale, touchingly told without excessive sentiment.

Change of Place, A (1994) (120mins) d: Donna Deitch s: Rosemary Anne Sisson, Jim Henshaw (based on the novel by Tracy Sinclair) : Richard Springfield, Andrea Roth, Geordie Johnson, Stephanie Beachman. A student at a prominent Canadian university has a twin sister, a troubled model working in Paris who is alcoholic and in desperate need of care. The student puts her sister in a home and goes to Paris to assume her modelling work. There, she must deal with the issues, including blackmail, that had driven her sister into despair. She also falls in love with an artist. A complicated chapter of events, finely etched with the ring of truth. (See: *Harlequin* series)

Changeling, The (1980) (107mins) (a Canadian-U.S. co-production of an American film) d: Peter Medak s: William Gray, Diana Maddox : George C. Scott, Trish Van Devere, Melvyn Douglas, Jean Marsh, John Colicos, Barry Morse, Helen Burns, Frances Hyland, Ruth Springford, Madeleine Thornton-Sherwood, Eric Christmas, Roberta Maxwell, Bernard Behrens. While small aspects of the seventies filming style might not hold up, *The Changeling* is an excellent horror/suspense story. After an accident kills his family, a classical musician moves into an old house and is contacted by a poltergeist. Motivated by the grief of loosing his child, he follows the clues left by this ghost who desperately wants the sordid and disturbing truth of its murder exposed. How scary can a film be without gore or fancy special-effects—this genre-classic will show you.

***Chanson pour Julie*:** see **Song for Julie, A**

Chaos and Desire: see *Turbulence des fluides, La*

Charlie Grant's War (1985) (130mins) d: Martin Lavut s: Anna Sandor : R.H. Thomson, Jan Rubes. Charles Grant was a Canadian who saved the lives of hundreds of Viennese Jews during World War II. He was caught by the Gestapo and sent to a concentration camp, where he was befriended by a Jewish man. This is a compelling and heartbreaking retelling of a very dark chapter in history.

Chasing Cain (2001) (90mins) d: Jerry Ciccoritti s: Andrew Rai Berzins : Peter Outerbridge, Alberta Watson, Emily Hampshire. In the Parkdale area of Toronto, two detectives investigate the murder of a Croatian woman who worked at an abortion clinic. They are led to a suspect, active in the pro-life movement, and this takes them into a seemingly impenetrable world of Balkan politics and prejudices. At times, the film is gripping, honest, exciting and a brave revelation of ethnic conflict. Toronto is seen and identified to good advantage. The settings are finely detailed and alive.

Chasing Rainbows (1988) (14hrs) d: William Fruet s: Douglas Bowie : Paul Gross, Michael Riley, Julie Stewart, Booth Savage, Lewis Gordon, Thomas Peacocke, Tony Van Bridge, Patricia Hamilton, Peter Boretski. This wonderfully dramatic and romantic film is a fascinating and beautifully dressed production set in Montréal during the period between the two World Wars. It is a movie in 10 parts each dealing with the lives of the rich and poor in a non-melodramatic way. The dialogue, production design, costumes and settings are a treat. A triumph for Bowie, Fruet and producer Mark Blandford. (The first Canadian film shot for tv in high definition.)

Chat dans le sac, Le: see **Cat in the Bag, The**

Château de cartes, Le: see **Castle of Cards, The**

Chats bottes, Les : see **Master Cats, The**

Chatwill's Verdict (Killer Instinct) (Baker County, U.S.A) (Trapped) (1982) (96mins) (a Canadian-American film) d: William Fruet s: John Beaird : Henry Silva, Nicholas Campbell, Barbara Gordon, Gina Dick, Joy Thompson, Ralph Benmergui, Allan Royal. When four college students camping at Chatwill's Village observe a brutal act of backwoods justice, they become prey to be hunted to death. A hackneyed and outdated cheapie. Sad to think that Fruet had to take it on.

Chautauqua Girl (1984) (120mins) d: Rob Iscove s: Jeannine Locke : Janet-Laine Green, Terence Kelly. In a small Alberta town in the 1920s, a young university student organizes a chautauqua, a small travelling arts festival. She catches the eye of a widowed farmer; they become acquainted, and he falls in love with her. Their relationship then becomes an on-and-off case of love's labours lost. An unusual two-character piece, well played and true to its roots.

Checkmate: see *Échec et mat*

Cheerful Tearful (1998) (97mins) d&s: Donna Brunsdale : Susan Bristow, Curt McKinstry, Douglas McLeod, Kevin Jones, Jarvis Hall. A film about a mixed-up young woman called Joan, who lives in a state of constant frustration; she cannot find her way on the road to happiness. Well intentioned and sympathetic, but somewhat exasperating to sit through.

Chemin de Damas, Le: see **Damascus Road, The**

Chevaux en hiver: see **Horses in Winter**

Chez Porky 2: see **Porky's II: The Next Day**

Chez Porky: see **Porky's**

Child on the Lake, A: see *Enfant sur le lac, L'*

Child Under a Leaf (1974) (88mins) (a Canadian-American Film) d&s: George Bloomfield : Dyan Cannon, Donald Pilon, Joseph Campanella, Micheline Lanctôt, Bud Knapp, Al Waxman, Sabina Maydelle. A foolish and boring film about a married woman, her lover, their love child and her jealous, violent husband.

Child, The (1994) (94mins) d: George Mihalka s: Kurt Wimmer : Emmet Walsh, Darlene Flugel. A baby is switched in a maternity ward for the child of a homicidal maniac. A most unpleasant picture, sensational and sordid.

Childhood Friend, A (*Une amie d'enfance*) (1978) (89mins) d: Francis Mankiewicz s: Louis Saia, Louise Roy : Pauline Martin, Pauline Lapointe, Jean-Guy Viau, Jean-Pierre Cartier. A slight but perceptive story of two childhood friends who meet after years of separation and find that their lives have changed too much for them to find friendship again. Lovely performances, beautiful direction by Mankiewicz.

Children of my Heart (2000) (120mins) d&s: Keith Ross Leckie (based on the novel *Médéric* by Gabrielle Roy) : Geneviève Désilets, Yani Gellman, Mark Ellis, Barbara Gordon, Geneviève Bujold, Michael Moriarty. Based on the author's true-life experience, this is a beautifully made film about a young and determined Quebec teacher who goes to a small Manitoba town after the Depression. She receives a frosty welcome from the staff and asked not to speak French. But she does, and wins the hearts of the children, soon talking about Canadian History with a portrait of George VI and the Union Jack on the wall. She becomes a reliable and well-liked member of the community. Several clever and some touching events come together to make a charming and very honest depiction of life and learning, with its triumphs and disappointments. While its heart is always in the right place, it doesn't blink at social weakness, and tells Roy's story with captivating creativity. The settings are authentic and the film opens and closes with a Canadian Pacific train arriving and leaving. Every character is well drawn and cast, making a winning ensemble of players. Genèvieve Desilets is a delightful discovery as the French teacher finding herself in an Anglo community. Geneviève Bujold, only seen in small roles these days, but always a pleasure, appears as the author writing her book. (Note 1: This is the fourth motion picture, set in Western rural schools.) (Note 2: There are dozens of films listed in this Index, in which child actors appear and they are all excellent and so real and true in their performances, which suggests we have a valuable resource of future actresses and actors for Canadian films yet to come.)

Chili's Blues (*C'était le 12 du 12 et Chili avait les Blues*) (1994) (100mins) d: Charles Binamé s: José Fréchette : Lucie Laurier, Roy Dupuis, Joëlle Morin,

Pierre Curzi, Fanny Louzier, Claude Gagnon. This gem of a picture, one of Binamé's best, is set in the waiting room of a snow-bound country railway station. A young man meets a young girl and saves her from suicide. They fall in love, and life takes on new meaning as they wait for the storm to pass and the tracks to be cleared. The arrival and departure of their train represents new understanding and a new beginning. Perhaps—or perhaps not! A fascinating movie with depth, compassion and no lack of quiet humour, accompanied by 1960's melodies from the juke box!

Chinese Chocolate (1995) (95mins) d&s: Yan Cui, Qi Chang (based on *Luo Niao* by Chang) : Diana Peng, Shirley Cui, James Purcell, Henry Wang. Two young Chinese women travelling on the same plane to Canada become friends. Upon arrival, they begin a series of affairs with men. A sincere but trite little film about fate, survival and the longing for love.

Chocolate Eclair (*Éclair au chocolat*) (1979) (106mins) d: Jean-Claude Lord s: Jean Salvy, Jean-Claude Lord (from the novel *Le voyageur mort* by Jean Santacroce) : Lise Thouin, Jean Belzil-Gascon, Jean-Louis Roux, Colin Fox, Danielle Panneton, Aubert Pallascio, Olivier Fillion, Valérie Deltour. A sensitive, entirely natural study of the young son of a single mother. The boy comes to love his absent father through the stories his mother tells. But one day, the fantasy ends and the boy's world changes. A winning and perceptive work.

Choices of the Heart: The Margaret Sanger Story (1994) (91mins) (a Canada-U.S. film) d: Paul Shapiro s: Matt Dorff : Dana Delaney, Yank Azman, Rod Steiger, Henry Czerny, Tom McCamus, Wayne Robson, Jeff Pustil, Kenneth Welsh. The true story of an American nurse, Margaret Sanger, who fought for women to have access to contraceptives in 1914. Done with skill and sensibility.

Christina (1974) (100mins) d: Paul Krasny s: Trevor Wallace : Barbara Parkins, Peter Haskell, James McEachin, Marlyn Mason, Barbara Gordon, Helen Shaver, Thomas Hauff. A woman in Vancouver offers an unemployed engineer $25,000 to become her husband—temporarily. He falls in love with her, but she disappears. The results are surprising. Above average.

Christmas Martian, The (*Le martien de Noël***)** (1971) (65mins) d: Bernard Gosselin s: Roch Carrier : Marcel Sabourin, Catherine Leduc, François Gosselin, Roland Chenail, Guy L'Écuyer, Paul Hébert, Louise Poulin-Roy, Paul Berval, Ernest Guimond, Yvan Canuel, Yvon Leroux. A delightful film for young children about a friendly Martian who lands in Québec's northern woods at Christmastime. He is discovered, lost and cold, by two children, who take care of him. Then, after a snowmobile chase by the villagers, he is sent on his way in his twinkling red spacecraft. A forerunner to *E.T.* (see: *Tales for All* series)

Christmas of Madame Beauchamp, The (*Le revanche noël de Madame Beauchamp***)** (1981) (87mins) d&s: Raphaël Lévy : Yvette Thout, Danielle Schneider, Jean Faubert, Marc Legault, Danièle Paradis. A simple, yet warm and sympathetic study of a rich and generous older woman who falls in love with a younger and self-absorbed man. She must then face the consequences. Beautifully acted by Yvette Thout and Jean Faubert.

Christmas Story, A (1983) (93mins) (a Canadian-American film) d: Bob Clark s: Jean Shepherd, Leigh Brown, Clark (based on Shepherd's book *In God We Trust, All Others Pay Cash*) : Melinda Dillon, Darren McGavin, Peter Billingsley, Ian Petrella, Tedde Moore, Colin Fox. Family life in a small American town where a young boy wants nothing more for Christmas than an airgun. Shepherd narrates in first person. Average entertainment. A second part, *It Runs in the Family*, was filmed entirely in the U.S. (also directed by Clark and later retitled *My Summer Story*).

Christopher's Movie Matinée (1969) (87mins) d: Mort Ransen : Graham Bourns, Jan Cassen, Malcolm Dean, Roger Dowker, Tom Evans, Doreen Foster, Lari Frolick, Cindy Glickman, Peter Keefe, Joyce Moore, Cathy Masmith, Harold Shore, Chris Whiteley, Ken Whiteley. The band: Darius Brubeck, Sandy Crawley, Amos Garrett, William Hawkins. This film about students, made primarily for them, would not normally be considered within the realm of public cinema. But the growth and appreciation of student filmmaking had become so widespread by the end of the 1960s that it was considered commercial in its own sphere. Campus exhibitions yielded profitable returns for low-budget productions such as this one. Here, there is no writing credit, since no script was used. In *cinéma-vérité* fashion, the content consists of moments in the lives of a group of Toronto students. The director, 25-year-old Mort Ransen, whose work with the NFB concerned the problems of youth—notably, *No Reason to Stay*, a dramatized documentary on pupils who drop out of school—intended to make a study of student behaviour and beliefs. The students, however, wanted to make the film themselves. Ransen and his crew let them have their way, providing token instructions on points of technique. The young people express their thoughts and feelings about themselves and society, and the causes of conflicts between them and the forces of authority. Nothing is resolved, confusion remains and life seems to have no direction. (see: *Flowers on a One-Way Street*)

Ciel est à nous, Le (Shooting Stars) (1997) (90mins) (a Canada-France co-production) d: Graham Guit s: Éric Névé, Graham Guit : Romane Bohringer, Melvil Poupaud, Jean-Philippe Ecoffey, Élodie Bouchez. Here we go again, to the murky underworld of drug dealers and double-crossers, with everyone trying to double-deal. Set, for the most part, in Paris, we also have a sub-plot revolving around the wrong briefcase. A routine reality piece.

Ciel sur la tête, Le (On Your Head) (2001) (104mins) d: André Melançon, Geneviève Lefebrve s: Geneviève Lefebrve : Arianne Maheu, Marc Messier, Céline Bonnier, Serge Dupire, David Boutin. A well-meaning, tender and moving film about a 10-year-old blind girl named Simone, who lives in an adult world. She has the gift of bringing happiness to a diverse set of characters whose lives are a catalogue of ills and uncertainties. Different, if not hard to take at times.

Cinderella and Me: see **I Was a Rat**

Circle Game, The (1994) (112mins) d&s: Brigitte Berman : Marnie McPhail, Renessa Blitz, Janet-Laine Green, Albert Schultz, Tom McCamus, Geordie Johnson, David Fox, Jayne Eastwood, Brooke Johnson, Dawn Greenhalgh. Brigitte Berman became known in film circles for her full-length documentaries on musicians Artie Shaw and Bix Beiderbecke. Here, she moves into fiction with a powerful story set in the world of nightclubs and jazz musicians. The main plot concerns the hopes and fears of two women (one an ambitious blues singer, the other a jazz pianist) trying to survive in Toronto's entertainment scene. Good listening!

Circle Man (1987) (87mins) d&s: Damian Lee : Vernon Wells, Sonja Belliveau, Franco Columbus. An aging Australian boxer, who has fallen on hard times and is no longer able to play the sport properly, ekes out a living in the underground world of bare-fist fighting. Set against some convincing we-don't-know-where backgrounds, the plot is as murky as the setting. Grim going.

Circle of Two (1980) (105mins) (a Canadian-American film) d: Jules Dassin s: Thomas Hedley (from Marie-Terese Baird's novel *A Lesson in Love*) : Richard Burton, Tatum O'Neal, Nuala Fitzgerald, Robin Gammell, Patricia Collins, Kate Reid, Pamela Hyatt, Maggie Morris, Leo Leyden. Burton plays an older artist who is platonically in love with a 16-year-old student. All very romantic and circumspect in accordance with the times; today, they would have been in bed! One of Dassin's forgettable pictures. The scenery is that of Toronto, but only residents would know it.

Circle, The (The Fraternity) (2001) (100mins) (a U.S.-Canada film) d: Sidney J. Furie s: Brian Hannah : Treat Williams, Robin Dunne, Gianpaolo Ventura, Daniel Enright, Gordon Currie, Malin Akerman. More familiar fraternity stuff in a campus thriller that fails to thrill when a mysterious murder upsets university life and throws suspicion on the head of the academy.

City Girl, The (1984) (85mins) (a Canadian-American film) d: Martha Coolidge s: Leonard-John Gates, Judith Thompson : Laura Harrington, Joe Mastroianni, Peter Riegert, Colleen Camp, Carole McGill. A young woman attempting to progress in her career as a pho-tographer finds herself in several mostly unsatisfying relationships with men eager to take advantage of her. Funny, serious and honestly observed.

City of Champions (1990) (70mins) d&s: Joseph Vismeg : Philip Zyp, Geraldine Carr, Kathryn Fraser, Marie Dame. This first film, quickly made on a low budget, is a delightfully free and entertaining adventure from Edmonton. It concerns three young people and their experiences in how money and love can draw individuals together, then push them apart.

City of Dark (1997) (122mins) d&s: Bruno Lázaro Pacheco : Carlo Rota, Lisa Ryder, Beatriz Pizano, Jean-Pierre Lefebvre, Jim Kinney. Yet another dismal science-fiction excursion. A scientist has created a computer program capable of scanning human brains and processing the information contained in memories and dreams. His work is the property of a huge multinational corporation. All is dark and dis-paraging, and confusion reigns supreme. What is the NFB doing wasting money on this tripe?

City on Fire (1979) (106mins) (a Canada-U.S. co-production) d: Alvin Rakoff s: Jack Hill : Barry Newman, Susan Clark, Henry Fonda, Shelley Winters, Leslie Nielsen, James Franciscus, Mavor Moore, Ava Gardner, Ken James, Donald Pilon, Cec Linder, Richard Donat, Hilary Labow. An embittered former worker sets fire to an oil refinery in Montréal (read: any big American city) in one of the most idi-otic films ever made, anywhere. A huge cast is good but goes up in the flames of mediocrity. A product of the Capital Cost Allowance program. (see *Capital Cost Allowance program*)

Claim, The (2000) (120mins) (a Canada-U.K. co-production) d: Michael Winterbottom s: Frank Cottrell Boyce (inspired by the novel *The Mayor of Casterbridge* by Thomas Hardy) : Peter Mullan, Wesley Bentley, Milla Jovovich, Nastassja Kinski, Sarah Polley, Julian Richings, Sean McGinley. Why anyone would want to take Hardy's sprawling 1886 novel, with its country bumpkins and rural way of life, and reformat it as a tale of love, greed and redemp-tion set in California at the time it became an American state? Despite some great moments, this film doesn't work, and interest in it flags. The story could have been told without trying to be Hardy. Sarah Polley ably provides Canadian content in this muddled co-production.

Clair obscur: see **Clear-Dark**

Claire: Tonight and Tomorrow (*Claire: cette nuit et demain*) (1985) (82mins) d&s: Nardo Castillo : Liliane Clune, Luc Matte, Nicole Leblanc, Maryse Pelletier, Margarita Stocker, François Cartier. One of life's passing moments of moral doubt. We meet an independent single woman who wants a child but does not want to be artificially inseminated. She vis-its an old boyfriend to discuss her need.

Clandestins (1997) (98mins) (a Canada-Switzerland co-production) d&s: Denis Chouinard, Nicolas Wadimoff : Christelle Sabas, Mauro Bellucci,

Miroslaw Baka, Jean-Luc Orofino, François Papineau, Hanane Rabman. A powerful and compelling film about a group of illegal stowaways on a cargo ship on its way to Canada. When the boat stops en route, the tired and hungry travellers come on deck to face the angry crew. This is a thought-provoking drama dealing with important social and political issues.

Class of 1984 (1982) (98mins) (a Canada-US Film) d: Mark L. Lester s: Tom Holland, John C.W. Saxton, Mark L. Lester : Perry King, Merrie Lynn Ross, Timothy Van Patten, Roddy McDowall, Al Waxman, Michael J. Fox, Lisa Langlois, David Gardner, Linda Sorensen. Another cheap, unpleasant entry in Hollywood's *Class of...* series, cynically exploiting the issues of crime and violence in schools and showing what high school life might be like in the future. This time, a teacher is hounded by a psychotic student. Some of this came true, but truth is not the concern here. Followed by *Class of 1999* in 1992.

Class Warfare 2001 (2000) (88mins) (a Canada-U.S. film) d: Richard Shepard s: George Finch : Kiele Sanchez, Lindsay McKeon, Robin Dunne, Wade Carpenter, David McGowan, Jessica Schreier. The winner of a lottery is murdered when an immoral teenager steals the ticket and runs away with it. A winning thriller, but over-doing the violence and bad language. Filmed in Vancouver.

Clean Hands (*Les mains nettes*) (1958) (73mins) (b/w) d: Claude Jutra s: Fernand Dansereau : Denise Provost, Jean Brousseau, Teddy-Burns Goulet. Another protest over working conditions. This time, the staff of a large company is angry about being reorganized and fearful of losing jobs. Working-class lives are depicted with sympathy and understanding. Jutra was later to become one of Québec's most successful and praised filmmakers.

Clean Machine, The (*Tirelire, combines & cie*) (1992) (90mins) d: Jean Beaudry s: Jacques Desjardins and Jean Beaudry : Vincent Bolduc, Pierre-Luc Brillant, Delphine Piperni, Alexandra Laverdière, Dorothée Berryman, Normand Chouinard, Denis Bouchard. Led by spoiled 12-year-old Charles, an enterprising group of children sets up a house and yard cleaning company to make money during the summer. Another youngster, Maggie, is a budding filmmaker doing a video commercial of their activities. However, each of the young entrepreneurs has his own reasons for participating, and the company soon finds itself in trouble. It is rare for a film to teach young people business management and ethics in an easygoing, honest and humorous way. This movie is natural, fresh and appealing. (See: *Tales for All* series)

Clean Up Squad, The: see **Hot Dogs**

Clear Cut (1991) (98mins) d: Richard Bugajski: Rob Forsyth (based on the novel *A Dream Like Mine* by M.T. Kelly) : Ronald Lea, Michael Hogan, Graham Greene, Rebecca Jenkins. This important film deals with land claims by native people in Northern Ontario and their struggles to keep the logging companies from stripping the forests. On a personal level, it brings a rebellious and militant native into deadly conflict with his lawyer and a mill owner. Anger leads to violence and the Ontario Provincial Police are called in to pacify the warring factions. However, some natives are shot, and melodrama takes over. This was the first movie Polish director Bugajski made after he came to Canada following the success of *Interrogation* (1989).

Clear-Dark (Clair obscur) (1988) (85mins) d: Bashar Shbib s: Marlyse Wilder, Marie-Nicole Simon, Bashar Shbib : Bobo Vian, Susan Eyton-Jones, Bashar Shbib, Paul Babiar, Attila Bertalan. A young singer returns to his village in Québec after an absence of many years. His presence alters the life of a local family. Shbib is in a calmer mood here.

Climb, The (1987) (90mins) d&s: Donald Shebib : Bruce Greenwood, James Hurdle, Kenneth Welsh, Kenneth Pogue, Thomas Hauff, Guy Bannerman. In 1953, a group of mountain climbers from Germany and Austria attempt to ascend the treacherous 26,000-foot Nanga Parbat mountain in the Himalayas. Incidents, mistakes and bad weather bring about clashes between the group leader and lead climber. A difficult film to make, but Shebib pulls it off with conviction. Epic adventure, with an undercurrent of political resentment. (Not to be confused with Shebib's *The Ascent*)

Close to Falling Asleep (*Trois pommes à côté du sommeil*) (1988) (91mins) d: Jacques Leduc s: Michel Langlois, Jacques Leduc : Normand Chouinard, Paule Baillargeon, Paule Marier, Josée Chaboillez, Guy Nadon. An introspective study of a freelance journalist on his 40th birthday and his encounters with the three women who have influenced his politics, passions and personal perceptions. As if this were not enough, he has a friend with whom he questions the meaning of life and the cosmos. A serious day, indeed.

Close to Home (1986) (95mins) d: Ric Beairsto s: Harvey Crossland, Ric Beairsto : Daniel Allman, Jillian Fargey, Anne Petrie. Davey Street in Vancouver is a notorious haunt of prostitutes, where young girls sell themselves and are badly treated, exploited and, sometimes, murdered. This compelling part-drama, part-documentary shows genuine concern. It never sacrifices the despair and degeneracy of these young people's lives for slick sensationalism or superficial social criticism. It is honest and deeply affecting.

Clown Murders, The (1976) (95mins) d&s: Martyn Burke : Stephen Young, Susan Keller, Lawrence Dane, John Candy, Gary Reineke, John Bayliss, Al Waxman, Michael Magee, Cec Linder, William Osler, Philip Craig. A clownish and clumsy attempt at doing an Agatha Christie at a boisterous Halloween party where a kidnapping takes place. John Candy makes one of his earliest movie appearances; his weight becomes a running joke!

Clumsy Klutz, The: see *Deux pieds dans la même bottine, Les*

Closer and Closer (1996) (89mins) (a U.S.-Canada film) d: Fred Gerber s: Matta Dorff : Kim Delaney, John J. York, Peter Outerbridge, Anthony Sherwood, Peter MacNeill. An unexpected and extraordinary film about a writer, a paraplegic, as a result of being attacked by a sex-maniac, who has published a book about serial killers of women. Now at home, where she moves deftly around in her wheelchair, she finds that she is being warned by an evil sounding voice over her complicated computer equipment, that he is the "classic gargoyle" she wrote about and that he will kill her and other women. This takes place entirely in the US (surprise) with the FBI and local police, intelligent and sympathetic characters for a change. On the whole it's a genuinely frightening, gripping study of psychological depth and awareness of human nature, very well made and superbly acted, set in an interesting home with fascinating electronic communications equipment.

Barbeque: A Love Story (1997) (97mins) d&s: Stacy Kirk : Peter Flemming, Babz Chula, Earl Pastko, Suzy Joachim, Deanna Milligan. Set in a trailer park in the southern U.S., where losers and unhappy misfits become embroiled in sex, betrayal and dissatisfaction. Not much to see or learn here.

Baree, Son of Kazan (1994) (96mins) d&s: Arnaud Selignac : Jeff Fahey, Neve Campbell. A sequel to *Kazan* in which a zoologist falls in love with a native woman. *(see Aventures du grand nord, Les and Kazan)*.

Barnone (1997) (118mins) d&s: Mark Tuit : William MacDonald, Cavan Cunningham, Anthony Dohm, Frank Topol, Kathleen Corbett. The insecure financial position of the owners of a Vancouver bar and restaurant provides a behind-the-counter look at the food services business. Human emotions come into play when the manager makes changes to the staff, and tensions play out between employees, management and regular clients. All quite revealing and convincingly served up by the cast and customers.

Baroness and the Pig, The (2002) (95mins) d&s: Michael Mackenzie (based on his play) : Patricia Clarkson, Caroline Dhavernas, Colm Feore, Bernard Hepton, Louise Marleau. Technology forms the foundation for this most unusual film. A wealthy American woman marries an English baron and moves to France, where she becomes fascinated with all things scientific and plunges herself into the world of art. Finding herself rejected by the upper classes, she brings a young country girl to the city and introduces her to a hostile society. The film itself is an advance in technology, being digital and shown in the cinema by satellite transmission and projected through a computer onto the screen: the way of the future!

Bastards (2003) (96mins) d&s: Mort Ransen : Liisa Repo Martell, Mort Ransen, Tygh Runyan. An experimental film, which at least has a story to tell, comprehensible and concerned. A retired man, Sam, whom we never see until the end, befriends a homeless young woman, who thinks that all men are 'bastards' and responsible for the mess the world is in. There are no sub-plots or cut-aways, the actors accept the cameras as just being around, living with them, and the audience discovers what is happening just as Sam does. Neither boring nor shallow, this comes within the Alan King sphere, but in a way that gives it its own form and style.

Clutch (1998) (85mins) d&s: Christopher Grismer : David Hewlett, Tanya Allen, David Fox, Gordon Michael Woolvett, Peter Spence, Ellen-Ray Hennessy, Tom Green, Carlo Rota. A thief who steals only rare books accidentally kills the owner of a house he is robbing. To dispose of the corpse, he enlists the help of a friend with a car. Of course, everything goes wrong. Referred to in current English lingo as a "hip" comedy, the film stretches its slender material to the breaking point. Many additional characters add to the confusion.

Cockroach That Ate Cincinnati, The (1996) (97mins) d: Michael McNamara s: Alan Williams : Alan Williams, Deborah Drakeford, Oliver Dennis. A couple of novice filmmakers decide to make a film in which Alan Williams, the British satirist and comic, will preserve his art for posterity. What follows is a record of Williams' funny, dry, despairing views on the world. At times, it becomes a somewhat tiresome rant. But it is funny watching the filmmakers filming!

Coeur au poing, Le: see **Streetheart**

Coeur de maman: see **Mother's Heart, A**

Coeur de nylon: see **Nylon Heart, A**

Coeur découvert, Le: see **Heart Exposed, The**

Coffin Affair, The (*L'affaire Coffin*) (1980) (106mins) d: Jean-Claude Labrecque s: Jacques Benoît (after the book by Jacques Hébert) : August Schellenberg, Yvon Dufour, Micheline Lanctôt, Jean-Marie Lemieux, Gabriel Arcand, Raymond Cloutier. This is a small-scale but dramatically effective retelling of the 1953 murder of three American hunters in the Gaspé forest. The police investigation becomes a political issue, and Wilbert Coffin is convicted and hanged for the murders in February 1956. There are reasons to believe he was innocent. A memorable film. See also: *Biographie: Jean Claude Labrecque* (2001) (60mins) Documentary by Jerome Labreque tracing the life and work of this distinguished cinematographer and director with scenes from many of his remarkable films.

Cold Blooded: see **Bad Faith**

Cold Comfort (1989) (88mins) d: Vic Sarin s: Richard Beattie, James Garrard, Elliot Sims (from his play) : Margaret Langrick, Maury Chaykin, Paul Gross, Jayne Eastwood, Ted Follows. A strange tow truck driver brings a stranded motorist home and presents him to his daughter! All is not well, however, between father and daughter, and life and death duel throughout their relationship. The first feature from noted cinematographer Vic Sarin. It begins as a drama of winter life on the prairies, then turns into a somewhat unconvincing horror film. Expertly photographed and well acted.

Cold Front (1989) (96mins) (a Canadian-American film) d: Paul Bnarbic (Allan Goldstein) s: Allan and Stefan Arngrim : Martin Sheen, Michael Ontkean, Beverly D'Angelo, Doug McGrath. A U.S. Drug Enforcement Agency officer comes to Vancouver to meet with his RCMP counterpart and work with him in tracking down terrorists. Strictly good relations here, lifeless and confusing.

Cold Journey (1976) (75mins) d: Martin Defalco s: David Jones : Johnny Yesno, Buckley Petawabano, Chief Dan George, Alphonse Dorion, Noel Starblanket, Guy L'Écuyer. In northern Saskatchewan, a native youth's unsuccessful attempts to integrate with white society leave him feeling alienated and ostracized. A disturbing portrait of a troubling situation.

Cold Sweat (1993) (95mins) d: Gail Harvey s: Richard Beattie : Ben Cross, Adam Baldwin, Shannon Tweed, Henry Czerny, Lenore Zann, Dave Thomas. An intriguing idea with some novel twists based on a story about a businessman who hires an assassin to murder his partner. But as the plot unfolds, the acting and direction fail to realize the possibilities of the narrative, and the result is ludicrous. The score, as with so many Canadian films, is inappropriate and breaks into silly songs to prop up the storyline.

Colder Kind of Death, A (2000) (120mins) d: Bradford Turner s: Andrew Wreggitt and R.B. Carney (based on the book by Gail Bowen) : Wendy Crewson, Victor Garber, Robin Dunne, Sugith Varughese. Joanne Kilbourn leaves the police force, when it fails to find her husband's murderer. She blames careless investigators. Then, when the police have enough evidence to arrest a prime suspect, he is murdered.. The dead suspect's wife is strangled with a scarf belonging to Kilbourn. The film is well plotted, exciting and provides enough suspense to keep audiences wondering what comes next. (See: *Mystery* series)

Collectionneur, Le (The Collector) (2001) (125mins) d: Jean Beaudin s: Chantal Cadieux, Jean Beaudin (based on the novel by Chrystine Brouillet) : Maude Guerin, Luc Picard, Lawrence Arcouette, Charles-Andre Bourassa, Christian Begin, Julie Menard. This is truly frightening study of a madman who kills women, cuts off their limbs and heads, and rejoins the pieces as exhibits. A young woman, a detective, is tracking him down. The film ends, having been an overlong and protracted horror. Yet it registers as one of the most incisive and truthful portrayals of an evil mind the screen has depicted.

Collector, The: see *Collectionneur, Le*

Collectors, The (1999) (101mins) (a Canadian-American film) d: Sidney J. Furie s: Robert Anton, David Penotti : Carl Alacchi, Allen Altman, Casper Van Dien, Daniel Pilon, Catherine Oxenberg. More crime as two hitmen, collecting unpaid debts, decide to try something that promises a bigger haul of cash. But a determined detective gets on their trail as she hunts them through city streets, here Montréal. The pace is fast, the tension high, and excitement accompanies the activities throughout.

Colombes, Les: see **Doves, The**

Columbus of Sex, The: My Secret Life (1969) (97mins) d: John Hofsess s: John Hofsess (based on the book *My Secret Life,* anon.) : Leon Jarvis, Patricia Murphy, Lyn Logan, Laurie Martin, Katharine Slobodin, Joan Vinell, Mary Jane Card, Ray Barker. An author working on his memoirs describes his lifelong pursuit of the perfect sexual experience. This is illustrated with shots of erotic sculpture and paintings of nudes and couples engaged in the act. It was made at McMaster University in Hamilton, Ontario, by a group of young cineastes, including Hofsess, Eugene Levy, Ivan Reitman and Dan Goldberg. They were arrested when they tried to show the film at the university, and the print was confiscated. Common sense later prevailed. (Shades of Larry Kent!)

Come l'America: see **Almost America**

Come Together (2001) (78mins) d&s: Jeff MacPherson : Tygh Runyan, Eryn Collins, Laura Harris. A small, light and pleasing romance comedy such as our filmmakers once made back in the '60s, this one brings us a young man who writes the greetings in birthday and other special-occasion cards. He loses his girlfriend, but meets another, who thinks he is an up-and-coming author. Delightful while it lasts. The title, is a poor choice for this charming portrayal,

Comics, The: see **Funny Farm, The**

Coming of Age (1983) (75mins) d: Jane Thompson s: Donald Martin : Jan Rubes, Marion Gilsenan, Jennifer Phipps, Bernard Behrens. A widowed woman takes in boarders to fill her empty days. Being alone, yet alive emotionally, she quite naturally falls in love with one of her residents. She also offers support to a man and his wife, who suffers from Alzheimer's disease. This is the director's first feature. Thompson felt the need "to shine a little light on a woman who had led an ordinary and uneventful life." A gem among our smaller films, with unforgettable images.

Coming Out Alive (1980) (90mins) d: Donald McBrearty s: John Kent Harrison : Helen Shaver, Scott Hylands, Christopher Crabbe, Michael Ironside, Winston Rekert, Doug McGrath, Monica Parker. A woman is desperate to find her kidnapped and handicapped son. She is shocked by the futile efforts of the police and a private detective and draws on her inner resources. She finds herself among frightening and unknown aspects of the criminal underworld. Tense and fast moving, with energy to spare. Look for Anne Ditchburn, Amelia Hall and Barbara Gordon in cameo roles.

Comme les six doigts de la main: see **Like the Six Fingers of a Hand**

Comme un voleur (Like a Thief) (1991) (83mins) d: Michel Langlois s: Marcel Beaulier, Michel Langlois : Andrée Lachapelle, Gildor Roy, Gilbert Sicotte, Lise Roy. A delicately written, made and acted meditation on life. A son visits his mother as she waits to die. He thinks about what she means to him and how much he loves her and wishes for more time together.

Comment faire l'amour avec un negre sans se fatiguer: see **How to Make Love to a Negro Without Getting Tired**

Comment ma mere accoucha de moi durant sa ménopause (How My Mother Was Giving Birth to Me During Menopause) (2001) (120mins) d&s: Sebastien Rose : Micheline Lanctôt, Paul Ahmarani, Sylvie Moreau, Lucie Laurier, Anne-Marie Cadieux, Patrick Huard. This, believe it or not, is a comedy such as only a Québec filmmaker would ever attempt. So one is not surprised to find the talented Micheline Lanctôt behind the scenes, bringing us a young man who is in no rush to wean himself from his mother's bosom. Thirty years later, he is still living in a woman's world. All quite likeable, really.

Comment savoir: see **Knowing to Learn**

Commercial Success, A: see **Q-bec My Love**

Common Bonds: see **Chain Dance**

Company of Strangers, The (Strangers in Good Company) (1990) (101mins) d: Cynthia Scott s: Gloria Demers : Beth Webber, Catherine Roach, Cissy Meddings, Constance Garneau, Mary Meigs, Michelle Sweeney, Winifred Holden. Elderly ladies, stranded on a bus in the countryside, learn to survive while they get to know each other. A spiritual experience—partly scripted, partly improvised—the film takes place without establishing identity. Perhaps the participants are merely passengers on their way to Heaven. And neither family members nor the owner of the bus on which they are travelling seem to be searching for them. Reality is not an issue here!

Comtesse de Baton Rouge, La: see **Countess of Baton Rouge, The**

Concièrgerie, La (The Caretaker's Lodge) (The Prison) (1997) (110mins) d: Michel Poulette s: Benoît Dutrizac, Michel Poulette : Serge Dupire, Michel Forget, Macha Grenon, Raymond Cloutier, David La Haye. An adroit murder melodrama about a detective on the trail of a killer and finding himself in a strange house of horrors called the Conciergerie. With some unexpected twists, this is a thriller with riveting moments.

Concrete Angels (1987) (97mins) d: Carlo Liconti s: Jim Purdy : Joseph DiMambro, Luke McKeehan, Dean Bosacki, Omie Craden. The year is 1964, and the Beatles are to give a concert in Toronto. A young Italian boy and his band of musicians are trying to win tickets to the concert. Lighthearted, enthusiastic and melodious.

Confessional, The (Le confessionnal) (1995) (100mins) (a Canada-U.K. co-production) d&s: Robert Lepage : Lothaire Bluteau, Patrick Goyette, Jean-Louis Millette, Kristin Scott-Thomas, Ron Burrage, Richard Fréchette, François Papineau, Marie Gignac, Normand Daneau, Anne-Marie Cadieux, Suzanne Clemont, Lynda Lepage-Beaulieu. The first feature film by the internationally known stage director Robert Lepage is an extraordinary work in every respect, set in Québec City and concerning questions of identity, religious faith and a family tragedy, both mysterious and profound. Cleverly filmed and inspired by Alfred Hitchcock's *I Confess*, shot in Québec City in 1952. A superior, spell-binding cinematic experience.

Confidences of the Night (L'amour blessé) (1975) (77mins) d&s: Jean-Pierre Lefebvre : Louise Cuerrier Voices: Gilles Proulx, Paule Baillargeon, Pierre Curzi, Frédérique Collin, Jean-Guy Moreau, Monique Mercure, Jocelyn Bérubé, Denis Morelle, Guy Thauvette, France Demer, Raymond Cloutier. A quiet evening in a room with a lonely lady listening to a talk show. The camera watches and the audience waits, and also listens. The atmosphere and use of natural sounds, however, is strikingly effective. Once again Lefebrve reveals deep feelings and sympathy for this lonely person whose only connection to the world is that of radio talk shows.

Confidential (1985) (95mins) d&s: Bruce Pittman : August Schellenberg, Neil Munro, Chapelle Jaffe. A low-budget, straightforward and tightly told incident about a newspaper reporter investigating an unsolved 40-year-old murder. Mostly flash without form, slick without substance, drab but not dull.

Connecting Lines (1990) (107mins) d&s: Mary Daniel : Myra French, David Brass, Daniel Lomas, Sara Wagner. A first film in which the filmmaker travels by train through the United States to discover Americans in a series of minimalist set pieces.

Conquest (1998) (92mins) (a Canada-U.K. co-production) d: Piers Haggard s: Rob Forsyth : Lothaire Bluteau, David Fox, Tara Fitzgerald, Monique Mercure, Eugene Lipinski, Daniel Macdonald. When Daisy MacDonald, a beautiful and mysterious English woman, drives her bright red sports car into the fading prairie town of Conquest, the surroundings suddenly brighten up. She falls in love with the bank manager, and the future of Conquest seems assured. Easy going, often charming, with a nice sense of place.

Conquête, La (1973) (96mins) d: Jacques Gagnon s: Michèle Lalonde : Michèle Rossignol, François Tassé, Marie Tifo, Gilles Renaud, Jocelyn Bérubé, Frédérique Collin. A couple meet and fall in love. Much soul searching ensues, with a happy ending being unlikely. Lots of talk about fears, failings and the pleasures of married life. Nicely cast, neatly filmed.

Conspiracy of Silence (1991) (200mins) d: Francis Mankiewicz s: Suzette Couture : Michelle St. John, Maury Chaykin, Dawn Greenhalgh, Carl Marotte. A searing, remarkable and unforgettable film from Mankiewicz and Couture about the actual 1971 killing of a native woman by a group of young white men in a cold, snowbound northern Manitoba town. Everyone in the community knew who commited the crime, but racism ran so deep that no one would tell the police.

Contrecoeur (1983) (95mins) d: Jean-Guy Noël s: Gilles Noël, Jean-Guy Noël : Monique Mercure, Anouk Simard, Raymond Cloutier, Gilbert Sicotte, Michel Forget. A whimsical piece about two women going to visit their husbands. They travel by tanker truck and become attached to the driver, with surprising results. A slight but charming glimpse of Québec society.

Convicted (1938) (55mins) (b/w) d: Leon Barsha s: Edgar Edwards (based on *Face Work* by Cornell Woolrich) : Rita Hayworth, Charles Quigley, Marc Lawrence, George McKay, Doreen MacGregor. A male nightclub singer is told his brother is about to leave town with a lady of ill repute. When the woman is murdered, the singer's brother is arrested before the real killer is discovered. A competent and mildly exciting thriller. (See: *British quota era films*)

Cool Sound From Hell, A (The Young and the Beat) (1959) (70mins) d&s: Sidney J. Furie : Anthony Ray, Kim Smith, Ronald Taylor, Madeleine Kronby, Alan Crowfoot, Murray Westgate, Tom Harvey, Walter Massey, Carolyn D'Annibale. A young man becomes disillusioned with the activities of the beat generation. Lively and knowingly, this low-budget, homemade-looking film captures his mood and feelings and those of the people around him. Few films at the time, even those from Hollywood, touched on young, unmarried couples living together. This is Furie's second film; it followed *A Dangerous Age*.

Cool Sound From Hell, A: see **Dangerous Age, A**

Cop (Heller) (1981) (65mins) d: Al Waxman s: Graham Woods : Lawrence Dane, Thomas Hauff, Susan Hogan, Meg Hogarth, Ken James, Len Doncheff, Henry Ramer, David Main. Here, we learn a great deal about a policeman's work and his life as a normal, ordinary man who endures much stress and strain on the job. When this film was made, audiences had probably seen or heard little on tv about the day-to-day activities of a police officer. Revealing, and never sensational.

Cord (Hide and Seek) (2000) (100mins) (a Canadian-American film) d: Sidney J. Furie s: Joel Hladecek and Yas Takata : Daryl Hannah, Jennifer Tilley, Bruce Greenwood, Vincent Gallo, Johanna

Black. A good thriller about a couple who want a baby. They kidnap a pregnant woman and make it seem that she has died, so no one goes looking for her. Seems unbelievable, but surprisingly it has so much tension and unexpected twists it will leave most audiences shattered. With so much odd behaviour going on these days, nothing seems unlikely.

Corde au cou, La (1966) (104mins) (b/w) d: Pierre Patry s: Claude Jasmin (from his novel) : Jacques Auger, Andreé Boucher, Gilbert Chénier, Rolland D'Amour, Henri Deyglun, Jean Duceppe, Camille Ducharme, Ronald France, Guy Godin, Ernest Guimond, Gaétan Labrèche, Andreé Lachapelle, Guy L'Écuyer, Richard Martin, Jean-Louis Millette, Denise Pelletier, Monique Sirois, Gabbi Sylvain. One night at a party, a young woman is murdered by her lover. He runs away on a long and tragic flight from justice. A gripping and well-told tale.

Cordélia (1980) (116mins) d: Jean Beaudin s: Marcel Sabourin, Jean Beaudin (from Pauline Cadieux's novel *La lampe dans la fenêtre*) : Louise Portal, Gaston Lepage, Pierre Gobeil, Gilbert Sicotte, Raymond Cloutier, Jean-Louis Roux, James Blendick, Rolland Bédard. In his second film, the director of *J.A. Martin, photographe*, deals with the true story of an unconventional young woman at the turn of the 20th century in Québec who was hanged for a murder she did not commit. Convincingly staged, with fine period settings, and beautifully played by Louise Portal. Otherwise, a somewhat slow and confined realization. Affecting, nonetheless.

Cornered (Corner, The) (2001) (88mins) d&s: Lee Broker (co-director Robert Crossman) : Domenic Cina, Alex Decosta, Paddy Braybrook, Lee Broker. A gloomy, tortured tale about desperate individuals living on a street corner. Punks, mafiosi, bookies, crap shooters and gamblers find themselves trapped in tangled webs of loves, loyalties and conflicting emotions, including the ambitions of a boxer. The film is well staged and acted, with depth and feeling, and never falls into shallow contrivance. The purpose of this film, we are told, is to pay tribute to the penniless characters who spend their time in the Crest Grill at Spadina and College Streets in Toronto.

Corporal Cameron of the North West Mounted Police: see **Cameron of the Royal**

Corps célestes, Les: see **Heavenly Bodies**

Corps et âme: see **Body and Soul**

Corps perdu, À (Straight to the Heart) (1988) (92mins) (a Canada-Switzerland co-production) d: Léa Pool s: Marcel Beaulieu, Michel Langlois, Léa Pool (based on the novel by Yves Navarre) : Mathias Habich, Johanne-Marie Tremblay, Michel Voita. Léa Pool tells the story of a middle-aged photojournalist who can no longer remain detached from the civil war horrors he witnesses in Nicaragua. The man returns to Montréal to suffer a self-imposed emotional exile. His attempt to find spiritual redemption is a long and tedious business; frankly, it is difficult to care about him.

Cosmos (1997) (100mins) d&s: Manon Briand, Marie-Julie Dallaire, Denis Villeneuve, André Turpin, Jennifer Alleyn, Arto Paragamian : Marie-Hélène Monpetit, Pascal Contamine, David La Haye, Marie-France Lambert, Alexis Martin. Seven short subjects are woven into a feature-length film by producer Roger Frappier working with a group of aspiring filmmakers. The seven different segments were shot in Montréal, including: *The Individual; The Technetium; Boost; Jules and Fanny; Aurore et crepuscule; Love, American-style;* and *Cosmos and Agriculture.* Uneven at times, but, on the whole, stylish, imaginative and promising.

Cosmos and Agriculture: see **Cosmos**
Côte est: see **East Coast**
Couleur encerclée, La: see **Encircled Colour, The**
Counterstrike (1993) (22 50-min episodes) (a Canada-U.K.-France-Italy co-production) d&s: various : Christopher Plummer, James Purcell, Simon MacCorkindale, Sophie Michaud, Cyrielle Clair, Tom Kneebone and others. This is an ambitious tv series about the exploits of an elite strike team engaged in counter-espionage and other secret-agent antics. It was filmed in Toronto and employed an army of Canadian actors and directors. Possibly the first series of its kind to be made in Canada, it is listed here for the record. Exciting and easy to take.

Countess of Baton Rouge, The (La Comtesse de Baton Rouge) (1997) (94mins) d&s: André Forcier : Robin Aubert, Geneviève Brouillette, Isabel Richer, David Boutin, Gaston Lepage. Decency prevails in André Forcier's personal story as a member of a "circus of happiness" when it travelled to Louisiana in 1968. As in most of the director's work, he uses cinematic techniques to move between place and time, past and present. Using flashbacks and other imaginative devices, including biographical references, he depicts the life of a young film student who falls in love with a bearded lady. This is a story filled with love and romance, working perfectly within its complicated but controlled structure, and continually surprising in its depth of passion and fantasy; it makes us painfully aware of a future that might have been.

Country on Your Chest, The: see *Pays dans la gorge, Le*
Coup at Daybreak, A (Coup d'état au petit matin) (1998) (97mins) (a Canada-Venezuela-Spain co-production) d: Carlos Azpurua s: Jose Ignacio Cabrujas : Ruddy Rodriguez, Gabriel Retes, Elba Escobar, Manuel Aranguiz. On the night of February 4, 1992, military rebels attempted a *coup d'état* in Venezuela. The film vividly and unsparingly shows the unrest, violence, fighting and death as witnessed by the citizens of Caracas and other towns, who were made prisoners in their homes.

Coup d'état au petit matin: see **Coup at Daybreak, A**
Coup d'état: see **Power Play**
Coup de grace, Le: see **Final Blow, The**

Coup de maître: see **Hot Touch**
Courage of Kavik the Wolf Dog, The (1980) (98mins) d: Peter Carter s: George Malko (based on the book *Kavik the Wolf Dog* by Walt Morey) : John Ireland, Ian McMillan, John Candy, Chris Wiggins, Johnny Yesno, Linda Sorensen, Irena Mayeska, Murray Westgate, Cec Linder, Sean McCann. Kavik, a champion racing dog, is injured in a plane crash. He walks more than 1,500 kilometres to find his owner. Lovely dog, lovely scenery. Filmed near Banff, Alberta, and Prince Rupert, B.C., and many other places in the north, it seems. Among the many wolves inhabiting our screen, this one is champion!

Courage to Love, The (Quadroon Ball) (1999) (90mins) (a Canada-U.S. film) d: Kari Skogland s: Heather Dale, Toni Ann Johnson : Vanessa Williams, David La Haye, Gil Bellows, Lisa Bronwyn Moore, Diahann Carroll, Jean-Louis Roux, Karen Williams, Cynda Williams. In the then French colony of Louisiana, a Créole woman is forbidden by the Catholic Church to teach and nurse slaves. Racism and religion are forcefully stated during a time of conquest and despair. Convincingly portrayed.

Court-Circuit (1983) (74mins) d: Jean-Claude Labrecque s: Guy Dufresne : Pascal Rollin, Monique Miller. The first film to be directed by the distinguished cinematographer Jean-Claude Labrecque is the first dramatized work to include a Canadian prime minister as one of the characters. Here, the PM is seen travelling to meet foreign politicians and sign several lucrative business contracts. Interesting political insights.

Covergirl (1984) (92mins) d: Jean-Claude Lord s: Charles Dennis : Jeff Conway, Irena Ferris, Cathie Shirriff, Roberta Leighton, Deborah Wakeham, Kenneth Welsh, William Hutt, Charles Dennis, Tiiu Leek, August Schellenberg, Christopher Newton, Henry Ramer, Charles Jolliffe. An early version of a now familiar subject, that of an attractive young woman's rise to prominence in the modelling profession. A provocative and penetrating portrayal of the superficial world of beauty and fashion. (Filmed in Toronto with almost every available actor, including several great names from the theatre.)

Covert Action (1986) (120mins) d: Les Rose s: Brian Damude, Barry Pearson : Art Hindle, Wendy Crewson. An RCMP officer and a government representative try to uncover a KGB plot to assassinate the Québec premier. Extremely good acting. The film steps carefully over difficult ground.

Cowboys and Indians (2003) (91mins) d: Norma Bailey s: Andrew Rai Berzins : Adam Beach, Eric Schweig, Currie Graham, Garry Chalk. The remarkable director, Norma Bailey, comes forward with a powerfully told story behind the shooting in 1988 of the Manitoba Native leader, J.J. Harper by Robert Cross, a Winnipeg Police Constable. Protests from the Aboriginal council revealed a cover-up by the force, and once again, the question, was this another example of a long-held racism. Affecting and questioning.

Cowboys Don't Cry (1987) (103mins) d&s: Anne Wheeler (based on the book of the same title by Marilyn Halvornson) : Ron White, Janet-Laine Green, Zachary Ansley, Rebecca Jenkins. Anne Wheeler's third feature film, following *A War Story,* has much to recommend it as a portrait of Canada's west and of a father who becomes a has-been rodeo rider and loses the affection of his son. Beautifully staged and carried out.

Cowboys Don't Cry: see **Bye Bye Blues**

Cowboyz (1988) (85mins) d&s: Peter Evanchuk : Len Corey, Hélène Lacelle, Jacques Couillard, Frank Cole. A minor movie of only passing interest about a country and western musician who drinks too much and, when intoxicated, thinks he's Hank Williams.

Coyote (1993) (99mins) (a Canada-France co-production) d: Richard Ciupka s: Michel Michaud, Richard Sadler, Louise-Anne Bouchard : Mitsou Gélinas, Patrick Labbé, Thierry Magnier, Jean-Claude Dreyfuss, François Massicotte, Claude Legault. Set against a stark suburban locale of dilapidated refineries and railway tracks, two lovers find themselves reflecting on the forceful desires of youth. An enjoyable film with a lively and likeable cast of young players.

Coyote Run (1996) (101mins) (a Canadian-American film) d: Shimon Dotan s: Rod Hewitt : Michael Paré, Macha Grenon, Peter Greene, Gilles Pelletier. A thriller set in a Vermont town where a group of ruffians and an underworld boss go on a rampage of murder, betrayal and revenge that ends—and none too soon—in Montréal.

Crabe dans la tête, Un (**A Crab in My Head**) (2001) (102mins) d&s: André Turpin : David La Haye, Isabelle Blais, Emmanuel Bilodeau, Chantal Giroux, Pascale Desrochers. An underwater photographer narrowly escapes drowning in the Indian Ocean and, after a time in hospital, returns home to Montréal to attend an exhibition of his work. An irritating young man with an easygoing charm, brittle sense of humour and an eye for the ladies, he spends time with an unpleasant businessman, drug dealers, a gay art gallery curator, a deaf girl and a female media critic. None of these individuals is of the slightest interest; they all live in large apartments filled with bright sunlight and lead colourful, lives without meaning. The roles are well played, but the script is superficial: the film goes nowhere. Turpin also photographed *August 32nd on Earth* (*Un 32 août sur terre*) and *Maelström*. This is his second feature film. His first is *Zigrail*.

Crack Me Up (1993) (76mins) d: Bashar Shbib s: Daphna Kastner, Maryse Wilder : Daphna Kastner, Tim Brazil, Mary Crosby, David Charles. Yet another of Shbib's low-budget sex comedies set and filmed in L.A. This one concerns an innocent, modern cowboy with a mission: to make the world a funnier,

more loving place with sex and more sex. Daphna Kastner remains as attractive as always. What would Shbib do without her?

Cracking India: see **Earth**

Craque la vie (**Life Blossoms**) (1994) (89mins) d: Jean Beaudin s: Monique Messier (from *Superdame* by Vibeke Gad and Lise Lotte Timmer) : Linda Sorgini, Guy Nadon, Annette Garant, Germain Houde. A woman with four children, an ill husband, a full-time job and pressing money matters is surrounded by friends and relatives whose lives are also filled with difficulties. This is a vivid portrait, convincingly presented, of the stress and pressures of contemporary society.

Crash (1996) (103mins) d&s: David Cronenberg (based on the novel by J.G. Ballard) : James Spader, Holly Hunter, Elias Koteas, Deborah Unger, Rosanna Arquette. An abomination about people having kinky sex after being injured in automobile accidents. Stupefying and soporific with preposterous sexual encounters, one involving the brutal mauling of a woman.

Crash (Breach of Trust) (1995) (95mins) (a Canadian-American film) d: Charles Wilkinson s: Gordon Basichis, Raul Inglis (from a story by Basichis) : Michael Biehn, Leilani Sarelle Ferrer, Matthew Craven, Kim Coates, Edward Lauter, Ben Ratner. In Vancouver, serving as Seattle, the leader of a drug mob is being tracked by an undercover FBI agent. There is blackmail, money laundering, murder, explosions, gunfire and car chases. (Not to be confused with Cronenberg's *Crash* 1996.)

Crazy Horse (She Drives Me Crazy) (Friends, Lovers & Lunatics) (1989) (90mins) d: Steve Withrow s: Michael Taav : Sheila McCarthy, Elias Koteas, Daniel Stern. Another unpleasant encounter in the country, where thugs hold a couple hostage in a cottage. Loud, tiresome and ugly. Sad to see such a waste of good players.

Crazy Manette and Cardboard Gods (*Manette: la folle et les dieux de carton*) (1964) (86mins) (b/w) d&s: Camil Adam : Mariette Lévesque, Léo Ilial, Lucille Papineau, Claire Berthiaume, Marthe Nadeau. A bleak yet honest account of a young woman who has been deceived and abandoned by so many men that she loses faith in herself and in society. Turning her back on all things cruel in her life, she finds true spirituality and self-knowledge by devoting herself to her young daughter. One becomes somewhat tired of this lady; but there is no denying that the director manages to hold it together, and Mariette Lévesque suffers gamely.

Crazy Moon (1986) (89mins) d: Allan Eastman s: Tom Berry, Stefan Wodoslawsky : Kiefer Sutherland, Vanessa Vaughan. A romantic tale about a love affair between an eccentric rich youth and a free-spirited young girl who is deaf. The moon is of little help.

Crazy Weekend, A (*Week-end en folie*) (1986) (78mins) d&s: Vincent Ciambrone : Nancy Blais,

Patrick Brosseau. Weird is the word for a Montréal professor who encourages a group of students to seduce his daughters while he and his wife enjoy a holiday by the lake. Forget it.

Creeper, The: see **Rituals**

Crême glacée, chocolat et autres consolations **(Ice Cream, Chocolate and other Consolations)** (2001) (97mins) d&s: Julie Hivon : Isabelle Brouillette, Danny Gilmour, Jacinthe René, Dorothée Berryman, Clermont Jolicoeur, France Castel. Amber, Suzie and Judith are friends. Their lives are lived in periodic episodes, in different acts as though they were living a play. But there isn't much to play with, and their lives fall apart. So will members of the audience.

Cri de la nuit, Le: see **Cry in the Night, A**

Cries in the Night: see **Funeral Home**

Crime d'Ovide Plouffe, Le: see **Crime of Ovide Plouffe, The**

Crime of Ovide Plouffe, The (*Le crime d'Ovide Plouffe*) (*Les Plouffe, II*) (1984) (107mins) (a Canada-France co-production) d: Denys Arcand s: Roger Lemelin, Denys Arcand (from the novel by Lemelin) : Gabriel Arcand, Anne Létourneau, Jean Carmet, Véronique Jannot, Juliette Huot, Pierre Curzi, Louise Laparé, Denise Filiatrault, Serge Dupire, Donald Pilon, Roger Lebel, Dominique Michel, Marcel Leboeuf, Rémy Girard. This feature film is based on a six-hour tv miniseries co-produced with France. It is the story of Ovide and his relations with his lusty wife, Rita, and his demure would-be mistress, Marie. Family, work colleagues and other friends are also involved. It is set in Québec City during the early 1950s but contains few of the social and historical details found in Lemelin's novel. However, the film is consistently entertaining, affectionate and funny. (See: *Les Plouffe* [The Plouffe Family])

Crime Spree: see **Wanted**

Crime Wave (1985) (80mins) d&s: John Paizs : John Paizs, Eva Kovacs, Darrel Baran, Jeffery Owen Madden, Barbara MacDonald. A man who makes crime movies has a major obstacle to overcome. He can only write the beginnings and endings of his stories—not the part in the middle. So, he travels to Kansas to meet a script doctor. Sometimes funny, sometimes simply silly. This first film was made by Paizs in the early years of the Winnipeg Film Group.

Crimes of the Future (1970) (63mins) d&s: David Cronenberg : Ronald Mlodzik, Jon Lidolt, Paul Mulholland, Jack Messinger, Iain Ewing, Donald Owen, Kaspers Dzeguze, Bruce Martin, Brian Linehan, Willem Poolman, Udo Kasemets. Another imaginative picture-puzzle from the new avant-garde. A doctor tries to find a cure for an illness that kills young girls called "Rogue's Malady". The director's players became noted in future film work, one being Donald Owen.

Crimson Paradise, The: see **British Quota Era Films**

Crinoline Madness (*La folie des crinolines*) (1995) (93mins) d&s: Jean Gagné, Serge Gagné : Guy Thauvette, Sylvie Legault, Réynald Bouchard, Françoise Graton, Maryse Pigeon, Bernard Lalonde. The Gagné brothers have a good reputation in Québec as true independents, meaning they develop complicated storylines in their films. Here, the Vatican sends a cardinal to verify documents prepared by a committee seeking the beatification of a holy man. Rather thin bread. The subplots are more apt to confuse than enlighten audiences. In 1996, the Gagné brothers followed this film with *La marche a l'amour*, a documentary about Québec poet Gaston Miron.

A Crisis of Conscience: see *Siege de l'ame, Le*:

Critical Age, The (1923) (50mins: silent) (b/w) d: Henry MacRae s: Faith Green, Kenneth O'Hara (from Ralph Conner's book *Glengarry Schooldays*) : Pauline Garon, James Harrison, Wallace Ray, Raymond Peck, Alice May. A farmer's son saves the life of an MP's daughter. In return, the MP helps defeat a bill unfavourable to farmers. This was the first time politics was the subject of a Canadian film. Thoughtful and pleasing.

Croon Maury and Mrs. B. (International Title) (2003) (93mins) d: Hilary Pryor (aka Hilary Jones-Farrow) s: Carmel Suttor : Alexandra Stewart, John Kapelos, Ellie Harvie, Babz Chula. A woman in her mid-sixties falls in love with a man ten years younger, and finds life somewhat bitter-sweet at times, in which family troubles and the challenge of running a business, make for difficulties. But love does prevail, making this a rare and delightful picture, honest and never cloying; and how pleasant it is to see Alexandra Stewart again, after so many years away from the screen.

Cross Country (1983) (104mins) (a Canada-U.S. co-production) d: Paul Lynch s: John Hunter, William Gray (from Herbert Kastle's novel) : Richard Beymer, Nina Axelrod, Brent Carver, Michael Ironside, David Conner, George Sperdakos, Michael Kane, August Schellenberg, Paul Bradley, Roberta Weiss. A nasty, unremitting cross-country stream of rape, violence and murder.

Cross My Heart: see *Fracture du myocarde, La*

Crossbar (1979) (77mins) d: John Trent s: Keith Ross Leckie (based on the story *Crossbar* by Bill Boyle) : Brent Carver, Kim Cattrall, John Ireland, Kate Reid, Murray Westgate, Sean Sullivan, Sara Botsford, Tom Butler, Jan Muszynski. Based on the true story of a Canadian athlete who, after winning a medal for high-jumping at the summer Olympics in 1976, loses a leg in a farm accident. Refusing to give in, he trains to qualify for the 1980 Games. Well played and staged; an interesting companion picture to *The Terry Fox Story*.

Crossed Over (2001) (120mins) (a U.S.-Canada film) d: Bobby Roth s: John Wierick (based on the book *Crossed Over: A Murder–A Memoir* by Beverly

Lowry) : Diane Keaton, Maury Chaykin, Jennifer Jason Leigh. A mother finds it difficult to come to terms with the death of her young son in a hit-and-run traffic accident involving a woman driver. She fills a scrapbook with articles about female killers. Many audiences might think this a somewhat odd thing to do. She then meets a convicted murderess awaiting execution on death row in Texas. She is drawn to this woman without really knowing why and begins to visit her regularly. This leads to friendship. Despite the concern of her husband, she "learns to live again from a woman about to die."[1] Well done, but hard to swallow.

Crosswinds: see *Vents contraires*

Crowd Inside, The (1971) (103mins) d&s: Al Waxman : Geneviève Deloir, Alan Dean, Patricia Collins, Lee Broker, Ken James, Jack Creley, Al Waxman, Cosette Lee, Tom Harvey, Jayne Eastwood. This first film to be directed by the well-known actor Al Waxman is a credible attempt to explore and explain a young girl's self-discovery after living a nightmare of sex and drugs. Well played and thoughtfully treated.

Cruising Bar (**Meat Market**) (1989) (96mins) d: Robert Ménard s: Michel Côté, Claire Wojas, Robert Ménard : Michel Côté (as Charles the Peacock, Jerry the Bull, Georges the Worm, Patrick the Lion), Louise Marleau, Geneviève Rioux. In this very popular Québec film, Michel Côté plays four different characters in four amusing singles stories. He adopts different personalities, goes to bars and approaches women to see how they respond. He is clever and convincing, but the material, at times lets him down.

Crunch (1981) (91mins) (a Canadian-American film) d: Mark Warren s: Douglas Ditonto, Richard Sauer : John Vernon, Norman Fell, Robert Forster, Jean Walker, Dave Patrick, Lisa Schwartz. As the town prepares for the big football game between rivals City High and Johnson High, the behind-the-scenes scheming causes chaos. Thin, without humour or excitement. Mainly of interest to sporting types.

Cry From the Heart, A: see **Night Friend**

Cry in the Night, A (1996) (100 mins) d&s: Robin Spry : Perry King, Carol Clark, Annie Gorardot, Amy Fulsco. Rebecca-like tale of a wealthy painter who brings his Aamerican wife and children to his estate outside Montreal and terrorizes them. Hardly Hitchcock, closer to Stephen King

Cry in the Night, A (*Le cri de la nuit*) (1996) (82mins) d&s: Jean Beaudry : Pierre Curzi, Félix-Antoine Leroux, Louise Richer. A pretentious and contrived little story about a security guard (who likes to study the stars), his girlfriend and a student who is making a video. For reasons unknown, the film alternates between colour and black and white. Art for art's sake in the most modest of terms. But someone somewhere probably loves it!

Cry Woman (*Ku qi de nu ren*) (2002) (91mins) (a China-South Korea-France-Canada co-production) d: Liu Bingjian s: Liu and Deng Ye : Liao Qin, Wei Xingkun, Zhu Jiayue, Li Longjun, Wen Qing, Wu Shengli. Not without humour, this is a down-to-earth depiction of poor people in Beijing who make a desperate living out of numerous odd jobs. A married couple, the wife helps out by living as a professional mourner for the deceased of rich families. She cries without difficulty. This is a picture with something to say about a society far from ours, and makes of it a notable film.

Cube (1997) (91mins) d&s: Vincenzo Natali : Nicole deBoer, Nicky Guadagni, David Hewlett, Andrew Miller, Maurice Dean Wint, Wayne Robson, Julian Richings. Six travellers search for the *sortie* sign, as they try to escape from a giant cube hurtling through space. But every time they manage to get out, they find themselves in another cube. The characters make for very dull passengers; they lack depth and have little of interest to say. The French reportedly admire this film, possibly because it doesn't offer an explanation for these unpleasant frequent-flyer trips from nowhere to nowhere.

Cuervo, the Private Detective (*Cuervo*) (1990) (80mins) d: Carlos Ferrand s: Martin Girard, Carlos Ferrand : Kim Yaroshevskaya, Nelson Villagra, Elizabeth Chouvalidze. A senior citizen in Montréal hires a private detective to find her long-lost sister. The detective's search takes him to South America, but there is not much here in the way of suspense or excitement. An exercise in Italian-Québécois community diversity.

Cuisine rouge, La (**The Red Food**) (1980) (82mins) d&s: Paule Baillargeon, Frédérique Collin : Michèle Mercure, Han Masson, Catherine Brunelle, Marie Ouellet, Monique Mercure, Pierre Curzi. A group of waitresses working in a topless bar in Québec City find that life is not smooth or agreeable. The directors know their subject well and treat it with skill and concern.

Curé de village, Le: see **Village Priest, The**

Curse of Oak Island, The: see **Terra X**

Curse of the Viking Grave (1990) (97mins) d: Michael Scott s: Malcolm MacRury (from the novel by Farley Mowat) : Nicholas Shields, Gordon Tootoosis, Cedric Smith. A companion picture to *Lost in the Barrens*, this story is set in Manitoba in the 1930s. It concerns the adventures of teenagers who discover a Viking grave. Exciting family fare.

Cursed (1990) (88mins) d: Michel Arsenault s: Pierre Dalpé, Jean-Marc Félio : Ronald Lea, Catherine Colvey, Thomas Rack, Joy Boushel. The obsessed chemist is back with dark doings going on in his lab. A statue and its demonic inscriptions yield a formula for awful genetic experiments. Average horror.

Curtains (1983) (89mins) (a Canada-U.S. co-production) d: Richard Ciupka (Jonathan Stryker) s: Robert Guza, Jr. : John Vernon, Linda Thorson, Samantha Eggar, Anne Ditchburn, Lynne Griffin,

Sandee Currie, Lesleh Donaldson, Maury Chaykin, Booth Savage, Kate Lynch, William Marshall. A badly made horror film set in the ghostly old home of a film director, where six actresses have been invited for an audition. These curtains never open. The producer, Peter Simpson, had to shoot a new ending, but it didn't help. The director took an assumed name.

Curtis's Charm (1995) (80mins) d&s: John L'Écuyer (based on the short story by Jim Carroll) : Maurice Dean Wint, Callum Keith Rennie, Rachel Crawford, Aaron Tager, Barbara Barnes-Hopkins. This first feature by Ryerson film student John L'Écuyer was filmed in Toronto but set in an American çity slum. It concerns two drug addicts, one of whom is possessed by hallucinations and voodoo spells. Endorsed by Egoyan and Rozema, this low-budget effort shows considerable cinematographic talent and features a good cast. The opening scene in a drab café with the first-rate actor Callum Keith Rennie is the best. But the events and behaviour it depicts are likely to leave most audiences baffled.

Cyberjack (1995) (100mins) (a Canada-Japan co-production) d&s: Robert Lee : Michael Dudikoff, Brion James, Suki Kaiser, Jon Cuthbert, James Thom. In this wild, sci-fi nightmare where a deadly computer virus has infiltrated every aspect of human existence, Britain's Magic Camera Company transforms Vancouver into a city of the next century. Despite the visuals, the storyline follows the familiar clash between good and bad. And, yes, there's a mad scientist and his attractive daughter, who is ransomed in exchange for secret codes. A well-done formula film disguised with special effects.

Cyberjack (2003) (72mins) d: Jean Bourbonnais s: Michel Monty (from his play of the same title) : Stephane Demers, Michel-Andre Cardin. This is not a sensational sci-fi of the future piece of absurdity, but a compelling, fact-based study of the year 2020 where fetuses and cloned-organs are being traded on the stock markets of the world, while techno-phobes become in involved in cyber-crime. Frightening and, one imagines, all too true.

Cyberteens in Love (1994) (93mins) d&s: John Dowler (from the play by Matthew Dowler) : Martin Cummins, Justine Priestly, Hagan Beggs, Carole Henshall. Another prediction of a miserable future, as teenagers wander through control systems with a fear of all living things. Fair cast in routine material. Will there be a sequel to show us how they made out?

Damaged Lives (1933) (70mins) d: Edgar G. Ulmer s: Donald Davis, Edgar G. Ulmer : Diane Sinclair, Lyman Williams, George Irving, Almeda Fowler, Jason Robarts. In 1932, the Canadian Social Health Council in Ottawa paid Columbia Pictures in Hollywood to make this film about a businessman who contracts venereal disease and passes it on to

his wife. Intended only as a medical lesson about STDs, it played in theatres with separate showings for women and for men, with "doctors" giving brief lectures. New York censors banned the movie for four years. In many ways, it was the forerunner of the Toronto-made film *Sins of the Fathers* (1948). (Listed for the record.) (See: *From Nine to Nine*)

Damascus Road, The (*Le chemin de Damas*) (1988) (82mins) d: George Mihalka s: Marcel Beaulieu : Rémy Girard, Pascale Bussières, Jessica Barker, Markita Boies. A confusing tale of a country priest who goes to jail to save the daughters of an old friend and finds himself with a new congregation of his fellow prisoners. Difficult, but Rémy can always be relied on to pull things together.

Dame en couleurs, La: see **Woman of Colours, A**

Dames galantes (**Romantic Ladies**) (1990) (100mins) (a France-Italy-Canada co-production) d&s: Jean Charles Tacchella : Isabella Rossellini, Richard Bohringer, Marie-Christine Barrault, Laura Betti, Robin Renucci. A medieval costume comedy opening on a dark, dismal battlefield during Henry IV's France. We meet dying soldiers and joking sporty aristocrats, who indulge in comic capers. Soon they are in the king's palace for fun and games, where jesting and clowning among promiscuous ladies and cuckolded husbands jumps from one bed to another. There is one "gentleman," however, who finds time to write about the women he has loved. Otherwise, it's back to bed, with huffing and puffing and moans and groans—once they get out of those voluminous clothes. The repartee is supposed to be witty and romantic. It's so absurd, it defies belief. This version is spoken in English with an occasional subtitle.

Dan Candy's Law: see **Alien Thunder**

Dan Seurs du Mozambique, Les: see **Myth That Wouldn't Die**

Dance Goes On, The (1991) (95mins) d&s: Paul Almond : James Keach, Matthew Almond, Bryan Hennessey, Louise Marleau, Leslie Hope, Geneviève Bujold. A divorced father gets to know his adult son who has returned home to the Gaspé on a visit from Los Angeles. Paul Almond's son plays the part of a youth who comes from L.A. to Quebec's Gaspe region to see the farm he's inherited from his uncle. Somewhat biographical, with his mother, Genevieve, also being there. Interestingly, the location house being used is the same one in which Almond filmed *Isobel*, 1968, the first of his trilogy with Bujold when they were married. An introspective and endearing study of traditional rural family life. A pleasing return to film by Almond.

Dance Me Outside (1994) (87mins) d: Bruce McDonald (adapted from writings by W.P. Kinsella) s: Bruce McDonald, Don McKellar & John Frizzell : Ryan Black, Adam Beach, Jennifer Podemski, Michael Greyeyes, Lisa Lecroix. This comedy about native teenagers focuses on Silas and his dim-witted sidekick Frank, both grappling with decisions about girls and school. When an acquaintance is murdered, and the white perpetrator gets off lightly, all the teens struggle individually to deal with the crime and inequity. With genuinely funny moments, the film's weakness is in the script. The writers failed to develop the female character who goes through most profound change, and in so the climax falls flat.

Dancing in the Dark (1986) (98mins) d&s: Leon Marr (based on the novel by Joan Barfoot) : Martha Henry, Neil Munro, Rosemary Dunsmore, Richard Monette. An extraordinary first film telling the story of a woman who is devoted to her house and husband. When she learns he is having an affair with his secretary, she is emotionally destroyed and committed to a mental institution. What is unusual about this impressive and assured work is its Bressonian style, overlaid with a compellingly spoken diary told in a flashback technique. This gives the whole a highly individual approach. Events are narrated by the protagonist, beautifully played by stage actress Martha Henry.

Dancing in the Dark (1995) (93mins) (a U.S.-Canada film) d: William Corcoran s: Jacqueline Feather & David Seidler : Nicholas Campbell, Victoria Principal, Robert Vaughn, Geraint Wyn Davies, Kenneth Welsh, Robert Wagner. A heart rendering, compelling and truly remarkable study of souls in torment and relationships shattered, as a result of lies, anger and deception. A ballet instructor is attacked one day in her studio and almost raped by her husband's drunken father. The husband cannot believe her and as good as calls her a liar. What follows is a trail of devious acts taking her into a mental asylum, under the care of a crooked psychiatrist. It may sound like melodrama but it never falls into this mode, being so well-written, directed and acted. It's the *Gaslight* theme again but so very different this time around. (See also: *The Risen*.) (Not to be confused with *Dancing in the Dark* 1986 d: Leon Marr.)

Dancing on the Moon (*Viens danser sur la lune*) (1997) (90mins) d: Kit Hood s: Kevin Tierney, Jacqueline Manning-Albert (from her novel of the same name) : Dorothée Berryman, Nathalie Vansier, Michael Yarmush, Elisha Cuthbert, Martine Badgley, Joanne Côté, Serge Houde. Another delightful family film from Rock Demers. Maddie is thirteen and does not want to leave her childhood behind her. Her cheerful and no-nonsense aunt comes to visit her family, and from her she learns "never to let fear stop you from dancing on the moon". She talks to her stuffed toy animals (these scenes are animated by Brajax Polar). This is another of the Demers Tierney beautifully made family films, set in the countryside, kind and concerned and never superficial nor syrupy. The young people are knowing and winsome, with the photography radiantly catching the sensual innocence of the young girls. It also gives young audiences, and just a few older characters, something to mull over and form opinions. (See: *Tales for All* series)

Danger to Society, A (*Danger pour la société*) (1970) (65mins) d&s: Jean Martimbeau : Paolo Noël, Carole Lemaire, Rolland D'Amour, Rita Bibeau, Jacques Bilodeau. A tightly told and affecting story of a former convict in Québec who attempts to lead a new life with his wife and young daughter but is not being given a second chance by an intolerant society. He loses his job because of his criminal record and, desperate for money to support his family, robs a bank. He is caught and sent back to prison.

Dangereux, Les (2003) (108mins) d: Louis Saia s: Saia, Stephane Saint-Denis, Sylvain Ratte : Stephane Rousseau, Veronique Cloutier, Marc Messier, Pierre Labeau, Guy Nadon, Louise Portal, Michel Charrette. A disappointing, heavy-handed, action-packed comedy from the talented Saia, revolving around the kidnapping of a famous star called Roxanne. It took three scriptwriters, including the director, to produce this bullet ridden hit-men chaos.

Dangerous Age, A (1958) (70mins) d&s: Sidney J. Furie : Ben Piazza, Anne Pearson, Aileen Seaton, Kate Reid, Shane Rimmer, Sean Sullivan, Austin Willis, Barbara Hamilton, Lloyd Jones, Claude Rae. An unpretentious, romantic melodrama about a young couple's unsuccessful attempts to wed without their parents' consent. Filmed in Toronto, this honest little picture holds an important place in the development of English-language films in Canada. Sidney Furie was working at CBC-tv when he decided to make a feature film. There were no public funds available, so he financed the production with money from family and friends. After he made the film, he could not get it distributed or screened in Canada. So, he took it to London where the Rank organization showed it to favourable reviews on its Odeon circuit. Furie returned to Canada and made *A Cool Sound From Hell*. This movie received only limited showings here. He then returned to England, settled in London, and later made *The Ipcress File*, with Michael Baine the success of which led him firmly on the path to international filmmaking .

Dangerous Dreams (1986) (80mins) d: Richard Niquette s: Anna Coulombe : Pasquale Ruffolo, Sandra Dahlie-Goyer, Carlos Khandia. A young woman living in the Gaspé decides to become an actress and goes to Montréal to attend drama classes. But she is rebuffed wherever she turns and becomes frustrated by the people she meets. A pleasant little cameo familiar to the thespians among us.

Danny in the Sky (2002) (95mins) d: Denis Langlois s: Bertrand Lachance, Denis Langlois : Thierry Pepin, Veronique Jenkins, Jessie Beaulieu, Eric Cababa, Daniel Lorte, Caroline Portelance. An emotionally wrecked youth was never loved by his parents; his mother committed suicide, his father is a 'fag'. The young man tries to find himself by becoming a stripper; he appears in porno pictures and sells himself to both women and men—one client being his father. Miserable, ugly, violent and boring.

Dark Harbour (1997) (93mins) d: Peter Svatek s: Charles Adair With: Gillian Ferrabee, Pascal Gruselle, Roy Dupuis, Kristin Lehman, Rutger Hauer. This is a ghoulish melodrama about a family with a dark past in Holland; they move to New Brunswick in search of a cure for a rare congenital blood disease. Complications and weird goings-on keep the film moving.

Dark Side of the Heart, The (El lado oscuro del corazon) (1993) (127mins) (a Canada-Argentina co-production) d&s: Elisso Subiela With: André Melançon, Sandra Ballesteros, Dario Grandnetti, Nacha Guevara. A sentimental and erotic metaphor about a nightclub Cinderella and a mad poet. You must love in spite of life's wounds! Melançon seems somewhat lost in Argentina.

Darkness Falling (2002) (93mins) d: Dominc Shiach s: Colin D. Simpson, Brad Simpson & Wilson Coneybeare With: Janet Kidder, Jason Priestley, Paul Johansson, Patsy Kensit, Michael Back, Lara Daans. We meet several well and stylishly dressed, heavily made-up young women living in expensively furnished apartments. They are soon in nothing more than slips and bras, very suggestive and obviously living on ill-gotten gains and the men who hang around. One girl throws herself from the top of their building. Running through this tattered screenplay is sex and more sex, and we come to realize, now if not sooner, that we are in an S&M place of worship and practice, with chains, pornography, oh what pleasure! Two of everything please, at a time. More trash from producer Simpson's Norstar sex shop. Darkness cannot fall quickly enough.

Darkside, The (1986) (98mins) d: Constantino Magnatta s: Allan Magee, Matt Black With: Tony Galati, Cyndy Preston, John Tench, Charles Loriot. A gangster who made a porn video of a woman while she was drugged tries to take it from her. A nasty piece of work.

Darling Family, The (1994) (86mins) d: Alan Zweig s: Linda Griffiths (adapted from her play of the same title) With: Linda Griffiths, Alan Williams. A winning portrait of a romantic couple confronted with an unwanted pregnancy. Like the children in Peter Pan, the two lovers want to forget about the serious side of growing up and find a never-never land free from problems, frictions and tensions. After discussing their fears, they arrive at a higher level of understanding and acceptance. Well written and played by the lovely Linda Griffiths, who is ably supported by Alan Williams. Alan Zweig gives a static play the breath of cinema.

Dawson Patrol, The (1985) (75mins) d&s: Peter Kelly : George Robertson, Tim Henry, Neil Dainard.

In 1911, an attempt was made by the RCMP to open a new supply route to the Yukon. This small but concise depiction of the event shows the heroism and tragedy of this chapter in road building which lead to the famous Alaska Highway.

Day Breaks Once More (1995) (110mins) (b/w) (a Canada-France co-production) d: Andrea Smith s: William Break and Smith (from her novel) : Jane Smart, Bill Dull, Monica True, Atom Explosive, John Cronenburg. This film was many years in the making. It concerns a young man who hates his mother and joins the foreign legion, where he meets his father. Badly written and directed, this is another waste-of-time movie. The actors appear stunned by it all.

Day by Day: see **Grands enfants, Les**

Day Drift (1999) (82mins) d&s: Ryan Bonder : Jed Rees, Enuka Okuma, Jillian Fargey, Megan Leitch, Kurt Max Runte. A disillusioned, self-indulgent, unlikeable and bad-tempered photographer tries to overcome his difficulties to prepare for an upcoming exhibit of his work in a commercial gallery. With such a boring character, it's hard to care for or relate to anything he does.

Day in a Life, A (1999) (94mins) d: Jean Mercier s: Peter Doré : John Smith, Doris White, Jenny Moore. A gentle comedy about a group of seniors who feel that their lives are wasting away in a retirement home. They break out and start living again.

Day in a Taxi, A (Une journée en taxi) (1982) (85mins) (a Canada-France co-production) d: Robert Ménard s: Roger Fournier : Jean Yanne, Gilles Renaud, Monique Mercure, Yvon Dufour, Marie Tifo, Pauline Lapointe, Gilbert Sicotte. A dangerous and frustrating taxi ride through Montréal with a prisoner out on leave who is determined to kill the ex-friend who betrayed him. A brilliant and compelling crime piece from Ménard.

Day My Grandad Died, The (1976) (90mins) d: René Bonnière s: Michael John Nimchuk : Jan Rubes, Hanna Poznanska, Joan Karasevich, August Schellenberg, John Horton, Gary Reineke, Brian Smegal. A touching drama about a crusty Polish farmer in Manitoba during the Depression who, as old age approaches, makes peace with himself, his family and God.

Day Without Evidence, A (Ainsi soient-ils) (1970) (74mins) (b/w) d: Ivan Patry s: Louise Carrière, Jean Clairoux, Yves Patry : Dominique Lavigne, Chantale Aubré, Lise Brunet, Normand Bissonnette, Alain Morency. Once again we are in the streets and homes of Québec, and we discover more about families, friends and foes through a group of young individuals and their anxious search for personal identity. Absorbing and revealing.

Daydream Believers: The Monkees' Story (2000) (89mins) (a Canada-U.S. film) d: Neil Fearnley s: Ronald McGee : George Stanchev, Jeff Geddis, Aaron Lohr, L.B. Fisher and a great many more monkees. Everything you wanted to know about this musical group of rock-and-rollers, from tv screens to pop music charts. In spite of lots of movement, this film doesn't go anywhere. The Beatles bit is good, but a sense of time and place is otherwise absent.

De jour en jour: see **Few Days More, A**

De Varennes, Nana: see **Promised Land, The**

Dead Aviators (1998) (90mins) d: David Wellington s: Gail Collins, Semi Chellas : Lothaire Bluteau, Marsha Mason, Juliana Wimbles, Leslie Hope, Ben Cook, Eugene Lipinski, Brooke Johnson, Dan Left, James Allodi. Two children visit their grandmother in Porter's Point, Newfoundland, and meet the ghosts of two French airmen who died in the 1920s. The pilots were trying to beat Lindbergh across the Atlantic; but on their way to New York, their plane crashed in a nearby river. The children help the ghosts salvage their plane and continue on their journey. This is the briefest outline of an altogether unusual, fascinating and imaginative film, often quite moving and entrancing. A cinematic treasure.

Dead End (False Pretense) (1998) (93mins) d: Douglas Jackson s: Karl Schiffman : Eric Roberts, Jacob Tierney, Eliza Roberts, Jayne Heitmeyer, Jack Langedijk. Back to the old standby of the policeman accused of murdering his former wife who, in this story, was also a lady of the streets. The man is taking care of his troubled teenage son when he's arrested. Then—surprise—a policewoman comes to their aid. Not bad, as these melodramas come.

Dead End (*Le dernier souffle***)** (1999) (107mins) d: Richard Ciupka s: Joanne Arseneau : Luc Picard, Julien Poulin, Michel Goyette, Serge Houde, Lorne Brass, Linda Singer. Set mostly in Arkansas, this is a murky and improbable crime melodrama about a policeman whose brother is murdered. Nasty skinheads, Russian mobsters, a plaster mummy, terrorists and other brutal types all become part of this convoluted and contrived journey into evil. Horrible.

Dead Innocent (1996) (91mins) d: Sara Botsford s: Mort Phattigo : Geneviève Bujold, Jonathan Scarfe, Dolores Payne, Nancy Beatty, Graham Greene, Emily Hampshire. A tense and creepy thriller about a woman who comes home from work to find her cleaning lady dead and her daughter kidnapped. She discovers that her entire apartment has been wired, and she cannot move or work without being observed. How she overcomes this horror and meets the perpetrator makes for edge-of-the-seat excitement. Well structured and acted. (This was the first film directed by Sara Botsford.)

Dead of Night (Deathdream) (1974) (89mins) (a Canada-U.K. co-production) d: Bob Clark s: Alan Ormsby : John Marley, Lynn Carlin, Richard Backus, Henderson Forsythe, Anya Ormsby. A U.S. soldier who was thought to have died in the Vietnam war

suddenly returns home; but he is a stranger to his family. Just as well, because he has an unnatural thirst for blood—and anyone's will do. Unpleasant, and not nearly as brilliant as the classic horror film whose name it bears.

Dead Ringers (Alter Ego) (Twins) (1988) (115mins) d: David Cronenberg s: Norman Snider, David Cronenberg (based on the novel *Twins* by Bari Wood and Jack Geasland) : Jeremy Irons, Geneviève Bujold, Heidi von Palleske, Barbara Gordon, Shirley Douglas, Stephen Lack. This unpleasant film tells the unlikely story of twin gynecologists who fall in love with the same beautiful actress. She consults them separately, hoping to be treated for infertility. One of the doctors considers her as just another affair; the other finds their relationship deeply disturbing. This cold and clinical journey into the depths of depression would amount to little without Jeremy Irons' remarkable performance playing the two twins and Geneviève Bujold as the actress-patient. The most absurdly overpraised film of the year.

Dead Silence (1997) (99mins) (a Canadian-American film) d: Daniel Petrie s: Donald Stewart (based on the book by Jeffrey Deaver) : James Garner, Marlee Matlin, Lolita Davidovich, Charles Martin Smith, Kim Coates, Kenneth Welsh, James Villemaire. A bus filled with deaf teenagers and their teacher is commandeered by a group of vicious kidnappers. The FBI attempts to free the hostages. A tightly told, all-American thriller.

Dead Wrong (1983) (92mins) d: Len Kowalewich s: Ron Graham : Britt Ekland, Winston Rekert, Jackson Davies, Dale Wilson, Don MacKay. A tedious and unconvincing adventure story (filmed mainly in Mexico) about smuggling drugs from Columbia to Canada. The highly capable actor Winston Rekert is wasted here. Britt Ekland plays an undercover Mountie! Everything about this misbegotten project is dead wrong.

Dead Zone, The (1983) (103mins) d&s: David Cronenberg (from Stephen King's story) : Christopher Walken, Brooke Adams, Tom Skerritt, Herbert Lom, Anthony Zerbe, Colleen Dewhurst, Martin Sheen, Nicholas Campbell, Jackie Burroughs. Other than the *The Shining* and *Stand By Me* most adaptations from Stephen King's works are poor. *The Dead Zone* holds up. After a near fatal accident, a young man is possessed with the ability to tell a person's fate simply through physical contact. It's refreshing to see Christopher Walken not typecast as the eccentric villain. He gently and ominously captures the loneliness this new power brings. A great cast, including the almost forgotten Herbert Lom, carries the film with confidence, and second sight.

Deadbolt (1984) (120mins) (a Canadian-American film) d: Douglas Jackson s: Mara Trafficante, Frank

Rehwaldt : Justine Bateman, Adam Baldwin, Michèle Scarabelli, Cyndi Pass, Chris Mulkey, Colin Fox. A nasty, clumsy movie by greedy producers hoping to generate revenues in the American market. A student rents her apartment to a man who attacks and tortures anyone who gets in his way. She soon becomes a prisoner in her own home. Violent, unsubtle, another time-waster.

Deadend.com (2002) (150mins) d&s: S. Wyeth Clarkson (improvised) : the participation of Harold Amero, Nicole Raven, Adrian Rogers, Lita Chase. Neither documentary nor drama, this copy of tv's *Reality Survival* series follows several teens (often joined by others) in a confusing fits-and-starts journey into sex, attempted suicide, drugs, drinks and depravity. They drive across Canada and indulge in aimless conversations. Cinema imitating the worst of television.

Deadline (Anatomy of a Horror) (1980) (85mins) d: Mario Azzopardi s: Dick Oleksiak, Mario Azzopardi : Stephen Young, Sharon Masters, Marvin Goldhar, Jeannie Elias. A highly acclaimed writer of horror movies realizes that the true horror is the state of his own life and mind. The audience will feel the same way after watching this quite useless film!

Deadly Appearances (1999) (120mins) d: George Bloomfield s: R.B. Carney (from the novel by Gail Bowen) : Wendy Crewson, Victor Garber, Simon Callow, Robert Hays, Domini Blythe, Kevin Hicks, Noah Shebib, Joyce Gordon, Joanne Kilbourn. A policewoman and former wife of a politician, is astonished when she hears that her old friend, Andy Boychuk, has been arrested for the murder of a young woman. This brings her into an investigation headed by her former partner, Inspector Millard. The many complications that arise require rapt attention. The final result is seamless. (Saskatchewan was the setting for Bowen's mystery series, but the film takes place in an unidentified Ontario town, perhaps Kingston.) (See: *Mystery* series)

Deadly Arrangement (1998) (96mins) d: Michael Ironside s: John Kerigan : Michael Ironside, Currie Graham, Lori Petty. Detectives investigate the murder of one of their own and discover a mob-related conspiracy. Better than many other suspense thrillers. (To date this is actor Ironside's first and only film as a director.)

Deadly Companion: see **Double Negative**

Deadly Eyes (The Rats) (1982) (93mins) (a Canadian-American film) d: Robert Clouse s: Charles Eglee (from the book *The Rats* by James Herbert) : Sam Groom, Sara Botsford, Scatman Crothers, Lisa Langlois, Cec Linder, Michael Hogan. A silly horror film about an invasion of giant rats played by dachshunds, not very well!

Deadly Friends: The Nancy Eaton Story (2003) (120mins) (a Canada-U.K. co-production) d: Jerry Ciccoritti s: William Scoular : Jessica Pare, Alice Krige, Brendan Fletcher, Leslie Hope. Eaton's has gone, but the memories remain of the true-life murder, in 1948, of the family 23-year-old heiress by a 17-year-old friend from childhood, obsessed with her. This awful crime, which at this time were rare in Canada, shook the family who owned the great department store. This is a subject that could make a film much better than this one.

Deadly Harvest (1980) (86mins) d: Timothy Bond s: Martin Lager : Clint Walker, Nehemiah Persoff, Gary Davies, Kim Cattrall, Jim Henshaw, Dawn Greenhalgh, Cec Linder, Leo Leyden, Jan Rubes, Nuala Fitzgerald. It was disaster time at the movies, and Canadian producers played their part in the pursuit of box-office fortunes. This is one example of their efforts. The entire world faces starvation: Yawn!

Deadly Portrayal (2003) (90mins) (a Can-U.S. film) d: Jason Hreno s: Howard Friedlander : Andrew Jackson, Nicolette Sheridan, Robert Seelinger, Amanda Jane Tilson, Leni Parker. Opening with the familiar tiresome nude 'bed bonking' scene, complete with sighs and moans, suddenly a woman is murdered, and we flash forward 20 years. Set in Boston but filmed in Montreal, what follows is a dark, dreary and deadly picture in which a wife, while her husband is away, and much to the grief of their daughter, falls for her teacher. This was not a wise move. The final sequence however, does provide some suspense in an unexpected twist.

Deaf and Mute (1986) (72mins) d: Hunt Hoe s: Howard Tessler, Hunt Hoe : Armand Laroche, Tata Workman, Lory Berger. Here's one for the books. Two toughs—one deaf, the other mute—live in a rundown building and are used by the landlord to make life miserable for the other tenants. Set in Montréal. Some might detect traces of racism.

Deaf Man's Ear, The: see *Oreille d'un sourd, L'*

Deaf to the City (*Le sourd dans la ville*) (1987) (97 mins) (a Canada-Italy co-production) d: Mireille Dansereau s: Mireille Dansereau (from the novel by Marie-Claire Blais) : Béatrice Picard, Pierre Thériault, Guillaume Lemay-Thivierge. A bleak story to read, and an even bleaker film to watch, about the struggle of a group of social misfits, between life and death, comes to the screen in a remarkable study of tortured lives set among the shabby rooms of the *Hotel des Voyageurs* in Montreal.

Dear Father (*Caro Papa*) (1979) (106mins) (a Canadian-France-Italy-co-production) d: Dino Risi s: Bernardino Zapponi & Risi : Vittorio Gassman, Andree Lachapelle, Aurore Clement, Stefania Madia, John Franis Lane. A powerful millionaire discovers that his son is involved with terrorists in Rome and the shock of this and the events which follow bring dissention, fear and tagedy to dear father's family. Another co-production mish-mash.

Dear John (1988) (112mins) d&s: Catherine Ord : Valerie Buhagiar, Stanley Lake. Two prostitutes—

one a woman, the other a male transvestite—meet in Toronto. They become friends and pass good and bad times together. Unusual and watchable, with two well-drawn and played characters.

Death Bite (Spasms) (1983) (87mins) d: William Fruet s: Donald Enright, Michael Maryk, Brent Monahana (from the novel *Snake Bite* by Brent Monahan) : Peter Fonda, Oliver Reed, Kerrie Keane, Al Waxman, Marilyn Lightstone, George Bloomfield. Trying to create a telepathic relationship with a deadly serpent becomes a truly dreadful experience for a loony scientist and his followers—as well as anyone else unfortunate enough to find it, including the audience.

Death Goes North: see **British Quota Era Films**

Death of a Lumberjack (*La mort d'un boucheron*) (1973) (115mins) d&s: Gilles Carle : Carole Laure, Daniel Pilon, Denise Filiatrault, Willie Lamothe, Pauline Julien, Marcel Sabourin, J.-Léo Gagnon, Roger Lebel, Ernest Guimond, Jacques Gagné, Jacques Bouchard, Marcel Fournier. A humourous yet sad and violent account of a young woman from a small Québec village. She goes to Montréal to find her long-lost father, and we meet the people she encounters during her search. A typical Carle film: friendly, perceptive, sensually aware and never dull. Carole Laure is provocative and engaging; she went on to more important roles.

Death Ship (1980) (91mins) (a Canada-U.K. co-production) d: Alvin Rakoff s: John Robins : George Kennedy, Richard Crenna, Nick Mancuso, Sally Ann Howes, Kate Reid, Saul Rubinek. A luxury liner on a blissful voyage across the ocean collides with another vessel. Passengers flee the damaged luxury liner but find themselves being hunted and murdered. Was this voyage really necessary?

Death Target: see **Sentimental Reasons**

Death Warrant (1990) (111mins) (a Canadian-American film) d: Deran Serafian s: David Goyer : Jean-Claude Van Damme, Robert Guillaume, Cynthia Gibb, George Dickerson. An RCMP constable has gone undercover in a prison but is exposed by an inmate who recognizes him. Moderately exciting. But there's no Mountie uniform or other indication to identify this film as Canadian—which, of course, it isn't.

Death Weekend (House by the Lake) (1976) (89mins) d&s: William Fruet : Brenda Vaccaro, Don Stroud, Chuck Shamata, Richard Ayres, Kyle Edwards, Donald Cranberry, Ed McNamara. Two lovers at a weekend retreat are brutalized by four thugs. A nasty, violent and shoddy film. Vaccaro and Stroud seem truly agonized. Fruet deserves better.

Death Wish V: The Face of Death (1994) (96mins) (a U.S.-Canada film) d: Allan A. Goldstein s: Michael Colleary, Allan A. Goldstein (based on characters by Brian Garfiled) : Charles Bronson, Lesley-Anne Down, Michael Parks, Chuck Shamata, Robert Joy, Saul Rubinek, Kenneth Welsh, Erica Lancaster. Bronson's vigilante hero (Paul Kersey), after three

outings with Michael Winner and another with J. Lee Thompson, comes to Canada (or does he?) for his fifth and hopefully last time. Here his fiancée has her business activities threatened by the usual mobsters. A bad job all around.

Deathbed: see **Terminal Choice**

Deathdream: see **Dead of Night**

December (1978) (92mins) d: Jean-Paul Fugère s: Guy Dufresne : Paule Baillargeon, Jacques Godin. Alcoholism destroys a partnership between a country and western singer and a classical musician. Competent variation on a familiar theme.

Decline of the American Empire, The (*Le declin de l'empire Américan*) (1986) (101mins) d&s: Denys Arcand : Dominique Michel, Pierre Curzi, Rémy Girard, Louise Portal, Dorothée Berryman, Yves Jacques, Daniel Brière, Geneviève Rioux, Gabriel Arcand. A group of male and female university professors meet for dinner and talk about sex and sociology, their personal relationships and private fantasies. The conversation is witty, sharp, funny, furious, bright and bitchy. The film is a triumph for the players and Denys Arcand. It brought him the recognition at home and abroad he so richly deserved after making many distinguished but less-noticed movies. (see: *Barbarian Invasions, The*)

Decoy for Terror: see **Playgirl Killer**

Decoys (2003) (93mins) d: Matthew Hastings s: Hastings & Tom Berry : Corey Sevier, Stefanie von Pfetten, Kim Poirier, Meghan Ory. A preposterous film about sex crazed students in a small-town college, and of the strange behaviour of two pretty-girl transfer students from England. A dull and demented piece of nonsense.

Deeply (2000) (101mins) d&s: Sheri Elwood : Kirsten Dunst, Lynn Redgrave, Julia Brendler, Alberta Watson, Peter Donaldson, Brent Carver. A mother takes her emotionally upset teenager to a beautiful island in the Maritimes, hoping to restore a sense of beauty and happiness in her. The girl meets a withdrawn, elderly lady who has written an autobiography in the form of a fairy tale. In accordance with an ancient Viking curse, the fish in the ocean suddenly disappear, and the story becomes a story within a story. A good-looking film with lots of atmosphere, beauty and a feeling of magical intervention.

Defcon 4 (1984) (89mins) d&s: Paul Donovan : Lenore Zann, Maury Chaykin, Kate Lynch, Tim Choate, Kevin King. Three astronauts return to a ravished and impoverished Earth run by the new generation of slimy and evil punksters. We would all have been better off remaining in space.

Defy Gravity (1990) (120mins) d&s: Michael Gibson : R.H. Thomson, Karen Saunders, Chapelle Jaffe, Juno Mills Cockell, Simon Reynolds, Tracey Moore. A first feature attempting to deal with a difficult style: high comedy–drama. It relates the story of a manic inventor who alternates between good cheer and violent rage, and the effect of this behaviour on his family. The film doesn't always work but is enjoyable and serious nonetheless, with an excellent cast.

***Délivrez-nous du mal* (Deliver Us From Evil)** (1967) (82mins) (b/w) d&s: Jean-Claude Lord : Yvon Deschamps, Guy Godin, Catherine Bégin, Olivette Thibault, Jacques Bilodeau. This first film by Jean-Claude Lord is the story of a homosexual and his sister who are both in love with the same man. A cruel game ensues, which leads to misunderstandings, emotional turmoil, anger and attempts to marry others. Finally, this somewhat mixed-up melodrama turns to attempted murder by hired killers. One of the first Canadian films in which a 'gay' character was prominent, but not a very auspicious beginning for Jean-Claude Lord, who went on to make better films.

***Demoiselle sauvage, La* (The Wild Girl) (Wild Damsel)** (1991) (105mins) (a Canada-Swiss co-production) d: Léa Pool s: Laurent Gagliardi, Michel Langlois, Léa Pool : Patricia Tulasne, Mattias Habich, Roger Jendly, Michel Voita. A young Québec nurse working in Switzerland flees to the mountains to escape the police but is injured during the chase. Exhausted, she rests at the foot of a huge dam. An engineer finds her and takes care of her for the summer. They fall in love, but he is married with children to whom he must return. So, what will happen to her? As with nearly all Léa Pool's oeuvres, this film is a study of relationships. Little is expressed emotionally, and audiences must respond by making themselves a part of the lives they are watching. But for some, this is not enough, even when it is as sensitively acted and beautifully photographed as it is here.

***Dernier cri* (The Last Cry)** (1996) (82mins) (a Canada-France co-production) d: Jean-Marie Comeau s: Pierre Billon : Pierre Santini, Rémy Girard, Beata Nilska, Janine Sutto. A psychological thriller about political duplicity, cover-ups and scientific dishonesty when a biogeneticist is found dead in his Montréal office. Tense and tingling with well-drawn characters.

Dernier glacier, Le: see **Last Glacier, The**

Dernier havre, Le (1986) (81mins) d: Denyse Benoît, Robert Vanherweghem s: Monique Gervais (based on Benoît's adaptation of the novel *Le dernier havre* by Yves Thériault) : Paul Hébert, Louisette Dussault, Claude Gauthier, Robert Rivard. Filmed along some of Québec's most beautiful coastlines, this simple tale concerns the efforts of an old fisherman to convert an ancient boat into a magnificent fishing vessel. Satisfaction comes with accomplishment. His family, friends and some rogues and rascals fill out the background.

Dernier souffle, Le: see **Dead End**

Dernière condition, La (1982) (85mins) d&s: Michel Laflamme : Claude Prégent, Lisette Guertin, Yvon Bouchard, France Desjarlais, Raymond Poulin, Paul Barrette. A former actor, penniless and drunk and living in a rundown hotel in Montréal, inherits his wealthy uncle's estate. Thinking he will start a new life with his absent wife, he finds himself at the mercy of a duplicitous lawyer. A fine study of a man driven to desperation.

Dernières fiançailles, Les: see **Last Betrothal, The**

***Dernières fougères, Les* (The Last Ferns)** (1991) (93mins) d: Daniel Roussel s: Michel D'Astous : Andrée Lachapelle, Hélène Loiselle, Monique Mercure, Élise Guilbault, Anne-Marie Provencher. Five nuns living in a convent in Québec's lower St. Lawrence River valley share in each other's lives, dreams and secrets under the watchful eye of a mother superior who rejoices in the power she wields over them. A serious, sensible and disturbing portrait of troubled women, under religious rule.

Déroute, La: see **Mr. Aiello**

Deux actrices: see **Two Actresses**

Des amis pour la vie: see **Friends for Life**

***Des chiens dans la neige* (Dogs in the Snow)** (2001) (90mins) (a Canada-France co-production) d: Michel Welterlin s: Antoine Lacomblez and Welterlin : Marie-Josée Croze, Jean-Philippe Ecoffey, Romano Orzari, Anne Rousset, Antoine Lacomblez. A woman kills her unfaithful lover and unexpectedly comes face to face with mafia gangsters. She learns that her lover had been laundering money for them. She is swept up in their intrigue and murders and begins a life of lies and deceit. A rarity: a neat and tidy crime thriller.

Des pas sur la neige: see **Footsteps in the Snow**

Desert Blades: see **Escape from Iran: The Canadian Caper**

Deserters (1983) (91mins) d&s: Jack Darcus : Alan Scarfe, Dermot Hennelly, Jon Bryden, Barbara March, Robin Mossley, Ty Haller, Bob Metcalfe. Like its predecessors, Darcus' fourth film is dark, dreary and muddled. Yet, there are moments in this story that are compelling and ring true. A brutal U.S. Army sergeant is chasing two Vietnam War deserters who have fled to Canada. The proceedings are made even more persuasive by the excellent performances of Alan Scarfe, whose first film appearance was in Larry Kent's *Bitter Ash* (1963), and Barbara March. Very much a filmed stage play, set in a small dark house, it resembles a potted version of Tennessee Williams crossed with Terence Rattigan. Darcus had previously made *Great Coups of History* (1969), *Proxyhawks* (1970) and *Wolfpen Principle* (1974).

Desire (2000) (95mins) (a Canada-German co-production) d&s: Colleen Murphy : Katja Riemann, Zachary Bennett, Martin Donovan, Elizabeth Shepherd, Graham Greene, Alberta Watson, Maggie Huculak. A concert pianist meets and falls in love with a teacher who is working with police to find a missing schoolgirl. After a bright and pleasant opening, the storyline goes cold, and we get a long and tedious stretch. Loneliness and perversion are apparent, along with little clues telling us what the pianist, polite and passionate, is really up to. Murdering little girls! An interesting study that, in this case, loses its grip.

Desire in Motion (*Mouvements du désire*) (1994) (94mins) (a Canada-Swiss co-production) d&s: Léa Pool : Valérie Kaprisky, Jean-François Pichette, Jolianne L'Allier-Matteau, William Jacques. For once, here is something very Canadian from Léa Pool that actually comes to life with passion and feeling. A woman and her young daughter are travelling on the train from Montréal to Vancouver. The woman is leaving a broken marriage and hoping to find a new life in the west. The passing landscape— prairie plains to Rocky Mountains—provides a metaphor for transition and change. She meets a fellow passenger, a man going to visit his lady friend. The two become close, but nothing is certain in life, and a happy ending is not in the cards. The sound effects and photography are in the David Lean tradition, with train sequences well filmed, and the acting convincing.

Desjardins, His Life and Times (*La vie d'un homme*) (1991) (168mins) d: Richard Martin s: Robert Malenfant : René Gagnon, Annette Garant, Vincent Bilodeau, Denise Filiatrault. The beginning of the 20th century in Québec provides the background for this fine biography of Alphonse Desjardins, the founder of *Caisses Populaires Desjardins*. Perfectly acted by René Gagnon, with a convincing cast giving a living portrait of the customers of the *Caisses*.

Désoeuvrés, Les: see **Mis-Works, The**

Destiny to Order (1989) (97mins) d&s: Jim Purdy : Stephen Ouimette, Alberta Watson, Michael Ironside, Victoria Snow. Here's a good idea about the power of imagination: the characters in an author's latest novel come to life and hound him into reworking their lives so that they evolve in ways he had not envisioned. Unfortunately, some of this doesn't work. But what does holds a firm fascination.

Deux amis silencieux (**Dogs to the Rescue**) (**Two Silent Friends**) (1969) (85mins) (a Canada-Romania co-production) d&s: Paul Fritz-Nemeth : Anthony Kramreither, Dorin Dron, Draga Olteanu, Gheorghe Gima and the dogs, Toro and London. The stars in this children's film are the two dogs seen in the *Littlest Hobo* tv series. The dogs rescue a baby girl from wicked relatives who want to use her to obtain a family fortune. Heavily dubbed, and with a musical score bordering on a full symphony, charm and delicacy are drowned out.

Deux femmes en or: see **Two Women of Gold**

Deux pieds dans la même bottine, Les (**Two Feet in the Same Ankle Boot**) (**The Clumsy Klutz**) (1974) (87mins) d: Pierre Rose s: Aubrey Solomon : Claude Michaud, Louise Portal, Guy Provost, Gérard Vermette, Marcel Giguère, Raymond

Lévesque and many others. This comedy concerns the many unfortunate accidents that befall a clumsy but honest hero fashioned very much on the classic screen comedies of old. The police in this case, not quite the keystone cops suspect him of complicity with a group of bank robbers. The heroine comes to his aid, and all ends well. Refreshing.

Deux solitudes: see **Two Solitudes**

Deux super-dingues (**Heaven Help Us**) (1982) (92mins) d: Claude Castravelli s: Jacques Raymond : Jacques Raymond, Moe B. Bourbon, Joanne Morency, Riva Spier, Claudia Udy, Paul Delaney. A private detective runs an agency with three partners who die in a plane crash. Some important documents appear as if from nowhere, and angels come to his aid. An odd piece of whimsy, touched with humour and regret.

Devil at Four, The (*Le diable à quatre*) (1988) (79mins) d: Jacques Wilbrod s: Jean-Raymond Marcoux : Normand Chouinard, Lucie Laurier, Sylvie Legault, Sébastien Tougas. The peaceful life of a divorced architect and his son is shattered when he meets a new woman and her daughter. Slow but worthwhile. Good dialogue and performances.

Devil Likes Jewels, The and **Devil's Jewelry, The**: see *Diable aime les bijoux, Le*

Devil's Spawn, The: see **Hired Gun**

Diable à quatre, Le: see **Devil at Four, The**

Diable aime les bijoux, Le (**The Devil Likes Jewels**) (**The Devil's Jewellery**) (*Las joyas del diablo*) (1969) (85mins) (a Canada-Spain-Tunisia co-production) d: Jose Maria Elorrieta s: Jacques Audouy : Donald Lautrec, Michèle Torr, Angel Picazo, Vidal Molina, Nachal Pidal. A Canadian detective working with Interpol investigates a Spanish duke who is selling precious art objects illegally. After several misadventures, the detective bravely puts a stop to all this at the duke's castle. A determined yet sadly unconvincing thriller.

Diable est parmi nous, Le: see **Possession of Virginia, The**

Diamond Fleece, The (1992) (82mins) d: Albert Waxman s: Michael Norell : Ben Cross, Kate Nelligan, Brian Dennehy, David Huband, Ronald Lea, Janet-Laine Green, Gene Mack. A former jewel thief in Toronto is hired by the owner of an expensive diamond to protect it. When the policeman who had been responsible for jailing the thief finds out what he's up to now, he naturally thinks that the crook will be tempted to repeat his past. A well-acted and cleanly cut behavioural study.

Diamond Girl (1998) (120mins) d: Timothy Bond s: Charles Lazer (from the novel by Diana Palmer) : Jonathan Cake, Joely Collins, Kevin Otto, Royston Stoffels. A young woman working in a vineyard falls in love with her employer, but he remains distant. His brother arrives to help sell the business and falls in love with the young employee. Where matters of the heart are concerned, this story is nicely balanced with often touching insights. (See: *Harlequin* series)

Diana Kilmury: Teamster (1996) (92mins) d: Sturla Gunnarsson s: Anne Wheeler & J.W. Meadowfield : Barbara Williams, Nicholas Campbell, Robert Wisden, Stuart Margolin. Diana Kilmury was a truck driver from Vancouver. She was troubled by widespread deceit and corruption in the Teamsters' Union. She fought them with courage and conviction and won; but she paid dearly for defending truth and decency. Acted with a genuine sense of righteousness by Barbara Williams. Brilliantly made: the director's best work and a truly great film.

Digger (1993) (95mins) d: Robert Turner s: Rodney Gibbons : Adam Hann-Byrd, Joshua Jackson, Olympia Dukakis, Timothy Bottoms, Barbara Williams, Leslie Nielsen. A small, simple family story set among the moody mountains of Vancouver Island, passing for the U.S. It deals with a marriage breakdown, the death of an infant son, difficult relatives and two young boys, who form a close friendship based on a mutual love of nature. All a bit much, but honest, decent and well played.

Ding and Dong, The Film (1990) (96mins) d: Alain Chartrand s: Claude Meunier (based on a shared idea with Serge Thériault) : Claude Meunier, Serge Thériault, Raymond Bouchard, Sophie Faucher. The most successful film in Québec in the year it was released, this is a funny piece with two of the province's zaniest comedians: Serge Thériault and Claude Meunier. They play two poor actors who suddenly become millionaires and open their own theatre. The film was regarded by Québec critics as being somewhat vulgar, but the public rejoiced in it and the humour of the two comics, Ding and Dong.

Dinner at Fred's (1997) (94mins) d&s: Shawn Alex Thompson : Gil Bellows, Parker Posey, Kevin MacDonald, John Neville, Christopher Lloyd. A young man marries his boss's daughter. Over Christmas dinner, her family learns that he practises magic and will not let him leave until he has freed them from a bizarre curse. Not much nourishment in this underdone meal, although the visitors work hard.

Dinner's on the Table (1994) (78mins) d&s: John Ellis, Darcy Hoover : Daniel Chercover, Ron Obadia, Jim Lucas, Tamara Bick, Kirk Hudson, Wendy MacDonald. A prosthetics salesman loses his job and must cope with the pressures of looking for other work. An uneasy comedy with limited appeal, but the events shown reflect many of the difficulties of life such as this.

Dinosaur Hunter, The (2000) (90mins) d: Rick Stevenson s: Edwina Follows (based on the book *My Daniel* by Pamela Conrad) : Joely Collins, Enuka Okuma, Alison Pill, Christopher Plummer, Roberta Maxwell, R.H. Thomson, Simon MacCorkindale, William Switzer, Wendy Anderson, Shaun Johnston. A fresh, lively, charming film set on the prairies against convincing 30's settings, showing how two determined youngsters, a boy and girl, search for the skeleton of a dinosaur in Alberta to put into the museum. A hunter who plans to take the skeleton away to make some ready cash, blocks their way. Beautifully photographed, an entirely natural well-acted piece, it raises moral issues, brings in an entirely relevant, mistreated black girl, and while classed as a "family film", its substance lifts it above the run-of-the-mill.

Diplomatic Immunity (1991) (96mins) d: Sturla Gunnarsson s: Stephen Luca : Wendel Meldrum, Ofelia Medina, Michael Hogan, Michael Riley, Pedro Armendriz. Filmed in Mexico but supposedly set in El Salvador, this is a misplaced effort to offer solidarity to the oppressed people of Central America. It is immature and unbelievable in its telling of a Canadian aid plan gone wrong.

Dirty (1998) (94mins) d&s: Bruce Sweeney : Tom Scholte, Babz Chula, Benjamin Ratner, Nancy Spivak, Vincent Gale. Another dirty film: a loathsome household, dirty language, sex, violence, drugs, booze and blather. But veracity is lacking here, although actress Chula emerges as the real thing.

Dirty Tricks (1980) (94mins) (a Canada-U.S. co-production) d: Alvin Rakoff s: Thomas Gifford (from his book *The Glendower Legacy*) : Elliott Gould, Kate Jackson, Arthur Hill, Rich Little, John Juliani, Alberta Watson, Nicholas Campbell, Mavor Moore, Hugh Webster, Michael McNamara, Martin McNamara. A Harvard professor, played by Gould, gets involved with thieves trying to steal a valuable letter written by George Washington. A dead letter of a film from start to finish, in spite of a great cast.

Disappearance, The (1977) (101mins) (a Canada-U.K. co-production) d: Stuart Cooper s: Paul Mayersberg (from the novel *Echoes of Calandine* by Derek Marlowe) : Donald Sutherland, Francine Racette, David Hemmings, David Warner, John Hart, Virginia McKenna, Christopher Plummer, Peter Bowles. A distinguished group of actors cannot bring life or coherence to this much anticipated but muddled, over-directed and tiresome story of a crook searching for his lost wife. This film went wrong from the start. After it was screened at the San Sebastián Film Festival in April 1977, it was re-edited and a new score added. The film reappeared in Toronto in April 1983.

Dis-moi le si j'dérange (**Tell Me if I Bother or Disturb You**) (1989) (76mins) d: Daniel Roussel s: Janette Bertrand : Juliette Huot, Michel Jasmin, Ginette Reno. A 58-year-old woman who has been betrayed and abandoned by her husband, and whose children have grown up and left home, occupies her time by watching TV, making phone calls and talking to religious symbols. As her fear of living alone becomes intolerable and she is filled with despair, we wonder if she will find the strength and desire to survive. A dramatic study of a woman's anguish, perfectly depicted by Juliette Huot.

Distant Thunder (1988) (114mins) (a U.S.-Canadian film) d: Rick Rosenthal s: Robert Stitzel :

John Lithgow, Ralph Macchio, Kerrie Keane, Reb Brown, Janet Margolin. A sentimental story about a troubled Vietnam veteran, who lives alone in B.C., and his long-forgotten son who is searching for him. Predictable stuff.

Divided Loyalties (1989) (75mins) d: Mario Azzopardi s: Peter Jobin : Jack Langedijk, Tantoo Cardinal, Chris Wiggins. This is a most unusual Canadian film in that it deals with our history as an English colony. The film is based on the story of Joseph Brant, a native leader and British ally during the American War of Independence. Despite some lapses, it is a colourful, moving, stirring and vivid chronicle, magnificently photographed and acted with power and passion.

Divine Light: see **Screwball Academy**

Divine Ryans, The (1998) (106mins) d: Stephen Reynolds s: Wayne Johnston (from his novel of the same name) : Pete Postlethwaite, Robert Joy, Jordan Harvey, Wendel Meldrum, Mary Walsh, Marguerite MacNeil, Richard Boland, Geneviève Tessier. There is much to praise about this family drama concerning a young boy who tries to unravel the mystery of his father's sudden death. The film lives and breathes the air and life of Newfoundland. It is well acted and directed and sometimes funny, touched with feelings of sadness and regret, darkened by religious fervor and family faith in the church.

Diviners, The (1993) (116mins) d: Anne Wheeler s: Linda Svendsen (from the novel by Margaret Laurence) : Sonja Smits, Tom Jackson, Wayne Robson, Nicola Cavendish, Jennifer Podemski, Don Francks. This is the long-awaited film adaptation of Margaret Laurence's controversial and much acclaimed novel spanning five decades in the life of a determined woman who gave birth to an illegitimate daughter, coped with the difficulties of social conventions and became a successful writer. Exceptionally well made and acted.

Do You Want to Sleep With God? (*Voulez-vous coucher avec Dieu?*) (1972) (68mins) d&s: Jack Christie, Michael Hirsh, Patrick Loubert : Tuli Kupferberg, Abigail Rosen, George Ward, Johnny Champagne, Jason Rosen, Judith Merril. This piece of Toronto/N.Y.C. craziness has the doubtful distinction of being the first in a long line of unpleasant, so-called comedies giving a supposed "put down " of sex, racism and drugs, and anything else thrown up.

Document of Michael da Vida, The: see **Vida, La**

Dog Park (1998) (91mins) d&s: Bruce McCulloch : Natasha Henstridge, Luke Wilson, Kathleen Robertson, Janeane Garofalo, Bruce McCulloch, Kristen Lehman. More fallout from the *Kids in the Hall* tv series concerning dating between dog owners who meet in a park while walking their pets. It's all bad taste and bad sex jokes, with flat dialogue between uninteresting characters. There is little comedy and few romantic encounters.

Dog Who Stopped the War, The (*La guerre des tuques*) (1984) (88mins) d: André Melançon s: Danyèle Patenaude, Roger Lively : Cédric Jourde, Julien Élie. Charming and funny once the amusing events take hold, this is a bright and often tender comedy about a group of children who build a snow fort, divide themselves into two warring groups and play at war for their winter fun. The moral is found in the value of friendship and the belief in individual character. This was the first film in Rock Demers' famous children's series *Tales for All*. (See: *Tales for All* series)

Dogmatic (1996) (95mins) d: Neill Fearnley s: Zak : Michael Riley, Eugene Levy, Leila Kenzie. This pathetic piece of slapstick makes fun of a man who is struck by lightning and finds he has changed places with his dog. He now eats dog food and licks people he meets before shaking hands. Mind you, he had worked in advertising, so perhaps this is a just reward. And even his girlfriend, who likes dogs, leaves him. This is a dog of a film.

Dogpound Shuffle (1975) (96mins) d&s: Jeffrey Bloom : David Soul, Ron Moody, Scruffy the dog. A Vancouver man is jailed and separated from his small dog, who is taken to the pound. A friend of the man raises the money to get the dog out, the man is also released, and owner, friend and dog leave for Australia. Cheerful and likeable, with a laugh and a tear; a decent little family film.

Dogs to the Rescue: see **Deux amis silencieux**

Dollar, The (The Other Side of the River) (*La piastre*) (*L'autre bord du fleuve*) (1976) (83mins) d: Alain Chartrand s: Diane Cailhier, Alain Chartrand : Pierre Thériault, Claude Gauthier, Michèle Magny, Rachel Cailhier, Larissa Bhereur, J.-Léo Gagnon. Another in the growing number of Québec films dealing with characters trying to come to terms with their lives. Here, a businessman's happy existence ends abruptly, when his wife leaves him and he tries to make sense of his life.

Don Quichotte (2001) (114mins) d: Mario Rouleau, Dominic Champagne s: Wajdi Mouawad, Dominic Champagne : Rémy Girard, Edgar Fruitier, Normand Chouinard, Dominique Quesnel. This film is based on a play by Mouawad and Champagne, who were inspired by the classic novel *Don Quixote de la Mancha*, about a series of chivalric adventures, by Don Miguel de Cervantes. In the film version, Quixote and his faithful servant, Sancho Panza, wander among the beautiful sand dunes of Tadoussac, Québec, looking for windmills to tilt. The editing pattern makes the whole something far from Cervantes, but the spirit is there and it's not all champagne!

Don't Forget (*Je me souviens*) (1979) (65mins) d: Robin Spry s: Carmel Dumas : Len Cariou, Louise Marleau, Gilles Renaud, Michèle Mercure, Peter Jobin, Claude Préfontaine. The election of the Parti Québécois and its effect on friendships and an Anglophone-Francophone marriage are finely detailed with both moving and troubling aspects, as politics and society began to change in Québec, due to disturbing, political moves within the new government. This was Robin Spry's first film as a director. (See: *For the Record*)

Don't Forget to Wipe the Blood Off (two episodes of the tv series *Seaway*) (1966) (120mins) (a Canada-U.K. co-production) d: George McGowan s: Lindsay Galloway : Stephen Young, Gordon Pinsent, Ivor Barry, Charmion King, Lynda Day, Austin Willis. A film about shipping on the St. Lawrence Seaway and kidnapping and intrigue in and around Toronto harbour. Conventional stuff helped out by a good cast.

Don't Let It Kill You (*Il ne faut pas mourir pour ça*) (1968) (75mins) d: Jean-Pierre Lefebvre s: Marcel Sabourin, Jean-Pierre Lefebvre : Marcel Sabourin, Monique Champagne, Suzanne Grossman, Claudine Monfette, Lucille Bélanger, André Pagé, Denise Morelle, Gabbi Sylvain, Gaétan Labrèche, Fleur-Ange Laplante. Another story of a strange young man in Montréal, an amiable, innocent eccentric who wants to change many things—but they change him, instead. The narrative shows little evidence of his intentions, and most of the action—there is not much—remains perplexing. The pace is slow, without much camera movement or change of viewpoint, and the conversations are long. But the character of the young man, casually played by Marcel Sabourin (who wrote the script with Lefebvre), is interesting, and the ideas put forward are valid and worth consideration. The moments of wit, warmth and charm are all too rare. This is among the director's early work. He went on to make films considered classics of Canadian (Québec) cinema.

Don't Let the Angels Fall (1969) (98mins) (b/w) d: George Kaczender s: Timothy Findley, George Kaczender : Arthur Hill, Sharon Acker, Charmion King, Jonathan Michaelson, Monique Mercure, Michèle Magny, Andrée Lachapelle, John Kastner, Peter Desbarats, Ian Ireland, Madeleine Rozon, Gwyn MacKenzie, Eileen Clifford, Len Watt, Walter Massey. A well-made and acted film in which the theme of alienation is cleverly expressed in symbolic terms. It begins with the death of a dog. A close-up of a woman's hearing device is meant to show how estranged she is from her husband. The narrative is framed by a television program that is supposed to show the extent to which he is uninvolved in society. A female voice is heard, but no one is even seen. In May 1969, the movie became Canada's first dramatized feature shown in competition at the Cannes Film Festival.

Don't Say Anything: see *Ne dis rien*

Donnez-nous notre amour quotidien (In Love With Sex) (1974) (92mins) (a Canada-France-Italy co-production) d: Claude Pierson s: Huguette Boisvert : Paola Senatore, Lucretia Love, Mauro

Parenti, Jacques Biron, Yves Arcanel, Marie-France Borquet. This is prime melodrama about a young woman looking for love. We also meet other women, their doctors and playboys. An unpleasant and far-fetched sexual farrago. Should one expect anything more, however, from Claude Pierson?

Dortoir, Le: see **Cargo**

Dory (1965) (60mins) d&s: John Kozak : Donna Lewis, Roscoe Handford. A beautifully realized and touching portrait of two sisters, one of whom is mad, living alone on the Prairies. An early work from the Winnipeg Film Group.

Double Frame (1999) (90mins) d: Stefan Scaini s: Reginald Howe : Daniel Baldwin, Leslie Hope, James Remar. The police successfully undertake a drug bust, but one of the officers—the rotten apple .in the barrel—gets in over his head after he frames his partner. The police just love this kind of film, don't you know! Audiences will find they have been here before, and a repeat visit is hardly necessary.

Double Happiness (1994) (100mins) d&s: Mina Shum : Sandra Oh, Stephen Chang, Alannah Ong, Frances You, Callum Keith Rennie. Jade Li is an aspiring 22-year-old actress in Vancouver who walks a fine line between the expectations of her traditional Chinese family and the values of contemporary Canadian society. When her parents start arranging her love affairs, she ceases to be a dutiful daughter. She falls in love with a non-Chinese man and becomes a modern Western woman. A charming and comical first film.

Double Impasse: see **Keeping Track**

Double Negative (Deadly Companion) (1979) (96mins) d: George Bloomfield s: Thomas Hedley (from the novel *The Three Roads* by Ross Macdonald) : Michael Sarrazin, Susan Clark, Anthony Perkins, Howard Duff, Kate Reid, Al Waxman, Elizabeth Shepherd, Kenneth Welsh, Ken James, Lee Broker, John Candy, Douglas Campbell, Maury Chaykin, Joe Flaherty, David Gardner, Ron Hartmann, Michael Ironside, Eugene Levy, Kate Lynch, Sabina Maydelle, Catherine O'Hara, Dave Thomas. Almost every actor in Toronto, plus the usual Hollywoodites, seemed to be hired for this tired and overblown thriller about an anguished photojournalist searching for his wife's murderer. Talented actors, however, could not save the film from being flat, annoying and slow moving.

Double Take (1998) (86mins) (a Canada-US film) d: Mark L. Lester s: Edward and Ralph Rugoff : Craig Sheffer, Costas Mandylor, Brigitte Bako, Dan Lett, Maurice Godin. A witness who helped convict a murderer has doubts about whether he had identified the right man. And to his consternation, he discovers he is being drawn into a political scheme involving blackmail, Argentine rebels and violence. A nifty, original thriller, better than most, filmed in easily recognised Toronto TTC subway, but of course it isn't our city but New York.

Double Vision (1992) (91mins) (a Canada-France film) d: Robert Nights s: Mary Higgins Clark : Kim Cattrall, Gale Hansen, Christopher Lee, Macha Meril, Naveen Andrews. A suspenseful mystery concerning a medical student who travels from Montréal to London and passes herself off as her kinky missing twin sister. One is not always certain why. Telepathy, dreams, visions and dangers of various kinds keep things moving on the double.

Doulike2Watch.Com (2002) (90mins) d: Josh Levy s: Paul Bellini, Josh Levy : Sadie Leblanc, Troy Mundle, Paul DeBoy, Nina Arsenault, Daryn Jones. A group of six young people are hired to live for one year in a specially constructed house wired with hidden cameras linked to a computer mainframe. Web subscribers can watch for a fee. This takes place in real time over the running time of the film. Strictly for voyeurs.

Doux aveux, Les: see **Sweet Lies and Tender Oaths**

Douzieme Heure: see **Twelfth Hour, The**

Doves, The (Les colombes) (1972) (118mins) d&s: Jean-Claude Lord : Jean Besré, Lise Thouin, Jean Duceppe, Jean Coutu, Willie Lamothe. Family upsets, again, when a poor girl marries into wealth and becomes a successful singer, only to find that her husband resents her success, and his family starts to meddle in their affairs. Acute and well played.

Downtime (1985) (65mins) d: Greg Hanec s: Mitchell Brown : Maureen Gamalsetter, Tadriac O'Beirn, Ray Impey, Debbie Williamson. An early movie from the Winnipeg Film Group dealing with a familiar subject: the persistent worry among young people trying to make sense of their lives. Competently done.

Downtime (2001) (100mins) d&s: John Detwiler, Renée Duncan : Brendan Fletcher, Jessica Paré, Maurice Dean Wint. This is the story of an innocent young man who is not wise to the ways of the world. After leaving his dysfunctional family, he gets caught up in a net of deceit and is accused of a crime. A darkly surreal and thoughtful examination of a lost individual looking for love in all the wrong places.

Dr. Frankenstein on Campus: see **Flick**

Dr. Jekyll and Mr. Hyde (1999) (95mins) (a Canada-Australia film) d: Colin Budds s: Peter Lenkov : Adam Baldwin, Steve Bastoni, Chang Tseng, Jason Chong, Kira Clavell, Karen Cliché. How famous characters suffer when they fall into the hands of present-day filmmaking monsters! Here, the good doctor falls prey to utterly incomprehensible activities, when he is mistakenly identified as the "white tiger," an ancient Asian man of mystery. Robert Louis Stevenson would be appalled. So will audiences.

Dr. Lucille: The Lucille Teasdale Story (1999) (120mins) d: George Mihalka s: Rob Forsyth (inspired by *Un rêve ou la vie* by Michel Arseneault)

: Marina Orsini, Massimo Ghini, Louis Gossett Jr. Lucille Teasdale was born in Montréal in 1929 to a poverty stricken family and grew up determined to become a doctor: a difficult task in a profession then dominated by men. But she succeeded, and after working in Québec for many years went to Uganda with her doctor husband to care for the sick and train nurses and doctors. During the brutal regime of Idi Amin Dada, thousands died or became infected with hiv/aids. In treating the dying, Teasdale contracted HIV, and after returning to Montréal, died of aids in 1996. Along with Bethune and Osler, she is remembered as one of Canada's greatest medical doctors. Filmed in East Africa, this is a beautifully made and acted remembrance of her remarkable and frequently painful life. (See: *Signature* series)

Dr. Norman Bethune: see **Bethune**

Dracula: Pages From a Virgin's Diary (2003) (65mins) (b/w) d: Guy Maddin s: Maddin and Mark Godden : Tara Birtwhistle and the Winnipeg Ballet Company. This is described as a "new interpretation" of the famous, blood-drinking vampire. It seems to be a ballet of sorts, filmed on stage in soft focus and dark shadows, with the story considerably blurred. The dancing isn't much above twirls and jumps, while the unfortunate Mahler's music sounds like a bad Hollywood score played backwards. This is a work that should have remained on stage. What next, Dracula on skates? Religion comes into the ending with the heavenly choir. This muddled mess, which fails to communicate on any level and never seems to end, would give Bram Stoker nightmares. Nasty and "bloody" awful.

Draghoula (1994) (85mins) d&s: Bashar Shbib : Stephanie Seidle, Chris Lee, Robyn Lane, Victoria Barkoff, Bobo Vian. Shbib is at it again: blood, sex, fun and games, and all at Dracula's expense. Not that one would recognize our old fiend.

Dragonwheel (2002) (94mins) (a Canada-U.K. co-production) d&s: Trica Fish : Graham Gavine, Krista MacDonald, Andrew McCarthy, Rejean Cournoyer, Matthew Harris, Neil Matheson, William Wright. A woman (who manages a teen boy band) and a morose country man escape from their trying lives and go travelling between big cities. They fall in love and cling to each other, but cannot change their lives. Not very appealing people.

Draw! (1984) (98mins) (a Canada-U.S. co-production) d: Steven Hilliard Stern s: Stanley Mann : Kirk Douglas, James Coburn, Alexandra Bastedo, Graham Jarvis, Len Birman, Derek McGrath, Gerard Parkes, Linda Sorensen, Richard Donat, Stuart Gillard. This is a wretched pseudo-Western (filmed on Alberta's wide-open ranges passing as the U.S.). An aging outlaw is challenged by a former and now heavy-drinking lawman to one last shootout. Producer-distributor Harold Greenberg (in company with David Perlmutter, Garth Drabinsky and others) eagerly embraced the concept of the "international" (read: American) film in order to receive financial assistance from Telefilm Canada's ill-conceived Capital Cost Allowance program. *Draw!* is one of the many films that were financed using this tax shelter. (see *Capital Cost Allowance program*)

Drawing Flies (1996) (76mins) d&s: Matt Gissing, Malcolm Ingram : Jason Lee, Jason Mewes, Renée Humphrey, Carmen Lee, Martin Brooks. Five conceited young men from Toronto arrive in Vancouver to find some truths about themselves. After idling their time away in front of the tv and at parties, they go to an uncle's cottage in the wilderness to look for Bigfoot. A waste of time.

Dream Life (*La vie revée*) (1972) (85mins) d&s: Mireille Dansereau : Liliane Lemaître-Auger, Véronique Le Flaguais, Jean-François Guite, Guy Foucault, Marc Messier. Slight but tender romance about two women who work in a movie studio and discuss their love affairs in an objective, candid and sympathetic manner, worth the watching and listening to.

Dream Like Mine, A: see **Clear Cut**

Dream Man, The: see *Homme de rêve, L'*

Dream on the Run (1977) (82mins) d&s: John Edwards, Nicky Fylan : John Edwards, Nicky Fylan, Jack Lalonde, Gloria Gagnon, Susan Minas. Here we go again; a man comes out of prison, wants to rebuild his life, gets caught up in another crime and finds that his lady friend is also a small-time crook. Familiar stuff taking a familiar path.

Dream Storm: A North of 60 Mystery (2001) (120mins) d: Stacey Stewart i s: Andrew Wreggitt : Tina Keeper, Tom Jackson, Gordon Tootoosis, Peter Kelly Gaudreault, Tracey Cook, Dakota House. Filmed in Bragg Creek, Alberta, this mystery is based on the popular tv series *North of 60*. An RCMP corporal investigates several seemingly unrelated incidents, including a murder, an epidemic and a fire. In so doing, she finds new strength to carry on with her difficult personal life. An extremely well-made mystery with a difference; this film is not ashamed to look and feel Canadian. (See the companion films, *In the Blue Ground* and *Trial by Fire*.)

Dreams Beyond Memory (1987) (93mins) d&s: Andrzej Markiewicz : George Touliatos, Lisa Schrage. An old man meets a new tenant who has moved into his building: a younger woman with whom he falls in love. But to no avail and he sadly comes to realize that perfect romance is now an elusive dream. And so we leave him with thoughts, torments, crises and memories of other women. Sentimental and sincere.

Dream-Speaker (1976) (75mins) d: Claude Jutra s: Anne Cameron : Ian Tracey, George Clutesi, Jacques Hubert. Jutra's first English-language film, made in Toronto for CBC-TV, is a heartbreaking story of a disturbed adolescent who escapes from a mental institution in B.C. and flees into the forest. There, he meets a native shaman and a young boy.

They become friends, but tragedy dooms their relationship. Jutra's sensitivity towards his subject is apparent throughout.

Dreamtrips (2000) (97mins) (a Canada-Hong Kong co-production) d&s: Kal Ng : Jennifer Chan, Wayne Kwok, Gary Sze, Wan Chi Hong, Jamie Lau, Jane Show, Kal Ng, Damon Mason, Paul Fonoroff, Alex Lee. A young woman from Hong Kong who suffers from insomnia worries about the disappearance of her lover. One night, she learns about a secret virtual reality tv program. She steals a computer chip and is transported to a cyberworld, where she wanders through empty cityscapes. Murky and lost in morbid drowsiness. Audiences are likely to give up.

Drifting Downstream: see **Between Sweet and Salt Water**

Drive, She Said (1997) (103mins) d&s: Mina Shum : Moira Kelly, Josh Hamilton, Sebastion Spence, Lori Triolo, Peter Stebbings, Jim Byrnes. The subject matter here concerns criminal activity, sex and violence: a favourite mix of younger directors. After a promising opening sequence in which a teller is kidnapped during a bank robbery, the story goes on the road to nowhere. Our expectations quickly diminish as the plot loses its way in the failing narrative and collapses into a series of improbabilities.

Drive, The (1996) (75mins) d: Romy Goulem s: Adam Barken (from his play), Romy Goulem : Daniel Brochu, Fabrizio Filippo, Alain Goulem, Jayne Paterson. A tame little piece about three friends in Montréal who are abducted by a wild ex-convict. No one knows where they are going, either physically or emotionally, and one simply doesn't care what happens to them.

Drop Dead Gorgeous (Victim of Beauty) (1991) (90mins) (b/w) d: Paul Lynch s: Harriet Steinberg, Nolan Powers : Jennifer Rubin, Peter Outerbridge, Sally Kellerman, Stephen Shellen, Lindsay Merrithew. An attractive young teacher changes her life in this comedy-drama to become a model. But her boyfriends keep getting killed. This film drops dead as soon as it begins. A mystery-thriller that only occasionally comes to life.

Drying Up the Streets (1978) (86mins) d: Robin Spry s: Anna Cameron : Len Cariou, Don Francks, Calvin Butler, August Schellenberg, Jacques Hubert, Sarah Torgov, Jayne Eastwood, Frank Moore, Warren Davis, Hugh Webster, Sharry Flett. "They're drying up the streets" is a slang expression used by addicts when police prevent shipments of heroin and other drugs from reaching them. Among the tide of violent and often inaccurate films about drugs and the young people who use them, this film stands out as an honest, entirely believable story of an innocent young girl who gets caught up in Toronto's underworld. Robin Spry went on to become one of Canada's best filmmakers.

Drylanders (1963) (70mins) (b/w) d: Donald Haldane s: M. Charles Cohen, William Weintraub :

Frances Hyland, James B. Douglas, Lester Nixon, Mary Savage, William Fruet, Don Francks, Irene Mayeska. A gripping and powerful drama of family life on the Prairies during the great drought and Depression of the 1930s. In the early 1960s, voices in film were heard asking why the NFB had not changed its continual productions of documentary, long and short, by turning to dramatized feature films. The Board was hesitant to make this move because, as a government agency it could not step outside its mandate and make only theatrical films. However, it has always been called upon to fulfill Grierson's dictum of the NFB interpreting Canada to Canadians. With television making inroads into movie attendance, the Board finally thought the best way to begin making long narrative films was through television. *Drylanders* and its French-language companion piece, *The Merry World of Leopold Z,* were filmed with television in mind. But the CBC, always distant in its attitude toward the NFB, ignoring it and snubbing it, when it could have been one of its main supporters, failed to respond and rejected *Drylanders.* So much for being a Canadian public broadcaster! Tired of waiting for the CBC to change its mind, the NFB decided to try cinemas first. *Drylanders* opened in Swift Current, Saskatchewan, on September 25, 1963. After less than enthusiastic reviews, it drew small audiences who really didn't know what to make of it; the film was not like the glamorous movies they were used to seeing. Yet, it has survived over the years and can be seen many times without wearing out its appeal. It is quietly and beautifully acted by mostly unknown players at that time and strikingly effective in its photography, directed with skill and sympathy. An enduring portrait of Prairie life before and after World War II. It remains one of the few Canadian English-language dramatized movies that can truly be said to be Canadian in every way.

***Du pic au coeur* (From Spades to Hearts)** (2000) (85mins) d&s: Céline Baril : Karine Vanasse, Tobie Pelletier, Xavier Caféïne. A thin picture about a couple who have loved each other since childhood. He has a band, she sings. Love turns out to be a different experience. Appealing at times, but not very believable at others.

Du poil aux pattes: see **And When the CWAC's Go Marching On**

Due South (1994) (120mins) d: Fred Gerber s: Paul Haggis : Paul Gross, David Marciano, Wendel Meldrum, Gordon Pinsent, Ken Pogue, Chuck Shamata. An RCMP officer goes to Chicago to catch the man who murdered his father and becomes friends with the local policeman assigned to work with him. The story moves from Chicago to the Yukon. The tv series upon which the film is based was a tremendous success in Canada, the U.S. and the rest of the world. The red-coated Mountie played by Paul Gross became one of our first international stars. The tv show was aired for over five years, not forgetting Diefenbaker, the dog!

Duke, The (1999) (88mins) (a Canadian-American film) d: Philip Spink s: Craig Detweiler, Anne Vince, Robert Vince : John Neville, James Doohan, Courtnee Draper, Jeremy Maxwell, Justine Johnston, Judy Geeson. This children's comedy is set in England but was filmed in Victoria, B.C. It is a story of the members of the landed aristocracy, their concern for the poor, and the struggle to preserve a family estate. With a faithful dog and lots of antics and music, this is a fairy tale world depicted with charm and good humour.

Dukes, The (1998) (96mins) d: Rob King s: Peter Bryant : Michael Goorjian, David Lovgren, Chandra West, Jennifer Beals. The Dukes are a group of young men who play poker and basketball, drink and pursue women. An all-guy film, the group is at least bearable, and the whole is not without a knowing touch and a sense of humour.

Dulcima (1970) (90mins) d: Rudi Dorn s: Matthew Segal : Jackie Burroughs, John Colicos, Chuck Shamata. A beautifully made, touching and effective drama about a young girl who flees the monotony and tedium of life in a small Ontario town and finds herself working as a maid for a wealthy landowner. Predictable, but honest and appealing.

***Duo pour une soliste* (Duet for a Soloiste) (Duet for One)** (1998) (92mins) d: Mireille Dansereau s: Adapted by Anne Tognetti and Claude Baigneres (from the play by Tom Kempinski, inspired by the life of cellist Jacqueline du Pré) : Louise Marleau, Benoît Girard. Jacqueline du Pré died from multiple sclerosis. In this perfect cameo by Dansereau—a reflection of the kind of work she does so well in film—the terminally ill violinist struggles with her psychiatrist while trying to cope with the anguish of her life. Graphic and emotionally disturbing, this is a beautifully made and moving film.

Duplessis' Orphans (1999) (120mins) d: Johanne Prégent s: Jacques Savoie : Lawrence Arcouette, Joël Drapeau, Xavier Morin, Julien Poulin, Hélène Grégoire, Frédérique Collin. This is the harrowing story of three Québécois boys who were wrongfully declared mentally ill and subjected to unimaginable abuse and violence in asylums run by priests and nuns in the mid–20th century. Filmed with courage and honesty, this is one of the most heartbreaking and powerful social documentaries ever to emerge from Québec cinema. A gripping drama with fine performances all round.

Duration of the Day (*Le règne du jour*) (1967) (118mins) (b/w) d: Pierre Perrault : Alexis Tremblay, Léopold Tremblay, Raphaël Clément, Louis Brosse, Robert Martin, Louis Lemarchand, Marie Tremblay, Marie-Paule Tremblay. Filmed in the *cinéma-direct* method, this is less a motion picture than a filmed conversation. We follow Alexis Tremblay and his wife as they go to New York's aquarium to see the whale they caught in the previous film, *So That the World Goes On (Pour la suite du monde)* (1963). From there, they go to visit relatives in France. Refreshing and often warmly funny, the film is an intimate look at family life. It raises, once again, the question of the validity of the *cinéma-vérité* technique as the last word in realism. What are we to think when people being photographed become aware of the camera and modify their behaviour accordingly, or start to act for the filmmakers?

Dur-Dur (1981) (82mins) (a Canada-France-Italy co-production) d: Jean Luret s: Jean Girard : André Chazel, Elisabeth Bure, Gilbert Servien, Hubert Géral, Victoria Van. A man by the name of Clo-Clo leaves France accompanied by three young women. For reasons that are unclear, they are forced to stop on an island. What results is a number of farcical sexual situations juxtaposed with scenes of Clo-Clo's wife back in France and her encounters with several male friends. Unpleasant and disconnected.

Dust from Underground (*Poussière sur la ville*) (1965) (92mins) (b/w) d: Arthur Lamothe s: André Langevin (from his novel) : Guy Sanche, Michel Rossignol, Henri Norbert, Nicole Filion, Gilles Pelletier, Nicolas Doclin, Roland Chenail, Victor Désy, Paul Guèvremont, Pierre Dupuis, Rose Rey-Duzil, Réjane Desrameaux, Louisette Dussault. A story of a small-town doctor living in the frozen countryside with a bored and unfaithful wife. However, the film is not short on mood or atmosphere and, considering the climate, this at least makes the lack of warmth between the characters partly understandable. A Quebec rural film which takes on a situation still with us today.

Dying Fall (2002) (105mins) d&s: Will Fraser : Patrick Garrow, Jennifer Ross, Michael Pellerin, Val McDow, Thea Harvey. Here we go again: we're on the trail of another loser, this time a musician who thinks he's dying of cancer and becomes trapped in frustrations and bitterness. Along with this, he manages to suffer bouts of claustrophobia. Now and again, a flash of humour helps audiences through this darkening. A good cast manages to light the way.

Dying Hard (1978) (65mins) d: Donald Haldane s: Bill Gough (based on the book of the same name by Elliott Leyton) : Neil Munro, Clyde Rose, Claude Bede, Austin Davis, Estelle Wall and Newfoundland actors. Narrator: Norman DePoe. The fishing town of St. Lawrence, Newfoundland, enjoyed relative prosperity until it was almost obliterated by a tidal wave in 1929. But it came back to life with the nearby discovery of rich deposits of fluorspar, an element used to refine metal. Fishermen became miners and then began to suffer from silicosis. Alcan, the company operating the mine, then moved operations to Mexico, where fluorspar was cheaper. The move marked the end of St. Lawrence, where "a hundred men were dead and another hundred waited to die." A masterly work of social and historical significance. (See: *For the Record*)

Earth (1998) (108mins) (a Canada-India co-production) d&s: Deepa Mehta (based on the autobiography *Cracking India* by Bapsi Sidhwa) : Aamir Khan, Nandita Das, Rahul Khanna, Maia Sethna, Kitu Gidwani, Eric Peterson. The second part of Mehta's trilogy about Indian life and history, this film attempts to come to grips with the enormous subject of India's independence from Britain and the resulting conflict and hatred between India's various religious groups. Most of this comes to us through the perspective of an eight-year-old daughter of an affluent family. A frightening, moving and compelling film. (see: *Fire* and *Water*)

Earth to Drink, The (*La terre à boire*) (1964) (76mins) (b/w) d: Jean-Paul Bernier s: Patrick Straram : Geneviève Bujold, Pauline Julien, Patricia Nolan, Patrick Straram, Gilles Pelletier. Romance turns tragic when a Radio-Canada interviewer in Montréal becomes the victim of a fatal accident that was unintentionally brought about by a young female art student who had fallen in love with him. It provoked a wave of adverse comment from critics when it opened, describing it as immoral. This was Geneviève Bujold's second film, after *Amanita Pestilens*.

East Coast (*Côte est*) (1986) (80mins) d: Richard Niquette s: Lynda St-Arneault : Richard Bilodeau, Nathalie Leskiewiez, François Bessette. The streets of Montréal are battlegrounds for gang members fighting among themselves and carrying out sexual assaults on the female members of rival gangs. Social awareness or sensational rubbish? Montréal is known for its biker gang warfare, but is this an answer?

East End Hustle (1976) (91mins) d: Frank Vitale s: Allan Moyle : Andrée Pelletier, Anne-Marie Provencher, Miguel Fernandes, Allan Moyle, Beverly Murray and dozens of others. Underworld sleaze and sex in Montréal—a prostitute stands up to her pimp! Some may find this entertaining, others simply enervating. Lots of cameras looking for *verité!*

Eat Anything (1971) (90mins) d&s: Iain Ewing : Emily Steed, Judy Steed, Garfield Smith, Bo Diddley, David Livingston, Jack Litvack, Jackie Burroughs, Ian Carruthers, Clarke Mackey, Janet Good. For his second feature film, Iain Ewing has turned to questioning the meaning of life itself; he doesn't attempt to answer himself. Instead, he gathers together a group of friends, and the question-and-answer game begins, resulting in this mock documentary. Why are we here? Some viewers won't be for long; others may be fascinated.

Eau chaude, l'eau frette, L': see **Pacemaker and a Sidecar, A**

Échec et mat (Checkmate) (1994) (105mins) (a Canada-France-Tunisia co-production) d&s: Rachid Ferchiou : Jamil Ratib, Cherihane, Françoise Christophe. A not-much-of-anything script in which the president of a Middle East country is deposed when he is on an official visit to a neighbouring country. With his wife and *aide-de-camp*, he finds refuge in a nearby castle and is joined by his son and a lady friend.

Echo Lake (2000) (90mins) d: Richard Story s: Sally O'Neill, Richard Story : Todd Witham, Harrison Coe, Asja Pavlovic, Danielle DeWet. Two brothers go on a camping trip in the forests of B.C., and one is lost. The other is left to wonder what happened. What follows is an almost abstract, non-narrative film poem of which the director said, "I was interested in creating a world evoking a spiritual connection with our environment, souls, feelings and mysteries of life." Some moviegoers may well respond, but others will become lost.

Echoes in Crimson (1987) (77mins) d: Caryl Wickman s: Jan Franklin, Julian Roffman : Greg Evigan, Patricia Talbot, Joy Boushel, James Rae. Two friends visiting an art gallery become aware of strange activities that affect them and almost end their friendship. Naturally, the reasons are discovered and amends are made. (See: *Shades of Love series*)

Echoes of a Summer (1976) (99mins) (a Canada-U.S. film) d: Don Taylor s: Robert Joseph : Jodie Foster, Richard Harris, Lois Nettleton, Geraldine Fitzgerald, William Windom, Brad Savage. The parents of an 11-year-old girl dying of heart disease decide to take her to live in Mahone Bay, N.S. There is little Canadian about this artificial concoction. A great cast cannot give it substance.

Echoes of Calandine: see **Disappearance, The**

Éclair au chocolat: see **Chocolate Eclair**

Eclipse (1994) (95mins) (b/w) d&s: Jeremy Podeswa : Von Flores, John Gilbert, Pascale Montpetit, Manuel Aranguiz, Maria del Mar, Daniel MacIvor, Earl Pastko. Ten characters in search of beds and bodies are aroused after being infected with a strange excitement that affects people in Toronto during the week before the eclipse of the moon. Why this is happening is never clearly explained. This, Podeswa's first film, is a shabby exercise in sexual perversion. It has nothing in common with the beauty of Antonioni or Max Ophuls.

Eddie and the Cruisers Part II: Eddie Lives! (1989) (Part I, 1983) (103mins) d: Jean-Claude Lord s: Charles Zev Cohen, Rick Doering : Michael Paré, Marini Orsini, Bernie Coulson, Matthew Laurance, Michael Rhoades, Anthony Sherwood. Thick-ear melodrama about a rock musician who disappears after a car crash and begins a new life in Montréal as a construction worker. A terrible script with tired characters, but the music is not bad.

Edge of Hell, The: see **Rock 'n Roll Nightmare**

Edge of Madness (*Station sauvage*) (**A Wilderness Station**) (2003) (99mins) d: Anne Wheeler s: Wheeler & Charles Kristian Pitts (based on a short story *A Wilderness Station* by Alice Munro) : Caroline Dhavernas, Paul Johansson,

Corey Sevier, Brendan Fehr, Tantoo Cardinal, Corey Sevier, Jonas Chernick, Currie Graham, Peter Wingfield. A pitiful starving and half-mad 18-year-old girl arrives in Ontario in 1853 having barely survived in the wilderness, and confesses to having murdered her young husband. The best film from Wheeler in some time, is authentic, literate, faithful to its origins and beautifully made, acted and told.

Eete avec les fantomes, Un: see **Summer With the Ghosts**

Ego Tri: see **Ride Me**

Eileen Franklin Story, The: see **Fatal Memories**

Eisenstein (2000) (99mins) (a Canada-Germany co-production) d&s: Renny Bartlett : Simon McBurney, Raymond Coulthard, Jacqueline Mckenzie, Jonathon Hyde, Barnaby Kay. This is a deplorable film making a mockery of Eisenstein and his great films. It would take pages to describe the horrors it inflicts on this genius of early cinema. Filmed on locations in Russia, the Ukraine and Mexico, with a largely stiff-upper lip Brit cast; the best critical analysis of this mediocre work is the review by Dennis Harvey in *Variety* Sept 2000. Read it and weep.

El jardin del Eden (**The Garden of Eden**) (1994) (105mins) (a Canada-France-Mexico co-production) d: Maria Novara s: Maria and Beatriz Novara : Renée Coleman, Bruno Bichir, Gabriela Roel, Rosario Sagrav. Set in the Mexican border town of Tijuana, we meet a widow in her 30s with three children, a disillusioned American writer, his sister and various other odd characters. They all end up in the same hotel seeking solutions to their difficulties and trying to find something to do with their lives. None of this is terribly interesting. The garden is overgrown!

Eldorado (1995) (108mins) d&s: Charles Binamé : Pascale Bussières, Isabel Richer, Macha Limonchik, Pascale Montpetit, James Hyndman, Robert Brouillette, Claude Lamothe. Cast members collaborated and improvised with Binamé in trying to piece together newsreel-like coverage of what youths do on city streets in the guise of aimless Generation X "culture." Binamé stated his mission as an attempt to question our acceptance of the rigidity of production methods. Really!

Eleventh Child, The (*Nguol Thua*) (1998) (91mins) (a Canada-Vietnam-France co-production) d&s: Dai Sijie Tang : Akihiro Nishida, Tapa Sudana, Nguyen-Thé-Minh Chau, Nguyen, Hoa Thuy. The Eleventh child leaves China to return to his native village in Vietnam. The people there are trying to find a cure for leprosy and believe it will be found, when a man with five daughters and five sons appears on the scene. The man will kill the magical fish in the lake, and the villagers will eat its flesh and be cured. Tang is their man. A bit much for Western audiences, perhaps. The film is also another strange result of Telefilm Canada's mania for co-productions. Photographed by the Québec master Guy Dufaux.

Eleventh Special, The (*Onzième spéciale*) (1988) (80mins) d: Micheline Lanctôt s: Marie Perreault, Louise Roy : Sylvie-Catherine Beaudoin. A beautifully played, delicately treated and unsentimental cameo picture about an older woman whose life has become boring and empty. Surprisingly, and happily for her, she accepts an invitation to a friend's party and finds meaning in life again.

Eliza's Horoscope (1975) (120mins) d&s: Gordon Sheppard : Elizabeth Moorman, Lila Kedrova, Tommy Lee Jones, Pierre Byland, Marcel Sabourin, Richard Manual, Alanis Obomsawin. When this film was shot in the summer of 1970, the distributor, Warner Brothers, withdrew when the film's budget exceeded the original estimate. Work proceeded in stops and starts for the next four years, requiring the use of three directors of photography. Heavily allegorical and densely symbolic, the often abstract events in the film concern a young girl from a rural area who goes to Montréal to have a child. To find a father, she consults with an ancient Chinese astrologer, who reads her horoscope and predicts that she will meet the right man within the next 10 days. The girl attempts to make the prediction come true in a confusing search during which she meets a parade of characters as strange as herself. Thought provoking but somewhat obscure. An ambitious undertaking whose promise eluded the producers. (First shown at the Stratford Film Festival.)

Elizabeth Rex (2003) (93mins) d: Barbara Willis Sweete s: The play by Timothy Findley : Diane D'Aquila, Brent Carver, Peter Hutt, Bernard Hopkins, Joyce Campion, Keith Dinicol. This is a film of Findley's play in which he creates a fictional meeting between William Shakespeare and Queen Elizabeth I. This play was staged as part of the celebrations commemorating the 50th anniversary of Canada's Stratford Festival, where the author's career as writer-actor began during its first year. (Listed for the record.)

Elvis Gratton (1985) (89mins) d&s: Pierre Falardeau, Julien Poulin : Julian Poulin, Denise Mercier, Pierre Falardeau, Marie-Claude Dufour, Reynaud Fortin. The Elvis Story: A Montreal mechanic is also an Elvis Presley impersonator, as were, and still are, many others. When he wins an Elvis look-alike contest and travels south with his wife, his entire life changes. In 1981-3-5 three tv shorts he made were enormously popular. He had become a star through being Elvis. His real name was lost, but the Quebec public made him the great entertainer, took him to their hearts, and with this first feature film followed by *Le King des Kings, Miracle in Memphis: Elvis Gratton II* (1990) became tremendously wealthy, being the unchallenged hero of popular entertainment in Quebec. He never found the same success in the ROC or US.

***Embrasse-moi, c'est pour la vie* (Embrace Me, This Is for Life)** (1994) (80mins) d&s: Jean-Guy Noël : François Chénier, Michèle-Barbara Pelletier, Patrice Dubois, Dorothée Berryman, Tony Nardi. After an unhappy love affair, a much wiser young man decides to fall in love again—this time, for good. He finds the lady of his desire, but she is not as forthcoming. A delightful love story, although one is apt to feel some impatience with the protagonist. A rare combination of images, acting and words tell us what we need to know about love.

Emerald Tear, The (1988) (75mins) d: Mort Ransen s: George Arthur Bloom (story by Lisa Zisman) : Edward Marinaro, Leah Pinsent, Joan Henry, Ronald Lea. Romance and drama merge here as a reporter puts aside her professional ambitions to become something other then a scribe. In so doing, romance finds itself becoming lost at first—but not for long. (See *Shades of Love* series)

Emil and the Detectives: see **Angel Square**

Eminent Domain (1990) (102mins) (a Canada-Polish film) d: John Irvin s: Andzej Krakowski : Donald Sutherland, Anne Archer, Bernard Hepton, Paul Freeman, Jodhi May, Alice Barrett, Pip Torens. A Kafkaesque nightmare set in Poland during the Communist regime, where an official with all the perks and privileges of his office suddenly finds his comfortable life taken away from him without explanation. The future becomes dark and deadly. This is a gripping political thriller with suspense to spare.

***Empereur du Pérou, L'*: see **Odyssey of the Pacific**

***Emporte-moi* (Set Me Free)** (1998) (95mins) (a Canada-Swiss-Belgium co-production) d&s: Léa Pool : Karine Vanasse, Pascale Bussières, Anne-Marie Cadieux, Monique Mercure, Charlotte Christeler, Nancy Huston, Marie-Hélène Gagnon, Sébastien Burns. This film is memorable for the remarkable and deeply felt performance of Karine Vanasse as a 13-year-old schoolgirl struggling to cope with her parents' love-hate relationship.

***En vacances* (Summer Holidays)** (2000) (102mins) d: Yves Hanchar s: Jackie Cukier : Luc Picard, Catherine Hosmalin, Didier de Neck, Luigi Diberti. The story of three families during the summer holidays, this humanistic film has comedy, romance and drama. But it is all somewhat familiar, and we are rather glad not to have been on holiday with them.

Enchanted Village, The (*Le village enchanté*) (1956) (62mins) d&s: Marcel and Réal Racicot Animators: Laura Ledoux, Pierre Lanaud, Charles Hébert, Guy Parent. A chapel bell with magical qualities affects the lives of a group of Canadian pioneers clearing land in the wilderness. When the bell rings, the dry land yields a bountiful harvest, enemies are reconciled and a child brightens a lonely home. Beautifully done. Canada's first animated feature-length film. The authors devoted their spare time for six years in order to produce it. But it was not a success. Critics found the script and dramatic construction weak and the animation a pale imitation of Disney. (Listed here for the record.)

Encircled Colour, The (*La couleur encerclée*) (1986) (102mins) d&s: Jean and Serge Gagné : Jacques Rainville, Frédérique Collin, Paule Ducharme, Laurent Imbeault. This part-fiction and collage film tries to explain and parody the creative process when it is applied to business matters. Hard going at times, but certainly different and thoughtful.

Enfant d'eau, L': see **Water Child**

Enfant des appalaches, L' **(The Appalachian Child)** (1998) (95mins) d: Jean-Philippe Duval s: Pierre Billon : Christine Boisson, Mirianne Brûlé, Emmanuel Charest, Anne Dorval, Stéphane Demers. A young girl living in a village deep in the Laurentian Mountains suffers from a terminal illness. Determined to get well, she challenges herself by starting a collection of postcards that she vows will become the world's largest. Naturally, there are complications, but not to the detriment of this lovely, touching little film.

Enfant sur le lac, L' **(A Child on the Lake)** (1993) (78mins) d: Jacques Leduc s: Yvon Rivard : René Gagnon, Monique Lepage, Patricia Tulasne. A deeply affecting film about a "happily" married father who discovers that his wife is seeing another man. His life is temporarily destroyed, but memories of his mother, and a visit to the house where he was raised as a child, bring him peace of mind. His wife also returns to him. Effective and honest.

Ennemi, L': see **Full Blast**

Entre deux amours: see **Where Two Roads Cross**

Entre la mer et l'eau douce: see **Between Sweet and Salt Water**

Entre tu et vous **(Between "tu" and "you")** (1970) (65mins) (b/w) d&s: Jean-Pierre Lefebvre, Gilles Groulx : Pierre Harel, Paule Baillargeon, Dolores Monfette, Mano D'Amour, Denise Lafleur, Susan Kay. This is a film better seen after reading about the director's intentions. It is an unrewarding portrayal of the seduction of a woman by society, shown in seven sequences and separated by contemporary scenes of student protests depicted in negative process. This film was made during Lefebvre's hard-going and somewhat unrewarding period.

Enuff is Enuff (*J'ai mon voyage!*) (1973) (89mins) d: Denis Héroux s: Gilles Richer : Dominique Michel, Jean Lefebvre, Régis Simard, René Simard, Mylène Demongeot, Barrie Baldaro, Dave Broadfoot. A quaintly amusing and madcap film about a modern-day Jacques Cartier, who discovers Canada by car and cabin trailer with his wife and two sons in tow. They dream of the adventures the early explorers experienced, but find that times have changed. A funny, easygoing and very Canadian film in the best sense.

Équinoxe (1986) (83mins) d: Arthur Lamothe s: Gilles Carle and Pierre-Yves Pépin (based on the story *Équinoxe* by Pepin) : Jacques Godin, Ariane Frédérique, Marthe Mercure, André Melançon,

Marcel Sabourin, Luc Proulx. *Équinoxe* is another triumph of cinematography (Guy Dufaux) over script (Lamothe, Carle and Pepin), which in this case is yet another revenge plot, slow, lurid and unconvincing. After 30 years, a man returns to the Québec hinterland with his 12-year-old daughter. He holds a deeply felt resentment against an ex-friend who had betrayed him. The manner in which he searches for this man and works out his anxieties semms of little consequence to him.

Erik: see **One Man Out**

Ernie Game, The (1967) (88mins) d&s: Donald Owen : Alexis Kanner, Judith Gault, Jackie Burroughs, Derek May, Anna Cameron, Leonard Cohen, Louis Negin, Corinne Copnick, Roland D'Amour. A dull fellow playing a dull game. A fragmentary, non-story film about a shiftless young man in Montréal who is precariously close to insanity and unable to face life. He survives by imposing himself on two girls and talking of the things he plans to do but is incapable of accomplishing. We never really know him, particularly due to Kanner's self-indulgent performance. The two girls are from Owen's excellent earlier short film, *Notes for a Film About Donna and Gail*. Seen in retrospect, however, *The Ernie Game* presaged an entire generation of American and European films dealing with gloomy, uncertain and boring individuals. Compared with most of them, it holds up rather well.

Erotic Love Games (1971) (88mins) (a Canada-France-Italy co-production) d: Claude Pierson s: Huguette Boisvert : Christine Davray, Juliette Villard, Bernard Verley, Roger Hanin. The title tells all. Very agreeable, actually, although promises more than audiences get.

Erreur sur la personne **(The Wrong Person)** (1995) (90mins) d&s: Gilles Noël : Michel Côté, Macha Grenon, Paul Doucet, Robert Gravel, Luc Picard, Annik Hamel, Marie-Andree Corneille. An actress appearing in a stage production of *Miss Julie* doesn't earn enough money to live well, so she seduces wealthy men and steals their wallets, all the time in search of her own identity. A detective tracks her down, but she robs him, too. Nevertheless, they continue to see each other, and he discovers why she steals. What this has to do with Strindberg remains a mystery. Pretentious yet intriguing.

Escape from Iran: The Canadian Caper (Desert Blades) (1981) (100mins) d: Lamont Johnson s: Lionel Chetwynd : Gordon Pinsent, R.H. Thomson, Chris Wiggins, Diana Barrington, Robert Joy, James B. Douglas. A hurried yet inspired telling of the true story of how the Canadian ambassador to Tehran—Ken Taylor, splendidly portrayed by Gordon Pinsent—assisted besieged American embassy officials in their escape from Iran after the 1979 revolution that brought down the Pahlavi dynasty. An excellent cast under the distinguished direction of American Lamont Johnson.

Escape Velocity (1999) (90mins) (a Canada-Czech film) d: Lloyd Simandl s: Paul Birkett : Peter Outerbridge, Wendy Crewson, Pavel Bezdek, Patrick Bergin, Patrik Stanek, Michelle Beaudoin, Emil Linka. Another frightful sci-fi tri: disoriented space explorers find a frozen criminal and, after allowing him to thaw, must escape a passing star that is about to explode. What next? Don't expect too much.

Escort, The (L'escorte) (1996) (92mins) d&s: Denis Langlois : Robin Aubert, Paul-Antoine Taillefer, Éric Cabana, Marie Lefebvre, Patrice Coquereau. Two young gay men in a Québec town operate a restaurant but face bankruptcy. They hold a party, hoping their friends might invest in their enterprise. All that happens is that one of the partners goes off with another friend. These events are treated in terms of a calamity. Overwrought and emotionally and narratively confused.

Esprit du mal, L' (Spirit of Evil, The) (1954) (92mins) (b/w) d: Jean-Yves Bigras s: Louis Pelland (from an original story by Henri Deyglun) : Rosanna Seaborn, Denyse St-Pierre, Roger Garceau, Robert Rivard, Camille Ducharme, Pierre Valcour, Marthe Thiéry, Édouard Wooley, Christianne Ranger, Paul Blouin, Pierrette Lachance, Josée Vincent. A somewhat melodramatic, contrived and tearful piece about a conniving stepmother and her attempts to marry her daughter to the handicapped son of a wealthy family. This was the last Québec feature-fiction film for 10 years. Reissued in 1962.

Et du fils: see **In the Name of the Son**

Ete Avec Les Fantomes,Un: see **Summer With the Ghosts**

Eternal Husband, The (1997) (93mins) d&s: Chris Philpott (after the story by Dostoevsky) : Richard Hughes, Paul Babiak, Mireille Dumont, Emma Davey, Caroline Neilson, Sara Sahr, Peter Purvis, Gérard L'Écuyer. A brave attempt to film Dostoevsky's tangled and verbose tale of two men whose friendship falls apart due to misunderstandings resulting from too much drink, mistrust and an abyss of troubled emotions. The contemporary setting reduces the original to something less than the real thing.

Étienne Brûlé, gibier de potence: see **Immortal Scoundrel, The**

Eva Guerrilla (1987) (78mins) d: Jacqueline Levitin s: Anna Fuerstenberg, Jacqueline Levitin : Angela Roa, Carmen Férland. A chronicle about a Montréal journalist interviewing women from around the world who have served in guerrilla movements. A young Salvadorean is just one of her many subjects. But once you have heard her story, you've heard them all!

Évangéline (1913) (50mins, silent) (b/w) d: William Cavanaugh s: Marguerite Marquis (from Longfellow's poem) : Laura Lyman, John Carleton, Arthur Morrison, E.P. Sullivan. A good, well-acted picture about the expulsion of the Acadians and the love between Évangéline and Gabriel. Considered the first Canadian feature film. Remade in Hollywood with Delores Del Rio and director Edwin Carewe (1929).

Évangéline the Second (Évangéline Deusse) (1985) (82mins) d&s: Danièle Suissa : Viola Léger, Guy Provost, André Cailloux, Jean Lapointe. Yet another Québécois study of personal anguish and the search for happiness, as personified by an octogenarian living alone in Montréal. To lessen her feelings of loneliness, she becomes friends with three older folk who are as socially isolated as she. Very true, very sad.

Eve (2002) (76mins) d&s: Neil St. Clair : Inger Ebeltoft, Matt Scarborough. Opening with a quotation from Lord Byron, "I had a dream which was not all a dream," what we then see could possibly be called a poem on film. Eve seems to have little else to do but wander across deserts, through forests and past chunks of great rocks—wearing very little, it should be noted. But she runs into Adam and a couple of other naked men, to spend a few minutes of squirming in the sand or a pool. The photography is beautiful, and there are no flies, birds or animals to make a nuisance of themselves. And Eve never eats nor talks. More quotations from poets come on screen to help us through this wonderland. Its ultimate destiny, one feels, is a National Geographic tv series. And supporters of Kyoto will go into ecstasy over it. There are probably deep meanings to all this primitive existence, but Eve will take your mind away from thinking about it.

Event, The (2003) (110mins) d: Thom Fitzgerald s: Tim Marback, Steven Hillyer, Thom Fitzgerald : Parker Posey, Olympia Dukakis, Don McKeller, Sarah Polley, Brent Carver. An investigator in the DA's office in New York City is looking into a series of suspicious deaths of aid's patients. This is a mess of mystery, filmed partly in Fitzgerald's Halifax, NS, over-long and a waste of Polley, Carver, and time.

Events Leading up to My Death, The (1991) (89mins) d&s: William Robertson : John Allore, Peter MacNeill, Rosemary Radcliffe. A worthy attempt at satirizing an affluent suburban family whose members seldom see or speak to each other and are consumed by the neuroses of a materialistic society. They are a tiresome and uninteresting lot; the writing fails to sustain the premise, and the cast is not up to it.

Ever After All: see **Golden Apples of the Sun**

Every Person Is Guilty (1979) (65mins) d: Paul Almond s: Ralph Thomas (story and research by Roy McGregor) : Ken Pogue, Gerard Parkes, Lynne Griffin, Booth Savage, R.H. Thomson, Gilbert Sicotte. The title of this remarkable story of a mysterious event that occurred within Canada's Armed Forces is also found in the opening text of the Official Secrets Act: "...every person is guilty." In this case, the guilty party is a former journalist who discovers startling information while investigating an assault on his daughter. This sort of plot has been the backbone of many Hollywood B pictures. Here, we get a refreshing Canadian interpretation of the subject, with deeper treatment and characterization. (See: *For the Record*)

Eviction (*Evixion*) (1986) (83mins) d: Bashar Shbib s: Claire Nadon, Bashar Shbib : Stephen Reizes, Daphna Kastner, Roland Smith, Claire Nadon, Eric Gregor Pierce. Here's Shbib, again. After spending time in Florida, he's back in Montréal. He has left the swinging life in the sunshine to become a tenant facing eviction. But with his many friends, he fights to stay on.

Evil Judgement (1984) (93mins) d: Claude Castravelli s: Vittorio Montesano : Pamela Collyer, Nanette Workman, Jack Langedijk, Suzanne De Laurentis, Walter Massey. Not much going on here: a waitress witnesses the murders of her friend, who is a prostitute, and one of her clients. With her boyfriend, the waitress searches the streets of Montréal, trying to find the murderer. Heavy handed. One doesn't feel very much empathy for any of the characters in this film.

Evixion: see **Eviction**

Excalibur Kid, The (1998) (98mins) d: James Head s: Antony Anderson : Mak Fyfe, Serban Celea, Natalie Ester, Marius Florea, George Duta. A young lad is transported back to medieval England, where he becomes a pawn in an evil witch's plan to prevent King Arthur from ascending the throne. A slight and well-meaning family film but not one of Arthur's better times.

Exception to the Rule (1996) (96mins) (a Canada-German co-production) d: David Winning s: Shuky Levy, Shell Danielson : Kim Cattrall, Sean Young, Eric McCormack, William Devane. An unsettling, well-crafted drama about a happily married couple. Happy, that is, until the husband is seduced by a strange woman who threatens havoc unless he betrays his father-in-law. Complicated suspenseful and skilfully told with good characterization.

Execution of Raymond Graham, The (1985) (104mins) (a U.S.-Canada film) d: Daniel Petrie s: David Rintels & Mel Frohman : Jeff Fahey, Graham Beckel, George Dzundza, Alan Scarfe, Kate Reid, Linda Griffiths, Morgan Freeman, Laurie Metcalf, Neil Dainard, Ken Pogue, Philip Sterling, Karen Young, Joseph Sommer, Lois Smith, Linda Goranson. A superior film in every way, based on a true story and attempting to come to grips with the paths of justice and the moral and emotional travail suffered by individuals on both sides of a murder case. A family and lawyers try to clear a man of a murder he committed. The family of the murdered man wants to see him found guilty and executed. A great Canadian cast. (Petrie, a Canadian director in LA, returns to Toronto frequently to make his films).

Execution: see **Firing Squad**

Exhuming Mr. Rice: see **Mr. Rice's Secret**

Exile, The (*L'exil*) (1971) (86mins) d&s: Thomas Vamos : Albert Millaire, Anne Pauzé, Louis Aubert, Jean-Pierre Cartier, Bernard Gagnon. A Québec broadcaster is told he must simply read the news and stop giving his opinions. He resigns from his job and takes a new position far from city life in the Laurentian Mountains north of Montréal. His long-time girlfriend and lover goes with him, but their relationship breaks down. She leaves him to his utopian visions and returns to the city. A convincing and timely drama about what constitutes news and who controls it.

Exiles in Paradise (2001) (90mins) d&s: Wesley Lowe : Benita Ha, Dimitri Boudrine. The trials and tribulations of two immigrants to Canada who cooperate to find financial success. Blunt and rude but quite instructive, if not entertaining.

Exils (2002) (93mins) (a Canada-France co-production) d: Daniel Grou s: Philippe Soldevila, Robert Bellefeuille (based on their play of the same title) : Annie and France Larochelle. Identical twin sisters were separated at birth and remain unaware of each other's existence; yet following an idea which it is said, the other twin will sub-concioously carry out what the other will carry out even though far away from each other, they begin a wide-ranging search for their parents. This turns into the familiar trek among the customs of immigrant families and lives of Québec communities. It's the old story about searching for one's origins and identity. The twins are played by real life twins, and the whole is not without tenderness and humour.

Exit (1986) (100mins) d: Robert Ménard s: Monique Messier : Louise Marleau, Louise Portal, Michel Côté, John Wildman. Although beautifully acted, this "exit" is not easy to find. A a successful concert pianist finds her life and career adversely affected since her first love was killed as a result of her advice. She is now haunted by demons that intrude upon her new love affair. A long concert!

Exotica (1994) (102mins) d&s: Atom Egoyan : Bruce Greenwood, Mia Kirshner, Don McKellar, Arsinée Khanjian, Elias Koteas, Sarah Polley, Victor Garber, Calvin Green. Several characters become linked at a strip club called Exotica. They are a weird lot, including an auditor with a secret nightlife, an emotionally starved mother-to-be, and a pet shop owner who loves exotic beings, whether animal or human. In a supposedly deep study of human relationships, Egoyan becomes lost in a tide of confusion, resulting in a tedious film in which it is impossible to become invested in the characters.

Expect No Mercy (1995) (92mins) d: Zale Dalen s: Stephen Maunder : Billy Blanks, Jalal Merhi, Wolf Larson, Laurie Holden. A cyber criminal runs a virtual arts academy while sitting in front of a bank of mysterious computers. Two undercover agents enroll in the school to catch assassins who are posing as innocent students but are really out to take over the world with the aid of computer-trained villains. Zale Dalen (*Hounds of Notre Dame*) does his best with a none-too-convincing script.

Expecting (2002) (90mins) d: Deborah Day (story by Deborah Day, Cindy Stone and Karen Hill; dialogue improvised by the cast) : Colin Mochrie, Valerie Buhagiar, Angela Gei, Debra McGrath, Barbara Radecki, Karl Pruner, Tom Melissis, Derwin Jordan. A single, pregnant performance artist invites a wide-ranging circle of friends, family and lovers (past and present) to her Toronto loft to watch and participate in the home birth of her first child. It's anything but a quiet time for baby, as everyone visiting is beset by their own problems. Don't expect too much!

Exploring the Kinsey Report: see **One Plus One Explosion** (1969) (96mins) (a Canadian-American film) d: Jules Bricken s: Jules and Arlene Bricken : Donald Stroud, Gordon Thomson, Richard Conte, Michèle Chicoine, Robin Ward, Cec Linder, Sherry Mitchell, Len Doncheff, Douglas Campbell. After his brother is killed in the Vietnam War, a young man escapes the military draft in the U.S. by fleeing to Canada, where he becomes involved in criminal activities. Aided and abetted by Bing Crosby Productions and Meridian Films of Toronto, this was among the first of many awful "Canadian" films made as "international" movies based on their American financing, content and connections.

Explosion, L' **(The Hideout)** (1971) (93mins) (a Canada-France-Belgium co-production) d: Marc Simenon s: Alphonse Boudard : Mylène Demongeot, Frédéric de Pasquale, Michèle Richard, Richard Harrison, Mario David, Paul Préboist. In a comedy-thriller set in a Mediterranean resort, two crooks work out a new scheme for a hold-up. They manage to get away with precious jewels from a wealthy woman's yacht and go to Sicily to hide their loot. The ensuing complications occur over the space of years, making this a convoluted and seemingly interminable cops-and-robbers carry-on. Directed by the son of the famous author of crime thrillers, Georges Simenon. (Not to be confused with *The Explosion* by Jules Bricken.)

External Affairs (1999) (90mins) d: Peter Moss s: Jeremy Hole (from Timothy Findley's *The Stillborn Lover*) : Victor Garber, Henry Czerny, Kenneth Welsh, Domini Blythe, Louise Marleau, Pixie Bigelow. A well-acted and convincingly staged political piece about a Canadian ambassador to Moscow who is implicated in the murder of a student. Set during the Cold War, this is a subtle, brooding encounter between love and diplomacy.

Extraordinary Visitor (1998) (90mins) d&s: John W. Doyle : Mary Walsh, Andrew Jones, Raoul Bhaneja, Jordan Canning, Rick Boland, Greg Malone, Janet Michael, Bryan Hennessy, Ken Campbell, Maisie Rillie, Roger Maunder. Newfoundlanders have a great sense of humour,

and their comedies, along with many from Québec, have always been among the funniest. In this "send-up" of religion, with its collection of popular players, the humour is both broad and satirical. It begins with the arrival of St. John the Baptist in St. John's on a mission to save the world. St. John becomes a media sensation and soon has his own tv show. To his followers, he becomes the new messiah. The complications are many, sharp and hilarious.

Eye of the Beholder (1999) (107mins) (a Canada-U.K. co-production) d&s: Stephan Elliott (based on a novel by Marc Behm filmed in France as *Mortelle Randonnée* by Claude Miller in 1983) : Ewan McGregor, Ashley Judd, Patrick Bergin, k.d. Lang, Jason Priestley, Geneviève Bujold. A detective follows a runaway couple. After the woman murders the man, then tries to escape, complications, contrivances and psychological studies take over. Much patience is expected of audiences. One of heart-throb Ewan McGregor's earliest appearances.

Eyes of Hell: see **Mask, The**

Fabrication d'un meurtrier, La **(The Making of a Murderer)** (1996) (90mins) d&s: Isabelle Poissant : Pierre Chagnon, Denis Bouchard, Gabriel Arcand, Chantal Monfils, Dominique Pétin. Strange, indeed, is the telling of this tangled tale. In Bulgaria, a doctor has a patient suffering from severe amnesia, who returns to Montréal. This becomes the beginning of various love affairs and other activities. Altogether too much to follow and understand. One's sympathies are with the characters, but we get little in return.

Fabuleux voyage de l'ange, Le **(The Fabulous Voyage of the Angel)** (1991) (102mins) d: Jean-Pierre Lefebvre s: Normand Desjardins, Jean-Pierre Lefebvre : Daniel Lavoie, Marcel Sabourin, Sylvie-Marie Gagnon, Geneviève Grandbois, François Chénier. A charming and fanciful tale about a comic book writer in Montréal who drives a taxi by night to keep himself, his wife and 15-year-old daughter in fairly comfortable living conditions. When he receives a commission from a Japanese publisher to create a science fiction story about a driver of an intergalactic taxi, he uses his own life as a model. A typically warm, funny and delightful film from Lefebrve.

Facade (1970) (72mins) d&s: Larry Kent : Elizabeth Owen, Charles Smith, Julie Lachapelle, Julie Wildman. The remarkable young filmmaker Larry Kent followed *The Bitter Ash, Sweet Substitute* and *High* with this direct, simple, yet penetrating study of love and sex. A woman leaves her husband for a lover who awakens her in a way she had not previously known. She goes to New York and models for a while. The inherent superficiality of this life deceives her, and she returns to her husband. As always, Kent displays feeling and empathy for his characters. He understands the emptiness of sex without love.

Face Off (1971) (105mins) d: George McCowan s: George Robertson : Art Hindle, Trudy Young, Frank

Moore, Steve Pernie, Kay Hawtrey, George Eaton, Robin White, Perry Thompson, Austin Willis, John Vernon, Sean Sullivan, Vivian Reis, George Armstrong, Susan Douglas, Harold Ballard, Derek Sanderson. Hockey is Canada's leading sport, but few films are made about it. This love story with a hockey background is often trite and overly sentimental, yet it has about it an authentic air of what the sport means to Canadians, and its settings and performances cannot be faulted. *Face Off* was given a splashy opening on November 12, 1971, at the magnificent Odeon Carlton Cinema (since demolished) in Toronto next to Maple Leaf Gardens. Trudy Young was highly appealing, and a great future in film was predicted for her. (Our hockey didn't come into its own on the screen until *Les Boys* 1997).

Face Work: see **British Quota Era Films**

Fade to Black (2001) (81mins) d&s: Rohan Cecil Fernando : Fernando, Jean MacDonald, Mohan Fernando. A finely depicted story dealing with the life of a Sri Lankan family in Canada, including a young painter who is going blind, and his search for family and friends. A concerned humane study.

Fairy Tales & Pornography (2003) (77mins) d&s: Chris Philpott : Kelly Harms, Lindy Booth, Eric Peterson, Mimi Kuzk, Michael Ironside. Actually set and identified in the small Ontario town of Tweed, here we meet an idealistic legal-aid lawyer (is there such a lawyer today?) who is captivated by Laura, his client. Christmas is near, her case is postponed, the lawyer invites her to his family home for the holiday, after which it's back to court. The purpose of this slight piece is somewhat absent.

Falcon's Gold (1982) (96mins) (a Canadian-American film) d: Bob Schulz s: Olaf Pooley, Walter Bell : John Marley, Simon MacCorkindale, Louise Vallance, Blanca Guerra, George Touliatos, Roger Cudney. Set in a Mexican jungle, a noted archaeologist finds hidden treasures from a distant age; they possess strange powers that are a threat to the entire world. More nonsense about supernatural and alien influences. Filmed in Mexico City.

Fallen Knight (The Minion) (1998) (96mins) (a U.S.-Canada film) d: Jean-Marc Piche s: Matt Roe & Ripley Highsmith : Dolph Lundgren, Francoise Robertson, Roc Lafortune, Allen Altman, Andy Bradshaw, Michael Greyeyes, Don Francks. Totally unbelievable tall-story with a religious bent about God banishing Lucifer to Hell, guarded by a group of Knights Templars. Flash forward to New York where Lucifer's servatn, The Minion, has the key and wants to let Lucifer free. A chase ensues. To those among the audience who worry about what happened to Lucifer, here are some battered answers for them.

Falling Over Backwards (1990) (104mins) d&s: Mort Ransen : Saul Rubinek, Paul Soles, Julie St-Pierre, Carolyn Scott, Helen Hughes. A slight, over-long comedy-drama about a son in mid-life crisis who lives with his divorced, cantankerous father in

Montréal and falls in love with their vivacious young landlady. One feels for him.

Falling Through (2000) (90mins) (a Canada-France-Luxembourg co-production) d: Colin Bucksey s: Ian Corson, Nick Villiers : Peter Weller, James West, Roy Scheider, Marjo Baayen, Gordon Currie, Eric Conner, Judy Parfitt, Yekaterina Rednikova. An American immigration inspector investigates a black-market passport ring in Canada with alarming results. Topical, if not terrific.

Falling, The (2000) (95mins) d&s: Raul Sanchez Inglis (from his story) : Christopher Shyer, Nicole Oliver, Rob Lee. A trite minimalist drama about a love triangle involving a man, a woman and her former husband, a gloomy policeman. The relationships are described from the point of view of each character. It's hard to care about them. As is so often the case with poorly scripted films like this, the photography is better than the body of the picture.

Family of Strangers (1993) (90mins) d: Sheldon Larry s: William Gough & Anna Sander : Melissa Gilbert, Patty Duke Astin, Eric McCormack, William Shatner, Martha Gibson, Gordon Clapp, Chuck Shamata. A mother driving from home is overcome by blindness and runs into a bus stop shelter, narrowly missing school children. Her doctor tells here she must have an operation, but to do so he requires information about her parents to check the possibility of genetic transfer. The mystery begins when her father tells her she was adopted. Opening in Seattle the story moves to BC when she goes there to find her mother. A good script and convincing performances, with restrained direction, make this a sensible, serious drama, poignant, gripping and utterly believable. A b&w flashback to a high school party where the rape of her mother, then a teen-aged student, takes place in a dark, wooded park, is particularly well-shot and edited, using imagination rather than, as in today's films, it's a matter of 'showing everything'. This is one of the very good films produced by Robert Lantos.

Family Pack (*Que faisaient les femmes, pendant que l'homme marchait sur la lune?*) (2000) (101mins) (a Canada-France-Belgium-Swiss co-production) d&s: Christine Vander Stappen : Marie Bunel, Hélène Vincent, Tsilla Chelton, Mimie Mathy, Macha Grenon, Christian Grahay. A young woman studying medicine in Canada changes her career path to become a photographer so she can spend more time with her closest friend, who is a lesbian. The two women move to Europe, where they become part of a collection of outcasts who call themselves *artistes*. Looking for identities and facing family objections clutter up the activities. Tiresome and not very enlightening.

Family Reunion (1987) (98mins) d: Vic Sarin s: Avrum Jacobson : David Eisner, Rebecca Jenkins. An inventor living in Vancouver breaks off his engagement before leaving by train for a family reunion in Toronto. When he alights from the train with a young woman he met en route, his waiting family assumes that she is his fiancée, throwing everyone into a state of confusion. An enjoyable romantic comedy. Cinematographer Vic Sarin's first film as a director.

Family Viewing (1988) (86mins) d&s: Atom Egoyan : David Hemblen, Aidan Tierney, Arsinée Khanjian, Jeanne Sabourin, Gabrielle Rose, Selma Keklikian. This much-hailed film from the director of *Next of Kin* tells a fragmented story of a dislocated Toronto family, set against characters who move between a nursing home, a condominium, a telephone sex service and a hotel. Television, pornography, home movies and surveillance play their part in witnessing the breakdown and resolution of the various family members. Who wouldn't break-down after this lot? Cold, confusing and empty.

Famous Dead People (1999) (95mins) d: Eric Whalen s: Jason Carter, Myles Shane : Jason Carter, Caryl McKay. A psycho-drama in which two strangers become trapped in an ancient elevator over a long weekend holiday and find that their every move—what little they can do—is spied on by a video surveillance camera. A mystery-horror film with a difference. Often surprisingly gripping.

Fan's Notes, A (1972) (93mins) (a Canadian-American film) d: Eric Till s: William Kinsolving (based on the book of the same title by Frederick Earl Exley) : Jerry Orbach, Julia Anne Robinson, Burgess Meredith, Patricia Collins, Rosemary Murphy, Douglas Campbell, Jackie Burroughs, Gerard Parkes, Linda Goranson, Ken James, August Schellenberg. Well-made and acted drama set in the U.S. about a writer who loves baseball but suffers a mental breakdown as a result of his disillusionment over conformity within the game and the misplaced values of success.

Fan's Notes: see Gentle Sinners

Fancy Dancing (2002) (91mins) (a Canada-U.K. co-production) d&s: Brock Simpson : Jason Priestly, Tanya Allen, Ewen Bremner, Dave Foley, Deborah Odell, Dave Thomas. A composer living on money from a trust fund leads a bohemian life with wine, women and song and likes to involve his young son in these activities—until his former wife puts a stop to it. Big Band music helps to keep this light-hearted piece going.

Fandom: see Stardom

Fantastica (1980) (110mins) (a Canada-France co-production) d&s: Gilles Carle, Oscar Paul : Carole Laure, Lewis Furey, Serge Reggiani, Claudine Auger, John Vernon, Denise Filiatrault, Claude Blanchard, Donald Pilon, Carine Carlier, Gilbert Sicotte, Guy L'Écuyer, Pierre Curzi, J.-Léo Gagnon, Gilles Renaud. With music and songs by Lewis Furey, this ambitious film set in Québec from the imaginative Gilles Carle falls short of what it was intended to be: a loving and harmonious fantasy world of music and nature. Carle's vision is not entirely realized, and his story of travelling musicians and their concern for the environment seems implausible on any level. Not without charm, however; one responds to his concern and genuine feelings for life.

Fantômes des trois Madeleines, Les: see **Three Madeleines, The**

Fantômes étrangers: see **Foreign Ghosts**

Far Cry From Home, A (1980) (90mins) d: Gordon Pinsent s: Helen Weils, William Gough : Mary Anne MacDonald, Richard Monette. A passionate dramatization about wife abuse, powerfully and movingly portrayed at a time when in real life the subject was called "the silent crime." Gordon Pinsent's first film as director. (See: *For the Record*)

Far From You Sweetheart (*Juis suis loin de toi mignonne*) (1976) (109 mins) d&s: Claude Fournier : Gilles Renaud, Denis Drouin, Juliette Hout, Gilbert Sicotte, Denise Filiatrault, Dominique Michel. A dramatic-comedy romance set in a munitions factory in Montreal during WWII where couples meet, become friends then lovers and marry. Done with sympathy and feeling and set against a realistic wartime backdrop with an exceptional cast.

Far Shore, The (1976) (105mins) d: Joyce Wieland s: Brian Barney (original story by Joyce Wieland) : Céline Lomez, Frank Moore, Lawrence Benedict, Sean McCann, Charlotte Blunt, Susan Petrie, Jean Carignan, Leo Leyden, Murray Westgate, Rachel Barney. A well-meaning but simple and melodramatic story of a selfish husband, his misunderstood wife and an idealistic painter. Lots of brooding over love, life and art. An inappropriate score and stilted direction.

Fast Company (1979) (92mins) d: David Cronenberg s: Philip Savath, John Hunter, David Cronenberg : William Smith, Claudia Jennings, John Saxon, Nicholas Campbell, Cedric Smith, Don Francks, Neil Dainard. Cronenberg takes a break from his road to depravity to visit the race course in Edmonton. He returns with this ridiculous venture into hot cars, sabotage, scores to be settled and sex among smoke and noise.

Fast Food High (2003) (85mins) d: Nisha Ganatra s: Jackie May & Tessie Cameron : Kevin Tighe, Gil Bellows, Allison Pill, Sarah Gordon, Kyle Schmid, John White. Based on an actual event in Toronto, where a number of teenage students, working at a burger outlet attempted to form a union because of their low-pay and difficult working conditions, this film should have been a timely, acutely observed documentary-like study of this social subject. Instead it trashes the truth to become just another Hollywood high school musical caper, with a nasty manager and sexy students. Slick, silly and superficial.

Fast Runner, The: see Atanarjuat

Fatal Attraction: see Head On

Fatal Memories (The Eileen Franklin Story) (1992) (95mins) (a U.S.-Canada film) d: Daryl Duke s: Audrey Davis (based on the book *Once Upon a Memory* by Eileen Franklin) : Dean Stockwell, Shelley Long, Sara Botsford, Helen Shaver, Georgann Johnson. A true story about a woman in California who finds memories of sexual abuse come back to trouble her. She accuses her father as the man who violated her. At the time this film was made, its subject matter was seldom if ever brought into public attention. Now it has sadly become a commonplace and oft recurring phase in tv entertainment. (Daryl Duke was one of Canada's early directors who distinguished himself with his thoughtful and imaginative work.)

Father and Son: see *Pere et Fils*

Favourite Game, The (2003) (a Canada-U.S. film) d&s: Bernard Hébert : Sabine Karsenti, J.R. Bourne, Cary Lawrence, Michele-Barbara Pelletier, Daniel Brochu. A film based on Leonard Cohen's first novel written in 1963, about a character named Leo Breavman, an aspiring poet, lover, looking for the sensational through sex and poetry. In the book, 'Leo' was Lawrence. Under any name this is somewhat pointless, shallow piece about a man who doesn't know himself, lost in his own emptiness.

Fear X (2003) (91mins) (a Denmark-U.K.-Canada co-production) d: Nicolas Winding Refn s: Refn & Hubert Selby Jr. : John Turturro, Deborah Kara Unger, Stephen McIntyre, Willam Allen Young, Eugene M. Davis. Another (anywhere-nowhere) film where Canada's 'big country' is passed off as the flat lands of Wisconsin and Montana in this menacing study by the author of *Last Exit to Brooklyn*. Here a security guard goes on an obsessive search for his late wife's murderer. Good atmosphere and acting makes for an unusual psychological thriller. But Canadian it isn't!

Fearless (1999) (93mins) d: Charles Haskell s: Larry Mollin : Kavan Smith, Belinda Waymouth, Natalie Mendoza, Dean O'Gorman, Gregory Storm. A movie stuntman travels to New Zealand to join his sister and her over eager sports friends. He finds several surprises awaiting him. Minor and missable.

February 15, 1839: see *15 février 1839, meurt à douleur*

Felicia's Journey (1999) (104mins) d&s: Atom Egoyan (from the novel by William Trevor) : Bob Hoskins, Elaine Cassidy, Claire Benedict, Brid Brennan, Peter McDonald, Gerard McSorley, Arsinée Khanjian. A cold and formal story of unrequited love and murder, when a young Irish girl is put in "a family way" by a British soldier. She sets out for England to find him living in a drab northern town. She becomes enmeshed in the evil deeds of a serial killer, making this one of the most morally repugnant movies in an age of cinematic ugliness. The splendid actor Hoskins cannot save the film from being dreary and dull. A disappointment.

Femme de l'hôtel, La: see **Woman in Transit, A**

Femme de Pablo Ruiz, La (Pablo qui court) (On the Run) (1991) (90mins) d&s: Bernard Bergeron : Jean-François Pichette, Louise Laprade, Pierre Chagnon, Roland Smith. An aggressive thief robs an accordionist on the Montréal metro. They meet again and we are asked to believe they fall in love. He steals her savings but her son gives him the punishment he deserves. All rather pointless.

Femme de Pierre: see **Stone Woman, The**

Femme qui boit, La (The Woman Who Drinks) (2001) (90mins) d&s: Bernard Émond : Elyse Guilbault, Luc Picard, Michel Forget, Gilles Renaud, Lise Castonguay, Fanny Mallette. In documentary filmmaker Émond's first work of fiction, he gives us the tormented life of a woman who is ruined after her marriage falls apart after years of excessive drinking. We learn her story through flashbacks, and what at first appears to be a broken narrative ends as a whole of emotional intensity, with details that create a rare film of genuine tragedy.

Femmes savantes, Les (The Wise Women) (2001) (115mins) d: Isabelle Turcotte s: Nicole Marchand, adapted from the Molière play : Jacques-Henri Gagnon, Marie-Ginette Guay, Sylvie Cantin, Nadine Meloche. An adaptation of the Molière play, showing that, like many classics of stage and literature, this work's themes are universal and still pertinent. We are introduced to three women whose dilemma— whether to marry for love or convenience—obliges them to choose between the virtues of the heart and those of the mind. Beautifully done with grace and intelligence.

Femmes-enfant, Les: see **Girls**

Fenêtre, La: see **Window, The**

Festin des morts, Le: see **Mission of Fear**

Few Days More, A (De jour en jour) (1981) (98mins) d: Robert Desrosiers s: André Caron : Louise Turcot, Paul Hébert, Marc Messier. A small but significant and personal film about hospitalized cancer patients who bring support and understanding to each other.

Fierro ou l'été des secrets: see **Summer of the Colt**

15 Fevrier 1839 (February 15 1839) (2001) (113 mins) d&s: Pierre Falardeau : Luc Picard, Sylvie Drapeau, Denis Trudel, Frederic Gilles, Pierre Rivard. A film from the separatist Quebec filmmaker, Pierre Falardeau, dealing with the Rebellion of 1837 and the hanging of two of its leaders. Here history is judged by the mores of today. An approach that either creates reflection or comes off as propganada. You judge. Falardeau shines best in *Elvis Gratton* comedies.

15 Minutes: see **Stardom**

Fifth Season, The: see **Profile for Murder**

51st State, The: see **Formula 51**

Fighting Men, The (1977) (78mins) d: Donald Shebib s: Tony Sheer : Allan Royal, Robert Lalonde, David Ferry, Mavor Moore, Yvan Ponton, Michael Reynolds, Sara Botsford, Henry Beckman. A well-made, cleverly told story about life in the armed services, made fresh and interesting because it portrays the Canadian Armed Forces—which receive precious little attention from our filmmakers.

Fille du Maquignon, La (The Girl of Maquignon) (1990) (89mins) d: A. Mazouz s: Pierre-Yves Pépin : Andrea Parro, Emmanuel Charest, Réjean Lefrançois, Marcel Sabourin, Denise Filiatrault, Jocelyn Bérubé, Michel Côté. At the turn of the 19th century, in the picturesque Québec village of Maquignon, two young lovers on the verge of being wed stop to consider what their lives would be like within a society controlled by priests and the upper classes. A affecting "how times have changed" look back at Quebec society.

Fille impossible, Une: see **Short Change**

Filles de Caleb, Les: see **Being at Home With Claude**

Fils de Marie, Les: see **Marie's Sons**

Final Assignment (1980) (98mins) (a Canadian-American film) d: Paul Almond s: Mark Rosen (from the story by Gail Thomson) : Geneviève Bujold, Michael York, Burgess Meredith, Colleen Dewhurst, Michelle Mostovoy, Richard Gabourie, Len Doncheff, Alexandra Stewart, Jon Granik. With Montréal being passed off as Moscow, this is probably the worst spy film ever made. Badly written and acted, it concerns a television reporter (Bujold) who runs afoul of the KGB while investigating reports of medical experiments on children. A huge cast hardly knows which way to turn. This is not within Almond's forte.

Final Blow, The (The Finishing Stroke) (Le coup de grâce) (1965) (105mins) (b/w) (a Canada-France co-production) d&s: Jean Cayrol, Claude Durand : Danielle Darrieux, Michel Piccoli, Yves Létourneau, Jacqueline Laurent, Emmanuele Riva, Olivier Hussenot. A dark and arresting drama about a man in France who, having betrayed friends and others working in the Resistance movement during World War II, goes back to his hometown after the war and thinks he will return to a normal life. But his past deeds are discovered, and he pays the price for his actions.

Final Edition (1982) (65mins) d: Peter Rowe s: Tony Sheer : Alan Scarfe, Neil Munro, Donald Davis, Michael Hogan, Robert Clothier, Michael Reynolds, Juliana Saxton. The *Courier* is printing its last edition. We find ourselves in the busy newsroom of a big city newspaper. We move to the boardroom, where the newspaper's owners have decided to shut it down. An up-to-the-minute and forceful drama, released three months prior to the publication of the Royal Commission report on newspaper ownership by Peter Kent. (See: *For the Record*)

Finalemente (In the End) (1971) (87mins) d: Richard Martin s: Jean Amadou : Chantal Renaud, Jacques Riberolles, Monique Mercure, Jacques Famery, Andrée Boucher. A famous fashion photographer works with society's most beautiful women,

much to the envy of the waitress who brings him his morning coffee. He agrees to photograph her, and in doing so discovers a world very different from his phony world of fashion. Full of sophisticated irony and subtle wit.

Find the Lady (1976) (93mins) (a Canada-U.K. co-production) d: John Trent s: John Trent and David Main : Lawrence Dane, John Candy, Dick Emery, Mickey Rooney, Peter Cook, Alexandra Bastedo, Richard Monette, Ed McNamara, Bob Vincid. Described as a comedy, there's not much to laugh at in this sequel to *It Seemed Like a Good Idea at the Time*. Two inept police constables are on the trail of a kidnapped society lady who hardly seems worthy of being found, despite John Candy's efforts! Monette, of course, later found a home with Shakespeare. (A cast of clever comedians haven't much to work with)

Finding Mary March (1989) (90mins) d&s: Kenneth Pittman : Andrée Pelletier, Rick Boland, Tara Manual, Yvon Joe. This first feature, made entirely in Newfoundland, is a rare find indeed: a thoughtful, sensitive study of native life from the past. A city photographer is looking for artifacts from the extinct Beothuks. She hires a local man as her guide, but soon finds herself involved in a dispute between mining interests and the need to respect and preserve the past. The guide's young daughter is also troubled over the death of her mother, but through the study of mythology, she comes to understand her own doubts about life. None of this is pretentious or overdrawn, nor obvious, patronizing or superficial. It even brings in a touch of excitement, without becoming nonsensical, and several surprising developments. Only the Montréal Film Festival appears to have shown any interest in this remarkable film. (Pittman, regrettably is little-heard from today).

Fine Art of Murder, The: see **Still Life**

Finishing Stroke, The: see **Final Blow, The**

Finishing Touch: see **Your Ticket is no Longer Valid**

Fire (1996) (104mins) d&s: Deepa Mehta : Shabana Azmi, Nandita Das, Kulbushan Kharbanda, Jaaved Jaaferi, Ranjit Chowdhry, Kushal Rekhi. India, where two women trapped in loveless arranged marriages turn to each other for affection. This violates social practices and conventions, and the two become outcasts. An understanding work about the clash between Indian beliefs and Western ways concerning love and marriage. This film was banned in India, as the director should have known it would be, and the angry public destroyed cinemas showing it. (*Earth, Fire, Water* Mehta's Trilogy).

Firebird 2015 AD (1980) (97mins) (a Canadian-American film) d: David Robertson s: Barry Pearson : Darren McGaven, Doug McClure, George Touliatos, Mary Beth Rubens, Robert Wisden, Alex Diakun, Lee Broker, Barbara Williams. In the 21st century, there is a worldwide fuel shortage, which prompts the Department of Vehicle Control to ban all automobiles. But some drivers won't give up their beloved cars and, hence, find themselves at war with the police squad. This brings about rifts between family and friends. Slow and unconvincing.

Firing Squad (1990) (111mins) (a Canada-France co-production) d: Michel Andrieu s: Jeremy Hole (based on the novel *Execution* by Colin MacDougall) : Stephen Ouimette, Robin Renucci, Cedric Smith, David Hemblen, Charley Boorman. A Canadian officer is faced with a crisis of conscience when he is ordered to execute a fellow soldier in France during the Second World War. The soldier, arrested for murder, claims that he is innocent. One of the few films made about the Canadian Army, so seldom seen on the screen.

First Circle, The (1991) (240mins) (a Canada-France-Italy co-production) d: Sheldon Larry s: M. Charles Cohen (from the novel by Solzhenitsyn) : Christopher Plummer, Robert Powell, Corinne Touzet, Victor Garber. A disappointing adaptation of Solzhenitsyn's novel about a group of Soviet political prisoners on the outer edge of Stalin's inferno, the first circle of Dante's Hell. Filmed in and around Québec City.

First Hello, The: see **High Country, The**

First Offender (1987) (65mins) d&s: Timothy Bond : Yannick Bisson, Bernard Casey, Victor Erdos, Jennifer Dale, Brock Simpson. Freddy, who is 13 years old, enjoys his friendship with Ronald and thinks highly of him. Freddy is sadly disappointed when Ronald carries out a robbery and then turns around and blames him for it. This is a charming and meaningful film for the younger generation and one most parents would find worth seeing.

First Season, The (1988) (93mins) d: Ralph L. Thomas s: Brian Ross, Victor Nicolle : Kate Trotter, R.H. Thomson, Christianne Hirt. This perfect little picture dealing with a large subject deserves to be called a classic. When a fisherman working along the B.C. coast commits suicide, his wife is forced to rely on a neighbour, an angry Vietnam soldier, to bring in the regular catch. Life works itself out, of course, in this well-written, finely acted and thoughtful and dramatically engaging picture.

Fish Hawk (1979) (94mins) d: Donald Shebib s: Blanche Hanalis : Will Sampson, Don Francks, Charles Fields, Mary Pirie, Chris Wiggins, Kay Hawtrey, Ken James, Mavor Moore, Allan Royal, Murray Westgate. A likeable family film from Shebib about an alcoholic native who comes to mend his ways through his friendship with a trusting young farm boy. A heartfelt study of difference—in age, social background and behaviour.

Fish, Tale Soup (1997) (90mins) d&s: Annette Mangaard : Kathleen Laskey, John Jarvis, Rémy Girard, Dawn Greenhalgh, Michele Muzzi. A bad-taste soup of odds and ends concerning a wife who wants a child, her husband (who doesn't), and a strange refugee who comes to live with them. Everything goes cold and loses its taste.

Fishing Trip, The (1998) (84mins) d: Amnon Buchbinder s: M.A. Louretta : Jhene Erwin, Melissa Hood, Anna Henry, Jim Kinney. A gem of a first film about two sisters driving to their father's chalet in northern Ontario to confront him for having abused them as children; they hope to avert a similar fate from befalling their nephew, who is staying with him. Cleverly filmed, almost entirely in the moving car. Knowingly and brightly acted by a cast of young, unknown players. The end slips slightly into melodrama, as the women physically attack the father, but not sufficiently to weaken this absorbing film.

Five Senses, The (1999) (105mins) d&s: Jeremy Podeswa : Mary-Louise Parker, Pascale Bussières, Molly Parker, Gabrielle Rose, Daniel MacIvor, Brendan Fletcher. This is a misplaced drama about the five senses and the part they play in the lives of various characters over a three-day period after a young child disappears. Would have benefitted from a good dose of common sense.

Flag (1987) (106mins) d&s: Jacques Santi : Richard Bohringer, Pierre Arditi, Philippine Leroy-Beaulieu. A meaningless title for a drama about the chief inspector of a police unit fighting animal poachers, and his conflicts with his supervisor over the methods used to catch the offenders. A matter of pressing significance not given the depth it deserves.

Flaming Frontier (1958) (70mins) (a Canadian-American film) d: Sam Newfield s: Louis Stevens : Bruce Bennett, Jim Davis, Paisley Maxwell, Cec Linder, Peter Humphries, Ben Lennick, Larry Solway, Larry Mann, Shane Rimmer, Bill Walsh. A low-budget B-picture Western about a Métis army officer who averts a native uprising. (Quickly made at fast marching orders, this is the second CAN-U.S.-Film shot in Canada between Regal and Fox. See: *Wolf Dog*)

Fleur aux dents, La: see **Flower Between the Teeth, The**

Fleur bleue: see **Apprentice, The**

Fleurs sauvages, Le: see **Wild Flowers, The**

Flick (Dr. Frankenstein on Campus) (1970) (81mins) d: Gilbert Taylor s: William Marshall, David Cobb, Gilbert Taylor : Robin Ward, Austin Willis, Kathleen Sawyer, Sean Sullivan, Alfie Scopp, Tony Moffat-Lynch. Working on the premise that a low-budget horror picture about a known character never loses money, the producers of this film have our old friend Frankenstein and a university professor conducting research into the remote control of humans. Thrills and chills are adroitly managed, without the extremes of contemporary horror. Set in Toronto, yet! This was the second feature film to be partly financed by the newly formed Canadian Film Development Corp. (CFDC).

Flinch (1994) (88mins) (a U.S.-Canada film) d: George Erschbamer s: Neal and Tippi Dobrofsky :

Gina Gershon, Judd Nelson, Nick Mancuso, Frank Cassini, Marilyn Norry. Two people witness a murder and then find their own lives in danger because of what they have seen. The difference here is that the witnesses are two models working as live mannequins. Accompanied by violence, bad language and nudity, it leaves a nasty taste and is of little interest.

Florida, La (1993) (115mins) d: George Mihalka s: Suzette Couture : Rémy Girard, Pauline Lapointe, Gildor Roy, Margot Kidder, Raymond Bouchard. This is one of Québec's broad popular comedies and deals with a topical issue: the snowbirds, who spend their winters in Florida, and conflicts between them and the local Floridians. The director has taken a good script by the talented writer Suzette Couture and compromised it as a low, clumsy, overlong comedy about vulgar characters. The ever reliable Rémy Girard plays a Montréal bus driver who invests his life's savings in a small Florida motel with his quarreling family. Their efforts are thwarted by an artful real estate agent, played by the lively Margot Kidder. Buffoonery reigns throughout. It may please audiences in Québec, but it won't travel far.

Flower & Garnet (2002) (103mins) d&s: Keith Behrman : Callum Keith Rennie, Jane McGregor, Colin Roberts, Dov Tiefenbach, Kristen Thomson. A family story set in the quietly impressive distant countryside of a small western town, this film, remarkable in every way, tells of the lives of an eight-year-old boy, Garnet, and his 16-year-old sister, Flower. The two live with their troubled father, having grown up together since their mother died giving birth to Garnet. What could easily have been an overly sentimental, shallow and ordinary story is here acted out by an admirable cast of players, living through the emotional and psychological aspects of their lives. Moving, honest and compelling to watch. The best film to come from B.C. in many a year.

Flower Between the Teeth, The (*La fleur aux dents*) (1976) (86mins) d: Thomas Vamos s: Pierre Turgeon, Thomas Vamos (based on the novel *La fleur aux dents* by Gilles Archambeault) : Claude Jutra, Lise Lasalle, Anne Dandurand, Guy L'Écuyer. A down-to-earth domestic upset arises when a technician at a radio station decides to become a journalist, but finds his ambitions curtailed by his unmarried daughter's pregnancy and his wife's determination to live her own life free from conventional restraints. Introspective, with a convincing background.

Flower of Youth (That Tender Age, The Adolescents) (*La fleur de l'âge*) (*Les adolescentes*) (1967) (109mins in four parts) (b/w) d: Michel Brault s: Alec Pelletier : Part 1, Geneviève Bujold, Louise Marleau, Bernard Arcand; Part 2, Gian Vittorio Baldi; Part 3, Jean Rouch; Part 4, Hiroshi Teshigahara. Four pleasing, natural and honest sketches about growing up, learning and loving, in Québec with a visit to the winter carnival. (The film *Genevieve* is the Canada part)

Flowers on a One-Way Street (1968) (60mins) d&s: Robin Spry. Somewhat like a first cousin to *Christopher's Movie Matinée*, shown the following year, this film was also shot in Toronto's Yorkville district, then the home of the hippie movement. It concerns itself mainly with the confrontation that took place between the representatives of the Canadian Youth Council and those of City Hall, who opposed the council's request for closed streets and freedom from police harassment. An interesting social document.

Fly Away Home (1996) (107mins) d: Carroll Ballard s: Robert Rodat, Vince McKewin (based on the autobiography by William Lishman) : Jeff Daniels, Anna Paquin, Dana Delaney, Terry Kinney, Holter Graham, Jeremy Ratchford. This magical film is based on a true story. Strictly speaking, it is not a Canadian film, but deserves to be included here because it is set in Ontario with Canadian characters. William Lishman is widely known as the man who taught geese that have imprinted on people how to fly. The geese followed him in his ultralight plane as he flew down the migratory route from Canada to North Carolina. This is a truly captivating film about nature, family and triumph over tragedy. The behaviour of the geese shown here is based on the scientific research of the highly respected Canadian naturalist William Garrick. See also: ***Fly Away Home*** (1999) (60mins) Documentary about Bill Lishman who taught the geese to be themselves again. His marvelous biography became a distiguished film.

Fly, The (1986) (100mins) (a Canadian-American film) d: David Cronenberg s: Charles Edward Pogue, David Cronenberg : Jeff Goldblum, Geena Davis, John Getz, Joy Boushel. A scientist accidentally turns himself into a fly in this remake of the 1958 classic by Kurt Neumann. What allows *The Fly* to rise above Cronenburg's other gore-fest films is Goldblum's arresting performance. Captured is his initial horror of transmogrification, and then the eventual exhilaration as his mind is overtaken by the insect's view of life.

Flying (1986) (94mins) d: Paul Lynch s: John Sheppard : Olivia D'Abo, Rita Tushingham, Sean McCann, Renée Murphy, Keanu Reeves, Jessica Steen. With the help of a determined coach, a woman overcomes a leg injury to become a gymnast. Not much of anything. However, the film gave Keanu Reeves his start, and brought us Rita Tushingham, after a long absence.

Flying Sneaker, The (1992) (90mins) (a Canada-Czech Republic co-production) d: Bretislav Pojar s: Jiri Fried and Bretislav Pojar : Ludek Navratil, Katka Pokorna, Katerina Machackova, Jaromir Hanzlik. This delightful mix of live action and animation tells the simple, non-violent story of a lonely 11-year-old boy who dreams of the faraway places he sees on the postcards sent to him by his absent father, a ship's captain. One day, he receives a strange collection of cocoons from his father. One of them turns into a beautiful fairy, who befriends the boy and teaches him magic, with which he impresses his friends at school. In one act, he makes his sneaker fly. An imaginative marvel. (See: *Tales for All* series) **Folle embellie (Out of this World)** (2003) (105mins) (a Canada-Belgium-France co-production) d: Dominique Cabrera s: Antoine Montperrin & Cabrera : Miou-Miou, Jean-Pierre Leaud, Morgan Marinne, Gabriel Arcand, Pascale Montpetit. There have been many strange films about WWII, and here is yet another, about a group of wanderers in France who want to continue their lives of freedom. And so we get a family study, simple people finding themselves under difficult circumstances, with violence occupying the world around. Altogether too simple. Fortunately for them the German army passed on.

Food of the Gods II (1989) (91mins) d: Damian Lee s: Richard Bennett, Kim Brewster : Paul Coufos, Lisa Schrage, Colin Fox, Frank Moore, Jackie Burroughs. Another scientific experiment goes dreadfully wrong. This time, a pack of rats terrorizes a university campus. "Ratty" is the word for it. No true connection here with the first U.S. film—which was just as bad—or H.G. Wells.

Fool Proof (2003) (90mins) d&s: William Phillips : Ryan Reynolds, David Suchet, Kristen Booth, Joris Jarsky, James Allodi. Three friends club together to think out how, through today's high tech capabilities, they might get away with a daring heist. A gangster gets to hear about this, and blackmails them into carrying it out. And so, what it all amounts to is just another heist movie, pretentious but familiar, with guns blazing.

Fools Die Fast (1995) (90mins) (b/w) (a Canada-US film) d: James Purcell s: David Blackwood (based on his play) : Peter Outerbridge, Victor Ertmanis, Kate Greenhouse, Robert Morelli. More psychology, some of it off-kilter, set in a small Midwestern town in a diner during the 1950s. It concerns two lonely people: Eddie is a serial killer and Rhonda is a prostitute. They find a way out of their desolate lives through each other's love. But happiness is not in the cards. Not even with that dependable actor Peter Outerbridge does this troubling search make much sense.

Footsteps in the Snow (*Des pas sur la neige*) (1966) (91mins) d: Martin Green s: Dan Daniels : Meredith MacRae, Peter Kastner, Veronica Lake, Gary Plaxton, Gloria Carlin, Ovila Légaré. Young men are on the run in Montréal after being suspected of drug dealing and murder. Poorly plotted, slick and shallow. But, at least there's Veronica Lake. What's she doing here? Don't ask.

For Better, for Worse (*Pour le meilleur et pour le pire*) (1975) (117mins) d&s: Claude Jutra : Claude Jutra, Monique Miller, Monique Mercure, Pierre Dufresne, Gisèle Trépanier, Roger Garand, Paul Savoie. A deft, lively and whimsical comedy about love and marriage, romance and reality. Filmed with insight and imagination, with obvious pleasure on the part of Jutra and his cast.

For Life: see **Acts of Love (Series)**

For the Moment (1994) (120mins) d&s: Aaron Kim Johnston : Russell Crowe, Christianne Hirt, Wanda Cannon, Scott Craft, Peter Outerbridge, Sara McMillan. Set in Manitoba in 1942 at the time of the British Commonwealth Air Training Plan, this is an appealing and nostalgic wartime love story bringing a true sense of time and place and showing us a relatively unknown chapter in Canadian history. Australian actor Russell Crowe went on to become a popular and clever actor in Hollywood movies. Here, he plays a handsome Clark Gable figure, a dashing pilot who falls in love with a married woman whose husband is in the army. There are some impressive flying scenes—and astonishing, considering the low cost of this film. It puts many so-called "indies" to shame.

For the Record (Series) (1970–1989): A series of 60- and 90-minute films dealing with contemporary issues affecting the daily lives of Canadians. These journalistic dramas took current and pressing social issues and, through the mode of dramatic fiction, gave these subjects a human dimension. Each film strove to entertain, challenge and inform audiences with a fresh, provocative and often disturbing approach to these true-to-life stories, and did so with consistent success. See under their respective titles:

1: **Ada**	24: **Kathy Karuks Is**
2: **An Honourable Member**	**a Grizzly Bear**
3: **Becoming Laura, Blind**	**(Lakeswim)**
Faith	25: **Lyon's Den**
4: **Boy Next Door, The**	26: **Maintain the Right**
5: **By Reason of Insanity**	27: **Maria**
6: **Cementhead**	28: **Matter of Choice, A**
7: **Certain Practices**	29: **Moving Targets**
8: **Change of Heart**	30: **One of Our Own**
9: **Don't Forget (Je me**	31: **Out of Sight, Out**
souviens)	**of Mind**
10: **Dying Hard**	32: **Question of the**
11: **Every Person Is Guilty**	**Sixth, A**
12: **Far Cry From Home, A**	33: **Ready for Slaughter**
13: **Final Edition**	34: **Reasonable Force**
14: **Front Line, The**	36: **Rough Justice**
15: **Hank**	36: **Running Man**
16: **Harvest**	37: **Seer Was Here**
17: **Hide and Seek**	38: **Slim Obsession**
18: **High Card**	39: **Snowbirds**
19: **Home Coming**	40: **Someday Soon**
20: **I Love a Man in**	41: **Takeover**
Uniform	42: **Tar Sands, The**
21: **In This Corner**	43: **Thousand Moons, A**

For Those I Loved (*Au nom de tous les miens*) (1983) (150mins) (a Canada-France co-production) d: Robert Enrico s: Tony Sheer, Robert Enrico (based on the novel by Martin Gray and Max Gallo) : Michael York, Jacques Penot, Macha Meril, Helen Hughes, Brigitte Fossy, Cec Linder. The true story of Martin Gray, who wrote a book about his experiences in the Treblinka concentration camp. The film traces his story from the Warsaw ghetto and his role in the Polish resistance movement to his life in the U.S., where his book was published. A deeply moving film, well acted, directed and written, filled with unforgettable moments. (A welcome antidote to the obnoxious *Life Is Beautiful*).

For Those Who Hunt the Wounded Down (1996) (100mins) d: Norma Bailey s: David Adams Richards (from his novel of the same name) : Callum Keith Rennie, Brooke Johnson, Brent Stait, Michael Hogan, Maggie Huculak, Paul Jarrett, Kelly Fox. A former prisoner trying to start a new life with his wife and sick young son is dismayed when his ex–partner in crime returns to exact revenge. This is a forthright, compelling and compassionate study of human behaviour, beautifully made and acted.

Forbidden Journey (1950) (82mins) d: Richard Jarvis s: Cecil Maiden : Jan Rubes, Susan Douglas, Gerry Rowan, Richard Kronold, Max Shoub, Rupert Caplan, Blanch Gautier, John Colicos, Eleanor Stuart, Elizabeth Leese, Henry Ramer (narrator). Political melodrama about a fugitive from behind the Iron Curtain who gains illegal entry into Canada in order to reveal communist atrocities. A well-intentioned B-picture made in the late 1940s and early 1950s, when feature film making was almost impossible. Interestingly, several Québec films produced immediately after World War II were made by anglo-Québécois. But with all Canadian films at this time, they were seldom screened for more than a week—if that—and usually just in Montréal and Toronto. This picture introduced Czech opera singer Jan Rubes and his actress wife, Susan Douglas, to Canadian audiences. Both of them made strenuous efforts at great financial cost to support Canadian film production. Rubes became better known on the stage as a singer, and actor in many motion pictures up to 2,000.

Forbidden Love: The Unashamed Stories of Lesbian Lives (1992) (85mins) d&s: Aerlyn Weissman, Lynne Fernie : Lynne Adams, Stephanie Morganstern. Standing out from a more recent rash of 'gay' and lesbian films, this imaginative work is delightful, funny and sad. Several mature women recall the difficult days in Canada when being a lesbian meant living in a world of shame and guilt. Their recollections are cleverly intercut with dramatized scenes from the pulp novels of the time that dared to discuss the "third sex."

Ford: The Man and the Machine (1987) (200mins) d: Allan Eastman s: Robert Hamilton : Lynne Adams, Damir Andrei, Louis Gascon, Michael Ironside, Victor Knight, Hope Lange, Yves Langlois, Chas Lawther, Kenneth Pogue, Cliff Robertson, R.H. Thomson, Chris Wiggins, Jacob Tierney. "Henry and Edsel Ford keep company with Wilbur Chrysler and John and Horace Dodge". This is a fast-moving history of the early days of the auto industry and the Empire of the Ford company, whose Model T was the first car to be mass produced and popularly priced. A fascinating and beautifully made dramatized documentary. Not just for car buffs but the social historians, as well. The archival material is cleverly used, and takes us back to those days with a sense of wonder "how did they do it."

Foreign Body, A (*Sinon, oui*) (1997) (119mins) (a Canada-France co-production) d&s: Claire Simon : Catherine Mendez, Emmanuel Clarke, Lou Castel, Agnès Regolo, Claude Merlin. A riveting and thought-provoking film from Québec (via France), dealing with the place of women in society and their emotions, desires and resentments. We witness the strange behaviour of a married woman who tells everyone that she is pregnant, although she isn't, and who carries out the presumed condition until an extraordinary ending. Many details of family and other personal relationships are finely detailed and skillfully stated through the acting, dialogue and direction.

Foreign Ghosts (*Fantômes étrangers*) (1997) (135mins) (bw/col) d&s: Hunt Hoe : Bonnie Mak, Vaggos Evyenia, Camille Martinez, Walter Bryant, Nancy Snytar and others. Three interrelated stories of the lives of three young women who have come to Montréal to seek a new life in Canada. One is from China, another from Greece and the third from the Dominican Republic. We learn of their fears, frustrations and differences. Revealing and thoughtful.

Foreign Nights (1990) (90mins) d: Izidore K. Musallam s: Musallam & Alan Zweig, : Terri Hawkes, Dean Richards, Youssef Abed-Alnour. Set in Toronto, this is the now familiar situation of an immigrant father in a new country who refuses to let his daughter live like her friends and colleagues. Stodgy but not without feeling and honesty. A lovely performance by newcomer Terri Hawkes.

Formula 51 (The 51st State) (2002) (92mins) (a U.K.-U.S.-Canada co-production) d: Ronny Yu s: Stel Pavlou : Samuel L. Jackson, Nigel Whitmey, Robert Carlyle, Robert Jezek, Emily Mortimer, Meat Loaf, Sean Pertwee, Rhys Ifans. Starting in Los Angeles and then moving to Liverpool, U.K., this confusing plot concerns a massive drug deal that goes wrong, as does this pile of trash in which all the characters are loathsome, and whose dialogue is shouted entirely in four-letter words. The violence, car chases and smash-ups are non-stop. Samuel Jackson wears a kilt and appears to be playing bagpipes. The cost of this monstrosity was reported to be $35 million, and comes to an end in a mass shootout. Liverpool and the Beatles are dragged into this frenetic confusion.

Forteresse suspendue, La (The Hidden Fortress) (2001) (94mins) d&s: Roger Cantin : Matthew Dupuis, Roxanne Gaudette-Loiseau, Jérôme Leclerc-Couture, Isabelle Cyr, Patrick Labbé, Georges Brossard. Cantin, like Rock Demers, holds a special place in Québec cinema with his marvellous films for children. This one upholds the tradition as children join forces to play war games, the old-fashioned kind with funny hats, swords and shields. The children are a likeable lot, and the action swirls around the finding of a traitor in their midst. Good fun, with a moral purpose. (see *Tales For All* series)

Forteresse, La: see **Whispering City**

Fortune and Men's Eyes (1971) (102mins) d: Harvey Hart s: John Herbert (from his play of the same title) : Wendell Burton, Michael Greer, Zooey Hall, Danny Freedman, Lee Broker, Jim Barron, Hugh Webster, Tom Harvey, Jon Granik, Robert Goodier, Catherine Wiele. A well-meaning story attempting to show that what goes on in prison is a crime in itself. However, in telling of homosexuality in prison, the film becomes explosive as well as exploitive.

Fortune's Sweet Kiss (2002) (93mins) d&s: Daniel Nearing : Brooke D'Orsay, Monty Walden. There's no fortune here for audiences, nor a sweet kiss among the violence, nudity and bad language that seems to be the lot of a repulsive homicide detective and a disoriented daughter whose father raped her. He is murdered but the confused and complicated events amount to just another exploitation pic, set in yet another nowhere city.

Four Days (1999) (92mins) d: Curtis Wehrftitz s: Pinckney Benedict : Kevin Zegers, Lolita Davidovich, William Forsythe, Colm Meaney, Anne-Marie Cadieux, Patrick Goyette. A confusing crime melodrama about a bank robber, his son, a lonely woman and crooks out for revenge. All of this has something to do with fate and the struggle between good and evil. It is also related, somehow, to former bank robber Stephen Reid, who told his story in a novel.

Fourth Angel, The (2001) (96mins) (a U.S.-U.K.-Canada film) d: John Irvin s: Allen Scott (based on the novel by Robin Hunter) : Jeremy Irons, Forest Whitaker, Jason Priestley, Charlotte Rampling. A distinguished magazine editor working in London surprises his wife and children by sending them on holiday to India. In a sudden and terrifying attack, their plane is taken over by terrorists. In a botched rescue attempt, the police storm the aircraft after it lands, killing the man's wife and daughters. On returning to London, the writer is incredulous when he hears that the terrorists have been released. He begins his own investigation, which takes him into a maze of other criminals and indifferent politicians. Driven by hatred, grief and a burning desire for revenge, the writer takes justice into his own hands and becomes a killer. His suffering then becomes even more acute. This gripping, compelling and stomach-turning film is driven by Jeremy Irons' agonized and tormented performance, which never lets us go. Many in the audience will sympathize with his character, society is becoming tired of light sentences and lack of concern on the part of justices.

49th Parallel (The Invaders) (1941) (123mins) (107mins U.S.) (a U.K.-Canada film) d: Michael Powell s: Emeric Pressburger, Rodney Ackland : Anton Walbrook, Eric Portman, Leslie Howard, Raymond Massey, Laurence Olivier, Glynis Johns, Niall MacGinnis, Finlay Currie. A superb cast in a splendid and exciting World War II drama in which a Nazi soldier-sailor escapes to Canada after his U-boat is sunk off our Atlantic coast. As he travels across the country before being captured and attempts to cross into the U.S. at Niagara Falls, he meets many ordinary people who speak quietly for democracy in opposition to the totalitarian rule supported by the invader. Tense, pointed and politically apt at a crucial stage of the war.

Fous de Bassan, Les: see **In the Shadow of the Wind**

Fous de la moto, Les: see **Hog Wild**

Foxy Lady (1971) (84mins) d: Ivan Reitman s: Robert Sandler, Mathew Segal : Alan Gordon, Sylvia Feigel, Nicole Morin, Patrick Boxill, Andrea Martin, Cec Linder, Eric Clavering, Art Hindle, Marilyn Lightstone, Joan Fox. A kind-hearted young man falls in love with the richest girl in the world; life becomes an entirely different experience from what he has known. A minor sensation when it opened. (Reitman soon left for LA)

Fracture du myocarde, La (Cross My Heart) (1990) (70mins) d&s: Jacques Fansten : Sylvain Copans, Jacques Bonnaffe, Lucie Blossier, Jacques Brunet. After the death of his mother, a young boy who is afraid of being sent to an orphanage asks his friends to join him and keep her death a secret. What follows is a mix of comedy and sadness, as they learn about adult hypocrisy. Small but vital; a memorable film.

Frame-Up Blues (La danse du scorpion) (1991) (90mins) (a Canada-France co-production) d: Josée Dayan s: Robert Geoffrion and Gérard Carré : Kim Coates, Roberta Bizeau, Ronald Guttman. The Paris jazz scene provides a hot and seductive background to this thriller about a group of friends who sleep around. One of them is charged with murder. Good musical score. Makes a change from the usual fare.

Frankenstein '88: see **Vindicator, The**

Frankenstein and Me (1995) (91mins) d: Robert Tinnell s: David Sherman, Richard Goudreau : Burt Reynolds, Myriam Cyr, Jamieson Boulanger. A minor piece of work. Two young boys who are interested in stories of vampires, werewolves, mummies and other classic creatures from the horror movies discover a large box that—surprise!—contains the real Frankenstein. The boys take Frankie to an abandoned mine and plan to bring him back to life. Boris Karloff, where are you when we need you? And what is Burt Reynolds doing here? Don't ask. Our producers just love a Hollywood name, no matter how much it lacks lustre.

Fraternity, The: see **Circle, The**

Freakshow (1988) (97mins) d: Constantino Magnatta s: Robert Farmer : Audrey Landers, Peter Read, Don Gallagher. An unconvincing horror story about an opportunistic tv reporter who finds herself in an art gallery filled with peculiar people and strange exhibits. Pointless.

Freedom of the City, The (1976) (90mins) d: Eric Till s: Hugh Webster (from the play by Brian Friel) : Florence Paterson, Neil Munro, Mel Tuck. Written after Bloody Sunday in Londonderry, this play/film does not purport to provide a solution to the Northern Irish "Troubles". It concerns the victims of the terror, and how they are caught between overreaction, frustration, bitterness and fear. This splendid film echoes the playwright's cry: "Enough is enough, is enough is enough."

Freeloading (1981, but not shown until 1986) (84mins) (a Canadian-American film) d&s: Joe Sutherland : Richard Comar, Duke Edwards, Shelby Gregory, Tom MacDonald, Susan Hart, Arnie Hardt, Glen Wilkins. A strained and somewhat feeble comedy-satire about running a television station. Reporters, cameramen, producers and owners all bitch at each other and find fault with the system. Too thin to be truly enjoyable.

French Love (Un amour comme le nôtre) (1974) (87mins) (a Canada-France-Italy co-production) d: Andrée Marchand s: Elisabeth Leclair : Paola Senatore, Mauro Parenti, Lucretia Love, Jean-Michel Dhermay, Catherine Laurent, Jacques Grégori. A somewhat flat melodrama about a marriage that falls apart after the death of a child, and an unfaithful husband who is shot by his wife—all followed by a happy ending! Of little consequence.

French Revolution, The (1989) (337mins) (a Canada-France co-production) d&s: Robert Enrico, Richard T. Heffron : Klaus Maria Brandauer, Jane Seymour, François Cluzet, Jean-François Balmer, Andrzey Seweryn, Peter Ustinov, Sam Neill, Claudia Cardinale, Gabrielle Lazure, Christopher Lee. We're on familiar ground here: the years from 1789–1799 and the end of the French monarchy, the proclamation of the First Republic and the violence of the bloody Reign of Terror. It is compressed historically, of course, with confusion of name and place. Full of dastardly characters. Most players seem to relish their moment in history. (A film in two parts: *Années Lumières* and *Années Terribles*) A simple tale and

film, *A Tale of Two Cities* still seems more real.

French Without Dressing (1964) (77mins) d: Ted Leversuch s: Stanley Lipinski : Sharon Lynn, Laurie Darnell, Amanda Keeler, Jean Cavall, Lori Lane, Kathy Quinn, Roy Revere. A young man in Toronto goes to buy a new tv set and discovers that the latest model will show viewers whatever they would like to see. He doesn't buy the set but steps into it, selects a model from a group of nude beauties, and takes her away with him! Very funny at times, but an interesting idea is lost in awkward and heavy-handed treatment.

Frère André, Le: see **Brother André**

Friday the 13TH: see **Burning, The**

Friends at Last (1995) (91mins) (a U.S.-Canada film) d: John David Coles s: Susan Sandler : Colm Feore, Kathleen Turner, Julie Khaner, Sarah Paulson. A New York housewife tries to come to terms with the breakdown of her marriage to a newspaper columnist by getting him to agree to try again and make their marriage work. A troubling effective treatment of a life in change.

Friends for Life (Des amis pour la vie) (1988) (80mins) d: Alain Chartrand s: Diane Cailhier : Françoise Faucher, Paul Hébert, Roger Joubert, Jean Mathieu, Anaïs Goulet-Robitaille. All is trouble in an old-folks home in Montréal where a group of seniors have decided to live together to ease their loneliness. All goes well until anonymous letters arrive to upset the residents. This takes some sorting out, but calm eventually prevails. All quite human and convincing.

Friends, Lovers & Lunatics: see **Crazy Horse**

Fright: see **Visiting Hours**

From Nine to Nine (1936) (65mins) d: Edgar G. Ulmer s: Kenneth Duncan, Shirley Castle, Edgar G. Ulmer : Ruth Roland, Roland Drew, Doris Covert, Kenneth Duncan, Eugene Sigaloff. Three years after *Damaged Lives,* Edgar G. Ulmer, now something of a cult director for his German-style Hollywood films, came to Montréal to make this film at the new Associated Screen studios. The result was a passable B-picture detective story, using a few Canadian players, that reflects something about Canadian society. (See: *Damaged Lives*)

From Spades to Hearts: see **Du pic au Coeur**

Front Line, The (1985) (65mins) d: Douglas Jackson s: Ken Mitchell : Brent Carver, Monique Mercure. Faith and commitment come into play in this contemporary account of how a group of ordinary people campaigning for nuclear disarmament are forced to reconcile their inner convictions with the practical demands of life. A firm narrative seems to wander somewhat when a Roman Catholic priest appears on the scene and becomes involved with spiritual and personal relationships. As if this were not enough, the group runs into trouble when they confront the company manufacturing missile parts. A lot to take in, but all very relevant. (See: *For the Record*)

Frontière du crime **(Double Identity)** (1990) (92mins) (a Canada-France co-production) d: Yves Boisset s: Robert Geoffrion : Nick Mancuso, Leah Pinsent, Patrick Bauchau, Anne Létourneau. A former college professor has allowed his life to slip into a pattern of violence, crime and drugs. He lacks the strength to stop, until he meets and falls in love with a beautiful young woman and believes that he has put his old life behind him. But the world of crime will not let him go so easily. A smart, tight, well-told and well-played tale of darkness and despair.

Frontières **(Border Line)** (2003) (90mins) d&s: Francois Aubry : Heidi Gadzala, Nicholas Frichot, Karen Elkin, Jacques Turgeon, Aimee Lee. This is yet another film about disturbing dreams and images, all very fanciful and obscure. A photographer driving through a snowstorm picks up a hitchhiker whom he discovers suffers from mental illness. The weather worsens, she gives him some of her medication, and both fall into a drugged out nightmare. The moral here? Be wary of whom you pick up on the road!

Frost Bite (*La gélure*) (1968) (90mins) d: Michel Audy s: Claude Cabana, André Dionne, Michel Audy : Jean-Guy Bécotte, Raymond Lamothe, Danièle Panneton, Claude Rivard. A simple but effective story of love and romance set in an apartment belonging to a young student. He has been in love with one of his professors for many years; she is a woman who has given him precious insights into life and loyalty. He relives the past through flashbacks that summarize what he has learned. The ending is unexpected.

Frostfire (1995) (90mins) d: David Greene s: Marc Strange : Mosha Côté, Wendy Crewson, David Quamaniq, August Schmolzer. After a long absence, director David Greene returns with this unusual drama set in the Arctic. The action takes place in Yellowknife and Ottawa in a surprising story about the Inuit, Russian scientists and tv news reports. The tale is threaded together by politics, spying, intrigue, conspiracy and passions galore. James Bond would fit in here, although he might find it rather cold!

Fubar (2002) (95mins) d: Richard Glatzer and Wash West s: Wash West : Scott Gurney, Michael Cunio, Roxanne Day, David Lawrence, Paul Spence. This film seems to ride the heels of Chris Smith's cult American hit *American Movie* about Mark Borchardt's trials making a horror film in "white-trash" rural Wisconsin. Smith's film is touching and redemptive. Fubar is neither. But that's the point. The film, following the empty lives of two "white-trash" Canadians, is a mockumentary, meaning it's a faux documentary. When the "director" tries to delve into his subject's depths he only hits the shallow end, and at times gets humiliatingly sucked into the low-brow shenanigans. The performances are absolutely convincing in this film about nothing that goes no where—perhaps here, form and content reflect the grim reality.

Full Blast (*L'ennemi*) (1999) (92mins) d&s: Jean Rodrigue : David La Haye, Louise Portal, Martin Desgagné, Patrice Godin, Marie-Jo Thério. The setting is an unidentified Acadian town in New Brunswick, a background seldom seen in Canadian films. The logging factory has been closed by a strike. We meet some of the workers: idle young men with little on their minds but booze and sex (with men or women). Despair and boredom permeate the days. One of the most striking aspects of this dreary portrait is the dramatic photography. Ocean waves break furiously on the beach, dingy bars and clapboard houses take on lives of their own, leaving the occupants to rot in their weaknesses and uncertainties.

Full Circle: see **Haunting of Julia, The**

Full Disclosure: see **All the Fine Lines**

Fun (1993) (105mins) (a Canadian-American film) d: Rafal Zielinski s: James Bosley (from his novel) : Leslie Hope, William Moses, Alicia Witt, Renée Humphrey. Young suburban teens murder a trusting old lady, just for the "fun" of it. A disturbing commentary on social habits and influences, well played and responsible. But fun it is not, although the boys think so: this is what makes the film so frightening.

Funeral Home (Cries in the Night) (1982) (93mins) d: William Fruet s: Ida Nelson : Lesleh Donaldson, Eleanor Beecroft, Kay Hawtrey, Barry Morse, Doris Petrie, Peter Sturgess, Harvey Atkin. A teenage girl becomes concerned about the disappearance of guests from her grandmother's summer bed and breakfast and begins to investigate why. A quietly contrived fear and fright story with just the right touch of mystery.

Funeral in Berlin: see **Bullet to Beijing**

Funny Farm, The (The Comics) (1983) (95mins) d&s: Ronald Clark : as many as 50 comics. Almost a documentary of a young hopeful from Ohio who arrives in L.A. to become a professional comedian. We get a slow-moving parade of comics, most of whom are far from being funny—depending, of course, on one's sense of humour. Not much to laugh at.

Futur intérieur, Le **(The Interior Future)** (1982) (63mins) d&s: Yolaine Rouleau, Jean Chabot : Véronique O'Leary. A short and bitter drama reflecting on the condition of women in society. Although it is dated, as yesterday's expression of societal failure, it gives credit where credit is due and served as a valuable stepping stone into the future.

G-2 (1998) (91mins) d: Nick Rotundo s: James Best : Daniel Bernhardt, James Hong, Meeka Schiro. The latest incarnation of a mystic warrior searching for the sacred sword of Alexander the Great. Not at all interesting or even faintly resembling classic tales or times.

Gaia (1994) (85mins) d&s: Pierre Lang : Richard Guèvremont, Geneviève Rochette, Yvon Roy, Danièle Panneton, Bernard Ranger, Roger Tabra. A young physicist meets a mysterious actress, and they fall in love and begin an obsessive relationship. They discover that secrets bring about events belonging to the realm of black magic. And that's where they should have remained.

Galileo (1973) (145mins) d: Joseph Losey, play by Bertolt Brecht : Topol, John Gielgud, Edward Fox, Tom Conti, Michael Gough, Michel Lonsdale, Colin Blakeley, Georgia Brown, Clive Revill, Margaret Leighton, Judy Parfitt, Patrick Magee. Topol plays the scientist whose theories about the universe upset church and state. (See: *American Film Theatre Series*)

Gammick, La : see **Swindle, The**

Ganesh (Ordinary Magic) (1993) (100mins) d: Giles Walker s: Jefferson Lewis (based on the novel by Malcolm Bosse) : Glenne Headly, David Fox, Heath Lamberts, Ryan Reynolds, Paul Anka. Here, we recognize the town of Paris, Ontario, sandwiched between scenes filmed in Sri Lanka being passed off as India. A young boy comes to live with his cousin, but what this film is about is never quite clear. Tedium is followed by absurdity and sensationalism. Unexpectedly, an older Paul Anka makes an appearance.

Gapi (1982) (100mins) d: Paul Blouin s: Antonine Maillet (from her novel *Gapi et Sullivan*) : Gilles Pelletier, Guy Provost. Filmed in St. Peter's Harbour, P.E.I. A lighthouse keeper, although happy with his position, is envious of a friend who sails to faraway places. The lighthouse, however, is scheduled to be demolished. This will be hard to bear, but its demise will allow the keeper the freedom to travel. The two players touch a chord of response.

Garden of Anna, The: see *Jardin d'Anna, Le*

Garden of Eden, The: see *El jardin del Eden*

Garden, The (1991) (60mins) d: Will Dixon s: Bruce Edwards, Will Dixon : Jan Rubes, Scott Bremner. A delightful family tale of two children, an old man and his wonderful garden.

Garnet Princess, The (1987) (81mins) d: Danièle Suissa s: Julian Roffman : Liliane Clune, Jean Leclerc, Claire Roger, Yvette Brind'Amour. Romance and royalty go hand in hand, as a handsome prince tracks down a long-lost princess. A lovely fairy-tale fantasy. (See: *Shades of Love* series)

Gars des vues, Le: see **Man from the Movies, The**

Gas (1981) (93mins) (a Canadian-American film) d: Les Rose s: Richard Wolf : Donald Sutherland, Susan Anspach, Howie Mandel, Stirling Hayden, Sandee Curtis, Peter Aykroyd, Helen Shaver, Michael Hogan, Richard Donat, Walter Massey. An unbelievably silly and ridiculous piece about panic in the city when gas pumps run dry, leading, of course, to a never-ending stream of car crashes. A waste of actors, time and money.

Gaspard et fils (1988) (89mins) d: François Labonté s: Monique Proulx : Jacques Godin, Gaston Lepage, Monique Miller. An unusually frail and tiresome film from Québec. A domestic comedy about an eccentric father and his odd son; they think they have won a lottery, but have lost the winning ticket.

Gate, The (1987) (92mins) (a Canada-U.S. film) d: Tibor Takacs s: Michael Nankin : Stephen Dorff, Christa Denton, Louis Tripp, Kelly Eowan. Bored teenagers find the entrance to hell in their suburban back garden. But a few scary special effects cannot save this *Gate* from coming apart. Surprisingly, quite a few moviegoers, mostly teens, seemed anxious to know what hell was like and gave the film a boost at the box office. This led to a second dose, *The Gate II* (1992), but hell had cooled down in the meantime!

Gazi el banat: see **Adolescente sucré d'amour, L'**

Gélure, La: see **Frost Bite**

Gentle Sinners (1984) (120mins) d: Eric Till s: Ed Thomason : Ed McNamara, Christopher Earle, Kenneth Pogue, Jackie Burroughs. This movie reintroduced the quiet and distinguished director, Eric Till, who is best remembered for *A Fan's Notes* and *Hot Millions* (U.K.). Here, he brings to the screen the W.D. Valgardson novel about a 17-year-old boy who escapes from the stifling atmosphere of his childhood home to find freedom and love on his uncle's farm in Alberta. Beautifully done, with feeling and insight.

George's Island (1989) (89mins) d: Paul Donovan s: Maura O'Connell, Paul Donovan : Nathaniel Moreau, Sheila McCarthy, Maury Chaykin, Ian Bannen, Gary Reineke, Vicki Ridler, Brian Downey. Set among attractive scenery in Nova Scotia, this is a broad comedy involving a young boy, a frustrated teacher, a weak bureaucrat, a crusty old sailor and the ghost of Captain Kidd. They all have their moments!

Gerda (1992) (89mins) d&s: Brenda Longfellow : Diana Fajrasjsl, Francine Vézina, Donald Pilon, Sean McCann. Following the Gouzenko spy scare in the 1950s, Canada witnessed a second scandal: the somewhat ridiculous Gerda Munsinger affair, involving a glamorous but dull German playgirl who allegedly seduced the then minister of defence. This film doesn't seem to know what it wants to be—comedy, satire, drama or experimental—and is tacky, tedious and thoroughly banal.

Get Back: see **Between Friends**

Getting Married in Buffalo Jump (1990) (98mins) d: Eric Till s: John Frizzell (based on the novel by Susan Charlotte Haley) : Wendy Crewson, Paul Gross, Marion Gilsenan, Victoria Snow. Set in the foothills of Alberta, this is a pleasing and often funny and sophisticated look at a cynical lounge pianist from Toronto who goes west to run her father's farm. To help her with the work, she hires an old school friend of Ukrainian descent who proposes marriage. The complexities of love and the value of traditions are thoughtfully examined with humour and charm. A future star appears here: Paul Gross.

Ghost Mom (1993) (92mins) d: Dave Thomas s: Daniel Harris, Costantino Magnatta : Jean Stapleton, Geraint Wyn Davies, Shae D'Lyn, Denis Akiyama. A miserable and meddling old mother awaits with anticipation her life in the hereafter. After her death, she returns to earth to bring happiness to her son. It would seem that her departure would have brought about this happiness, but no, the film will have it otherwise. A good cast tries hard.

Ghostkeeper (1981) (88mins) (a Canadian-American film) d: James Makichuk s: Douglas MacLeod : Riva Spier, Murray Ord, Sheri McFadden, Georgie Collins, Bill Grove. Three young people are marooned in a snowbound mansion run by an old woman whose weird sons kill all strangers. Slight, predictable and pointless. Filmed in Alberta.

Giant Mine (1996) (120mins) d: Penelope Buitenhuis s: Martin O'Malley : Peter Outerbridge, Thomas Mitchell, Alberta Watson. The terrible 1992 mine disaster in Yellowknife, N.W.T., is compellingly dramatized in this documentary-like film. This landmark event in the history of Canadian labour politics was defined by the conflict between a Canadian company and American management, which eventually led to a vicious strike and murder. The town is closed down and becomes a battleground. Families divide and fear prevails. This vital film deserves to be shown as part of our industrial history. Everything about it is well done, and it has a shocking, lasting and truthful impact.

Giant Steps (1992) (95mins) d: Richard Rose s: Greg Dummett, Paul Quarrington : Billy Dee Williams, Ranee Lee, Kristina Nicoll, Michael Mahonen, Ted Dykstra, Robyn Stevan, Don McKellar, Peter Wildman. A talented trumpet player who dreams of playing jazz becomes involved with a bawdy group of musicians, their lady loves, and the various scams they set in motion. A lively musical background keeps a tattered tribe moving among the manipulators, while others attempt to reclaim the joys of music. This was stage director Richard Rose's first film.

Gina (1975) (95mins) d&s: Denys Arcand : Céline Lomez, Claude Blanchard, Frédérique Collin, Serge Thériault, Gabriel Arcand, Jocelyn Bérubé, Andre Gagnon, Carol Faucher, Paule Baillargeon, Dorothée Berryman, Denise Filiatrault, Donald Pilon, Marcel Sabourin. Based partly on Denys Arcand's experiences as a documentary filmmaker, this film is an ironic study of a unit shooting a film about conditions in a strike-bound Québec textile factory. Told in violent and symbolic terms, this is a strangely moving, disturbing and critical statement about individuals and their pursuits. With this film, Denys Arcand moved from documentary into dramatized narrative films and made his reputation as our leading filmmaker. Also appearing in this film are the actors and artists who were to become the future celebrities of Québec cinema.

Ginger Snaps (2000) (107mins) d: John Fawcett s: Karen Walton : Emily Perkins, Katharine Isabelle, Kris Lemche, Mimi Rogers, Jesse Moss, Danielle Hampton. A truly wretched concoction in which a snarling, evil, hideous and hardly ever seen monster—supposedly a werewolf, but having nothing in common with its Universal cousins—tears people into bloody pieces. Two teenage sisters who are tired of their meaningless suburban life are victims. Once torn, the victim is infected and turned into a werewolf. And so it goes, on and on. Clumsy, crude and ugly, this film is frightening only in making us feel physically ill when realizing to what depths of depravity the cinema has sunk. (Followed by a sequel just as bad).

Ginger Snaps: The Sequel (2003) (95mins) d: Brett Sullivan s: Megan Martin : Emily Perkins, Katharine Isabelle, Tatiana Maslany, Eric Johnson, Janet Kidder, Brendan Fletcher. The director of the first film, John Fawcett, becomes one of the several producers of this sequel. More nonsense about werewolves. One was enough.

Giornata particolare ,Una **(A Special Day)** (1977) (106mins) (a Canada-Italy co-production) d: Ettore Scola s: Ruggero Maccari, Claude Fournier, Maurizio Constanzo, Ettore Scola : Sophia Loren, Marcello Mastroianni, John Vernon, Françoise Berd, Nicole Magny. A pleasant but trifling film about two lonely people who meet the year before World War II—one a frumpy housewife, the other a troubled homosexual. Delicately done, but being described as a Canadian film was the joke of the year. Telefilm's co-production mania even more silly than it already was.

Girl in Blue, The: see **U-Turn**

Girl Is a Girl, A (1999) (87mins) d: Reginald Harkema s: Angus Fraser, Reginald Herkema : Andrew McIntyre, Paige Morrison, Laurie Baranyay, Aeryn Twidle, Jo-Ann MacDonald. A young man living in Vancouver is searching for the perfect woman. He goes from one to another, always finding a flaw that rules them out as the perfect partner. All these characters are more like caricatures.

Girl King (2002) (80mins) d&s: Ilena Pietrobruno : Chrystal Donbrath-Zinga, Michael-Ann Conner, Raven Courtney, Victoria Deschanel. A one-woman film made for gay-lesbian audiences, this is a meandering piece of experimental junk. There is no story here to be described, other than the presence of three characters who seem to be pirates. Why and what, don't ask although deep meanings and symbolic significance will no doubt be discovered by the film's supporters and certain critics.

Girl of Maquignon, The: see *Fille du Maquignon, La*

Girl Who Married a Ghost, The (2003) (83mins) d&s: Sandra Sawatzky : Janna Jo Scheunhage, Jerry Longboat, Wendy Walker, Carol Greyeyes,

Michael Lawrenchuck. The good-looking daughter of a Native chief living on an island, finds that her father (not wanting her to be involved with any men around) attacks a shama who had visited her. From here on we go into a spiritual world, where the daughter leaves with the shaman, who turns into a ghost, as a pile of bones on the beach. The whole calamity, she is also pregnant, is indeed a pile of Native nonsense.

Girls (Les femmes-enfant) (1980) (95mins) (a Canada-France-Germany co-production) d: Just Jaeckin s: Jean-Luc Voulfow, Just Jaeckin : Anne Parillaud, Zoe Chauveau, Charlotte Walior, Isabelle Mejias, Louise Marleau. Four young teenage students and their coming-of-age difficulties, dilemmas, hopes and joys. By the director of *Emmanuelle*. Lively and assured.

Give Us Our Daily Love: see *Soleil des autres, Le*

Gladiator Cop (1994) (a U.S.-Canada film) d&s: Nick Rotundo : Frank Anderson, Dan Carter, Eugene Clark, Heather Gillan, Lorenzo Lamas, George Touliatos. Secret killing fights are going on underground. A policeman tries to find out who is behind them and takes the name Gladiator One. The audience must then suffer the most boring and ridiculous story about Alexander the Great's ancient sword. A time waster. But then why should we expect anything more from producer and part scriptwriter Nicolas Stiliadis?

Glendower Legacy, The: see **Dirty Tricks**

Glengarry Schooldays: see **Critical Age, The**

Global Heresy (Rock My World) (2002) (106mins) (a U.K.-Canada co-production) d: Sidney J. Furie s: Mark Mills : Peter O'Toole, Joan Plowright, Alicia Silverstone, Lochlyn Munro, Jaimz Woolvett. A comedy about class and cash, two British aristocrats have fallen on hard times and decide to put their dilapidated castle up for rent. They must pass themselves off as butler and housekeeper and are decidedly alarmed when they hear their first tenant is America's loudest and much enjoyed rock band Global Heresy. With knowing players, the games, romance and music make this an entertaining piece of make-believe.

Glory Enough for All (1988) (197 mins) d: Eric Till s: Grahame Woods (based on two books by Michael Bliss) : R.H. Thomson, Robert Visden, John Woodvine, Martha Henry, Michael Zeiniker. A splendid, well-acted, sensitive and intelligent biography of two pioneer doctors, Drs. Frederick Banting and Charles Best, who discovered insulin. It was filmed where much this took place, at the University of Toronto where the two doctors studied and worked.

Gobital (1975) (86mins) d&s: René Brodeur : Ginette Marcotte, Denis Jacques, Robert Desfonds, Madeleine Gignac, Louise Trudel, Roger Vachon. Another look at the terrible future awaiting us. *Gobital* is a universe that looks like a giant concentration camp, where the citizens are forced to undergo genetic experiments. Heaven forbid. This is not a subject for si-fi entertainment.

God's Crucible (1921) (60mins-silent) (b/w) d: Henry MacRae s: Faith Green, Ralph Conner (from his book *The Foreigner*) : Gaston Glass, Wilton Lackaye, Ann Sutherland, Gladys Coburn. Russians settling around Winnipeg suffer hostility from the resident Canadians. A simple, well-done social statement.

Goin' Down the Road (1970) (87mins) d: Donald Shebib s: William Fruet, Donald Shebib : Doug McGrath, Paul Bradley, Jayne Eastwood, Nicole Morin, Pierre LaRoche, Gayle Chernin, Ted Sugar, Don Steinhouse, Ron Martin. With few exceptions, the filmmakers of any country late in establishing itself with its own dramatized cinema must, of necessity, endure a long and vexing period during which their films fail to find a public large enough to make them financially successful. This was the situation in Canada from late 1960s; film after film came and went, frequently receiving praise abroad but finding little at home. Experienced observers knew that nothing would change until a certain film came along that, for a number of reasons, would catch fire on its opening, intriguing the public and suddenly making Canadian films a professional reality and a fact of life. This long-awaited moment finally arrived with Don Shebib's *Goin' Down the Road,* which opened to impressive grosses in Toronto and ran for a year without the supposed benefits of a New York premiere or as an entry in a European festival. Ironically, this success was achieved with a simple drama about working-class life. It was made for around $87,000 by 32-year-old Donald Shebib, who trained in the documentary school of the University of California and at the CBC and found recognition in 1969 for his now classic 45-minute study of old soldiers called *Good Times, Bad Times*. This first feature is a pleasure to watch and refreshingly free of the fashions, fads and familiar hang-ups of youth-oriented cinema at the time. Written by Shebib and William Fruet (who appeared in *Drylanders*), the story concerns two simple Maritimer provincials who leave their poverty-stricken region and take to the road, which leads them to Toronto. In the big city, they feel sure they will find work, money and a better life. Without education or skills of any kind, they come to realise they are doomed to a useless existence even worse than what they have left behind. In the end, they leave as they began. Still on the road they head west, still exuberant, still hoping to find a new life. This very human and compassionate film with its many genuinely funny moments (notably the wedding), was made under difficult conditions by a determined young filmmaker who, with his first feature film, found well-deserved success and made the road easier for others. Together with Claude Jutra's *Mon Oncle Antoine,* which arrived a few months later, *Goin' Down the Road* still appears on the critics' list among the top ten Canadian films, and deservedly so.

Going Back (2002) (117mins) (a U.S.-Vietnam-Philippines-Canada co-production) d: Sidney J. Furie s: Greg Mellot (from a story by Furie) : Casper Van Dien, Jaimz Woolvett, Carre Otis, Bobby Hosea, Scott Taylor. A striking, powerful and penetrating war film set in Vietnam, where several veterans of the U.S. Echo Company return to describe to a television reporter what they went through. This must have been a very difficult film to make, but the director pulls it off ably. Bound to stir up controversy in its depiction of this debatable war. (Note: the film opened at the time of huge political crisis as President George W. Bush prepared to go to war against Saddam Hussein and Iraq.)

Going Berserk (1983) (84mins) (a Canada-U.S. production) d: David Steinberg s: Dana Olsen and David Steinberg : John Candy, Joe Flaherty, Eugene Levy, Alley Mills, Pat Hingle, Dixie Carter. A dolt of a young man expects to marry the daughter of a pompous U.S. congressman. A cast of popular comedians is unable to raise a single laugh in this inept film.

Going to Kansas City (1998) (97mins) (a Canada-Finland co-production) d: Pekka Mandert s: Morrie Ruvinski (from a story by Mandert and Tony MacNabb) : Mikko Nousiainen, Melissa Galianos, Michael Ironside, Susie Almgren, Mark Camacho. A Finnish exchange student, a musician, goes to the American Midwest. He wants to play in a blues band but finds himself living with a farming family. There are the usual expressions of distrust and dislike of strangers. He becomes friendly with a waitress and is then accused of taking part in a robbery. What follows goes off track, but, on the whole, this is a pleasant, sharp and likeable film with funny moments, well played and photographed. Filmed in Québec.

Golden Apples of the Sun (Ever After All) (1973) (80mins) d: Barrie Angus McLean, Kristin Weingartner : Percy Harkness, Elizabeth Suzuki, Derek Lamb, Leon Morenzie. A first film, in the experimental mode, about a boy and a girl wandering the woods and finding surrealism, sex and uncertainties as to what it all means. So will most audiences.

Golden Fiddles (1991) (180mins) (a Canada-Australia co-production) d: Claude Fournier s: Sheila Sibley (based on the novel by Mary Grant Bruce) : Kate Nelligan, John Bache, Rachel Friend, Charles Mayer, Cameron Daddo, Pippa Grandison, Hamish Fletcher. Canada goes down under to give us a tale of an outback family living on their failing farm during the Depression. Their lives change dramatically when they become rich from a large inheritance. But, as we all know, money is the root of all evil, and this absorbing tale goes on to prove it. Kate Nelligan is marvellous as always.

Golden Will: The Silken Laumann Story (1997) (91mins) d: Eric Till s: Joy Fielding : Nancy Anne Sakovich, Dylan Neal, Kate Trotter, Cedric Smith, Susan Hogan. Canada's outstanding Olympic sculler, Silken Laumann, overcame injury and other personal setbacks to become one of the world's best female rowers. Unfortunately, this chapter in her life is reduced to a sentimental travesty in this film. It is well made but suffers from editing decisions made by CTV.

Goldenrod (1976) (98mins) d: Harvey Hart s: Lionel Chetwynd : Tony Lo Bianco, Donald Pleasence, Gloria Carlin, Will Darrow, Donnelly Rhodes, Ed McNamara, Andrew Ian McMillan. After an injury, a rodeo rider in Calgary loses his confidence and his job and slips into depression. A striking performance from Donnelly Rhodes, ably supported by Donald Pleasence.

Goldirocks (2003) (94mins) d&s: Paula Tiberius : Sasha Ormond, Greg Legros, Laura Kim, Dru Viergever, Domminick Abrams, Megan Dunlop. A young and oversexed girl is obsessed with rock-and-roll. She joins a trio of musicians, runs into difficulties, and who would believe it, finds that success comes from becoming your own rock-and-roll hero. So there! Mainly for other rock-and-rollers.

Gone to Glory (*Partis pour la gloire*) (1975) (103mins) d&s: Clément Perron : Serge L'Italien, Rachel Cailhier, Jacques Thisdale, André Melançon, Yolande Roy, Jean-Marie Lemieux. A disturbing film about the people of a small Québec town; they were not interested in World War II, nor the invasion of France, and opposed conscription and wanted nothing to do with the army. They even refused to help the military police find draft dodgers.

Good Day, Mr. Gauguin: see *Bonjour, monsieur Gauguin*

Good Luck, Jennifer Gagnon: see **Homecoming, The**

Good Place to Come From, A: see **Today I Am a Fountain Pen**

Good Riddance (*Les bons débarras*) (1980) (116mins) d: Francis Mankiewicz s: Réjean Ducharme : Charlotte Laurier, Marie Tifo, Germain Houde, Louise Marleau. A 13-year-old girl living in a dilapidated old house in the Laurentian Mountains north of Montréal is deeply attached to her mother but fears losing her to the affections of an uncle and a local policeman. A deeply moving study of family relations as seen through the eyes of the anguished daughter. Perfectly acted, with an unforgettable performance by Charlotte Laurier. A masterly work from Mankiewicz.

Good Times, Bad Times: see **Goin' Down the Road**

Goodbye Neighbours and Wives: see **Summerlust**

Goodbye, See You Monday (*Au revoir, à lundi*) (1979) (103mins) (a Canada-France co-production) d: Maurice Dugowson s: Roger Fournier, Maurice Dugowson (from Fournier's novel *Moi, mon corps, mon âme*) : Carole Laure, Miou-Miou, Claude Brasseur, David Birney, Frank Moore, Gabriel Arcand, Denise Filiatrault, Murray Westgate, Gilbert Sicotte, J.-Léo Gagnon, Lewis Furey. Living alone in Montréal, two women become involved in love affairs with married men. Their few pleasures are diminished by the disappointments they must suffer in these unequal relationships. This film is much superior to those being made at the same time in Hollywood about unconventional affairs and the changing patterns of love and marriage. Although the pace is somewhat slow and the treatment unimaginative, the situations and the talented cast give it a direct appeal and emotional depth.

Grand Bill, The (*Le gros Bill*) (1949) (90mins) d: René Delacroix s: Jean Palardy : Ginette Letondal, Yves Henry, Juliette Béliveau, Maurice Gauvin, Paul Guèvremont, Amanda Alarie, Lise Villeneuve, Jean-Claude Robillard, Amanda Laforet. Bill, a Texan, comes to Québec to claim a farm he has inherited from his father. Unable to speak French, he runs into difficulties with the townspeople. An amusing and often piquant portrayal of the frustrations arising from language barriers, taking place at a time when the subject itself was not the issue it has since become.

Grand day, Le: see **Big Day, The**

Grand film ordinaire, Le: see **Great Ordinary Movie, The**

Grand Larceny (1991) (93mins) d: Stephen Surjik s: Douglas Bowie : Jennifer Dale, Robert Joy, Kenneth Welsh, Victor Garber. In 1901, a confidence lady escapes from prison and tries to retrieve her ill-gotten gains. She is assisted by two of her former associates. A fitting sequel to *Love and Larceny*.

Grand logement, Un: see **Large Abode, A**

Grand Recess, The (*La grande récré*) (1976) (96mins) (a Canada-France co-production) d: Claude Pierson s: Huguette Boisvert : Michel Galabru, Jacques Préboist, Paul Préboist, Roger Carel, Monique Tarbes. In Paris, a gang of young boys, playful and inventive, have built a shelter on a vacant lot from boards and bricks. Here, they hold their "committee meetings." One day, all their stuff is out on the street, and promoters announce the construction of a new building. The gang begins a struggle to preserve their place in a campaign that takes them to the president of France. All a bit far-fetched, but good humoured.

Grand Rock, Le : see **Big Rock, the Big Man, The**

Grand sabordage, Le: see **Big Sabotage, The**

Grand serpent du monde, Le **(The Great World Serpent)** (1999) (99mins) d: Yves Dion s: Monique Proulx : Murray Head, Zoé Traverse, Louise Portal, Gabriel Arcand, Elyzebeth Walling, Jean-Pierre Bergeron, June Wallack, Jacques Languirand. A Montréal bus driver endlessly follows the same urban route, day and night, putting up with a mix of passengers—some boring, others eccentric. He, himself, is devoted to Jack Kerouac's *On the Road* and plans to go to the American West and Mexico to rediscover his lost youth. One day, a young woman who is also reading Kerouac's book gets on his bus. Will she be the woman for him? This truly wonderful film does work on many levels, with the plain or misty scenes of the bus creating a captivating sense of poetry and atmosphere. Beautifully acted within a memorable piece of work.

Grand zélé, Le **(The Great Zeal)** (1993) (84mins) d: Roger Cantin s: Claude Lalonde, Pierre Lamothe : Marc Labrèche, Raymond Cloutier, Gérard Poirier. This is intended to be a comedy: a young office employee is conscientious and capable, but his boss doesn't think he works enough. Deeply hurt, the young man decides to live in his office and work constantly. But this doesn't please the boss either, who tries all kinds of tricks to get rid of him. Stretched. Not quite Harold Lloyd.

Grande récré, La: see **Grand Recess, The**

Grande séduction, La (2003) (110mins) d: Jean-Francois Pouliot s: Ken Scott : Raymond Bouchard, David Boutin, Pierre Collin, Benoit Briere, Rita Lafontaine, Lucie Laurier. A small port village in Quebec is facing poverty due to the lack of fish. It tries to get a multi-national company to open a factory. But they also need a doctor, and this leads to a rift over having to decide what decision to make. Lively and topical perhaps, but who can care or any of these characters? The director's long career has been in the production of commercials for tv. It shows.

Grandpa and Frank: see **Home to Stay**

Grands enfants, Les **(Day by Day)** (1980) (83mins) d&s: Paul Tana : Gilbert Sicotte, Julie Vincent, Robert Gravel, Jean Mathieu, Rita Lafontaine, Amulette Garneau, Roger Turcotte, Pauline Martin, Claude Gai. A light romance about a man who falls in love with a beautiful florist and buys flowers from her, then gives them back as a sign of his affection. Where this leads to is ultimately funny and charming.

Gratien (1989) (75mins) d: Bruno Laliberté s: Céline Bourgault, Bruno Laliberté : Jocelyn Bédard, Céline Bourgault, Hélène Laliberté, Gilles Turmel. A husband informs his wife that their marriage has become monotonous: they need to do something about their lives. After considering a variety of options, the husband finally decides that his current life and wife are the best of all possible worlds. It seems that we have been this way before. Another look at domestic matters.

Graveyard Shift (1987) (89mins) d&s: Jerry Ciccoritti : Cliff Stoker, Silvio Oliviero, Dorin Ferber, Helen Papas, Martin Bochner. Yet another misfire about Dracula. Here we meet a cab driver vampire who enjoys working the night shift because it's easier to find victims. Set in New York in the 1980s, this film has atmosphere but not much to sustain it.

Understudy: see **Graveyard Shift II**

Graveyard Story (1989) (90mins) (a Canadian-American film) d&s: B.D. Benedick : John Ireland, Adrian Paul, Cayle Chemin. A psychiatrist living in the Niagara region of Ontario is haunted by a vision of a little girl buried in a nearby cemetery. A private detective finds out why. Conventional but nifty and decently told.

Great Big Thing, A (1968) (83mins) (a Canada-U.S. co-production) d: Eric Till s: Terence Heffernan : Reni Santoni, Louise Latraverse, Paul Sand, Marcy Plotnick, Gerard Parkes, François Yves Carpentier, Roberta Maxwell, Leon Pownall, Heath Lamberts. Similar in many ways to Donald Owen's *The Ernie Game,* this was yet another in the growing line of plotless, unresolved movies about disoriented youth. Here we meet a 23-year-old who, while not entirely unlikeable or even criminal, is irresponsible, unreliable, annoyed with the world and unable to know himself or come to terms with life. This was Eric Till's first Canadian film after leaving the U.K.

Great Chess Movie, The (*Jouer sa vie*) (1982) (80mins) d&s: Gilles Carle : Anatoly Karpov, Viktor Korchnoi, Bobby Fischer. Carle provides us with some wonderfully candid portraits of chess masters Bobby Fischer, Viktor Korchnoi, Anatoly Karpov and others. An informative film made more enjoyable by Carle's fascination with the game. A witty and engaging drama-documenary study of the great names of international chess. Like the principal pieces on the black-and-white board, they are analyzed by the pawns, a group of grand masters. Fernando Arrabal goes deeper with the commentary looking at the players' personal eccentricities, suggesting religious, sexual, and psychological motivations. Scenes from the movies showing actors at the game are cleverly interspersed, making a witty and humourous compilation of a most unusual screen subject. Narrators: Pascal Rollin (French) Bondfield Marcoux (English)

Great Coups of History (1969) (81mins) d&s: Jack Darcus : Delphine Harvey, Ellis Pryce-Jones, Janie Cassie, Ted Sutton. A charming romance-drama set in Vancouver about a young boy who learns of love from an older woman.

Great Coups of History: see **Deserters**

Great Goose Caper, The (2003) (85mins) d: Nicholas Kendall s: Charles Dennis : Chevy Chase, Kari Matchett, Joan Plowright, James Purefoy, Max Morrow, Isabella Fink. On his way home from school one day, a likeable young boy, who is dumb, meets a magical talking goose. He and other friends think up an elaborate plan to save the goose from being cooked. A fairytale, winning, charming and well made. Chevy Chase and John Plowright make welcome appearances.

Great Land of Small, The (*C'est pas parce qu'on est petit qu'on peut pas être grand!*) (1987) (93mins) (a Canada-Czech Republic co-production) d&s: Vojtech Jasny : Karin Elkin, Michael Blouin. Two children from New York travel with their mother to spend a long weekend with their grandparents in Canada. There, they encounter an invisible being, Fritz, who has had his magical gold stolen. The children journey with Fritz through the rainbow to the Great Land of Small, where they meet some very strange and interesting characters and get into a lot of trouble. A tale filled with humour, special effects and magical encounters. (See: *Tales for All* series)

Great Ordinary Movie, The (Joan of Arc Is Alive and Well and Living in Québec) (*Le grand film ordinaire***)** (1971) (78mins) d&s: Roger Frappier : Raymond Cloutier, Paule Baillargeon, Jocelyn Bérubé, Claude Laroche, Suzanne Garceau, Guy Thauvette. A filmed record of the presentation of the play *T'es pas tannée, Jeanne d'Arc* by the theatre troupe *Le Grand Cirque Ordinaire,* with fictional scenes added. Combining documentary with fiction this fascinating chapter of theatrical history questions the part and place of the acting fraternity in Quebec at the time of the tumultuous social changes which took place in the province during the 1960's.

Great Shadow, The (1920) (50mins-silent) (b/w) d: Harley Knoles s: Eve Unsell : Tyrone Power Sr., Donald Hall, Dorothy Bernard, John Rutherford. A war story about the rising power of Bolshevism. An early appearance of politic subject matter. The first film to be made at the newly opened studio in Trenton, Ontario.

Great World Serpent, The: see **Grand serpent du monde, Le**

Great Zeal, The: see *Grand zélé, Le*

Greening of Ian Elliot, The (1991) (90mins) d: Stacey Curtis s: Jeannine Locke : Anthony Bekenn, Carol Sinclair, Helen Carscallen, Gary Reineke, Joseph Ziegler. Elliot is a newly ordained United Church minister from Toronto assigned to a small Saskatchewan farming community. He is struck by the beauty of the place, "so silent on the prairie, austere and unaltered." But he finds the people in turmoil over a proposed power project, a dam that will destroy their river valley. The minister will join the opposition, but he must also deal with an aspect of his personal life that adds to the air of controversy: he is homosexual. The environment, morality and social change are among the concerns affecting the townspeople. This film is a beautifully rendered work bringing to the screen a fascinating side of Canadian life. This was the last of many noteworthy films made for CBC by Jeannine Locke. The shabby treatment meted out to her and this film brought about her resignation in the face of timorous programmers who disliked its controversial elements: implied criticism of the Rafferty-Alameda project and the inclusion of a homosexual. By this time, the CBC had entered a phase during which it preferred American programs to Canadian. In chasing ratings, the CBC abandoned its mandate.

Grelots rouges, sanglots bleus: see **Red Bells, Blue Tears**

Grenouille et la baleine, La: see **Tadpole and the Whale**

Grey Fox, The (1982) (91mins) d: Phillip Borsos s: John Hunter : Richard Farnsworth, Jackie Burroughs, Wayne Robson, Ken Pogue, Timothy Webber, David Petersen, Gary Reineke, Sean Sullivan. A graceful, beautifully photographed, real and romantic biography of Bill Miner, the American train robber who came to Canada at the turn of the 19th century to ply his "trade." He had been chased out of the U.S. after spending 30 years in prison there. Gentle and intelligently told, it is a refreshing glimpse into history, set against the magnificent scenery of British Columbia. Splendid performances from Farnsworth and Burroughs. This picture marked a second beginning to creative filmmaking outside of Québec after the *Goin' Down the Road* (1970) period faded out. But our hopes were dashed once again.

Grey Owl (1999) (117mins) (a Canada-U.K. co-production) d: Richard Attenborough s: William Nicholson : Pierce Brosnan, Annie Galipeau, Nathaniel Arcand, Vlasta Vrana, David Fox, Charles Powell, Stephanie Cole, Renée Asherson, Stewart Bick, Graham Greene. One of the most endearing and enduring stories in Canada's history is that of Grey Owl, an Englishman named Archibald Belaney who transformed his life and pretended to be a native. At a time when native life fascinated the public, Grey Owl became an early celebrity figure on the lecture circuit here and in the U.K. Attenborough brings this remarkable life to the screen with deep feeling, understanding and veracity. Brosnan is surprisingly good as Grey Owl, and the supporting players give winning performances. Among its more memorable moments is the scene where Grey Owl returns to England to visit his sisters, who did not know of his masquerade as a native. They are intrigued that he would go to work and live in such an exotic and beautiful land as Canada. Belaney–Grey Owl's double life was not discovered until his death in 1938. A very human and perceptive work from the distinguished Attenborough.

Grizzly Falls (2000) (94mins) (a Canada-U.K. co-production) d: Stewart Raffill s: Richard Beattie (from a story by Stuart Margolin) : Daniel Clark, Bryan Brown, Tom Jackson, Oliver Tobias, Richard Harris, Brock Simpson. An innocent fable about children and bears set in Canada's Rocky Mountains. It has adventures galore but not much excitement as it follows familiar paths, along which the tired cast limps from one scene to another. Only the bears seem to be at home, and only in the movies are they so unfailingly friendly. The cast does all that's required of it, and the background score, as in almost every other Canadian film, is much too intrusive.

Grocer's Wife, The (1991) (104 mins) d&s: John Pozer : Simon Webb, Andrea Rankin, Susinn McFarlen, Nicola Cavendish, Leroy Schultz. A low-budget first film strikingly photographed in black and white and set among the industrial smokestacks of Trail, British Columbia (although it is not identified). We are introduced to a dull fellow who spends his days checking emissions and his evenings tending to his domineering mother. The grocer's wife and a B-circuit stripper also complicate his life. There are laughs along the way, and the concept is imaginative, but events never quite live up to their promise. Neither did Pozer, who, though highly praised by some critics, seems not to have moved beyond this flash in the pan!

Gros Bill, Le: see **Grand Bill, The**

Gross Misconduct (1992) (120mins) d: Atom Egoyan s: Paul Gross (from the book by Martin O'Malley) : Daniel Kash, Peter McNeil, Linda Goranson, Douglas Hughes, Lenore Zann. The life of Brian "Spinner" Spencer, the celebrated Canadian hockey player, was marked by infidelity, drugs and murder. The director and writer have adapted this true story into a convincing and brutally realistic meditation on the excesses of human behaviour brought about by hockey's need for constant demonstrations of masculinity. Divided into brief chapters, this is essentially a tawdry tale delineating Spencer's ambitious career, bringing out the tragedy and pathos of an ill-spent life. Paul Gross went on to become a highly popular and talented star and writer in television.

Grub-Stake, The (1922) (90mins: silent with intertitles) d&s: Nell Shipman : Walt Whitman, Alfred Allen, Lilian Leighton, Nell Shipman. Canada's pioneering actress and filmmaker portrays a woman living in the far north who becomes tired of her unreliable husband. She travels to the Klondike to make her own life and, ultimately, a fortune. A fascinating early silent film in which a woman speaks up for herself and refuses to be treated like a vassal. A piece teeming with history and humanity. One of several films made by or starring the lovely and intelligent Nell Shipman.

Guardian Angel, The: see *Ange gardien, L'*

Guardian, The (1999) (91mins) d: Gerry Lively s: Daniel Greenberg (from his novel) : Frank Zagarino, Stellina Rusich, Bryan Genesse. A bodyguard protecting a wealthy businessman becomes a suspect when murders begin to take place around him. Not to cast aspersions on individuals, but one does wonder, sometimes, about these security guards. The action and the thrills are not well stirred.

Guêpe, La: see **Wasp, The**

Guerre des toques, La: see **Dog Who Stopped the War, The**

Guerre du feu, La: see **Quest for Fire**

Guilt By Association (2002) (95mins) (a U.S.-Canada film) d: Graeme Campbell s: Alan Hines : Alberta Watson, Mercedes Ruehl, Karen Clave. A film based on an actual event. The severity of drug laws in the US in this particular case, result in a mother of two young children being sent to prison for ten years because she never reported to the police that her live-in lover grew, smoked and sold marihuana. She never smoked it herself and had come to the point when she no longer allowed the man to enter her house. Although she, her friends and family fought tirelessly for her release she endured a nightmare, then to find that her son, now grown up was smoking pot. President Clinton secured the release of many of these women. This is a first-rate, honest and aching drama of life inside and outside prison, deeply felt with a heart-breaking performance by Alberta Watson. The ending, however, is weakened by an obtrusive score. This is one of the very few worthy Canadian-American films. (Note: Not to be confused with *The Guilty*, 2000).

Guilty, The (2000) (107mins) d: Anthony Waller s: William Davies (based on the book of the same title by Simon Burke) : William Pullman, Gabrielle Anwar, Devon Sawa, Angela Featherstone, Joanne Whalley, Ken Tremblett, Jaimz Woolvett, Darcy Belsher. A convoluted picture about a slippery married lawyer, his craven ambitions, nasty moments with women and involvement in criminal activities. It manages to bring about a surprising turn at the end, but is otherwise guilty of following a hackneyed brief.

Guitar (*Guitare*) (1974) (90mins) d: Richard Lavoie s: Jocelyn Sheehy, Richard Lavoie : Roy Witham, Manon Ares, Patrice Drouin, Richard Isabel, Paul Piché, Jocelyn Sheehy. A myth, a poem, a dream. Some children find an old man alone on an island and listen to his stories of life. He then dies peacefully, and the children bury him. Only in Québec could a film like this be made today with such kindness, love and feeling.

Guitarman (1994) (93mins) d: Will Dixon s: Hart Hanson, Will Dixon : Nicholas Campbell, Donnelly Rhodes, Shawn Ashmore, Andrea Martin, Suzy Joachim. A family fairy tale hatched on the Saskatchewan prairies, where people struggling to make a living in the dust bowl are suddenly confronted with a travelling musician, who makes a deal with the mayor to save the crops. The mayor is a crook, and the musician retaliates by becoming the Pied Piper to take the children away. Rhodes and Campbell bring this fetching social study believably to life.

Gun Runner, The (1984) (92mins) d: Nardo Castillo s: Arnie Gelbart : Kevin Costner, Sara Botsford, Paul Soles, Gerard Parkes, Ronald Lea, Mitch Martin, Aline Van Dine, Ruth Danan, Larry Lewis. An idealistic young Canadian returns home from China during the '20s to obtain guns for the Chinese Rebellion. He becomes involved with smugglers—not of drugs this time, but of liquor! How Canadian! Unfortunately, the proceedings become tiresome and unconvincing. This was one of Costner's very early films, which he managed to survive. His later

fame brought it out on video in 1989. Paul Soles recalls his character was based and modelled on the legendary Sam Brofman.

Gust of Panic, A: see *Petit vent de panique, Un*

H (Heroin and Hell) (1990) (90mins) d&s: Darrell Wasyk : Martin Neufeld, Pascale Montpetit. A relentless first-film melodrama showing the disintegration of two heroin addicts locked in a dreary basement room in a struggle to break their habit. This is an enterprising low-budget production with only two characters, who seem to be actually living their roles. It will leave most audiences uninvolved and without sympathy. When first shown, the film was hailed by critics as a masterpiece and the director as a genius. After being recognized with awards he and his film didn't deserve, Wasyk made *Mustard Bath* (1993). We haven't heard from him since.

Habitat (1995) (110mins) (a Canada-Netherlands co-production) d&s: René Daalder : Balthazar Getty, Tcheky Karyo, Alice Krige, Kenneth Welsh, Laura Harris. The ozone layer is so seriously depleted that the sun's rays are deadly. A teenager resists the burning because his father, a famous geneticist, has found ways of protecting people. But there are horrors ahead. The special effects are good, but the story could send one to sleep.

Halfback of Notre Dame, The (1994) (120mins) d: René Bonnière s: Richard Clark, Mark Trafficante, Michael McClary : Gabriel Hogan, Emmanuelle Vaugier, Allen Cutler, Scott Hylands, Sandra Nelson, Nicole Parker. A portrait of high school life seen through the lens of the Victor Hugo classic. Here, the hunchback is a very large football-playing kid, and his own little Esmeralda is a French transfer student. The taunting crowds are played by other students. And so it goes, with parallels all the way to the bell tower. The spirit is there, but emotional appeal doesn't run deep. Nice to see Bonnière still directing.

Halfway House: see *Babylone*

Hall, Chipman: see **Bayo**

Handmaid's Tale, The (1990) (109mins) (a U.S.-U.K.-German co-production) (Listed for the record) d: Volker Schlondorff s: Harold Pinter (based on the novel of the same title by Margaret Atwood) : Natasha Richardson, Faye Dunaway, Robert Duvall, David Dukes, Aidan Quinn, Elizabeth McGovern, Victoria Tennant, Blanche Baker. A far-fetched story about a "new world" where women are forced to become child bearers for a new, pure generation. A sterile film only slightly better than the book.

Handyman, The (*L'homme à tout faire*) (1980) (99mins) d&s: Micheline Lanctôt : Jocelyn Bérubé, Andrée Pelletier, Paul Dion, Gilles Renaud, Marcel Sabourin. In her first film as director, the talented actress Micheline Lanctôt tells a charming story of an affluent and bored suburban housewife who breaks the heart of her amorous handyman. It is played with just the right touch of romance and longing and is a delight from beginning to end.

Hanging Garden, The (1997) (91mins) d&s: Thom Fitzgerald : Chris Leavens, Kerry Fox, Seana McKenna, Troy Veinotte, Sarah Polley, Peter MacNeill. This complicated narrative is neither well devised nor told. A gay man returns home, from where we are never told, to attend his sister's wedding. His brother-in-law-to-be is bisexual—and a previous lover. They rendezvous the night before the wedding. The sister seems to know of this relationship, but it doesn't appear to bother her. There is no one in this dysfunctional family to believe in or relate to, except the put-upon wife and mother. At the end, the brother leaves—to go nowhere, apparently. Filmed in Nova Scotia.

Hank (1977) (65mins) d: Donald Haldane s: Donald Bailey, Ralph Thomas : Robert Warner, Florence Paterson, Richard Donat, Mina E. Mina, Budd Knapp, Chuck Shamata. The title character is an honest middle-aged man with a successful fresh-produce business and a fairly contented family life. When he tries to bring his establishment up to date, he finds himself in conflict with big business and big labour. This leads to violence, and Hank's life is shattered. A brave and timely film stating the issues (that are still with us) loud and clear. (See: *For the Record*)

Hank Williams: The Show He Never Gave (1982) (86mins) d: David Acomba s: Maynard Collins (from his play) : Sneezy Waters, Dixie Seatle, Sean McCann, Sean Hewitt, Kay Hawtrey, George Essery, Jackie Washington. A lively and enjoyable musical in which Sneezy does as much as might be expected, playing Hank Williams with affection and admiration.

Happy Birthday Gemini (1980) (107mins) (a Canadian-American film) d: Richard Benner s: : Madeline Kahn, Rita Moreno, Robert Viharo, Alan Rosenberg, Sarah Holcomb, David Marshall Grant, Timothy Jenkins. The popular Broadway play by Albert Innaurato concerning a young man worried about his sexual identity makes a somewhat flat and colourless transfer to the screen.

Happy Birthday to Me (1981) (108mins) d: J. Lee Thompson s: Timothy Bond, Peter Jobin, John Saxton (from his story) : Melissa Sue Anderson, Glenn Ford, Lawrence Dane, Sharon Acker, Frances Hyland, Tracy Bregman, Jack Blum, Matthew Craven, Lenore Zann, Lisa Langlois, Walter Massey, Victor Knight, Louis del Grande, Murray Westgate. A gory bucket of blood and murder about a student who is thought to have killed off several classmates because they killed her mother several years earlier. A nasty piece of nonsense. The director has done better things.

Happy Christmas, Miss King (1999) (87mins) d: Stefan Scaini s: Raymond Storey : Jackie Burroughs, Lally Cadeau, Mag Ruffman, Cedric Smith, Zachary Bennett. With the First World War as a backdrop, the entire King family prepares for a traditional Christmas dinner. Their happiness is marred when they learn that a son is reported missing in action. The daughter, worried that her Christmas

concert will fail, collapses. A pleasant, moving and honest recreation of times gone by.

Happy Days (Beckett on Film series) (2000) (79mins) (a Canada-Ireland co-production) d: Patricia Rozema s: the play by Samuel Beckett : Rosaleen Linehan, Richard Johnson. A wife and husband sit in the desert for hours, she buried in sand and chattering on about nothing that makes sense. We are expected to consider this a depiction of an awful and typical marriage. Beckett disciples will worship it. Heathens will walk out. The director said she was pleased to have served "the great master." (See *Krapp's Last Tape*)

Happy Memories (Old Memories) (Les beaux souvenirs) (1981) (114mins) d: Francis Mankiewicz s: Réjean Ducharme : Monique Spaziani, Julie Vincent, Paul Hébert, R.H. Thomson, Rémy Girard. A strange, brooding, yet compelling narrative, told in fragments that finally come together, about a young woman who returns to her family home outside Québec City. She finds herself ignored by her father in favour of her sister, who has moved into her former bedroom and removed all traces in the house of their dead mother. The sister is also possessed by an odd passion for her father. The past slowly reappears, and the various pieces make up an absorbing family study.

Hard Core Logo (1996) (94mins) d: Bruce McDonald s: Noel Baker (based on the novel by Michael Turner) : Hugh Dillon, Callum Keith Rennie, John Pyper-Ferguson, Bernie Coulson, Julian Richings. A mock documentary about the reunion of a Vancouver punk band travelling across Canada, as filmed by McDonald. The band members are mostly an unpleasant lot, playing unpleasant punkster pulp, with the usual quota of foul language.

Hard Feelings (1981) (110mins) (a Canada-U.S. co-production) d: Daryl Duke s: W.D. Richter, John Herzfeld (from the novel by Don Bredes) : Carl Marotte, Charlaine Woodward, Grand Bush, Vincent Bufano, Allan Katz, Lisa Langlois, Walter Massey. Set in the 1960s with an American background, this is a finely made film. One of the first about a difficult relationship between a young white boy and a black girl attending the same school. Difficulties and prejudice are all around them.

Hard Part Begins, The (1973) (86mins) d: Paul Lynch s: John Hunter : Donnelly Rhodes, Nancy Belle Fuller, Paul Bradley, Linda Sorenson, Robert Hawkins, Doug McGrath, Les Carlson, Neil Vipond, Sean Sullivan, Eric Clavering. An honest and perceptive film with realistic settings and a strong emotional appeal. About a down-and-out country and western singer travelling around the small towns of Ontario. An arresting study into character and motivation, almost, as time goes by, an historic picture of Ontario places.

Hard to Forget (So Hard to Forget) (1998) (120mins) d: Vic Sarin s: Gerald Wexler (from the novel by Evelyn Crowe) : Polly Shannon, Timothy

FEATURE FILM GUIDE

Dutton, Nicholas Campbell, Lois Maxwell. A loving woman is murdered by her husband, who appears to have gotten away with it. But a private detective looking for evidence to prove that the husband was the murderer suddenly sees the woman's picture in an advertisement for Africa. He decides to visit to see what's going on. His discoveries make a gripping tale of romance and jealousy. (See: *Harlequin* series)

Harlequin Series (CTV-Alliance-Atlantis): See under respective titles:
1: **Another Woman**
2: **At the Midnight Hour**
3: **Awakening, The**
4: **Broken Lullaby**
5: **Change of Place, A**
6: **Diamond Girl**
7: **Hard to Forget (So Hard to Forget)**
8: **Loving Evangeline**
9: **Recipe for Revenge**
10: **This Matter of Marriage**
11: **Treacherous Beauties**
12: **Waiting Game**

Harmoney (1999) (90mins) d: Naomi Hiltz s: Jonathan Hiltz : Corey Feldman, Maestro Fresh Wes, Scott Speedman, Mart Donato, Ivan Segal, Jordan Knight, The Persuasions. During the boy band phenomenon of the 1990s, we are taken behind the scenes to meet Harmoney, a young pop group that has found fame and fortune. The members have now forgotten why they wanted to be singers. Great for those who dig this stuff.

Harmony Cats (1993) (100mins) d: Sandy Wilson s: David King : Kim Coates, Jim Byrnes, Lisa Brokop. The director of *My American Cousin* goes on the road with a lively musical entertainment. A snobbish classical violinist first loses his job with the Vancouver Symphony, then his girlfriend, and then his apartment. He goes on tour as a bass player with a country and western band and evolves into a warm and loving soul. Good fun.

Haro (1994) (89mins) d&s: Michael Kezin : Gregory Merrick, Penny Hetherington, Bee Farquhar. A boy is unable to cope with his mother's suffering as she deteriorates due to Alzheimer's disease. A caring film considering issues of memories and mortality, what is real, and what is illusion.

Harry Tracy, Desperado (1981) (107mins) (a Canadian-American film) d: William A. Graham s: David Lee Henry : Bruce Dern, Helen Shaver, Michael Gwynne, Gordon Lightfoot, Jacques Hubert, Daphne Goldrick, Fred Diehl. American Western life is vividly recreated in Port Alberni, B.C., and Canmore, Alberta, to tell this saga of an outlaw who lives as he pleases. Well played, but the Mounties are missing, of course. A familiar chapter from the Old West.

Harry's Case (2000) (120mins) d: Stephen Williams s: Peter Lauterman : Brian Markinson, Adam Beach, Sherry Miller, Janet-Laine Green, Kim Schraner, Thomas Melisis, Conrad Dunn, Mark Lutz, Dianne Debassige. A down-and-out lawyer who has become a private investigator is debarred after being falsely accused of bribing a witness. Murder, embezzlement and betrayal. This is a dark, taut and often chilling look into crime and its consequences.

Harvest (1981) (65mins) d: Giles Walker s: Rob Forsyth : Jan Rubes, David McIlwraith, Lally Cadeau, Peter Dvorsky, Charles Joliffe, Layne Coleman. This film is based on an actual controversy on the Prairies during the 1980s, brought about by the complicated plots, plans and payments by the provincial government related to the purchase of lands for a uranium refinery. A Mennonite farmer and his neighbours are involved, and conflicts run deep. A fine dramatization of true-life events. (Not to be confused with *Harvest*, a one-hour film of the contemporary opera by Raymond and Beverly Pannell, directed by John Thomson with Claude Corbeil and Cindy Girling, that draws its inspiration from the struggle of migrant workers against their exploitation by a union organizer.) (See: *For the Record*)

Harvest (1993) (90mins) d: Michael Scott s: Malcolm MacRury : Ted Shackelford, Ron White, Rebecca Jenkins, Kenneth Pogue. Manitoba could be anywhere in the rural Midwest in this reasonably authentic story of a family farm in distress, winding its way along the road to a predictably simplistic outcome.

Hasards ou coïncidences (1998)(120mins) (a Canada-France co-production) d&s: Claude Lelouch : Alessandra Martines, Geoffrey Holder, Pierre Arditi, Véronique Moreau, David La Haye, France Castel. "Myriam danced like a swan in Venice, Rome, Milan," writes Lelouch. "She had beauty and grace, and her life was a fairy tale." Missing, however, was what she craved the most: love. Lelouch, the writer, proceeds to make amends, and soon we are drenched in his special kind of romance, with the usual sticky music on the soundtrack.

Hathi (1998) (97mins) d&s: Philippe Gautier : Jamedar Sabu Saab, Kawadi Makbul, Noorullah, Pyare Jan, Begum Jamila. A beautiful and compassionate study of the elephant in India. It brings home to audiences the vanishing world of these wonderful creatures and the mahouts who care for them as their forests are destroyed. Based on real-life events and eyewitness accounts, this film, upholding the great Flaherty tradition, is another caring picture from producer Rock Demers (see: *Tales for All*).

Hatley High (2003) (90mins) d: Phil Price s: Myles Hainsworth : Nicolas Wright, Rachelle Lefevre, Nwamiko Madden, Paul Van Dyck, James Woods, Morgan Kelly, Ilona Elkin. A new student in town quickly becomes popular with other students after joining a chess club, getting involved here and there with this and that, including becoming part of a filmmaking team shooting grade-b horror movies. All well and good, but is it possible to see such a story without a gun being produced? No.

Haunting Harmony, A (1993) (60mins) (a U.K.-Canada film) d: Alvin Rakoff s: Fiona McHugh : Nathaniel Moreau, Jean-Marc Perret, Frank Middlemass, Francesca Annis, John Hallam. A young schoolboy from Canada is befriended by the 400-year-old ghost of a Welsh choirboy. Slight but sensible with just the right dose of fright.

Haunting of Julia, The (Full Circle) (1976) (96mins) (a Canada-U.K. co-production) d: Richard Loncraine s: David Humphries, Harry Bromley Davenport (from Peter Straub's novel *Julia*) : Mia Farrow, Keir Dullea, Tom Conti, Jill Bennett, Robin Gammell, Cathleen Nesbit, Anna Wing, Edward Hardwicke, Nigel Havers, Mary Morris. A great cast in a haunted house where a woman—who has witnessed the death of her daughter—is troubled by a wandering and troubled spirit, possessing strange powers, an occult thriller not laking in thrills.

Haunting of Lisa, The (1995) (99mins) d: Donald McBrearty s: Donald Henry : Cheryl Ladd, Staci Keanan, Duncan Regehr, Amilia Robinson, Wayne Northrop, Kate Lynch, Toni Rosata. Innocent fun turns into a dangerous game when a young girl realizes the truth about the man she is dating. One of the better efforts in the school of suspense and social studies.

Haute surveillance : see **Black Mirror**

Have Mercy (1999) (85mins) d&s: Anaïs Granofsky : Alisa Weiger, Clark Johnson, Jackie Burroughs. A patient at a psychiatric hospital is persuaded against her will to join in the presentation of a supposedly therapeutic talent show for tv. The ever reliable Burroughs rises to the occasion, even though audiences might find it hard to do so. In questionable taste.

Haven (2001) (240 mins) (a Canada-U.S. co-production) d: John Gray s: Suzette Couture (based on the book by Ruth Gruber) : Natasha Richardson, Hal Holbrook, Martin Landau, Anne Bancroft, Bruce Greenwood, Henry Czerny, Colm Feore, Robert Joy, Daniel Kash, Sheila McCarthy, Janet-Laine Green, Kenneth Welsh. An ambitious attempt to portray the real-life journey of 1,000 Jewish refugees from Germany to America during World War II, escorted by Ruth Gruber, a young Jewish journalist. At times, the human and political aspects of this great movement are complicated in the sprawling narrative, which has many affecting moments. Filmed mainly in Toronto.

Hawk's Vengeance (1997) (96mins) d: Marc F. Voizard s: Michael Ellis : Gary Daniel, Jayne Heitmeyer, Cass Magda, George Chiang, Catherine Blythe. A British soldier (or policeman, wearing an odd uniform) comes to an unidentified American city, actually filmed in the less known streets of Montréal, in search of his stepbrother's killers. He meets an

attractive woman, a police detective; she disappears for a while, during which time he becomes involved in constant violence with skinheads and a gang of Chinese criminals, one of whom becomes his friend. Not bad and interesting to see the criminal scene through the eyes of "a copper" from 'over there'.

Hayseed (1997) (90mins) d&s: Andrew Hayes, Joshua Levy : Jamie Shannon, Elva Mai Hoover, Maria Vacratsis, Mark McKinney, Sarain Boylen, Scott Thompson, cameos by Bruce LaBruce and Daniel MacIvor. A rarity: a pleasant, amusing comedy that finds its humour without going into the toilet. Two innocents up from the country visit that unknown place called "Toronto" and are astonished, pleased or put off by what they find in the big city. Made by students using their credit cards and loans from their parents, this is a low-budget fairy-tale romp and a welcome change from other films claiming to be comedies.

Head of Normande St. Onge, The (*La tête de Normande St-Onge*) (1975) d: Gilles Carle s: Ben Barzman, Gilles Carle : Carole Laure, Reynald Bouchard, Raymond Cloutier, Carmen Giroux, Gaétan Guimond, J.-Léo Gagnon, Anne-Marie Ducharme, Renée Girard, Denys Arcand, Yves Massicotte, Marcelle Pallascio, Robert Gravel, Jean Comtois, Gil Laroche. A girl, trying to understand the supposed insanity of her mother, falls victim to her own kind of mental aberrations. With the exception of the dream sequences, which represent Carle at his most extreme and self-indulgent, this is a film of tenderness, humour and sympathy. With fine backgrounds and character delineation.

Head On (Fatal Attraction) (1980) (98mins) d: Michael Grant s: James Sanderson, Paul Illidge : Sally Kellerman, Stephen Lack, John Huston, Lawrence Dane, Sandra Scott, Robert Silverman. An uneasy mix of comedy and drama as two people who meet after a traffic accident bring their sex fantasies to life. It tries hard to make sense but gives up when it does not. However, we are spared the excesses of Cronenberg's *Crash*.

Heads or Tails (*Pile ou face*) (1971) (96mins) d: Roger Fournier s: Gérald Tassé : Nathalie Naubert, Jean Coutu, Diane Arcand, Monique Bélisle, Patricia Foster. Snow. skiing and sex in the Laurentian Mountains as four couples have a happy reunion—even though the partner swapping doesn't work out. Another of Québec's likeable and not-so-innocent bedside stories.

Heads or Tales: see *J'en suis*

Heart Exposed, The (*Le coeur découvert*) (1986) (107mins) d: Jean-Yves Laforce s: Michel Tremblay : Gilles Renaud, Michel Poirier. A simple look at life through the relationship between an actor and a teacher, whose love for each other is complicated by a five-year-old son. Tremblay is at his best in the underplayed simplicity of this script. Set naturally in Montréal, but a bit overlong.

Heart of America: Homeroom (2003) (87mins) (a Canada-Germany co-production) d: Uwe Boll s: Robert Dean Klein (from story by Boll) : Jurgen Prochnow, Elisabeth Rosen, Michael Belyea, Clint Howard, Elisabeth Howard. A dreadful film in bad-taste and incompetence which uses the tragedy of the Littleton and Columbine School shootings to make from them a sensational exploitation piece of entertainment, both painfully silly and cheap. (Filmed in Vancouver in tandem with *House of the Dead*.)

Heart of Stone: see *Homme et son pêché, Un*

Heart of the Sun (1998) (95mins) d: Francis Damberger s: Kim Hogan (from Betty Lambert's play *Jennie's Story*) : Christianne Hirt, Shaun Johnston, Michael Riley, Merrilyn Gann, Graham Greene. Stylishly adapted from a play about Alberta's forced sterilization program begun in 1900, this is a sympathetic and compelling story about a young woman, happily married, who yearns for a family. Through a series of flashbacks, we discover why she will never carry her own child. Filmed near Medicine Hat, Alberta, the landscape is striking.

Heart: The Marilyn Bell Story (2000) (90mins) d: Manon Briand s: Karen Walton : Caroline Dhavernas, Ron White, Amy Sloan, Chip Chuipka. A title like this is enough to turn away most audiences. A pity because the life of the record-setting swimmer Marilyn Bell, who at age 16 became the first person to swim across Lake Ontario from Toronto, is well told. Bell also completed what was then the longest marathon swim in history, after overcoming a number of formidable obstacles. With a fine actress, a good script and a director who avoids bathos, this is a memorable film about a time that holds many happy memories for Canadians.

Heartaches (1981) (93mins) d: Donald Shebib s: Terence Hefferman : Margot Kidder, Annie Potts, Robert Carradine, Winston Rekert, George Touliatos, Maureen Fitzgerald. An amusing trifle about a pregnant young woman on a bus trip to Toronto. She has left her husband and meets another woman who is a laugh a minute—and she is looking for a laugh. A good cast makes this an enjoyable trip.

Heartbreak (*L'arrache-coeur***)** (1979) (92mins) d&s: Mireille Dansereau : Louise Marleau, Françoise Faucher, Michel Mondie, Anne Létourneau, Guy Godin, Gilbert Comtois. A sensitively told story of a difficult love-hate relationship between a mother and her daughter. Played with deep feeling and understanding by Louise Marleau and Françoise Faucher. Mireille Dansereau's first film as writer-director.

Heat Line, The (*La ligne de chaleur***)** (1987) (90mins) d: Hubert-Yves Rose s: Micheline Lanctôt and Rose : Gabriel Arcand, Simon Gonzalez. A drama in which a divorced man flees the Québec winter and takes his son to Florida to bring back his dead father's car. On the road back, various adventures befall them, while the father comes to think back on his life and family relationships. A difficult theme almost lost in the monotony.

Heater (1999) (87mins) d&s: Terence Odette : Gary Farmer, Stephen Ouimette, Tina Keeper. A tale of two homeless men living on the cold winter streets of Winnipeg and of the friendship that develops between them. This slight and largely improvised film pays its respects to those who find themselves in desperate situations.

Heatwave Lasted Four Days, The (1973) (80mins) d&s: Douglas Jackson : Gordon Pinsent, Alexandra Stewart, Lawrence Dane, Domini Blythe, Al Waxman, Ron Hartmann, Judy Ann Davies, Jon Granik, Joan Blackman, Jean-Roger Périard, Frank Perry, Ken James, Walter Massey. A Montréal television cameraman accidentally witnesses a heroin deal and finds himself involved with the underworld. A taut and tightly told contemporary drama, giving a Canadian view of criminal life.

Heaven Before I Die (1997) (95mins) d&s: Izadore K. Musallam : Andy Velasquez Jr., Giancarlo Giannini, Joanna Pacula, Omar Sharif, Leonard Cohen. A young man living in Palestine is made to feel different from others due to a defect in his feet. He walks like Charlie Chaplin. So he emigrates to Canada, where everyone is "equal." He meets a thief who teaches him how to survive and a prophet who gives him advice. Well, heaven comes in many forms, and this one is certainly different and close to home (ours, that is).

Heaven Help Us: see *Deux super-dingues*

Heaven on Earth (1987) (120mins) d: Allan Kroeker s: Margaret Atwood, Peter Pearson : Sian Leisa Davies, Amos Crawley, R.H. Thomson, Huw Davies. In rural Ontario in 1911, various farms are ready for the influx of orphaned children coming to Canada from England to start a new life. This film follows the lives of a brother and sister who, like the other children, find joy or sadness with the kind and not-so-kind farmers. A film that lingers long in memory.

Heavenly Bodies (1985) (89mins) d&s: Lawrence Dane : Cynthia Dale, Richard Rebiere, Walter George Alton, Linda Sorensen, Cec Linder, Micki Moore, Sean Sullivan, Murray Westgate, Laura Henry, Stuart Stone. A sex-and-aerobics musical taking place among the workout girls on a Chicago TV station. Hard to take. (not to be confused with *Les Corps Celestes*)

Heavenly Bodies (*Les corps célestes***)** (1973) (104mins) (a Canada-France co-production) d: Gilles Carle s: Arthur Lamothe, Gilles Carle : Donald Pilon, Carole Laure, Micheline Lanctôt, Judi McDonald, Sheila Charlesworth, Claudie Verdant, Dominique Charron, Yves Barrette. A slight but lively comedy with serious undertones about a pimp who arrives in a small Québec mining town with seven prostitutes and plans to open a brothel and enjoy himself on the proceeds. The coming of World War II changes his plans. Typically Carle, the film ranges from great moments to silly sequences but seldom leaves audiences unmoved. It's fascinating to look back on the performances of Micheline Lanctôt and Carole Laure in their films of this period.

Heis, The: see **Hostile Force**

Hell Bent (1994) (83mins) d&s: John Kozak : Danial Sprintz, Kevin Doerksen, Alison Northcott. A disturbing film that tries to come to grips with adolescents who, when left to their own devices by apathetic parents, seek escape from the bleak winter of Winnipeg by unleashing violence and cruelties not hitherto suspected of them: bullying of other children, petty thievery, rages against teachers, and exploits more daring than those tried before. Knowingly acted by three young players living within a grim nocturnal landscape, this well-intentioned film has no answers—but then neither does anyone else, it seems, in these unsettling times.

Heller: see **Cop**

Hemingway vs Callaghan (2003) (in two 120mins part) d: Michael DeCarlo s: Malcolm MacRury : Robin Dunne, Vincent Walsh, Gordon Pinsent, Aida Turturro. And so Hemingway went to Paris and wrote for the *Toronto Star* and met Canadian writer Morley Callaghan. On returning to Canada, they became good friends, and one spurred the other in their writing endeavours. Their time together culminated in a boxing match refereed by F. Scott Fitzgerald. Hemingway returned to New York. The *Star* gets a lot of attention.

Henri (1986) (91mins) d: François Labonté s: Jacques Jacob : Éric Brisebois, Jacques Godin, Lucie Laurier. An appealing cameo about a 15-year-old boy who is determined to win the marathon in the Québec village of Marie-Beauce, even though his mother has recently died and his father shows little interest in the race. Done with delicacy and affection.

Henry and Verlin (1994) (87mins) d&s: Gary Ledbetter : Gary Farmer, Keegan MacIntosh, Nancy Beatty, Robert Joy, Joan Orenstein, Eric Peterson, Margot Kidder, David Cronenberg, Wilfred Bray A likeable film marked by exceptional performances. The setting is an Ontario farm during the Depression, where an autistic boy and his uncle, a giant of a man with a childlike mind, become good friends. Based on true incidents in the life of the writer, this is oddly affecting, natural and honest in the telling. Margot Kidder strikes a wrong note as an irascible old lady.

Herd, The (1998) (100mins) d: Paul Lynch s: Nicholas McKinney, Paul Lynch : Dennis Allen, James Allodi, Colm Feore, David Hemblen, Douglas Lennox, Don McKellar, Mark McKinney, Graham Greene. This film documents the epic journey of a 62-year-old Laplander, Andrew Bahr, who was hired by the Canadian government in 1929 to escort 3,000 reindeer from Alaska to the Mackenzie River delta in the Northwest Territories. Bahr planned to take 18 months, but due to weather conditions and the decisions of misguided civil servants it took six years.

The director takes the role of Bahr, and most of the actors play bureaucrats. The film captures the atmosphere of the far north but is somewhat lacking in reindeer; the herd has declined in numbers over the intervening years.

Here Am I (1999) (72mins) (b/w) d&s: Joshua Dorsey, Douglas Naimer : Ivailo Tsvetkov, Ivailo Christov, Josef Sergichiev. A pretentious two-person first work by Dorsey and Naimer directing, producing, writing and photographing "the soul of a foreign landscape," in this instance, the Balkans. Made during a 20-month visit to Bulgaria, this is the story of a 19TH-century horseman who destroyed and burned villages in his search for a sacred text. His banished clan and murdered family were not permitted to read the text because its "purity" was beyond their understanding. Some audiences might feel the same way, but others may find murky meanings in this undeniably well made low-budget effort.

Here I Will Nest (1941) (90mins) (b/w with colour insert) d: Melburn Turner s: Hilda Hooke Smith (from her play of the same title) : John Burton, Robina Richardson, George Simpson, Mary Ashwell. Filmed in London, Ontario, this simple, homemade, low-budget film pays tribute to the 19TH-century British pioneer Col. Thomas Talbot, who founded the Talbot Settlements in Ontario. Rather like looking at pictures in a history book.

Here's to Life! (The Old Hats) (2000) (95mins) (a Canada-U.S. co-production) d&s: Arne Olsen : Eric McCormack, James Whitmore, Ossie Davis, Marya Delver, Kim Hunter. A young retirement home administrator whose accountant has "cooked the books" is blackmailed by three angry clients into taking them on a trip to Vancouver with all expenses paid. This is a nauseating, sticky mixture of characters and contrivances. It gives Golden Agers a bad name. And what a pity Kim Hunter was not offered something better than this for which to come out of retirement; but she succeeds in being a genuine and likeable character.

Heroin and Hell: see **H**

Hersenschimmen (Mind Shadows) (1987) (112mins) (a Dutch-Canadian film) d&s: Heddy Honigman (based on the novel of the same name by J. Bernlef) : Joop Admiraal, Marja Kok. This film is a finely made and absorbing tragedy, set in Halifax, Nova Scotia, about a Dutch-born businessman suffering from Alzheimer's disease who cannot tell the past from the present.

Heures précieuses, Les: see **Precious Hours, The**

Hey Babe! (1984) (100mins) d: Rafal Zielinski s: Edith Rey, Rafal Zielinski, an Arthur Vronka project. : Buddy Hackett, Yasmine Bleeth, Henry Gamer, Maruska Stankova, Denise Proulx. Set and filmed mainly in New York, this is an easygoing, lively and colourful musical comedy, about a young and ambitious girl who wants to be in show business and the friends who help her.

Hey, Happy! (2000) (75mins) d&s: Noam Gonick : Jeremie Yuen, Craig Aftanas, Clayton Godson, Johnny Simone. A strictly nothing picture set in an industrial section of Winnipeg where survivors of an environmental disaster—we don't know of what kind—are living. They cavort in the ruins and engage in sick sex activities and are, without doubt, among the most loathsome and boring collection of inhabitants imaginable. Nothing much to be happy about here. A waste of time.

Hidden Fortress, The: see *Forteresse suspendue, La*

Hide and Seek (1984) (60mins) d: René Bonnière s: Barrie Wexler Long : Robert Martin, Ingrid Veninger, David Patrick, John Friesen, Alan Scarfe. The chilling story of a brilliant computer expert whose invention penetrates the security system of a nuclear power station, with sinister results. Ominous and omnipotent. (See: *For the Record*)

Hide and Seek, The (1983): see **Adolescence of P-1**

Hide and Seek (2000): see **Cord**

Hideout, The: see *Explosion, L'*

High (1968) (80mins) (b/w/col) d&s: Larry Kent : Astri Thorvik, Lanny Beckman, Melinda McCracken, Janet Amos. At the Montréal Film Festival, held in September 1967 in association with Expo 67, this picture was scheduled to be shown as part of a series devoted to Canadian films. But at the last moment, a licence was refused by Québec censors. Largely improvised, and with the fragmentary narrative that was standard back then, High concerns a group of young people whose lives are without purpose and who indulge in a dreary round of pot, sex and petty crime. When Kent moved from Vancouver to Montréal, he began to lose his touch later, much to our regret.

High Card (1982) (65mins) d: William Gough s: Anna Sandor : Chuck Shamata, Helen Hughes, Beth Amos, Céline Lomez, Sean Sullivan, Jack Mather. A light and romantic story about the misuse of credit cards. A cheerful photographer who enjoys living well must face the realization that his debts are ruining his professional life. He turns to his girlfriend, who is exasperated by his behaviour. In the end, life is no longer a laughing matter. (See: *For the Record*)

High Country, The (The First Hello) (1981) (98mins) d: Harvey Hart s: Bud Townsend : Timothy Bottoms, Linda Purl, George Sims, James Lawrence, Bill Berry, Walter Mills. An inept chase melodrama with two obnoxious jailbirds on the run through the mountains, trying to escape the police. Filmed at Banff and Canmore, Alberta, and Invermere, B.C.

High Stakes (1986) (80mins) d&s: Larry Kent : David Foley, Roberta Weiss. In the early 1980s, a messenger boy working at a Vancouver tv station becomes involved with a gangster's moll and a real-life murder mystery. Above-average crime melodrama.

High: see **Facade**

High-Ballin' (1978) (100mins) (a Canadian-American film) d: Peter Carter s: Paul Edwards : Peter Fonda, Jerry Reed, Helen Shaver, Chris Wiggins, David Ferry, Harvey Atkin, Christopher Langevin, Len Doncheff, Kay Hawtrey, Michael Hogan, Cec Linder. Another silly pseudo-American melodrama about conflict between violent truck drivers and goons. Helen Shaver warms things up in one of her earliest screen appearances.

Higher Education (1986) (92mins) d: John Sheppard s: Daniel Nathanson, John Sheppard : Kevin Hicks, Isabelle Mejias, Stephen Black, Maury Chaykin. An art student in Toronto shares a room with the son of a local Mafioso and must learn, with the help of his girlfriend, how to cope with the son's bodyguard. Inconsequential.

Highpoint (1980) (88mins) (a Canadian-American film) d: Peter Carter s: Richard Guttman, Ian Sutherland : Richard Harris, Christopher Plummer, Beverly D'Angelo, Kate Reid, Peter Donat, Saul Rubinek, Robin Gammell, Maury Chaykin, Ken James, Eric House. An accountant becomes mixed up with the CIA and international intrigue. This results in never-ending chases, including a poorly staged fall from the CN Tower. Trite and confused, a waste of time and talent.

Highway 61 (1992) (110mins) d: Bruce McDonald s: Don McKellar : Don McKellar, Valerie Buhagiar, Earl Pastko, Peter Breck, Jello Biafra, Arthur Bergmann, Tracy Wright. Beginning in Northern Ontario, this film takes its audience on a crazy journey to New Orleans in an old Chrysler with a coffin on top. Rude, crude and unpleasant for the most part, the film has many admirers who think that McDonald and company are saviours of Canadian cinema. Their minds, however, are more attuned to a life that is American rather than Canadian; otherwise, why not make this journey to Vancouver?

Highway of Heartaches (1994) (86mins) d&s: Gregory Wild : Barbara Chamberlain, Pat Patterson, Willie Taylor, Dusty Ryane, Christy Russell. The director has described his film as a country and western musical melodrama, providing a satirical comment on the conservative Christian right wing and its hypocrisy when denouncing changing lifestyles and beliefs. Here, Wynona-Sue Turnpike becomes a victim of far-right scorn and oppression as she becomes a star. All this makes for a highly indigestible tract set to twangy music.

Highwayman, The (1999) (90mins) d: Keoni Waxman s: Richard Beattie : Stephen McHattie, Laura Harris, Gordon Michael Woolvett, Bernie Coulson, Jason Priestley, Louis Gossett Jr. A complicated springboard for unbelievable sequences violent, comic and boring, in a plot that almost defies description: lunatics rob banks, a man is framed for fraud, his wife is tired of living in substandard housing, and vicious landladies evict tenants while the protagonists search for the true meaning of love and family! Bring back the masked robber on his faithful horse, sword by his side!

Hired Gun (The Devil's Spawn) (The Last Gunfighter) (1959) (61mins) (b/w) d&s: Lindsay Shonteff : Don Borisenko, Tess Tory, Jay Shannon, Art Jenoff, Ken James, Gordon Clark, James Beggs, Michael Zenon, Jim Peddie, Ed Holmes, Bill Williams, Al Waxman. A gunfighter is hired by farmers to stop the molestation of their women by cowboys from a large ranch in the district. But the hired gun is killed by a farmer whose wife he had seduced. This B picture filmed at the new Meridian Studio in Toronto for $25,000 was considered a bad joke. However, it helped Lindsay Shonteff get to London and begin a career there, just as *A Dangerous Age* launched Sidney Furie on a career in England. (Unfortunatly we have heard little of his activities compared to the well-know names who went to LA)

Hiroshima (1996) (195mins) (a Canada-Japan co-production) d: Roger Spottiswoode, Koreyoshi Kurahara s: John Hopkins, Toshira Ishido : Kenneth Welsh, Tatsuo Matsumura, Wesley Addy, Kohji Takahashi. A great Canadian film in the finest dramatic documentary tradition, it vividly and grimly portrays the events leading up to the decision made by the Allies to bring an end to the Second World War in the Pacific by dropping the atom bomb on Japan. Historical figures and world events are related in a clear and accurate representation through newsreels and clever writing by John Hopkins. Produced by Robin Spry, the perfectionist, and directed by the remarkable Roger Spottiswoode, with a marvellous performance by Kenneth Welsh as President Truman, this is a film for the ages. It brings history alive as only the screen can do. The contributions made by the Japanese partners are considerable.

Histoire de chasse: see **Story of the Hunt, The**

Histoire de Pen (Inside) (2002) (120mins) d: Michel Jette s: Leo Lévesque, Michel Jette : Emmanuel Auger, Karyne Lemieux, David Boutin, Paul Dion, Dominic Darceuil. Life behind bars is a favourite subject for many Québec filmmakers, so there is nothing new in this brutal conflict between prisoners. When Harvey Hart's film of Herbert's play *Fortune and Men's Eyes* opened in 1971, its publicity carried this catch phrase: "What goes on in prison is a crime." In this new film, the crime is that committed by the writer-directors in betraying the art and craft of the cinema by making films about prisons, such as this one, soaked in a muddled narrative of violence and brutality. If all the prisoners in real life smashed each other up with the fighting we see, they would all be dead within a week, and prisons would be empty! So what are we seeing? Societal truths or bloodthirsty entertainment?

Histoire des trios, L': see **Story of the Three, A**

Histoire inventée, Une (An Imaginary Tale) (1990) (91mins) d: André Forcier s: Jacques Marcotte, André Forcier : France Castel, Marc Gélinas, Jean Lapointe, Louise Marleau, Charlotte Laurier. A strange collection of Fellini-like characters wind their way through this comedy-tragedy of theatrical and musical life, with jealousy, love and revenge occupying time and attention under circumstances both real and imaginary. Beautiful Florence has always loved Gaston, the aging musician, but her young daughter eventually wins his heart. The complications involving the rest of the group take on a surreal note and, eventually, a somewhat tiresome whimsy. But that's Forcier for you!

Histoires d'Eve: see **Book of Eve**

Histoires d'hiver: see **Winter Stories**

Hit and Run: see **Hitting Home**

Hitler: The Rise of Evil (2003) (4hrs in 2 parts) (a U.S.-Canada film) d: Christian Duguay s: John Pielmeier & G. Ross Parker : Robert Carlyle, Stockard Channing, Jena Malone, Julianna Margulies, Matthew Modine, Liev Schreiber, Peter Stormare, Peter O'Toole, Zoe Telford. The question arises, do we really want to see and hear anything more about Hitler? It was asked by many individuals, even those who made this extraordinary film. Opening at the time of the defeat (one hopes) of another murderous dictator, Saddam Hussein—it could be said to be timely—it is not, however about the persecution of the Jews and other peoples and individuals, there are no camps, no plots or battles, just the madman, and he is played with unflinching intensity, from the shabby little corporal to the cunning, raving goose stepping heiling "leader" bent on creating the 'pure' Germany, and conquering the rest of the world. There have been many Hitlers portrayed on the screen, most were accurate, but Robert Carlyle's performance is unforgettable. It goes much deeper than a moustache and uniform. And so, when we want future generations to know who Hitler was, this film will go well with the newsreels and documentaries. (Filmed in Prague standing in for Munich.)

Hitting Home (Obsessed) (1989) (103mins) d: Robin Spry s: Douglas Bowie (based on the book *Hit and Run* by Tom Alderman) : Kerrie Keane, Daniel Pilon, Max Middleton, Saul Rubinek, Lynne Griffin, Alan Thicke, Colleen Dewhurst. First-rate, well-directed story of a mother frustrated in her attempts to get a hit-and-run driver who killed her son extradited from the U.S. to face justice in Canada. Engrossing and different.

Hiver bleu, L': see **Blue Winter**

Hiver de Tourmente, Un **(A Winter of Torment)** (1999) (90mins) d: Bernard Favre s: Marcel Beaulieu and others : Thierry Fortineau, Marie-France Monette, Alexandre Mérineau, Audrey Laurin, Geneviève Rioux. Tearful doses of courage, maturity, love, death, loneliness, illness, and pregnancy—all this at home with a 16-year-old daughter and her stressed-out father. Done quietly and delicately.

Hochelaga (2000) (130mins) d&s: Michel Jetté : Dominic Darceuil, David Boutin, Ronald Houle, Michel Charette, Jean-Nicolas Verreault. Murder, robbery, drug dealing, violence and intimidation among the biker gangs of Montréal and other Canadian cities. These gangs get away with it all because the courts do not convict, except in Québec. After all, these hoodlums have rights! There is need for a serious film depicting this dreadful situation, but this is not it. In fact, it revels in the sensationalism inherent in the subject matter. Bikers will love it.

Hockey Night (1984) (77mins) d: Paul Shapiro s: Martin Harbury : Megan Follows, Rick Moranis, Gail Young. A boys' hockey team in a small Canadian town finally accepts a female goalie. The team's coach then finds he has a number of issues he must confront. Largely of interest to see Megan Follows at the beginning of her rewarding career, when she was also acting in the role of Anne Shirley in the *Anne of Green Gables* tv series. We must not forget Moranis, either!

Hog Wild (Les fous de la moto) (1980) (97mins) d: Les Rose s: Andrew Peter Marin : Patti D'Arbanville, Michael Biehn, Tony Tosato, Angelo Rizacos, Martin Doyle, Matthew Craven, Sean McCann. A flat, low-grade comedy about boorish bikers who enjoy harassing teenagers. Not much to laugh about.

Hold on, Papa!: see **What the Hell Are They Complaining About?**

Hold-Up (1985) (114mins) (a Canada-France co-production) d: Alexandre Arcady s: Francis Veber, Daniel St-Hamont, Alexandre Arcady (based on the novel *Quick Change* by Jay Cronley) : Jean-Paul Belmondo, Guy Marchand, Jacques Villeret, Kim Cattrall, Karen Racicot, Jean-Pierre Marielle. A man dressed as a clown robs a Montréal bank and escapes with his accomplices to the city's Mirabel airport. There's not much originality here. Belmondo should have remained in Paris.

Hollow Point (1997) (102mins) (a Canadian-American film) d: Sidney J. Furie s: Robert Geoffrion, James H. Stewart : Thomas Ian Griffith, Tia Carrere, John Lithgow, Donald Sutherland. A routine action-adventure set in an American city in which two rival law enforcement officers, both on the trail of a criminal mastermind, find themselves in a mutually destructive struggle. The actors play this out with a confidence that makes the whole seem better than it is.

Hollywood Productions (series): In conjunction with Regal films, Canadian distributor then, these two films were filmed entirely in Canada in 1960 and 1961. See under respective titles: *Canadians, The* (by Fox) and *Wild Dog of the North* (by Disney).

Home (2002) (70mins) d&s: Phyllis Katrapani : Francois Papineau, Jacinte Lague, Atanas Katrapani. This film about home is really a halfway house, as it mixes fiction with documentary, or the other way around, in an examination of what home means to different people in different places. Not without interest, but what is real or imagined?

Home Movie (1992) (93mins) d: Frederick Frame s: Peter Bryant : John Pyper-Ferguson, Ian Tracey, Suki Kaier, Kerry Sandomirsky, Venus Terzo. One of the few indigenous films to come from American-oriented B.C. (Others include *Impolite* and *The Portrait*.) This is a bright and stylish low-budget joke on the juxtaposition of reality and make-believe; some friends attempt to produce a film within a film and become hopelessly confused with what they are doing and who they have become.

Home Team (1999) (91mins) d: Allan Goldstein s: Paul Knowles : Steve Guttenberg, Larry Day, Sophie Lorain, Tyler Hynes, Michael Perron, Derek Lebrero. Underprivileged children fight to keep their foster home from being closed by playing a big soccer match against children from wealthy families. A poignant family drama.

Home to Stay (1978) (75mins) (a Canada-U.S. co-production) d: Delbert Mann s: Suzanne Clauser (based on the book *Grandpa and Frank* by Janet Majerus) : Henry Fonda, Michael McGuire, Frances Hyland, Kristen Vigard, David Stambaugh, Pixie Bigelow, Louis del Grande, Trudy Young, Doris Petrie, Eleanor Beecroft, James Morris, Sandra Scott. A father has grown old and senile. While taking care of him, his son finds his own life falling apart. Beautifully acted.

Homecoming, The (Good Luck, Jennifer Gagnon) (1978) (65mins) d: Gilles Carle s: B.A. Cameron : August Schellenberg, Lesleh Donaldson, Donald Granbery, David Hemblen, David Frank, Gladys Taylor. A Métis rodeo rider travels the western circuit with his young daughter and a close friend. While riding in Ontario, they all meet and stay with his parents. Their close friendship gives the daughter an awareness of her native roots. Gilles Carle described this as "a different kind of love story about a new kind of family." This is his first English-language film.

Homer (1970) (89mins) (a Canadian-American film) d: John Trent s: Claude Harz : Don Scardino, Alex Nicol, Tisa Farrow, Tim Henry, Tom Harvey, Arch McDonell, Ralph Endersby, Murray Westgate, Mona O'Hearn, Trudy Young. Filmed in Schomberg, Ontario, passing for the U.S., this is a feeble tale of a young man in conflict with everyone in his life.

Homme à tout faire, L': see **Handyman, The**

Homme de ma vie, L' (The Man in My Life) (1993) (98mins) (a Canada-France co-production) d&s: Jean-Charles Tacchella : Maria de Meideiros, Thierry Fortineau, Anne Létourneau, Jean-Pierre Bacri. A slight but delightful romantic comedy set in a French town about a good-looking young woman who cannot find a job. This takes a bit of believing. Then she meets a bookseller who is out of tune with society and wins him over. But wait, there must be a subtext. Will wealth and success take away her illusions and love? Don't expect an answer.

Homme de rêve, L' (The Dream Man) (1991) (83mins) d: Robert Ménard s: Claire Wojas : Rita Lafontaine, Michel Dumont, Claude Gauthier. A woman in her 50s takes care of her depressed husband and her 20-year-old son who can't keep a job. She works as a housekeeper for wealthy people, and this gives her the opportunity to dream about beautiful lives and romantic men. One day, a stranger enters her life, and he is not an illusion. What now? A lovely little dream of a film.

Homme et son pêché, Un (Séraphin) (A Man and His Sin) (1949) (112mins) (b/w) d: Paul Gury s: Claude-Henri Grignon (from his popular radio play) : Hector Charland, Nicole Germain, Guy Provost, Henri Poitras, Suzanne Avon, George Alexander, Ovila Légaré. Incidents in the family life of the miser Séraphin and his wife, Donalda. A highly popular radio serial with Québec audiences of the time, taking place in Sainte Adele, Quebec in 1889, this film version is mostly talk with little action, but is very real and not without warmth and charm during a time when life was simple and settled and very much family-based. The popularity led to **Séraphin** (1950) (105mins) (b/w) d: Jean Boisvert. s: Claude-Henri Grignon. The further adventures of Séraphin the miser. Gossip and scandal galore. See also *Séraphin (*2002).

Homme idéal, L': see **Ideal Man, The**

Homme nu, L': see **Atanarjuat: The Fast Runner**

Homme perché: see **Bean Pole Man, The**

Homme renversé, L' (1987) (97mins) d: Yves Dion s: René Gingras, Yves Dion : André Lacoste, Yves Gagné, Johanne Seymour. A piffling little nothing set in Montréal about three men who spend time wondering what it means to be male.

Homme sur les quais, L': see **Man on the Shore, The**

Honeymoon (1996) (89mins) d&s: Joan Carr-Wiggin : Stephen Shellen, Anthony Ulc, Thomas Cavanagh, Pascale Bussières, Elaine Lakeman, Susan Wilkey. A woman's honeymoon at a waterfront hideaway is disrupted by a homeless man who announces that he's going to perform a miracle. The mysterious stranger becomes a catalyst in the romantic misadventures of the honeymooners and their friends. Hearts are broken and mended, individuals fall in love with the unlikeliest people, and an unexpected event reminds everyone that life itself is a miracle.

Honeymoon (Lune de miel) (1985) (101mins) (a Canada-France co-production) d: Patrick Jamain s: Philippe Setbon, Robert Geoffrion, Patrick Jamain : Nathalie Baye, Richard Berry, John Shea, Peter Donat, Cec Linder, Ken Roberts, Henry Gamer. Danger, drugs and despair in New York and elsewhere. Not much substance here, and what there is doesn't amount to much.

Honourable Member, An (1982) (65mins) d: Donald Brittain s: Roy MacGregor : Fiona Reid, John Marley, Patricia Hamilton, Donald Francks, Hugh Webster, Mavor Moore, Eric House, Gerard Parkes. An ambitious young member of parliament receives a phone call from the prime minister. She has been given a cabinet portfolio. She becomes the only woman in the cabinet, and the course of her political career changes. This gives us a very good idea of what goes on behind those massive doors of Parliament and in the sanctums beyond. (See: *For the Record*)

Horses in Winter (Chevaux en hiver) (1988) (87mins) d&s: Rick Raxlen : Jacob Tierney, Erin Whittaker, Colin Kish, Elizabeth Bellm, Vicki Barkoff. A tired and overworked 40-year-old family man looks back with nostalgia to the time when he was an innocent eight-year-old and enjoyed his summers in the country with horses and friends. A beautiful film acted and told with delicacy and understanding.

Horsey (1997) (89mins) d&s: Kirsten Clarkson : Holly Ferguson, Todd Kerns, Ryan Robbins, Victoria Deschanel, Madeleine Kipling. A young painter is trying to find her way in life but is unable to make decisions or fully understand her conflicting emotions. She meets a man who seems to be the man of her dreams, but he is insufferable and unreliable and complicates her life. Good performances hold this somewhat tiresome chronicle together.

Hostile Advances: The Kerry Ellison Story (1996) (97mins) (a U.S-Canada film) d: Allan Kroeker s: Layce Gardner : Victor Garber, Real Andrews, Ron Hartman, Rena Sofer, Sean McCann, Maria Ricossa, Patricia Gage, Don Francks, Bernard Behrens. Yet another based-on-a-true-story drama, in which an American woman working in the IRS sued a fellow worker for sexual harassment, the outcome of which suit set a legal precedent. Done with honesty and depth of feeling, and set against appropriate backgrounds.

Hostile Force (The Heist) (1996) (98mins) (a Canada-German co-production) d: Michael Kennedy s: Michael January : Andrew McCarthy, Wolf Larson, Cynthia Geary, Cali Timmins, Hannes Jaenicke. Two years after a fierce encounter between the police, one a woman, and a gang of insane louts holding up a drugstore in an unnamed US city, we move forward two years and find the policewoman working for a security company held up by another murderous gang which takes all the staff hostage. But it's the audience who is taken hostage here in one of the longest robbery attempts probably ever filmed, being tedious, tiresome and all quite useless as drama or entertainment. The final moments are given over to the usual truck and car chase, filled with gunfire and explosions, filmed in Vancouver.

Hot Dogs (Clean Up Squad, The) (1980) (97mins) d: Claude Fournier s: Marie-José Raymond, Claude Fournier : Harry Reems, Nicole Morin, Geoffrey Bowes, Daniel Pilon, Fiona Reid, Guy L'Écuyer. One expects another teenage picture of vulgar behaviour, but no; these hot dogs are members of a morality squad trying to rid Montréal of its sinners. A hit-and-miss comedy, creaking all the way. An odd piece from Fournier.

Hot Millions: see **Gentle Sinners**

Hot Touch (Coup de maître) (1982) (92mins) (a Canada-U.S. co-production) d: Roger Vadim s: Lionel Chetwynd : Wayne Rogers, Marie-France Pisier, Lloyd Bochner, Samantha Eggar, Patrick MacNee, Gloria Carlin, Melvyn Douglas, James B. Douglas. An art forger in New York buys a Picasso, which he and his friend intend to reproduce. They are almost caught but flee to Montréal, where they carry out another robbery. A pleasant trifle with some very human characters, directed by a restrained Vadim.

Hotel New Hampshire (1984) (110mins) d&s: Tony Richardson : Rob Lowe, Jodie Foster, Beau Bridges, Amanda Plummer. This American film was shot in Québec. It is absurd to call this a Canadian film, listed here solely to show how ridiculous this period had become for "Canadian" production with support from Telefilm. (See: *Louisiana*)

Hound of the Baskervilles, The (2000) (90mins) d: Rodney Gibbons s: Joseph Wiesenfeld (from Arthur Conan Doyle's story) : Matthew Frewer, Kenneth Welsh, Jason London. Filmed seven times previously, is there anyone who hasn't read or seen Sir Arthur Conan Doyle's most famous Sherlock Holmes mystery? This is the story of the demon dog with glowing red eyes that haunts the Baskerville estate on the misty moors of Devonshire. This first Canadian version takes its place along with the best of the others. Montréal doubles convincingly for Baker Street and the dark winding lanes of old London. (See: *Sherlock Holmes* series)

Hounds of Notre Dame, The (1981) (95mins) d: Zale Dalen s: Ken Mitchell : Thomas Peacocke, Frances Hyland, Barry Morse, Lawrence Reese, Lenore Zann, David Ferry, Phil Ridley. An affectionate and lively depiction of 36 hours in the life of the legendary Father Athol Murray, founder of Notre Dame College in Regina. Set on the post-Depression Prairies with the clouds of war looming large over a poverty-stricken community. A remarkable and memorable first film. It was part of that wonderful era when new young filmmakers like Shebib, Jutra, Owen, Rowe, Borsos and Kent were making truly Canadian films.

Hounds of Notre Dame: see **Expect No Mercy**

House (1995) (85mins) d&s: Laurie Lynd (based on a play by MacIvor) : Daniel MacIvor, Patricia Collins, Stephen Ouimette. Three very good actors attempt courageously but fruitlessly to make something out of this tangled script divided into ten vignettes. It is set in a church, where a disturbed young man spews out the violent and paranoid story of his life.

House by the Lake: see **Death Weekend**

House in Order, A (La maison en ordre) (1936) (55mins) d: Gordon Sparling s: Peggy Miller, Gordon Sparling : Cecil Nichol, John Pratt, Mildred Mitchell, Jack Clifford. Partly sponsored by the Shell Oil Company, with some humour and not too much of a hard sell when showing the workings of its service stations. John Pratt is an asset to the proceedings. Gordon Sparling was one of the leading pioneers in Canadian filmmaking.

House of Light, The (La chambre blanche) (1969) (78mins) (b/w) d: Jean-Pierre Lefebvre : Marcel Sabourin, Michèle Magny. Another film from productive and highly individualistic Jean-Pierre Lefebvre. This is a stylistic, ritualistic, beautifully staged and composed black and white study of a man and his wife. It is set against mainly snowy landscapes seen through their window. Told with an ambiguity and lack of narrative concern then typical of Lefebvre, it is an ode to love, beauty, honour and to the conscience and contradictions of human nature.

House of Lovers (La maison des amants) (1972) (82mins) (a Canada-France co-production) d: Jean-Paul Sassy s: Patrick Cummings : Anna Gaël, Benoît Girard, Jean Leclerc, Paula Stromberg, Julie Wildman. A pornographic picture woven around a young woman who escapes from a psychiatric institution and takes refuge in the home of a sex-crazed architect. Sex and madness ensue in confused but graphic measure.

House of Luk (2000) (114mins) d: Derek Diorio s: Dan Lalande : Pierre Brault, John Ng, Dan Lalande, Michael Moriarty, Lorraine Ansell, Pat Morita. The *House of Luk* is a Chinese restaurant in Montréal (or Ottawa) where three regular customers, businessmen, come to eat and discuss the difficulties that make them anxious and uncertain. More characters appear, a lesbian is invited in, and so it goes, not without a sense of humour and winning moments, but more of a filmed play.

House of Pain (1995) (79mins) d&s: Mike Hoolboom : Kika Thorne, Charles Costello, Janieta Eyre, Paul Couillard, Andrew Wilson. This is another in-the-gutter work from the experimental filmmaker Hoolboom. Here, he creates images of life and death through rituals, games and pastimes between hetero and homosexual partners. The whole is so depraved, degenerate, dissolute and repugnant. Financed by the Ontario Arts Council.

House of the Dead (2003) (90mins) (a Canada-Germany co-production) d: Uwe Boll s: Mark Altman, Dave Parker : Jonathan Cherry, Tyron Leitso, Clint Howard, Ona Grauer, Jurgen Prochnow. Based on the Sega videogame, this mess defies description as a film although possibly addicts on the game might make something of its stupid, loud and violent confusion and carnage. Sad that the cinema sinks this low for a so-called video story. Filmed in Vancouver.

House on Turk Street, The (2002) (103mins) (a Canada-US-German co-production) d: Bob Rafelson s: Christopher Canaan and Steve Barancik (based on the story by Dashiell Hammett) : Samuel L. Jackson, Milla Jovovich, Stellan Skarsgard, Douglas Hutchison, Joss Ackland, Grace Zabriskie, Jonathan Higgins. Hammett's story about a group of mixed characters planning a robbery is brought up to date in time, place and individual relationships. The story is complicated and lacking any sense of excitement or credibility. This is yet another example of Telefilm misplacing our money in a co-production, with the only Canadian content being when three of the crooks make a run for it over the Canadian border.

House That Hides the Town, The (*La maison qui empêche de voir la ville***)** (1975) (125mins) d&s: Michel Audy : Carmen Jolin, Jean Beaudry, Luc Alarie, Claude Lemieux, Jean-Pierre Masse. A slight, dark and strange exposé of family relationships involving a dead child, a brother and sister, and another woman. A tangled, compelling, yet fascinating study of human nature. Set in a small Québec town.

House With a View of the Sea, A (*Una casa con vista al mar***)** (2001) (93mins) (a Canada-Venezuela-Spain co-production) d&s: Alberto Arveto : Gabriel Arcand, Imanol Arias, Leandro Arvelo, Alejo Felipe. A recently widowed farmer living in the Andes takes his son to the seashore, where they believe his wife, the boy's mother, had once visited. A photograph of her in such a place is the only picture they have to remind them of her. Justly described by its director as "a melancholy tale."

Housekeeper, The (Judgement in Stone) (1986) (102mins) d: Ousama Rawi s: Elaine Waisglass (based on the novel *A Judgement in Stone* by Ruth Rendell) : Rita Tushingham, Ross Petty, Shelley Peterson, Jackie Burroughs, Tom Kneebone, Jessica Stern, Jonathan Crombie. The splendid actress Rita Tushingham is seen here as a repressed, psychotic and illiterate young woman from England. She goes to work as a housekeeper, but the results are tragic. In the book, she goes to the U.S.; in the film, she is in Toronto. It doesn't quite come off.

How My Mother Was Giving Birth to Me During Menopause: see *Comment ma mere accoucha de moi durant sa menopause*

How to Make Love to a Negro Without Getting Tired (*Comment faire l'amour avec un nègre sans se fatiguer***)** (1989) (100mins) d: Jacques Wilbrod Benoît s: Dany Laferrière, Richard Sadler (based on Laferrière's novel of the same name) : Isaach de Bankole, Roberta Bizeau, Maka Kotto. Needless to say, the title hasn't much in common with the story: a lighthearted comedy full of amusing incidents and insights about two black immigrants living in a small apartment in the heart of Montréal.

One of the characters is writing a book, which becomes the film. It plays on reverse racist and sexual stereotypes.

Hue and Cry: see **Angel Square**

Human Misery, The: see **At the Autumn of Life**

Humongous (1982) (93mins) d: Paul Lynch s: William Gray : Janet Julian, David Wallace, Janit Baldwin, John Wildman. A raving man-beast kills off a group of youths stranded on an island. A horrible subject, and difficult to see in the darkness of this slow picture; which is just as well, perhaps, with one hackneyed situation following the next.

Hunchback's Diary, A: see *Journal d'un bossu, Le*

Hurt (2002) (92mins) d&s: Steve Dimarco : Terra Vnese, Stephanie Nikolaidis, Andrew Martin Smith. For once, we have a decent film about 16-year-olds friends, who come from violent, broken, neglectful homes—that is not all sex, drinks, drugs and swearing. One feels concern and sorrow for these characters, and the tragedy of their lives is almost total. A sensitive, knowing film.

Hurt Penguins (1992) (98mins) d: Robert Bergman, Myra Field s: Myra Field : Michele Muzzi, Daniel Kash, George King, Myra Field, Denny Doherty, Ian Thomas. A romantic and stylish comedy about a married couple: two rock-and-roll musicians who are going nowhere in their careers. When a wealthy businessman comes into their lives, they have a chance to sign a deal with a recording company. In order to get the contract, the wife plans to seduce and marry the millionaire, then divorce him. Manners, morals and ethics play an important part in this likeable look at the world of pop music.

Hush Little Baby (Mother of Pearl) (1993) (91mins) (a U.S.-Canada film) d: Jorge Montesi s: Julie Moskowitz, Gary Stephens : Wendel Meldrum, Diane Ladd, Geraint Wyn Davies, Illya Woloshyn, Paul Soles. A woman tracks down her daughter 35 years after she, the mother, was sent to a mental home for trying to kill the child. This is a serious film, with a fine, poignant and remarkable story, beautifully acted and so well told, a frightening depiction of mental illness, without extremes of violence. (although filmed in unidentified Toronto, it's set in the US for no good reason, yet remains a first-class Canadian film.)

Hustler White (1996) (80mins) d&s: Bruce LaBruce, Rick Castro : Tony Ward, Bruce LaBruce, Kevin Scott, Ivar Johnson, and others. A homoerotic piece of manure, aimless and offensive in its depiction of hustler life in L.A. There is no narrative as such, just odd scenes described as comic and satiric, which this picture is not.

I Confess: see **Confessional, The**

I Don't Love You: see *Je n'aime que toi*

I Have the Right to Pleasure (*J'ai droit au plaisir***)** (1975) (86mins) (a Canada-France co-production) d: Claude Pierson s: Elisabeth Leclair : Laure Cottereau, Michel Forget, Anne Sand, Frédéric

Duré, Alain Saury, Francoise Becarrie, Rosine Amand, Donald Juin. A delicate cameo in which a 16-year-old daughter is desperate for company and attention after the divorce of her parents. Her mother finds another lover who has no time for the daughter. She falls into minor crime, makes her way to the US, and marries an American. Slight, but with the ring of truth and touched by tenderness.

I Heard the Owl Call My Name (1973) (75mins) (a Canada-U.S. film) d: Daryl Duke s: Gerald DiPego (based on the book of the same title by Margaret Craven) : Tom Courtenay. A interesting piece from Duke filled with meaning and understanding. A priest living in a B.C. native village has a fatal illness. He finds a spiritual relationship with the inhabitants, and this helps him prepare to meet his death.

I Love a Man in Uniform (1984) (60mins) d: Donald McBrearty s: John Frizzell : Kenneth Welsh, Denis Forest, Dixie Seatle, Tim Webber, Tom Butler. This forceful and thoughtful drama portrays the dilemma of a policeman trying to fulfill his responsibilities when confronted with local teens who have nothing to do but hang out in doughnut shops and get into mischief. Mistrust, hatred and violence surface, and the policeman finds himself in a quandary. (Not to be confused with David Wellington's film of the same title.) (See: *For the Record*)

I Love a Man in Uniform (1993) (99mins) d&s: David Wellington : Tom McCamus, Brigitte Bako, David Hemblen, Kevin Tighe. A Canadian film, wanting to be American, about a mild-mannered bank clerk who spends his spare time portraying a policeman in a US tv crime series being shot on location in Toronto. One day, he fails to turn in his uniform to the costume department (very unlikely that he would be allowed to get away with this), and wearing the uniform goes out on the streets and passes himself off as a real policeman—an American, of course. The sordidness of his life drives him into a moral fervour and finally to suicide. All very shallow, difficult to believe and critically overrated at the time it opened.

I Love You (Je t'aime) (1974) (90mins) d&s: Pierre Duceppe : Jeanne Moreau, Roseline Hoffman, Jean Duceppe, Lionel Villeneuve, Jean-René Ouellet, Willie Lamothe, Rose Rey-Duzil, Jacques Bilodeau. A passion pit of romance and murder results when a woman from France arrives to live in a small Québec town. She meets with her pregnant daughter and lover, who promptly falls for her, with fatal results. Glossy and well acted, but silly.

I Marry or I Don't Marry: see *J'me Marie, j'me Marie*

I, Maureen (1980) (101mins) d&s: Janine Manatis (from Elizabeth Spencer's short story) : Colleen Collins, Diane Bigelow, Robert Crone, Sandra Shuman, Brian Damude, Keith Leckie, Michael Ironside, Barry Greenwald, Joan Hutton. A slight but affecting story of a woman trapped in a difficult marriage. When her husband apparently dies in an acci-

dent, she begins to think of herself and what life means to her. When her husband reappears, she adapts herself to a new existence. Interesting character portrayals; a thoughtful and honest treatment of human feelings and emotions.

I Miss You, Hugs and Kisses (1978) (87mins) d&s: Murray Markowitz : Elke Sommer, Donald Pilon, Chuck Shamata, Cindy Girling, George Touliatos, Cec Linder, Linda Sorensen, Susan Hogan, Larry Solway. Apparently based on the true story of a wealthy Hungarian-Canadian businessman involved in murdering his wife: she had an insurance policy and he had a mistress. Some tense moments and chills along the way.

I Was a Rat (Cinderella and Me) (When I Was a Rat) (2001) (102mins) (a Canada-U.K. co-production) d: Laurie Lynd s: Richard Carpenter : Brenda Fricker, Katie Blake, Stephen Ouimette, Calum Worthy, James Millard, Don McKellar, Tom Conti, Ned Beatty, Sheila McCarthy, Edward Fox. A lovely fairy tale about a rat who is reincarnated as a page-boy to royalty and how he recollects amusing anecdotes from his past. Novel and amusing. A good public relations piece for a disliked species. Marvelous characters and settings of Victorian London.

I Won't Dance (1992) (92mins) d: Hunt Hoe s: Loren Edizel, Hunt Hoe : Camille Martinez, Frank Schorpion, Carlo Essagian, Bianca Paradis. There is not much time in this film for anyone to dance. A fortune teller and a small-time crook flee Costa Rica for Canada. They become involved with other desperate characters and the RCMP when their drug-smuggling activities are discovered. This all takes place in Montréal, where we could all find better things to do than sit through this time-waster.

I'm Going to Get You…Elliot Boy (1971) (92mins) (a Canadian-American film) d: Edward Forsyth s: Jerry Thomas, Edward Forsyth : Ross Stephanson, Maureen McGill, Jeremy Hart, Edward Blessington. A sordid pseudo-American film about a bank robber who is released from prison and kills his girlfriend. Filmed in Edmonton—with few saving moments.

I've Heard the Mermaids Singing (1987) (81mins) d&s: Patricia Rozema : Sheila McCarthy, Paule Baillargeon, Ann-Marie MacDonald. Sheila McCarthy plays an engaging, perky yet naive woman in her 30s. She's an amateur photographer who describes herself as being "organizationally inept." She has flights of fancy in which she dreams of another life. Through the likeable owner of a small, sophisticated art gallery (Paule Baillargeon), she discovers the real world and its hypocrisies. Rozema uses various popular techniques—video to stills, colour and black and white, flashes and fall-outs and a broken narrative—and assembles them in an experimental and controlled way. But the film is held together by the marvellous performance of Sheila McCarthy. Made on a budget of $35,000, this is also a tribute to Donald Haig, producer of *Dancing* *in the Dark,* who encouraged filmmakers like Rozema. It received tremendous acclaim when shown at Cannes.

Ice Cream, Chocolate and other Consolations: see *Crème glacée, chocolat et autres consolations*

Ice Men, The (2001) (100mins) d: Thom Best s: Michael MacLennan : David Hewlett, Martin Cummins, Brandy Ledford, Gregory Spottiswood, James Thomas, Ian Tracey. Some 20-something male friends take a winter holiday at a cottage and attempt to come to grips with themselves and their lives. In baring their souls, they come to realize who they are and to accept their place in society. All very high flown and strictly for men only.

Ideal Man, The (*L'homme idéal***)** (1996) (110mins) d: Georges Mihalka s: Sylvia Pilon, Daniaile Jarry : Marie-Lise Pilote, Roy Dupuis, Macha Grenon, Joe Bocan, Francine Ruel, Denis Bouchard, Patrice L'Écuyer, Jean-Marie Lapointe, Rémy Girard, Jean Leclerc, Martin Drainville, Rita Lafontaine. This Québec comedy rises above most others to provide audiences with an almost continuous run of amusing situations and downright funny encounters concerning love, sex and odd relationships, without falling into continuous crudity. Much of the credit goes to the popular local comedienne Marie-Lise Pilote, in her first film. It enjoyed phenomenal success in Québec.

If You Could See What I Hear (1982) (102mins) d: Eric Till s: Stuart Gillard (from the book by Tom Sullivan and Derek Gill) : Marc Singer, R.H. Thomson, Sarah Torgov, Douglas Campbell, Helen Burns, Harvey Atkin, Tony Van Bridge, Jack Creley, David Gardner, Gary Reineke, Hugh Webster, Nonnie Griffin, Robert DesRoches, Shari Belafonte. An overlong biography of the blind singer-composer Tom Sullivan. Well intended, it has its moments, but tedium ultimately sets in.

Il était une fois dans l'est: see **Once Upon a Time in the East**

Il était une guerre: see **There Once Was a War**

Il ne faut pas mourir pour ça: see **Don't Let It Kill You**

Île de Sable, L' **(Sable Island)** (1999) (105mins) d: Johanne Prégent s: Gilles Desjardins, Johanne Prégent : Caroline Dhavernas, Sébastien Huberdeau, Anick Lemay, Marie Tifo, Geneviève Désilets. Another delicate portrayal of a juvenile in emotional turmoil and the complications that make her life stressful and hard to understand. A daughter sees her mother die, then discovers she is pregnant and her boyfriend unpredictable. Together they travel to Sable Island seeking a life and love together. Believable characters, portrayed with sympathy and concern.

Ile jaune, L': see **Yellow Island, The**

Ils sont nus **(We Are all Naked)** (1966) (87mins) (b/w) (a Canada-France co-production) d: Claudè Pierson s: Huguette Boisvert, Jack Curtis : Jacques Norman, Alain Saury, Rita Maiden, Catherine Ribeiro, Gérard Dessalles, Isabelle Pierson. Of course, everyone is naked. What else to expect from Pierson, the sex peddler?

Imaginary Tale, An: see *Histoire inventée, Une*

Immortal Scoundrel, The (*Étienne Brûlé, gibier de potence***)** (1952) (102mins) d: Melburn Turner s: Jeannette Downing (adapted from the book *The Immortal Scoundrel* by J.H. Cranston) : Paul Dupuis, Jacques Auger, Ginette Letondal, Paulette Deguise, Gabriel Gascon, Guy Hoffman, Donald McGill, Peter Jennings, Pierre Rondeau, Réal Lemieux, Madeleine Lévesque. A disappointing attempt to tell the story of Étienne Brûlé, an early French explorer and protégé of Samuel Champlain. This was the first full-length Canadian film in colour (Kodachrome).

Immortels, Les **(The Immortals)** (2003) (98mins) d: Paul Tinen s: Marc Bisaillon : Guillaume Lemay-Thivierge, Jean Lapointe, Isabelle Lemme, Pascal Parent, Andre Ouellette, Manon Brunelle, Olivier Maher. The 'immortels' is a group of musicians in a small working-class town, who meet up with a once famous musician from the golden-age of jazz. They join forces and share their passion for music. This is a delightful excursion into that seldom seen genre today, the screen musical.

Impolite (1992) (95mins) d: David Hauka s: Michael McKinley : Robert Wisden, Heidi von Palleske, Jill Tweed, Stuart Margolin, Christopher Plummer. A once respected reporter has slipped down the ranks and is writing obits, due to drink and despair. He is given the opportunity to redeem himself when he investigates the strange death of a wealthy businessman. In discovering the truth, the reporter finds himself again. Good location shooting, interesting performances and pertinent observations of the *demi-monde*.

Impossible Elephant, The (2001) (95mins) d: Martin Wood s: Robert Cooper : Nicholas Lea, Alex Doduk, Mia Sara, Mark Rendak. This is a truly delightful, marvellous and funny film about a baby elephant. He is freed from the zoo by a young boy who takes him home and to school, with uproarious results. Never strained, always natural, with nicely stated observations about children finding love and friendship. All performances, including that of the elephant, are pleasing.

Improper Channels (1981) (92mins) (a Canadian-US film) d: Eric Till s: Ian Sutherland, Morrie Rúvinsky : Alan Arkin, Mariette Hartley, Sarah Stevens, Monica Parker, Leslie Yeo, Ruth Springford, Eric Clavering, Gillie Fenwick, Luba Goy, Joyce Gordon, Kate Lynch, Harry Ditson. An overly caring social worker accuses an eccentric architect of child abuse. An uneasy mixture of comedy and drama, but a good cast and script sees it through.

In Celebration (1975) (110mins) d: Lindsay Anderson, play by David Storey : Alan Bates, James Bolam, Brian Cox, Bill Owen, Constance Chapman,

Gabrielle Day. Three brothers return to the coal-mining town of their birth to attend the 40th anniversary of their parents. It turns into a harrowing and suspenseful drama. (See: *American Film Theatre Series*)

In Her Defense (In Self Defense) (1998) (97mins) (a Canadian-US film) d: Sidney Furie s: Marc Lynn, Jeffrey Rosenbaun : Sophie Lorain, Marlee Matlin, Michael Dudikoff, Maurice Arsenault, David Attis, John Ball, Daniel Pilon, Rob Pinnock, Eric Theriault, Yves Turbide, Doug Sutherland. An intriguing interplay of relationships; a thoughtful excursion into the law and how it lends itself to the most unlikely situations. A lawyer in love with a married deaf woman shoots her husband. The police think the wife murdered him, and she expects her lawyer lover to defend her. The result comes about with considerable tension and suspense.

In Love With Sex: see *Donnez-nous notre amour quotidian*

In Praise of Older Women (1978) (110mins) d: George Kaczender s: Paul Gottlieb (based on the book of the same title by Stephen Vizinczey) : Tom Berenger, Karen Black, Susan Strasberg, Helen Shaver, Ann MacDonald, Marilyn Lightstone, Alexandra Stewart, Alberta Watson, Louise Marleau, Mignon Elkins, Jon Granik, Budd Knapp, Michael Kirby, Julie Wildman, narrated by Henry Ramer. A trite soft-core sex film about a young woman-crazed Hungarian (badly miscast with the American actor Tom Berenger) who arrives in Montréal to continue his "adventures" with every woman he meets. At the time, it gave our censors something to loudly denounce.

In Self Defense: see **In Her Defense**

In the Belly of a Dragon (*Dans le ventre du dragon*) (1989) (102mins) d: Yves Simoneau s: Pierre Revelin, Marcel Beaulieu, Yves Simoneau : David La Haye, Marie Tifo, Rémy Girard, Michel Côté, Pierre Curzi, Monique Mercure. Here the director mixes comedy, drama, action and adventure in an uneven blend and almost succeeds, despite trying to be so many things at once. The belly of the dragon is a huge, menacing research centre. The protagonist is a simple "everyman" who delivers door-to-door advertising flyers and decides to undergo dangerous drug research for which he thinks he will be highly paid. He is rescued by his friends in comical Laurel-and-Hardy-type circumstances. As one would expect from Simoneau, the force of imagery employed in the camera techniques is impressive.

In the Blue Ground (1999) (120mins) d: Alan Simmonds s: Andrew Wreggitt : Tina Keeper, Peter Kelly Gaudreault, Tracey Cook, Robert Bockstael. An absolutely first-rate thriller (born out of the tv series *North of 60*) set against the spectacular scenery of the Canadian west. An RCMP corporal and her partner find themselves unexpectedly caught up in strange crimes and emotional conflicts when a nurse is kidnapped and terrorized. The well-worn Mountie adventure genre here takes on a new life.

In the Dead of Space (Space Fury) (2000) (92mins) (a Canada-U.S. film) d: Eli Necakov s: Vincent Monton : Michael Paré, George Chuvalo, Lisa Bingley, Stacie Fox, Nenad Petrovic. Two American astronauts on one of their periodic space trips collide with a Russian space station and find themselves part of a terrorist plot. Badly done, and believe it or not, there's nudity. So exciting—in space, yet!

In the End: see *Finalemente*

In the Land of Zom (*Au pays de Zom*) (1983) (77mins) d&s: Gilles Groulx : Joseph Rouleau, Charles Trudeau, René Racine, Françoise Berd, Christiane Alarie, Michèle Mercure, Jack Fisher, Denis Sawyer, Michel Bouchard. An authentic surrealistic musical fantasy about powerful worldly figures who become ordinary people. Effectively played and sung by Joseph Rouleau, with music by Jacques Hétu.

In the Name of the Son (*Et du fils*) (1972) (84mins) d&s: Raymond Garceau : Ovila Légaré, Jacques Godin, Réjean Lefrançois, Jocelyn Bérubé, Paule Baillargeon. An absorbing and concerned story of a family thinking about selling the farm where they live (on a small island in the St. Lawrence River) to Americans. Will it become a hunt club?

In the Shadow of the Wind (*Les fous de Bassan*) (1986) (83mins) d: Yves Simoneau s: Sheldon Chad (from the novel by Anne Hébert) : Steve Banner, Charlotte Valandrey, Laure Marsac. This film is unlike Simoneau's two previous pictures in that it leaves city life and criminal elements far behind to take us to Griffin Creek, an isolated community on the lonely Québec coastline. There, all the inhabitants are related, and two cousins disappear during an outing on the beach. Suspicion flies in a cloud of sex and sin in this overripe melodrama. The action is counterpointed in a triumph of cinematography with crashing waves and crying seagulls.

In This Corner (1986) (60mins) d: Atom Egoyan s: Paul Gross : Robert Wisden, Patrick Tierney, Brenda Bazinet, Sean McCann, Cedric Smith. A young champion boxer unknowingly gets involved with an Irish terrorist. Sports and politics are knowingly brought together in a boxing film like no other. A promising early work by both the director and writer. (See: *For the Record*)

Inbreaker, The (1974) (90mins) d: George McCowan s: Jacob Zilber, W. Sigurgierson : Johnny Crawford, Johnny Yesno, Christopher George, Wendy Sparrow, Leonard George. A likeable drama set against the beautiful scenery of Alert Bay and Port Hardy. A student from Calgary works with native people in their fishing boats. Set against the Pacific deep-sea fishing business, this is an apt social saga.

Incompris, L' (Misunderstood) (1997) (90mins) (a Canada-France co-production) d: Pierre Gang s: Christian Fournier : Pierre Malet, Jérôme Leclerc-

Couture, Alexis Delvecchio, Louisette Dussault, Pascale Montpetit, Gabriel Sabourin. A beautifully told story of a man who has difficulty relating to his two sons when his wife, their mother, dies. The dramatic treatment makes the human sadness permeating this story very real.

Incredible Adventures of Marco Polo, The (1998) (97mins) (a Canada-U.K.-U.S. film) d: George Erschbamer s: J. Hugh Benson : Oliver Reed, Jack Palance, Donald Diamond, Cas Anvar, John Hallam, Herbert Lom. No, this film has nothing to do with Marco. He is long gone. It is the story of his son, who goes looking for his father's trade route to China. Another case of "was this journey really necessary?" These travellers are a dull lot.

Incredible Journey, The (1963) (80mins) (an Canada-US film) d: Fletcher Markle s: James Algar, Sheila Burnford (from her novel of the same name) : Émile Genest, John Drainie, Tommy Tweed, Sandra Scott, Robert Christie This now classic Disney film tells of a journey made by three pets—two dogs and a cat. They travel 250 miles together to join their owners. Wonderfully well done under Canadian director Fletcher Markle who, on the strength of his success, was invited to work in Hollywood. The film was one of the first in which several of our most distinguished stage and radio actors were seen on film and the first English-track film to have a Quebec actor in the cast. Disney remade this film in 1993 under the title *Homeward Bound: The Incredible Journey,* but much of the original charm was lost when the animals were given human voices to talk to us about their trip. A sequel followed, *Homeward Bound II: Lost in San Francisco* (1996). Neither was filmed in Canada.

Incredible Mrs Ritchie, The (2003) (102mins) (a Canada-U.K. co-production) d&s: Paul Johanasson : Gena Rowlands, James Caan, Nick Cassevettes, Leslie Hope, Brenda James, Kevin Zegart, Cameron Chaddo. We've come a long way from Richard Brooks' *Blackboard Jungle* (1973), when we see this latest film about juvenile delinquency in schools, and how, over the years that have passed, society has slipped into depravity. This new film opens with a group of students standing around in a circle while another youth viciously and repeatedly smashes his fist into the other's face. The bully goes home to a father who beats his mother, while a brother and sister are terrified. With a life like this, the youth slips away to Mrs. Ritchie's Secret Garden, where she grows beautiful plants and flowers and talks to him. This is an appealing and thoughtful work, leaving audiences to think once again about today's morals and morass. Gena and James make welcome re-appearances.

Incroyable vérité, L': see **No Blame**

Incubus (1981) (92mins) (a Canadian-US film) d: John Hough s: Sandor Stern (from the book by Ray Russell) : John Ireland, John Cassavetes, Kerrie

Keane, Helen Hughes, Harry Ditson, Neil Dainard, Eric Flannery, Duncan McIntosh. A badly made horror-thriller about sex murders in a small Wisconsin town. Unremittingly repulsive and a waste of talented Cassavetes and Ireland.

Indigo Autumn (1987) (80mins) d&s: Stuart Gillard : Marc Singer, Lisa Schrage, Jayne Eastwood, Linda O'Dwyer. In this romantic piece, a woman throws off the shadows in her life and discovers a new love. A quiet and pleasing picture. (See: *Shades of Love* series)

Individual, The: see **Cosmos**

Inertia (2001) (100mins) d&s: Sean Garrity : Jonas Chernick, Gordon Tanner, Sarah Constible, Micheline Marchildon. A contrived and unlikely attempt at comedy—described as being anti-romantic—and played by four young urban types whose romantic desires are quite different from what they might have expected. Meaningless and motionless, this film lives up to its title and remains unchanged.

Inferno: see **Pilgrim**

Initiation, The (*L'initiation*) (1970) (94mins) d: Denis Héroux s: Yves Thériault : Chantal Renaud, Danielle Ouimet, Jacques Riberolles, Gilles Chartrand, Céline Lomez, Louise Turcot. Two friends at the Université de Montréal search for sexual fulfillment. Sometimes funny, but mostly rather silly.

Inside Out (1979) (97mins) d: Graham Parker s: Munro Scott : Carole Laure, John Juliani, Ratch Wallace, Linda Goranson, Colin Fox, David Hemblen, Carole Taylor, John Evans. A World War II spy story, unusual because it concerns the Canadian Army and our soldiers for a change. Two of them organize escape routes for pilots whose planes have been shot down over France. Stirring, exciting, well told and played out by a believable cast.

Inside: see *Histoire de Pen*

Insurance Man From Ingersoll, The (1976) (65mins) d&s: Peter Pearson (from the play by Norman Hartley) : Michael Magee, Araby Lockhart, Charlotte Blunt, Warren Davis, David Gardner, Mavor Moore, George Sperdakos. A powerful story of political chicanery at Queen's Park, the Ontario legislature, following the discovery of a link between a corrupt labour union and the government party. The film has a raw force and air of reality that was welcomed by audiences, who had never seen anything like this exposure of local Canadian politics on our screens. (See: *For the Record*)

Interior Future, The: see *Futur intérieur, Le*

International Title: see **Croon Maury and Mrs. B.**

Interrogation of Michael Crowe, The (2002) (90mins) (a U.S.-Canada film) d: Donald McBrearty s: Alan Hines : Mark Rendall, Ally Sheedy, Hannah Lochner, Michael Riley. A 14-year-old boy is being cruelly interrogated by police in California over the murder of his 12-year-old sister. He was innocent. The acting is very fine, in particular by the youth playing Michael, who must express the turmoil of being emotionally torn between parents and police. This film is the second feature to be made by the U.S. company, Court TV following *Guilt by Association*, a series distinguished by strong crime and social justice issues, based on actual cases such as this one. Since this film was made, legislation has been passed requiring that all juvenile interrogations be taped. This crime drama is much superior to the many others based on actual cases, that seem presently to be taking over our screens.

Interrogation: see **Clear Cut**

Intimate Power (Blind Trust) (*Pouvoir intime*) (1985) (95mins) d&s: Yves Simoneau : Pierre Curzi, Marie Tifo, Jacques Godin, Jean-Louis Millette, Robert Gravel, Éric Brisebois, Jacques Lussier. A superior film in every respect in which a group of crooks holds up an armoured truck. They had planned their heist well, but a hitch develops, leaving them unable to get at the money. As they wait, they realize that from being so cocksure, they have been reduced to the losers, not the winners, in one of life's desperate gambles. In action, mood, excitement and style, this is the kind of film almost never made in Canada. The highly talented Simoneau later went to Hollywood, where he distinguished himself with many exceptional films, notably *The Last Flight of Amelia Earhart*.

Intimate Relations (1995) (102mins) (a Canada-U.K. co-production) d&s: Philip Goodhew : Julie Walters, Rupert Graves, Matthew Walker, Laura Sadler. A marvellously funny, yet touching comedy-drama about a housewife in a provincial English town who seduces her boarder. Her 14-year-old daughter discovers what's going on and wants to become part of the affair. All does not end well. This is an entirely British picture with no Canadian participation, although it was made as a Telefilm co-production initiative.

Into the Fire (1987) (93mins) d: Graeme Campbell s: Jessie Ballard : Susan Anspach, Olivia d'Abo, Art Hindle. A lodge owner in wintry northern Canada likes to seduce some of her guests, who interest her. This results in a familiar sex-murder thriller that is not too hard to figure out.

Into the Fire: see **Legend of Wolf Lodge, The**

Intruder, The (1981) (91mins) d: David Eustace s: Norman Fox : Pita Oliver, Gerard Jordan, James B. Douglas, Tony Fletcher, Gordon Thomson, Jackie Burroughs, Kay Hawtrey, Len Doncheff. Another small town, another evil stranger, and murder, once again. This is mild as these things go, predictable and tedious, but a good cast makes the most of it.

Invaders, The: see **49th Parallel**

Invasions Barbares, Les: see **Barbarian Invasions, The**

Invention de l'amour, L': see **Invention of Love, The**

Invention of Love, The (*L'invention de l'amour*)

(2000) (90mins) d: Claude Demers s: Pierre Fedele, Claude Demers : David La Haye, Pascale Montpetit, Delphine Brodeur, Andreas Apergis, Irene Stamou. A happily married woman with a caring, good-looking husband and a loving child, falls under the influence of an odious, unshaven, mentally disturbed young writer and becomes a slave to indecorous sexual behaviour. Steamy and silly portrait of immature adults.

Investigation (2002) (92mins) (a Canada-U.K. co-production) d: Anne Wheeler s: Bruce Smith : Nick Lea, Reece Dinsdale, Lochlyn Munro, David Warner, Paul Cover. Anne Wheeler is back in form with producers Bernard Zuckerman and Wendy Hill-Tout with this tightly told and frightening retelling of the murders committed by Clifford Olsen, Canada's most notorious serial killer. The film gives us the disturbing news that back in 1981, when Olsen was considered a prime suspect in the killings, he got away due to red tape and misinformation, and carried out his additional murders. This is a first-class hard hitting film.

Invincible (2001) (120mins) (a Canada-US co-production) d: Jefery Levy s: Michael Brandt, Derek Haas, Jefery Levy : Tory Kittles, Byron Mann, Billy Zane, Stacy Oversier, Dominic Purcell. A martial arts drama cooked up by Mel Gibson and colleagues follows four modern-day warriors who learn they have been pre-destined from birth to defeat the Shadow Men, an army of dark angels determined to destroy the world. Lots of kick-boxing and flying through the air. It's exciting, beautiful to watch and steeped in operatic myth. Everything an audience interested in tae-kwon-do would want.

Invitation (2000) (65mins) d&s: Samir Rehum : Anais Granofsky, Stefan Brogen. Three roomies throw a crowded, cramped, noisy, lively bust-up with assorted friends, with one photographing the event—for future pleasure, one assumes. They should have saved the film and gone home early.

Iron Eagle (1986) (119mins) (a Canada-Israel co-production) d: Sidney J. Furie s: Kevin Elders, Sidney Furie : Mark Humphrey, Stuart Margolin, Alan Scarfe, Sharon Brandon, David Suchet. An 18-year-old pilot commandeers a fighter jet and flies to the Middle East to attempt to save his father, who has been taken prisoner during hostilities. In dangerous skies over war-torn grounds, this film is ethically, politically and creatively disturbing, and not for a moment worth watching. Followed by three sequels, which are best not mentioned. Sidney makes the most of things from his shell-shocked scripts.

Iron Road (2002) (125mins) d&s: Barry Pearson (based on the opera of the same name by Chan Ka Nin and Mark Brownell) : Siu Ta, Mike Shara, Cedric Smith, Charmaine Lau, Dwight McFee. A teenaged boy working in a Hong Kong fireworks factory in 1882 leaves to come to Canada to search for his long-lost father and finds himself working on the building of the railway, passed off here as the Nichol Construction Company. He turns out to be a girl, who falls in love with the son of the company's owner. A fascinating story.

Isaac Littlefeathers (1984) (95mins) d: Les Rose s: Barry Pearson, Les Rose : Lou Jacobi, Scott Hylands, William Korbut, George Clutesi, Lynda Mason Green, Michelle Thrush. A well-meaning, yet uneasily contrived drama concerning a native and a Jewish schoolboy, and their relations with their families and the inhabitants of a small town in western Canada.

Isabel (1968) (108mins) d&s: Paul Almond : Geneviève Bujold, Marc Strange, Gerard Parkes, Elton Hayes, Edie Kerr, Al Waxman, Ratch Wallace, Lynden Bechervaise, Eric Clavering, Rob Hayes, Donald J. Dow. A young girl returns to her home in the isolated Gaspé region of Québec and becomes aware of strange influences at work around her. Beautifully photographed, sensitively acted and directed, splendidly brooding and atmospheric, this first feature by former CBC-tv director Paul Almond tells a fascinating tale of suppressed sex, subjective fears and psychotic fantasies. (See: *Act of the Heart* and *Journey*)

Isis From the 8th Rang (*Isis au 8*) (1972) (65mins) d&s: Alain Chartrand : Jean-Pierre Cantin, Marie-Andrée Chartrand, Raymond Bélisle, Henri Herbert, Gilles Desrochers. Isis wants out of the crowded and noisy city and goes to live in a small house in the country to raise goats. But this is no refuge for him, either, and the cold Québec winter brings on his wife's death and other misfortunes. Expertly told and played, one feels a good scotch would have made things better for Isis, not to mention the audience.

Isla the Tigress of Siberia (1977) (92mins) d: Jean Lafleur s: Marven McGara : Dyanne Thorne, Michel Morin, Jean-Guy Latour, Michel Maillot, Henry Gamer, Tony Angelo. Complicated and far-fetched post-war spy melodrama set in Montréal, where a survivor from Stalin's regime meets the woman who was in charge of the camp where he was imprisoned. Now undercover, she kidnaps the man, and the familiar chase and search prevails.

Island Love Song (1987) (75mins) d: Vic Sarin s: Jeannine Locke : Gordon Clapp, Ann-Marie MacDonald. Filmed against the marvellous scenery of Cape Breton Island a young man's father dies, and he has to cope with family responsibilities and find a way to live with the woman he loves. Sensitive and relevant.

It Can't Be Winter, We Haven't Had Summer Yet (*Ça peut pas être l'hiver, on n'a même pas eu d'été*) (1981) (87mins) d&s: Louise Carré : Charlotte Boisjoli, Jacques Galipeau, Céline Lomez, Mireille Thibault, Serge Bélair. Somewhat along the same lines as *Madame Beauchamp,* this is a modest yet affecting study of a recently widowed woman. She suddenly realizes that she has been living only for her selfish husband and her eight children. She decides to break away from family constraints and live her own life. A splendid and touching performance from Charlotte Boisjoli.

It Happened in Canada (1961) (96mins) (b/w) d&s: Luigi Petrucci : Nello Zordan, Gisela Zdunek, Dedena Morello, Pino Ubaldo. In this production by enthusiastic non-professionals, Rita, a young Italian teacher, comes to Canada to meet the man her parents have arranged for her to marry. He is a 45-year-old widower. She falls in love with his handsome nephew. Nicely told. Petrucci had studied at film school in Rome and worked for eight years in Canada as a salesman to save enough money to make this film. The actors were all local amateurs. It was photographed entirely in Toronto, on a very low budget, and took almost two years.

It Seemed Like a Good Idea at the Time (1975) (97mins) d: John Trent s: David Main, John Trent : Anthony Newley, Stefanie Powers, Isaac Hayes, Lloyd Bochner, Yvonne De Carlo, Henry Ramer, Lawrence Dane, John Candy, Robert Silverman, Roy Wordsworth. A husband set on winning back his ex-wife tries to ruin her new romantic associations in what appears to be a modern version of the Keystone Cops. It ends up being far from a good idea or a fun comedy, but the players are a wonderful lot and it's a pleasure to see Yvonne De Carlo, after a long absence. (One of the seldom mentioned Canadians in Hollywood) (see: *Find the Lady*)

It's a Wonderful Love (*C'est ben beau l'amour*) (1971) (87mins) (b/w) d&s: Marc Daigle : Ann Brockmann, Michel Janvier, Lina Sauvageau, Christian Sasseville. In a small Québec town, six boys and girls talk about liberty, love, work, sex and religion. Their main interest, however, is the birth of a child. A natural and pleasing portrait of interesting, concerned and intelligent young people that has the ring of truth.

It's Not Jacques Cartier's Fault (*C'est pas la faute à Jacques Cartier*) (1968) (87mins) d&s: Clément Perron, Georges Dufaux : Jacques Desrosiers, Michèle Chicoine, Mary Gay, Michael Devine, Paul Buissonneau, Paul Hébert, Lisette Gervais. An early work from Perron and Dufaux, this is a funny and winning trip as three American tourists and their guide discover Québec. Filled with moments of comedy, banality, love and satire. The actuality of it all creates a wonderful atmosphere.

It's Your Turn, Laura Cadieux (*C't à ton tour, Laura Cadieux*) (1998) (92mins) d&s: Denise Filiatrault (adapted from the novel by Michel Tremblay) : Ginette Reno, Pierrette Robitaille, Denise Dubois, Samuel Landry, Adèle Reinhardt. The accomplished, talented and lovely actress turned director Denise Filiatrault gives us a bittersweet comedy about three overweight ladies who meet each week at the doctor's office, where they escape loneliness and solitude by gossiping and joking around.

When one woman's child disappears, a parade of mishaps and misunderstandings ensues. Marvellous location photography around Montréal. The performances are honest; when one woman says she hates mirrors, we know she speaks the truth. (Followed by a sequel, see *Laura Cadieux, La Suite*)

Ivy League Killers (The Fast Ones) (1959) (70mins) (b/w) d: William Davidson s: Norman Klenman : Don Borisenko, Don Francks, Barbara Bricker, Barry Lavender, Patrick Desmond, Jean Templeton, Martin Lager, Jon Ringham, John Paris, Igors Gavon, George Carron, Rolf Carston, Art Jenoff, Boyd Jackson, the Black Diamond Riders. A group of rich, idle youths think up the perfect crime through which to demonstrate their superiority over a rival motorcycle gang. But they underestimate their victims and find themselves involved with the police. A small picture that played an important part in the beginnings of filmmaking in Toronto. It wasn't shown until five years after its completion because a cinema could not be found, to play it.

IXE-13 (1972) (114mins) d&s: Jacques Godbout : Louise Forestier, André Dubois, Carole Laure, Diane Arcand, Susan Kay, Luce Guilbeault, Jean-Guy Moreau. An often funny but somewhat strained version of a Québec comic strip super-spy hero of the 1950s. A large cast does its best to be cartoonish.

J.A. Martin, Photographer (*J.A. Martin, photographe*) (1977) (101mins) d&s: Jean Beaudin : Marcel Sabourin, Monique Mercure, Jean Lapointe, Yvan Canuel, Guy L'Écuyer, Luce Guilbeault, Denis Drouin, Walter Massey, Henry Ramer, Éric Gaudry. Rose-Aimée decides to leave her five children at home with an aunt and accompany her husband on his annual summer tour as an itinerant country photographer. In their horse and wagon, they travel country roads and rediscover the love they once knew. This is a beautifully acted and memorable turn-of-the-19th-century study of nature, longing and love.

J'ai droit au plaisir: see **I Have the Right to Pleasure**
J'ai mon voyage!: see **Enuff is Enuff**
J'aime, j'aime pas **(Love Me, Love Me Not)** (1995) (89mins) d: Sylvie Groulx s: Jacques Marcotte, Sylvie Groulx : Lucie Laurier, Dominic Darceuil, Rémi Laurin-Ouellette, Patrice Dubois, Caroline Néron, Patrick Labbé. The director, known for her compelling documentaries, here remains on the social scene but tells her story in dramatized form with young players. The life depicted so unerringly is that of Winnie, a 17-year-old single mother, and her attempts at overcoming difficulties in bringing up her baby. Refusing to be caught in a life of dull routine, she accepts a friend's offer of a starring role in his next video. An intense and passionate relationship develops, where reality and fiction become increasingly confused. Winnie, with a shy, seductive charm, is played by Lucie Laurier—so appealing in *Chili's Blues*—who gives a near perfect performance. Intimate and often moving.

J'en suis **(Heads or Tales)** (1997) (103mins) d: Claude Fournier s: Marie-José Raymond, Claude Fournier : Roy Dupuis, Patrick Huard, Arielle Dombasle, Charlotte Laurier. A somewhat strained and overlong comedy about two brilliant architects whose company closes down, leaving them without work. One joins the National Theatre School, and the other finds a job in the antiques trade but realizes that to be successful, it would be a help to be gay. Therefore, he must pretend to be gay. This brings about troubles with his wife, and he begins to think he might be gay. It all becomes somewhat drawn out, despite a few funny moments.

J'me Marie, J'me Marie **(I Marry or I Don't Marry) (A Reflection on a Marriage)** (1974) (81mins) d&s: Mireille Dansereau, Anne-Claire Poirier : Francine Larivée, Linda Gaboriau, Jocelyne Lepage, Tanya MacKay. Two of Québec's leading filmmakers get together with four other independently minded women to discuss and play out their feelings and emotions on marriage and their choices in becoming wives and mothers with responsibilities. A loss of freedoms becomes apparent. Thoughtful and sympathetic, understanding and fully cognizant of the traditional designs of life.

Jack and Jill (1998) (84mins) d&s: John Kalangis : John Kalangis, Shauna MacDonald, Kathryn Zenna, Scott Gibson, Tara Johnson. A silly, lightweight comedy-romance—a Kalangis ego trip—about Jack, a young man who changes his mind about getting married. Naturally, Jill is upset. In spite of a few minor diversions, Jack and Jill tumble haplessly downhill from start to finish.

Jack Higgins' Midnight Man: see **Midnight Man**
Jack London Story, The: see **Klondike Fever**
Jack of Hearts (1993) (92mins) (b/w) d&s: Cynthia Roberts : Andrew Scorer, Kirsten Johnson, Edward Fielding, Valerie Buhagiar, Cindy Beattie. Assisted by the brilliant Doctor Mustapha, a wealthy recluse artificially protects his body against the ravages of old age. Too many family complications make this a minor horror in the mad-scientist genre.

Jacob Two-Two Meets the Hooded Fang (1977) (80mins) d: Theodore Flicker s: Flicker (from Mordecai Richler's novel) : Alex Karras, Stephen Rosenberg, Guy L'Ecuyer, Joy Coghill, Earl Pennington, Claude Gaik, Walter Massey, John Wildman. Richler's engaging little fantasy for children is marred by heavy handed treatment and poor production values.

Jacob Two-Two Meets the Hooded Fang (1999) (95mins) d: George Bloomfield s: Tim Burns : Gary Busey, Mark McKinney, Miranda Richardson, Maury Chaykin. Mordecai Richler's engaging fantasy for children and family is about a boy who dreams he's sent to a children's prison and gets into trouble with the Hooded Fang. As in the original film, an American actor was brought in to play the Fang; there are obviously no Canadian actors sufficiently skilled to play this role! This second version is a little better than its predecessor.

Jacques and November (*Jacques et novembre*) (1984) (71mins) d: François Bouvier s: Jean Beaudry : Jean Beaudry, Carole Fréchette, Marie Cantin, Pierre Rousseau, Reine France, Jean Mathieu, Louise Richer, Pat Gagnon, José Ledoux. This modest Québec film is unusual. In semi-documentary fashion, it tells of the last months of a young man (portrayed by Beaudry) dying of cancer. An enthusiastic movie buff, he decides to make a film about his life, his friends and his death. By no means a gloomy or heavy chronicle, it is filled with humour and sympathy.

Jacques Brel Is Alive and Well and Living in Paris (1975) (97mins) (a Canada-France co-production) d: Denis Héroux s: Eric Blaw, Mort Shuman, Jacques Brel (from the stage production) : Elly Stone, Mort Shuman, Joe Masiell, Jacques Brel, Annick Berger, and complete cast. A delightful filmed record of the popular musical revue with its 26 songs on life, love, war and death by the Belgian singer. No story or dialogue, just the music. Made for the *American Film Theatre* series of filmed stage works. Although not a UK-US production like the other five of the series, it is directed by a Canadian. (See: *American Film Theatre Series*)

Jacques et novembre: see **Jacques and November**

Jailbait! (2000) (94mins) (a Canada-U.S. film) d: Allan Moyle s: Timothy Garrick, Scott Russell : Kevin Mundy, Mary Gross, Matt Frewer, Reagan Pasternak. A high school football ruffian forces himself on a trailer park attendant and is charged with raping her. A media match ensues. And this is served up as a comedy. Give us a break from such bait! Not to be confused with U.S. film *Jailbait* (1994) by Rafal Zielinski.

***Jardin d'Anna, Le* (The Garden of Anna)** (1994) (78mins) d: Alain Chartrand s: Diane Cailhier : Danielle Proulx, Jessica Barker, Roger Léger, Vincent Bolduc. Twelve-year-old Anna has leukemia and, in time, it will prove fatal. This is a heartfelt study of what this means to her family.

Je me souviens: see **Don't Forget**

***Je n'Aime que toi* (I Don't Love You)** (2003) (90mins) d&s: Claude Fournier : Michel Forget, Noemie Godin-Vigneau, Dorothy Berryman, Jean-Nicolas Verreault, France Castel, Normand Chouinard, Louis-Jose Houde. A novelist is finding it difficult to finish his new book. At his favourite café one day, he is recognized by a young woman and admirer of his books. She tells him all about her life, he makes her story part of the book he is writing. He falls madly in love with her. Then she disappears, he searches for her, cannot find her and falls into deep despair. This is a beautiful love story, a genuinely romantic film, spellbinding from start to finish. The director knows his characters, knows what a situa-tion like this can do to one who has loved and lost.

Je t'aime: see **I Love You**

Jean-François-Xavier de... (1971) (85mins) d&s: Michel Audy : Danièle Panneton, Jean Isabelle, Paul Tompson, René Bouchard, René de Cotret, André Panneton. Three names, three faces personify the triple image of a liberated man and his death after a life of carrying a certain guilt over his love for a woman. An unusual study in thoughts and feelings, with dignity and understanding.

Jeanne d'Arc: see **Joan of Arc**

Jenifer Estess Story, The (2001) (120mins) (a U.S.-Canada film) d: Jane Alexander s: David Marshall Grant, Geoffrey Nauffts, Patricia Resnick : Laura San Giacomo, Jane Kaczmarck, Annabella Sciorra, Jane Alexander, Edie Falco, Rob Morrow. This is a documentary-style telling of a true story about a New York theatre producer, Jenifer Estess, who was struck down by Amyotrophic Lateral Sclerosis (ALS) at the peak of her success. Her family discovered there was no cure for the disease and so created Project ALS, a non-profit organiza-tion that raises money to promote stem cell research. Although severely disabled, Miss Estess worked on this film. A sensible and serious picture avoiding fake sentimentality.

Jennie's Story: see **Heart of the Sun**

Jerome's Secret: see ***Secret de Jerome, Le***

Jerry and Tom (1998) (94mins) d: Saul Rubinek s: Rick Cleveland : Joseph Mantegna, Sam Rockwell, Maury Chaykin, Ted Danson, Charles Durning, William Macy, Peter Rigert. A film more American than Canadian from actor Rubinek in his first time out as director. He might have chosen a better story than this dubious piece about two used car sales-men who work as hired killers by night. They take this job very lightly and laugh about the murders they commit. It's unfunny, unpleasant and unneces-sary. Find a better tale next time, Saul.

***Jésus de Montréal* (Jesus of Montréal)** (1989) (119mins) d&s: Denys Arcand : Lothaire Bluteau, Catherine Wilkening, Johanne-Marie Tremblay, Rémy Girard, Robert Lepage, Gilles Pelletier, Marie-Christine Barrault. Denys Arcand's second and also triumphant film after *Decline of the American Empire* is a wise, perceptive and both funny and moving morality tale about an eager troupe of actors who come together at the request of a priest to stage the church's annual Passion Play but in a more present day interpretation. The result does not please the religious authorities; and no wonder as Arcand deft-ly and humorously spans a wide range of comment on religious hypocrisy, rampant commercialism, media sensationalism, bureaucracy, but never in the tired and stilted way these subjects are frequently dealt with in screen satire. The actor who plays Jesus, and might be taken a martyr, is a triumph for Lothaire Bluteau, who went on to star in many inter-national films. Also in the cast is Robert Lepage, actor and writer, who later made his own controversial religious drama, *The Confessional*. Denys Arcand plays a judge, proving that he is both a good actor as well as a great director. He was given a special Jury Award at Cannes for this film where it was extremely well received.

Jesus' Son (1999) (198mins) d: Alison Maclean s: Elizabeth Cuthrell, David Urrutia, Oren Moverman (from the book by Denis Johnson) : Billy Crudup, Jack Black, Robert Michael, Torben Brooks, Dierdre Lewis, Jimmy Moffit, Samantha Morton. Too many cooks spoil a broth; too many writers spoil a script. As is the case here of a young man known as f***head who becomes addicted to heroin and thieving. But while working in a hospital, he discovers that by touching patients they feel better. There are probably deep meanings about religion and faith buried in this unpleasant film, but they are hardly likely to atrract many converts.

Jet Boy (2001) (105mins) d&s: David Schultz : Dylan Walsh, Kelly Rowan, Branden Nadon. A familiar theme, but this time the boy in search of his father is a 13-year-old street hustler whose mother, dead from a heroin overdose, has left him alone in the world. Meeting a male drifter with a car, he travels with him to Vancouver. On the way, they stop at the driver's home, and what happens next should give audiences a surprise. Different and well above average.

Jeune fille à la fenêtre, Une **(The Young Girl at the Window)** (2001) (90mins) d: Francis Leclerc s: Marcel Beaulieu : Fanny Mallette, Evelyn Rompré, Daniel Parent, Louis-David Morasse, Richard Fagon, Rosa Hugues Frénette, Evelyn Rompré, Richard Fagon, Rosa Zacharie. A gem. This wonderful film takes us back to 1925, when a young musician decides to move to the city to study piano. She finds a garret apartment and begins a new life where no one knows her and where, within the artistic groups of this time, she realizes her dreams and ambitions. Beautifully set and fashioned, the period is brought engagingly to life.

Jeune magicien, Le: see **Young Magician, The**

Jeunes Québécoises, Les **(The Younger Generation)** (1980) (100mins) d: Claude Castravelli s: Vittorio Montesano : Jacques Robert, Isa Bell, Suzanne Clément, Victor Pugliano, Elizabeth Grandpré, Carole Meilleur. Eight students, four young women and four young men, go to one of their houses—while the parents are away—to explore amorous adventures. When the parents return, they become involved in the goings-on. Set in Montréal, this is an unbelievable and unpleasant sex comedy from Quebec.

Jeux de pouvoir: see **Power Games**

Jewel (2000) (120mins) (a Canadian-UK co-production) d: Paul Shapiro s: Susan Cooper (based on the novel by Bret Lott) : Farrah Fawcett, Patrick Bergin, Cicely Tyson, Ashley Wolfe, Robin Dunne, Geoffrey Bowes. The time is WWII in Mississippi (actually filmed mostly in Mississauga) where a poor Southern woman with a family of four finds herself pregnant again. After a difficult birth she is told that her child has Down's Syndrome. Life is hard and fraught with peril. Everyone is poor and medicine expensive. Unintentionally it's a case for state medicine. While not without emotional depth, the whole is sadly a bit of a weary trudge over familiar territory.

Jeweller's Shop, The (1988) (94mins) (a Canada-France-Italy co-production) d: Michael Anderson s: Jeff Andrus (based on an original script by Mario Di Nardo, developed from the book of the same name by Karol Wojtyla) : Burt Lancaster, Daniel Olbryscki. A jeweller in Cracow sells engagement rings for betrothed couples. A priest works to unite and counsel young marrieds in Poland and, later, in Montréal. A slight play written by Pope Jean Paul II in his younger years.

Jigsaw (Angry Man, An) (*L'homme en colère*) (1979) (97mins) (a Canada-France co-production) d: Claude Pinoteau s: Charles Israël, Jean-Claude Carrière, Claude Pinoteau : Lino Ventura, Angie Dickinson, Laurent Malet, Chris Wiggins, Hollis McLaren, R.H. Thomson, Donald Pleasence, Pierre Curzi, John Wildman, Walter Massey, Sydney Banks, Murray Westgate. A man moves from Paris to Montréal to search for his son who is involved in the drug trade and finds, instead, a beautiful woman. A subtle and insouciant romance-drama. (Not to be confused with Fletcher Markle's 1968 U.S. film of the same title)

Jinnah on Crime (2002) (90mins) d: Brad Turner s: Don Hauka, Margaret Bard, Bartley Bard : Dhirendra, Pamela Sinha, Chistian Bocher, Emily Holmes. The remains of a cremated body are found in a pizza oven. A crime reporter discovers that the police are after the wrong man. His revelations put the lives of himself and his family in peril—from outraged Pizza Pizza owners, no doubt.

Jinnah On Crime–White Knight, Black Widow (2003) (90mins) d: Brad Turner s: Don Hauka, Margaret Bard, Bartley Bard : Dhirenda, Pamela Sinha, Christian Bocher, Janet Wright. A businessman's career becomes even more complicated after he becomes involved in the strange death of a high-living Vancouver stock promoter. But he must keep up with the activities on the market, and attempt to clear his name of murder. This is all rather stale stuff, notable only because the businessman is played by a black actor and this is actually a Canadian movie filmed in Vancouver; a lone effort among all the US films shot there, and which the film agencies lovingly describe as Canadian.

Joan of Arc (*Jeanne d'Arc*) (1999) (240mins) (a Canada-U.S. film) d: Christian Duguay s: Michael Alexander Miller, Ronald Parker : Leelee Sobieski, Jacqueline Bisset, Powers Boothe, Neil Patrick Harris, Maury Chaykin, Shirley MacLaine, Peter

O'Toole, Peter Strauss, Maximilian Schell, Ronald White, Jaimz Woolvett, Jiri Trnka and around five thousand clergy, soldiers, peasants and others managed by 12 assistant directors! Lots of talk, smoke, fire, Barbarian Brits, battle and, let's not forget, prayers in this umpteenth version of the girl who hears voices. Extremely well acted, with marvellously authentic production values and a literate script.

Joan of Arc Is Alive and Well and Living in Québec: see **Great Ordinary Movie, The**

Joe's So Mean to Josephine (1997) (89mins) d&s: Peter Wellington : Eric Thal, Sarah Polley, Don McKellar, Waneta Storms, Dixie Seatle. Girl meets boy in a rock 'n' roll bar, but the two never expect to see each other again. Well, surprise, he's a telephone company repairman who comes to her home to fix the phone. So, girl falls for her rock companion; but she is rather "upper," and he is definitely "lower." When she tries to end their brief encounter, he refuses, being something of a lout who will never understand a woman. A neat little piece of work done with some feeling and insight.

Joe's Wedding (1996) (100mins) d: Michael Kennedy s: Tony Johnston, John Dolin : Kate Vernon, Tammy Isbell, David Hewlett, Aidan Devine. A half-baked and seriously overlong comedy about romance and big business and how the latter takes the shine off the former. Antics galore but few laughs.

John and the Missus (1986) (90mins) d&s: Gordon Pinsent (based on his novel of the same name) : Gordon Pinsent, Jackie Burroughs. This is the film Pinsent had been trying to make for ten years. From the original screenplay, it became a novel, a stage play, a radio program and, finally, a film. It is beautiful to look at and finely acted, a fanciful, romantic, poetic and leisurely collection of observations and memories. The characters' wonderful old boat drifts along the Newfoundland coastline, depicting family and industrial life there in the early 1960s, when the provincial government decided to close down isolated communities and resettle the inhabitants elsewhere. It has a rare serenity about it. Quite captivating.

John Woo's Once a Thief (1997) (120mins) d: John Woo s: Glenn Davis, William Laurin : Sandrine Holt, Ivan Sergei, Nicholas Lea, Jennifer Dale. Two fugitives flee their Hong Kong Triad family and are reluctantly recruited by a clandestine crime-fighting unit—we're not sure where—and sent to work with a former policeman. Enter their estranged adopted brother, who hunts them down for leaving "the family." We've seen it all before, laced here with Woo's trademark violence.

Johnny (1999) (85mins) (a Canada-US co-production) d&s: Carl Bessai : Chris Martin, Gema Zamprogna, Vanessa Shaver, Kris Lemche, Clinton Walker. Johnny, an unpleasant and manipulative young man, leads a group of confused squeegee kids who live desperate lives on the snowy city streets. He takes control and begins to make a film about their lives, bending them brutally to his will. A tortured, twisted "experiment"; the actors would all have been better off washing windshields.

Johnny Belinda (1977) (120mins) d: Norman Campbell s: (based on the play of the same name by Elmer Harris) : Amanda Wilcox, William Cole, Donald McManus, Barbara Hamilton. A young woman who cannot hear or speak is raped in a Maritime village by a local fisherman. Later, she has a child she calls Johnny. Was it really necessary for CBC-tv to remake this famous (1948) Warner Brothers picture? It is well enough done; the subject of rape was taboo at this time in films and tv.

Johnny Greyeyes (2001) (78mins) d&s: Jorge Manuel Manzano : Gail Maurice, Columpa Bob, Jonathan Fisher, Gloria May Eshkibok, Georgina Lightning, Shirley Cheechoo, Marion Devries. A small picture, but a telling portrait of a resilient native woman serving time in the prison for women in Kingston, Ontario. Her name is Johnny, but she is very much a woman. She looks back over her journey through a fractured life; with her release date near, she finds herself finally possessed with a sense of spiritual purpose and a resolution to make peace with herself.

Johnny Mnemonic (1995) (98mins) (a Canadian-American film) d: Robert Longo s: William Gibson (from his short story) : Keanu Reeves, Takeshi, Ice-T, Dina Meyer, Udo Kier, Denis Akiyama, Donald Francks, Barbara Sukowa. Johnny is a 21st-century mnemonic courier who dumps his memory bank for chip-enhanced data-storage capacity in this trashy high-tech film that looks like a video game gone mad, in a world of unrelieved grimness. Elaborate computer graphics are mostly alarming.

Johnny Shortwave (1995) (95mins) (b/w) d&s: Michael Bockner : Emmanuel Mark, John Tench, Mona Matteo, Valerie Buhagiar. A young, unemployed man tires of watching what he believes to be the destruction of Canada by big business and corrupt politicians. He starts up a rogue radio station to broadcast directly to the people, urging them to revolt against the system and assert their rights. The Department of Communications sends secret agents to destroy him. Several unusual characters pass through his clandestine world. A dark and genuinely frightening thriller that makes the worldwide protests against globalization seem uncannily relevant.

Jos Carbone (1975) (75mins) d&s: Hugues Tremblay (from the novel by Jacques Benoît) : Katerine Mousseau, Jacques Benoît, Han Masson, Yves Barrette, Jean-Pierre Saulnier, Raymond Bélisle. Once again, the world has been reduced to nothingness, with little human life remaining. There is only the weight of bestial subsistence. Thank goodness it's only a movie—and not a very good one at that.

Joshua Then and Now (1985) (126mins) d: Ted Kotcheff s: Mordecai Richler (from his novel) : James Woods, Gabrielle Lazure, Alan Arkin, Michael

Sarrazin, Linda Sorensen, Alan Scarfe, Ken Campbell, Kate Trotter, Alexander Knox, Henry Beckman, Chuck Shamata, Robert Joy, Harvey Atkin, Gordon Woolvet, Linda Smith. Working under impossible pressures to make a $12-million feature and tv series from Mordecai Richler's novel about the misadventures of a sardonic author, Ted Kotcheff has made an alternately witty and strained film that is fine until Joshua grows up and becomes James Woods, who is unable to cope with the complex character.

Jouer sa vie: see **Great Chess Movie, The**

Jour S, Le: see **S Day**

Jour se leve c'est, Le: see **Day Breaks Once More**

Journal d'un bossu, Le (**A Hunchback's Diary**) (1993) (100mins) (a Canada-Russia-Poland-German co-production) d: Jan Kidawa-Blonski s: Jacek Kondracki, Zenon Olejniczak, Jan Kidawa-Blonski : Olaf Lubaszenko, Edward Linde Lubaszenko, Linda Buguskaw, Trybala Marzena and others. A grim, almost documentary-like chronicle tracing the history of the Polish people from 1939 to the 1990s. Divided into five dramas: conception, infancy, adolescence, maturity and finale. Complicated, dark and weighty, but compelling and revealing nonetheless.

Journée en taxi, Une: see **Day in a Taxi, A**

Journey (1972) (88mins) d&s: Paul Almond : Geneviève Bujold, John Vernon, George Sperdakos, Elton Hayes, Luke Gibson, Gale Garnett, Judith Gault, Ratch Wallace. The life depicted here takes place outside the normal frame of space and time. It begins with a girl floating down the deep and mysterious Saguenay River. She is rescued by a man who carries her back to his community in the wilderness, called Undersky. Its inhabitants live in houses and wear clothes they have made themselves, living off the land they have cultivated. There, the girl, a lonely person who cannot make friends, begins to come back to life, to speak and move. She falls in love with the man. But her presence provokes strange, dark deeds that mar the happiness of the commune. There is nothing for the girl to do but return to the river, where, once again, she floats away into another world. *Journey* was described by Almond as being the last of his trilogy, which includes *Isabel* and *Act of the Heart*, but it is difficult to find a relationship between them. At times, the awesomely beautiful, mist-shrouded region of Tadoussac, Québec, seems to be enough to sustain the film. But eventually, the metaphorical and unfathomable tale drowns in its incomprehensible screenplay. The marvellous acting abilities of John Vernon and Geneviève Bujold are of considerable benefit here. (See: *Isabel* and *Act of the Heart*.)

Journey Into Darkness: The Bruce Curtis Story (1990) (89mins) (A Canada-U.S. co-production) d: Graeme Campbell s: Keith Ross Leickie : Simon Reynolds, Jaimz Woolvett, Dawn Greenhalgh, Kenneth Welsh. This is another in the ever growing series of films based on true-life crime stories. Bruce Curtis was a young Canadian visiting the U.S. who was involved in the murder of his friend's parents. Curtis received a 20-year sentence for the crime. The first part of the film is about the murder; the second concerns his parents' long struggle to have him return to Canada. Well acted, although the characters could have been made more interesting.

Journey Into Fear (1975) (103mins) (a Canadian-American film) d: Daniel Mann s: Trevor Wallace : Sam Waterston, Zero Mostel, Yvette Mimieux, Scott Marlowe, Ian McShane, Joseph Wiseman, Shelley Winters, Stanley Holloway, Donald Pleasence, Vincent Price, Jackie Cooper. A second-rate remake of the 1942 Norman Foster–Orson Welles original as based on Eric Ambler's exciting novel about a research geologist who becomes involved in international intrigue in Europe while smuggling munitions into Turkey. Good location shooting and a good cast, but an unsatisfying journey.

Joy (1983) (101mins) (a Canada-France co-production) d: Serge Bergon s: Marie-Françoise Hans, Christian Charrière, Serge Bergon, Robert Geoffrion (based on the book by Joy Laurey) : Claudia Udy, Gérard-Antoine Huart, Agnès Torrent, Elisabeth Mortensen, Kenneth Welsh. Joy is a free-and-easy photographic model who seems to have everything life provides. However, she is not entirely satisfied and cannot love the men who swoon over her because her heart belongs to Daddy—although she may have given him more than her heart. Poor Joy, awash in soft-core slush.

Joyas del diablo, Las: see *Diable aime les bijoux, Le*

Joyeux calvaire (**Poverty and Other Delights**) (1997) (105mins) (a Canada-France co-production) d: Denys Arcand s: Denys Arcand, Yves Pelletier (based on Pelltier's novel *J'en suis*): Claire Richard, Gaston Lepage, Benoît Brière, Chantal Baril, Roger Blay, André Melançon, René-Richard Cyr. Arcand gives us a glimpse into how street people survive and what they think and feel about themselves. But this is no preachy, sentimental on-the-street documentary but a funny and wise observation seen through the eyes of a long-time wanderer who becomes a friend to a newcomer. We find that life is what you make of it, even on the streets.

Judgement in Stone: see **Housekeeper, The**

Juiced (1999) (93mins) d&s: Katie Tallo : Susan Brooks, Kate Hurman, Anne Lishman, Paul Rainville, Robert Marinier, Thomas Michael. This film is about a day and a night in the life of a waitress named Syd, a self-styled "slice of life served up hot and gravy." Of interest as a well-documented account of what it means to be living such a life.

Juis suis loin de toi mignonne: see **Far From You Sweetheart**

Jules and Fanny: see **Cosmos**

Julia Has Two Lovers (1990) (88mins) d: Bashar Shbib s: Daphna Kastner : Daphna Kastner, David Duchovny, David Charles, Tim Ray, Clare Bancroft. Julia lives on the beach in Venice, California, and must decide whether to continue in her seemingly drab, normal life or risk everything for the possibility of passion. A contemporary look at relationships in the 1990s. Shbib, judging by his other films, should know all about this.

Julia: see **Acts of Love (series)**

Julie and Me and Julie Again: see *Revoir Julie*

Julie Darling (1982) (100mins) (a Canada-German co-production) d: Paul Nicolas s: Lutz Schaarwachter, Paul Nicolas : Anthony Franciosa, Sybil Danning, Isabelle Mejias, Paul Hubbard, Cindy Girling. Filmed mostly in German, this is a tired and unpleasant thriller about a teenage daughter who loves Daddy and kills his second wife.

Julie Walking Home (2002) (120mins) (a Canada-German-Poland co-production) d: Agnieszka Holland s: Arlene Sarner, Roman Gren, Agnieszka Holland : Miranda Otto, William Fichtner, Lothaire Bluteau, Ryan Smith, Bianca Crudo, Jerzy Nowak. A family drama of familiar incidents: infidelity, a child with cancer, and other emotional disturbances. A thin, confused, empty and disappointing work from the heretofore distinguished Polish filmmaker.

July Group, The (1981) (90mins) d: George McCowan s: Lister Sinclair (based on the novel by Stanley Ellin) : Nicholas Campbell, Chapelle Jaffe, Kenneth Pogue, Sarah Torgov, Calvin Butler, Maury Chaykin, Jefferson Mappin. Timely when it was made and even more so today. This film is a sombre, part controversial, part religious drama about a confrontation between a family of peace-loving Quakers and a band of ruthless terrorists. Sinclair said, "It is about courage, not heroics." Quakers believe no one has the right to kill for a belief, but everybody has the right to die for one; eloquently stated here with a great cast.

Jungleground (1995) (88mins) (a Canadian-American film) d: Don Allan s: Michael Stokes : Roddy Piper, Torri Higginson, J.R. Bourne, Peter Williams, Rachel Wilson. Jungleground is presumably the underground of an American city. Punks are everywhere, buildings are decrepit, crime is rampant, brutal gang war rules, bullets fly and cars are aflame in a darkness that seems eternal. A love affair between a policeman and a dancer lightens this pit of depravity all too briefly. An odious film.

Junior (1985) (86mins) d: Jim Hanley s: Don Carmody, John Maxwell : Suzanne DeLaurentis, Linda Singer, Jeremy Ratchford, Michael McKeever, Ken Roberts. Here we go again. Two men released from prison are determined to lead better lives, but after settling down in a quiet neighbourhood, they find themselves being terrorized in their new home, initially by persons unknown to them. This soon changes for the worst. Tired, crude and predictable. (Not to be confused with Ivan Reitman's *Junior*, 1994)

Jusqu'au coeur: see **Straight to the Heart**

Jusqu'au cou: see **Over My Head**

Just a Game (*Rien qu'un jeu*) (1983) (101mins) d: Brigitte Sauriol s: Monique Messier, Brigitte Sauriol : Marie Tifo, Raymond Cloutier, Jennifer Grenier, Julie Mongeau, Julie Desjardins, Lothaire Bluteau. This is a deeply observed, understated and eloquent study of the silent agony of a daughter forced into an incestuous relationship with her father. When she finally refuses to continue, he turns his attention to his younger daughter. The wife makes matters worse by blaming the girls and excusing the father's behaviour to hide her own weaknesses. The whole is well acted, rings entirely true, and accurately reflects the situation with sadness and dispair.. At this time, the fathers were rarely brought to trial. Lothaire Bluteau makes his first screen appearance here.

Just Jessie (1981) (75mins) d&s: Bert Salzman : Hollis McLaren, Nicholas Campbell, Irena Mayeska, Sydney Brown, Maury Chaykin. A young woman living on Prince Edward Island dreams of becoming a ballet dancer but is in love with a fisherman. Should she leave or remain in the little town? Refreshing and nicely portrayed.

Justice (1998) (120mins) d: Richard Lewis s: Alyson Feltes : Julie Khaner, Gary Farmer, Stéphane Archambault, Deanna Milligan, Sean McCann, Martha Burns, Gregory Ellwand, Shawn Doyle, Serge Houde, Barbara Eve Harris. Canada's filmmakers have long been loathe to make movies about our political systems, parties and provocations, unlike the Americans who have made their political background a mainstay of their stories. Two constables are abducted and murdered in gang-style executions. Fanatical revolutionaries are suspected. A third policeman, determined to stop the terrorists, finds his efforts thwarted by further abductions. A brave and penetrating plot about Québec *séparatistes* and the disintegration of Canada. Events go off in all directions, with so many subplots that the whole would have crashed had it not been for a great cast, script and direction, as well as a moving intensity in depicting the issues raised in a thoughtful and concerned narrative.

Justice Denied (1989) (98mins) d&s: Paul Cowan : Billy Merasty, Wayne Robson, Thomas Peacocke, Troy Adama, Daniel MacIvor, Peter MacNeill. This is a hard-hitting, convincing, but sometimes flawed retelling of the case of Donald Marshall, a 17-year-old Micmac in Sydney, Nova Scotia, who was imprisoned for a murder he didn't commit—a shameful instance of justice blinded by racism. Many years later, he was given his freedom.

Justice Express (1990) (92mins) (a Canada-France co-production) d: Richard Martin s: Pierre Billon : Jean Leclerc, David Jalil, Liliane Clune. Some weighty matters get off lightly in this none-too-well-realized story of diplomats, mistresses and terrorists in Québec City. Where is Bond when we need him?

Justine (*Justine De Sade*) (1972) (99mins) (a Canada-France-Italy co-production) d: Claude Pierson s: Huguette Boisvert (based on *Justine ou les malheurs de la vertu* by the Marquis De Sade) : Alice Arno, France Verdier, Mauro Parenti, Franco Fantasia. This tin-pot telling of Sade's famous novel, is disappointing on every level.

Justine de Sade: see **Justine**

Justocoeur: see **Until the Heart**

K2 2001: see *Karmina 2: L'enfer de Chabot*

Kabloonak (Nanook) (1994) (105mins) (A Canada-France co-production) d&s: Claude Massot : Charles Dance, Adamie Inukpuk, Seporah Q. Ungalaaq, Matthew Jaw-Saviakjuk, Natar Ungalaaq. More French than Canadian, this is a brilliant piece of filmmaking re-constucting the arrival in Port Harrison in 1920 of the Irish-American explorer Robert Flaherty, who became a pioneer of the documentary film. The result of his visit was *Nanook of the North*, one of the greatest and appealing documentaries in the history of film and still shown somewhere in the world every week, telling the story of an Eskimo and his family, capturing the essence of primitive man's struggle for survival against the hostile forces of nature. Kabloonak (*The Stranger*) tells the epic story with skill and fidelity. Massot cannot bring either Nanook or Flaherty back, but Nanook is played be Nanook's grandson, Adamie Inukpuk being uncannily believable and Flaherty by the exceptional actor Charles Dance with sensitivity and understanding. In Flaherty's day, everything was black and white, this time, we see in colour, magnificently photographed with drama and beauty, the surroundings which made life so hard for the Eskimo of those times. A complelling and humanistic document. Flahert's visual poetry is omnipresent.

Kalamazoo (1988) (84mins) d: Marc-André Forcier s: Jacques Marcotte, Marc-André Forcier : Rémy Girard, Marie Tifo, Tony Nardi. A tale of a retired botanist in Montréal who falls in love with an illusory woman, a dual role beautifully played by Marie Tifo.

Kamouraska (1973) (123mins) (a Canada-France co-production) d: Claude Jutra s: Claude Jutra, Anne Hébert (based on her novel) : Geneviève Bujold, Richard Jordan, Philippe Léotard, Suzie Baillargeon, Marcel Cuvelier. A romantic and passionate tale set in Québec in 1839, concerning a wife who relives her past while tending her dying husband. Jutra's film is astonishing in its sweep, power and beauty, and the characters are subtly delineated. The depiction of the past is detailed and vivid.

Kanada (1993) (65mins) d&s: Mike Hoolboom : Babz Chula, Gabrielle Rose. A silly attempt at satire in the experimental vein, foreseeing Canada engaged in a long-running civil war. A hit-and-miss proposition.

Kanadiana (2000) (85mins) d&s: Jon Einarsson Gustafsson : Tom Schioler, Robert Ryder, Christie Wilkes. Two brutal young hoods steal diamonds from a courier and drive out of town. We are in wintry Winnipeg and the surrounding countryside. The policeman who pursues the robbers is clearly from the RCMP. Short, sharp and above average for this kind of plot.

Karmen Gel (2001) (86mins) (a Canada-France-Senegal co-production) d&s: Joseph Gai Ramaka : Djeinaba Diop Gai, Magaye Adama Niang, Stephanie Biddle, Thierno Ndiaye Dos, El Hadji Ndiaye. Set in Senegal on a picturesque coastline near a desolate prison. The entire population of this film (described as a black retelling of Bizet's *Carmen*) spends its time singing about love, talking about love, having sex and giving forth enough platitudes about love and life to fill a book. Everyone is impressively and lavishly dressed in colourful clothes set against stages worthy of a Hollywood musical, with everyone whirling about—dancing, prancing and preening—like proverbial dervishes. The timeless issues of love and freedom seem to have lost their way here.

Karmina (1998) (100mins) d: Gabriel Pelletier s: Ann Burke, Yves Pelletier (based on an idea by Burke) : Isabelle Cyr, Robert Brouillette, Gildor Roy, Yves Pelletier, France Castel. A wonderfully funny story about Karmina, a 140-year-old vampire who is tired of family and friends and flees Transylvania for Canada, where she is warmly welcomed by a customs officer. Here, she meets other vampires and becomes involved in various incidents, speaking a clunky kind of French with a certain degree of sophistication. All of this is done with a touch of Gothic horror in sets and costumes. A most unusual but winning concoction with a cast wholeheartedly enjoying itself, as does the audience.

***Karmina 2: L'enfer de Chabot* (K2 2001)** (2001) (97mins) d: Gabriel Pelletier s: Gabriel and Yves Pelletier : Robert Brouillette, Isabelle Cyr, Yves Pelletier, Gildor Roy, Diane Lavallee, Sylvie Léonard. A group of vampires has lost a special potion that has allowed them to behave like humans. They go on a mad search and scramble to find it before they go back to being vampires again. Quite funny and well played along its bloody trail. Not as entertaining as Pelletier's *Karmina*.

Kart Racer (2002) (89mins) (a U.S.-Canada film) d: Stuart Gillard s: Nicholas Dibella : Randy Quaid, Will Rothhaar, David Gallagher. Two boys race their go-karts around their neighbourhood, disregarding their safety and that of the people they pass. The father of one of the boys, who has previously shown no interest in his son's life, resolves to help the boy enter the regional championships of go-karting and, in future, to spend more time with him. A family film that, hopefully, will find its audience on tv. A welcome antidote to the usual violent movies.

Kate Morris, Vice President (1984) (90mins) d: Danièle Suissa s: John Saxton : Kate Trotter, Sean

McCann, Barbara Gordon, Scott Hylands, Marc Strange, Norma Edwards. A dramatic portrayal of the career difficulties a dynamic young corporate executive faces because she is a woman. Her co-workers are all men, and because they are forced to recognize that a woman at work is their equal, they treat her with hostility and anger. Sympathetic, unbiased and enlightened for its time. (See: *For the Record*)

Kathy Karuks Is a Grizzly Bear (Lakeswim) (1976) (65mins) d: Peter Pearson s: Ralph Thomas : Dixie Seatle, Lesley Angus, Donnelly Rhodes, Rudy Lipp, Inta Purvs, cameos by Ben Wicks, Dini Petty, Red Burnett. In Estonian, *"karuks"* means grizzly bear. This is a fitting metaphor for this film about the tenacity, determination and lasting courage of the youngest swimmer ever to attempt to cross Lake Ontario. True to life, it makes an emotionally charged drama tinged with suspense and charm. (See: *For the Record*)

Katryn's Place (2002) (86mins) d: B. de Burgh s: James Galwey, from a story by Jeanne Kassir : Pascale Montpetit, Eric Goulem, France Arbour, Angelo Cadet, Chip Chuipka, Marthe Turgeon. 'Katryn's' place is one of acute depression—for her—as we follow the misery and misfortunes of a young working-class immigrant woman. She is struggling to put her life in order after all else, from love to trying to stay alive, has failed. It makes an impression right enough, but enough is often too much.

Kavik the Wolf Dog: see **Courage of Kavik the Wolf Dog, The**

Kayla (1998) (96mins) d: Nicholas Kendall s: Peter Behrens (based on the novel by Elizabeth Van Steenwik) : Tod Fennell, Henry Czerny, Meredith Henderson, Bronwen Booth, Carl Marotte, Brian Dooley. Set against Québec winter landscapes, this period piece for children is about a boy as he trains his wolf-like dog to compete in a big race. Here, there are several far from familiar twists. Family relationships are a bother, of course. Overall, a welcome relief from the mostly awful fare masquerading as children's films.(Other than those from Montreal),

Kazan (1994) (97mins) d&s: Arnaud Selignac : Jeff Fahey, Sophie Duez. A dog has become a trained killer. A man who cares about the animal decides to "tame" him back to his original state. A small but contemporary undertaking set against the great Rockies, with difficulties to overcome, and prejudiced people to deal with. (see *Baree, Son of Kazan*)

Keep an Eye on the Trombone (*L'assassin jouait du trombone***)** (1992) (100mins) d&s: Roger Cantin : Germain Houde, Anaïs Goulet-Robitaille, Raymond Bouchard. A family comedy about an out-of-work actor who becomes a security guard at a film studio that refuses to employ him. Various misfits, including Countess Skinhead and the Tattooed Man, think the guard has bumped off the studio owners and will do each of them in, too. The original French-language version may be funnier than this laboured dubbed English version.

Keep It in the Family (1973) (91mins) d: Larry Kent s: Edward Stewart : Patricia Gage, John Gavin, Adrienne La Russa, Allan McRae, Kenneth Dight, Gillie Fenwick, Michael Kirby, Julie Wildman, Barrie Baldaro. Silly domestic sex comedy in which a young married couple, annoyed by the refusal of their parents to subsidize their extravagant way of life, plans to seduce their parents in revenge. Overall, a bit too much to take.

Keeper, The (1975) (88mins) d&s: T.Y Drake (based on the novel of the same name by Donald Wilson and David Curnick) : Christopher Lee, Tell Schreiber, Sally Gray, Ross Vezerian, Christian Bruyère. Feeble comic horror tale about the keeper of an insane asylum who wants to become all powerful by killing the heirs of wealthy people and taking control of the fortunes. Barely worth watching.

Keeping the Promise (1997) (120mins) d: Sheldon Larry s: Gerald DiPego (based on the novel *Sign of the Beaver* by Elizabeth George Speare) : Keith Carradine, Gordon Tootoosis, Annette O'Toole, Brendan Fletcher. Filmed in Penetanguishene, Ontario, but set in Maine. In the 1770s, the Hallowell family pursues its dream of a better life by moving to Maine. During the harsh winter that follows, the family is torn apart by loneliness and disease but finds some comfort with a Penobscot Indian. Believable and above average for this sort of pioneer portrayal.

Keeping Track (Double Impasse) (1987) (102mins) d: Robin Spry s: Jamie Brown (based on a story *Amtrak* by Spry and Brown) : Margot Kidder, Michael Sarrazin, Donald Pilon, Alan Scarfe. Two strangers on a train witness a robbery followed by gunfire. They work together to find out what happened and, in so doing, become involved with the RCMP and the KGB. A neat little thriller well played by Sarrazin and Kidder, who make an engaging couple.

Keiko (1979) (95mins) (a Canada-Japan co-production) d&s: Claude Gagnon : Junko Wakashiba, Akiko Kitamura, Takuma Ikeuchi. A film in Japanese about Japan made by a *gaijin* (foreigner). Gagnon moved from Montréal to Japan and lived there for 10 years, marrying Yuri Yoshimura, who became his co-producer. This intimate, personal low-budget film concerns the place of women in Japanese society, as seen through the life of Keiko and her discovery of love.

Kelly (Touch the Wind) (1981) (94mins) d: Christopher Chapman s: Robert Logan : Robert Logan, Twyla-Dawn Vokins, George Clutesi, Elaine Nalee, Douglas Lennox, Alec Willows. Chapman, one of Canada's outstanding documentary filmmakers, takes on his first feature and is defeated by an inane story in which a wealthy young girl is tamed by the outdoor life—to say nothing of interference by producers. Filmed in Alberta being passed off as Alaska!

Kevin of the North (2001) (102mins) (a Canada-U.K. co-production) d: Bob Spiers s: William Osborne : Leslie Nielsen, Natasha Henstridge, Skeet Ulrich, Rik Mayall, Lochlyn Munro. During the first section of this film, two years in the making, audiences may well experience feelings of delight in watching, at last, a genuine comedy based somewhat on the classics of olden years in which a young innocent finds himself the target of scoundrels, but manages to outwit them. Unfortunately this is all there is to cheer about. After a vicious scene in which the heroine beats and smashes the hero into his car, with a violence which is stomach turning all under the guise of comedy, the film lumbers into its main plot set against the snows and mountains of Alaska, read Vancouver, and taking place in an interminable dog sled race which our hero must win in order to qualify for his dead grandfather's fortune left to him in his will. This so-called comedy now gets thoroughly out-of-control by becoming preposterous in the extreme; loud, unpleasant, and over-the-top in all aspects of nastiness and humour, filled with crude lavatory-jokes and ghastly, violent humour. We couldn't care whether he wins the race or not. There is no one to relate to. This is a pity. The likeable leads would be a pleasing couple, even Neilsen makes something of his character as a conniving lawyer, but like everything else in this film becomes over-loaded. The only genuine likeable creatures here are the dogs, and much to the credit of one of them, it refused to urinate on the hero's face, as called for in the tattered script.

KGB: The Secret War (1984) (90mins) (a Canada-U.S. film) d: Dwight Little s: Sandra Bailey, Dwight Little : Michael Billington, Denise Dubarry, Sally Kellerman, Michael Ansara, Walter Gotell. A KGB spy becomes involved with an American woman both in love and war. The cold war finally gives them the big freeze! A fair look at times past in politics and peace.

Khaled (2002) (95mins) d&s: Asghar Massombagi : Michael D'Ascenzo, Michael Kanev, Normand Bissonnette, Michèle Duquet, Lynne Deragon. Khaled is a quiet and well-behaved immigrant boy who has been trained by his mother to keep himself to himself and not to become involved with people who might harm him. They live in a run-down Toronto apartment building. When his mother suddenly dies he keeps her death a secret, afraid he'll be returned to an abusive foster home. This is a moving, beautifully acted, and realistic portrayal of a difficult life. It is the best film of consequence to emerge from the Canadian Film Centre's production programme. (*Of interest is the fact that shortly after the release of this film a similar situation was reported from London, UK, in which a young boy was left alone when his mother disappeared and he continued to live while making excuses for her absence.*)

Kid Brother, The (1987) (100mins) (a Canada-U.S.-Japan co-production) d&s: Claude Gagnon : Kenny Easterday, Caitlin Clarke, Liane Curtis, Zack Grenier. Thirteen-year-old Kenny Easterday, a Pennsylvania boy who has no legs or torso, is relaxed and cheerful in this part-fiction, part-documentary story of his life. Hailed as a Canadian film, it is an American story financed by Japanese interests. (The film has enjoyed its greatest success in Japan.) Only the writer-director is Canadian.

Kid Sentiment (1967) (87mins) d&s: Jacques Godbout, Ghislaine Godbout : Andrée Cousineau, François Guy, Michèle Mercure, Louis Parizeau, Jacques Languirand, François Jasmin. Compared to more contemporary films about young people, this Québec picture has great charm and sensitivity. Two teenage boys meet two friendly young girls, and they decide to make a night of it, for their first time. Wise beyond their years, they contemplate life, politics, affection and learning. A concerned and thoughtful film from Godbout at the NFB, which couldn't make a film of this calibre today—no matter how it tried.

Kid Tougas, The: see **Little Tougas**

Kid Who Couldn't Miss, The (1982) (80mins) d&s: Paul Cowan : Eric Peterson. Based partly on the play *Billy Bishop Goes to War* by John Gray, this is a likeable, revealing and sympathetic study of Canada's flying hero of the Great War. Includes scenes from newsreels and interviews with people who knew Bishop. The film proved controversial when it opened, with the director being accused of not giving Bishop his due.

Kid, The (1997) (90mins) d: John Hamilton s: Seymour Blicker : Rod Steiger, Jeff Saumier, Ray Aranha, Jane Wheeler. A young man with a passion for boxing starts training with an aging former boxer but does not tell his parents because he knows they would not approve. Charlie where are you?

Kidnapping of Baby John Doe, The (The Baby John Doe) (1985) (90mins) d&s: Peter Gerretsen : Jayne Eastwood, George Millenbach, Geoffrey Bowes, Janet-Laine Green, Helen Hughes, Barbara Gordon, Kenneth James, Chuck Shamata. Criminal act or mission of mercy? A severely mentally handicapped newborn infant, left by his parents to die in a hospital, is kidnapped by a sympathetic nurse. After the baby is saved by an operation, nurse Jane attempts to smuggle him back into the hospital, where she is arrested and charged with kidnapping. After a heart-rending court scene, the baby is returned to his natural parents. A thoughtful, concerned and absorbing social document.

Kidnapping of the President, The (1980) (113mins) (a Canadian-American film) d: George Mendeluk s: Richard Murphy (based on Charles Templeton's novel) : William Shatner, Hal Holbrook, Van Johnson, Ava Gardner, Gary Reineke, Maury Chaykin, Cindy Girling, Elizabeth Shepherd, Jackie Burroughs, Lynda Mason Green. Third World terrorists kidnap the American president. A film hailed by the "international clique" as a great Canadian breakthrough into the U.S. market. Shot mainly in Toronto, on a huge budget with herds of American players, it is topical but tepid and false.

Kids in the Hall: Brain Candy (1996) (96mins) d: Kelly Makin s: Bruce McCulloch and four other "Kids" : Bruce McCulloch, Mark McKinney, Scott Thompson, Kevin McDonald, David Foley, Jackie Harris. For their first film, the Kids produced (in their words) "a comedy about depression... a story of a scientist's rise and fall at the hands of a manipulative corporation... and a social comedy about a mythical drug that moves through society and changes it." The drug theme thins down the comedy somewhat.

Kids in the Hall: see **Dog Park**

Kids of the Round Table (1995) (88mins) d: Robert Tinnell s: David Sherman : Malcolm McDowell, Johnny Morina, Michael Ironside, Roc Lafortune, Renée Simard. Well, well—good old King Arthur's knights are back again. This time, they entrance a group of kids who find Arthur's sword. Of course, there are lots of nasties around who fall before the power of the sword. In a spiritual ending, the power is revealed as nothing more than one's own inner strength. Hard not to like a film such as this.

Kill (1969) (84mins) d&s: Iain Ewing : Clara Mayer, Daisy Waterman, Howard Cronis, Iain Ewing. A first film by a University of Toronto student, this is a strange, dark examination of life and death. Three characters talk and behave in ways that are meaningful and absurd. It still finds room to be thoughtful about contemporary society.

Killer (Bulletproof Heart) (1994) (96mins) (a Canada-U.S. film) d: Mark Malone s: Gordon Melbourne : Anthony LaPaglia, Mimi Rogers, Matt Craven, Peter Boyle, Monika Schnarre, Joseph Maher. How Canada became involved with this cheap Hollywood gangster film is a leading question. Canadian participation in it appears to be nil. A prosperous hit man is not prepared to knock out a victim who wants to die. What happens next is of little interest.

Killer Image (1992) (95mins) d: David Winning s: Jaron Summers, Rudy Barichello, David Winning : M. Emmet Walsh, John Pyper-Ferguson, Michael Ironside, Krista Errickson. The director's second feature is a stylish exploitation movie about a corrupt U.S. senator and his psycho-killer brother—who are opposed by two other brothers, both of whom are photographers. Although set in Calgary, the film deliberately looks American.

Killer Instinct: see **Chatwill's Verdict**

Killing 'Em Softly: see **Man in 5A, The**

Killing Moon (1998) (88mins) (a Canada-U.S. film) d: John Bradshaw s: Tony Johnston : Kim Coates, Penelope Ann Miller, Daniel Baldwin, Diana Salvatore, Daniel Kash, Peter Outerbridge. A mysterious virus is found on a plane during a flight to Hawaii. Back on the ground, a scientist and his mysterious colleague have terrifying plans. Well done and frightening in its implications.

Killing Spring, A (2001) (120mins) d: Stephen Williams s: Jeremy Hole, Janet MacLean (from the novel by Gail Bowen) : Wendy Crewson, Shawn Doyle, Tom Keaton, Val Massey. When the dean of journalism at a college in eastern Canada is found dead of asphyxiation in an apparent attempt at auto-erotic suffocation, former police officer Joanne Kilbourn is brought in to investigate. Much to her surprise, she finds herself in a murky world of kinky sex, academic jealousies and ruthless ambitions at many levels. Soon after, the body count begins to multiply as Kilbourn finds herself at risk from a villain desperate to avoid being exposed as both a fraud and a killer. Chills and thrills abound, cleverly set out and followed up. The late *Inspector Morse* would have relished it. (See: *Mystery* series)

King Chronicle, The: Parts 1, 2 and 3 (1988) (300mins) d&s: Donald Brittain : Sean McCann. William Lyon Mackenzie King's legacy has a fascinating hold on Canada. He was prime minister for 22 years, longer than any other. This three-part dramatic series by Canada's master documentarist, Donald Brittain, recreates the period, the man, his personal life and political controversies with insight, humour and a keen understanding of human nature. Sean McCann gives a splendidly evocative performance of the man, our truly remarkable prime minister.

King of Fire (*Adramelech*) (1985) (80mins) d&s: Pierre Grégoire : Jacques Allard, Jean Petitclerc, Benoît Aumais, Roger Larue. A static and theatrical study of a dresser working on a play adapted from the Faust legend. After a while, he seems to become the Devil himself. Unfortunately, the film also leaves us very much in the dark.

King of Friday Night, The (1985) (88mins) d&s: Andrew Gosling : Eric Peterson, Frank MacKay, Geoffrey Bowes. Set in a Nova Scotia town, this three-character piece is a lively musical history of Screaming John, the "Ghost of Rock and Roll," whose presence provides the film with a reason to say something valid on the challenges life presents to the teenage generation.

King Solomon's Treasure (1979) (88mins) (a Canadian-British film) d: Alvin Rakoff s: Colin Turner & Allan Pryor (from the book *Allan Quartermain* by Rider Haggard) : John Colicos, David McCallum, Patrick MacNee, Britt Ekland, Yvon Dufour, Wilfred Hyde-White, Ken Gampu, John Quentin, Véronique Béliveau, Fiona Fraser. Three men search for treasures and dinosaurs in Africa. They find a Phoenician princess (which explains Britt Ekland's presence). Haggard would have been horrified! The producer should have stayed with the original story, and we might all have become richer.

King's Gambit (1985) (90mins) d: Carol Moore-Ede s: Donny Young : Robin Gammell. In this unusual and striking little film, we get a marvellous performance by Robin Gammell as Prime Minister Mackenzie King. He captures the man's eccentricities and sensible observations. Here, King comes to terms with a constitutional crisis during the mid-1920s.

King's Plate, The: see **British Quota Era Films**

Kingdom or the Asylum, The (Le royaume ou l'asile) (1989) (95mins) d&s: Jean and Serge Gagné : Roger Léger, Luc Proulx, Geneviève Rioux. On the road to the Saguenay, a motorcyclist meets a young woman, and they talk and think out loud about the differences between the 1960s and the 1980s. Nothing moves into high gear.

Kings and Desperate Men (1981) (118mins) d: Alexis Kanner s: Edmund Ward, Alexis Kanner : Patrick McGoohan, Alexis Kanner, Andrea Marcovicci, Margaret Trudeau, Budd Knapp, David Patrick, Robin Spry, Jean-Pierre Brown, Frank Moore, Neil Vipond, August Schellenberg. A talk-show host has his program disrupted when terrorists shout him down and demand the release of a comrade. As an ego trip for Kanner (*The Ernie Game*), who seems to have done everything during the making of this film, it's all rather feeble. Margaret Trudeau's first movie appearance.

Kingsgate (1989) (110mins) d&s: Jack Darcus : Christopher Plummer, Roberta Maxwell, Duncan Fraser, Elizabeth Dancoes, Allan Scarfe. Domestic warfare between the super-sophisticates: a tired professor, a cynical airline pilot, a tipsy wife, a super-cilious writer and a young student. This makes for a tiresome, brittle, unfunny film, although there are some laughs here and there.

Kinsey Report, The: see **One Plus One**

Kirby's Gander: see **Wings of Chance**

Kiss, The (1988) (98mins) (a Canadian-American film) d: Pen Densham s: Stephen Volk : Joanna Pacula, Meredith Salenger, Nicholas Kilbertus, Mimi Kuzyk, Jan Rubes. A terrible curse is passed on from one generation to the next by a woman-to-woman kiss. Not much fright in this tame horror.

Kissed (1996) (78mins) d: Lynne Stopkewich s: Angus Fraser, Lynne Stopkewich : Molly Parker, Peter Outerbridge, Jay Brazeau, Natasha Morley. A young necrophiliac goes to work as an embalmer at a funeral home. Soon, she experiences hot sexual desires for sex with the cold, dead, decaying males in her care. No wonder her boyfriend commits suicide. A ghoulish piece of depravity.

Kissinger and Nixon (1994) (120mins) d: Daniel Petrie s: Lionel Chetwynd (based on the book *Kissinger: A Biography* by Walter Isaacson) : Ron Silver, Beau Bridges, Matt Frewer, Ron White, George Takei, Kenneth Welsh. Daniel Petrie has translated Chetwynd's screenplay into a gripping and startling look at a chapter of history. Trying to depict the dynamics between Kissinger and Nixon during negotiations to end the Vietnam War could not have been an easy task. There are faults here, but not to the detriment of the whole. Ron Silver's Kissinger brings out the darkness of this man of mystery.

Kitchen Party (1997) (92mins) d&s: Gary Burns : Scott Speedman, Laura Harris, Gillian Barber, Kevin McNulty, Sarah Strange, Tygh Runyan. Wealthy, bored Alberta teenagers throw a party while their parents are being entertained at a neighbour's soiree. Supposedly a social satire, the whole is as tiresome as the characters portrayed. A few moments of humour may be found.

Klondike Fever (The Jack London Story) (1979) (118mins) d: Peter Carter s: Martin Lager, Charles Israel (from the book by Jack London) : Jeff East, Rod Steiger, Angie Dickinson, Lorne Greene, Barry Morse, Gordon Pinsent, Robin Gammell, Lisa Langlois, Michael Hogan. Adventures in Alaska, the Chilkoot Pass, Skagway, and into Dawson City during the Gold Rush days. Lively and colourful, filmed throughout B.C., with a cast of old reliables taking it in their stride—or, rather, in their sleighs.

Knock! Knock! (1985) (62mins) d: Bruce McDonald s: Daniel Brooks, Bruce McDonald : Daniel Brooks, Christie MacFadyen, Atom Egoyan, Donald Nijboer, Adrienne Mitchell, Kevan Buss. Cross Egoyan with McDonald and what have we? An obscurantist being driven mad by a punkster, with neither quite knowing what the other is doing. Luckily, it's too brief to venture far into tedium and boredom. A curio for the curious.

Knowing to Learn (Comment savoir) (1965) (71mins) d: Claude Jutra s: Jean Lemoyne : various students. An attempt to explain the effectiveness of technology in the classroom. Good for its time. As archival material showing us earlier efforts in technological advancement, this film is invaluable—like much of the NFB's work at the time. Furthermore, it brought a later-to-be-distinguished filmmaker, Claude Jutra, into our awareness.

Kootenai Brown: see **Showdown at Williams Creek**

Krapp's Last Tape (Beckett on Film series) (2000) (58mins) (a Canada-Ireland co-production) d: Atom Egoyan s: the play by Samuel Beckett : John Hurt. A feeble old man shambles around his dirty office lost in thought about his wasted, empty life. Beckett, the playwright, has many admirers, who consider him one of the theatre's great writers. He also has many detractors, who find his work is all much ado about nothingness and unbearable to sit through. So, those who like Beckett will like this film. Egoyan has simply filmed the play. It suits him well, being cold, boring and static. (See: *Happy Days*)

Ku qi de nu ren: see **Cry Woman**

Kurt Vonnegut's Harrison Bergeron (2000) (90mins) d: Bruce Pittman s: Arthur Crimm (based on Vonnegut's short story) : Sean Astin, Miranda DePencier, Christopher Plummer, Diana Reis, Buck Henry, Eugene Levy, Howard Mandel, Andrea Martin, Nigel Bennett, Peter Boretski. It is 2053, and there has been an official decree that the population must wear metallic headbands to receive electronic impulses designed to stifle synaptic signals, thus turning society into a mass of stupid people. To avoid this fate, a student tries desperately to underachieve in his studies. Spirited and properly frightening.

L'automne de la vie, À: see **At the Autumn of Life**
La croisée des chemins, À: see **Where Two Roads Cross**

Labour of Love (1985) (120mins) d&s: Richard Neilsen : Tom Butler, Michèle Scarabelli, Jim Bearden, Maury Chaykin. A union organizer is sent from Ottawa to Miramichi, New Brunswick, to negotiate on behalf of a group of mechanics who have gone on strike. A disturbing and revealing chronicle of union activities. Although not a documentary, it follows in the best of our documentary traditions.

Lac de la lune, Le (The Lake of the Moon) (1994) (90mins) d&s: Michel Jetté : Guy Provencher, Ronald Houle, Raymond Royer, André Lacoste, Claude Gai. Another introspective study detailing an old man's ruminations as he leaves the hospice he's been living in to think about life and death, dreams and reality. Among the many films treating the same kind of subject matter, this one is also very worthy.

Ladies Room (1999) (90mins) (a Canada-U.K. co-production) d: Gabriella Cristiani s: Leila Basen, Andrée Pelletier, Geneviève Lefebvre, Natalina Di Leandro, Amanda Roberts (based on an idea by Tony Roman) : John Malkovich, Lorraine Bracco, Greta Scacchi, Veronica Ferres, Molly Parker, Greg Thomey, Nanette Workman, Charlott Pitts, Adrianna Plitz, Amanda Roberts. The proceedings are set in a women's washroom in the theatre and opera, where actresses meet to gossip and bare their souls, thus giving the audience an insight into the way women think about their own lives, men, sex and motivations. In spite of all the lovely never-lost-for-words ladies, the result is flat, tiresome and of limited interest.

Lado oscuro del corazon, El: see **Dark Side of the Heart, The**

La-haut (Up There on the Mountain) (2002) (110mins) (b/w) (a Canada-France co-production) d: Pierre Schoendoerffer s: Pierre and Ludovic Schoendoerffer : Florence Darel, Bruno Cremer, Claude Rich, Jacques Perrin, Gérard Oury. In Paris, a young reporter begins an investigation into the psychological and historical aspects relating to the sudden disappearance of a filmmaker in the mountains of Thailand. Through the testimonies of many who knew him, the politics of the situation bring about some startling revelations. Another impressive work from Schoendoerffer, who has been working with such themes in his movies since 1956.

Lake of the Moon, The: see **Lac de la lune, Le**

Lakeboat (2000) (98mins) (a Canada-U.S. film) d: Joseph Mantegna s: David Mamet : Charles Durning, Peter Falk, Robert Forster, Roberta Angelica, Saul Rubinek. Actor Mantegna's first film as director is from a script by David Mamet about a college student learning of life from the world-weary crew of a freighter on the Great Lakes, whom he joins in his desire to learn more about people, their outlooks, and behaviour. Said to be a memoir of Mamet's own early days, this is an unusual film taking a voyage through a seafaring discovery of self and meaning.

Lakeswim: see **Kathy Karuks Is a Grizzly Bear**
Lampe dans la fenêtre, La: see **Cordélia**

Lana in Love (1991) (89mins) d: Bashar Shbib s: Daphna Kastner : Daphna Kastner, Clark Gregg, Ivan E. Roth, Susan Eyton-Jones. Lana puts an ad in the personals. She was expecting a doctor, but instead, Marty, a cocky, beer-guzzling plumber, shows up. She thinks he's the doctor that responded to her ad—a bit off the wall, with a tool kit and name patch on his shirt, but why be choosy? And Marty thinks a beautiful young woman is attempting to seduce him. When the real doctor makes his house call, life for Lana becomes even more complex. What follows is a hilarious affair of failed romance and twisted human relationships. With a good screenplay, this emerged as one of Bashar's better efforts.

Lantern Hill (1990) (109mins) (a Canada-U.S. co-production) d: Kevin Sullivan s: Fiona McHugh (based on Lucy Maud Montgomery's story *Jane of Lantern Hill*) : Mairon Bennett, Sam Waterston, Patrica Phillips, Zoe Caldwell, Colleen Dewhurst. Kevin Sullivan returns to in Lucy Maud Montgomery's *Green Gables* country, this time with the simple drama of a daughter who discovers that her father, whom she thought dead, is alive and working as a writer on Prince Edward Island. The light shines brightly here.

LAPD: To Protect and Serve (2001) (97mins) (a U.S.-Canada film) d: Edward Anders s: B.J. Davis, Rob Neighbors : Dennis Hopper, Michael Madsen, Charles Durning, Marc Singer, Wayne Crawford, Brenda James. Here we go again, with the underworld crooks and the crooked policemen. Audiences should be protected from this kind of sensational stuff. Filmed mostly in Toronto being passed off as Los Angeles, this is a tribute to "the most respected police force on the continent." It no doubt has many honest and efficient constables, but so do Canadian police forces, will there ever be a time when we'll make films identitfying Canadian police forces? Other than the RCMP of course!

Lapse of Memory: see *Mémoire tronquée*

Large Abode, A (Un grand logement) (1978) (61mins) (b/w) d&s: Mario Bolduc : Mario Davignon, Claire Bourbonnais, Geneviève Solomon, Nicole St-Pierre, Claude Champagne, Marie-Ginette Guay, Serge Dompierre. Concerned social-issue drama about a Québec family trying desperately to find a home, while working with a group reviewing housing requirements in their community.

Larose, Pierrot and Luce (Larose, Pierrot et Luce) (1982) (105mins) d&s: Claude Gagnon : Richard Niquette, Lou Matte, Louise Portal, Céline

Jacques. Three friends decide to turn away from the daily grind and rebuild a house left to one of them by his grandmother. A gentle and likeable film of personal discovery.

Last Act of Martin Weston, The (1971) (96mins) (a Canada-Czech co-production) d&s: Michael Jacot : Jon Granik, Milena Dvorska, Al Waxman, Nuala Fitzgerald. Filmed in Prague, a minor mystery about an engineer who rigs up his suicide, but we never really find out why. Bizarre and befuddled.

Last Betrothal, The (Les dernières fiançailles) (1973) (91mins) d&s: Jean-Pierre Lefebvre : Marthe Nadeau, J.-Léo Gagnon, Marcel Sabourin. Armand Tremblay, 78, and his wife, 75, have lived together for more than fifty years on a piece of land they cleared themselves. Their solitude is almost total, and their days are filled with the simple repetitive acts of working, eating, and sleeping. The film closes with their deaths. This is an unexpectedly tender, evocative, and entirely beautiful, moving, study portraying an ordinary existence as one of happiness and serenity, conveyed by Lefebvre's style of long takes, slow panning shots, and as a remarkable observant of real time.

Last Chapter (Biker Wars) (2002) (180 mins) (In 3 parts) d: Richard Roy s: Luc Dionne : Roy Dupuis, Michael Ironside, Marina Orsini. A frightening account of how the Quebec biker gang, *Hell's Angels*, invaded and expanded in Ontario in the late 2000. (Wrongly described as a sub-culture, even a culture, rather than what they are, deadly criminal elements destroying the society). This is otherwise an accurate portrait of deadly monsters from their clothing to their financial success, dirty deeds, comtempt for the police and their connection to the underworld and the Mafia. At times confusing, but a strong production never-the-less, calling by inference, for a stronger arm in justice.

Last Chase, The (1980) (105mins) (a Canada-U.S. film) d: Martyn Burke s: Burke, Christopher Crowe (from his story) : Lee Majors, Christopher Makepeace, Burgess Meredith, Alexandra Stewart, George Touliatos, Harvey Atkin, Hugh Webster, Trudy Young, Moses Znaimer, Douglas Lennox, Robert Christie. Travel by car has come to a stop as a result of the scarcity of oil. Twenty years later, a former racing car driver crosses the States as a symbol of freedom once oil supplies resume. This vehicle should never have left the garage. Its cast of passengers deserved a better trip.

Last Cry, The: see *Dernier cri*

Last Ferns, The: see *Dernières fougères, Les*

Last Glacier, The (Le dernier glacier) (1984) (84mins) d&s: Jacques Leduc, Roger Frappier : Robert Gravel, Louise Laprade, Martin Dumont, Michel Rivard, Marie St-Onge, Renato Battisti. Fiction blended with documentary makes this film a dramatic and moving depiction of the emotional and economic effect of the local iron ore mine's closure on the people of Shefferville, Québec.

Last Gunfighter, The: see **Hired Gun**

Last Night (1998) (94mins) d&s: Don McKellar : Don McKellar, Sandra Oh, Callum Keith Rennie, Sarah Polley, Geneviève Bujold, David Cronenberg. An exasperating and silly concoction of incidents in the lives of a disparate group of individuals in Toronto on the evening of the last day of the world. They seem to be interested in nothing other than turning over a streetcar and trying out new variations of sexual activity. They are all so dull that one couple commits suicide just seconds before the end. Why bother? The one good scene in these absurdly futile proceedings belongs to the delightful Geneviève Bujold, who, understandably, seems anxious to get away.

Last Run, The: see **Proud Rider, The**

Last Season, The (1987) (168mins) d: Alan Winton King s: Roy MacGregor (based on his novel of the same title) : Booth Savage, John Colicos, Eric Peterson. The dark side of hockey. A Polish-Canadian player from Northern Ontario has found his fame through the use of ugly force and violence. His career collapses and he returns home to his father, where his life is bedevilled by uncertainties and fantasies, leading to an early death. A study of human frailty perfectly realised.

Last Stop, The (1999) (92mins) (a Canada-US film) d: Mark Malone s: Bart Summer : Adam Beach, Jurgen Prochnow, Rose McGowan. An odd group of people find themselves snowbound in a café in Colorado. Is anyone surprised when a murder mystery begins to emerge between cups of coffee and piles of snow?

Last Straw, The (1987) (98mins) d: Giles Walker s: David Wilson, Giles Walker : Sam Grana, Beverley Murray, Stefan Wodoslawsky, Christine Pak, Walter Martin, Patricia Phillips, Maurice Podbrey. This is the sequel to *90 Days*, in which Alex Rossi, the sperm donor, becomes a natural resource for women. Unfunny and unpleasant.

Last Supper, The (1994) (95mins) d: Cynthia Roberts s: Hillar Liitoja (adapted from his play) : Ken McDougall, Jack Nicholsen, Daniel MacIvor. Ken McDougall, re-playing his stage role, takes the part of Chris, a brilliant dancer who is terminally ill with aids and confined to his bed. He stages the final moments of his life and with his lover relives some of their happy times together. Filmed in real time, he died after the completion of the film. Cynthia Roberts takes us on a dignified and visceral visit.

Last Train Home, The (1990) (95mins) d: Randy Bradshaw s: Jeremy Hole : Noam Zylberman, Ron White, Nick Mancuso. Some familiar faces are to be found hanging around for the last train, which never seems to come, as the famous Mountie, Inspector Sam Steele, continues his search for a father and son who are suspected of being murderers. This train's journey lacks excitement, and could be more involving.

Last Wedding, The (2001) (100mins) d&s: Bruce Sweeney : Benjamin Ratner, Frida Betrani, Thomas Scholte, Nancy Sivak, Vincent Gale, Molly Parker, Babz Chula. After a promising opening in which a mother is helping her daughter decide what kind of gown she should buy for her wedding, this clumsily improvised film degenerates into an unpleasant and ugly portrayal of the collapse of the marriages of three couples into an orgy of screaming, fighting, and fornication in a four-letter life. Without heart or depth, with minds in the gutter instead. Could this be a last film, perhaps? Praise be that Virginia and Edward endure!

Last Winter, The (1989) (104mins) d&s: Aaron Kim Johnston : Gerard Parkes, Joshua Murray, David Ferry, Wanda Cannon. Set in rural Manitoba in the mid-1950s, this is another sentimental family story in which a young boy is distressed by his father's plans to leave the country to seek a better life in the city. Naturally and imaginatively told.

Lathe of Heaven (2002) (120mins) (a U.S.-Canada film) d: Philip Haas s: Alan Sharp (based on the novel by Ursula K. LeGuin) : Lukas Haas, James Caan, Lisa Bonet, David Strathairn, Sheila McCarthy. A mild-mannered man is cursed with the ability to alter reality through dreams. This drives him to the brink of suicide. Whatever he dreams about at night becomes real for him the next day. Far from being just another sci-fi nightmare, this is a thoughtful consideration of love in a world that is ever changing and how, for some, trusting one's heart and mind becomes a form of philosophy that endures above all else. Well characterized and stated.

Latitude 55 (1982) (102mins) d: John Juliani s: Sharon Riis, John Juliani : Andrée Pelletier, August Schellenberg. A two-character play on film intended to be a philosophical study of a strange encounter between a young woman, the cultural representative for Alberta, and a Polish potato farmer who might also be a mystic. Interesting but the exploration becomes somewhat trying.

Laura Cadieux, la Suite (Laura's Back!) (2000) (99mins) d&s: Denise Filiatrault : Ginette Reno, Pierrette Robitaille, Denise Dubois, Dominique Michel, Adele Reinhart, Raymond Bouchard, Martin Drainville, Samuel Landry. When we first met Laura and her friends in their doctor's waiting room talking about their lives as overweight women, there was little joy to be found, yet their humour was high, sharp, funny and observant. And now they are back. Laura has won a trip on a cruise ship going down the St. Lawrence River. It is her 55th birthday, and all her friends buy tickets to accompany her. What follows is a truly joyful picture, sometimes perhaps a little too happy, but never so much as to spoil this mar-vellous film by the marvellous Denise Filiatrault. All roles, including those of the captain and the captain of a Russian ship, are perfectly cast, and Ginette Reno excels as the mother and wife. There are honest moments of affection and feelings in this high comedy, and the colours, music, scenery, atmosphere and passengers are captivating. (see: *It's Your Turn, Laura Cadieux*)

Laura Laur (1988) (92mins) d&s: Brigitte Sauriol (based on the novel by Suzanne Jacob) : Paula de Vasconcelos, Dominique Briand, Éric Cabana, André Lacoste. Who is the mysterious, complex, elusive, beautiful and unruly Laura? Her impenetrable character, whom those she mixes with find fascinating, remains an enigma. Audiences would probably like to find out why, but answers are not forthcoming. A good cast in an attractive but trying film.

Laura's Back!: see *Laura Cadieux, La Suite*

Laure Gaudreault: A Remarkable Woman (Rencontre avec une femme remarquable: Laure Gaudreault) (1983) (89mins) d&s: Iolande Cadrin-Rossignol : Louisette Dussault, Nicholas Marier, Marie Michaud, Lise Castonguay, Marie-France Desrochers, Joanne Edmond. A well-made and dedicated study of the life of Laure Gaudreault (played superbly by Louisette Dussault), a journalist, teacher and union organizer in Montréal during the 1930s, and of her work for the women's movement, and improved conditions for rural teachers.

Law of Enclosures, The (2000) (111mins) d&s: John Greyson (from the novel by Dale Peck) : Sarah Polley, Brendan Fletcher, Diane Ladd, Sean McCann, Kristen Thomson, Rob Stefaniuk, Shirley Douglas, Victor Cowie. Sandwiched between the oil wells of Sarnia, Ontario, and the Persian Gulf War on television, this is an odd story, being the director's first move from "gay" films to so-called conventional screen drama. We go back to 1991 to meet a young teenage couple: a pleasant girl and an odi-ous-looking boy who is said to have AIDS but then doesn't have it. The two find they have been given the gift of life together when the boy finds out that he only had a tumour, cured by an operation. In the meantime, we see the good people of Sarnia gathering for their annual Biggest Kiss contest. All very dour and somewhat desperate. There are truths here and there, and much boredom in between. A good cast keeps the whole from breaking up.

Law of the Jungle: see **Street Law**

Leaving Metropolis (2002) (90mins) d&s: Brad Fraser (based on his play *Poor Super Man*) : Troy Ruptash, Vincent Corazza, Lynda Boyd, Cherilee Taylor, Thom Allison. A somewhat tiresome and predictable carry-on about a group of assorted characters whose tangled, messy lives revolve around meetings in a café. We come to hear about their various emotional, medical, sexual and other confusions. Hardly worth the visit.

Lebedyne ozero-zona: see **Swan Lake: The Zone**

Left-hand Side of the Fridge, The (*La moitié gauche du frigo***)** (2000) (89mins) d&s: Philippe Falardeau : Paul Ahmarani, Stéphane Demers, Geneviève Néron. Antoine, a would-be film director, decides to make a *cinéma-vérité* record of the daily life of his roommate Christophe, who has been out of work for three months. Soon Antoine is wandering away from *vérité* to help shape his friend's life so that it becomes more a fiction, with the director finding he's actually making a documentary about himself—or at least it seems this way. This is a lovely little film, cool and wise and funny with a lot to say about human nature as it manifests itself in the life and work of two friends. Maybe the best Québec film of the year.

Legal Memory (1992) (80mins) d&s: Lisa Steele, Kim Tomczak : Lisa Steele, Rosy Frier Dryden, Geoff Naylor. In a style blending documentary and narrative techniques with experimental overtones, this unusual film takes the form of an inquiry into the life of a man convicted of murder and who became the last man to be hanged in British Columbia, in 1959.

Legend of Kootenai Brown, The (1990) (100mins) d: Allan Kroeker s: John Gray : Donnelly Rhodes, Tom Burlinson, Michelle Thrush, Stephen Miller, John Pyper-Ferguson. Films about Canada's fascinating western history are few and far between. All the more regrettable, then, that this true story of John Brown, an Anglo-Irishman who joined the gold rush to seek his fortune, doesn't come to life as vividly as one would expect. The narrative is often confusing and hard to believe, the rewarding moments few in number.

Legend of Sleepy Hollow, The (1999) (120mins) d: Pierre Gang s: Joe Wiesenfeld : Brent Carver, Rachelle Lefevre, Paul Lemelin, Michael Perron, Dawn Daen Ford. Ichabod Crane, a Yankee wanderer, arrives in Sleepy Hollow and becomes the new schoolmaster. He meets Katrina and loves her, but also her money. But the local blacksmith also loves Katrina, and to scare Ichabod away, he dresses as the legendary Headless Horseman. But it's the real ghost who appears and drives Ichabod away. The legend lives again, and this charming and delightful version should be around for some time.

Legend of Wolf Lodge, The (Into the Fire) (1989) (88mins) d: Graeme Campbell s: Jessie Ballard : Susan Anspach, Art Hindle, Lee Montgomery. A stable mate to *Caribe*, this is a puerile piece of worn-out plot in the horror and evil category.

Legends of the North (1996) (95mins) (a Canada-France film) d: René Manzor s: Robert Geoffrion : Randy Quaid, Sandrine Holt, Georges Corraface, Serge Houde, Macha Grenon, John Dunn-Hill. Three mismatched partners go into the remote parts of the Yukon to search for a legendary lake of gold. Cold and unconvincing, a tiresome journey from a Jack London story.

Legends of the North (series): see *Aventures du grand nord, Les*

Léger vertige, Un: see *Part des choses, La*

Len Deighton's Bullet to Beijing: see **Bullet to Beijing**

Léolo (1992) (107mins) d&s: Jean-Claude Lauzon : Maxime Collin, Ginette Reno, Julien Guiomar, Giuditta del Vecchio, Pierre Bourgault, Roland Blouin This beautifully filmed, semi-autobiography by Lauzon is about his family life set in Quebec. As Léolo tries to make sense of his eccentric family, expressed is both the wretchedly-absurd and touching aspects of growing up. Lauzon nearly ruins it though, with an offensive scene involving Leolo impregnating a cat. Why? And how unnecessary.

Leopard in the Snow (1978) (94mins) (a Canada-U.K. co-production) d: Gerry O'Hara s: Ann Mather, Jill Hyem (from the novel by Ann Mather) : Keir Dullea, Susan Penhaligon, Kenneth More, Billie Whitelaw, Jeremy Kemp, Yvonne Manners, Gordon Thomson. Keir Dullea, the favourite American actor of Canadian producers at this time, leads a cast of British players through this first movie produced by the publishers of Harlequin paperbacks, the romantic story of an English girl who falls for an American. For those who read the book, it's all love on the screen.

Lesson in Love, A: see **Circle of Two**

Let Me Go: see *Tu as crié*

Let's Talk About Love (*Parlez-nous d'amour***)** (1976) (127mins) d: Jean-Claude Lord s: Michel Tremblay, Jean-Claude Lord : Jacques Boulanger, Benoît Girard, Claude Michaud, Monique Mercure, Denis Drouin, Guy L'Écuyer, Gabriel Arcand, Pierre Curzi, Henry Gamer and 80 others. A somewhat far-fetched comedy about a popular host of a tv talk show for women who finds himself being destroyed by his own popularity. Tremblay's fine mind is everywhere, however, when the exploitation, greed and cynicism of television producers becomes apparent.

Letter From New France, A (*Le trésor de Nouvelle France***)** (1979) (88mins) d&s: Vincent Davy : Louis-Charles Chartrand, Catherine Dufourd, Éric Leclercq, Sophie Maheu, Daniel Scott, Madeleine Barbulée. Five Québécois children work together trying to find a lost treasure of gold coins. With the help of an elderly native man, they find the box that held the coins, but it is empty, the coins having been sent to France. Disappointed, they begin looking for further treasures. A charming and enthusiastic children's film.

Liar's Edge (1992) (95mins) (a Canada-U.S. film) d&s: Ron Oliver : Nick Sheilds, David Keith, Shannon Tweed, Joseph Bottoms, Christopher Plummer. A realistic if somewhat overdone melodrama set on the seedy edges of Niagara Falls and concerning a family living in a trailer and hoping for better things. Violence, however, is the order of the day.

Liens de sang, Les: see **Blood Relatives**

Lies My Father Told Me (1975) (103mins) d: Jan Kadar s: Ted Allan (from his original story) : Yossi Yadin, Len Birman, Marilyn Lightstone, Jeffrey Lynas, Ted Allan, Barbara Chilcott, Henry Ramer, Carole Lazare, Rolland Bédard, Raymond Benoît, Bertrand Gagnon, Guy L'Écuyer, E.M. Margolese, Les Nirenberg, Howard Ryshpan, Jean Dubost, Judith Gault, Sylvie Heppel, Victor Knight, Diana Leblanc, Harry Mayerovitch, David Raboy, Norman Taviss, Ruth Thomas. A young boy remembers his youth and grandfather in old Montréal. Overly sentimental and unevenly directed with compromises made in editing and post-production, this film is nonetheless sensitive and intelligent. It is a wonder, however, that the film was finished at all. Started with great optimism and much fanfare with the signing of Czech director Jan Kadar, the film went over budget, started and stopped, and was in and out of production for three years before its premiere—and was then received with mixed blessings!

Life, A (1988) (75mins) d&s: Frank Cole : Anne Miquet, Heather O'Dwyer, Abderranhmane Ghris, Mr. and Mrs. Fred Howard. In this self-examination, Frank Cole goes deeply into his study of life and death, which he experienced in preparing to walk across the Sahara in 1985. Certainly well off the beaten track!

Life After Love (*La vie après l'amour*) (2000) (105mins) d: Gabriel Pelletier s: Kenneth Scott : Norman Helms, Patrick Huard, Yves Jacques, Denis Mercier, Kenneth Scott, Sylvie Léonard, Guylaine Tremblay. After twenty years of a seemingly blissful marriage, a wife decides to leave her husband. This is a blow for him, and what follows is an often very funny chronicle of what he does to give meaning to his new life. Soon he feels madness overtaking him when it seems his wife will return to become part of his life again. Refreshing, different and under the laughs and disappointments may be found an unerring understanding of life.

Life and Times of Alonzo Boyd, The (1982) (97mins) d: Leslie Rose s: Gordon Pinsent : Gordon Pinsent, Mary Ann McDonald, Karen Kennedy, Jack Langhorn. A dramatized documentary in which the talented actor-writer Gordon Pinsent plays both narrator and principal character in this unusually structured, effective retelling of the exploits of the Boyd gang, who robbed Toronto banks in the early 1950s. Gripping, with authentic locations.

Life and Times of Chester-Angus Ramsgood, The (1971) (60mins) d&s: David Curnick : Robert Matson, Mary Beth McGuffin, Michael Storeoff, Judi Sommer, Craig Peterson, Janet Pollack. Broad and flat-out minor sex comedy filmed in Vancouver about friends and lovers, misunderstandings and difficult relationships. Passable.

Life Before This, The (1999) (94mins) d: Jerry Ciccoritti s: Semi Chellas : Catherine O'Hara, Joe Pantoliano, Sarah Polley, Steven Rea. A neighbourhood café is filled with strangers who, it seems, are in search of a plot, but they can't find it and nor can we. But every choice they make may well lead to their death. Who cares? Slick and superficial

Life Blossoms: see *Craque la vie*

Life Classes (1987) (117mins) d&s: William MacGillivray : Jacinta Cormier. Set in Nova Scotia, this is a marvellous film introducing us to Mary Cameron and her growth from a quiet girl in a small and sleepy town to a lively artist in the city. On the way, she makes some pertinent discoveries about working within a selfish technological society. This is also a biting comment on what passes as art today. Jacinta Cormier strikes the right notes throughout. A long film which never falters.

Lifeforce Experiment, (The Breakthrough) (1994) (a Canada-U.K. co-production) (120mins) d: Piers Haggard s: Mike Hodges, Gerard MacDonald (based on the novella *Breakthrough* by Daphne du Maurier) : Donald Sutherland, Mimi Kuzyk, Corin Nemec, Haley Reynolds, Miguel Fernandes. A CIA agent arrives one dark night on a sea-pounded coast to a collection of strange yet impressive futuristic buildings. Her assignmentis to meet with scientists, to find out what they are up to. She almost immediately becomes part of their strange experiments. The chief, our very own Donald, hiding behind a massive beard, is amicable, makes her comfortable on a couch and puts her in a trance. His studio is a maze of screens, super computers, strange pictures, soft voices giving instructions, and more "things to come" stuff than H.G. Wells ever thought of. Her brain appears on the screens, and from them shadowy shapes emerge as the computers begin to visualise in pictures the thoughts and memories going through her mind. What this is all about, he explains to her, are not to be thought of as intrusive computer techniques, but the capture, from people facing death, of the energy of the life force, a new source of immortality, and so on … well, it may be bunk, but it cannot be denied that it is frightening and altogether plausible. The special effects serve the story well and are remarkable, with first rate acting and creation of atmosphere. Filming was done in Montreal and Nova Scotia. Need one add, being passed off as Europe. The agent's name is Jessica but this is not "Murder She Wrote."

Life in the Balance (2001) (95mins) (a U.S.-Canada film) d: Adam Weissman s: Paul Koval : Stewart Bick, Bo Derek, Jonathan Higgins, Bruce Boxleitner. A convoluted piece about a lawyer addicted to prescription drugs who gets the chance to redeem her reputation when hired to defend a man in prison awaiting execution for murder. Set in the U.S., of course. Nothing really matters from beginning to end. The law is very dry here.

Life Is Beautiful: see *For Those I Loved*

Lifeline to Victory (1993) (95mins) d: Eric Till s: Tony Sheer : Michael Riley, Simon Reynolds. There are few films made about Canada's armed forces, during war or peace. This is a particularly welcome telling that tells of the corvette HMCS Fireweed on its maiden voyage from Halifax, Nova Scotia, to Liverpool during World War II, and the difficulties that befell the inexperienced crew. Made to coincide with the 50th anniversary of the Battle of the Atlantic, it is a gripping and forceful chronicle from the past that leaves us with much to admire about dedication to duty.

Life of a Hero, The (*La vie d'un héros*) (1994) (104mins) d&s: Micheline Lanctôt : Gilbert Sicotte, Véronique Le Flaguais, Marie Cantin, Christopher MacCabe, Erwin Potitt. An extremely controversial film from the distinguished Lanctôt that did not sit well with many viewers. Set on a farm in the Eastern Townships of Québec during World War II, where a German POW is sent to work, the director attempts to explore the strange effects this arrogant yet sympathetically portrayed German soldier has on three generations of Québec women. Told with flashbacks, the narrative becomes confused and the sentiments perverse. The director's view of this difficult period is ambiguous.

Life of Charles Pathé, The: see *Ou le roman de*

Life of Willie Lamothe (Documentary) (60mins) d: Jean Beaudin. Five 60-minute films called Willie. In remembrance of this tremendously popular singer-musician with the people of Quebec, and played here by another popular country music star, Luc Guerin. Lamothe appeared in many Quebec films.

Life With Billy (1993) (90mins) d: Paul Donovan s: John Frizzell, Judith Thompson : Stephen McHattie, Nancy Beatty. The true and disturbing account of a woman in an abusive marriage who has killed her husband. Her trial in Liverpool, Nova Scotia, brought to light the extent of family violence and made legal history when she was found not guilty. The film is concerned mainly with the trial, but shows in flashback the events leading to the death of Billy Stafford. Troubling, direct and touching in its realism.

Lift, The (1965) (85mins) d&s: Burton Krancer : Job Stewart, Helen Ryan, Holly Doone, Alistair Williamson, Shirley Rogers. Made by Julius Rascheff (a Bulgarian) and Diederik d'Ailly (a Frenchman), both living in Toronto and who had made *Lydia* (in Greece), Gordon Pinsent's first film. Next, they went to London with European money and an American director to make *The Lift*, which one might call the typical hybrid Canadian film. An absurd and chaotic story of sex and deceit in London among a group of womanizing businessmen and innocent young women. The location photography by Rascheff is the picture's main attraction. In the end, it went nowhere, and Rascheff and d'Ailly left Canada to teach filmmaking in the U.S. See: *Lydia*.

Light Vertigo, A: see *Part des choses, La*

Lightheaded: see *Léger vertige, Un*

Lighthouse (1989) (90mins) d: Paul Tucker s: Boon Collins : Ryan Michael, Deborah Wakeham. A loving couple takes a holiday at a remote lighthouse on the BC coast. Much to their consternation, they find themselves possessed by the souls of two previous lovers who were murdered there. A chilly thriller, with not much light!

Lightly: see **Bayo**

Lights of My City (*Lumières de ma ville*) (1950) (126mins) d: Jean-Yves Bigras s: Jean-Marie Poirier : Guy Maufette, Huguette Oligny, Pierre Berval, Monique Leyrac, Albert Duquesne, Maurice Gauvin, Denyse Proulx. A lighthearted and amusing romance dealing with the affairs of a nightclub singer, a composer, and an author, in an attempt to create a touch of easygoing post-war entertainment.

Ligne de chaleur, La: see **Heat Line, The**

Ligne interdite: see **Phone Call, The**

Like a Thief: see *Comme un voleur*

Like the Six Fingers of a Hand (*Comme les six doigts de la main*) (1978) (74mins) d&s: André Melançon : Éric Beauséjour, Philippe Bouchard, Caroline Larouche, Daniel Murray. Actor Melançon wrote and directed this minimalist story about a group of no-goods, with the newest member of their gang spying on an old man in his house.

Lilac Dream (1987) (74mins) d: Marc Voizard s: Julian Roffman : Dack Rambo, Susan Almgren, Walter Massey, Arthur Grosser. A young man suffering from amnesia is very much in love with a woman, and all is going well between them, with romance brightening his days—until, that is, the wife he had forgotten comes back into his life. But true love will always find a way! (See: *Shades of Love* series)

Lilies (1996) (95mins) d: John Greyson s: Michel-Marc Bouchard, Linda Gaboriau : Jason Cadieux, Brent Carver, Alexander Chapman, Ian D. Clark, Gary Farmer. In 1952, Bishop Bilodeau is called to hear an aging prisoner's confession concerning three youths in 1912. When he hears their names, the Bishop recognizes his own life story. Other prisoners then perform a play about what actually happened, and the Bishop begins, trance-like, to move back and forward between the stage and the village where the events described took place. If only it was this straightforward. This complicated, unbelievable and impossible concoction is notable mainly for some frequently beautiful photography.

Lilly (1993) (105mins) (b/w) d&s: David Marcoux (based on his play) : Shelly Long, Deanne Judson, Shirley Cui. An odd story about a young Asian girl who goes to the police to claim the body of a murdered man, insisting that he was her lover. The evidence shows, however, that the girl may have been the murderer. The intentions here are better than the results.

Limites du ciel, Les: see **Sky's the Limit, The**

Lion of Oz (2000) (75mins) d: Timothy Deacon s: Roger Baum (based on his novel of the same title and *The Badge of Courage*, with credit to Frank Baum) : Timothy Curry, Lynn Redgrave, Jason Priestly. A circus lion is awarded a Badge of Courage and, together with his admirers and followers, he goes off to see the Wizard. A pleasing family film, but one misses Bert Lahr.

Lions for Breakfast (1975) (98mins) d: William Davidson s: Martin Lager : Danny Forbes, Jim Henshaw, Jan Rubes, Susan Petrie, Paul Bradley, William Osler, Frank Moore. Two brothers go searching in the Ontario countryside looking for a change to their lives. A highly enjoyable film for young audiences.

Lip Service (2001) (93mins) (a Canada-U.S. film) d&s: Graeme Campbell : Stewart Bick, Peter Outerbridge, Gail O'Grady. A slight showbiz plot about a music producer who signs up a tantalizing but no-talent singer and then discovers a singing star. Pleasant, if somewhat piffling.

List, The (2000) (91mins) (a U.S.-Canada film) d: Sylvain Guy s: Marcel Giroux, Sylvain Guy : Madchen Amick, Roc Lafortune, Ben Gazzara, Catherine Blythe, Ryan O'Neal, Romano Orzari, Daniel Pilon. A sex-thrill piece, somewhat on the dull side, about a call girl who blackmails her wealthy client after she is arrested for solicitation. No lack of bad language. (Note: This comic strip chronicle is a remake, in English, using Hollywood players, of *Black List (Liste noire)* (1995) also filmed in Montréal. It is the first Québec (French-language) film to be remade in English with U.S. actors set in the US). See *Black List*.

Listen to the City (1984) (77mins) d&s: Ron Mann (from the story by Bill Schroeder) Authors, filmmakers and artists talking about life and work in general. Interesting to hear what they have to say. Imaginative editing.

Lit, Le (The Bed) (*Le plumard en folie*) (1974) (87mins) (a Canada-France co-production) d&s: Jacques Lemoine : Alice Sapritch, Michel Galabru, Jean Lefebvre, Anna Gael, Willie Lamothe, Denise Filiatrault. This is a bed unlike all others. One day, the bed breaks down under the rough treatment it receives from uncouth guests. A new one is ordered and, being a living character, the old bed settles down and tells the pretty maid about all the people who slept on him/her, from amorous young teenagers to the old and grumpy and the many in between. As a comedy, it's a welcome laughable change.

Little Aurore's Tragedy (*La petite Aurore, l'enfant martyre*) (1952) (102mins) d: Jean-Yves Bigras s: Émile Asselin : Yvonne Laflame, Lucie Mitchell, Paul Desmarteaux, Jeannette Bertrand, Jean Lajeunesse, Roch Poulin, J.-Léo Gagnon, Lucie Poitras, Adrien Laurion, Andrée Poitras, Pierrette Legard. A wrenching psychological study of a woman's hatred of her stepchild, based on an actual case in which a child was cruelly murdered after years of suffering and torture. The opening of this remarkable and honest film was supposed to have been on November 10, 1951, but was cancelled

when the family involved obtained an injunction against its showing. It finally opened on April 25, 1952, at Montréal's Saint-Denis cinema, where nearly all Québec-made films opened during the formative years of the 1950s.

Little Boy Blues (2000) (75mins) d: David Gonella s: Aaron Pearl : Patrick Stevenson, Aaron Pearl, Christopher Shyer, Chris Bradford, Adam Beach, Rebecca Harker. Set in Saskatchewan, four brawling, smoking, drinking, swearing, fighting young men leave by van to travel to B.C. to find a place for themselves in today's society. One of them goes mad, and not to wonder. It's a nightmare of a journey, which the actors play to the hilt, and few audiences are likely to enjoy.

Little Canadian, The (1955) (74mins) d&s: Melburn Turner : Wallace Havelock Robb, Robert Agar, Diane MacMillan, Edythe Millman, Ronald Grant, Gary Evani, Margaret Shortliffe, George Grant, Airlie Robb, Allan Anderson, William Angus, Kerrie Meek, Kevin Robert, David William. Rustic comedy about an eccentric writer living in the country and a youth who marries his daughter. All rather limp and predictable, but another well-intentioned 1950s effort to make films in Ontario. Filmed around Kingston.

Little Criminals (1996) (120mins) d: Stephen Surjik s: Dennis Foon : Brendan Fletcher, Myles Ferguson. One of the first social portraits of crimes committed by children, this dark commentary and observation follows two 11-year-old boys on a rampage of arson, theft and vandalism. Unrelentingly grim, it raises many questions. The answers, difficult to come by, perhaps, are not to be found here. Vancouver is the background, but only if audiences recognize it.

Little Girl Who Lives Down the Lane, The (1977) (94mins) (a Canada-France co-production) d: Nicolas Gessner s: Laird Koenig (from his novel) : Jodie Foster, Alexis Smith, Martin Sheen, Mort Shuman, Scott Jacoby, Julie Wildman. Another in the growing number, at this time, of pseudo-American tax-shelter films, this one a complicated murder mystery about a 13-year-old girl, her strange father, and a child-molesting son, with nasty complications. Immoral and immaterial. Filmed in the countryside around Knowlton, Québec.

Little Kidnappers, The (1990) (94mins) (a Canada-U.S. co-production) d: Donald Shebib s: Coralee Elliott : Charlton Heston, Bruce Greenwood, Leo Wheatly, Charles Miller, Patricia Gage, Leah Pinsent. A story about two young orphaned boys who find a baby and keep it when their grandfather refuses to let them have a dog. Set in Nova Scotia. The original *Kidnappers* was a hugely popular British film made in 1953, and partially shot in Canada.. To remake it was an unenviable task. Under the circumstances, the result is agreeable, but with a lost charm.

Little Man Abroad, A (*Tilom Aletranje: le petit homme a l'étranger*) (1989) (90mins) d&s: Fayolle Jean : Pyrrhus Dessaint, Numa Innocent, Yole

Lablanc, Francis Nelson. A documentary-like drama about the dreams, hopes, fears and challenges of peasant Haitian immigrants to Québec.

Little One Is Coming Soon, The (Le p'tit vient vite) (1972) (96mins) d: Louis-Georges Carrier s: Yvon Deschamps : Yvon Deschamps, Denise Filiatrault, Janine Suto, Hélène Loiselle, Denis Drouin, Magali Noël, Juliette Huot, Jacques Bilodeau. A married couple have a baby only eight months after their marriage, and they worry about what his boss, the wife's father, will think of such behaviour. A mild but engaging comedy based on Georges Feydeau's farcical play of manners, *Léonie est en avance*.

Little Tougas (The Kid Tougas) (Ti-Cul Tougas) (1976) (83mins) d&s: Jean-Guy Noël : Micheline Lanctôt, Suzanne Garceau, Claude Maher, Gilbert Sicotte, Louise Forestier, Guy L'Écuyer, Gabriel Arcand. Low-key robbery drama about a man who steals thousands of dollars from a project payroll in a business enterprise. He leaves with his girlfriend and another man turns up to retrieve the cash, but they tell him they do not have it, leading to a restrained pursuit from the Îles de la Madeleine to Prince Edward Island and on to California. Here, matters come to a deadly confrontation. Handily done.

Little White Lies (1988) (75mins) d: Susan Martin s: Marilyn Lightstone : Duncan Regehr, Linda Smith, Susan Almgren, Bernard Behrens. A young detective uses her life savings to buy a ticket to Rome. On the flight over, she meets a doctor. For reasons not revealed until late in the plot, they fall in love but lie about their professions. When they return, they must hide their little white lies and not let either know who's who, out of fear they will lose each other. Amusing and romantic. (See: *Shades of Love* series)

Littlest Hobo: see *Deux amis silencieux*

Live Bait (1995) (84mins) d&s: Bruce Sweeney : Tom Scholte, Micki Maunsell, Babz Chula, Kevin McNulty, Jay Brazeau, David Lovgren, Laara Sadiq. A charming and original picture from a young Vancouver filmmaker who studied with Mike Leigh, this is a tale of summer life in the well-to-do suburbs, concerning a young man who gets nowhere with the girls of his age, but then meets an older woman who teaches him about love and sex. (The title is unfair to the film).

Live Through This (2000) (60mins) (a Canada-U.S. co-production) d: John L'Écuyer s: George Huang, Bernard Lechowick (from a story by Karen Krenas and Brian Strause) : Jane McGregor, Jessica Welch, Sarah Manninen, Tom Lock, Matthew Carey, Bruce Dinsmore, David Nerman, Jennifer Dale, Ronald Lea. A well-written and characterized drama revolving around young people and their love of popular music. A reunion tour brings the younger ones back together with parents and others. Altogether, this is

an enjoyable film with Jennifer Dale once again proving her worth as a solo artist who has been battling her own demons.

Lives of Girls and Women, The (1996) (120mins) d: Ronald Wilson s: Charles K. Pitts, Kelly Rebar (based on the novel by Alice Munro) : Tanya Allen, Wendy Crewson, Kate Hennig, Liisa Repo-Martell, Dean McDermott. The coming of age of a young woman growing up in the repressive surroundings of 1940s small-town Ontario. This is a gentle statement about a teenager who suffers the embarrassment of having a mother whose views are far ahead of her time. One of Canada's literary treasures is given sympathetic and affecting treatment here.

Loi du cochon, La (The Pig's Law) (2001) (95mins) d: Erik Canuel s: Joanne Arseneau : Isabel Richer, Sylvain Marcel, Catherine Trudeau, Jean-Nicolas Verreault, Stéphane Demers, Marie Brassard. A 27-year-old woman is a compulsive gambler. She grows marijuana for two criminals on land that includes a pigsty inherited from her father. She hopes to make money from the harvest to pay debts at the bank and secure her ownership of the property. There are countless other complications. This is the director's first film, and in his words, it has "touched on important themes in human relationships while not losing its genuine sense of entertainment." Sorry to disagree, but "entertainment"? This unpleasant picture is one of incessant depravity, violence and brutality. All characters but one are ugly, coarse and quarrelsome. In the film is in French, so the usual flood of F-words comes to us in English subtitles. Watch *Act of Grace*, instead.

Lola (2001) (97 min) d&s: Carl Bessai : Sabrina Grdevich, Colm Feore, Ian Tracey, Joanna Going, Janet Wright. The second installment of Bessai's soon-to-be trilogy (see *Johnny*). A flighty and irresponsible Lola struggles to find a focus in life. An argument with her exasperated boyfriend makes for an encounter with a free-spirited girl. Along comes an intriguing twist and Lola embarks on an adventure into self-realization. Characters and dialogue ring true. Courageously subtle.

Lola Zipper (1991) (91mins) (a Canada-France co-production) d&s: Ilan Duran Cohen : Judith Reval, Jean-Paul Comart, Arielle Dombasle, François Perrot, Tom Rack. A young man working in a show business office in Paris is dismissed on grounds of incompetence. To show his bosses what he is capable of, he takes one of the young performers who failed to find a job, Lola Zipper, and makes a star of her. Superficially pleasant.

Lolo's Child (2002) (85mins) d&s: Romeo Candido : Romeo Candido, Stephanie Comilang, Jayson Camat, Steven Comilang, Yvette Leano. A one-man-band multi-cultural Filipino-Canadian melo-drama and comedy, with music, ti moves around a clan's epic wake for a dead patriarch. Rivalries, relatives, fantasies, and karaoke moments, keep this strange tableau with lots of technical tricks, from dissolving into empty exuberance.

Lone Eagle: see **Blood of the Hunter**

Long Day's Journey Into Night (1996) (174mins) d: David Wellington : Martha Henry, William Hutt, Tom McCamus, Peter Donaldson, Martha Burns. The Stratford (Ontario) Festival production of the Eugene O'Neill play concerning the trials and tribulations of the Tyrone family comes to the screen with its superlative original cast. When a film record is made of a play, it is usually filmed during a performance or at one specially staged without an audience. Whatever the circumstances, the film director plans out the angles and close-ups and uses cameras accordingly and as unobtrusively as possible, should an audience be present. David Wellington decided to build an expensive set in a studio, with the original actors moving in under his direction. In what sense then does this become a film of the original performance? Not at all. So we end up with half a journey into night. Even stranger, Wellington decides to use wide screen when the obvious market for such a film is television. With O'Neill hardly being a box-office draw, the film drew a small cinema audience and then became squashed for TV. The best that can be said is that the cast is, of course, magnificent, but the spark of theatre creativity is considerably muted. This entire enterprise is an expensive failure. See also: *A Long Day's Journey* (1990) (60mins) Documentary by David Langer about the life and work of actress Martha Henry.

Long Life, Happiness & Prosperity (2002) (95 mins) d: Mina Shum s: Dennis Foon, Mina Shum : Sandra Oh, Tsai Chin, Ric Young, Chang Tseng, Valerie Tian. Set in the Chinese community of Vancouver, this intimate film based on magic-realism involves a drama of many characters, including a 12-year-old girl who tries Taoist magic to improve her single mother's financial situation and romantic prospects. A nicely told and played-out story of hope and faith in a troubled world.

Long Live France (Vive la France) (1970) (80mins) (b/w) d&s: Raymond Garceau : Léopold Castonguay, Camille Desjardins, Rémi Émond, Antonio Ouellette. This light and enjoyable satire revolves around a professor from France who comes to a small Québec town and who appears strange to the people he meets, in his speech, manners and behaviour. Good humour and charm temper the mocking tone.

Long Road Home, The (1988) (120mins) (a Canadian-American film) d: William Johnston s: Dan Datree : Denis Forest, Kelly Rowan, Gareth Bennett. An American who has received his draft notice for Vietnam comes north to Canada as a camp counsellor. He suffers a crisis of conscience in his political confrontations with his campers—somewhat contrived and far-fetched. Filmed in Ontario's Algonquin Park.

Looking for Eternity (Portion d'éternité) (1989) (96mins) d&s: Robert Favreau : Danielle Proulx, Marc Messier, Paul Savoie, Patricia Nolan. Starts out as an interesting story about a childless couple who try the new experiments in artificial insemination. The expensive clinic in which this takes place, however, is not what it seems, and soon we are into the machinations of drug companies and scientists. The plot then becomes a cousin to Frankenstein, several times removed, and with a lack of realism.

Looking for Leonard (2002) (90mins) d&s: Steven Clark, Matt Bissonnette : Joel Bissonnette, Benjamin Ratner, Darcy Belshar, Gabriel Gascon, Kim Huffman Justin Pierce, Molly Parker. Filmed in Montréal, four absurd young men walk endlessly along drab streets, visiting empty apartments, talking a lot of drivel in stilted conversations. Where is Cohen? The audience would like to know. He comes on screen in a couple of brief old news clips and that's it. This mishmash about absolutely nothing is an insult to Leonard Cohen.

Looking for Miracles (1989) (103mins) d: Kevin Sullivan s: Stuart McLean, Kevin Sullivan : Gregory Spottiswood, Joseph Flaherty, Patricia Gage, Zachary Bennett. A sentimental but honest depression-era, coming-of-age family tale taking place against an idyllic summer background in northern Ontario.

Loose Ends: see **Screwball Academy**

***Los Naufragos* (The Lost Ones)** (1994) (118mins) (a Canada-France-Chile co-production) d&s: Miguel Littin : Marcelo Romo, Luis Alarcon, Valentina Vargas, Bastian Bodenhofer. A tortured tale about a Chilean exile who leaves Canada to return to his native country after the revolution. Society is still in a state of crisis. Who to trust? Who were the victims? Who were the executioners? For the exile, his life has become a journey in search of himself. In many ways a valiant film.

Losin' It (Tijuana) (1983) (99mins) d: Curtis Lee Hanson s: B.W.L. Norton : Tom Cruise, Jackie Earle Haley, John Stockwell, Shelley Long, John Navin, Henry Darrow, Hector Elias. The usual witless, tasteless, vulgar excursion into what purports to be teenage sex frolics. Debases characters and audiences alike. Filmed in Mexico.

Lost and Delirious (2000) (98mins) d: Léa Pool s: Judith Thompson, Léa Pool (from the novel *The Wives of Bath* by Susan Swan) : Piper Perabo, Jessica Paré, Mischa Barton, Jackie Burroughs, Graham Greene, Mimi Kuzyk, Luke Kirby. This film is the director's first on which she worked with a script she did not write. Not that the difference is all that noticeable in this overwrought, cloying romance set in a boarding school for girls in which emotional torment and lesbian love seems to take up more time than learning. Handsome, well made and acted, it's nevertheless hard to take seriously. (Graham takes care of the gardens, while Jackie 'digs' the girls!)

Lost in Manhattan: see **Sue Lost in Manhattan**

Lost in the Barrens (1990) (112mins) d: Michael Scott s: Keith Ross Leckie (based on Farley Mowat's novel of the same name) : Evan Adams, Nicholas Shields, Lee Campbell, Grahame Greene. This companion picture to *Curse of the Viking Grave*, from Mowat's adventure story, is about two boys who find themselves alone during a terrible episode in the arctic wilderness. Good family fare convincingly acted and set against beautifully photographed arctic scenery.

Lost Ones, The: see *Los naufragos*

Lost Words (*Les mots perdus*) (1993) (87mins) d &s: Marcel Simard : Rita Dell, Myriam Belhadj, Anne-Dominique Staehli, John Dobrynine. The lives of the four protagonists in this unusual film have been shattered by aphasia, a mysterious condition that results from physical trauma. Simard shows us how his characters find themselves again. A fascinating and moving chronicle on par with his *Love-moi* and *Le grande monde*. Each deals with medical matters from a social and educational point of view, in a humane and understanding way.

Lost World, The (1992) (97mins) (a U.K.-U.S.-Canada film) d: Timothy Bond s: Peter Welbeck (from the novel by Arthur Conan Doyle) : John Rhys-Davies, David Warner, Eric McCormack, Nathania Stanford, Darren Peter Mercer, Tamara Gorski, Kate Egan. This is a handsomely mounted and pleasantly spoken semi-classic representation of Conan Doyle's famous story of the discovery of a lost continent, with friendly dinasours and other strange creatures, both human and animal. In today's politically correct society much of what's here is taboo. This won't make it into Black History Month. (Note: This is version number 6 and following its release and a number of truly awful versions have been flying off and on tv. Surprisingly, the well-written screenplay of this Victorian-era story is marred by the use of the banal modern comment, 'no problem' spoken by the young lad on the expedition. An inside joke?

Lost! (1986) (95mins) d&s: Peter Rowe : Michael Hogan, Kenneth Welsh, Helen Shaver. Based on the true story by Thomas Thompson telling of a fundamentalist minister whose obsession with God's will drives him to sea in a trimaran, bound for Costa Rica from Vancouver, with his brother and pregnant sister-in-law. Capsized in a terrible storm, they are lost for 74 days, during which the conflicts between the three, both spiritual and physical, make this sea voyage somewhat different and better than many others.

Lottery Ticket, The: see *Petite fille particulière, Une*

Lotus Eaters, The (1993) (100mins) d: Paul Shapiro s: Peggy Thompson : Sheila McCarthy, R.H. Thomson, Michèle-Barbara Pelletier, Frances Hyland, Paul Soles, Aloka McLean, Tara Fredrick. This is another successful study in "nothing ever happens" domestic family relations, and like *My American Cousin*, it's set in B.C. in the 1960s. The family in this case lives placidly on a beautiful, rugged island. Life is not without heartbreak for the wife and children, when the father falls in love with the new teacher from Québec. Charming, funny, sad and sensitively played with disarming naturalism by the children and adults.

Louis XIX, le roi des ondes (Louis 19, King of the Airwaves) (1994) (95mins) d: Michel Poulette s: Émile Gaudreault, Sylvie Bouchard, Michel Michaud : Martin Drainville, Agathe de la Fontaine, Dominique Michel, Patricia Tulasne, Gilbert Lachance, Jean L'Italien, Yves Jacques, Benoît Brière. A highly successful and consistently amusing Québec comedy about a dull everyman who spends his leisure time watching popular television, and then becomes a media celebrity when every minute of his life is shown on tv as a result of his winning a contest. Provides a lighthearted opportunity to make fun of television's power to misrepresent so much of what it feeds to its audience.(Remade in Hollywood as *Ed TV*, 1999).

Louisa May Alcott's Little Men (1998) (98mins) (an American-Canadian film) d: Rodney Gibbons s: Mark Evan Schwartz (based on the novel by Louisa May Alcott) : Michael Caloz, Mariel Hemingway, Ben Cook, Ricky Mabe, Chris Sarandon, Gabrielle Boni, Michael Tarmoush. A straightforward condensed version of the story of two urchins who are befriended by a kindly benefactor and go to live at the happy, peaceful school of Plumfield. The message is about valour and ethics and family relationships, all well said and acted here, but not as engrossing as its famous companion book and film, *Little Women*.

Louisiana (1993) (186mins) (a Canada-France co-production) d: Jacques Demy, Philippe de Broca s: Étienne Perier, Dominique Fabre, with Charles E. Israel (based on the books *Louisiane* and *Fausse Rivière* by Maurice Denuzière) : Margot Kidder, Ian Charleson, Victor Lanoux, Andrea Ferreol, Len Cariou, Raymond Pellegrin, Lloyd Bochner, Kenneth Pogue, Corinne Marchand, Akosua Busia and hundreds more! A sprawling canvas of history and its principal players, looking somewhat like an ersatz GWTW. Filmed largely in Québec on a budget of $15 million, it was one of Canada's great movie mistakes, as a result of hunting for the international market!. A feature film and six-hour tv film.

Love and Death on Long Island (1997) (93mins) (a Canada-U.K. co-production) d&s: Richard Kwietniowski (adapted from the novel by Gilbert Adair) : John Hurt, Jason Priestley, Maury Chaykin, Fiona Loewi, Sheila Hancock. An erudite British writer in London goes into the wrong film at a multiplex and finds himself watching a teenage sex comedy. He becomes infatuated with the star and cannot rest until he finds him, living on Long Island, where he experiences a new world of love. Hurt is apt and funny as the somewhat dazed professor, and Jason Priestley acquits himself well in this delightful and clever film. Nova Scotia stands in for Long Island not too convincingly.

Love and Greed (1992) (79mins) d&s: Bashar Shbib : Frank Bruynbrock, Melissa White, Dick Monday, Lori Eastside. Uncle Leo leaves his fortune to his nephew Robert and wife Alex with one catch: they must have a baby within a year. Trouble is, they hate each other and their new mates, Ted and Suzie, who are not happy, either. The foursome and a witness move into Leo's estate for a madcap week-long romp of sex, love and the pursuit of the almighty dollar. (Shbib loses himself here).

Love and Hate (The Story of Colin and Joan Thatcher) (1989) (193mins) d: Francis Mankiewicz s: Suzette Couture (based on the book *A Canadian Tragedy* by Maggie Siggins) : Kate Nelligan, Kenneth Welsh. The true story of a wealthy Saskatchewan businessman who murdered his wife and was sentenced to life in prison. Grim, starkly realistic, and a thoroughly professional work as befits the skills of Couture, Mankiewicz and the cast. There is not a hint of sensationalism here. A truly important picture.

Love and Human Remains (Unidentified Human Remains and the True Nature of Love) (1994) (100mins) d: Denys Arcand s: Brad Fraser (from his play) : Thomas Gibson, Ruth Marshall, Cameron Bancroft, Mia Kirshner, Joanne Vannicola, Matthew Ferguson, Rick Roberts, Bernard Arcand. A disappointing black comedy, supposedly symbolic of the 1990s, follows two friends—a witty, cynical actor turned waiter, and an optimistic and romantic book reviewer—who are searching for the meaning of love. In trying to make sense of today's society, they discover someone they know is a serial killer. This is Arcand's first film in English. He did his best with a shallow script, which gives the film a few memorable scenes, but the whole defeats him.

Love and Larceny (1985) (149mins) d: Rob Iscove s: Douglas Bowie : Jennifer Dale, Douglas Rain, Brent Carver. This is a skilfully written and directed biography of Betsy Bigley, the turn-of-the-century Canadian confidence trickster, vividly portrayed by Jennifer Dale. Full of life and spirit and capturing the era with a fine sense of style. See also *Grand Larceny*.

Love and Murder (1988) (86mins) (a Canada-U.S. film) d&s: Steven Hilliard Stern : Todd Waring, Kathleen Laskey. A man secretly photographs his female neighbours and witnesses the death of one of them. The murderer and the police then come after him. Predictable and contrived.

Love and Murder (1999) (120mins) d: George Bloomfield s: R.B. Carney (from the novel by Gail Bowen) : Wendy Crewson, Victor Garber, Caroline Goodall. When Sally Love, a renowned visual artist, opens an exhibit of her work, she finds her ex-husband and owner of the gallery bludgeoned to death.

She calls her old friend, Joanne Kilburn, a former policewoman, to investigate the murder. From here, one thing leads to another in an intriguing whodunit with Inspector Millard. (See: *Mystery* series)

Love at First Sight (1974) (85mins) d&s: Rex Bromfield : Mary Anne McDonald, Dan Aykroyd, Jane Mallett, George Murray, Barry Morse, Mignon Elkins, Alan Anderson, Beth Amos. In this, his first screen appearance, Dan Aykroyd plays a blind man who meets and falls in love with a young woman. Simple and predictable, but at times affecting, with many of our notable actors of this time.

Love Come Down (2000) (99mins) d&s: Clement Virgo : Larenz Tate, Deborah Cox, Martin Cummins, Rainbow Sun Francks, Kenneth Welsh, Sarah Polley, Peter Williams, Jennifer Dale. After a promising opening, this picture of family troubles among a black family in Toronto simply falls apart as violence, abuse and ugliness take over. There's not much love going anywhere here. The director has taken on too much, leaving us swamped and confused.

Love From the Market Place: see **Acts of Love Series**

Love in a Four Letter World (*Viens, mon amour*) (1970) (92mins) d: John Sone s: Arthur Voronka, John Sone : Michael Kane, Helen White, André Laurence, Cayle Chermin, Monique Mercure, Candy Greene. Two young men open a music store next to a film editor and his sculptor wife and daughter. Sex soon enters the scene, and the games in bed begin. (Mild however, compared with what we see today and the better for it.)

Love in Canada (1979) (103mins) (in Hindi) d: S. Ramanathan s: Sheora Singh : Vinod Mehra, Moushimi. A portrayal of East Indian–Canadian family troubles and misunderstandings between generations. Filmed at Niagara, this is enterprising fare for new Canadian East-Indian audiences.

Love Letters: A Romantic Trilogy (2001) (95mins) (a U.S.-Canada film) d: Frank A. Caruso s: Robert Antidormi, Frank A. Caruso : Brian Frank, Kathy Shower, Norma Jean Jones, Meeka Majic, Albert Caverlin. A successful novelist asks her friends to talk about their intimate sex lives and reveal their secrets. For those who expect a story, there isn't one. What an audience gets, and indeed some may want, is straight Pornography. The friends become engaged in sexual activity, with great cries of torment and final agony, lots of bare bodies heaving around in bed and crawling over each other, up against walls, on the floor, with everyone quarrelling, their lives falling apart. And all this going on in green and pleasant Muskoka?

Love Me (*Love-moi*) (1991) (90mins) d&s: Marcel Simard : Germain Houde, Paule Baillargeon, Mario St-Amand, Denis Bouchard, Stéphane Demers and others. A young man is assassinated in the street on an ordinary day in a working-class Montréal neighbourhood. This event is the starting point for Simard to move into a sociological study of the ways of justice as eight youths go on trial. A thoughtful consideration about right and wrong, represented by the arbiters of many professions involved in this autopsy on violence. Well stated and acted.

Love Me, Love Me Not: see *J'aime, j'aime pas*

Love on the Nose (1978) (79mins) d: George Bloomfield s: John Smith : Saul Rubinek, Al Waxman, Joseph Silver. At the close of the Depression era in Montréal an idealistic socialist, desperate for work, takes a job that turns out to be a cover for gambling and prostitution. Trying to be true to his beliefs, he runs afoul of the crooks running the joints. A gripping social drama.

Love on Your Birthday: see **Acts of Love (Series)**

Love Songs: see *Paroles et musique*

Love That Boy (2002) (95mins) d: Andrea Dorfman s: Jennifer Deyell, Andrea Dorfman : Nadia Litz, Adrien Dixon, Nikki Barnett, P.J. Crosby, Dax Ravina. A slight and simple teenage story involving a girl who, not wanting to be alone at graduation, looks for a boyfriend. She falls in love with him, although difficulties arise when she discovers he's only 14. A welcome change from the usual worn-out depiction of student lives and loves. A decent, likeable and honest portrayal.

Love, American-style: see **Cosmos**

Love: see **Acts of Love (series)**

Love-moi: see **Love Me**

Lover's Exile, The (1981) (87mins) (a Canadian-Japanese film) d&s: Marty Gross : Tamao Yoshida, Minnosuke Yoshida, Kanjuro Kiritake, Oritayu Takemoto, Enza Tsuruzawa, Koshijidayu Takemoto, Seiji Tsuruzawa, Mojidayu Takemoto, Kinshi Nozawa (this is the play *Meido No Hikayaku* [*The Courier to Hell*] by Monzoemon Chikamatsu). A faithful re-creation of the Bunraku Theatrical Ensemble of Osaka, filmed with imagination and admiration. Marty Gross is noted for his Japanese-Candians films.

Loving and Laughing (1971) (97mins) d: John Sone s: Martin Bronstein Lively : André Lawrence, Céline Lomez, Michèle Mercure, Julie Wildman, Walter Massey, Jimmy Tapp, Mignon Elkins. Sex comedy about young people, hippies and their communes. Shallow, shameless, but lively.

Loving Evangeline (1998) (120mins) d: Timothy Bond s: Charles Lazer (based on the novel by Linda Howard) : Nick Mancuso, Kelly Rowan, Shari Belafone, Winston Rekert. Big business comes into play here, set against an industrial background in Nova Scotia. When a rich company president dies, a struggle ensues over inheritance rights with the shadow of murder bringing a chill to the romantic side of the events. Well played with the proceedings unfolding in an engaging and intriguing way. (See: *Harlequin* series)

Low Self-Esteem Girl (2000) (96mins) d&s: Blaine Thurier : Corrina Hammond, Rob McBeth, Cindy Wolde, Carl Newman, Ted Dave, Howard Reid,

James Dawes. Based on a cartoon by the writer and director and filmed on digital video this doubtful enterprise opens with such stimulating dialogue as "you're a f*cking piece of sh*t" and "let's f*ck," with a sickening near-naked rough-and-tumble. And that's the end of the self-esteem issue. We then proceed on a slumming trip into the contemporary lifestyle of a group of teenagers. We meet young men who never shave and women of questionable morals. Life may be this awful, but this film, set in Vancouver, is badly written, muddled in its plotting, and confused in its characterization. There is a religious encounter: send up or serious? We don't know. Forget it.

Low Visibility (1984) (99mins) d&s: Patricia Gruben : Larry Lillo, David Petersen, Penelope Stella, Robert Metcalfe, Jerry Wasserman, Sue Astley, Brenda Robins. Vancouver experimental filmmaker Gruben has here a narrative of sorts, portraying a man wandering alone on the roadside of a snowy mountain, waving his arms and shouting into space. Taken into care, he refuses to explain what has happened to him. Today, few would pay any attention to him, but here the entire phalanx of media, medical and law representatives build an elaborate net of speculation and investigation. A tricky piece of work but often funny and always perceptive.

Loyalties (1985) (98mins) (a Canada-U.K. co-production) d: Anne Wheeler s: Sharon Riis : Susan Wooldridge, Kenneth Welsh, Tantoo Cardinal, Vera Martin, Christopher Barrington-Leigh. A psychological drama about a British couple forced to leave England and who came to Canada to live in a remote town in Alberta. The husband is a sex offender with a history of assaulting women. He rapes their housekeeper and his wife calls the police. Effective, well acted and provocative in its revelations relating to human behaviour. A difficult subject clearly stated and directed.

Loyalties: see **Bye Bye Blues**

Luc ou la part des choses: see **Luke or the Part of Things**

Lucien Brouillard (1983) (90mins) d&s: Bruno Carrière : Pierre Curzi, Roger Blay, Marie Tifo, Paul Savoie, Jean Duceppe, Frédérique Collin. To the working-class people of a Montréal neighbourhood, Lucien Brouillard is a hero. Injustice and political and legal trickery are the objects of his rage and he eventually gets sent to prison. His saviour is a childhood friend who has become a lawyer and is determined to join the ruling political party that Lucien so despises. Both a psychological thriller and a perceptive social drama, this unusual film, which is only thinly disguised when it comes to describing the Québec social scene, is marred when the character of Lucien becomes so unlikeable that audiences are likely to lose patience with him.

Luck (2003) (91mins) d&s: Peter Wellington : Luke Kirby, Sarah Polley, Jed Rees, Sergio Di Zio,

Noam Jenkins. Set against one of the great moments of Canada's sport history, the Canada-Russia hockey series in 1972, we soon meet a group of free-spirited student 'underachievers' whose lives do not seem to be much connected with glory, as with heartache.

Luck of Ginger Coffey, The (1964) (100mins) (b/w) d: Irvin Kershner s: Brian Moore (from his novel of the same name) : Robert Shaw, Mary Ure, Liam Redmond, Tom Harvey, Libby McClintock, Leo Leyden, Powys Thomas, Tom Kneebone, Leslie Yeo, Vern Chapman, Paul Guèvremont, Barry Stewart, Arch McDonell, Ovila Légaré, Jacques Godin, Maurice Beaupré, Sydney Brown, Juliette Huot, Paul Hébert, Barney McManus, Clarence Goodhue. How a likable Irish immigrant attempts to find a job in Montréal and a new understanding with his wife. An absorbing and often funny and truthful study of individuals struggling to make a new life in a new country, marvellously acted by the legion of Canadian actors of the time. With a distinct Canadian character and atmosphere, this picture represented a brave step forward into feature filmmaking by F.R. (Budge) Crawley, who had distinguished himself in documentary filmmaking in Ottawa in the early 1940s. Seen today, it is still fascinating to travel along Montréal streets. A highly contemporary film when made, this is now a perfect period piece.

Lucky Girl (2000) (120mins) d: John Fawcett s: Grame Manson : Elisha Cuthbert, Sherry Miller, Evan Sabba, Gregory Ellwand. A disturbing social commentary about teenagers' lives, moving away from drugs, drink and sex, and into gambling. Penny, who aims for more than pennies, cannot stop. She wins a little and loses a lot and becomes the victim of a loan shark. A dramatization based on conversations and research. Revealing, and thoughtful. (See: *Signature series*)

Lucky Star, The (*La belle étoile*) (1980) (111mins) d: Max Fischer s: Jack Rosenthal, Max Fischer (from a story by Roland Topor) : Rod Steiger, Louise Fletcher, Lou Jacobi, Brett Marx, Yvon Dufour, Helen Hughes, Isabelle Mejias, Jean Gascon, Guy L'Écuyer, Michèle Mercure. Set in war-torn Holland, this story concerns a 13-year-old Jewish boy who loves and lives Western movies and admires the sheriff's gold star. When he is forced by the Nazis to wear the yellow star identifying him as a Jew, he imagines he is a courageous sheriff and, buying a gun, goes into the countryside and captures a German colonel. His parents are taken to a concentration camp. It is hard to believe this: a cheap Western out of the horror of the Holocaust.

Luke or the Part of Things (*Luc ou la part des choses*) (1982) (91mins) d: Michel Audy s: Jean Lemay, Michel Audy : Pierre Normandin, Éric Boulay, Alain Thiffault, Lynda Bistodeau, Germain Lemay, Rollande Lambert. The trials and tribulations of a teenager who goes to work in a garage to support his family, and then discovers he is homosexual, which leads to attempted suicide and depression. A friend shows him the way out. A sensitive study made at a time when such topics were almost taboo.

Lulu (1995) (90mins) d&s: Srinivas Krishna : Kim Lieu, Clark Johnson, Michael Rhoades, Manuel Aranguiz, Peter Breck, Saeed Jaffrey. Lulu is a Vietnamese mail-order bride, mysterious and exotic. She works behind a cosmetics counter and is troubled by her past, her present and her traditional parents. She also becomes mixed up with three rascally men. Not even the presence of the great Indian actor, Saeed Jaffrey is enough to save this inept and confusing film.

Lumières de ma ville: see **Lights of My City**

Lunch with Charles (2001) (102mins) (a Canada-Hong Kong co-production) d&s: Michael Parker : Sean Lau, Nicholas Lea, Yjeresa Lee, Bif Naked, Philip Granger, Tom Scholte, Francoise Yip, Peter Wilds, Simon Kendall, Shannon Saunders. This first Canada-Hong Kong film is a romantic comedy set against the majesty of B.C. mountains. A group of colourful characters, somewhat lacking a story to tell, have a good time with rock and pop music as they attempt to sort out all manner of difficulties. Appealing and certainly entertaining with its multicultural threads. Charles is not the prince of course.

Lune de miel: see **Honeymoon**

Luther (1973) (95mins) d: Guy Green, play by John Osborne : Stacy Keach, Julian Glover, Robert Stephens, Patrick Magee, Hugh Griffith, Judi Dench, Alan Badel. The founder of the Protestant Reformation here becomes the subject of an appraisal and affirmation of a dedicated human being, biting and keen, from a modernist playwright. (See: American Film Theatre Series)

Lyddie (1995) (120mins) (a Canada-U.K. co-production) d: Stefan Scaini s: Maggie Wadek, Katherine Peterson (from her novel) : Tanya Allen, Christianne Hirt, Thomas Georgeson, Patricia Keen, Simon James. A British tale moved to Saskatchewan passing for Cornwall, Ontario. This takes place in the 1860s and tells the story of Lyddie Worthen, a young woman forced to fend for herself as she goes from a backwoods farm into the new industrial age and begins a journey of self discovery. Beautifully made and acted and engaging throughout.

Lydia (1964) (85mins) d: Diederik d'Ailly s: Burton Krancer, Julius Rascheff, Diederik d'Ailly (from Stratis Myrivilis' book Our Lady the Siren) : Gordon Pinsent, Anna Hagan, Benentino Costa, Malena Anousaki. A love story filmed on location in Greece. Gordon Pinsent (in his first film) plays an American with an incurable illness who visits a Greek island to find peace. He also finds love, which is related to a local legend, but gives up the girl because he has no future. Pinsent is excellent and this film started him on a highly successful career as an actor on screen, stage and television. Rascheff and d'Ailly came from Europe, determined to make films. This was their first and (almost) only production. It went nowhere and eventually they became film production teachers in the U.S. See *Lift, The.*

Lyon's Den (1983) (65mins) d: Graham Parker s: Tony Sheer : James Blendick, Barbara Williams, Mary Bellows, Mogeus Gander, Mary Pirie, Christopher Langevin, Tedde Moore. The subject of manipulative and selective journalism becomes a personal crisis for a crusading tv journalist, Peter Lyon. While producing a show on teenage vandalism, he finds that his own children are part of a gang destroying homes in his neighbourhood. What does his profession expect of him now? Compelling and thoughtful. (See: *For the Record*)

M. Butterfly (1993) (100mins) d: David Cronenberg s: David Henry Hwang (based on his play) : Jeremy Irons, John Lone, Ian Richardson, Anabel Leventon. The far-fetched and said to be true tale that a French diplomat in China during the 1960s conducted an 18-year affair with a man he always thought was a woman simply cannot be believed on film—not the way Cronenberg tells it. And in choosing a British actor to play the Frenchman, and John Lone to play Song Liling, disbelief becomes even greater. There is no emotion or understanding of any kind between them to suggest that this relationship was possible.

M.V.P.: Most Valuable Primate (2000) (92mins) (a U.S.-Canada film) d: Robert Vince s: Ann and Robert Vince : Russell Ferrier, Rick Ducommun, Oliver Muirhead, Kevin Zegers, Jamie Renee Smith, Lomax Study. An adorable chimp (aren't they all?) escapes from a medical laboratory and eventually finds a home with a hockey-loving family in B.C. The chimp is only too happy to join in the fun and games. A family film with a difference. A bit too cute at times, but these chimps know how to make audiences laugh.

M.V.P. 2: Most Valuable Primate (2001) (86mins) d: Robert Vince s: Elan Mastai, Robert Vince : Cameron Bancroft, Richard Karn, Robert Costanzo, Dolores Drake, Jacqui Kaese. More of the same; this time the chimp, having been such a success playing hockey, is thrown out by jealous players and takes up skateboarding. Whether Jack the chimp is real or not, he and other animals are treated with love and respect.

M.V.P. 3 (2003) (90mins) d: Robert Vince s: Anne and Robert Vince : Devin Douglas Drewitz, Trevor Wright, Karina MacKenzie, Anna McRoberts, Robert Tinkler. The further adventures of Jack the chimp, now in danger of wearing out his welcome.

M'en revenant par les épinettes: see **Passing Through the Pine Trees**

Ma Murray (1983) (90mins) d: Philip Keatley s: based on the play Ma! by Eric Nicol : Joy Coghill and John Milligan as Margaret and George Murray. A more-or-less filmed play of the life and work of the legendary Margaret "Ma" Murray, the founder and

editor of a pioneering weekly newspaper in Lillooet, B.C. Keatley, whose excellent work in tv has gone largely unnoticed, brings this tableau convincingly to life with great performances by the two players.

Mad About Mambo (2000) (92mins) (a Canada-U.K. film) d&s: John Forte : Keri Russell, William Ash, Brian Cox. A young soccer player takes up mambo dancing to improve his sense of rhythm. But with all those girls mamboing away, who needs football? An odd film with some good moments of music and dance.

Madame B (1986) (112mins) d: Jean-Yves Laforce s: François Tassé (loosely based on the novel *Madame Bovary* by Gustave Flaubert) : Louise Marleau, Dominique Briand, Sophie Clément. A woman is frustrated by the oppressive atmosphere of her small Québec village. That's about as close as it comes to Flaubert in this version.

Madame Brouette (2002) (104mins) (a Canada-Senegal-France co-production) d: Moussa Sene Absa s: Gilles Desjardins, Moussa Absa : Ousseynou Diop, Rokhaya Niang, Aoubacar Sadikh. Set in Dakar, a divorced woman known as Mrs. Wheelbarrow makes a difficult living pushing her cart through the market and dreaming of a better life. But fate has other plans for her, not all of which bring her happiness. Produced by Rock Demers (see: *Tales for All* series). One can see the appeal of this subject for him, and as one would expect of Demers, it is a fine film.

Madeleine Is... (1971) (90mins) d&s: Sylvia Spring : Nicola Lipman, John Juliani, Wayne Robson, Gordon Robertson, Margot Chapman. A first film, simple, slight but sincere in its depiction of a young girl who, surrounded by unhealthy elements, struggles to find herself (An important entry into B.C. filmmaking) (the first Canadian contemporary feature film to be directed by a woman).

Madly in Love: *see Amoureux fou*

Maelström (2000) (88mins) d&s: Denis Villeneuve : Marie-Josée Croze, Jean-Nicolas Verreault, Stephanie Morgenstern, Pierre Lebeau. This dreary, depressing and repugnant film opens with a monstrous, ancient fish being carved up. This fish's voice comments throughout, saying who knows what, about a spoiled and totally uninteresting young woman whose life has become chaotic after a traffic accident. The maelstrom here is in the script and direction. A critically over-praised film.

Magician's House, The (1999) (in two 83-minute parts) (a Canada-U.K. co-production) d: Paul Lynch s: William Corlett : Ian Richardson, Sian Phillips, Neil Pearson, Jennifer Saunders, Kati Stuart. A group of likeable children in search of adventure come across a marvellous magician in an old English mansion. Familiar stuff in an enchanting new set of clothes and circumstances.

Magnificent Blue, The (*Bleue, la magnifique***)** (1990) (83mins) d: Pierre Mignot s: Louise Matteau,

Claire Wojas : Denise Filiatrault, Geneviève Rioux. A young country and western singer takes pity on and becomes friends with a Montréal bag lady. A strange little chapter on human kindness, and fans of this kind of music will like the generous time devoted to the popular songs the singer specializes in.

Mahoney's Last Stand (1976) (108mins) d: Harvey Hart s: Terence Heffernan, Alexis Kanner : Alexis Kanner, Maud Adams, Sam Waterston, Diana Leblanc, Ed McNamara, Hugh Watson. Kanner takes an ego trip into the countryside with his boring "Ernie" character in hopes of making a living from the land. There are complications, of course, but it's hard to care for any of this unbelievable material.

Maids, The (1975) (95mins) d: Christopher Miles, play by Jean Genet : Glenda Jackson, Susannah York, Vivien Merchant, Mark Burns. Two maids hate their mistress, rubbish to many, remarkable to the few. This is one work that should have remained on stage. (See: *American Film Theatre Series*)

Mains nettes, Les: see **Clean Hands**

Maintain the Right (1982) (65mins) d: Leslie Rose s: Tony Sheer : Nicholas Campbell, Laurie J. Brown, Michael Hogan, Frank Adamson, Stephen Lack, Douglas Leiterman, Neil Dainard, Shirley Douglas, Richard Donat. Unusual drama about a police constable who finds that he must choose between honesty toward the woman he loves and loyalty to his superiors when she decides to charge the RCMP because she is certain it was one of the force's undercover agents who broke into the offices of the labour organization where she works. A moral dilemma well thought out, stated and portrayed, without violence, brutality or ugliness. (See: *For the Record*)

Maison des amants, La: see **House of Lovers**

Maison en ordre, La: see **House in Order, A**

Maison qui empêche de voir la ville, La: see **House That Hides the Town, The**

Maîtres anciens (Old Masters) (1998) (85mins) d: Olivier Asselin s: Denis Marleau (based on the novel by Thomas Bernhard) : Gabriel Gascon, Pierre Collin, Pierre Lebeau, Henri Chassé, Alexis Martin, Marie Michaud. A theatrical work about a testy old man who has spent his life loving, criticizing and hating the arts. "Life without art is sad, but art without life is nothing." This is a genuinely human drama, and it speaks well of the performances which maintain opinions and beliefs.

Maîtresse, La: see **And I Love You Dearly**

Major Crime (1998) (140mins) d: Bradford Turner s: Steve Lucas : Michael Moriarty, David Cubitt, Megan Follows, Nicholas Campbell. A child disappears, and three police officers attempt to bring a child molester to justice. Their efforts are hampered by bureaucracy, lack of support and uncooperative witnesses. This is a well thought out and searing indictment of the manner in which justice is subverted so familiar to us all, reflecting accurately the lack of common sense so prevalent today in our courts of law.

Make Mine Chartreuse (1987) (82mins) d: James Kaufman s: Gilles Savard : Joseph Bottoms, Catherine Colvey, Russell Gordon, Sheena Larkin. Romance isn't what it used to be until two lovers, she in office work and he in business, come to terms with private life and working hours, and attempt to bring passion back into their lives—with rewarding results. (See: *Shades of Love series*)

Making Love in St. Pierre (2003) (90mins) d: John Vatcher s: Ken Pittman : Nicole Underhay, Allan Howco, Cherie Ouellet, Aiden Flynn. A Newfoundland film, set in 1993, where a young fisherman, unable to work because of diminishing cod from the oceans, takes up his girlfriend's suggestion to holiday in Halifax. They end up however, on the French island of St. Pierre, where making loves seems to be no different from making love anywhere else. A likeable film, but little more. Interestingly, the writer and producer of it, Ken Pittman, once made several of the best films ever to come from Newfoundland. Since then he has spent the years since 1994 making tv commercials and music videos. A great loss to the cinema.

Malarek: A Street Kid Who Made It (1988) (100mins) d: Roger Cardinal s: Avrum Jackson (based on the book *Hey, Malarek* by Victor Malarek) : Elias Koteas (as Malarek), Kerrie Keane, Al Waxman, Michael Sarrazin, Kahil Kam. An honest semi-documentary about a crusading journalist in Montréal, a former juvenile delinquent, working against odds and the establishment, in uncovering a miscarriage of justice and proving his honesty and courage.

Mâles, Les: see **Men, The**

Malicious (1995) (92mins) d: Ian Corsan s: George Saunders : Molly Ringwald, John Vernon, Patrick McGaw, Mimi Kuzyk, Sarah Lassez. In this suspense thriller, a college baseball hero is seduced by an admiring and aggressive fan who takes things too far for comfort. Steamy and wild but hardly a good home game.

Mama's Going to Buy You a Mockingbird (1987) (97mins) d: Sandy Wilson s: Anna Sandor (based on the novel by Jean Little) : Linda Griffiths, Geoffrey Bowes, Louis Tripp, Marsha Moreau. A fragile but sensitively explored and stated portrayal of a wife and two children attempting to come to terms with the death of the father.

Man and His Sin, A: see *Homme et son péché, Un*

Man Called Intrepid, A (1979) (128mins) (three two-hour episodes for tv edited into one feature film) (a Canada-U.K. co-production) d: Peter Carter s: David Ambrose (based on the book of the same title by Sir William Stephenson) : David Niven, Michael York, Barbara Hershey, Paul Harding, Flora Robson, Gayle Hunnicut, Renee Asherson, Ken James, Robin Gammell, Chris Wiggins, Colin Fox, Larry

Reynolds, Donald Pilon, with Ferdy Mayne as Sir Alexander Korda, Nigel Stock as Winston Churchill, Ken James as Sir Edgar Hoover. The wealthy Canadian Sir William Stephenson is seen at work developing his espionage network with the Allies during World War II, with the enemy being vanquished during many encounters. One of the most successful Canadian productions of this kind.

Man from Glengarry, The (1920) (60mins-silent) (b/w) d: Henry MacRae s: Faith Green, Kenneth O'Hara (from Ralph Conner's book of the same name) : Anders Randolph, Warner Richmond, Marion Swayne, Frank Badgley, Pauline Garon. Murder, rivalry and revenge in a lumber camp in northern Ontario. Well done for its time. A review of the day commented favourably on the absence of snow!

Man from the Movies, The (Le gars des vues) (1976) (149mins) d&s: Jean-Pierre Lefebvre : Claudette Chapdelaine, Roger Cantin, Alain Gendreau, Suzanne Éthier, Ivanhoe Viens. The inventive Lefebvre casts his net wide here as he goes in search of visions of truth and fantasy to show how images and themes are developed, how they are used, and what they mean. Thoughtful, weighty and revealing.

Man in 5A, The (Killing 'Em Softly) (1982) (81mins) d: Max Fischer s: Leila Basen, Max Fischer (from Laird Koenig's book The Neighbour [La Porte En Face] : George Segal, Irene Cara, Joyce Gordon, Andrew Martin, Nicholas Campbell, Clark Johnson. A peculiar tale about an unemployed stage hand in Montréal who kills the manager of a rock band because he had killed his neighbour's dog. A young singer falls in love with him. There's more! But none of it really matters.

Man in My Life, The: see **Homme de ma vie, L'**

Man in the Attic, The (1994) (120mins) (a Canada-U.S. film) d: Graeme Campbell s: Duane Poole, Tom Swale (from the story by Norman Winski) : Anne Archer, Len Cariou, Neil Patrick Harris, Alex Carter, Deborah Drakeford, Tedde Moore. Inspired by a true story that began in Milwaukee against the backdrop of World War I and, later, Prohibition, it chronicles the love affair of a married woman and her young lover, whom she hides in the attic of her home for over twenty years until the unsuspecting husband finally discovers him. The outcome is madness and murder. Shot almost entirely in Toronto, this compelling, remarkable and incredulous film, so well made and acted in its portrayal of obsessive love, becomes one of the few movies one can term unforgettable.

Man Inside, The (1975) (95mins) (a Canada-U.S. co-production) d: Gerald Mayer s: Tony Sheer : James Franciscus, Jacques Godin, Stefanie Powers, Len Birman, Allan Royal, John Horton, Ken James, Donald Davis, Lynne Griffin. An undercover RCMP officer in Toronto tracks down a gang of drug peddlers. Moderately good. A great cast has little to work with.

Man on the Shore, The (L'homme sur les quais) (1993) (106mins) (a Canada-Haiti-France co-production) d&s: Raoul Peck : Jennifer Zubar, Toto Bissainthe, Jean-Michel Martial, Patrick Rameau, Mirielle Metellus. A detailed and affecting picture of Papa Doc Duvalier's dictatorship of Haiti in the 1960s, where torture, massacre and repression are endemic, and communities fall apart under violence and terror. Events are seen through the eyes of a child. An honest and painful film.

Man Who Guards the Greenhouse, The (1988) (84mins) d: Marc Voizard s: George Arthur Bloom : Christopher Cazenove, Rebecca Dewey, Louise Vallance, Bob Piedalue. A writer leaves her romantic world to look at life as it exists around her and to find a way of reconciling her two lovers. Of course, it ends with understanding and peace of mind. Amusing and diverting. (See: Shades of Love series)

Man, a Woman and a Bank, A (1979) (101mins) (a Canada-U.S. film) d: Noel Black s: Raynold Gideon, Bruce Evans, Stuart Margolin (based on the story by Gideon and Evans) : Donald Sutherland, Brooke Adams, Paul Mazursky, Allan Magicovsky, Leigh Hamilton. A bank heist, but this time no shoot-ups: computer manipulation instead. Easy going with a likeable cast. Look for director Mazursky, who is seldom behind the cameras these days.

Manette: la folle et les dieux de carton: see **Crazy Manette and Cardboard Gods**

Manhattan Shakedown: see **British Quota Era**

Manipulateur, Le: see **Artificial Lies**

Manteau, Le: see **Overcoat, The**

Mansfield Park (1998) (108mins) (a Canada-U.S.-U.K. co-production) d&s: Patricia Rozema (from Jane Austen's novel) : Frances O'Conner, Embeth Davidtz, Harold Pinter, Lindsay Duncan, Sheila Gish, James Purefoy, Justine Waddell, Hugh Bonneville, Victoria Hamilton. Fanny Brice is sent to live with her wealthy relations at Mansfield Park. She has always felt a debt of gratitude toward her aunt and her wealthy family, but is always being reminded that she is out of her class. So far, so good for Jane. But now the director gives us some comically surreal teenage writings to construct her view of the original passionate story. Splendid acting and lovely backgrounds cannot disguise this adaptation from being anything other than a misrepresenation.

Manuel: A Son by Choice (Manuel, le fils emprunté) (1990) (79mins) d: François Labonté s: Gerald Wexler : Francisco Rabal, Kim Yaroshevskaya, Nuno Da Costa, Luiz Saraiva. A 12-year-old Portuguese boy in Montréal runs away from his father and goes to live with an old man, a friend of the family who had fought in the Spanish Civil War. The moral dilemma his teachings create for the boy makes for a thoughtful, sparing and entirely convincing study of immigrant life and the influencing of an adolescent.

Manuscrit érotique, Le (A Romantic Scenario) (2002) (90mins) d&s: Jean-Pierre Lefebvre : Lyne Riel, Christiane Drolet, Sylvie Moreau, Francois Papineau, Liane Simard, Leo Bosse. Lefebvre's constant themes, to love and be loved, run through this slight but acutely observed study of a young woman who works for a publishing company. One day she realizes that a manuscript she is reading concerns a young woman who has experienced and survived a love affair similar to her own. Beautifully done.

Many Trials of One Jane Doe, The (2002) (120mins) d: Jerry Ciccoritti s: Karen Walton : Wendy Crewson, Steven Mackintosh, Gary Lewis, Sarah Constible, Jacob Tierney, Eric Peterson. This is a commendable film that, unfortunately, gets lost in its own confusions and those of the many characters involved as it attempts to tell the true-life story of a woman who was raped in 1987 in Toronto. As the years pass, her anger remains undiminished, and she decides to sue the Toronto police for failing to warn her and the women in her neighbourhood that a rapist was living among them. She also found the police and the legal system to be sexist and uncaring. Unfortunately, after the powerful opening scenes showing Jane's (Wendy Crewson) terrible mental and physical agony after the assault, throughout the remainder of the film it is difficult to feel any sympathy for her as she fiercely pursues her objective. Neither can we feel tension or excitement over the outcome of the case; it's just too tangled. However, it is a welcome change to see a Canadian court and legal proceedings, rather than an American setting.

Map of the Human Heart (1993) (126 mins) (a Canada-U.K.-Australia-France co-production) d&s: Vincent Ward : Patrick Bergin, Anne Parillaud, Jason Scott Lee, John Cusack, Robert Joamie, Annie Galipeau, Jeanne Moreau, Ben Mendelson, Clotilde Couran. Like *Black Robe*, this is a magnificent Canada-Australia co-production moving between the Arctic, Montréal and London, detailing the lives of an Inuit man and a Cree woman from childhood to old age. This is a brilliant piece of cinema almost beyond description; filled with beauty, mythology, love and dreams, it places Vincent Ward among the finest and most daring of filmmakers. His is an unfailing imagination at work creating unforgettable characters caught up in gripping events both simple and momentous. The human heart has seldom been mapped so eloquently and with such feeling.

Marais, Le (The Marsh) (2002) (85mins) d&s: Kim Nguyen : Gregory Hlady, Paul Ahmarani, Gabriel Gascon, Jennifer Morehouse. In 19TH-century Eastern Europe, a nomadic family wanders from town to town meeting rejection from their compatriots, the Turks. They finally take up residence on the edge of a marsh, home of demons, monsters and goblins. When a murder is committed, the peasants suspect them. A very strange subject, set against very strange backgrounds; superstitious and eventually very tiresome.

Marchands du silence, Les (The Merchants of Silence) (1994) (85mins) (a Canada-France-Brazil co-production) d: François Labonté s: Christine Miller and others : Julie Vincent, Didier Flamand, Betty Lago, Gaston Lepage. This work was filmed in Brazil in the terrible world of abandoned street children. A social worker from Québec becomes involved with a kidnapping and other cruel activities. The faces of the children haunt us throughout this daring film.

Marche a l'amour, La: see **Crinoline Madness**

Marcheurs de la Nuit, Les: see **Cain**

Margaret Sanger Story, The: see **Choices of the Heart**

Margaret's Museum (1995) (114mins) (a Canada-U.K. co-production) d: Mort Ransen s: Gerald Wexler, Mort Ransen (based on short stories by Sheldon Currie) : Helena Bonham Carter, Kate Nelligan, Clive Russell, Andrea Morris, Kenneth Welsh. A moving chronicle of a woman's struggle to find a better life for herself, set against the coal mines of Nova Scotia during the late 1940s. As Margaret, Helena Bonham Carter's performance is extraordinary, deeply aware and emotionally compelling. Too bad the surprise ending rings false with the rest of the film's realistic portrayal. Kate Nelligan is marvellous as the overworked mother. The entire cast is to be applauded.

Marguerite Volant (1996) (65mins) d: Charles Binamé s: Jacques Jacob, Monique Messier : Catherine Sénart, Michael Sapieha, Normand D'Amour, Gilbert Sicotte, Marie Tifo, Pascale Bussières, Pierre Curzi, Pascale Monpetit. A fascinating love story set in 1763, when Québec has been ceded to the British. The daughter of a seigneur falls in love with French and British officers during this time of passions, treachery and intrigue among the nobility. Production values are marvellous and the cast walks straight out of history.

Maria (1977) (65mins) (b/w) d: Allan King s: Rick Salutin : Diane d'Aquila. In a garment factory in Toronto, Maria, a courageous Italian immigrant, sets out to form and organize a union to bring peace among women immigrant workers, who are exploited by men and management alike. A rare dramatic film for its time, venturing into the living conditions of immigrant workers with fairness, insight and sympathy. (See: *For the Record*)

Maria Chapdelaine (1983) (107mins) (a Canada-France co-production) d: Gilles Carle s: Guy Fournier, Gilles Carle (based on Louis Hémon's once popular story of pioneer life in Québec) : Carole Laure, Nick Mancuso, Pierre Curzi, Donald Lautrec, Claude Rich, Amulette Garneau, Gilbert Sicotte, Marie Tifo, Guy L'Écuyer, Rock Demers, and many others. In spite of Carle's several clever directorial devices, he fails to bring events to life or to create romantic and emotional depth in the characters. In particular, the young lovers look too old for their roles, the settings are not convincing, and the period feels wrong. It seems that Carle, afraid of being called old-fashioned for bringing an old-fashioned book to the screen, has no fashion at all, resulting in a film without style or spirit. This is the third version of Maria Chapdelaine. The first, in 1934, was a French film shot mainly in Québec by the distinguished French director Julien Duvivier, and starring the popular French players Jean Gabin, Madeleine Renaud and Suzanne Desprès. The second version of Maria Chapdelaine, in 1950, was a British film shot mainly in Québec by the well-known French director Marc Allegret and starring a mixed French-British cast, including Michèle Morgan, Kieron Moore, Françoise Rosay, Jack Watling and Phillipe Lemaire. Also known as *The Naked Heart.*

Mariages (Marriages) (2001) (95mins) d&s: Catherine Martin : Marieve Bertrand, Guylaine Tremblay, Mirianne Brûlé, Hélène Loiselle, David Boutin, Markita Boies. Set in Québec during Victorian times, this is a dark portrayal of the life forced upon women by the church, society and state. Sometimes, these women's lives must have seemed beyond endurance; they were frustrated, exploited, and expected to bear endless numbers of children. Set in forested country, a 20-year-old woman finds her life has fallen into two parts, one of cold austerity that concealed feeling and passion, the other filled with desire and vibrant intensity. A first feature taking its time to unfold, this film creates another world with authentic and sombre tones and beliefs.

Marie in the City (Marie s'en va-t-en ville) (1987) (75mins) d&s: Marquise Lepage : Geneviève Lenoir, Frédèrique Collin. This is a compelling and intelligent study of the relationship between a 13-year-old girl who has run away from home and an aging and disillusioned prostitute on the streets of Montréal. An affection and companionship develops between them that is cleverly and delicately treated, never falling into the trite or familiar. A memorable and affecting work.

Marie s'en va-t-en ville: see **Marie in the City**

Marie's Sons (Les fils de Marie) (2002) (100mins) (a Canada-France co-production) d: Carole Laure s: Pascal Arnold, Carole Laure : Carole Laure, Jean-Marc Barr, Felix Lajeunesse-Guy, Danny Gilmour, Daniel Desjardins An odd and trying picture about mostly unlikeable people. This is a first film as director for actress Carole Laure, who appears to be suffering from a Gilles Carle hangover. It's about a bereaved woman whose husband and teenage son have been killed in a car crash. She now seeks a boy her son's age to mother. This could have been a story with emotional and psychological depth and appeal. Instead, as knowing critics pointed out at

Cannes, where this picture was shown in the Critics' Week, it invokes comparison with Kieslowski's *Three Colours: Blue*, to its detriment.

Marie-Anne (1978) (87mins) d: Martin Walters s: George Salverson (based on the novel Marie-Anne by Marjorie Mousan) : Andrée Pelletier, John Juliani, Tantoo Martin, Gordon Tootoosis. A simple yet telling story of Marie-Anne, the first white woman to travel to Fort Edmonton, and who later became the grandmother of Louis Riel. Beautifully played by Pelletier.

Marilyn Bell Story, The: see **Heart**

Marine Life (2000) (95mins) d: Anne Wheeler s: Lori Lansens, Rob Forsyth (based on the book by Linda Svendsen) : Cybill Shepherd, Peter Outerbridge, Alexandra Purvis, Gabrielle Miller, Michael Hogan. This is a shambling, untidy and altogether tiresome depiction of life with a broken-down family. We see through the eyes of the film's only likeable character, a 12-year-old daughter with a divorced mother, whose new companion is also rough-and-ready, who wonders who will give her the love she so desperately craves. Set on the waterfront in Vancouver, the only attractive place in the film. Cybill Shepherd was brought up from L.A. to play a pianist because, obviously, there are no Canadians who can sing as badly as she does as a barroom entertainer.

Mario (1984) (98mins) d: Jean Beaudin s: Arlette Dion, Jacques Paris, Jean Beaudin : Xavier Norman Petermann, Francis Reddy, Nathalie Chalifor, Jacques Godin, Marcel Sabourin. Based on Claude Jasmin's novel, *La Sablière*, and set in the Îles de la Madeleine, this is a beautifully filmed fable of two young brothers. The innocence, affection and fantasy in their lives lead to their destruction when a young woman appears.

Marion Bridge (2002) (95mins) d: Wiebke von Carolsfeld s: Daniel MacIvor (adapted from his play) : Molly Parker, Rebecca Jenkins, Stacy Smith, Ellen Page, Marguerite McNeail. A compassionate film concerning three sisters bound together yet torn apart by a family secret, in their rural home in Cape Breton. When they meet to care for their dying mother, the youngest is determined they will face up to what happened and accept it—or else. This is a marvellous, perceptive, beautifully acted portrayal of women in crisis.

Mark of Cain, The (1984) (90mins) d: Bruce Pittman s: John Sheppard (and Peter Colley from his play) : Robin Ward, Wendy Crewson, August Schellenberg, Deborah Grover, Anthony Parr. A complicated and often harrowing piece about identical twin boys who were adopted and raised by an extremely religious couple. After murdering a young girl, one of the boys ends up in an institution for the criminally insane. The other marries and enjoys a contented life until murder most foul raises its ugly head again. A gripping study of minds gone mad.

Marriage Bed, The (1986) (99mins) d: Martin Lavut s: Anna Sandor (from the novel of the same title by

Constance Beresford-Howe) : Linda Griffiths, Layne Coleman, R.H. Thomson, Jan Rubes, Martha Gibson, Sheila McCarthy. A pregnant wife is abandoned by her dull and irresponsible husband. It's Christmastime and, rather than give in to melancholy, she makes up her mind to appreciate her home and children and make the most out of being alive. Beautifully stated and played with just the right amount of family warmth and sentiment.

Marriages: see *Mariages*

Married Life: The Movie (2000) (120mins) d&s: Kenneth Finkleman : Ken Finkleman, Robert Cait, Mark Farrell, Wayne Flemming, Karen Hines, Jeremy Hotz, Rosemary Radcliffe. Finkleman plays himself, a film director, in this superficial satire of television that portrays the marriage of a young couple as part of a new reality tv series. Based on his previous television work in this form.

Marsh, The: see *Marais, Le*

Martha, Ruth and Edie (1987) (91mins) d: Norma Bailey, Deepa Mehta Saltzman, Danièle Suissa s: Anna Sandor, Barbara O'Kelly, Janet MacLean (based on works by Alice Munro, Cynthia Flood, Betty Lambert) : Jennifer Dale, Margaret Langrick, Andrea Martin. Three accomplished actresses are at their charming best in three stories about the lives of three women who, after a chance meeting, feel much better about themselves.

Ma*rtien de Noël, Le*: see **Christmas Martian, The**

Martin's Day (1984) (98mins) (a Canada-U.S. film) d: Alan Gibson s: Chris Bryant : Richard Harris, Justin Henry, Karen Black, James Coburn, Lindsay Wagner, John Ireland. A cast of mostly American players can do little with this silly story of an escaped prisoner who kidnaps a young boy and then befriends him. A time waster in every respect.

Mary and Joseph: A Story of Faith (1979) (152mins) (a Canada-German-Israel co-production) d: Eric Till s: Carmen Culver : Blanche Baker, Jeff East, Colleen Dewhurst, Stephen McHattie, Lloyd Bochner, Marilyn Lightstone, Murray Matheson. A slow-moving depiction of Joseph and Mary's life together before the birth of you know who. The director does his best with a somewhat lacklustre script among the expected sets, costumes and locales. The cast is not always as convincing.

Mary Silliman's War (1994) (93mins) (a Canadian-American film) d: Steven Surjik s: Steven Schechter : Nancy Palk, Richard Donat. Filmed in Nova Scotia, passing for Connecticut at the time of the American Revolution, the pregnant Mary Silliman, wife of the state attorney, sees him taken to New York as a prisoner of the British. We see the revolution through Mary's eyes and through her diaries and memoirs. This is a quietly compelling and authentic piece of history nicely told, filmed and acted, without anger.

Masala (1992) (105mins) d&s: Srinivas Krishna : Krishna, Zohra Segal, Saeed Jaffrey, Sakina Jaffrey, Madhuri Bhatia. A multicultural muddle set among an East Indian family in Toronto and straining credibility as neither good comedy nor melodrama. A case of a first-time filmmaker doing too much and, in the bargain, wasting the talents of the international actor Saeed Jaffrey.

Masculine Mystique, The (1984) (87mins) d&s: John Smith, Giles Walker, David Wilson : Stefan Wodoslawsky, Char Davies, Eleanor MacKinnon, Felice Grana, Stefanie Grana, Mort Ransen. A look at four men, each of whom has failed one way or the other in his relationships with women. What do women want? What is feminism? How can men live with the "modern woman" and her claim to liberation? From what? Interesting, perceptive, amusing and annoying, and a great discussion piece for its time.

Mask, The (Eyes of Hell) (1961) (83mins) d: Julian Roffman s: Frank Taubes (and others) : Paul Stevens, Claudette Nevins, Bill Walker, Anne Collings, Martin Lavut, Jim Moran. With sequences in 3-D, the novelty at the time, using techniques devised at Britain's National Research Centre, with work by the once-famed montage expert Slavko Vorkapich) A psychiatrist is visited by a man who claims to have committed a murder while under the influence of a mask unearthed in South America. Though the psychiatrist is skeptical, he experiences fearful hallucinations and a compulsion to strangle his receptionist. When a colleague demands tests of the mask under his supervision, and his fiancée threatens to tell the police, the psychiatrist goes berserk. The police eventually overcome him as he tries to strangle his fiancée, and the mask is returned to the museum. A highly colourful melodramatic pastiche anxiously contrived to make the most of the 3-D process, a technique all the rage in Hollywood at the time. (The mask used may be seen at the Toronto Film Reference Library.) (It was originally donated to the Ontario Film Institute by Julian Roffman.)

Master Cats, The (Les chats bottes) (1971) (90mins) d: Claude Fournier s: Marie-José Raymond, Claude Fournier : Donald Pilon, Donald Lautrec, Louise Turcot, Jacques Famery, Andrée Lalonde, Katerine Mousseau. Only in Québec could Canadian filmmakers think up something so romantically outlandish as this comedy about a couple of men who live mainly on the kindness of women. Their friendship is threatened when one man finds that he loves them all! Lots of fun in a loving way.

Master of Images, The (1972) (79mins) d&s: Byron Black : Byron Black, Neils Ashby, Tony White, Bruce Macdonald, June Boe, Gloria Rothwell. Byron Black came to Vancouver from California in the late 1960s and established a name for himself with experimental films that few people seemed to like or understand. This venture into fiction is supposedly about a nutty spiritual master who is making a film about strange people who come to him for spiritual enlightenment. It sank out of sight after it opened, and the infinity movement Black espoused went with it.

Matin dans une forêt de pins: see **Morning in the Pine Forest**

Matin, une vi, Un: see **Morning Man, The**

Matinée (1989) (90mins) d&s: Richard Martin : Ron White, Gillian Barber, Jeff Schultz. For once, a genuine horror story, imaginatively filmed and set in a Vancouver cinema where the Horror Film Festival leads to murder most foul. All the usual suspects make this an exciting and gripping film. It deserved more showings and reviews.

Matins infidèles, Les: see **Unfaithful Mornings**

Matou, Le: see **Alley Cat, The**

Matroni and Me (*Matroni et moi*) (1999) (102mins) d: Jean-Philippe Duval s: Alexis Martin, Jean-Philippe Duval (based on the play by Martin) : Alexis Martin, Guylaine Tremblay, Gary Boudreault, Pierre Lebeau, Maude Guérin, Pierre Curzi. A talkative play becomes a tiring film about a dull intellectual who comes into conflict with Mafia toughs. Supposedly a comedy, the funny and tender moments are hard to find. And isn't everyone fed up with the Mafia? Dashing camera work and techniques cannot atone for a pointless story.

Matter of Choice, A (1978) (90mins) d: Francis Mankiewicz s: B.A. Cameron, Cam Hubert : Roberta Maxwell, Fiona Reid, Neil Dainard, Gary Reineke, Michael Ironside. A distressing, agonizing drama looking at the violent crime of rape. A woman is raped by an acquaintance. She is humiliated, repulsed and alienated and turns to her friends for comfort. This is not a sensational treatment for sex-seeking audiences but a concerned view of a terrible crime. (Note: Francis Mankiewicz is the third director from Montréal to join Gilles Carle and Claude Jutra in bringing their skills to English-language filmmaking.) (See: *For the Record*)

Matter of Life, A (*Question de vie*) (1971) (65mins) d&s: André Théberge : Frédérique Collin, Alain Gélinas, Josée Beauregard, Valda Dalton, Rejane Desramrant. After being abandoned by her worthless husband, a young mother in Montréal must work in a clothing factory to support herself and her children. She suffers a mental breakdown and struggles to persevere within a society that pays little heed to those carrying on a lonely struggle for survival. Still a timely subject, movingly depicted and filmed as a fictional narrative containing the truth and looks of a documentary.

Matthew Shepard Story, The (2001) (120mins) (a U.S.-Canada film) d: Roger Spottiswoode s: John Wierick, Jacob Krueger : Shane Meier, Paul Robbins, Philip Edolls, Sam Waterston, Stockard Channing. Two men, brutally murder a University of Wyoming student, simply because he was homosexual. The murderers were caught and put on trial. The student's parents asked the court not to apply the death penalty but, instead, to use the trial as an attempt to end the cycle of hatred by making as many people as possible take notice of hate crimes. A worthy ambition of an actual event, if not entirely successful, but the film never loses sight of the depth and seriousness of its subject.

Matusalem (1993) (108mins) d&s: Roger Cantin : Marc Labrèche, Émile Proulx-Cloutier, Maxime Collin, Steve Gendron, Jessica Barker. A cheerful family film, this is a boisterous adventure tale of a 17th-century pirate ghost who seeks the help of a present-day young boy to end a curse placed upon him by an evil spirit. Caribbean pirate activities are colourfully staged against Cuban and Québec backgrounds.

***Matusalem II, le dernier des Beauchesne* (Matusalem II: The Last of the Beauchesne)** (1996) (100mins) d&s: Roger Cantin : Marc Labrèche, Émile Proulx-Cloutier, Steve Gendron, Marie-France Monette. Another of Cantin's popular family fantasies, this one about the further adventures of Oliver, who, every year on his birthday, finds a door opens and takes him into a mysterious past. Costumes, performances, design and effects are well done, but the treatment heavy-handed. This time around a group of children go time-travelling back to the days of pirates and derring-do in the tropics. The first of these fantasy films by Roger Cantin was a tremendous financial success in Quebec, but this one won't catch on as did Pt.1. There is too much violence, and falls between being a family or grown-up film. The *Matusalem* is a diamond.

Maudite galette, La: see **That Darned Loot**

Maudits sauvages, Les: see **Those Damned Savages**

Max (1994) (95mins) d&s: Charles Wilkinson : R.H. Thomson, Denise Crosby, Walter Dalton, Garwin Sanford, Fabio Wilkinson. A placid Vancouver family has grown tired of the daily rat race and its anxieties. They have a young son fatally ill from environmental pollution and decide to move into the interior of B.C. to start over again in a rural home. The father, searching desperately for the perfect unspoiled surroundings, is brought to the point of his own destruction. The son is, in real life, the son of the director. The performances have the depth and despair of characters who find that life has become intolerable for them. A thoughtful and provocative piece.

Max (2001) (105mins) (a Hungary-U.K.-Canada co-production) d&s: Menno Meyjes : John Cusack, Leelee Sobieski, Noah Taylor, Ulrich Thomsen, Molly Parker, Janet Guzman. This is a handsome film set in Munich just after World War I and filled with high-class Europeans given to pseudo-sophisticated discussions about art, politics and paintings. The principal characters here are a retiring Jewish art dealer and an obviously lower-class former army corporal named Adolf Hitler, who rages with frustration over his attempts at painting and drawing. He also claims that the Jews are successful because of the purity of their blood. The art dealer tries to help him by exhibiting his work. This is not successful, leading to the emergence of the Fuhrer as we will soon know him, when he gives a rabble-rousing speech addressing a crowd and condemning the Jews. This prompts several thugs to go out into the winter snow and beat the art dealer to death. It's all very well to say, "We must remember," but this glib "history" we could do without.

Maxwell's Dream (1999) (78mins) (b/w) d&s: David Clark : Andy Curtis, Mark David Stewart, Darcy Dunlop. An interesting and poignant sci-fi drama with a serious purpose. A hapless private detective is investigating the suicide of a sperm-bank operator and becomes involved in an astronomer's strange dream experiments. A far-reaching treatment with a nod to academic study, but nicely underlined with a sense of the comedic. (Note: Not to be confused with *Maxwell's Demon,* 1968, an animated film by James Duesing about "existence shaped by environment.")

Mayday (1996) (94mins) (a Canada-France co-production) d: Jean-Louis Daniel s: Robert Gauthier, Alain Berliner : Carl Marotte, Macha Grenon, Bruno Wolkowitch, Jochen Nickel. You might never have heard of them, but the Canadian army's search and rescue units save lives regularly across our treacherous and unforgiving landscape. The group of four depicted here also has personal worries and cares outside of army life. What Hollywood does for the U.S. Armed Forces, this film does exceptionally for ours.

Mayor of Casterbridge, The: see **Claim, The**

Mazes and Monsters (1982) (100mins) (a Canada-U.S. film) d: Steven Hilliard Stern s: Tom Lazarus (based on Rona Jaffe's book *Dungeons and Dragons*) : Tom Hanks, Wendy Crewson, David Wallace, Chris Makepeace, Lloyd Bochner, Peter Donat, Murray Hamilton, Susan Strasberg. Four university students become involved with game playing in a medieval world of fantasy, fright and fear. Engrossingly and cleverly done.

Me (1974) (82mins) d: John Palmer s: Barry Pearson (based on the play by Martin Kinch) : Brenda Donohue, Chapelle Jaffe, Stephen Markle, William Webster. A play about a violent relationship between a writer and his lovers. Simple but deep and not easily forgotten. (First shown at the Stratford (Ontario) Film Festival, 1974)

Me and My Shadows (2000) (240mins) (a Canada-U.S. film) d: Robert Allan Ackerman s: Robert L. Freedman (based on the book of the same title by Lorna Luft) : Judy Davis, Victor Garber, Hugh Laurie, John Benjamin Hickey, Tammy Blanchard, Sonja Smits, Marsha Mason, Jayne Eastwood, Daniel Kash and Al Waxman. A splendid, deeply moving and definitive portrait of the famous, complex and often misunderstood actress and singer Judy Garland, and her daughter Lorna. This poignant dramatization of their lives also conveys the magic that made Garland so special. With 30 songs, and the late Al Waxman doing a fairly accurate Louis B. Mayer, and Judy Davis being marvellous as Judy.

Meat Market: see **Cruising Bar**

Meatballs (1979) (94mins) (a Canada-U.S. film) d: Ivan Reitman s: Dan Goldberg and others : Bill Murray, Harvey Atkin, Kate Lynch, Cindy Girling, Chris Makepeace, Michael Kirby, Larry Solway. A coming-of-age comedy with all the typical summer camp antics. Billy Murray is excellently cast as the sly, wise-cracking councilor whose unique and rather twisted way of viewing the world helps an innocent adolescent (Chris Makepeace) discover self-confidence.

Meatballs, Part II (1984) (87mins) (a Canada-U.S. film) d: Ken Wiederhorn s: Bruce Singer : Richard Mulligan, John Menatti, Hamilton Camp, Kim Richards, Tammy Taylor, Misty Rowe. The dumbsters are back, this time mixed up in a boxing match with a nearby camp. If the protagonists lose, their camp will be finished. Awful.

Meatballs, Part III: The Climax (1987) (94mins) (a Canada-U.S. film) d: George Mendeluk s: Michael Pascornek, Bradley Kesden : Sally Kellerman, Patrick Dempsey, Al Waxman, Isabelle Mejias, Shannon Tweed, Ian Taylor, George Buza, Maury Chaykin. A lousy cook-up about a dead porno star and a teenage creep. Thoroughly indigestible.

Meatballs, Part IV (1992) (84mins) (a Canadian-American film) d&s: Bob Logan : Corey Feldman, Jack Nance, Sarah Douglas. Summer camp nonsense once again, deplorable, despicable and rife with nudity and foul language. The balls, stale at the start, are now a mouldy mess.

Méchant party **(The Party from Hell)** (2000) (78mins) d&s: Mario Chabot : David La Haye, Roc Lafortune, Paul-Patrick Charbonneau, Tony Conte, Lise Dion, Catherine Sénart. It's Halloween night in Montréal and one young man going to a romantic rendezvous with the woman of his dreams, falls in with another man dressed like a jester, who behaves coarsely and loudly. They proceed from one seedy bar to another in a film that has not one redeeming feature. A time waster from beginning to end.

Medicine River (1993) (94mins) d: Stuart Margolin s: Thomas King, Ann MacNaughton (adapted from King's first novel of the same name) : Graham Greene, Tom Jackson, Janet-Laine Green, Sheila Tousey. A young Cree photographer returns from Toronto to the Prairies, near Medicine River, to discover his people and his past. Insightful, humorous and appealing.

Medium Blues (1985) (78mins) d: Michel Préfontaine s: Carmel Dumas, Michel Préfontaine : Marthe Turgeon, Hélène Lasnier, Guy Vauthier, Gilbert Beaumont, Lise Grégoire. Recently separated from her lover, an active and successful Montréal businesswoman finds loneliness becoming a constant blight upon her life. Her unhappiness deepens when her former partner, who is pregnant, no longer has time for her.

Megantic Outlaw, The (1971) (90mins) d&s: Ron Kelly : Gary McKeehan, Lloyd Bochner, Sydney Brown, Neil Dainard, Jon Granik, Carole Lazare, Jane Mallett, Ratch Wallace, David Hughes, Harry Finlay, Ralph Endersby, William Nunn. A striking drama based on the true story of a young outlaw in Québec's Eastern Townships. In the late 19th century, a farmer's son is accused of barn burning and becomes a fugitive. He hides within the community until he is hunted as a murderer and finally shot while surrendering, believing in the law's willingness to let him off lightly. Brings the period convincingly to life.

Melanie (1982) (107mins) (a Canada-U.S. film) d: Rex Bromfield s: Robert Guza, Richard Paluck (story: Michael Green) : Glynnis O'Conner, Paul Sorvino, Burton Cummings, Trudy Young, Don Johnson. Cummings plays a has-been rock star who helps a woman from Arkansas regain custody of her young boy from her former husband. The score is washed by tears, but the sincerity of the whole prevents a flood.

Melting Pot, The (1975) (102mins) d&s: Deke Miles, Lesley Gibbs (based on the story by Romeo Jacobucci) : Peter Jacob, Richard Fullerton, Camilo Jubarbal, Max Scheindel, Kimberly Smith. This is dramatic feature film that wants to be a documentary and ends up an uncomfortable hybrid in its record of the great Winnipeg floods in 1950, and the arrival of two young Americans, dodging the draft, who pitch in to help the locals hold back the great waters.

Même sang, Un (The Same Blood) (1994) (78mins) d&s: Michel Langlois : Andrée Lachapelle, Mario Saint-Amant, Fabien Dupuis, Jean-René Ouellet. One autumn evening in Montréal, a mother is stabbed by her son. She refuses to charge him, but under interrogation the son confesses to his father and the police. No one believes him, and he is left with a terrible secret that might well destroy the family. A tragic family drama, done with conviction and understanding.

Mémoire battante (1983) (168mins) d&s: Arthur Lamothe : Gabriel Arcand. The life of the Jesuit missionary Père Paul Le Jeune is shown in a mix of documentary film and dramatized sequences, with Gabriel Arcand taking the part of the missionary. One has to be something of a missionary to live through this unconventional film.

Mémoire tronquée (Lapse of Memory) (1990) (90mins) (A Canada-France co-production) d: Patrick Dewolf s: Philippe le Guay, John Frizzell, Patrick Dewolf (from Robert Cormier's book I'm the Cheese) : John Hurt, Marthe Keller, Matthew MacKay, Kathleen Robertson, Marion Peterson. A tidy, ambitious thriller-romance about a boy who suffers a canoe accident and loses his memory, but is helped by a psychiatrist to get it back. We learn that the boy's family changed its name and left New York City after his father brought a huge case of corruption to light. The attempt to begin a new, different life confuses the boy. Complicated but certainly not run of the mill.

Memoirs (1984) (83mins) d: Bashar Shbib s: John Beckett Wimbs (based on his play Memoirs of Johnny Daze) : Philip Baylaucq, Norma-Jean Sanders, Julia Gilmore, Michel Gagnon, Claire Nadon. Hardly a year passes without the irrepressible Shbib bringing out another of his distant cousins to Warhol. This time, a writer becomes involved with an art addict, who meets a new artist, who leads to another... And so it goes, a colourful tribe of no depth, but good for an hour's entertainment. This time, Shbib shuns Florida for Montréal.

Memories Unlocked (Souvenirs intimes) (1999) (118mins) d: Jean Beaudin s: Monique Proulx (based on her novel Homme invisible à la fenêtre) : James Hyndman, Pascale Bussières, Pierre-Luc Brillant, Yves Jacques, Louise Portal, Marcel Sabourin. Max, a painter who lost his legs in an accident years ago, works in his loft surrounded by friends. We meet the women he loves, from the past and the present, and a mysterious voice that haunts his nights with phone calls. A mixture somewhat typical of Beaudin's work: a blend of charm, wit, frankness, tedium and interesting characters.

Memory Run (Synapse) (1995) (89mins) (a Canada-U.S. film) d: Allan Goldstein s: David Gottlieb, Allan Goldstein : Karen Duffy, Barry Morse, Matt McCoy, Torri Higginson, Saul Rubinek, Chris Makepeace, Lynne Cormack. In the year 2015, the search for immortality is over. Those who benefit from the new technology will wake up to a youthful new life. However, the rest of mankind must exist in a living hell. Pity us, please; no more of this!

Men of Means (1999) (101mins) d: George Mendeluk s: Shane Perez : Raymond Serra, Austin Pendleton, Kaela Dobkin, Tony Cucci, Michael Pare, Rodd Baker. A football player has ruined his own career by his behaviour, and now he must decide to make a new life on his own or to join and run with the mob. Behind the scenes manipulations smartly depicted in shadows and shame.

Men With Brooms (2002) (98mins) d: Paul Gross s: John Krizanc, Paul Quarrington, Paul Gross : James Allodi, Peter Outerbridge, Jed Rees, Paul Gross, Leslie Nielsen, Molly Parker, Polly Shannon. What we hoped would be a delightful, honest and affectionate comedy about the thousands of decent Canadians for whom the sport of curling is an integral part of their lives turns out to be a crawl along the gutter of sexual slime, foul language and crude behaviour. The likeable, talented and good-looking actor Paul Gross is part producer, writer, director and star, and has been quoted as saying, "I didn't know what the hell I was doing." But then what else could be expected from working with producer low-taste Lantos? A final hymn of praise for the sport comes too late to redeem this wretched concoction. As for Leslie Nielsen, he might just as well have stayed at home. (And please let's not bracket this with *The Full Monty*.) (Locations: Sudbury and Toronto.)

Men With Guns (1996) (90mins) d: Kari Skogland s: Lachy Hulme : Donal Logue, Gregory Sporleder, Callum Keith Rennie, Paul Sorvino, Max Perlich, Joseph Griffin, Derek Ritschel, William MacDonald. An irresponsible, tortured and terribly told tale about men who live marginally and become involved with drug dealers, hoping to make quick money. It wallows in violence and mayhem, ugly and sensational for its own sake. Pity to see the exceptional actor Callum Keith Rennie mired in this muck.

Men, The (*Les mâles*) (1971) (113mins) d&s: Gilles Carle : Donald Pilon, René Blouin, Andrée Pelletier, Katerine Mousseau, Guy L'Écuyer, J.-Léo Gagnon, Marc Gélinas, Denise Lafleur, Michèle Latraverse, Jacques Bilodeau, Paul Gauthier, Robert DesRoches. Backwoods comedy of two clods in the wilderness who have abandoned civilization and one day decide to hunt for a woman. With its local jokes and provincial references, *Les mâles* was a runaway success in Québec. Carle, as usual, goes from one extreme to another, and in this case he dredges for humour, sex and sympathy among the boisterous working class, much to their delight, as witnessed by the box-office returns.

Ménace, La (Backlash) (1977) (117mins) (a Canada-France co-production) d: Alain Corneau s: Daniel Boulanger, Alain Corneau : Yves Montand, Carole Laure, Marie Dubois, Roger Muni, Jean-François Balmer, Bob Hughes, Michel Ruhi, Ion Katzman. A complicated and not terribly convincing plot about the death of a woman in love with a man who leaves her. He then implicates himself in the death to save another woman he loves. On escaping to Canada, he fakes his own death. Stretched to the breaking point, the menace doesn't go far.

Merchants of Silence, The: see *Marchands du silence, Les*

Merry Wives of Tobias Rouke, The (1972) (77mins) d: John Board s: George Mendeluk, Arthur Slabotsky : Paul Bradley, Henry Beckman, Judith Gault, Linda Sorensen, Ratch Wallace, Samuel Jephcott, Guy Sanvido, Earl Pomerantz. In spite of a stable of talented actors, this rural comedy doesn't quite take off. It concerns a travelling salesman in the west and his somewhat doubtful schemes involving wives and wealth.

Merry World of Léopold Z, The (*La vie heureuse de Léopold Z*) (1965) (70mins) d&s: Gilles Carles : Guy L'Écuyer, Paul Hébert, Suzanne Valery, Monique Joly, Jacques Poulin, André Gagnon. Léopold, a plump, amiable, happily married man,

drives a snowplow for the city of Montréal. It is Christmas Eve, and the snow is falling heavily. Between cleaning streets, he takes out a loan, buys his wife a fur coat, and takes care of his cousin, a nightclub singer. Throughout his long and tiring day, he is watched by his foreman, who suspects he is up to other things. This is a lively, spirited, deftly handled comedy with serious undertones. It is an auspicious beginning for Gilles Carle. (See: *Drylanders*)

Mesmer (1994) (102mins) (a Canada-U.K.-German co-production) d: Roger Spottiswoode s: Dennis Potter : Alan Rickman, Amanda Ooms, Jan Rubes, Gillian Barge, David Hemblen. A compelling, splendidly acted, written and directed biographical study of the life and achievements in medicine of Franz Anton Mesmer, one of the most successful originators of dynamic psychology (superbly played here by Alan Rickman.).

Meurtre en musique (Murder and Music) (1994) (92mins) d: Gabriel Pelletier s: Suzanne Aubry : Joseph Boca, Serge Dupire, Claude Léveillée, Marcel Sabourin, Yves Jacques, Sonia Laplante. Well-plotted and suspenseful thriller set in a nightclub where a popular singer and her songwriter lover of 15 years end their relationship because she has fallen in love with her pianist. One day, the songwriter is murdered. The investigation takes some surprising turns in this romantic and colourful yarn.

Mi Vida Sin Mi: see **My Life Without Me**

Michelle Apartments, The (1995) (91mins) d: John Pozer s: Ross Weber John Pozer : Henry Czerny, Mary Elizabeth Rubens, Daniel Kash, Peter Outerbridge, Nancy Beatty, David Calderisi, Ian D. Clark. A macabre and ultimately tedious comedy fantasy about a government auditor (a wasted Henry Czerny) sent to investigate a corrupt chemical company in an imaginary industrial town.

Midday Sun, The (1989) (93mins) d&s: Lulu Keating : Isabelle Mejias, George Seremba, Robert Bockstael, Jackie Burroughs. A well-intentioned but unconvincing account of a young Canadian woman on her first visit to a former British colony in Africa, and whose naive perceptions of social habits and political ways lands her in trouble with the authorities.

Middle-Age Crazy (1980) (97mins) (a Canada-U.S. film) d: John Trent s: Carl Kleinschmit : Bruce Dern, Ann Margret, Graham Jarvis, Eric Christmas, Deborah Wakeham. A husband reaching his 40th birthday finds himself in a mid-life crisis and exchanges his wife for a young cheerleader, among other peculiar acts. A comedy often hitting its marks with sympathy for the subject matter.

Middlemen (2000) (100mins) d: Kevin Speckmaier s: Robert Petrovicz, Kevin Speckmaier : James Hutson, Kirsten Robek, Byron Lucas, Philip Maurice Hayes, Jay Brazeau, Blu Mankuma. This is a low-point thriller that spends all of its time explaining how everyone who is dead at the film's opening came to be this way. Set against low-life Vancouver settings, this is a dreary work trying hard to make the dead interesting, but who refuse to come to life.

Midnight Magic (1988) (81 mins) d: George Mihalka s: Tannis Korbin : James Wilder, Jennifer Dale, Stuart Gillard. A psychologist whose life is on the slow side is invigorated by a young man who comes to him for counselling. What an unusual break for these over-worked practioners! The mental troubles here are easily dispersed with. (See *Shades of Love* series)

Midnight Man (Jack Higgins' *Midnight Man*) (1995) (95mins) (parts 1&2) (a Canada-U.K.-U.S.-Luxembourg film) d: Lawrence Gordon-Clark s: Jurgen Wolff, Jack Higgins (from his novels *Eye of the Storm* and *On Dangerous Ground*) : Rob Lowe, Kenneth Cranham, Deborah Moore, Hannes Jaenicke, Daphne Cheung, Michael Sarrazin. A former Secret Agent, now married, and retired, goes back to being his former self to work with the army, police and other agents to save the Royal Family form being assassinated. This is a preposterous, loud and exceedingly violent, confused and forgettable piece of work.

Midnight Witness (1992) (89mins) (a U.S.-Canada film) d&s: Peter Foldy : Jan-Michael Vincent, Karen Mongrieff, Paul Johansson, Maxwell Caulfield, Zoe Kelli Simon, Andy Romano. Here we are: back with corrupt policemen who seem to have committed a murder, and who were videotaped by a passing couple. Now the police, realizing they have been caught on tape, go looking for the couple. A routine production, only just slightly above average.

Midwife's Tale, A: The Discovery of Martha Ballad (1996) (88mins) (a Canadian-American film) d: Richard Rogers s: Laurie Cohn-Leavitt : Kalulani Lee, Laurel Ulrich. A true story set in a small town in Maine concerning an ordinary woman who is reading the diary of a midwife during a time of social change and religious conflict. Somewhat fusty at times but very human and often quite moving.

Mild Vertigo, A: see *Léger vertige, Un*

Mile Zero (Point Zero) (2001) (92mins) d: Andrew Currie s: Michael Melski : Michael Riley, Sabrina Grdevich, Conner Widdows. Filmed against Vancouver's mountain landscapes, a computer programmer's life goes off-screen when his wife and young child leave him. After a number of flashbacks dealing with then and now, he goes to live alone in the wilderness, trying to believe that his life and marriage will return to the way it was. Nicely said and done with warmth and understanding.

Milgaard (1998) (92mins) d: Stephen Williams s: Keith Ross Leckie, Alan Difiore : Ian Tracey, Gabrielle Rose. Is there anyone in Canada who does not know about David Milgaard, the man sentenced to prison for a murder he claimed he did not commit? His mother spent years of her life and a fortune in legal costs fighting for his freedom, which eventually came. This film is that story, very well

done, and looking at the emotional and physical toll paid by his mother.

Milk and Honey (1988) (89mins) d: Rebecca Yates s: Glen Salzman, Trevor Rhone : Josette Simon, Richard Mills, Lyman Ward, Djanet Sears. Much was expected from this film about a Jamaican family in Toronto and its difficulties with immigration officials. It turned out to be disappointing, in spite of a sensitive and understanding performance by Josette Simon. (see *Signature Series*)

Millennium (1988) (110mins) d: Michael Anderson s: John Varley (from his story *Air Raid*) : Kris Kristofferson, Cheryl Ladd, Victoria Snow, Daniel Travanti, Brent Carver. A small-scale, effective and original piece of science fiction about a daring mission into Earth's past in order to save its future. Gripping and intriguing.

Millennium Queen 2000: see **Battle Queen 2020**

Million Dollar Babies (1995) (240 mins) d: Christian Duguay s: Suzette Couture (based on the novel *Time of their Lives: The Dionne Tragedy* by John Nihmey and Stuart Foxman) : Roy Dupuis, Céline Bonnier, Sean McCann, Rémy Girard, Monique Spaziani, James B. Douglas, Ginette Reno, Domini Blythe, Kate Nelligan, Martin Drainville, Pierre Curzi, Marcel Sabourin, Beau Bridges as Dr. Dafoe. In 1934, during the Depression, an extraordinary event made news around the world when a mother of an impoverished family in a small northern Ontario town gave birth to five identical girls, who became known as the Dionne quintuplets. With the family unable to care for the babies, the province built them a special home, but the publicity and the throng of visiting tourists almost destroyed their lives. This film recreates the period and the people involved, with dissent and desperation in authentic detail. (Note: The real-life American doctor Allan Dafoe, played here by Bridges, was portrayed in the 1936 RKO film, *The Country Doctor*, some of which was shot at the location.)

Mills of Power, The: see *Tisserands du pouvoir, Les*

Mind Field (1989) (95mins) d: Jean-Claude Lord s: William Deverell : Michael Ironside, Lisa Langlois, Christopher Plummer, Stefan Wodoslawsky. Vaguely based on mind control experiments carried out by the CIA in Montréal, this interpretation attempts to make a *policier* out of the matter, in which a detective and a lawyer race against time to expose the deadly cover-up. Different and fast-moving.

Mind Shadows: see **Hersenschimmen**

Mindstorm (2001) (97mins) (a U.S.-Canada film) d: Richard Pepin s: Paul Birkett, Michael Derbas, Richard Pepin : Antonio Sabato Jr., Emmanuelle Vaugier, Clarence Williams III, Michael Moriarty, Michael Ironside, Eric Roberts, Sarah Carter. A psychic conducts an investigation into the disappearance of a U.S. senator. She finds that the dangerous cult responsible also reveals to her aspects of her own past, some of which are highly disturbing. It's different, which is something to think about between the car chases, gunfire and explosions, the hallmarks of this kind-of-Canadian film.

Miracle in Memphis (1999) (103mins) d: Pierre Falardeau s: Julien Poulin, Pierre Falardeau : Julien Poulin, Yves Trudel, Barry Blake. An out-of-control monster of a man, a Frankenstein who has been dead for three days, comes back to life in Memphis. The media makes a never-ending show about this miracle, whose name is Elvis Gratton, and he becomes a metaphor for show business and an international celebrity. This is one of a series of Elvis films that have been wildly popular with Québec audiences, resulting in gold mines at box offices.

Mirage, Le (The Mirage) (1992) (100mins) d&s: Jean-Claude Guiguet (based on a short story by Thomas Mann) : Louise Marleau, Fabienne Babe, Véronique Silver, Marco Hofschneider, Christopher Scarbeck. A 50-year-old woman believes she can recapture her youth by discovering someone to love. She is suddenly possessed by a consuming passion for a young American, a friend of her son. But not even the beauty of Lake Geneva (Lac Léman) and its surroundings can sustain this love for long and, with her family to consider, the woman soon shows signs of a strange physical weariness. Typically Québécois, both poignant and romantic, and touched with the sadness of love.

Misanthrope, Le (1966) (95mins) (b/w) d: Louis-Georges Carrier s: Raymond Boucher (after the play by Molière) : Guy Provost, Albert Millaire, Andrée Lachapelle, Guy Hoffman, Elizabeth Le Sieur, Denise Provost. A film record of a stage performance of Molière's popular satire of society's misdeeds, produced by Québec's film office and ministry of education. Well acted and effectively filmed, it was possibly the first play to be transferred to film in Canada. Many of the performers went on to become part of the thriving school of actors who appear regularly in Québec movies.

Misbegotten (1997) (96mins) (a U.S.-Canada film) d: Mark L. Lester s: Larry Cohen, James Gabriel Berman (from his novel) : Kevin Dillon, Robert Lewis, Nick Mancuso, Matthew Walker, Lysette Anthony. A man with blood on his hands wants very much to become a father. He has donated his sperm to a lab. When he hears that a woman is pregnant, he goes looking for her. Peculiar indeed. Audiences take warning. We never know these days where making a baby will take us!!

Misdeal: see **Best Revenge**

Misère humaine, La: see **At the Autumn of Life**

Misery Harbour (1999) (102mins) (a Canada-Norway-Sweden co-production) d: Nils Gaup s: Kenny Sanders, Sigve Endresen : Nikolaj Coster, Coster Waldau, Stuart Graham, Anneke von der Lippe, Graham Greene, Bjorn Floberg, Hywel Bennett, Margot Finley, Stig Hoffmeyer, Lars Goran Persson, Mats Helin. This film begins well at an elegant dinner with gentlemen and beautiful women. A young writer is taunted by an acerbic critic over a book by the writer called *Misery Harbour*, in which a man is killed. The critic wants to know if the writer believes that any man can be driven to kill, including himself, followed by more highfalutin dialogue. We now find the writer, much younger, is a lowly working-class youth living with his family among the roughs around smoking ironworks. He escapes by going to sea as a crew member of a sailing ship bound for Newfoundland, with a captain and crew who make Captain Bligh seem benevolent. The ship soon finds it heavy going, and so does the film, as it becomes an ugly, absurd, contrived and confused melodrama with its share of sex and brutality. The writer swims ashore at Deadman's Point and goes to work in a fish packing plant, then a lumber camp. What is he writing? What is he imagining? What is real? Newfoundlanders and their lives appear to be grossly exaggerated. This is a film running just under two hours that seemed more like four.

Miss Moscou (1992) (82mins) (a Canada-Swiss co-production) d: Gilles Carle s: Lev and Alexandre Shar Gorodsky, Gilles Carle : Chlöé Ste-Marie, Renée Faure, Michel Côté. The ever questing Carle goes to Moscow and visits an apartment where he meets a group of eight residents who discuss their lives with an old friend visiting from Canada. Revealing and appealing.

Mission of Fear (*Le festin des morts*) (1965) (80mins) (b/w) d: Fernand Dansereau s: Alex Pelletier (narrator Hubert Loiselle) : Alain Cuny, Jean-Guy Sabourin, Jacques Godin, Jean-Louis Millette, Albert Millaire, Yves Létourneau, Monique Mercure, Maurice Tremblay, Jacques Kasma, François Guillier, Ginette Letondal, Janine Sutto, Jean Perraud, Marcel Sabourin. A stark, unadorned and philosophical statement about the martyrdom of Jesuit missionaries among the Huron, 1611 to 1760. Contains some murky observations about courage, death and religion, but certainly there has never been a motion picture depicting the clash between the first colonists and the natives, as this grim and gripping re-creation does.

Misunderstood: see *Incompris, L'*

Mis-Works, The (*Les désoeuvrés*) (1959) (60mins) (b/w) d&s: René Bail : Roger Tremblay, Régent Tremblay, Michel Pelland, Serge Guenette. Three young people live in a small Québec village. One quiet afternoon, they decide to borrow an uncle's truck to take a trip into the woods. After driving around somewhat aimlessly, the truck gets stuck in muddy tracks, they free it, and return to the village. Now they must offer explanations as to why they did this. The film is divided into three parts: *The Judges*, *Guilty Ones* and *Indifferents*. How times have changed; these days, the youths would have stolen the truck and disappeared. The director calls the film a documentary but Jean-Pierre Lefebvre, who reviewed it, says "it is a reconstruction of reality". Either way, it accomplishes its intended purpose and is a valuable, if small, social document.

Mob Story (1987) (95mins) d: Gabriel and Jancarlo Markiew s: Gabriel and Jancarlo Markiews. David Flaherty : John Vernon, Kate Vernon, Margot Kidder, A sister's home in snow-swept Winnipeg becomes the refuge for her brother, an aging mobster being pursued by young gangsters of previous acquaintance. Vernon, as usual, deserves better. Second rate and insubstantial.

Moi, mon corps, mon âme: see **Goodbye, See You Monday**

Moitié gauche du frigo, La: see **Left-hand Side of the Fridge, The**

Mon amie Max (1993) (107mins) d: Michel Brault s: Jefferson Lewis : Geneviève Bujold, Marthe Keller, Rita Lafontaine. A slow-moving story of a middle-aged classical pianist, Marie-Alexandrine, who returns to Québec City after a 25-year absence to renew an old friendship and to find a long-lost son. An extended flashback shows us their younger years and how life begins to go wrong. The characters could have been more credible and appealing.

Mon amie Pierrette: see **My Friend Pierrette**

Mon enfance a Montréal: see **My Childhood in Montréal**

Mon oeil **(My Eye)** (1971) (87mins) d&s: Jean-Pierre Lefebvre : Raoul Duguay, Katia Bellange, Janou Furtado, Andrée Paul, Denys Arcand, Yvon Malette. The ever facetious but sensible Jean-Pierre pokes fun at our consumer society in this witty black comedy about a young man who can watch eight tv shows at the same time, believing himself to be each of the characters on the tiny screen that dominates his life. Yet another Québec comedy dealing with tv and its viewers, as in *Louis 19, King of the Airwaves*. Denys Arcand makes a welcome appearance.

Mon oncle Antoine: see **My Uncle Antoine**

Monkeys in the Attic (1974) (80mins) d: Morley Markson s: John Palmer, Morley Markson : Jackie Burroughs, Victor Garber, Louis del Grande, Jess Walton, Jim Henshaw. A weird and overblown domestic imbroglio involving characters living a strained fantasy life.

Montréal Blues (1972) (100mins) A collective work by Raymond Cloutier, Pascal Gélinas and Claude Laroche in which over 20 members of the *Grand cirque ordinaire* decide to open a restaurant and live communally. (Listed for the record)

Montréal Flight 871: see **YUL 871**

Montréal Main (1974) (88mins) (b/w) d: Frank Vitale s: John Sutherland (dialogue improvised by a non-professional cast) : Frank Vitale, Allan Moyle, John Sutherland, Dave Sutherland, Anne Sutherland, Peter Brawley, Pam Marchant, Jackie Holden,

Stephen Lack, Tony Booth, Janet Walczewski, George MacKenzie, Maggie Gunston, Leonard Coleman, Suzy Lake. A well-intentioned but depressing story about a relationship between a mature man and an adolescent boy, set in an artists' colony in Montréal in which everyone is thoroughly unhappy about life. A low-budget homemade effort. Allan Moyle and Frank Vitale reappeared in 1999 with *Pump up the Volume*.

Montréal Sextet (*Montréal vu par***)** (1991) (100mins) d: Denys Arcand, Atom Egoyan, Michel Brault, Patricia Rozema, Léa Pool, Jacques Leduc s: by the directors. A collection of sketches by well-known directors in special tribute to Montréal's 350th anniversary, celebrated in 1992. Denys Arcand leads off with *Seen from Elsewhere*, a witty and moving party episode where a married woman (Guylaine St-Onge) suddenly reveals to her husband a rapturous infatuation thirty years earlier. Atom Egoyan follows with, believe it or not, a funny episode. *Passing Through*, has a traveller (Maury Chaykin) find his way around the city with the aid of pictograms, a satire on the language situation. Michel Brault is next with the touching *The Last Game*, a tale of an elderly couple (Hélène Loiselle and Jean Mathieu) attending what will be their last hockey game together. Léa Pool's *Rispondetemi* is the familiar story of the victim of a car accident (Anne Dorval) reliving moments of her life in the ambulance on the way to hospital. Patricia Rozema picks things up in *Desperanto* with Sheila McCarthy as the ingenuous visitor from Toronto hoping to find a weekend romance. Jacques Leduc's episode, *The Canvas of Time*, about the first mayor of Montréal, was deemed not to fit in with the other stories in this sextet and was originally omitted, but later restored. The whole was produced and put together by Denise Robert.

Montréal vu par: see **Montréal Sextet**

Moody Beach (1990) (94mins) d&s: Richard Roy : Michel Côté, Claire Nebout, Philip Spensley, Andrée Lachapelle. A first feature in which a middle-aged man leaves his job in Montréal to live in his late mother's house in Florida. There he meets a free-spirited French girl who has taken up residence. Their subsequent association, far from being romantic, is tedious, moody and monotonous.

Moonshine (*Au clair de la lune***)** (1982) (90mins) d&s: André Forcier : Michel Côté, Guy L'Écuyer, Lucie Miville, Gaston Lepage, Marcel Fournier, J.-Léo Gagnon, Rose Turcotte, Gilles Lafleur. A sad and funny tale of a strange friendship between a former bowling champion (now a sandwich board man) and an albino, who spends his time living in dreams. Abstract and illusionary, the behaviour is always thoughtful and lively.

More Joy in Heaven (1975) (97mins) d&s: Ronald Weyman (based on the novel by Morley Callaghan) : John Vernon, Linda Goranson, Budd Knapp, Bill

Kemp. A rewarding low-budget attempt at bringing Callaghan's novel to the screen, concerning a former prisoner becoming involved with a priest, a politician and a waitress, all of them using him to further their own interests.

More to Love (2000) (93mins) d: Paul Lynch s: Shirley McCann : Maxwell Caulfield, Louise Werner, Kristen Farraro, Claudine de Jong, Rosemary Doyle, Galen Ireland, Jim McAleesa, Julie Watson, Stephen King. A sensitively told story about an overweight young woman lacking confidence in herself who finally decides to live a "better" life. She meets a dashing young chap at a nightclub and finds love at last. Affecting and honest.

Morning! (1992) (81mins) d: Derek Banasik s: William Gallacher : Michael Hannigan, Andrew Moodie, Dawn Gilmour, Kris Ryan. During the late 1950s and early 1960s, the CIA secretly co-sponsored psychiatric experiments at Montréal's Allan Memorial Institute, subjecting Canadian patients to radical treatments later described as "cruel and barbarous." Many of the victims sued for compensation. This film attempts to relate what happened to some of them. One an actor has lost his memory as a result of experiments being carried out at his brother's laboratory. He goes to work for two mute women at their cottage in northern Ontario; they were also harmed by the experiments. Eventually, the actor is brutally murdered by government agents who are destroying all signs of the research. Somewhat hard to believe. Morning is also listed as *Morningside*.

Morning in the Pine Forest (*Matin dans une forêt de pins*) (1998) (110mins) (a Canada-Latvia co-production) d&s: Mara Ravins-Janis : Helene Kozlova, Eva Juhnevica, Anna Heinrihsone, Aldis Berzins, Janis Berzins, Guntis Vindulis Kalejs. Six young people in a battered car take a journey between past and present in Latvia. On the way, they become introspective and serious about their relationships with the world. It's a long and pretentious trip, at times heavy going for most audiences.

Morning Man, The (*Un matin, une vie*) (1986) (100mins) d: Danièle Suissa s: Wallace Clarke : Bruno Doyon, Kerrie Keane, Alan Fawcett, Mark Strange, Walter Massey. A surprisingly compelling film based on an actual event, about an escaped and wounded prisoner assisted by a young woman who cares for him. With her help, he starts a new life as a radio morning man in a small Québec town. Naturally, they fall in love, but a detective is searching for him, and the future bodes ill. Marvellous performance by Kerrie Keane.

Morrison Murders, The (1997) (120mins) (a Canada-U.S. film) d: Christopher Thomson s: Keith Ross Leckie : Jonathan Scarfe, John Corbett, Tanya Allen, Gordon Clapp, Maya McLaughlin. Set in Georgia, this film was motivated by the true story of two brothers who resolve to find the murderer of their parents. Then one sibling discovers that his other brother is guilty of it and works with the police in the agonizing process of convicting him. All very well and good, but could we not have left this to the Americans to film?

Mort d'un boucheron, La: see **Death of a Lumberjack**

Morte amoureuse, La (1997) (84mins) d&s: Alain Vézina : Luc Pilon, Virginie Dubois, Denise Bouchard, Yvan Roy, Pierre Mailloux, Pierre Ricard. A newly ordained young priest falls deeply in love with a beautiful young woman. Bad enough that he's a priest, but even worse when he discovers that she is a young vampire. Then, foolishly, he tries through his love for her to enter her immortal world. "This is not just another Dracula," said the director, "but a mixture of popular folkloric elements within the symbolic framework of the St. Lawrence River." But this is still very familiar stuff to horror fans with nothing much to set it apart from all the others in the same genre. (Perhaps residents along the St. Lawrence should watch out.)

Mortelle Amnesie: see **Shadows of the Past**

Mortelle Randonnée: see **Eye of the Beholder**

Morvern Callar (2002) (97mins) (a U.K.-Canada co-production) d: Lynne Ramsay s: Liana Dognini, Lynne Ramsay (based on the novel by Alan Warner) : Samantha Morton, Kathleen McDermott, Raife Patrick Burchell, Daniel Cadan, Carolyn Calder. Scottish writer, director Ramsay has, with her sixth feature, made an absorbing psychological (although plotless) work in which a young woman, Morvern Callar, finds her boyfriend dead. But this is no crime of detection tale. Far from it. A most unusual film, it is difficult to describe: a dreamlike, free-flowing study of an ingenuous, distant, sometimes spaced-out young woman with few friends finding her way in the world. This could be called a true experimental film; it shows up many others of present day as being of little worth.

Môtel Hélène (1999) (111mins) (b/w/col) d: René-Richard Cyr s: Serge Boucher, René-Richard Cyr : François Papineau, Maude Guérin, Stéphane Gagnon. Twenty-nine scenes present 29 moments in the life of a village, the principal character being Joan, a 25-year-old woman who, beneath her light-hearted exterior, is filled with the pain of life. Described as being a crude, explicit and straightforward voice of Québec. Audiences there might find it rewarding. Others elsewhere will wonder.

Môtel St-Laurent (1998) (82mins) (b/w) d: Pascal Maeder s: William Eastwood, Pascal Maeder : Anna Papadakos, Jerry Snell. A couple meet, fall magically in love and drive toward the sea in search of adventure. Their car breaks down and they find an old motel where they can stay overnight. The owner is writing a book. The young woman reads it and discovers that all the people staying in the motel, including themselves, are not real at all and are just characters in his book. A fascinating journey into the occult in an intriguing, unusual little film.

Mother of Pearl: see **Hush Little Baby**

Mother's Heart, A (*Coeur de maman*) (1953) (112mins) d&s: René Delacroix (from a play by Henri Deyglun) : Jeanne Demons, Rosanna Seaborn, Denyse St-Pierre, Jean-Paul Dugas, Paul Guévremont, Paul Desmarteaux, Jean-Paul Kingsley, Yvonne Laflamme, Henri Norbert, Rose Ouellette. A sorrowful family drama about the trials of a mother, following the death of her husband. Her son, who is her only means of support, is sent to prison after being falsely accused of a crime his father had committed. Absorbing character study elevates this film above a routine domestic existential story. A classic of its time. (An early Quebec film produced by Frontier, distributed by Renaissance, by Richard J. Jarvis).

Mother's Meat, Freud's Flesh (1984) (92mins) d&s: Demetri Demetrios : Esther Vargas, Demetri Demetrios, Claire Nadon, Michel Gagnon, Christian Dufault. A minimalist, lacklustre and undernourished script about pornography, mother love, and other unlikely and hard-to-understand matters. A waste of time.

Mothers and Daughters (1992) (90mins) d: Larry Kent s: Larry and Linda Jarosiewicz : Mary Peach, Clair Sims, Rebecca Nelson, Gordon Day, Aaron Tager, Libby Barrett. A mother-daughter relationship, with its misunderstandings and long simmering resentments, is explored with humour, insight and understanding—marred, unfortunately, by an ending arrived at by several false steps and unlikely turns. This film is notable, too, for bringing back to the screen the long absent and lovely South African actress Mary Peach.

Mots perdu, Les: see **Lost Words**

Mourir à tue-tête: see **Scream for Silence, A Showdown**

Mourir pour vivre: see **To Kill to Live**

Mourning Suit, The (1976) (85mins) d: Leonard Yakir s: Joe Wiesenfeld, Leonard Yakir : Allan Moyle, Norman Taviss, Brenda Donohue, Henry Gamer. Set in Winnipeg, this is a slow but honest tale of a Jewish tailor and his beliefs, contrasted with the negative outlook of a young man. Perceptive and engaging.

Mouvements du desire: see **Desire in Motion**

Moving Targets (1983) (65mins) d: John Trent s: Ian Sutherland : Allan Royal, Brenda Bazinet, David Clement, James B. Douglas, David McIlwraith, David Ferry. This is a very fine one-man story about an individual who battles bureaucrats in the public interest. On this occasion, an exhausted senior air traffic controller is working with outdated and faulty radar equipment that jeopardizes the safety of Canadian airspace. Thanks to this film, the situation was corrected when government officials finally took notice of the problem. (See: *For the Record*).

Mr. Aiello (*La déroute*) (1998) (111mins) d: Paul Tana s: Bruno Ramirez, Paul Tana, Tony Nardi : Tony Nardi, Michèle-Barbara Pelletier. This very operatic story follows a wealthy Italian businessman in Montréal as he becomes increasingly isolated from his family. Impressive and portrayed with sympathy and understanding.

Mr. Nice Guy (1986) (91mins) d: Henry Wolfond s: Mark Breslin, Henry Wolfond : Michael Macdonald, Joe Silver, Jan Smithers, Harvey Atkin, Keith Knight. A security guard turned mercenary faces up to a local gang out for revenge. This is presented as comedy. Laughs are hard to come by.

Mr. Patman (1981) (105mins) (a Canada-U.S. film) d: John Guillermin s: Thomas Hedley : James Coburn, Kate Nelligan, Candy Cane, Michael Kirby, Jan Rubes, Hugh Webster, Kenneth Wickes, Lois Maxwell. A film in trouble from the beginning (among the first of the tax shelter "international" films), it was poorly conceived and carried out, detailing the story of a psycho ward orderly and the convoluted incidents taking place around him. After completion, the picture was drastically cut and re-edited to no avail.

Mr. Rice's Secret (Exhuming Mr. Rice) (2000) (113mins) (a Canada-U.S. fim) d: Nicholas Kendall s: J.H. Wyman : Kevin Blatch, David Bowie, William Switzer, Teryl Rothery, Garwin Sanford. A terminally ill boy's life is saved when his deceased 400-year-old friend or teacher, Mr. Rice, shows him the way to find a magical life potion. Bowie appears for about five minutes. The story stretches credulity to the limits. Utterly absurd and frequently ugly.

Ms. Bear (1999) (95mins) (a Canada-U.S. film) d: Paul Ziller s: Antony Anderson, Paul Ziller : Ed Begley Jr., Kaitlyn Burke, Kimberly Warnat, Natja Jamaan, Shaun Johnston, Dennis Arduini, Devin Drewitz, Arthur Brauss. A rewarding family adventure set against the impressive mountains of B.C. about a young girl, her friendship with an orphaned bear cub, and her efforts with friends to save the bear from an animal trafficking ring that means a certain death in Asia. (See: the companion picture *Bear With Me*)

Ms. Bear: see **Bear With Me**

Mule and the Emeralds, The (*La mule et les émeraudes*) (1995) (94mins) d&s: Bashar Shbib : Frédéric Duval, Pascal Auclair, Susila Maraviglia, Claude Larivière. Yet another in the stream of B-pictures turned out regularly in Florida and Montréal by the inexhaustible Bashar Shbib. This one concerns a series of confusing complications in which a great chase is carried out by a mix of characters looking out for five stolen emeralds. Murder and romance receive a fair share of the often flat proceedings.

Mule et les émeraudes, La: see **Mule and the Emeralds, The**

Murder and Music: see *Meurtre en musique*

Murder by Decree (1979) (123mins) (a Canada-U.K. co-production) d: Bob Clark s: John Hopkins (from the book *The Ripper File* by Elwyn Jones and John Lloyd) : Christopher Plummer, James Mason, David Hemmings, Susan Clark, Anthony Quayle,

John Gielgud, Frank Finlay, Donald Sutherland, Geneviève Bujold, Chris Wiggins, Tedde Moore. Bob Clark, does poorly by Sherlock Holmes as the great detective investigates the murder of prostitutes by Jack the Ripper. The picture is saved by the marvellous portrayals of Holmes and Watson by Plummer and Mason and firm support by a huge cast of distinguished British actors. Filmed in London.

Murder by Phone (Bells) (1982) (80mins) d: Michael Anderson s: John Kent Harrison : Richard Chamberlain, John Houseman, Sara Botsford, Robin Gammell, Gary Reineke, Barry Morse, Alan Scarfe, James B. Douglas, Kenneth Pogue, Neil Munro, Colin Fox, Luba Goy, Lenore Zann, Clare Coulter, George R. Robertson. The efforts of a highly skilled director, Michael Anderson, are wasted in this horror story of a murderer who telephones his victims and kills them with a lethal long-distance attachment.

Murder Is News: see **British Quota Era Films**

Murder Most Likely (1999) (120mins) d: Alex Chapple s: Rob Forsyth and R.B. Carney (from the book *The Judas Kiss* by Michael Harris) : Paul Gross, William Davis, Marie-Josée Croze, Kim Huffman, Janine Thériault, Beau Starr. Another Canadian true crime comes to the screen, this one about Patrick Kelly, a former undercover RCMP officer who was convicted in 1984 of throwing his wife from the balcony of their apartment at Toronto's Palace Pier. Kelly claimed that he was innocent; the film shows us that he was not, but it somehow seems to want us to believe his version. Gross lives up to his challenging role. (See: *Mystery* series)

Murder Seen (2000) (93mins) d: Robert King s: Marilyn Webber : Timothy Bottoms, Nicole Eggert. A botany student in Montréal uses her psychic powers to unravel a frightening crime. Better than most so-called thrillers. Tightly told where every minute counts.

Murder Sees the Light (1987) (120mins) d: Harvey Hart s: Howard Engel (based on his novel of the same title; the fourth book in the Benny Cooperman series and the second to be filmed) : Saul Rubinek, Kenneth Welsh, Janet-Laine Green, Donald Lake, Joan Orenstein, Maryanne Macdonald, Gary Reineke, Graham Greene (an early role). Back on his own turf in Grantham (St. Catharines), Ontario, detective Benny Cooperman is a bit of a bumbler. But when he is sent to Algonquin Park, he comes into his own upon discovering an illegal gold mine and a satanic cult involved in murders in the woods. Well done, gripping and intelligent. (See: *The Suicide Murders*)·

Muses orphelines, Les: see **Orphan Muses, The**

Music of the Spheres, The (1984) (80mins) d: Philip Jackson s: Gabrielle de Montmolin, Philip Jackson : Anne Dansereau, Peter Brikmanis, Jacques Couture, Ken Lemaire, Kenneth Gordon. In a city that was Toronto, a computer-based technology governs and controls all life in the 21st century. A "beast" machine is on guard and will not permit the intrusion of alien supreme beings, who are part of the "music from the spheres." Good special effects hide the more muddled pieces of the narrative. All done in Philip Jackson's well-known experimental mode.

Must Be Santa (1999) (120 mins) d: Bradford Turner s: Douglas Bowie : Arnold Pinnock, Dabney Coleman, Deanna Milligan, Keenan MacWilliam, Gerard Parkes, Joe Flaherty. A Christmas fantasy in which a black man finds himself playing Santa Claus, taking the place of a white man. Includes many other twists and turns involving children, the police and parents, most of them agitated and attempting to be funny under lively circumstances. A good script by Douglas Bowie seems to have lost some charm under the weight of magic effects.

Mustang (1975) (95mins) d: Marcel Lefebvre, Yves Gélinas s: Gilles Gauthier, Marcel Lefebvre : Willie Lamothe, Claude Blanchard, Luce Guilbeault, Albert Millaire, Marcel Sabourin, Andrée Pelletier. A lively and colourful tale about a small Québec town, its annual rodeo, and how the violence of the Old (American) West pervades some of the participants.

Mustard Bath (1993) (108mins) d&s: Darrell Wasyk : Michael Riley, Martha Henry, Eddy Grant, Alissa Trotz, Tantoo Cardinal A young medical student returns to Guyana after the death of his mother in search of a geographical and psychological stability to his life. What follows is a boring, wearying, meaningless amount of twaddle and pretentious posturing. Martha Henry seems to have wandered in by mistake.

Mutagen (1987) (96mins) d: Eli Necakov s: Terry Gadsden, Eli Necakov : Simon Richards, Jackie Samuda. Possibly one of the earliest sci-fi melodramas to present us with a weird tale of DNA manipulation by a genetic scientist. Of course, it doesn't work, but leads to several murders that the doctor's experimental subjects may have something to do with. Doesn't live up to its promise.

My American Cousin (1985) (90mins) d&s: Sandy Wilson : Margaret Langrick, John Wildman, Richard Donat, Babz Chula, Terry Moore. Coming after several years of tiresome teenage sex comedies from Canada and Hollywood, this memoir of Sandy Wilson's youth in B.C. is refreshing, funny and nicely observed. Set in the 1950s, her cousin from California arrives in his red convertable to spend the summer with her family. A gem that found wide popular appeal, it is a classic with her opening words from her diary "Nothing ever happens." being oft quoted.

My Bloody Valentine (1981) (91mins) (a Canadian-American film) d: George Mihalka s: John Beaird : Paul Kelman, Lori Hallier, Neil Affleck, Don Francks, Cynthia Dale. A thoroughly unpleasant horror film in which a murderous coal miner in the U.S. town of Valentine Bluffs sends candy boxes containing bloody human hearts to his next victims. Awful.

My Childhood in Montréal (*Mon enfance a Montréal*) (1971) (64mins) (b/w) d& S: Jean Chabot : Marc Hébert, Véronique Vilbert, Robert Rivard,

Carole Laure, Paul Guévremont, Nana de Varennes. A documentary-looking dramatized story about a poverty-stricken young family in Montréal as seen through the questioning eyes of a child. Authentic and disturbing.

My Daniel: see **Dinosaur Hunter, The**

My Dog Vincent (1997) (85mins) d&s: Michael McGowan : Chuck Campbell, Ben Carlson, Gavin Crawford, Kyle Downs, Fiona Byrne, Zerha Leverman. Another comedy involving three young men in their early twenties, each working an ordinary job while trying to run a Vincent Price fan club and find a woman to love. Light and refreshing at times but drags to a slow finish.

My Eye: see *Mon oeil*

My Father's Angel (West of Sarajevo) (1999) (86mins) d: Davor Marjanovic s: Frank Borg : Brendan Fletcher, Tony Nardi, Tygh Runyan, Timothy Weber, Lynda Boyd, Vanessa King, Asja Pavlovic. A disturbing chronicle of hatred, anger and violence between Muslim and Serb immigrants living in Vancouver. The film opens with horrific scenes from the BBC graphically depicting the war in Bosnia, and then moves to Canada where superstitions and customs have been brought to the new land. The whole presents an unsettling look at the divisions that mark our society for the worst. The actors are unfailingly believable and the direction is clear and unflinching.

My Five Wives (2000) (100mins) (a Canada-U.S. film) d: Sidney J. Furie s: Rodney Dangerfield, Harry Basil : Rodney Dangerfield, Andrew Dice Clay, John Byner, Molly Shannon, Jerry Stiller, Judy Taylor, Angelika Baran. Rodney. Dangerfield's successful comedy comes to the screen with its good humour intact as it tells of a rich American real estate developer, several times divorced, who joins a friend to build a ski resort in Utah (actually filmed in the Maritimes). They soon find themselves involved with local religions that forbid everything except a man having several wives. Other complications pile upon one another. Expertly carried off by Dangerfield and the supporting players.

My Friend Pierrette (Mon amie Pierrette) (1969) (68mins) (b/w) d&s: Jean-Pierre Lefebvre : Francine Mathieu, Yves Marchand, Gérard Fortier, Anne Fortier, Madeleine Thibault, Raoul Duguay. Lefebvre's fourth film takes us one step further into understanding life in Québec. Here, he shows us the generational differences within a family, their children, their friends and relatives, in a series of encounters in a world that is becoming increasingly ugly.

My Kind of Town (1984) (78mins) d&s: Charles Wilkinson : Peter Smith, Martina Schliessler, John Cooper, Martin Paul, Michael Marks. This was the discovery of the year. A low-budget first film from Vancouver, it tells a pleasing story of two likeable young people who try to save a dying lumber town by painting the place with murals to attract tourists.

The narrative falters at times but never fails to charm. Wilkinson, unfortunately, was not so lucky with his following films.

My Life Without Me (Mi vida sin mi) (2003) (106mins) d&s: Isabel Coixet : Sarah Polley, Scott Speedman, Deborah Harry, Mark Ruffalo, Amanda Plummer, Alfred Molina. A sentimental but beautifully and honestly told story of a lovely young wife and mother, living in a rundown trailer in the backyard of her mother's suburban home in Vancouver, who is told by her doctor that she will shortly die from cancer. Set against finely detailed backgrounds among a group of interesting characters, she prepares herself and the children for her death. This will not be a critic's favourite, but most audiences will find it a genuinely moving film with Sarah Polley once again proving her worth as a great young actress.

My Little Devil (2000) (88mins) (a Canada-India co-production) d&s: Gopi Desai : Om Puri, Rushabh, Patni, Pooja Batra, Satyajit Sharma. Tells of the life of a young, motherless boy at a boarding school in India and of his experiences in human relations. This is a touching, truthful and tender telling of growing up, the whole strengthened by the presence of the great actor Om Puri, last seen in *Such a Long Journey*. (see *Tales For All* series)

My Little Eye (2002) (95mins) (a U.K.-Canada co-production) d: Marc Evans : David Hilton, James Watkins : Sean C.W. Johnson, Kris Lemche, Stephen O'Reilly, Laura Regan, Jennifer Sky, Bradley Cooper, Nick Mennell. Filmed in Nova Scotia, five young people are given permission to live in an isolated house for six months and agree to have every moment of their lives filmed. If anyone leaves, the prize of $1 million is lost. Shades of deplorable survival tv. Spending five minutes with them would be enough.

My Mother's Ghost (1996) (95mins) d: Elise Swerhone s: Heather Conkie : Elisabeth Rosen, Gabrielle Rose, Barry Flatman, Janet Wright, Barna Moricz, Gordon Tootoosis. A grief-stricken family mourns a lost son, moves into the Double Oak Ranch, and struggles to make it a successful business. The daughter begins to see ghosts; a similar tragedy had afflicted another family a hundred years earlier. Simple, straightforward and winningly portrayed.

My Pleasure Is My Business (1975) (94mins) d: Al Waxman s: Alvin Boretz : Xaviera Hollander, Henry Ramer, Colin Fox, George Sperdakos, Michael Kirby, Jayne Eastwood, Sydney Brown, Robert Goodier, Dinah Christie, Jackie Burroughs. Toronto welcomes the sensation of the day, the Happy Hooker. She didn't remain for long, and neither did this picture. Actor Waxman's first film as a director. A short and happy caper.

My Script Doctor (1997) (92mins) d&s: Nick Curcin : Valerie Buhagiar, Simon Richards, Martha Ferguson, Ken Puley. A very odd piece, probably only to be fully understood by those working in film. After many years away from making films, Alex Gull makes a comeback with the assistance of a script doctor, a writer or producer who rewrites weak scripts. Alex begins a relationship with him that fails and on reflecting that her script is a reflection of her current situation, she loses her grip on reality. Hard to become involved or to sympathize with.

My Secret Life: see **Columbus of Sex, The: My Secret Life**

My Summer Story: see **Christmas Story, A**

My Summer Vacation (1996) (95mins) (b/w/col, 16mm) d&s: Sky Gilbert : Clinton Walker, Christofer Williamson, Daniel MacIvor, Sky Gilbert, Ann Holloway and others. A formless, mildly diverting, pseudo-documentary work following the various ins and outs of gay life. Several lost-looking characters give filmed interviews while keeping an eye open for partners. Casually made and not very edifying.

My Uncle Antoine (Mon oncle Antoine) (Silent Night) (1971) (110mins) d: Claude Jutra s: Clément Perron, Claude Jutra : Jacques Gagnon, Lyne Champagne, Jean Duceppe, Monique Mercure, Lionel Villeneuve, Olivette Thibault, Hélène Loiselle, Claude Jutra, René Salvatore, Jean Dubost, Benoît Marcoux, Dominique Joly, Michel Talbot, Lise Talbot, Siméon Dallaire, Sydney Harris, Roger Garand. Claude Jutra, like many filmmakers, started his career by trying new techniques and abstractions in form and style, but found that narrative and characterization were more important than manipulations of people and camera for the sake of experiment. *My Uncle Antoine* is his best film and one of the finest Canadian films of this period. The familiar story of a village boy growing into manhood and discovering the world and his family anew is beautifully told and acted. Its eternal truths make it a compelling and thought-provoking family drama. Taking place in the 1940s, the depicted values, behaviour and morality of a small Québec town are conveyed effortlessly, honestly and in terms both deeply emotional and realistic. This film, coming out as it did at the same time as *Goin' Down the Road*, marked a new beginning for Canadian films in both English and French. Like Shebib's film, Jutra's *Mon oncle Antoine* has remained at the top of the critics' best film list. (See: *Goin' Down the Road*)

Mystérieuse Mademoiselle C, La (The Mysterious Lady Charlotte) (The Mysterious Miss C.) (2001) (95mins) d: Richard Ciupka s: Jacques Bonin : Gildor Roy, Marie-Chantal Perron, Eve Lemieux, Maxime Dumontier, Félix-Antoine Despatie. A strange but charming schoolyard comedy about a substitute teacher, a woman with many unconventional ways and passions, who teaches her unruly students the pleasures of reading. When they discover that the principal has emptied the school library and intends to use it as his own office, they join in the struggle to save their library. A warm, funny, spontaneous and caring film about the younger generation.

Mystery (CTV series): Detective Joanne Kilbourn by author Gail Bowen. See under respective titles:
1: **Bookfair Murders**
2: **Colder Kind of Death, A**
3: **Deadly Appearances**
4: **Killing**
5: **Spring, A,**
6: **Love and Murder**
7: **Murder Most Likely**
8: **Torso: The Evelyn Dick Story**
9: **Verdict in Blood**
10: **Wandering Soul Murders, The**

Mystery of the Million Dollar Hockey Puck (1975) (88mins) d&s: Jean Lafleur, Peter Svatek : Michael MacDonald, Angele Knight, Jean-Louis Millette, Kurt Schiegl. Two orphans from Chicoutimi foil crooks who have hidden stolen diamonds in a hockey puck the Montréal Canadiens will use in the Forum. A likeable children's film that breathes the heart and appeal of Canadian hockey.

Myth of the Male Orgasm, The (1993) (90mins) d: John Hamilton s: David Reckziegel, John Hamilton : Bruce Dinsmore, Miranda de Pencier, Mark Camacho, Burke Lawrence, Ruth Marshall. Three young professional men who live together in Montréal and delight in chasing women attend a survey conducted by women to determine men's feelings about them. Excessively talkative, some words are well said, but mostly it is sheer silliness.

Myth That Wouldn't Die (Danseurs du Mozambique, Les) (1991) (92mins) (a Canada-France co-production) d: Philippe Lefebvre s: Guy Mullally, Richard Oleksiak, Donald Martin : Thierry Lhermitte, Erin Gray, Jacques Francois, Marc De Jonge, Anne Letournea. A valuable statue is stolen from a French hotel. A writer of suspense stories staying at the hotel, finds herself involved in a strange mystery after making an attempt to discover who took the statue. A thriller with a different look, attractively filmed in the French countryside. (The French title is the name of the collection of statues being auctioned.)

Naked Flame, The (1964) (88mins) (a Canada-U.S. film) d: Lawrence Matanski s: Everett Dennis : Dennis O'Keefe, Kasey Rogers, Al Ruscio, Linda Bennett, Robert Howay, Robert Gibb, Colin Hamilton, John Bruce. A truly terrible film with five Hollywood players as characters exploiting the Doukhobor community of Alberta in a sensational story about murder and rape. A complicated and confusing storyline.

Naked Lunch (1992) (115mins) d&s: David Cronenberg (from the novel by William S. Burroughs) : Peter Weller, Judy Davis, Ian Holm, Julian Sands, Monique Mercure, Roy Scheider. An ugly, empty and ultimately tiresome interpretation of Burroughs' meandering memories of life as a drug user. Accompanied by horrid creatures, lacking the faintest glimmer of humanity, and acted out with a wooden incomprehension by a wasted talented cast.

Nanook: see **Kabloonak**

Nashville Bound (1996) (115mins) d&s: Frank Spinney : Frank Spinney, Mike Johnson, Audley Pineo, Alvin Cox, Rod Saunders. A one-man-band film in which Frank Spinney did everything. We meet four country musician friends from Nova Scotia who are on their way to Nashville to collect a songwriting award. Their plane crashes in the wilderness and they spend weeks in dire distress. Deserves an A for effort.

Nasty Burgers (1994) (68mins) d&s: James Motluk : Gary Harper, Jack Cruickshank, Richard Guttman. Two brothers use their inheritance to open a burger joint. They manage to keep it going in an under-cooked comedy, with the works. Lots of violence and bad language.

National Lampoon's Last Resort (1994) (91mins) (a Canada-U.S. film) d: Rafal Zeilinski s: Patrick Labyorteaux, Damian Lee : Corey Feldman, Corey Haim, Maureen Flannigan, Demetra Hampton, Robert Mandan. When two virtual reality characters are asked to save a financially depressed theme park, everything goes from bad to worse.

Nature of Nicholas, The (2002) (100mins) d&s: Jeff Erbach : Jeff Sutton, David Turnbull, Ardith Boxall, Tom McCamus, Robert Hucalak, Katherine Lee Raymond, Samantha Hill. An accomplished work about a difficult subject, here the troubles of a family tormented by metaphysical horror with surrealist overtones. Hard to describe, this work must be seen to experience the various meanings within the film's compelling and abstract atmosphere. A director to watch.

Naufragés du Labrador, Les (Stranded in Labrador) (1991) (83mins) d: François Floquet s: Marcel Dubé : Ian Ireland, Jean L'Italien, Jean Faubert. In 1939, a bush pilot is flying a business-man and an engineer to Labrador. The plane is forced to land and the three men find shelter in a miners' camp. But the weather worsens and rescue does not come. The three men, who talk about their lives and feelings, come to realize that they are facing death. An altogether chilly experience.

Ne dis rien (Don't Say Anything) (2001) (82mins) d&s: Simon Lacombe : Patrick Labbé, Marie-France Marcotte, Dominique Lamy, Marcel Sabourin. After a failed love affair, a municipal worker in Montréal wanders the city at night stealing cars and searching for a new roommate. He decides to move and installs a camera in his apartment to see the people who leave messages for him. He meets Lisa, who soon moves in with him. Now they must suffer the pain of ridding themselves of past memories. Will they learn to love again? Perhaps you won't want to sit around long enough to find out.

Né pour l'enfer: see **Born for Hell**

Nearest to Heaven (Au plus pres du paradis) (2002) (100mins) (a France-Spain-Canada co-production) d: Tonie Marshall s: Tonie Marshall, Anne Louise Trividic (from a story by Marshall) : Catherine Deneuve, William Hurt, Bernard Le Coq, Helene Fillieres, Patrice Chereau. "Heaven" seems popular in movie titles this year, but this one is perhaps more on the attempted romance side. This, however, is about all one can say about the tedious comings and goings of a painter in New York City, at the Empire State Building—which is supposed to be closer to heaven than anywhere else. She is looking for a lost love, inspired by having seen Cary Grant and Deborah Kerr in Leo McCarey's 1957 romance *An Affair to Remember,* no doubt on tv and ruined by commercials. This tepid new version is not likely to be around as long.

Neg', Le (The Negro) (2002) (95mins) d&s: Robert Morin : Iannicko N'Doua-Legare, Robin Aubert, Emmanuel Bilodeau, Jean-Guy Bouchard, Rene-Daniel Dubois, Suzanne Lemoine. A black teenager living in a Québec village destroys a woman's lawn ornament. A crowd gathers, old animosities return and the boy is accidentally shot by a policeman. An investigation follows in which many contradictory views of what actually happened are given. This is not a racist film, but one making a brave and power-ful statement about race relations and attitudes. When it opened in Montréal, a black youth group condemned the posters and wanted them removed from public view. The producer rightfully refused and told them he would not change the film's title, either.

Neige a fondu sur la Manicouagan, La: see **Snow Has Melted on the Manicouagan, The**

Neighbour, The (1993) (93mins) d: Rodney Gibbons s: Kurt Wimmer : Linda Kozlowski, Ronald Lea, Benjamin Shirinian, Rod Steiger, Sean McCann, Jane Wheeler. A young couple buy an old villa. Their psychopathic neighbour thinks the wife is really his dead mother. Complications soon arise in this supernatural nightmare, part thriller, some-times enjoyable.

Nelligan: see **Ange noir, L'**

Nenette (The Young Girl) (1991) (85mins) d: André Melançon s: Andrée and Louise Pelletier : Gisèle Schmidt, Andrée Pelletier. A touching vignette about a young woman who finds life somewhat dull with her doctor husband. Being adopted, she decides to find her birth mother. Two women come to her, each claiming to be her mother. What is she to do? Portrayed with sympathy and understanding.

Neon Palace, The: A '50s and '60s Trip (1971) (102mins) d&s: Peter Rowe : Judy Soroka, Peter Whittal, Steven Sherriff, Jack Wolowick, Adrienne Horswill, Moira Armour, Gino Empry, Susan Feldman. Journeying to Niagara Falls, Wasaga Beach and Crystal Beach, Ontario, this bright, live-ly, colourful first film is a fast-paced mix of laughter, life and music. It put Rowe on the road to filmmaking, illustrating how slight western entertainment had become.

Neptune Factor, The (The Neptune Disaster) (An Undersea Odyssey) (1973) (98mins) (a Canadian production of an American film) d: Daniel Petrie s: Jack De Witt : Ben Gazzara, Yvette Mimieux, Walter Pidgeon, Ernest Borgnine, Chris Wiggins, Donnelly Rhodes, Stuart Gillard, Kenneth Pogue, Frank Perry, Joan Gregson. A submarine descends to the ocean floor to rescue three men trapped by an earthquake. It's all wet! (Devised to take advantage of the ruinous Capital Cost Allowance Act, which made vast profits for Canadian producers who never made indigenous Canadian films.)

Nest of Shadows (1976) (60mins) d&s: Jim Bird : Louise Renfret, Ralph Endersby, Bonnie Brooks, Doug McGrath, Art Hindle, Mary Haney, John Friesen. An unwed teenage mother is expecting her second child. Her young lover, a mechanic struggling to make enough to care for them, promises that they will soon be married. A social worker attempts to save the young woman from the brink of collapse. An affecting and honestly presented social drama.

Net Worth (1997) (120mins) d: Jerry Ciccoritti s: Donald Truckey, Philip Savath, David Cruise, Alison Griffiths (based on the book by Cruise and Griffiths) : Kevin Conway, Hugh Thompson, David Mucci, Carl Marotte, R.H. Thomson, Robin Gammell, Dan Lett, Richard Donat, Michael Reynolds, Al Waxman, Aidan Devine. A brave, true and dramatic telling of the struggles and efforts of hockey players who fought to organize a players' association in 1956. Al Waxman is in his element as the manipulative general manager.

Never Cry Wolf (1983) (105mins) (a Canada-U.S. film) d: Carroll Ballard s: Curtis Hanson, Sam Hamm, Richard Kletter (based on the novel by Farley Mowat) : Charles Martin Smith, Brian Dennehy, Zachary Ittimangnaq, Samson Jorah. A beautiful and striking film about Mowat's (played by Smith) journeys in the Arctic. While studying the behaviour and ways of wolves, he discovered much about himself.

Never Talk to Strangers (1995) (102mins) (a Canada-U.S. film) d: Peter Hall s: Lewis Green, Jordan Rush : Rebecca de Mornay, Antonio Banderas, Dennis Miller, Len Cariou, Beau Starr, Eugene Lipinski, Harry Dean Stanton. A psychologist who has made a long study of the minds of criminals, not much interested in women, suddenly becomes deeply attracted to one who fascinates him with her mysterious ways. Terrifying incidents take place that are unexplained until the end is near. Not much to be thrilled about and a disappointment from Peter Hall, of theatre fame. But he gets the best from his cast members.

Never Too Late (1996) (96mins) d: Giles Walker s: Donald Martin : Olympia Dukakis, Cloris Leachman, Jan Rubes, Jean Lapointe, Corey Haim, Matthew Craven. A group of elderly friends living in a retirement home discover that the manager is fiddling with the books and keeping money rightly belonging to the deceased. They take on the roles of detectives to bring the rascal to justice. A pleasing blend of easygoing humour touched with drama and gentility.

Never Trust an Honest Thief (Going for Broke) (1979) (120mins) d: George McCowan, Zale Magder s: Carl DeSantis, Phyllis Camesanoi, Joel and Neil Cohen : Orson Welles, Michael Murphy, Michele Finney, Henry Ramer, Kenneth Pogue, Alfie Scopp, Kenneth Welsh, Doris Petrie, Mavor Moore, Tom Harvey, Ken James, Diane Polly, Sharon Dyer, Jon Granik, Marvin Goldhar. The script goes broke very early in this convoluted ramble among lower-level crooks, con men and their women. It revolves around a fat, alcoholic border town sheriff (played by Welles). This film received a ton of media coverage while it was filming in Georgetown, Ontario, because of Welles' presence. It ended up being much revised and edited and hardly ever shown.

New Blood (1999) (91mins) (a Canada-U.K. film) d&s: Michael Hurst : John Hurt, Nick Moran, Carrie-Anne Moss. A kidnapping goes wrong and results in severe complications for a woman undergoing a heart transplant. Much of this is accompanied by violence and rough language. It's hard to care about the outcome of this strangled thriller.

New Shoes (1990) (80mins) d&s: Ann Marie Fleming : Ann Marie Fleming, Valerie Buhagiar, Alex MacKenzie, Madge Roberts. A first feature in which Emily, a feminist filmmaker, tries to discover why a man would buy new shoes before killing his lover and then himself. A slight and inconsequential film.

New Waterford Girl (1999) (97mins) d: Allan Moyle s: Tricia Fish : Liane Balaban, Mary Walsh, Nicholas Campbell, Tara Spencer-Nairn, Andrew McCarthy, Cathy Moriarty. Sue desires to escape her working-class home in a rundown town in Cape Breton and travel to New York to study. As she struggles with the decision a new girl moves into the neighbourhood, providing fresh air and fresh perspective. Nicholas Campbell and Mary Walsh are perfect as the tired and sometimes short-tempered parents. All in all, real and appealing characters rendered by a well-written first-time script. Of course, we cannot let the film go without the obligatory couple of American players: Andrew McCarthy and Cathy Moriarty. The impressive aspect to *Waterford* (shades of Anne-Marie MacDonald) is the stunning photography of the town and its surroundings, the atmosphere, the surging sea, the beaches—so consistent and so marvellously Canadian.

Next of Kin (1984) (72mins) d&s: Atom Egoyan : Patrick Tierney, Berge Fazlian, Arsinée Khanjian, Andrew Coyne, Margaret Loreys. A stimulating first film by the director in which a repressed youth is taken to a family counsellor for therapy. He then meets and goes to live with a cheerful Armenian family.

Nez rouge **(Red Nose)** (2003) (110mins) d: Erik Canuel s: Sylvie Pilon & Sylvie Desrosiers : Patrick Huard, Michele Barbara Pelletier, Pierre Lebeau, Caroline Dhavernas, Jean L'Italien, Frederic De Grandpre, Sylvain Marcel. A Christmas-time romantic comedy about a book critic who falls madly in love with a young writer. But she cannot forget the bad review he wrote about her first piece of writing. And her first novel is about to be published. Critics beware; it could happen to you! A pleasing and witty film, with a rare charm and appeal.

Nguol Thua: see **Eleventh Child, The**

Night Friend (A Cry From the Heart) (1987) (90mins) d&s: Peter Gerretsen : Chuck Shamata, Heather Kjollesdal. A priest tries to save a young prostitute on the streets of Toronto. His experience convinces him that the church should play a more active role in caring for teenage street people. A study both concerned and moral, and bringing in timely observations about a failing society.

Night in America, A (*Une nuit en Amérique*) (1975) (93mins) d: Jean Chabot s: Jean-Pierre Plant, Jean Chabot : Robert Rivard, Jill Frappier, Jocelyne Goyette, Reynald Bouchard, Guy L'Écuyer, Carol Facher. Murder-mystery drama set in Montréal where a physician from Hungary arrives and is promptly murdered. His wife and a young girl become involved before detectives appear. Unusual fare for a Canadian film and while not exactly a *Poirier*, it never loses its grip.

Night Magic (1985) (95mins) (a Canada-France co-production) d: Lewis Furey s: Leonard Cohen, Lewis Furey : Nick Mancuso, Carole Laure, Stéphane Audran, Barbara Harris, Frank Augustyn. A musical fantasy about a company of music hall singers and dancers, one of whom is an angel. Familiar consequences arise when it comes to matters of the heart. The music, which should carry this make-believe, is undistinguished and repetitive.

Night of the Dribbler (1990) (88mins) d: Jack Bravman s: Maurice Thevenet : Fred Travalena, Gregory Calpakis, Flavia Carrozzi, Cynthia Mantel. The halls of a suburban high school are haunted by a mysterious and brutal killer known as the "Dribbler" (for his trademark habit of dribbling a basketball as he pursues his next victim). A minor thriller about murder in a secondary school, unintentionally foretelling what has become a dreadful reality.

Night of the Flood (*La nuit du déluge*) (1996) (91mins) d&s: Bernard Hebert : Geneviève Rochette, Julie McClemens, Jacques Godin, Anne Barry, Kenneth Gould, Mireille Lablanc, Maryse Poulin. Floods of mythological stuff here as the world's population is washed away, leaving, it seems, only a pregnant woman floating around in a box. There is narration but no dialogue. Spirits, symbolism and dreams abound, as well as balletic dance sequences. The cameras whirl around and the editing tries to follow. It rains a lot.

Night of the High Tide, The (*La notte dell'alta marea*) (1976) (95mins) (a Canada-Italy co-production) d: Luigi Scattini s: Claude Fournier, Luigi Scattini (based on the book by Alfredo Todisco) : Anthony Steel, Annie Belle, Pam Grier, Hugo Pratt, Alain Montpetit. Set in wintery Montréal and under the sunny skies of Martinique, this is a love story amidst a sea of beautiful girls involved in modelling and advertising agency work. A handsome older man falls passionately in love with a strange, alluring and inviting young model, who makes his life one of desire and despair. Beneath the sexual encounters lies a well-written and understanding screenplay about the many sides of an imperfect relationship. The voodoo bits, however, are hard to take.

Night of the Wedding: see *Nuit de noces*

Night Shift, The: see *Shift de nuit, Le*

Night with Hortense, The (*La nuit avec Hortense*) (1987) (76mins) d&s: Jean Chabot : Carole Laure, Lothaire Bluteau, Marcel Sabourin. A dreamy piece of broken romance concerning a man who has failed in love and decides to give up Montréal for Chicago to start fresh. But he unexpectedly meets a woman who rekindles his will to live and love again. Eloquent, yet sad.

Night Zoo: see *Zoo la nuit, Un*

Nightingales and the Bells (*Le rossignol et les cloches*) (1952) (92mins) (b/w) d: René Delacroix s: Joseph Schull : Gérard Barbeau, Nicole Germain, Jean Coutu, Clément Latour, Hector Charland, Juliette Béliveau, Juliette Huot, Ovila Légaré. Musical comedy about the efforts of a village priest to raise money to buy new bells for the local church. Another simple and appealing story about life in Québec before the Quiet Revolution.

Nightmare, The (*Cauchemar*) (1979) (102mins) d&s: Françoise Daigle, Jean-Claude Filion, François Milord, Yvan Roy : Jean Bélanger, Diane Landry, Charles Goulet, Lucie Beaulieu, Sylvain Dionne, Nicole Marquis. Contains four stories, in which a simple beach party turns into a nightmare. Seven students out for a good time die one by one in the most horrible way. A detective, Inspector Beaulieu, is put on the case. But the mystery is only cleared up after a series of sensational events, including student demonstrations, explosions and armed intervention. Not without interest but quite muddled.

Nights Below Station Street (1997) (90mins) d: Norma Bailey s: David Adams Richards (from his novel of the same title) : Liisa Repo-Martell, Michael Hogan, Lynda Boyd, Marnie McPhail, Brent Stait, Michael McPhaden. Skilled filmmaker Norma Bailey has made a touching drama of working-class life with its sadness and moments of humour. We see here the strained relations between parents and their bright and perceptive daughter. The result is a truly remarkable film from the west, well written and played, and achingly true.

Nightwaves (2002) (90mins) (a U.S.-Canada film) d: James Kaufman s: Melissa J. Pelletier : Sherilyn Fenn, David Nerman. A convoluted thriller about a reporter whose husband was killed in a road accident and who later begins to listen to his phone messages and comes to believe that he was actually murdered. Hardly surprising! Filmed in Montreal passing as Massachusetts, US. Set against the American Justice System.

Nikki, Wild Dog of the North (*Nomades Du Nord*) (1961) (75mins) (a Canada-U.S. film) d: Jack Couffer, Donald Haldane s: Ralph Wright, Winston Hibler (from James Oliver Curwood's novel *Nomads of the North*) : Jean Coutu, Émile Genest, Uriel Luft, Robert Rivard, Jim Barron. A Disney Studios production filmed in Banff and Calgary about trappers and their animals, including Nikki, who is forced to become a fighting dog. Beautifully shot and convincingly staged.

Nine B (1986) (98mins) d: James Swan s: Grahame Woods (from a story by Donald Hunter) : Robert Wisden. Based on the true story of Donald Hunter, a British teacher, one of the first, who taught school in Fort Nelson, B.C. Robert Wisden gives a convincing performance as Hunter. Set against an historical background both informative and exciting.

19 Months (2002) (77mins) d&s: Randall Cole : Benjamin Ratner, Angela Vint, Kari Matchett, Sergio DiZio, Carolyn Taylor, Chuck Shamata. A tedious attempt to describe romantic love. A loving couple decides to part; but to escape the heartbreak that usually accompanies such an event, they try a "new and better way of breaking up." This is filmed for them by a documentary crew, watching their every move. This leads to jealousy and desperation.

90 Days (1985) (100mins) d&s: Giles Walker : Stefan Wodoslawsky, Christine Pak, Sam Grana, Fernanda Tavares, Daisy de Bellefeuille. Supposedly a sequel to Walker's *The Masculine Mystique* (1984), two of the characters return here: one to wed a mail-order Korean bride, often charming, the other to become a donor to a sperm bank. In doubtful taste.

***90 jours, Les* (90 Days)** (1959) (99mins) d: Louis Portugais s: Gérard Pelletier : Jean Doyon, Béatrice Picard, Teddy Burns-Goulet, René Mathieu, Guy L'Écuyer. A small town in Québec finds its daily life turned upside down when workers in a local factory go on strike to be given more control over their working conditions. A well done drama conveying a deep sense of social unrest and the working class. (This feature consists of four parts from *Panoramique*, a 26-part tv series made by the NFB for Radio-Canada [CBC].) Not to be confused with *90 Days* (1985) by Giles Walker.

No (1998) (85mins) d&s: Robert Lepage (taken from his play *The Seven Branches of the River Ota* : Anne-Marie Cadieux, Marie Brassard, Marie Gignac, Richard Fréchette, Alexis Martin. The film opens in Osaka during the 1970 World's Fair. An actress from Montréal finds herself living a 24-hour period in which her life becomes confused and complicated by a number of events culminating with her discovery that she is pregnant. Her lover is not too interested. This, Lepage's third film after *The Confessional* and *The Polygraph*, is a fascinating if incoherent narrative soaked in symbolism, coincidences, politics and psychology, leaving the spectator to wonder what Lepage's stand might be, particularly with regard to "yes" or "no" in the Québec referendum. He gives a filmic sense to theatrical work and leaves us all with something to think about.

No Alibi (2000) (92mins) d&s: Bruce Pittman : Dean Cain, Eric Roberts, Lexa Doig. Bruce Pittman returns to features and brings some semblance of reality to this suspense-thriller about a successful businessman who is lured into a criminal situation when his brother borrows his car to take vengeance on a vicious crook. Pittman knows how to put this familiar stuff into a new portfolio.

No Angel (1992) (99mins) d&s: Frank Caruso : Domenic Cuzzorea, Susan Hamann, Lynn Blackadar. A young woman with a captivating personality turns many lives upside-down as she goes from one relationship to another, finding no satisfaction and learning little. A decent effort with winning moments, but cannot sustain its length.

No Apologies (1990) (90mins) d&s: Ken Pittman : Barrie Dunn, Bryan Hennessey, Maisie Rillie, Tony Quinn, Kenneth Mercer, Mary Lewis, Frances Nickle, Frank O'Flaherty, Richard Nercer. An uncharacteristically pessimistic film from Newfoundland. Set in a company town, it concerns a filmmaker back from the Third World who finds conditions at home as depressing as those he had just left. An examination of nationalism and social justice through family relationships, the story manages to bring back a sense of humour for the final scenes. A remarkable and pleasing picture.

No Blame (*L'incroyable vérité*) (1988) (89mins) (a Canada-France co-production) d: Danièle Suissa s: Gordon Stoddard (based on a story by Donald Martin and Danièle Suissa) : Helen Shaver, Stephen Macht. A happy, successful married woman with a child discovers during her second pregnancy that she is carrying the aids virus. Who is to blame? Recriminations, doubts, despair and anxieties follow. A timely subject well stated and responsible.

No Game Without Sun: see **Time Zero**

No Holiday for Idols (*Pas de vacances pour les idoles*) (1965) (85mins) (b/w) d: Denis Heroux s: Noël Vallerand : Joël Denis, Albert Millaire, Suzanne Lévesque, Marcel Cabay, Jacques Godin. A world-of-show-business story in which Michel, a young singer working in a club as a waiter, finds himself courted by television—which brings him great success. He and his young starlet lover, Sophie, attract the attention of a rich impresario, who uses him as a carrier of heroin for Toronto. Michel extracts himself from this and returns to Montréal to Sophie and continuing success in the world of pop music. This was the first film as the director of the of celebrated cinematographer Jean-Claude Labrecque.

No Looking Back: see **Out of the Blue**

No More Monkeys Jumpin' on the Bed (2000) (76mins) (b/w) d&s: Ross Weber : Tom Scholte, Nancy Sivak, Can Cronin, Erik Whittaker, Babz Chula. In b&w and seemingly improvised, this is supposedly about twenty-somethings, flat characters and their constricted lives. Do we get to know them? No. Do we need to know them? No. They sit around talking about nothing in particular. There are one or two pleasing moments. They are probably true to life, but who needs to waste time with them? Only those who made this misbegotten effort.

No Reason to Stay: see **Christopher's Movie Matinée**

No Surrender (1985) (102mins) (a Canada-U.K. co-production) d: Peter Smith s: Alan Bleasdale : Michael Angelis, Avis Bunnage, James Ellis, Tom Georgeson, Bernard Hill, Ray McAnally, Mark Mulholland, Joanne Whalley. A violent, rousing, hilarious farce about the miseries and glories of political passions in old age. Three busloads of elderly pensioners are brought to a seedy nightclub in Liverpool on New Year's Eve as part of a practical joke. The groups include Irish Protestants and Irish Catholics. With a punk-rock band, lots of arguments over pints and strong, colourful performances, it all ends up being a highly enjoyable experience. Not that peace was declared!

Nobody Makes Me Cry (Between Friends) (1983) (100mins) (a Canada-U.S. film) d: Lou Antonio s: Shelley List (from her novel) : Elizabeth Taylor, Carol Burnett, Barbara Bush, Stephen Young, Henry Ramer, Bruce Grey, Chuck Shamata, Lally Cadeau A hard-to-believe and silly story of two *divorcées* looking for husbands. The stars have difficulty shining here.

Nobody Waved Goodbye (1964) (80mins) d&s: Donald Owen : Peter Kastner, Julie Biggs, Claude Rae, Charmion King, Toby Tarnow, Ron Taylor, Robert Hill, Jack Beer, Sean Sullivan, Lynne Gorman, Ivor Barry, Norman Ettlinger, John Vernon. A funny and sad depiction of Peter, charming and impulsive, who leaves home to escape his nagging and materialiastic middle-class parents, only to discover that the world outside can be just as harsh and intolerant. This was intended to be a short documentary. Owen, with the support of Grant McLean, then the NFB Commissioner, turned his original story into a feature-length drama that found its place as one of the most important films in the evolution of English-language track motion pictures. It was the start of recognizably Canadian indigenous filmmaking, all too soon snuffed out by Telefilm's Capital Cost Allowance program, which oversaw the making of mostly dreadful Canadian-American films. (Se: Owen's 1984 sequel, *Unfinished Business*) (see Capital Cost Allowance program)

Noces de papier, Les: see **Paper Wedding**

Noël et Juliette (1973) (87mins) d&s: Michel Bouchard : Reynald Bouchard, Esther Auger, Micheline Lanctôt, Jean-Pierre Plant, J.-Léo Gagnon, Frédérique Collin. An inconsequential story about a man who loves animals, loses his lady companion because of them and then meets a suicidal woman. Micheline Lanctôt went on to better films.

Nomades Du Nord: see **Nikki, Wild Dog of the North**

Noncensus (1964) (80mins) d&s: John P. Fitzgerald, Colin Fox : Vincent Marino, Arthur Macri, Janet Amos, Agnes Fisher, Eric Holzwarth, Don di Novo, Vanya Franck, Dermot Grice, Carol Bradshaw, Beth Amos, Chris Wiggins, Judith Coates, Heath Lamberts, Sylvia Shawn, Edward J. Kelly, Stella Chadwick, Trudi Wiggins. This treasure from the archives was aptly described by John Fitzgerald as "a mad comedy about Toronto, a city full of absurdities," an apt description of this work of comedy and character with a cast of wonderful names from the past. Not to be equalled today. Never vulgar, cheap or ugly, but genuinely satirical and also kind.

Noroc (1999) (91mins) d: Marc Retaileau s: Robert French, Marc Retaileau : Peter Lacroix, Gina Chiarelli, Jay Brazeau, Alan Peterson, Babz Chula. A Romanian refugee photographer makes a living in Vancouver as a night watchman. His waterfront world is one of bored teenagers, vandals, pimps, druggies and weird artists, all looking for a life. An unpleasant picture for its own sake, and little more.

North of Pittsburgh (1992) (98mins) d: Richard Martin s: Jeff Schultz : Viveca Lindfors, Jeff Schultz. This disappointing film from the director of *Matinée* would be better titled South of Sault Ste. Marie, as little of it takes place in Ontario. Set in 1975, it concerns the wanderings of a widowed grandmother and her grandson, who come to understand each other as they drive the drab and darkened streets of Pittsburgh, trying to get the coal mining company where her husband once worked to pay her a pension.

North Station: see *Station nord*

Not Another Love Story (1979) (62mins) d&s: John Bradshaw : Paul Fitzgerald, Janis Allen, Elizabeth Landsdell. Said to be Ryerson University's first feature film from the film and photography school, this slight and fractured story of a man confused in his relationships with women makes a good start.

Not Just a Dirty Little Movie (1985) (97mins) d&s: Jack Darcus : Victor Ertmanis, Duncan Fraser, Gale Garnett, Alan Scarfe, Ian White. A European director making his first film this side of the Atlantic meets an unemployed actor desperate for work and a simple but good-natured actress; they agree to play in an adult film about a vampire nymphomaniac. A comic satire of the world of porno pictures, expertly done by the imaginative Darcus.

Not Me! (*Sous-sol*) (1996) (90mins) d&s: Pierre Gang : Louise Portal, Richard Mofatt, Isabelle Pascoe, Patrice Godin, Daniel Gadouas. A different coming-of-age portrayal concerning an 11-year-old boy deeply attached to his mother who watches his parents make love one night and confuses what he sees and hears with acts of violence and cruelty. For the young René, life is never quite the same as he becomes involved with emotional issues of his own. A beautifully made and acted study of innocence lost.

Nothing (2003) (90mins) d: Vincenzo Natali s: The Drews : David Hewlett, Andrew Miller, Andrew Lowery, Marie-Josee Croze, Gordon Pinsent. Two of life's losers, friends and roommates, find they have the power to make anything they hate, along with life's pretty frustrations, disappear. One wishes this silly nothing film would disappear.

Nothing Personal (1980) (96mins) (a Canada-U.S. co-production) d: George Bloomfield s: Robert Kaufman : Donald Sutherland, Suzanne Somers, Lawrence Dane, Roscoe Lee Browne, Dabney Coleman, Sean McCann, Chief Dan George, John Dehner, Gary Reineke, Sean Sullivan, Catherine O'Hara, Douglas Campbell, Patricia Collins, Hugh Webster, Robert Christie, Jane Mallet, Maury Chaykin, Heath Lamberts, Joe Flaherty, David Perlmutter, Eugene Levy, Sandy Webster, Jack Duffy, Peter Sturgess. In her first movie, Suzanne Somers plays a lawyer assisting professor Sutherland in his campaign to stop the slaughter of baby seals. Some charm and expression of concern, supported by a huge cast of Canadian regulars. Makes its point and knows when to stop.

Nothing to Lose (1994) (95mins) (a U.S.-Canada film) d&s: Izidore K. Musallam : Alexandra Paul, Youssef Abed-Alnour, Paul Gleason, Michael V. Gazzo, David Campbell, Mariliese Rizzardo. A father of an immigrant family in Montreal is killed by criminals, along with his family, but a son survives. Feeling he has nothing more to lose, he takes on the Mafia and wages his own war on them. Taut and plausible, set against convincing rundown surroundings. (The final film of Michael Gazzo.)

Nothing Too Good for a Cowboy (1998) (120mins) d: Kari Skogland s: David Barlow, Charles Lazer (based on books by Rich Hobson) : Chad Willett, Ted Atherton, Sarah Chalke, Dan MacDonald. Something new in Canadian films: a Western. Set in British Columbia, it tells the well-known story of a man who possessed the world's largest cattle ranch, a million-acre spread in the interior of B.C. in the late 1930s on the eve of World War II. A Vancouver debutante falls in love with him and joins him in running his enormous property. Well-plotted with some sharp dialogue and well-played by experienced

actors, this is a highly enjoyable film. Its success led to a tv series. Good to see Skogland getting away from guns, blood and sex.

Notre-Dame of the Mouise (*Notre-Dame de la Mouise*) (1941) (95mins) (b&w) (a Canada-France-Dutch film) d: Robert Peguy s: Grégoire Leclos, René Delacroix, Robert Peguy (after the book *Le Christ dans la banlieue* by Pierre Lhande : François Rozet, Georges Rollin, René Sarvil, Odette Joyeux, Édouard Delmont. This unusual and heartfelt early Québec film is the result of fifteen years of missionary reports from the Montréal suburb of *Notre-Dame de la Mouise*.

Notte dell'alta marea, La: see **Night of the High Tide, The**

***Nous deux, À* (An Adventure for Two)** (1979) (112mins) (a Canada-France co-production) d&s: Claude Lelouch : Jacques Dutronc, Catherine Deneuve, Jacques Villeret, Paul Preboist, Émile Genest. A woman and her mobster boyfriend go on the run after police uncover her blackmailing activities. An uneven mix of romance and thrills.

Now and Forever (2001) (99mins) d: Robert Clark s: William Boyle : Mia Kirshner, Adam Beach, Gordon Tootoosis, Theresa Russell. A native boy and small-town girl in Saskatoon are good friends in their local school. The boy has grown very fond of her, but she wants to escape small-town life and considers leaving with another young man, who is charming but sinister. The native boy tries to protect her, but succeeds only in driving her away. The film arrives at a sharp climax that changes everything and everyone. A different teen drama with a sense of despair.

Now That April's Here (1958) (85mins) (b/w) d: William Davidson s: Norman Klenman (from four short stories by Morley Callaghan), introduced by Raymond Massey *Silk Stockings:* Don Borisenko, Judy Welch, Beth Amos, Michael Mann, Sheila Billings, Pam d'Orsay *Rocking Chair:* John Drainie, Katherine Blake, Alan Hood, Art Jenoff *The Rejected One:* Tony Grey, Nancy Lou Gill, Fred Diehl, Paisley Maxwell, Josephine Barrington *A Sick Call:* Walter Massey, Georges Toupin, Kathy McNeil, Anna Collings, Rolf Carston *Silk Stockings* is about a shy young boy attracted to his landlady's daughter. He buys her a pair of stockings for her birthday, but when she wears them to go out with her boyfriend, he attempts to stop her. *Rocking Chair* tells of a widower and his lonely life. His ex-wife's close friend, an unmarried woman, tries to befriend him and make him forget the past. *The Rejected One* is about a young man from a reserved family who falls in love with a simple shopgirl. We see her first meeting with his family. *A Sick Call,* the final story, is concerned with a husband who opposes the visit of a priest to his sick wife, fearing that the church will come between them. These are lovely and telling vignettes, all of which deal quietly with love, loneliness and seemingly timid characters who have never come to terms with life. Their latest and perhaps only contact with another human being always seems to fail them. This film was the first feature from the partnership of Bill Davidson and Norman Klenman, though they had earlier made several documentaries and worked as a writer-director team for the CBC. They purchased the film rights to Callaghan's four stories (published in the collection *Now That April's Here*, 1936) in July 1957, began casting in November and shooting on February 1, 1958. During the four-week shooting schedule, they filmed entirely on location with interiors shot in a variety of homes and buildings. The production cost $75,000.

Now Where Are You? (*Où êtes-vous, donc?*) (1969) (95mins) d&s: Gilles Groulx : Christian Bernard, Georges Dor, Danielle Jourdan, Stéphane Venne. Two men drive around in an old Jaguar and visit St-Hyacinthe and Montréal in a search to understand why the world is becoming so unliveable. This is a search and destroy mission with the target being the Québécois, but frankly, most audiences may well wonder what Groulx is getting at. This film asks questions about commercialism, but doesn't come up with all the answers, although finding them is an entertaining social exploration.

Nowhere in Sight (2000) (93mins) (a Canada-U.S. film) d: Douglas Jackson s: James Lemmo : Helen Shaver, Andrew McCarthy, Richard Jutras, Christopher Heyerdahl. A young woman who has been recently blinded in a traffic accident must try to defend herself against a pair of bullies who attack her while her lover is away on business. The whole is an odd tale to tell.

Nowhere to Hide (1987) (90mins) d: Mario Azzopardi s: Alex Rebar, George Goldsmith : Amy Madigan, Daniel Hugh Kelly, Robin MacEachern, Michael Ironside, John Colicos. A U.S. marine is killed while investigating the cause of several helicopter crashes. His wife then becomes the target of the murderers. An agreeable time waster.

Nuit avec Hortense, La: see **Night with Hortense, The**

Nuit de noces (**Night of the Wedding**) (2001) (90mins) d: Émile Gaudreault s: Marc Brunet, Émile Gaudreault : François Morency, Geneviève Brouillette, Pierrette Robitaille, Yves Jacques, Michel Courtemanche, René-Richard Cyr, Diane Lavallée. A young Québécois couple wins a free trip to Niagara Falls and decides to go and get married there. Family and friends go along, too, so it's not surprising that the marriage is called off. The couple soon tires of this strange city—who wouldn't?—and their romantic notions about love and marriage begin to lose their appeal in this very popular comedy.

Nuit du deluge, La: see **Night of the Flood**

Nuit en Amérique, Une: see **Night in America, A**

Nuremberg (2000) (240mins) (a Canada-U.K.-U.S. film) d: Yves Simoneau s: David W. Rintels (based on the book *Nuremberg: Infamy on Trial* by Joseph Persico) : Alec Baldwin, Jill Hennessy, Michael Ironside, Matthew Craven, Len Cariou, Herbert Knaup, Colm Feore, Robert Joy, Charlotte Gainsbourg, Max Von Sydow, Christopher Plummer. While Stanley Kramer made a better film in 1961, *Judgment at Nuremberg,* there is much to recommend this new version an event which cannot be portrayed too often in the study of history. And for those who may not know or have forgotten, Nuremberg, a town in Germany, is where 21 members of the Nazi High Command were tried by the allies for the horrific war crimes committed under their leadership.

Nylon Heart, A (*Coeur de nylon*) (1989) (74mins) d: Michel Poulette s: Jean Barbeau : Yves Desgagnés, Guillaume Lemay-Thivierge. A tramp on the streets of Montréal always carries a small suitcase; this catches the eye of a young runaway. The two become strange bedfellows. A somewhat dreary drama with flat performances.

O or the Invisible Infant (*O ou l'invisible enfant*) (1971) (67mins) d&s: Raoul Duguay : Raoul Duguay, Michèle Magny, Paule Baillargeon, Gilles Renaud, Guy Boivin. The first film of Raoul Duguay concerns a family group that spends much time thinking and talking about the nature of life and how the contemporary world developed. Didactic.

Obachan's Garden (2001) (94mins) d&s: Linda Ohama : non-actors and some dramatic re-creations by actors Concerns the life of Hiroshima-born Asayo Murakami, who came to Canada in 1923 and lived through many social and family upsets. A graphic testament to one woman's strength and spirit, and a record of Canada's changing years.

Obsessed: see **Hitting Home**

Obstruction of Justice (1995) (85mins) d: Ron Hulme s: John Richards : Sara Botsford, Richard Zeman, Alan Fawcett. A lacklustre whodunit about the murder of a policeman's wife. Is one of the husband's friends the murderer? The police believe it was a random break-in, but then a lead suggests that perhaps the husband did the foul deed! This is hardly a spine-tingler.

October (*Octobre*) (1994) (97mins) d&s: Pierre Falardeau (based on the book by Francis Simard *Pour en finir avec octobre*) : Hugo Dubé, Luc Picard, Pierre Rivard, Denis Trudel, Serge Houde. Four terrorists, members of the FLQ, kidnap Pierre Laporte, minister of labour, murder him and conceal his body in the trunk of their car. This bloody time became known as the October Crisis when James Cross, the British trade commissioner to Montréal, was also kidnapped. The director, known for his separatist beliefs, treats these happenings as a heroic undertaking in the name of freedom. This wretched piece of propaganda lauding terrorism is undeniably well made and so becomes even more disturbing. For the excellent documentary about the topic see:

Action: The October Crisis of 1970 (1974) (87mins) d&s: Robin Spry. A strong and gripping feature-length documentary delving into the sources and rise of the separatist movement in Québec, from the death of Duplessis to the October Crisis. Three-quarters of the film deals with the events in October 1970, beginning with the kidnapping of James Cross, the British Trade Commissioner, in Montréal. The protagonists involved in this drama are the politicians: Trudeau, Bourassa, Lévesque, Drapeau, Douglas, Lemieux and others. The film closes at the end of 1970 with the arrest of Pierre Laporte's murderers.

Odd Balls (1984) (92mins) d: Miklos Lente s: Edward Naha : Foster Brooks, Michael MacDonald, Konnie Krome, Walter Wodchis, Milan Cheylov. A summer camp story set near Beaverton, Ontario, but supposedly in the U.S. The usual antics, involving lots of nerdy characters, soon begin to pall.

Odyssee d'Alice Tremblay, L' (**Alice's Odyssey**) (2002) (101mins) d: Denise Filiatrault s: Sylvie Lussier, Pierre Poirier : Sophie Lorain, Martin Drainville, Pierrette Robitaille, Marc Beland, Marc Labreche, Mitsou. This monster of a musical comedy—reinterpreting for adults the delightful fairy tales beloved by children—becomes a distasteful portrait of sexual activity from one tale to the next. Snow White, for example, has a different dwarf to bed every night. This clumsy, witless, heavy-handed farrago turns everything it touches into ugliness and violence. Sadly, the redoubtable Filiatrault has come a cropper here.

Odyssey of the Pacific (**L'Empereur du Pérou**) (1982) (81mins) (a Canada-France co-production) d: Fernando Arrabal s: Roger Lemelin, Fernando Arrabal : Mickey Rooney, Anick Starr, Jonathan Starr, Monique Mercure, Guy Hoffman, Jean-Louis Roux, André Melançon. A retired railway worker in France lives in an abandoned railway station and befriends a group of homeless children. Odd but appealing. Finding Rooney here is a surprize.

Oedipus Rex (1956) (87mins) d: Tyrone Guthrie : Douglas Campbell, Eleanor Stuart, Robert Goodier, Donald Davis, Eric House, Tony van Bridge, Douglas Rain, William Hutt, Naomi Cameron, Barbara Franklin, Gertrude Tyas, Robert Christie, Roland Bull, Edward Follows, Bruno Gerussi, David Gardner, Edward Holmes, Richard Howard, Roland Hewgill, James Manser, Louis Negin, Grant Reddick, William Shatner, Bruce Swerdfager, Neil Vipond. Based on the Greek tragedy by Sophocles and the English translation by William Butler Yeats. The son of a king kills his father in error and marries his mother. On becoming king, he discovers the truth of his situation, puts out his eyes and ends his life wandering in exile. A highly effective straight-from-stage-to-screen version, performed at the Shakespearean Festival in Stratford, Ontario, in 1955. With original masks and costumes by Tanya Moiseiwitsch and score by Louis Applebaum and nearly every great Canadian actor who made Stratford famous. Tom Patterson saw the value of filming Stratford's plays for posterity and as a record of the festival's achievements and began with this version of *Oedipus Rex*. But other plays were filmed only intermittently, until the coming of Robin Phillips in 1980 who decided that everything would be filmed. That this too rarely happened due to union demands, a reluctant CBC and other considerations, is to be deplored.

Of the Fields, Lately (1975) (90mins) d: Mike Newell s: David French (from his play of the same title) : R.H. Thomson, Gerard Parkes, Florence Paterson, Sean Sullivan. The Mercer family moved to Toronto from Newfoundland sixteen years ago. A deeply felt and human study of Newfoundland arising out of the author's own experience. (Note: Mike Newell's first film. He returned to the U.K. and became a leading director.)

Of Unknown Origin (1983) (90mins) (a Canada-U.S. co-production) d: George Pan Cosmatos s: Brian Taggert : Peter Weller, Jennifer Dale, Lawrence Dane, Kenneth Welsh, Louis del Grande, Shannon Tweed, Maury Chaykin. A businessman who has taken a temporary apartment while working in New York City is being driven mad by a giant rat. Why? Hard to know. A companion picture, you could say, to that other ratty Canadian-U.S. picture, *The Rats* or *Deadly Eyes*.

Off Your Rocker (1982) (92mins) (a Canadian-American film) d: Morley Markson, Larry Pall s: Samuel Warren-Joseph, Morley Markson (from Warren-Joseph's story) : Milton Berle, Red Buttons, Lou Jacobi, Dorothy Malone, Helen Shaver, Sharon Acker, Helen Hughes, Helen Burns, Sean McCann, Paul Kligman, Michael Ironside, Peter Sturgess. An unfunny comedy set in a retirement home, where the residents go on the warpath when a developer threatens to take over the home for a big-business venture. The tenants would pass as close cousins to Hal Roach comics. And why not; the film was produced by Hal Roach International!

Offering, The (1966) (80mins) (b/w) d: David Secter s: Martin Lager : Kee Faun, Ratch Wallace, Ellen Yamasaki, Marvin Goldhar, Gene Mark. The 23-year-old director of *Winter Kept Us Warm*, the University of Toronto film that brought him a measure of recognition, raised some $50,000 to make this, his second film. While a brave effort, it fails due to its script and a lack of knowledge of his subject. The weak story concerns a romance between a Chinese dancer, who is a member of the visiting Peking Opera Company, and a stagehand at the theatre where she appears. The film's saving grace is bright black and white photography of Toronto.

Office Party (1988) (90mins) d: George Mihalka s: Stephen Zoler (based on the novel of the same title by Michael Gilbert) : David Warner, Michael Ironside,

Jayne Eastwood, Kate Vernon. A mild-mannered accountant takes his fellow workers hostage in an unnamed American city. Very soon all are quarrelling among themselves and descending into a state of primitive violence. Unsavoury and predictable.

Oh, If Only My Monk Would Want (*Ah! Si mon moine voulait*) (1973) (92mins) (a Canada-France co-production) d: Claude Pierson s: Huguette Boisvert : Gilles Latulippe, Jean-Marie Proslier, Louise Turcot, Marcel Sabourin, Guy Hoffman, Rita Lafontaine. A mediocre movie consisting of sketches about monks and nuns, a farmer and a seductive widow, and ridiculous religious characters. All is set against scatological references, out-of-place irreverences and indecent images. A comedy stuffed with a continuous stream of unfunny moments.

Oh, What a Night (1992) (91mins) d: Eric Till s: Richard Nielson : Corey Haim, Barbara Williams, Keir Dullea, Geneviève Bujold, Robbie Coltrane, Andrew Miller. This silly title (suggesting a sex comedy, for box office appeal) masks a sensitively told, charming, yet down-to-earth study of rural life concerning domestic discord, disaffected juveniles and a youth who is initiated into manhood. The closing sequence has the look and restraint of the best silent cinema.

Ohama, Linda: see **Obachan's Garden**

OK Liberty (*Ok…Laliberté*) (1973) (112mins) d: Marcel Carrière s: Jean Morin, : Jacques Godin, Luce Guilbeault, Jean Lapointe, Lucille Papineau, Denise Proulx, Denis Drouin, Marcel Carrière. A paper-thin piece of whimsy about a man without means who falls in love with a woman who lifts his spirit, and joins him in becoming a hold-up robber. A truly funny piece.

Old Country Where Rimbaud Died, The (*Le vieux pays où Rimbaud est mort*) (1977) (113mins) (a Canada-France co-production) d: Jean-Pierre Lefebvre s: Marielle Amiel, Jean-Pierre Lefebvre : Marcel Sabourin, Anouk Ferjac, Myriam Boyer, Roger Blin, Germaine Delbat, François Perrot, Mark Lesser. Jean-Pierre Lefebvre went to France to make this film, a statement about what a Québécois feels on returning to the land of his ancestors. It is a visit of discovery and the revelations are simple, charming, sometimes happy but often sad. It is perhaps too slight, but the intent and the illusion are there.

Old Hats, The: see **Here's to Life!**

Old Masters: see *Maîtres anciens*

Old Memories, The: see **Happy Memories**

On Est Loin Du Soleil (*One is Far From the Sun*) (*The Brother Andre and the Sun*) (1971) (80 mins) d: Jacques Leduc s: Robert Tremblay : Marthe Nadeau, J-Leo Gagnon, Pierre Curzi, Marcel Sabourin, Willie Lamothe, Claude Jutra, Reynald Bouchard. This is a most unusual biographical study of a once famous man in the life of Quebec, Alfred Bessette (1845-1937), who became known as Brother Andre, whose ministrations at the Saint-

Joseph Oratory made him seem like a 'miracle man' to the poor and needy and deeply religious people of the province. A remarkable document in trying to come to terms with religion in a meaningful and aesthetic analysis of sociology, simplicity and spirituality. Convincing and complex and authentically characterized. (Jutra fits in very well as the doctor.)

On est loin du soleil: see **We Are Far From the Sun**

On Hostile Ground (2000) (120mins) (a Canadian-American film) d: Mario Azzopardi s: Brian Ross (from the story by Brent Reed, Sharon Cobb and Brian Ross) : John Corbett, Jessica Steen, Brittany Daniel, Andrew Kraulis, Peter Stebbings. Just like the disaster film of yesteryear, where huge calamities took place on Earth, not in space, this exciting story concerns the appearance of sinkholes in the road. In this case, the famous New Orleans Mardi Gras all but disappears when the road collapses. A geologist discovers it's not so much the weather, but unnatural causes doing the damage. Great special effects make a "gripping disaster" all too real!

On My Own (1992) (93mins) (a Canada-Italy-Australia co-production) d: Antonio Tibaldi s: Gill Dennis, John Frizzell, Antonio Tibaldi : Judy Davis, Matthew Ferguson, David McIlwraith, Jan Rubes, Michele Melega, Colin Fox. Here an Italian director has created an observant and impressionistic study of a young boy's troubled life, brought about by the separation of his parents and the mysterious behaviour of his mother. Set in wintertime in an exclusive boarding school in Ontario and on the Toronto–Kingston train. Beautifully acted and photographed.

On n'engraisse pas les cochons a l'eau Claire: see **Pigs Are Seldom Clean**

On the Nose (2001) (105mins) (a Canada-Ireland co-production) d: David Caffrey s: Tony Philpott : Robbie Coltrane, Brenda Blethyn, Dan Aykroyd, Eanna MacLiam, Zara Turner. A somewhat far-fetched but delightful comedy about a janitor who bets on the horses and loses all the money he had set aside for his daughter's university education. Then he finds the head of an ancient Australian aborigine that, when the sun shines in the right place, provides the numbers of winning horses. A nice, tight group of comedians makes this all seem quite probable, mixed in with a stable of other funny incidents.

On the Run (*Pablo qui court*) (1993) (80mins) d&s: Bernard Bergeron : Jean-François Pichette, Louise Laprade. Another shallow, shorthand series of jumps and cuts of life in the gutter. This time, a petty thief lives on the kindness of others, mostly women.

On the Run: see *Femme de Pablo Ruiz, La*

On Their Knees (2001) (85mins) d&s: Anaïs Granofsky : Anaïs Granofsky, Ingrid Veninger, Ram Fakeer, Julian Richings, Maury Chaykin, Jackie Burroughs. Two sisters—one black, the other white, same mother but different fathers—pack their dead grandmother in ice and put her in an old ice cream truck. They set out from Toronto to drive her to her hometown for burial, somewhere, it seems, in Northern Ontario. They cheat, steal money and quarrel to keep themselves going. When they arrive at the grandmother's family home, all celebrate and attempt to bring a sense of conviction to this tattered tale. Was this journey really necessary?

On Your Head: see *Ciel sur la tête, Le*

Once (1981) (84mins) s: d: Gordon Pinsent s: Donald Harron : Charmion King, Leslie Toth. A widowed woman living on her own provides a young student with room and board. One of several interesting small films made for the CBC by leading actors of the time. Pinsent's first film as a director, working with the comedian Donald Harron as the writer.

Once in a Blue Moon (1995) (96mins) d&s: Philip Spink : Cody Serpa, Simon Baker, Deanna Milligan, Mike MacDonald, Cheryl Wilson. The director, who has specialized in tv films for children, has set this family story in 1967, Canada's centennial year. There are the expected ups and downs between parents and children. Principally, Peter and Sam decide to build a rocket and to make it fly. Everyone in the cast works hard to make this domestic world likeable, but it lacks charm and depth. Filmed in Vancouver.

Once Upon a Memory: see **Fatal Memories**

Once Upon a Time in the East (*Il était une fois dans l'est*) (1974) (101mins) d: André Brassard s: Michel Tremblay, André Brassard : Denise Filiatrault, Michelle Rossignol, Frédérique Collin, Sophie Clément, Gilles Renaud, André Montmorency, Manda Parent, Amulette Garneau, Claude Gai, Denis Drouin, Rita Lafontaine, Jean Archambault. Characters from plays written by Michel Tremblay, with strange and desperate patterns of behaviour, come together in the lively and sordid night world of Montréal's east end. A good deal of truth, a knowing insight into hearts and minds and some rousing performances make the sensational aspects of the activity depicted here very real and touched with tragedy.

One Heart Broken Into Song (1998) (90mins) d: Clement Virgo s: George Elliott Clarke : Linette Robinson, Rainbow Sun (real name Don Francks), Eugene Clark, Arden Bess, Jeremiah Sparks, Tara Baxter, Djanet Sears, Troy Adams. During and after the American Civil War, many black people came to Canada and settled in Halifax, Nova Scotia, where they built a village called Africville. The story takes place in the 1930s and concerns two young lovers who come to Africville to make a new life, which soon becomes tragic when the realities of everyday existence defeat them. This is a gentle, well-meaning film that brings home the difficulties at that time, facing black people in a mostly white society.

100 Days in the Jungle (2002) (90mins) d: Sturla Gunnarsson s: Sean O'Byrne : Michael Riley, Aidan Devine, Jonathan Scarfe, Adrien Dorval, Hugh Thompson, Brendan Fletcher, Brian Markinson. A vivid semi-documentary reliving a harrowing real-life event that happened in Ecuador in 1999 when a group of Canadian technicians working for an oil company were abducted by bandits for ransom. They survived 100 days of a frightening ordeal in the jungle on the border between Ecuador and Colombia before being rescued. Although audiences know the outcome, this is still a gripping, powerful and moving film.

100% Bio (Hundred Percent Biography) (2003) (101mins) d: Claude Fortin s: Serge Laprade & Fortin : Serge Laprade, Claude Fortin, Michel Mongeau, Aline Caron, Brigitte Lacasse, Gaston L'Heureux, Martin Soucy. This is a film about Quebec's television history, where two men, one a tv host, the other a once famous filmmaker, both opposites, who meet over the making of a proposed biography about the other, find to their consternation there is a lack of archival material to make such a programme. All somewhat pretentious but mesmerizing in its memories of the once new 'show business'.

125 Rooms of Comfort (1974) (80mins) (b/w) d&s: Patrick Loubert : Tim Henry, Jackie Burroughs, Sean Sullivan, Robert Silverman, Michael Lewis, Jackie Crossland, Marcia Diamond. The 125 rooms of comfort are in the Grand Central Hotel, St. Thomas, Ontario. The owner dies and the manager wants to sell it, but the son of the owner refuses to give his permission. This causes upsets both serious and amusing that keep this likeable little film moving along among the mixed collection of guests!

One is Far From the Sun: see *On Est Loin Du Soleil*

One Magic Christmas (1985) (88mins) (a Canada-U.S. co-production) d: Phillip Borsos s: Thomas Meehan : Mary Steenburgen, Harry Dean Stanton, Gary Basaraba, Elizabeth Harnois, Arthur Hill, Wayne Robson, Jan Rubes, Elias Koteas, Sarah Polley, Michelle Meyrink, Robbie Magwood. A sentimental tale about a mother who has lost the Christmas spirit due to hardship and woe. But Santa and his guardian angel discuss the matter with the mother's 12-year-old daughter—Sarah Polley in her first film appearance—and all is well for the holiday. No specific setting, but a red mailbox may be fleetingly seen. An honest piece as one would expect from the late Phillip Borsos.

One Man (1977) (88mins) d: Robin Spry s: Peter Pearson, Peter Madden, Robin Spry : Len Cariou, Jayne Eastwood, Carole Lazare, Barry Morse, August Schellenberg, Jean Lapointe, Sean Sullivan, Terry Haig, Marc Legault, Danny Freedman, Gilles Renaud, Bob Girolami, Jacques Godin, Larry Kent, Budd Knapp, Victor Knight. A compelling and concerned drama in which a Montréal tv reporter tries to expose a factory owner whose plant emits dangerous pollutants causing the death of children. The reporter then finds himself and his family threatened by corporate and political interests. Much of what this film has to say later came true with the discovery of the contamination of the Love Canal in Niagara Falls, New York. With fine performances and clever direction, this was Robin Spry's first dramatized feature film made at the NFB.

One Man Out (Erik) (1989) (90mins) (a U.S.-Canada film) d&s: Michael Kennedy : Stephen McHattie, Deborah Van Valkenburgh, Cecilia Tijeriha, Michael Champion. In Central America a soldier of fortune, together with a crusading journalist, fights drug runners, with several close calls they persue and work hard to put a stop to their deadly activities. It all seems to be a losing battle which, mildly exciting , soon loses interest as well.

One Night Only (1986) (86mins) d: Timothy Bond s: John Kent Harrison : Lenore Zann, Helene Udy, Taborah Johnson, Kenneth James. Fortunately, this contemporary sex comedy doesn't last for more than one night. We witness the often sordid events in the life of a young law student who, in need of tuition money, becomes involved in parties with call girls, drink, hockey players, their groupies and many other unsavoury companions. A 16-year-old cousin is also hanging around. In the end, we find we have not cared for anybody in this picture. It gives no depth to its characters.

One Night Stand (1978) (93mins) d: Allan Winton King s: Carol Bolt (based on her play) : Chapelle Jaffe, Brent Carver, Dinah Christie, Susan Hogan, Mina E. Mina, Len Doncheff, Robert Silverman, Pixie Bigelow, Don Daynard, Rough Trade. A spine-chilling dance of death for an unsuspecting lady and a psychopathic killer. Angry and hurt because her boyfriend stood her up on her birthday, Daisy goes to a discotheque and picks up a man called Rafe. She comes home with him on her arm and locks herself into a nightmare. Thus begins this truly great film by Allan King, which never resorts to sensationalism for its own sake.

One of Our Own (1977) (65mins) d: William Fruet s: Florrie Adelson : David McFarlane, David Gardner, Colleen Collins, Kay Hawtrey, Josh Orwin, Terry Cherniak. A sensitive and imaginative consideration of the life of a teenager afflicted with Down's Syndrome. Many years later, the same boy, now an adult, appeared on the tv program *Man Alive* to talk about his attempts to become an actor. (See: *For the Record*)

One Plus One (The Kinsey Report) (Exploring the Kinsey Report) (1961) (114mins) (a Canada-U.S. co-production) d&s: Arch Oboler (based on his play *Mrs. Kingsley's Report*) The film is in six parts. It stars Leo G. Carroll and features different actors in the various stories. *Honeymoon:* Hilda Brauner, William Taylor *Homecoming:* Kate Reid, Ernest Graves, Richard Janver *The Divorcee:* June Duprez, Austin Willis, Douglas Rain *Average Man:* Jane Rose, Truman Smith *Baby:* Rita Gardner, Jack Betts. Professor Logan addresses a symposium on

the Kinsey Report on male and female sexual behaviour. As he discusses the various statistics, individual members of the audience reflect on their personal experiences. In *Honeymoon,* a newly married couple wonder if they were right to have had premarital sex. They decide their actions were justified because the world might have ended before they married. In *Homecoming,* a lonely wife feels she is growing old and passionless through the continued absence of her husband on business. When he returns home after a long trip, she confesses that, although she loves him deeply, her loneliness has led to her infidelity with another man. In *The Divorcée,* a *divorcée* is taken advantage of by a distinguished middle-aged playboy. In *Average Man,* an overweight businessman regrets that he is not represented in the statistics in the Kinsey Report and sets out to taste the forbidden fruit. He meets a former girlfriend and tries to seduce her, but she has to babysit her grandchildren. In *Baby,* a young wife dares not tell her husband she is pregnant and tries to secure an illegal abortion. The film ends with *Lecture Hall,* a general discussion by members of the symposium. This was an unusually frank subject for its time, but the treatment renders the entire project foolish in the extreme. It was hardly ever shown in cinemas.

One Who Sees the Hours, The (Celui qui voit les heures) (1985) (73mins) d&s: Pierre Goupil : Ginette Boivin, Frédérique Collin, Serge Gagné, Régis Gauthier, Pierre Goupil. The nephew of the director tells how his uncle wanted to make a big-screen version of George Orwell's *1984* but was refused and now suffers the same doubts as Winston, the book's leading character. However, he manages to transform Montréal into "Alphaville" and after many disappointments makes the film he is watching now, the one the audience is looking at. The characters are held prisoners by their environment which constantly fades away leaving them in almost total isolation, and the director and protagonists in torments of doubt and alienation. It would probably be difficult for even Orwell to read all this, but some audiences might want to dive in and bring out what they want to know. Close to being an experimental film.

Only God Knows (1974) (95mins) d: Peter Pearson s: Paul Wayne : Gordon Pinsent, John Beck, Paul Hecht, Tisa Farrow, Toby Tarnow, Peter Sturgess, Pamela Hyatt, Cec Linder, George Touliatos, Lawrence Dane, Mary Long. Three priests run a drug rehabilitation centre. In need of money, they accept a donation from a mobster, who dies before delivering it. So, the ministers go to his home to steal it. Lots of laughs in the tradition of the famous British *Carry On* series.

Only Thing You Know, The (1971) (82mins) d&s: Clarke Mackey : Ann Knox, John Denos, Allan Royal, Linda Huffman, Iain Ewing, Hugh McIntyre,

Eileen McIntyre, Ellen Rosenburg, Gilbert Sauvé, Douglas Mackey, Theresa Lee-Horbatiuk, Becky Shechter, Eleanor MacKay, Howard Cronis. A remarkable first feature about a young girl, dissatisfied at home with her tiresome parents, who falls in love with her schoolteacher but finds that genuine romance and affection are hard to come by. While a good deal of improvisation is noticeable, the sensitive depiction of the subject matter and the insights it reveals into the girl's nature are honest and affecting. Ann Knox's performance is unforgettable, and MacKay's direction and dialogue is thoughtful and imaginative.

Onzième spéciale: see **Eleventh Special, The**

Opération beurre de pinottes: see **Peanut Butter Solution, The**

Operation Overthrow: see **Power Play**

Oranges of Israel, The (*Valse à trois)* (1974) (90mins) d: Fernand Rivard s: Andreanne Foucault (from the book *The Oranges of Israel* by Michelle Guérin) : Ian Ireland, Karin Schubert, Paule Bélanger, Laurier Lapierre. A pregnant girl comes between a couple living in Montréal. A slight, yet sometimes appealing story told with more words than images.

Orders, The (*Les ordres*) (1974) (107mins) (b/w/col) d&s: Michel Brault : Jean Lapointe, Hélène Loiselle, Guy Provost, Claude Gauthier, Louise Forestier, Amulette Garneau, Louise Latraverse, Sophie Clément, J.-Léo Gagnon, Jose Rettino, Guy Bélanger. An affecting dramatized account of the dreadful experiences of individuals taken to prison in Montréal under the War Measures Act during the October Crisis of 1970—most guilty, some innocent. The film captures honestly and fairly the humiliation of the innocent who became caught up in the backlash of a violent terrorist activity. Brault was also behind the camera.

Ordinary Magic: see **Ganesh**

Ordinary People (*Ti-peuple*) (1971) (82mins) d&s: Fernand Bélanger : Yves Angrignon, Elizabeth Bart, Gilbert Roudier, Joanne Roudier. Two young and idealistic individuals look for work but find themselves out of step with their materialistic society. They come to think of themselves as being foreign among people they thought of as friends. Another acute and knowing portrait of contemporary Québec life.

Ordinary Tenderness (*Tendresse ordinaire*) (1973) (82mins) d: Jacques Leduc s: Robert Tremblay : Esther Auger, Jocelyn Bérubé, Jean-Pierre Bourque, Luce Guilbeault, J.-Léo Gagnon, Tiffany Lee. A wife and her friend wait for her husband to return from his winter of work at a mine in Shefferville, Québec. Again, reality and mixed emotion are breathed into the ordinary things in life within a seemingly quiet and dull existence.

***Oreille d'un sourd, L'* (The Deaf Man's Ear)** (1996) (83mins) d&s: Mario Bolduc : Marcel Sabourin, Micheline Lanctôt, Luc Proulx, Paul Hébert. A black comedy with a mixed bag of likeable and nasty characters: a man and his mistress, a wife and children, a father-in-law and others, set against colourful and humorous backgrounds from bingo to bathroom.

Orphan Muses, The (*Les muses orphelines*) (2000) (107mins) d: Robert Favreau s: Gilles Desjardins (based on the play by Michel-Marc Bouchard) : Marina Orsini, Céline Bonnier, Fanny Mallette, Stéphane Demers, Louise Portal. After a mad, dangerous car ride through the darkened countryside, several young family members arrive at home to join a party to mark the 20ᵀᴴ anniversary since the death of their parents, with fireworks, much noise, music, and memories, some of them touching on family secrets, and the fact that their mother had run away with a Spaniard. This seemed to have a lasting effect on a 25-year-old daughter who has become demented and headstrong. In this role, Celine Bonnier gives a mesmerizing performance in torment, sustained, deeply affecting, and believable.

Other Kingdom, The (1985) (180mins) d: Vic Sarin s: Jeannine Locke : Leueen Willoughby, Terence Kelly, Helen Carscallen. Set in a hospital ward, this was possibly the first dramatisied film to concern itself with the subject of breast cancer. The distinguished cinematographer Vic Sarin, in his first film as director, treats his subject with sensitivity and understanding. The cast is admirable.

Other Side of the Law (Outside the Law) (1994) (95mins) d&s: Gilles Carle : Brigitte Boucher, Jurgen Prochnow, Yves Renier, Xavier Deluc, Maggie Castle. Life among European settlers in Québec, apparently rather dull and predictable, with romance and murder on the river and into the trees. (see *Aventures du grand nord, Les*)

Other Side of the River, The: see **Dollar, The**

Où êtes-vous, donc?: see **Now Where Are You?**

***Ou le roman de Charles Pathé* (The Life of Charles Pathé)** (1994) (104mins) (a Canada-France-Belgium co-production) d: Jacques Rouffio s: Jean Gruault, Jacques Rouffio : Didier Bezace, Yves Jacques, Isabelle Lajeunesse, Gérard Loussine, Ronny Coutteure, Ronald Guttman, Alain Fromager. The producer Rock Demers, noted for his love of cinema, put together this captivating dramatized documentary of the life, times and inventions of the great film pioneer Charles Pathé. The company that bears his name is still active today. No cineaste should be without this document, and it should be a boon to teachers of film history.

Out of Sight, Out of Mind (The Seventh Circle) (1983) (65mins) d: Zale Dalen s: Martin Lager (based on a story by Roy Moore) : Robert Joy, Nicholas Campbell, Graham Greene, Hardee T. Lineham, Denis Forest, Richard Donat, Layne Coleman, Bruce Swerdfager. This is a thoughtful, studied and compelling portrait of social violence and the way the courts deal with psychopaths. A doctor just out of school goes to a mental hospital to attempt to cure the criminally insane. He works in a twisted world of distrust, violence and hopelessness. A painfully true and controversial subject. (See: *For the Record*)

Out of the Blue (No Looking Back) (1980) (94mins) (a Canada-U.S. film) d: Dennis Hopper s: Leonard Yakir, Brenda Nielson : Linda Manz, Dennis Hopper, Raymond Burr, Sharon Farrell, Donald Gordon. A dismal melodrama about bikers and junkies in B.C. With Hopper's name to promote, the film was given a mass critical reception, but even this could not turn trash into treasure.

Outcast (1991) (93mins) d: Roman Buchok s: Brian Iger : John Trench, Peter Read. In this minor horror, an abused misfit makes an evil pact with something supernatural; only his young daughter can help. A better script might have done the job in a more interesting manner.

Outrageous! (1977) (100mins) d&s: Richard Benner (based on the short story *Making It From Butterfly Ward* by Margaret Gibson) : Craig Russell, Hollis McLaren, Richert Easley, Allan Moyle, Andrée Pelletier, Helen Shaver, Martha Gibson, Helen Hughes, Michael Ironside. A lively, human, and often moving account of the relationship between a female impersonator and a schizophrenic girl, told with humour and believability. Craig Russell was quite a celebrity at the time, and the film was among the first Toronto-made movies to draw large audiences and do well at the box office. The sequel followed a year later.

Outside Chance of Maximillian Glick, The (1988) (96mins) d: Allan Goldstein s: Phil Savath (based on the novel of the same title by Morley Torgov) : Noam Zylberman, Fairuza Balk, Saul Rubinek, Jan Rubes, Susan Douglas. Max is a 12-year-old boy who isn't sure that he wants to be Jewish in the small prairie town of Beauséjour, Manitoba. The arrival of a lively rabbi changes his outlook and that of the community. Funny and sad, the film tends to limp from scene to scene, but is enlivened by Saul Rubinek's knowing performance as the rabbi.

Outside the Law: see **Other Side of the Law**

Over My Head (*Jusqu'au cou*) (1964) (74mins) (b/w) d&s: Denis Héroux : Édith de Villers, Raymond Levasseur, Guy Dufresne, Renée Lescop, Bernard Landry. A second film from Héroux, who later became well known for his sex comedies. A student falls in love with a woman who turns out to be his father's mistress. This leads to a great many complications, most of them political and romantic. One of the first films by students of the Université de Montréal. Enjoyable. Where are all these students today?

Overcoat, The (*Le manteau*) (2002) (85mins) d&s: Morris Panych (no dialogue) : Peter Anderson, Wendy Gorling, Colin Heath, Cyndi Mason. A filmed version of the play inspired by the famed Gogol short story and set to music by Shostakovich. This study of a poor man who tries to survive the taunts of society becomes a meaningful cameo played by the original cast seen in the play. The story is interpreted through music and movements.

Overnight (1985) (96mins) d&s: Jack Darcus : Gale Garnett, Alan Scarfe, Victor Ertmanis, Tedde Moore, Duncan Fraser, Ian White. An actor desperate for money becomes involved in the making of pornographic films. He is helped by a European director who has also fallen on hard times. Intended to be a spoof of conventional filmmaking, it is not funny enough and too silly to be true. Darcus misses out this time.

Owning Mahowny (2001) (107mins) (a Canada-U.K. co-production) d: Richard Kwietniowski s: Maurice Chauvet : Philip Seymour Hoffman, Minnie Driver, Maury Chaykin, John Hurt. Remember the largest single-handed bank fraud in Canadian history? Well, this is the story. The year is 1982, and Brian Mahowny has been appointed credit manager of a major bank in Toronto. He is frugal to a fault, with none of the usual vices except one: a gambling habit. With backgrounds ranging over Toronto, Las Vegas and Atlantic City, this production never goes wrong, as did Mahowny!

P'tit vient vite, Le: see **Little One Is Coming Soon, The**

Pablo qui court: see *Femme de Pablo Ruiz, La*

Pacemaker and a Sidecar, A (*L'eau chaude, l'eau frette*) (1997) (92mins) d: André Forcier s: Jacques Marcotte, André Forcier : Jean Lapointe, Jean-Pierre Bergeron, Sophie Clément, Louise Gagnon, Guy L'Écuyer, J.-Léo Gagnon, Carole Laure, Francine Grimaldi. In a dumpy, rowdy rooming house in Montréal with its shady inhabitants, a mother becomes involved in the murder of a loan shark, after she has borrowed money from him to buy her daughter a pacemaker. Everything is somewhat overdone and overstated.

Paint Cans (1994) (93mins) d&s: Paul Donovan (from his novel of the same title) : Chas Lawther, Robyn Stevan, Bruce Greenwood, Nigel Bennett, Don Francks, Ann Marie MacDonald, Andy Jones, Martha Burns, Paul Donovan, worn down, frustrated and exasperated in his dealings with government funding agencies (such as Telefilm, CBC, Ontario Film Development Corp.), was driven to write a novel, which became this film. It provides a mainly humorous exposé of what goes on between rogue film producers, deluded bureaucrats and overly ambitious directors. Halifax, Nova Scotia, has become as well known as St. John's, Newfoundland, as a centre of irreverent and scathing humour with such locally produced tv programs as *The Royal Canadian Air Farce*, *Codco* and *This Hour Has Twenty-Two Minutes*. *Paint Cans,* by Paul and Michael Donovan, lives up to this tradition. Chas Lawther is just right as a morose official at "The Film Financing Agency of Canada" who gets dragged into a succession of political intrigues and romantic disasters that end in murder, with millions spent and no films made. Apart from flaws here and there, this is a marvellous comic melodrama that hits home with bite and satisfaction.

Painted Angels (1998) (108mins) (a Canada-U.K. co-production) d: Jon Sanders s: Anna Mottram, Jon Sanders : Brenda Fricker, Kelly McGillis, Meret Becker, Bronagh Gallagher, Lisa Jakub, Anna Mottram. Set in Saskatchewan in the 1870s, this gem of a film tells of the hardship, heartache and struggles of five women who work as prostitutes in a frontier brothel. More portrait than dramatized narrative, but effective nonetheless. The settings and period details are brought so expertly to life that one feels transported into the past. The treatment of the women by the crude men, the tragedy, misery and loveless lives, about which are never sentimentalized but depicted with honesty and intensity. This is a part of our history about which we see and hear little. The actresses are all memorable.

Palais Royale (1988) (100mins) d: Martin Lavut s: David Daniels, Hugh Graham, Lawrence Zack : Kim Cattrall, Matthew Craven, Dean Stockwell, Michael Hogan. A clerk in a Toronto advertising agency during the 1950s falls for a gorgeous girl on a cigarette poster. Finding her draws him into a strange world of gangsters, guns and murder. A good try for something new in Canadian films, though it doesn't quite come off. All is resolved, however, in Toronto's Palais Royale dance pavilion, where the carefree music and energetic dancing create a wonderful atmosphere of a time passed.

Pale Face: see *Visage pâle*

Pale Saints (1997) (90mins) d&s: Joel Wyner : Sean Patrick Flanery, Michael Riley, Saul Rubinek, Maury Chaykin, Rachel Crawford, Gordon Pinsent. A piece of violent tripe from the Norstar factory about small-time hoods, mobsters, murder and double-dealing, all so confused that even seasoned actors struggling with the plot, including the ever reliable Pinsent, go down in gloom and doom.

Panic (*Panique***)** (1977) (97mins) d: Jean-Claude Lord s: Jean Salvy : Paule Baillargeon, Jean Coutu, Gabriel Arcand, J.-Léo Gagnon, Pierre Thériault, Jacques Thisdale. A well-done film from Lord, unknowingly foretelling what happens when a town finds its water poisoned.

Panic Bodies (1998) (70mins) d: Mike Hoolboom : Ed Johnson, Tom Chomont, Kathryn Ramey, Jason Broughton, Moucle Blackout, Janieta Ryre, Steve Sanguedolce. Apparently working without a script, the experimental filmmaker Hoolboom has thought up a six-part journey—small trips would be a better description—that creates a blueprint for love and death in our new century. Aids, death, sexuality, memory, spirituality, split screens and pop culture images—there seems to be no end to this confused and tangled wandering through mind and body.

Panique: see **Panic**

Paper People, The (1967) (90mins) d: David Gardner s: Timothy Findley : Marc Strange, Marigold Charlesworth, Lucy Warner, Robin Ward, Kate Reid, Hilary Vernon, Brett Somers, Sabina Maydelle, Clifford Trevor, Stevie Wise, Ed McGibbon, Claudette Houchen, Liza Creighton, Adam Ludwig, Don McGill. An eccentric, willful and selfish artist makes paper sculptures of people he doesn't like and then burns them. This frequently silly, pretentious and ambiguous film draws great strength from the remarkable acting performances by the entire cast, notably Marc Strange (the moody young man later seen in *Isabel*) and from the vivid and imaginative direction of David Gardner, who makes much of Timothy Findley's erratic script. At the time, Findley, who also wrote *Don't Let the Angels Fall,* was one of Canada's most promising and skillful young writers; he later found recognition for his novels and the film version of one of them, *The Wars* (1982). This was the CBC's first feature film production under its own auspices.

Paper Wedding (*Les noces de papier***)** (1989) (87mins) d: Michel Brault s: Jefferson Lewis : Geneviève Bujold, Manuel Aranguiz, Dorothée Berryman, Gilbert Sicotte, Jean Mathieu. Geneviève Bujold appeared in Brault's first feature film as a director, *Entre la mer et l'eau douce* in 1968 (and Denys Arcand's first screenplay). Now 20 years later she returns to Montréal from L.A. to play a solitary 40-year-old university professor and mistress to a married Hungarian businessman who finds her life lacking a sense of purpose. She has come to help her sister, a lawyer, with a difficult immigration case. She reluctantly agrees to a marriage of convenience with a Chilean refugee to give him the right to live in Canada. It is purely a business matter; she has no feelings for him and they will go their separate ways until a divorce can be arranged. But it doesn't turn out to be as easy as this; they are watched by immigration officials, tested repeatedly on their knowledge of each other and, as a result of being thrown together, actually fall in love. This is a familiar plot device that we have seen before, yet it is utterly convincing and conveyed in subdued tones with a sense of grace, beauty and tenderness. It is in every way a remarkable piece of cinema, with near perfect performances by all concerned. It was poorly remade in Hollywood under the title *Green Card* with Gérard Dépardieu and Andie MacDowell (director Peter Weir, 1990).

Paperback Hero (1973) (94mins) d: Peter Pearson s: Leslie Rose, Barry Pearson : Keir Dullea, Elizabeth Ashley, John Beck, Dayle Haddon, Franz Russell, George R. Robertson, Margot Lamarre, Ted Follows, Linda Sorenson. A far-fetched Western about a skirt-chasing hockey hero who shoots up the town whenever he pleases. Set against a timely hockey background. One of the few early Canadian films to take hockey as their subject. This was the time when Canada's producers couldn't get enough of

Hollywood's Keir Dullea (*Black Christmas, Welcome to Blood City, Full Circle, Leopard in the Snow*).

Paperboy, The (1994) (93mins) d: Douglas Jackson s: David Peckinpah : Alexandra Paul, Marc Marut, Brigid Tierney, William Katt, James Rae, Frances Bay, Krista Errickson. A paperboy murders an old lady. He tries to make friends with the family, but they banish him from their lives. He then begins to terrorize them. We've come across these "bad seeds" before on film; this one is believable and holds the interest, but the cruelty is hard to take.

Papillon Bleu, Le : see **Blue Butterfly, The**

Par le sang des autres: see **By the Blood of Others**

Paradise (1982) (99mins) (a Canada-Israel co-production) d&s: Stuart Gillard : Willie Aames, Phoebe Cates, Tuvia Tavi, Neil Vipond. Shot in Israel, with sex on the sand instead of in the sea. A feeble reworking of *The Blue Lagoon*, with a touch of *Arabian Nights*.

Parallels (1980) (92mins) d: Mark Schoenberg s: Jaron Summers, Mark Schoenberg : David Fox, Joan Hurley, Judith Mabey, Gerard LePage, David Ferry. About a priest who feels he is losing touch with the church and its people. Includes several interesting views and opinions about the place of religion in people's lives. Told with feeling and concern.

Parasite Murders (Shivers) (They Came from Within) (1975) (87mins) d&s: David Cronenberg : Susan Petrie, Barrie Baldaro, Julie Wildman, Joy Coghill. Sex-hungry parasites infect the inhabitants of a high-rise apartment, leaving a trail of gory violence. This was the first of Cronenberg's twisted, puerile pictures, which regrettably have given him a cult status among certain critics.

Parce que Pourquoi: see **Because Why**

Paris or Somewhere (1995) (95mins) d: Bradford Turner s: Lee Gowan (adapted from John Synge's *The Playboy of the Western World*) : Callum Keith Rennie, Molly Parker, Christopher Owens, Charlene Fernetz, Francis Damberger, John Vernon. If one forgets about Synge and accepts this mishmash of murder, intrigue, romance and comedy taking place in a lonely corner of the Canadian prairies, then this film probably qualifies as minor entertainment.

Paris, France (1993) (112mins) d: Gérard Ciccoritti s: Tom Walmsley : Leslie Hope, Peter Outerbridge, Victor Ertmanis, Dan Lett, Raoul Trujillo. A relentless tale of sexual perversion among the so-called literati and involving a young novelist, her failed publisher-husband (who believes that John Lennon is calling from the grave) and a stranger who lives for sex. This is a shallow film about unpleasant, unlikeable and foolish characters: a descent into bad taste.

Park Is Mine, The (1986) (101mins) (a Canadian-American film) d: Steven Hilliard Stern s: Lyle Gorch : Tommy Lee Jones, Helen Shaver, Yaphet Kotto, Lawrence Dane, Gale Garnett, Tom Harvey, George Bloomfield, Eric Peterson, Louis DiBianco. New York's Central Park police station is blown up by two Vietnam veterans who are unable to adapt to society. One of them commits suicide, and the other continues their plan to take over the park. He doesn't get far. A somewhat far-fetched cry against wars is weakened by the sense of disbelief it creates.

Parlez-nous d'amour: see **Let's Talk About Love**

Paroles et musique **(Love Songs)** (1985) (108mins) (A Canada- France co-production) d&s: Élie Chouraqui : Catherine Deneuve, Richard Anconina, Christopher Lambert, Jacques Perrin, Nick Mancuso, Dayle Haddon and many others. With music by Michel Legrand, this is a part-doc, part-fic parade of love songs and their singers. Some of the songs create a dreamy, romantic mood.

Parsley Days (2000) (76mins) d&s: Andrea Dorfman : Megan Dunlop, Mike Le Blanc, Maria MacLean, Kenneth Harrington, Marcia Connolly. A young couple who have been together for five years and seem to have a perfect relationship part company when the woman realizes that she has fallen out of love with her man. Life becomes more complicated when she discovers she is pregnant. Not wanting to have an abortion, she begins eating parsley all day long with every meal because it is supposed to induce a miscarriage. This film, which began with some charm, now becomes a mess, having something to do with a need for independence. But with so much parsley everywhere, it's difficult to know what's going on. The director, who is also the cinematographer, is sometimes lost in the green stuff and it isn't money at the box-office, unfortuunately.

Part des choses, La **(Un léger vertige) (A Part of Things) (A Light Vertigo)** (1991) (80mins) d: Diane Poitras s: Michel Langois, Diane Poitras : Paul Savoie, Raymond Legault, Dulcinée Langfelder, Marie Laberge, Emmanuelle Tétreault. This is a small film with much to say: both pertinent and engrossing. A divorced baby-boomer worries about his daughter. They discuss her social values compared to those that prevailed when he was a teenager, and he finds himself thinking about the choices he has made in his own life. A thoughtful, retrospective piece.

Part of Things, A: see *Part des choses, La*

Parting: see **Acts of Love (Series)**

Partis pour la gloire: see **Gone to Glory**

Partners (1976) (97mins) d: Donald Owen s: Norman Snider, Don Owen : Denholm Elliott, Hollis McLaren, Michael Margotta, Lee Broker, Judith Gault, Robert Silverman, Irene Mayeska, Robert Warner, Lorraine Foreman, Don McGill, Jackie Burroughs, Heath Lamberts, Sandy Webster, Dale Wilson, Eric Clavering. An uneven mixture in which an American multinational firm tries to take over an established, family-owned Canadian paper company. The younger members of the new and the old, American and Canadian, meet and fall in love. The American longs for tradition, the girl's father dies, and now the story becomes much too cluttered to be convincing. Winning performances by a likeable cast and good production values with caring direction by Don Owen.

Partners 'n Love (1992) (96mins) d: Eugene Levy s: Josh Goldstein, Jonathan Prince : Eugene Levy, Jayne Eastwood, Colin Fox, John Hemphill, Linda Kash, John James, Debra McGrath, E.M. Margolese. A lighthearted comedy about a divorced couple who think about reconciling when they find out their divorce wasn't legal. Because they must come to terms over the swimwear company they own, it takes many amusing incidents before they end up together. Made at a time when swearing was not everyone's second word and violence the only solution, this is a film that could be a play. It is lively, attractive and well played.

Party from Hell, The: see *Méchant party*

Party, The (*Party, Le***)** (1990) (103mins) d&s: Pierre Falardeau : Charlotte Laurier, Benoît Dagenais, Julien Poulin, Lou Babin. A well-made and convincingly played prison melodrama, but sordid and sensational in its depiction of a concert for the inmates given by a group of burlesque entertainers and of the brutal goings-on behind the scenes. Supposedly a film about hope and freedom, the characters are so sketchily drawn one feels nothing for them.

Pas de jeu sans soleil: see **Time Zero**

Pas de vacances pour les idoles: see **No Holiday for Idols**

Paspébiac: The Games Country (*Paspébiac: Terre des Jeux***)** (1985) (97mins) d: Jean-Yves Laforce s: Jean-Marie Lelièvre : Juliette Petrie, Carl Béchard. A young doctor travels to the Gaspé to visit his dying Micmac grandmother; the past becomes the present. Intimate and revealing.

Passage des hommes libres **(Passage of Free Men)** (1996) (95mins) (a Canada-France-Venezuela co-production) d&s: Luis Armando Roche : Roy Dupuis, Christian Vadim, Carlos Cruz, Dora Mazzone. The German naturalist Alexander von Humboldt is writing an account of his life's work when news reaches him that his closest friend, the medical doctor Aimé Bonpland, has died. Von Humboldt begins thinking back over their time spent together in South America. An unusual, fascinating and engrossing chronicle about the lives of two distinguished 19TH-century scientists.

Passage of Free Men: see *Passage des hommes libres*

Passage to Ottawa, A (2002) (90mins) d: Gaurav Seth s: Jameel Khaja : Nabil Mehta, Amy Sobol, James Codrington, Ivan Smith, Franceen Brodkin. This pleasing partly true story concerns an eight-year-old boy who is sent from India to stay with an uncle's family in Ottawa. There are family difficulties, but the boy finds life wonderful when he meets a tourist boat captain, an African-Canadian, and listens to his tales. He has yet to grasp the fact that his mother is dying back in India. Imagine: it takes an Indian filmmaker, through striking location scenes, to show us Canada's capital, a city we seldom see in our own films. Sympathetic, touching, funny and honest.

Passengers (1981) (90mins) d: Vic Sarin s: Rob Forsyth : Lally Cadeau, Scott Hylands, John Evans, Alberta Watson. A married couple's harmonious life together is weakened by dissent when the husband becomes reluctant to follow his wife when she is offered a new career in New York. She, however, had followed him across Canada in his work. Well spoken and told with depth and feeling, a study in disillusionment.

Passing Through the Pine Trees (*M'en revenant par les épinettes***)** (1977) (95mins) d&s: François Brault : Gilles Schetagne, Nathalie Gascon, Marc Poitras, Julien Poulin, Lionel Racine. A touching tale of a lonely man going mad in his isolation, who is supported only by a faithful companion. Strong performances in a movie of deep melancholy.

Passion (2001) (105mins) d&s: Zale Dalen : Mike Harrison, Jennifer Baker, Tim Johnson, Nicole Busby, Dale McEachren, Jacqui Kaese. This often strange but enjoyable sex comedy is about a widowed owner of an antique shop, who has a series of extraordinary encounters with young women. Low budget but enthusiastic and filmed in Nanaimo, B.C. Pleasing to have Zale Dalen back on film from tv.

Passion and Paradise (1989) (240mins) (a U.S.-U.K.-Canada co-production) d: Harvey Hart s: Andrew Laskos (from the book *Who Killed Sir Harry Oakes* by James Leasor) with added parts by David Reid : Armand Assante, Catherine Mary Stewart, Rod Steiger, Mariette Hartley, Kevin McCarthy, Michael Sarrazin, Linda Griffiths, Wayne Rogers, Andrew Ray. The wealthy mine owner Sir Harry Oakes died in his home in the Bahamas in 1943, the victim of an unsolved murder. Much has been written and filmed about Oakes and his murder, and this big picture keeps its audience on the alert as it brings up all the facts and fancies about who, what, when, where and why. Good performances from a well-chosen cast, all sleuthing against the attractive Bahamas backgrounds. Other versions of this story have been made for tv, notably a *Scales of Justice* episode. (Note: this was Harvey Hart's last film.)

Past Perfect (2002) (82mins) d&s: Daniel MacIvor : Rebecca Jenkins, Maury Chaykin, Daniel MacIvor, Marie Brassard. Flying between Halifax and Vancouver, a man and a woman fall in love. Two years later, they are now a couple living in Halifax, their lives one of crisis. Don't take this flight; the on-board movie would have been better than this boring, pretentious, dreary concoction.

Pasta King of the Caribbean, The (1999) (77mins) d&s: Sharon Cavanagh : Berni Stapleton, Michael Jones. A woman's husband has disappeared, but never mind: her brother-in-law turns up to take his place. He's a cook of sorts and makes "sexy" pasta. But it's hardly strong enough to sustain this peculiar picture.

Pathfinder, The (1996) (105mins) d: Donald Shebib s: James Mitchell, Thomas W. Lynch : Kevin Dillon, Graham Greene, Laurie Holden, Jaimz Woolvett, Michael Hogan, Frances Hyland, Russell Means, Stacy Keach. This historical saga is the fourth story in James Fenimore Cooper's series of *Leatherstocking* tales relating the drama of the struggle between the French and the British with their respective Indian allies for a contested northern wilderness during the 18th century. Among the many participants is the sub-plot of a native boy and his friendship with his adopted father. Brought off with spirit and imagination.

Paths of the World, The (Les allées de la terre) (1973) (71mins) d&s: André Théberge : Frédérique Collin, Pierre Curzi, Robert DesRoches, André Melançon, Jacques Bilodeau, Gilbert Sicotte, Amulette Garneau. A husband returns to Montréal from a business trip to Paris to find that both he and his wife begin to feel disturbed by the outside world, but do not seem to know why. Thought provoking yet inconclusive.

Patricia and Jean-Baptiste (1966) (85mins) d&s: Jean-Pierre Lefebvre : Patricia Kaden-Lacroix, Henri-Mathieu Kaden, Richard Lacroix, Jean-Pierre Lefebvre. In this, one of his earlier works, the idiosyncratic Lefebvre sets out his style and approach in examining the lives of immigrants and their communities.

Pays dans la gorge, Le (The Country on Your Chest) (1999) (94mins) d: Gilles Noël, Serge Denoncourt s: Simon Fortin : Louise Marleau, Andrée Lachapelle, Julie McClemens, Catherine Sénart. A most unusual but striking and tender account of the relationship between a young singing student and her teacher. This teacher had known the student's sister, who had become one of the major voices of British opera at the end of the 19th century. The music and splendid backgrounds recalling Queen Victoria's times make this an impressive journey into the past.

Peacekeeper, The (1997) (100mins) (a U.S.-Canada film) d: Frederic Forestier s: Robert Geoffrion, Dan Mirvish, James H. Stewart : Dolph Lundgren, Michael Sarrazin, Montel Williams, Roy Scheider, Monika Schnarre. A lot of nonsense about a U.S. Air Force pilot assigned to keep an eye on the president's missile launcher. He must have closed it one day, because terrorists steal the launcher away, and the pilot must risk all to retrieve it. Very unexciting.

Peacekeepers (1997) (120mins) d: Brad Turner s: Peter White : Gabriel Hogan, Jeremy Ratchford, Larissa Laskin, Tom Butler. Much was expected of this film about Canadian soldiers as UN peacekeepers in war-torn Croatia. But what do we get? Tons of explosions and all the clichés of average Hollywood war films. A great opportunity sadly aimed in the wrong direction.

Peanut Butter Solution, The (Opération beurre de pinottes) (1985) (94mins) d&s: Michael Rubbo : Matthew MacKay, Helen Hughes, Patricia Thompson (theme songs performed by Céline Dion. The second of Rock Demers' series of family films, this is a spellbinding romp and fantasy about a bald-headed boy who finds that peanut butter makes his hair grow. A modern fable relating to childhood's early fears about being different. Done with fun, charm, wonderful imagery and fascinating children. (See: *Tales for All* series)

Peau blanche, La (White Skin) (2003) (90mins) d: Daniel Roby s: Joel Champetier & Roby : Marc Paquet, Frederic Pierre, Marianne Farley, Jessica Malka, Julie Lebreton, Jou Joù Turenne, Lise Roy. Two young men in their apartment, one decides to find a prostitute, she has red hair, he gets his throat cut. But the living friend gets involved with another red head. And so it goes, 'dark and deadly'. All quite pointless and painful to watch.

Peau et les os, La (Skin and Bones) (1988) (89mins) d: Johanne Prégent s: Monique Gignac, Johanne Prégent : Hélène Bélanger, Sylvie-Catherine Beaudoin, Louise Turcot. Two young women living in Montréal suffer from anorexia: one attempts to escape adolescence, the other wants to be "closer to God." This is a subject seldom dealt with in films other than documentary. Serious and relevant, teens could learn much from it.

Peep (1984) (77mins) d&s: Jack Cunningham (from his play *See No Evil*) : Lois Maxwell, Donald Harron, Allan McRae, Robin Cameron. A wife and husband take in two boarders; before long, the husband has seduced them. The wife has written this in her diary. A character arises from the diary to control her and drive her to take revenge on her husband. Much of this comes to us through the latest technique known as "Image Control".

Père Chopin (1945) (109mins) (b/w) d: Fedor Ozep s: Jean Desprez : Madeleine Ozeray, François Rozet, Pierre Durand, Guy Moufette, Ginette Letondal, Louis Rolland, Janine Sutto, Ovila Légaré, Paul Guèvremont, Rolland D'Amour, J.-Léo Gagnon. A comedy-drama with music about two brothers from France who live in Québec. One plays the organ and is very poor; the other is a financier and is very rich. All kinds of domestic misunderstandings and incidents occur before a satisfactory resolution is reached and life is made smoother for both brothers. Somewhat broad but quaintly appealing, with a pleasing musical background. Among the first post-WWII Québec films.

Père et fils (Father and Son) (2003) (96mins) (a Canada-France co-production) d: Michel Boujenah s: Pascal Elbe, Edmond Bensimon & Boujenah : Philippe Noiret, Charles Berling, Pascal Elbe, Bruno Putzulu, Marie Tifo, Genevieve Brouillette, Pierre Lebeau.

Three writers and a good cast find it hard to make fresh this slight story of a 70-year-old father, whose children never visit him until he is felled by ill health and sent to a hospital. He suggests that while waiting for a serious operation in three weeks time, they all go on holiday together. Of course this doesn't work out as intended. A knowing human study, but might induce a 'so what' attitude on the part of audiences.

Perfect Man, The (1993) (94mins) d&s: Wendy Hill-Tout : Michelle Little, Phyllis Diller, Garwin Sanford. A comedy from Calgary about love, living together, marriage and planning a family. It involves a commercial artist who wants to be a painter; she drops her boyfriend to take up with a gallery owner who just might be her "perfect man." Described as a wickedly candid portrayal of what young women really think of guys, sex, careers and success, with a distinctive female point of view. Unfortunately, none of this makes it the "perfect film."

Perfect Pie (2002) (92mins) d: Barbara Willis Sweete s: Judith Thompson (from her play) : Wendy Crewson, Barbara Williams, Tom McCamus, Alison Pill, Rachel McAdams, Jennifer Pisana, Brittany Bristow, Kay Hawtrey, David Gardner. The effective opening to this notable picture makes it a rarity among Canadian films. A speeding locomotive thunders by, while two young girls who have placed a penny on the track watch through the bushes. The two girls grow up as good friends; one becomes an opera singer, the other stays on the family farm. This is a beautifully made, directed and acted film identifying itself as taking place in rural Ontario. Of course, the past holds a terrible event: one of the women is raped. We care about these women and their difficult lives. One is not quite sure, however, where the pie comes into it!

Perfect Son, The (2000) (93mins) d&s: Leonard Farlinger : Colm Feore, David Cubitt, Chandra West. Two brothers attend the funeral of their father. One is a writer whose life is a mess; the other is a calm and experienced lawyer. One brother then admits to the other that he's homosexual and has aids. The two brothers now find a new and loving relationship before death claims the older man. The melodramatic tendencies of the screenplay, however, let the actors down in spite of their good performances, leaving audiences unmoved by the outcome.

Perfect Timing (1984) (86mins) d: René Bonnière s: William DeSeta : Stephen Markle, Michele Scarabelli, Paul Boretski, Mary Beth Rubens, Kelly Craig, Michael Rudder. Details the life of a famous fashion photographer in Montréal, whose outlook changes when he meets a strange sculptor and punk rocker. A lot of bunk, actually. Not what we expect from Bonnière.

Perfectly Normal (1990) (104mins) (a Canada-U.K. co-production) d: Yves Simoneau s: Eugene Lipinski, Paul Quarrington : Michael Riley, Robbie Coltrane, Deborah Duchene, Kenneth Welsh. Much was expected from this co-production, but the material, fanciful and quaint, is too slight to sustain the comic antics of Robbie Coltrane, who plays a shady entrepreneur with a love of food and opera who makes friends with a shy young man working in a small-town Ontario brewery. Like beer, the film soon goes flat. But it did have its supporters, and the opera house restaurant raised some laughs. Simoneau went on to a successful career in L.A.

Perpetrators of the Crime (1999) (85mins) d: John Hamilton s: Max Sartor : Tori Spelling, Victoria Sanchez, William Davis, Bruce Dinsmore, Mark Burgess, Sean Devine, Danny Strong. A trio of incompetent college students decide to kidnap a woman but capture the wrong one. Unexpectedly very funny, this is an often clever black comedy, whih does not make light of the crime.

Personal Exemptions (1988) (90mins) d: Peter Rowe s: Madeleine Hombert : Nanette Fabray. A tax investigator's honesty and belief in her work brings about the collapse of her son's business. An interesting look at financial affairs, adding up.

Persuasions, The: see **Harmoney** (1999)

***Petit vent de panique, Un* (A Gust of Panic)** (2000) (92mins) d: Pierre Gréco s: Marc Robitaille, Pierre Gréco : Marie-Johanne Boucher, Martin Laroche, Geneviève Bilodeau, Pierre Powers. Two brothers and a sister living together in a quiet district of Québec City lead a fairly simple life until they become involved in two murders committed in their neighbourhood. They assist in finding the murderer but it is possible that he is the wrong suspect. A thriller as quiet as its setting but intelligently done.

Petite Aurore, l'enfant martyre, La: see **Little Aurore's Tragedy**

***Petite fille particulière, Une* (The Lottery Ticket)** (1995) (90mins) d: Jean-Pierre Prevost s: Pierre Billon : Jacques Perrin, Alexandra Vandernoot, Geneviève Morin-Dupont, Monique Spaziani, André Melançon. This is a beautiful little film about a young woman, Lucie, who lives alone and has won the lottery, but puts the money in the bank. Then she meets a young girl who has Down's syndrome. She cannot talk but Lucie talks to her and tells her about her life. The mother of the girl leaves her frequently with Lucie, who finds a new life for herself. Sensitively portrayed and acted, this is a winning ticket.

Phantom Life, A (*La vie fantôme*) (1992) (98mins) d: Jacques Leduc s: Yvon Rivard, Jacques Leduc (based on the novel by Danièle Gallenare) : Pascale Bussières, Élise Guilbault, Ron Lee, Johanne Marie Tremblay, Tobie Pelletier. This is the familiar story of the happily married man with a lovely wife and two engaging children who meets and falls passionately in love with a younger woman. Gradually, she longs for more of his time, and the complications of being together drive them apart. Splendid acting.

Phobia (1980) (90mins) d: John Huston s: Lewis Lehman, Jimmy Sangster, Peter Bellwood : Paul

Michael Glaser, Susan Hogan, John Colicos, David Bolt, Patricia Collins, Lisa Langlois, Neil Vipond, Alexandra Stewart, Kenneth Welsh. Savaged by critics when first released, this gripping account of a psychiatrist who murders his patients is perfectly valid: it has happened. Huston, filming in Toronto, made this work with insight and skill, cleverly directing a cast of talented Canadian players.

Phone Call, The (*Ligne interdite*) (1989) (91mins) d: Allan Goldstein s: Donald Martin : Michael Sarrazin, Ronald Lea. A businessman is traced by a mentally unbalanced former convict who invades his life and terrorizes his family. This is a call that should never have been made. Illogical and unpleasant, only average in treatment.

Pianist, The (1991) (113mins) d&s: Claude Gagnon : Gail Travers, Macha Grenon, Eiji Okuda, Dorothée Berryman, Maury Chaykin. A lush, expensive, sentimental tearjerker of immense banality moving uronto, Montréal and Vancouver and in which two young girls fall helplessly in love with a Japanese pianist.

Piano Man's Daughter, The (2000) (90mins) d&s: Kevin Sullivan (based on the novel by Timothy Findley) : Allan Price, Stockard Channing, Isabella Fink, Wendy Crewson, Dixie Seatle, R.H. Thomson. A pianist in a 1930s swing band leads a swinging life, too, with tragic results for his daughter. A welcome change from sex and swearing. A commendable adaptation of Findley's novel.

Piastre, La: see **Dollar, The**

Picture Claire (2001) (90mins) d: Bruce McDonald s: Semi Chellas : Juliette Lewis, Gina Gershon, Callum Keith Rennie, Kelly Harms, Camilla Rutherford, Mickey Rourke. A chaotic and haphazard piece of work attempting to show a young Québécoise in Toronto who is unable to speak English and looking for her photographer boyfriend, whom she met in Montréal. She becomes involved in a bewildering set of circumstances, conveyed in a disorganized flood of split-screen images, thumping music, car chases, various kinds of thugs and utter confusion. And why is an American cast in the role of a woman from Québec? A 10 million dollar indulgence which went nowhere.

Pictures at the Beach (1990) (70mins) d&s: Aaron Shuster : Paul Babiak, Catherine Kuhn, Bob Bidaman, Ann Curran. A first feature about seven spoiled, discontented Toronto yuppies spending a Sunday at the beach. They share common problems: not enough money, sex or time. This is a well-intentioned picture, but the conversations do not make these characters worth the time we spend with them.

Piege d'Issoudun, Le **(Trapped in Issoudun)** (2002) (85mins) d&s: Micheline Lanctôt : Sylvie Drapeau, Frederick de Grandpre, Shanie Beauchamp, Pierre-Luc Lafontaine, Ghislain Tremblay. A 40-year-old woman kills her two children and tries to kill herself in a car accident. A

policeman, understanding the full horror of what she has done, helps her carry out her wish to die. This is not what we have come to expect from Lanctôt; it is a hard work to take, or to comprehend, but it is happening often in real life today.

Pigs Are Seldom Clean (*On n'engraisse pas les cochons a l'eau claire*) (1973) (112mins) d&s: Jean-Pierre Lefebvre : Jean-René Ouellet, Jean-Pierre Saulnier, Marthe Nadeau, J.-Léo Gagnon, Denys Arcand. A surprisingly violent and messy film from the indefatigable Lefebvre about the police, students, drugs, rape and murder, set in Hull (now Gatineau), Québec. This film strays far from the director's usual gentle and sympathetic studies of people's lives. Had this worked, it could have been a searing social study.

Pile ou face: see **Heads or Tails**

Pilgrim (Inferno) (1999) (94mins) (a Canada-U.K.-Mexico co-production) d&s: Harley Cokliss : Gloria Reuben, Julian Busio, Ray Liotta, Armin Mueller-Stahl. A man suffering from loss of memory in the desert awakes one day to learn that he has a criminal record and many enemies anxious to find him and give him a permanent blackout. A hot and tidy thriller made bearable by Mueller-Stahl.

Pin (1988) (103mins) d&s: Sandor Stern (based on the novel by Andrew Neiderman) : David Hewlett, Cyndy Preston. An unlikely story of mystery and imagination in which a doctor's son grows up thinking that his father's anatomical model is alive. His sister doesn't understand it, and neither will the audience. Listless and silly all round.

Pinball Summer (1980) (102mins) (U.S. title: *Pick-up Summer*, 1980, 92mins) d: George Mihalka s: Richard Zelniker (based on the story *Pinball Summer* by Fred Fox) : Michael Zelniker, Carl Marotte, Karen Stephen, Helene Udy, Tom Kovacs . Teenagers live it up with pinball, drinking, drugs and sex. This wretched concoction looks unashamedly American. Thankfully, it didn't spawn a series.

Pin-Pon, The Film (*Pin-Pon, Le film*) (1999) (80mins) d: Ghyslaine Côté s: Paul Thinel, Paule Marier : Thomas Graton, Yves Soutière, Philippe Lambert, Julien Poulin. Pin and Pon are two firemen (popular heroes of a Québec tv series for children) who go on holiday to camp in the countryside. A thin tale follows, involving a circus family, fishing and playing in the sand. All good natured and probably pleasing for the youngsters with its songs and funny moments.

Pit Pony (1998) (92mins) d: Eric Till s: Heather Conkie (based on Joyce Barkhouse's book of the same name) : Ben Rose-Davis, Gabriel Hogan, Jennie Raymond, Richard Donat. There was a time between the two world wars when more than 10,000 boys worked in the coal mines of Nova Scotia. This film tells of one who, after the death of his father and brother in a mine accident, works to support his family—a task made easier by his friendship with a pony that gives him strength and courage. Pleasingly well done and set against authentic backgrounds.

Pit, The: see **Teddy**

Plague, The (1979) (88mins) d&s: Ed Hunt, Barry Pearson : Kate Reid, Céline Lomez, Daniel Pilon, Michael Reynolds, Brenda Donohue, Barbara Gordon. New and deadly germs are on the loose, but one couldn't care less what happens to the characters who become infected. Well acted, but an unbelievable, bone-aching bore.

Planet of Junior Brown, The (1997) (91mins) d: Clement Virgo s: Cameron Bailey, Clement Virgo (based on Virginia Hamilton's novel) : Lynn Whitfield, Martin Villafana, Rainbow Sun Francks, Sarah Polley, Clark Johnson, Margot Kidder. Junior Brown is an overweight black teenager who loves food and music. His unstable mother destroyed his piano in a fit of madness, so instead, he thumps out his lessons on his teacher's dining-room table. In the basement of his school, he and the janitor have built a model of the solar system, with Junior as the tenth planet. Watching it, he imagines himself lost in the music of the spheres. Slender and sometimes uncertain of itself, this is a patched piece, yet oddly moving at times.

Plans mystèrieux, Les: see **Ti-Ken Madeleines**

Plastic Mile, The (1969) (85mins) d: Morrie Ruvinsky s: Philip Surguy, Morrie Ruvinsky : Jace Vander veen, Pia Shandel, Beverlee Miller, Sylvia Spring, Stanley Fox, Shelly Sachs, Mark Perry, Nelson Holland, D'Arcy Devine. An unpleasant film-maker cannot deal with life's pressures and his wife's pregnancy, so he begins a love affair with an actress. Some audiences will find this bold; others will be bored. At the Vancouver Film Festival in 1969, the censor board banned its showing.

Platinum (1997) (120mins) (a Canada-U.S. film) d: Bruce McDonald s: Leopold St. Pierre, Paul Risacher : Robert Cavanah, Pascale Bussières, Tanya Allen, Jessica Webb, Stewart Bick, Jackie Burroughs. This film is for anyone interested in the behind-the-scenes activities and working methods of music recording companies—and what erstwhile singers and musicians go through trying to find their place in the world of pop music. Many groups and individual singers provide the musical accompaniment. One of McDonald's better films.

Playgirl Killer (Decoy for Terror) (1965) (85mins) d&s: Erick Santamaria (based on a story by William and Henry Kerwin) : William Kerwin, Jean Christopher, Neil Sedaka, Andrée Champagne, Mary Lou Collins. A nasty piece of work about an artist who murders his models and preserves them in a freezer.

Pleasure Palace (Angela) (1973) (91mins) d&s: Ed Hunt : Janice Duval, Nicki Fylan, Tom Celli, Vicki Gabereau, Susan Garret, Art Roberts. A model working in Toronto is in love with a client who is being blackmailed by her employer. The couple attempt to rid themselves of him. Of absolutely no interest or appeal.

Plouffe, II, Les: see **Crime of Ovide Plouffe, The**

Plouffe, Les **(The Plouffe Family)** (1981) (245 mins) d: Gilles Carle s: Roger Lemelin (based on his novel), Gilles Carle : Émile Genest, Juliette Huot, Denise Filiatrault, Gabriel Arcand and others. Carle's *Les Plouffe* is something of a surprise in many ways. With his *Fantastica* being disliked by many critics and not finding much success in the cinemas, it might well have been some time before he worked again. But one of the strengths of filmmaking in Québec is that real talent is never buried for long. Carle found great success with this film, which is an affectionate scrapbook of scenes of life in Québec before and during World War II. We are given a poignant look at a bygone generation, quaint and humorous in its outlook and ways, scolded by church and state and defiant of *les anglais*. Based on an extremely popular radio series written by Roger Lemelin during the time in which the film is set, the life depicted here comes back to charm audiences as a wonderfully warm and nostalgic memory. There are about three versions of *Les Plouffe*. The original four-hour version that opened in Québec City was followed by a shorter version for general release by Denys Arcand, and a two-hour version, all with English subtitles. A six-hour version was later shown on television. (See: *The Crime of Ovide Plouffe*)

Point of No Return (1976) (83mins) d&s: Edward Hunt : Nicky Fylan, Susan Petrie, Eli Rill, Cec Linder, Gary McKeehan, Susan Minas. A small piece of low-budget nonsense about a man trying to find out how his brother died and being led into a suspicious world of research and UFOs.

Point Zero: see **Mile Zero**

Poison (Tease) (1999) (93mins) (a Canada-Germany film) d: Dennis Berry s: Andreas Grunberg, Dennis Berry : Rosanna Arquette, Mandy Shaffer, Michael Des Barres, Jurgen Prochnow, Thomas Kretschmann. A timid thriller about a wealthy widow who suspects that her daughter is responsible for a number of mysterious deaths among family and friends. Not much to become thrilled about.

Pomme, la queue et les pépins, La: see **Apple, the Stem and the Seeds, The**

Polygraph, Le (1996) (106 mins) d & s: Robert Lepage : Marie Brassard, Patrick Goyette. Lucie Champagne is given the role of the victim, Marie-Claire, in a film about a true unsolved murder. By coincidence Lucie's neighbour, Francois, was the real victim's boyfriend. He is still a suspect in the continuing investigation and is unsure of his own innocence. Results of his polygraph test (lie-detector) create dramatic tension, and the "film within the film" draws its own conclusions on who the perpetrator is. Lepage's second film is a fascinating piece.

Population of One, A (1980) (90mins) d: Robert Sherrin s: Anna Sandor (from the book by Constance Beresford-Howe) : Dixie Seatle, Tony Van Bridge, R.H. Thomson, Kate Lynch, Jonathan Welsh, Nicholas Campbell. A shy young woman arrives in Toronto determined to find a teaching position and, perhaps, fall in love. Working in the English department at the university, she meets a gallery of professors and students who keep life moving between bouts of comedy and the search for knowledge. Worthy and well dressed with a fine cast of players, all chasing the charm of the moment.

Porky's (Chez Porky) (1981) (98mins) (a Canada-U.S. film) d&s: Bob Clark : Dan Monahan, Mark Herrier, Wyatt Knight, Roger Wilson, Kim Cattrall, Doug McGrath, Susan Clark, Art Hindle, Alex Karras, Eric Christmas, Don Daynard, Kaki Hunter. Gross comedy of students who take a trip to Florida, involving girls, booze, sex and everything vulgar. It paid off at the box office and, like *Meatballs,* set the stage for a *Porky* family series. The media and film trade remind us, with great pride every time *Porky's* is mentioned, that it is Canada's highest-grossing film ever!

Porky's II: The Next Day (Chez Porky 2) (1983) (95mins) (a Canada-U.S. film) d&s: Bob Clark and others : Dan Monahan, Wyatt Knight, Mark Herrier, Roger Wilson, Kaki Hunter, Art Hindle, Eric Christmas, Nancy Parsons. The usual garbage is still around and getting dirtier as the teens take on a new set of escapades best not talked about.

Porky's Revenge (Revanche de Porky, La) (1985) (92mins) (a Canada-U.S. film) d: James Komack s: Ziggy Steinberg : Dan Monahan, Wyatt Knight, Mark Herrier, Kaki Hunter, Nancy Parsons, Eric Christmas. Everyone's getting older and the plots even more so with the same stupidity, profanity and cheap laughs. Thankfully, this was the end of *Porky's.*

Pornographe, Le (The Pornographer) (2001) (111mins) (a Canada-France co-production) d&s: Bertrand Bonello : Jean-Pierre Léaud, Jérémie Renier, Dominique Blanc, Thibault De Montalembert. This film asks us to feel some sympathy for the producer of hard-core porn films when he decides to give it up and find a more meaningful life. This doesn't mean, however, that we miss out on seeing just what kind of films he made. An ill-begotten enterprise.

Portes tournantes, Les (The Revolving Doors) (1988) (101mins) (a Canada-France co-production) d: Francis Mankiewicz s: Jacques Savoie, Francis Mankiewicz (based on Savoie's book) : Monique Spaziani, François Methe, Gabriel Arcand, Miou-Miou. A film of lightness, charm and affection, tinged in its latter half with the more sombre tones brought about by the contrast between youth and old age. A young girl from a country home in Québec leaves her large family to work as a pianist in a cinema in a nearby town. But when movies with sound arrive, she is out of work. She marries the son of a wealthy family, and her life takes on a slow and claustrophobic existence robbed of its former pleasure and enjoyment. After the birth of her son, she leaves him with the family and goes to New York to pursue a career in music. These events are interspersed with scenes of the present as her son, now a married but separated man with his own curious young son, reads his mother's diary. Cleverly written, devised and filmed by Francis Mankiewicz with a faultless cast of players and a genuine-sounding silent-film score by François Dompierre, this is an astutely rendered work on the human necessity of coming to terms with the pain of contradictory parental behaviour.

Portion d'éternité: see **Looking for Eternity**

Portrait for Murder: see **Rendering, The**

Portrait, The (1992) (100mins) d&s: Jack Darcus : Alan Scarfe, Barbara March, Gwyneth Walsh, Serge Houde, Gabrielle Rose. A sensibly written dissertation on art and artists cleverly dramatized against the constricted background of a painter's studio. Impressively played, the film concerns three women who complicate the life of an artist searching for perfection.

Portrait, The: see **Home Movie**

Posers (2002) (80mins) d&s: Katie Tallo : Jessica Pare, Sarain Boylan, Stefanie Von Pfetten, Emily Hampshire, Adam Beach. Four girlfriends dancing in a disco become involved in the murder of one of them. Jealousy, vengeance, detachment, passion and love are all here in what is described as an "unapologetic portrayal of the female dynamic." It is also one we could do without.

Position de l'escargot, La: see **Snail's Point of View, A**

Possession of Virginia, The (Le diable est parmi nous) (1972) (91mins) d: Jean Beaudin s: John Dunning, André Link : Louise Marleau, Daniel Pilon, Danielle Ouimet, Jacques Famery, Henri Norbert, Rose Rey-Duzil. Something better from the Dunning-Link sex factory: a melodrama of murder, magic and romance.

Possible Worlds (2000) (93mins) d: Robert Lepage s: John Mighton (from his play of the same title) : Tom McCamus, Tilda Swinton, Sean McCann, Rick Miller, Gabriel Gascon. Robert Lepage's fourth film is not as easily understood as his first three because it is an enigmatic and surreal examination of the boundaries of consciousness. The central character is a charming, well-dressed and well-mannered middle-aged man who finds himself slipping between other lives he has lived, and those of other people including attractive women he has known, without quite comprehending what the essential nature of personal identity means. This borders on exsistentialism, intreguing but finally as dry as dust. We are cheered up only in the sequences featuring the long-established and remarkable actor Sean McCann, who is brought in to investigate the murder of a man whose brain was removed. The cast finds its way determinedly, but we aren't rewarded with a satisfactory whole. The players are a likeable lot to watch and listen to and, although the backgrounds are sombre, there is an elegance to the entire film.

Post Concussion (1999) (80mins) d&s: Daniel Yoon : Daniel Yoon, Jennifer Welch, Michael Hohmeyer, Niloufar Talebi, C.B. Yoon. A management consultant advising financial corporations is struck by a car and suffers a head trauma with dizzying and confusing after-effects. A semi-autobiographical film produced, written, directed, photographed and edited by Yoon (who also plays the leading character) in spite of his ill health. This might well explain the baffling nature of the film.

Post Mortem (1999) (92mins) d&s: Louis Bélanger : Gabriel Arcand, Sylvie Moreau, Hélène Loiselle. Living in Montréal, Linda is a good mother by day and a bad girl at night: she goes out with "johns" and bashes them on the head, stealing their money and credit cards. One night, she is assaulted and dies. Taken to the morgue, she comes back to life, and the mortician confesses his love for her. She thinks he had raped her while dead. She moves to the country with her daughter, and morgue man writes letters to her. The director tells us these are the lives of lonely, unhappy people cut off from society and just trying to survive—so there! Audiences may have a difficult time carrying out their own post-mortems on this well-acted but somewhat confusing and far-fetched film.

Postière, La (The Postmistress) (1992) (90mins) d: Gilles Carle s: Jean-Marie Estève, Gilles Carle : Chlöé Ste-Marie, Michèle Richard, Nicolas-François Rives, Steve Gendron, Michel Barrette. This renowned director's first cinema film since *La Guêpe* (The Wasp) is sadly unfunny and flat. It is a tired hash of small-town Québécois stock comedy characters and a postmistress who is determined to win over the man she loves but who does not respond. Entertaining, at times, in its silliness.

Postmistress, The: see *Postière, La*

Pots casses, Les (Broken Dishes) (1994) (90mins) d: François Bouvier s: Gilles Desjardins : Gilbert Sicotte, Marie Tifo, Marc Messier, Louise Deslières, Jean-Marc Parent. A novelist and a stockbroker have been married for 20 years. She is famous and emotional; he is cold and reserved, but secretly likes to write. One day, she writes a thriller and comes to believe that the character she has devised might reveal her secret self. Her character murders her husband. She burns the manuscript and flees from her husband. Once she has found herself again, she returns to him and a new reality. A finely wrought piece with a sensitively enacted duo.

Pour la suite du monde: see **So That The World Goes On** see **Duration of the Day**

Pour le meilleur et pour le pire: see **For Better, for Worse**

Pourquoi l'étrange Monsieur Zolock s'intéressait-il tant à la bande dessinée: see **Why Is the Strange Mr. Zolock So Interested in Comic Strips?**

Pousse mais pousse égal: see **Push but Push Reasonably**

Poussière sur la ville: see **Dust from Underground**

Pouvoir intime: see **Intimate Power**

Poverty and Other Delights: see *Joyeux calvaire*

Powder Heads (1980) (85mins) d: John Anderson s: Michael French : David Ferry, Gordon Marriott, William Samples, Catherine Stewart, Donald Goodspeed. A comedy about four skiers who hijack the tour bus of born-again Christians to visit ski hills, discos and hot tubs on their way to Sun Valley, Idaho. Filmed also in Jasper, Alberta, this humourous treatment of hijacking may have seemed funny when made, but not now.

Power Games (*Jeux de pouvoir*) (1990) (87mins) d: Mychel Arsenault s: Jean-Marc Félio : Richard Zeman, Dorian Clark, Marc Ruel, Kenneth Roberts, Macha Grenon. Teenagers training for the national championships of the Power Commando Games find themselves trapped inside the territory of the Pot Growers, a ruthless band of marijuana producers. Against the powerful weapons of their captors, all the teenagers have are the fake bullets of their play guns. Although they desperately fight for their lives, the battle ends with the Pot Growers eliminating each of the teenagers in a terrible bloodbath. But what is the point? Is all logic put aside for a senseless and bloody ending? Or is it to be dismissed as sci-fi sensationalism?

Power of Attorney (1995) (97mins) (a U.S.-Canada film) d: Howard Himelstein s: George Erschbamer, Jeff Barmash : Danny Aiello, Elias Koteas, Rae Dawn Chong, Cindy Cowan, Roger Wilson, Nina Siemasko. It is doubtful whether lawyers well trained either in the legalities of law and the ways of corruption would make anything out of the ramshackle plot of this clumsy piece of work in which an attorney leaves his job as a public prosecutor to join a crooked organization. He then finds himself defending the boss of the mob, or so it seems. Violence ensues, of course. There is nothing here in character or deed that one can relate to. Set in New York (filmed in Vancouver) under the US Justice System.

Power Play (*Coup d'état*) (State of Shock) (Operation Overthrow) (1978) (102mins) (a Canada-U.K. co-production) d&s: Martyn Burke (based on the book *Coup d'état* by Edward Luttvak) : Peter O'Toole, David Hemmings, Donald Pleasance, Barry Morse, Jon Granik, George Touliatos, Marcella St-Amant, Gary Reineke, Chuck Shamata, Harvey Atkin, August Schellenberg, Alberta Watson, Peter Sturgess, Robert Goodier, Sandra Scott, Sandy Crawley. A tired and unconvincing plot about a revolution in a South American country. Flat, dramatically speaking, lacking in suspense and setting but packed with a great cast. It's the revolution that does them in.

Precious Hours, The (*Les heures précieuses*) (1989) (84mins) d: Mireille Goulet, Marie Laberge s:

Marie Laberge : Paule Baillargeon, Martine Beaulne. Surrounded by family, friends and sympathetic medics, patients suffering from terminal illnesses live out their final weeks in a special hospital in Montréal. Part documentary, part drama, this is a sympathetic and caring study of the end of life.

Preludes (2000) (76mins) Ten short films, made by Canadian filmmakers to hail the Toronto International Film Festival on its 25th anniversary, have been laced together to make a whole piece. The best of these instantly forgettable ego items is Jean-Pierre Lefebvre's lively, witty and beautifully photographed contribution called *See You in Toronto*. (The others are by Atom Egoyan, David Cronenberg, Patricia Rozema, Guy Maddin, Don McKellar, Jeremy Podeswa, Anne Wheeler, Michael Snow, Mike Jones)

Prescription for Murder: see **Taking Care**

Présence des ombres, La **(The Presence of Shadows)** (1996) (90mins) d: Marc Voizard s: Pierre Billon : Patrice L'Écuyer, Isabelle Renaud, Denis Mercier, Patricia Tulasne. A woman who believes she is possessed by the spirit of a 19th-century nun commits suicide. A specialist trying to understand multiple personalities, who had fallen in love with her, is startled when he later meets an alluring woman who looks almost exactly like the dead woman. This begins a spiral of murder and deception. Based on Boileau-Narcejac's novel *Sueurs froides,* which inspired Hitchcock's unforgettable *Vertigo.* Hitchcock would have found this film compelling and worthy, no doubt, of approbation.

Pressure Point (2000) (94mins) d: Eric Weston s: William Lee : Jeff Wincott, Michael Madson. A family going on holiday in their trailer home fears the worst when criminals take over. This is everybody's worst nightmare when they take to the roads these days. And this film makes it seem all too real.

Primo Baby (1989) (110mins) d&s: Eda Lishman : Esther Purves-Smith, Duncan Regehr, Janet-Laine Green. A rebellious 15-year-old is placed in a foster home with a wealthy racehorse owner in Calgary and trains a half-blind racehorse to become a winner. The horse is not the only handicap in this unconvincing film.

Princes in Exile (1990) (103mins) d: Giles Walker s: Joe Wiesenfeld (based on the novel of the same title by Mark Schreiber) : Zachary Ansley, Nicholas Shields, Alexander Chapman, Stacie Mistysyn, Chuck Shamata. A drama with a documentary look. Camp Hawkins is a summer retreat for children and young people with cancer. The young players give a good account of themselves as their characters face up to their fatal disease with fortitude and good humour.

Prison, The: see *Conciergerie, La*

Private Capital, The (1988) (144mins) d: Donald McBrearty s: Jeannine Locke (based on the book by Sandra Gwyn) : Martha Burns, Gordon Clapp. A stunningly well-produced, written and acted recreation of Ottawa at the time of the Boer War. The film is set against an intriguing background of politics and heartaches, of romance and despair, and of personalities well known in our history. The past is faithfully and compellingly brought back to life.

Probable Cause (Sleepless) (1994) (90mins) (a Canada-U.S. film) d: Paul Ziller s: Hal Salwen, Paul Ziller : Kate Vernon, Michael Ironside, James Downing, David Neale, David McNally. Policemen are being murdered in the city (not a Canadian one, of course). One detective heads the investigation but is hampered by charges of sexual abuse, while his new partner, a woman trying to cope with constant fatigue, is also a suspect. An unsavoury mixture. Vernon and Ironside make an interesting couple. They deserved to have their own series.

Prodigious Hickey, The (1987) (90mins) d: Rob Iscove s: Jan Jaffe Kahn (from *The Lawrenceville Stories*) : Zach Galligan, Robert Joy, Tony Van Bridge, Damir Andrey, Stephen Baldwin, David Foley. A nostalgic and pleasing drama based on Owen Johnson's *Saturday Evening Post* short stories, filmed in Toronto about a group of boys at a private prep school. We follow their pranks and pursuits, which wear down the staff. Creates a longing for the old days when boys would be boys and not monsters.

Profile for Murder (The Fifth Season) (1997) (95mins) (a U.S.-Canada film) d: David Winning s: Steve Fisher : Lance Henriksen, Jeff Wincott, Jason Nash. An attractive man finds women to have sex with; soon three of them are found stabbed to death. A psychiatrist hired by the police to investigate these murders develops fantasies when she is investigating a suspect. Unpleasant and unconvincing, a third-rate thriller.

Project Grizzly (1996) (72mins) d&s: Peter Lynch : Troy James Hurtubise. A North Bay, Ontario, scrap-metal dealer who hunted bears and survived an attack by one of them is determined to make a suit to protect himself while he seeks a confrontation with bears to study them. He spends thousands of dollars making a high-tech piece of apparatus, and he tests it by getting himself hit by a truck and beaten by baseball bats, among other doings. That such silly behaviour should be the subject of an expensive NFB film is beyond belief. A short comedy had been made earlier, and the subject should have been left there. Yet many critics thought this version was somehow praiseworthy, being a rumination on the behaviour of man! Nonsense. This particular one is not worth one frame of film.

Prologue (1970) (88mins) (b/w) d: Robin Spry s: Michael Malus : John Robb, Elaine Malus, Gary Rader, Peter Cullen, Henry Gamer, Victor Knight. A sympathetic and thoughtful first feature from the distinguished Robin Spry. Made in the documentary form, this film concerns 1960s flower children in Montréal and Lachute, Québec, pacifists and the

Chicago riots, set against attempts to publish an underground newspaper. A bit wearying, but a valuable document of its time.

Prom Night (1980) (91mins) (a Canadian-American film) d: Paul Lynch s: William Gray, John Hunter : Leslie Nielsen, Jamie Lee Curtis, Robert Silverman, George Touliatos, Casey Stevens, Antoinette Bower, David Gardner, Beth Amos, Joy Thompson. A group of high school students suspected of murdering a little girl several years earlier is menaced by a deadly killer. Cheap and awful and progenitor of three more.

Prom Night II: Hello Mary Lou (1987) (96mins) (a Canadian-American film) d: Bruce Pittman s: Ron Oliver : Lisa Schrage, Michael Ironside, Richard Monette, Wendy Lyon, Justin Louis, Terri Hawkes. The spirit of a murdered prom queen provides tame thrills and chills.

Prom Night III: The Last Kiss (1989) (97mins) (a Canadian-American film) d&s: Ron Oliver : Tom Conlon, Cyndy Preston, David Stratton, Courtney Taylor, Dyland Neal. Yet another prom queen back from the dead. Better had she remained in her grave.

Prom Night IV: Deliver Us From Evil (1992) (95mins) (a Canadian-American film) d: Clay Borris s: Richard Beattie : Nikki de Boer, Alden Kane, Joy Tanner, Ken McGregor, Brock Simpson, James Carver. Psychotic priest murders tiresome teens in an isolated holiday home. Deliver us from any more of this.

Prom, The (1991) (50 mins) d: Bradford Turner s: David Barlow : Stacie Mistysyn, Jaimz Woolvett, Sean Roberts, Nikki de Boer, Kathleen Robertson. A very rare film, indeed: a charming and delightful comedy about the misadventures of two likeable teenagers and their attempts to get to their high school prom.

Promise the Moon (1997) (90mins) d: Kenneth Jubenvill s: Kevin Sullivan, Peter Behrens : Henry Czerny, Shawn Ashmore, Gloria May Eshkibok, Colette Stevenson, In western Canada during the 1920s, a ranch hand is sent by his boss to track down his abandoned son and train him to run the family's cattle ranch. This he does, and during this time he meets a dignified woman, a newcomer, who teaches him how to run a business. She becomes his partner, and the two stand together in the face of powerful business interests working to take over their ranch. A welcome and likeably done twist on the conventional Western.

Promised Land, The (Les brûlés) (1958) (111mins) d&s: Bernard Devlin (based on the novel *Nuages sur les brûlés [Clouds over the Clearing]* by Hervé Biron) : Jean Lajeunesse, J.-Léo Gagnon, Leclerc, Rolland D'Amour, Rolland Bédard, René Caron, Camille Ducharme, Georges Toupin, Félix Pierre Dufresne, Georges Bouvier, Henri Poulin, Nana de Varennes. An interesting re-creation in dramatized form of the story of the settlement of the Abitibi region of Québec during the Depression years of the 1930s.

The new community must suffer fires, storms and social difficulties before an established order is created with the building of homes, a church and school. Faithful and fascinating.

Propos de la femme, À: see **All About Women**

Protection (2000) (80 mins) (made for the tv series *Panoramique*) d&s: Bruce Spangler : Nancy Sivak, Jillian Fargey, William MacDonald, Hiro Kanagawa. A social worker has seen misery and tragedy for five years: children who have been battered and sexually abused, mothers who love their children but have lost the ability to care for them, lives shattered by financial ruin, men who have been in and out of prison for drugs and assault. But even more chilling is the "system," with its managers and bureaucrats who take care of themselves and remain indifferent to the suffering they are supposed to alleviate. This graphically drawn and convincingly acted film is heartbreaking and easily the best to come from British Columbia in many years.

Proud Rider, The (The Last Run) (1972) (76mins) d&s: Chester Stocki : Art Hindle, Karen Gregory, Michael Bell, Ted Anderson, Jack Oliffe, Loni Lane. Motorcycle melodrama filmed in Oshawa, Ontario, about a youth with emotional problems and tangled friendships. Average.

Proxyhawks (1970) (75mins) d&s: Jack Darcus : Susan Spencer, Jack Darcus, Edward Hutchings, Lesley Rachuk, Barry Jones. Darcus's second film shows us the beginning of his care and consideration for animals. A humane work. (see also *Deserters*)

Psychic (1991) (92mins) (a Canada-U.S. film) d: George Mihalka s: Mark McQuade, Paul Koval : Catherine Mary Stewart, Michael Nouri, Zach Galligan, Susan Horton, Ken James, Andrea Roth. Attended by a flurry of coarse language, nudity and violence, a young man with supposedly psychic powers attempts to use them to stop a serial killer from finding his victims. Nothing to get excited about.

Psycho Girls (1986) (92mins) d: Jerry Ciccoritti s: Michael Bockner : John Haslett Cuff, Rose Graham, Silvio Oliviero, Darlene Mignacco, Giorgio DiCicco, Agi Gallus. Opening in 1966, two young parents are murdered by one of their daughters, who gives them a poisoned meal on their anniversary. Fifteen years later, the daughter escapes from the asylum to which she had been committed to seek revenge on her sister, who was the real killer. A most unpleasant and shallow picture.

Public Domain (2003) (90mins) d&s: Kris Lefcoe : Nichole deBoer, Nadia Litz, Mike Beaver, Don McKellar, Lindy Booth, Jason Jones, Dov Tiefenbach. A tv games show, 'Public Domain', awards money to individuals who must show they are truly alone in the world, must suffer accordingly, and have experienced agonizing defeats. Three finalists come forward, one pimps, another obsessed with the eighties, another an agoraphobic man. This would be rubbish on tv, it is no less so on film.

Pudding chômeur **(Bread Pudding)** (1996) (100mins) d&s: Gilles Carle : Chlöé Ste-Marie, François Léveillé, Sylvie Potvin, Robert Gravel, France Arbour. Four friends escape from the mafia and go among the poor in an adventure that Carle describes as a "satirical and cynical comedy" that makes a mockery of the happiness-through-faith practices preached by church and other organizations at the expense of the down-and-outers. Knowing Carle is to know what a deeply felt work this is.

Punch (2002) (90mins) d&s: Guy Bennett : Michael Riley, Sonja Bennett, Meredith McGeachie, Marcia Laskowski, Mercedes de la Zerda. In an unpleasant opening, we meet a teenage girl who is passionately and sexually in love with her father. She becomes furiously jealous when another woman enters his life. The script then falls into a pit of depravity in which more women become involved in a brutal and vicious encounter, fighting, punching and swearing at each other. They ought to have turned on the writer-director for making such a worthless film.

Push but Push Reasonably (Scarlatina) (*Pousse mais pousse égal*) (1975) (93mins) d: Denis Héroux s: Marcel Gamache : Gilles Latulippe, Céline Lomez, Denis Drouin, Yves Létourneau, Huguette Oligny, Janine Suto. Inconsequential piece about an ineffective young man working in a Montréal hospital. His girlfriend helped him get the job because her father is the head of the hospital board. Her parents do what they can to put an end to the relationship, but to no avail.

Pygmalion (1983) (80mins) (a Canada-U.S. film) d: Alan Cooke s: the play by George Bernard Shaw : Peter O'Toole, Margot Kidder, Helen Beavis, Donald Ewer, Frances Hyland, Nancy Kerr, John Standing. Ronald White. This now almost unknown film brings to tv G.B. Shaw's classic play about a Victorian professor who makes a bet that he can teach a Cockney girl how to speak "proper" English and become a lady. He succeeds, as everyone who saw *My Fair Lady* knows! A fascinating work taking us back to the early years of films made for showing on tv. This was an Astral pay-tv production for First Choice in association with 20th Century Fox tv. It was shot in one week at the Glen-Warren studios (now CFTO in Toronto) on a $1-million budget, with terrific sets and costumes. Margot Kidder, the bright and breezy Canadian actress, is delightful as Eliza, and Peter O'Toole is in his element as Professor Higgins. This thoughtful and dedicated work, with its great cast, makes for excellent tv. (original film 1938) d: Anthony Asquith : Lesile Howard, Wendy Hiller . The musical 1962 d: George Cukor : Rex Harrison, Audry Hepburn)

Pyx, The (1973) (111mins) d: Harvey Hart s: Robert Schlitt (from a novel by John Buell) : Karen Black, Christopher Plummer, Donald Pilon, Jean-Louis Roux, Yvette Brind'Amour, Jacques Godin, Lee Broker, Terry Haig, Robin Gammell, Louise Finfret, Julie Wildman, Francine Morand, Gerard Parkes, Henry Ramer, Marcel Fournier. The strange and troubling tale of a beautiful call girl who becomes involved in religious hocus-pocus. A well-made but ridiculous film, mixing horror, science fiction and murder. A first cousin, far removed, to *Rosemary's Baby*.

Q-bec My Love (A Commercial Success) (1970) (77mins) (b/w) d&s: Jean-Pierre Lafebvre : Anne Lauriault, Jean-Pierre Cartier, Larry Kent, Denis Payne, André Caron, Judith Paré, Raoul Duguay. Among Québec's many vigorous and determined moviemakers, none has achieved a widespread reputation quite so quickly as Jean-Pierre Lefebvre. It's only fair to point out, however, that he did so mainly by making baffling and convoluted films that his many supporters could not help but talk about. He was not likely to find a mass and responsive audience. This film is rather like a scrapbook of bits and pieces of unrelated scenes in a nonmusical revue. Satirical and contemporary, the scenes are paraded in a hit-or-miss fashion, some very funny, others tedious, dull and childlike, accompanied by a jumble of sounds and words, tricks and tomfoolery. Scenes appear to have been added at random until feature-length time was achieved. The whole abounds in bare breasts, bottoms, pubic hair and copulation. While the uninitiated were trying to puzzle it out, Lefebvre, one suspects, was laughing quietly up his sleeve. In his later films, Lefebvre proved himself a caring, concerned and humanistic filmmaker of narrative skill with a deep understanding of life and an appreciation of meaningful relationships.

Quadroon Ball: see **Courage to Love, The**

Quand hurlent les loups: see **When Wolves Howl**

Quand je serai parti vous vivrez encore: see **When I'm Gone You'll Still Be Alive**

Quarantaine, La **(Beyond Forty)** (1982) (105mins) d: Anne-Claire Poirier s: Marthe Blackburn, Anne-Claire Poirier : Monique Mercure, Jacques Godin, Roger Blay, Luce Guilbeault, Michèle Rossignol, Patricia Nolan, Louise Rémy, Benoît Girard, Pierre Thériault, Pierre Gobeil, Aubert Pallascio. Ten childhood friends, now forty years older, meet at one of their old haunts in a small town in Québec to talk about what has happened to them in the intervening years. It is a night of revelations. Some of the characters have prospered, others have failed; some have found happiness, others have known tragedy. The film is made up entirely of conversation, which ranges from the amusing to the dramatic, yet movement and change is always evident. The whole is held together by the marvellous ensemble acting, the direction and the very real expression of feelings and emotions. With this marvellous movie, coming after several timely pictures of social significance, *La quarantaine* brought Poirier into the top rank of Canada's filmmakers.

Quarantine (1989) (97mins) d&s: Charles Wilkinson : Beatrice Boepple, Garwin Sanford, Jerry

Wasserman, Tom McBeath. Futuristic nonsense about a plague infecting a police state in cyber time in a city that resembles Vancouver. The authorities decide to quarantine the victims. One expected better from Wilkinson. (The fact that the year 2003 brought a disease–SARS–to Toronto doesn't make this any better.) (Not to be confused with Anne-Claire Poirier's *La Quarantaine*)

Quarrel, The (1990) (88mins) d: Eli Cohen s: David Brandes (from the story by Chaim Grade) : R.H. Thomson, Saul Rubinek. This odd film from the Israeli director of *The Summer of Aviya* is a well-acted two-part conversation taking place during a walk in Montréal's Mount Royal park between Chaim and Hersh, two Jews who passionately debate their religious beliefs. To some, it is a case of much ado about an unnecessary state of anguish; to those who believe, it will be difficult and disturbing.

Que faisaient les femmes, pendant que l'homme marchait sur la lune?: see **Family Pack**

Québec Operation Lambda (1985) (88mins) d&s: Marc Degryse : Louise Noel, Marcel Roy. We are in the year 2014 and a group of foreign journalists and filmmakers attending a conference in Montréal is startled when a plot is uncovered in which Québec is planning to break up North America. An interesting spin into speculation, but the imaginations at work here are not quite up to the full significance of such a calamity. But in the chaos that ensues, a young man and woman find love.

Québec-Canada 1995 (1983) (90mins) d&s: John McGreevy : Jackie Burroughs, Martha Henry, John Neville, Kenneth Welsh. It is seldom that politics, particularly controversial subjects, form the basis of any of our film and tv projects. Here, John McGreevy jumps in head first with a clever look into the future as it was when this work was filmed. A seasoned cast wrestles with the aftermath of the referendum, under which Québec has gone its own way and now wants to "liberate" francophones in the rest of Canada.

Québec-Montréal (2002) (104mins) d: Ricardo Trogi s: Jean-Philippe Pearson, Patrice Robitaille, Ricardo Trogi : Patrice Robitaille, Jean-Philippe Pearson, Stepane Breton, Francois Létourneau, Isabelle Blais, Julie Le Breton, Pierre-Francois Legendre. We follow two cars on the highway between one city and another. In one, three youths talk constantly about sex, threesome sex in particular. In the other car, a youth chews open-mouthed all the time while trying to convince his girlfriend he cannot live without her. Characters such as this are not worthy of having films made about them. This is a boring trip.

Quelque chose d'organique: see **Something Organic**

Quelques arpents de neige: see **Rebels 1837, The**

Quest for Fire (*La guerre du feu*) (1981) (100mins) (a Canada-France co-production) d: Jean-Jacques Annaud s: Gérard Brach (with special languages by Anthony Burgess and bodily movements by Desmond Morris) : Everett McGill, Ron Perlman, Rae Dawn Chong, Naseer and Nameer El-Kadi and many others. Pretty silly business about prehistoric tribes being attacked by apes and wolves and losing its fire in the process. Sometimes fascinating but mostly, life is a drag. Filmed in Kenya, Iceland and Scotland as well as in Ontario and Alberta's badlands. The epic that wasn't.

Question de vie See: **A Matter of Life**

Question of Loving, A (*Qui à tiré sur les histoires d'amour?*) (1986) (92mins) d&s: Louise Carré : Monique Mercure, Guylaine Normandin, A slow, quiet, fragile tale set in a small Québec town during a summer meeting of a mother and daughter, who discuss life's illusions and longings. Beautifully done.

Question of Privilege, A (1998) (97mins) (a Canada-U.S. film) d: Rick Stevenson s: David Schultz : Jessica Steen, David Keith, Wendy Crewson, Christopher Lee Fassbinder, Benjamin Ratner, Michael Ironside, Nick Mancuso. Married lawyers find themselves on opposite sides of a controversial murder case involving four youths who rape and kill a young girl. Described as a mystery, the only mystery here is why this film was made.

Question of the Sixth, A (1981) (65mins) d: Graham Parker s: Grahame Woods : Lawrence Dane, Maureen McRae, Kenneth James, Joan Karasevich, Jan Chamberlain, David Storey, Larry Reynolds. The Sixth is, of course, the sixth commandment: thou shalt not kill. In this case, it becomes an intense and painful issue concerning a middle-aged farmer who is told he is dying of cancer. Wishing to die with dignity, he asks his brother to help him end his life. The brother refuses. Many audiences were shocked by this film. Euthanasia was hardly ever mentioned in public when this film was produced. A concerned drama told with sympathy and understanding, neither condoning nor condemning. (See: *For the Record*)

Qui à tiré sur les histoires d'amour?: see **Question of Loving, A**

Quick Change: see **Hold-Up**

Quiconque meurt, meurt à douleur (**Whoever Dies, Dies in Pain**) (1998) (90mins) d&s: Robert Morin : Alain Claude, Sylvie Jacques. The title is taken from a line by the 15TH-century French poet François Villon. It's doubtful, however, that he would identify his telling of pain with this reality-based crime concoction where police raid a drug dealer's premises with a tv cameraman following. The junkies are armed, and the cameraman and the police are taken hostage. And so it goes. All too true, unfortunately, for society, and staged with a disturbing sense of agony.

Quiet Day in Belfast, A (1973) (87mins) d: Milad Bessada s: Jack Gray (based on a play of the same name by Andrew Angus Dalrymple) : Barry Foster,

Margot Kidder, Sean McCann, Leo Leyden, Mel Tuck, Joyce Campion, Sean Mulcahy, Gillie Fenwick. This is an unusual story, filmed on location in Ireland with the "Troubles" as context, revolving around a small betting shop and its varied customers. Lively, provocative and humorous, Margot Kidder is excellent in her dual role as the characters of Bridgit and Thelma.

Rabid (Rage) (1977) (90mins) d&s: David Cronenberg : Marilyn Chambers, Frank Moore, Joe Silver, Patricia Gage, Allan Moyle, Robert Silverman. A nasty, loathsome piece of tripe about a blood-sucking lady who infects Toronto with her thirst. The director should have been among the first victims.

Race for Freedom: The Underground Railroad (1993) (120mins) (a Canada-U.S. co-production) d: Donald McBrearty s: Diana Braithwaite, Nancy Trites Bodkin, Peter Mohan : Michael Riley, Dawn Lewis, Courtney B. Vance, Janet Bailey, Ron White. In 1850, the U.S. proclaimed the Fugitive Slave Act, under which runaway slaves from the south could be captured in the slave-free states of the north. To escape, over 3,000 refugees trekked to Ontario using designated places to hide along the way. This became known as the Underground Railway. In this story about four of them, sentimentality is minimal, but the result is a drama that would have benefitted from a deeper historical reality.

Rafales: see **Blizzard, The**

Raffle, The (1994) (100mins) d: Gavin Wilding s: John Fairley : Robert Dawson, Jennifer Clement, Nicholas Lee, Mark Hamill, Babz Chula, Callum Keith Rennie. Very rarely does a film as good as this one open so badly. A clumsy, boorish beginning for what becomes a wonderful 'once upon a time romance'. It all begins with three young men, friends and free-wheeling, who raffle off a date with a beautiful woman. What follows is a delightful, funny, lively, colourful, romp against out-door amusements, the airport, and other pleasing places. (X-Files fans will find Nicholas Lea is his first lead role.)

Rage: see **Rabid**

Ragtime Summer (Age of Innocence) (1977) (100mins) (a Canada-U.K. co-production) d: Alan Bridges s: Ratch Wallace : David Warner, Trudy Young, Honor Blackman, Cec Linder, Jon Granik, Lois Maxwell. A hot summer in 1921 in a quiet Ontario town is disrupted by the arrival of a new science teacher from England. A slight story with well-drawn characters, this is told with quiet conviction against a recognizable background.

Rainbow (1995) (98mins) (a Canada-U.K. film) d: Bob Hoskins s: Ashley and Robert Sidaway : Willie Lavendahl, Bob Hoskins, Jack Fisher, Jacob Tierney, Susan Glover, Jane Gilchrist, Lisa Moore. A film that might never have been made had it not been for the single-minded determination of Bob Hoskins to raise the money for it. Shot in Oxford, England, and Montréal. Hoskins also directs and, for the second time, plays another of his many-faceted characters; here he portrays a magician among a group of children who follow the curve of a rainbow and steal its gold, draining the world of its colour. A highlight for audiences young and old is the scene showing the remorseful children riding the rainbow. Few families will not respond to this colourful film. (Not to be confused with Ken Russell's Rainbow 1989)

Rainbow Boys, The (1973) (92mins) d&s: Gerald Potterton : Donald Pleasence, Kate Reid, Don Calfa. Outdoor comedy, filmed against the rugged beauty of British Columbia, concerning a comical gold miner and his attempts to find a lost mine with two looney friends. Broad and at times boring but not without appealing moments. Reid and Pleasence make quite the couple.

Rainy Day Woman (1970) (83mins) (b/w) d&s: Ronald Hallis : Helen Keenan, Ashley Murray, John Roston, Julie Wildman, Beverley Light, Linda Henry, Sven Jurshevski. This story revolves around a childless couple whose relationship has deteriorated to the point of frustration and lack of communication. The wife prefers the company of her younger brother. Her husband finds companionship of a different nature. He is discovered by his wife and, in a seemingly perverse change of behaviour, she begins to find her way again. Worth watching.

Random Passage (2001) (480mins) (a Canada-Ireland co-production) d: John N. Smith s: Des Walsh (based on the novels Random Passage and Waiting for Time by Bernice Morgan) : Colm Meaney, Aoife McMahon, Deborah Pollitt, Daniel Payne, Brenda Devine, Michael Sapieha, Jessica Paré, Mary Walsh, Andy Jones. Here we have sailing ships making their way across the Atlantic in olden days, carrying either mutinous crews, slaves or immigrants. The opening of this panoramic drama provides a taste of the suffering, and eventual success, of the varied passengers travelling in the miserable lower decks. Among them is a young Irish orphan woman from a London workhouse coming to find a new and better life in Newfoundland. She finds herself sold into service and sent to the isolated fishing station of Cape Random. There she becomes one of a collection of exiles and joins the struggle to escape the past and seek a better life. This, of course, is the beginning of lots of 'bad things' happening to everyone, set against the dramatic surging backdrop of the restless ocean. This is a gripping, well-acted re-creation of history, intense, sometimes beautiful, and very much the Newfoundland we have come to know so well. It has taken its rocks lately on the screen, what with Misery Harbour, Rare Birds, and The Shipping News. Announcing the making of this film, CBC said that "bringing Random Passage to television audiences is very important for us." This, however, didn't prevent the incompetents sheltered at CBC, our 'public broadcaster' from tearing this "important" movie to pieces with constant interruptions for commercials and program promotions. The film and its viewers also suffered survival pangs.

Rape of a Sweet Young Girl, The (*Le viol d'une jeune fille douce*) (1968) (83mins) d&s: Gilles Carle : Julie Lachapelle, Jacques Cohen, Daniel Pilon, Katerine Mousseau, Donald Pilon, André Gagnon, Jacques Chenail, Susan Kay, Claude Jutra, Larry Kent, Guy Marcenay, Arnie Gelbart, Francine Monette, Jacques Charest, Michèle Dion, Yves Langlois. This film is Gilles Carle's second feature, an independent production made by his own company. It is supposed to be a comedy, but black or white, there's nothing funny about its sketchy story. There is little point or purpose to be found here, apart from some occasionally humorous and apt statements in the dialogue, which seem to indicate that Carle is attempting to reference the way life and people continually "rape" each other in the metaphysical sense.

Rare Birds (2001) (90mins) d: Sturla Gunnarsson s: Edward Richie (based on his novel of the same title) : William Hurt, Molly Parker, Andy Jones. The owner of a restaurant along the scenic coastline of Newfoundland may have to close down the business because his customers are few and far between. To get birdwatchers and tourists to visit, he tells everyone in the community that he has seen an Auk (a bird that is now extinct) in the vicinity. Not without a sense of humour in portraying the owner's attempts to safeguard his future, it is not as funny as one had hoped—a lame duck that, like the Auk, doesn't fly.

Rat Tales (1987) (68mins) d: Peter Cambell s: Francis Damberger : John Vernon, Dave McNally, Larry Farley, Dan Lehmann. The supervisor of an Edmonton rat exterminating company is a World War II veteran. His wartime experiences have unhinged him psychologically and he is becoming a danger to his staff and clients alike. Weird is the word for it, with John Vernon stuck in yet another oddity.

Rats (1999) (72mins) d&s: Jacques Holender : David Hemblen, Torri Higginson, David Fox, Earl Pastko, Colette Stevenson, Peter St. Laurent, John Gilbert, Lally Cadeau, Edward Fielding. This film's subtitle should be "The frustrations of a filmmaker." In this, the oddest of the odd, a documentary filmmaker recalls events in his life that drove him into madness, beginning with his home becoming infested with rats. After a number of distractions while finding funding, he decides to make a documentary about rats, only to suffer their return to his home and then to discover that someone has already made such a film. A nightmare in many ways! (For *Rats* 1982 see *Deadly Eyes*)

Rats and Rabbits (2000) (91mins) d: Lewis Furey s: Pascal Arnold, Lewis Furey (based on the play by George F. Walker) : Carole Laure, Paul Ahmarani, Nigel Bennett. A nasty tale about a group of misfits living in a ghetto who find unwanted attention when the mayor of the city is assassinated. "Which city?" you may well ask, in vain. A deplorable piece of work in every direction.

Rats, The (1982): see **Deadly Eyes**

Raye Makhfi: see **Secret Ballot**

Reach for the Sky (*La championne*) (1991) (92mins) (a Canada-Romania co-production) d: Elisabeta Bostan s: Vasilica Istrate, Rock Demers, Elisabeta Bostan : Izabela Moldovan. The latest in Rock Demers' series *Tales for All* is different in that it has no Canadian characters this time, preferring to remain in Romania and take us into the world of youngsters training to become gymnasts. Their difficulties, disappointments, home lives and achievements are authentically dramatized. (See: *Tales for All* series)

Ready for Slaughter (1983) (65mins) d: Allan King s: Roy MacGregor : Gordon Pinsent, Diana Belshaw, Mavor Moore, Pat Cull, Layne Coleman, Booth Savage, Winston Carroll. Looking at lives on the farms of Canada during the recession of 1981–83, this concerned study asks, "Was it the cattle or the farmers being slaughtered?" This film was not only controversial for what it was saying but also for showing—the first time on tv, the producers claimed—the difficult birth of a calf that has "turned" inside its mother. Filmed in Ontario. (See: *For the Record*)

Real Howard Spitz, The (1998) (102mins) (a Canada-U.K. co-production) d: Vadim Jean s: Jurgen Wolff : Kelsey Grammer, Amanda Donohoe, Geneviève Tessier, Joseph Rutten, Patrick McKenna, Kay Tremblay, David Christofel. This family comedy set in the U.S. but filmed in Nova Scotia concerns a bad-tempered writer who gives up on seedy fiction and begins to write stories for children, even though he dislikes them, and finds himself at last a successful author. There are many complications along the line, of course; most of them fail to lift proceedings above the mundane.

Reality Survival: see **Deadend.com**

Reasonable Force (1983) (65mins) d: Peter Rowe s: Brian Kit McLeod, Peter Lower : Deepa Mehta, Abdul Merali, Lee Taylor, Douglas Greenall, Michael Dyson, Pawanjit Bains, Sushma Sardana, Philip Quatermain. Inspired by an actual incident, we see how a farming family is harassed and threatened simply for being different. A reasonable, calm and carefully considered treatment of racism. (See: *For the Record*)

Rebels 1837, The (*Quelques arpents de neige*) (1972) (94mins) d: Denis Héroux s: Marcel Lefebvre : Daniel Pilon, Christine Olivier, Mylène Demongeot, Rose-Rey Duzil, Jean Coutu, Bertrand Gagnon, Dave Broadfoot, Barrie Baldaro. Once again Pilon is on the run, this time during the 1837 Rebellion, and again his wife is shot—by the British, it seems. Another slipshod treatment of history. (See: *Two Wise Men, The* [*Les smattes*])

Réception, La (1989) (91mins) d&s: Robert Morin (based on the novel *Ten Little Indians* by Agatha

Christie) : Carole Dalcourt, Antoine Zarzour. Ten people are invited to a remote manor by a mysterious host and one by one the guests disappear. Miss Marple couldn't solve this one and Miss Christie would be horrified!

Recipe for Revenge (1998) (120mins) d: Stacey Stewart Curtis s: Jennifer Black, Peter Lauterman (based on the novel *Bullets Over Boise* by Kristin Gabriel) : Kim Huffman, Alex Carter, Corbin Bernsen, Stephen J.M. Sisk, Hugh Thompson. Unusual tale about a woman with a catering business who, in helping out a friend, becomes involved in a murder mystery with the police and several suspects. A romantic crime-drama with believable backgrounds and winning moments. (See: *Harlequin* series)

Reckless Disregard (1985) (105mins) (a Canadian-U.S film) d: Harvey Hart s: Charles Haas : Tess Harper, Leslie Nielsen, Ronny Cox, Roger Abbott, Sean McCann, Kate Lynch. A television reporter is put on trial, accused of libelling a doctor, who claims the reporter presented, on his tv program, a bogus prescription signed by the doctor. Weak medicine here.

Recommendation for Mercy (1975) (91mins) d: Murray Markowitz s: Fabian Jennings, Joe Wiesenfeld, Murray Markowitz : Andrew Skidd, Robb Judd, Mike Upmalis, Karen Martin, Michele Fansett. A true story of a crime of passion in an Ontario town makes a tacky movie. A welcome change, however, to be in a Canadian court of law.

Recorded Live (1982) (82mins) (b/w) d&s: Michael Korican, Andrew Rowsome, Almerinda Travassos : Natalia Kuzmyn, Allen Blumenthal, Liza Soroka, Robert Mills, Margaret Moores. Set against a background of activity by the recording group False Kolours, a young and penniless painter becomes involved when she begins to distribute bootleg videotapes. She becomes dubious about her way of living and earning money. The subject was all quite new for its time but hardly inspiring or refreshing.

Recruits (1987) (90mins) d: Rafal Zielinski s: Charles Wiener, B. Roderick (from an idea by Maurice Smith) : Douglas Annear, Stephen Osmond. At a resort in Ontario, a corrupt police chief hires an incompetent group of mixed individuals to staff the police force. Hopeless.

Red (1969) (101mins) d: Gilles Carle s: Ennio Flaiano, Gilles Carle : Daniel Pilon, Geneviève Deloir, Fernande Giroux, Donald Pilon, Gratien Gélinas, Paul Gauthier, Claude Michaud, Yvon Dufour, Raymond Cloutier, Frank Héron, Jacques Bilodeau, André Lejeune, Céline Bernier. A strange collaboration between Gilles Carle and the Italian writer Flaiano has resulted in a film that sounds French, looks Italian and follows the violent traditions of American cinema. The story of a homeless, restless, rootless young man who is part native, part Québécois concerns his violent encounters with women and the establishment until his heavily sym-

bolic death. Well shot and acted, the film takes Carle further into professionalism, but away from a true reflection of French-Canadian society. This was the first film, and one of the few, in which Famous Players, the leading Canadian cinema circuit then owned by Paramount, invested money.

Red Bells, Blue Tears (*Grelots rouges, sanglots bleus***)** (1987) (76mins) d: Pierre Harel s: Hélène Gagnon, Pierre Harel : Magdalena Gaudreault, Luc Matte, Pierre Harel. A filmmaker in Montréal has parted company with his girlfriend, who is a painter and script writer. While making a film from her last script, the director carefully analyzes it in an attempt to discover why their relationship has failed. Another introspective examination of the human condition. Simple yet effective.

Red Blooded 2 (1996) (86mins) (a Canadian-American film) d: David Blyth s: Nicolas Stiladis : Kari Salin, Kristoffer Ryan Winters, Burt Young, Nicholas Pasco, David Keith. A low-budget blood-gore-and-sex atrocity, a sequel to *Red Blooded American Girl*. It's a thoroughly revolting clutch of cliches in murder, rape, violence and bad language, to say nothing about bad performances.

Red Deer (2000) (109mins) d&s: Anthony Couture : James Hutson, Amber Rothwell, Loreya Montayne, Awaovieyi Agie, Joseph Procyk. This is a film in which nothing happens among a small group of disconnected characters set within a few buildings, a small motel, alongside a highway on which distant, fast-moving cars and other vehicles stream from somewhere to nowhere. References to Canada in this town in Alberta are minimal. One scene in a supermarket has a large sign describing itself as Canada's "favourite store", but Canada is covered over by a poster. Relations between the individuals here, coming and going, are slight, although they are not an unlikeable lot, including a bookseller who goes mad and throws his books around. Overall no doubt this is supposed to be taken as a study in meditation and observation of the dull lives of uninteresting beings. Tedious in the extreme, yet it has some style although of little substance. To its credit, however, there is no violence, filthy language or sex; and the players do well with what they have to work on.

Red Eyes (Accidental Truths) (*Les yeux rouges***) (***Les verités accidentelles***)** (1983) (90mins) d&s: Yves Simoneau : Marie Tifo, Jean-Marie Lemieux, Pierre Curzi, Raymond Bouchard, Rémy Girard, Denise Proulx. For once a *policier* from a Canadian point of view as a police officer in Québec City tracks down a *voyeur* known as "Red Eyes." A nifty, scary tale, dramatically realized and splendidly acted.

Red Food, The: see *Cuisine rouge, La*

Red Green's Duct Tape Forever (2002) (92mins) d: Eric Till s: Steve Smith : Steve Smith, Patrick McKenna, Wayne Robson, Graham Greene, Melissa Dimarco, Lawrence Dane, Fiona Reid, Sheila McCarthy, Dave Broadfoot, Jayne Eastwood.

(These 'stalwarts' are joined by 30 other players.) Based on the long-running and enormously popular throughout Canada and the U.S., television comedy series *The Red Green Show* was first aired on CHCH-tv Hamilton, in 1990, and subsequently on the CBC, this, their first film, like the weekly series, is set in Northern Ontario in Possum Lodge, "145 beer stores from Toronto." The comic antics of the regulars come into play when the residents of the lodge struggle to raise money to save it from an evil land baron. To obtain the money, they enter a duct tape sculpture contest in Minneapolis, with their rendition of a giant goose. What follows is a good, earthy, knock-about comedy that cannot fail to please the tv show's fan club of over a million enthusiastic members. (Thousands of them in the U.S.)

Red Hot (1993) (95mins) (a Canada-U.S. film) d: Paul Haggis s: Michael Maurer, Paul Haggis : Donald Sutherland, Balthazar Getty, Carla Gugino, Ian Niklas, Armin Mueller-Stahl, Hugh O'Conor. In Russia in the 1950's a youngster is introduced to rock-and-roll music and finds himself in trouble with the authorities who consider the music as being pagan and a threat to society. This is neither a red nor a hot film, the title meaning Red for Russia and Hot for popular music. It's an odd, gentle, slight and slow little movie filmed in Latvia, a love story about two young lovers, both concert pianists, with the boy smuggling in copies of Western popular music from the West. They escape to Copenhagen. Don't blink or you will miss Sutherland and Mueller-Stahl, who haven't been given much to do but it's pleasing to see them, like this film as a whole.

Red Nose: see *Nez rouge*

Red River (*Rivière Rouge*) (1996) (180mins) (a Canada-France co-production) d: Yves Boisset s: Michel Leviant, Philippe Lopes-Curval, Yves Boisset : Christophe Malavoy, Claudia Koll, Eric Schweig, Gordon Pinsent, Nick Mancuso. Here we are again, on the prairies, through the forests, with the trappers and the untamed land of western Canada at the turn of the century. An adventurer and his Métis friend also have love affairs to contend with in the Red River settlement. Familiar though it may be, there is a freshness about the film that gives it an authentic feeling.

Red Violin, The (*Le violon rouge*) (1998) (131mins) (a Canada-Italy co-production) d: François Girard s: Don McKellar : Samuel L. Jackson, Don McKellar, Carlo Cecchi, Irene Grazioli, Jean-Luc Bideau, Christoph Koncz, Jason Flemyng, Greta Scacchi, Sylvia Chang, Liu Zi Feng, Colm Feore, Monique Mercure, Sandra Oh. A sometimes confused, often bizarre, narrative trying to follow the fortunes of a 300-year-old cursed violin from Italy to Vienna, London, Montréal, China and finally New York to be auctioned, in a most unlikely conclusion. Depressing and frustrating, decent but dull in spite of colourful backgrounds, lavish costumes and a score by John Corigliano.

Reflection on a Marriage, A: see *J'me Marie, j'me Marie*

Regeneration (1988) (87mins) d&s: Russel Stephens : John Anderson, Marek Cieszewski, Suzanne Ristic, Dermot Hennelly. Yet another high-tech experiment goes wrong, this time with the first person brought back to life inside a computer-television machine. Nonsense, numb-dumb and poorly made.

Regeneration (1996) (110mins) (a Canada-U.K. co-production) d: Gilles MacKinnon s: Allan Scott (based on a novel by Pat Barker) : Kelly MacDonald, James Bolam, Hans Matheson, Ewan Stewart, Andy Serkis, Jonathan Pryce, James Wilby, Jonny Lee Miller, Stuart Bunce, Tanya Allen. A beautifully acted film telling the story of the relationships developed between Siegfried Sasson, Wilfred Owen and Dr. William Rivers while they are being treated by a psychiatrist at Craiglockhart Military Hospital in Edinburgh during World War I. The horror of the war in the trenches is brought home to us with a reality that is hard to bear. A film to be remembered.

Regina (2002) (95mins) (a Canada-Iceland co-production) d: Maria Sigurdardottir s: Margret Ornolfsdottirsjon : Sigurbjorg Alma Ingolfsdottir, Benedikt Clausen, Baltasar Kormakur, Halldora Geirhardsdottir, Bjorn Ingi Hilmarsson, Solveig Arnarsdottir, Rurik Haraldsson. A charming story about a widowed mother's 10-year-old daughter who, alone in the home during summer with little to do, decides to find her mother a soul mate. She does, and then reveals her likeable singing voice, which leads everyone to fall under her spell and makes her summer one of pleasure rather than emptiness. Filmed in Iceland, it's a family musical comedy, fresh and engaging as a summer breeze. (See: *Tales for All* series)

Règne du jour, Le: see **Duration of the Day**

Reincarnate, The (1971) (90mins) d: Donald Haldane s: Seeleg Lester : Jack Creley, Trudy Young, Hugh Webster, Colin Fox, Stuart Gillard, Marcia Diamond. A confused and talkative attempt at reincarnation, mixed up with black magic and virgin sacrifice, all taking place in a small Ontario town. Laughable and ridiculous.

Réjeanne Padovani (1973) (94mins) d: Denys Arcand s: Jacques Benoît, Denys Arcand : Jean Lajeunesse, Luce Guilbeault, Roger Lebel, Margo MacKinnon, Jean-Pierre Lefebvre, Frédérique Collin, Pierre Thériault, Gabriel Arcand, Henry Ramer, Céline Lomez, Paule Baillargeon, Jean-Pierre Saulnier, André Melançon, Julien Poulin, Bernard Gosselin, Jacques Leduc, Roger Frappier, Michel Bouchard, Denys Arcand, Marguerite Duparc. A forthright provocative drama about corruption in Québec in the construction business, with strong political overtones and caustic comments about businesspeople and their deals with governments. Arcand controls a huge cast and a complicated scenario with skill and a wicked sense of humour. Truly a remarkable achievement.

Relative Fear (1994) (90mins) (a Canadian-American film) d: George Mihalka s: Kurt Wimmer : Darlanne Fluegel, James Brolin, M. Emmett Walsh, Denise Crosby, Matthew Dupuis. A feeble variation of *Bad Seed* set in an American city and played by a mostly American cast. A young boy is obsessed with tv's The Crime Channel and those who taunt him die mysteriously. False notes predominate in a thin attempt at horror.

Reluctant Angel (1997) (103mins) d: John Helliker s: Denise O'Rourke : Megan Follows, Jaimz Woolvett, James Gallanders, Martin Villafana, Anne Marie Loder, Victor Ertmanis. Jason, a small-time criminal and con man keeps his girlfriend, who is tired of his scams, by promising to get her a gallery showing of her art. She leaves him and meets Donald, and they fall in love but he has a drinking problem. She devotes herself to saving him from himself, but Jason comes back to put an end to the relationship. Melodrama, over-long, routine and predictable, but not without feeling thanks to Megan Follows, in one of her early roles.

Remembering Mel (1986) (78mins) d: Douglas Harris s: Laurence Raskin, Douglas Harris : Robert Kolomeir, Arthur Holden, Jim Connolly, Guy Laprade, Natalie Timoschuk. A director is making a documentary film about a man whose life has been a losing proposition. This film also seems to have lost its way. No, it's not about the Mayor of Toronto!

Rencontre avec une femme remarquable: Laure Gaudreault: see **Laure Gaudreault: A Remarkable Woman**

Rendering, The (Portrait for Murder) (2002) (91mins) (a Canada-U.S. film) d: Peter Svatek s: David Amann : John Brennan, Peter Outerbridge, Shannen Doherty, Tammy Isbell, Conrad Pia, Sean Devine. When a woman's husband is falsely accused for a crime he had no part of, her past comes back to haunt her. This is a rare compact, first-rate thriller, frightening and strikingly photographed. Good acting. Agatha Christie would have enjoyed it!

Reno and the Doc (1984) (88mins) d&s: Charles Dennis : Kenneth Welsh, Henry Ramer, Linda Griffiths, Gene Mack. Silly attempt at a scatter-brained comedy set on the ski slopes of the Rocky Mountains. The accomplished Kenneth Welsh is wasted, as are Henry Ramer and the lovely Linda Griffiths.

Répétition, La **(The Repetition)** (2001) (95mins) (a Canada-France co-production) d&s: Catherine Corsini : Emmanuelle Béart, Pascale Bussières, Dani Levy, Jean-Pierre Kalfon, Sami Bouajila. Surely one of the most complicated relationships ever depicted on the screen as two women who were firm friends in the past meet again ten years later to discover their true feelings for each other. All this goes on set against a stage background and in a dentist's office. All a bit much and well done, but confusing, dismal and Louise Brooks and *Lulu* are even dragged in!

Replikator (1994) (96mins) d: Philip Jackson s: Michelle Bellevose : Michael St.Gerard, David Hemblen, Brigette Bako, Ronald Lea, Erica Ehm, Ned Beatty. We are in the 21st century with a vengence as a policeman and two cyberites attempt to stop two ruthless criminals from using technology which duplicates all humans, the worst of us included and use them to control the world. Exciting sci-fi not so outlandish as some of its counterparts. Done well by the dependable Jackson.

Requiem for a Handsome Bastard (*Requiem pour un beau sans-coeur***)** (1992) (93mins) d&s: Robert Morin : Gildor Roy, Jean-Guy Bouchard, Brigette Paguette, Sabrina Boudot, Klimbo, Stéphane Côté, France Arbour. A brutal thief and murderer with no redeeming qualities escapes from prison to take revenge on those who put him there. The flash and fury of experimental video techniques and a subjective camera, with few cross-cuts to the characters, leads to considerable confusion as to what is actually happening and why.

Retour de l'Immaculée Conception, Le **(The Return of the Immaculate Conception)** (1970) (86mins) (b&w) d&s: André Forcier : Julie Lachapelle, Fernand Roy, Jacques Chenail, Jacques Marcotte. Forcier goes to the east end of Montréal to film disenchanted youths who find it hard to believe that life has anything to offer. Provocative, concerned and observant.

Retour des aventuriers du timbre perdu, Le: see **Return of Tommy Tricker, The**

Return of Ben Casey, The (1988) (93mins) (a Canada-U.S. film) d: Joseph L. Scanlan s: Barry Oringer : Vince Edwards, Lynda Mason Green, Barbara Eve Harris, Harry Landers, Gwynyth Walsh, Al Waxman. Based on the earlier and popular tv series. This new picture, which stands on its own as a likeable and well-made film, brings back Dr. Casey, the expert brain surgeon, to resume his practice at County Hospital after being away for several years helping in distant countries. He finds that he is not actually welcome, due to professional jealousy. The following events are thoughtful, well detailed, often touching and poignant. The film is not afraid to speak out about doctors' fees in many U.S. hospitals, and lawyers and relatives who sue hospitals and doctors on the slightest pretext. The cast is a pleasure to be with.

Return of the Immaculate Conception, The: see *Retour de l'immaculée conception, Le*

Return of Tommy Tricker, The (*Le retour des aventuriers du timbre perdu***)** (1994) (97mins) d&s: Michael Rubbo : Michael Stevens, Joshawa Mathers, Heather Goodsell, Adele Gray, Tommy Pierre Tutangata, Paul Nichols, Andrew Bauer-Gador.

Tommy and his friends are determined to free the mysterious lad held prisoner on Canada's famous Bluenose stamp. Their journey takes them as far away as the Cook Islands. Lots of adventures, laughs and obstacles to overcome. A worthy sequel to the first Tommy Tricker journey. (See: *Tales for All series*)

Return to Kandahar (2002) (60mins) d&s: Moshen Makhmalbaf. Partly a semi-fictionalized re-construction of the real-life attempts by Canadian journalist, Nelofer Pazira, who, born in Afghanistan, goes back to visit friends after the war on the Taliban. Revealing, telling and disturbing in its portrait of a regime which toppled the World Trade Center and continues to threaten the world. Note: This portrait was followed by the documentary *Kandahar* (2003) in which Nelofer Pazira co-directs with Paul Jay, in depicting her continuing mission to find a childhood friend. Leaving Kabul, she travels across the desert talking with individuals about life since the Allied Forces went to war to crush the Islamic fundamentalists. A truly horrifying journey.

Revanche de Porky, La: see **Porky's Revenge**
Revanche noël de Madame Beauchamp, Le: see **Christmas of Madame Beauchamp, The**
Revenge of the Lady in Black, The: see *Vengeance de la femme en noir, La*

Revenge of the Land (2000) (240 mins) d: John N. Smith s: Sharon Riis (based on the book by Maggie Siggins) : Chandra West, Kenneth Welsh, Sean Gallagher, Jennifer Dale, Henry Woolf. A turn-of-the-century epic, set in Saskatchewan. We first meet the Carmichaels and the Hawkes, who live in a rough prairie town called Promise. They work the land in an exhausting struggle to survive. The Hawkes have done well and live in luxury, in an expensively furnished house, eating the best food accompanied by fine wines. Was life in the Dust Bowl really like this? An ambitious undertaking, the film is somewhat cluttered with characters who talk and talk except when bouncing around in bed. One rather wishes they would go out and get some ploughing done. As always, Kenneth Welsh can be depended upon to provide the nasty moments.

Revenge of the Radioactive Reporter (1992) (85mins) d&s: Craig Pryce : David Scammell, Kathryn Boese, Derrick Strange. A comic strip sci-fi world of evil and corruption at the local nuclear power plant. The machinations of the dastardly president lead to an inquisitive reporter being dumped into a bubbling vat of radioactive waste. He emerges a nuclear mutant with unusual powers and goes after the villains in an orgy of revenge. Not quite funny enough.

Revoir Julie (See Julie Again) (Julie and Me) (1998) (92mins) d&s: Jeanne Crépeau : Dominique Leduc, Stephanie Morganstern, Marcel Sabourin, Murielle Dutil, Lucille Bélair. Juliet drives to Québec to see her old friend Julie again. Their relationship is over; they haven't seen each other for 15 years, and they try to come to terms with their often difficult love affair. Juliet kisses her and as in the past, Julie cannot accept it. A film of slender moments with a quiet charm and thoughtful issues. Several vignettes in animation bring a gentle sense of humour to it as a whole. Filmed in Eastern Townships.

Revolutionaries, The (*Le révolutionnaire***)** (1965) (72mins) (b/w) d&s: Jean-Pierre Lefebvre : Louis St-Pierre, Louise Rasselet, Alain Chartrand, Robert Daudelin, Michel Gauthier, René Goulet, Pierre Hébert, Camil Houle, Richard Lacroix, Jacques Monette. This first film of Jean-Pierre Lefebvre was shot in a few weeks on 16mm with hardly enough cash to buy raw stock. As such it comes off fairly well and is frequently commendable, but falls victim to obvious shortcomings such as not enough cross-cutting, shots held too long, a complete lack of characterization, awkwardness, and uncertainty. The minimalist story is intended to be a comic look at a group of youths who call themselves "revolutionaries for a free Québec" and go into the cold, snowbound countryside to an old house for training purposes. This kind of activity soon palls and they end by accidentally eliminating each other. The treatment wavers between satire and seriousness, and results in considerable monotony and some foolishness. However, a sequence depicting a brief history of Canada filled in with scratchy animation effects is ingeniously done. This marked the beginning of the career of Jean-Pierre Lefebvre, a truly independent artist whose outlook on life marks him as a highly principled creator of films of love, beauty and kindness. ("Revolutionaries" caused a bit of a stir at the Montreal Film Festival of 1965).

Révolutions, d'ébats amoureux, éperdus, douloureux (Revolutions...Forever and Ever) (1984) (69mins) d&s: Jean-Marc Larivière : Brigitte Haentjens, Sylvie Lacombe, Martha Wheaton, Louis Nolan. Three women live together, redecorating their new apartment and sharing daily activities: watching tv, preparing meals and reading the papers and journals. More didactic than dialectic.

Revolving Doors, The: see *Portes tournantes, Les*

Rhino Brothers, The (2002) (99mins) d: Dwayne Beaver s: Rudy Thauberger : Gabrielle Rose, Curt Bechdholt, William MacDonald, Alistair Abell, Deanna Milligan, Heather McCarthy. This first film creates a vivid and disturbing portrayal of hockey and the men who play it, reflecting what many people have come to think about the greed and violence of our national obsession. Set in B.C., the film throws us in with a hockey-mad family encouraged by a fanatical mother, who continually urges her sons on to greater achievements. To no avail: they are swallowed up by shoving, swearing, shouting, bloodied louts whose cunning and brutality are truly revolting. *Les Boys* are much to be preferred to this mob.

Ribo ou 'le soleil sauvage' (a Canada-Cameroun co-production) (1978) (93mins) d&s: Roger Racine, Joseph Henri Nama, Louise Darios : Suzanne

Bandolo, Dieudonné Ond Ond, Daniel Ndo, Roger Manga, Pierre Elong Based on the opera *Le mariage de Ribo* by Joseph Henri Nama, a curio listed for the record.

Ride Me (Ego Trip) (1995) (85mins) d: Bashar Shbib s: David Cohen, Bashar Shbib : Bianca Rossini, Frederick Duval, Clark Gregg, Adam Coleman Howard, Colleen Coffey, Christina Beck, Robyn Rosenfeld. Bashar is directing in Las Vegas, one of his favourite playgrounds with girls, gangsters and lots of sex. The manager of a casino prepares a romantic dinner for an assorted starring cast of friends. One, is upset that her lover doesn't turn up to ask her to marry him, as he promised. A detective comes on the scene to sort out a murder-suicide. All very lively and entertaining.

Ride, The (2000) (120mins) d: Steven DiMarco s: Paul Dreskin : Al Waxman, Yaphet Kotto, Ronald White, Alison Sealy-Smith, Carolyn Goff, Vik Sahay, Tony Munch, Rachel Crawford, Vincent Corazza. Driving a taxi in North America is said to be the most dangerous way of making a living. This film sets out to prove it in a sensational, foul-mouthed, raw and murderous chronicle of incidents, the sum total of which should convince the public to never set foot in a taxi again. The producer calls this film "our Sopranos". Perish the thought that it might be "our Torontonians"! (Not to be confused with *Ride Me*).

Riders: see **Steal**

Riel (1979) (146mins) d: George Bloomfield s: Roy Moore : Raymond Cloutier, Roger Blay, Christopher Plummer, Jean-Louis Roux, Marcel Sabourin, Arthur Hill, William Shatner, Leslie Nielsen, Barry Morse, Lloyd Bochner, Donald Harron, John Neville, Claude Jutra, Don Francks, Normand Chouinard, Chris Wiggins, Budd Knapp, Kenneth Welsh, James Bradford, Lee Broker, Maury Chaykin, Pierre Curzi, Neil Dainard, Brenda Donohue, Ken James, Robert Lavoie, Ed McNamara, Gary Reineke, August Schellenberg, Gladys Taylor, Dave Thomas, Tony Van Bridge, Paxton Whitehead. There is much to admire in this depiction of the life of Louis Riel, one of Canada's most debatable historical figures, but excessive length and confusing characters and events leave a somewhat shadowed portrait. For the most part, however, it is a powerful and compelling work. This was an immense undertaking by CBC-tv with a huge cast consisting of many of Canada's prominent actors. The excitement and speculation surrounding the film's production and opening was intense and widespread; true to the Canadian nature, everyone expected it to be a disaster. Instead, it was a remarkable accomplishment in costumes, sets, acting, writing and direction. The actual filming took only three months at the Kleinberg studio outside Toronto. Editing and post-production was another matter! Simply stated, the script got lost under the weight of the logistics. But it certainly could never be made today with Riel being subject to revisionism. First showing Ontario Film Theatre, Ontario Film Institute with filmakers and cast meme-bers in attendance, Toronto, April 9, 1979, Rideau Hall, Ottawa, April 11, 1979, CBC and Radio Canada TV Pt.1 April 15, 1979, CBC & Radio Canada TV Pt.2 April 17, 1979.

Rien qu'un jeu: see **Just a Game**

Rip-Off (1971) (88mins) d: Donald Shebib s: William Fruet : Don Scardino, Ralph Endersby, Mike Kukulewich, Peter Gross, Susan Petrie, Hugh Webster, Maxine Miller, Susan Conway, August Schellenberg, Tedde Moore. This film followed Shebib's immensely popular *Goin' Down the Road*, and much was expected of it. Four high-school friends go away for a weekend in the country and attempt to start a commune with a rock band and a movie camera. They find that nothing works and life is not simple. Light-hearted and socially concerned. A promising second film.

Ripper: Letter from Hell (2001) (115mins) d: John Eyres s: Pat Bermel : Kelly Brook, Bruce Payne, Jurgen Prochnow, A.J. Cook. Emmanuelle, a student doing research into the minds of serial killers, is haunted by her own horrific past when she meets a former stalker. Much too long, and far too many slashings and unpleasant sex talk.

Risen, The (2003) (90mins) d: Jeff Beesley s: Jim Osborne : Alberta Watson, Eugene Lipinski, Peter Outerbridge, Helen Shaver, Wendy Anderson, Daniel Massey. The wife of a headmaster at a private school decides to terminate her pregnancy. Complications set in, her life is at risk, and she is left with a loss of memory. She is haunted by nightmares and hallucinations, and sees death around her. Her sister finding that traditional surgery is not working decides to turn to the supernatural to help the sister back to normal. A near death experience, hence *The Risen*. Unusual in some ways, disturbing and mysterious in others. Done well, but not always convincing, and often confusing. With a miserable monster of a husband and a suspicious psychiatrist, this film runs along the same lines as *Dancing in the Dark* (1995).

Rituals (The Creeper) (1977) (99mins) (a Canada-U.S. co-production) d: Peter Carter s: Ian Sutherland : Hal Holbrook, Lawrence Dane, Robin Gammell, Ken James, Gary Reineke, Jack Creley, Murray Westgate, Michael Zenon. Violence in the wild patterned after *Deliverance* as five doctors hike into northern Ontario wilderness to go fishing, only to fall victims to brutal attacks that leave them struggling to survive. As gory and unpleasant as they come.

Rivière rouge: see **Red River**

Road to Saddle River (1994) (105mins) d&s: Francis Damberger : Paul Jarrett, Paul Coeur, Michael Hogan. A young immigrant from Europe goes on a comic journey through the western provinces to find the land "where the river runs clear, the grass is green, and the sky is blue as far as the eye can see." Simple humour, striking scenery.

Roadkill (1989) (80mins) d: Bruce McDonald s: Don McKellar, Bruce McDonald : Valerie Buhagiar, Don McKellar, Gary Quigley, Larry Hudson, Bruce McDonald. A "just for a lark" first film, freewheeling and often foolish, but refreshing in its attempt to capture the flavour of pop culture and its followers. A timid assistant goes out on the road for a rock promoter to find out what happened to a touring band of musicians lost in the wilds of Ontario. Uneven, unfinished, but spontaneous.

Rock 'n Roll Nightmare (The Edge of Hell) (1987) (83mins) d: John Fasano s: Jon-Mikl Thor : John Triton. In a remote Ontario farmhouse an evil invisible force kills off a family. Years later a rock band becomes caught by the same power when it begins to use the farmhouse to practice in. Pretty stale stuff.

Rock My World: see **Global Heresy**

Roger and Elvis (1993) (83mins) d&s: Donald Terry : Scott Armstrong, Kate Fallon, Glenn Martin, Roger Martin, Edwin Fuller. A mishmash of ideas gone wrong about a gang of drug dealers and a group of odd friends. Set against Elvis paraphernalia shops, golf courses, video games and drug deals. Described as a black comedy, it blacks out early.

Roller Coaster (1999) (90mins) d&s: Scott Smith : Brendan Fletcher, Kett Turton, Crystal Buble, Brent Glenen, Sean Amsing, David Lovgren. Five teenagers living narrow and empty lives visit a shabby closed-down-for-the-winter amusement park in Vancouver and start smoking, drinking and being sick while discussing what to do with their lives. One commits suicide by falling from the roller coaster and the pals walk away and leave her as though she didn't matter. Monotonous, annoying and empty.

Romantic Ladies: see *Dames galantes*

Romantic Scenario, A: see *Manuscrit érotique, Le*

Rookies (1990) (93mins) d: Paul Shapiro s: Jeffrey Cohen, Paul Shapiro : Yannick Bisson, Peter MacNeill, Christianne Hirt, Ian Tracey. A simple, well-made film about Canada's favourite sport, concerning a 17-year-old hockey player from a small northern Ontario town who comes to prove himself with the Oshawa Blades. Natural and appealing, with lively scenes on the rink and thoughtful consequences for the participants.

Room for a Stranger (1968) (85mins) (b/w) d: Edward Leversuch s: Stanley Lipinski : Jean Christopher, Bruce Gray, Sean Sullivan, Brian Hedley-James, Faith Gardiner, Jean Cavall. About a man who is an utter rotter and lives off unfortunate women whom he then blackmails, this film earns a place in our movie history on the grounds that the director made no bones out of announcing it was a sex-exploitation film. It was possibly our first porno picture, the nude shots in which had some critics up in arms. An MP complained, questions were asked in the House of Commons, and the Toronto police investigated, but to their credit found the sex orgy scenes "acceptable by modern standards." They obviously enjoyed it! Critics declared it "appalling," "mediocre," and "terrible," with "awful acting" and so on. It opened in Toronto five years after all the commotion had died down.

Rose Cafe, The (1987) (75mins) d: Danièle Suissa s: Julian Roffman : Parker Stevenson, Linda Smith, Damir Andrei, Browen Mantel. A familiar yet still endearing love story in which two high-school classmates meet later in life and find that there is still magic between them whenever they are together. They open a cafe that becomes a success, after some misunderstandings. (See: *Shades of Love* series)

Roses in December (1965) (80mins) (b/w) (unfinished) d&s: Graham Gordon : Leigh Warton, Ann Campbell, Marty Cohen, Dawn Ballentyne, Joan Busat, Stephen DePahk and others. A former air force officer from the U.K. living in Toronto gives up his acting career to become a businessman, falls in love with a younger woman, and faces many setbacks, especially when he re-opens the Winter Garden in the Loews' Cinema to present a tribute to Charlie Chaplin. But his on-screen difficulties are insignificant compared to those of Graham Gordon, who toiled for years trying to raise the money to make and finish this picture. It was one of the first features to be made in post-war Toronto, and money was simply not available. The CFDC let him down, but he would not give up. (some shooting was done in Casa Loma). The result still holds a continuing appeal.

Rossignol et les cloches, Le: see **Nightingales and the Bells**

Rough Justice (1984) (65mins) d: Peter Yalden-Thomas s: Donald Truckey : Peter Dvorsky, Garrick Hagon. A disturbing portrayal of child abuse and how child abusers exploit the system. We see the points of view of the defence, prosecution, victim and molestor. (See: *For the Record*)

Rowdyman, The (1972) (95mins) d: Peter Carter s: Gordon Pinsent : Gordon Pinsent, Frank Converse, Will Geer, Linda Goranson, Sabina Maydelle, Ted Henley, Estelle Wall, Stuart Gillard, Austin Davis, Dawn Greenhalgh, Murray Westgate, Tess Ewing, Jonathan White, Dan MacDonald, Doug McGrath. Gordon Pinsent is one of Canada's finest and best-known actors and, like many of his fellow artists, he was anxious to get films made to provide more opportunities for himself and his colleagues. With his own life and Newfoundland in mind, he wrote this screenplay about a forthright, boisterous, independent, fun-loving rascal who finds himself ultimately alone in society. Made entirely on location in Newfoundland, with Peter Carter directing his first feature, and with the veteran producer F.R. Crawley making this venture possible, the result is a sharply observed study of the simple life and its island people. There are many marvellous moments, and the whole has a charm and energy that carries it over the thinner parts. Pinsent is truly a tremendous presence on film, television, and stage and is a gifted writer and director. He has never let the system get him down. When rebuffed by the small minds in high places, he comes back time and time again with another worthy project. The final shot of him giving a joyful jump as he walks away, has become a famous "still picture".

Rowing Through (1996) (116mins) (a Canada-Japan film) d: Masato Harada s: Will Aitken, Masato Harada, David Halberstam (from his book) : Colin Ferguson, Helen Shaver, Leslie Hope, Kenneth Welsh, Peter Murnik, Claude Genest, James Hyndman, Andrew Tarbet, Michiko Gada. A riveting story of a remarkable athlete, a rower, who is racing against time. Cut off from the 1980 Olympics in Moscow, he continues his efforts to be as good as the younger rowers. Exceptionally well done with an unexpected ending.

Royal Bonbon (2002) (85mins) (a France-Canada-Haiti co-production) d&s: Charles Najman : Dominique Batraville, Verlus Delorme, Ambroise Thompson, Erol Josue, Anne-Louise Mesadieu. Haiti's past as a black republic is evoked by showing it through the mad delusions of Henri Roi Christophe, a former slave who became a 'liberator'. The people of Haiti will probably be the only audiences to know what exactly is going on in this plodding, poorly etched, theatrical picture.

Royal Journey (1952) (65mins) d: David Bairstow Technical credits: Tom Daly, Grant McLean, Gerald Graham and others. Narrator Lorne Greene. This historic film is best described in the words of Gerald Graham: "External Affairs was advised that Queen Elizabeth and Prince Philip would tour Canada in the late fall of 1951. There was no Canadian colour television network to supply national coverage of the event so NFB was called in to provide theatrical film coverage. Arthur Irwin, newly arrived Film Commissioner requested an immediate response from the producer, Tom Daly and me on how this could be accomplished. The main problem was choice of a suitable colour film process for this purpose. Technicolor, the standard theatrical system, was excellent but required cumbersome 3-strip cameras plus use of their crews and consultant who would have overriding control of shooting conditions. Fine for a large studio with a contained shooting environment but hopeless for a subject which could neither be scripted nor directed. Fortunately, the NFB Technical Research Division had been experimenting with a number of 35mm colour film systems which appeared at the close of World War II. Tests had been made on Ansco Color, Dufaycolor, Cinecolor, Gevacolor and Ferrania color, the major commercial systems available at that time. All had shown inconsistent colour quality. Luckily, in 1951, we had started assessing a new Kodak product,

Ektachrome, which looked promising. It was a neg/pos process which could produce duplicate negatives for alternate language versions and archival storage. However, it was still a research laboratory product not yet generally released on the open market. Tom and I recommended this untried colour system to Arthur Irwin, who did not know or trust NFB personnel at that time. We got a reluctant approval with the inference that heads would roll in the event of failure. On the technical side the first step was to obtain meteorological records covering late fall weather patterns along the route for the preceding five years. As anticipated the prospects were ominous, rain, fog, overcast skies and possibly snow could be expected across Canada. So, our planning tests were conducted mainly during variable weather conditions. After all, any colour process would look good on a sunny autumn day so why waste film confirming this fact! The Royal Visit was shot by a superb crew of NFB cameramen supervised by Grant McLean. Two teams leapfrogged each other along the itinerary so that we could catch both arrivals and departures of the Royal Couple. Exposed camera negatives were returned by courier to Ottawa on Trans Canada Airlines and were then escorted by Fin Quinn or one of the other technical staff members to and from the Duart Laboratory in New York. As the first processed rushes arrived back in Ottawa it was apparent that we had a winner and Arthur Irwin began to breathe again. Since the final assembly would simply follow the itinerary in chronological sequences editing and development of the commentary could proceed as the rushes came in. This speeded up the timetable for negative cutting, opticals, titles and track laying for final sound recording significantly. Within ten days after the departure of the Royal Couple release prints were being shown in all major Canadian theatres. To top off this stellar team performance, with the help of the Canadian Air Force, a jet fighter delivered presentation copies to Buckingham Palace before the royal yacht *Britannia* docked in England. *Royal Journey* was the Board's first feature length production; it was seen by over two million people within two months of release, and it recovered all production costs and yielded a profit. The title appears in the *Book of Firsts* (Melvin Harris), where it is confirmed as the first use of Eastman Kodak's negative/positive colour film in a theatrical feature. Of more significance to the NFB staff, its favourable reception as Canada's sole means of international visual communication was a major factor in saving the Board from possible dissolution in the Massey Royal Commission's Report on Development in the Arts, Letters and Sciences." (Gerald Graham was Director of Technical Operations and research at the NFB 1944–1964. He is the author of *Canadian Film Technology* (1896–1986), published by the Associated University Press.) *Royal Journey* has taken its place as one of the great documentaries in the history of the Canadian film/documentary and the NFB)

Royal Scandal, The (2001) (120mins) d: Rodney Gibbons s: Joe Wiesenfeld (from the book by Sir Arthur Conan Doyle) : Matthew Frewer, R.H. Thomson, Kenneth Welsh, Robin Wilcox, Liliana Komorowska, Seann Gallagher, Daniel Brochu. Holmes and Watson are back in London (Montréal serves well as Baker Street) after their India adventure. They promptly become involved with royalty when the prince of Bohemia asks for assistance after finding compromising pictures of himself with a wily beauty. Holmes has little time for this, but faithful to his calling, he discovers that there's more than meets an eye in a photograph. Fascinating, with dry humour and a good plot, of course. (See: *Sherlock Holmes* series)

Royaume ou l'asile, Le: see **Kingdom or the Asylum, The**

Rub & Tug (2002) (90mins) d: Soo Lyu s: Edward Stanulis, Soo Lyu : Don McKellar, Kira Clavell, Tara Spencer-Nairn, Lindy Booth. An unpleasant sex comedy set in a male massage parlour, where the owner discovers that three of his girls are providing "full service" to the customers. He hires a manager who also becomes caught up in this boring, sordid portrayal of women, although the actresses who agreed to play their roles obviously didn't think so. Audiences for this film will need a bath afterwards, not a massage.

Rubber Carpet (1995) (82mins) (b/w) d: John May s: Suzanne Bolch : Jonathan Wilson, Judy Coffey, Peter Coffey, Richard Sali, Barry Stevens, Tina Lalka. More character studies with lessons on morality. Seen through the eyes of a café dish washer and his two friends. Effective, if not a complete success in touching on work-day routine.

Rubber Gun, The (1977) (86mins) d: Allan Moyle s: Stephen Lack, John Laing, Allan Moyle : Stephen Lack, Allan Moyle, Pam Holmes-Robert, Pierre Robert, Peter Brawley. A co-operative, self-indulgent, semi-biographical study of a peculiar art dealer, played somewhat self-consciously by Stephen Lack, and his involvement with a group of drug users.

Rude (1995) (88mins) d&s: Clement Virgo : Maurice Dean Wint, Rachel Crawford, Clark Johnson, Richard Chevolleau, Sharon Lewis, Melanie Nicholls-King, Stephen Shellen. A first feature by Jamaican filmmakers in Toronto depicting three characters trapped in the low-life of the city's downtown district. Somewhat murky in its unfolding, the characters are lively if not always clear. The imaginative stylization provides an impressive look to the whole. "Rude" is a provacative, peculiar, baleful lady d.j. on a local "private" radio station. All sin and redemption.

Ruffian, The (1983) (108mins) (a Canada-France co-production) d: Jose Giovanni s: Jose Giovanni (based on his novel *Le Ruffian*) : Lino Ventura,

Bernard Giraudeau, Claudia Cardinale, Beatrix Van Til, Pierre Frag, August Schellenberg. Outdoor drama set in the Canadian north where a gold miner lives through conflicts between other miners and then travels to Montréal to use the money he has made to care for a friend in need of medical attention. He then returns to the gold mines to continue working. An unusual depiction of immigrant life, sympathetic and revealing.

Run for it, Lola! (*Sauve-toi, Lola*) (1986) (106mins) d: Michel Drach s: Jacques Kirsner (based on the book of the same title by Ania Francos) : Carole Laure, Jeanne Moreau, Dominique Labourier. A small but telling personal drama about a lawyer who learns that she has cancer, and leaves her journalist lover to concentrate on restoring her health. It could run faster.

Running (1979) (101mins) (a Canadian-American film) d&s: Steven Hilliard Stern : Michael Douglas, Susan Anspach, Lawrence Dane, Eugene Levy, Chuck Shamata, Trudy Young, Murray Westgate. An unemployed American father of two comes to Canada to compete at the Montréal Olympics. Absurd melodrama straining for laughs as it runs. One of the several films made by producers taking advantage of the Capital Cost Allowance Act.

Running Brave (1983) (106mins) d: D.S. Everett (Donald Shebib) s: Henry Bean, Shirley Hendryx : Robby Benson, Pat Hingle, Claudia Cron, Jeff McCracken, August Schellenberg, Denis Lacroix, Graham Greene, Margo Kane, George Clutesi, Maurice Wolfe, Francis Damberger, Thomas Peacocke. On October 14, 1964, in Tokyo, Japan, Lieutenant Billy Mills, an American Indian running for the U.S. Marine Corps, edged out world record holders Ron Clark of Australia and Mohamed Gammoudi of Tunisia to win the gold medal in the 10,000-metre run. The race was regarded by many as the most remarkable result in the history of the Olympic Games. To date, Mills remains the only American to have won that event. This is a Canadian film financed by the Ermineskin Band of Cree, who saw in the story an opportunity to depict their history in a positive light. It was filmed entirely in Alberta, with Drumheller being used for the South Dakota reservation and the University of Alberta in Edmonton serving as the University of Kansas. Edmonton's Commonwealth Stadium was used to recreate the famous race. The story strikes a commendable balance between sports and social situations relating to the poverty and discrimination borne by the Indians. But many individuals question whether or not the $8 million spent by the Cree could not have been better used to improve the present day way of life of Canada's native peoples. (Donald Shebib did not agree with producer Ira Englander's final version and had his name removed from the credits, but the film remains a tribute to Shebib's remarkable direction.)

Running Man (1980) (65mins) d: Donald Brittain s: Anna Sandor : Chuck Shamata, Barbara Gordon, Dennis Hayes, Donald Scanlan, Colm Feore, David Field, Linda Sorenson, Kate Trotter. A married high-school teacher who is the father of two children and deeply in love with his wife has tried for most of his adult life to deny the fact that he is homosexual. He knows that he must finally learn to face reality and to deal with it, within himself, in his work, and with his wife. A moving and compassionate work. This was the first dramatic film to be directed by documentary filmmaker Donald Brittain. At the time of filming, he made the following observation: "This fictional film gives the director the responsibility of creating the reality of the life he is showing. With documentary the director stays in the background and lets the reality unfold before him. Now I can impose a presence." (See: *For the Record*)

Running Time (1978) (80mins) d&s: Mort Ransen : Jackie Burroughs, David Balser, Gerard Parkes, Richard Raxlen, Ken James, Sandy Webster, Ryan Larkin, Judith Gault, Larry Kent. An uncertain mixture of comedy and music involving an old lady in Montréal, a group of young schoolboys and the eccentric behaviour of middle-aged friends. (An earlier treatment perhaps of the theme of the later film *Touched* by Ransen in 1999?)

Rupert's Land (1998) (94mins) d: Jonathan Tammuz s: Graeme Manson : Samuel West, Ian Tracey, George Wendt, Susan Hogan, Gabrielle Miller, William MacDonald. Rupert, a somewhat formal British lawyer, and his half-brother Dale, a loveable fisherman, drive on a three-day trip from Vancouver to the town of Prince Rupert to attend their father's funeral. On their way they meet a motley crew of bizarre drinking and drug-taking characters who are meant, it seems, to be funny. The scenery is beautiful and makes the trip worthwhile.

Ruth (1994) (75mins) d&s: François Delisle : Ariane Frédérique, Frédéric Teyssier, Emmanuel Bilodeau, Micheline Lanctôt. Ruth is a bored, headstrong and impulsive teenager (aren't they all?) living in a drab town in Québec who goes to live with her journalist brother and then falls in love with his best friend. Middling and uneven.

Ryan's Babe (2000) (87mins) d: Ray Ramayya s: Mel Goldman : William Lavasseur, Alix Hitching, Katherine Rossini. A young man drives out of town to escape his troubles with girlfriends only to find himself in a series of mishaps. Ridiculous and boring beyond belief.

S Day (*Le jour S*) (1984) (87mins) d&s: Jean-Pierre Lefebvre : Pierre Curzi, Marie Tifo, Marcel Sabourin, Simon Esterez, Benoît Castel. Think of "S" says Jean-Pierre Lefebvre, as in "smile," "satire," "symbol," "surrealism," "sexuality." One morning, the hero, Jean-Baptiste, is eagerly awaiting his girlfriend, Claire, an actress who is returning that same evening to Montréal after shooting a TV commercial in Toronto. Jean-Baptiste has nothing special to do but contemplate the approach of his fortieth birthday and he falls into a mood of introspection. His thoughts centre on his relations with women and, so preoccupied, he goes walking and in all innocence provokes a series of meetings and events. Before the day is over, the coincidences multiply, reviving the fantasies of his childhood, his adolescence, his first marriage and divorce, until finally he is reunited with Claire and brought back to the present. Once again, Lefebvre takes an ordinary man and some commonplace thoughts and spins them into a likeable and affecting revue touching on the pleasures and banality of life. Marie Tifo is delightful playing all the women he encounters.

Sable Island: see *Île de Sable, L'*

Sacrifice, The (*La sacrifiée*) (1955) (94mins) (b/w) d: Benjamin Bélisle s: Paul Gauthier : Pierrette Gosselin, Denise Bourque, Thérèse Bourque, René Gamache, Jean Morin. A young woman is secretly in love with a young doctor, who has similar undeclared feelings for her. However, her sister is jealous of this relationship and wants to destroy it, so she declares her own love for the doctor. This complicates matters and the other sister leaves for a convent. Shot on location in 16mm in Chicoutimi, Jonquière, L'Ilset-sur-Mer, Montmagny, and in the main centres of Lac St-Jean and Abitibi in the autumn and winter of 1955, this was very much a co-operative venture, although Bélisle financed the whole production. It was both his and Gauthier's first feature, designed more as a learning project than a film that would be released. It was shot when those involved could take time away from their regular jobs and consequently was quite difficult to make. Bélisle has made only one other feature, *L'amour du couple* (1973).

Sadness of the Moon: see **Skin Deep**

Sadness, Reduced to Go (*Tristesse modèle réduit*) (1987) (83mins) d&s: Robert Morin : Vincent Leduc, Marcia Pilote. A small two-character film about family relations. A mentally handicapped young man is encouraged by the family's servant to develop feelings of independence. Feeling much better as a result of this encouragement, he leaves his family. Convincingly played out in suburban Montréal. A simple, direct, affecting portrayal.

Saint Jude (2000) (93mins) d: John L'Écuyer s: Heather O'Neil : Nicholas Campbell, Raymond Cloutier, Bernie Coulson, Liane Balaban, Louise Portal, Victoria Sanchez. Loose girls and leering men in Montréal's underground of drugs, sex and violence. Nicholas Campbell, always to be relied upon to provide truthful performances, appears here as an unpleasant father with designs on his daughter. With its narrative of muddled and shapeless conversations, the film crawls along, flounders and eventually falls apart. Some knowing performances here and there cannot save this saint from ultimate obscurity.

Saint Monica (2002) (82mins) d&s: Terrance Odette : Genevieve Buechner, Clare Coulter, Maurizio Terrazzano, Brigitte Bako, Krista Bridges. Set in Toronto's Portuguese community, this slight story brings us a 10-year-old girl living with a shouting mother and an indifferent uncle. The girl attends church and wants to be an archangel in the church procession. When she is not chosen, she steals the pair of immense wings she would wear, and then loses them on a streetcar. Now she meets a tiresome homeless woman she believes is the Virgin Mary. One thing slowly leads to another, but it's hard to become caught up in any of it. The Vatican would probably disagree.

Salem Witch Trials (2001) (240mins) (a U.S.-Canada film) d: Joseph Sargent s: Maria Nation : Kirstie Alley, Henry Czerny, Jay Sanders, Susan Coyne, Gloria Reuben, Alan Bates, Rebecca De Mornay, Peter Ustinov, Shirley MacLaine. Arthur Miller's classic play *The Crucible*, 1953 about the Salem witch hunts, came to the screen in a French-German version in 1956 and in the first American version in 1996. This latest version tells its own story minus Miller but stays very close to what happened in Salem when a child's affliction with fits and convulsions sent the Puritans looking to religion and the supernatural for answers bringing about the hunt for "witches" all women who are hanged, murdered and drowned. This is a fine rendition and telling of this black chapter in history and one in which so many events happening today bear a terrible likeness to this portrait if mass hysteria in the name of religion. The cast is exemplary.

Sally Fieldgood and Co. (1975) (82mins) d: Boon Collins s: Barry Pearson, Boon Collins : Hagan Beggs, Liza Creighton, Lee Broker, Valerie Ambrose, Brian Brown, Anne Cameron. Set in British Columbia, this is a colourful and lusty pioneer times comedy about a prostitute who travels between mining camps in her horse-drawn carriage. Just about every situation one can think of turns up to add to the merriment.

Sally Marshall Is Not An Alien (1999) (97mins) (a Canada-Australia co-production) d: Mario Andreacchio s: Robert Geoffrion, Amanda McKay (based on her novel) : Helen Neville, Natalie Vansier, Thea Gumbert, Glenn McMillan, Danielle de Grossi . A film about children for children. A new family arrives next door and are soon thought to be from another planet because they are a bit unusual. The setting is Adelaide, South Australia, and the message of tolerance and understanding is effectively conveyed.

Salt Water Moose (1996) (98mins) d: Stuart Margolin : Timothy Dalton, Lolita Davidovich, Johnny Morina, Katharine Isobel. A reliable cast in a slight film about a family who leave Toronto to spend summer with grandmother in Nova Scotia. Bobby meets Jo and agrees to help her capture a young female moose and sail her over to Rock Island to keep company with a lonely bull moose. Tax credits come into the game somewhere, and bull or no bull, the producer is hardly likely to be left stranded. A perfect family film.

Salut! J.W. (1981) (87mins) d&s: Ian Ireland : Ian Ireland, Louise Laparé, Nathalie Naubert, Marcel Sabourin, Anouk Simard, Claire Pimparé. In this clever and unusual treatment of the eternal triangle, we find a number of sad yet amusing twists when an actor whose marriage has recently ended falls in love with an actress appearing with him in a film. She loves him too, and soon they go to dinner at the home of his best friend, whose lover turns out to be the ex-mistress of the actress' husband. Quite moving in trying to come to terms with whom we love and why.

Salut, Victor! (1988) (84mins) d: Anne-Claire Poirier s: Marthe Blackburn, Anne-Claire Poirier (based on the novel *Matthew and Chauncey* by Edward Phillips) : Jean-Louis Roux, Jacques Godin, Julie Vincent, Murielle Dutil. Two homosexuals living in a senior citizens' home in Montréal are opposites to each other in their characters and manners; one is open and impudent, the other quiet and repressed. After getting to know each other they become firm friends. An honest and understanding study, well played and developed.

Sam and Me (1991) (94mins) d: Deepa Mehta s: Ranjit Chowdhry : Ranjit Chowdhry, Peter Boretski, Heath Lamberts, Kulbushan Kharbanda, Javed Jafri. A family flare-up concerning a nephew of an overbearing East Indian doctor who comes to Toronto to take care of an elderly Jewish man, considered to be awkward to manage. The entire film is awkwardly managed.

Same Blood, The: see *Même sang, Un*

Samuel Lount (1985) (96mins) d: Laurence Keane s: Philip Savath, Laurence Keane : R.H. Thomson, Linda Griffiths, Cedric Smith, Donald Davis, Christopher Newton, Richard Donat, David Fox, Booth Savage. Samuel Lount was a pioneer, a blacksmith and a pacifist. All would have been well for him and his family had he not joined the 1837 Rebellion, in which he lost his life, leaving his hard-working wife Elizabeth to keep a primitive home together. Filmed where the events occurred around Hamilton and Niagara-on-the-Lake, Ontario, this is more a statement of fact than a dramatized chapter of history. Cedric Smith as William Lyon Mackenzie provides us with a portrait of one of our prime ministers to add to the meagre library of Canadian PMs on film. And Linda Griffiths is fine as Elizabeth Lount.

Sang des autres, Le: see **Blood of Others, The**

Sang du chasseur , Le: see **Blood of the Hunter**

Sanity Clause (1990) (98mins) d: George McCowan s: Neil Ross, Louis del Grande : Louis del Grande, Martha Gibson, Booth Savage, Susan Roman. When the residents are thrown out of a group home for mentally ill people, the couple who manage and administer the premises go searching for new homes and justice for one tenant who had his invention stolen. A comedy under these circumstances might seem in bad taste, but the cast, led by comedian Del Grande, manages to keep it human and caring.

Sarabande (1997) (56mins) d&s: Atom Egoyan : Yo Yo Ma, Lori Singer, Arsinée Khanjian, Jan Rubes, Don McKellar, George Sperdakos, David Hemblem. Made as part of a series of six short films under the generic title Yo Yo Ma. Inspired by Bach, this film by Egoyan tells a fictional story about a number of incidents taking place with the arrival in Toronto of Yo Yo Ma. Somewhat strained and only just managing to keep the audience's attention for its brief running time. Bach's Suite No. 4 for cello holds it together. Unusual but hardly inspiring.

Saracen, The (La Sarrasine) (1991) (105mins) (a Canada-Italy co-production) d: Paul Tana s: Bruno Ramirez, Paul Tana : Enrica Maria Modugno, Tony Nardi, Jean Lapointe, Gilbert Sicotte. Set in Montréal in 1904, this melodramatic retelling of the conflict and struggle between Italian immigrants and French Canadians concerns an Italian tailor unfairly accused of the murder of a Québécois shopkeeper. The tailor's wife refuses to return to Sicily, preferring Québec in spite of the social strife. Well played and compelling with the ring of truth despite the treatment.

Saturday's Passage (1969) (89mins) d&s: Edward Bridgewater : Russ Waller, Marvel Cairns, Bert De Vries, Gordon Robertson, John Macdonald. An ambitious film made at Queen's University in Kingston, Ontario, by a group of students and included here as it might well be termed the beginning of student feature-film making. A futuristic story of an enormous catastrophe that destroys the people of the world except for a few who escape to the countryside to live off the land. An early warning perhaps. A bit overdone but good for its time.

Sauve-toi, Lola: see **Run for it, Lola!**

Savage Autumn, The: see *Automne sauvage, L'*

Savage Messiah (2001) (120mins) (a Canada-UK-German co-production) d: Mario Azzopardi s: Sharon Riis (based on the novel of the same name by Paul Kaihla and Ross Laver) : Polly Walker, Luc Picard, Isabelle Blais, Isabelle Cyr, Julie Larochelle, Pascale Montpetit, Elizabeth Robinson, Domini Blythe. This extraordinary motion picture, easily among the best Canadian films, tells the true story of a religious fanatic, abusive and diabolical, in a Quebec-Onartio town and countryside, who commanded his harem of eight 'wives' along with 26 children, and tormented and tortured them with physical, and sexual and psychological abuse. It's so well made and acted it fills the spectator with horror and despair over what this madman got away with for so long. Justice was blind, 'he's not such a bad fellow', loves to laugh and drink, all in the name of God, the social workers looked the other way, all but one who having lived through a violent marriage herself, tire-

lessly keeps after 'Moses'as he called himself, and at last brings him to trial. He receives a life sentence, but is deemed suitable for early parole. It all defies credibility and common sense. This is a great film, with powerful, deeply moving performances. Another memorable achievement by producer, Bernard Zukerman. It is not Moses alone this story deals with, but the causes which drove lonely women into his treacherous embrace. Luc Picard is cunning and frightening as he was in *The Collector*.

Say Nothing (2001) (94mins) (a U.S.-Canada film) d: Allan Moyle s: Madeline Sunshine : Nastassja Kinski, William Baldwin, Hart Bochner, Michelle Duquet, Jordy Benattar. A slow-moving thriller about a wife, husband and children, and a boss who slept with the wife while she was on holiday in Miami. For this, he arranges for the husband to get a top job in the firm. Miami looks very colourful and that's about it.

Scandale (1982) (96mins) d: George Mihalka s: Robert Geoffrion : Sophie Lorain, Alpha Boucher, Gilbert Comtois, François Trottier, Nanette Workman. A low-budget quickie made to cash in on the alleged use of video equipment by the staff of the Québec legislature to make a porno picture. At first a very funny spoof, it turns sour when hard-core performance is introduced.

Scanner Cop (1994) (94mins) (a Canadian-American film) d: Pierre David s: John Bryant, George Saunders : Daniel Quinn, Darlanne Fluegel, Richard Grove, Mark Rolston, Richard Lynch, Hilary Shepard, James Horon. More excuses to blow people up. A "scanner" since childhood is afraid his powers will destroy him and goes after an evil scientist who is making it possible for people to kill policemen. Awful and, like its victims, brainless.

Scanner Cop II: Volkin's Revenge: see **Scanners: The Showdown**

Scanners (1981) (103mins) (a Canada-U.S. film) d&s: David Cronenberg : Jennifer O'Neill, Stephen Lack, Patrick McGoohan, Lawrence Dane, Michael Ironside, Robert Silverman, Lee Broker, Mavor Moore, Louis del Grande, Victor Knight, Chuck Shamata. Scanners are superbrain scientists who track down the bad ones and blow up their heads. Ugly, bloody, messy and morbid. Followed by a chain of worse examples.

Scanners II: The New Order (1991) (105mins) (a Canada-U.S. film) d: Christian Duguay s: B.J. Nelson : David Hewlett, Deborah Raffin, Yvan Ponton, Isabelle Mejias, Tom Butler, Raoul Trujillo. Police join forces with the scientists to trap scanners. More of the same, but Cronenberg not involved in this or any of the following.

Scanners III: The Takeover (1992) (101mins) (a Canada-U.S. film) d: Christian Duguay s: B.J. Nelson : Liliana Komorowska, Valerie Valois, Daniel Pilon, Colin Fox, Claire Cellucci, Michael Copeman, Steve Parrish. A new drug turns good scanners into bad ones. Telekinetic tripe bathed in blood.

Scanners: The Showdown (Scanner Cop II: Volkin's Revenge) (1994) (95mins) (a Canadian-American film) d: Steve Barnett s: B.J. Nelson : Daniel Quinn, Patrick Kilpatrick, Khrystyne Haje, Stephen Mendel, Robert Forster, Brenda Swanson. Attempting to pick up from where *Scanner Cop* blew up, we now have scanners sucking the life out of other scanners. Anyone who can enjoy this needs a scan badly. Horrid, heartless, and hellish. David C., what hast thou brought upon us!

Scar Tissue (2002) (120mins) d: Peter Moss s: Dennis Foon (from Michael Ignatieff's novel) : Roberta Maxwell, Aidan Devine, Shawn Doyle, Paul Hecht. This is a searching, affecting and sensitively depicted portrayal of a mother's struggle with Alzheimer's. Once an acclaimed artist, she ceased painting at the height of her success, without understanding why. Her son is a doctor, who feels that she is following her mother and grandmother—who died from the same disease. Her brother hopes that this is not to be. The tragedy deepens when the father of the family, worn down by anxiety, suffers a heart attack and dies. The complications do not end here, however, and the torments continue to take their toll. This is not melodrama, but concerned and sensitive drama, beautifully acted and honestly depicted with a message that is not to be ignored.

Scarlatina: see **Push but Push Reasonably**

School's Out! The Degrassi Feature (1992) (93mins) d: Kit Hood s: Yan Moore : Pat Mastroianni, Stacie Mistysyn and others. A slight feature film based on the over-praised tv series. It deals with the lives and antics of students in a school set in an ethnic neighbourhood that never lets on it's in Toronto.

Scoop (1978) (60mins) d: Anthony Perris s: Douglas Bowie : Scott Hylands, Lloyd Bochner, Deborah Templeton, Sabina Maydelle, David Stein, Moses Znaimer, Marvin Goldhar. A ruthless journalist steals evidence from another journalist that incriminates the wife of a cabinet minister in a hit-and-run accident that left a young girl paralyzed. The minister has set his sights on becoming the next premier and a scandal such as this would rule him out of the running. The journalist, as a price for silence, blackmails the minister into giving him an important position on his staff. A disturbing look at what goes on behind the scenes in politics and publishing. All too true one fears.

Scorn (2000) (120mins) d: Sturla Gunnarsson s: Andrew Rai Berzins (based on the book *Such a Good Boy* by Lisa Hobbs Birnie) : Eric Johnson, Brendan Fletcher, Bill Switzer. Recounts the actual case in which a mentally ill teenager obsessed with taking over the country of Brunei enlists two friends to help him murder his mother and grandmother to collect an inheritance. Intelligently written, with powerful performances, imaginative direction, and frightening in the extreme that such a crime was possible.

Scream for Silence, A (*Mourir à tue-tête***)** (1979) (95mins) d&s: Anne-Claire Poirier : Julie Vincent, Germain Houde, Paul Savoie, Monique Miller, Micheline Lanctôt, Louise Portal. Anne-Claire Poirier dramatizes the effects and consequences of rape. Intense, powerful and deeply moving.

Scream of Stone (*Terro Torra***)** (1991) (95mins) (a Canada-France-German-Italian-Swiss co-production) d: Werner Herzog s: Hans-Ulrich Kienner, Walter Saxer, Robert Geoffrion : Donald Sutherland, Vittorio Mezzogiorno, Stefan Glowacz, Mathilda May, Al Waxman, Gunilla Karlzen, Brad Dourif, Werner Herzog. In this Euro-pudd-mish-mash by the over-rated German director, Herzog, our Donald, with waxed moustache, a tired face, and wearing a loosely fitting big black coat, plays a conniving tv journalist who starts a rivalry between two world-famous mountain climbers to discover the best of the two. Filmed in Argentina, the setting is Patagonia. Most of the mountain climbing is studio work adroitly mixed with the real thing and deftly edited to provide audiences with expected chills. Perhaps a study in fear, but strictly for mountain climbers, otherwise a big bore. One hears a lot about the silence of being in the mountains. Not here, this film has the noisiest soundtrack, ending with great doses of Wagner's *Tristan and Isolda*. The cast is almost entirely Euro and we care nothing for any of them.

Screamers (1995) (107mins) d: Christian Duguay s: Dan O'Bannon (from the story *Second Variety* by Philip Dick) : Peter Weller, Roy Dupuis, Jennifer Rubin, Andrew Lauer, Charles Powell, Ronald White, Michael Caloz, Liliana Komorowska. A better-than-average sci-fi horror in which "screamers," self-creating robots, are out to kill the survivors from a distant planet devastated by war. Lots of thrills and action, all very convincing, except for the closing events.

Screwball Academy (Divine Light) (Loose Ends) (1986) (87mins) d: John Blanchard s: David Mitchell, Michael Paseornek, Charles Dennis : Colleen Camp, Kenneth Welsh, Christine Cattell, Charles Dennis, Damian Lee, Henry Ramer, Shirley Douglas, Sonja Smits. A feeble teenage comedy taking place on a beach with predictable laugh and leer results. The first of the *Meatballs* imitations. Good players working with thin material.

Screwballs (1983) (80mins) (a Canadian-American film) d: Rafal Zielinski s: Linda Shayne, Jim Wynorski : Peter Keleghan, Kent Deuters, Linda Speciale, Alan Deveau, Linda Shayne. A witless, tasteless, vulgar excursion into teenage sex antics with boys leering at girls' breasts.

Screwballs II: Loose Screws (1985) (92mins) (a Canadian-American film) d: Rafal Zielinski s: Michael Cory : Bryan Genesse, Lance Van der Kolk, Alan Deveau, Karen Wood, Annie McAuley, Liz Green More of the same; debases characters and audiences alike.

Sea People (1999) (92mins) (a Canadian-American film) d: Vic Sarin s: Christopher Hawthorne, Wendy

Biller : Hume Cronyn, Joan Gregson, Tegan Moss, Shawn Roberts, Don McKellar. A 14-year-old girl living in a small town in Nova Scotia dreams of fulfilling her ambition to swim the English Channel. She meets a mysterious couple who have a magical relationship with the sea, and her life changes as a result. An odd family film not without charm and poignancy.

Sea Wolf, The (1993) (95 mins) (a U.S.-Canada film) d: Michael Anderson s: Andrew J. Fenady (from the book by Jack London) : Charles Bronson, Christopher Reeves, Catherine Mary Stewart, Len Cariou, Clive Revill. Yet another version of the London story: a writer has an accident with his boat, and he and a lady companion are saved by Captain Wolf Larsen, who turns out to be a dangerous psycho. Anderson has difficulty trying to catch up with Curtiz and Edward G. (1941)

Search and Destroy (1979) (93mins) (a Canada-U.S. co-production) d: William Fruet s: Donald Enright : Perry King, Donald Stroud, Tisa Farrow, George Kennedy, Park Jong Soo. A former South Vietnamese official plots to take revenge for U.S. involvement in the Vietnam War by taking it out on two American soldiers. Gives us a different look at this conflict but could have used more drama and drive.

Searching for Diana (1992) (95mins) d: Milad Bessada s: Maissa Bessada-Patton, Milad Bessada : Diana Calenti, Brett Halsey, Janet Richardson, Jan Filips, Corinne Conley. A fairy-tale dance film alternating between Canada and Egypt in which a beautiful dancer is inspired by her mysterious visions. Dreamy and well intentioned but hardly convincing.

Seasons in the Sun (1986) (74mins) d: Ain Sooder s: Joan Bachman-Singer : Kathryn Witt, John Ireland, Carol Bagdasarian, Michael Vale, John Quade, Maxine Nunes, Terry Jacks. Suffering from a serious disease, a man is told he has half a chance of surviving the next 18 months. To make the most of his limited future he moves to the country where he becomes a tool of espionage agents. Firmly done with winning performances and a neat script.

Seat of the Soul, The (Crisis of Conscience, A) (Le siege de l'âme) (1997) (101mins) d&s: Olivier Asselin : Emmanuel Bilodeau, Lucille Fluet, Remy Girard, Ronald Houle, Luc Durand. At the end of the 19TH century, in a gloomy city where death is on everyone's mind, a young researcher dreams of and believes in the existence of the soul. One day a mummy is found, its heart still beating. From then on it's an existential frenzy. A brave, bold film the likes of which we have never seen before, and being decidedly out of this world, while still being a part of it, gives the audience a great deal to think about. Marvelously well done in atmosphere, place and character. This is not run-of-the-mill sci-fi junk.

Seaway: see **Don't Forget to Wipe the Blood Off**

Second Skin (2000) (95mins) (a Canada-U.K.-S.

Africa co-production) d: Darrell Roodt s: John Lau : Peter Fonda, Angus MacFadyen, Natasha Henstridge, Liam Waite, Norman Anstey, André Jacobs. A new girl comes to town (which one we are never told) and is promptly hit by a car and loses her memory. The owner of a bookstore becomes drawn into a deadly scandal, part of the woman's mysterious past, with gangsters galore. The mystery is, how ever did this get made?

Second Wind (1976) (93mins) d: Donald Shebib s: Hal Ackerman : James Naughton, Lindsay Wagner, Kenneth Pogue, Tedde Moore, Tom Harvey, Louis del Grande, Gerard Parkes, Jonathan Welsh, Cec Linder, Allan Levson, Robert Goodier. A stylish film nicely played out from Shebib, but one with little wind as we meet an American couple in Toronto whose marriage isn't working because the husband goes out running. The script also runs away, becoming slight and superficial with no answer to the questions it poses.

Secondary High (2003) (90mins) d&s: Pat Mills, Emily Halfon & Hazel Bell-Koski : Alyson Richards, Bubba, Catherine Bertin, Daniel Levesque, Katy Gilliam, Pat Mills. A film about being gay from Ryerson University students telling three separate stories. Absurdist and surreal humour abounds, bewildering, and muddled, involving a class-size collection of crazy youths whose efforts to entertain are mostly in vain. The last part however, where they appear as an all-girl punk band called appropriately enough Six Healthy Fists, is funny, enjoyable, lively and listenable.

Secret Ballot (Raye Makhfi) (2001) (105mins) (a Canada-Italy-Iran-Swiss co-production) d&s: Babak Payami : Nassim Abdi, Cyrus Abidi, Youssef Habashi, Farrokh Shojail, Gholbahar Janghali. There's not much here to reflect any Canadian content, but nevertheless this is a delightful film finding the funny side to voting in Iran. The film reflects the simplicity of a fairy tale but with the underlying awareness that finding a path to introduce democracy into a once totalitarian state is difficult and still dangerous.

Secret de banlieue, Un (The Secret of a Suburb) (2002) (90mins) d: Louis Choquette s: Annie Pierard, Bernard Dansereau : Jean-Francois Pichette, Élise Guilbault, Roxanne Loiseau, Joannie Lemay, Louisette Dussault, Josee Deschenes. More tangled lives and emotional torment—this time concerning teenage girls, their parents, criss-cross relationships, anguish, fear and sexual temptations. At first it seems to be another Bad Seed brat, but no, it is a father suffering from madness who becomes the key. But as nearly always in a Québec movie, all this is genuine, heartfelt and absorbing to watch. The cast knows what is expected of it and comes through with conviction.

Secret de Jérôme, Le: see **Secret of Jerome, The**

Secret Laughter of Women, The (1999) (99mins) (a Canada-U.K. co-production) d: Peter Schwabach s: O.O. Sagay : Colin Firth, Nia Long, Fissy Roberts, Caroline Goodall, Dan Lett, Joke Jacobs, Ariyon Bakare, Joy Elias Rilwan, Hakim Kae-Kazim, Bella Enahoro, Rakie Ayola. Not much if any Canadian content here as we find ourselves in the home of an English comic-book writer on the French Riviera where he begins an affair with a young Nigerian woman to the dismay of her family and friends. The secret laughter is hard to hear.

Secret Life of Algernon, The (1996) (104mins) (a Canadian-American film) d: Charles Jarrott s: John Cullum, John Gray (adapted from Russell Greenan's novel) : John Cullum, Carrie-Anne Moss, Charles Durning, Hrant Alianak, Kay Hawtrey, Ivan Van Hecke. Filmed mainly in New Brunswick, this is an exotic tale steeped in Egyptology. Algernon lives a quiet and reclusive life in the home of his great-grandfather (a famous Egyptian explorer) who is buried in a graveyard behind his house. When an old friend of Algernon turns up with tales about fabulous treasures, his life falls apart. Part comedy and drama, well paced and acted with no mummies, and certainly different.

Secret Nation (1991) (110mins) d: Michael Jones s: Edward Riche : Cathy Jones, Mary Walsh, Michael Wade, Rick Mercer, Ron Hynes. Canada's famous and outspoken CODCO comedy group, working out of Newfoundland and enjoying great success on stage and television, has made its second film (the first was *The Adventure of Faustus Bidgood*). *Secret Nation* is a political thriller, set in 1949, that supposes that the British and Canadian governments conspired to make certain that when Newfoundland voted to become Canada's tenth province, the vote would be in favour of Confederation. Well acted and skilfully contrived for the most part, with pertinent observations on the personal and national conflicts involved, it unfortunately collapses into comic absurdity.

Secret of a Suburb, The: see *Secret de banlieue ,Un*

Secret of Jerome (Jerome's Secret) (*Le secret de Jérôme*) (1994) (99mins) d&s: Phil Comeau : Myriam Cyr, Germain Houde, Rémy Girard, Denis Lapalme, Andrea Parro, Viola Léger, Lionel Doucette, Neil Thompson. This is the first Acadian feature-length film, based on a mysterious folk tale in which a mute, young, legless man is found on a beach in September 1863. He is taken in by Jean, known as the Corsican, and his brave, childless, high-spirited wife. Soon she and Jean are at odds over the stranger in their home. This is a striking film, free from melodrama, both humorous and dramatic, well acted and showing a society unknown to us.

Secret of Nandy, The (1991) (92mins) d: Danièle Suissa s: Pierre Billon, Donald Martin : Bibi Andersson, Michael Sarrazin, Marc de Jonge, Claudine Auger, Yvette Brind'Amour. Two sisters lived on the Nandy estate, one died. Now, the remaining one still living in the house finds herself being haunt-ed by objects, messages, phone calls and all the spooky moments that come with haunted houses. She is forced to unravel the frightening secret of the past. On the whole, a peaceful ghost story rather than slashers at work. Good cast and atmosphere.

Secret Patrol: see **British Quota Era Films**

Secrets of Chinatown: see **British Quota Era Films**

Seducing Maarya (1999) (107mins) d&s: Hunt Hoe : Nandana Sen, Cas Anvar, Vijay Mehta, Ryan Hollyman, Mohan Agashe. The widowed father of an East Indian family in Montréal finds the "perfect Indian woman" for his Canadian-born son and arranges the marriage. To the father's dismay, the son turns out to be gay and doesn't respond to his wife. The father finds that he himself is in love with her. What next? Family problems know no bounds! Passable, but it's hard to believe.

Seductio (1987) (80mins) d&s: Bashar Shbib : Kathy Horner, Attila Bertalan, Susan Eyton-Jones, Mark Ettlinger. Bashar goes overboard again, this time with an unbalanced woman and friends making a video about seduction and death. For what it is supposed to be, which is in itself a puzzle, this film makes its way creating a sense of doom!

Seeds of Doubt (1997) (93mins) d: Peter Foldy s: David Wiechorek : Peter Coyote, Alberta Watson, Joseph Lando, Colin Fox, Frank Moore. A newspaper reporter is convinced that an artist in prison for murdering a beautiful model is innocent. Her campaigning gets him released but then more murders follow and she becomes a target. But in the background lurks an unknown factor: a detective who thinks the artist was guilty. Or was he? The seeds of doubt take their time to sprout. A good cast does its best with a difficult story.

Seer Was Here (1978) (60mins) d: Claude Jutra s: Donald Bailey, Claude Jutra : Saul Rubinek, Robert Forsythe, Mina E. Mina, Eric Peterson, Martin Short, David Hemblen. Filmed at the Prince Rupert penitentiary in B.C., we meet a mischievous young convict with an unusual sense of humour who brings an element of warmth and humanity to the lives of his fellow prisoners. A clever mixture of sadness and satire, with a touch of Jutra's special comedy. (See: *For the Record*)

Seetha and Carole (1997) (90mins) d&s: Ray Ramayya : Archana, Robert Crowe, P.L. Narayana, Paul Noiles. A married couple have a perfect life in Saskatchewan but a child has not been a part of it. Desperate, they seek a child overseas and find a little boy to adopt in India. But this turns out to be a risky and complicated undertaking and bringing him back to Canada proves to be difficult. Love and compassion bring about a happy ending.

Seizure (Tango Macabre) (1974) (95mins) (a Canada-U.S. co-production) d: Oliver Stone s: Edward Mann, Oliver Stone : Jonathan Frid, Martine Beswick, Joseph Sirola, Christina Pickles, Hervé Villechaize, Mary Woronov, Troy Donahue. Oliver

Stone's first feature is a nightmarish, convoluted horror about a writer and his family who are terrorized by a deadly game forced upon them by three evildoers who might be figments of the imagination—or might be their very own next door neighbours. Much to be preferred to what passes as horror today! Filmed in Québec.

Sensations (1973) (98mins) d&s: Robert Séguin : Marie-Josée Longchamps, Robert DesRoches, Hugo Champagne, André Allaire, Denise Andrieu, Suzanne Langlois, Jacques Bilodeau, Pat Gagnon. A woman and her child are taken hostage by a convict who has escaped from jail in Montreal and is running from the police. They cannot speak to each other because they do not understand one another's language, leading to a violent confrontation. A carefully thought out and sensitively played psychological study of human behaviour under stress.

Senses, The (1996) (425mins) d&s: Bashar Shbib and others : Bashar Shbib and others A compilation work of five 85-minute films, each based on one of the five senses: taste, sight, smell, touch and hearing. A provocative and original interpretation very much in the vein of Shbib's other films. The films are as follows: *Hot Sauce* (Taste), *Taxi to L.A.* (Sight), *The Perfumer* (Smell), *Strictly Spanking* (Touch), *Panic* (Hearing). (Not to be confused with Jeremy Podeswa's 1998 film *The Five Senses*.)

Sentimental Reasons (Death Target) (1984) (90mins) d: Jorge Montesi s: Montesi & Peter Haynes : Jorge Montesi, Elaine Lukeman, Peter Haynes, Arvi Liimatainen, Israel Manchild. Strange friendships are born out of blood and violence. Fifteen years ago, three men fought together in central Africa as mercenaries. But what is it that still makes Alex, Peter and Helmut feel inextricably linked? At first it's a matter of conflict over oil rights. Negotiations fail and the three friends find their lives come crashing down upon them. An unusual and gripping drama with a fascinating backdrop.

Separate Vacations (1986) (90mins) d: Michael Anderson s: Robert Kaufman (based on the novel of the same title by Eric Webber) : Jennifer Dale, David Naughton, Harvey Atkin, Rebecca Jones, Lally Cadeau, Susan Almgren, Mark Keyloun, Blanca Guerra. A married architect goes off to Puerto Vallarta for sex in the sun, leaving his upset wife and children at a ski resort. He finds nothing, but in the wily Canadian way, there's often more sex in the snow, and the wife, well played by Jennifer Dale, doesn't do so badly after all. Minor but often hilarious.

Separation (1978) (150mins) d: George McGowan s: Sandor Stern (based on the novel by Richard Rohmer) : Émile Genest, Monique Lepage. A first-rate, exciting and brilliant political drama arising from the Canadian government's intention to bring in two million British immigrants. This film is a rarity: about Canadian politics and politicians.

Sept fois par jour: see **Seven Times a Day**

Sept jours de simon labrosse, Les **(The September Days of Simon)** (2003) (92mins) d: Jean Bouronnais s: Carole Frechette (based on her play) : Daniel Parent, Sophie Vajda, Philippe Cousineau. Simon, a young man, is looking for a job both meaningful and emotionally satisfying for himself as well as others. He has two friends – a poet and a young woman. They might well feel concerned about him, but it's hardly likely an audience at this film will. How very boring.

Séraphin (1950) listed within *Homme et son pêché, Un* (*Séraphin*) (1949)

Séraphin **(Heart of Stone) (A Man and His Sin)** (2002) (128mins) d: Charles Biname s: Pierre Billon, Charles Biname (based on the novel *Un homme et son pêché* by Claude-Henri Grignon, 1933) : Pierre Lebeau, Karine Vanasse, Roy Dupuis, Remy Girard, Céline Bonnier, Marie Tifo, Robert Lalonde. It's been a long time since the screen has seen such a ripe and 'over the top' melodrama as this 'out of control' adaptation of Claude-Henri Grignon's classic story about pioneers in a forest outpost, St. Adele in the 1890's. Once a hugely popular radio series in Quebec, it was followed by a notable film in two parts (see note). This new version opens with the 'obligatory' sex scene, and gets around to the love story about Donalda and Alexis. They plan to marry, but she is forced instead to marry the cruel and sex-starved miser, Seraphin. Misery is piled on misery with everything about this film, from its characters, their clothes, their behaviour, and the direction, being tiresomely unreal. One feels nothing for any of them, not even the young lovers. To liven up this cardboard depiction of an unbelievable existence, a horse pulling logs is brutally treated and seemingly shot. The score, like the film, is overblown. Quebec audiences, however, have thought differently, as the film has made over $20 million at the box office. (Note: Originally filmed by Paul L'Anglais, *Un homme et son Peche* in 1949 with follow-up *Séraphin* in 1950).

Set Me Free: see *Emporte-moi*

Seul ou avec d'autres **(Alone or With Others)** (1962) (65mins) (b/w) d: Denys Arcand s: Stéphane Venne, Denys Arcand : Nicole Braun, Pierre Létourneau, Marie-José Raymond, Michelle Boulizon (and the comedy team *Les Cyniques*) A film combining the styles and techniques of the "new wave" and *cinéma-vérité* movements to reveal the lives of several students who talk into the camera about their thoughts and difficulties, and with others enacting roles. This was Arcand's first film made with the assistance of his friends Michel Brault, Denis Héroux, Gilles Groulx and Bernard Gosselin. After this, he went to the NFB to begin a career during which he made many accomplished films.

Seven Streams of the River Ota, The (1998) (65mins) d: Francis Leclerc s: Robert Lepage,

Francis Leclerc : Reine Yusa, Patrick Goyette, Anne-Marie Cadieux, Benoît Goulin and others. A meditation by Lepage about the people of Hiroshima painfully recovering from the atomic bomb that destroyed the city and ended World War II. (Note: Michel Duchesne made a documentary about Lepage's work, *The Seven Faces of Robert Lepage* (1998), including the films *The Confessional* and *The Polygraph*.

Seven Times a Day (*Sept fois par jour*) (1971) (87mins) (a Canada-Israel co-production) d: Denis Héroux s: Ted Allan (after his novel *The Woman Luli Sent Me*) : Rosanna Schiaffino, Jean Coutu, Dalia Friedland, Avner Hizkyau, Suzanne Valery. A silly sex comedy filmed in Israel about an architect from Québec who becomes worried about his over-capacity for sex.

Seventh Circle, The: see *Out of Sight, Out of Mind*

Sex Among the Stars (*Le sexe des étoiles*) (1993) (100mins) d: Paule Baillargeon s: Monique Proulx (from her novel of the same name) : Marianne-Coquellcot Mercier, Denis Mercier, Tobie Pelletier, Sylvie Drapeau, Luc Picard. A young teenage girl is disturbed by the confusions of growing up. She spends most of her time looking at the stars and longing for the return of her father. Now he does reappear but as a transsexual! This makes her even more confused, and no wonder! Then her loving mother sends him away and she learns that life means having to make difficult decisions. The film takes some sitting through, but the daughter is most engaging. Québec's directors seem to enjoy making films about troubled minds and painful relationships. A difficult subject treated with intelligence and good taste.

Sex and the Lonely Woman (1966) (84mins) d: Ted Leversuch s: Margot Stevens : Susanna Grossen, Sergio Regules, Ron Boni, Freddie Deakin, Israel Bak, George Bayar. The neglected wife of a prison commandant in South America falls in love with an escaped convict. Many steamy encounters and nasty events follow, leading to murder. Awful. Filmed in Uruguay. Tourists will think twice whether to visit or not!

Sex and the Single Sailor (1967) (90mins) (b/w) d&s: Ernest Reid : Theodorous Roubanis, Keti Papanika, Keti Chloe, Dimitri Karystinos, Jane Galani, Rita Dalton, Hank Smith, Bob Green. Filmed in Greece. A companion picture by Reid to *Mother Goes Greek,* also filmed in Greece. Family comedies about going on holidays.

Sex in the Snow (*Après-ski*) (1971) (104mins) d: Roger Cardinal s: Pierre Brousseau, Roger Cardinal : Daniel Pilon, Mariette Lévesque, Céline Lomez, Robert Arcand, Francine Grimaldi. It's not what happens during the skiing, but what takes place in the chalets afterwards. Yet another in Québec's skin-flick school: all tease, somewhat tame, but always cheerful.

Sexe des étoiles, Le: see **Sex Among the Stars**

Shabbat Shalom (1994) (83mins) d: Michel Brault s: Gilles Desjardins : Gilbert Sicotte, Robert Brouillette, Françoise Robertson, Marie Philippe, Michel Daigegt. Set in Montréal, this is a rare excursion into the life of a community of Hasidic Jews. Conflict arises when they seek to have the zoning rules changed, permitting them to build a new synagogue. The project is rejected and the mayor's idealistic son discovers for himself the realities of religious prejudice.

Shades of Love (series): (Astral-First Choice) (Produced by Julian Roffman) See under respective titles:
1: **Ballerina and the Blues**
2: **Champagne for Two**
3: **Echoes in Crimson**
4: **Emerald Tear, The**
5: **Garnet Princess, The**
6: **Indigo Autumn**
7: **Lilac Dream**
8: **Little White Lies**
9: **Make Mine Chartreuse**
10: **Man Who Guards the Greenhouse, The**
11: **Midnight Magic**
12: **Moonlight Flight**
13: **Rose Café, The**
14: **Sincerely Violet**
15: **Sunset Court**
16: **Tangerine Taxi**

Shadow Dancing (1988) (102mins) d: Lewis Furey s: Christine Foster : Nadine Van Der Velde, Christopher Plummer, James Kee, John Colicos. A shadowy musical drama about a young dancer possessed by the spirit of a former dancer who appears to have remained in residence in the old theatre in which she works. Christopher Plummer, lurking in the wings, seems to know all about it.

Shadow Lake (2000) (120mins) d: Carl Alexander Goldstein s: Paula J. Smith : Graham Greene, Frederic Forrest, Joy Tanner, Shirley Douglas, Gabriel Hogan. Uxbridge, Ontario, is faced with a murder mystery when a man's body is found in a frozen lake. Two policemen and a wife and daughter are involved. It's wintertime, of course, and the officers have to cope not only with finding out "whodunit," but also with finding their way through the snow. In this respect we have a marvellously cold, Canadian background. Not many thrillers have such a setting. Different, holding attention throughout.

Shadow of the Hawk (1976) (92mins) d: Daryl Duke, George McCowan s: Norman Thaddeus Vane (from his book), Herbert Wright : Jan-Michael Vincent, Marilyn Hassett, Chief Dan George, Pia Shandel, Marianne Jones, Jacques Hubert. A successful Métis businessman living in Vancouver has forgotten his heritage and is called upon by his grandfather to help defeat a mystical evil power tormenting the reserve. More of a nightmare than a revelation.

Shadow of the Wolf: see **Agaguk,**

Shadows of the Past (*Mortelle Amnesie*) (1991) (a Canda-U.S.-France Film) (92mins) d: Gabriel

Pelletier s: David Preston : Nicholas Campbell, Victoria Barkoff, Erika Anderson, Richard Berry, Pierre Auger, Lorne Brass, Heidi von Palleske. A man suffering from loss of memory is disturbed when he finds out that secret agents are looking for him. He doesn't know why. Neither will the audience. The shadows here are dark indeed.

Shape of Things to Come, The (1979) (98mins) d: George McCowan s: Martin Lager (from the book by H.G. Wells) : Jack Palance, Carol Lynley, John Ireland, Barry Morse, Nicholas Campbell, Eddie Benton, Lynda Mason. Green Earth has been destroyed and a few survivors are living dangerously on the moon. H.G. Wells would have a fit. Better to look for the 1936 classic, *Things to Come*, rather than the things in this new version.

She Drives Me Crazy: see **Crazy Horse**

She's So Young and Knows All!: see **There's Nothing Wrong With Being Good to Yourself**

Sheep Calls and Shoplifters (1995) (75mins) d: Attila Bertalan s: Deborah Van Slet : Deborah Van Slet. A vanity piece made up of a series of monologues, stories and statistics illustrating and commenting on the absurdities of the world around us; this film narrowly escapes being called one of them. There are times when it informs and entertains, although not everything that is grotesque can be accepted through laughter and derision.

Sheldon Kennedy Story, The (1999) (120mins) d: Norma Bailey s: Suzette Couture : Noel Fisher, Polly Shannon, Robert Wisden, Jonathan Scarfe. The story of the hope and healing of Sheldon Kennedy who, as a young hockey player in Calgary, suffered sexual abuse from his hockey coach and found the courage to come forward and tell of it publicly. His revelations (and those of others) shook the world of hockey in Canada. Intelligent writing, acting and direction lift this entry in the "true story of" genre above the ordinary. Not to be confused with the documentary *Sheldon: A story of human courage*.

Shelley (Turned Out) (1987) (80mins) d&s: Christian Bruyere : Robyn Stevan, Ian Tracey, Ramona Klein. Teenager Shelley finally runs away from her home in Vancouver after being sexually abused by her mother's new man. On the run, Shelley makes friends with a pimp and a prostitute. Yet another twist on a familiar situation. Done with care but not much new to tell. One hopes its message reaches teen audiences as both a lesson and a warning.

Shellgame (1986) (120mins) d: Peter Yalden-Thomson s: William Deverell : Brenda Robins, Germain Houde, Tony Rosato. A somewhat long-winded walk into the criminal underworld of Toronto where a defense attorney finds herself defending a murderer. Complications arise, of course. This look at Canadian justice is a welcome relief from U.S. stories.

Shepherd Park: see **Turning Paige**

Sherlock Holmes (CTV Muse Enterprises series): See under respective titles:
1: **The Hound of the Baskervilles**
2: **The Case of the Whitechapel Vampire**
3: **The Sign of Four**
4: **The Royal Scandal**

Shift de nuit, Le **(The Night Shift)** (1979) (90mins) d&s: Mario Bolduc : Marie-Ginnette Guay, Camille Bergeron, Paul Bélanger, Sylvie Rousseau, Normand Poire. On the night shift, we meet a student, a caretaker and a mechanic in Montréal during the summer of 1978. Around these three and their companions we see the life of the district in all its moods, anxieties and small moments of satisfaction. All very human and real.

Shipping News, The (2001) (111mins) (a U.S.-U.K.-Canada film) d: Lasse Hallstrom s: Robert Nelson-Jacobs (based on the novel by Annie Proulx) : Kevin Spacey, Julianne Moore, Judi Dench, Cate Blanchett, Pete Postlethwaite, Scott Glenn, Rhys Ifans, Gordon Pinsent, Robert Joy. A U.S. producer and writer, a Swedish director, a British cinematographer, with an international cast, make heavy weather out of a confusing story about an unlucky American marked by life who returns to his native Newfoundland to find love and deliverance from damnation. No good news here, except for the appearance of Gordon Pinsent. (Shot in Newfoundland and Nova Scotia.)

Shirley Pimple in the John Wayne Temple (1999) (100mins) d&s: Demetrios Estdelacropolis : Chelsea McIsaac, Rick Trembles, Nettie Harris. Impossible to describe and difficult to watch, this experimental film was ten years in the making and brings us Shirley Pimple as the representative of the John Wayne Institute. (Whatever this is!) Audiences make of this what they may.

Shivers: see **Parasite Murders**

Shoemaker (1997) (80mins) d: Colleen Murphy s: Jaan Kolk : Randy Hughson, Alberta Watson, Hardee Lineham, Carl Marotte, George Buza, Ellen Ray Hennessy. A fragile and timid man, a shoe repairer by trade, attempts on many occasions to find romance. One day a lively, knowing and kind woman comes to his shop and it seems that a relationship might result but, alas, it doesn't turn out this way. The film observes every nuance of how its characters think and feel, and brings about a depth of compassion for their sense of loneliness and isolation. Humour and honesty prevail to make the whole a gentle portrait of life.

Shoot (1976) (98mins) (a Canadian-American film) d: Harvey Hart s: Dick Berg (from the novel by Douglas Fairbairn) : Cliff Robertson, Ernest Borgnine, Kate Reid, Helen Shaver, Gloria Carlin, Ed McNamara, Sydney Brown, Henry Silva, James Blendick. Filmed in Ontario passing as the U.S., an extraordinarily silly film about American hunters who shoot at each other as though they were opposing armies in combat. Presented as an anti-gun story, it is anything but!

Shopping for Fangs (1996) (90mins) (an American-Canadian film) d&s: Quentin Lee, Justin Lin : Radmar Jao, Jeanne Chin, Clint Jung, Lela Lee, John Cho. This muddled hybrid offers what it thinks is something for everyone as it scrambles through a an empty life of melodrama, murder, horror and sex. We follow three lonely outlandish characters in their quest for identity and a purpose for living. Sloppy and silly cinema. Filmed entirely in California.

Short Change (*Une fille impossible*) (1989) (103mins) d: Nicholas Kinsey s: Jacques Hardy, Nicholas Kinsey : Frank Pellegrino, George Touliatos, Shannon Lawson. A muddle about an Iranian working as a security guard in Canada. When his devout Muslim uncle arrives for a visit, he demands that his nephew find him a wife so that he can remain in Canada. The security guard catches a woman shoplifting who turns out to be the perfect mate. Trying to find a way through this could induce a headache.

Shot in the Face (2002) (93mins) d: David Hansen s: Jaymie Hansen : Bruce Ramsay, Katherine Isabelle, Nicholas Lea, Benjamin Ratner, John Cassini, Frank Cassini. Noted for several interesting documentaries, this director (whose first feature this is) comes from working on music video–tv stuff. It shows. The main character here is an unlikeable nonconformist, who likes all the things decent people abhor. After being involved in a robbery, he meets a woman who helps him adjust to our intolerant society. He's hardly worth bothering about, like this film.

Shot Through the Heart (1998) (112mins) (a Canada-U.K.-Hungary co-production) d: David Attwood s: Guy Hibbert (based on *Details* magazine article "Anti-Sniper" by John Falk) : Vincent Perez, Linus Roache, Lia Williams, Lothaire Bluteau. Based on a true relationship, this is a well-told and believable study of two friends who are torn apart by the racial conflicts in war-torn Sarajevo. One friend becomes a marksman to kill off snipers as they move into his district. A double-cross becomes apparent and events turn into murder, agony and despair. A graphic representation of a horrible time.

Showdown at Williams Creek (Kootenai Brown) (1991) (97mins) d: Allan Kroeker s: John Gray : Tom Burlinson, Donelly Rhodes, Michelle Thrush, John Pyper Ferguson, Alex Bruhanski, Raymond Burr. Set in the Northwest Territories during pioneer years, this true story tells of the agonies of a former British army officer who is on trial for murder. Set against the racism, hatred and greed of the times. A finely crafted and well-acted historical drama.

Shower, The (1992) (85mins) d: Gail Harvey s: Richard Beattie, Gail Harvey : Brent Carver, Kate Lynch, Janet-Laine Green. Lightweight sex comedy where everything goes awry at a party for a bride-to-be. Brent Carver survived to go on to better things!

Shrew in the Park, The (2000) (90mins) d: (and adaptation) Andrew Honor. Here, the director follows his group of community players as they prepare *The Taming of the Shrew* as a "Shakespeare in the Park" performance. They work hard and do everything from the first to final curtain, yet the entire text of the Bard's farce is the film's only dialogue. While the actors on screen are not always doing what's in the play, each scene is devised to tell both stories at once. The play, for the actors, is everything, and their daily stress is lightened through their satisfaction in giving their all to the stage. Well, Shakespeare has survived many interpretations, but he would undoubtedly have understood this one. It's a clever and imaginative production.

Si belles **(So Pretty)** (1994) (82mins) d: Jean-Pierre Gariépy s: Suzanne Mancini-Gagner : Marie-Josée Picard, Geneviève L'Allier-Matteau, Michel Laperrière, Louison Danis. Lynne lives with her eight-year-old daughter, her only company. It has been this way since the girl was very young. Coping has not always been easy. Then two men enter her life and each one wants to live with her, help her, and do their best for Lynne and the little girl. But Lynne isn't sure she wants to complicate her life with another person. She wants to be self-sufficient and meet the challenge of survival. An interesting look at making decisions about one's life.

Siamoises, Les **(The Siamese Twins)** (1999) (80mins) d&s: Isabelle Hayeur : Isabelle Blais, Jessica Barker, Stéphane Demers, René Gagnon. A convoluted study of twin sisters and their neurotic mother living in a subsidized housing unit. Their problems with life are severe and psychological, leading to a death trap. Hard to see the point or purpose of this picture. It tells us nothing really, we just watch and that's it.

Siège (1983) (84mins) d: Paul Donovan, Maura O'Connell s: Paul Donovan (based on an idea by Marc Vautour) : Tom Nardini, Brenda Bazinet, Douglas Lennox, Darel Haney, Terry-David Despres, Jeff Pustil, Jack Blum, Keith Knight, Brad Wadden, Gary Dempster, Tricia Fish A violent melodrama set in Halifax, Nova Scotia, based on the 42-day police strike in 1982.

Siège de l'âme, Le: see **Seat of the Soul, The**

Sign of Four, The (2001) (120mins) d: Rodney Gibbons s: Joe Wiesenfeld (from the book by Sir Arthur Conan Doyle) : Matthew Frewer, Kenneth Welsh, Sophie Lorain, Marcel Jeannin, Michel Perron, Edward Yankie. Dr. Watson becomes infatuated with a young governess who has been receiving a rare and lustrous pearl every year from an anonymous benefactor. We go to India in 1856, where British soldiers are fighting rebel attacks in Sepoy, and are shown how this all began. Captivating and highly enjoyable. (See: *Sherlock Holmes* series)

Feature Film Guide

Signature (CTV series): See under respective titles:
1: **After the Harvest (Wild Geese)**
2: **Blessed Stranger: After Flight 111**
3: **David Milgaard Story, The**
4: **Dr. Lucille: The Lucille Teasdale Story**
5: **Lucky Girl**
6: **Milk and Honey**
7: **Tagged: The Jonathan Wamback Story**
8: **Stolen Miracle**

Silence (1997) (100mins) d: Jack Darcus s: Hank Schachte : August Schellenberg, Alan Scarfe, Annick Obonsawin, James Nicholas, Joy Coghill, Lynn Johnson, Terence Kelly, Tulkweemult. Set on a remote native reserve, this is a minimalist family story given originality by virtue of its unusual background with characters not much seen on the screen. Well caught in Darcus' studied manner.

Silence des fusils, Le: see **Silencing the Guns**

Silence nous guette, Le (**Silence Is Watching Us**) (2002) (90mins) d&s: Nathalie Saint-Pierre : Alexandre Agostini, Frederic Desager, Marianne Cote-Olijnik. A brief encounter between a lonely street photographer and a lonely woman in Montréal brings about a strange relationship between them, which works because the woman's daughter reminds the photographer of his dead daughter. Is there a psychiatrist in the house?

Silence of Adultery, The (1995) (94mins) d: Steven Hilliard Stern s: Susan Rhineheart : Kate Jackson, Art Hindle, Patricia Gage, Robert Desiderio, Kristin Fairlie, Tori McPetrie, Kevin Zeg. A woman, her husband and children, live in the country, own and ride horses, and in all ways lead a perfect life. But for the wife, with her husband away at work, life can be unrewarding. Until she meets the veterinary doctor who helps to care for the horses; and an affair begins between them. This is a rare film indeed, beautifully detailed and emotionally expressed, acted with feeling and understanding, interestingly done, without going to extremes. One of the rare gems in Canadian filmmaking.

Silence of the North (1981) (93mins) (a Canada-U.S. film) d: Allan Winton King s: Patricia Knop (from the book by Frederickson & East) : Ellen Burstyn, Tom Skerritt, Gordon Pinsent, Colin Fox, Chapelle Jaffe, Thomas Hauff, Kenneth Pogue, Larry Reynolds, Tom Harvey, Ken Babb, Janet Amos, Robert Clothier, Ken James, Murray Westgate, Kay Hawtrey, Booth Savage, Lynda Mason Green, Sean Sullivan, Tom McEwan. Based on a true story, Burstyn plays Olive Frederickson, who falls in love with a trapper and moves to Canada to face catastrophes, the cold and the inhospitable environment. Filmed in British Columbia, this was Allan King's first feature, which he directed expertly and with imagination. Previously known for his documentaries. Allan added his middle name Winton to the credits to avoid confusion with the American Allan King. This film was made in Canada and financed by Universal Films in a move intended to dilute the criticism of Hollywood's domination of Canadian cinemas.

Silencer, The (1999) (92mins) (A U.S.-Canada film) d: Robert Lee s: Charles Case : Michael Dudikoff, Gabrielle Miller, Brennan Elliott, Terence Kelly, Colin Cunningham, Peter LaCroix. An FBI agent fakes his own death and comes back with a new identity, ready to take on his next assignment. Let's hope we are not around to hear about it. Thin stuff.

Silencing the Guns (*Le silence des fusils*) (1996) (97mins) d: Arthur Lamothe s: Jean Beaudry, Arthur Lamothe : Michèle Audette, Jacques Perrin, Gabriel Gascon, Louisette Dussault, Marco Bacon, Jean Harvey, Hugo Dubé. A scientist has gone to northern Québec to carry out research on whales, but accidentally becomes involved in the discovery of the bodies of two drowned fishermen. Finding the answers to this mystery takes him into a society corrupted by racism, leading him to examine his own principles. A finely told and acted chronicle dealing with politics and power.

Silent Cradle (1998) (96mins) d: Paul Ziller s: David Schultz : Lorraine Bracco, Margot Kidder, John Heard. A pregnant woman who gives birth is later told by the hospital that she lost the baby. The mother-to-be in question is a reporter—bad luck for a hospital trying to cover up a crooked adoption agency!

Silent Hunter (1993) (93mins) d&s: Fred Williamson : Miles O'Keefe, Fred Williams. An undercover policeman in Montréal sees his family slaughtered by sadistic robbers. Stunned, he goes to live in a remote cabin in an attempt to heal his shattered life. An unusual and moving study in grief and emotional turmoil.

Silent Love, A (2003) (100mins) (a Can-Mexico film) d: Federico Hidalgo s: Hidalgo & Paulina Robles : Noel Burton, Vanessa Bauche, Suzanna Salazar, Maka Kotto, Carmen Salinas. Set in Mexico and spoken in Spanish, French and English, this is about romance gone wrong when a teacher from Montreal falls in love with a young Mexican woman but she demands, as a condition of marriage, that her mother comes also to the wedding. With the ceremony hardly over, the teacher falls in love with his mother-in-law, and returns with her to Mexico, leaving the young wife alone, except for hope! Well, what next? Not terribly appealing.

Silent Night, Evil Nights: see **Black Christmas**
Silent Night: see **My Uncle Antoine**
Silent Partner, The (1978) (106mins) d: Daryl Duke s: Curtis Lee Hanson (based on the novel *Think of a Number* by Anders Bodelsen) : Elliott Gould, Christopher Plummer, Susannah York, Céline Lomez, Michael Kirby, Kenneth Pogue, John Candy, Sean Sullivan, Jack Duffy, Nuala FitzGerald, Charlotte Blunt, Sandy Crawley, Sue Lumsden, Jack Duffy. A gifted director gives credibility to this brutal depiction

of a bank robbery, carried out in Toronto by such unlikely citizens as Elliott Gould and Susannah York. This film was greatly over-praised by many critics.

Silent Witness: What a Child Saw (1994) (90mins) d: Bruce Pittman s: Paris Qualles : Amir Jamal Williams; Mia Corf, Clark Johnson. A young boy is the only witness to a gang murder, and the murderers, including his brother, know that he saw them. Tense and touching, with several outstanding revelations about how the American justice system can be subverted when laywers clash.

Simon and the Dream Hunters (*Simon et les nuages*) (1990) (82mins) d&s: Roger Cantin : Hugolin Chevrette-Landesque. A beautiful and likeable children's film about Simon, who dreams day and night about a land where all the animals that have become extinct or been killed off still live. And so he and his friends travel throughout Québec looking for this distant land where all the animals, big and small, remain.

Simon et les nuages: see **Simon and the Dream Hunters**

Sincerely Violet (1987) (86mins) d: Mort Ransen; James Kaufman s: Julian Roffman : Simon MacCorkindale, Patricia Phillips, Barbara Jones, Joan Heney. Deception—to tell or not to tell? Two lovers find that disclosure strengthens their relationship and their love actually flourishes. But how many times can this be so? The past is put aside and true romance wins hearts and seems safe for the days ahead. Pleasing to watch. (See: *Shades of Love* series)

Singing the Bones (2001) (88mins) d&s: Gordon Halloran (from the novel by Caitlin Hicks) : Caitlin Hicks, Edward White, Brenda Menard. An unusual and thoughtful chronicle about three pregnant women, each from a different station in life. A doctor warns of dangerous complications. From here, strange dreams, secrets and the possible death of a baby bring about a clash of beliefs. Set on Canada's west coast. A doctor's tale with a difference!

Sinon, oui: see **Foreign Body, A**

Sins of the Fathers (1948) (94mins) (b/w) d: Phil Rosen s: Gordon Burwash : Austin Willis, Joy LaFleur, John Pratt, Phyllis Carter, Suzanne Avon, Frank Heron, Mary Barclay, Gerald Rowan, Norman Traviss, Robert Goodier, Gordon Burwash. An anti-venereal disease melodrama set in a small Canadian town. The censor boards of the time required this film to be shown on alternate nights to women only and to men only. It had to be introduced on stage by a doctor who, accompanied by slide illustrations, spoke of the evils of sexually transmitted diseases. Hence, actor Austin Willis playing the doctor!

Sister Blue (2001) (96mins) d: Douglas Greenall : Stacy Fair, Clare Lapinskie, Bruce Dawson, Matthew Harrison. A compact tale about two sisters who remember an abandoned farmhouse and keep dark secrets from the men in their lives. There are other awful echoes and we are left wondering if life

will get any better or worse. An ensemble cast fits into this subject with quiet assurance.

Sitting in Limbo (1985) (95mins) d: John Smith s: David Wilson, John Smith : Fabian Gibbs, Pat Dillon, Sylvie Clarke, Debbie Grant. This is a low-budget feature film for the most part, depicting the everyday lives of black teenagers in Montréal. Characters and events are frequently real and touching, but the whole at times tends to wander. Shot by Smith for the NFB in documentary style. This is an honest and revealing work by the talented Smith, who has moved easily from documentary to drama over the years and became widely recognized in 1993 for *The Boys of St.Vincent*.

Size of Watermelons, The (1996) (82mins) d: Kari Skogland s: Rob Stefaniuk : Paul Rudd, Donal Loogue, Donovan Leitch, Ione Skye, Marissa Ribisi, Adam West. This film goes to Venice Beach, California, where three losers try to make a documentary film. The result is described as a comedy, unfortunately a feeble one. It seems that all involved were simply looking for time off in the sun.

Skate (Blades of Courage) (1987) (99mins) d: Randy Bradshaw s: Suzette Couture : Christianne Hirt, Colm Feore, Stuart Hughes. This interesting story, both psychologically and dramatically, concerns a young figure skater in Toronto who is controlled and almost destroyed by her demanding coach. Another fine script by the remarkable Couture.

Skin and Bones: see *Peau et les os, La*

Skin Deep (Sadness of the Moon) (1995) (81mins) d: Midi Onodera s: Barbara O'Kelly, Midi Onodera : Natsuka Ohama, Alex Koyamo, Keram Malicki-Sanchez, Christopher Black. Midi Onodera's first feature film examines the issues surrounding perceptions of sexuality and gender. Sympathetic and perceptive, this film led the way in feminist consciousness of previously unheard of subject matter. Still one of the best of its kind.

Skip Tracer (1977) (94mins) d&s: Zale Dalen : David Petersen, John Lazarus, Rudy Szabo, Sue Astley A gem. A first feature by Zale Dalen of considerable force, power and poignancy concerning a man who comes to despise himself for his work as a debt collector for a Vancouver agency. One of the first, and still few, indigenous films to be made in British Columbia, and now rightly regarded as one of our classics.

Sky's the Limit, The (*Les limites du ciel*) (1986) (81mins) d: Yvan Dubuc s: Yvan Dubuc : Charlotte Morin, Ginette Allaire. At a lighthearted summer party in Maniwaki, Québec, the guests begin to discuss their love stories, with the relationship between one couple proving to be of unusual interest. Very talkative.

Slavers, The (1984) (96mins) d&s: Larry Kent : Sheenan Graham, Kevin McGrath, James Sheridan, Dennis O'Conner, David Spencer. A slight piece from Larry Kent about a young man who goes to the rescue of a young woman kidnapped in Montréal. A large matter rendered somewhat minor.

Sleep Walkers, The (Les somnambules) (1986) (79mins) d: Robert Desrosiers s: Jacques Lazure : Anne Bédard, Pierre Curzi. A strange world here in which music lulls the living into a state of sleepwalking pain and pleasure. A survivor wanting to protect herself from this music associates with two strangers and their mini-bus studio, where they insulate themselves with rock, played at full volume. All rather unnerving.

Sleeping Dogs Lie (1999) (120mins) d: Stefan Scaini s: Raymond Storey (inspired by the book *The Strange Case of Ambrose Small* by Fred McClement) : Wendy Crewson, Joel Keller, Michael Murphy, Art Hindle, Leon Pownall, Leslie Yeo, Shannon Lawson, Cedric Smith, Eric Peterson. This is the somewhat suspect story of Toronto millionaire Ambrose Small, who disappeared without a trace during the 1920s and was never found. Set in Toronto, at the time described as "a cesspool of corrupt upper-classes and politicians, religious conflict between Protestant and Catholics, and drugs and prostitutes." Ambrose and his various women make a confusing patchwork. Still, it's a fascinating picture showing how we can Hollywood our history.

Sleepless: see **Probable Cause**

Sleeproom, The (1998) (240mins) d: Anne Wheeler s: Bruce Smith (based on the book *In the Sleep Room: The Story of the Brainwashing Experiments in Canada* by Anne Collins) : Leon Pownall, Eric Peterson, Nicola Cavendish, Daniel Kash, Nicholas Campbell, Gabrielle Rose, Emmanuel Bilodeau. The late doctor Ewen Cameron, the director of Montréal's Allan Memorial Institute for psychiatric treatment, became obsessed in the late 1950s with developing a radical cure for mental illness using drug-induced sleep lasting weeks at a time. Twenty-five years later, nine psychologically shattered patients learned that they had been guinea pigs in the doctor's barbaric tests funded by the CIA. This is their story, cleverly told with composite characters, dramatized documentary and a certain amount of controversy.

Slim Obsession (1984) (65mins) d: Donald Shebib s: Martin Lager, Janet Kranz : Susan Wright, Paul Kelman. An overweight schoolteacher risks her marriage, career and life after she begins to live on a diet that becomes an obsession of frightening proportions. (See: *For the Record*)

Slipstream (1973) (93mins) d: David Acomba s: William Fruet : Luke Askew, Patti Oatman, Eli Rill, Scott Hylands, Danny Friedman. A reclusive disc-jockey broadcasts hard-rock music over the spacious and lonely plains of Alberta, taking a jaundiced view of life and love. Beautifully photographed but dramatically confused.

Slow Burn (1989) (100mins) (a Canada-U.K. co-production) d: John Eyres s: Steven Lister : William Smith, Anthony James, Ivan Rogers, Scott Anderson, Mellisa Conroy. Filmed under the title "Brothers In Arms" but changed to "Slow Burn" when the producers found another film being shown with that name, this is not likely to find its way anywhere under any title. Filmed in Vancouver, which is passed off unconvincingly as New York City, this is a dark and dismal piece of gangster double-cross. A prelude shows the murder of a family by a thug. He spares the young son. A great mistake. The audience must endure his determination to take revenge. Watching this film, an empty exercise in violence seems to take an eternity.

Slow Run (1969) (80mins) (b&w) d&s: Larry Kardish : Jane Austen, David Flower, Bruce Gorden, Pat Jones, Heather Sim, Rita Stein, Melvyn Green. A young Canadian living in New York City is about to move elsewhere but stops to think of all his free and romantic times in New York. All very much confused. Kardish went on to play an important role at the MOMA Film Library in NYC.

Small Pleasures (1993) (85mins) d&s: Keith Lock, Qi Guang : Lily Zhang, Reimonna Sheng, Phillip Mackenzie, Andy X. Xu. A likeable first feature set in Toronto's Chinatown concerning the difficulties and delights of a family from Beijing coming to terms with a new society.

Smattes, Les: see **Two Wise Men, The**

Smoked Lizard Lips (1991) (95mins) d&s: M. Bruce Duggan : Simon Magana, Andrée Pelletier, Kyle McCulloch, Victor Cowie, Margaret Anne MacLeod, Greg Klymkiw A well-intentioned but not-funny-enough comedy revolving around the misadventures of a South American dictator in exile in a small town outside Winnipeg.

Snail's Point of View, A (La position de l'escargot) (1998) (100mins) (a Canada-France co-production) d&s: Michka Saal : Mirella Tomassini, Victor Lanoux, Henri Chassé, Dino Tavarone, Pascale Montpetit, Judes-Antoine. Jarda Myriam, a 28-year-old Jewish woman who emigrates from Tunisia to Montréal, goes from one crisis to another in her new life, having difficulties with friends, family and lovers alike. Another study in human relationships and the agony of those who suffer from simply being alive. Competently realized by a capable cast.

SnakeEater (1990) (95mins) (a Canadian-American film) d: George Erschbamer s: John Dunning, Michael Paseornek : Lorenzo Lamas, Josie Bell, Robert Scott, Ronnie Hawkins. The Snake Eaters are a biker gang in Montréal who kidnap and kill the sister of a former marine, now working as an undercover detective.

SnakeEater II: The Drug Buster (1990) (92mins) (a Canadian-American film) d: George Erschbamer s: John Dunning and Michael Paseornek : Lorenzo Lamas, Michele Scarabelli, Larry Scott, Harvey Atkin. This time around, an undercover policeman teams up with a young boy from the ghetto to close down the crack houses and exterminate the drug lords. All the usual action, dialogue and gun-play.

SnakeEater III: The Revenge (His Law) (1992) (95mins) (a Canadian-American film) d: George Erschbamer s: John Dunning, Glenn Duncan (from his novel *Rafferty's Rules*) : Lorenzo Lamas, Scott "Bam Bam" Bigelow, Minor Mustain, Tracey Cook, Holly Chester. The policeman, now known as "Soldier," is under suspension for his unorthodox crime fighting. He's reinstated because of his caring methods in saving street kids from drugs. He kills the local pushers and is once again charged. The audience is with him as the drug merchants are blown away.

Sneakers (Spring Fever) (1982) (99mins) d: Joseph Scanlan s: Stuart Gillard, Fred Stefan : Carling Bassett, Susan Anton, Frank Converse, Jessica Walter. Filmed in Florida where two 13-year-old tennis players find themselves under intolerable strain and pressure to be great at the game. A film made by the Bassett family to show the progress of their daughter. Likeable enough. (Not to be confused with *Sneakers* [1992] with Robert Redford.)

Snow Has Melted on the Manicouagan, The (*La neige a fondu sur la Manicouagan***)** (1965) (95mins) (b/w) d&s: Arthur Lamothe : Monique Miller, Gilles Vigneault, Margot Campbell, Jean Doyen. An atmospheric mood piece photographed in the winter at the giant dam built by Hydro-Québec in the northern wilds of the province. The story concerns a worker's wife, who is bored with her dreary existence in the wilderness. She walks around in the snow recalling how she met her husband, then goes to the landing field to catch a departing plane. But she remains when her husband tells her how much his work means to him. This moving and very humanistic tale represents the NFB at its best.

Snow Walker, The (2002) (110mins) d&s: Charles Martin Smith (based on the short story *Walk Well My Brother* by Farley Mowat) With Barry Pepper, Annabella Piugattuk, James Cromwell, Jon Gries, Robin Dunne, Kiersten Warren. A bush pilot crashes in a remote area of Canada's Arctic. A young Inuit woman, a passenger, shows him how to survive and adapt to the surroundings. Told in the spirit of a *Boys' Own Paper* adventure, competent and sensible.

Snowbirds (1981) (65mins) d: Peter Pearson s: Margaret Atwood : Doris Petrie, Neil Dainard, Jayne Eastwood, Cicely Thomson, Robert Christie, Budd Knapp. A romantic and gently humorous story about a lively, willful senior citizen whose husband has died. She finds herself at the mercy of her determined daughter, who insists that mother sell her house and move into a retirement home. She is saved when she meets an itinerant camper who comes into her life, romance blooms and she begins an independent life with him in his trailer. Charming and well played. (See: *For the Record*)

So Faraway and Blue (2001) (78mins) d&s: Roy Cross : Nicole Eliopoulos, Daniel Giverin, Julie Ménard, Bradley Moss. A homeless young girl in Montréal spends her days following strangers. Abandoned by her family, she looks for love and courage and tries to satisfy her desires. Still hoping to find her father one day, she finds instead a man from Alberta looking for his missing daughter. The two of them join forces and they wander on their way. The slight narrative feels deeply and holds a certain appeal.

So Hard to Forget: see **Hard to Forget**

So Pretty: see **Si belles**

So That the World Goes On (*Pour la suite du monde***)** (1963) (105mins) (b/w) d&s: Pierre Perrault, Michel Brault : Léopold Tremblay, Alexis Tremblay, Abel Harvey, Louis Harvey, Joachim Harvey. This film tells of the people of the Île-aux-Coudres (an island in the St. Lawrence, 100 kilometres downstream from Québec City) and their attempts to revive the hunting of the Beluga whale. Among the customs revived with this endeavour are the Lent festivities, the auction sales for the benefit of souls in Purgatory, and the jigs and customs dating back to the discovery of Canada by Europeans. (See: *Moon Trap; Acadia, Acadia; End of Summer*)

Society's Child (2001) (90mins) d: Pierre Gang s: Dennis Foon : Jessica Steen, Hugh Thompson, Margot Kidder, Melanie Nicholls-King. A slight but significant portrait of a 10-year-old girl diagnosed with Rett Syndrome, a rare neurological disorder. It is a terrible struggle for her to walk and talk, yet her personality is bright with a range of expression. Her mother learns all she can about this illness and challenges the medical authorities about their treatment of her daughter. A deeply moving and entirely credible film from Winnipeg.

Sodbusters (1995) (98mins) (a Canadian-American film) d: Eugene Levy s: John Hemphill, Eugene Levy : Kris Kristofferson, John Vernon, Wendel Meldrum, Max Gail, John Hemphill. In 1875, the simple folk of Marble Hat, Colorado, are working their land, building homes and looking forward to a better future. But the railway is coming and the land grabbers are out to make their profits at the people's expense. But then a mysterious stranger arrives named Destiny. If all this seems familiar, perhaps it is, the picture supposedly being a "comic tribute to all the classic westerns that pit the good against the bad." Not quite.

Soho (1994) (90mins) d: Jean-Phillipe Duval s: José Fréchette : Pascale Montpetit, Dominique Darceuil, Rita Lafontaine. Soho is the name of a 30-year-old woman who has enjoyed living on the fringe with odd and colourful characters who, like herself, live from day to day and believe that tomorrow they will become celebrities as writers, performers or musicians. Their wait may be long! But they are an enjoyable group.

Soleil des autres, Le (The Sun of the Others) (Give Us Our Daily Love) (1979) (70mins) (b/w) d&s: Jean Faucher : Françoise Faucher, Gérard

Poirier, Liette Desjardins, Nicole Caron, Monique Champagne. A sentimental drama about an architect who divorces his wife to marry a younger woman. This second marriage, however, doesn't work out, and he goes to see his former wife again. When she finds him unchanged, selfish, and flighty as before, she commits suicide. Like the marriage it depicts, this film doesn't work, either.

Soleil se leve en retard, Le: see **Sun Rises Late, The**

Solitaire (1991) (107mins) d&s: Francis Damberger : Paul Coeur, Michael Hogan, Valerie Pearson, Lee Royce. Talkative yet affecting study of three former friends who meet in a drab bar on Christmas Eve in a western town, after a separation of 25 years, and recall what they wanted to be and reflect on what they have become. A small gem.

Solitude (2001) (89mins) d: Robin Schlaht s: Connie Gault, Robin Schlaht : Lothaire Bluteau, Vanessa Martinez, Wendy Anderson, Eugene Lipinski, William Hugli, Michael O'Brien, Michel Marchildon, Bruce McKay. We are in a rural monastery with a monk and two women on a spiritual retreat. All three are looking for answers to questions of faith and purpose. What follows is a thoughtful discussion about religion, love and identity, underlined by the belief that there is no faith without doubt. An unusual film requiring a patient and understanding audience.

Some Do It for Money: see **All in Good Taste**

Someday Soon (1977) (65mins) d: Donald Haldane s: Rudy Wiebe, Barry Pearson : John Vernon, George Waight, Kelly Parker, Kyla Bemner, Deborah Kipp, John Pierce. Filmed on location in southern Manitoba, where contaminated water from the recently opened billion-dollar Garrison irrigation project in North Dakota swept across Manitoba farmland. A group of desperate Canadian farmers, when their cries for help brought none from the provincial or federal governments, found themselves a leader and sought action before their land was lost for generations. This is a minor masterwork bringing major concerns dramatically to life. (See: *For the Record*)

Something About Love (1988) (93mins) d: Tom Berry s: Stefan Wodoslawsky, Tom Berry : Stefan Wodoslawsky, Jan Rubes, Jennifer Dale. A Canadian working in television in Los Angeles returns to his home in Cape Breton, Nova Scotia, to visit his father, whose mind is deteriorating with Alzheimer's disease but who refuses to admit that he is no longer competent to manage his affairs. An interesting but somewhat lifeless confrontation between father and son.

Something More (1999) (98mins) d: Rob King s: Peter Bryant : Michael Goorjian, Chandra West, David Lovgren, Thomas Cavanaugh, Jennifer Beals. The emotional problems of lost and aimless suburbanites who find life to be without meaning, are hon-estly portrayed in this sometimes funny film, at times tedious. The actors are recognizeably what they represent. Filmed in Regina.

Something Organic (*Quelque chose d'organique*) (1998) (89mins) d&s: Bertrand Bonello : Romane Bohringer, Laurent Lucas, Charlotte Laurier. A tenderly told, haunting and realistic portrayal of a youthful marriage in Montréal between two immigrants and their Greek-French families. Emotionally unsettling, often strange and sad, this is a perceptive and true-to-life description.

Something's Rotten (1978) (75mins) d: Harvey Frost s: Norman Fox : Charlotte Blunt, Geoffrey Bowes, Trudy Weiss, Christopher Barry, Cec Linder, Irene Hogan, Charles Jolliffe, Harvey Sokolov. A queen misuses her powers in this feeble thriller played out within a central European monarchy. A misplaced picture if there ever was one.

Somnambules, Les: see **Sleep Walkers, The**

Son copain: see **Unknown From Montréal, The**

Sonatine (1984) (90mins) d&s: Micheline Lanctôt : Pascale Bussières, Marcia Pilote, Kliment Demtchev, Pierre Fauteux. Two lonely young girls find that the world is filled with aloof and indifferent people, including their parents. The girls decide to commit suicide in public to attract attention to themselves in death, if not in life. But, events rob them of this satisfaction. A strange, haunting, fascinating film held together with great skill by the director, with an astonishing flow of images set within buses and subway trains, and divided into three parts. This was Micheline Lanctôt's second film, following the enjoyable *The Handyman*. A perceptive and understanding work.

Song for Julie, A (*Chanson pour Julie*) (1976) (92mins) d: Jacques Vallée s: Michel Garneau, Jacques Vallée : Anne Dandurand, Jean-Pierre Ferland, Danielle Roy, Valerie Pannaccio, Jacques Thisdale. A woman about to give birth returns to the past in her daydreams to recall places, people and passions during her life in Montréal, all revealed in a series of expertly mounted flashbacks.

Song of Hiawatha, The (1996) (95mins) (a Canadian-American film) d: Jeffrey Shore s: Earl Wallace : Graham Greene, Lightfoot, Gordon Tootoosis, Irene Bedard, David Strathairn. Adapted from the Longfellow poem, we hear the tale of a priest and a fur trader who travel into the woods to meet the legendary Ojibway chief. Different and deserving.

Song Spinner, The (1996) (95mins) d: Randy Bradshaw s: Pauline Lebel : Patti LuPone, John Neville, Brent Carver, Meredith Henderson, Wendel Meldrum, David Hemblen. An elegant and captivating tale, part fable and part love story about children in the land of Shanrilan who are not allowed to sing or talk, until the mysterious Zantalallia comes along with her magic box and produces beautiful songs and music. With an engaging cast.

Sonia (1986) (57mins) d&s: Paule Baillargeon : Kim Yaroshevskaya, Lothaire Bluteau, Marc Messier, Blanche Baillargeon, Paule Baillargeon. Sonia, at the prime of her artistic and professional life, with no anxieties or stress, finds herself suffering from Alzheimer's disease. The relationship between her and her daughter Roxanne is the subject of this sensitive and affecting study.

Soul Investigator, The (Stories of Chide the Wind) (1994) (82mins) d&s: Kal Ng : Edwin Cheung, Patrick Cho, Alice Ng, Edmond Chu. A dark attempt to create an Everyman character who searches for a cure for the spiritual and physical malaise he sees in the world around him. He wanders through the dark silent skyscrapers of a seemingly abandoned city, bleak and alien, strikingly photographed in black and white with bursts of colour. A ghost story with Confucius lurking around somewhere, perhaps; many audiences may find it baffling and not a little boring.

Soul Survivor (1995) (89mins) d&s: Stephen Williams : Peter Williams, David Smith, George Harris, Judith Scott, Clark Johnson. A young Jamaican-Canadian in Toronto is looking for a better life and a little more money than his current job in a beauty salon and goes to work for a local club owner and loan shark. Despite the young man's determination to stay clear of the club's criminal activities, he does become involved and soon finds himself in a dilemma over love and loyalty. This film was much heralded as a positive example of the skill and talent of young Jamaican artists in Toronto. Direction and performances are assured.

Sourd dans la ville, Le: see **Deaf to the City**

Sous les draps, les étoiles **(Stargazing and Other Passions) (Stars Under the Sheets)** (1989) (90mins) d&s: Jean-Pierre Gariépy : Guy Thauvette, Marie-Josée Gauthier, Marcel Sabourin, Joseph Cazalet, Gilles Renaud. A former astronomer returns to Montréal from South America and falls passionately in love with a dark-eyed woman while visiting a strange and surreal cafe. An affair develops and what begins in a pit of passion soon becomes baffling and disturbing as his past keeps breaking up the future. A sinister and stylish thriller.

Sous-sol: see **Not Me!**

South of Wawa (1991) (93mins) d: Robert Boyd s: Lori Lansens : Catherine Fitch, Rebecca Jenkins, Andrew Miller, Scott Renderer. It's a continuing disappointment in Canadian films when a story clearly identifies the town where the story takes place and then fails to take advantage of the setting. Opening in Stayner, Ontario, and taking place mostly in a coffee-and-donut cafe, and the homes of its two waitresses, the untidy screenplay reflects little of the town and its people as one waitress leaves for Toronto to attend a concert.

South Pacific, 1942 (1981) (85mins) d&s: Paul Donovan : Alan MacGillivray, Janet MacMillan, Bob Backen, Mahar Boutros, Lynette Louise, Bill Papps. A misplaced clumsy comedy set during World War II when a Canadian submarine becomes involved with German and Japanese naval ships. The film is as incompetent as the crew. This was Donovan's first film. His following films were an improvement.

Souvenirs intimes: see **Memories Unlocked**

Space Fury: see **In the Dead of Space**

Spacehunters: Adventures in the Forbidden Zone (1983) (90mins) (in 3-D) d: Lamont Johnson s: David Preston : Peter Strauss, Molly Ringwald, Ernest Hudson, Andrea Marcovicci, Michael Ironside, Deborah Platt. The Spacehunter in question roams the barren surface of a faraway planet trying to rescue three women being held captive by a horrid mutant. Tedious and unpleasant, made more so by the inferior 3-D process.

Spanish Fly (1975) (85mins) (a Canada-U.K. co-production) d: Robert Kellet, Robert Ryerson : Leslie Phillips, Terry Thomas, Graham Armitage, Nadiuska, Sue Lloyd, Frank Thornton. Two popular British comedians, Thomas and Phillips, are all but lost trying to make funny this feeble jaunt to Minorca to photograph scantily dressed models among other antics. Almost nothing about this is Canadian except the producers applying for their tax benefits.

Sparkle (1998) (82mins) d&s: Jeff Beesley : Wendy Anderson, Jake Roberts, Bradley Turton. What happens to three teens after leaving school? One to succeed, one to become pregnant another always being taken advantage of. Life is dull; so is this film, with no sparkle, no doubt the point of the picture.

Spasms: see **Death Bite**

Speaking Parts (1989) (92 mins) d&s: Atom Egoyan : Arsinée Khanjian, Michael McManus, Gabrielle Rose, Tony Nardi, David Hemblen, Patricia Collins. Once again this director is balancing on the fine line that exists between individuals as they are and they way they appear to others. Set against a background of communication by television, with masturbation and video during the writing of a screenplay on a family relationship. For the most part dense, deadly and dull.

Special Day, A: see *Giornata particolare, Una*

Special Delivery (1982) (65mins) d: Randolph Bradshaw s: Keith Ross Leckie : Wanda Cannon, Jonathan Welsh, David McIlwraith, Mary Long, Barbara Gordon. A woman's decision to have a natural childbirth is opposed by her husband, a medical researcher. This conflict threatens to destroy their marriage, and the subject of a woman's right to decide these matters comes to the fore.

Special Inspector: see **British Quota Era Films**

Special Magnum (Strange Shadows in an Empty Room) (1977) (99mins) (a Canada-Italy co-production) d&s: Alberto de Martino : Stuart Whitman, John Saxon, Martin Landau, Tisa Farrow, Carole Laure, Jean Leclerc, Gayle Hunnicutt, Jean Marchand,

Julie Wildman. A police officer travels from Toronto to Montréal to attend his sister's funeral and find her murderer. A colossal waste of time and money on yet another of our overblown co-productions.

Sphinx, The (1995) (100mins) d: Louis Saia s: Marc Messier : Marc Messier, Céline Bonnier, Serge Thériault, Eric Hoziel, Vittorio Rossi, Sylvie Drapeau. A comedy populated by many favourite Québec comedians, this is an uneven mix of laughs woven around a peculiar tale of a husband who leaves his wife and children for an erotic dancer. Too long and underdeveloped, bringing in the usual drug, mobster and partying scenes. This would be dull indeed without its rocking, lively music.

Spider (2002) (98mins) (a U.K.-Canada co-production) d: David Cronenberg s: Patrick McGrath (based on his novel) : Ralph Fiennes, Miranda Richardson, Gabriel Byrne, Bradley Hall, Lynn Redgrave, John Neville, Gary Reineke, Philip Craig. After a long period in a mental institution, a placid, lost-in-the-past man suffering from severe mental illness returns to East End London, where he grew up. The sights, sounds and smells of those streets begin to awaken deeply buried memories of his childhood, and Spider sees himself as a little boy. This engrossing, stark, never depressing but so very honest and deeply moving film simply cannot be faulted. The camera work, editing, the London locations, and the brilliant acting performances are mesmerizing and unforgettable. Like the best moments of great silent cinema, the scenes where Spider, gaunt, grim and dark, appears to see himself as a small boy, moving around the house with his parents, are so quietly dramatic as to seem to be nightmares. And what an opening shot: the train pulls into Victoria station, the passengers all hurry away and thin out, and there, standing in his worn suit, body seeming to crumble, is Spider. But most important of all is that Cronenberg, after a career of self-indulgent, nasty-minded mediocre movies, has emerged as a true director, one who finally seems to understand the literacy of cinema and the eye of the camera. Perhaps he should go back to the U.K. and make more films. As for the present, *Spider* will not be forgotten.

Spike of Love (1994) (93mins) (a U.S.-Canada film) d&s: Steve DiMarco : Dyanne DiMarco, Ronald Lea, Tony Munch, Gerry Quigley. A vague young man is studying to become a priest through a correspondence course. All around him, various 'chicks', and other awful characters, are fornicating and playing kinky games, with psychos out for vengeance, looking at the severed head of a murder victim, a noxious, contemptible picture.

Spirit of Evil, The: see *Esprit du mal, L'*

Spirit Rider (1993) (75mins) (b/w/col) d: Michael Scott s: Mary Ellen Lang Collura (based on her novel *Winners*) : Herbie Barnes, Adam Beach, Graham Greene, Michelle St. John, Tantoo Cardinal, Tom Jackson, Gordon Tootoosis. Set in Manitoba, this handsomely mounted and well-executed story depicts a recalcitrant 16-year-old native boy within the repatriation government program, in which he is made to learn about life away from the reservation. On his return 14 years later, he wants nothing more to do with his past. This courageous little film makes a case for the benefits of self-determination. Well played and often affecting, it is naturally acted and believably played out. It compares well with the companion pictures, such as *Lost in the Barrens* and *The Curse of the Viking Grave,* by Farley Mowat.

Spreading Ground, The (2000) (100mins) d: Derek Vanlint s: Mark Katsumi, Nakamura : Dennis Hopper, Leslie Hope, Frederic Forrest, Tom McCamus, Elizabeth Shepherd, Chuck Shamata, David Dunbar. This promising thriller about detectives hunting down the elusive murderer of young girls is minimalist and bland following all the conventions.

Spring Fever: see **Sneakers**

Squamish Five, The (1988) (98mins) d: Paul Donovan s: Ken Gass : Robyn Stevan, Michael McManus, Albert Schultz, David McLeod, Nicky Guadagni. This excellent film is based on the actual bombing of Litton Industries in Toronto in 1982 by a misguided left-wing group protesting Canada's part in the "arms race". This dark, sometimes funny and entirely compelling re-enactment, with some fictional overtones in characterization, is one of the few dramatized films made in this country to concern itself with political and social unrest.

Stag (1997) (92mins) d: Gavin Wilding s: Evan Tylor, Pat Bermel (based on a story by Jason Schombing) : Andrew McCarthy, John Stockwell, Kevin Dillon, Taylor Dayne, Mario van Peebles, Ben Gazzara. A group of loud and drunken young men are attending a stag party in a friend's home. One of the strippers brought in for entertainment is killed. Disorder then takes over as efforts are made to hide the crime from the police. Drinks, drugs and degeneracy.

Stalking of Laurie Show, The (2000) (120mins) d: Norma Bailey s: Jennifer Salt : Jennifer Finnigan, Marnette Patterson, Rel Hunt, Mary-Margaret Humes. Another of the slight yet devastating stories based on an event which is news in today's media and forgotten by next week. Laurie, a teenage girl, and her mother leave Canada to live in a small town in Pennsylvania where the daughter is terrorized and eventually murdered by a classmate jealous of the attention her boyfriend is giving to the "new girl" in school. Poignant and true in the telling.

Stallion (1988) (90mins) (a Canada-France co-production) d: Mohamed Benayat s: Elisabeth Leclair, Mohamed Benayat : Charles Mayer, Frédérique Feder. A man leaves his boring life in Paris, goes to Montréal to save his sister from a life of prostitution, and fulfills his dream of living on a ranch in Arizona. Pretty silly business all round.

Stampede: see **British Quota Era Films**

Star Is Lost, A (1974) (75mins) d: John Howe s: Don Arioli, John Howe : Tiiu Leek, Don Arioli, Les Nirenberg, Ken James, Jack Creley, Eric House, Al Waxman, Tom Harvey, Barrie Baldaro, Michele Craig, Grant Munro, J.-Léo Gagnon. An inexperienced star disappears after being mismanaged by her boyfriend. An ambitious attempt by the NFB to make a musical with melodies by director Howe, in which the music and the comedy simply doesn't jell and all is lost. Tiiu Leek was the talk of the town for some time, then she appeared only to disappear.

Stardom (15 Minutes) (Fandom) (2000) (102mins) (a Canada-France co-production) d: Denys Arcand s: Jacob Potashnik, Denys Arcand : Jessica Paré, Dan Aykroyd, Charles Berling, Robert Lepage, Thomas Gibson, Frank Langella, Camille Rutherford. A small-town girl in Cornwall, Ontario, becomes a famous model in this stinging satire, biting comedy perfect parody of the mindless people who inhabit television, not forgetting the foolish fashion designers, the shams who call themselves artists, and the crafty politicians, and synthetic media types, mixed with the publis's obseesion with celebrity. It is a broad and detailed canvas only a genius such as Arcand could fill with telling images and knowing performances. Yet above all and throughout it's an appreciation of beauty surviving in a society in which life imitates art, art imitates life, and the media imitates anything and everything. Flawlessly played by a splendid cast.

Stargazing and Other Passions: see *Sous les draps, les étoiles*

Starlight (1995) (100mins) d: Jonathon Kay s: Michael St. Gerard, John Smith, Jonathon Kay : Rae Dawn Chong, Billy Wirth, Willie Nelson, Deborah Wakeham, Jim Byrnes, Alex Daikun. A sci-fi melodrama-romance set in the Rocky Mountains in which a lonely man—a half-alien son of a cosmonaut from Pleiades—meets a beautiful geneticist from the same planet who wants to take him back with her. They have fallen in love, but he doesn't want to leave and she cannot stay. Will their union bring about a new breed of mankind? We can only hope not. Magical at times but hard to believe.

Stars Under the Sheets: see *Sous les draps, les étoiles*

Starship Invasions (1977) (89mins) (a Canadian-American film) d&s: Ed Hunt : Robert Vaughn, Christopher Lee, Daniel Pilon, Tiiu Leek, Helen Shaver, Sean McCann, Victoria Johnson, Henry Ramer, Gordon Thomson. Good and bad aliens battle over who will rule the Earth. Good cast floats around in poor script and awful special effects. Space travel has improved somewhat since this invasion.

State of Shock: see **Power Play**

State Park (1987) (94mins) d: Rafal Zielinski s: Neal Noble : Kim Myers, Isabelle Mejias, Jennifer Inch. Three young women, long-time friends, are on a camping trip in Parc du Mont-Tremblant, Québec, when they discover signs of a probable ecological disaster. Nothing much happens as a result of their find.

Station nord (North Station) (2002) (111mins) d: Jean-Claude Lord s: Daniel Morin, Denyse Benoît : Benoît Briere, Xavier Morin-Lefort, Roxanne Gaudette-Loiseau, Catherine Florent, Lansana Kourouma. An unusual and delightful family Christmas film from the veteran Jean-Claude Lord. This is about a 14-year-old mailman who is taken to Santa's workshop by a young elf to be in charge of the mail for the North Pole. There are complications, of course, but magic brings about the happy ending. Beautifully told, dressed and photographed.

Stations (1983) (86mins) d&s: William MacGillivray : Michael Jones, Richard Boland, Andy Jones, Mary Walsh, Libby Davies, Patricia Kipping. After failing his training to be a priest, a young man becomes a tv journalist. One of his first assignments is to travel by train across Canada to find out for himself people's opinions about religion. As most of the participants in this film belong to the lively, out-spoken school of Newfoundland comedy, there are quite naturally a great many laughs on the journey, and the scenery is marvellous.

St-Denis dans le temps: see Battle of St. Denis... Yesterday, Today, The

Steal (Riders) (2002) (86mins) (a Canada-France co-production) d: Gerard Pires s: Mark Ezra : Stephen Dorff, Natasha Henstridge, Bruce Payne, Steven Berkoff, Karen Cliché, Cle Bennett, Steven McCarthy. An untidy crime melodrama about a gang of young thieves, a crooked policeman, and the mob and heists here, there and everywhere. Nothing new here.

Stereo (1969) (65mins) (b&w) d&s: David Cronenberg : Ronald Mlodzik, Iain Ewing, Jack Messinger, Clara Mayer, Paul Mulholland, Arlene Mlodzik, Glenn McCauley. Cronenberg's first film. An experimental portrait of the schizophrenic nature of man and the world he inhabits. The film was submitted to the 1969 Canadian Film Awards but was rejected, much to the director's fury, by the pre-selection committee on the grounds that it was totally confusing, pointless and couldn't be considered as being a feature film. Filmed in Toronto.

Stiletto Dance (2000) (98mins) d: Mario Azzopardi s: Alfonse Ruggiero : Eric Roberts, Romano Orzari, Shawn Doyle, Brett Porter, Lucie Laurier. A far-fetched work of muddled mayhem in which two undercover policemen who hear about the sale of nuclear arms have a hard time stopping it. It requires, naturally, constant violence and bad language.

Still Life (Still Life: The Fine Art of Murder) (1990) (82mins) d: Graeme Campbell s: Dean Parisot, Michael Taav : Jason Gedrick, Jessica Steen, Stephen Shellen, Gary Farmer, Sam Malkin, Beverly Murray. We are in Manhattan's Lower East Side and as this is supposed to be a horror film, a serial killer is on the loose—one who has taken a liking to the world of art. A horror in more ways than one.

Stillborn Lover, The: see **External Affairs**

Stolen Heart (1998) (95mins) d&s: Terry O'Brien : Lisa Ryder, Randy Hughson, Gary Farmer, Christopher Healey, James Gatto, Shirley McQueen, Meghan Toll. A low-budget timely little film with good intentions, but not entirely satisfactory result in raising the important questions and issues of parents' rights to see and perhaps take care again of their children who have been placed in custody.

Stolen Miracle (2001) (120mins) d: Norma Bailey s: Peter Lauterman, Shelley Eriksen : Leslie Hope, Hugh Thompson, Marnie McPhail, Nola Augustson, Dean McDermott, Gabriel Hogan. Based on the real-life story of a startling occurrence at Christmas 1993 when a newborn child was abducted from the maternity ward of a small-town Ontario hospital, which remains unnamed in the film—no doubt due to fear of a lawsuit. Effective, appealing and highly charged. (See: *Signature* series)

Stone Coats (1997) (78mins) d&s: Rolf Schrader : Carrie Schiffler, Lyle St. Goddard, Friedrich Mayr, Brennan Elliott. A man who has lived most of his life on the streets begins to search anxiously for his girlfriend, who has disappeared. Helped by a long-time hooker, life becomes even more complicated. A little film with a lot to say, without amounting to much by finishing time.

Stone Cold Dead (1979) (100mins) (a Canada-US film) d&s: George Mendeluk (from the book *The Sin Sniper* by Hugh Garner) : Richard Crenna, Paul Williams, Linda Sorensen, Belinda Montgomery, Chuck Shamata, Andrée Cousineau, Alberta Watson, Monique Mercure, Frank Moore, Jennifer Dale, Paul Bradley, Michael Ironside, Nicky Fylan. Steamy melodrama about a Toronto detective searching for a modern-day Jack the Ripper who shoots prostitutes. The detective is also determined to arrest the pushy pimps and devious drug dealers. Toronto by night comes out looking very dark and dirty. A good cast brings some sense of meaning to the goings-on.

Stone Woman, The (*Femme de pierre*) (1990) (86mins) d&s: Jean Salvy : Louise Marleau, Gilles Renaud, Pascale Bussières, Patrick Labbé. In a small Québec town, a mother distraught over the death of her son from food poisoning tragically destroys her marriage and her life. A dark portrait with the incomparable Marleau.

Stop (1971) (85mins) d: Jean Beaudin s: Clément Perron : Raymond Bouchard, Danielle Naud, Marie Tifo. Another *Stop the World I Want to Get Off*, more likely to evoke the response "Stop the film, I want to get out!" Once again, the story of people destroying themselves for materialistic purposes, and who are unable to commit to or communicate with each other, all heavily laced with solemn sex both real and imagined. This film should have stopped before it started.

Stories of Chide the Wind: see **Soul Investigator, The**

Stork Derby, The (2001) (120mins) d: Mario Azzopardi s: Karyn Nolan (based on the book *Bearing the Burden: The Great Toronto Stork Derby, 1926-1938*, by Elizabeth Wilton) : Megan Follows, Pascale Montpetit, R.H. Thomson, John Neville, Eric Peterson, Ellen David, Janine Thériault, Terry Simpson. A wealthy never-married lawyer, Charles Millar, dies in Toronto in 1926 and bequeaths a million dollars to the Toronto woman who can give birth to the highest number of babies in the ten years after his death. This news makes headlines around the world and creates a media frenzy known as the "Great Toronto Stork Derby", a *Toronto Daily Star*–sponsored race, with coverage spanning more than ten years and culminating in a sensational court case. This film captures the time and the topic simply marvellously and takes us back to these now-distant times in Toronto.

Storm (1985) (96mins) d&s: David Winning : David Palfy, Tom Schioler, Sam Kane, Harry Freedman, Lawrence Elion. A compact little drama from Alberta in which a couple taking a walk in the woods encounters a gang of thieves. Some violence but taken all together, nothing to get worked up about.

Story of Colin and Joan Thatcher, The: see **Love and Hate**

Story of Dr. Louise, The (*Docteur Louise*) (1949) (100mins) (b&w) (a Canada-France-film) d: Paul Vandenberghe & Rene Delacroix s: Maurice Jacquemont, Aloysius Vachet, Jean-Louis Bouquet : Madeleine Robinson, Jean Davy, Line Noro, Henri Poitras, Suzanne Avon, Jean-Louis Roux. A young woman doctor, at a time when women as doctors were opposed by the medical profession, doctor Louise found her difficulties doubled in the antagonistic Quebec country town where she opens a practice and the people show their resentment over her appearance. (This was one of the several feature films to be made in Quebec after WWII, by the pioneering company Renaissance.) (Alexandre De Sevre)

Story of the Hunt, The (*Histoire de chasse*) (1990) (106mins) d: Louis-Georges Carrier s: Jean-Marie Poupart : Jean-René Ouellet, Michel Daigle, Hélène Major, Monique Mercure. Two friends—one a taxi driver, the other a magazine editor—meet after being apart for 25 years. While the somewhat proper editor leads a steady life, the taxi driver creates his own life as he drives around all and every day. These differences lead not to a clearly defined destination but to tragedy, murder and further complications that change their lives. A fascinating kaleidoscope of places, events, human emotions, desires and failures. A "road film" with deep differences from the conventional routes!

Story of the Three, A (*L'histoire des trois*) (1989) (74mins) (b&w) d: Jean-Claude Labrecque s: Lise Létourneau, Carmel Dumas : Jean-Pierre Goyer,

Francine Laurendeau, Bruno Meloche. Going back to 1958, this little politico-drama recalls the incident when three students attempted to see Premier Maurice Duplessis to express their worry and fears over the lack of opportunities to attend university. Passionate in its pleading.

Straight to the Heart (*Justocoeur*) (1969) (92mins) d&s: Jean-Pierre Lefebvre : Robert Charlebois, Claudine Monfette, Claudette Robitaille, Paul Berval, Denis Drouin, Pierre Dufresne, Luc Granger, Gaetan Labrèche, Louise Dionne, Pierrette Lavigueur. A young man's message is this: no matter what society does to destroy the individual, to murder his soul, it cannot conquer his heart. Our life, says Lefebvre, is science fiction. There is much talk of destiny, parallel lives, the mystery of existence, the matter of choice, the effect of advertising on individuals, love and death, the bomb and abortion. All too true, but also like life, overwhelming.

Strange and Rich (1994) (95mins) d: Arvi Liimatainen s: Roy Sallows : Ron White, Michele Goodger, Christine MacInnis, Larry Musser, Jan Wood, Eugene Lipinski. A small town is wracked by doubts and fears when a new police chief arrives and finds himself in conflict with the sergeant; a suspicious death and an escaped convict make matters worse. The frustrations of the characters are well caught against real-life backgrounds.

Strange Blues of Cowboy Red, The (1995) (85mins) d: Rick Raxlen s: Brenda Newman, Rick Raxlen : Terry Haig, Debra Weiner, Chloé Rose, Kristine Demers, Susan Raxlen, Glen Lemesieur, Ray Condo, Leni Parker. The memories of Red, a young Canadian boy who grew up watching cowboy films in the '50s, are woven into the lives of Roy Rogers, Dale Evans and Trigger. As a man, Red travels into the desert searching for the "Cowboy Code." A biographical film, the director calls this a "poetic and personal meditation on the moral values of this time in his life and their effect on him in his role as father, husband, artist and English Québecker." Movie buffs might pass over much of this to enjoy the shots from Roy's films and tv and from a rare silent movie, *The Irish Gringo*.

Strange Brew (1983) (90mins) d&s: Dave Thomas, Rick Moranis : Dave Thomas, Rick Moranis, Max Von Sydow, Paul Dooley, Lynne Griffin, Angus MacInnes, Douglas Campbell, Tom Harvey, Brian McConnachie, Len Doncheff, Jill Frappier, David Beard, Thick Wilson, Mel Blanc (voice of Mr. McKenzie), Eric House. This is such an innocuous concoction that it is hard to find fault with its lack of brilliance or drive when it comes to adding up the laughs in this slight but entirely amiable comedy. The film introduces to the screen the two Canadian "hosers," brothers who became well known on the small screen, with a host of fellow comedians, in SCTV. Here we have the story of a mad brewer who plans to take over the world with his newly brewed and potent beer. The brothers, in their bumbling way, soon put an end to his ambitions. However, there is enough good humour to sustain the whole, and audiences abroad will be introduced for the first time to the big socio-cultural Canadian joke in which "hosers" are identified by their liking for plaid clothing, toques, earmuffs, an infinite capacity for back bacon and beer, and the habit of ending every comment with the query "Eh?" They have undoubtedly created a national characteristic, one that some Canadians prefer to ignore. This film has the distinction of being one of the first of the very few Canadian films to be distributed by a major American company, in this instance MGM.

Strange Horizons (1992) (83mins) d&s: Philip Jackson : David Ferry, Olga Prokhorova. Weird and weak amalgamation of science fiction, black humour, alcohol, drugs and spaced-out characters in an alien world in the 23rd century.

Strange Shadows in an Empty Room: see **Special Magnum**

Stranger in the House: see **Black Christmas**

Stranger in Town (1998) (94mins) d: Stuart Margolin s: John Hopkins : Harry Hamlin, Shaun Johnston, Rebecca Jenkins, Dixie Seatle, Graham Greene, Trevor Blumas, Alison Pill. In this suspenseful drama, a suspicious son investigates a local murder to see if his mother's new heartthrob is guilty of it. A good cast keeps interest high.

Strangers in Good Company: see **Company of Strangers, The**

Strass Café (1980) (65 mins) d: Léa Pool s: Luc Caron, Léa Pool : Céline Lacoste, Luc Caron, Léa Pool, Antoinette Ammann, Yvei Champagne, Louise Ladouceur. The first of Léa Pool's Canadian films. Of it she has said that *Strass Café* is, "...a place within me. Neither Québec nor Switzerland; the story of the encounter of two beings. Never seen, living through their solitudes. A door for the imaginary world. To let the emptiness reach ourselves. Only then we shall create." And this set the pattern for her films that followed.

Street Law (Law of the Jungle) (1995) (98mins) (a Canada-U.S. film) d&s: Damian Lee : Paco Christian Prieto, Jeff Wincott, Christina Cox, Richard Yearwood, Michael Copeman. The trials and tribulations of a martial arts–trained lawyer and what happens to him when he is forced to pay off a loan shark. This is one cause that should never have come to court. Violent martial arts rule here.

Streetheart (*Le coeur au poing*) (1998) (100mins) d: Charles Binamé s: Monique Proulx, Charles Binamé : Pascale Montpetit, Anne-Marie Cadieux, Guy Nadon, Guylaine Tremblay. A dark and touching drama about two sisters, one who is not quite of this world and offers herself to strangers for one hour. Some people react in disbelief and reject her; others show compassion, and some think only of sex. This is a woman who feels too deeply and expects too much from life. Her sister tries to bring her down to earth but she has her own disappointments to contend with. Binamé tells the story with understanding and sensitivity and the two actresses are perfect in their roles.

Strike! (1998) (110mins) (a Canadian-American film) d&s: Sarah Kernochan : Lynn Redgrave, Gaby Hoffman, Kirsten Dunst, Monica Keena, Merritt Wever. Toronto, anytown U.S.A, is the background to this ridiculously named film set in an all-women boarding school that becomes co-ed, around 1963. The following confrontations between the sexes leads to a series of disasters both amusing, frank and forced, but nicely recreate the tunes and times of the 1960s. Sex, of course, is everywhere dispensed by a cast of college girls.

Striker's Mountain (1985) (98mins) d: Alan Simmonds s: Peter White, Wendy Wacko : August Schellenberg, Leslie Nielsen, Mimi Kuzyk, Bruce Greenwood, Jessica Steen, Robin Gammell, Thomas Peacocke, Booth Savage, Francis Damberger. In Jasper National Park, Alberta, a businessman who runs a helicopter skiing attraction finds himself in conflict with a developer who wants to buy the enterprise and build a large resort. Different and daring, with an early screen appearance by Bruce Greenwood.

Striking Poses (1999) (93mins) (a Canada-U.S. film) d: Gail Harvey s: Michael Stokes : Joseph Griffin, Colm Feore, Shannen Doherty, Diane D'Aquila, Tamara Gorski, Janet-Laine Green, Aidan Devine. A photographer for a sensational tabloid finds herself on the other side of the page when a psychotic stalker (aren't they all?) begins to move into her private life and threatens to murder her. We've seen it before but the director gives it a new life.

Stuart Bliss (1998) (88mins) (a Canadian-American film) d: Neil Grieve s: Michael Zelniker : Michael Zelniker, Dea Lawrence, Hoke Howell, Derek McGrath, Ania Suli. Stuart Bliss' world begins to fall apart when his frustrated wife walks out on him. This domestic comedy drama has its moments now and then, but on the whole it's a life without bliss that begins to weary.

Stuff (1999) (87mins) d&s: James & Rebecca Dunnison : Max Danger, Sandra Guérard, Joe Sather, Maureen Burgoyne, Winston Spear, Russell Oliver, Irene Leonetti. An off-the-wall, fly by night, loose and lively comedy the likes of which have never before appeared on and torn up Canadian movie screens. It's about many deeds, antics and absurdities revolving around the strange behaviour of a loopy young orderly in a Toronto hospital. He lives in the basement of his mother's home. She is paranoid and very nasty, so he murders her and tries to bury her in the yard, all the while strange events wind their quirky way among his stuff of life, which is far from being the staff of life, and of which there is

entirely too much.While not always pleasant, it was not meant to be, it is much to be preferred to what passes for comedy on the stage and screen today.

Suburban Legend (1995) (64mins) d&s: Jay Ferguson : Stuart Burchill, Jenny Whiteley, Mike Varley, Christopher Robinson, Vanessa Slater. A study of a young man who resorts to tv and pornography to learn about sex. Years later at university, with his parents still refusing to discuss the subject, he learns that he cannot deal with simple problems or communicate effectively with women. A legend this certainly is not. He's just a tiresome young man in a tedious film.

Suburbanators, The (1995) (87mins) d&s: Gary Burns : Joel McNichol, Stephen Spender, Stewart Burdett, Jacob Banigan, Jihad Traya. Bored youth in Calgary seek out something to do in this largely improvised and uninteresting anti-drama set in cars, homes and city streets. Only one brief incident, in which a youth describes his efforts to get a job, is genuinely funny.

Such a Long Journey (1998) (113mins) (a Canada-India co-production) d: Sturla Gunnarsson s: Sooni Taraporevala (from the novel by Rohinton Mistry) : Roshan Seth, Om Puri, Soni Radzan, Naseeruddinn Shah, Pearl Padamsee, Ranjit Chowdhry. Set in Bombay in 1971, the year India went to war over the creation of Bangladesh, the social upheaval is seen through the eyes of an honest, industrious bank clerk, a man dedicated to his family and whose principles are compromised by terrorist activities. An excellent cast of Indian players, set against authentic backgrounds, make this a thoughtful and honest film, but lacking the empathy a talented Indian filmmaker would have brought to it.

Sucre amer (1997) (90mins) (a Canada-France co-production) d&s: Christian Lara : Jean-Michel Martial, Marie Verdi, Gabriel Gascon, Maka Kotto. Major figures from history are brought together to serve on a "court of history" to decide whether or not a legendary figure in the history of Guadeloupe—Ignace, who fought against the armies of Napoléon—should receive a new and fair trial. Of limited appeal but not without interest.

Sudden Fury (1975) (91mins) d&s: Brian Damude : Dominic Hogan, Gay Rowan, Dan Hennessy, Hollis McLaren, David Yorston, Sean McCann, Eric Clavering, Robin Ward. Set in the Ontario countryside during summertime, this effectively told and cleverly filmed low-budget picture concerns a husband whose work is failing, whose wife is unfaithful, and who, on a car journey northwards, becomes thoroughly demented when his wife refuses to give him money to buy land in a real-estate scheme. An accident gives the husband an opportunity to leave his wife to die. A sympathetic young man comes along and attempts to save her. By the time this straightforward but ingenious tale has finished, the innocent man is the murderer.

Suddenly Naked (2001) (105mins) d: Anne Wheeler s: Elyse Friedman : Wendy Crewson, Peter Coyote, Joe Cobden. The scene is set for a love affair between two writers: a 20-year-old man and a 40-year-old woman. At first, she cannot admit her love either to herself or to her friends, thinking him too young. With much bad language, their association carries on among the superficial lives and activities of characters in film and television. However, it must be said that Wendy Crewson, with energy to spare, makes her unlikeable character credible. Otherwise, there is no one here to relate to, feel sympathy for, or find interest in. This film could have shown a very real and affecting relationship; instead it enjoys its excesses at the expense of honesty.

Sue Lost in Manhattan (Sue) (1997) (87mins) (a U.S.-Canada film) d&s: Amos Kollek : Anna Levine, Tahnee Welch, Matthew Powers, Tracee Ellis Ross. An out-of-work and troubled woman living in a sleazy New York City hotel desperately seeks companionship as she tries to cope with her descent into madness. Honest, depressing and deeply moving.

Suicide Murders, The (1986) (98mins) d: Graham Parker s: Howard Engel (based on the novel of the same title) : Saul Rubinek, Richard Donat, Sherry Flett, Helen Hughes, Gerard Parkes, Michael Hogan, Tanya Jacobs. Detective Benny Cooperman has been hired to follow a land developer, who apparently kills himself. The detective then tries to convince the police that there is more to this small-town suicide than meets the eye. Tense and exciting, this is very much a different view of crime in Canada. This was the first of Howard Engel's 10-volume series of Benny Cooperman books. (See: *Murder Sees the Light*)

Summer (2002) (89mins) d: Phil Price s: Myles Hainsworth : Joe Cobden, Karen Cliché, Michael Rubenfeld, Amy Sloane. Three friends graduate from college and gather by a pool to begin a summer of fun. They are a disagreeable, unlikeable lot, given to bad language and silly comments such as 'lick-a-dick' and 'I have a small penis'. Just when one feels 'enough is enough' the film improves when they all go north to cottage country to begin writing a magazine. Other friends arrive, sex is in the air, and in the bed, but they become likeable, with more sense than expected, and where they find that the 'course of true love does not run true'. The end appears to come about with a beautifully staged and oddly moving moment at a concert where one of the girls sings 'silly bitch', an appealing song which sums up what trying to become an actress is about. The film loses its spell after this and limps to a contrived ending. One welcome touch throughout however is they all don't hesitate to say they are 'from Toronto'. And it's good to see, if only briefly, Victor Knight again.

Summer Holidays: see *En vacances*

Summer of the Colt (*Fierro ou l'été des secrets*) (1989) (100mins) (a Canada-Argentina co-production) d: André Melançon s: Geneviève Lefebvre, Rodolfo Otero (from his novel) : Hector Alterio, China Zorrilla, Alexandra London-Thompson, Juan de Benedictus. A simple but compelling story by Otero set against beautiful scenery surrounding a family ranch. Here, 12-year-old Martin, his friend, brother and sister come from Buenos Aires to visit their grandfather. There are hundreds of beautiful horses to be ridden and enjoyed—a family tradition that has taught the children to become aware of the land and to love nature. Family complications cast a shadow, but at the end the children are happily looking forward to next summer. A delightful, aware and honest film made with skill and sensitivity. (See: *Tales for All* series)

Summer of the Monkeys (1998) (100mins) (a Canadian-American film) d: Michael Anderson s: Greg Taylor, Jim Strain : Leslie Hope, Michael Ontkean, Wilford Brimley, Katie Stuart, Don Francks, André Thérien, Melissa Thomson. A 14-year-old boy is working in his grandfather's store to save money to buy a pony. One day he finds a group of monkeys who have escaped from a circus. He takes them back and is given reward money. He can now work on his father's farm and help care for his younger sister and still buy his pony. A charming tale beautifully brought to the screen by Michael Anderson. Not a false tear is shed.

Summer With the Ghosts (*Un été avec les fantômes*) (2002) (85mins) (a Canada-Austria co-production) d: Bernd Neuburger s: Nadja Selich : Sarah-Jeanne Labrose, Nikola Culka, Ron Lea, Karl Merkatz, Richard Jutras. A ten-year-old girl goes to Austria from Montreal to spend time with her father who is making a film in a ghostly medieval castle. But something is going wrong. With the help of an Austrian boy, they uncover the ghosts of five nuns buried alive 500 years ago for daring to dance during the night. Another of Rock Demers' international family films should find an appreciative audience. (See: *Tales for All* series)

Summer's Children (1979) (82mins) d: Julius Kohanyi s: Jim Osborne : Tom Hauff, Paully Jardine, Don Francks, Kate Lynch, Ken James, Patricia Collins, Kay Hawtrey, Michael Ironside. A first feature by a former short-film maker showing considerable feeling, ability and appeal in this portraying of a brother-and-sister love affair set in Toronto, discreet to the point of sometimes becoming tiring.

Summerlust (Goodbye Neighbours and Wives) (1973) (77mins) d&s: William and Jean Kowalchuk : Gray Johnson, Chris Little, Terri Toth, Tamara Edwards, Susan Sachs. A lively film made in Burleigh Falls, Ontario, by young hopefuls (the Kowalchuks and Larry Strauss) in the years when raising money for even the most modest of films was almost impossible. But they managed it, and made this picture about young people having fun at a picnic party. When it was all done, the Kowalchuks said they wanted their following films to make Toronto's streets and scenery as familiar on our screens as Los Angeles and California have become through Hollywood films. But regrettably, life didn't work out this way for our movies.

Sun of the Others, The: see *Soleil des autres, Le*

Sun Rises Late, The (*Le soleil se leve en retard***)** (1977) (112mins) d: André Brassard s: Michel Tremblay, André Brassard : Rita Lafontaine, Yvon Deschamps, Denise Filiatrault, Huguette Oligny, Claude Gai, Paule Baillargeon. A touching description of a 30-year-old unmarried woman whose previous unhappy relationship with a man makes it difficult for her to love again. Insightful and sympathetic. This is the kind of delicate story Québec filmmakers manage so well, and dialogue by Tremblay is an asset to the cast and the screenplay.

Sunday in the Country (1975) (92mins) (a Canada-U.K. co-production) d: John Trent s: Robert Maxwell, John Trent (from a story by David Main) : Ernest Borgnine, Michael J. Pollard, Hollis McLaren, Louis Zorich, Cec Linder, Vladimir Valenta, Al Waxman, Tim Henry, Murray Westgate, Ralph Endersby, Susan Petrie, Ratch Wallace, Mark Walker, Gary Reineke, Eric Clavering, David Hughes, Carl Banas, Franz Russell, Ruth Springford, Alan King, Laddie Dennis, Joan Hurley, Winnifred Springbett, Jonathan White, Jim Barron. A contrived and bloody melodrama about a farmer and his terrible vengeance on three bank robbers. This film marked the beginning of Canada's pseudo-American film period (the setting is supposedly the U.S.) with American actors in the leads.

Sunset Court (1988) (76mins) d: Marc Voizard s: George Arthur Bloom : Ted Wass, Elizabeth Bellm, George Robertson, Caird Urquhart Tennis anyone? A dedicated tennis player finds that her passion to win becomes greater than her passion to love. There are games on both sides of the net, but a draw finally calms things somewhat. (See: *Shades of Love* series)

Sunshine (1999) (180mins) (a Canada-U.K.-Hungary-German co-production) d: Istvan Szabo s: Istvan Szabo and Israel Horovitz : Ralph Fiennes, Rachel Weisz, Rosemary Harris, Jennifer Ehle, Deborah Kara Unger, Molly Parker, William Hurt. A magnificent and personal epic spanning three generations of the Sonnenscheins, a Hungarian Jewish family. The splendid Fiennes plays a different role in each generation as the disturbing and horrifying events of the past century encircle and trap the family in this brave film. It met with considerable resistance when shown in Hungary.

Super 8 (1994) (106mins) (b/w) d&s: Bruce LaBruce : Bruce LaBruce, Liza LaMonica, Mikey Mike, Klaus von Brucker, Buddy Cole, Scott Thompson. Described by his punkster friends as a leading avant-garde filmmaker, Bruce LaBruce, here playing himself (could he possibly ever be anyone else?), wanders through the past thirty years to collect and portray a sick stream of queer art and pornographic cinema, in a pastiche of uncontrolled wallowing in sex and sluttishness. A jumble-jungle of old new black and white–and that's it!

Super Star (1999) (81mins) (a U.S.-Canada film) d: Bruce McCulloch s: Molly Shannon, Steve Koren : Molly Shannon, Elaine Hendrix, Will Ferrell, Glynis Johns, Tom Green, Rob Stefaniuk. A plain high-school girl believes her feelings of being unwanted will change if only she could become a star in a talent contest and make a date with a popular boy. Trivial from start to finish. A pity to see the long absent and wonderful Glynis Johns return to this.

Superdame: see *Craque la vie*

Supreme Kid, The (1976) (88mins) d&s: Peter Bryant : Frank Moore, Jim Henshaw, Don Granbery, Helen Shaver. A likeable but overlong tale about discontented students wandering through British Columbia in search of themselves.

Sur Le Seuil **(Under the Sky)** (2003) (97mins) d: Eric Tessier s: Patrick Senecal & Tessier : Michel Cote, Patrick Huard, Catherine Florent, Albert Millaire. A murder-mystery in which a policeman kills children; a writer of horror stories then tries to commit suicide; no one knows why until a tired-of-it-all psychiatrist, starts to put the facts together taking the murders into terrifying events. Hardly *Inspector Morse*, but a welcome entry into this style of thriller, not much seen on film today having been banished to tv.

Surfacing (1981) (88mins) d: Claude Jutra s: Bernard Gordon (based on the novel by Margaret Atwood) : Joseph Bottoms, Kathleen Beller, R.H. Thomson, Margaret Dragu, Michael Ironside, James Buller, Larry Schwartz, Diane Bigelow. Atwood's novel is here turned into an American-looking film with two American actors who are out of place in a murky transposition of the original story. What was intended as an examination of thoughts, feelings and the innermost fears of human abstractionism becomes a meaningless, coarse and sour depiction of a daughter's search in the northern backwoods for her missing father. Not one of Jutra's finest films, but not entirely his fault.

Surrogate (1984) (100mins) d: Don Carmody s: Don Carmody and Robert Geoffrion : Carole Laure, Art Hindle, Shannon Tweed, Michael Ironside, Jim Bailey, Marilyn Lightstone, Jackie Burroughs, Gary Reineke. A car dealer in Montréal suffers from uncontrollable rages and forgetfulness. When he goes with his wife to see a psychiatrist, they become involved in a series of mysterious murders. An appalling exploitation picture wallowing in sex and violence and wasting a good cast.

Suspended Life: The Charming Story of the Adolescent Sugar Love: see *Adolescente sucré d'amour, L*

Suspicious Minds (1996) (94mins) d: Alain Zaloum s: Brenda Newman, Alain Zaloum : Patrick Bergin, Jayne Heitmeyer, Vittorio Rossi, Gary Busey, Daniel

Pilon, Liliana Komorowska, Ellen David, Bruce Dinsmore. A private detective is hired by a lumber tycoon to follow his beautiful but unfaithful wife. Murder quickly comes into play with an investigation plagued with difficulties. Not bad but the script bogs down under the sub-plots.

Suspicious River (2000) (92mins) d&s: Lynne Stopkewich (based on the novel of the same title by Laura Kasischke) : Molly Parker, Callum Keith Rennie, Joel Bissonnette, Deanna Milligan. In the director's previous film, the execretory *Kissed,* Molly Parker had sex with dead men. In this second film, she has sex with a procession of live men. She plays a receptionist at a motel in misty, mountainous B.C. being passed off as the U.S. with American money and flags. For an extra $60 or more she services men who register for a stay. The servicing leaves little to the imagination. What she wants the money for is never explained, and neither is anything else involving a husband, a little girl and an unfaithful mother. Finally, as the film ends in her utter degradation, she speaks her thoughts, saying she has at last "found love" or words to this effect. This dull, shallow work is an obscenity. Why is the river suspicious? Who knows? The title should be "Suspicious Pornography."

Suzanne (1980) (114mins) d: Robin Spry s: Robin Spry, Ronald Sutherland (based on his novel *Snow Lark*) : Jennifer Dale, Winston Rekert, Gabriel Arcand, Kenneth Pogue, Michelle Rossignol, Marianne McIsaac, Michael Ironside, Gina Dick, Pierre Curzi, Gordon Thompson, Helen Hughes, Adam Chase. Set against the background of the working-class world of Montréal during the early 1950s. A young girl finds herself attracted to men, used and left by them, and finally marries a man she does not love to give a home and father to the child she carries by a petty criminal—her true but doomed lover. Robustly played and forcefully told, it is poignant without false emotions and compellingly directed, with unforgettable performances by Winston Rekert and Jennifer Dale. A memorable Canadian film in every way.

Swan Lake: The Zone (*Lebedyne ozero-zona***)** (1996) (96mins) (a Canada-Ukraine co-production) d: Yuri Illienko s: Serge Paradjanov, Yuri Illienko : Victor Solovyow, Liudmyla Yefymenko, Pylyp Illienko, Maya Bukhakova. A man escapes from a notorious prison three days before the end of his sentence. He finds refuge in a huge hammer and sickle monument. The escaped convict is discovered there by a woman, the mother of a boy who uses the same monument as his second home. The woman nurses the prisoner back to health inside the monument. They fall in love. The boy, jealous of his mother's affection for the stranger, betrays the man, who is captured and returned to prison. Very much a Russian film, this is a compelling, haunting, unforgettable motion picture about man's fate.

Swann (1996) (97mins) (a Canada-U.K. co-produc-tion) d: Anna Benson Gyles s: David Young (based on the novel by Carol Shields) : Miranda Richardson, Brenda Fricker, Michael Ontkean, David Cubitt, Sean Hewitt, Sean McCann, John Neville. A famous author arrives in a rural Ontario community to unravel the secrets of Mary Swann, an obscure poet found murdered on her husband's farm. Whatever virtues were found in the novel are sadly absent in this confused, meandering and life-less screen version, which lacks any sense of mys-tery or meaning. Its poetic overtones are decidedly blurred. The actresses involved also seem bewil-dered by the perplexing events.

Sweet and the Bitter, The (1962) (87mins) (b/w) d&s: James Clavell : Yoko Tani, Paul Richards, Torin Thatcher, Jane Mallett, Dale Ishimoto, Verlie Cooter, Teru Shimada, Audrey Kniveton, Sam Payne, Peter Hayworth, David Hushes, Reg McReynolds. A love story about a Japanese girl and a Canadian boy, set in Vancouver. There was no release in North America due to legal difficulties. James Clavell later found fame as the author of *Shogun* and other novels.

Sweet Angel Mine (1996) (85mins) (a Canada-U.K. co-production) d: Curtis Radclyffe s: Sue Maheu, Tim Willocks : Oliver Milburn, Margaret Langrick, Anna Massey, Alberta Watson. A slight yet absorbing ghost story set in Nova Scotia where a young man is travelling around on his motorcycle looking for his long-lost father. The people he meets in small com-munities are secretive and not at all helpful. Suddenly he finds himself in the presence of a young and unaffected young woman living in the proverbial old dark house with her protective mother who, floating around ghost-like, promptly exerts a strange power over the young man. And no wonder! As played by the compelling Alberta Watson, who could resist her? The story, like the ghost, tends to drift away but leaves us with a surprise outcome that gives the audience something to think about.

Sweet Hereafter, The (1996) (120mins) d&s: Atom Egoyan (based on the novel by Russell Banks) : Sarah Polley, Bruce Greenwood, Ian Holm, Arsinée Khanjian, Tom McCamus, Maury Chaykin. Filmed against the Rocky Mountains of British Columbia but without any reference to B.C. The narrative con-cerns a lawyer who arrives from nowhere, as do characters in other Egoyan films. No one he speaks to asks him where he comes from or about his cre-dentials. We are repeatedly told that he has come to serve the community, which we never see—never a main street, never a town, only a car wash. The sor-rowful parents he has come to assist, who have lost children in a school bus accident, are hard to believe. The dialogue is, for the most part, meaning-less and repetitive. The characters have little depth or identity. Slow, tedious and tiresome.

Sweet Killing (1993) (90mins) (a Canada-France-U.K. co-production) d: Eddy Matalon s: Dominique Roulet, Eddy Matalon (based on Angus Hall's novel *Qualthrough*) : Anthony Higgins, Leslie Hope, F. Murray Abraham, Michael Ironside. A black comedy treatment of the familiar "perfect murder" situation, but bringing together the guilty person with many others who were involved, leading to frightening results. An average piece of killing, neither sweet or sour.

Sweet Lies and Tender Oaths (*Les doux aveux*) (1982) (90mins) d&s: Fernand Dansereau : Hélène Loiselle, Marcel Sabourin, Geneviève Brassard, Gilbert Turp, André Melançon. This is a delightful four-part two-generations study of an eccentric grandmother who leaves the home of her nagging daughter, finds her own place to live, and meets an equally eccentric older man who becomes her friend. Perfectly acted and lightly directed.

Sweet Movie (1974) (96mins) (a Canada-France-Germany co-production) d&s: Dusan Makavejev : Carole Laure, John Vernon, Pierre Clementi, Anna Prucnal, Jane Mallet, Don Arioli, Sami Frey. By the time Makavejev arrived in Canada, his reputation as a daring artist when it comes to a realistic portrayal of sex was well known among cineastes and critics, and much was expected from his work here. A surreal comedy and satire on the Cold War, communism and the sale of a virgin bride to a wealthy businessman. Uneven but funny, serious and sensual.

Sweet Substitute (Caressed) (1964) (90mins) (b/w) d&s: Larry Kent : Robert Howay, Carol Pastinsky, Angela Gann, Lanny Beckman, Robert Silverman, Bill Hartley, Mitzi Hurd, Virginia Dunsaith. A teenage boy can't concentrate on his studies because he is obsessed with sex. A pleasant, plain girl satisfies his demands and sees him through his scholarship, but becomes pregnant as a result. He then abandons her and becomes engaged to a socially acceptable, but less accessible woman. Yet another of Larry Kent's forward-looking no-budget views of sexual relationships—the type of film that aroused the fury of censor boards but might seem all too ordinary today, but no less honest and aware.

Sweet Substitute: see **Facade**

Sweet Teenager Love, The: see *Adolescente sucré d'amour, L'*

Sweeter Song, A (1976) (91mins) d: Allan Eastman s: Jim Henshaw, Allan Eastman : Jim Henshaw, Susan Petrie, Susan Hogan, Nick Mancuso, Lise Granik, David Main, Douglas Fetherling. A pleasant and gentle film about a sports photographer who must choose between two women who care for him. Likeable cast and never maudlin.

Swindle, The (*La gammick*) (1974) (86mins) d: Jacques Godbout s: Pierre Turgeon, Jacques Godbout : Marc Legault, Pierre Gobeil, Dorothée Berryman, Gilbert Chénier, Ronald Wilson, Denis Drouin, Rita Lafontaine. An unusual film from Godbout. An exciting, penetrating and effective portrayal of the activities of the mob in Montréal. Frightening in its revelations.

Switch in Time, A (1987) (100mins) d&s: Paul Donovan : Tom McCamus, Laurie Paton, Jacques Lussier, David Hemblen. A daring attempt to make a comedy by fusing the present with the past, which doesn't quite come off. At a technical institute in Geneva, an eccentric genius locks himself into the control room of an experimental laboratory and brings about a violent explosion that throws him back into the years of the Roman Empire. He will now do to the ancient Romans what he was attempting to achieve at the Institute. With some laughs along the way, one is left with the feeling that none of it really matters.

Switching Channels (1988) (105mins) (U.S.-Canadian film) d: Ted Kotcheff s: Jonathan Reynolds : Kathleen Turner, Burt Reynolds, Christopher Reeve, Albert S. Waxman, Kenneth James, Monica Parker. A surprisingly and effective and smartly satirical remake of the successful play and film, *The Front Page* by Ben Hecht and Charles MacArthur. Taken away from the newspaper world it now fits well into the satellite-tv age, where a reporter announces her departure from the network to marry a wealthy man, finding herself at odds with her former husband. A sensible comedy from the old days which brightens up an unfunny present.

Sword of Gideon (1986) (148mins) (a Canada-U.K. co-production) d: Michael Anderson s: Chris Bryant (from *Vengeance*, a book by George Jonas) : Steven Bauer, Michael York, Rod Steiger, Colleen Dewhurst, Robert Joy, Leslie Hope, Laurent Malet, Lino Ventura. A U.S. commando officer is chosen to lead an anti-terrorist team to avenge the massacre of Israeli athletes at the Munich Olympics. A well-written, intelligent and suspenseful film with a convincing cast knowingly directed.

Swordsman, The (1993) (97mins) (a Canadian-American film) d: Michael Kennedy s: Palo Alvarez : Lorenzo Lamas, Claire Stansfield, Michael Champion, Nicholas Pasco, Raoul Trujillo. Found in Greece, the sword of Alexander is sent to New York. The owner of it becomes invincible. When someone promptly steals the sword and kills a security guard, a female witness is hunted by the killer and the police provide her with protection. (Audiences shold be protected too from seeing this inane stuff.)

Sylvan Lake Summer (1991) (96mins) d: Peter Campbell s: Donald Truckey : Robyn Stevan, Christianne Hirt, Johanna Newmarch, Allan Grant, Shawn Clements, Spencer Rochfort, Lochlyn Munro, Andrew Rhodes, Christine McInnis. Summer cottages are as much a part of Canadian life as hockey, swimming and boating, but they seldom find themselves portrayed on the screen. In this unusual film the cottages are in Alberta and managed by the mother of her teenage who must adjust to a new life, in which her mother loses one lover and finds another. Romantic, sunny, perceptive and with much to laugh at through the tears.

Symposium (1996) (80mins) d&s: Nik Sheehan : Byron Ayanoglu, Brad Fraser, Gerald Hannon, Tomson Highway, Donald Martin, Charles Pachter, Stan Persky, Patricia Rozema, Nik Sheehan, Scott Symons. All of the above express their views in a symposium, inspired by none other than Plato, on the meaning and nature of love from a contemporary Canadian perspective. The host is Adrian Childe, a fictional filmmaker who takes the audience on a journey into the hearts and minds of the "symposiasts." Some might think it better than watching scenery flying by.

Synapse: see **Memory Run**

T'es belle, Jeanne: see **You Are Beautiful Jeanne**

T'es pas tannée, Jeanne d'Arc: see **Great Ordinary Movie, The**

Tadpole and the Whale (***La grenouille et la baleine***) (1988) (90mins) d: Jean-Claude Lord : Fanny Lauzier, Marina Orsini, Jean Lajeunesse, Lise Thouin, Denis Forest. Known as Tadpole, Daphne is as much at home in the water as she is on land. Because of her highly developed sense of hearing, she can hear the songs of the humpback whales that frequent her shores in summer and who seem to respond to the sounds of her flute. This is the touching story of an exceptionally sensitive young girl who knew how to sing with the whales. (See: *Tales for All* series)

Tagged: The Jonathan Wamback Story (2002) (120mins) d: John L'Écuyer s: Elizabeth Stewart, Michael Amo : Tyler Hynes, Marnie McPhail, Ron White, Janet-Laine Green, Christopher Jacot, Charlotte Sullivan. In June 1999, student Jonathan Wamback was savagely beaten by a group of his fellow students and came close to dying. He went into a coma and, with the help of his parents, fought a long and wrenching battle to regain his health. He still endures seizures, great pain and suffering. Among the many such films detailing violence in today's schools, this particular picture is faithful, honest, penetrating and deeply affecting. And once again we wonder about justice today, when the victims have fewer rights than the accused. The acting and treatment cannot be faulted. (See: *Signature* series)

Tail Lights Fade (1999) (87mins) d: Malcolm Ingram s: Matt Gissing : Denise Richards, Breckin Meyer, Jake Busey, Tanya Allen, Elizabeth Berkley, Jaimz Woolvett, Lisa Marie. Yet another in the list of road movies in which a group of dizzy young things argue their way across Canada with a confused and worn-out script, swearing and complaining, dealing drugs and having sex. The tail lights here faded out before the journey began.

Take Her by Surprise (1967) (80mins) b-w (a Can-U.S. film) d: Rudi Dorn s: John Somerset : Joan Armstrong, Nuel Beckett, Paul Negri, Peter Adamson, Dara Wells. Another version of the stand-by murder mystery about a husband who arranges to have his wife killed. A mindless soft-core sex film with endless shots of women undressing, it lacks any redeeming qualities and is clumsy and gratuitous with an empty plot set in the Ontario countryside.

Take It All: see ***Tout prendre, À***

Takeover (1981) (90mins) d: Peter Rowe s: Rob Forsyth : John Ireland, Allan Royal, Michael Hogan, Susan Petrie, David Main. Filmed in Toronto and Calgary, this ambitious and hard-hitting drama concerns a businessman involved in the intrigue and manipulative practices surrounding a corporate takeover. As head of a family business he must also contend with the plans of his ambitious son. A rare venture, for Canadian film, into the high-flying and often corrupt world of big business. (See: *For the Record*)

Taking Care (Prescription for Murder) (1987) (87mins) d: Clarke Mackey s: Rebecca Schechter (based on a piece by June Callwood) : Kate Lynch, Janet Amos, Saul Rubinek. This is the director's first film since the remarkable *The Only Thing You Know* (1971). During the intervening years he has worked as an editor and taught filmmaking. He returns with an auspicious semi-documentary, keenly observed and well acted, set in a Toronto hospital and based on the real-life situation of a nurse charged with murdering her patients.

Tale of Teeka, The (1999) (90mins) d: Tim Southam s: Michael Marc Vouchard (English text by Linda Gaboriau) : Brent Carver, Maxime Desbiens. A cautionary tale looking at the hereditary nature of family violence. A man returns to his father's abandoned family farm to come to grips with his unloving past. Teeka is a white goose, and together the two seek an escape from daily beatings and humiliations by going into an imaginary world of adventures. Beautifully done with feeling and affection.

Tales for All (series): films produced by Rock Demers with his company Productions La Fête, beginning in 1984 and consisting of 23 films, is unique in the history of Canadian film in that the works maintained a standard of excellence that is truly remarkable. The films incorporate freshness, imagination, humour and genuine emotional appeal, and are never preachy or patronizing in their portrayal of moral issues. See under respective titles:

1: **Bach and Broccoli**
2: **Bye Bye Red Riding Hood**
3: **Case of the Witch Who Wasn't, The**
4: **Christmas Martian, The** (***Le martien de Noël***)
5: **Clean Machine, The**
6: **Dancing on the Moon**
7: **Dog Who Stopped the War, The**
8: **Flying Sneaker, The**
8: ***Forteresse suspendue, La*** (**Hidden Fortress, The**)
9: **Great Land of Small, The**
10: **Hathi**
11: **My Little Devil**
12: **Peanut Butter Solution, The**
13: **Reach for the Sky**
15: **Regina**

16: **Return of Tommy Tricker, The**

17: **Summer of the Colt**

18: **Summer with the Ghosts**

19: **Tadpole and the Whale**

20: **Tommy Tricker and the Stamp Traveller**

21: **Vincent and Me**

22: **Young Magician, The**

23: **Whiskers**

Tales From the Gimli Hospital (1988) (72mins) (b/w) d&s: Guy Maddin : Kyle McCulloch, Michael Gottli, Angela Heck. Two men share a bedroom in the crowded hospital of Gimli, Manitoba, during a smallpox epidemic at the turn of the century. The writer-director's murky, surreal interpretation of the events that follow suggests there is talent waiting to be used for a better purpose.

Tales of the Wild: see *Aventures du grand nord, Les*

Tangerine Taxi (1988) (75mins) d: Mort Ransen s: Lennette Horton, Mort Ransen : Marshall Colt, Roberta Weiss, Steven Marshall, Joan Heney, Raymond Belisle, Perry Schneiderman. An easygoing and delightful plot revolving around a taxi driver and the events that take place in the lives of many of his passengers. A pleasing drive through an atmosphere of romance and happiness. (See: *Shakes of Love* series)

Tango Macabre: see **Seizure**

Tanya's Island (1980) (89mins) d: Alfred Sole s: Pierre Brousseau : Dede Winters, Mariette Lévesque, Richard Sargent, Don McCloud. A beautiful Toronto model fantasizes that she is marooned on a tropical island with her boyfriend and meets a half-human creature. Beauty feels sorry for the beast and 'King Kong' finally gets the girl. Weird is the word for it.

Tanzi (1987) (112mins) d: Bernard Picard s: Claire Luckham : France Labrie. An oddity from Montréal about the daughter of a wrestling family. After her husband leaves her for another woman, she decides to become a wrestler herself. Hardly earth shaking but disturbing to audiences who are not keen on seeing women in the ring, wrestling or boxing.

Tar Angel: see *Ange de goudron, L'*

Tar Sands, The (1977) (60mins) d: Peter Pearson s: Ralph Thomas, Peter Pearson, Peter Rowe (based in part on the book of the same title by Larry Pratt) : Kenneth Welsh, George Touliatos, Kenneth Pogue, Dr. Morton Shulman, Mavor Moore. This drama, based solidly on fact, is about the pressure that forced the federal and Alberta governments to make a deal with four major American oil companies involved in the controversial Syncrude project— under which taxpayers put up $1.87 billion in cash and tax credits, for only a 30 per cent return. This film was delayed for over six months due to legal considerations. (See:*For the Record*)

Task Force (2000) (120mins) d: Richard Ciupka s: Wayne Grigsby : Alex Carter, Richard Robitaille, Patrick Goyette, Clark Johnson. A chronicle based on a true story of a policeman in Montréal who is appalled to find that a powerful drug dealer is at work in the city. Together with the RCMP, he launches a daring operation to put the dealer out of business. Good behind-the-scenes portrayal of a difficult life for the police. A gripping thriller woven in a web of deceit and betrayal encompassing Holland, Belgium, Spain, the U.S. and Pakistan. Familiar, but deadly in its energy, insight and intelligent portrayal.

Taureau (1972) (97mins) d&s: Clément Perron : André Melançon, Monique Lepage, Michèle Magny, Louise Portal, Marcel Sabourin, Jacques Bilodeau, André Cartier, Yvan Canvet, Marguerite Lemir, Denis Drouin, Anne Létourneau, Marthe Mercure, Roger Gosselin, Germain DeBlois, Benoît Thibault. The writer of Jutra's *My Uncle Antoine,* Clément Perron, turns to writing and directing in this film, a somewhat sensational and derivative tale of lust and life in a village of demented souls in Québec.

Tax-Shelter Era: see **Capital Cost Allowance Films**

Tease: see **Poison**

Technetium, The: see **Cosmos**

Tectonic Plates (1992) (100mins) d: Peter Mettler s: Based on Robert Lepage's stage presentation : Robert Lepage, Marie Gignac. Described as a purely cinematic interpretation of the geological metaphor of tectonic plates applied to human relationships, this film, about a Québécois art historian who leaves her troubled and unfulfilled love affair to visit Venice, appears to be nothing other than an excuse for a number of performance players to portray lost souls in a lost cause, whatever that might be!

Teddy (The Pit) (1980) (99mins) (a Canada-U.S. film) d: Lewis Lehman s: Ian Stuart : Sammy Snyders, Jeanne Elias, John Stoneham, Richard Alden, Sonja Smits, John C. Bassett. A 12-year-old autistic boy's teddy bear brings about the demise of a small western U.S. town with the aid of his creatures the Tra-la-logs. Somewhat nasty and off-putting.

Tek War: Tek Justice (1994) (100mins) d: Jerry Ciccoritti s: Morgan Gendel, James Mack : Greg Evigan, Eugene Clark, Torri Higginson, William Shatner, Jacob Tierney, Barbara Eve Harris. A detective in the future sci-fi world is arrested for the murder of his former wife's husband. He refuses to let the authorities investigate, leading to complications brought about by living in this new society. Interesting, forceful, and amusing to see the involvement of *Star Trek's* Shatner.

Tell Me if I Bother or Disturb You: see *Dis-moi le si j'dérange*

Tell Me My Name (1977) (78mins) (a Canada-U.S. co-production) d: Delbert Mann s: Joanna Lee (based on the book of the same name by Mary Carter) : Arthur Hill, Barbara Barrie, Barnard Hughes, Valerie Mahaffey, Murray Westgate, Dawn Greenhalgh. A young girl searches for her parents after being told that she was adopted. The distinguished American director Delbert Mann makes the most of somewhat thin material with pleasing results.

Tell Me That You Love Me (1983) (95mins) (a Canada-Israel co-production) d: Tzipi Trope s: Sandra Kolber, Tzipi Trope : Nick Mancuso, Belinda Montgomery, Barbara Williams, Kenneth Welsh, Andrée Pelletier. A protracted, poorly written and unreal story of a failed marriage set against affluent Tel Aviv backgrounds.

Temps d'une chasse, Le: see **Time of the Hunt, The, The**

Temps d'une vie, Le **(The Times of Our Life)** (1998) (90mins) d: René-Richard Cyr s: Based on the play by Robert Lepage : Sylvie Drapeau, Henri Chassé, Jean-François Pichette, Luc Proulx, Gary Boudreault, Stéphane Jacques. Writer Lepage believes that "no matter how unique we are, how particular our lives are, we are all ultimately children of our forefathers. My story of a woman is shared by so many in Québec and elsewhere whose ordinary lives were marked by simple joys and sorrows which, endured, ensured the survival of a people rooted in the land." His play, now an absorbing film, has been performed more than 500 times in Canada and Europe.

Temps de l'avant, Le: see **Before the Time comes**

Temps zero, Le: see **Time Zero**

Temptation of Big Bear, The: see **Big Bear**

Ten Girls Ago (1962) (95mins) (an American-Canadian film) d: Harold Daniels s: Peter Farrow : Buster Keaton, Bert Lahr, Risella Bain, Jan Miner, Diane Scaville, Beth Jones, Marguerite Gray, Austin Willis, Eric Clavering. An American musical-comedy satire on the television business with Canadian financing, filmed at the Lakeshore Studios in Toronto.(Released, but showings very few.)

Tendresse ordinaire: see **Ordinary Tenderness**

Terminal Choice (Deathbed) (1985) (95mins) (a Canadian-American film) d: Sheldon Larry s: Neal Bell (based on the story *Terminal Choice* by Peter Lawrence) : Don Francks, Joe Spano, David McCallum, Robert Joy, Diane Venora, Nicholas Campbell, Ellen Barkin, Chapelle Jaffe, Clare Coulter, Martha Gibson, Chas Lawther, Tom Harvey. A good cast can do little to lift this messy medical drama off the operating table in attempts to find out who is using a high-tech system to kill certain patients in a medical clinic. A private investigator finally discovers whodunit.

Terminal City Ricochet (1990) (95mins) d: Zale Dalen s: Philip Savath and others : Mark Bennett, Peter Breck, Germain Houde, Jello Biafra. A satire on what the world might well become: deadly space junk rains from the sky, the streets are glutted with obsolete consumer goods and environmental decay is everywhere. Much more could have been made of the party of Cultural Resistance Against Happy Face Fascism, but with five writers on the screenplay, something was lost.

Termini Station (1990) (107mins) d: Allan Winton King s: Colleen Murphy : Megan Follows, Gordon Clapp, Debra McGrath, Gordon Pinsent, Colleen Dewhurst. Set in the bleak winter streets of Kirkland Lake, Ontario, a young teenage prostitute, driven by family problems and social disadvantages, attempts to cope with her own life and that of her alcoholic mother. For the most part it is a riveting portrait of desperate people, marred at times by overtones of melodrama but the reality of the whole remains true and affecting.

Terra X (The Curse of Oak Island) (1997) (55mins) d: Eric Till s: Mark Finnan, Robert Linnell : David Renton, Rhonda MacLean, Mark Finnan. Part drama, part documentary, this unusual film tells us the story of Oak Island, Nova Scotia's strange depression in the ground that has mystified thousands of visitors, treasure seekers and geologists over the years. And as the film closes, yet another research vessel with state-of-the-art scientific equipment pulls in to continue the search for answers.

Terre à boire, La: see **Earth to Drink, The**

Terror Train (1980) (97mins) (a Canadian-American film) d: Roger Spottiswoode s: T.Y. Drake : Ben Johnson, Jamie Lee Curtis, Hart Bochner, David Copperfield, Derek MacKinnon, Victor Knight. Frat boys hire a train for an all-night graduation party soon to be ruined by the appearance of a former member who was emotionally marked in a previous initiation party. With everyone in frightening masks, with slashing and blood everywhere, this is mass horror and no mystery. Good train photography and movement provide dramatic moments. An early film from the Canadian director Spottiswoode.

Terry Fox Story, The (1983) (98mins) d: Ralph Thomas s: Edward Hume : Robert Duvall, Eric Fryer (Terry Fox), Michael Zelniker, Chris Makepeace, Rosalind Chao, Elva Mai Hoover, Frank Adamson, Marie McCann, R.H. Thomson, Saul Rubinek, Gary Darycott, Matthew Craven, Chuck Shamata, Patrick Watson, Robert DesRoches. Terry Fox was a young Canadian who lost a leg to cancer and, determined to make the most of his life, chose to run across Canada to raise money for medical research. His heroic undertaking is shown here with documentary-like realism, chronicled with honesty and insight.

Terry Fox Story, The: see **Crossbar**

Tête de Normande St-Onge, La: see **Head of Normande St. Onge, The**

That Cold Day in the Park (1969) (107mins) (a Canada-U.S. film) d: Robert Altman s: Gillian Freeman (based on the novel by Richard Miles) : Sandy Dennis, Michael Burns, Luana Anders. This is one of Altman's films best forgotten, in which a frustrated spinster takes in a young man she meets in the park and gives vent to suppressed sexuality. Although this film is classified in B.C. as being Canadian, it is not. It was filmed in Vancouver and uses some Canadian actors. Altman

returned to Vancouver in 1971 to film the more successful *McCabe and Mrs. Miller.*.

That Darned Loot (*La maudite galette*) (1972)
(108mins) d: Denys Arcand s: Jacques Benoît : Luce
Guilbeault, Marcel Sabourin, René Caron, J.-Léo
Gagnon, Gabriel Arcand, Jean-Pierre Saulnier,
Maurice Gauvin, Andrée Lalonde, Suzanne Valéry,
Julien Lippe, Hélène Loiselle and Denys Arcand.
Had it moved a little faster and talked a little less,
this would have been a superior crime thriller with a
neat twist ending making it suitable for wide popular
exhibition. A wickedly black film about a poor
plumber and his family, their hired hand and lodger,
and of the robbery and murder of a rich old uncle.
Unfortunately, the director is dedicated to long
Godard-ish sequences that slow the pace, introduce
tedium, and blunt the satirical ending. The film's
observations about human nature, however, are
deadly accurate. With this film Arcand consolidated
his position as one of Canada's foremost directors.

That Was a Film: see **This Is a Film**

That's My Baby (1984) (96mins) d&s: Edie Yolles,
John Bradshaw : Timothy Webber, Sonja Smits,
Lenore Zann, Derek McGrath, Kate Trotter, Matthew
Craven, Frank Moore. A run-of-the-mill comedy
about male motherhood in Toronto with a talented
cast of players enjoying themselves in spite of the
picture's inadequacies.

The Brother Andre and the Sun: see *On Est Loin Du Soleil*

There Once Was a War (*Il était une guerre*) (1958)
(95mins) (b/w) d: Louis Portugais s: Réginald
Boisvert : Aimé Major, Hélène Loiselle, J.-Léo
Gagnon, Lucie Poitras. Episodes in the life of a
young man in Québec during World War II, in which
he tries to avoid conscription, marries quickly, works
in a munitions factory, but cannot avoid military service, goes overseas, and then, with the war over,
comes home where picking up civilian and married
life has its setbacks and disappointments. An interesting look at lives during this period. Revealing and
aware of the issues involved. (compiled from five
parts of the tv series *Panoramaorisue*)

**There's Always a Way to Get There (*Y a toujours
moyen de moyenner!*)** (1973) (92mins) d: Denis
Héroux s: Marcel Lefebvre : Jean-Guy Moreau,
Yvan Ducharme, Willie Lamothe, Dominique
Michel, Danielle Ouimet. The mental and emotional
misgivings of a bank teller whose life seems to be
caught up in white lies and family unrest. Perceptive
and disturbing.

**There's Nothing Wrong With Being Good to
Yourself (*Y a pas d'mal à se faire du bien*) (She's
So Young and Knows All!) (*C'est jeune et ça sait
tout!*)** (1974) (83mins) (a Canada-France co-pro-
duction) d: Claude Mulot s: Michel Lebrun, Jean
Curtelin, Claude Mulot : Jean Lefebvre, Françoise
Lemieux, Darry Cowl, Andrée Cousineau, Céline
Bernier, Danielle Ouimet, Suzanne Langlois. After

finding the sexual revolution something of a sham,
a Montréal husband and wife return home to
resume their happy marriage and find new strength
in their quiet existence. Slim, slender, but insightful
and revealing in emotions, thoughts and feelings.
Funny and charming.

**Thetford in the Middle of Our Life (*Thetford au
milieu de notre vie*)** (1980) (84mins) d: Fernand
Dansereau, Iolande Cadrin-Rossignol s: Bertrand
Bergeron and others : Lucille Drouin, Théo Gagné,
André Plante, Georges Dionne. A union leader and
his wife struggle to keep their marriage together at
the Thetford Mines in Québec (where we once met
Uncle Antoine) while trying to cope with the social
and economic issues in a town completely owned
and run by the mining company. A moving drama of
working-class life carefully detailed and portrayed.

They Came from Within: see **Parasite Murders**

Thick As Thieves (1990) (91mins) d&s: Steven
DiMarco : David Quigley, Carolyn Dunn, Amber-Lea
Weston, Karl Pruner. An uneven first feature about a
brother and sister's life of crime and its complications.

Things to Do on a Saturday Night (1998) (95mins)
d: Norman Fassbender s: Scott McPherson,
Norman Fassbender : David McNally, Kate Ryan,
Mark Gibbon, Ken Brown. This melodrama set in
Edmonton is about several characters who have
made a mess of their lives by becoming involved in
crime, treachery, some sex and lots of muddle.
Absolutely empty. All the wrong things to do on a
Saturday night.

Third Walker, The (1980) (85mins) (a Canadian-
American film) d: Teri McLuhan s: Robert Thom :
Colleen Dewhurst, William Shatner, Frank Moore,
Monique Mercure, Andrée Pelletier, Marshall
McLuhan (voice of the judge). Twins are separated
by mistake at birth and grow up with different fami-
lies in opposite social conditions. All somewhat
murky and indistinct. This is the first feature film
made by Marshall McLuhan's daughter Teri. He was
annoyed when it failed to win a CFA award."The
Americans think more of it than you do," he said.
(Teri later received a U.S. award.)

32 août sur terre, Un: see ***Crabe dans la tête, Un***

Thirty-two Short Films About Glenn Gould (1994)
(92mins) d&s: Francois Girard and Donald McKellar
: Colm Feore. The life of the enigmatic pianist Glenn
Gould, who many consider a genius, is captured
here in a thoughtful study modelled on Bach's
Goldberg Variations, one of Gould's most successful
recordings. There are the expected interviews with
family and friends and several dramatized
sequences of episodes in Gould's life. Colm Feore is
outstanding in his portrayal of the musician.

This Is a Film (That Was a Film) (1989) (96mins)
(b/w/col) (a Canada-U.K. co-production) d: Robert
White s: Arthur Rogers (based on his novel of the
same name) : James Greer, Sally Smith, Arthur
Tracy, William Rogers. A romantic drama concerning

two teens and their efforts to marry against their parents' wishes. Well done and affecting. Set in Toronto. Shades of Sidney Furies' *A Dangerous Age.*

This Is My Father (1998) (120mins) (a Canada-Ireland co-production) d&s: Paul Quinn : Aidan Quinn, James Caan, John Cusack, Stephen Rea, Jacob Tierney. Another of the "who are we and where do we come from?" studies in discovering ourselves. This time around a high school teacher decides to take a trip to Ireland with his nephew to visit his family. Passable entertainment helped along by the beauty of the Irish countryside.

This Matter of Marriage (1998) (120mins) d: Bradford Turner s: Peter Lauterman, Debbie Macomber (from her novel) : Leslie Hope, Richard Peters, Sherry Miller, Natasha Greenblatt. Two architects in their mid-thirties decide the time has come to find partners in life. One meets a wealthy developer; the other finds that the man she has dreamt about lives next door. An interesting play of thoughts, feelings and emotions, expressed by likeable characters. (See: *Harlequin* series)

Those Damned Savages (*Les maudits sauvages***)** (1971) (115mins) d&s: Jean-Pierre Lefebvre : Pierre Dufresne, Nicole Filion, Rachel Cailhier, Jacques Thisdale, Denise Morelle, Marcel Sabourin, Roger Garceau, Gaétan Labrèche, Denis André. In his first film in colour, Lefebvre attempts to "repossess," or make contemporary, certain historical facts and characters and place them in the present to show us that society's attitudes, particularly towards humanity, have not changed. These observations revolve around a native woman and a trapper, with the action wandering between 1670 and 1970 settings. The belief that life is an "eternal tragicomedy" is hardly original, but Lefebvre succeeds in restating it, by putting it all into a different context.

Thousand Moons, A (1977) (65mins) d: Gilles Carle s: Mort Forer : Adeline Coppaway, James Buller, Ronald Morey, Robert Silverman, Carole Laure, Nick Mancuso. More than a thousand moons have come and gone since a Métis matriarch was born, far from the squalor in Toronto where she now lives with her son. Knowing that her death is imminent, she must return to her distant birthplace to be welcomed by the spirits of her ancestors. This is a gentle, compassionate love story told in contrasts of darkness and light. Carle said on completion of the film, "I wanted to see if it could be interesting without murders, car crashes and violence. It could and it is." (Note: This was Gilles Carle's first English-language film.) (See: *For the Record*)

Thousand Wonders of the Universe, The (1997) (83mins) (a Canada-France co-production) d: Jean-Michel Roux s: Régine Abadia, Alexis Galmont, Jean-Michel Roux : Tcheky Karyo, Julie Delpy, Feodor Atkine, James Hyndman, Guy Nadon, Pascale Bussières. A sci-fi fantasy piece opening with scenes showing all of humanity awaiting in fear and despair an invasion by aliens. People vanish, nasty creatures appear, and all seems lost. The actors do their best but are clearly lost in this gruesome concoction. Not many wonders here.

Three and a Half (*Trois et demi***)** (2002) (90mins) d: Boris Mojsovski s: Ryan Redford, Mike Thorn, Boris Mojsovski : Kim Huffman, Donald Allison, Barbara Gordon, Walter Alza, Santino Buda, Emily Taylor. Following unreadable "artistic" title credits, this film opens with a sequence never before seen in a Canadian film; passengers on the Toronto subway, with shots from the front window showing it moving through the tunnels. Of course it is not identified as being in Toronto. Three so-called artists live in decaying apartments buried in their own untidiness. All are emotional wrecks saying nothing and wear a minimum of clothes. An older man appears, a professor with beard and smoking a pipe who walks around looking blankly at life. A woman keeps breaking a window to get the repairman back. Is this all penance for dishonouring their bodies and burying themselves in lust? One of them is brought to Jesus after watching a religious programme on tv. Audiences can read what they want to believe in this piffle supposedly about materialism, choice and desire, but it's not very interesting spending time with these tiresome characters. Some English subtitles tell us that they are apparently foreigners. The film closes with everyone black on the subway, going who knows where! The money for this, not surprisingly, came from the trough known as "multiculturalism."

Three by Paizs (1984) (87mins) d&s: John Paizs : John Paizs, Dean Dacko, John Harvie, Kathy Driscoll, George Toles. *The Obsession of Billy Botski* sees Nick, the hero, fascinated with a dream girl from the '60s. In *Springtime in Greenland,* Nick dislikes his beer-guzzling acquaintances. In *The International Spy,* Nick becomes a super agent bent on getting a top-secret microchip out of the reach of a multi-millionaire. Nick is possibly Paizs himself. Another early work from the Winnipeg Film Group.

Three Madeleines, The (*Les fantômes des trois Madeleines***)** (1999) (81mins) (b/w) (a Canada-France co-production) d&s: Guylaine Dionne : Sylvie Drapeau, France Arbour, Isadora Galwey, Kathleen Fortin, Maxim Gaudette, Isabelle Blais, Monique Joly, Luc Proulx, Jean-Guy Bouchard, Patrick Goyette. Three generations of Québec women whose names are variations of Madeleine take a car trip to the Gaspé. A narrator's singsong voice carries on at tiresome length about dreams and memories accompanied by classical and choral music. Scenery provides welcome distractions.

Three More Days (1995) (86mins) d: Peter Gerretsen s: Rebecca Mauro : Naomi Krayker, James Murray, Frank Scott, Mary Johanna. Alone on a farm in Saskatchewan, with only her bed-ridden father for company, a woman is left with memories of a man she met in Toronto and the frustration of not knowing if they will meet again. An intimate love story sensitively told touching on the emotional aspects of dependence and absence.

Three Roads, The: see **Double Negative**

Three Women in Love: see *Trois femmes, un amour*

Three-Card Monte (1978) (92mins) d: Les Rose s: Richard Gabourie : Richard Gabourie, Christopher Langevin, Lynne Cavanagh, Valerie Warburton, John Rutter, Sean McCann. An excellent first feature written, produced and acted by Richard Gabourie about a small-time swindler and card player in Toronto who cares for a 12-year-old orphan boy. Poignant with sombre street photography and sharp dialogue, this is an unusual and impressive achievement.

Threshold (1981) (97mins) (a Canadian-American film) d: Richard Pearce s: James Salter : Donald Sutherland, John Marley, Sharon Acker, Mare Winningham, Jeff Goldblum, Jan Muszynski, Stuart Gillard, Mavor Moore, Lally Cadeau, Ralph Benmergui, Eric Clavering, Tom Harvey, Ken James, Robert Joy, Kate Trotter, Murray Westgate. An uncertain telling of the first artificial heart transplant in the U.S. For a film about life and hearts, it's a lifeless body without heart in which Sutherland, as the famous surgeon, gives the impression he is thinking of other matters.

Thrillkill (1984) (96mins) d&s: Anthony Kramreither, Anthony D'Andrea : Robin Ward, Gina Massey, Frank Moore, Laura Robinson, Diana Reis, Eugene Clark. A far-fetched video game of mystery and death leading the participants into a world of electronic murder. Too dumb to be disturbing.

Ticket to Heaven (1981) (109mins) d: Ralph Thomas s: Anne Cameron, Ralph Thomas (adapted from *Moonwebs*, a novel by Josh Freed) : Nick Mancuso, Saul Rubinek, Meg Foster, Kim Cattrall, R.H. Thomson, Jennifer Dale, Guy Boyd, Dixie Seatle, Robert Joy, Stephen Markle, Timothy Webber, Paul Soles, Harvey Atkin, Patrick Brymer, Michael Zelnicker, Marcia Diamond, Doris Petrie, Josh Freed and others. A frightening and outspoken first feature depicting the inside workings of a religious cult in San Francisco that attracts emotionally deprived youth and forces them into following its beliefs and where a Toronto youth, down-hearted at the ending of a love affair, becomes indoctrinated by the cult. The parents kidnap their own son in order to free him from the clutches of the businessman who is making money at the expense of the followers. The one weakness of this film, shot in the documentary style of television, lies in its failure to convince us that the young man could have so easily been taken in by the cult. Otherwise gripping, authentic and well played out.

Ti-Cul Tougas: see **Little Tougas**

Tiens-toi bien après les oreilles à Papa: see **What the Hell Are They Complaining About?**

Tijuana: see **Losin' It**

Ti-Ken (*Les plans mystèrieux*) (1965) (92mins) d&s: Roger Laliberté : Anthony Tremblay, Jacques Provost, William Gagné, Ève-Marie. Minor spy melodrama about a Canadian invention being stolen and taken to Moscow. Not likely.

Till Death Do Us Part (1982) (85mins) d: Timothy Bond s: Peter Jobin, Timothy Bond : Claude Jutra, James Keach, Helen Hughes, Jack Creley, Toby Tarnow, Candace O'Conner. Jutra turns up here as a psychiatrist who invites three couples to a weekend of intense marital therapy at his remote mansion in the countryside outside Montréal. This encounter turns the plot into a murder mystery, all rather murky in more ways than one. Jutra seems to enjoy it!

Tilom Aletranje: le petit homme a l'étranger: see **Little Man Abroad, A**

Time of the Hunt, The (*Le temps d'une chasse*) (1972) (90mins) d&s: Francis Mankiewicz : Guy L'Écuyer, Marcel Sabourin, Pierre Dufresne, Olivier Lécuyer, Luce Guilbeault, Frédérique Collin, Monique Mercure. Francis Mankiewicz's first film was among the first important works of the new Québec cinema. Set almost entirely outdoors, it concerns three men who leave Montréal at dawn to go on a weekend hunting trip. They are crude men who must rid themselves of the frustrations of domestic life by proving their virility in a desperately cheerful attempt to find an animal to kill, a woman to sleep with, and friends to get drunk with. They succeed in none of their desires and find only increased despair and emptiness in their lives. Here is one of those rare films that never takes a false step nor contains an unnecessary scene. Achingly real, beautifully written, honest and perceptive, it never compromises or exploits the weakness and despair of its characters. The cast is superb, the technique imaginative and unobtrusive.

Time of Zero, A: see **Pas de jeu sans soleil**

Time Zero (No Game Without Sun) (*Le temps zéro*) (*Pas de jeu sans soleil*) (1972) (73mins) d&s: Claude Bérubé : Francine Vernac, Michel Laprise. A two-character play in which Hélène and François, who work together in an office, come to discover each other's likes and dislikes, outlook on life and desires for peace and stability, and fall deeply in love. But is it too good to last? To spend almost an hour with them is a test for the players. One does not forget them!

Times of Our Life, The: see **Temps d'une vie, Le**

Ti-mine Bernie pis la gang: see **Bernie and the Gang**

Timing (1985) (77mins) d&s: Eric Weinthal : Heather-Lynne Meacock, Eric Weinthal, Tom Melisis, Alice Lafléche, Nancy Bell, Michael Kopsa, Denyse Karn, Christiane Vaillancourt. An actor falls in love with a divorced actress, but they part company when she goes to L.A. to work. But they come together again in Toronto finding the spirit of romance as it once was by playing in a production of *Romeo and Juliet*. Trust Shakespeare to come to the rescue!

Tin Flute, The (Bonheur d'occasion) (1983) (123mins) d: Claude Fournier s: Anne Cameron (based on Gabrielle Roy's popular novel *Bonheur d'occasion* [Second-hand Happiness] published in 1945) : Marilyn Lightstone, Mireille Deyglun, Michel Forget, Pierre Chagnon, Martin Neufeld, Charlotte Laurier, Linda Sorgini. The book was one of the first to depict life among the working-class people of Québec. Times were hard, the Depression was ending, World War II was near. The film brings vividly to life the story of a family as it goes through the cycle of life and death, heartbreak and unemployment. The settings are drab but lively, and the streets and buildings re-create the impression of the 1930s. The author's theme of the erosion of human faith and values in the face of poverty and industrialization comes through with poignancy and purpose. This cinema version seems at times inconsistent in the telling, having been edited down to its present running time from a five-hour version for television. See also: **Gabrielle Roy** (1990) (60mins) Documentary by Lea Pool about this distinguished writer and the film of her novel, *The Tin Flute*.

Tinamer (1987) (83mins) d&s: Jean-Guy Noel (based on the novel *L'amelanchier* by Jacques Ferron) : Gilles Vigneault, Louise Portal, Sarah-Jeanne Salvy. A fanciful and talkative tale of childhood dreams and family conflicts recalled by a woman attending her mother's funeral in Montréal. Sadness, tears and the touch of truth.

Ti-peuple: see **Ordinary People**

Tirelire, combines & cie: see **Clean Machine, The Tiresia** (2003) (112mins) (a Canada-France co-production) d&s: Bertrand Bonello : Laurent Lucas, Clara Choveaux, Thiago Teles, Celia Catalifo. A transsexual man in Paris is turned into half-man, half-woman when he is denied his hormone injections. Now he can see into the future but offends the church with his predictions. A laughable and silly film which makes no sense at any level.

Tisserands du pouvoir, Les (The Mills of Power, Parts 1 and 2) (1988) (135mins) d: Claude Fournier s: Michel Cournot, Claude Fournier : Gratien Gélinas, Michel Forget, Gabrielle Lazure, Madeleine Robinson. This is an ambitious two-part cinema-tv feature that takes on more than it can mill. This sprawling historical saga concerns French-Canadians who left the barren farms of Québec to seek a better life in the textile mills of New England at the turn of the century. A struggling family is contrasted with a wealthy family from France who owns the mills. Uneven and not as convincing as one would like.

Tit-Coq (1953) (101mins) (b/w) d: René Delacroix s: Gratien Gélinas (from his play of the same name) : Gratien Gélinas, Monique Miller, Fred Barry, Paul Dupuis, Denise Pelletier, Clément Latour, Juliette Béliveau, Amanda Alarie, George Alexander, Jean Duceppe, Corinne Conley, Henri Poitras. Tit-Coq, a shy, unhappy little man, without friends and self-conscious over his illegitimate birth, finds unexpected happiness in his love for Marie-Ange. But while he is away during the war, her parents persuade her to marry another man. On his return, Tit-Coq again finds himself alone in the world. The importance of this film for Québec and the rest of Canada cannot be overstated. Based on Gélinas' highly popular play, the film actually questioned the Establishment, particularly the Church, and gave the populace reason to speak up and begin to change the social pattern they had lived under. (The first Quebec film to be shown outside the province, at the Avenue Theatre on Eglinton Ave. in Toronto with English subtitles, 1954)

Title Shot (1980) (88mins) d: Les Rose s: John Saxton, Richard Gabourie (story) : Tony Curtis, Richard Gabourie, Susan Hogan, Allan Royal, Jack Duffy, Sean McCann, Michael Hogan, Larry Solway. A disappointing film from Gabourie about a charming, cunning underworld crook (Tony Curtis from Hollywood) who devises a way of using his network of computers to predict the winners of athletic events and becomes wealthy with his scam. All quite boring, actually, with unlikeable characters.

To Be Sixteen (Avoir 16 ans) (1979) (125mins) d&s: Jean-Pierre Lefebvre : Yves Benoît, Louise Choquette, Aubert Pallascio, Lise L'Heureux. A long, involving and penetrating study and examination by the always-concerned Lefebvre of a rebellious young teenager who is taken to an institution for delinquents where he is oppressed by his father and the authorities. A valuable social chronicle, set in Montréal.

To Catch a Killer (1991) (240mins) (a Canadian-American film) d: Eric Till s: Jud Kinberg : Brian Dennehy, Michael Riley, Meg Foster, Tony deSantis. This dramatization of the Wayne Gacy serial killings is a superior, quiet, unsensational gripping depiction of the police work that brought him to justice.

To Kill the King (1974) (86mins) (a Canadian-American film) d: George McCowan s: Tom Cole, Bernard Eisman, Rod Sheldon (from the novel *Holocaust* by A. McCall): Patrick O'Neal, Susan Tyrrell, Barry Morse, Ken James, Robert Goodier, Jack Mather, Murray Westgate, Claude Rae, Cec Linder, Lance Henriksen. A contrived melodrama in which the U.S. President is assassinated on a visit to Toronto, although, not to worry, it's being passed off as usual as an American city.

To Kill to Live (Mourir pour vivre) (1973) (94mins) d: Franco Vigliante s: Robert Bourges : Diane Lanies, Serge Gottraud, Robert Curotte, Rosy Opez. A muddled and confusing mix-up in which the director of this film goes to a party and begins talking to guests about his difficulties making films. This becomes tiresome and in fact one woman dies as a result of it all. Self-indulgent and empty.

To the Rhythm of My Heart (Au rythme de mon coeur) (1983) (80mins) d&s: Jean-Pierre Lefebvre

Before filming Le jour "S," the remarkable and truly independent Lefebvre made this affecting semi-documentary that grew out of his many trips across Canada to visit workshops, seminars and festivals. Much of this is related to the death of his wife and collaborator, Marguerite Duparc. Narrated by Lefebvre.

To Walk with Lions (1999) (108mins) (a Canada-U.K. co-production) d: Carl Schultz s: Sharon Buckingham & Keith Ross Leckie : Richard Harris, John Michie, Ian Bannen, Kerry Fox, Hugh Quarshie. A sequel to Born Free (1966) brings a moving performance by Richard Harris as George Adamson, Kenya's dedicated conservationist and his struggles to preserve his compound from deadly poachers, corrupt game wardens and encroaching civilization. The lions and their surroundings are beautifully filmed. A brave and inspiring picture for a subject that will never find a happy ending.

Toby McTeague (1986) (96mins) d: Jean-Claude Lord s: Jamie Brown (based on the book of the same title by Jeff Maguire and Djordje Milicevic) : Winston Rekert, Yannick Bisson, Stephanie Morganstern, George Clutesi. Set in the impressive snows of northern Québec, this endearing family film concerns an adolescent boy whose mother has died. Once he accepts this, he goes out to rescue his bush-pilot father from a plane crash and then drives his dog team to victory in the championship race. Lively, exciting and affirmative.

Today I Am a Fountain Pen (A Good Place to Come From) (1980) (90mins) d: Robert Sherrin s: Israel Horowitz (based on short stories by Morley Torgov) : Allan Levson, Hollis McLaren, Harvey Atkin, Ralph Benmergui. A young boy now in his teens looks back over Jewish life in Sault Ste. Marie during the 1930s and '40s. The essence and humour of Torgov's writing comes faithfully to life.

Today or Never (Aujourd'hui ou jamais) (1998) (105mins) d&s: Jean-Pierre Lefebvre : Marcel Sabourin, Claude Blanchard, Julie Ménard, Micheline Lanctôt, Jean-Pierre Ronfard. This is yet another of Lefebvre's quiet, beautiful portraits of individuals who have known sadness and joy and survived emotional and physical torments. Abel, who has wanted to fly since he was a child, runs a small airfield but cannot bring himself to fly after the death of his best friend and co-pilot in a plane crash. The arrival of a bright and attractive young aviatrix changes his outlook on life. There is nothing forced or false in the telling of this gossamer-like story, with its sunny, spring background, and one is enveloped in Lefebvre's characteristic warmth and compassion.

Tokyo Cowboy (1994) (94mins) d: Kathy Garneau s: Caroline Adderson : Christianne Hirt, Janne Mortil, Hiromoto Ida, Alec Willows, Anna Ferguson. A pleasant and amusing romantic comedy about a young Japanese man who comes to British Columbia to take up the life of a cowboy and marry a lovely cowgirl. But the maid of his dreams doesn't want to be a cowgirl, which leads to frustration and disillusionment. Nicely done with appealing performances. Marvellously entertaining.

Tom Alone (1989) (120mins) d&s: Jeremy Hole : Noam Zylberman, Gordon Tootoosis, Nick Mancuso, Ned Beatty. An episode in the fascinating history of the building of the trans-Canada railway. In a true story set in the 19TH century, a 15-year-old boy follows his father (who had been falsely accused of a murder in Toronto) west. On the way, he meets the now-famous RCMP inspector Sam Steele and Cornelius Van Horne, the builder of the railway (although Beatty is not everyone's idea of Van Horne). The boy finally finds his father. Faithful to the times and genuinely exciting.

Tom Stone: For the Money (2002) (120mins) d: Stuart Margolin s: Andrew Wreggitt : Chris William Martin, Janet Kidder, Stuart Margolin, Terence Kelly, Nola Augustson, Carmen Moore, Timothy Webber, Art Hindle, Donnelly Rhodes, Preston Manning. In Calgary, a suspicious accident puts Tom, a young oil rig worker, into hospital. Marina, an RCMP constable, waits for him and then places him undercover at the rig to find out what really happened. The two of them discover an elaborate oil investment plot. Another accident sends Tom and Marina to investigate the company in its other dubious activities. Or so it seems. This opening to a massive CBC-tv series came along on a tide of publicity for Calgary, where it was filmed, and based on every conceivable event associated with money, justice, greed, crime, loyalty and betrayal and love, all set against giant buildings and the Rocky Mountains. Quite a stampede, in fact, but on the whole it is interesting and engaging. Well acted and carried off.

Tommy Tricker and the Stamp Traveller (Les aventuriers du timbre perdu) (1988) (101mins) d&s: Michael Rubbo : Lucas Evans, Anthony Rogers, Jill Stanley, Andrew Whitehead. Young Ralph shares his father's passion for collecting stamps. One day, he makes the mistake of trading one of his father's most precious stamps to clever Tommy Tricker and a whole series of misadventures ensues as he tries to get his hands on a worthy replacement. Ralph soon finds himself on a delightfully perilous journey aboard a postage stamp heading for Australia with a totally unexpected stopover in China. An exotic and exhilarating fantasy. (See: Tales for All series)

Tomorrow Never Comes (1978) (107 mins) (a Canada-U.K. co-production) d: Peter Collinson s: Sydney Banks, David Pursall, Jack Seddon : Oliver Reed, Susan George, John Osborne, Raymond Burr, John Ireland, Stephen McHattie, Richard Donat, Cec Linder, Jayne Eastwood, Walter Massey. Filmed in a Québec tourist town, a policeman, possibly corrupt, gets into a struggle with a young man who goes beserk when he discovers his girlfriend has been unfaithful. Not of much interest to the tourists, but an exceptional cast manages to provide us with many good moments.

Too Much Is Enough: see *Trop c'est assez*

Too Much Sex (1999) (87mins) d&s: Andrew Ainsworth ; Michael McMurty, Janet Kidder, Christine Donato, Murray Furrow, Diane Flacks, Christie McFadden, Joan Henry. A randy hairdresser, while in bed with his 390th woman, is called to heaven. His guardian angel sends him back with a warning that the next woman will be his last unless he recognizes the difference between sex with love and sex without. Intended to be a risqué romantic comedy, this is foolish, flat and strained.

Too Outrageous (1987) (105mins) d&s: Richard Benner : Craig Russell, Hollis McLaren. The sequel to *Outrageous* lacks the power that came from the novel used for the first film and is only fitfully entertaining as Robin Turner and Liza return from New York to Toronto.

Tools of the Devil (1985) (65mins) d: Peter Yalden-Thomson s: Donald Truckey : Marc Strange, Heath Lamberts, Garry Stevens, Diana Belshaw, John Friesen, Wayne Best, Lubomir Mykytiuk, Cordelia Strube, Patrick Brymer, Gordon Clapp, Ralph Endersby. A thickly populated but highly engrossing drama about political chicanery and journalistic ethics, involving reporters and politicians. What it all comes down to is the question of who controls public perceptions of events and information—the press or the politicians? Thoughtful, knowing, and familiar with the Tools. (See: *For the Record*)

Top of His Head, The (1989) (110mins) d&s: Peter Mettler : Stephen Ouimette, Christie MacFadyen, Gary Reineke. This was the first feature film from cinematographer-experimentalist Peter Mettler and is an exercise in avant-garde comedy about a satellite dish salesman. His promising future changes when he meets a black-haired, blue-eyed, radical social activist beauty and is transformed by her ideas of what life should be. This makes a different, demanding excursion into existentialism.

Top of the Food Chain (1999) (99mins) d: John Paizs s: Phil Bedard, Larry Lalonde : Campbell Scott, Fiona Loewi, Nigel Bennett, Tom Everett Scott, Hardee Lineham. Spare on wit and imagination, this sci-fi spoof, which brings in an atomic scientist to find out what strange creature is eating the people of the town, is flat, foolish and feeble.

Torso: The Evelyn Dick Story (2000) (120mins) d: Alex Chapple s: Dennis Foon (based on the book of the same name by Marjorie Freeman Campbell) : Kathleen Robertson, Victor Garber, Brenda Fricker, John Henry Canavan, Callum Keith Rennie, Hannah Lochner, Jonathan Pitts. In Hamilton, Ontario, in 1946, a group of children made a gruesome discovery when they came upon a man's torso—all that remained of streetcar conductor John Dick. His wife, Evelyn, was convicted of his murder and sentenced to be hanged. An ambitious young lawyer has the

verdict overturned when he proves the police investigation was faulty. But then a search of Evelyn's house uncovers the remains of a baby boy. This is a compelling film of one of Canada's most lurid and sensational murders. (See: *Mystery* series)

Touch and Go (2002) (100mins) d: Scott Simpson s: Michael Melski : Jeff Douglas, Patricia Zentilli, Stephen Sharkey, Cassie MacDonald, Karen Beverly, Ellen Page, Glen Grant. Yet another interpretation of a character trying to come to terms with himself and what he has become. A 28-year-old man—charming and good looking, with many friends, an enjoyable summer job, money in the bank, good health and more—tries not to accept becoming older. But finally he begins his fight for freedom from his fears. It's difficult to care about this man or even like him. A good try, but slim and superficial.

Touch of Murder, A (1990) (80mins) d&s: David Wellington : Chuck Shamata, Nicholas Kilbertus, Ronald Lea, Jon Cuthbert. David Wellington's first feature is about a young man who has the power to tell the background and history of anything he touches and examines. This, of course, is a power that may lead to trouble—even murder. A nifty little work of imagination.

Touch the Wind: see **Kelly**

Touched (1999) (103mins) d&s: Mort Ransen, Joan Hopper-Ransen : Lynn Redgrave, Tygh Runyan, Lolita Davidovich, Maury Chaykin, Ian Tracey. Filmed on location in Keremeos, B.C., Redgrave is cast as a hard-drinking, aging widow living on the native reserve of her late husband. She doesn't get along with her daughter and life is generally bleak. One morning she goes to her barn and there finds a politically correct Peter Pan who falls in love with her. So begins their May-September romance. Far from being touched, it's all rather humdrum.

Touching Wild Horses (2002) (90mins) (a Canada-U.K.-German co-production) d: Eleanore Lindo s: Murray McRae : Jane Seymour, Mark Randall, Andrew Tarbet, Charles Martin Smith, Gloria Slade. An 11-year-old boy whose family has been killed in a traffic accident is sent to live with his aunt on remote Sable Island. She studies a protected herd of wild horses and does not take kindly, at first, to having to care for a youngster. Although we know that this will change (as it does, and the horses become part of their relationship), this is not an overly sentimentalized storybook tale but a convincing, well-acted, beautifully photographed portrayal of a world-weary older woman and an eager-to-learn young boy. The horses are great, too, and the score by *Inspector Morse*'s talented Barrington Pheloung is perfection. One can relate to every aspect of this portrait.

Tout feu, tout femme: see **Woman Inflamed, A**

Tout prendre, À (Take It All) (The Way It Goes) (1963) (98mins) d&s: Claude Jutra : Claude Jutra, Johanne Herelle, Victor Desy, Tania Fedor, Guy

Hoffman, Monique Mercure, Monique Joly. Claude Jutra portrays his failed love affair with Johanne, a model, in a personal film of a real-life experience. This was his first film—somewhat haphazard and frank beyond the usual boundaries—and made with very little money before there were funding agencies. The film made Jutra's name and he went on to become one of Canada's leading directors. (This film made a stir at the Montreal Film Festival, at its first showing, due to Johanne being a black woman.)

Traces (1978) (80mins) d&s: Régis Tremblay : Régis Tremblay, Natalie Suzanne, Roger Lambert, Anna Charest, Jean Rodrigue, Natalie Truchon. A "one-man-band" film about two childhood friends who meet again as adults. Odd and slow moving.

Tracker, The (1999) (95mins) d: Jeff Schechter s: Robert Geoffrion : Casper Van Dien, Françoise Robertson, Russell Wong. A former New York policeman living in Montréal becomes caught up in a battle between two underworld gangs in the course of trying to help his old friend track down his kidnapped sister. This scenario sets up what follows: long stretches of martial arts combat, fist fights, gun battles, car chases and crashes. We've seen it all before.

Tragic Diary of Zero, the Fool, The (1970) (75mins) d&s: Morley Markson (based on an outline by Daniel Grigg and Penelope) : Gerald Cogan, Penelope the Poet, Daniel Grigg, Natasha Dudarev, Robert Ladouceur, Beverly Webster. A poetess, her would-be lover, and her fool set about to project their fantasies onto film, and are in confrontation with the filmmaker who has his own point of view about the three of them and their relationship. He sees them as futile, over-verbose and silly, and it is only through the Fool that he is able to express a sense of truth about these characters. As the film opens, the three are playing roles, but as the film moves on, the line between role-playing and direct expression is blurred, as the characters seem to become more real, even though their actions become more fantastic. The director, the invisible force who is the magician, is very much a part of the action even though he is not seen on camera. His presence is felt because the actors act not just at his command, but also directly in relation to him. Much more than simply an experimental film, there are individuals here to think about as they search for their sense of reality. We are left with a lot to think about and discuss. One of the players, Robert Ladouceur, held an important position at the NFB for many years.

Train of Dreams (1987) (88mins) d: John Smith s: Sally Bochner s: Jason St. Amour, Marcella Santa Maria, Fred Ward, Christopher Neil. John N. Smith made this National Film Board semi-documentary that improvises, quite convincingly for most of its length, the social drama of a teenager whose violent behaviour on the streets of Montréal leads to his arrest and confinement in a correctional centre. The cast is made up of non-professionals.

Tramp at the Door (1985) (80mins) d&s: Allan Kroeker (based on the story *"Un vagabond frappe à notre porte"* by Gabrielle Roy) : August Schellenberg, Monique Mercure, Ed McNamara, Eric Peterson, Jean-Louis Hébert, Joanna Schellenberg. In a small town in Manitoba in the 1930s a stranger suddenly appears at the door of a French-Canadian family. He tells them he is a long-lost cousin from Québec. But they soon discover, to their disappointment, that he is not the man he claims to be. A charming little story, highly watchable.

Trapped in Issoudun: see *Piège d'Issoudun, Le*

Trapped: see **Chatwill's Verdict**

Traveller, The (1989) (120mins) d: Bruno Lázaro Pacheco s: Jean-Pierre Lefebvre, Bruno Lázaro Pacheco : Lewis Morrison, Ginette St-Denis, Denise Brillon. Once again we are drawn into the dreams and torments of childhood and visions of images of the past, this time in the life of a successful dealer of Pacific Northwest Indian masks. On a business trip, he is mysteriously lost. There are times when it seems he might be better off not found. What is the independent-minded Lefebvre doing here?

Treacherous Beauties (1994) (120mins) d: Charles Jarrott s: Jim Henshaw (based on the novel by Charyl Emerson) : Emma Samms, Bruce Greenwood, Ronald White, Catherine Oxenberg. A photographer hears that her brother has been shot dead at a horse-rearing farm. She decides to visit the scene of the crime and while there, much to her terror, she uncovers a murky conspiracy. A thriller with a difference, holding steady interest. (See: *Harlequin* series)

Treasure Island (2001) (94mins) (a Canada-U.K. co-production) d&s: Peter Rowe (based on Robert Louis Stevenson's novel) : Jack Palance, Kevin Zegers, Patrick Bergen, Walter Sparrow, David Robb. Jim Hawkins and Long John Silver are back in this tepid telling of Stevenson's famous pirate yarn. (Note: This is the 5th version. Robert Newton, we still miss you!)

Tree of Hands, The: see **Betty Fisher and Other Stories**

Treed Murray (2001) (90mins) d&s: William Phillips : David Hewlett, Aaron Ashmore, Cle Bennett, Kevin Duhaney, Jessica Greco. This is a film that begins with promise and then falls apart. Murray is a white, middle-aged, middle-class advertising executive. One morning, while walking through the park, he is set upon by a group of young, working-class thugs. To escape, Murray climbs a tree and stays there while they scream and shout at each other in a vocabulary consisting entirely of foul four-letter words. One gets shot, and blood is everywhere. This contrived clash of classes attempts to make a social statement about the rich and the poor, where goodness may be found among the bad and evil is rife among the good.

Trésor de Nouvelle France, Le: see **Letter From New France, A**

Trial and Error (1993) (91mins) (a U.S.-Can film) d: Mark Sobel s: Andrew Peter Marin, Rick Way & others : Helen Shaver, Tim Matheson, Alicia Clarke, Sean McCann, Maurice Dean Wint, Pam Hyatt, David Gardner, Michael J. Reynolds, Page Fletcher, Gene Mack. A study of conscience, portraying an earnest American prosecutor who puts his career at risk when he discovers that in a previous murder case he sent an innocent man to jail. Now the real killer emerges to threaten the lawyer's wife. Gripping and believable.

Trial at Fortitude Bay (1994) (93mins) d: Vic Sarin s: Keith Ross Leckie : Lolita Davidovich, Henry Czerny, Raoul Trujillo, Marcel Sabourin, Robert Ito. This is a gripping, thought-provoking story revealing how Canada's justice system came into conflict with an Inuit community over the crime and punishment of a 19-year-old man accused of sexual assault. He is defended by a young, white, female lawyer from Upper Canada who comes to realize that in defending her client's best interests, she is working on a very different social structure. This is an exceptional film with great performances by an excellent cast. The director is also known as one of Canada's best cinematographers.

Trial by Fire: A North of 60 Mystery (2002) (160 mins) d: Francis Damberger s: Andrew Wreggitt (a feature film based on the successful tv series *North of 60*) : Tina Keeper, Tracey Cook, Tom Jackson, Peter Kelly-Gaudreault. A new lodge in the town of Lynx River burns down, leaving a corpse in the ashes. An RCMP officer starts an investigation of corruption in Yellowknife as the evidence mounts against her brother, who is about to become premier of the Northwest Territories. Brave investigating here, and the end comes not with the usual car chases but with a fatal boat chase across Great Slave Lake. It's rewarding to find a good melodrama such as this actually taking place in Canada rather than somewhere south of the border.

Trial by Vengeance (1989) (81mins) d&s: Dean Lewis : Andres Aspergis, Walker Bonshor, Linda Singer, Laird Stevens. After a policeman posing as a drug user arrests a trafficker, two murders follow. The detective becomes involved when one of the victims is found to be a friend. Although he finds the murderer, the latter commits suicide, leaving the detective with difficulties to resolve. A well-made genre film with the chilly atmosphere of a good street thriller.

Tribe of Joseph (2002) (99mins) (a Canada-U.S. film) d&s: Cleetche : Steven Grayhm, Shuan Johnson, Karen de Zilva.Wandering the deep, dark forests and moutnains of BC, a group of religiously maniacal young men with bows and arrows kill deer and grizzlies. Called the Tribe of Joseph, they look like early aboriginals, and are lead by their Lord and Master who claims to be the Messiah. They go into small towns and entice boys with troubled parental relations, into theforest where they are ruthlessly indoctrinated. Their behavior is so murderous, the Lord himself would be horrified. One woman is there, who must suffer too, from child-birth. Weird is the word for it; the Stone Age was holiday compared with this. It's horrible; there are small truths, and it is well-done. It's purpose? To warn us all of cults which are flourishing around the world today.

Tribute (1980) (124mins) (a Canadian-American film) d: Bob Clark s: Bernard Slade (from his play of the same title) : Jack Lemmon, Robby Benson, Lee Remick, John Marley, Kim Cattrall, Gale Garnett, Colleen Dewhurst. Jack Lemmon in an overwrought performance as a New York theatrical agent dying of cancer. Mawkish, poorly directed, heavy going.

Trick or Treat (2001) (90mins) d: Marc Cayer s: Jean-Marc Dalpé : Pierre Curzi, David Boutin, Maxime Dénommé, Jean-Marc Dalpé. A teen who has become a victim of school bullies goes out and gets a gun from a small-time gangster and meets another juvenile delinquent. So begins yet another and familiar depiction of teen torment. That old reliable, Pierre Curzi, should have remained at home. Wavers between being shallow and serious.

Triggermen (2000) (96mins) (a Canada-U.K. co-production) d: John Bradshaw s: Tony Johnston : Donnie Wahlberg, Neil Morrisey, Adrian Dunbar, Claire Forlani, Amanda Plummer, Michael Rappaport, Saul Rubinek, Pete Postlethwaite. A nasty piece of supposedly comic crime about low-class Brits in Chicago—a group of fools, killers, bikers and drunks. A waste of time, with a wasted cast.

Trilogie Marseillaise, La (2001) (three parts, 90 mins each) d: Nicholas Ribowski s: Jacques Nahoum : Roger Hanin, Gaela Le Devehat, Lenie Scoffie, Éric Poulin. Three of the great French films of the 1930s were known collectively as the *Pagnol Trilogy*. All were written by Marcel Pagnol and the trilogy consisted of *Marius* (1931, directed by Alexander Korda), *Fanny* (1932, directed by Marc Allegret), and *Cesar* (1936, directed by Pagnol) with all three using the same actors. The films depicted a simple but deeply affecting chronicle of provincial life in Marselilles. Now we have a new version filmed in Quebec that attempts the impossible: to remake these classic films. It is not the same Pagnol, even though this new film is described as being inspired by the original. It is adequate but nothing more. (Note: The trilogy formed the basis of the successful American play and film *Fanny*, 1961, directed by Joshua Logan, with Leslie Caron, Maurice Chevalier and Charles Boyer.)

Trinity (2002) (85mins) d&s: Gary Boulton-Brown : Lucy Akhurst Tom McAmus, Stephen Moyer. A three-hand sci-fi thriller about three characters who become involved in secret genetic experiments. Deceit and betrayal, murder and love affairs are packed in here with surprisingly satisfying results.

Trip to Serendipity, A (1992) (80mins) d&s: Nancy Marano : Donna Larson, James Bell, David Brindle, Patrick Brown. A pleasing, unusual modern-day fairy tale filmed in Calgary about a young woman rediscovering herself through her love of dance.

Tristesse modèle réduit: see Sadness, Reduced to Go

Trois et demi: see Three and a Half

Trois femmes, un amour (Three Women in Love) (1994) (95mins) d: Robert Favreau s: Guy Fourier, Caroline Mitchell, Dominique Lancelôt : Élizabeth Bourgine, Andrée Lachapelle, Judith-Emmanuelle Lussier, Serge Dupire. Mathieu and Claire have been living together and are very much in love. They get married and their happiness is complete. The next day he goes out in the morning to the bakery and is knocked down, sending him into a deep coma. The families come to visit and during the endless vigil that follows, they fall apart. Perceptive and affecting.

Trois pommes à côté du sommeil: see Close to Falling Asleep

Trouble (1996) (103mins) d&s: Paul DiStefano : Tom Smith, Trevor Leigh, Ian Coulter, Patrick Gorman. Two 28-year-old best friends with minimal prospects of achieving much in life decide to rob a bank van. They almost get away with it, but are pursued by other criminals after the same swag. This is a likeable first feature low-bugetpicture that is not exploitative and is often quite funny.

Trouble Makers (Trouble-fête) (1964) (87mins) d: Pierre Patry s: Jean-Claude Lord, Pierre Patry : Percy Rodriguez, Henri Tremblay, Yves Corbeil, Jean-Louis Paris, Jean-Paul Brodeur, Jean-Pierre Souriol, Chantal Rousseau, Denis André, Vallon Legendre, Maurice Beaupré, José Ledoux, Lucie Poitras, Camille Ducharme, Jean Duceppe, Roland Chenail. A college student in Montréal revolts against the authorities, his family, and his friends in his struggle to find a meaning to his existence. Patry moves fast, packs in his actors, and falls into melodrama, but with some meaningful moments about student awareness of self.

Trouble-fête: see Trouble Makers

Truckin' (1972) (89mins) d&s: Peter Hitchcock, John Carroll : Evan Garber, Ryan Trash, Liz Martiniak, Willie McKay. Part documentary, part fiction, this is a record of the Festival Express as it crossed Canada in the late'60s. A communal living experience for those taking the trip.

Trudeau (2002) (480mins) d: Jerry Ciccoritti s: Wayne Grigsby : Colm Feore, Polly Shannon, R.H. Thomson, Raymond Bouchard, Raymond Cloutier, John Neville, Donald McKellar, Geraint Wyn Davies, Karl Pruner, Aidan Devine, David McIlWraith, Eric Peterson, Robert Bockstael, Luc Proulx, Sara Botsford, Ronald White, Jeremy Akerman, Jean Marchand, Guy Richer, Peter Outerbridge, Patrick McKenna. Well, Raymond Massey could play Lincoln, Kenneth Walsh Truman, (Hiroshima),

Ronald Silver Kissinger, Robert Christie John A. MacDonald, among the many Canadian actors who have played statesmen and politicians, but with all due respect to Colm Feore's brave attempt to play Trudeau, the result is unconvincing, with Pt.1 of this botched, confusing, often inaccurate survey of the Trudeau years looking like a True Romance novelette, with the desperate time of the FLQ crisis falling like a damp squid. Pt.2, the constitutional crisis is turned into a bankers' extended lunch hour, where keeping track of who the players were portraying is almost impossible. This film, like Trudeau himself, has no depth, but this does not make it an effective or gripping portrayal. The narrative lacks a backbone. Feore presents at first a likeable young man in his own right, who now and then bears a shadow of someone we once knew; but a flower in his buttonhole, a prime minister does not make. Trudeau defeats him in this jumble of flash, fizzle and edited newsreel bits, making use of a small army of actors and accompanied by an entirely inappropriate score. Trudeau can only be seen for what he was in a skilfully created documentary made up of film taken over his life and career, with a well-written, beautifully-spoken narration. Donald Brittain, where are you now we need you? Media critics went into ecstasy over this present production. Recommended reading, however, is Robert Fulford "CBC's Trudeau fails to capture the man and his times," National Post, April 3/02; Paul Wells "Trudeau myth not something that can be simplified," National Post, April 4/02. Recommended documentary, see: Pierre Elliott Trudeau: Memoirs (1993) (5 one-hour parts) (b/w) d: Brian McKenna s: Terence McKenna : Pierre Elliot Trudeau. This superlative documentary made by Rock Demers and Kevin Tierney's Productions la fete gives us a deeply absorbing, cleverly put together, revealing survey of Trudeau's life, times, and years in Parliament. In this film, culled from thousands of feet of newsreel coverage and interviews, the man's personality and shortcomings, characteristics and comments—both wise and inane—provide a stunning portrait of a prime minister who most certainly can be called different, among the many other complimentary and angry things said of him. There is certainly no difficulty in recognizing the other politicians who surrounded him.

True Confections (1991) (95mins) d&s: Gail Singer : Leslie Hope, Kyle McCulloch, Jill Riley, Judah Katz, Chandra West. Three friends, Verna, Norma and Carol, have grown up Jewish in Winnipeg during the 1950s. The friends have been advised by their traditional families to find husbands and settle down to family life with children. A series of incidents follows: some funny and delightful, others more sad and reflective. Questions about facing up to life are wisely answered by a knowing grandmother. An enjoyable, nicely played-out lesson in living. The director, noted for documentaries, makes her first dramatic film here.

True Nature of Bernadette, The (La vraie nature de Bernadette) (1972) (96mins) d&s: Gilles Carle : Micheline Lanctôt, Donald Pilon, Réynald Bouchard, Maurice Beaupré, Ernest Guimond, Julien Lippe, Robert Rivard, Willie Lamothe, Jacques Bilodeau, Robert des Roches, Paul Gauthier, Yves Gélinas, Suzanne Langlois, Lucie Mitchell. Bernadette is a young wife and mother who leaves her city home and family to find freedom and purity in the fresh clean air of country life. Taking over an old farm, she also provides sexual gratification for a variety of men. She persuades a mute, abandoned child to speak and finds a horde of handicapped villagers at her door begging for a miracle cure. Meanwhile, two of her visitors turn on her household with guns, a young boy is shot, and farmers dump their produce on the highway in a revolt that is never really explained. While Gilles Carle's vitality as a filmmaker never seems to flag, he often doesn't give himself enough time to work out or properly motivate his screenplays. Fortunately, he has injected a good deal of comedy into the proceedings here and is helped considerably by the appealing performance of Micheline Lanctôt. The whole seems to have wandered into Bunuel's world.

Trust in Me (1995) (96mins) d: William Corcoran s: Hart Hanson, Matthew MacLeod : Carrie Graham, Sandra Nelson, Ian Tracey, Duncan Fraser, Stacy Keach. A formidable, stark and unsettling drama about a policeman working undercover among Vancouver's warring gangs while trying to come to terms with his failing marriage and the fact that the bikers' leader once saved his life. Skilfully done and gripping.

Tu as crié (Let Me Go) (1997) (98mins) d: Anne-Claire Poirier s: Anne-Claire Poirier with Marie-Claire Blais. This documentary is so much a work of personal anguish it cannot go without being included here. It is about what happened to filmmaker Anne-Claire Poirier when she discovered that her 20-something daughter, a heroin addict and prostitute, was found strangled to death in a Montréal alley. What we see, feel and hear throughout casts a shadow over society and social services as Anne-Claire searches for the meaning of what has happened. An unforgettable, agonizing experience reaching out to audiences, who also feel deeply involved in this tragedy.

Tu brûles, tu brûles: see **You Are Warm, You Are Warm**

Tuesday, Wednesday (1987) (82mins) d: Jon Pedersen s: Jon Pedersen, David Adams Richards (based on his story) : Phillip Blayney, Liz Dufresne. A first-feature from a New Brunswick director who sets his story in Fredericton and tells a serious, forceful and often moving tale of the loneliness and despair of a reformed alcoholic attempting to make amends for the child he killed while driving drunk.

Tulips (1981) (93mins) (a Canadian-American film) d: Rex Bromfield, Al Waxman s: Henry Olek : Gable Kaplan, Bernadette Peters, Henry Gibson, Al Waxman, Sean McCann. A feeble romance in which two characters who do not know each other attempt to commit suicide, then meet and fall in love. No flowers please.

Tunes a Plenty (1989) (103mins) d&s: Greg Hanec : Greg Hanec, Ray Impey. A garage band in Winnipeg insists on playing only its own original music. Apparently, this is upsetting to the fans. The likeable music finds it difficult to sustain the over-long running time. An early effort from the ambitious Winnipeg Film Group.

Tunnel (2000) (94 mins) a U.S.-Can film d: Daniel Baldwin s: Tony Johnston : Daniel Baldwin, Kim Coates, Mark Camacho, Audrey Benoît, Rob Ferguson. A former SAS agent with a thief as his accomplice struggles to keep breathing as the air runs out in a maze of abandoned mine tunnels where they have gone to steal a fortune in diamonds. As the air runs out, so does the story. A movie as bad as they come. (Not to be confused with Maurice Elvey's The Tunnel, 1935).

Turbulence des fluides, La (Chaos and Desire) (2002) (113mins) (a Canada-France co-production) d&s: Manon Briand : Pascale Bussieres, Julie Gayet, Jean-Nicolas Verreault, Geneviève Bujold, Vincent Bilodeau. Manon Briand's second film following Two Seconds bears out the promise of her previous work, with this new film cleverly combining science, mystery and romance in a spellbinding narrative. For the past week in a small bay in northern Québec, the tides have stopped coming in. A Québec seismologist, an independent young woman, working in Tokyo returns home on a scientific mission to try to find out why this has happened, bringing trouble and discontent to the residents. In tracking down clues, we are held by this convincing mixture of science and uncertainty. And not unexpectedly, romance finds its place quite naturally in this unusual film, in which Canada, at last, is shown playing an international role. The use of complicated computers and scientific methods effectively creates atmosphere. Very different and provoking.

Turnabout (1987) (70mins) d&s: Donald Owen : Jane Gibson, Judith Gault. Owen makes a welcome return with this delightful, sensible comedy about two women, one rich, the other not, who change places and take on different sets of wardrobes and social values. Lightly but sharply observed and engagingly played. A film gem.

Turned Out: see **Shelley**

Turning April (1996) (100mins) (a Canada-Australia co-production) d: Geoffrey Bennett s: James Nichol : Tushka Bergen, Aaron Blabey, Kenneth Welsh, Judi Farr, Christopher Morsely. Although partly financed by Telefilm and the OFDC, this is more an Australian than Canadian picture. Drama, comedy, romance and adventure each play a somewhat confusing part in this predictable story of kidnapping, revenge and child molestation. In spite of this over-crowding, it turns out better than expected.

Turning Paige (Shepherd Park) (2002) (112mins) d: Robert Cuffley s: Jason Long, Robert Cuffley : Katharine Isabelle, Nicholas Campbell, Brendon Fletcher, Torri Higginson, Philip DeWilde, Nikki Barnett. Filmed in Moncton, Alberta (but easily passing as Toronto during a snowy winter), we find ourselves with a failed father, intractable daughter, who wants to be a writer, and violent son driving themselves into a frenzy of recrimination over their past life and the death of the mother, who drank too much. Undeniably well done, but ultimately over-long, tiresome and mired in deepest depression. The atmosphere and the look of a domestic household is expertly caught in the production design, and very few Canadian films look and sound so completely in character as this one.

Turning to Stone (1986) (98mins) d: Eric Till s: Judith Thompson (based on her novel) : Shirley Douglas, Nicky Guardagni, Jackie Richardson, Anne Anglin, Bernard Behrens. Produced by actor John Kastner and brilliantly directed by Till from Thompson's expert screenplay, the story concerns a young woman who is sent to Kingston's penitentiary for women for smuggling drugs, and how she comes to adjust herself to the realities of prison life. Splendid performances in a film that does not wallow in sensationalism.

Twelfth Hour, The (*La douzième heure*) (1966) (70mins) (b/w) d&s: Jean Martimbeau : Guy Provencher, Guy Hoffman, Henri Norbert, Ovila Légaré, Pierre Chouinard. A one-man film, with Martimbeau doing almost everything. A mild but telling crime melodrama about two men in Montréal, one who inherits money, leading to murder and recriminations.

20th Century Chocolate Cake, A (1983) (70mins) d: Lois Siegel s: Gregory Van Riel : Gregory Van Riel, Charles Fisch, Jeannine Lasker, Stephen Lack, Peter Brawley, Kevin Tierney. More doc than fic, this is a trip through a world of gay, lesbian and trans-vestite characters. Not a long journey and of interest to those who find the surroundings congenial. Lois Siegel has made an illustrious career discovering such unseen worlds.

24 Poses (2002) (90mins) d: René-Richard Cyr s: Serge Boucher : Guylaine Tremblay, Michel Dumont, Roger Leger, Louison Danis. Richard is celebrating his 40TH birthday with his wife Nicole and family and friends. It is summertime and there are eight characters here, and all would seem to be right in their lives. But such is not the case, as most of them (as with so many individuals in life) try to ignore the issues that cloud their everyday being. When tragedy strikes, all illusions fall away. This is a perceptive, clearly stated drama, beautifully written and acted, and filled with understanding.

24 Store, The (1990) (75mins) d&s: Brian Stockton : Dawn Kasborf-Stinson, Spyro Egarhos, Marsha Herle, Brian Stockton. A winning small-scale comedy-drama set against the backdrop of a suburban convenience store in Regina, observing many of the characters who drop in to shop.

Twice Upon a Yesterday (1998) (91mins) (a Canada-U.K. co-production) d: Maria Ripoll s: Rafa Russo : Douglas Henshall, Lena Headey, Mark Strong, Penelope Cruz, Elizabeth McGovern, Gustavo Salmerone. In this romantic drama, an unfaithful actor in London is given a supernatural second chance with his girlfriend. But life still doesn't turn out as planned. A strange but fetching and melancholic film.

Twilight of the Ice Nymphs (1997) (100mins) d: Guy Maddin s: George Toles : Pascale Bussières, Shelley Duvall, Frank Gorshin, Alice Krige, R.H. Thomson. Mandragora is a surreal place where the sun never sets. Its inhabitants all seem sex-struck. This is Maddin's fourth experimental film and his supporters will find any number of hidden meanings to make this twilight less deep.

Twin Sisters (1993) (92mins) d: Tom Berry s: David Preston : Stepfanie Kramer, Susan Almgren, Frederic Forrest, James Brolin. Here we go again: the beautiful young woman with looks, money, poise and a loving husband one day discovers her sister is missing and has become a call girl. This fills her with dread. The audience is likely to feel even worse.

Twins: see **Dead Ringers**

Two Actresses (*Deux actrices*) (1993) (95mins) d&s: Micheline Lanctôt : Pascale Bussières, Pascale Paroissien, Louise Latraverse, François Delisle, Suzanne Garceau. Solange is a daycare worker married to Charles, a student. The uneventful pattern of their lives is broken with the arrival of Fabienne, who claims to be Solange's long-lost sister. At first Fabienne brings happiness, but her unpredictable behaviour places a strain on Charles and Solange's relationship. Highly emotional, unconventional and honest, the volatile relationship between the two sisters is tempered by the inclusion of videotape sequences showing the two actresses discussing their lives and the roles they are playing. This drama of trust and reconciliation is yet another tribute to Micheline Lanctôt's filmmaking capabilities, which so often bring touching insights into women's life experiences.

Two Brothers, a Girl and a Gun (1993) (93mins) d&s: William Hornecker : Shaun Johnston, Kim Hogan, David Everhart. A nasty piece of low-budget sensationalism, low-life sex and violence with two lovers on a motorcycle—the girl on the run from the police—heading out across the prairie to the family farm and its difficulties. Strident, empty and repelling.

Two Feet in the Same Ankle Boot: see *Deux pieds dans la même bottine, Les*

Two Men (1988) (96mins) d: Gordon Pinsent s: Anna Sandor : John Vernon, Jan Rubes. Another excellent work from Sandor and Pinsent. This time their story is about a Hungarian immigrant living in Toronto who runs into a man he believes was responsible for the deaths of his family in Auschwitz.Once again, history brings back the awful past.

Two or Three Words (1999) (78mins) d&s: Evan Georgiades : Scott McCord, David Sutcliffe, Noam Jenkins, John Kalangis. A neurotic man living in Toronto is dropped by his girlfriend, leaving him to ponder the meaning of his life. A boring drama.

Two Seconds (2 secondes) (1998) (100mins) d&s: Manon Briand : Charlotte Laurier, Dino Tavarone, Yves Pelletier, Louise Forestier, André Brassard, Pascal Auclair, Jessica MacKenzie, Denis Trudel. Laurie, a young bicycle racer, hesitates for two seconds before the start of a race, and this convinces her that she has lost her skill and she retires from the sport, instead becoming a bicycle courier in downtown Montréal. Her fears are psychological; her need to speed is still within her. On a visit to a bicycle shop to have her wheels checked, she meets a gruff old Italian who was himself once a champion bicycle racer. He shows her how every triumph is relative to certain aspects of life, and a deep friendship grows between them. This is a lovely, thoughtful film with great location shots of Laurie riding in heavy traffic. Laurie is beautifully played by Charlotte Laurier, the unforgettable 12-year-old Manon in Francis Mankiewicz's classic film *Les bons débarras* (1980). She has appeared in many other films since then, never losing her appeal as a remarkable actress.

Two Silent Friends: see *Deux amis silencieux*

Two Solitudes (Deux solitudes) (1978) (116mins) d&s: Lionel Chetwynd : Jean-Pierre Aumont, Stacy Keach, Gloria Carlin, Chris Wiggins, Claude Jutra, Budd Knapp, Murray Westgate, Walter Massey, Pierre Trudeau. Much was expected from this film of Hugh MacLennan's brilliant novel about French-English relations in Québec during World War I. But an inexperienced director with a disappointing script and a poorly cast American actor, Stacy Keach, makes a mockery of the book on film. An important opportunity lost, and never tried again.

Two Summers (2002) (118mins) d&s: Bruce Lapointe : Matthew Harbour, Frank Fontaine, Chip Chuipka, Robert Crooks, Sheena Larkin. A young boy whose mother has died is left alone during the summer by his jet-set father, in the care of his grandfather. The usual and expected family misunderstandings arise, none of which can ease the tedium of watching this well-meaning but trudging, drama.

Two Thousand and None (2000) (90mins) d&s: Arto Paragamian : John Turturro, Oleg Kisseliov, Katherine Borowitz, Julian Richings, Vanya Rose, Carl Alacchi, Pascale Devigne. This peculiar picture opens promisingly with scenes of a successful pale-ontologist making the most important fossil discovery of his career. He returns home to an appointment with his doctor, who tells him that due to a brain disease he has only five weeks to live. In confronting his own mortality, he becomes involved in a string of absurd activities. Uneven, obscure and more fossil than fundament.

2001: A Space Travesty (2001) (98mins) (a Canada-German co-production) d: Allan A. Goldstein s: Alan Shearman, Francesco Lucente : Leslie Nielsen, Ophelie Winter, Ezio Greggio, Peter Egan, Alexandra Kamp-Groeneveld. The American president is kidnapped by aliens and replaced by a clone. A spoof that only splutters. The original, *2001*, although wildly overpraised, doesn't deserve this. We are left wishing that this ugly, sex-ridden and expensive production could be returned to space, never to be seen again.

2103: The Deadly Wake (1996) (100mins) (a Canada-U.K. co-production) d: Philip Jackson s: Andrew Dowler, Doug Bagot, Timothy Lee : Malcolm McDowell, Michael Pare, Heidi von Palleske, Gwynyth Walsh, Hal Eisen, McKenzie Gray. A superior sci-fi journey set in 2103 about a corporate state called Proxate that wants to join the UN. Difficulties arise when Proxate sends a futuristic freighter loaded with deadly toxic waste to a third world country for disposal. Visually impressive.

Two Wise Men, The (Les smattes) (1972) (86mins) d: Jean-Claude Labrecque s: Clément Perron, Jean-Claude Labrecque : Donald Pilon, Daniel Pilon, Louise Laparé, Marcel Martel, Marcel Sabourin. Two brothers living in the Gaspé region of Québec are ordered to leave and be resettled by the government. They run for cover and hide in the woods, but the wife of one is shot. Notable as being cinematographer Jean-Claude Labrecque's first film as a director in a story that makes it possible for the real-life brothers of Donald and Daniel Pilon to work together. (See: *The Rebels 1837*)

Two Women of Gold (Deux femmes en or) (1970) (107mins) d: Claude Fournier s: Marie-Jose Raymond, Claude Fournier : Monique Mercure, Louise Turcot, Marcel Sabourin, Donald Pilon, Donald Lautrec, Jean Lapointe, Janine Suto. A very funny sex comedy. A modern version of wives who pay the tradesmen with favours instead of money. The financial success of this picture played a significant part in bringing Québec cinema back into steady production after a lapse of several years. A remarkable accomplishment by Claude Fournier, who does it all: writing, direction, editing and cinematography.

Tyler (1977) (82mins) d: Ralph L. Thomas s: Roy MacGregor : R.H. Thomson, Murray Westgate, Kay Hawtrey. A trifle about a son who wants to buy his father's farm but cannot raise the money required. A training experience for R.H. Thomson.

Ultimatum (1975) (126mins) d&s: Jean-Pierre Lefebvre : Francine Morand, Jean-René Ouellet,

Dominique Cobello. Charlotte and Arthur are becoming adults and begin to discover that the world around them is one of little civility or consideration. They search within themselves for feelings of love and liberation to bring them freedom from the imperfect world around them. A pessimistic study by the thoughtful Lefebvre.

Uncanny, The (1977) (89mins) (a Canada-U.K. co-production) d: Denis Héroux s: Michel Parry : Peter Cushing, Alexandra Stewart, Ray Milland, Donald Pilon, Chloé Franks, Donald Pleasance, Samantha Eggar, Jean Leclerc, Katrina Holden, Susan Penhaligon, John Vernon, Joan Greenwood, Roland Culver, Sean McCann. An important cast tries to bring some sense of reality to this silly co-production about cats conspiring to take revenge on humans, in three episodes, taking place in a Québec family home. What a waste of a great cast. The cats survive. The audience won't.

Uncles, The (2000) (94mins) d&s: Jim Allodi : Chris Owens, Tara Rosling, Kelly Harms, Veronica Hurnik, Dino Tavarone. A confused drama about an Italian family in Toronto's Little Italy. We find two brothers whose father walked out on the family, leaving them to take care of their mother and a simple sister who steals other mothers' babies. John, the elder, has a job in a restaurant, and he falls in love with the boss' daughter. This leads to complications when he realizes that he will now be not only a father, brother and son, but also the provider for two women. Quite complicated, particularly when it comes to getting the sister pregnant, hoping that once she has her own baby she will stop taking others'. None of this is very deep or affecting. In fact, it's somewhat tedious, and doesn't quite ring true.

Uncut (1997) (91mins) d&s: John Greyson : Matthew Ferguson, Michael Achtman, Damon D'Oliveira, Maria Reidstra, Daniel MacIvor. In this miserable mess of a picture, Greyson, a filmmaker and video artist, somehow manages to drag into the considering of copyright laws a tract on circumcision and the former prime minister Pierre Trudeau. This film should have been cut before it started.

Under the Piano (1998) (120mins) d: Stefan Scaini s: Blair Ferguson : Amanda Plummer, Megan Follows, Teresa Stratas, John Juliani, James Carroll. Another true story, but unlike so many others, this film never sinks into sentimentality. *Under the Piano* is a masterwork that never found a public and was ignored by the critics. It is difficult to even describe it without a sigh in response. It is about a faded opera star, Regina Basilio (Teresa Stratas), whose desire for adulation and control has destroyed her relationship with her two daughters; one is autistic, the other musically gifted. Poignant and deeply moving, the expression of the various emotions and related feelings of the characters is never false and the writing, direction and honest performances cannot be faulted.

Under the Sky: see *Sur Le Seuil*

Undergrads, The (1985) (102mins) (a Canadian-American film) d: Steven Hilliard Stern s: Paul Shapiro (story by Michael Weisman) : Art Carney, Jackie Burroughs, Chris Makepeace, Len Birman, Alfie Scopp, Dawn Greenhalgh, Lesleh Donaldson, Angela Fusco, Gary Farmer, Ronald James, Peter Spence. Canadian produced, and filmed in Toronto passing as an American city, this Disney film is all about an elderly father placed in a retirement home and his grandson and friends who are going to college. Our players are first-rate; the rest is what is generally known as "solid entertainment for the family."

Understanding Bliss (1990) (80mins) d: William MacGillivray s: Kathryn Cochran, William MacGillivray : Catherine Grant, Bryan Hennessey, Rosemary House. MacGillivray (*Life Classes*) is one of the Atlantic provinces' most interesting and talented directors. In this study of human emotions, he shows the complex relationship between an academic who has come to Newfoundland to give a public reading of Katherine Mansfield's *Bliss*, and her lover, a professor at the university. A lovely, sad and compelling encounter.

Understudy, The: Graveyard Shift II (1988) (90mins) d&s: Jerry Ciccoritti : Wendy Gazelle, Mark Soper, Silvio Oliviero, Ilse Von Glatz, Tim Kelleher, Lesley Kelly. As usual, the sequel isn't as good as (or should we say "as bad as"?) the original. This time our vampire goes on the set of a film about vampires and manages to get his nightly drink in spite of confusion all around. (See: *Graveyard Shift*)

Undertaker's Wedding, The (1996) (86mins) d&s: John Bradshaw : Adrien Brody, Jeff Wincott, Kari Wuhrer, Holly Gagnier, Burt Young, Darren Andrea, Paul Amo, Steve Bloom. Familiar fare about an undertaker trying to find a wife and fend off the mob, while getting involved in all manner of miseries, murder and misunderstandings. Tired and predictable.

Undivided Attention (1987) (107mins) d&s: Christopher Gallagher : Barrie Jones, Merika Talve, Christopher Gallagher, Wren Jackson. Another story taking a young couple across Canada in a small sports car. More self-indulgent journeying in which we are expected to experience a cinematic metaphor to help us understand and make sense of what we see or think we see. Not much time to look at the scenery.

Unexpected Phantom, The: see **Apparition, The**

Unfaithful Mornings (Les matins infidèles) (1988) (85mins) d&s: Jean Beaudry : Denis Bouchard, Jean Beaudry, Violaine Forest, Laurent Faubert-Bouvier, Louise Richer, Nathalie Coupal. Two friends (one a writer, the other a photographer) decide to undertake a strange project. Every morning at 8:00, the photographer takes a picture of the street corner where they live while the writer starts a novel based on the photos of the unchanging corner. Differences of opinion and personal problems intrude. The street corner loses its significance, if it ever had any. Tedious and boring.

Unfinished Business (1984) (99mins) d&s: Donald Owen : Isabelle Mejias, Peter Spence, Peter Kastner, Julie Biggs, Chuck Shamata. Owen has gone back to the characters he made famous two decades ago in *Nobody Waved Goodbye*. Peter and Julie, 18 years removed from their own troubled adolescence, married and now divorced, are disappointed with what has become of their lives and are at a loss to know how to cope with their sullen and resentful 17-year-old daughter. There are some very good individual scenes, but the whole too often seems to amount to news and social studies.

Unidentified Human Remains and the True Nature of Love: see **Love and Human Remains**

Unknown From Montréal, The (*Son copain*) (1950) (110mins) (a Canada-France co-production) (b/w) d: Jean Devaivre s: Charles Exbrayat, Jean Devaivre, Ted Allan : René Dory, Patricia Roc, Paul Dupuis, Alan Mills, Guy Maufette, Armand Leguet, Jacques Langevin, Albert Dinan. A first-rate chase-melodrama set in Paris and Québec City involving an RCMP officer whose friend is an acquaintance of a supposed murderer whom the RCMP seek to arrest. In two versions, English and French, with the same cast. Patricia Roc, an accomplished English actress under contract to the J. Arthur Rank Organization, was chosen by producer Paul L'Anglais to play opposite Paul Dupuis, who himself went to England to appear in several films. Possibly the first Canada-France co-production.

Unsaid, The (2001) (109mins) (a Canada-U.S. film) d: Tom McLoughlin s: Miguel Tejada-Flores, Scott Williams (story by Christopher Murphey) : Andy Garcia, Vincent Kartheiser, Linda Cardellini, Trevor Blumas, Teri Polo, Sam Bottoms. A melodrama concerning a wealthy psychologist living in Kansas who has taken to writing books and giving talks in an effort to end the depression he has fallen into since the suicide of his 16-year-old son. Ensuing developments bring about a murder and related sinister events. Saskatchewan's prairies stand in for Kansas. The end result might well do with some analysis.

Until the Heart (*Jusqu'au coeur*) (1980) (93mins) d&s: Mary Stephen : Corinne Lanselle, Michel Voletti, Michel Rocher, Mathieu Carrière, Nadia Vasil, Andrée Pelletier. Another well-meaning but peculiar tale about a sensitive man who hates war and the temptations around him. With his companion, Mouffe, he gives way to romanticism and his life ends as they sit in the park awaiting the arrival of Martians to establish a new order and bring solutions to the problems we humans have brought upon ourselves. Many good moments sensitively interpreted.

Up There on the Mountain: see *La-haut*

Ups and Downs (1983) (97mins) d: Paul Almond s: Lewis Evans, Paul Almond : Colin Skinner, Andrew Sabiston, Gavin Brannon, Leslie Hope, Margo Nesbit, Alison Kemble, Sandy Gauthier. Filmed in Vancouver by Almond (*Isabel*, *Act of the Heart*, *Journey*) and written in part by him, this slight film concerning the daily lives of spoiled children in a private school is pleasant and likeable, but somewhat lacking in identity, insight, and purpose.

Urban Safari (1995) (94mins) (a Canada-Swiss co-production) d: Reto Salimbeni s: James J. Desmarais : David Naughton, Linda Kash, Jay Brazeau, Donnelly Rhodes, Andrea Nemeth, Teryl Rothery. With four writers, this little farce misses out in its tv sitcom formula about a New York family who invent a holiday in Africa in their attempt to keep up with the Joneses. Nice to see the return of Donnelly Rhodes, who has been away too long, but better to have missed this one, perhaps.

Urinal (1988) (100mins) d&s: John Greyson : Pauline Carey, Paul Bettis, George Spevlin, Keltie Creed. A group of dead artists are summoned like ghosts to a mysterious garden of dead sculptors to discuss the practices of Ontario's police forces in the way they patrol public toilets looking for sexual activity among gay men. Acclaimed as hilarious and brave from one viewpoint, but as tiresome and boring on the other.

Utilities (1981) (94mins) d: Harvey Hart s: James Kouf, David Greenwalt, Carl Manning : Robert Hays, Brooke Adams, John Marley, Helen Burns, Lee Broker, Jan Rubes, Helene Winston, Jane Mallett, Toby Tarnow, Heath Lamberts, Beth Amos, Larry Solway, George Touliatos, Ken James, Robert Christie. A social worker tired of the poor service his community is getting from the gas, oil, electric and phone companies begins a protest movement. Supposedly a satiric comedy, both the satire and the laughs are noticeably absent—poor service from the producers!

U-Turn (The Girl in Blue) (1973) (98mins) d: George Kaczender s: Douglas Bowie, George Kaczender : David Selby, Maud Adams, Gay Rowan, William Osler, Diane Dewey, Michael Kirby. A sad young lawyer is so struck by a pretty girl he meets at the ferry that he spends the next two years in a desperate search for her. He finds her, but learns that she is married with children. After leaving her, he feels more unhappy than he did before. Romantic, often touching, but wearying. After many short films at the National Film Board and the feature *Don't Let the Angels Fall*, this was Kaczender's first independent film, working with John Kemeny and cameraman Mike Lente, all three from Hungary.

Vacant Lot, The (1989) (103mins) d&s: William MacGillivray : Grant Fullerton, Trudi Peterson. The 'Vacant Lot' is an all-female rock band. The youngest member is 17-year-old Trudy, from a broken home, obsessed with memories of a father who abandoned her, she meets a 42-year-old rock guitarist whose career is at its end. He joins the band, and after further periods of despair, they manage to strike a harmonious note together. Interesting characterization and Nova Scotian backgrounds put a new face on familiar material.

Valentine's Day (1994) (80mins) d&s: Mike Hoolboom : Babz Chula, Gabrielle Rose. This is a film that disintegrates as fast as its subject. Canada is at war, but a war fought on television, and is a nation in decay symbolized by the devastation of the AIDS plague. Two women in a shabby, dirty old apartment make love, cook, eat, watch tv, and console each other over the demise of the CBC—the only note of truth and comedy in this wildly out-of-control experimental nightmare.

Valérie (1969) (97mins) (b/w) d: Denis Héroux s: Louis Gauthier : Danielle Ouimet, Guy Godin, Michel Paje, Yvon Ducharme, Claude Préfontaine, Andrée Flamand, Kim Wilcox, Pierre Paquette, Hugo Gélinas, Henri Norbert, Clémence Desrochers. With *Valérie* Denis Héroux joined the sex film game with financially rewarding results. Héroux, who made films for the NFB and CBC for several years, independently slapped together a film so simple and naïve that its chances of success seemed nonexistent. But it was this very simplicity (and a low production budget) that was responsible, in part, for the film's success. Valérie, a simple, physically well-endowed woman, flees a convent, becomes a topless dancer, takes to the money-making world of high-class call girls, and actually ends by finding true love with an artist (the father of a small son) who is madly in love with her and prepared to forget her follies. The first of several "skin flick" romantic comedies made by Cinepix with great success. These films were considered bold and sexy and there had never before been others like them in the heavily censored provinces. Today the would be intercourse-uninterrupted.

Valse à trios: see **Oranges of Israel, The**

Varian's War (2001) (122mins) (a Canada-U.K. co-production) d&s: Lionel Chetwynd : William Hurt, Julia Ormond, Matthew Craven, Maury Chaykin, Alan Arkin, Lyn Redgrave, Rémy Girard, Walter Massey, Dorothée Berryman. The true story of American Varian Fry who planned and carried out the escape of about 2000 artists and intellectuals from Nazi persecution in Vichy, France, during World War II. A magnificently set and acted film, both poignant and troubling. The tension slips slightly when it comes time to cross the border. Otherwise this is a film of lasting power and significance. (Production note: Executive-produced by Barbra Streisand, the Earl of Wessex and veteran Montréal filmmaker Kevin Tierney.)

Various Positions (2002) (90mins) d&s: Ori Kowarsky : Tygh Runyan, Carly Pope, L. Harvey Gould, Marie Stillin, Michael Suchanek, Terry Chen. A simple romance-comedy about a Jewish student and his difficulties with his Orthodox family when he falls in love with a flirty, pretty, non-Jewish girl at his school. The familiar complications come over in a winning way.

Vautours, Les: see **Vultures, The**

Vengeance de la femme en noir, La (The Revenge of the Lady in Black) (1996) (100mins) d&s: Roger Cantin : Germain Houde, Julie St-Pierre, Anaïs Goulet-Robitaille, Raymond Bouchard. This comedy is a follow-up to Cantin's *Keep an Eye on the Trombone* and once again Augustin Marleau, the actor who was working as a security guard, finds himself in trouble. He decides to return to acting but his life is just one misadventure after another. The humour is broad with several genuinely funny moments.

Vent de galerne (The Wind From Galerne) (1991) (100mins) (a Canada-France co-production) d: Bernard Favre s: Claude Nedjar, Bernard Favre : Jean-François Casabonne, Charlotte Laurier, Jean-François Blanchard, Francis Reddy. A cumbersome love and death tale set around the French Revolution in the Vendée countryside where priests are found guilty of refusing to swear allegiance to the Republic. Average cloak and dagger melodrama.

Vent du Wyoming, Le: see **Wind From Wyoming, A**

Vents contraires (Crosswinds) (1995) (90mins) d: Allen Goldstein s: Robert Geoffrion, Nancy Heikin-Pépin : David Soul, Daniel Pilon, Grace de Capitani, Carl Marotte, Jean-François Blanchard, Danielle Schneider, André Champagne. A murky thick-ear melodrama, with the usual shooting, police-car crashes, shouting and fighting in which a group of individuals are being held hostage on a boat on the Great lakes by a gang of drug dealers. One wishes they would sink and save us from the violent and bloody ending.

Vercingétorix (2001) (120mins) (a Canada-France co-production) d&s: Jacques Dorfman : Christopher Lambert, Klaus Maria Brandauer, Max Von Sydow, Ines Sastre. With seemingly no Canadian talent involved in this tattered telling of French history, one wonders why Telefilm put money into it. A semi-serious semi-epic series of scenes involving the Romans in Gaul and all the French heroes who opposed them. We even meet Julius Caesar and, of course, the impossible-to-pronounce Vercingétorix.

Verdict in Blood (2001) (120mins) d: Stephen Williams s: Jeremy Hole, Janet MacLean (from the novel by Gail Bowen) : Wendy Crewson, Shawn Doyle, Robert Davi, Sally Kellerman. Judge Marcia Blackwell has reduced her severe jail sentences to community service work. But this leads to her murder during a robbery, thought to have been carried out by a dangerous young man caught assaulting a woman, whom she had released after he had been brought to trial. Detective Joanne Kilbourn is convinced that the reason the judge experienced a change of heart is the key to finding the reason for her death. The high standard in creating mystery, excitement and suspense set by this series is well maintained here. (See: *Mystery* series)

Verités accidentelles, Les: see **Red Eyes**

Vicky (1973) (90mins) d: René Bonnière s: Grahame Woods (based on his play) : Jackie Burroughs, Michael Reynolds, Julie Amato, Sean Sullivan, James Bearden. This is the second part of a film about the murder of two young children by their mentally disturbed mother. Part one is entitled *12 1/2 Cents*. A difficult subject, but written and acted with sympathy and understanding. (See: *For the Record*)

Victim of Beauty: see **Drop Dead Gorgeous**

Vida, La **(The Document of Michael da Vida)** (1965) (75mins) d&s: Daniel Singer, Jim Salt : Peter Montgomery. Made in a basement room at Simon Fraser University (the film brought about the creation of the university's film school), this one-student work is a thoughtful, reflective little picture bridging youth to old age as an elderly man sitting in his garage among piles of movie cans thinks back over his attempts to make a documentary film. He ponders his life and how he gave up the woman he loved because he had given his life to his film. Not terribly encouraging to students who want to make a career in filmmaking, but humorous and quite wise from one so young.

Videodrome (1983) (90mins) (a Canadian-American film) d&s: David Cronenberg : James Woods, Sonja Smits, Deborah Harry, Peter Dvorsky, Les Carlson, Jack Creley, Lynne Gorman, Lally Cadeau, Kay Hawtrey, Jayne Eastwood. An exceedingly unpleasant work in which the director digs deep into an exploration of technology. Slow and silly with bodies being destroyed all over the place.

Vie après l'amour, La: see **Life After Love**

Vie d'ange: see **Angel Life**

Vie d'un héros, La: see **Life of a Hero, The**

Vie d'un homme, La: see **Desjardins, His Life and Times**

Vie fantôme, La: see **Phantom Life, A**

Vie heureuse de Léopold Z, La: see **Merry World of Léopold Z, The**

Vie revée, La: see **Dream Life**

Viens danser sur la lune: see **Dancing on the Moon**

Viens, mon amour: see **Love in a Four Letter World**

Vieux pays où Rimbaud est mor't Le: see **Old Country Where Rimbaud Died, The**

Vigil, The (1998) (82mins) d&s: Justin MacGregor : Damon Johnson, Donny Lucas, Allan Franz, Trevor White, Tahina Awan, Jane Spence, Brendan Beiser, William MacDonald. A group of 20-somethings pile into a Winnebago and drive from Lethbridge, Alberta, to Seattle to join the vigil being held there to pay tribute to Kurt Cobain, lead singer for the band Nirvana, who had committed suicide. The year is 1994. The ups and downs of the journey, strained

relations and other incidents make up the story. Hard going for anyone unfamiliar with the lifestyle and its hero.

Viking, The (1931) (80mins) (b/w) d: George Melford s: Varick Frissell : Charles Starrett, Louise Huntington, Capt. Bob Bartlett, Arthur Vinton; introduction by Sir Wilfred Grenfell. A great and memorable film in every respect, mixing fiction and documentary and set against the turbulent seas off Newfoundland during the annual seal hunt. Two fishermen in love with the same woman are lost in the huge ice floes during a blizzard. One makes his way back to land, eventually to find the church and his lover. This church still stands in St. John's, with a plaque mentioning the film. The photography of the raging seas and the men looking for seals is gripping and awesome. Frissell, the American producer and scientist, took the print back to Hollywood for final work, and it was decided that more scenes were required. The *Viking* put out to sea again and exploded, with the deaths of 27 men. This was Canada's first sound film, and the print was lost for years until producer Ralph Ellis, then an NFB representative, was visiting St. John's and happened to come across it in a freezer. He then sent it to the National Film Archives in Ottawa. A film that can be seen repeatedly without losing its tremendous appeal. See also: *White Thunder* (NFB 2001) (52mins) Compelling documentary by Victoria King about the making of Frisell's feature film *The Viking*, using historic footage with journal accounts and interviews.

Village enchanté, Le: see **Enchanted Village, The**

Village Priest, The (*Le curé de village***)** (1949) (88mins) (b/w) d: Richard Jarvis s: Robert Choquette (based on his radio play) : Ovila Légaré, Lise Roy, Denis Drouin, Paul Guèvremont, Camille Ducharme, Guy Mauffete, Eugène Daignault, Jeanne Quintal, Blanche Gautier, Juliette Huot, Jeannette Teasdale. A tale of a Québec village priest who is the religious head, counsellor, and final authority in the community. Based on a highly successful radio series. Seen today, this film is a revealing chronicle of what life was like in Québec before the Quiet Revolution brought about changes. This was the second beginning of Paul L'Anglais' brave attempts to start a regular production of films in Quebec during the aftermath of World War II. He failed in this respect but laid the foundations for those who followed. (See: *Whispering City*)

Ville jolie: see *Amanita pestilens*

Vincent and Me (*Vincent et moi***)** (1990) (100mins) (a Canada-France co-production) d&s: Michael Rubbo : Nina Petronzio, Christopher Forrest, Paul Klerk, Andrée Pelletier, Tcheky Karyo. This is a thoroughly likeable and beautifully made work of imagination and fact about a young student from western Canada who, inspired by the paintings of Van Gogh, goes to Montréal to study art. In time, she goes to

France, dreams of meeting him and confronts a den of forgers in Amsterdam. A good fairy story acted convincingly with charm, humour and naturalism. A triumph for director-writer Michael Rubbo, who also painted and drew the convincing Van Goghs used. (See: *Tales for All* series)

Vindicator, The (Frankenstein '88) (1986) (92mins) (a Canada-U.S. co-production) d: Jean-Claude Lord s: Edith Rey, David Preston : David McIlwraith, Teri Austin, Richard Cox, Pam Grier, Maury Chaykin, Lynda Mason Green. Scientists working on experiments in space come up with a frightening metal monster and so, once again, Frankenstein lives for today but not for long. Above-average excursion into horror sci-fi.

Viol d'une jeune fille douce, Le: see **Rape of a Sweet Young Girl, The**

Violet (2000) (105mins) d&s: Rosemary House : Andrew Younghusband, Bryan Hennessey, Peter MacNeill, Barry Newhook, Jody Richardson, Gerry Murphy, Mary Walsh, Susan Kent, Bernard Stapleton. Violet is a single woman of 55 whose few remaining family members are brought together to spend time in her house sitting around outside, drinking and talking about nothing in particular. For the opening 15 minutes, Mary Walsh as Violet manages to hold our attention, but once the other mostly unsavoury characters intrude, the film becomes a disaster and for the most part unwatchable. There was a time when remarkable films were made in Newfoundland. This is not one of them.

Violette Nozière (1978) (123mins) (a Canada-France co-production) d&s: Claude Chabrol : Isabelle Huppert, Stéphane Audran, Jean Carmet, Jean-François Garreaud, Lisa Langlois, Bernadette Lafont. Based on a case in France in which a 14-year-old girl led a double life and poisoned her parents. This is a slow-paced film from Chabrol, but one with enough poignancy and shudders to make it memorable.

Violon rouge, Le: see **Red Violin, The**

Virginia's Run (2003) (102mins) (a U.S.-Canada film) d: Peter Markle s: Markle & Valarie Trapp : Gabriel Byrne, Joanne Whalley, Lindze Letherman, Kevin Zegers, Rachel Skarsten, Robert Guy Miranda. A father who cannot accept the death of his wife, thrown from her horse, forbids his daughter, who has inherited her love of horses from her mother, to have anything to do with riding or taking care of horses. Ignoring his opposition, and an objectionable young man, the daughter meets a new and sympathetic trainer, and against all odds wins an important endurance race. A film which will have a hard time riding for critics' approval, but a winning, genuine and appealing picture nonetheless.

Visage pâle **(Pale Face)** (1986) (103mins) (a Canada-Japan co-production) d&s: Claude Gagnon : Luc Matte, Denis Lacroix, Allison Odjig, Guy Thauvette, Gilbert Sicotte. A former Montréal

Canadiens hockey player working as a waiter in Montréal takes a holiday and is attacked by local thugs. A native man comes to his aid but is killed while taking the hockey player back to the reserve for safety. His sister sees what happens and takes the athlete into her care. A small but telling chapter, one supposes, in breaking down discrimination.

Visiting Hours (Fright) (1982) (104mins) (a Canadian-American film) d: Jean-Claude Lord s: Brian Taggert : Michael Ironside, Lee Grant, Linda Purl, William Shatner, Lenore Zann, Harvey Atkin, Helen Hughes, Victor Knight, Sylvia Lennick. Horror junk about a demented patient on the loose in a mental hospital and stalking a tv journalist. The horror here is how so many talented people could become involved in this contrived fantasy. Tiresome nonsense and expensive at that.

Visitor, The (1974) (96mins) d&s: John Wright : Pia Shandel, Eric Peterson, Hetty Clews, Alan Robertson, Patricia Vickers, Scott Hylands. Another oddity in the Canadian film parade. This time, a student in a small town close to Heritage Park in Calgary rents a home and finds herself visited by a ghostlike character from the past. Unbelievably, the two fall in love, and she wisely runs away. Pia Shandel found publicity galore in real life as a beautiful model who married a rich businessman centuries older than she. All very odd indeed.

Vita Cane (1994) (111mins) d&s: Carlo Liconti : Tony Nardi, Janet-Laine Green, Joseph DiMambro. Painfully unfunny sex comedy-drama set in a deserted northern town concerning a charmless Italian hairdresser who has a different woman to sleep with every night of the week. Monotonous and tiresome.

Vive la France: see **Long Live France**

Vivid (1996) (85mins) d&s: Evan Georgiades : Stephen Shellen, Kari Salin, Ilene Kristen. Filmed entirely in a painter's one-studio apartment. The painter involved can only create while rolling around on a paint-drenched canvas on the floor while having sex with his girlfriend. And that's it. Stultifying.

Voitures d'eau, Les: see **Water Cars**

Voleur de caméra, Le: see **Camera Thief, The**

Voulez-vous coucher avec Dieu?: see **Do You Want to Sleep With God?**

Voyageur mort, Le: see **Chocolate Eclair**

Voyageurs d'été, Les: see **Wings in the Wilderness**

Vraie nature de Bernadette, La: see **True Nature of Bernadette, The**

Vulture, The (1967) (91mins) (a Canadian film made in the U.K.) d&s: Lawrence Huntington : Akim Tamiroff, Broderick Crawford, Robert Hutton, Diane Clare, Philip Friend, Gordon Tanner. Another odd attempt to get feature-film production going in English-speaking Canada at this time. This was not the way to do it. A tattered tale of villagers tormented by a vulture with a human head. Stilted, laughable sci-fi for those who will believe anything. (Part b&w.)

Vultures, The (Les vautours) (1975) (91mins) d: Jean-Claude Labrecque s: Robert Gurik, Jacques Jacob (original idea by Jean-Claude Labrecque) : Gilbert Sicotte, Monique Mercure, Carmen Tremblay, Amulette Garneau, Gabriel Arcand, Paule Baillargeon, Jacques Bilodeau, Raymond Cloutier, Jean Duceppe, Robert Gravel, Georges Proulx, Rita Lafontaine, Roger Lebel, Guy L'Écuyer, Gilles Pelletier, Denise Proulx, Anne-Marie Provencher, Jean-Pierre Saulnier. A young man becomes an unwitting pawn in an artful political game played out during the regime of Premier Maurice Duplessis of Québec. A shadowy and thoughtful film about human relationships, individual selfishness and political deception. This was one of cinematographer Jean-Claude Labrecque's early films as director. (See: Years of Dreams and Revolt)

Waiting for Caroline (1967) (85mins) d: Ron Kelly s: George C. Robertson, Ron Kelly : Alexandra Stewart, Robert Howay, François Tassé, Sharon Acker, William Needles, Aileen Seaton, Paul Guèvremont, Daniel Gadouas, Lucie Poitras, Monique Mercure, Reg McReynolds, Paul Buissonneau. Ron Kelly, who established his reputation with his interesting work for the CBC and NFB in documentary and television, entered feature-film making with Waiting for Caroline, a beautifully made, expensively mounted piece of romantic melodrama concerning a woman and her love for two men: one from Québec and one from British Columbia. It is a somewhat boring business waiting for Caroline to make up her mind and decide between the two. This was the first of two co-productions between the CBC and the NFB, the other being Don Owen's The Ernie Game (see under this title). Both films went well over their budgets, which gave the CBC the opportunity to cancel their arrangement. Had the two organizations found a way to work in harmony, the long period during which so many Canadian films languished unseen due to the lack of cinema exhibition would never have come to pass.

Waiting for Michelangelo (1995) (93mins) (a Canada-Swiss co-production) d: Curt Truninger s: Margit Ritzmann, Curt Truninger : Renée Coleman, Roy Dupuis, Rick Roberts, Jeremy Chance, Michael Adam, Ruth Marshall. A piece of stale Swiss cheese in which a Toronto tv journalist finally meets a man she can love, but then on a trip to Lucerne falls for another man who returns with her. Now she has two, and what's to be done about it? The script is not of much help. Well-played romantic piffle.

Waiting for the Parade (1984) (90mins) d: Robin Phillips s: John Murrell (based on his play of the same name) : Martha Henry, Susan Wright, Sheila McCarthy, Donna Goodhand, Carole Shelley. In a factory in Calgary in 1940, five women work on the homefront during World War II, all waiting for the war to end and their men to come home. Stage director Phillips turns a poignant play into a fluid film with a great cast.

Waiting Game, The (1998) (120mins) d: Vic Sarin s: Barbara O'Kelly (based on the novel by Jayne Ann Krentz) : Chris Potter, Chandra West, Paula Abdul, Art Hindle, Jonathan Crombie, John Pyper-Ferguson, Shaun Clarke, Pedro Salvin, Christine Munroe. Two youths who have been best friends since college days mount their first art show in a small New England town. When women and two enigmatic men enter the picture, both mystery and romance result. A nicely told and pleasingly acted piece. (See: Harlequin series)

Walk Backwards (2001) (95mins) d&s: Laurie Maria Baranyay : Laurie Maria Baranyay, Phillip Powers, Edith Baranyay, Andrew McIntyre. A young woman meets a youth in the park and they have unsatisfying sex on a bench. He then lets loose a string of obscenities and mocks and bullies her, calling her a bitch and more. She then goes home to a fairly cheerful family where her sister asks her why she continues to see "that prick." She leaves again, walks the night streets, and we gather that she is trying to face up to the truth about herself and put her life back in order. Part biographical, it's hard going for everyone.

Walls (1984) (88mins) d: Tom Shandel s: Christian Bruyère (from his play of the same name) : Winston Rekert, Alan Scarfe, Andrée Pelletier, John Wright, Lloyd Berry. A prison drama based on a true hostage incident in a British Columbia penitentiary in 1975. Taken from a stage play and given life and meaning by a splendid cast and clever direction.

Wandering Soul Murders, The (2000) (120mins) d: Bradford Turner s: Andrew Wreggitt and R.B. Carney (based on the novel by Gail Bowen) : Wendy Crewson, Cynthia Gibb, Victor Garber, Robin Dunne, Jayne Eastwood. Joanne Kilbourn, the former police officer, and Inspector Philip Millard join forces here when one of Kilbourn's daughter's employees is found murdered. We hear sexist attitudes on the part of the police balanced by a more understanding outlook on the part of the women involved. Well paced and frequently exciting with depth and keen understanding. One wonders what Detective Frost might have done with a difficult situation such as this. (See: Mystery series)

Wanted (Crime Spree) (2003) (99mins) (a Canada-U.K. co-production) d&s: Brad Mirman : Gerard Depardieu, Johnny Hallyday, Renaud, Harvey Keitel, Abe Vigoda, Richard Bohringer, Said Taghmaoui, Stephane Freiss, Albert Dray, Joanne Kelly. A hybrid if there ever was under these co-prods, here we have another crime caper contrived for laughs in which a group of French criminals go to Chicago, after stealing a painting in Paris, to break into the safe of a wealthy couple who collect jewels. Here they bungle the job and very thing that can go wrong does so, leading to complications with the law. The cast switches easily from French to English. Once again, following the musical, Toronto stands in for Chicago. The film is supposed to be a send-up comedy, but quickly sinks instead.

War Between Us, The (1995) (93mins) d: Anne Wheeler s: Sharon Gibbon : Shannon Lawson, Mieko Ouchi, Robert Wisden, Ian Tracey, Robert Ito, Juno Ruddell, Edmond Kata. Taking up the controversy over the internment of Japanese residents living on Canada's west coast during World War II, Anne Wheeler's understanding, humanistic and well-reasoned chronicle of this troubled period is seen through the life of the uprooted Kawashima family. Eventually, the film becomes the story of the friendship between two women, and the symbol of better times ahead. Wheeler has again, with an excellent screenplay, created a masterpiece of significant social drama—a fitting addition to her two previous and unforgettable wartime films, *A War Story* and *Bye Bye Blues*.

War Boy, The (Point of Escape) (1985) (86mins) d: Allan Eastman s: Julius Kohanyi : Helen Shaver, Kenneth Welsh, Ingrid Venninger, Jason Hopley, Derrick Hart. An honest and moving story of a young boy's struggle to escape the perils of World War II. This family drama, set in central Europe, traces his adventures as he attempts to escape the Nazi juggernaut. Tense and terrifying.

War Bride, The (2001) (120mins) (a Canada-U.K. co-production) d: Lyndon Chubbuck s: Angela Workman : Anna Friel, Brenda Fricker, Molly Parker, Aden Young, Julie Cox, Loren Dean. A young woman in London during World War II falls in love with a Canadian soldier. They are married, he goes into battle, and she and a friend come to Canada, where she finds that she has escaped the air raids only to suffer isolation. loneliness and a miserable mother-in-law. on the Alberta prairies. Lively scenes of crowded trains arriving out of the west, and the authentic feel of wartime London, but all somewhat uneven in the telling.

War Brides (1980) (105mins) d: Martin Lavut s: Grahame Woods : Elizabeth Richardson, Sharry Flett, Sonja Smits, Wendy Crewson. With World War II over, four war brides from Britain and Germany all meet on the train from Halifax to Toronto to join their husbands and begin a new life, and we share with them their joys and disappointments. Well done, with feeling, conviction, and fine period settings and atmosphere. See also: *The War Brides: From Romance to Reality* (2001) (45mins) Documentary by Anne Hainsworth about the women who married Canadian soldiers in Britain during WWII and came to live in Canada. A lively and nostalgic post-war record.

War Story, A (1981) (82mins) d&s: Anne Wheeler This first film by the now-distinguished director Anne Wheeler is a clever mix of documentary and drama telling of the shocking captivity of her father, Dr. Benjamin Wheeler (played by David Edney), in a Japanese prisoner of war camp, and how he took care of hundreds of British and Canadian soldiers suffering agonies under brutal treatment by the Japanese army. The story is taken from Dr. Wheeler's diaries, which are read off-screen by the director and Donald Sutherland.

War Story, A: see **Cowboys Don't Cry**

Warrendale (1967) (100mins) (b/w) d&s: Allan King Although commissioned by the CBC, the Corporation refused to show this film because the children portrayed used then-forbidden four-letter words. It was shown instead at the New Yorker Cinema, Toronto. This *cinéma-direct* study of disturbed children, at a home in Toronto called Warrendale, shows the special treatment devised for them by the home's director. No attempt is made to impose a dramatic story on the events of the day. Quite by chance, as the filmmakers were at work, the home's cook, much-liked by the children, died suddenly and added a drama not envisioned by the director. There is no commentary, and the picture has a vital, disturbing effect on audiences leading them to wonder perhaps what parents are doing to their children in the age of psychotics and psychiatrists. Chosen as the first feature to be presented by the New Cinema Club in London May 1967.

Warrior Spirit (1994) (94mins) (a Canada-France-U.S. co-production) d&s: René Manzor (from stories by James Oliver Curwood) : Allan Musy, Byron Chief-Moon, Lukas Haas, Jimmy Herman, Jessica Welch. An Indian boy, Wabi, attending boarding school, is harassed by other students. He leaves the school and his best friend Rod to return to the Yukon. When he hears that Rod has also left the school because his parents cannot afford the fees, he offers Rob work as a fur trapper. Fortunately for the animals, the boys hear that gold is to be found in the mountains, so off they go. Moderately entertaining with history thrown in. (see *Aventures du grand nord, Les*)

Warriors (1994) (100mins) (a Canada-Israel co-production) d: Shimon Dotan s: Alexander Epstein, Benjamin Gold : Michael Paré, Griffith Brewer, Gary Busey, Liz MacRae, Wendii Fulford, Catherine MacKenzie. Yet another violent action-melodrama, this time about a U.S. special forces agent who, falsely imprisoned, escapes and goes on the run managing to avoid being recaptured until the final reckoning. A Victoria, B.C., critic summed it up succinctly as being "really bad, even for a Canadian film!"

Wars, The (1983) (120mins) d: Robin Phillips s: Timothy Findley (based on his novel) : Brent Carver, Martha Henry, William Hutt, Anne-Marie MacDonald, Jackie Burroughs, Jean Leclerc, Domini Blythe, Alan Scarfe, Margaret Tyzack, Barbara Budd, Shirley Douglas, Jeff Hyslop, Leo Leyden, Clare Coulter, Hardee Lineham and others.

The first Canadian film of stage director Robin Phillips, much fought-over during production, comes to the screen as a stilted, pretentious, and cumbersome portrayal of an upper-class Toronto family and their son who goes to the western front during World War I. The army of splendid actors recruited for this could-be epic, fights a losing battle with the script.(see also *Paper People, The*)

Wasaga (1994) (90mins) d&s: Judith Doyle : Louise Liliefeldt, Tracy Wright, Daniel MacIvor, Andrew Paterson. A home movie masquerading as a dramatized documentary dealing with the lakeside town of Wasaga, Ontario, past and present, as seen through the eyes of an artist and dead certain to put anyone off from ever travelling there!

Washed Up (2002) (90mins) d&s: Michael DeCarlo : Cameron Mathison, Liisa Repo-Martell, Jennifer Baxter, Sabrina Grdevich, Deborah Pollitt, Jackie Burroughs, Randy Hughson. After a brief, light and colourful opening with two lovers on the beach, this then foul-minded film introduces a sex-starved old woman, two ugly old men, and a group of sex-crazy beach bimbos—whom we are expected to accept as lifeguards, with no lives to save other than their own, perhaps. Everyone becomes involved in possibly the filthiest Canadian film to find its way into a cinema. It's trash and should be washed down the nearest sewer.

Wasp, The (La guêpe) (1986) (87mins) d: Gilles Carle s: Camille Coudari, Gilles Carle : Chlöé Ste-Marie, Warren Peace, Donald Pilon. Try as one might, it is difficult to find any justification for Gilles Carle's confused tale of corruption and violence. A well-to-do aviatrix sees her two young sons killed in a car accident by a powerful millionaire and his wife, who get lawyers to lie for them and are acquitted of the crime.

Watchers (1988) (92mins) (a Canadian-American film) d: Jon Hess s: Damian Lee, William Freed (from the novel by Dean Koontz) : Corey Haim, Michael Ironside, Barbara Williams, Lala, Duncan Fraser, Dale Wilson. More experiments, this time arising from a laboratory explosion on a military research project, resulting in the creation of a super-intelligent monster of a dog. Barely worth watching.

Watchers II (1990) (97mins) (a Canadian-American film) d: Thierry Notz s: Henry Dominic : Marc Singer, Tracy Scoggins, Thomas Foster, Jonathan Farwell, Mary Woronov. Einstein, the horrible dog, is chased by another monster born of the same experiment carried out in No. 1. Everything is much the same as in No. 1—awful.

Watchers III (1994) (80mins) (a Canadian-American film) d: Jeremy Stamford s: Michael Palmer : Wings Hauser, Gregory Scott-Cummins, Daryl Roach, John Lindton, Lolita Ronalds. One of the scientists involved in these experiments feels sorry for the animals and he arranges for animal rights activists to steal them away. About time, too. There were other *Watchers* watching later, including *Watchers Reborn* but unable to claim a Canadian cloak.

Watchtower, The (2001) (101mins) (a U.S.-Canada film) d: George Mihalka s: Rod Browning, Robert Geoffrion : Tom Berenger, Eli Gabay, Tygh Runyan, Ralph J. Alderman, Rachel Haywood, Elizabeth Carol Savenkoff. A stranger comes to a small fishing port in South Carolina and becomes friends with a brother and sister. The town is attractive, by the sea and the rocks, with a prevailing sense of atmosphere and authentic settings. The woman falls for the stranger, who torments the brother to the point of mental illness. The whole is too slow and talkative for its own good. The actors are from the school of "deliberate performance." There really is no point or purpose to this fishy enterprise.

Water Cars (Les voitures d'eau) (1970) (110mins) d&s: Pierre Perrault : Laurent Tremblay and his sons Aurèle and Yvan, Éloi Perron, Nerée Harvey, Joachim Harvey, Léopold Tremblay, Alexis Tremblay, Louis Harvey. This is the third of Perrault's *cinéma-vérité* studies of the Tremblay family, who live on an island and speak an ancient form of French. This time, the family and friends are involved in building a magnificent wooden boat in the way in which their ancestors would have done. Gentle, amusing, tender and kind, this is a poetic film about rugged and independent people, beautifully observed and a social document for all time.

Water Child (L'enfant d'eau) (1995) (107mins) d: Robert Ménard s: Claire Wojas : David La Haye, Marie-France Monette, Gilbert Sicotte, Monique Spaziani, Danielle Proulx. Emile at 15 is an attractive young man but mentally still a child. On a holiday trip to the Bahamas, his plane crashes and he's washed ashore with 12-year-old Cendrine. He soothes her fears and together in their solitude they become lovers. A wide-ranging study of conflicting emotions at many levels, and the need for love and companionship. Portrayed with delicacy and understanding.

Water Damage (1999) (84mins) d: Murray Battle s: Tony Johnston : Daniel Baldwin, Roberta Maxwell, Leslie Hope, Eugene Lipinski, Dean Stockwell, Mimi Kuzyk, John Neville, Peter Keleghan. A father is in a state of shock after hearing that his son has been killed in an accident at a swimming pool. He tries to get his life in order and go on living, only to find to his despair and disbelief that his past is full of secrets and sordid deeds he cannot remember. This film is also best forgotten.

Water Game, The (2002) (106mins) d&s: John Bolton : Rochelle Greenwood, Dawn Perkins, Ben Eberhard, Edmond Wong, Kristina Copeland. An overlong, overpopulated picture of hordes of teens and their mostly obnoxious behaviour. The title refers to a new interpretation of the game of tag, bringing in giant water guns. Dialogue is mumbled, but at least there's no violence; there is, of course, lots of sex. Mostly tiresome and of little value in its representation of teenage behaviour.

Way It Goes, The: see *Tout prendre, À*

Way to Meet Single Women, The (1985) (91mins) d: Randy Bradshaw s: Allan Katz : Allan Katz, Nancy Cser, Tony de Santis. A man living in Montréal has only one interest in life, and that is to meet and seduce single women. That's the best that can be said of it. At least he doesn't break up homes by chasing married women. Or does he? Unpleasant and shallow.

Waydowntown (2000) (87mins) d: Gary Burns s: James Martin, Gary Burns : Fabrizio Filippo, Don McKellar, Marya Delver, Gordon Currie, Jennifer Clement, Tobias Godson. Workers in one of Calgary's many tall towers of office buildings, connected by pathways and tunnels, devise ways to find their way out of the maze of passages and to relieve the madness and confinement they feel being trapped in this strange, cold, metallic world. Often funny but stretched past its originality, moving into silly sex and foul language. (30 mins would have been enough.)

Wayne's World 2 (1993) (94mins) (a Canada-U.S. film) d: Stephen Surjik s: Mike Myers, Bonnie Turner, Terry Turner : Mike Myers, Dana Carvey, Christopher Walken, Tia Carrere, Ralph Brown, Kim Basinger. This sequel to *Wayne's World* (1992, 95mins, d: Penelope Spheeris, same cast as above) brings back the party boys from *Saturday Night Live* to put on a marathon rock concert in Aurora. All the usual bits and pieces, some funny, others flat.

We All Fall Down (2000) (92mins) d&s: Martin Cummins : Darcy Belsher, Martin Cummins, Francoise Robertson, Helen Shaver, Nicholas Campbell, Barry Pepper. Prostitutes, junkies, the homeless, days of drugs and sex, obscene characters, filthy language and violence in Vancouver's downtown east side. In this partly autobiographical film, the director plays himself recalling his own struggle to free himself from drugs. It's all sexsation and exploitation. It's difficult to care about any of the characters.

We Are all Naked: see *Ils sont nus*

We Are Far From the Sun (*On est loin du soleil*) (1971) (79mins) (b/w) d: Jacques Leduc s: Robert Tremblay : Marthe Nadeau, J.-Léo Gagnon, Réynald Bouchard, Pierre Curzi, Marcel Sabourin, Claude Jutra. Far from the sun in Montréal is a married couple struggling to keep their family together under adversity and despair. Finely detailed and much alive.

We the Jury (1996) (120mins) (a-canada-U.S.-film) d: Sturla Gunnarsson s: Philip Rosenberg : Kelly McGillis, Christopher Plummer, Lauren Hutton, Nicholas Campbell, Roberta Maxwell, George Touliatos, David Hemblen, Rachael Crawford, and others. A vast army of mostly Canadian performers amassed to serve on this jury, all about a popular tv talk show host accused of the murder of her philandering husband. Battled out in the jury room with considerable insight, thoughtfulness and moral concern.

Wedding in White (1972) (106mins) d&s: William Fruet (based on his play) : Donald Pleasence, Carol Kane, Doris Petrie, Leo Phillips, Paul Bradley, Doug McGrath, Christine Thomas, Bonnie Carol Case, David Hughes. William Fruet's first film is his strong adaptation of his play of the same name about a Scottish Presbyterian family in Toronto during World War II. Essentially a study of small-minded people living in small, dingy homes, in which a daughter is made pregnant by the beer-drinking friend of her brother, home on leave from the army. The film sensitively and knowingly depicts the bleak outlook and attitudes of hopeless people unaware of the possibility of a better life. Marvellously well acted, accurately written and observed, frequently moving, and only occasionally overmagnified. Terrible-tempered Donald Pleasence and a resigned Doris Petrie as the parents are drawn from life itself and the re-creation of the period is claustrophobically depressing. This picture is part of the trio, including *Goin' Down the Road* and *My Uncle Antoine,* that formed the encouraging beginning to a new era of Canadian films beginning in the '70s.

Week-end en folie: see **Crazy Weekend, A**

Weep No More My Lady (1992) (91mins) d: Michel Andrieu s: Leila Basen, Michel Andrieu : Daniel J. Travanti, Kristin Scott-Thomas, Shelley Winters, Stephane Audran, Robin Renucci. Part of the Mary Higgins Clark collection of novels. A wealthy businessman comes between sisters, who bring their sibling rivalry to murderous stages. An interesting combination of suspense, passion and sympathy.

Weight of Water, The (2000) (130mins) (a Canadian-American film) d: Kathryn Bigelow s: Alice Arlen, Christopher Kyle (based on the novel by Anita Shreve) : Sean Penn, Catherine McCormack, Elizabeth Hurley, Josh Lucas, Sarah Polley. Said to be inspired by a true story, this tale of deceit, malice and desire takes place in New Hampshire where a photojournalist and her husband investigate a crime that happened in the 1800s. Why they do so is not fully explained as we go from past and present. Average.

Welcome to Blood City (1977) (96mins) (a Canada-U.K. co-production) d: Peter Sasdy s: Michael Winder, Stephen Schneck : Jack Palance, Keir Dullea, Samantha Eggar, Hollis McLaren, Chris Wiggins, Barry Morse, Allan Royal, Henry Ramer, Ken James, Sydney Brown, Larry Reynolds, Gary Reineke, Jack Creley, Chuck Shamata, Eric Clavering, Shelley Peterson, Neil Dainard. If nothing else, once getting past the Hollywood names, this film gave several weeks' work to almost our entire acting fraternity. The first Anglo-Canadian co-production gets off to a bad start with this poorly written nonsense about a fascist group kidnapping individuals and transporting them through computer electronics to a western outpost (a Kleinberg, Ontario ranch) where they are valued by the number of people they murder. Confused and ridiculous but with good performances from the hard-put cast.

Welcome to Canada (1989) (87mins) d: John Smith s: Sam Grana, John Smith : Madonna Hawkins, Charlene Bruff, Brendan Foley, Noreen Power. In 1987, a group of Tamils calling themselves refugees landed mysteriously on Canada's east coast. They had been put ashore in small boats from the ship that had brought them to Canada. But this film is only "inspired" by the incident, and while it looks like a documentary, it is not. It contains several natural character studies and conversations between Tamils and Newfoundlanders, which may or may not have taken place, but of the furor and controversy this incident created, the film has nothing to say.

Welcome to the Freakshow (2001) (98mins) d: Thom Fitzgerald s: Lori Lansens : Victoria Sanchez, Tim Curry, Grace Jones, Lesley Ann Warren, Darlene Cates, Dov Tiefenbach. A woman suffering from a rare genetic disorder that covers her with hair leads a life as a wolf-girl in a circus. A young man's mother has a formula that soon takes care of this condition, but as a normal woman, she cannot rid herself of her wolf-girl past. Weird but hardly wonderful, Tod Browning would certainly be freaked out.

Welcome to the Parade (1986) (85mins) d&s: Stuart Clarfield : Alan Powell, Jane Sowerby. A spoiled son of a wealthy family leaves home, becomes involved with a prostitute and her child, and after seeing something of the seamier side of life, goes home a wiser youth. It lacks a lot, but as a first-effort York University student film, it's better than many being done today.

Wendy (1971) (85mins) d: Fred Fox s: Les Thomas : Wendy Stark, Muerdine McCreath, Allen Hustak, Judy Mazurik, Terry Bowerman, Vic Pell, Janet McLane, Reni Aug, Ron Lowe. An ambitious little film made by an enthusiastic group of students at the University of Saskatchewan and dealing naturally with student life, containing a strong moral centre and flashes of genuine talent in acting and directing—all made with their own money.

Westray (2001) (80mins) d&s: Paul Cowan : Townspeople. A film that seems to want to be both truth and fiction loses its way in telling the story of the Westray coal mine disaster in Nova Scotia that killed 26 men in 1992. Told in a series of confused images and a plethora of dialogue heard on and off-screen, by characters who *might* be survivors, and who *might* have been there, but perhaps are actors just talking about it. This is far from being what true documentary should be and leaves us dissatisfied with many unanswered questions.

West of Sarajevo: see **My Father's Angel**

Whale Music (1994) (107mins) d: Richard Lewis s: Paul Quarrington (based on his book) : Maury Chaykin, Cyndy Preston, Jennifer Dale, Paul Gross, Kenneth Welsh. A romantic comedy that loses both comedy and romance in a strained story about a once well-known rock musician now living in obscurity in a seaside mansion in B.C. who meets a young runaway woman from Toronto who becomes his saviour and friend, perhaps. He's obsessed with composing his masterwork: a huge piece for the listening pleasure of the whales. From what we hear of this, one doubts the whales will find it appealing. This is about redemption and coming face to face with life. It is difficult to become involved with these characters.

What the Hell Are They Complaining About?) (Hold on, Papa!) (*Tiens-toi bien après les oreilles à Papa*) (1971) (102mins) D: Jean Bissonettes s: Gilles Richer ' : Dave Broadfoot, Claude Michaud, Yvon Deschamps, Suzanne Lévesque, Jean Leclerc, Hélène Loiselle, Walter Massey, Jimmy Tapp. An amusing and cheerful situation comedy about the efforts of a bright-eyed French-Canadian secretary working for a British insurance company in Montréal. A fun, hit-and-miss piece benefitting immeasurably from the comic capers of Dave Broadfoot.

What We Have Here Is a People Problem (1976) (60mins) d: Francis Mankiewicz s: Michael Mercer : Heath Lamberts, George Waight, Sandy Webster, Kenneth Pogue, Paul Bradley, Mia Anderson. A powerful chronicle about a defiant farmer who refuses to leave his land despite an official expropriation notice ordering him to do so. A lawyer who comes to persuade him that he must obey the law comes to suspect that civic progress, in this case, is a matter of political gain for a provincial minister. Powerful and highly probable. Another highly disturbing film from Mankiewicz.

What's Your Verdict? (1995) (92mins) d&s: Anthony Metchie : Roger Cross, Tom Pickett, Michelle Lonsdale-Smith, Judith Maxie, Alvin Sanders. Three strangers meet a drug addict and persuade him to reform and bring his life back to normal. As a morality play, it makes its points about dealing with one's problems and not hiding them from others. Much of this takes place in a courtroom with a black judge impressively wearing a traditional black wig. Made in Vancouver, this film is mainly an opportunity for black actors to show off their talents. The director too, is from Nigeria.

Wheat Soup (1987) (75mins) d&s: Brian Stockton : Shaf Hussain, Brian Stockton. A wheat farmer in Saskatchewan is the only one to survive a nuclear holocaust. He decides to leave his farm and on his travels he meets a wheat poacher. Once enemies, they now try to make the best of their new situation. Talky but intelligent.

When Billie Beat Bobby (2001) (120mins) (a Canadian-American film) d&s: Jane Anderson : Holly Hunter, Ron Silver, Matthew Letscher, Robert Gunton, Jacqueline McKenzie, Caitlin Martin, Vincent Van Patten. Based on the actual event of the 1973 "male versus female tennis match" seen around the world. Billie Jean King fought for the rights of women tennis players, attempting to emerge from under the shadow of men. Well played.

When I Was a Rat: see **I Was a Rat**

When I Will Be Gone (*L'âge de braise*) (1998) (98mins) d: Jacques Leduc s: Jacques Marcotte, Jacques Leduc : Annie Girardot, France Castel, Michel Ghorayeb, Sheile Rose, Domini Blythe, Widemir Normil, Pascale Bussières. This is a sad tale about an elegant and deeply troubled woman (beautifully played by Annie Girardot) at odds with life and preparing herself for death. Touching, wise and thoughtful.

When I'll Be Gone: see **When I'm Gone You'll Still Be Alive**

When I'm Gone You'll Still Be Alive (When I'll Be Gone) (*Quand je serai parti vous vivrez encore*) (1999) (120mins) d&s: Michel Brault : Francis Reddy, David Boutin, Pierre Lebeau, Micheline Lançtôt, James Bradford, Noël Burton. Michel Brault has made many films as director and cinematographer to his credit, but this overblown historical melodrama is not one of them. The film seems to have been made for the purpose of furthering his separatist sentiments. It's all one-dimensional, out to score political points, poorly characterized and slow.

When Night Is Falling (1995) (94mins) d&s: Patricia Rozema : Pascale Bussières, Rachel Crawford, Henry Czerny, Don McKellar, Tracy Wright, David Fox. A passionately tale about a love affair between two women: a prim, religious college teacher and a circus performer. A reserved minister who is the boyfriend of the teacher loses out in this poorly written, flatly filmed flirt with an existence none of the characters had experienced before.

When Tomorrow Dies (1965) (87mins) (b/w) d: Larry Kent s: Robert Harlow, Larry Kent : Patricia Gage, Douglas Campbell, Neil Dainard, Lanny Beckman, Nikki Cole, Diane Filer, Desmond Smiley, Helen Milligan, Francesca Long, Rex Owen, Louise Payne, Patricia Wilson, Caroline Kennedy. A young housewife and mother finds that her daily existence has become dull and empty as both her husband and children are too taken up with their own affairs to bother with her. Feeling alone and rejected, she goes back to studying in an attempt to brighten her life. She meets a professor and finds him attractive, but after a brief liaison she knows that life with him would be no different than with her husband. For her,

tomorrow will be just like today. This was the last of Kent's trio of perceptive studies of sexual conflicts made in Vancouver.

When Wolves Howl (*Quand hurlent les loups***)** (1973) (79mins) d&s: André Lafferrere : Francine Robert, Jean-Pierre Saulnier, Richard Vigneault, Isabelle Forte, Louise Brosseau. A convict discharged from prison in Montréal cannot adjust to ordinary life and decides to break the law again in order to return to prison. An interesting if somewhat tedious look at social issues.

Where the Heart Is (1985) (65mins) d: Carol Moore-Ede s: Suzette Couture : Margo Kane, Tantoo Martin, Paul Stanley, Graham Greene, Shirley Cheechoo, Chas Lawther, Eric Herbert. This is the story of one native woman who married an American, had a small child, and was told she was no longer welcome on her reserve. This drama deals forcefully and affectingly with the issue of native women's rights. What happens here was taking place regularly on reserves. (See: *For the Record*)

Where the Spirit Lives (1989) (65mins) d: Bruce Pittman s: Keith Ross Leckie : Michelle St. John, Anne-Marie MacDonald, Heather Hess, Ron White. During the 1930s native children were taken away from their homes by government decree and sent to Christian schools. The children were treated badly and denied their traditional values. This film, a change of pace for its director, movingly recalls this period with the story of Amelia, a young Blackfoot girl, and her brother, who went through this chapter of change. Moody and enhanced by fine performances.

Where Two Roads Cross (Between Two Loves) (*À la croisée des chemins*) (*Entre deux amours*) (1943) (97mins) (b/w) d&s: Jean-Marie Poitevin : Paul Guèvremont, Denise Pelletier, Rose Rey-Duzil, Denis Drouin, Jean Fontaine. In this film record sponsored by the Foreign Missions Society of Québec, a wealthy young man decides to leave his family and fiancee to become a missionary. This low-key drama is enhanced by scenes of China photographed by the director when he visited this then little known country in the mid-1930s. Of particular interest are the flashbacks when he's looking back over the beliefs, spiritual matters and family ties of life in Québec, before it became the restless society.

Whiskers (1997) (95mins) d: James Kaufman s: Wendy Biller, Christopher Hawthorne : Brent Carver, Michael Caloz, Laurel Paetz, Stephen Adams, Monique Mercure, Suzanne Cloutier, Jacob Tierney. This truly magical film in the Tierney-Demers tradition of exceptional family screen stories begins with a shy 10-year-old boy who decides to transform his friendly cat, Whiskers, into a human. This results in adventures both hilarious and touching as the young lad learns what it means to be a best friend, to cherish your family, and to believe in oneself. A pleasure throughout. (*Tales for All* series.)

Whisper to a Scream (1988) (96mins) d: Robert Bergman s: Bergman & Jerry Ciccoritti : Nadia Capone, Yaphet Kotto, Lawrence Bayne. An incomprehensible study, part horrow, part experimental, of a group of artists in turmoil seeking 'perfection in their work.' It hardly seems worth it!

Whispering City (*La forteresse*) (1947) (98mins) (b/w) d: Fedor Ozep s: Rian Jones, Leonard Lee (from an original story by George Zuckerman and Michael Lennox) : Paul Dupuis, Nicole Germain, Jacques Auger, Mimi d'Estée, John Pratt, Lucie Poitras, Joy Lafleur, George Alexander, Henri Poitras. Pathological and romantic crime melodrama concerning the homicidal machinations of a patron of classical music. While *Bush Pilot*, a simple, inexpensive production was marking the beginning of post-World War II filmmaking in Toronto, producer Paul L'Anglais embarked on a vastly larger and more difficult project, *La forteresse*, in Montréal. The film's budget was said to reach the $1M mark, with Hollywood's European director, Fedor Ozep, on board. The film was large, elaborate and difficult to make. The reviews were not kind, and it failed dismally at the box office. The two versions, one French, the other English, were shot under the same title with three Hollywood players, Helmut Dantine, Paul Lukas and Mary Anderson, changing places with the Québec leads.

Whispers (1990) (94mins) d: Douglas Jackson s: Anita Doohan (from the story by Dean Koontz) : Victoria Tennant, Jean Leclerc, Chris Sarandon, Peter MacNeill, Linda Sorensen, Eric Christmas. A thriller turning on a murdered man who suddenly turns up alive, much to the puzzlement of the police. Predictable yet both amusing and chilling.

Whistle Down the Wind: see **Boys' Club, The**

White Lies (1998) (120mins) d: Kari Skogland s: Dennis Foon : Sarah Polley, Albert Schultz, Tanya Allen, Joseph Kell, Lynn Redgrave, Jonathan Scarfe. The subject here is the complicated matter of free speech versus the expression of racial hatred, lies and false accusation, revolving around the world of neo-Nazism in print and on the Internet. Cleverly and vividly dramatized, this is the story of a student who becomes caught up in the "National Identity Movement," made up of hate rock music, hate propaganda, drugs, sex and violence. Thoughtful and frightening in the extreme.

White Light (1991) (97mins) d: Al Waxman s: Ron Base : Martha Henry, Martin Cove, Alison Hossack. A heavy-handed excursion into a detective's afterlife experience in which he meets a beautiful woman. Upon his return to the living, he searches for her. Not very compelling. Do we care whether he finds her or not? This is not *Vertigo*.

White Road, The (1929) (60mins–silent, with English inter-titles) (b/w) d&s: George Thorne Booth : Marjorie Horsfall, Jolynine Gilliere, Frederick Mann, Ernest Sidney, Ivor Danish. A story about a Canadian girl who saves the life of a Chinese boy while she is visiting China. Years later he repays her when he comes to Toronto. (An Ontario Film Co. production filmed in Toronto with actors from the Hart House Theatre.)

White Room (1989) (91mins) d&s: Patricia Rozema : Maurice Godin, Barbara Gordon, Margot Kidder, Kate Nelligan, Sheila McCarthy. A would-be writer and sometime voyeur sees a popular singer murdered. At the funeral he meets her mysterious friend, who invites him to her home. From here on the narrative turns into fantasy and confusion but, according to the filmmaker, it has much to do with feminism and the destructive effects of media attention on our private lives. The film has a nice finish to it, and what lies beneath is open to interpretation.

White Skin: see *Peau Blanche, La*

White Tiger (1995) (93mins) d: Richard Martin s: Gordon Melbourne, Roy Shallows, Don Woodman (based on story by Bev Logan) : Gary Daniels, Matthew Craven, Cary-Hiroyuki Tagawa. A secret agent takes on two opposing criminal bodies to avenge his partner's murder. All rather ho-hum.

Who Has Seen the Wind (1977) (102mins) d: Allan King s: Patricia Watson (from the novel by W.O. Mitchell) : Brian Painchaud, Douglas Junor, Gordon Pinsent, Chapelle Jaffe, Jose Ferrer, Charmion King, David Gardner, Patricia Hamilton, Helen Shaver, Thomas Hauff, Gerard Parkes, Nan Stewart, Cedric Smith, Hugh Webster, Ed McNamara. A difficult book to film about a boy's growing-up period on the Saskatchewan prairies during the Depression, and his growing awareness of life and death. This film version is lovely, light and lyrical, and beautifully acted by an understanding cast of players. Jose Ferrer's role could just as easily have been played by a Canadian actor but he was, you see, the box-office name so loved by our producers.

Whodunit (1986) (92mins) d&s: Aiken Scherberger : Wendy Crewson, David Ferry, Keith Knight, Robert Benson, Jack Duffy, Nick Nichols, Gerry Pearson. A far cry from Abbot and Costello, we find ourselves in Honey Harbour on Georgian Bay, Ontario, where a reporter is investigating a murder that happened 25 years ago. The daughter of the murdered man is also looking into "whodunit." A minor mystery, made bearable by a clever cast.

Whoever Dies, Dies in Pain: see *Quiconque meurt*

Whole of the Moon, The (1996) (100mins) (a Canada-New Zealand co-production) d: Ian Mune s: Richard Lymposs, Ian Mune (based on a story by Lymposs) : Toby Fisher, Nikki Si'Ulepa, Pascale Bussières. In Auckland, a young boy with a passion for skating is involved in an accident and while being treated, doctors discover that he has cancer. He finds friendship with another cancer patient, a street-wise girl, and together they conquer their fears and decide to make a life together. Appealing and believable.

Whole Shebang, The (2001) (96mins) (a Canada-U.S. film) d: George Zaloom s: Jeff Rothberg, George Zaloom : Stanley Tucci, Bridget Fonda, Giancarlo Giannini, Talia Shire, Jo Champa, Anna Maria Alberghetti, Anthony DeSanto, Alexander Milani. More of an Italian comedy-romance than anything from Hollywood, and filmed in Vancouver passed off as New Jersey with other scenes filmed in Naples, the complicated plot concerns a manufacturer of fireworks who blows himself up during a display. This throws his large family into fits of frenzy and hysterics, laughs and love affairs that fizz more than they illuminate. (Note: George Zaloom made the documentaries *Heart of Darkness: A Filmmaker's Apocalypse* and *Frank Capra: An American Dream*.)

Whose Child Is This? The War for Baby Jessica (1993) (75mins) (a U.S.-Canada film) d: John Kent Harrison s: Based on the DeBoers' version of the case, and the *New Yorker* magazine article by Lucinda Franks : Susan Dey, Michael Ontkean, Amanda Plummer, David Keith. Millions of people watched on TV as two-year-old Jessica Deboer was taken from the home of her foster parents after a long and acrimonious court battle with her birth parents. Children's rights issues are at the heart of this truly wrenching, well-played drama in which parents' rights groups, social agencies and the legal system come in for examination. Where, we wonder, is Jessica now?

Why Is the Strange Mr. Zolock So Interested in Comic Strips? (*Pourquoi l'étrange Monsieur Zolock s'intéressait-il tant à la bande dessinée*) (1983) (70mins) d: Yves Simoneau s: Marie-Loup Simon : Michel Rivard, Jean-Louis Millette, Yves Desgagnés, Paul Colpron, Jasmine Desjardins. A lively and colourful look at the work of French-speaking cartoonists in France and Belgium. Of interest as one of the talented Simoneau's first films.

Why Rock the Boat? (1974) (112mins) d: John Howe s: William Weintraub (based on his novel) : Stuart Gillard, Ken James, Tiiu Leek, Henry Beckman, Budd Knapp, Sean Sullivan, Patricia Gage, Ruben Moreno, Cec Linder, Henry Ramer, Barrie Baldaro, J.-Léo Gagnon, Patricia Hamilton. A fresh, gentle, and witty comedy about a young reporter who goes to work on a Montréal newspaper in the 1940s, only to lose his innocence and discover the facts of life. Based on the actual experiences of the writer William Weintraub, Stuart Gillard is perfect in the leading role. A genuine portrayal of "English" Montréal, based on working at the *Gazette*, this film captures a sense of place seldom found in English-track Canadian films. Stuart Gillard went on to work in New York and L.A. and found a measure of success there.

Why Shoot the Teacher (1977) (99mins) d: Silvio Narizzano s: James DeFelice (based on Max Braithwaite's book) : Bud Cort, Samantha Eggar, Chris Wiggins, Gary Reineke, John Friesen, Michael J. Reynolds, Kenneth Griffith. A well acted, directed, and photographed adaptation of Braithwaite's humorous and episodic novel about a young teacher trying to cope with the loneliness of a Saskatchewan prairie school in winter, and the economic poverty of the Depression. Among the mixed Can-U.K.-U.S. players, Bud Cort is miscast, unfortunately, as the inexperienced young man. Silvio Narizzano, a noted CBC-tv director, moved on to London where he worked for BBC television and in feature films.

Wicked Minds (2002) (92mins) (a U.S.-Can-film) d: Jason Hreno s: Turi Meyer, Al Septien : Angie Everhart, Andrew Walker, Winston Rekert, Amy Sloan, Frank Schorpion. A tidy and acceptable thriller about a young man who returns home and finds his father has remarried. Within a few days, the father is murdered. Whodidit? It's worth finding out.

Wild Damsel, The: see *Demoiselle sauvage, La*:

Wild Dogs, The (2002) (97mins) d&s: Thom Fitzgerald : Rachel Blanchard, Visinel Burcea, Mihai Calota, Marcel Ungurianu, Thom Fitzgerald, David Hayman, Geraint Wyn Davies, Alberta Watson. In present-day Bucharest, among the tourists and new residents, is a Canadian pornographer, a diplomat's wife and a dog catcher. They all risk being there because of their involvement in the struggles of abandoned children, Gypsies, beggars and stray dogs, all of whom roam the streets. This is a dreadful film without energy, point or purpose. Fitzgerald, who plays the pornographer, should have remained home.

Wilderness Station, A: see **Edge of Madness**

Wild Flowers, The (*Les fleurs sauvages*) (1982) (152mins) d&s: Jean-Pierre Lefebvre : Marthe Nadeau, Michèle Magny, Pierre Curzi, Éric Beauséjour, Claudia Aubin. A perceptive and understanding look at a family's life observed during the summer when, for a week, the wife's mother comes on her annual visit. The little irritants, tensions, conflicts, and joys are accurately told, together with moments of happiness and the sadness of time passing. A gentle portrait of human relations in an idyllic setting as only Lefebvre could portray with such depth and feeling.

Wild Geese: see **After the Harvest**

Wild Girl, The: see *Demoiselle sauvage, La*

Wild Horse Hank (1979) (94mins) (a Can-U.S. film) d: Eric Till s: James Lee Barrett (from the book *The Wild Horse Killers* by Mel Ellis) : Linda Blair, Richard Crenna, Helen Hughes, Michael Wincott, Al Waxman, Gordon Tapp, Hardee Lineham, Gary Reineke, W.O. Mitchell. Another tax-concession period film shot mainly in Alberta passing as the U.S. A young woman devoted to horses leads a campaign to stop the butchering of wild horses for dog food. Well staged and directed by Eric Till with affecting performances by a cast obviously sympathetic to the subject.

Willing Voyeur, The (1996) (77mins) d&s: Richard Kerr : Hadley Obodiac, Kaya McGreggor, Iain Maclean, Jake Roberts, Dean Cooney. Described as a "post-modern murder-mystery," in a Regina of the future. Apart from some interesting visual composition, what we see is simply baffling, not over "whodunit" but "what does it all mean?"

Win, Again! (1998) (120mins) d: Eric Till s: Gordon Pinsent : Gordon Pinsent, Gabrielle Rose, Michael Riley, Leah Pinsent, Eric Peterson, Laurence Dane. A beautifully written and acted story set in Nova Scotia about a movie projectionist who has been on the run for many years following his wrongful conviction for murder. On returning home his expected happiness is dulled by the complications that arise as he tries to pick up his life where he left off. He finds that relationships with his family are not so easy to resolve. Disarming, sad, honest and humorous, this is another splendid work from the remarkable Pinsent and Eric Till.

Wind at My Back (2001) (120mins) d: Stefan Scani s: John Boni : Kathryn Greenwood, Andrew Jackson, Shirley Douglas, Laura Bruneau, James Carroll, Dylan Provencher, Tyrone Savage. This film marks the end of the successful *Wind at my Back* tv series that chronicled the lives and loves of the Bailey family of New Bedford, whose high spirits and eccentricities were set against the turbulent and difficult days of the 1930s. We are given a lasting portrait of Canadian life at that time, with places, characters and themes clearly being Canada and not somewhere south of the border. Backgrounds, settings, performances, costumes and dialogue bring conviction to the narratives. As with all Kevin Sullivan and Stefan Scaini films, the attention to the setting and strength of the dramatic structures cannot be faulted.

Wind From Galerne, The: see *Vent de galerne*

Wind From Wyoming, A (*Le vent du Wyoming*) (1994) (100mins) (a Canada-France co-production) d&s: André Forcier : François Cluzet, Sarah-Jeanne Salvy, France Castel, Michel Côté, Marc Messier. The wind from Wyoming blows into Québec in the form of a writer who soon finds himself caught in the many and convoluted cruel deceptions of love within a tormented Québec family. Passions run high and the cast finds its way through some pretty surrealistic material from Forcier.

Windigo (1994) (97mins) d&s: Robert Morin : Donald Morin, Guy Nadon, Nathalie Coupal, Michel Laperrière, Richard Kistabish. A First Nations group living in northern Québec declares its independence from Canada as a result of what it considers to be the exploitation of their land by a mining company. Up the river comes an old boat appropriately called "Pickle" with a group of politicians and a television

news cameraman. It is through the lens of his camera that we view the arguments associated with this crisis. This film expresses genuine concern over the never-ending debate about the rights and place of native peoples in Canada. This is possibly the first Canadian dramatized film to attempt to portray this subject and as such is most welcome. Some critics have rushed in to rank it with the Joseph Conrad novel, *Heart of Darkness*, and Coppola's *Apocalypse, Now*, but this is too much.

Window, The (*La fenêtre*) (1992) (90mins) d&s: Monique Champagne : Anne Létourneau, Jean-François Balmer, Albert Millaire, Monique Mercure. A subjective study of a young careerwoman who has success and financial independence but is haunted by ghosts from her past life. Now pregnant by her Italian lover, she leaves him to start a new existence. An absorbing and understanding character portrayal.

Wings in the Wilderness (*Les voyageurs d'été*) (1975) (90mins) d: Robert Ryan s: Martin Laser : Dan Gibson, Ralph Ellis Narr: Lorna Greene, Bert Devitt, Ronald France. When Canadian naturalist Dan Gibson came across two newly hatched Canada geese, just minutes old, he encountered the phenomenon naturalists call "imprinting" on humans. The goslings, emerging from their shells, "imprinted" or attached themselves to the first large moving object they saw. Usually this would be their mother, but in this instance, it was a very surprised Dan Gibson. Filmed in super slow motion at 400 frames per second, these magnificent birds are pure poetry in motion as they fill the screen in full flight, with every graceful movement shown in astonishing close-ups. Twenty years later, U.S. filmmaker Carroll Ballard came to Canada and filmed this story with some changes under the title *Fly Away Home*.

Wings of Chance (Kirby's Gander) (1961) (76mins) d: Edward Dew s: Patrick Whyte (based on the novel *Kirby's Gander* by John Patrick Gillese) : Jim Brown, Frances Rafferty, Patrick Whyte, Richard Trotter. Two Canadian bush pilots are in love with the same woman. One crashes in the far north, but devises a way to send his position by using geese. He is saved and wins the hand of the lady he loves. Colourful, spectacular, human and exciting, this was one of the few Canadian films at this time to be taken for distribution in the U.S. (by Universal-International). Shades of *Bush Pilot*! Filmed in Edmonton and on location in Jasper National Park.

Winnings of Frankie Walls, The (1980) (65mins) d: Martin Lavut s: Rob Forsyth : Al Waxman, Samantha Langevin, Chapelle Jaffe. A middle-aged labourer and father of three children is suddenly laid off. Unskilled and uneducated, he struggles to find work in a society that has deemed his work experience obsolete. One of the most perfect and telling dramas during this period of Canadian filmmaking, Waxman himself described it well when he spoke of it as being his *Rocky* but whereas Rocky's victory was a fairy tale, Frankie Walls' is realistic and he triumphs over circumstances in a way that we can all understand and aspire to. (See: *For the Record*)

Winter Kept Us Warm (1965) (81mins) (b/w) d&s: David Secter : John Labow, Henry Tarvainen, Joy Tepperman, Janet Amos, Iain Ewing, Jack Messinger, Larry Greenspan, Sol Mandlsohn, George Appleby. A University of Toronto and Ryerson student film, *Winter Kept Us Warm* convincingly expresses the feeling of post-adolescent torment of a secret love. It is a psychological study of two boys: one a sensitive new student from the country, the other the confident man on campus. Contrary to convention, it is the older boy who falls in love with the younger one, making the point that it is often the quiet misfit who is more secure than the brash and friendly fellow. This intelligent student film, possibly the first in Canada to touch on homosexual love, is made with skill and imagination, and is well acted and absorbing. Secter did not do as well with his second film, *The Offering*, and left for New York to take up a career in photography.

Winter Lily (1998) (90mins) d: Roshell Bissett s: Ryosuke Aoike : Dorothée Berryman, Danny Gilmour, Kimberly Laferrie, Chris McCabe, Peter Beland, Philip LaMaistre. Another variation on the haunted house theme with a young photographer who stops at a B&B in the New England countryside (naturally, being a Canadian film the setting is American) and finds himself haunted by the unseen presence of a daughter who is nowhere to be found. Nice try with a good cast but slow and contrived.

Winter of Torment, A: see *Hiver de tourmente, Un*

Winter Stories (Histoires d'hiver) (1999) (105mins) d: François Bouvier s: François Bouvier, Marc Robitaille (based on his novel of the same name) : Joel Drapeau-Dalpé, Denis Bouchard, Luc Guérin, Diane Lavallée, Suzanne Champagne, Sylvie Legault. Canada's national sport is the gist of this genuinely human and knowing family film in which a boy growing up in Montréal is fascinated by the hockey games of the city's team. With this beautifully observed study of friends, fathers and family relationships we find, minus hockey, a companion piece to Jutra's legendary *Mon Oncle Antoine*.

Winter Tan, A (1988) (91 mins) d: Jackie Burroughs s: Jackie Burroughs : Louise Clark, John Frizzell, John Walker, Aerlyn Weissman. This collective work is set in Mexico and based on the letters that the American woman Maryse Holder wrote to a friend in Toronto describing her sexual activities and feelings about the men she had affairs with. This desperate, useless search for a lasting love culminated in her murder. Jackie Burroughs, acting out the letters as dialogue spoken mostly to herself, gives such an intense, deeply felt and understanding portrait of this empty, tiresome character that it softens the ugly and sordid nature of the whole.

Wise Women, The: see **Femmes savantes, Les**

Wishmaster 1 (1997) (90mins) (a U.S.-Canada-film) d: Robert Kurtzman : Tammy Lauren, Andrew Divoff, Chris Memmon, Wendy Benson. The beginning of murky mythology, gory story and prophecy.

Wishmaster 2 (credited to Wes Craven) appears to be lost! Doubtful if anyone will miss it.

Wishmaster 3: Beyond the Gates of Hell (2001) (89mins) (a U.S.-Can film) d: Chris Angel s: Alex Wright : Jason Connery, A.J. Cook, Tobias Mehler, Emmanuelle Vaugier, Aaron Smolinski, Louisette Geiss. In this minor horror, an evil spirit, Djinn, escapes from his 'mysterical' tomb when an unsuspecting student releases it on campus. Can you imagine what follows? Lots of violence, rotten language and nudity.

Wishmaster 4: The Prophecy Fulfilled (2002) (91mins) (a U.S.-Canada film) d: Chris Angel s: John Benjamin Martin, Peter Atkins. : Jason Thompson, Victor Webster, Michael Trucco, Tara Spencer-Naim, Kimberley Huire. The last of this horror series opens with the every-so-familiar scene of young man and girl arriving home, clothes come off, clumsy kisses, nude on the bed, let the "bonking begin". The Djinn materializes, an evil spirit of some kind born from the fires of earth's beginnings, or some such twaddle. The events are predictable and oh so boring "give me your soul and your wish will be granted". Desperation. 'Love and trust are only words if you can't back them up'. The result, a truly ugly, bloody, horrid film: just like its predecessors.

Witchboard I (1985) (78mins) d&s: Kevin Tenny : Todd Allen, Clare Bristol, Burke Byrnes.

Witchboard II (1993) (75mins) d&s: Kevin Tenny : Ami Dolenz, Christopher Michael Moore, Laraine Newman, Timothy Gibbs. (More of the same.)

Witchboard III: The Possession (1995) (75mins) (a U.S.-Canada film) d: Peter Svatek s: Kevin Tenny, John Ezrine : David Nerman, Locky Lambert, Donna Sarrasin, Cedric Smith, Danette MacKay. The third in a commonplace series in which a husband suspected by his wife to be a demon fights for his sanity. The connection between these routine low-budget excursions into evil is the Ouija Board.

With Friends Like These (Avec des amis) (1990) (82mins) d&s: Christopher Malazorewicz and others : Marc Ruel, Deirdre Fitzsimmons, Michael Burns, Beth Lachance. A trilogy of terror stories: a creature at home, a car that runs itself, a dream date that becomes a nightmare, and other scary bits. Nothing special.

Without Malice (2000) (82mins) (a Canada-U.S. film) d: Rob King s: Peter Layton : Jennifer Beals, Corey Haim, Craig Sheffer, Gabrielle Anwar, Adam Harrington. Two Americans find themselves in trouble while hunting in Ontario during a weekend that turns deadly. Serves them right. The film dies earlier.

Wolf Dog (1958) (69mins) (a Canadian-American film) d: Sam Newfield s: Louis Stevens : Jim Davis,

Allison Hayes, Tony Brown, Austin Willis, Lloyd Chester, Sydney Brown. Once again farmers and ranchers battle for land on the Canadian prairies (filmed in Ontario!) and once again an ex-con tries to start a new life with the help of Prince, the dog. One of the first Hollywood B-films to be made in co-operation with a local Canadian company, in this instance, Twentieth-Century Fox with Regal Film of Toronto. (See: *Flaming Frontier*)

Wolf Girl (2001) (75mins) (a Canada-U.S. film) d: Thom Fitzgerald s: Lori Lansens : Victoria Sanchez, Tim Curry, Lesley Ann Warren, Darlene Cates, Grace Jones. A young woman has grown hair from head to toe. She lives as a wolf girl with a traveling freak show, an object of amusement to a crude public. This tripe is not only dreadful but an insult to the classic silent film by Todd Browning, *Freaks* (1932)—about a traveling sideshow filled with nature's misfits but still a humane and fascinating work.

Wolfpen Principle (1974) (85mins) d&s: Jack Darcus : Vladimir Valenta, Lawrence Brown, Doris Chilcott, Wayne Robson, Helen Shaver. Darcus, the experimental filmmaker whose work has never been inaccessible although rather dense at times, has been one of the few mainstays in B.C.'s film production scene. This time around the central character is a middle-aged businessman who finds his wife boring and goes on nightly visits to the zoo to commune with the wolves. A native asks him to help release the animals but they fail. From this the man draws strength to try and mend his home life. Good for the wolves but hard on audiences!

Woman Hunted, A (2003) (98mins) (a Can-US film) d&s: Morris Ruvinsky : Alexandre Pal, Lynda Ashbury, Maxim Roy, Jonathan Higgins. A kind and caring wife and mother with two young children has become addicted to narcotics as a result of her marriage breakup. Her children are taken away until she can prove to be free of the habit. The strain of being away from the children brings on a mental breakdown. If this were not enough she is raped by a popular hockey player. She fights back and he is killed. The outcome of this is surprising. A thriller so much better than the stream of violent, ugly movies being made and calling themselves thrillers. And a pleasant change in the scene when she cannot get her car out of a ditch, to hear her say 'damn it'. Acting, direction and settings are first rate, but of course the place where it is supposed to be happening is the US, but Montreal is where it was actually filmed.

Woman in the Cage, The: see **Angel in a Cage**

Woman in Transit, A (*La femme de l'hôtel*) (1984) (89 mins) d: Léa Pool s: Michel Langlois, Robert Gurik, Léa Pool : Louise Marleau, Paule Baillargeon, Marthe Turgeon, Serge Dupire, Celine LaCoste. Andrea Richler is making a film in Montréal during the bitter cold of winter when she meets Estelle, a woman who might have been the character whose story she is telling. The world of shadows and illusions created around the woman makes an obscure film, yet one of frosty beauty and introspective despair. Estelle, the most interesting person, remains in the background.

Woman Inflamed, A (*Tout feu, tout femme*) (1975) (87mins) d&s: Gilles Richer : Jean Lapointe, Andrée Boucher, Denis Drouin, Guy L'Écuyer, Jacques Bilodeau, Suzanne Langlois. A timid young fireman in Montréal rescues a young woman from a fire in her apartment and she falls in love with him. Delightful and charming.

Woman Inside, The (1981) (94mins) (a U.S.-Canada film) d: Joseph Van Winkle s: Steve Fisher & Winkle : Gloria Manon, Dane Clark, Joan Blondell, Michael Champion, Marlene Tracy. At a time when sex-changes were hardly mentioned, this nervous look at such a taboo subject comes about because a former soldier in the Vietnam war comes home in a shaky state to undertake such an operation. Feeble, dreadful and silly, it's sadly the last film of the delightful Hollywood star, Joan Blondell.

Woman of Colours, A (*La dame en couleurs*) (1985) (111mins) d: Claude Jutra s: Louise Rinfret : Guillaume Lemay-Thivierge, Ariane Frédérique, François Methe, Mario Spenard, Charlotte Laurier, Paule Baillargeon, Rita Lafontaine, Monique Mercure. Jutra's range of interests in humankind rests here for a time to observe the orphans housed in an asylum in Montréal during the 1940s. A penetrating dramatization of this period.

Woman Wanted (1999) (98mins) d: Kiefer Sutherland, (Alan Smithee) s: Joanna McClelland Glass (from her novel) : Holly Hunter, Michael Moriarty, Kiefer Sutherland, Victor Cowie, Shirley Douglas, Joanna McClelland Glass, Sean McCann. A love-triangle story which ambles along with a certain grace and sophistication about a woman who goes to work as a cook and maid at a rambling old house near Yale University. There she meets a widower and his son and eventually has affairs with both. Oh well, it all becomes rather wearying. (Sutherland had his name removed from the credits because of a dispute between him and the producer over the editing. Hence Smithee comes to the rescue once again!)

Woman Who Drinks, The: see **Femme qui boit, La**

Women in Love: see **Amoureuses, Les**

Women Without Wings (2002) (109mins) d&s: Nicholas Kinsey : Katya Gardner, Micheline Lanctôt, Lowell Gasoi, Besa Imani. An esoteric tale about an Albanian woman living in Canada who, being unable to make up her mind which of two lovers she should marry, chucks it all and goes back to the mountains of Albania, where she becomes an avowed virgin and lives as a man. An honest film for those who want to suffer it.

World Pup: see **Air Bud**

World Traveler (2001) (104mins) (a Canada-U.S. film) d&s: Bart Freundlich : Billy Crudup, Julianne

Moore, Clevant Derricks, David Keith, Liane Balaban. Being on the road has become something of a tiresome journey in the movies, and this road movie is no exception. The roads, of course, are not Canadian, and go through Alabama and Oregon. Taking the journey this time is an architect who suddenly, without any good reason, drives away from home, family, son, wife, everyone, on his way west. He stops for odd jobs and drinks, meets various strange individuals, both male and female, and goes slumming to places he's never been, experiencing activities he's never been a part of before. Murky symbolism fogs up much of this exploration.

Wounded (1996) (98mins) (a Can-U.S. film) d: Richard Martin s: Harry Longstreet : Madchen Amick, Graham Greene, Adrian Pasdar, Jim Beaver, Richard Joseph Paul, Daniel Kash, Kelly Benson. Set in remote areas of the Rocky Mountains, this is the story of federal game wardens and their struggles with poachers who are killing the great grizzlies. There are also emotional difficulties to contend with between the several characters involved. A thoughtful and gripping look into unusual lives, with some consideration for the unfortunate bears.

Wow (1970) (95mins) d&s: Claude Jutra : Danielle Bail, Philippe Dubé, Michèle Mercure, Dave Gold, Philippe Raoul, Monique Simard, François Jasmin. Dealing in a supposedly comic way with would-be anarchists, this is Jutra's first film to disappoint many of his followers. Fast-paced, lively and colourful—an imagination run riot—the content is too close to home to be considered funny. (Jean-Phillippe Duval made the documentary *Wow II* in 2002, to bring Jutray's film 'up-to-date'.)

Wozeck: Out of the Fire (1992) (90mins) d: George Bloomfield s: Malcolm MacRury : JohnVernon, Dominic Zamprogna, Christianne Hirt, Patricia Collins, Michael Hogan, Ted Follows. Some twenty years after *Wozeck,* the immensely popular tv series, finished, the popular coroner returns home after working in a medical clinic in Africa, and finds that he must confront several contentious issues from his past. To sum up the audience sentiment about this film, almost everyone said that it was great to see John Vernon back again, and in such an intriguing story.

Wrong Guy, The (1998) (87mins) d: David Steinberg s: Dave Foley, David Higgins, Jay Kogen : Dave Foley, Jennifer Tilly, David Higgins, Colm Feore, Joe Flaherty. Dave Foley was a member of the comedy group on tv, 'The Kids in the Hall'. This is one of the leftover skits he wrote, which is sometimes funny but mostly absurd about odd characters known as "nerds" and their misadventures. Fast but futile.

Wrong Number (2001) (90mins) (a Canada-U.S.A. film) d&s: Robert Middleton : David Lipper, Brigitte Bako, Karen Cliché, Eric Roberts. Violence, bad language and sexual goings-on result in murder on the stock exchange. No wonder Wall Street has the jitters.

Wrong Person, The: see **Erreur sur la personne**

Wrong Woman, The (1995) (90mins) d: Douglas Jackson s: Douglas Soesbe : Chelsea Field, Nancy McKeon, Michele Scarabelli, Dorothée Berryman, Serge Houde, Dawn Greenhalgh, Richard Jutras. A temporary secretary, on returning to her office one day, is accused of having murdered her boss, with whom she was having an affair. A pocketbook crime thriller, neatly told with several interesting insights into behaviour, played out with lively performances.

Xchange (2000) (100mins) d: Allan Moyle s: Christopher Pelham : Kyle MacLachlan, Stephen Baldwin, Pascale Bussières, Kim Coates, Sean Devine, Janet Kidder. Technology has advanced to the point where it can save travellers time simply by transporting their minds to a body waiting at a chosen destination. But then, one day, a man's body is hijacked by corporate terrorists. Hard to believe a word of it although this film tries hard to make it seem possible.

X-Rated (1994) (92mins) d: Kit Hood s: Susin Nielsen, Paul Aitken : Gordon-Michael Woolvett, Stacie Mistysyn, Billy Merasty, Marcia Laskowski, Joel Bissonnette, Dean Paras. Take a shabby apartment building and throw in a bunch of 20-somethings, including hippies, gay roommates, a bike courier, bizarre retro store owners, someone who lurks, and others from here and there, and this is supposed to result in an offbeat romantic comedy. Far from it!

Xtro II: The Second Encounter (1991) (93mins) d: Harry Bromley Davenport s: John Curtis, Edward Kovach, Stephen Lister, Robert Smith : Jan-Michael Vincent, Paul Koslo, Tara Buckman, Jano Frandsen. A fierce monster breaks loose from an experimental centre of inter-dimensional travel buried deep underground. The monster does what monsters do in this feeble piece of sci-fi horror. (Note: The same director made Xtro I in the U.K. in 1983 and this follow-up in Canada. It has no connection with the previous picture.)

Y a pas d'mal à se faire du bien: see **There's Nothing Wrong With Being Good to Yourself**

Y a toujours moyen de moyenner!: see **There's Always a Way to Get There**

Year of the Sheep (1997) (77mins) d: John Detwiler, Renee Duncan : Patrushka Sarakola, Vieslav Krystyn. A zoologist from a former communist country and his fiancée, a doctor, are finally together after a long separation and are free to be themselves. In their small Toronto apartment they try to create a normal life but they lack the will or understanding to know themselves or what it is they now want from life. Audiences will feel only exasperation.

Years of Dreams and Revolt (Les années de rêves) (1984) (96mins) d: Jean-Claude Labrecque s: Robert Gurik, Marie Laberge, Jean-Claude Labrecque (based on his story) : Anne-Marie Provencher, Gilbert Sicotte, Monique Mercure, Amulette Garneau, Carmen Tremblay. Jean-Claude

Labrecque continues his social history of Québec as seen through the eyes of a single family—a story he began in *Les Vautours* in 1974. Many of the family characters, including the three aunts, are back, and the whole is not lacking in passion and feeling, yet strangely it remains somewhat empty in spite of the creator's affinity with the period and the events set against it.

Years, The: see *Années, Les*

Yellow Island, The (*L'île jaune*) (1975) (78mins) (b/w) d&s: Jean Cousineau : Frédérique Collin, Michel Sébastien, Jean-Pierre Saulnier, Denise Morelle, Francine Morand, Jean-Pierre Lefebvre. Strange little story about a brother and sister living in Montréal who are forced to leave their home when the police inform the neighbours that the two are not to be trusted. Could they be in an unhealthy union? Slight but perceptive and often touching.

Yellow Wedding (1998) (95mins) d: Qi Chang, Jan Cui s: Yan Cui, Jin Xiao Peng, Qi Chang : Liu Xin, Edmund Chen, David Oren Ward, Craig Wasson, Victoria Snow, Annie Szanosi, Karyn Dwyer. A tangled tale of the troubled family of a psychiatrist and a beautiful Chinese girl who refuses to speak. The doctor also has a breakdown! Rife with betrayal and tragedy. There are some good moments for these Chinese immigrants, whose film this is, but the whole wears rather thin.

Yellowknife (2002) (118mins) d&s: Rodrigue Jean : Sebastien Huberdeau, Helene Florent, Patsy Gallant, Philippe Clement. A well-made and acted yet repugnant picture about a wildly demented young woman (we never know why) and a youth, who takes her away from a small hospital. They go on the road to Yellowknife (we are never told why), and on the way they pick up two youths, who seem normal at first glance—but not for long. From one of them we learn, later, that the couple are brother and sister. Incest is not a part of the following proceedings, but there is no lack of masturbation, sighing, writhing, gasping and genital close-ups, making one wonder if they will ever get to their destination. The film is spoken in English, with a smattering of French subtitled in English. Yet the story is reluctant to tell us where they are along the road and doesn't identify anything much among the diners and gas stations usually shown at night, with dancing, discos and dives, group rapings and stops for more sex and violence. A crooked policeman comes into the mix, the force not identified. And Patsy Gallant, with her torch songs, seems almost normal in her appearances. We know that characters like this do exist, but it would be better to see this life through a responsible treatment by a distinguished documentarian than by a cash-hungry producer.

Yesterday (1981) (98mins) (a Canadian-American film) d: Larry Kent s: Bill LaMond, John Dunning : Vincent Van Patten, Claire Pimpare, Eddie Albert, Cloris Leachman, Nicholas Campbell, Gerard Parkes. Above-average melodrama about an American in Montréal who falls in love with an art student, goes off to Vietnam (leaving her pregnant), and comes back wounded, to further complications in their lives.

Yeux rouges, Les: see **Red Eyes**

You Are Beautiful Jeanne (*T'es belle, Jeanne*) (1988) (82mins) d: Robert Ménard s: Claire Wojas, Robert Ménard : Marie Tifo, Pierre Curzi, Michel Côté. Three actors are perfectly cast in this sensitive story of individuals in a Montréal hospital who are coming to terms with serious disabilities. Shines with love and hope.

You Are Warm, You Are Warm (*Tu brûles, tu brûles*) (1973) (94mins) d&s: Jean-Guy Noel : Gabriel Arcand, Louise Francoeur, Guy L'Écuyer, Raymond Lévesque, Pierre Curzi, Janine Lebel. A fireman in a small Québec village decides to leave his life behind and live alone in the wilderness. Not finding peace of mind, he goes to Montréal, where he finds nothing but disillusionment. We leave him to continue sorting out his future plans. A slight but significant study of an individual coming to terms with where and how he wants to spend his life.

You Can Thank Me Later (1998) (110mins) d: Shimon Dotan s: Oren Safdie : Ellen Burstyn, Geneviève Bujold, Amanda Plummer, Mary McDonnell, Ted Levine, Marc Blum, Jacob Tierney, Macha Grenon. The Cooperberg family reluctantly meet at the hospital to await the results of their father's surgery. We soon learn that the daughters, living under incessant criticism from their mother, have become mentally unbalanced. So are the lovers, friends and strange men who troop through their lives. Everyone in this life is a mess, and so is this film despite the well-intentioned efforts of the leading ladies.

You've Come a Long Way, Katie (1981) (153mins) d: Vic Sarin s: Jeannine Locke, Jay Telfer : Lally Cadeau. The first film to be directed by the distinguished cinematographer Vic Sarin. The main thread in the narrative is a fine performance by Cadeau as a talk-show host going under as a result of too much booze and too many tranquilizers.

Young and the Beat, The: see **Cool Sound From Hell, A**

Young Catherine (1990) (240mins) (a Canada-U.K.-U.S.S.R. co-production) d: Michael Anderson s: Christopher Bryant : Julia Ormond, Vanessa Redgrave, Christopher Plummer, Marthe Keller, Franco Nero, Maximilian Schell, Mark Frankel, Reece Dinsdale, and others. We follow 16-year-old Princess Sophie of Anhalt-Zerbst from her arrival in Russia as "goods on approval" in a marriage contract, through treacherous political and sexual intrigue at the court of Empress Elizabeth, and finally, to her bittersweet ascent to the throne as "Catherine the Great." In between, of course, we have a gallery of figures in history with all the plotting, planning and scheming, the heroic moves and moments of happiness and exultation. A beautifully made film with an accomplished and inspired cast commanded by a director who knows how to make an epic like this come to life. Filmed exclusively in and around the palaces of Leningrad.

Young Girl at the Window The: see *Jeune fille à la fenêtre, Une*

Young Girl, The: see *Nenette*

Young Magician, The (*Le jeune magicien***)** (1987) (99mins) (a Canada-Poland co-production) d&s: Waldemar Dziki : Rusty Jedman, Edward Garson. A 12-year-old boy dreams of becoming a magician. One day, he finds he possesses magical powers: he can move objects without touching them. But to his and his parents' great concern, he doesn't have total control over this power. After several mishaps and with the help of a new friend, he learns to master his power and ultimately uses it to save his entire city from destruction. Captivating and humorous. (See: *Tales for All* series)

Younger Generation The: see *Jeunes Québécoises, Les*

YUL 871 (Montréal Flight 871) (1966) (70mins) (b/w) d&s: Jacques Godbout : Charles Denner, Andrée Lachapelle, Francine Landry, Paul Buissonneau, Jean Duceppe, Jacques Desrosiers, Jacques Normand, Louise Marleau, Claude Préfontaine. The tale of a French man on a two-day business trip to Montréal who brings with him memories of his childhood. He searches for relatives living in the city and meets a woman with whom he stays the night before flying back to Paris. A touching but talkative romantic memory.

Zacharia Farted (1998) (110mins) d: Michael Rohl s: Colin Cunningham : Colin Cunningham, Benjamin Ratner, Madison Graie, Betty Linde, Erndt Harth, Willie John Hanna. A mechanic finds he spends as much time diagnosing his clients as he spends working on the vehicles themselves. He tires of life and goes fishing with his best friend. In the country they find an unmarked grave and spend their time travelling around in search of information to tell them who is buried in it. This among other things. All rather confused in its comedic touches with never a whiff from Zach (who-he you may well ask).

Zebra Lounge (2001) (93mins) d: Kari Skogland s: Claire and Monte Montgomery : Kristy Swanson, Stephen Baldwin, Brandy Ledford, Daniel Magder, Cameron Daddo, Dara Perlmutter. Cheap and tawdry titillation plot in which a jaded suburban couple decide to spice up their sex lives by joining a couple of prostitutes to discover what they are missing. Their new companions have other tricks in their bags, none of them worth watching.

Zero Patience (1993) (100mins) d&s: John Greyson : John Robinson, Normand Fauteux, Dianne Heatherington, Richardo Keens-Douglas, Bernard Behrens. A superficial and muddled musical comedy worked around AIDS and the controversial "Patient Zero" theory that holds that a French-Canadian airline steward first brought the disease to North America. The hijinks are mostly unattractive, and what the film is supposed to be saying about the subject in question is hard to discern.

Zigrail (1995) (78mins) d&s: André Turpin : André Charlebois, Dorothée Berryman, Arianne Cordeau, Sonia Vigneault, Armand Turpin. A 20-something "don't know what to do with my life" Gen X-er decides to travel from Montréal to Istanbul on a motorcycle to meet up with his pregnant girlfriend. Not a journey many audiences will find illuminating.

Zoo la nuit, Un (A Zoo, by Night) (1987) (116mins) d&s: Jean-Claude Lauzon : Gilles Maheu, Germain Houde, Roger Le Bel, Denys Arcand, Lynne Adams, Lorne Brass. This controversial film falls into two parts: the first being cold, calculated and brutally violent; the second being problematic and sentimental, with the final sequence at the zoo, where an elephant is shot, being unnecessary. A slick crime story along the lines of *Miami Vice* (Lauzon lived and worked in the States and the influence is obvious), it concerns a recently released criminal with some hidden loot and two corrupt policemen who are determined to get it from him. The film's unremitting black mood lightens when the ex-prisoner establishes a new relationship with his ailing father, played by the distinguished actor Roger Le Bel, whose tranquil fishing scenes in the beautiful Québec countryside provide a symbolic contrast to his son's underworld existence. The whole film is infused with a driving, stylish energy, which holds up remarkably well until the false ending. By then the film seems over-long and morally immature. Gilles Maheu playing the part of Marcel is entirely convincing, and the supporting cast is appropriately loathsome in its seamy, sordid behaviour. Roger Frappier (who was involved with *The Decline of the American Empire*) has added another controversial film to his impressive list of credits.

Aames, Willie: Paradise (1982)

Abadia, Régine: Thousand Wonders of the Universe, The (1997)

Abbas, Hiam: *Ange de goudron, L'* (Tar Angel) (2001)

Abbott, Roger: Reckless Disregard (1985)

Abbott, Simon: Beyond Suspicion (1993)

Abboud, Hanane: *Autour de la maison rose* (Around the Pink House) (1999)

Abdi, Nassim: Secret Ballot (*Raye Makhfi*) (2001)

Abdul, Paula: Waiting Game, The (1998)

Abed-Alnour, Youssef: Foreign Nights (1990), Nothing to Lose (1994)

Abell, Alistair: Rhino Brothers, The (2002)

Abidi, Cyrus: Secret Ballot (*Raye Makhfi*) (2001)

Abkarian, Simon: Ararat (2002)

Abraham, F. Murray: Sweet Killing (1993)

Abrams, Domminick: Goldirocks (2003)

Absa, Moussa Sene: *Madame Brouette* (2002)

Achtman, Michael: Uncut (1997)

Acker, Sharon: Act of the Heart (1970), Don't Let the Angels Fall (1969), Happy Birthday to Me (1981), Off Your Rocker (1982), Threshold (1981), Waiting for Caroline (1967)

Ackerman, Hal: Second Wind (1976)

Ackerman, Robert Allan: Me and My Shadows (2000)

Ackland, Joss: House on Turk Street, The (2002)

Ackland, Rodney: 49th Parallel (The Invaders) (1941)

Acomba, David: Hank Williams: The Show He Never Gave (1982), Slipstream (1973)

Adair, Charles: Dark Harbour (1997)

Adam, Camil: Crazy Manette and Cardboard Gods (*Manette: la folle et les dieux de carton*) (1964)

Adam, Michael: Waiting for Michelangelo (1995)

Adama, Troy: Justice Denied (1989)

Adamiam, Ashot: Calendar (1993)

Adams, Brooke: Dead Zone, The (1983), Man, a Woman and a Bank, A (1979), Utilities (1981),

Adams, Evan: Lost in the Barrens (1990)

Adams, Ian: Agent of Influence (2002), Bad Faith (Cold Blooded) (1999), Lost in the Barrens (1990)

Adams, E. Riley: Agent of Influence (2002)

Adams, Lynne: Carpenter, The (1987), Forbidden Love: The Unashamed Stories of Lesbian Lives (1992) Ford: The Man and the Machine (1987), Zoo la nuit,Un (A Zoo, by Night) (1987)

Adams, Maud: Mahoney's Last Stand (1976), U-Turn (The Girl in Blue) (1973)

Adams, Stephen: Whiskers (1997)

Adams, Troy: One Heart Broken Into Song (1998)

Adamson, Frank: Artichoke (1978), Maintain the Right (1982), Terry Fox Story, The (1983)

Adamson, Peter: Take Her by Surprise (1967)

Adderson, Caroline: Tokyo Cowboy (1994)

Addy, Wesley: Hiroshima (1996)

Adelson, Florrie: One of Our Own (1977)

Admiraal, Joop: Hersenschimmen (Mind Shadows) (1987)

Affleck, Neil: My Bloody Valentine (1981)

Aftanas, Craig: Hey, Happy! (2000)

Agar, Robert: Little Canadian, The (1955)

Agashe, Mohan: Seducing Maarya (1999)

Agie, Awaovieyi: Red Deer (2000)

Agostini, Alexandre: *Silence nous guette, Le* (2002)

Ahmarani, Paul: *Au fil de l'eau* (By the Riverside) (2002), *Comment ma mère accoucha de moi durant sa ménopause* (How My Mother Was Giving Birth to Me During Menopause) (2001), Left-hand Side of the Fridge, The (2000), *Marais, Le* (2002), Rats and Rabbits (2000)

Agnieszka, Holland: Julie Walking Home (2002)

Aiello, Danny: Brooklyn State of Mind, A (1997), Power of Attorney (1995)

Aimée, Anouk: *Bethune: The Making of a Hero* (1990), see Bethune (1977)

Ainsworth, Andrew: Too Much Sex (1999)

Aitken, Paul: X-Rated (1994)

Aitken, Will: Rowing Through (1996)

Akerman, Jeremy: Trudeau (2002)

Akerman, Malin: Circle, The (The Fraternity) (2001)

Akhurst, Lucy: Trinity (2002)

Akin, Philip: Airborne (1998), Certain Practices (1979)

Akiyama, Denis: Ghost Mom (1993), Johnny Mnemonic (1995)

Aktouf, Karina: *Casablancais, Les* (The Casablancans) (1998)

Alacchi, Carl: Collectors, The (1999), Two Thousand and None (2000)

Alarcon, Luis: *Los Naufragos* (1994)

Alarie, Amanda: Grand Bill, The (*Le gros Bill*) (1949), *Tit-Coq* (1953)

Alarie, Christiane: In the Land of Zom (1983)

Alarie, Luc: House That Hides the Town, The (*La maison qui empêche de voir la ville*) (1975)

Alberghetti, Anna Maria: Whole Shebang, The (2001)

Albert, Eddie: Yesterday (1981)

Alden, Richard: Teddy (The Pit) (1980)

Alderman, Ralph J.: Watchtower, The (2001)

Alexander, George: *Homme et son péché, Un* (*Séraphin*) (A Man and His Sin) (1949), *Tit-Coq* (1953), Whispering City (*La forteresse*) (1947)

Alexander, Jane: Jenifer Estess Story, The (2001)

Alexandre, Marlène: All About Women (*À propos de la femme*) (1969)

Algar, James: Incredible Journey, The (1963)

Alianak, Hrant: By Reason of Insanity (1982), Secret Life of Algernon, The (1996)

Allaire, André: Sensations (1973)

Allaire, Ginette: Sky's the Limit, The (*Les limites du ciel*) (1986)

Allan, Don: Jungleground (1995)

Allan, Ted: Bethune (1977), Lies My Father Told Me (1975), Seven Times a Day (*Sept fois par jour*) (1971), Unknown From Montréal, The (*Son copain*) (1950)

Allard, Jacques: King of Fire (1985)

Allen, Alfred: Grub-Stake, The (1922)

Allen, Dennis: Herd, The (1998)

Allen, Janis: Not Another Love Story (1979)

Allen, Michelle: And When the CWAC's Go Marching On (*Du poil aux pattes*) (1985)

Allen, Patrick: Bullet to Beijing (Len Deighton's Bullet to Beijing) (1995)

Allen, Randi: Cathy's Curse (1977)

Allen, Tanya: Clutch (1998), Fancy Dancing (2002), Lives of Girls and Women, The (1996), Lyddie (1995), Morrison Murders, The (1997), Platinum (1997), Regeneration (1996), Tail Lights Fade (1999), White Lies (1998)

Allen, Todd: Witchboard I (1985)

Alley, Kirstie: Salem Witch Trials (2001)

Alleyn, Jennifer: Cosmos (1997)

Allison, Donald: Three and a Half (*Trois et demi*) (2002)

Allison, Thom: Leaving Metropolis (2002)

Allman, Daniel: Close to Home (1986)

Allodi, James: Dead Aviators (1998), Fool Proof (2003), Herd, The (1998), Men With Brooms (2002), Uncles, The (2000)

Allore, John: Events Leading up to My Death, The (1991)

Allyson, June: Blackout (1978)

Almgren, Susan: Going to Kansas City (1998), Lilac Dream (1987), Little White Lies (1988), Separate Vacations (1986), Twin Sisters (1993)

Almond, Matthew: Dance Goes On, The (1991)

Almond, Paul: Act of the Heart (1970), Dance Goes On, The (1991), Every Person Is Guilty (1979), Final Assignment (1980), Isabel (1968), Journey (1972), Ups and Downs (1983)

Alonso, Maria Conchita: Blackheart (1997)

Alpay, David: Ararat (2002)

Alterio, Hector: Summer of the Colt (*Fierro ou l'été des secrets*) (1989)

Altman, Allen: Collectors, The (1999), Fallen Knight (The Minion) (1998)

Altman, Mark: House of the Dead (2003)

Altman, Robert: That Cold Day in the Park (1969)

Alton, Walter George: Heavenly Bodies (1985)

Alvarez, Palo: Swordsman, The (1993)

Alza, Walter: Three and a Half (*Trois et demi*) (2002)

Amand, Rosine: I Have the Right to Pleasure (*J'ai droit au plaisir*) (1975)

Amadou, Jean: *Finalemente* (In the End) (1971)

Amann, David: Rendering, The (2002)

Amato, Julie: Vicky (1973)

Amber, France Castel: *Crême glacée, chocolat et autres consolations* (2001)

Ambrose, David: Man Called Intrepid, A (1979)

Ambrose, Valerie: Sally Fieldgood and Co. (1975)

Amero, Harold: Deadend.com (2002)

Amick, Madchen: List, The (2000), Wounded (1996)

Amiel, Marielle: Old Country Where Rimbaud Died, The (1977)

Ammann, Antoinette: *Strass Café* (1980)

Amo, Michael: Blessed Stranger: After Flight 111 (2001), Tagged: The Jonathan Wamback Story (2002)

Amo, Paul: Undertaker's Wedding, The (1996)

Amos, Beth: High Card (1982), Love at First Sight (1974), Noncensus (1964), Now That April's Here (1958), Prom Night (1980), Utilities (1981)

Amos, Janet: Ada (1981), High (1968), Noncensus (1964), Silence of the North (1981), Taking Care (Prescription for Murder) (1987), Winter Kept Us Warm (1965)

Amsing, Sean: Roller Coaster (1999)

Anconina, Richard: *Paroles et musique* (1985)

Anders, Edward: LAPD: To Protect and Serve (2001)

Anders, Luana: That Cold Day in the Park (1969)

Anderson, Alan: Love at First Sight (1974)

Anderson, Allan: Little Canadian, The (1955)

Anderson, Antony: Excalibur Kid, The (1998), Ms. Bear (1999)

Anderson, Erika: Shadows of the Past (1991)

Anderson, Frank: Gladiator Cop (1994)

Anderson, Jane: When Billie Beat Bobby (2001)

Anderson, John: Powder Heads (1980), Regeneration (1988)

Anderson, Lindsay: In Celebration (1975)

Anderson, Melissa Sue: Happy Birthday to Me (1981)

Anderson, Melody: Boy in Blue, The (1986)

Anderson, Mia: What We Have Here Is a People Problem (1976)

Anderson, Michael: Jeweller's Shop, The (1988), Millennium (1988), Murder by Phone (1982), Sea Wolf, The (1993), Separate Vacations (1986), Summer of the Monkeys (1998), Sword of Gideon (1986), Young Catherine (1990)

Anderson, Peter: Captains Courageous (1996), Overcoat, The (*Le manteau*) (2002)

Anderson, Scott: Slow Burn (1989)

Anderson, Ted: Proud Rider, The (The Last Run) (1972)

Anderson, Wendy: Dinosaur Hunter, The (2000), Risen, The (2003), Solitude (2001), Sparkle (1998)

Andersson, Bibi: Secret of Nandy, The (1991)

Andraos, Asma: *Autour de la maison rose* (Around the Pink House) (1999)

André, Denis: Those Damned Savages (*Les maudits sauvages*) (1971), Trouble Makers (*Trouble-fête*) (1964)

Andrea, Darren: Undertaker's Wedding, The (1996)

Andreacchio, Mario: Sally Marshall Is Not An Alien (1999)

Andrei, Damir: Ford: The Man and the Machine (1987), Prodigious Hickey, The (1987), Rose Cafe, The (1987),

Andreiuci, Freddy: Bounty Hunters (1996)

Andrey, Damir: Prodigious Hickey, The (1987)

Andrews, Naveen: Double Vision (1992)

Andrews, Real: Hostile Advances: The Kerry Ellison Story (1996)

Andrieu, Denise: Sensations (1973)

Andrieu, Michel: Firing Squad (1990), Weep No More My Lady (1992)

Andrus, Jeff: Jeweller's Shop, The (1988)

Angel, Chris: Wishmaster 3: Beyond the Gates of Hell (2001), Wishmaster 4: The Prophecy Fulfilled (2002)

Angelica, Roberta: Lakeboat (2000)

Angélil, René: Apparition, The (The Unexpected Phantom*)* (1972)

Angelis, Michael: No Surrender (1985)

Angelo, Tony: Isla the Tigress of Siberia (1977)

Angilirq, Paul Apak : Atanarjuat: The Fast Runner (*L'homme nu*) (2000)

Anglin, Anne: Accident at Memorial Stadium, The (1983), Ada (1981), Turning to Stone (1986)

Angrignon, Yves: Ordinary People (*Ti-peuple*) (1971)

Angus, Lesley: Kathy Karuks Is a Grizzly Bear (1976)

Angus, William: Little Canadian, The (1955)

Anka, Paul: Ganesh (Ordinary Magic) (1993)

Annaud, Jean-Jacques: Quest for Fire (*La guerre du feu*) (1981)

Annear, Douglas: Recruits (1987)

Annis, Francesca: Haunting Harmony, A (1993)

Ann-Margret: Middle-Age Crazy (1980)

Anousaki, Malena: Lydia (1964)

Ansara, Michael: KGB: The Secret War (1984)

Ansell, Lorraine: House of Luk (2000)

Ansley, Zachary: Cowboys Don't Cry (1987), Princes in Exile (1990)

Anspach, Susan: Gas (1981), Into the Fire (1987),

Legend of Wolf Lodge, The (1988), Running (1979)

Anstey, Norman: Second Skin (2000)

Anthony, Lysette: Misbegotten (1997)

Antidormi, Robert: Love Letters: A Romantic Trilogy (2001)

Antoine, Geneviève Néron: Left-hand Side of the Fridge, The (2000)

Anton, Robert: Collectors, The (1999)

Anton, Susan: Sneakers (Spring Fever) (1982)

Antonio, Lou: Nobody Makes Me Cry (Between Friends) (1983)

Anvar, Cas: Incredible Adventures of Marco Polo, The (1998), Seducing Maarya (1999)

Anwar, Gabrielle: Guilty, The (2000), Without Malice (2000)

Aoike, Ryosuke: Winter Lily (1998)

Apergis, Andreas: Invention of Love, The (2000)

Appleby, George: Winter Kept Us Warm (1965)

Aranguiz, Manuel: Coup at Daybreak, A (*Coup d'état au petit matin*) (1998), Eclipse (1994), Lulu (1995), Paper Wedding (*Les noces de papier*) (1989),

Aranha, Ray: Kid, The (1997)

Arbour, France: Bach and Broccoli (*Bach et bottine*) (1986), Bean Pole Man, The (*Homme perché*) (1996), Katryn's Place (2002), *Pudding chômeur* (Bread Pudding) (1996), Requiem for a Handsome Bastard (*Requiem pour un beau sans-coeur*) (1992), Three Madeleines, The (*Les fantômes des trois Madeleines*) (1999)

Arcady, Alexandre: Hold-Up (1985)

Arcand, Bernard: Flower of Youth (That Tender Age, The Adolescents) (*La fleur de l'âge*) (*Les adolescentes*) (1967), Love and Human Remains (Unidentified Human Remains and the True Nature of Love) (1994)

Arcand, Denys: Barbarian Invasions, The (*Invasions Barbares, Les*) (2003), Between Sweet and Salt Water (Drifting Downstream) (*Entre la mer et l'eau douce*) (1967), Crime of Ovide Plouffe, The (*Le crime d'Ovide Plouffe*) (*Les Plouffe, II*) (1984), Decline of the American Empire, The (*Le declin de l'empire Américain*) (1986), Gina (1975), Head of Normande St. Onge, The (*La tête de Normande St-Onge*) (1975), *Jésus de Montréal* (1989), Joyeux calvaire (1997), Love and Human Remains (Unidentified Human Remains and the True Nature of Love) (1994), *Mon oeil* (My Eye) (1971), Montréal Sextet (1991), Pigs Are Seldom Clean (*On n'engraisse pas les cochons a l'eau claire*) (1973), *Réjeanne Padovani* (1973), *Seul ou avec d'autres* (Alone or With Others) (1962), Stardom (15 Minutes) (2000), That Darned Loot

Arcand, Denys continued:
(*La maudite galette*) (1972) *De l'art et la maniere chez Denys Arcand (Arcand, Actors and Filmmaking)* (2000) (80mins) A revealing and fascinating documentary by Georges Dufaux (noted cinematographer) taking us behind the scenes as Denys Arcand, Canada's pre-eminent director, is filming Stardom showing us his creativity and work with actors.

Arcand, Diane: Heads or Tails (*Pile ou face*) (1971), IXE-13 (1972)

Arcand, Gabriel: Agnes of God (1985), *Ange noir, L'* (The Black Angel) (Nelligan) (1991), Blood of the Hunter (*Sang du chasseur, Le*) (Lone Eagle) (1995), Coffin Affair, The (*L'affaire Coffin*) (1980), Crime of Ovide Plouffe, The (*Le crime d'Ovide Plouffe*) (*Les Plouffe, II*) (1984), Decline of the American Empire, The (*Le declin de l'empire Américain*) (1986), *Fabrication d'un meurtrier, La* (The Making of a Murderer) (1996), *Folle Embellie* (Out of this World) (2003), Gina (1975), Goodbye, See You Monday (*Au revoir, à lundi*) (1979), *Grand serpent du monde, Le* (The Great World Serpent) (1999), Heat Line, The (*La ligne de chaleur*) (1987), House With a View of the Sea, A (*Una casa con vista al mar*) (2001), Let's Talk About Love (1976), Little Tougas (1976), *Mémoire battante* (1983), Panic (*Panique*) (1977), *Plouffe, Les* (The Plouffe Family) (1981), *Portes tournantes, Les* (The Revolving Doors) (1988), Post Mortem (1999), *Réjeanne Padovani* (1973), *Sang du chasseur, Le* (1995), Suzanne (1980), That Darned Loot (*La maudite galette*) (1972), Vultures, The (*Les vautours*) (1975), You Are Warm, You Are Warm (*Tu brûles, tu brûles*) (1973)

Arcand, Hélène Loiselle: That Darned Loot (1972)

Arcand, Nathaniel: Grey Owl (1999)

Arcand, Robert: Sex in the Snow (*Après-ski*) (1971)

Arcanel, Yves: *Donnez-nous notre amour quotidien* (In Love With Sex) (1974)

Archambault, Jean: Once Upon a Time in the East (*Il était une fois dans l'est*) (1974)

Archambault, Stéphane: Justice (1998)

Archana: Seetha and Carole (1997)

Archer, Anne: Art of War, The (2000), Eminent Domain (1990), Man in the Attic, The (1994)

Arcouette, Lawrence: *Collectionneur, Le* (2001), Duplessis' Orphans (1999)

Arditi, Pierre: Flag (1987), *Hasards ou coïncidences* (1998)

Arduini, Dennis: Ms. Bear (1999)

Ares, Manon: Guitar (*Guitare*) (1974)

Arias, Imanol: House With a View of the Sea, A (*Una casa con vista al mar*) (2001)

Arioli, Don: Star Is Lost, A (1974), Sweet Movie (1974)

Arkin, Alan: Improper Channels (1981), Joshua Then and Now (1985), Varian's War (2001)

Arlen, Alice: Weight of Water, The (2000)

Arling, Charles: Back to God's Country (1919)

Armendriz, Pedro: Diplomatic Immunity (1991)

Armitage, Graham: Spanish Fly (1975)

Armour, Moira: Neon Palace, The: A '50s and '60s Trip (1971)

Armstrong, George: Face Off (1971)

Armstrong, Joan: Take Her by Surprise (1967)

Armstrong, Scott: Roger and Elvis (1993)

Arnarsdottir, Solveig: Regina (2002)

Arnatiaq, Peter: Atanarjuat: The Fast Runner (*L'homme nu*) (2000)

Arngrim, Allan: Cold Front (1989)

Arngrim, Stefan: Cold Front (1989)

Arno, Alice: Justine (1972)

Arnold, Pascal: Rats and Rabbits (2000), Marie's Sons (*Les fils de Marie*) (2002)

Arquette, Rosanna: Crash (1996), Poison (1999)

Arrabal, Fernando: Odyssey of the Pacific (*L'Empereur du Pérou*) (1982)

Arsenault, Maurice: In Her Defense (1998)

Arsenault, Michel: Cursed (1990)

Arsenault, Mychel: Power Games (1990)

Arsenault, Nina: Doulike2Watch.Com (2002)

Arseneau, Joanne: Dead End (*Le dernier souffle*) (1999), Loi du cochon, La (2001)

Arvelo, Leandro: House With a View of the Sea, A (*Una casa con vista al mar*) (2001)

Arveto, Alberto: House With a View of the Sea, A (*Una casa con vista al mar*) (2001)

Ash, William: Mad About Mambo (2000)

Ashbury, Lynda: Woman Hunted, A (2003)

Ashby, Neils: Master of Images, The (1972)

Asherson, Renée: Grey Owl (1999), Man Called Intrepid, A (1979)

Ashley, Elizabeth: Paperback Hero (1973)

Ashmore, Aaron: Treed Murray (2001)

Ashmore, Shawn: Guitarman (1994), Promise the Moon (1997)

Ashwell, Mary: Here I Will Nest (1941)

Askew, Luke: Slipstream (1973)

Asner, Edward: Case of Libel, A (1985)

Aspergis, Andres: Trial by Vengeance (1989)

Assad, Khadija: *Casablancais, Les* (The Casablancans) (1998)

Assante, Armand: Passion and Paradise (1989)

Asselin, Émile: Little Aurore's Tragedy (*La petite Aurore, l'enfant martyre*) (1952)

Asselin, Olivier: *Maîtres anciens* (1998), Seat of the Soul, The (*Le siege de l'ame*) (1997)

Astin, Patty Duke: By Design (1981), Family of Strangers (1993)

Astin, Sean: Boy Meets Girl (1998), Kurt Vonnegut's Harrison Bergeron (2000)

Astley, Sue: Low Visibility (1984), Skip Tracer (1977)

Atherton, Ted: Nothing Too Good for a Cowboy (1998)

Atkin, Harvey: All in Good Taste (1983), If You Could See What I Hear (1982), High-Ballin' (1978), Funeral Home (Cries in the Night) (1982), Joshua Then and Now (1985), Last Chase, The (1980), Meatballs (1979), Mr. Nice Guy (1986), My Little Eye (2002), Power Play (*Coup d'état*) (State of Shock) (Operation Overthrow) (1978), Separate Vacations (1986), SnakeEater II: The Drug Buster (1990), Ticket to Heaven (1981), Today I Am a Fountain Pen (A Good Place to Come From) (1980), Visiting Hours (Fright) (1982)

Atkine, Feodor: Thousand Wonders of the Universe, The (1997)

Atkins, Peter: Wishmaster 4: The Prophecy Fulfilled (2002)

Attenborough, Richard: Grey Owl (1999)

Attis, David: In Her Defense (1998)

Attwood, David: Shot Through the Heart (1998)

Atwell, Gerry: Barbara James (2001)

Atwood, Margaret: Heaven on Earth (1987), Snowbirds (1981)

Aubert, Louis: Exile, The (*L'exil*) (1971)

Aubert, Robin: Countess of Baton Rouge, The (*La Comtesse de Baton Rouge*) (1997), Escort, The (*L'escorte*) (1996), *Neg', Le* (2002)

Aubin, Claudia: Wild Flowers, The (*Les fleurs sauvages*) (1982)

Aubré, Chantale: Day Without Evidence, A (*Ainsi soient-ils*) (1970)

Aubry, Francois: *Frontières* (Border Line) (2003)

Aubry, Suzanne: *Meurtre en musique* (1994)

Auclair, Pascal: Mule and the Emeralds, The (1995), Two Seconds (*2 secondes*) (1998)

Audette, Michèle: Silencing the Guns (1996)

Audouy, Jacques: *Diable aime les bijoux, Le* (The Devil Likes Jewels) (The Devil's Jewellery) (*Las joyas del diablo*) (1969)

Audran, Stéphane: Bay Boy, The (1984), Blood of Others, The (*Le sang des autres*) (1984), Blood Relatives (*Les liens de sang*) (1978), Night Magic (1985), *Violette Nozière* (1978), Weep No More My Lady (1992)

Audy, Michel: Body and Soul (*Corps et âme*) (1971), Frost Bite (*La gélure*) (1968), House That Hides

the Town, The (*La maison qui empêche de voir la ville*) (1975), Jean-François-Xavier de... (1971), Luke or the Part of Things (1982)

Aug, Reni: Wendy (1966)

Auger, Claudine: Fantastica (1980), Secret of Nandy, The (1991), Whispering City (1947)

Auger, Emmanuel: *Histoire de Pen* (Inside) (2002)

Auger, Esther: *Corde au cou, La* (1966), Immortal Scoundrel, The (*Étienne Brûlé, gibier de potence*) (1952), *Noël et Juliette* (1973), Ordinary Tenderness (*Tendresse ordinaire*) (1973), Whispering City (*La forteresse*) (1947)

Auger, Pierre: Shadows of the Past (1991)

Augustson, Nola: Stolen Miracle (2001), Tom Stone: For the Money (2002)

Augustyn, Frank: Night Magic (1985)

Aumais, Benoît: King of Fire (1985)

Aumont, Jean-Pierre: Blackout (Blackout in New York) (1978), Two Solitudes (*Deux solitudes*) (1978), Blood of Others, The (*Le sang des autres*) (1984)

Auréfil, Marie-Christine: All About Women (*À propos de la femme*) (1969)

Austen, Jane: Slow Run (1969)

Austin, Teri: Vindicator, The (1986)

Avon, Suzanne: Story of Dr. Louise, The (1949), *Homme et son pêché, Un* (*Séraphin*) (A Man and His Sin) (1949), Sins of the Fathers (1948)

Awan, Tahina: Vigil, The (1998)

Axelrod, Nina: Cross Country (1983)

Ayanoglu, Byron: Symposium (1996)

Aykroyd, Dan: Arrow, The (1997), Love at First Sight (1974), On the Nose (2001), Stardom (15 Minutes) (Fandom) (2000)

Aykroyd, Peter: Gas (1981)

Aylward, Alan: Chain Dance (1991)

Ayola, Rakie: Secret Laughter of Women, The (1999)

Ayotte, Dominique: Beat (1976)

Ayre, Kristian: Bear With Me (2000)

Ayres, Leah: Burning, The (1981)

Ayres, Richard: Death Weekend (House by the Lake) (1976)

Azman, Yank: Choices of the Heart: The Margaret Sanger Story (1994)

Aznavour, Charles: Ararat (2002)

Azzopardi, Mario: Deadline (Anatomy of a Horror) (1980), Divided Loyalties (1989), Nowhere to Hide (1987), On Hostile Ground (2000), Savage Messiah (2001), Stiletto Dance (2000), Stork Derby, The (2001)

Azpurua, Carlos: Coup at Daybreak, A (*Coup d'État au petit matin*) (1998)

Baayen, Marjo: Falling Through (2000)

Babb, Ken: Silence of the North (1981)

Babe, Fabienne: *Mirage, Le* (1992)

Babiak, Paul: Clear-Dark (1988), Eternal Husband, The (1997), Pictures at the Beach (1990)

Babiar, Paul: Clear-Dark (*Clair obscur*) (1988)

Babin, Lou: Party, The (Party, Le) (1990)

Bache, John: Alexander Bell: The Sound and the Silence (1991), Golden Fiddles (1991)

Bachman-Singer, Joan: Seasons in the Sun (1986)

Back, Michael: Darkness Falling (2002)

Backen, Bob: South Pacific, 1942 (1981)

Backer, Brian: Burning, The (1981)

Backus, Richard: Dead of Night (1974)

Bacon, Marco: Silencing the Guns (1996)

Bacri, Jean-Pierre: *Homme de ma vie, L'* (The Man in My Life) (1993)

Badel, Alan: Luther (1973)

Badgley, Frank: Man from Glengarry, The (1920)

Badgley, Martine: Dancing on the Moon (*Viens danser sur la lune*) (1997)

Baer, Édouard: Betty Fisher and Other Stories (*Betty Fisher et autres histoires*) (2001)

Bagdasarian, Carol: Seasons in the Sun (1986)

Bagot, Doug: 2103: The Deadly Wake (1996)

Baigneres, Claude: *Duo pour une soliste* (Duet for a Soloiste) (Duet for One) (1998)

Bail, Danielle: Wow (1970)

Bail, René: Mis-Works, The (1959)

Bailey, Cameron: Planet of Junior Brown, The (1997)

Bailey, Donald: Hank (1977), Seer Was Here (1978)

Bailey, Janet: Race for Freedom: The Underground Railroad (1993)

Bailey, Jim: Surrogate (1984)

Bailey, Norma: Bordertown Café (1991),Cowboys and Indians (2003), For Those Who Hunt the Wounded Down (1996), Martha, Ruth and Edie (1987), Nights Below Station Street (1997), Sheldon Kennedy Story, The (1999), Stalking of Laurie Show, The (2000), Stolen Miracle (2001)

Bailey, Sandra: KGB: The Secret War (1984)

Bailey, Sidney: Capture of Karna Small, The (1987)

Baillargeon, Blanche: Sonia (1986)

Baillargeon, Paule: Angel Life (*Vie d'ange*) (1979), August 32nd on Earth (*Un 32 août sur terre*) (1998), Before the Time Comes (*Le temps de l'avant*) (1975), Close to Falling Asleep (*Trois pommes à côté du sommeil*) (1988), Confidences of the Night (*L'amour blessé*) (1975), *Cuisine rouge, La* (The Red Food) (1980), December (1978), *Entre tu et vous* (Between "tu" and "you") (1970), Gina (1975), Great Ordinary Movie, The (Joan of Arc Is Alive and Well and Living in Québec) (*Le grand film ordinaire*) (1971), In the Name of the Son (1972), I've Heard the Mermaids Singing (1987), Love Me (1991), O or the Invisible Infant (*O ou l'invisible enfant*) (1971), Panic (*Panique*) (1977), Precious Hours, The (*Les heures précieuses*) (1989), Réjeanne Padovani (1973), Sex Among the Stars (*Le sexe des étoiles*) (1993), Sonia (1986), Sun Rises Late, The (*Le soleil se leve en retard*) (1977), Vultures, The (*Les vautours*) (1975), Woman in Transit, A (*La femme de l'hôtel*) (1984), Woman of Colours, A (*La dame en couleurs*) (1985)

Baillargeon, Suzie: Kamouraska (1973)

Bain, Risella: Ten Girls Ago (1962)

Bains, Pawanjit: Reasonable Force (1983)

Bairnsfather, Bruce: Carry on Sergeant (1927–1928)

Bairstow, David: Royal Journey (1952)

Bak, Israel: Sex and the Lonely Woman (1966)

Baka, Miroslaw: Clandestins (1997)

Bakare, Ariyon: Secret Laughter of Women, The (1999)

Baker, Blanche: Mary and Joseph: A Story of Faith (1979), Handmaid's Tale, The (1990)

Baker, Jennifer: Passion (2001)

Baker, Noel: Hard Core Logo (1996)

Baker, Rodd: Men of Means (1999)

Baker, Simon: Once in a Blue Moon (1995)

Baker, William: Battle Queen 2020 (Millennium Queen 2000) (2000)

Bako, Brigitte: Double Take (1998), I Love a Man in Uniform (1993), Replikator (1994), Saint Monica (2002), Wrong Number (2001)

Balaban, Liane: After the Harvest (Wild Geese) (2000), New Waterford Girl (1999), Saint Jude (2000), World Traveler (2001)

Baldaro, Barrie: Apprenticeship of Duddy Kravitz, The (1974), Enuff is Enuff (*J'ai mon voyage!*) (1973), Keep It in the Family (1973), Parasite Murders (Shivers) (They Came from Within) (1975), Rebels 1837, The (*Quelques arpents de neige*) (1972), Star Is Lost, A (1974), Why Rock the Boat? (1974)

Baldi, Gian Vittorio: Flower of Youth (That Tender Age, The Adolescents) (*La fleur de l'âge*) (*Les adolescentes*) (1967)

Baldwin, Adam: Cold Sweat (1993), Deadbolt (1984), Dr. Jekyll and Mr. Hyde (1999), Sonia (1986)

Baldwin, Alec: Nuremberg (2000)

Baldwin, Daniel: Double Frame (1999), Killing Moon (1998)), Tunnel (2000), Water Damage (1999)

Baldwin, Janit: Humongous (1982)

Baldwin, Stephen: Prodigious Hickey, The (1987), Xchange (2000), Zebra Lounge (2001)

Baldwin,William: Say Nothing (2001)

Bale, Christian: American Psycho (2000)

Balinet, René: *Alégria* (1998)

Balk, Fairuza: Outside Chance of Maximillian Glick, The (1988)

Ball, John: In Her Defense (1998)

Ballard, Carroll: Fly Away Home (1996), Never Cry Wolf (1983),

Ballard, Harold: Face Off (1971)

Ballard, Jeffrey: Air Bud: Seventh Inning Fetch (2002)

Ballard, Jessie: Into the Fire (1987), Legend of Wolf Lodge, The (1988)

Ballentyne, Dawn: Roses in December (1965)

Ballesteros, Sandra: Dark Side of the Heart, The (*El lado oscuro del corazon*) (1993)

Balmer, Jean-François: French Revolution, The (1989), *Ménace, La* (1977), Window, The (*La fenêtre*) (1992)

Balser, David: Running Time (1978)

Banas, Carl: Sunday in the Country (1975)

Banasik, Derek: Morning! (1992)

Bancroft, Anne: Agnes of God (1985), Haven (2001)

Bancroft, Cameron: Anything For Love (1992), Love and Human Remains (Unidentified Human Remains and the True Nature of Love) (1994), M.V.P. 2: Most Valuable Primate (2001)

Bancroft, Clare: Julia Has Two Lovers (1990)

Banderas, Antonio: Never Talk to Strangers (1995)

Bandol, Doru: Because Why (*Parce que Pourquoi*) (1993)

Bandolo, Suzanne: *Ribo ou 'le soleil sauvage'* (1978)

Banigan, Jacob: Suburbanators, The (1995)

Banks, Sydney: Blood Relatives (*Les liens de sang*) (1978), Jigsaw (Angry Man, An) (*L'homme en colère*) (1979), Tomorrow Never Comes (1978)

Bannen, Ian: Alexander Bell: The Sound and the Silence (1991), George's Island (1989), To Walk with Lions (1999)

Banner, Steve: In the Shadow of the Wind (1986)

Bannerman, Bill: Air Bud: World Pup (2000)

Bannerman, Guy: Climb, The (1987)

Baran, Angelika: My Five Wives (2000)

Baran, Darrel: Crime Wave (1985)

Barancik, Steve: House on Turk Street, The (2002)

Baranyay, Edith: Walk Backwards (2001)

Baranyay, Laurie Maria: Girl Is a Girl, A (1999), Walk Backwards (2001)

Barbeau, Gérard: Nightingales and the Bells (*Le rossignol et les cloches*) (1952)

Barbeau, Jean: Nylon Heart, A (*Coeur de nylon*) (1989)

Barber, Gillian: Kitchen Party (1997), Matinée (1989)

Barbulée, Madeleine: *Bob Million: Le jackpot de la planète* (Bob Million and His World Jackpot) (1997), Letter From New France, A (1979)

Barclay, Mary: Sins of the Fathers (1948)

Bard, Bartley: Jinnah on Crime (2002), Jinnah On Crime – White Knight, Black Widow (2003)

Bard, Margaret: Jinnah on Crime (2002), Jinnah On Crime – White Knight, Black Widow (2003)

Bardeaux, Michelle: American Boyfriends (1989)

Barge, Gillian: Mesmer (1994)

Barichello, Rudy: *Alégria* (1998), Killer Image (1992)

Baril, Céline: Absent One, The (1997), *Du pic au coeur* (From Spades to Hearts) (2000)

Baril, Chantal: *Joyeux calvaire* (1997)

Barken, Adam: Drive, The (1996)

Barker, Jessica: Bananas From Sunny Québec (1993), Damascus Road, The (*Le chemin de Damas*) (1988), *Matusalem* (1993), *Siamoises, Les* (The Siamese Twins) (1999)

Barker, Jessica: *Amoureux fou* (Madly in Love) (1991), *Jardin d'Anna, Le* (1994)

Barker, Ray: Columbus of Sex, The: My Secret Life (1969)

Barkin, Ellen: Terminal Choice (Deathbed) (1985)

Barkoff, Victoria: Draghoula (1994), Horses in Winter (*Chevaux en hiver*) (1988), Shadows of the Past (1991)

Barlow, David: Nothing Too Good for a Cowboy (1998), Prom, The (1991)

Barmash, Jeffrey: Bounty Hunters (1996), Power of Attorney (1995)

Barnes, Herbie: Spirit Rider (1993)

Barnes-Hopkins, Barbara: Curtis's Charm (1995)

Barnett, Nikki: Love That Boy (2002), Turning Paige (Shepherd Park) (2002)

Barnett, Panchetta: Another Planet (2000)

Barnett, Steve: Scanners: The Showdown (Scanner Cop II: Volkin's Revenge) (1994)

Barney, Brian: Far Shore, The (1976)

Barney, Pamela: Black Christmas (Silent Night, Evil Nights) (Stranger in the House) (1974)

Barney, Rachel: Far Shore, The (1976)

Barr, Jean-Marc: Marie's Sons (*Les fils de Marie*) (2002)

Barra, Gemma: And I Love You Dearly (*La maîtresse*) (1973)

Barrault, Marie-Christine: *Dames galantes* (Romantic Ladies) (1990)

Barrett, Alice: Eminent Domain (1990)

Barrett, James Lee: Wild Horse Hank (1979)

Barrett, Libby : Mothers and Daughters (1992)

Barrette, Michel: *Boys, Les* (The Boys) (1997), *Postière, La* (The Postmistress) (1992)

Barrette, Paul: *Dernière condition, La* (1982)

Barrette, Yves: Heavenly Bodies (*Les corps célestes*) (1973), Jos Carbone (1975)

Barrie, Barbara: Tell Me My Name (1977)

Barrington, Diana: Ambush at Iroquois Pass (1979), Escape from Iran: The Canadian Caper (1981)

Barrington, Josephine: Now That April's Here (1958)

Barrington-Leigh, Christopher: Loyalties (1985)

Barron, Jim: Fortune and Men's Eyes (1971), Nikki, Wild Dog of the North (1961), Sunday in the Country (1975)

Barry, Anne: Night of the Flood (1996)

Barry, Christopher: Something's Rotten (1978)

Barry, Fred: *Tit-Coq* (1953)

Barry, Ivor: Don't Forget to Wipe the Blood Off (two episodes of the TV series *Seaway*) (1966), Nobody Waved Goodbye (1964)

Barry, Simon Davis: Art of War, The (2000)

Barsha, Leon: Convicted (1938)

Bart, Elizabeth: Ordinary People (*Ti-peuple*) (1971)

Bartlett, Renny: Eisenstein (2000)

Bartlett, Capt. Bob: Viking, The (1931)

Barton, Mischa: Lost and Delirious (2000)

Barzman, Ben: Head of Normande St. Onge, The (*La tête de Normande St-Onge*) (1975)

Basara, Svetislav: Boomerang (2002)

Basaraba, Gary: One Magic Christmas (1985)

Base, Ron: White Light (1991)

Basen, Leila: Ladies Room (1999), Man in 5A, The (1982), Your Ticket Is no Longer Valid (Finishing Touch) (1982), Weep No More My Lady (1992)

Basichis, Gordon: Crash (Breach of Trust) (1995)

Basil, Harry: My Five Wives (2000)

Basinger, Kim: Wayne's World 2 (1993)

Bassam, Hala: *Adolescente sucré d'amour, L'* (1985)

Bassett, Carling: Sneakers (Spring Fever) (1982)

Bassett, John C.: Teddy (The Pit) (1980)

Bastedo, Alexandra: Draw! (1984), Find the Lady (1976)

Bastoni, Steve: Dr. Jekyll and Mr. Hyde (1999)

Bateman, Justine: Another Woman (1994), Deadbolt (1984)

Bates, Alan: Butley (1974), In Celebration (1975), Salem Witch Trials (2001)

Batra, Pooja: My Little Devil (2000)

Batraville, Dominique: Royal Bonbon (2002)

Battisti, Renato: Last Glacier, The (1984)

Battle, Murray: April One (1994), Water Damage (1999)

Bauchau, Patrick: *Frontière du crime* (Double Identity) (1990)

Bauche, Vanessa: Silent Love, A (2003)

Bauer-Gador, Andrew: Return of Tommy Tricker, The (1994)

Bauer, Steven: Sword of Gideon (1986)

Baum, Roger: Lion of Oz (2000)

Baxter, Jennifer: Washed Up (2002)

Baxter, Tara: One Heart Broken Into Song (1998)

Bay, Frances: Paperboy, The (1994)

Bayar, George: Sex and the Lonely Woman (1966)

Baye, Nathalie: Honeymoon (*Lune de miel*) (1985)

Baylaucq, Philip: Memoirs (1984)

Bayliss, John: Clown Murders, The (1976)

Bayne, Lawrence: Whisper to a Scream (1988)

Bazinet, Brenda: In This Corner (1986), Moving Targets (1983), Siege (1983)

Beach, Adam: Art of Woo, The (2001), Cadillac Girls (1993), Cowboys and Indians (2003), Dance Me Outside (1994), Last Stop, The (1999), Little Boy Blues (2000), Harry's Case (2000), Now and Forever (2001), Posers (2002), Spirit Rider (1993)

Beach, Wayne: Art of War, The (2000)

Beachman, Stephanie: Change of Place, A (1994)

Beaird, John: Chatwill's Verdict (Killer Instinct) (Trapped) (1982), My Bloody Valentine (1981)

Beairsto, Ric: Close to Home (1986)

Beals, Jennifer: Dukes, The (1998), Something More (1999), Without Malice (2000)

Bean, Henry: Running Brave (1983)

Bean, Sean: Airborne (1998)

Beard, David: Strange Brew (1983)

Bearden, James: Labour of Love (1985), Vicky (1973)

Béart, Emmanuelle: *Répétition, La* (2001)

Beattie, Cindy: Jack of Hearts (1993)

Beattie, Richard: Blindside (1986), Cold Comfort (1989), Cold Sweat (1993), Grizzly Falls (2000), Highwayman, The (1999), Prom Night IV: Deliver Us From Evil (1992), Shower, The (1992)

Beatty, Nancy: Dead Innocent (1996), Henry and Verlin (1994), Life With Billy (1993), Michelle Apartments, The (1995)

Beatty, Ned: Angel Square (Angel Street) (1990), I Was a Rat (Cinderella and Me) (2001), Replikator (1994), Tom Alone (1989)

Beauchamp, Shanie: Piege d'Issoudun, Le (2002)

Beauchemin, Yves: Alley Cat, The (1985)

Beaudin, Jean: Alley Cat, The (*Le matou*) (1985), Being at Home With Claude (1992), Collectionneur, Le (The Collector) (2001), Cordélia (1980), Craque la vie (Life Blossoms) (1994), J.A. Martin, Photographer (1977), Mario (1984), Memories Unlocked (1999), Life of Willie Lamothe (Documentary), Possession of Virginia, The (1972), Stop (1971)

Beaudoin, Michelle: Escape Velocity (1999)

Beaudoin, Sylvie-Catherine: Bombardier (1992), Eleventh Special, The (*Onzième spéciale*) (1988), *Peau et les os, La* (1988)

Beaudry, Jean: Case of the Witch Who Wasn't, The (*Pas de répit pour Mélanie*) (1990), Clean

Machine, The (*Tirelire, combines & cie*) (1992), Cry in the Night, A (*Le cri de la nuit*) (1996), House That Hides the Town, The (*La maison qui empêche de voir la ville*) (1975), Jacques and November (1984), Silencing the Guns (*Le silence des fusils*) (1996), Unfaithful Mornings (*Les matins infidèles*) (1988)

Beaulier, Marcel: *Comme un voleur* (1991)

Beaulieu, Jessie: Danny in the Sky (2002)

Beaulieu, Lucie: Nightmare, The (1979)

Beaulieu, Marcel: *Corps perdu, À* (Straight to the Heart) (1988), *Autre homme, Un* (Another Man) (1991), Damascus Road, The (*Le chemin de Damas*) (1988), *Hiver de tourmente, Un* (A Winter of Torment) (1999), In the Belly of a Dragon (1989), *Jeune fille à la fenêtre, Une* (2001)

Beaulne, Martine: *Albertine, en cinq temps* (Albertine in Five Times) (1999), Precious Hours, The (*Les heures précieuses*) (1989)

Beaumont, Gilbert: Medium Blues (1985)

Beaupré, Maurice: Luck of Ginger Coffey, The (1964), Trouble Makers (*Trouble-fête*) (1964), True Nature of Bernadette, The (*La vraie nature de Bernadette*) (1972)

Beauregard, Josée: Matter of Life, A (1971)

Beauséjour, Éric: Like the Six Fingers of a Hand (1978), Wild Flowers, The (*Les fleurs sauvages*) (1982)

Beaver, Dwayne: Rhino Brothers, The (2002)

Beaver, Jim: Wounded (1996)

Beaver, Mike: Public Domain (2003)

Beavis, Helen: Pygmalion (1983)

Becarrie, Francoise: Have the Right to Pleasure (*J'ai droit au plaisir*) (1975)

Béchard, Carl: Paspébiac: The Games Country (*Paspébiac: Terre des Jeux*) (1985)

Bechdholt, Curt: Rhino Brothers, The (2002)

Bechervaise, Lynden: Isabel (1968)

Beck, Christina: Ride Me (Ego Trip) (1995)

Beck, John: Only God Knows (1974), Paperback Hero (1973)

Beckel, Graham: Execution of Raymond Graham, The (1985)

Becker, Meret: Painted Angels (1998)

Beckett, Nuel: Take Her by Surprise (1967)

Beckman, Henry: Between Friends (Get Back) (1973), Blood and Guts (1978), Brood, The (1979), Fighting Men, The (1977), Joshua Then and Now (1985), Merry Wives of Tobias Rouke, The (1972), Why Rock the Boat? (1974)

Beckman, Lanny: High (1968), Sweet Substitute (Caressed) (1964), When Tomorrow Dies (1965)

Bécotte, Jean-Guy: Frost Bite (*La gélure*) (1968)

Bédard, Anne: Sleep Walkers, The (*Les somnambules*) (1986)

Bedard, Irene: Song of Hiawatha, The (1996)

Bédard, Jocelyn: *Gratien* (1989)

Bedard, Phil: Top of the Food Chain (1999)

Bédard, Rolland: *Cordélia* (1980), Lies My Father Told Me (1975), Promised Land, The (*Les brûlés*) (1958)

Bede, Claude: Dying Hard (1978)

Bedelia, Bonnie: Between Friends (Get Back) (1973)

Bederman, Michael: Bust a Move (1993)

Bednarski, Andrew: Blue Man, The (1985)

Beecroft, David: Awakening, The (1995)

Beecroft, Eleanor: Atlantic City, U.S.A (1980), Funeral Home (Cries in the Night) (1982), Home to Stay (1978)

Beer, Jack: Nobody Waved Goodbye (1964)

Beesley, Jeff: Borderline Normal (2000), Risen, The (2003), Sparkle (1998)

Beggs, Hagan: Cyberteens in Love (1994), Sally Fieldgood and Co. (1975)

Beggs, James: Hired Gun (The Devil's Spawn) (The Last Gunfighter) (1959)

Bégin, Catherine: Beautiful Sundays (*Les beaux dimanches*) (1974), *Délivrez-nous du mal* (Deliver Us From Evil) (1967)

Bégin, Christian: *Collectionneur, Le* (The Collector) (2001)

Begley Jr., Ed: Anthrax (2001), Ms. Bear (1999)

Behrens, Bernard: Changeling, The (1980), Coming of Age (1983), Hostile Advances: The Kerry Ellison Story (1996), Little White Lies (1988), Turning to Stone (1986), Zero Patience (1993)

Behrens, Peter: Cadillac Girls (1993), Kayla (1998), Promise the Moon (1997)

Behrman, Keith: Flower & Garnet (2002)

Beiderbecke, Bix: Circle Game, The (1994)

Beiser, Brendan: Vigil, The (1998)

Bekenn, Anthony: Greening of Ian Elliot, The (1991)

Belafone, Shari: Loving Evangeline (1998)

Belafonte, Shari: If You Could See What I Hear (1982)

Bélair, Lucille: *Revoir Julie* (See Julie Again) (Julie and Me) (1998)

Bélair, Madeleine: Autobiography of an Amateur Filmmaker, The (*L'autobiographe amateur*) (1999), Camera Thief, The (*Le voleur de caméra*) (1993)

Bélair, Serge: It Can't Be Winter, We Haven't Had Summer Yet (1981)

Béland, Marc: Beauty of Women, The (*La beauté des femmes*) (1994), *Odyssée d'Alice Tremblay, L'* (2002)

Beland, Peter: Winter Lily (1998)

Béland, Réal: Apple, the Stem and the Seeds, The (*La pomme, la queue et les pépins*) (1974)

Bélanger, Fernand: Ordinary People (1971)

Bélanger, Guy: Orders, The (*Les ordres*) (1974)

Bélanger, Hélène: *Peau et les os, La* (Skin and Bones) (1988)

Bélanger, Jean: Nightmare, The (*Cauchemar*) (1979)

Bélanger, Louis: Post Mortem (1999)

Bélanger, Lucille: Don't Let It Kill You (*Il ne faut pas mourir pour ça*) (1968)

Bélanger, Paule: Oranges of Israel, The (*Valse à trois*) (1974), Shift de nuit, Le (1979)

Belhadj, Myriam: Lost Words (1993)

Bélisle, Benjamin: Sacrifice, The (1955)

Bélisle, Monique: Heads or Tails (*Pile ou face*) (1971)

Bélisle, Raymond: Isis From the 8th Rang (1972), Jos Carbone (1975), Tangerine Taxi (1988)

Béliveau, Juliette: Grand Bill, The (*Le gros Bill*) (1949), Nightingales and the Bells (*Le rossignol et les cloches*) (1952), *Tit-Coq* (1953)

Béliveau, Véronique: King Solomon's Treasure (1979)

Bell, Isa: *Jeunes Québécoises, Les* (1980)

Bell, James: Trip to Serendipity, A (1992)

Bell, Josie: SnakeEater (1990)

Bell, Michael: Proud Rider, The (1972)

Bell, Nancy: Timing (1985)

Bell, Neal: Terminal Choice (Deathbed) (1985)

Bell, Walter: Falcon's Gold (1982)

Bellange, Katia: *Mon oeil* (My Eye) (1971)

Belle, Annie: Night of the High Tide, The (*La notte dell'alta marea*) (1976)

Bellefeuille, Robert: *Exils* (2002)

Beller, Kathleen: Surfacing (1981)

Bellevose, Michelle: Replikator (1994)

Bellini, Paul: Doulike2Watch.Com (2002)

Belliveau, Sonja: Circle Man (1987)

Bell-Koski, Hazel: Secondary High (2003)

Bellm, Elizabeth: Horses in Winter (*Chevaux en hiver*) (1988), Sunset Court (1988)

Bellows, Gil: Assistant, The (1996), Courage to Love, The (Quadroon Ball) (1999), Dinner at Fred's (1997)

Bellows, Mary: Lyon's Den (1983)

Bellucci, Mauro: *Clandestins* (1997)

Bellwood, Peter: Phobia (1980)

Belmondo, Jean-Paul: Hold-Up (1985)

Belshaw, Diana: Ready for Slaughter (1983), Tools of the Devil (1985)

Belsher, Darcy: Guilty, The (2000), Looking for Leonard (2002), We All Fall Down (2000)

Belyea, Michael: Heart of America: Homeroom (2003)

Belzil-Gascon, Jean: Chocolate Eclair (*Éclair au chocolat*) (1979)

Bemner, Kyla: Someday Soon (1977)

Benard, Michael: Alias Will James (1988)

Benattar, Jordy: Say Nothing (2001)

Benayat, Mohamed: Stallion (1988)

Benedick, B.D.: Graveyard Story (1989)

Benedict, Claire: Felicia's Journey (1999)

Benedict, Lawrence: Far Shore, The (1976)

Benedict, Pinckney: Four Days (1999)

Benmergui, Ralph: By Design (1981), Chatwill's Verdict (Killer Instinct) (Trapped) (1982), Threshold (1981), Today I Am a Fountain Pen (A Good Place to Come From) (1980)

Benmoussa, Salah Eddine: *Casablancais, Les* (The Casablancans) (1998)

Benner, Richard: Happy Birthday Gemini (1980), Outrageous! (1977), Too Outrageous (1987)

Bennett, Bruce: Flaming Frontier (1958)

Bennett, Cle: Steal (2002), Treed Murray (2001)

Bennett, Gareth: Long Road Home, The (1988)

Bennett, Geoffrey: Turning April (1996)

Bennett, Guy: Punch (2002)

Bennett, Hywel: Misery Harbour (1999)

Bennett, Jill: Haunting of Julia, The (1976)

Bennett, Linda: Naked Flame, The (1964)

Bennett, Mairon: Lantern Hill (1990)

Bennett, Mark: Terminal City Ricochet (1990)

Bennett, Nigel: Kurt Vonnegut's Harrison Bergeron (2000), Paint Cans (1994), Rats and Rabbits (2000), Top of the Food Chain (1999)

Bennett, Richard: Food of the Gods II (1989)

Bennett, Sonja: Punch (2002)

Bennett, Zachary: Bay of Love and Sorrows, The (2002), Desire (2000), Happy Christmas, Miss King (1999), Looking for Miracles (1989)

Benoît, Audrey: Tunnel (2000)

Benoît, Denyse: Beautiful Facade, A (*La belle apparence*) (1979), *Dernier havre, Le* (1986), *Station nord* (North Station) (2002)

Benoît, Jacques Wilbrod: Coffin Affair, The (*L'affaire Coffin*) (1980), How to Make Love to a Negro Without Getting Tired (*Comment faire l'amour avec un nègre sans se fatiguer*) (1989), Jos Carbone (1975), *Réjeanne Padovani* (1973), That Darned Loot (*La maudite galette*) (1972)

Benoît, Jean-Louis: *Arthur Rimbaud: L'homme aux semelles de vent* (1995)

Benoît, Raymond: Lies My Father Told Me (1975)

Benoît, Yves: To Be Sixteen (*Avoir 16 ans*) (1979)

Bensimon, Edmond: *Père et Fils* (2003)

Benson, J. Hugh: Incredible Adventures of Marco Polo, The (1998)

Benson, Kelly: Wounded (1996)

Benson, Robby: Tribute (1980), Running Brave

(1983), Whodunit (1986)

Benson, Wendy: Wishmaster 1 (1997)

Bentley, Wesley: Claim, The (2000)

Benton, Eddie: Shape of Things to Come, The (1979)

Benton, Susanne: That Cold Day in the Park (1969)

Berd, Françoise: Beautiful Facade, A (*La belle apparence*) (1979), *Giornata particolare, Una* (1977), In the Land of Zom (1983)

Berenger, Tom: In Praise of Older Women (1978), Watchtower, The (2001)

Beresford, Bruce: Black Robe (1991)

Berg, Dick: Shoot (1976)

Bergen, Patrick: Treasure Island (2001)

Bergen, Tushka: Turning April (1996)

Berger, Annick: Jacques Brel Is Alive and Well and Living in Paris (1975)

Berger, Deborah: Born for Hell (*Né pour l'enfer*) (1976)

Berger, Lory: Deaf and Mute (1986)

Bergeron, Annick: Beauty of Pandora, The (*La beauté de Pandore*) (2000)

Bergeron, Bernard: *Femme de Pablo Ruiz, La* (*Pablo qui court*) (On the Run) (1991), On the Run (*Pablo qui court*) (1993)

Bergeron, Bertrand: Thetford in the Middle of Our Life (*Thetford au milieu de notre vie*) (1980)

Bergeron, Camille: *Shift de nuit, Le* (The Night Shift) (1979)

Bergeron, Jean-Pierre: *Grand serpent du monde, Le* (The Great World Serpent) (1999), Pacemaker and a Sidecar, A (*L'eau chaude, l'eau frette*) (1997)

Bergin, Patrick: Escape Velocity (1999), Eye of the Beholder (1999), Map of the Human Heart (1993), Jewel (2000), Suspicious Minds (1996)

Bergman, Robert: Hurt Penguins (1992), Whisper to a Scream (1988)

Bergmann, Arthur: Highway 61 (1992)

Bergon, Serge: Joy (1983)

Berkley, Elizabeth: Tail Lights Fade (1999)

Berkoff, Steven: Steal (Riders) (2002)

Berle, Milton: Off Your Rocker (1982)

Berliner, Alain: Mayday (1996)

Berling, Charles: *Père et fils* (Father and Son) (2003), Stardom (15 Minutes) (Fandom) (2000)

Berman, Brigitte: Circle Game, The (1994)

Berman, James Gabriel: Misbegotten (1997)

Bermel, Pat: Stag (1997), Ripper: Letter from Hell (2001)

Bernard, Christian: Now Where Are You? (*Où êtes-vous, donc?*) (1969)

Bernard, Denis: Bombardier (1992)

Bernard, Dorothy: Great Shadow, The (1920)

Bernhardt, Daniel: G-2 (1998)

Bernier, Céline: Apprentice, The (*Fleur bleue*) (1971), Red (1969), There's Nothing Wrong With Being Good to Yourself (*Y a pas d'mal à se faire du bien*) (She's So Young and Knows All!) (*C'est jeune et ça sait tout!*) (1974)

Bernier, Jean-Paul: Cat in the Bag, The (*Le chat dans le sac*) (1964), Earth to Drink, The (*La terre à boire*) (1964)

Bernsen, Corbin: Borderline Normal (2000), Recipe for Revenge (1998)

Berry, Bill: High Country, The (The First Hello) (1981)

Berry, Dennis: Poison (Tease) (1999)

Berry, Lloyd: Walls (1984)

Berry, Richard: Honeymoon (*Lune de miel*) (1985), Shadows of the Past (1991), Something About Love (1988), Twin Sisters (1993)

Berry, Tom: Amityville Curse, The (1990), Crazy Moon (1986), Decoys (2003), Something About Love (1988)

Berryman, Dorothée: *Autre homme, Un* (Another Man) (1991), Back Stab (1990), Barbarian Invasions, The (*Invasions Barbares, Les*) (2003), Beauty of Women, The (*La beauté des femmes*) (1994), Bombardier (1992), Café Olé (2000), Clean Machine, The (*Tirelire, combines & cie*) (1992), *Crème glacée, chocolat et autres consolations* (Ice Cream, Chocolate and other Consolations) (2001), Dancing on the Moon (*Viens danser sur la lune*) (1997), Decline of the American Empire, The (*Le declin de l'empire Américain*) (1986), *Embrasse-moi, c'est pour la vie* (Embrace Me, This Is for Life) (1994), Gina (1975), *Je n'aime que toi* (I Don't Love You) (2003), Paper Wedding (*Les noces de papier*) (1989), Pianist, The (1991), Swindle, The (*La gammick*) (1974), Winter Lily (1998), Wrong Woman, The (1995), Varian's War (2001), Zigrail (1995)

Berryman, Gilbert: Paper Wedding (*Les noces de papier*) (1989)

Berthiaume, Claire: Crazy Manette and Cardboard Gods (*Manette: la folle et les dieux de carton*) (1964)

Bertalan, Attila: Between the Moon and Montevideo (2000), Clear-Dark (*Clair obscur*) (1988), Seductio (1987), Sheep Calls and Shoplifters (1995)

Berti, Dehl: Bullies (1986)

Bertin, Catherine: Secondary High (2003)

Berto, Juliet: *Adolescente sucré d'amour, L'* (1985)

Bertrand, Janette: Little Aurore's Tragedy (*La petite Aurore, l'enfant martyre*) (1952) *Dis-moi le si j'dérange* (1989)

Bertrand, Marieve: *Mariages* (2001)

Bérubé, Claude: Time Zero (No Game Without Sun) (*Le temps zéro*) (*Pas de jeu sans soleil*) (1972)

Bérubé, Jocelyn: Absence, The (*L'absence*) (1976), *Barbaloune* (2002), Confidences of the Night (*L'amour blessé*) (1975), *Conquête, La* (1973), *Fille du Maquignon, La* (The Girl of Maquignon) (1990), Gina (1975), Great Ordinary Movie, The (Joan of Arc Is Alive and Well and Living in Québec) (*Le grand film ordinaire*) (1971), Handyman, The (*L'homme à tout faire*) (1980), In the Name of the Son (1972), Ordinary Tenderness (*Tendresse ordinaire*) (1973)

Berval, Paul: Apprentice, The (*Fleur bleue*) (1971), Christmas Martian, The (*Le martien de Noël*) (1971), Straight to the Heart (1969)

Berval, Pierre: Lights of My City (1950)

Berzins, Aldis: Morning in the Pine Forest (1998)

Berzins, Andrew Rai: Blood and Donuts (1995), Chasing Cain (2001), Scorn (2000)

Berzins, Janis: Morning in the Pine Forest (1998)

Besré, Jean: Doves, The (*Les colombes*) (1972)

Bess, Arden: One Heart Broken Into Song (1998)

Bessada, Milad: Quiet Day in Belfast, A (1973), Searching for Diana (1992)

Bessada-Patton, Maissa: Searching for Diana (1992)

Bessai, Carl: Johnny (1999), Lola (2001)

Bessette, François: East Coast (*Côte est*) (1986)

Best, James: G-2 (1998)

Best, Thom: Ice Men, The (2001)

Best, Wayne: Tools of the Devil (1985)

Beswick, Martine: Seizure (Tango Macabre) (1974)

Betrani, Frida: Last Wedding, The (2001)

Betti, Laura: *Dames galantes* (1990)

Bettis, Paul: Urinal (1988)

Betts, Jack: Bloody Brood, The (1959), One Plus One (The Kinsey Report) (Exploring the Kinsey Report) (1961)

Beverly, Karen: Touch and Go (2002)

Beymer, Richard: Cross Country (1983)

Bezace, Didier: *Ou le roman de Charles Pathé* (The Life of Charles Pathé) (1995)

Bezdek, Pavel: Escape Velocity (1999)

Bhaneja, Raoul: Extraordinary Visitor (1998)

Bhatia, Madhuri: Masala (1992)

Bhereur, Larissa: Dollar, The (The Other Side of the River) (*L'autre bord du fleuve*) (1976)

Biafra, Jello: Highway 61 (1992), Terminal City Ricochet (1990)

Bianco, Tony Lo: Goldenrod (1976)

Bibeau, Rita: Danger to Society, A (1970)

Bichir, Bruno: *El jardin del Eden* (The Garden of Eden) (1994)

Bick, Stewart: Artificial Lies (*Le manipulateur*) (2000), Blind Terror (2000), Grey Owl (1999), Life in the Balance (2001), Lip Service (2001), Platinum (1997)

Bick, Tamara: Dinner's on the Table (1994)

Bidaman, Bob: Pictures at the Beach (1990)

Biddle, Stephanie: Karmen Gel (2001)

Bideau, Jean-Luc: Red Violin, The (1998)

Biehn, Michael: Art of War, The (2000), Blood of the Hunter (*Sang du chasseur, Le*) (Lone Eagle) (1995), Crash (Breach of Trust) (1995), Hog Wild (*Les fous de la moto*) (1980), *Sang du chasseur, Le* (1995)

Bigelow, Diane: I, Maureen (1980), Surfacing (1981)

Bigelow, Kathryn: Weight of Water, The (2000)

Bigelow, Pixie: External Affairs (1999), Home to Stay (1978), One Night Stand (1978)

Bigelow, Scott "Bam Bam": SnakeEater III: The Revenge (1992)

Biggs, Julie: Nobody Waved Goodbye (1964), Unfinished Business (1984)

Bigras, Jean-Yves: *Esprit du mal, L'* (Spirit of Evil, The) (1954), Lights of My City (1950), Little Aurore's Tragedy (1952)

Biller, Wendy: Sea People (1999), Whiskers (1997)

Billings, Sheila: Now That April's Here (1958)

Billingsley, Peter: Christmas Story, A (1983)

Billington, Michael: KGB: The Secret War (1984)

Billon, Pierre: *Dernier cri* (The Last Cry) (1996), *Enfant des appalaches, L'* (The Appalachian Child) (1998), Justice Express (1990), *Petite fille particulière, Une* (The Lottery Ticket) (1995), *Présence des ombres, La* (The Presence of Shadows) (1996), Secret of Nandy, The (1991), *Séraphin* (Heart of Stone) (A Man and His Sin) (2002)

Bilodeau, Emmanuel: *Crabe dans la tête, Un* (A Crab in My Head) (2001), *Neg', Le* (2002), Ruth (1994), Seat of the Soul, The (A Crisis of Conscience) (*Siège de l'âme, Le*) (1997), Sleeproom, The (1998)

Bilodeau, Geneviève: *Petit vent de panique, Un* (2000)

Bilodeau, Jacques: *Aventures d'une jeune veuve, Les* (1974), Big Rock, the Big Man, The (*Le Grand Rock*) (1969), Danger to Society, A (*Danger pour la société*) (1970), *Délivrez-nous du mal* (Deliver Us From Evil) (1967), I Love You (1974), Little One Is Coming Soon, The (1972), Men, The (1971), Paths of the World, The (*Les allées de la terre*) (1973), Red (1969), Sensations (1973), Taureau (1972), True Nature of Bernadette, The (*La vraie nature de Bernadette*) (1972), Vultures, The (*Les vautours*) (1975), Woman Inflamed, A (*Tout feu, tout femme*) (1975)

Bilodeau, Richard: East Coast (*Côte est*) (1986)

DIRECTORS, SCRIPTWRITERS & ACTORS

Bilodeau, Vincent: Bilan (2003), Desjardins, His Life and Times (*La vie d'un homme*) (1991), *Turbulence des fluides, La* (Chaos and Desire) (2002)

Binamé, Charles: *Autre homme, Un* (Another Man) (1991), Beauty of Pandora, The (*La beauté de Pandore*) (2000), Chili's Blues (*C'était le 12 du 12 et Chili avait les Blues*) (1994), Eldorado (1995), *Séraphin* (Heart of Stone) (A Man and His Sin) (2002), *Marguerite Volant* (1996), Streetheart (*Le coeur au poing*) (1998)

Bingjian, Liu: Cry Woman (*Ku qi de nu ren*) (2002)

Bingley, Lisa: In the Dead of Space (2000)

Bird, Brian: Captive Heart: The James Mink Story (1996)

Bird, Jim: Nest of Shadows (1976)

Birkett, Paul: Escape Velocity (1999), Mindstorm (2001)

Birman, Len: Draw! (1984), Lies My Father Told Me (1975), Man Inside, The (1975), Undergrads, The (1985)

Birney, David: Goodbye, See You Monday (1979)

Biron, Jacques: *Donnez-nous notre amour quotidien* (In Love With Sex) (1974)

Birtwhistle, Tara: Dracula: Pages From a Virgin's Diary (2003)

Bisaillon, Marc: Immortal Scoundrel, The (*Étienne Brûlé, gibier de potence*) (1952)

Bishop, Kirsten: Champagne for Two (1987)

Bishopric, Thor: Breaking All the Rules (1985)

Bissainthe, Toto: Man on the Shore, The (1993)

Bisset, Jacqueline: Joan of Arc (1999)

Bissett, Roshell: Winter Lily (1998)

Bisson, Yannick: Brothers by Choice (1985), First Offender (1987), Rookies (1990), Toby McTeague (1986)

Bissonettes, Jean: What the Hell Are They Complaining About?) (Hold on, Papa!) (*Tiens-toi bien après les oreilles à Papa*) (1971)

Bissonnette, Joel: Boulevard (1994), Century Hotel (2001), Looking for Leonard (2002), Suspicious River (2000), X-Rated (1994)

Bissonnette, Matthew: Looking for Leonard (2002)

Bissonnette, Normand: Day Without Evidence, A (*Ainsi soient-ils*) (1970), Khaled (2002)

Bistodeau, Lynda: Luke or the Part of Things (1982)

Bizeau, Roberta: Frame-Up Blues (*La danse du scorpion*) (1991), How to Make Love to a Negro Without Getting Tired (*Comment faire l'amour avec un nègre sans se fatiguer*) (1989)

Blabey, Aaron: Turning April (1996)

Black, Byron: Master of Images, The (1972)

Black, Christopher: Skin Deep (Sadness of the Moon) (1995)

Black, Ian: Big Bear (1988)

Black, Jennifer: Recipe for Revenge (1998)

Black, Johanna: Cord (Hide and Seek) (2000)

Black, Karen: Blue Man, The (1985), In Praise of Older Women (1978), Martin's Day (1984), Pyx, The (1973)

Black, Matt: Darkside, The (1986)

Black, Noel: Man, a Woman and a Bank, A (1979)

Black, Ryan: Dance Me Outside (1994)

Black, Stephen: Higher Education (1986)

Blackadar, Lynn: No Angel (1992)

Blackburn, Marthe: Before the Time Comes (*Le temps de l'avant*) (1975), Quarantaine, La (Beyond Forty)(1982), Salut, Victor! (1988)

Blackburn, Nicole: Carnival in Free Fall (*Carnaval en chute libre*) (1966)

Blackburn, Richard: By Reason of Insanity (1982)

Blackman, Honor: Ragtime Summer (Age of Innocence) (1977)

Blackman, Joan: Heatwave Lasted Four Days, The (1973)

Blackout, Moucle: Panic Bodies (1998)

Blackwood, David: Fools Die Fast (1995)

Blackwood, John: Adolescence of P-I, The (Hide and Seek) (1983)

Blain, Manon: Cat in the Bag, The (*Le chat dans le sac*) (1964)

Blair, Linda: Wild Horse Hank (1979)

Blair, Lucille: Bar Salon (1974)

Blais, Isabelle: Crabe dans la tête, Un (A Crab in My Head) (2001), Québec-Montréal (2002), Savage Messiah (2001), *Siamoises, Les* (The Siamese Twins) (1999), Three Madeleines, The (*Les fantômes des trois Madeleines*) (1999)

Blais, Nancy: Crazy Weekend, A (*Week-end en folie*) (1986)

Blake, Barry: Miracle in Memphis (1999)

Blake, Katherine: I Was a Rat (Cinderella and Me) (When I Was a Rat) (2001), Now That April's Here (1958)

Blakeley, Colin: Galileo (1973)

Blanc, Dominique: *Pornographe, Le* (The Pornographer) (2001)

Blanc, Mel: Strange Brew (1983)

Blancard, Jarred: Boys' Club, The (1996)

Blanchard, André: *Alisée* (1991), Beat (1976), Blue Winter (*L'hiver bleu*) (1980)

Blanchard, Claude: Blizzard, The (*Rafales*) (1990), Fantastica (1980), Gina (1975), Mustang (1975), Today or Never (*Aujourd'hui ou jamais*) (1998)

Blanchard, Jean-François: *Vent de galerne* (The Wind From Galerne) (1991), *Vents contraires* (Crosswinds) (1995)

Blanchard, John: Screwball Academy (Divine Light) (Loose Ends) (1986)

Blanchard, Rachel: Wild Dogs, The (2002)

Blanchard, Tammy: Me and My Shadows (2000)

Blanchett, Cate: Shipping News, The (2001)

Blandford, Mark: Chasing Rainbows (1988)

Blanks, Billy: Expect No Mercy (1995)

Blasberg, Joel: Breach of Faith: A Family of Cops II (1996)

Blatch, Kevin: Mr. Rice's Secret (2000)

Blaw, Eric: Jacques Brel Is Alive and Well and Living in Paris (1975)

Blay, Roger: *Quarantaine, La* (Beyond Forty) (1982), *Joyeux calvaire* (1997), *Lucien Brouillard* (1983), *Riel* (1979)

Blayney, Phillip: Tuesday, Wednesday (1987)

Bleasdale, Alan: No Surrender (1985)

Bleeth, Yasmine: Hey Babe! (1984)

Blendick, James: *Cordélia* (1980), Lyon's Den (1983), Shoot (1976)

Blessington, Edward: I'm Going to Get You...Elliot Boy (1971)

Blethyn, Brenda: On the Nose (2001)

Blicker, Seymour: Kid, The (1997)

Blier, Bernard: By the Blood of Others (*Par le sang des autres*) (1974)

Blin, Roger: Old Country Where Rimbaud Died, The (*Le vieux pays où Rimbaud est mort*) (1977)

Blitz, Renessa: Circle Game, The (1994)

Blondell, Joan: Woman Inside, The (1981)

Bloom, Claire: Book of Eve (*Histoires d'Eve*) (2002)

Bloom, George Arthur: Emerald Tear, The (1988), Man Who Guards the Greenhouse, The (1988), Sunset Court (1988)

Bloom, Jeffrey: Dogpound Shuffle (1975)

Bloom, Steve: Undertaker's Wedding, The (1996)

Bloomfield, Angela: Bonjour, Timothy (1995)

Bloomfield, George: Awakening, The (1995), Child Under a Leaf (1974), Deadly Appearances (1999), Death Bite (Spasms) (1983), Double Negative (1979), Jacob Two Two Meets the Hooded Fang (1999), Love and Murder (1999), Love on the Nose (1978), Nothing Personal (1980), Park Is Mine, The (1986), *Riel* (1979), Wozeck: Out of the Fire (1992)

Blossier, Lucie: *Fracture du myocarde, La* (Cross My Heart) (1990)

Blossom, Roberts: Candy Mountain (1987)

Blouin, Michael: Great Land of Small, The (*C'est pas parce qu'on est petit qu'on peut pas être grand!*) (1987)

Blouin, Paul: *Esprit du mal, L'* (Spirit of Evil, The) (1954), Gapi (1982)

Blouin, René: Men, The (1971)

Blouin, Roland: *Léolo* (1992)

Blum, Jack: Babyface (1998), Happy Birthday to Me (1981), Siege (1983)

Blum, Marc: You Can Thank Me Later (1998)

Blumas, Trevor: Stranger in Town (1998), Unsaid, The (2001)

Blumenthal, Allen: Recorded Live (1982)

Blunt, Charlotte: Far Shore, The (1976), Insurance Man From Ingersoll, The (1976), Silent Partner, The (1978), Something's Rotten (1978)

Bluteau, Lothaire: Black Robe (1991), *Bonjour, monsieur Gauguin* (Good Day, Mr. Gauguin) (1989), Confessional, The (*Le confessionnal*) (1995), Conquest (1998), Dead Aviators (1998), *Jésus de Montréal* (1989), Julie Walking Home (2002), Just a Game (1983), Night with Hortense, The (*La nuit avec Hortense*) (1987), Shot Through the Heart (1998), Solitude (2001), Sonia (1986)

Blyth, David: Red Blooded 2 (1996)

Blythe, Catherine: Hawk's Vengeance (1997), List, The (2000)

Blythe, Domini: Deadly Appearances (1999), External Affairs (1999), Heatwave Lasted Four Days, The (1973), Million Dollar Babies (1995), Savage Messiah (2001), Wars, The (1983), When I Will Be Gone (*L'âge de braise*) (1998)

Bnarbic, Paul: Cold Front (1989)

Boakar, Uttara: Burning Season, The (1993)

Board, John: Merry Wives of Tobias Rouke, The (1972)

Bobb, Columpa: Johnny Greyeyes (2001)

Boca, Joseph: *Meurtre en musique* (1994)

Bocan, Joe: Ideal Man, The (*L'homme idéal*) (1996)

Bocher, Christian: Jinnah on Crime (2002), Jinnah On Crime – White Knight, Black Widow (2003)

Bochner, Hart: Say Nothing (2001), Terror Train (1980)

Bochner, Lloyd: Hot Touch (1982), It Seemed Like a Good Idea at the Time (1975), Louisiana (1993), Mary and Joseph: A Story of Faith (1979), Mazes and Monsters (1982), Megantic Outlaw, The (1971), *Riel* (1979), Scoop (1978)

Bochner, Martin: Graveyard Shift (1987)

Bochner, Sally: Train of Dreams (1987)

Bockner, Michael: Johnny Shortwave (1995), Psycho Girls (1986)

Bockstael, Robert: In the Blue Ground (1999), Midday Sun, The (1989), Trudeau (2002)

Bodenhofer, Bastian: *Los Naufragos* (1994)

Bodkin, Nancy Trites: Race for Freedom: The Underground Railroad (1993)

Boe, June: Master of Images, The (1972)

Boepple, Beatrice: Quarantine (1989)

Boese, Kathryn: Revenge of the Radioactive Reporter (1992)

Bohringer, Richard: *Dames galantes* (1990), Flag (1987), Wanted (Crime Spree) (2003)

Bohringer, Romane: Ciel est à nous, Le (Shooting

Stars) (1997), Something Organic (*Quelque chose d'organique*) (1998)

Boies, Markita: Damascus Road, The (*Le chemin de Damas*) (1988), *Mariages* (2001)

Boisjoli, Charlotte: Awakening, The (*L'amour humain*) (1970), It Can't Be Winter, We Haven't Had Summer Yet (1981)

Boisset, Yves: *Frontière du crime* (Double Identity) (1990), Red River (*Rivière Rouge*) (1996)

Boisson, Christine: Born for Hell (*Né pour l'enfer*) (1976), *Enfant des appalaches, L'* (The Appalachian Child) (1998)

Boisvert, Huguette: All About Women (*À propos de la femme*) (1969), *Donnez-nous notre amour quotidien* (In Love With Sex) (1974), Erotic Love Games (1971), Grand Recess, The (*La grande récré*) (1976), *Ils sont nus* (1966), *Justine* (1972), Oh, If Only My Monk Would Want (*Ah! Si mon moine voulait*) (1973)

Boisvert, Jean: *Séraphin* (1950)

Boisvert, Marthe: Castle of Cards, The (*Le château de cartes*) (1980)

Boisvert, Réginald: There Once Was a War (*Il était une guerre*) (1958)

Boivin, Denis: *Attache ta tuque* (2003)

Boivin, Ginette: One Who Sees the Hours, The (*Celui qui voit les heures*) (1985)

Boivin, Guy: O or the Invisible Infant (*O ou l'invisible enfant*) (1971)

Boivin, Régis: Camera Thief, The (*Le voleur de caméra*) (1993)

Bolam, James: In Celebration (1975), Regeneration (1996)

Boland, Richard: Divine Ryans, The (1998), Extraordinary Visitor (1998), Finding Mary March (1989), Stations (1983)

Bolch, Suzanne: Rubber Carpet (1995)

Bolduc, Mario: Large Abode, A (1978), *Oreille d'un sourd, L'* (The Deaf Man's Ear) (1996), *Shift de nuit, Le* (The Night Shift) (1979)

Bolduc, Vincent: Case of the Witch Who Wasn't, The (*Pas de répit pour Mélanie*) (1990), Clean Machine, The (*Tirelire, combines & cie*) (1992), *Jardin d'Anna, Le* (1994)

Boles, Markita: *Années, Les* (The Years) (1997)

Boll, Uwe: Heart of America: Homeroom (2003), House of the Dead (2003)

Bolt, Carol: One Night Stand (1978)

Bolt, David: Phobia (1980)

Bolton, John: Water Game, The (2002)

Bombardier, Denise: *Amanita pestilens* (1963), Between Sweet and Salt Water (Drifting Downstream) (*Entre la mer et l'eau douce*) (1967)

Bombardier, Louise: *Années, Les* (1997)

Bond, Samantha: Bookfair Murders, The (1999)

Bond, Timothy: Deadly Harvest (1980), Diamond Girl (1998), First Offender (1987), Happy Birthday to Me (1981), Lost World, The (1992), Loving Evangeline (1998), Till Death Do Us Part (1982), One Night Only (1986)

Bonder, Ryan: Day Drift (1999)

Bonello, Bertrand: *Pornographe, Le* (The Pornographer) (2001), Something Organic (*Quelque chose d'organique*) (1998)

Bonello, Bertrand: Tiresia (2003)

Bonet, Lisa: Lathe of Heaven (2002)

Boni, Gabrielle: Louisa May Alcott's Little Men (1998)

Boni, John: Wind at My Back (2001)

Boni, Ron: Sex and the Lonely Woman (1966)

Bonin, Jacques: *Mystérieuse Mademoiselle C, La* (2001)

Jacques, Bonnaff: *Fracture du myocarde, La* (Cross My Heart) (1990)

Bonnariage, Manu: Babylone (Halfway House) (1991)

Bonneville, Hugh: Mansfield Park (1998)

Bonnier, Céline: *Ababouinée* (1994), Caboose (1996), *Ciel sur la tête, Le* (On Your Head) (2001), Million Dollar Babies (1995), Orphan Muses, The (*Les muses orphelines*) (2000), *Séraphin* (Heart of Stone) (A Man and His Sin) (2002), Sphinx, The (1995)

Bonnière, René: Adolescence of P-I, The (Hide and Seek) (1983), *Amanita pestilens* (1963), Day My Grandad Died, The (1976), Halfback of Notre Dame, The (1994), Perfect Timing (1984), Vicky (1973)

Bonshor, Walker: Trial by Vengeance (1989)

Boorman, Charley: Firing Squad (1990)

Booth, Bronwen: Babel (1999), Kayla (1998)

Booth, George Thorne: White Road, The (1929)

Booth, Kristen: Burn: The Robert Wraight Story (2003), Fool Proof (2003)

Booth, Lindy: Century Hotel (2001), Fairy Tales & Pornography (2003), Public Domain (2003), Rub & Tug (2002)

Booth, Tara: Century Hotel (2001)

Booth, Tony: Montréal Main (1974)

Boothe, Powers: Joan of Arc (1999)

Boretski, Paul: Canada's Sweetheart: The Saga of Hal C. Banks (1985), Chasing Rainbows (1988), Perfect Timing (1984), Sam and Me (1991)

Boretski, Peter: Chasing Rainbows (1988), Kurt Vonnegut's Harrison Bergeron (2000)

Boretz, Alvin: My Pleasure Is My Business (1975)

Borg, Frank: My Father's Angel (1999)

Borgnine, Ernest: Neptune Factor, The (The Neptune Disaster) (1973), Shoot (1976), Sunday in the Country (1975)

Borich, Milan: Bonjour, Timothy (1995)

Borisenko, Don: Hired Gun (The Devil's Spawn) (1959), Ivy League Killers (The Fast Ones) (1959), Now That April's Here (1958)

Borowitz, Katherine: Two Thousand and None (2000)

Borquet, Marie-France: *Donnez-nous notre amour quotidien* (In Love With Sex) (1974)

Borris, Clay: Alligator Shoes (1981), Prom Night IV: Deliver Us From Evil (1992)

Borris, Gary: Alligator Shoes (1981)

Borsos, Phillip: *Bethune: The Making of a Hero* (1990) see Bethune (1977), Grey Fox, The (1982), One Magic Christmas (1985)

Bosacki, Dean: Concrete Angels (1987)

Bosley, James: Fun (1993)

Bosse, Leo: *Le manuscrit érotique* (2002)

Bossé, Réal: *Bouteille, La* (The Bottle) (2000)

Bostan, Elisabeta: Reach for the Sky (1991)

Bostjancic, William: Battle Queen 2020 (Millennium Queen 2000) (2000)

Botsford, Sara: Arrow, The (1997), By Design (1981), Crossbar (1979), Dead Innocent (1996), Deadly Eyes (The Rats) (1982), Fatal Memories (The Eileen Franklin Story) (1992), Fighting Men, The (1977), Gun Runner, The (1984), Murder by Phone (1982), Obstruction of Justice (1995), Trudeau (2002)

Bottoms, Joseph: Liar's Edge (1992), Make Mine Chartreuse (1987), Surfacing (1981)

Bottoms, Sam: Unsaid, The (2001)

Bottoms, Timothy: Digger (1993), High Country, The (The First Hello) (1981), Murder Seen (2000)

Bou Nassar, Joseph: *Autour de la maison rose* (Around the Pink House) (1999)

Bouajila, Sami: *Répétition, La* (2001)

Bouchard, Denis: *Autre homme, Un* (Another Man) (1991), Blizzard, The (*Rafales*) (1990), Castle of Cards, The (*Le château de cartes*) (1980), Clean Machine, The (*Tirelire, combines & cie*) (1992), Ideal Man, The (*L'homme idéal*) (1996), *Fabrication d'un meurtrier, La* (The Making of a Murderer) (1996), Love Me (1991), *Morte amoureuse, La* (1997), Trudeau (2002), Unfaithful Mornings (*Les matins infidèles*) (1988), Winter Stories (*Histoires d'hiver*) (1999)

Bouchard, Francis: Adventures of Ti-ken, The (1961)

Bouchard, Guy: Carnival in Free Fall (1966)

Bouchard, Jacquelin: *Années, Les* (1997)

Bouchard, Jacques: Death of a Lumberjack (*La mort d'un boucheron*) (1973)

Bouchard, Jean-Guy: *Neg', Le* (2002), Requiem for a Handsome Bastard (*Requiem pour un beau sans-coeur*) (1992), Three Madeleines, The (*Les fantômes des trois Madeleines*) (1999)

Bouchard, Louise-Anne: Claim, The (2000), Coyote (1993)

Bouchard, Michel: In the Land of Zom (1983), *Noël et Juliette* (1973), *Réjeanne Padovani* (1973)

Bouchard, Michel-Marc: Lilies (1996)

Bouchard, Philippe: Like the Six Fingers of a Hand (1978)

Bouchard, Raymond: *Automne sauvage, L'* (The Savage Autumn) (1992), Ding and Dong, The Film (1990), Florida, La (1993), *Grande séduction, La* (2003), *Laura Cadieux, la Suite* (2000), Keep an Eye on the Trombone (1992), Red Eyes (Accidental Truths) (*Les yeux rouges*) (*Les vérités accidentelles*) (1983), Stop (1971), Vengeance de la femme en noir, La (The Revenge of the Lady in Black) (1996)

Bouchard, René: *Jean-François-Xavier de…* (1971)

Bouchard, Réynald: Crinoline Madness (*La folie des crinolines*) (1995), Head of Normande St. Onge, The (*La tête de Normande St-Onge*) (1975), Night in America, A (*Une nuit en Amérique*) (1975), *Noël et Juliette* (1973), True Nature of Bernadette, The (*La vraie nature de Bernadette*) (1972), We Are Far From the Sun (*On est loin du soleil*) (1971)

Bouchard, Sylvie: *Louis XIX, le roi des ondes* (1994)

Bouchard, Yvon: *Dernière condition, La* (1982)

Boucher, Alpha: Scandale (1982)

Boucher, Andreé: *Corde au cou, La* (1966), Finalemente (In the End) (1971), Woman Inflamed, A (*Tout feu, tout femme*) (1975)

Boucher, Brigitte: Other Side of the Law (Outside the Law) (1994)

Boucher, Marie-Johanne: *Petit vent de panique, Un* (A Gust of Panic) (2000)

Boucher, Raymond: *Misanthrope, Le* (1966)

Boucher, Serge: 24 Poses (2002), *Môtel Hélène* (1999)

Bouchez, Élodie: *Ciel est à nous, Le* (1997)

Boudard, Alphonse: *Explosion, L'* (1971)

Boudot, Sabrina: Requiem for a Handsome Bastard (*Requiem pour un beau sans-coeur*) (1992)

Boudreault, Gary: Beauty of Pandora, The (*La beauté de Pandore*) (2000), Matroni and Me (1999), *Temps d'une vie, Le* (The Times of Our Life) (1998)

Boudrine, Dimitri: Exiles in Paradise (2001)

Boujenah, Michel: *Père et Fils* (Father and Son) (2003)

Boulanger, Daniel: *Ménace, La* (1977)

Boulanger, Jacques: Let's Talk About Love (1976)

Boulanger, Jamieson: Frankenstein and Me (1995)

Boulay, Éric: Luke or the Part of Things (1982)

Boulizon, Michelle: *Seul ou avec d'autres* (Alone or With Others) (1962)

Boulton-Brown, Gary: Trinity (2002)

Bourassa, Charles-André: *Collectionneur, Le* (The Collector) (2001)

Bouquet, Jean-Louis: Story of Dr. Louise, The (Docteur Louise) (1949)

Bourbon, Moe B.: *Deux super-dingues* (Heaven Help Us) (1982)

Bourbonnais, Claire: Large Abode, A (1978)

Bourbonnais, Jean: Cyberjack (2003)

Bourgault, Céline: *Gratien* (1989)

Bourgault, Pierre: *Léolo* (1992)

Bourges, Robert: To Kill to Live (*Mourir pour vivre*) (1973)

Bourgine, Élizabeth: *Trois femmes, un amour* (Three Women in Love) (1994)

Bourlakova, Anastasia: *Attache ta tuque* (2003)

Bourne, J.R.: Favourite Game, The (2003), Jungleground (1995)

Bourns, Graham: Christopher's Movie Matinée (1969)

Bouronnais, Jean: *Sept Jours de Simon Labrosse, Les* (The September Days of Simon) (2003)

Bourque, Denise: Sacrifice, The (*La sacrifiée*) (1955)

Bourque, Jean-Pierre: Ordinary Tenderness (*Tendresse ordinaire*) (1973)

Bourque, Sylvie: Black List (*Liste noire*) (1995)

Bourque, Thérèse: Sacrifice, The (1955)

Boushel, Joy: Cursed (1990), Echoes in Crimson (1987), Fly, The (1986)

Boutin, David: *Ciel sur la tête, Le* (On Your Head) (2001), Countess of Baton Rouge, The (*La Comtesse de Baton Rouge*) (1997), *Grande séduction, La* (2003), *Histoire de Pen* (Inside) (2002), Hochelaga (2000), *Mariages* (2001), Trick or Treat (2001), When I'm Gone You'll Still Be Alive (When I'll Be Gone) (*Quand je serai parti vous vivrez encore*) (1999)

Boutros, Mahar: South Pacific, 1942 (1981)

Bouvier, François: Jacques and November (1984), *Pots cassés, Les* (Broken Dishes) (1994), Winter Stories (*Histoires d'hiver*) (1999)

Bouvier, Georges: Promised Land, The (*Les brûlés*) (1958)

Bower, Antoinette: Prom Night (1980)

Bowerman, Terry: Wendy (1966)

Bowes, Geoffrey: Hot Dogs (Clean Up Squad, The) (1980), Jewel (2000), Kidnapping of Baby John Doe, The (1985), King of Friday Night, The (1985), Mama's Going to Buy You a Mockingbird (1987), Something's Rotten (1978)

Bowie, David: Mr. Rice's Secret (2000)

Bowie, Douglas: Boy in Blue, The (1986), Chasing Rainbows (1988), Grand Larceny (1991), Hitting Home (Obsessed) (1989), Love and Larceny (1985), Must Be Santa (1999), Scoop (1978), U-Turn (The Girl in Blue) (1973)

Bowles, Peter: Disappearance, The (1977)

Boxall, Ardith: Nature of Nicholas, The (2002)

Boxill, Patrick: Foxy Lady (1971)

Boxleitner, Bruce: Life in the Balance (2001)

Boyce, Frank Cottrell: Claim, The (2000)

Boyd, Guy: Ticket to Heaven (1981)

Boyd, Lynda: Leaving Metropolis (2002), My Father's Angel (West of Sarajevo) (1999), Nights Below Station Street (1997)

Boyd, Robert: South of Wawa (1991)

Boyer, Myriam: Born for Hell (*Né pour l'enfer*) (1976), Old Country Where Rimbaud Died, The (*Le vieux pays où Rimbaud est mort*) (1977)

Boylan, Sarain: Posers (2002)

Boyle, Peter: Killer (1994)

Boyle, William: Now and Forever (2001)

Boylen, Sarain: Hayseed (1997)

Bozovic, Petar: Boomerang (2002)

Bracco, Lorraine: Ladies Room (1999), Silent Cradle (1998)

Brach, Gérard: *Adolescente sucré d'amour, L'* (1985), Quest for Fire (*La guerre du feu*) (1981)

Bradford, Chris: Little Boy Blues (2000)

Bradford, James: *Riel* (1979), When I'm Gone You'll Still Be Alive (When I'll Be Gone) (*Quand je serai parti vous vivrez encore*) (1999)

Bradley, Paul: Cross Country (1983), Goin' Down the Road (1970), Hard Part Begins, The (1973), Lions for Breakfast (1975), Merry Wives of Tobias Rouke, The (1972), Stone Cold Dead (1979), Wedding in White (1972), What We Have Here Is a People Problem (1976)

Bradshaw, Andy: Fallen Knight (The Minion) (1998)

Bradshaw, Carol: Noncensus (1964)

Bradshaw, John: All the Fine Lines (Full Disclosure) (1999), Big Slice, The (1991), Killing Moon (1998), Not Another Love Story (1979), That's My Baby (1984), Triggermen (2000), Undertaker's Wedding, The (1996)

Bradshaw, Randy: Bad Faith (Cold Blooded) (1999), Last Train Home, The (1990), Skate (Blades of Courage) (1987), Song Spinner, The (1996), Special Delivery (1982), Way to Meet Single Women, The (1985)

Braithwaite, Diana: Race for Freedom: The Underground Railroad (1993)

Braithwaite, Jacen: Bust a Move (1993)

Brand, Maurice: Birds of Prey (1985)

Brandauer, Klaus Maria: Between Strangers (2002), French Revolution, The (1989), *Vercingétorix* (2001)

Brandes, David: Quarrel, The (1990)

Brandon, Sharon: Iron Eagle (1986)

Brandt, Michael: Invincible (2001)

Brannon, Gavin: Ups and Downs (1983)

Brass, David: Connecting Lines (1990)

Brass, Lorne: Dead End (*Le dernier souffle*) (1999), Shadows of the Past (1991), *Zoo la nuit, Un* (A Zoo, by Night) (1987)

Brassard, André: Once Upon a Time in the East (*Il était une fois dans l'est*) (1974), Sun Rises Late, The (*Le soleil se leve en retard*) (1977), Two Seconds (*2 secondes*) (1998)

Brassard, Geneviève: Sweet Lies and Tender Oaths (*Les doux aveux*) (1982)

Brassard, Marie: *Loi du cochon, La* (2001), No (1998), Past Perfect (2002), *Polygraph, Le* (1996)

Brasseur, Claude: Goodbye, See You Monday (*Au revoir, à lundi*) (1979), *Polygraph, Le* (1996)

Brault, François: Flower of Youth (That Tender Age, The Adolescents) (*La fleur de l'âge*) (*Les adolescentes*) (1967), Orders, The (*Les ordres*) (1974), Paper Wedding (*Les noces de papier*) (1989), Passing Through the Pine Trees (*M'en revenant par les épinettes*) (1977), Shabbat Shalom (1994), So That the World Goes On (*Pour la suite du monde*) (1963), When I'm Gone You'll Still Be Alive (When I'll Be Gone) (*Quand je serai parti vous vivrez encore*) (1999)

Brault, Michel: Between Sweet and Salt Water (Drifting Downstream) (*Entre la mer et l'eau douce*) (1967), Flower of Youth (That Tender Age, The Adolescents) (*La fleur de l'âge*) (*Les adolescentes*) (1967), *Mon amie Max* (1993), *Montréal Sextet* (1991), So That the World Goes On (*Pour la suite du monde*)(1963), When I'm Gone You'll Still Be Alive (When I'll Be Gone) (Quand je serai parti vous vivrez encore) (1999)

Brault, Pierre: House of Luk (2000)

Braun, Nicole: *Seul ou avec d'autres* (1962)

Brauner, Hilda: One Plus One (The Kinsey Report) (Exploring the Kinsey Report) (1961)

Brauss, Arthur: Ms. Bear (1999)

Bravman, Jack: Night of the Dribbler (1990)

Brawley, Peter: 20th Century Chocolate Cake, A (1983), Montréal Main (1974), Rubber Gun, The (1977)

Bray, Wilfred: Henry and Verlin (1994)

Braybrook, Paddy: Cornered (Corner, The) (2001)

Brazeau, Jay: Air Bud: Seventh Inning Fetch (2002), Better Than Chocolate (1999), Middlemen (2000), Kissed (1996), Live Bait (1995), Noroc (1999), Urban Safari (1995)

Brazil, Tim: Crack Me Up (1993)

Break, William: Day Breaks Once More (1995)

Bréard, Roland: Absent One, The (1997)

Breck, Peter: Highway 61 (1992), Lulu (1995), Terminal City Ricochet (1990)

Bregman, Tracy: Happy Birthday to Me (1981)

Brel, Jacques: Jacques Brel Is Alive and Well and Living in Paris (1975)

Bremner, Ewen: Fancy Dancing (2002)

Bremner, Scott: Garden, The (1991)

Brendler, Julia: Deeply (2000)

Brennan, Brid: Felicia's Journey (1999)

Brennan, John: Rendering, The (2002)

Breslin, Mark: Mr. Nice Guy (1986)

Breton, Stepane: Québec-Montréal (2002)

Brett, Delia: American Boyfriends (1989)

Brewer, Griffith: Warriors (1994)

Brewster, Kim: Food of the Gods II (1989)

Breznahan, Tom: Brain, The (1988)

Briand, Dominique: *Laura Laur* (1988), Madame B (1986)

Briand, Manon: Cosmos (1997), Heart: The Marilyn Bell Story (2000), *Turbulence des fluides, La* (Chaos and Desire) (2002), Two Seconds (*2 secondes*) (1998)

Bricken, Arlene: Explosion (1969)

Bricken, Jules: Explosion (1969)

Bricker, Barbara: Ivy League Killers (1959)

Bridges, Alan: Ragtime Summer (1977)

Bridges, Beau: Hotel New Hampshire (1984), Kissinger and Nixon (1994), Million Dollar Babies (1995)

Bridges, Krista: Saint Monica (2002)

Bridges, Lloyd: Bear Island (1979)

Bridgewater, Edward: Saturday's Passage (1969)

Brière, Benoît: Angelo, Fredo and Roméo (1996), *Grande Séduction, La* (2003), *Joyeux calvaire* (1997), *Louis XIX, le roi des ondes* (1994), *Station nord* (North Station) (2002)

Brière, Daniel: Decline of the American Empire, The (*Le declin de l'empire Américain*) (1986)

Brigitte, Sauriol: Absence, The (*L'absence*) (1976)

Brikmanis, Peter: Music of the Spheres, The (1984)

Brillant, Pierre-Luc: Clean Machine, The (1992), Memories Unlocked (1999)

Brillon, Denise: Traveller, The (1989)

Brimley, Wilford: Summer of the Monkeys (1998)

Brind'Amour, Yvette: Garnet Princess, The (1987), Pyx, The (1973), Secret of Nandy, The (1991)

Brindle, David: Trip to Serendipity, A (1992)

Brisebois, Éric: Henri (1986), Intimate Power (1985)

Brisebois, René: *Boys II, Les* (The Boys II) (1998)

Bristol, Clare: Witchboard I (1985)

Bristow, Brittany: Perfect Pie (2002)

Bristow, Susan: Cheerful Tearful (1998)

Brittain, Donald: Accident at Memorial Stadium, The (1983), Bethune (1965), Canada's Sweetheart: The Saga of Hal C. Banks (1985), Honourable Member, An (1982), King Chronicle, The (1988), Running Man (1980)

Broadfoot, Dave: Enuff is Enuff (*J'ai mon voyage!*) (1973), What the Hell Are They Complaining About?) (Hold on, Papa!) (*Tiens-toi bien après les oreilles à Papa*) (1971), Rebels 1837, The (*Quelques arpents de neige*) (1972), Red Green's Duct Tape Forever (2002)

Broca, Philippe de: Louisiana (1993)

Brochu, Daniel: Drive, The (1996), Favourite Game, The (2003), Royal Scandal, The (2001)

Brockman, Ann: It's a Wonderful Love (*C'est bien beau l'amour*)(1971)

Brodeur, Delphine: Invention of Love, The (2000)

Brodeur, Jean-Paul: Trouble Makers (1964)

Brodeur, René: Gobital (1975)

Brodkin, Franceen: Passage to Ottawa, A (2002)

Brody, Adrien: Undertaker's Wedding, The (1996)

Brogen, Stefan: Invitation (2000)

Broker, Lee: Cornered (Corner, The) (2001), Crowd Inside, The (1971), Double Negative (Deadly Companion) (1979), Firebird 2015 AD (1980), Fortune and Men's Eyes (1971), Partners (1976), Pyx, The (1973), *Riel* (1979), Sally Fieldgood and Co. (1975), Scanners (1981), Utilities (1981)

Brokop, Lisa: Harmony Cats (1993)

Brolin, James: Back Stab (1990), Relative Fear (1994), Twin Sisters (1993)

Bromfield, Rex: Café Romeo (1992), Love at First Sight (1974), Melanie (1982), Tulips (1981)

Bronson, Charles: Breach of Faith: A Family of Cops II (1996), Death Wish V: The Face of Death (1994), Sea Wolf, The (1993)

Bronstein, Martin: Loving and Laughing (1971)

Brook, Kelly: Ripper: Letter from Hell (2001)

Brooker, Blake: Bad Money (1999)

Brooks, Bonnie: Nest of Shadows (1976)

Brooks, Daniel: Knock! Knock! (1985)

Brooks, Foster: Odd Balls (1984)

Brooks, Martin: Drawing Flies (1996)

Brooks, Susan: Juiced (1999)

Brooks, Torben: Jesus' Son (1999)

Brosnan, Pierce: Grey Owl (1999)

Brossard, Georges: *Forteresse suspendue, La* (The Hidden Fortress) (2001)

Brosse, Louis: Duration of the Day (1967)

Brosseau, Louise: When Wolves Howl (*Quand hurlent les loups*) (1973)

Brosseau, Patrick: Crazy Weekend, A (*Week-end en folie*) (1986)

Broughton, Jason: Panic Bodies (1998)

Brouillette, Geneviève: Black List (*Liste noire*) (1995), Countess of Baton Rouge, The (*La Comtesse de Baton Rouge*) (1997), *Nuit de noces* (Night of the Wedding) (2001), *Père et Fils* (Father and Son) (2003)

Brouillette, Isabelle: *Crême glacée, chocolat et autres consolations* (Ice Cream, Chocolate and other Consolations) (2001)

Brouillette, Richard: *Trop c'est assez* (Too Much Is Enough) (1996)

Brouillette, Robert: Eldorado (1995), Karmina (1998), *Karmina 2: L'enfer de Chabot* (K2 2001) (2001), Shabbat Shalom (1994)

Brousseau, Jean: Clean Hands (*Les mains nettes*) (1958)

Brousseau, Pierre: Sex in the Snow (*Après-ski*) (1971), Tanya's Island (1980)

Brown, Brian: Sally Fieldgood and Co. (1975)

Brown, Bryan: Grizzly Falls (2000)

Brown, Christene: Another Planet (2000)

Brown, Georgia: Galileo (1973)

Brown, Jamie: Keeping Track (1987), Toby McTeague (1986)

Brown, Jean-Pierre: Kings and Desperate Men (1981)

Brown, Jim: Wings of Chance (1961)

Brown, Ken: Things to Do on a Saturday Night (1998)

Brown, Laurie J.: Maintain the Right (1982)

Brown, Lawrence: Wolfpen Principle (1974)

Brown, Leigh: Christmas Story, A (1983)

Brown, Lois: Bingo Robbers, The (2000)

Brown, Marcia: Another Planet (2000)

Brown, Mitchell: Downtime (1985)

Brown, Patrick: Trip to Serendipity, A (1992)

Brown, Philip: Bitter Ash, The (1963)

Brown, Ralph: Wayne's World 2 (1993)

Brown, Reb: Distant Thunder (1988)

Brown, Sydney: Just Jessie (1981), Luck of Ginger Coffey, The (1964), Megantic Outlaw, The (1971), My Pleasure Is My Business (1975), Shoot (1976), Welcome to Blood City (1977), Wolf Dog (1958)

Brown, Tony: Wolf Dog (1958)

Browne, Roscoe Lee: Nothing Personal (1980)

Browning, Rod: Watchtower, The (2001)

Brubeck, Darius: Christopher's Movie Matinée (1969)

Bruce, Christopher: Black Swan (2002)

Bruce, John: Naked Flame, The (1964)

Bruff, Charlene: Welcome to Canada (1989)

Bruhanski, Alex: Showdown at Williams Creek (Kootenai Brown) (1991)

Brûlé, Mirianne: *Enfant des appalaches, L'* (The Appalachian Child) (1998), *Mariages* (2001)

Bruneau, Laura: Wind at My Back (2001)

Brunelle, Manon: Immortal Scoundrel, The (*Étienne Brûlé, gibier de potence*) (1952)

Brunelle, Catherine: *Cuisine rouge, La* (1980)

Brunet, Jacques: *Fracture du myocarde, La* (Cross My Heart) (1990)

Brunet, Lise: Day Without Evidence, A (*Ainsi soient-ils*) (1970)

Brunet, Marc: *Nuit de noces* (Night of the Wedding) (2001)

Brunsdale, Donna: Cheerful Tearful (1998)

Bruyère, Christian: Keeper, The (1975), Shelley (Turned Out) (1987), Walls (1984)

Bruynbrock, Frank: Love and Greed (1992)

Bryan, Anne: And When the CWAC's Go Marching On (*Du poil aux pattes*) (1985)

Bryant, Christopher: Martin's Day (1984), Sword of Gideon (1986), Young Catherine (1990)

Bryant, John: Scanner Cop (1994)

Bryant, Peter: Dukes, The (1998), Home Movie (1992), Something More (1999), Supreme Kid, The (1976)

Bryant, Walter: Foreign Ghosts (*Fantômes étrangers*) (1997)

Bryden, Jon: Deserters (1983)

Brydon, William: Bloody Brood, The (1959)

Brymer, Patrick: Ticket to Heaven (1981), Tools of the Devil (1985)

Bryne, Gabriel: Virginia's Run (2003)

Bubba: Secondary High (2003)

Buble, Crystal: Roller Coaster (1999)

Buchbinder, Amnon: Fishing Trip, The (1998)

Buchok, Roman: Outcast (1991)

Buckler, Hugh: Carry on Sergeant (1927–1928)

Buckingham, Sharon: To Walk with Lions (1999)

Buckman, Tara: Xtro II: The Second Encounter (1991)

Bucksey, Colin: Falling Through (2000)

Buda, Santino: Three and a Half (2002)

Budd, Barbara: Wars, The (1983)

Budds, Colin: Dr. Jekyll and Mr. Hyde (1999)

Buechner, Genevieve: Saint Monica (2002)

Bufano, Vincent: Hard Feelings (1981)

Bugajski, Richard: Clear Cut (1991)

Buguskaw, Linda: *Journal d'un bossu, Le* (1993)

Buhagiar, Valerie: Dear John (1988), Expecting (2002), Highway 61 (1992), Jack of Hearts (1993), Johnny Shortwave (1995), Roadkill (1989), My Script Doctor (1997), New Shoes (1990)

Buissonneau, Paul: It's Not Jacques Cartier's Fault (1968), Waiting for Caroline (1967), YUL 871 (Montréal Flight 871) (1966)

Buitenhuis, Penelope: Boulevard (1994), Giant Mine (1996)

Bujold, Geneviève: Act of the Heart (1970), *Amanita pestilens* (1963), Between Sweet and Salt Water (Drifting Downstream) (*Entre la mer et l'eau douce*) (1967), Bookfair Murders, The (1999), Children of my Heart (2000), Dance Goes On, The (1991), Dead Innocent (1996), Dead Ringers (Alter Ego) (Twins) (1988), Earth to Drink, The (*La terre à boire*) (1964), Eye of the Beholder (1999), Final Assignment (1980), Flower of Youth (That Tender Age, The Adolescents) (*La fleur de l'âge*) (*Les adolescentes*) (1967), Isabel (1968), Journey (1972), Kamouraska (1973), Last Night (1998), *Mon amie Max* (1993), Murder by Decree (1979), Oh, What a Night (1992), Paper Wedding (*Les noces de papier*) (1989), *Turbulence des fluides, La* (Chaos and Desire) (2002), You Can Thank Me Later (1998)

Bukhakova, Maya: Swan Lake: The Zone (1996)

Bull, Roland: Oedipus Rex (1956)

Buller, James: Thousand Moons, A (1977), Surfacing (1981)

Bunce, Stuart: Regeneration (1996)

Bunel, Marie: Family Pack (*Que faisaient les femmes, pendant que l'homme marchait sur la lune?*) (2000)

Bunnage, Avis: No Surrender (1985)

Burcea, Visinel: Wild Dogs, The (2002)

Burchell, Raife Patrick: Morvern Callar (2002)

Burchill, Stuart: Suburban Legend (1995)

Burdett, Stewart: Suburbanators, The (1995)

Bure, Elisabeth: *Dur-Dur* (1981)

Burgess, Gaye: Best of Both Worlds (1983)

Burgess, Mark: Perpetrators of the Crime (1999)

Burgh, B. de: Katryn's Place (2002)

Burgoyne, Maureen: Stuff (1999)

Burke, Ann: Karmina (1998)

Burke, Kaitlyn: Bear With Me (2000), Ms. Bear (1999)

Burke, Martyn: Clown Murders, The (1976), Last Chase, The (1980), Play (*Coup d'état*) (State of Shock) (Operation Overthrow) (1978)

Burlinson, Tom: Legend of Kootenai Brown, The (1990), Showdown at Williams Creek (Kootenai Brown) (1991)

Burnett, Carol: Nobody Makes Me Cry (Between Friends) (1983)

Burnett, Red: Kathy Karuks Is a Grizzly Bear (1976)

Burnford, Sheila: Incredible Journey, The (1963)

Burns, Gary: Kitchen Party (1997), Suburbanators, The (1995), Waydowntown (2000)

Burns, Helen: Catsplay (1977), Changeling, The (1980), If You Could See What I Hear (1982), Utilities (1981), Off Your Rocker (1982)

Burns, Mark: Maids, The (1975)

Burns, Martha: Justice (1998), Long Day's Journey Into Night (1996), Paint Cans (1994), Private Capital, The (1988)

Burns, Michael: That Cold Day in the Park (1969), With Friends Like These (Avec des amis) (1990)

Burns, Sébastien: Emporte-moi (Set Me Free) (1998)

Burns, Tim: Jacob Two Two Meets the Hooded Fang (1999)

Burns-Goulet, Teddy: 90 jours, Les (90 Days) (1959), Mains nettes, Les (1957)

Burr, Raymond: Out of the Blue (No Looking Back) (1980), Showdown at Williams Creek (Kootenai Brown) (1991), Tomorrow Never Comes (1978)

Burrage, Ron: Confessional, The (Le confessionnal) (1995)

Burroughs, Jackie: 125 Rooms of Comfort (1974), Anne of Green Gables (1985), Careful (1992), Dead Zone, The (1983), Dulcima (1970), Eat Anything (1971), Ernie Game, The (1967), Fan's Notes, A (1972), Food of the Gods II (1989), Gentle Sinners (1984), Grey Fox, The (1982), Happy Christmas, Miss King (1999), Have Mercy (1999), Housekeeper, The (Judgement in Stone) (1986), John and the Missus (1986), Intruder, The (1981), Kidnapping of the President, The (1980), Lost and Delirious (2000), Midday Sun, The (1989), Monkeys in the Attic (1974), My Pleasure Is My Business (1975), On Their Knees (2001), Partners (1976), Platinum (1997), Québec-Canada 1995 (1983), Running Time (1978), Surrogate (1984), Undergrads, The (1985), Vicky (1973), Wars, The (1983), Washed Up (2002), Winter Tan, A (1988)

Burstyn, Ellen: Silence of the North (1981), You Can Thank Me Later (1998)

Burton, John: Here I Will Nest (1941)

Burton, Noël: Silent Love, A (2003), When I'm Gone You'll Still Be Alive (When I'll Be Gone) (Quand je serai parti vous vivrez encore) (1999)

Burton, Richard: Circle of Two (1980)

Burton, Wendell: Fortune and Men's Eyes (1971)

Burwash, Gordon: Bush Pilot (1946), Sins of the Fathers (1948)

Busat, Joan: Roses in December (1965)

Busby, Nicole: Passion (2001)

Busey, Gary: Canvas, artiste et voleur (Canvas) (1993), Jacob Two Two Meets the Hooded Fang (1999), Suspicious Minds (1996), Warriors (1994)

Busey, Jake: Tail Lights Fade (1999)

Bush, Barbara: Nobody Makes Me Cry (1983)

Bush, Grand: Hard Feelings (1981)

Busia, Akosua: Louisiana (1993)

Busio, Julian: Pilgrim (Inferno) (1999)

Buss, Kevan: Knock! Knock! (1985)

Bussières, Pascale: August 32nd on Earth (Un 32 août sur terre) (1998), Beauty of Pandora, The (La beauté de Pandore) (2000), Between the Moon and Montevideo (2000), Blue Butterfly, The (Papillon Bleu, Le) (2003), Bouteille, La (The Bottle) (2000), Damascus Road, The (Le chemin de Damas) (1988), Eldorado (1995), Emporte-moi (Set Me Free) (1998), Five Senses, The (1999), Honeymoon (1996), Marguerite Volant (1996), Memories Unlocked (1999), Phantom Life, A (1992) (1992), Platinum (1997), Répétition, La (The Repetition) (2001), Sonatine (1984), Stone Woman, The (Femme de pierre) (1990), Thousand Wonders of the Universe, The (1997), Turbulence des fluides, La (Chaos and Desire) (2002), Twilight of the Ice Nymphs (1997), Two Actresses (1993), When I Will Be Gone (L'âge de braise) (1998), When Night Is Falling (1995), Whole of the Moon, The (1996), Xchange (2000)

Butler, Calvin: Drying Up the Streets (1978), July Group, The (1981)

Butler, David: Bear Island (1979)

Butler, Tom: Cementhead (1979), Crossbar (1979), I Love a Man in Uniform (1984), Labour of Love (1985), Peacekeepers (1997), Scanners II: The New Order (1991)

Buttons, Red: Off Your Rocker (1982)

Buza, George: Meatballs, Part III: The Climax (1987), Shoemaker (1997)

Bydwell, Glenn: Ballerina and the Blues, The (1987)

Byland, Pierre: Eliza's Horoscope (1975)

Byner, John: My Five Wives (2000)

Byrne, Fiona: My Dog Vincent (1997)

Byrne, Gabriel: Virginia's Run (2003), Spider (2002)

Byrne, Michael: Butley (1974)

Byrnes, Burke: Witchboard I (1985)

Byrnes, Jim: Drive, She Said (1997), Harmony Cats (1993)

Caan, James: Incredible Mrs Ritchie, The (2003), Lathe of Heaven (2002), This Is My Father (1998)

Cababa, Éric: Danny in the Sky (2002), Escort, The (L'escorte) (1996)

Cabana, Claude: Frost Bite (La gélure) (1968)

Cabana, Éric: Laura Laur (1988)

Cabay, Marcel: No Holiday for Idols (Pas de vacances pour les idoles) (1965)

Cabrujas, Jose Ignacio: Coup at Daybreak, A (Coup d'état au petit matin) (1998)

A Century of Canadian Cinema

Cadan, Daniel: Morvern Callar (2002)
Cadeau, Lally: *Emporte-moi* (Set Me Free) (1998), Four Days (1999), Harvest (1981), Happy Christmas, Miss King (1999), Nobody Makes Me Cry (Between Friends) (1983), Passengers (1981), Rats (1999), Separate Vacations (1986), Threshold (1981), You've Come a Long Way, Katie (1981), Videodrome (1983)
Cadet, Angelo: Katryn's Place (2002)
Cadieux, Anne-Marie: *Comment ma mère accoucha de moi durant sa ménopause* (How My Mother Was Giving Birth to Me During Menopause) (2001), Confessional, The (1995), *Emporte-moi* (Set Me Free) (1998), Four Days (1999), No (1998), Seven Streams of the River Ota, The (1998), Streetheart (*Le coeur au poing*) (1998)
Cadieux, Chantal: *Collectionneur, Le* (2001)
Cadieux, Jason: Lilies (1996)
Cadrin-Rossignol, Iolande: Laure Gaudreault: A Remarkable Woman (1983), Thetford in the Middle of Our Life (1980)
Caféïne, Xavier: *Du pic au coeur* (2000)
Caffrey, David: On the Nose (2001)
Cage, Nicholas: Boy in Blue, The (1986)
Cailhier, Diane: Dollar, The (The Other Side of the River) (*La piastre*) (*L'autre bord du fleuve*) (1976), Friends for Life (1988)
Cailhier, Diane: *Jardin d'Anna, Le* (1994)
Cailhier, Rachel: Dollar, The (The Other Side of the River) (*La piastre*) (*L'autre bord du fleuve*) (1976), Gone to Glory (*Partis pour la gloire*) (1975), Those Damned Savages (*Les maudits sauvages*) (1971)
Cailloux, André: Évangéline the Second (1985)
Cain, Dean: No Alibi (2000)
Caine, Michael: Bullet to Beijing (1995)
Cairns, Marvel: Saturday's Passage (1969)
Cait, Robert: Married Life: The Movie (2000)
Cake, Jonathan: Diamond Girl (1998)
Calder, Carolyn: Morvern Callar (2002)
Calderisi, David: Michelle Apartments, The (1995)
Caldwell, Zoe: Lantern Hill (1990)
Calenti, Diana: Searching for Diana (1992)
Calfa, Don: Rainbow Boys, The (1973)
Callow, Simon: Deadly Appearances (1999)
Calota, Mihai: Wild Dogs, The (2002)
Caloz, Michael: Louisa May Alcott's Little Men (1998), Screamers (1995), Whiskers (1997)
Calpakis, Gregory: Night of the Dribbler (1990)
Camacho, Mark: Going to Kansas City (1998), Myth of the Male Orgasm, The (1993), Tunnel (2000)
Camat, Jayson: Lolo's Child (2002)
Cambell, Peter: Rat Tales (1987)
Cambron, Kathia: Barbaloune (2002)

Cambron, Valentine: Barbaloune (2002)
Cameron, Anna: Cadillac Girls (1993), Drying Up the Streets (1978), Ernie Game, The (1967)
Cameron, Anne: Dream-Speaker (1976), Drying Up the Streets (1978), Sally Fieldgood and Co. (1975), Ticket to Heaven (1981), Tin Flute, The (*Bonheur d'occasion*) (1983)
Cameron, B.A.: Homecoming, The (1978), Matter of Choice, A (1978)
Cameron, Naomi: Oedipus Rex (1956)
Cameron, Robin: Peep (1984)
Cameron, Tessie: Fast Food High (2003)
Camesanoi, Phyllis: Never Trust an Honest Thief (Going for Broke) (1979)
Camirand, François: Angelo, Fredo and Roméo (1996), *Boys II, Les* (The Boys II) (1998)
Camp, Colleen: City Girl, The (1984), Screwball Academy (Divine Light) (Loose Ends) (1986)
Camp, Hamilton: Meatballs, Part II (1984)
Campanella, Joseph: Café Romeo (1992), Child Under a Leaf (1974)
Campbell, Ann: Roses in December (1965)
Campbell, Chuck: My Dog Vincent (1997)
Campbell, David: Nothing to Lose (1994)
Campbell, Douglas: Double Negative (Deadly Companion) (1979), Explosion (1969), Fan's Notes, A (1972), If You Could See What I Hear (1982), Nothing Personal (1980), Oedipus Rex (1956), Strange Brew (1983), When Tomorrow Dies (1965)
Campbell, Graeme: Built By Association (2002), Into the Fire (1987), Journey Into Darkness: The Bruce Curtis Story (1990), Legend of Wolf Lodge, The (1988), Lip Service (2001), Man in the Attic, The (1994), Still Life (Still Life: The Fine Art of Murder) (1990)
Campbell, Ken: Extraordinary Visitor (1998), Joshua Then and Now (1985)
Campbell, Lee: Lost in the Barrens (1990)
Campbell, Margot: *Au fil de l'eau* (By the Riverside) (2002), Snow Has Melted on the Manicouagan, The (1965)
Campbell, Neve: Baree, Son of Kazan (1994)
Campbell, Nicholas: For Life (see Acts of Love Series) (1980), All the Fine Lines (Full Disclosure) (1999), Amateur, The (1981), Boozecan (1995), Bordertown Café (1991), Boys' Club, The (1996), Brood, The (1979), Butterbox Babies (1995), Certain Fury (1985), Champagne for Two (1987), Chatwill's Verdict (Killer Instinct) (Baker County, U.S.A) (Trapped) (1982), Dancing in the Dark (1995), Dead Zone, The (1983), Diana Kilmury: Teamster (1996), Dirty Tricks (1980), Fast Company (1979),

Going Home (1987), Guitarman (1994), Hard to Forget (So Hard to Forget) (1998), July Group, The (1981), Just Jessie (1981), Maintain the Right (1982), Major Crime (1998), Man in 5A, The (1982), New Waterford Girl (1999), Out of Sight, Out of Mind (The Seventh Circle) (1983), Population of One, A (1980), Saint Jude (2000), Shadows of the Past (1991), Shape of Things to Come, The (1979), Sleeproom, The (1998), Terminal Choice (Deathbed) (1985), Turning Paige (Shepherd Park) (2002), We All Fall Down (2000), We the Jury (1996), Yesterday (1981)

Campbell, Norman: Johnny Belinda (1977)

Campbell, Peter: Sylvan Lake Summer (1991)

Campbell, Sarah: Change of Heart (1993)

Campbell, Sterling: Bush Pilot (1946)

Campbell, Torquil: Bay of Love and Sorrows, The (2002)

Campion, Joyce: Elizabeth Rex (2003), Quiet Day in Belfast, A (1973)

Canaan, Christopher: House on Turk Street, The (2002)

Canavan, John Henry: Torso: The Evelyn Dick Story (2000)

Candido, Romeo: Lolo's Child (2002)

Candy, John: Clown Murders, The (1976), Courage of Kavik the Wolf Dog, The (1980), Double Negative (Deadly Companion) (1979), Find the Lady (1976), Going Berserk (1983), It Seemed Like a Good Idea at the Time (1975), Partner, The (1978), Silent Partner, The (1978)

Cane, Candy: Mr. Patman (1981)

Canning, Jordan: Extraordinary Visitor (1998)

Cannon, Dyan: Child Under a Leaf (1974)

Cannon, Wanda: For the Moment (1994), Last Winter, The (1989), Special Delivery (1982)

Cantin, Jean-Pierre: Isis From the 8th Rang (1972)

Cantin, Lea Marie: Amoureuses, Les (1993), Blanche and the Night (1989)

Cantin, Marie: Jacques and November (1984), Life of a Hero, The (La vie d'un héros) (1994)

Cantin, Roger: Forteresse suspendue, La (The Hidden Fortress) (2001), Grand zélé, Le (The Great Zeal) (1993), Keep an Eye on the Trombone (1992), Man from the Movies, The (1976), Matusalem (1993), Matusalem II, le dernier des Beauchesne (1996), Simon and the Dream Hunters (Simon et les nuages) (1990), Vengeance de la femme en noir, La (1996)

Cantin, Sylvie: Femmes savantes, Les (The Wise Women) (2001)

Cantois, Gilbert: Autre homme, Un (1991)

Canuel, Erik: Loi du cochon, La (The Pig's Law) (2001) Nez rouge (Red Nose) (2003)

Canuel, Yvan: Christmas Martian, The (Le martien de Noël) (1971), J.A. Martin, Photographer (1977), Taureau (1972)

Canvet, Yvan: Taureau (1972)

Caplan, Rupert: Forbidden Journey (1950)

Capone, Nadia: Whisper to a Scream (1988)

Cara, Irene: Busted Up (1986), Certain Fury (1985), Man in 5A, The (1982)

Carcano, Alvaro: Pilgrim (Inferno) (1999)

Card, Mary Jane: Columbus of Sex, The: My Secret Life (1969)

Cardellini, Linda: Unsaid, The (2001)

Cardi, Louise: Carry on Sergeant (1927–1928)

Cardin, Michel-Andre: Cyberjack (2003)

Cardinal, Gil: Big Bear (1988)

Cardinal, Roger: Apparition, The (The Unexpected Phantom) (1972), Malarek: A Street Kid Who Made It (1988), Sex in the Snow (1971)

Cardinal, Tantoo: Big Bear (1988), Black Robe (1991), Divided Loyalties (1989), Loyalties (1985), Edge of Madness (Station Sauvage) (Wilderness Station) (2003), Mustard Bath (1993), Spirit Rider (1993)

Cardinale, Claudia: French Revolution, The (1989), Ruffian, The (1983)

Carel, Roger: Grand Recess, The (1976)

Carey, Matthew: Live Through This (2000)

Carey, Pauline: Urinal (1988)

Carignan, Jean: Far Shore, The (1976)

Cariou, Len: Don't Forget (Je me souviens) (1979), Drying Up the Streets (1978), Louisiana (1993), Man in the Attic, The (1994), Never Talk to Strangers (1995), Nuremberg (2000), One Man (1977), Sea Wolf, The (1993)

Carle, Gilles: Angel and the Woman, The (L'ange et la femme) (1977), Death of a Lumberjack (La mort d'un boucheron) (1973), Équinoxe (1986), Fantastica (1980), Great Chess Movie, The (Jouer sa vie) (1982), Head of Normande St. Onge, The (La tête de Normande St-Onge) (1975), Heavenly Bodies (Les corps célestes) (1973), Homecoming, The (Good Luck, Jennifer Gagnon) (1978), Maria Chapdelaine (1983), Men, The (1971), Merry World of Léopold Z, The (1965), Miss Moscou (1992), Other Side of the Law (Outside the Law) (1994), Plouffe, Les (The Plouffe Family) (1981), Postière, La (The Postmistress) (1992), Pudding chômeur (Bread Pudding) (1996), Rape of a Sweet Young Girl, The (Le viol d'une jeune fille douce) (1968), Red (1969), Thousand Moons, A (1977),True Nature of Bernadette, The (La vraie nature de Bernadette) (1972), Wasp, The (La guêpe) (1986), Gilles Carle-Moi jme fais mon cinema

Carle, Gilles continued:
(1999) (75mins) Documentary about his career with excerpts from his 29 feature films and 23 documentaries.

Carleton, John: Évangéline (1913)

Carlier, Carine: Fantastica (1980)

Carlin, Gloria: Footsteps in the Snow (*Des pas sur la neige*) (1966), Goldenrod (1976), Hot Touch (*Coup de maître*) (1982), Shoot (1976), Two Solitudes (*Deux solitudes*) (1978)

Carlin, Lynn: Dead of Night (Deathdream) (1974)

Carlson, Ben: My Dog Vincent (1997)

Carlson, Les: Adolescence of P-1, The (Hide and Seek) (1983), Hard Part Begins, The (1973), Videodrome (1983)

Carlyle, Robert: Formula 51 (The 51ST State) (2002), Hitler: The Rise of Evil (2003)

Carmet, Jean: Crime of Ovide Plouffe, The (*Le crime d'Ovide Plouffe*) (*Les Plouffe, II*) (1984), Alley Cat, The (*Le matou*) (1985), *Violette Nozière* (1978)

Carmody, Don: Junior (1985), Surrogate (1984)

Carney, Art: Undergrads, The (1985)

Carney, R.B.: Colder Kind of Death, A (2000), Deadly Appearances (1999), Love and Murder (1999), Murder Most Likely (1999), Wandering Soul Murders, The (2000)

Carolsfeld, Wiebke von: Marion Bridge (2002)

Caron, Aline: 100% Bio (Hundred Percent Biography) (2003)

Caron, André: Few Days More, A (*De jour en jour*) (1981), Q-bec My Love (1970)

Caron, Léon: Adventures of Ti-ken, The (1961)

Caron, Luc: *Strass Café* (1980)

Caron, Nicole: *Soleil des autres, Le* (The Sun of the Others) (Give Us Our Daily Love) (1979)

Caron, René: Promised Land, The (*Les brûlés*) (1958), That Darned Loot (1972)

Carpenter, Randall: Cannibal Girls (1973)

Carpenter, Richard: I Was a Rat (Cinderella and Me) (When I Was a Rat) (2001)

Carpenter, Wade: Class Warfare 2001 (2000)

Carpentier, François Yves: Great Big Thing, A (1968)

Carr, Geraldine: City of Champions (1990)

Carr, Joe: Bush Pilot (1946)

Carradine, Keith: Keeping the Promise (1997)

Carradine, Robert: Blackout (Blackout in New York) (1978), Heartaches (1981)

Carré, Gérard: Frame-Up Blues (*La danse du scorpion*) (1991), Fortune and Men's Eyes (1971)

Carré, Louise: Before the Time Comes (*Le temps de l'avant*) (1975), It Can't Be Winter, We Haven't Had Summer Yet (1981), Question of Loving, A (*Qui à tiré sur les histoires d'amour?*) (1986)

Carrere, Tia: Hollow Point (1997), Wayne's World 2 (1993)

Carrier, Louis-Georges: Little One Is Coming Soon, The (1972), *Misanthrope, Le* (1966), Story of the Hunt, The (*Histoire de chasse*) (1990)

Carrier, Roch: Christmas Martian, The (*Le martien de Noël*) (1971)

Carrière, Bruno: *Lucien Brouillard* (1983)

Carrière, Jean-Claude: Black Mirror (*Haute surveillance*) (1981), Jigsaw (Angry Man, An) (*L'homme en colère*) (1979), Carrière, Louise: Day Without Evidence, A (1970)

Carrière, Marcel: Battle of St. Denis… Yesterday, Today, The (*St-Denis dans le temps*) (1969), Bernie and the Gang (1977), OK Liberty (*Ok…Laliberté*) (1973)

Carrière, Mathieu: Bay Boy, The (1984), Born for Hell (*Né pour l'enfer*) (1976), Until the Heart (*Jusqu'au coeur*) (1980)

Carroll, Diahann: Courage to Love, The (1999)

Carroll, James: Under the Piano (1998), Wind at My Back (2001)

Carroll, John: Truckin' (1972)

Carroll, Leo G.: One Plus One (1961)

Carroll, Winston: Blood and Donuts (1995), Ready for Slaughter (1983)

Carron, George: Ivy League Killers (1959)

Carrozzi, Flavia: Night of the Dribbler (1990)

Carruthers, Ian: Eat Anything (1971)

Carr-Wiggin, Joan: Honeymoon (1996)

Carscallen, Helen: Greening of Ian Elliot, The (1991), Other Kingdom, The (1985)

Carston, Rolf: Bloody Brood, The (1959), Ivy League Killers (The Fast Ones) (1959), Now That April's Here (1958)

Carter, Alex: Man in the Attic, The (1994), Recipe for Revenge (1998), Task Force (2000)

Carter, Dan: Gladiator Cop (1994)

Carter, Dixie: Going Berserk (1983)

Carter, Donovan: Battle of St. Denis… Yesterday, Today, The (*St-Denis dans le temps*) (1969)

Carter, Helena Bonham: Margaret's Museum (1995)

Carter, Jason: Famous Dead People (1999)

Carter, Peter: Courage of Kavik the Wolf Dog, The (1980), High-Ballin' (1978), Highpoint (1980), Klondike Fever (1979), Man Called Intrepid, A (1979), Rituals (The Creeper) (1977), Rowdyman, The (1972)

Carter, Phyllis: Sins of the Fathers (1948)

Carter, Sarah: Mindstorm (2001)

Cartier, André: Taureau (1972)

Cartier, François: Claire: Tonight and Tomorrow (*Claire: cette nuit et demain*) (1985)

Cartier, Jean-Pierre: Apprentice, The (*Fleur bleue*)

(1971), Childhood Friend, A (1978), Exile, The (1971), Q-bec My Love (1970)

Caruso, Frank A.: Love Letters: A Romantic Trilogy (2001), No Angel (1992)

Carver, Brent: Ararat (2002), Balls Up (1998), Cross Country (1983), Crossbar (1979), Deeply (2000), Elizabeth Rex (2003), Event, The (2003), Front Line, The (1985), Legend of Sleepy Hollow, The (1999), Lilies (1996), Love and Larceny (1985), Millennium (1988), One Night Stand (1978), Shower, The (1992), Song Spinner, The (1996), Tale of Teeka, The (1999), Wars, The (1983), Whiskers (1997)

Carver, James: Prom Night IV: Deliver Us From Evil (1992)

Carvey, Dana: Wayne's World 2 (1993)

Casabonne, Jean-François: Beauty of Pandora, The (La beauté de Pandore) (2000), Vent de galerne (The Wind From Galerne) (1991)

Case, Bonnie Carol: Wedding in White (1972)

Case, Charles: Silencer, The (1999)

Casey, Bernard: First Offender (1987)

Cassavetes, John: Incubus (1981)

Cassel, Seymour: Burial Society, The (2002)

Cassen, Jan: Christopher's Movie Matinée (1969)

Cassevettes, Nick: Incredible Mrs Ritchie, The (2003)

Cassidy, Elaine: Bay of Love and Sorrows, The (2002), Felicia's Journey (1999)

Cassidy, Joanna: Anthrax (2001)

Cassie, Janie: Great Coups of History (1969)

Cassini, Frank: Flinch (1994), Shot in the Face (2002)

Cassini, John: Shot in the Face (2002)

Castel, Benoît: S Day (Le jour S) (1984)

Castel, France: Crême glacée, chocolat et autres consolations (Ice Cream, Chocolate and other Consolations) (2001), Blanche and the Night (Blanche et la nuit) (1989), Hasards ou coïncidences (1998), Histoire inventée, Une (An Imaginary Tale) (1990), Je n'aime que toi (I Don't Love You) (2003), Karmina (1998), When I Will Be Gone (L'âge de braise) (1998), Wind From Wyoming, A (Le vent du Wyoming) (1994)

Castel, Lou: Foreign Body, A (Sinon, oui) (1997)

Castillo, Nardo: Claire: Tonight and Tomorrow (Claire: cette nuit et demain) (1985), Gun Runner, The (1984)

Castillo, Patricia: Pilgrim (Inferno) (1999)

Castle, Maggie: Other Side of the Law (Outside the Law) (1994)

Castle, Shirley: From Nine to Nine (1936)

Castonguay, Julie: Cabaret neiges noires (1997)

Castonguay, Léopold: Long Live France (1970)

Castonguay, Lise: Femme qui boit, La (The Woman Who Drinks) (2001), Laure Gaudreault: A Remarkable Woman (1983)

Castravelli, Claude: Anomaly (Anomie) (1973), Deux super-dingues (Heaven Help Us) (1982), Evil Judgement (1984), Jeunes québécoises, Les (The Younger Generation)(1980)

Castro, Rick: Hustler White (1996)

Catalifo, Celia: Tiresia (2003)

Cates, Darlene: Welcome to the Freakshow (2001), Wolf Girl (2001)

Cates, Phoebe: Paradise (1982)

Cattell, Christine: Bedroom Eyes (1984), Screwball Academy (Divine Light) (Loose Ends) (1986)

Cattrall, Kim: Brown Bread Sandwiches (1990), Crossbar (1979), Deadly Harvest (1980), Double Vision (1992), Exception to the Rule (1996), Hold-Up (1985), Palais Royale (1988), Porky's (Chez Porky) (1981), Ticket to Heaven (1981), Tribute (1980)

Caulfield, Maxwell: Midnight Witness (1992), More to Love (2000)

Cavall, Jean: French Without Dressing (1964), Room for a Stranger (1968)

Cavanagh, Lynne: Three-Card Monte (1978)

Cavanagh, Sharon: Pasta King of the Caribbean, The (1999)

Cavanagh, Thomas: Honeymoon (1996)

Cavanah, Robert: Platinum (1997)

Cavanaugh, Thomas: Something More (1999)

Cavanaugh, William: Évangéline (1913)

Cavendish, Nicola: Diviners, The (1993), Grocer's Wife, The (1991), Sleeproom, The (1998)

Caverlin, Albert: Love Letters: A Romantic Trilogy (2001)

Cayer, Marc: Trick or Treat (2001)

Cayrol, Jean: Final Blow, The (The Finishing Stroke) (Le coup de grâce) (1965)

Cazalet, Joseph: Sous les draps, les étoiles (Stargazing and Other Passions) (Stars Under the Sheets) (1989)

Cazenove, Christopher: Man Who Guards the Greenhouse, The (1988)

Cecchi, Carlo: Red Violin, The (Le violon rouge) (1998)

Celea, Serban: Excalibur Kid, The (1998)

Celli, Tom: Pleasure Palace (Angela) (1973)

Cellucci, Claire: Scanners III: The Takeover (1992)

Chaboillez, Josée: Close to Falling Asleep (Trois pommes à côté du sommeil) (1988)

Charbonneau, Paul-Patrick: Méchant party (2000)

Chabot, Jean: Futur intérieur, Le (The Interior Future) (1982), Night in America, A (Une nuit en Amérique) (1975), Night with Hortense, The (La nuit avec Hortense) (1987), My Childhood in Montréal (Mon enfance a Montréal) (1971)

Chabot, Mario: *Méchant party* (2000)

Chabrol, Claude: Blood of Others, The (*Le sang des autres*) (1984), Blood Relatives (*Les liens de sang*) (1978), *Violette Nozière* (1978)

Chad, Sheldon: In the Shadow of the Wind (1986)

Chaddo, Cameron: Incredible Mrs Ritchie, The (2003)

Chadwick, June: Back Stab (1990)

Chadwick, Stella: Noncensus (1964)

Chagnon, Pierre: *Fabrication d'un meurtrier, La* (The Making of a Murderer) (1996), *Femme de Pablo Ruiz, La* (*Pablo qui court*) (On the Run) (1991), Tin Flute, The (*Bonheur d'occasion*) (1983)

Chalifor, Nathalie: Mario (1984)

Chalk, Garry: Cowboys and Indians (2003)

Chalke, Sarah: Nothing Too Good for a Cowboy (1998)

Chamberlain, Barbara: Highway of Heartaches (1994)

Chamberlain, Jan: Question of the Sixth, A (1981)

Chamberlain, Richard: Murder by Phone (1982)

Chambers, Marilyn: Rabid (Rage) (1977)

Champa, Jo: Whole Shebang, The (2001)

Champagne, André: Black List (*Liste noire*) (1995), Playgirl Killer (Decoy for Terror) (1965), *Vents contraires* (Crosswinds) (1995)

Champagne, Claude: Large Abode, A (1978)

Champagne, Dominic: *Cabaret neiges noires* (1997), Don Quichotte (2001)

Champagne, Hugo: Sensations (1973)

Champagne, Johnny: Do You Want to Sleep With God? (*Voulez-vous coucher avec Dieu?*) (1972)

Champagne, Joseph: *Boîte à soleil, La* (The Box of the Sun) (1988)

Champagne, Louis: *Bouteille, La* (The Bottle) (2000)

Champagne, Lyne: My Uncle Antoine (1971)

Champagne, Monique: Don't Let It Kill You (*Il ne faut pas mourir pour ça*) (1968), *Soleil des autres, Le* (The Sun of the Others) (Give Us Our Daily Love) (1979), Window, The (*La fenêtre*) (1992)

Champagne, Suzanne: Winter Stories (*Histoires d'hiver*) (1999)

Champagne, Yvei: *Strass Café* (1980)

Champetier, Joel: *Peau Blanche, La* (White Skin) (2003)

Champion, Michael: One Man Out (Erik) (1989), Swordsman, The (1993), Woman Inside, The (1981)

Chan, Jennifer: Dreamtrips (2000)

Chance, Jeremy: Waiting for Michelangelo (1995)

Chang, Qi: Chinese Chocolate (1995), Yellow Wedding (1998)

Chang, Stephen: Double Happiness (1994)

Chang, Sylvia: Red Violin, The (1998)

Channing, Stockard: Hitler: The Rise of Evil (2003), Matthew Shepard Story, The (2001), Piano Man's Daughter, The (2000)

Chao, Rosalind: Terry Fox Story, The (1983)

Chapdelaine, Claudette: Man from the Movies, The (1976)

Chaplin, Geraldine: Buster's Bedroom (1991)

Chaplin, Tamara: Ballerina and the Blues, The (1987)

Chapman, Alexander: Lilies (1996), Princes in Exile (1990)

Chapman, Christopher: Kelly (1981)

Chapman, Constance: In Celebration (1975)

Chapman, Margot: Madeleine Is... (1971)

Chapman, Vern: Luck of Ginger Coffey, The (1964)

Chapple, Alex: Murder Most Likely (1999), Torso: The Evelyn Dick Story (2000)

Charbonneau, Paul-Patrick: *Méchant party* (2000)

Charest, Anna: Traces (1978)

Charest, Emmanuel: *Enfant des appalaches, L'* (The Appalachian Child) (1998), *Fille du Maquignon, La* (The Girl of Maquignon) (1990)

Charest, Jacques: Rape of a Sweet Young Girl, The (*Le viol d'une jeune fille douce*) (1968)

Charette, Michel: Hochelaga (2000)

Charland, Hector: *Homme et son pêché, Un* (A Man and His Sin) (1949), Nightingales and the Bells (*Le rossignol et les cloches*) (1952)

Charlebois, André: Zigrail (1995)

Charlebois, Robert: Between Sweet and Salt Water (Drifting Downstream) (*Entre la mer et l'eau douce*) (1967), Straight to the Heart (1969)

Charles, David: Crack Me Up (1993), Julia Has Two Lovers (1990)

Charleson, Ian: Louisiana (1993)

Charlesworth, Marigold: Paper People, The (1967)

Charlesworth, Sheila: Heavenly Bodies (1973)

Charrette, Michel: *Dangereux, Les* (2003)

Charrière, Christian: Joy (1983)

Charron, Dominique: Heavenly Bodies (1973)

Charron, Mireille: Autobiography of an Amateur Filmmaker, The (1999)

Chartrand, Alain: Ding and Dong, The Film (1990), Dollar, The (The Other Side of the River) (*La piastre*) (*L'autre bord du fleuve*) (1976), Friends for Life (*Des amis pour la vie*) (1988), Isis From the 8th Rang (1972), *Jardin d'Anna, Le* (1994), Revolutionaries, The (1965)

Chartrand, Gilles: Initiation, The (1970)

Chartrand, Louis-Charles: Letter From New France, A (1979)

Chartrand, Madeleine: Bar Salon (1974)

Chartrand, Marie-Andrée: Isis From the 8th Rang (1972)

Chase, Adam: Suzanne (1980)

Chase, Chevy: Great Goose Caper, The (2003)

Chase, David: Almost Grown (1987)

Chase, Lita: Deadend.com (2002)

Chasle, Véronie Quinn: *Aline et Michel* (Aline) (1992)

Chassé, Henri: Bilan (2003), *Maîtres anciens* (1998), Snail's Point of View, A (*La position de l'escargot*) (1998), *Temps d'une vie, Le* (The Times of Our Life) (1998)

Chatterji, Moushumi: Bollywood/Hollywood (2002)

Chau, Nguyen-Thé-Minh: Eleventh Child, The (*Nguol Thua*) (1998)

Chauveau, Zoe: Girls (*Les femmes-enfant*) (1980)

Chauvet, Maurice: Owning Mahowny (2001)

Chaykin, Maury: Adjuster, The (1991), Art of War, The (2000), Brethren (1976), Buried on Sunday (1993), Camilla (1994), Canada's Sweetheart: The Saga of Hal C. Banks (1985), Caribe (1988), Cold Comfort (1989), Conspiracy of Silence (1991), Crossed Over (2001), Curtains (1983), Defcon 4 (1984), Double Negative (Deadly Companion) (1979), George's Island (1989), Higher Education (1986), Highpoint (1980), Jacob Two Two Meets the Hooded Fang (1999), Jerry and Tom (1998), Joan of Arc (1999), July Group, The (1981), Just Jessie (1981), Kidnapping of the President, The (1980), Labour of Love (1985), Love and Death on Long Island (1997), Meatballs, Part III: The Climax (1987), Montréal Sextet (1991), Nothing Personal (1980), Of Unknown Origin (1983), On Touched (1999), On Their Knees (2001), Owning Mahowny (2001), Pale Saints (1997), Past Perfect (2002), Pianist, The (1991), *Riel* (1979), Sweet Hereafter, The (1996), Varian's War (2001), Vindicator, The (Frankenstein '88) (1986), Whale Music (1994)

Chazel, André: *Dur-Dur* (1981)

Cheechoo, Greta: Bear Walker (Backroads) (2000)

Cheechoo, Shirley: Bear Walker (Backroads) (2000), Johnny Greyeyes (2001), Where the Heart Is (1985)

Cheezo, Marianne: *Attache ta tuque* (2003)

Cheezo, Wally: *Attache ta tuque* (2003)

Chellas, Semi: Dead Aviators (1998), Life Before This, The (1999), Picture Claire (2001)

Chelton, Tsilla: Family Pack (*Que faisaient les femmes, pendant que l'homme marchait sur la lune?*) (2000)

Chemin, Cayle: Graveyard Story (1989)

Chen, Edmund: Yellow Wedding (1998)

Chen, Terry: Various Positions (2002)

Chenail, Jacques: Rape of a Sweet Young Girl, The (*Le viol d'une jeune fille douce*) (1968), *Retour de l'Immaculée Conception, Le* (The Return of the Immaculate Conception) (1970)

Chenail, Roland: Christmas Martian, The (*Le martien de Noël*) (1971), Dust from Underground (*Poussière sur la ville*) (1965), Trouble Makers (*Trouble-fête*) (1964)

Chénier, François: *Embrasse-moi, c'est pour la vie* (Embrace Me, This Is for Life) (1994), *Fabuleux voyage de l'ange, Le* (The Fabulous Voyage of the Angel) (1991)

Chénier, Gilbert: *Corde au cou, La* (1966), Swindle, The (*La gammick*) (1974)

Chénier, Michel: Blue Winter (*L'hiver bleu*) (1980)

Chercover, Daniel: Dinner's on the Table (1994)

Chereau, Patrice: Nearest to Heaven (*Au plus pres du paradis*) (2002)

Cherihane: *Échec et mat* (Checkmate) (1994),

Chermin, Cayle: Love in a Four Letter World (1970)

Cherniak, Terry: One of Our Own (1977)

Chernick, Jonas: Edge of Madness (*Station Sauvage*) (2003), Inertia (2001)

Chernin, Gayle: Goin' Down the Road (1970)

Cherrie, Michael: Angel in a Cage (1998)

Cherry, Jonathan: House of the Dead (2003)

Chesler, Lewis: Bear With Me (2000)

Chester, Holly: SnakeEater III: The Revenge (1992)

Chester, Lloyd: Wolf Dog (1958)

Chetwynd, Lionel: Apprenticeship of Duddy Kravitz, The (1974), Escape from Iran: The Canadian Caper (Desert Blades) (1981), Goldenrod (1976), Hot Touch (*Coup de maître*) (1982), Kissinger and Nixon (1994), Two Solitudes (*Deux solitudes*) (1978), Varian's War (2001)

Cheung, Daphne: Midnight Man (1995)

Cheung, Edwin: Soul Investigator, The (Stories of Chide the Wind) (1994)

Chevolleau, Richard: Rude (1995)

Chevrette-Landesque, Hugolin: Simon and the Dream Hunters (*Simon et les nuages*) (1990)

Cheylov, Milan: Odd Balls (1984)

Chiang, George: Hawk's Vengeance (1997)

Chiarelli, Gina: Noroc (1999)

Chicoine, Michèle: Explosion (1969), It's Not Jacques Cartier's Fault (1968)

Chief-Moon, Byron: Almost America (*Come l'America*) (2001), Warrior Spirit (1994)

Chilcott, Barbara: Lies My Father Told Me (1975)

Chilcott, Doris: Wolfpen Principle (1974)

Chin, Jeanne: Shopping for Fangs (1996)

Chin, Tsai: Long Life, Happiness & Prosperity (2002)

Chloé, Franks: Uncanny, The (1977)

Chloé, Keti: Sex and the Single Sailor (1967)

Cho, John: Shopping for Fangs (1996)

Cho, Patrick: Soul Investigator, The (Stories of Chide the Wind) (1994)

Choate, Tim: Defcon 4 (1984)

Chomont, Tom: Panic Bodies (1998)

Chong, Jason: Dr. Jekyll and Mr. Hyde (1999)

Chong, Rae Dawn: Boulevard (1994), Chain Dance (Common Bonds) (1991), Power of Attorney (1995), Quest for Fire (1981), Starlight (1995)

Choquette, Louis: To Be Sixteen (*Avoir 16 ans*) (1979), *Secret de banlieue, Un* (The Secret of a Suburb) (2002)

Choquette, Robert: Village Priest, The (*Le curé de village*) (1949)

Chouinard, Denis: *Ange de goudron, L'* (Tar Angel) (2001), *Clandestins* (1997)

Chouinard, Normand: Clean Machine, The (*Tirelire, combines & cie*) (1992), Close to Falling Asleep (*Trois pommes à côté du sommeil*) (1988), Devil at Four, The (1988), Don Quichotte (2001), *Je n'aime que toi* (2003), *Riel* (1979)

Chouinard, Pierre: Twelfth Hour, The (1966)

Chouinard, Yvan: At the Autumn of Life (The Human Misery) (*À l'automne de la vie*) (*La misère humaine*) (1987)

Chouraqui, Élie: *Paroles et musique* (1985)

Chouvalidze, Elizabeth: Cuervo, the Private Detective (1990)

Choveaux, Clara: Tiresia (2003)

Chowdhry, Ranjit: Bollywood/Hollywood (2002), Fire (1996), Sam and Me (1991), Such a Long Journey (1998)

Christeler, Charlotte: *Emporte-moi* (1998)

Christie, Dinah: My Pleasure Is My Business (1975), One Night Stand (1978)

Christie, Jack: Do You Want to Sleep With God? (*Voulez-vous coucher avec Dieu?*) (1972)

Christie, Robert: Artichoke (1978), Bloody Brood, The (1959), Bush Pilot (1946), Incredible Journey, The (1963), Last Chase, The (1980), Oedipus Rex (1956), Nothing Personal (1980), Snowbirds (1981), Utilities (1981)

Christmas, Eric: Air Bud (1997), Challengers, The (1990), Changeling, The (1980), Middle-Age Crazy (1980), Porky's (*Chez Porky*) (1981), Porky's II: The Next Day (*Chez Porky 2*) (1983), Porky's Revenge (*Revanche de Porky, La*) (1985), Whispers (1990)

Christofel, David: Real Howard Spitz, The (1998)

Christophe, Françoise: *Échec et mat* (1994)

Christopher, Jean: Playgirl Killer (Decoy for Terror) (1965), Room for a Stranger (1968)

Christov, Ivailo: Here Am I (1999)

Chu, Edmond: Soul Investigator, The (Stories of Chide the Wind) (1994)

Chubbuck, Lyndon: War Bride, The (2001)

Chuipka, Chip: Katryn's Place (2002), Heart: The Marilyn Bell Story (2000), Two Summers (2002)

Chula, Babz: Barbeque: A Love Story (1997), Croon Maury and Mrs. B. (International Title) (2003), Dirty (1998), My American Cousin (1985), Kanada (1993), Last Wedding, The (2001), Live Bait (1995), No More Monkeys Jumpin' on the Bed (2000), Noroc (1999), Raffle, The (1994), Valentine's Day (1994)

Churchill, Adrian: Bob's Garage (2001)

Chuvalo, George: In the Dead of Space (2000)

Ciambrone, Vincent: Crazy Weekend, A (*Week-end en folie*) (1986)

Ciccoritti, Gérard: Paris, France (1993)

Ciccoritti, Jerry: Boy Meets Girl (1998), Chasing Cain (2001), Deadly Friends: The Nancy Eaton Story (2003), Graveyard Shift (1987), Understudy, The: Graveyard Shift II (1988), Life Before This, The (1999), Many Trials of One Jane Doe, The (2002), Net Worth (1997), Psycho Girls (1986) Tek War: Tek Justice (1994), Trudeau (2002), Whisper to a Scream (1988)

Cieszewski, Marek: Regeneration (1988)

Cina, Domenic: Cornered (Corner, The) (2001)

Ciupka, Richard: Coyote (1993), Curtains (1983), Dead End (1999), *Mystérieuse Mademoiselle C, La* (2001), Task Force (2000)

Clair, Cyrielle: Counterstrike (1993)

Clairoux, Jean: Day Without Evidence, A (*Ainsi soient-ils*) (1970)

Clapp, Gordon: Family of Strangers (1993), Island Love Song (1987), Morrison Murders,The (1997), Private Capital, The (1988), Tools of the Devil (1985), Termini Station (1990)

Clare, Diane: Vulture, The (1967)

Clarfield, Stuart: Welcome to the Parade (1986)

Clark, Bob: Black Christmas (Silent Night, Evil Nights) (Stranger in the House) (1974), Breaking Point (1976), Christmas Story, A (1983), Dead of Night (Deathdream) (1974), Murder by Decree (1979), Porky's (*Chez Porky*) (1981), Porky's II: The Next Day (*Chez Porky 2*) (1983), Tribute (1980)

Clark, Carol: Cry in the Night, A (1996)

Clark, Dane: Woman Inside, The (1981)

Clark, Daniel: Grizzly Falls (2000)

Clark, David: Maxwell's Dream (1999)

Clark, Dorian: Power Games (1990)

Clark, Eugene: Gladiator Cop (1994), One Heart Broken Into Song (1998), Tek War: Tek Justice (1994), Thrillkill (1984)

Clark, Gordon: Hired Gun (The Devil's Spawn) (The Last Gunfighter) (1959)

Clark, Ian D.: Lilies (1996), Michelle Apartments, The (1995)

Clark, Lawrence Gordon: Midnight Man (1995)

Clark, Louise: Winter Tan, A (1988)

Clark, Mary Higgins: Double Vision (1992)

Clark, Richard: Halfback of Notre Dame, The (1994)

Clark, Robert: Now and Forever (2001)

Clark, Ronald: Funny Farm, The (The Comics) (1983)

Clark, Steven: Looking for Leonard (2002)

Clark, Susan: Butterbox Babies (1995), City on Fire (1979), Double Negative (Deadly Companion) (1979), Murder by Decree (1979), Porky's (*Chez Porky*) (1981)

Clarke, Alicia: Trial and Error (1993)

Clarke, Caitlin: Kid Brother, The (1987)

Clarke, Emmanuel: Foreign Body, A (*Sinon, oui*) (1997)

Clarke, George Elliott: One Heart Broken Into Song (1998)

Clarke, Scott: Bob's Garage (2001)

Clarke, Shaun: Waiting Game, The (1998)

Clarke, Sylvie: Sitting in Limbo (1985)

Clarke, Wallace: Morning Man, The (1986)

Clarkson, Helene: Blood and Donuts (1995)

Clarkson, Kirsten: Horsey (1997)

Clarkson, Patricia: Baroness and the Pig, The (2002)

Clarkson, S. Wyeth: Deadend.com (2002)

Claude, Alain: *Quiconque meurt, meurt à douleur* (Whoever Dies, Dies in Pain) (1998)

Clausen, Benedikt: Regina (2002)

Clauser, Suzanne: Home to Stay (1978)

Clave, Karen: Built By Association (2002)

Clavell, James: Sweet and the Bitter, The (1962)

Clavell, Kira: Dr. Jekyll and Mr. Hyde (1999), Rub & Tug (2002)

Clavering, Eric: Welcome to Blood City (1977), Foxy Lady (1971), Hard Part Begins, The (1973), Improper Channels (1981), Isabel (1968), Partners (1976), Sudden Fury (1975), Sunday in the Country (1975), Ten Girls Ago (1962), Threshold (1981)

Clay, Andrew Dice: My Five Wives (2000)

Clayton, Hannah: Black Swan (2002)

Cleetche: Tribe of Joseph (2001)

Clement, Aurore: Dear Father (*Caro Papa*) (1979)

Clement, David: Moving Targets (1983)

Clement, Jennifer: Raffle, The (1994), Waydowntown (2000)

Clement, Philippe: Yellowknife (2002)

Clément, Raphaël: Duration of the Day (*Le règne du jour*) (1967)

Clément, Sophie: *Albertine, en cinq temps* (1999), Madame B (1986), Once Upon a Time in the East (*Il était une fois dans l'est*) (1974), Orders, The (*Les ordres*) (1974), Pacemaker and a Sidecar, A (*L'eau chaude, l'eau frette*) (1997)

Clément, Suzanne:*Jeunes québécoises, Les* (The Younger Generation) (1980)

Clementi, Pierre: Sweet Movie (1974)

Clements, Shawn: Sylvan Lake Summer (1991)

Clémont, Suzanne: Confessional, The (*Le confessionnal*) (1995)

Cleveland, Rick: Jerry and Tom (1998)

Clews, Hetty: Visitor, The (1974)

Cliché, Karen: Dr. Jekyll and Mr. Hyde (1999), Steal (Riders) (2002), Summer (2002), Wrong Number (2001)

Clifford, Eileen: Don't Let the Angels Fall (1969)

Clifford, Jack: House in Order, A (*La maison en ordre*) (1936)

Clothier, Robert: Final Edition (1982), Silence of the North (1981)

Clouse, Robert: Deadly Eyes (The Rats) (1982)

Cloutier, Raymond: Black List (*Liste noire*) (1995), *Montréal Blues* (1972), Coffin Affair, The (*L'affaire Coffin*) (1980), Confidences of the Night (*L'amour blessé*) (1975). *Concièrgerie, La* (The Caretaker's Lodge) (The Prison) (1997), *Contrecoeur* (1983), *Cordélia* (1980), *Grand zélé, Le* (The Great Zeal) (1993), Great Ordinary Movie, The (Joan of Arc Is Alive and Well and Living in Québec) (*Le grand film ordinaire*) (1971), Head of Normande St. Onge, The (*La tête de Normande St-Onge*) (1975), Just a Game (1983), Red (1969), *Riel* (1979), Saint Jude (2000), Trudeau (2002), Vultures, The (*Les vautours*) (1975)

Cloutier, Suzanne: Whiskers (1997)

Cloutier, Veronique: *Dangereux, Les* (2003)

Clune, Liliane: Claire: Tonight and Tomorrow (*Claire: cette nuit et demain*) (1985), Garnet Princess, The (1987)

Clune, Liliane: Justice Express (1990)

Clutesi, George: Dream-Speaker (1976), Isaac Littlefeathers (1984), Kelly (Touch the Wind) (1981), Running Brave (1983), Toby McTeague (1986)

Cluzet, François: *Ababouinée* (1994), French Revolution, The (1989), Wind From Wyoming, A (*Le vent du Wyoming*) (1994)

Coates, Judith: Noncensus (1964)

Coates, Kim: Airborne (1998), All the Fine Lines (Full Disclosure) (1999), Amityville Curse, The (1990), Crash (Breach of Trust) (1995), Dead Silence (1997), Frame-Up Blues (*La danse du scorpion*) (1991), Harmony Cats (1993), Killing Moon (1998), Tunnel (2000), Xchange (2000)

Cobb, David: Flick (Dr. Frankenstein on Campus) (1970)

Cobden, Joe: Suddenly Naked (2001), Summer (2002)

Cobello, Dominique: Ultimatum (1975)

Coburn, Gladys: God's Crucible (1921)

Coburn, James: Draw! (1984), Martin's Day (1984), Mr. Patman (1981)

Cochran, Kathryn: Understanding Bliss (1990)

Cochran, Steve: Back to God's Country (1953)

Cockell, Juno Mills: Defy Gravity (1990)

Cokliss, Harley: Pilgrim (Inferno) (1999)

Codrington, James: Passage to Ottawa, A (2002)

Coe, Harrison: Echo Lake (2000)

Coeur, Paul: Solitaire (1991), Road to Saddle River (1994)

Coffey, Colleen: Ride Me (Ego Trip) (1995)

Coffey, Judy: Rubber Carpet (1995)

Coffey, Peter: Rubber Carpet (1995)

Cogan, Gerald: Tragic Diary of Zero, the Fool, The (1970)

Coghill, Joy: Change of Heart (1984), Jacob Two-Two Meets the Hooded Fang (1977), Ma Murray (1983), Parasite Murders (Shivers) (1975), Silence (1997)

Cohen, Annette: Love on Your Birthday (see Acts of Love Series) (1980)

Cohen, Ari: Archangel (1990)

Cohen, Charles Zev: Eddie and the Cruisers Part II: Eddie Lives! (1989)

Cohen, David: Ride Me (Ego Trip) (1995)

Cohen, Eli: Quarrel, The (1990)

Cohen, Ilan Duran: Lola Zipper (1991)

Cohen, Jacques: Rape of a Sweet Young Girl, The (Le viol d'une jeune fille douce) (1968)

Cohen, Jeffrey: Rookies (1990)

Cohen, Joel: Never Trust an Honest Thief (Going for Broke) (1979)

Cohen, Larry: Burnt Eden (1997), Misbegotten (1997)

Cohen, Leonard: Ernie Game, The (1967), Heaven Before I Die (1997), Night Magic (1985)

Cohen, M. Charles: Drylanders (1963), First Circle, The (1991)

Cohen, Marty: Roses in December (1965)

Cohen, Neil: Never Trust an Honest Thief (Going for Broke) (1979)

Cohn-Leavitt, Laurie: Midwife's Tale, A: The Discovery of Martha Ballad (1996)

Coixet, Isabel: My Life Without Me (Mi Vida Sin Mi) (2003)

Cokeliss, Harley: Pilgrim (Inferno) (1999)

Colbert, Paul: Butler's Night Off, The (1948)

Cole, Buddy: Super 8 (1994)

Cole, Frank: Cowboyz (1988), Life, A (1988)

Cole, Nikki: When Tomorrow Dies (1965)

Cole, Randall: 19 Months (2002)

Cole, Stephanie: Grey Owl (1999)

Cole, Tom: To Kill the King (1974)

Cole, William: Johnny Belinda (1977)

Coleman, Dabney: Must Be Santa (1999), Nothing Personal (1980)

Coleman, Layne: Blue City Slammers (1987), Harvest (1981), Marriage Bed, The (1986), Out of Sight, Out of Mind (The Seventh Circle) (1983), Ready for Slaughter (1983)

Coleman, Leonard: Montréal Main (1974)

Coleman, Renée: El jardin del Eden (The Garden of Eden) (1994), Waiting for Michelangelo (1995)

Coles, John David: Friends at Last (1995)

Colicos, John: Breaking Point (1976), Changeling, The (1980), Dulcima (1970), Forbidden Journey (1950), King Solomon's Treasure (1979), Last Season, The (1987), Nowhere to Hide (1987), Phobia (1980), Shadow Dancing (1988)

Colleary, Michael: Death Wish V: The Face of Death (1994)

Colley, Peter: Mark of Cain, The (1984)

Collin, Frédérique: Absence, The (L'absence) (1976), Au fil de l'eau (By the Riverside) (2002), Confidences of the Night (L'amour blessé) (1975), Conquête, La (1973), Cuisine rouge, La (The Red Food) (1980), Duplessis' Orphans (1999), Encircled Colour, The (La couleur encerclée) (1986), Gina (1975), Lucien Brouillard (1983), Marie in the City (1987), Matter of Life, A (1971), Noël et Juliette (1973), Once Upon a Time in the East (Il était une fois dans l'est) (1974), One Who Sees the Hours, The (Celui qui voit les heures) (1985), Paths of the World, The (Les allées de la terre) (1973), Réjeanne Padovani (1973), Time of the Hunt, The (Le temps d'une chasse) (1972), Yellow Island, The (L'île jaune) (1975)

Collin, Maxime: Léolo (1992), Matusalem (1993)

Collin, Pierre: Grande Séduction, La (2003), Maîtres anciens (1998)

Collings, Anne: Bloody Brood, The (1959), Mask, The (1961), Now That April's Here (1958)

Collins, Boon: Abducted (1985), Lighthouse (1989), Sally Fieldgood and Co. (1975)

Collins, Colleen: I, Maureen (1980), One of Our Own (1977)

Collins, Eryn: Come Together (2001)

Collins, Gail: Dead Aviators (1998)

Collins, Georgie: Ghostkeeper (1981)

Collins, Joely: Diamond Girl (1998), Dinosaur Hunter, The (2000)

Collins, Mary Lou: Playgirl Killer (Decoy for Terror) (1965)

Collins, Maynard: Hank Williams: The Show He Never Gave (1982)

Collins, Patricia: Artichoke (1978), Bear Island (1979), By Reason of Insanity (1982), Circle of Two (1980), Crowd Inside, The (1971), Fan's Notes, A (1972), House (1995), Nothing Personal (1980), Phobia (1980), Speaking Parts (1989), Summer's Children (1979), Wozeck: Out of the Fire (1992)

Collinson, Peter: Tomorrow Never Comes (1978)

Collura, Mary Ellen Lang: Spirit Rider (1993)

Collyer, Pamela: Bye Bye Red Riding Hood (*Bye bye, chaperon rouge*) (1989), Evil Judgement (1984)

Colpron, Paul: Why Is the Strange Mr. Zolock So Interested in Comic Strips? (*Pourquoi l'étrange Monsieur Zolock s'intéressait-il tant à la bande dessinée*)(1983)

Colt, Marshall: Tangerine Taxi (1988)

Coltrane, Robbie: Perfectly Normal (1990), Oh, What a Night (1992), On the Nose (2001)

Columbus, Franco: Circle Man (1987)

Colvey, Catherine: Cursed (1990), Make Mine Chartreuse (1987)

Comar, Richard: Freeloading (1986)

Comart, Jean-Paul: Lola Zipper (1991)

Comeau, Jean-Marie: *Dernier cri* (1996)

Comeau, Phil: Secret of Jerome, The (1994)

Comilang, Stephanie: Lolo's Child (2002)

Comilang, Steven: Lolo's Child (2002)

Comtois, Gilbert: Heartbreak (*L'arrache-coeur*) (1979), Scandale (1982)

Comtois, Jean: Angel and the Woman, The (*L'ange et la femme*) (1977), Head of Normande St. Onge, The (1975)

Condo, Ray: Strange Blues of Cowboy Red, The (1995)

Coneybeare, Wilson: Darkness Falling (2002)

Conkie, Heather: My Mother's Ghost (1996), Pit Pony (1998)

Conley, Corinne: Butterbox Babies (1995), *Tit-Coq* (1953), Searching for Diana (1992)

Conlon, Tom: Prom Night III: The Last Kiss (1989)

Conner, David: Cross Country (1983)

Conner, Eric: Falling Through (2000)

Conner, Michael-Ann: Girl King (2002)

Conner, Ralph: Cameron of the Royal Mounted (1921), Critical Age, The (1923), God's Crucible (1921)

Conners, Mike: Armen and Bullik (1993)

Connery, Jason: Bullet to Beijing (Len Deighton's Bullet to Beijing) (1995), Wishmaster 3: Beyond the Gates of Hell (2001)

Connolly, Jim: Remembering Mel (1986)

Connolly, Marcia: Parsley Days (2000)

Conroy, Mellisa: Slow Burn (1989)

Constanzo, Maurizio: *giornata particolare, Una* (1977)

Constible, Sarah: Inertia (2001), Many Trials of One Jane Doe, The (2002), Many Trials of One Jane Doe, The (2003)

Contamine, Pascal: Cosmos (1997)

Conte, Richard: Explosion (1969)

Conte, Tony: *Méchant party* (2000)

Conti, Tom: Galileo (1973), Haunting of Julia, The (Full Circle) (1976),I Was a Rat (Cinderella and Me) (When I Was a Rat) (2001)

Converse, Frank: Anne of Green Gables: The Continuing Story (Series) (1985-1999), Rowdyman, The (1972), Sneakers (1982)

Conway, Jeff: Covergirl (1984)

Conway, Kevin: Net Worth (1997)

Conway, Susan: Rip-Off (1971)

Conway, Tom: Air Bud: Golden Receiver (1998)

Cook, A.J.: Ripper: Letter from Hell (2001), Wishmaster 3: Beyond the Gates of Hell (2001)

Cook, Ben: Dead Aviators (1998), Louisa May Alcott's Little Men (1998)

Cook, Peter: Find the Lady (1976)

Cook, Tracey: Dream Storm: A North of 60 Mystery (2001), In the Blue Ground (1999), SnakeEater III: The Revenge (1992), Trial by Fire: A North of 60 Mystery)

Cooke, Alan: Armen and Bullik (1993), Pygmalion (1983)

Coolidge, Martha: City Girl, The (1984)

Cooney, Dean: Willing Voyeur, The (1996)

Cooper, Bradley: My Little Eye (2002)

Cooper, Jackie: Journey Into Fear (1975)

Cooper, John: My Kind of Town (1984)

Cooper, Robert: Impossible Elephant, The (2001)

Cooper, Stuart: Disappearance, The (1977)

Cooper, Susan: Jewel (2000)

Coopersmith, Jerome: American Christmas Carol, An (1979)

Cooter, Verlie: Sweet and the Bitter, The (1962)

Copans, Sylvain: *Fracture du myocarde, La* (1990)

Copeland, Kristina: Water Game, The (2002)

Copeman, Michael: Scanners III: The Takeover (1992), Street Law (Law of the Jungle) (1995)

Copnick, Corinne: Ernie Game, The (1967)

Coppaway, Adeline: Thousand Moons, A (1977)

Copperfield, David: Terror Train (1980)

Coquereau, Patrice: Escort, The (*L'escorte*) (1996)

Corazza, Vincent: Leaving Metropolis (2002), Ride, The (2000)

Corbeil, Yves: Trouble Makers (*Trouble-fête*) (1964)

Corbett, John: Morrison Murders, The (1997), On Hostile Ground (2000)

Corbett, Kathleen: Barnone (1997)

Corcoran, William: Dancing in the Dark (1995), Trust in Me (1995)

Cordeau, Arianne: Zigrail (1995)

Corder, Sharon: Babyface (1998)

Corey, Len: Cowboyz (1988)

Corf, Mia: Silent Witness: What a Child Saw (1994)

Corlett, William: Magician's House, The (1999)

Cormack, Lynne: Memory Run (1995)

Corman, Roger: Avalanche Alley (2001)

Cormier, Jacinta: Life Classes (1987)

Corneau, Alain: *Ménace, La* (1977)

Corneille, Marie-Andree: *Erreur sur la personne* (The Wrong Person) (1995)

Corraface, Georges: Legends of the North (1996)

Corsan, Ian: Malicious (1995)

Corsini, Catherine: *Répétition, La* (2001)

Corson, Ian: Falling Through (2000)

Cort, Bud: Why Shoot the Teacher (1977)

Cortese, Valentina: Buster's Bedroom (1991)

Cory, Michael: Screwballs II: Loose Screws (1985)

Cosmatos, George Pan: Of Unknown Origin (1983)

Costa, Benentino: Lydia (1964)

Costa, Nuno Da: Manuel: A Son by Choice (1990)

Costanzo, Robert: M.V.P. 2: Most Valuable Primate (2001)

Costello, Charles: House of Pain (1995)

Coster, Nikolaj: Misery Harbour (1999)

Costner, Kevin: Gun Runner, The (1984)

Côté, Ghyslaine: Pin-Pon, The Film (1999)

Côté, Joanne: *Ange gardien, L'* (The Guardian Angel) (1978), Blue Man, The (1985), Dancing on the Moon (*Viens danser sur la lune*) (1997)

Côté, Michel: *Ababouinée* (1994), Black List (*Liste noire*) (1995), *Cruising Bar* (Meat Market) (1989), *Erreur sur la personne* (The Wrong Person) (1995), Exit (1986), *Fille du Maquignon, La* (The Girl of Maquignon) (1990), In the Belly of a Dragon (1989), *Miss Moscou* (1992), Moody Beach (1990), Moonshine (1982), *Sur Le Seuil* (Under the Sky) (2003), You Are Beautiful Jeanne (*T'es belle, Jeanne*) (1988), Wind From Wyoming, A (*Le vent du Wyoming*) (1994)

Côté, Mosha: Frostfire (1995)

Côté, Stéphane: Requiem for a Handsome Bastard (*Requiem pour un beau sans-coeur*) (1992)

Cote-Olijnik, Marianne: *Silence nous guette, Le* (2002)

Cotret, René de: *Jean-François-Xavier de...* (1971)

Cottereau, Laure: I Have the Right to Pleasure (*J'ai droit au plaisir*) (1975)

Coudari, Camille: Wasp, The (*La guêpe*) (1986)

Couffer, Jack: Nikki, Wild Dog of the North (1961)

Coufos, Paul: Busted Up (1986), Food of the Gods II (1989)

Couillard, Jacques: Cowboyz (1988)

Couillard, Paul: House of Pain (1995)

Coulombe, Anna: Dangerous Dreams (1986)

Coulon, Patrick: Apprentice, The (1971)

Coulson, Bernie: Eddie and the Cruisers Part II: Eddie Lives! (1989), Hard Core Logo (1996), Highwayman, The (1999), Saint Jude (2000)

Coulter, Clare: By Design (1981), Murder by Phone (1982), Saint Monica (2002), Terminal Choice (Deathbed) (1985), Wars, The (1983)

Coulter, Ian: Trouble (1996)

Coulthard, Raymond: Eisenstein (2000)

Coupal, Nathalie: Unfaithful Mornings (*Les matins infidèles*) (1988), Windigo (1994)

Couran, Clotilde: Map of the Human Heart (1993)

Cournot, Michel: *Tisserands du pouvoir, Les* (1988)

Cournoyer, Rejean: Dragonwheel (2002)

Courtemanche, Michel: *Nuit de noces* (2001)

Courtenay, Tom: I Heard the Owl Call My Name (1973)

Courtney, Raven: Girl King (2002)

Cousineau, Andrée: Kid Sentiment (1967), There's Nothing Wrong With Being Good to Yourself (*Y a pas d'mal à se faire du bien*) (She's So Young and Knows All!) (1974)

Cousineau, Jean: Stone Cold Dead (1979), Yellow Island, The (*L'île jaune*) (1975)

Cousineau, Philippe: *Sept Jours de Simon Labrosse, Les* (2003)

Coutteure, Ronny: *Ou le roman de Charles Pathé* (The Life of Charles Pathé) (1995)

Coutu, Angele: Book of Eve (*Histoires d'Eve*) (2002)

Coutu, Jean: And I Love You Dearly (*La maîtresse*) (1973), Apparition, The (The Unexpected Phantom) (1972), Doves, The (*Les colombes*) (1972), Heads or Tails (*Pile ou face*) (1971), Nightingales and the Bells (*Le rossignol et les cloches*) (1952), Nikki, Wild Dog of the North (1961), Seven Times a Day (*Sept fois par jour*) (1971), Rebels 1837, The (*Quelques arpents de neige*) (1972), Panic (*Panique*) (1977)

Couture, Anthony: Red Deer (2000)

Couture, Jacques: Music of the Spheres, The (1984)

Couture, Suzette: After the Harvest (Wild Geese) (2000), Conspiracy of Silence (1991), *Florida, La* (1993), Haven (2001), Love and Hate (1989), Million Dollar Babies (1995), Sheldon Kennedy Story, The (1999), Skate (Blades of Courage) (1987), Where the Heart Is (1985)

Cove, Martin: White Light (1991)

Cover, Paul: Investigation (2002)

Covert, Doris: From Nine to Nine (1936)

Cowan, Cindy: Power of Attorney (1995)

Cowan, Paul: Justice Denied (1989), Kid Who Couldn't Miss, The (1982), Westray (2001)

Cowie, Victor: Law of Enclosures, The (2000), Smoked Lizard Lips (1991), Woman Wanted (1999)

Cowl, Darry: There's Nothing Wrong With Being Good to Yourself (*Y a pas d'mal à se faire du bien*) (She's So Young and Knows All!) (*C'est jeune et ça sait tout!*) (1974)

Cox, Alvin: Nashville Bound (1996)

Cox, Brian: In Celebration (1975), Mad About Mambo (2000)

Cox, Christina: Better Than Chocolate (1999), Street Law (Law of the Jungle) (1995)

Cox, Deborah: Love Come Down (2000)

Cox, Julie: *Alégria* (1998), War Bride, The (2001)

Cox, Paul: Careful (1992)

Cox, Richard: Vindicator, The (1986)

Cox, Ronny: Reckless Disregard (1985)

Coyne, Andrew: Next of Kin (1984)

Coyne, Susan: Salem Witch Trials (2001)

Coyote, Peter: Seeds of Doubt (1997), Suddenly Naked (2001)

Crabbe, Christopher: Coming Out Alive (1980)

Craden, Omie: Concrete Angels (1987).

Craft, Scott: For the Moment (1994)

Craig, Kelly: Perfect Timing (1984)

Craig, Michele: Star Is Lost, A (1974)

Craig, Philip: Clown Murders, The (1976), Spider (2002)

Cranberry, Donald: Death Weekend (House by the Lake) (1976)

Cranham, Kenneth: Midnight Man (1995)

Craven, Matthew: Crash (Breach of Trust) (1995), Happy Birthday to Me (1981), Hog Wild (*Les fous de la moto*) (1980), Killer (1994), Never Too Late (1996), Nuremberg (2000), *Palais Royale* (1988), Terry Fox Story, The (1983), That's My Baby (1984), Varian's War (2001), White Tiger (1995)

Crawford, Broderick: Vulture, The (1967)

Crawford, Gavin: My Dog Vincent (1997)

Crawford, Johnny: Inbreaker, The (1974)

Crawford, Rachael: Pale Saints (1997), Ride, The (2000), Rude (1995), We the Jury (1996), When Night Is Falling (1995)

Crawford, Rachel: Captive Heart: The James Mink Story (1996), Curtis's Charm (1995), When Night Is Falling (1995)

Crawford, Wayne: LAPD: To Protect and Serve (2001)

Crawley, Amos: Heaven on Earth (1987)

Crawley, F.R. (Budge): *Amanita pestilens* (1963), *Budge: The One True Happiness of F.R. Budge Crawley* (2003) (53mins) By Michael Ostroff, Seaton Findlay. Narrator: Don Franks. With original and archive footage, film clips, photographs, and interviews with those who knew him in the world of film and the arts, this excellent documentary shows us his life and career from the famous shorts, The Mask & Newfoundland Scene, to dramatized films such as The Luck of Ginger Coffey, and much more of this pioneer's impact on Canadian film.

Crawley, Sandy: Christopher's Movie Matinée (1969), Power Play (*Coup d'état*) (State of Shock) (Operation Overthrow) (1978), Silent Partner, The (1978)

Creed, Keltie: Urinal (1988)

Creighton, Liza: Paper People, The (1967), Sally Fieldgood and Co. (1975)

Creley, Jack: Alien Thunder (Dan Candy's Law) (1973), All in Good Taste (1983), Crowd Inside, The (1971), If You Could See What I Hear (1982), Reincarnate, The (1971), Rituals (The Creeper) (1977), Star Is Lost, A (1974), Till Death Do Us Part (1982), Videodrome (1983), Welcome to Blood City (1977)

Cremer, Bruno: *La-haut* (2002)

Crenna, Richard: Death Ship (1980), Stone Cold Dead (1979), Wild Horse Hank (1979)

Crépeau, Jeanne: *Revoir Julie* (See Julie Again) (Julie and Me) (1998),War Brides (1980), Whodunit (1986)

Crête, Stéphane: *Bouteille, La* (The Bottle) (2000)

Crewson, Wendy: At the End of the Day: The Sue Rodriguez Story (1998), Better Than Chocolate (1999), Between Strangers (2002), Colder Kind of Death, A (2000), Covert Action (1986), Deadly Appearances (1999), Escape Velocity (1999), Frostfire (1995), Getting Married in Buffalo Jump (1990), Killing Spring, A (2001), Lives of Girls and Women, The (1996), Love and Murder (1999), Many Trials of One Jane Doe, The (2002), Mark of Cain, The (1984), Mazes and Monsters (1982), Perfect Pie (2002), Piano Man's Daughter, The (2000), Question of Privilege, A (1998), Sleeping Dogs Lie (1999), Suddenly Naked (2001), Verdict in Blood (2001), Wandering Soul Murders, The (2000), War Brides (1980), Whodunit (1986)

Cronenburg, John: Day Breaks Once More (1995)

Crimm, Arthur: Kurt Vonnegut's Harrison Bergeron (2000)

Cristiani, Gabriella: Ladies Room (1999)

Critch, Mark: Anchor Zone (1994)

Croft, William: Bullies (1986)

Crombie, Jonathan: Anne of Green Gables (1985), Anne of Green Gables: The Continuing Story (1985-1999), Bullies (1986), Café Romeo (1992), Housekeeper, The (Judgement in Stone) (1986), Waiting Game, The (1998)

Cromwell, James: Snow Walker, The (2002)

Cron, Claudia: Running Brave (1983)

Crone, Robert: I, Maureen (1980)

Cronenberg, David: Blood and Donuts (1995), Brood, The (1979), Crash (1996), Crimes of the Future (1970), Day Breaks Once More (1995), Dead Ringers (Alter Ego) (Twins) (1988), Dead Zone, The (1983), Fast Company (1979), Fly, The (1986), Henry and Verlin (1994), Last Night (1998), M. Butterfly (1993), Stereo (1969), Naked Lunch (1992), Parasite Murders (Shivers) (They Came from Within) (1975), Preludes (2000), Rabid (Rage) (1977), Scanners (1981), Spider (2002), Stereo (1969), Videodrome (1983)

Cronin, Can: No More Monkeys Jumpin'on the Bed (2000)

Cronis, Howard: Kill (1969), Only Thing You Know, The (1971)

Cronyn, Hume: Camilla (1994), Sea People (1999)

Crooks, Robert: Two Summers (2002)

Crosby, Denise: Max (1994), Relative Fear (1994)

Crosby, Mary: Crack Me Up (1993)

Crosby, P.J.: Love That Boy (2002)

Cross, Ben: Ascent, The (1994), Cold Sweat (1993), Diamond Fleece, The (1992)

Cross, Roger: Beyond Suspicion (1993), What's Your Verdict? (1995)

Cross, Roy: So Faraway and Blue (2001)

Crossland, Harvey: Burning Season, The (1993), Close to Home (1986)

Crossland, Jackie: 125 Rooms of Comfort (1974)

Crossman, Robert: Cornered (Corner, The) (2001)

Crothers, Scatman: Deadly Eyes (The Rats) (1982)

Crowe, Christopher: Last Chase, The (1980)

Crowe, Robert: Seetha and Carole (1997)

Crowe, Russell: For the Moment (1994)

Crowfoot, Alan: Cool Sound From Hell, A (The Young and the Beat) (1959)

Croze, Marie-Josee: Ararat (2002), Des chiens dans la neige (Dogs in the Snow) (2001), Maelström (2000), Murder Most Likely (1999), Croze

Croze, Marie-Josée: Barbarian Invasions, The (Invasions Barbares, Les) (2003), Des chiens dans la neige (Dogs in the Snow) (2001)

Crudo, Bianca: Julie Walking Home (2002)

Crudup, Billy: Jesus' Son (1999), World Traveler (2001)

Cruickshank, Jack: Nasty Burgers (1994)

Cruickshank, Laura: Buying Time (1988)

Cruise, David: Net Worth (1997)

Cruise, Tom: Losin' It (1983)

Cruz, Carlos: Passage des hommes libres (Passage of Free Men) (1996)

Cruz, Penelope: Twice Upon a Yesterday (1998)

Cser, Nancy: Way to Meet Single Women, The (1985)

Cubitt, David: Major Crime (1998), Perfect Son, The (2000), Swann (1996)

Cucci, Tony: Men of Means (1999)

Cucinotta, Maria Grazia: Brooklyn State of Mind, A (1997)

Cudney, Roger: Falcon's Gold (1982)

Cuerrier, Louise: Confidences of the Night (L'amour blessé) (1975)

Cuff, John Haslett: Psycho Girls (1986)

Cuffley, Robert: Turning Paige (Shepherd Park) (2002)

Cui, Jan: Yellow Wedding (1998)

Cui, Shirley: Chinese Chocolate (1995), Lilly (1993)

Cui, Yan: Chinese Chocolate (1995)

Cukier, Jackie: En vacances (2000)

Culka, Nikola: Summer With the Ghosts (Un été avec les fantômes) (2002)

Cull, Pat: Ready for Slaughter (1983)

Cullen, Becky: Bullies (1986)

Cullen, Peter: Prologue (1970)

Cullum, John: Secret Life of Algernon, The (1996)

Culp, Robert: Breaking Point (1976)

Culver, Carmen: Mary and Joseph: A Story of Faith (1979)

Culver, Roland: Uncanny, The (1977)

Cummings, Burton: Melanie (1982)

Cummings, Irving: Cameron of the Royal Mounted (1921)

Cummings, Patrick: House of Lovers (La maison des amants) (1972)

Cummins, Martin: Cyberteens in Love (1994), Ice Men, The (2001), Love Come Down (2000), We All Fall Down (2000)

Cunio, Michael: Fubar (2002)

Cunningham, Cavan: Barnone (1997)

Cunningham, Colin: Zacharia Farted (1998), Silencer, The (1999)

Cunningham, Tracy: Blue City Slammers (1987)

Cunningham, Jack: Peep (1984)

Cuny, Alain: Mission of Fear (1965)

Curcin, Nick: My Script Doctor (1997)

Curnick, David: Life and Times of Chester-Angus Ramsgood, The (1971)

Curotte, Robert: To Kill to Live (Mourir pour vivre) (1973)

Curran, Ann: Pictures at the Beach (1990)

Currie, Finlay: 49th Parallel (The Invaders) (1941)

Currie, Gordon: Blood and Donuts (1995), Circle, The (The Fraternity) (2001), Falling Through (2000), Waydowntown (2000)

Currie, Andrew: Mile Zero (2001)

Currie, Sandee: Curtains (1983)

Curry, Tim: Lion of Oz (2000), Welcome to the Freakshow (2001), Wolf Girl (2001)

Curtelin, Jean: There's Nothing Wrong With Being Good to Yourself (*Y a pas d'mal à se faire du bien*) (She's So Young and Knows All!) (*C'est jeune et ça sait tout!*) (1974)

Curtis, Andy: Maxwell's Dream (1999)

Curtis, Jack: *Ils sont nus* (1966)

Curtis, Jamie Lee: Prom Night (1980), Terror Train (1980)

Curtis, John: Xtro II: The Second Encounter (1991)

Curtis, Liane: Kid Brother, The (1987)

Curtis, Sandee: Gas (1981)

Curtis, Stacey Stewart: Dream Storm: A North of 60 Mystery (2001), Greening of Ian Elliot, The (1991), Recipe for Revenge (1998)

Curtis, Tony: Title Shot (1980)

Curwood, James Oliver: Back to God's Country (1919)

Curzi, Pierre: *Babylone* (Halfway House) (1991), Barbarian Invasions, The (*Invasions Barbares, Les*) (2003), Bulldozer (1974), Chili's Blues (*C'était le 12 du 12 et Chili avait les Blues*) (1994), Confidences of the Night (*L'amour blessé*) (1975), Crime of Ovide Plouffe, The (*Le crime d'Ovide Plouffe*) (*Les Plouffe, II*) (1984), Cry in the Night, A (*Le cri de la nuit*) (1996), *Cuisine rouge, La* (The Red Food) (1980), Decline of the American Empire, The (*Le declin de l'empire Américain*) (1986), Fantastica (1980), Jigsaw (Angry Man, An) (*L'homme en colère*) (1979), In the Belly of a Dragon (1989), Intimate Power (1985), Let's Talk About Love (1976), *Lucien Brouillard* (1983), *Marguerite Volant* (1996), *Maria Chapdelaine* (1983), Matroni and Me (1999), Million Dollar Babies (1995), Paths of the World, The (*Les allées de la terre*) (1973), Red Eyes (Accidental Truths) (*Les yeux rouges*) (*Les vérités accidentelles*) (1983), Riel (1979), S Day (*Le jour S*) (1984), Sleep Walkers, The (*Les somnambules*) (1986), Suzanne (1980), Trick or Treat (2001), We Are Far From the Sun (*On est loin du soleil*) (1971), Wild Flowers, The (*Les fleurs sauvages*) (1982), You Are Beautiful Jeanne (*T'es belle, Jeanne*) (1988), You Are Warm, You Are Warm (*Tu brûles, tu brûles*) (1973)

Cusack, John: Map of the Human Heart (1993), Max (2001), This Is My Father (1998)

Cushing, Peter: Uncanny, The (1977)

Cuthbert, Elisha: Believe (2000), Dancing on the Moon (1997), Lucky Girl (2000)

Cuthbert, Jon: Cyberjack (1995), Touch of Murder, A (1990)

Cuthrell, Elizabeth: Jesus' Son (1999)

Cutler, Allen: Halfback of Notre Dame, The (1994)

Cuvelier, Marcel: Kamouraska (1973)

Cuzzorea, Domenic: No Angel (1992)

Cyr, Isabelle: *Forteresse suspendue, La* (The Hidden Fortress) (2001), *Karmina 2: L'enfer de Chabot* (K2 2001) (2001), Karmina (1998), Savage Messiah (2001)

Cyr, Myriam: Frankenstein and Me (1995), Secret of Jerome, The (*Le secret de Jérôme*) (1994)

Cyr, René-Richard: 24 Poses (2002), *Joyeux calvaire* (Poverty and Other Delights) (1997), *Môtel Hélène* (1999), Nuit de noces (Night of the Wedding) (2001), *Temps d'une vie, Le* (The Times of Our Life) (1998)

Czerny, Henry: Almost America (*Come l'America*) (2001), Anchor Zone (1994), Boys of St. Vincent, The (1992), Choices of the Heart: The Margaret Sanger Story (1994), Cold Sweat (1993), External Affairs (1999), Haven (2001), Kayla (1998), Michelle Apartments, The (1995), Promise the Moon (1997), Salem Witch Trials (2001), Trial at Fortitude Bay (1994), When Night Is Falling (1995)

D'Abo, Olivia: Bullies (1986), Flying (1986), Into the Fire (1987)

D'Ailly, Diederik: Lydia (1964)

D'Amour, Mano: *Entre tu et vous* (Between "tu" and "you") (1970)

D'Amour, Normand: *Marguerite Volant* (1996)

D'Amour, Rolland: *Corde au cou, La* (1966), Danger to Society, A (*Danger pour la société*) (1970), Ernie Game, The (1967), *Père Chopin* (1945), Promised Land, The (*Les brûlés*) (1958)

D'Andrea, Anthony: Thrillkill (1984)

D'Angelo, Beverly: Cold Front (1989), Highpoint (1980)

D'Annibale, Carolyn: Cool Sound From Hell, A (The Young and the Beat) (1959)

D'Aquila, Diane: Elizabeth Rex (2003), Maria (1977), Striking Poses (1999)

D'Arbanville, Patti: Hog Wild (1980)

D'Ascenzo, Michael: Khaled (2002)

D'Astous, Michel: *Dernières fougères, Les* (The Last Ferns) (1991)

D'Estée, Mimi: Whispering City (*La forteresse*) (1947)

D'Lyn, Shae: Ghost Mom (1993)

D'Oliveira, Damon: Angel in a Cage (1998), Uncut (1997)

D'Or, Daniel: Battle Queen 2020 (Millennium Queen 2000) (2000)

D'Or, Georges: Now Where Are You? (1969)

D'Orsay, Brooke: Fortune's Sweet Kiss (2002)

D'Orsay, Pam: Now That April's Here (1958)

Da, Guo: *Bethune: The Making of a Hero* (1990) see Bethune (1977)

Daalder, René: Habitat (1995)

Daans, Lara: Darkness Falling (2002)

Dacko, Dean: Three by Paizs (1984)

Daddo, Cameron: Anne of Green Gables: The Continuing Story (1985-1999), Anthrax (2001), Golden Fiddles (1991), Zebra Lounge (2001)

Dafoe, Willem: American Psycho (2000)

Dagenais, Benoît: Party, The (*Party, Le*) (1990)

Dahlie-Goyer, Sandra: Dangerous Dreams (1986)

Daigle, Françoise: Nightmare, The (*Cauchemar*) (1979)

Daigle, Marc: It's a Wonderful Love (*C'est bien beau l'amour*) (1971), Story of the Hunt, The (*Histoire de chasse*) (1990)

Daignault, Eugène: Village Priest, The (*Le curé de village*) (1949)

Daikun, Alex: Starlight (1995)

Dainard, Neil: Becoming Laura (1982), Dawson Patrol, The (1985), Execution of Raymond Graham, The (1985), Fast Company (1979), Incubus (1981), Maintain the Right (1982), Matter of Choice, A (1978), Megantic Outlaw, The (1971), *Riel* (1979), Snowbirds (1981), Welcome to Blood City (1977), When Tomorrow Dies (1965)

Dalcourt, Carole: *Réception, La* (1989)

Dale, Cynthia: At the Midnight Hour (1995), Boy in Blue, The (1986), Heavenly Bodies (1985), My Bloody Valentine (1981)

Dale, Heather: Blood and Donuts (1995), Courage to Love, The (Quadroon Ball) (1999)

Dale, Holly: Blood and Donuts (1995)

Dale, Jennifer: Adjuster, The (1991), Broken Lullaby (1994), Cadillac Girls (1993), First Offender (1987), John Woo's Once a Thief (1997), Grand Larceny (1991), Live Through This (2000), Love and Larceny (1985), Love Come Down (2000), Martha, Ruth and Edie (1987), Midnight Magic (1988), Of Unknown Origin (1983), Suzanne (1980), Revenge of the Land (2000), Separate Vacations (1986), Something About Love (1988), Stone Cold Dead (1979), Ticket to Heaven (1981), Whale Music (1994), Your Ticket Is no Longer Valid (1982)

Dalen, Zale: Expect No Mercy (1995), Hounds of Notre Dame, The (1981), Out of Sight, Out of Mind (The Seventh Circle) (1983), Passion (2001), Skip Tracer (1977), Terminal City Ricochet (1990)

Daley, Sandy: Another Planet (2000)

Dallaire, Marie-Julie: Cosmos (1997)

Dallaire, Siméon: My Uncle Antoine (1971)

Dallesandro, Joe: Beefcake (1999)

Dalmain, Jean: Act of the Heart (1970),

Dalpé, Jean-Marc: Trick or Treat (2001)

Dalpé, Pierre: Cursed (1990)

Dalton, Rita: Sex and the Single Sailor (1967)

Dalton, Timothy: Salt Water Moose (1996)

Dalton, Valda: Matter of Life, A (1971)

Dalton, Walter: Max (1994)

Daly, Timothy: Almost Grown (1987)

Daly, Tom: Royal Journey (1952)

Damberger, Francis: Heart of the Sun (1998), Paris or Somewhere (1995), Rat Tales (1987), Road to Saddle River (1994), Running Brave (1983), Solitaire (1991), Striker's Mountain (1985), Trial by Fire: A North of 60 Mystery

Dame, Marie: City of Champions (1990)

Damude, Brian: Covert Action (1986), I, Maureen (1980), Sudden Fury (1975)

Danan, Ruth: Gun Runner, The (1984)

Dance, Charles: Kabloonak (1994)

Dancoes, Elizabeth: Kingsgate (1989)

Dandurand, Anne: Flower Between the Teeth, The (*La fleur aux dents*) (1976), Song for Julie, A (*Chanson pour Julie*) (1976)

Dane, Lawrence: Acts of Love (series) see: Julia (1980), Bear Island (1979), Case of Libel, A (1985), Clown Murders, The (1976), Cop (Heller) (1981), Find the Lady (1976), Happy Birthday to Me (1981), Head On (Fatal Attraction) (1980), Heatwave Lasted Four Days, The (1973), Heavenly Bodies (1985), Julia (see Acts of Love) (1980), It Seemed Like a Good Idea at the Time (1975), Nothing Personal (1980), Of Unknown Origin (1983), Only God Knows (1974), Park Is Mine, The (1986), Question of the Sixth, A (1981), Red Green's Duct Tape Forever (2002), Rituals (The Creeper) (1977), Running (1979), Scanners (1981), Win, Again! (1998)

Daneau, Normand: Confessional, The (1995)

Danger, Max: Stuff (1999)

Dangerfield, Rodney: My Five Wives (2000)

Daniel, Brittany: On Hostile Ground (2000)

Daniel, Gary: Hawk's Vengeance (1997)

Daniel, Jean-Louis: Mayday (1996)

Daniel, Mary: Connecting Lines (1990)

Daniels, Daniel: Footsteps in the Snow (1966)

Daniels, David: *Palais Royale* (1988)

Daniels, Gary: White Tiger (1995)

Daniels, Harold: Ten Girls Ago (1962)

Daniels, Jeff: Fly Away Home (1996)

Danielson, Shell: Exception to the Rule (1996)

Danis, Louison: *Si belles* (So Pretty) (1994), 24 Poses (2002)

Danish, Ivor: White Road, The (1929)

Danning, Sybil: Julie Darling (1982)

Dansereau, Anne: Music of the Spheres, The (1984)

Dansereau, Bernard: Thetford in the Middle of Our Life (*Thetford au milieu de notre vie*) (1980), *Secret de banlieue, Un* (The Secret of a Suburb) (2002), Sweet Lies and Tender Oaths (*Les doux aveux*) (1982)

Dansereau, Fernand: Clean Hands (*Les mains nettes*) (1958), *Mains nettes, Les* (1957), Mission of Fear (1965), Sweet Lies and Tender Oaths (Les doux aveux) (1982)

Dansereau, Jean: Big Sabotage, The (*Le grand sabordage*) (1973)

Dansereau, Mireille: Deaf to the City (*Le sourd dans la ville*) (1987), Dream Life (*La vie revée*) (1972), *Duo pour une soliste* (Duet for a Soloiste) (1998), Heartbreak (*L'arrache-coeur*) (1979), *J'me Marie, J'me Marie* (1974)

Danson, Ted: Jerry and Tom (1998)

Danza, Tony: Brooklyn State of Mind, A (1997)

Darceuil, Dominic: *Histoire de Pen* (Inside) (2002), Hochelaga (2000), *J'aime, j'aime pas* (1995)

Darceuil, Dominique: Soho (1994)

Darcus, Jack: Deserters (1983), Great Coups of History (1969), Kingsgate (1989), Not Just a Dirty Little Movie (1985), Overnight (1985), Portrait, The (1992) Proxyhawks (1970), Silence (1997), Wolfpen Principle (1974)

Darel, Florence: *La-haut* (2002)

Darios, Louise: *Ribo ou 'le soleil sauvage'* (1978)

Darling, W. Scott: Bush Pilot (1946)

Darnell, Laurie: French Without Dressing (1964)

Darrieux, Danielle: Final Blow, The (The Finishing Stroke) (*Le coup de grâce*) (1965)

Darrow, Henry: Losin' It (1983)

Darrow, Will: Goldenrod (1976)

Darycott, Gary: Terry Fox Story, The (1983)

Das, Nandita: Earth (1998), Fire (1996)

Dassin, Jules: Circle of Two (1980)

Datree, Dan: Long Road Home, The (1988)

Daudelin, Robert: Revolutionaries, The (*Le révolutionnaire*) (1965)

Dugay, Christian: Adrift (1993)

Dave, Ted: Low Self-Esteem Girl (2000)

Davenport, Harry Bromley: Haunting of Julia, The (Full Circle) (1976), Xtro II: The Second Encounter (1991)

Davey, Emma: Eternal Husband, The (1997)

Davi, Robert: Verdict in Blood (2001)

David, Carole: Alias Will James (1988)

David, Clark: Maxwell's Dream (1999)

David, Daniel: Alias Will James (1988)

David, Ellen: Suspicious Minds (1996), Stork Derby, The (2001)

David, Lou: Burning, The (1981)

David, Mario: *Explosion, L'* (The Hideout) (1971)

David, Pierre: Scanner Cop (1994)

David, Stewart Mark: Maxwell's Dream (1999)

David, William: Anthrax (2001)

David, Wilson: Last Straw, The (1987)

Davidovich, Lolita: Blindside (1986), Dead Silence (1997), Four Days (1999), Salt Water Moose (1996), Trial at Fortitude Bay (1994), Touched (1999)

Davidson, William: Ivy League Killers (The Fast Ones) (1959), Lions for Breakfast (1975), Now That April's Here (1958)

Davidtz, Embeth: Mansfield Park (1998)

Davies, Char: Masculine Mystique, The (1984)

Davies, Gary: Deadly Harvest (1980)

Davies, Geraint Wyn: Ambush at Iroquois Pass (1979), Hush Little Baby (Mother of Pearl) (1993), Ghost Mom (1993),Trudeau (2002), Wild Dogs, The (2002)

Davies, Huw: Heaven on Earth (1987)

Davies, Jackson: Dead Wrong (1983)

Davies, Judy Ann: Heatwave Lasted Four Days, The (1973)

Davies, Libby: Stations (1983)

Davies, Sian Leisa: Heaven on Earth (1987)

Davies, William: Guilty, The (2000)

Davignon, Mario: Large Abode, A (1978)

Davis, Audrey: Fatal Memories (The Eileen Franklin Story) (1992)

Davis, Austin: Dying Hard (1978), Rowdyman, The (1972)

Davis, B.J.: LAPD: To Protect and Serve (2001)

Davis, Donald: Agency (1980), Damaged Lives (1933), Final Edition (1982), Man Inside, The (1975), Oedipus Rex (1956), Samuel Lount (1985)

Davis, Dorothy: Apprentice, The (*Fleur bleue*) (1971)

Davis, Eugene: M. Fear X (2003)

Davis, Geena: Fly, The (1986)

Davis, Glenn: John Woo's Once a Thief (1997)

Davis, Jim: Flaming Frontier (1958), Wolf Dog (1958)

Davis, Judy: Me and My Shadows (2000), Naked Lunch (1992), On My Own (1992)

Davis, Kristin: Blacktop (2000)

Davis, Ossie: Here's To Life (The Old Hats) (2000)

Davis, Warren: Drying Up the Streets (1978), Insurance Man From Ingersoll, The (1976)

Davis, William: Murder Most Likely (1999), Perpetrators of the Crime (1999)

Davray, Christine: Erotic Love Games (1971)

Davy, Jean: Story of Dr. Louise, The (1949)

Davy, Vincent: Letter From New France, A (1979)

Dawes, James: Low Self-Esteem Girl (2000)

Dawson, Bruce: Sister Blue (2001)

Dawson, George: Big Meat Eater (1982)

Dawson, Robert: Raffle, The (1994)

Day, Deborah: Expecting (2002)

Day, Gabrielle: In Celebration (1975)

Day, Gordon: Mothers and Daughters (1992)

Day, Larry: Home Team (1999)

Day, Lynda: Don't Forget to Wipe the Blood Off (1966)

Day, Roxanne: Fubar (2002)

Dayan, Josée: Frame-Up Blues (*La danse du scorpion*) (1991)

Daynard, Don: One Night Stand (1978), Porky's (*Chez Porky*) (1981)

Dayne, Taylor: Stag (1997)

De Bankole, Isaach: How to Make Love to a Negro Without Getting Tired (*Comment faire l'amour avec un nègre sans se fatiguer*) (1989)

De Bellefeuille, Daisy: 90 Days (1985)

De Benedictus, Juan: Summer of the Colt (1989)

De Boer, Nikki: Prom, The (1991), Prom Night IV: Deliver Us From Evil (1992)

De Capitani, Grace: *Vents contraires* (Crosswinds) (1995)

De Carlo, Yvonne: It Seemed Like a Good Idea at the Time (1975)

De Grandpre, Frederic: *Nez Rouge* (2003)

De Grossi, Danielle: Sally Marshall Is Not An Alien (1999)

De Jong, Claudine: More to Love (2000)

De Jonge, Marc: Myth That Wouldn't Die (*Dan Seurs du Mozambique, Les*) (1991), Secret of Nandy, The (1991)

De la Fontaine, Agathe: *Louis XIX, le roi des ondes* (1994)

De la Zerda, Mercedes: Punch (2002)

De Alberto, Martino: Special Magnum (Strange Shadows in an Empty Room) (1977)

De Medeiros, Maria: Babel (1999)

De Pencier, Miranda : Myth of the Male Orgasm, The (1993)

De Montalembert, Thibault: *Pornographe, Le* (The Pornographer) (2001)

De Mornay, Rebecca: Never Talk to Strangers (1995), Salem Witch Trials (2001)

De Neck, Didier: *En vacances* (2000)

De Pasquale, Frédéric: *Explosion, L'* (1971)

De Santis, Tony: To Catch a Killer (1991), Way to Meet Single Women, The (1985)

De Varennes, Nana: Apprentice, The (*Fleur bleue*) (1971), My Childhood in Montréal (*Mon enfance à Montréal*) (1971), Promised Land, The (1958)

De Veillers, John: Ascent, The (1994)

De Villers, Édith: Over My Head (1964)

De Vries, Bert: Saturday's Passage (1969)

De Wiel, Alexa: August and July (1973)

De Witt, Jack: Neptune Factor, The (1973)

De Zilva, Karen: Tribe of Joseph (2001)

Deacon, Timothy: Lion of Oz (2000)

Deakin, Freddie: Sex and the Lonely Woman (1966)

Dean, Alan: Crowd Inside, The (1971)

Rubes, Anthony Dean: Amityville Curse, The (1990)

Dean, Jason: Canada's Sweetheart: The Saga of Hal C. Banks (1985)

Dean, Loren: War Bride, The (2001)

Dean, Malcolm: Christopher's Movie Matinée (1969)

Deban, Frédéric: *Babylone* (Halfway House) (1991)

Debassige, Dianne: Harry's Case (2000)

DeBlois, Germain: Taureau (1972)

DeBoer, Nichole: Public Domain (2003)

DeBoer, Nicole: Cube (1997)

DeBoy, Paul: Doulike2Watch.Com (2002)

DeCarlo, Michael: Hemingway vs Callaghan (2003), Washed Up (2002)

Decosta, Alex: Cornered (Corner, The) (2001)

Dee, Ruby: Captive Heart: The James Mink Story (1996)

Defalco, Martin: Cold Journey (1976)

DeFelice, James: Why Shoot the Teacher (1977)

Degryse, Marc: Québec Operation Lambda (1985)

Deguise, Paulette: Immortal Scoundrel, The (1952)

Dehner, John: Canadians, The (1961), Nothing Personal (1980)

Deitch, Donna: Change of Place, A (1994)

Del Grande, Louis: Atlantic City, U.S.A (1980), Buried on Sunday (1993), Happy Birthday to Me (1981), Home to Stay (1978), Monkeys in the Attic (1974), Of Unknown Origin (1983), Sanity Clause (1990), Second Wind (1976), Scanners (1981)

Del Mar, Maria: Eclipse (1994)

Delacroix, René: Grand Bill, The (*Le gros Bill*) (1949), Mother's Heart, A (1953), Notre-Dame of the Mouise (*Notre-Dame de la Mouise*) (1941), Nightingales and the Bells (*Le rossignol et les cloches*) (1952), Tit-Coq (1953), Story of Dr. Louise, The (Docteur Louise) (1949)

Delaney, Kim: Closer and Closer (1996)

Delaney, Dana: Choices of the Heart: The Margaret Sanger Story (1994), Fly Away Home (1996)

Delaney, Paul: *Deux super-dingues* (Heaven Help Us) (1982)

DeLaurentis, Suzanne: Evil Judgement (1984), Junior (1985)

Delbat, Germaine: Old Country Where Rimbaud Died, The (1977)

Delisle, François: Ruth (1994), Two Actresses (*Deux actrices*) (1993)

Dell, Howard: Beyond Suspicion (1993)

Dell, Rita: Lost Words (1993)

Delmont, Édouard: Notre-Dame of the Mouise (*Notre-Dame de la Mouise*) (1941)

Deloir, Geneviève: Crowd Inside, The (1971), Red (1969)

Delorme, Gilles Philippe: Battle of St. Denis... Yesterday, Today, The (1969)

Delorme, Verlus: Royal Bonbon (2002)

Delpy, Julie: Thousand Wonders of the Universe, The (1997)

Deltour, Valérie: Chocolate Eclair (1979)

Deluc, Xavier: Other Side of the Law (1994)

Delvecchio, Alexis: *Incompris, L'* (1997)

Delver, Marya: Better Than Chocolate (1999), Here's To Life (The Old Hats) (2000), Waydowntown (2000)

Demer, France: Confidences of the Night (*L'amour blessé*) (1975)

Demers, Claude: Invention of Love, The (2000)

Demers, Gloria: Company of Strangers, The (Strangers in Good Company) (1990)

Demers, Kristine: Strange Blues of Cowboy Red, The (1995)

Demers, Rock: Hathi (1998), *Maria Chapdelaine* (1983), Reach for the Sky (*La championne*) (1991)

Demers, Stéphane: Cyberjack (2003), *Enfant des appalaches, L'* (The Appalachian Child) (1998), Left-hand Side of the Fridge, The (2000), *Loi du cochon, La* (The Pig's Law) (2001), Love Me (1991), *Siamoises, Les* (The Siamese Twins) (1999), Orphan Muses, The (*Les muses orphelines*) (2000)

Demetrios, Demetri: Mother's Meat, Freud's Flesh (1984)

Demongeot, Mylène: By the Blood of Others (*Par le sang des autres*) (1974), Enuff is Enuff (*J'ai mon voyage!*) (1973), *Explosion, L'* (The Hideout) (1971), Rebels 1837, The (*Quelques arpents de neige*) (1972)

Demons, Jeanne: Mother's Heart, A (1953)

Dempsey, Patrick: Meatballs, Part III: The Climax (1987)

Dempster, Gary: Siege (1983)

Demtchev, Kliment: *Sonatine* (1984)

Demy, Jacques: Louisiana (1993)

Dench, Judi: Luther (1973), Shipping News, The (2001)

Deneuve, Catherine: Nearest to Heaven (*Au plus près du paradis*) (2002), *Nous deux, À* (An Adventure for Two) (1979), *Paroles et musique* (Love Songs) (1985)

Denis, Joël: No Holiday for Idols (*Pas de vacances pour les idoles*) (1965)

Denker, Henry: Case of Libel, A (1985)

Dennehy, Brian: Diamond Fleece, The (1992), Never Cry Wolf (1983), To Catch a Killer (1991)

Denner, Charles: YUL 871 (Montréal Flight 871) (1966), Reno and the Doc (1984), Screwball Academy (Divine Light) (Loose Ends) (1986)

Dennis, Charles: Covergirl (1984), Great Goose Caper, The (2003), Reno and the Doc (1984), Screwball Academy (1986)

Dennis, Everett: Naked Flame, The (1964)

Dennis, Gill: On My Own (1992)

Dennis, Laddie: Sunday in the Country (1975)

Dennis, Oliver: Cockroach That Ate Cincinnati, The (1996)

Dennis, Sandy: That Cold Day in the Park (1969)

Dénommé, Maxime: Trick or Treat (2001)

Denoncourt, Serge: *Pays dans la gorge, Le* (The Country on Your Chest) (1999)

Denos, John: Only Thing You Know, The (1971)

Densham, Pen: Kiss, The (1988)

Denton, Christa: Gate, The (1987)

DePahk, Stephen: Roses in December (1965)

Depardieu, Gerard: Between Strangers (2002), Wanted (Crime Spree) (2003)

DePencier, Miranda: Kurt Vonnegut's Harrison Bergeron (2000)

DePoe, Norman: Dying Hard (1978)

Deragon, Lynne: Khaled (2002)

Derbas, Michael: Mindstorm (2001)

Derek, Bo: Life in the Balance (2001)

Deret, Jean-Claude: Aurora Borealis (*Une aurore boréale*) (1981)

Dermer, Robert: Acts of Love (Love) (The Black Cat in the Black Mouse Socks) (1980)

Dern, Bruce: Harry Tracy, Desperado (1981), Middle-Age Crazy (1980)

Derricks, Clevant: World Traveler (2001)

Des Barres, Michael: Poison (Tease) (1999)

Des Roches, Robert: True Nature of Bernadette, The (*La vraie nature de Bernadette*) (1972)

Desager, Frederic: *Silence nous guette, Le* (2002)

Desai, Gopi: My Little Devil (2000)

DeSantis, Carl: Never Trust an Honest Thief (Going for Broke) (1979)

DeSanto, Anthony: Whole Shebang, The (2001)

DeSanto, Daniel: Brown Bread Sandwiches (1990)

Desbarats, Peter: Don't Let the Angels Fall (1969)

Desbiens, Maxime: Tale of Teeka, The (1999)

Deschamps, Yvon: *Délivrez-nous du mal* (Deliver Us From Evil) (1967), Little One Is Coming Soon, The (1972), Sun Rises Late, The (*Le soleil se lève en retard*) (1977), What the Hell Are They Complaining About?) (Hold on, Papa!) (1971)

Deschanel, Victoria: Girl King (2002), Horsey (1997)

Deschenes, Josée: *Secret de banlieue, Un* (The Secret of a Suburb) (2002)

DeSeta, William: Perfect Timing (1984)

Desfonds, Robert: Gobital (1975)

Desgagné, Martin: Full Blast (*L'ennemi*) (1999)

Desgagnés, Yves: Nylon Heart, A (*Coeur de nylon*) (1989), Why Is the Strange Mr. Zolock So Interested in Comic Strips? (*Pourquoi l'étrange Monsieur Zolock s'intéressait-il tant à la bande dessinée*) (1983)

Desiderio, Robert: Silence of Adultery, The (1995)

Désilets, Geneviève: Children of my Heart (2000), *Île de Sable, L'* (1999)

Desjardins, Camille: Long Live France (1970)

Desjardins, Daniel: Marie's Sons (*Les fils de Marie*) (2002)

Desjardins, Gilles: *Bilan* (2003), *Île de Sable, L'* (1999), *Madame Brouette* (2002), Orphan Muses, The (*Les muses orphelines*) (2000), *Pots cassés, Les* (Broken Dishes) (1994), Shabbat Shalom (1994)

Desjardins, Jacques: Clean Machine, The (*Tirelire, combines & cie*) (1992)

Desjardins, Jasmine: Why Is the Strange Mr. Zolock So Interested in Comic Strips?

Desjardins, Julie: Just a Game (1983)

Desjardins, Liette: *Soleil des autres, Le* (The Sun of the Others) (Give Us Our Daily Love) (1979)

Desjardins, Normand: *Fabuleux voyage de l'ange, Le* (The Fabulous Voyage of the Angel) (1991)

Desjarlais, France: *Dernière condition, La* (1982)

Deslières, Louise: *Pots cassés, Les* (Broken Dishes) (1994)

Desmarais, James J.: Urban Safari (1995)

Desmarestz, Erick: *Bob Million: Le jackpot de la planète* (1997)

Desmarteaux, Paul: Little Aurore's Tragedy (*La petite Aurore, l'enfant martyre*) (1952)

Desmond, Patrick: Ivy League Killers Ones) (1959)

Despatie, Félix-Antoine: *Mystérieuse Mademoiselle C, La* (2001)

Despres, Terry-David: Siege (1983)

Desprez, Jean: *Père Chopin* (1945)

Desramrant, Réjane: Matter of Life, A (1971)

Desrameaux, Réjane: Dust from Underground (*Poussière sur la ville*) (1965)

DesRochers, Alain: *Bouteille, La* (The Bottle) (2000)

Desrochers, Clémence: *Valérie* (1969)

Desrochers, Gilles: Isis From the 8th Rang (1972)

Desrochers, Marie-France: Laure Ga Remarkable Woman (1983)

Desrochers, Pascale: *Crabe dans la tête, Un* (A Crab in My Head) (2001)

DesRoches, Robert: If You Could See What I Hear (1982), Men, The (1971), Paths of the World, The (*Les allées de la terre*) (1973), Sensations (1973), Terry Fox Story, The (1983)

Desrosiers, Jacques: It's Not Jacques Cartier's Fault (1968)

Desrosiers, Robert: Few Days More, A (*De jour en jour*) (1981), Sleep Walkers, The (*Les somnambules*) (1986), YUL 871 (1966)

Desrosiers, Sylvie: *Nez Rouge* (Red Nose) (2003)

Dessaint, Pyrrhus: Little Man Abroad, A (1989)

Dessalles, Gérard: *Ils sont nus* (1966)

Désy, Victor: Dust from Underground (*Poussière sur la ville*) (1965), *Tout prendre, À* (Take It All) (1963)

Detmers, Maruschka: Armen and Bullik (1993)

Detweiler, Craig: Duke, The (1999)

Detwiler, John: Downtime (2001), Year of the Sheep (1997)

Deuters, Kent: Screwballs (1983)

Devaivre, Jean: Unknown From Montréal, The (*Son copain*) (1950)

Devane, William: Exception to the Rule (1996)

Deveau, Alan: Screwballs (1983), Screwballs II: Loose Screws (1985)

Deverell, William: Mind Field (1989), Shellgame (1986)

Devigne, Pascale: Two Thousand and None (2000)

Devine, Aidan: 100 Days in the Jungle (2002), Arrow, The (1997), Joe's Wedding (1996), Net Worth (1997), Scar Tissue (2002), Striking Poses (1999), Trudeau (2002)

Devine, Brenda: Random Passage (2001)

Devine, D'Arcy: Plastic Mile, The (1969)

Devine, Michael: It's Not Jacques Cartier's Fault (1968)

Devine, Sean: Perpetrators of the Crime (1999), Rendering, The (2002), Xchange (2000)

Devitt, Bert: Wings in the Wilderness (1975)

Devlin, Bernard: Promised Land, The (1958)

Devries, Marion: Johnny Greyeyes (2001)

Dew, Edward: Wings of Chance (1961)

DeWet, Danielle: Echo Lake (2000)

Dewey, Diane: U-Turn (The Girl in Blue) (1973)

Dewey, Rebecca: Man Who Guards the Greenhouse, The (1988)

Dewhurst, Colleen: Anne of Green Gables (1985), Anne of Green Gables: The Continuing Story (Series) (1985-1999), Dead Zone, The (1983), Final Assignment (1980), Hitting Home (Obsessed) (1989), Lantern Hill (1990), Mary and Joseph: A Story of Faith (1979), Sword of Gideon (1986), Termini Station (1990), Third Walker, The (1980), Tribute (1980)

DeWilde, Philip: Turning Paige (2002)

Dewolf, Patrick: *Mémoire tronquée* (1990)

Deyell, Jennifer: Love That Boy (2002)

INDEX: DIRECTORS, SCRIPTWRITERS & ACTORS

Doering, Rick: Eddie and the Cruisers Part II: Eddie Lives! (1989)

Doerksen, Kevin: Hell Bent (1994)

Dognini, Liana: Morvern Callar (2002)

Doherty, Denny: Hurt Penguins (1992)

Doherty, Shannen: Another Day (2001), Striking Poses (1999), Rendering, The (2002)

Dohm, Anthony: Barnone (1997)

Doig, Lexa: No Alibi (2000)

Dolenz, Ami: Witchboard II (1993)

Dolin, John: Joe's Wedding (1996)

Dombasle, Arielle: *J'en suis* (1997), Lola Zipper (1991)

Dominic, Henry: Watchers II (1990)

Dominique, Cabrera: *Folle embellie* (2003)

Dompierre, Serge: Large Abode, A (1978)

Donahue, Troy: Seizure (Tango Macabre) (1974)

Donald, Martin: Never Too Late (1996)

Donaldson, Lesleh: Ambush at Iroquois Pass (1979), Curtains (1983), Funeral Home (Cries in the Night) (1982), Undergrads, The (1985)

Donaldson, Peter: Deeply (2000), Funeral Home (Cries in the Night) (1982), Homecoming, The (1978), Long Day's Journey Into Night (1996), Undergrads, The (1985)

Donat, Peter: Bay Boy, The (1984), Highpoint (1980), Honeymoon (1985), Mazes and Monsters (1982)

Donat, Richard: City on Fire (1979), Draw! (1984), Gas (1981), Hank (1977), Maintain the Right (1982), Mary Silliman's War (1994), My American Cousin (1985), Net Worth (1997), Out of Sight, Out of Mind (The Seventh Circle) (1983), Pit Pony (1998), Samuel Lount (1985), Suicide Murders, The (1986), Tomorrow Never Comes (1978)

Donato, Christine: Too Much Sex (1999)

Donato, Marc: Blue Butterfly, The (2003)

Donatro, Mart: Harmoney (1999)

Donbrath-Zinga, Chrystal:

Donato, Marc: Blue Butterfly, The (2003)

Donatro, Mart: Harmoney (1999)

Donbrath-Zinga, Chrystal: Girl King (2002)

Doncheff, Len: Cop (Heller) (1981), Explosion (1969), Final Assignment (1980), High-Ballin' (1978), Intruder, The (1981), One Night Stand (1978), Strange Brew (1983)

Donkin, Eric: Agency (1980)

Donnadieu, Bernard-Pierre: Agaguk (Shadow of the Wolf) (1993), Caboose (1996)

Donohoe, Amanda: Real Howard Spitz, The (1998)

Donohue, Brenda: Me (1974), Mourning Suit, The (1976), Plague, The (1979), *Riel* (1979)

Donovan, Martin: Desire (2000)

Donovan, Paul: Buried on Sunday (1993), Caribe (1988), Defcon 4 (1984), George's Island (1989), Life With Billy (1993), Paint Cans (1994), Siege (1983), South Pacific, 1942 (1981), Squamish Five, The (1988), Switch in Time, A (1987)

Doohan, Anita: Whispers (1990)

Doohan, James: Duke, The (1999)

Dooley, Brian: Boys of St. Vincent, The (1992), Kayla (1998)

Dooley, Paul: Strange Brew (1983)

Doone, Holly: Lift, The (1965)

Doré, Peter: Day in a Life, A (1999)

Dorff, Matt: Choices of the Heart: The Margaret Sanger Story (1994), Closer and Closer (1996)

Dorff, Stephen: Gate, The (1987), Steal (2002)

Dorfman, Andrea: Love That Boy (2002), Parsley Days (2000)

Jacques Dorfmann: *Vercingétorix* (2001)

Dorion, Alphonse: Cold Journey (1976)

Dorn, Rudi: Dulcima (1970), Take Her by Surprise (1967)

Dorner, Françoise: Black Mirror (1981)

Dorsey, Joshua: Here Am I (1999)

Dorval, Adrien: 100 Days in the Jungle (2002)

Dorval, Anne: *Enfant des appalaches, L'* (1998), Montréal Sextet (1991)

Dory, René: Unknown From Montréal, The (1950)

Dos, Thierno Ndiaye: Karmen Gei (2001)

Dotan, Shimon: Coyote Run (1996), You Can Thank Me Later (1998), Warriors (1994)

Doucet, Paul: *Erreur sur la personne* (1995)

Doucette, Lionel: Secret of Jerome, The (1994)

Douglas, James B.: All in Good Taste (1983), American Christmas Carol, An (1979), Bedroom Eyes (1984), Boy in Blue, The (1986), Drylanders (1963), Escape from Iran: The Canadian Caper (1981), Hot Touch (*Coup de maître*) (1982), Intruder, The (1981), Million Dollar Babies (1995), Moving Targets (1983), Murder by Phone (1982)

Douglas, Jeff: Touch and Go (2002)

Douglas, Kirk: Draw! (1984)

Douglas, Melvyn: Changeling, The (1980), Hot Touch (*Coup de maître*) (1982)

Douglas, Michael: Running (1979)

Douglas, Mike: Birds of Prey (1985)

Douglas, Sarah: Meatballs, Part IV (1992)

Douglas, Shirley: Dead Ringers (1988), Forbidden Journey (1950), Law of Enclosures, The (2000), Maintain the Right (1982), Screwball Academy (1986), Shadow Lake (2000), Turning to Stone (1986), Wars, The (1983), Wind at My Back (2001), Woman Wanted (1999)

Douglas, Susan: Face Off (1971), Forbidden Journey (1950), Outside Chance of Maximillian Glick, The (1988)

Dourif, Brad: Chain Dance (Common Bonds) (1991), Scream of Stone (*Terro Torra*) (1991)

Dow, J. Donald: Isabel (1968)

Dowd, Nancy: For Life (see Acts of Love Series) (1980)

Dowker, Roger: Christopher's Movie Matinée (1969)

Dowler, Andrew: 2103: The Deadly Wake (1996)

Dowler, John: Cyberteens in Love (1994)

Down, Alisen: Bad Money (1999)

Down, Lesley-Anne: Death Wish V: The Face of Death (1994)

Downey, Brian: George's Island (1989)

Downing, James: Probable Cause (Sleepless) (1994)

Downing, Jeannette: Immortal Scoundrel, The (*Étienne Brûlé, gibier de potence*) (1952)

Downs, Kyle: My Dog Vincent (1997)

Doyen, Jean: Snow Has Melted on the Manicouagan, The (*La neige a fondu sur la Manicouagan*) (1965)

Doyle, John W.: Extraordinary Visitor (1998)

Doyle, Judith: Wasaga (1994)

Doyle, Martin: Hog Wild (*Les fous de la moto*) (1980)

Doyle, Rosemary: More to Love (2000)

Doyle, Shawn: Babyface (1998), Justice (1998), Killing Spring, A (2001), Scar Tissue (2002), Stiletto Dance (2000), Verdict in Blood (2001)

Doyon, Bruno: Morning Man, The (1986)

Doyon, Jean: 90 jours, Les (90 Days) (1959)

Dr. John: Candy Mountain (1987)

Drabinsky, Garth: Draw! (1984)

Drach, Michel: Run for it, Lola! (*Sauve-toi, Lola*) (1986)

Dragone, Franco: *Alégria* (1998)

Dragu, Margaret: The Black Cat in the Black Mouse Socks (see Acts of Love) (1980), Surfacing (1981)

Drainie, John: Incredible Journey, The (1963), Now That April's Here (1958)

Drainville, Martin: Angelo, Fredo and Roméo (1996), Ideal Man, The (*L'homme idéal*) (1996), *Laura Cadieux, la Suite* (2000), *Louis XIX, le roi des ondes* (1994), Million Dollar Babies (1995), *Odyssée d'Alice Tremblay, L'* (2002)

Drake, Dolores: M.V.P. 2: Most Valuable Primate (2001)

Drake, T.Y.: Keeper, The (1975), Terror Train (1980)

Drakeford, Deborah: Cockroach That Ate Cincinnati, The (1996), Man in the Attic, The (1994)

Drapeau, Joël: Duplessis' Orphans (1999)

Drapeau, Sylvie: *15 février 1839* (February 15, 1839) (2001), *Piège d'Issoudun, Le* (Trapped in Issoudun) (2002), Sex Among the Stars (*Le sexe des étoiles*) (1993), Sphinx, The (1995), *Temps d'une vie, Le* (The Times of Our Life)

(1998), Three Madeleines, The (*Les fantômes des trois Madeleines* (1999)

Drapeau-Dalpé, Joel: Winter Stories (1999)

Draper, Courtnee: Duke, The (1999)

Dray, Albert: Wanted (Crime Spree) (2003)

Dreskin, Paul: Ride, The (2000)

Drew, Roland: From Nine to Nine (1936)

Drewitz, Devin Douglas: M.V.P. 3 (2003), Ms. Bear (1999)

Dreyfuss, Jean-Claude: Coyote (1993)

Dreyfuss, Richard: Apprenticeship of Duddy Kravitz, The (1974)

Driscoll, Kathy: Three by Paizs (1984)

Driver, Minnie: Owning Mahowny (2001)

Drolet, Christiane: *Le manuscrit érotique* (2002)

Dron, Dorin: *Deux amis silencieux* (Dogs to the Rescue) (Two Silent Friends) (1969)

Drouin, Denis: Apple, the Stem and the Seeds, The (*La pomme, la queue et les pépins*) (1974), *Aventures d'une jeune veuve, Les* (1974), Far From You Sweetheart (*Juis suis loin de toi mignonne*) (1976), J.A. Martin, Photographer (*J.A. Martin, photographe*) (1977), Let's Talk About Love (*Parlez-nous d'amour*) (1976), Little One Is Coming Soon, The (*Le p'tit vient vite*) (1972), OK Liberty (*Ok…Laliberté*) (1973), Once Upon a Time in the East (*Il était une fois dans l'est*) (1974), Push but Push Reasonably (*Scarlatina*) (*Pousse mais pousse égal*) (1975), Straight to the Heart (*Jusqu'au coeur*) (1969), Swindle, The (*La gammick*) (1974), Taureau (1972), Where Two Roads Cross (Between Two Loves) (*À la croisée des chemins*) (*Entre deux amours*) (1943), Woman Inflamed, A (*Tout feu, tout femme*) (1975), Village Priest, The (1949)

Drouin, Lucille: Thetford in the Middle of Our Life (*Thetford au milieu de notre vie*) (1980)

Drouin, Patrice: Guitar (*Guitare*) (1974)

Druxman, Michael: Battle Queen 2020 (Millennium Queen 2000) (2000)

Dryden, Rosy Frier: Legal Memory (1992)

Dubarry, Denise: KGB: The Secret War (1984)

Dubé, Hugo: October (*Octobre*) (1994), Silencing the Guns (*Le silence des fusils*) (1996)

Dubé, Marcel: Beautiful Sundays (*Les beaux dimanches*) (1974), Between Sweet and Salt Water (Drifting Downstream) (*Entre la mer et l'eau douce*) (1967), *Naufragés du Labrador, Les* (Stranded in Labrador) (1991)

Dubé, Philippe: Wow (1970)

Dubois, André: *Aventures d'une jeune veuve, Les* (1974), IXE-13 (1972)

Dubois, Denise: It's Your Turn, Laura Cadieux (1998), *Laura Cadieux, la Suite* (2000)

Dubois, Marie: *Ménace, La* (1977)

Dubois, Patrice: *Embrasse-moi, c'est pour la vie* (1994), *J'aime, j'aime pas* (1995)

Dubois, Rene-Daniel: *Neg', Le* (2002)

Dubois, Virginie: *Morte amoureuse, La* (1997)

Dubos, Jean: Lies My Father Told Me (1975), My Uncle Antoine (1971)

Dubrowolska, Gosia: Careful (1992)

Dubuc, Yvan: Sky's the Limit, The (1986)

Duceppe, Jean: Act of the Heart (1970), Alien Thunder (Dan Candy's Law) (1973), Beautiful Sundays (*Les, beaux dimanches*) (1974), Bingo (1974), *Corde au cou, La* (1966), Doves, The (*Les colombes*) (1972), I Love You (*Je t'aime*) (1974), *Lucien Brouillard* (1983), My Uncle Antoine (1971), *Tit-Coq* (1953), Trouble Makers (*Trouble-fête*) (1964), YUL 871 (Montréal Flight 871) (1966), Vultures, The (1975)

Duceppe, Pierre: I Love You (*Je t'aime*) (1974)

Ducharme, Anne-Marie: Beautiful Facade, A (*La belle apparence*) (1979), Bernie and the Gang (*Ti-mine Bernie pis la gang*) (1977), Good Riddance (*Les bons débarras*) (1980), Head of Normande St. Onge, The (1975)

Ducharme, Camille: *Corde au cou, La* (1966), *Esprit du mal, L'* (Spirit of Evil, The) (1954), Promised Land, The (*Les brûlés*) (1958), Trouble Makers (*Trouble-fête*) (1964), Village Priest, The (*Le curé de village*) (1949)

Ducharme, Paule: Encircled Colour, The (*La couleur encerclée*) (1986)

Ducharme, Réjean: Good Riddance (1980), Happy Memories (*Les beaux souvenirs*) (1981)

Ducharme, Yvan: There's Always a Way to Get There (1973)

Ducharme, Yvon: *Valérie* (1969)

Duchene, Deborah: Perfectly Normal (1990)

Duchovny, David: Julia Has Two Lovers (1990)

Ducommun, Rick: M.V.P.: Most Valuable Primate (2000)

Dudarev, Natasha: Tragic Diary of Zero, the Fool, The (1970)

Dudikoff, Michael: Bounty Hunters (1996), Cyberjack (1995), In Her Defense (1998), Silencer, The (1999)

Duez, Sophie: Kazan (1994)

Dufault, Christian: Mother's Meat, Freud's Flesh (1984)

Dufaux, Georges: It's Not Jacques Cartier's Fault (1968)

Dufaux, Guy: Eleventh Child, The (1998)

Duff, Howard: Double Negative (Deadly Companion) (1979)

Duffy, Jack: Blackheart (1997), Nothing Personal (1980), Silent Partner, The (1978), Title Shot (1980), Whodunit (1986)

Duffy, Karen: Memory Run (1995)

Dufour, Marie-Claude: Elvis Gratton (1985)

Dufour, Yvon: Beautiful Sundays (*Les beaux dimanches*) (1974), Cain (1965), Coffin Affair, The (*L'affaire Coffin*) (1980), Day in a Taxi, A (1982), King Solomon's Treasure (1979), Lucky Star, The (1980), Red (1969)

Dufourd, Catherine: Letter From New France, A (1979)

Dufresne, Félix Pierre: Promised Land, The (*Les brûlés*) (1958)

Dufresne, Guy: Brother André (*Le frère André*) (1987), Court-Circuit (1983), December (1978), Over My Head (*Jusqu'au cou*) (1964)

Dufresne, Liz: Tuesday, Wednesday (1987)

Dufresne, Nicolas: Before the Time Comes (*Le temps de l'avant*) (1975)

Dufresne, Pierre: And I Love You Dearly (*La maîtresse*) (1973), For Better, for Worse (*Pour le meilleur et pour le pire*) (1975), Straight to the Heart (*Jusqu'au coeur*) (1969), Those Damned Savages (*Les maudits sauvages*) (1971), Time of the Hunt, The (1972)

Dugas, Jean-Paul: Mother's Heart, A (1953)

Duggan, M. Bruce: Smoked Lizard Lips (1991)

Dugowson, Maurice: Goodbye, See You Monday (*Au revoir, à lundi*) (1979)

Duguay, Christian: Art of War, The (2000), Adrift (1993), Hitler: The Rise of Evil (2003), Joan of Arc (1999), Million Dollar Babies (1995), Scanners II: The New Order (1991), Scanners III: The Takeover (1992), Screamers (1995)

Duguay, Raoul: *Mon oeil* (My Eye) (1971), My Friend Pierrette (1969), O or the Invisible Infant(1971), Q-bec My Love (1970)

Duhaney, Kevin: Treed Murray (2001)

Dukakis, Olympia: Digger (1993), Event, The

Duke, Daryl: Fatal Memories (The Eileen Franklin Story) (1992), Hard Feelings (1981), I Heard the Owl Call My Name (1973), Shadow of the Hawk (1976), Silent Partner, The (1978)

Duke, Patty: Family of Strangers (1993)

Dukes, David: Handmaid's Tale, The (1990)

Dull, Bill: Day Breaks Once More (1995)

Dullea, Keir: Black Christmas (1974), Haunting of Julia, The (Full Circle) (1976), Leopard in the Snow (1978), Paperback Hero (1973), Welcome to Blood City (1977), Oh, What a Night (1992)

Dumas, Carmel: Don't Forget (*Je me souviens*) (1979), Medium Blues (1985), Story of the Three, A (*L'histoire des trois*) (1989)

Dummett, Greg: Giant Steps (1992)

Dumont, Martin: Last Glacier, The (1984)

Dumont, Michel: 24 Poses (2002), Cargo (1990), Homme de rêve, L' (The Dream Man) (1991)

Dumont, Mireille: Eternal Husband, The (1997)

Dumontier, Maxime: Mystérieuse Mademoiselle C, La (2001)

Dunaway, Faye: Handmaid's Tale, The (1990)

Dunbar, Adrian: Triggermen (2000)

Dunbar, David: Spreading Ground, The (2000)

Duncan, Glenn: SnakeEater III: The Revenge (1992)

Duncan, Kenneth: From Nine to Nine (1936)

Duncan, Lindsay: Mansfield Park (1998)

Duncan, Renée: Downtime (2001), Year of the Sheep (1997)

Dunlop, Darcy: Maxwell's Dream (1999)

Dunlop, Megan: Goldirocks (2003), Parsley Days (2000)

Dunn, Barrie: No Apologies (1990)

Dunn, Carolyn: Breaking All the Rules (1985), Thick As Thieves (1990)

Dunn, Conrad: Harry's Case (2000)

Dunne, Robin: Borderline Normal (2000), Circle, The (The Fraternity) (2001), Class Warfare 2001 (2000), Colder Kind of Death, A (2000), Hemingway vs Callaghan (2003), Jewel (2000), Snow Walker, The (2002), Wandering Soul Murders, The (2000)

Dunn-Hill, John: Because Why (Parce que pourquoi) (1993), Legends of the North (1996)

Dunning, John: Possession of Virginia, The (Le diable est parmi nous) (1972), SnakeEater (1990), SnakeEater II: The Drug Buster (1990), SnakeEater III: The Revenge (1992), Yesterday 1981)

Dunnison, James: Stuff (1999)

Dunnision, Rebecca: Stuff (1999)

Dunsaith, Virginia: Sweet Substitute (1964)

Dunsmore, Rosemary: Blind Faith (1982), Dancing in the Dark (1986)

Dunst, Kirsten: Deeply (2000), Strike! (1998)

Duparc, Marguerite: Réjeanne Padovani (1973)

Dupire, Serge: Alley Cat, The (Le matou) (1985), Automne sauvage, L' (The Savage Autumn) (1992), Ciel sur la tête, Le (On Your Head) (2001), Concièrgerie, La (The Caretaker's Lodge) (The Prison) (1997), Crime of Ovide Plouffe, The (Le crime d'Ovide Plouffe) (Les Plouffe, II) (1984), Meurtre en musique (1994), Trois femmes, un amour (Three Women in Love) (1994), Woman in Transit, A (La femme de l'hôtel) (1984),

Duprez, June: One Plus One (The Kinsey Report) (Exploring the Kinsey Report) (1961)

Dupuis, Fabien: Même sang, Un (The Same Blood) (1994)

Dupuis, Matthew: Forteresse suspendue, La (The Hidden Fortress) (2001), Relative Fear (1994)

Dupuis, Paul: Immortal Scoundrel, The (Étienne Brûlé, gibier de potence) (1952), Tit-Coq (1953), Unknown From Montréal, The (Son copain) (1950), Whispering City (La forteresse) (1947)

Dupuis, Pierre: Dust from Underground (Poussière sur la ville) (1965)

Dupuis, Roy: Being at Home With Claude (1992), Cap Tourmente (Cape Torment) (1993), Chili's Blues (C'était le 12 du 12 et Chili avait les Blues) (1994), Dark Harbour (1997), Ideal Man, The (L'homme idéal) (1996), J'en suis (1997), Last Chapter (Biker Wars) (2002), Million Dollar Babies (1995), Screamers (1995), Passage des hommes libres (Passage of Free Men) (1996), Waiting for Michelangelo (1995), Séraphin (Heart of Stone) (A Man and His Sin) (2002)

Duquesne, Albert: Lights of My City (1950)

Duquet, Michèle: Khaled (2002)

Duquet, Michelle: Say Nothing (2001)

Durand, Claude: Final Blow, The (The Finishing Stroke) (Le coup de grâce) (1965)

Durand, Luc: The Seat of the Soul (A Crisis of Conscience) (Siège de l'âme, Le) (1997)

Durand, Pierre: Père Chopin (1945)

Duré, Frédéric: I Have the Right to Pleasure (J'ai droit au plaisir) (1975)

Durning, Charles: Jerry and Tom (1998), Lakeboat (2000), LAPD: To Protect and Serve (2001), Secret Life of Algernon, The (1996)

Dussault, J.-Yves: Celebrations, The (1979)

Dussault, Louisette: Big Day, The (Le grand day) (1988), Dernier havre, Le (1986), Dust from Underground (Poussière sur la ville) (1965), Incompris, L' (1997), Laure Gaudreault: A Remarkable Woman (1983), Secret de banlieue, Un (2002), (Le silence des fusils) (1996)

Duta, George: Excalibur Kid, The (1998)

Dutan, Mathieu: Another Planet (2000)

Dutil, Murielle: Revoir Julie (See Julie Again) (Julie and Me) (1998), Salut, Victor! (1988)

Dutrizac, Benoît: Concièrgerie, La (The Caretaker's Lodge) (The Prison) (1997)

Dutronc, Jacques: Nous deux, À (1979)

Dutton, Timothy: Hard to Forget (1998

Duval, Frédéric: Mule and the Emeralds, The (1995), Ride Me (Ego Trip) (1995)

Duval, Janice: Pleasure Palace (Angela) (1973)

Duval, Jean-Philippe: Enfant des appalaches, L' (The Appalachian Child) (1998), Matroni and Me (1999), Soho (1994)

Duvall, Robert: Handmaid's Tale, The (1990), Terry Fox Story, The (1983)

Duvall, Shelley: Twilight of the Ice Nymphs (1997)

Duzil, Rose-Rey: Rebels 1837, The (1972)

Dvorska, Milena: Last Act of Martin Weston, The (1971)

Dvorsky, Peter: Harvest (1981), Rough Justice (1984), Videodrome (1983)

Dwyer, Karyn: Yellow Wedding (1998)

Dyer, Sharon: Never Trust an Honest Thief (Going for Broke) (1979)

Dykstra, Ted: Black Swan (2002), Boy in Blue, The (1986), Giant Steps (1992)

Dyson, Michael: Reasonable Force (1983)

Dzeguze, Kaspers: Crimes of the Future (1970)

Dziki, Waldemar: Young Magician, The (1987)

Dzundza, George: Execution of Raymond Graham, The (1985)

Eames, David: By Design (1981)

Earle, Christopher: Gentle Sinners (1984)

Easley, Richert: Outrageous! (1977)

East, Jeff: Klondike Fever (1979), Mary and Joseph: A Story of Faith (1979)

Easterday, Kenny: Kid Brother, The (1987)

Eastman, Allan: Crazy Moon (1986), Ford: The Man and the Machine (1987), Sweeter Song, A (1976), Videodrome (1983), War Boy, The (1985)

Easto, Barbara: Boîte à soleil, La (1988)

Eastside, Lori: Love and Greed (1992)

Eastwood, Jayne: Ada (1981), Back to Beulah (1974), Circle Game, The (1994), Cold Comfort (1989), Crowd Inside, The (1971), Drying Up the Streets (1978), Goin' Down the Road (1970), Indigo Autumn (1987), Kidnapping of Baby John Doe, The (The Baby John Doe) (1985), Me and My Shadows (2000), My Pleasure Is My Business (1975), Office Party (1988), One Man (1977), Partners 'n Love (1992), Red Green's Duct Tape Forever (2002), Tomorrow Never Comes (1978), Snowbirds (1981), Videodrome (1983), Wandering Soul Murders, The (2000)

Eastwood, William: Môtel St-Laurent (1998)

Eaton, George: Face Off (1971)

Ebeltoft, Inger: Eve (2002)

Eberhard, Ben: Water Game, The (2002)

Ecoffey, Jean-Philippe: Ciel est à nous, Le (1997), Des chiens dans la neige (2001)

Eddy, Michael Alan: Bedroom Eyes (1984)

Edizel, Loren: I Won't Dance (1992)

Edmond, James: Black Christmas (Silent Night, Evil Nights) (Stranger in the House) (1974)

Edmond, Joanne: Laure Gaudreault: A Remarkable Woman (1983)

Edney, David: War Story, A (1981)

Edolls, Philip: Matthew Shepard Story, The (2001)

Edwards, Bruce: Garden, The (1991)

Edwards, Duke: Freeloading (1986)

Edwards, Edgar: Convicted (1938)

Edwards, John: Dream on the Run (1977)

Edwards, Kyle: Death Weekend (1976)

Edwards, Neville: Case of the Whitechapel Vampire, The (2001)

Edwards, Norma: Kate Morris, Vice President (1984)

Edwards, Paul: High-Ballin' (1978)

Edwards, Tamara: Summerlust (1973)

Edwards, Vince: Return of Ben Casey, The (1988)

Egan, Kate: Lost World, The (1992)

Egan, Peter: 2001: A Space Travesty (2001)

Egarhos, Spyro: 24 Store, The (1990)

Eggar, Samantha: Brood, The (1979), Curtains (1983), Hot Touch (Coup de maître) (1982), Uncanny, The (1977), Welcome to Blood City (1977), Why Shoot the Teacher (1977)

Eggert, Nicole: Anything For Love (1992), Murder Seen (2000)

Eglee, Charles: Deadly Eyes (The Rats) (1982)

Egoyan, Atom: Adjuster, The (1991), Ararat (2002), Calendar (1993), Exotica (1994), Family Viewing (1988), Felicia's Journey (1999), Gross Misconduct (1992), In This Corner (1986), Knock! Knock! (1985), Krapp's Last Tape (Beckett on Film series) (2000), Montréal Sextet (1991), Next of Kin (1984), Preludes (2000), Sarabande (1997), Speaking Parts (1989), Sweet Hereafter, The (1996)

Ehle, Jennifer: Sunshine (1999)

Ehm, Erica: Replikator (1994)

Eisen, Hal: 2103: The Deadly Wake (1996)

Eisman, Bernard: To Kill the King (1974)

Eisner, David: Family Reunion (1987)

Ekland, Britt: Dead Wrong (1983), King Solomon's Treasure (1979)

Elbe, Pascal: Père et Fils (Father and Son) (2003)

Elder, Linda: Birds of Prey (1985)

Elders, Kevin: Iron Eagle (1986)

Elias, Hector: Losin' It (1983)

Elias, Jeannie: Deadline (Anatomy of a Horror) (1980), Teddy (The Pit) (1980)

Élie, Julien: Dog Who Stopped the War, The (La guerre des tuques) (1984)

Elion, Lawrence: Storm (1985)

Eliopoulos, Nicole: So Faraway and Blue (2001)

Eliot, Jonathan: After the Harvest (Wild Geese) (2000)

El-Kadi, Nameer: Quest for Fire (La guerre du feu) (1981)

El-Kadi, Naseer: Quest for Fire (*La guerre du feu*) (1981)

Elkin, Ilona: Hatley High (2003)

Elkin, Karin: *Frontières* (Border Line) (2003), Great Land of Small, The (*C'est pas parce qu'on est petit qu'on peut pas être grand!*) (1987)

Elkins, Mignon: Loving and Laughing (1971), Love at First Sight (1974), In Praise of Older Women (1978)

Elliott, Brennan: Stone Coats (1997), Silencer, The (1999)

Elliott, Coralee: Little Kidnappers, The (1990)

Elliott, Denholm: Apprenticeship of Duddy Kravitz, The (1974), Partners (1976)

Elliott, Stephan: Eye of the Beholder (1999)

Ellis, James: No Surrender (1985)

Ellis, John: Dinner's on the Table (1994)

Ellis, Mark: Children of my Heart (2000)

Ellis, Michael: Hawk's Vengeance (1997)

Ellis, Ralph: Wings in the Wilderness (1975)

Ellis, Tracee: Sue Lost in Manhattan (Sue) (1997)

Ellwand, Gregory: Justice (1998), Lucky Girl (2000)

Elong, Pierre: *Ribo ou 'le soleil sauvage'* (1978)

Elorrieta, Jose Maria: *Diable aime les bijoux, Le* (The Devil Likes Jewels) (The Devil's Jewellery) (*Las joyas del diablo*) (1969)

Elwood, Sheri: Deeply (2000)

Emery, Dick: Find the Lady (1976)

Émond, Bernard: *Femme qui boit, La* (The Woman Who Drinks) (2001)

Émond, Rémi: Long Live France (1970)

Empry, Gino: Neon Palace, The: A '50s and '60s Trip (1971)

Enahoro, Bella: Secret Laughter of Women, The

Endersby, Ralph: Challengers, The (1990), Homer (1970), Megantic Outlaw, The (1971), Nest of Shadows (1976), Rip-Off (1971), Sunday in the Country (1975), Tools of the Devil (1985)

Endrade, Steven: Challengers, The (1990)

Endresen, Sigve: Misery Harbour (1999)

Engel, Howard: Murder Sees the Light (1987), Suicide Murders, The (1986)

Engel, Susan: Butley (1974)

Enrico, Robert: For Those I Loved (*Au nom de tous les miens*) (1983), French Revolution, The (1989)

Enright, Donald: Circle, The (The Fraternity) (2001), Search and Destroy (1979)

Eowan, Kelly: Gate, The (1987)

Epstein, Alexander: Warriors (1994)

Epstein, Yan: *Arthur Rimbaud: L'homme aux semelles de vent* (1995)

Erbach, Jeff: Nature of Nicholas, The (2002)

Erdos, Victor: First Offender (1987)

Eriksen, Kaj-Erik: Captains Courageous (1996)

Eriksen, Shelley: Burn: The Robert Wraight Story (2003), Stolen Miracle (2001)

Erlich, Alan: Balls Up (1998)

Errickson, Krista: Killer Image (1992), Paperboy, The (1994)

Erschbamer, George: Bounty Hunters (1996), Flinch (1994), Incredible Adventures of Marco Polo, The (1998), Power of Attorney (1995), SnakeEater (1990), SnakeEater II: The Drug Buster (1990), SnakeEater III: The Revenge (1992)

Ertmanis, Victor: Fools Die Fast (1995), Not Just a Dirty Little Movie (1985), Overnight (1985), Paris, France (1993), Reluctant Angel (1997)

Erwin, Jhene: Fishing Trip, The (1998)

Escobar, Elba: Coup at Daybreak, A (*Coup d'état au petit matin*) (1998)

Eshkibok, Gloria May: Johnny Greyeyes (2001), Promise the Moon (1997)

Essagian, Carlo: I Won't Dance (1992)

Essery, George: Hank Williams: The Show He Never Gave (1982)

Estdelacropolis, Demetrios: Shirley Pimple in the John Wayne Temple (1999)

Ester, Natalie: Excalibur Kid, The (1998)

Esterez, Simon: *Boîte à soleil, La* (The Box of the Sun) (1988), S Day (*Le jour 'S'*) (1984)

Estève, Jean-Marie: *Postière, La* (The Postmistress) (1992)

Éthier, Suzanne: Man from the Movies, The (1976)

Ettlinger, Mark: Seductio (1987)

Ettlinger, Norman: Nobody Waved Goodbye (1964)

Eustace, David: Intruder, The (1981)

Evanchuk, Peter: Cowboyz (1988)

Evani, Gary: Little Canadian, The (1955)

Evans, Bill: Airport In (1996)

Evans, Bruce: Man, a Woman and a Bank, A (1979)

Evans, John: Inside Out (1979), Passengers (1981)

Evans, Lewis: Ups and Downs (1983)

Evans, Lucas: Tommy Tricker and the Stamp Traveller (1988)

Evans, Marc: My Little Eye (2002)

Evans, Matt John: Black Swan (2002)

Evans, Tom: Christopher's Movie Matinée (1969)

Everett, D. S.: Running Brave (1983)

Everhart, Angie: Wicked Minds (2002)

Everhart, David: Two Brothers, a Girl and a Gun (1993)

Evigan, Greg: Echoes in Crimson (1987), Tek War: Tek Justice (1994)

Evyenia, Vaggos: Foreign Ghosts (1997)

Ewer, Donald: Pygmalion (1983)

Ewing, Iain: Crimes of the Future (1970), Eat Anything (1971), Kill (1969), Only Thing You

Ewing, Iain continued:
Know, The (1971), Rowdyman, The (1972), Stereo (1969), Winter Kept Us Warm (1965)

Ewing, Tess: Rowdyman, The (1972)

Exbrayat, Charles: Unknown From Montréal, The (*Son copain*) (1950)

Explosive, Atom: Day Breaks Once More (1995)

Eyre, Janieta: House of Pain (1995)

Eyres, John: Ripper: Letter from Hell (2001), Slow Burn (1989)

Eyton-Jones, Susan: Clear-Dark (*Clair obscur*) (1988), Lana in Love (1991), Seductio (1987)

Ezra, Mark: Steal (Riders) (2002)

Ezrine, John: Witchboard III: The Possession (1995)

Fabray, Nanette: Personal Exemptions (1988)

Fabre, Dominique: Louisiana (1993)

Facher, Carol: Night in America, A (*Une nuit en Amérique*) (1975)

Faedette, Giselle: Autumn Born (1979)

Fagon, Richard: *Jeune fille à la fenêtre, Une* (2001)

Fahey, Jeff: Baree, Son of Kazan (1994), Execution of Raymond Graham, The (1985), Kazan (1994)

Fair, Stacy: Sister Blue (2001)

Fairley, John: Raffle, The (1994)

Fairlie, Kristin: Silence of Adultery, The (1995)

Fajrasjsl, Diana: Gerda (1992)

Fakeer, Ram: On Their Knees (2001)

Falardeau, Pierre: *15 février 1839* (2001), Elvis Gratton (1985), Left-hand Side of the Fridge, The (2000), Miracle in Memphis (1999), October (1994), Party, The (*Party, Le*) (1990)

Falco, Edie: Jenifer Estess Story, The (2001)

Falcon, André: *Ange gardien, L'* (1978)

Falk, Peter: Bloody Brood, The (1959), Lakeboat (2000)

Fallana, Leroy: Butler's Night Off, The (1948)

Fallon, Kate: Roger and Elvis (1993)

Famery, Jacques: *Finalemente* (In the End) (1971), Master Cats, The (1971), Possession of Virginia, The (*Le diable est parmi nous*) (1972)

Fani, Leonora: Born for Hell (*Né pour l'enfer*) (1976)

Fansett, Michele: Recommendation for Mercy (1975)

Fansten, Jacques: *Fracture du myocarde, La* (Cross My Heart) (1990)

Fantasia, Franco: Justine (1972)

Fargey, Jillian: Close to Home (1986), Day Drift (1999), Protection (2000)

Farley, Larry: Rat Tales (1987)

Farley, Marianne: *Peau Blanche, La* (2003)

Farlinger, Leonard: Perfect Son, The (2000)

Farmer, Gary: Heater (1999), Henry and Verlin (1994), Justice (1998), Lilies (1996),

Undergrads, The (1985), Still Life (Still Life: The Fine Art of Murder) (1990), Stolen Heart (1998)

Farmer, Robert: Freakshow (1988)

Farnsworth, Richard: Anne of Green Gables (1985), Anne of Green Gables: The Continuing Story (Series) (1985-1999), Grey Fox, The (1982)

Farquhar, Bee: Haro (1994)

Farr, Judi: Turning April (1996)

Farraro, Kristen: More to Love (2000)

Farrell, Mark: Married Life: The Movie (2000)

Farrell, Sharon: Out of the Blue (1980)

Farrow, Mia: Haunting of Julia, The (1976)

Farrow, Peter: Ten Girls Ago (1962)

Farrow, Tisa: Homer (1970), Only God Knows (1974), Search and Destroy (1979), Special Magnum (1977)

Farwell, Jonathan: Watchers II (1990)

Fasano, John: Rock 'n Roll Nightmare (The Edge of Hell) (1987)

Fassbender, Norman: Things to Do on a Saturday Night (1998)

Fassbinder, Christopher Lee: Question of Privilege, A (1998)

Faubert, Jean: Christmas of Madame Beauchamp, The (*Le revanche noël de Madame Beauchamp*) (1981), Naufragés du Labrador, Les (Stranded in Labrador) (1991)

Faubert-Bouvier, Laurent: Unfaithful Mornings (*Les matins infidèles*) (1988)

Faucher, Carol: Gina (1975)

Faucher, Françoise: Friends for Life (*Des amis pour la vie*) (1988), Heartbreak (*L'arrache-coeur*) (1979), *Soleil des autres, Le* (The Sun of the Others) (Give Us Our Daily Love) (1979)

Faucher, Jean: *Soleil des autres, Le* (The Sun of the Others) (Give Us Our Daily Love) (1979)

Faucher, Sophie: Ding and Dong, The Film (1990)

Faun, Kee: Offering, The (1966)

Faure, Renée: *Miss Moscou* (1992)

Fauteux, Normand: Zero Patience (1993)

Fauteux, Pierre: *Sonatine* (1984)

Favre, Bernard: *Hiver de tourmente, Un* (A Winter of Torment) (1999), *Vent de galerne* (The Wind From Galerne) (1991)

Favreau, Robert: *Ange noir, L'* (The Black Angel) (Nelligan) (1991), Looking for Eternity (1989), Orphan Muses, The (*Les muses orphelines*) (2000), *Trois femmes, un amour* (1994)

Fawcett, Alan: Morning Man, The (1986), Obstruction of Justice (1995)

Fawcett, Farrah: Jewel (2000)

Fawcett, John: Boys' Club, The (1996), Ginger Snaps (2000), Lucky Girl (2000)

Fazlian, Berge: Next of Kin (1984)

Fearnley, Neil: Daydream Believers: The Monkees' Story (2000), Dogmatic (1996)

Feather, Jacqueline: Dancing in the Dark (1995)

Featherstone, Angela: Breach of Faith: A Family of Cops II (1996), Guilty, The (2000)

Fedele, Pierre: Invention of Love, The (2000)

Feder, Frédérique: Stallion (1988)

Fedor, Tania: *Tout prendre, À* (Take It All) (The Way It Goes) (1963)

Fehr, Brendan: Edge of Madness (*Station sauvage*) (Wilderness Station) (2003)

Feigel, Sylvia: Foxy Lady (1971)

Feldman, Corey: Harmoney (1999), Meatballs, Part IV (1992), National Lampoon's Last Resort (1994)

Feldman, Susan: Neon Palace, The: A '50s and '60s Trip (1971)

Félio, Jean-Marc: Cursed (1990), Power Games (*Jeux de pouvoir*) (1990)

Felipe, Alejo: House With a View of the Sea, A (*Una casa con vista al mar*) (2001)

Fell, Norman: Crunch (1981)

Feltes, Alyson: Justice (1998)

Fenady, Andrew J.: Sea Wolf, The (1993)

Feng, Liu Zi: Red Violin, The (*Le violon rouge*) (1998)

Fenn, Sherilyn: Nightwaves (2002)

Fennell, Tod: Kayla (1998)

Fenwick, Gillie: Improper Channels (1981), Keep It in the Family (1973), Quiet Day in Belfast, A (1973)

Fenwick, Moya: Catsplay (1977)

Feore, Colm: Airborne (1998), Baroness and the Pig, The (2002), Beautiful Dreamers (1990), Bethune: The Making of a Hero (1990) see Bethune (1977), Century Hotel (2001), Friends at Last (1995), Haven (2001), Herd, The (1998), Lola (2001), Nuremberg (2000), Running Man (1980), Skate (Blades of Courage) (1987), Perfect Son, The (2000), Red Violin, The (*Le violon rouge*) (1998), Striking Poses (1999), Thirty-two Short Films About Glenn Gould (1994), Trudeau (2002), Wrong Guy, The (1998)

Ferber, Dorin: Graveyard Shift (1987)

Ferchiou, Rachid: *Échec et mat* (Checkmate) (1994)

Ferguson, Anna: Tokyo Cowboy (1994)

Ferguson, Blair: Under the Piano (1998)

Ferguson, Colin: Rowing Through (1996)

Ferguson, Holly: Horsey (1997)

Ferguson, Jay: Suburban Legend (1995)

Ferguson, John Pyper: Showdown at Williams Creek (Kootenai Brown) (1991)

Ferguson, Martha: My Script Doctor (1997)

Ferguson, Matthew: Love and Human Remains (Unidentified Human Remains and the True Nature of Love) (1994), On My Own (1992), Uncut (1997)

Ferguson, Myles: Little Criminals (1996)

Ferguson, Rob: Tunnel (2000)

Ferilli, Sabrina: Almost America (*Come l'America*) (2001)

Ferjac, Anouk: Old Country Where Rimbaud Died, The (*Le vieux pays où Rimbaud est mort*) (1977)

Férland, Carmen: Eva Guerrilla (1987)

Ferland, Jean-Pierre: Song for Julie, A (*Chanson pour Julie*) (1976)

Ferlatte, Sylvie: Brother André (*Le frère André*) (1987)

Fernandes, Miguel: East End Hustle (1976), Lifeforce Experiment (1994)

Fernandez, Raul: Anything For Love (1992)

Fernando, Mohan: Fade to Black (2001)

Fernando, Rohan Cecil: Fade to Black (2001)

Fernetz, Charlene: Paris or Somewhere (1995)

Fernie, Lynne: Forbidden Love: The Unashamed Stories of Lesbian Lives (1992)

Ferrabee, Gillian: Dark Harbour (1997)

Ferrand, Carlos: Cuervo, the Private Detective (1990)

Ferrier, Russell: M.V.P.: Most Valuable Primate (2000)

Ferrell, Will: Super Star (1999)

Ferreol, Andrea: Louisiana (1993)

Ferrer, Jose: Who Has Seen the Wind (1977)

Ferrer, Leilani Sarelle: Crash (Breach of Trust) (1995)

Ferres, Veronica: Ladies Room (1999)

Ferri, Claudia: Artificial Lies (2000)

Ferris, Irena: Covergirl (1984)

Ferrucci, Francesco: Beyond Suspicion (1993)

Ferry, David: Breach of Faith: A Family of Cops II (1996), Fighting Men, The (1977), High-Ballin' (1978), Hounds of Notre Dame, The (1981), Last Winter, The (1989), Moving Targets (1983), Parallels (1980), Powder Heads (1980), Strange Horizons (1992), Whodunit (1986)

Fetherling, Douglas: Sweeter Song, A (1976)

Fichtner, William: Julie Walking Home (2002)

Field, Chelsea: Wrong Woman, The (1995)

Field, David: Running Man (1980)

Field, Myra: Hurt Penguins (1992)

Fielding, Edward: Jack of Hearts (1993), Rats (1999)

Fielding, Joy: Golden Will: The Silken Laumann Story (1997)

Fields, Charles: Fish Hawk (1979)

Fiennes, Ralph: Spider (2002), Sunshine (1999)

Filer, Diane: When Tomorrow Dies (1965)

Filiatrault, Denise: *Adolescente sucré d'amour, L'* (1985), *Alisée* (1991), Beautiful Sundays (*Les beaux dimanches*) (1974), By the Blood of Others (*Par le sang des autres*) (1974), Crime of Ovide Plouffe, The (*Le crime d'Ovide Plouffe* (*Les Plouffe, II*) (1984), Death of a Lumberjack (*La mort d'un boucheron*) (1973), Fantastica (1980), Far From You Sweetheart (*Juis suis loin de toi mignonne*) (1976), *Fille du Maquignon, La* (The Girl of Maquignon) (1990), Gina (1975), Goodbye, See You Monday (*Au revoir, à lundi*) (1979), It's Your Turn, Laura Cadieux (1998), *Laura Cadieux, La Suite* (2000), *Lit, Le* (1974), Little One Is Coming Soon, The (1972), Magnificent Blue, The (*Bleue, la magnifique*) (1990), *Odyssée d'Alice Tremblay, L'* (2002), Once Upon a Time in the East (*Il était une fois dans l'est*) (1974), *Plouffe, Les* (The Plouffe Family) (1981), Sun Rises Late, The (*Le soleil se leve en retard*) (1977)

Filion, Jean-Claude: Nightmare, The (1979)

Filion, Nicole: Those Damned Savages (*Les maudits sauvages*) (1971), Dust from Underground (*Poussière sur la ville*) (1965)

Filippo, Fabrizio: Drive, The (1996), Waydowntown (2000)

Filips, Jan: Searching for Diana (1992)

Fillières, Hélène: Nearest to Heaven (2002)

Fillion, Olivier: Chocolate Eclair (1979)

Finch, George: Class Warfare 2001 (2000)

Findley, Timothy: Catsplay (1977), Don't Let the Angels Fall (1969), Piano Man's Daughter, The (2000), External Affairs (1999), Paper People, The (1967), Wars, The (1983)

Finfret, Louise: Pyx, The (1973)

Fink, Isabella: Great Goose Caper, The (2003), Piano Man's Daughter, The (2000)

Finkleman, Kenneth: Married Life: The Movie (2000)

Finlay, Frank: Murder by Decree (1979)

Finlay, Harry: Megantic Outlaw, The (1971)

Finley, Margot: Misery Harbour (1999)

Finnan, Mark: Terra X (The Curse of Oak Island) (1997)

Finnegan, Joan: Best Damn Fiddler From Calabogie to Kaladar, The (1968)

Finney, Michele: Never Trust an Honest Thief (Going for Broke) (1979)

Finnigan, Jennifer: Stalking of Laurie Show, The (2000)

Firth, Colin: Secret Laughter of Women, The (1999)

Fisch, Charles: 20th Century Chocolate Cake, A (1983)

Fischer, Bobby: Great Chess Movie, The (*Jouer sa vie*) (1982)

Fischer, Max: Lucky Star, The (1980), Man in 5A, The (1982)

Fiset, Steve: Apprentice, The (*Fleur bleue*) (1971)

Fish, Tricia: Dragonwheel (2002), New Waterford Girl (1999), Siege (1983)

Fisher, Agnes: Noncensus (1964)

Fisher, Jack: In the Land of Zom (1983), Rainbow (1995)

Fisher, Jonathan: Johnny Greyeyes (2001)

Fisher, L.B.: Daydream Believers: The Monkees' Story (2000)

Fisher, Noel: Sheldon Kennedy Story, The (1999)

Fisher, Steve: Profile for Murder (The Fifth Season) (1997), Woman Inside, The (1981)

Fisher, Toby: Whole of the Moon, The (1996)

Fitch, Catherine: Butterbox Babies (1995), South of Wawa (1991)

Fitzgerald, Thom: Event, The (2003)

Fitzgerald, Geraldine: Echoes of a Summer (1976)

Fitzgerald, John P: Noncensus (1964)

Fitzgerald, Maureen: Heartaches (1981), Love From the Market Place (see Acts of Love) (1980)

Fitzgerald, Nuala: Brood, The (1979), Circle of Two (1980), Deadly Harvest (1980), Last Act of Martin Weston, The (1971), Silent Partner, The (1978)

Fitzgerald, Paul: Not Another Love Story (1979)

Fitzgerald, Tara: Conquest (1998)

Fitzgerald, Thom: Beefcake (1999), Event, The (2003), Hanging Garden, The (1997), Welcome to the Freakshow (2001), Wild Dogs, The (2002), Wolf Girl (2001)

Fitzpatrick, Richard: Brethren (1976)

Fitzsimmons, Deirdre: With Friends Like These (*Avec des amis*) (1990)

Flacks, Diane: Too Much Sex (1999)

Flaherty, David: Mob Story (1987)

Flaherty, Joe: Double Negative (1979), Going Berserk (1983), Looking for Miracles (1989), Must Be Santa (1999), Nothing Personal (1980), Wrong Guy, The (1998)

Flaiano, Ennio: Red (1969)

Flamand, Andrée: *Valérie* (1969)

Flamand, Didier: *Marchands du silence, Les* (1994)

Flanery, Sean Patrick: Pale Saints (1997)

Flannery, Eric: Incubus (1981)

Flannigan, Maureen: National Lampoon's Last Resort (1994)

Flashner, Graham: Adrift (1993)

Flatman, Barry: My Mother's Ghost (1996)

Fleming, Ann Marie: New Shoes (1990)

Fleming, William: Buried on Sunday (1993)

Flemming, Peter: Barbeque: A Love Story (1997)

Flemming, Wayne: Married Life: The Movie (2000)

Flemyng, Jason: Red Violin, The (1998)

Fletcher, Brendan: 100 Days in the Jungle (2002), Deadly Friends: The Nancy Eaton Story (2003), Downtime (2001), Five Senses, The (1999), Ginger Snaps: The Sequel (2003), Keeping the Promise (1997), Law of Enclosures, The (2000), Little Criminals (1996), My Father's Angel (West of Sarajevo) (1999), Roller Coaster (1999), Scorn (2000), Turning Paige (Shepherd Park) (2002)

Fletcher, Hamish: Golden Fiddles (1991)

Fletcher, Louise: Lucky Star, The (1980)

Fletcher, Page: Trial and Error (1993)

Fletcher, Tony: Intruder, The (1981)

Flett, Sharry: Drying Up the Streets (1978), War Brides (1980), Suicide Murders, The (1986)

Flicker, Theodore: Jacob Two-Two Meets the Hooded Fang (1977)

Floberg, Bjorn: Misery Harbour (1999)

Floquet, François: Naufragés du Labrador, Les (Stranded in Labrador) (1991)

Florea, Marius: Excalibur Kid, The (1998)

Florent, Catherine: Sur Le Seuil (Under the Sky) (2003), Station nord (North Station) (2002)

Florent, Helene: Yellowknife (2002)

Flores, Von: Eclipse (1994)

Flower, David: Slow Run (1969)

Fluegel, Darlanne: Relative Fear (1994), Scanner Cop (1994)

Fluet, Janine: Bingo (1974)

Fluet, Lucille: The Seat of the Soul (A Crisis of Conscience) (Siège de l'âme, Le) (1997)

Flugel, Darlene: Child, The (1994)

Flynn, Aiden: Making Love in St. Pierre (2003)

Foldy, Peter: Midnight Witness (1992), Seeds of Doubt (1997)

Foley, Brendan: Welcome to Canada (1989)

Foley, Dave: Fancy Dancing (2002), High Stakes (1986), Kids in the Hall: Brain Candy (1996), Prodigious Hickey, The (1987), Wrong Guy, The (1998)

Edward Follows: Oedipus Rex (1956)

Follows, Edwina: Dinosaur Hunter, The (2000)

Follows, Megan: Anne of Green Gables (1985), Anne of Green Gables: The Continuing Story (Series)(1985-1999), Hockey Night (1984), Major Crime (1998), Termini Station (1990), Reluctant Angel (1997), Stork Derby, The (2001), Under the Piano (1998)

Follows, Ted: Cold Comfort (1989), Oedipus Rex (1956), Paperback Hero (1973), Wozeck: Out of the Fire (1992)

Fonda, Bridget: Camilla (1994), Whole Shebang, The (2001)

Fonda, Henry: City on Fire (1979), Home to Stay (1978)

Fonda, Jane: Agnes of God (1985)

Fonda, Peter: Certain Fury (1985), Death Bite (Spasms) (1983), High-Ballin' (1978), Second Skin (2000)

Fonoroff, Paul: Dreamtrips (2000)

Fontaine, Frank: Two Summers (2002)

Fontaine, Jean: Where Two Roads Cross (Between Two Loves) (À la croisée des chemins) (Entre deux amours) (1943)

Fontaine, Jean-Louis: Attache ta tuque (2003)

Fontaine, Marie-Hélène: Canada's Sweetheart: The Saga of Hal C. Banks (1985)

Foon, Dennis: Little Criminals (1996), Long Life, Happiness & Prosperity(2002), Lies (1998), Scar Tissue (2002), Society's Child (2001), Torso: The Evelyn Dick Story (2000), White Lies (1998)

Forbes, Danny: Lions for Breakfast (1975)

Forcier, André: Ababouinée (1994), Bar Salon (1974), Countess of Baton Rouge, The (La Comtesse de Baton Rouge) (1997), Histoire inventée, Une (An Imaginary Tale) (1990), I Love a Man in Uniform (1984), Moonshine (1982), Pacemaker and a Sidecar, A (L'eau chaude, l'eau frette) (1997), Retour de l'immaculée conception, Le (The Return of the Immaculate Conception) (1970), Wind From Wyoming, A (Le vent du Wyoming) (1994)

Forcier, Jacques Marcotte: Retour de l'immaculée conception, Le (The Return of the Immaculate Conception) (1970)

Forcier, Marc-André: Kalamazoo (1988)

Ford, Dawn Daen: Legend of Sleepy Hollow, The (1999)

Ford, Glenn: Happy Birthday to Me (1981)

Foreman, Lorraine: Partners (1976)

Forer, Mort: Thousand Moons, A (1977)

Forest, Denis: I Love a Man in Uniform (1984), Long Road Home, The (1988), Out of Sight, Out of Mind (The Seventh Circle) (1983), Tadpole and the Whale (La grenouille et la baleine) (1988)

Forest, Violaine: Unfaithful Mornings (Les matins infidèles) (1988)

Forestier, Frederic: Peacekeeper, The (1997)

Forestier, Louise: IXE-13 (1972), Little Tougas (1976), Orders, The (Les ordres) (1974), Two Seconds (2 secondes) (1998)

Forget, Michel: Concièrgerie, La (The Caretaker's Lodge) (The Prison) (1997), Contrecoeur (1983), Femme qui boit, La (The Woman Who Drinks) (2001), I Have the Right to Pleasure (J'ai droit au plaisir) (1975), Je n'aime que toi (I Don't Love You) (2003), Tin Flute, The (Bonheur d'occasion) (1983), Tisserands du pouvoir, Les (The Mills of Power) (1988)

Forlani, Claire: Triggermen (2000)

Forrest, Christopher: Vincent and Me (1990)

Forrest, Frederic: Shadow Lake (2000), Spreading Ground, The (2000), Twin Sisters (1993)

Forster, Robert: Crunch (1981), Lakeboat (2000), Scanners: The Showdown (Scanner Cop II: Volkin's Revenge) (1994)

Forsyth, Edward: I'm Going to Get You...Elliot Boy (1971)

Forsyth, Rob: Becoming Laura (1982), Clear Cut (1991), Conquest (1998), Dr. Lucille: The Lucille Teasdale Story (1999), Harvest (1981), Lakeboat (2000), Marine Life (2000), Murder Most Likely (1999), Passengers (1981), Seer Was Here (1978), Winnings of Frankie Walls, The (1980), Takeover (1981)

Forsythe, Henderson: Dead of Night (1974)

Forsythe, William: Four Days (1999)

Forte, Isabelle: When Wolves Howl (Quand hurlent les loups) (1973)

Forte, John: Mad About Mambo (2000)

Fortier, Anne: My Friend Pierrette (1969)

Fortier, Gérard: My Friend Pierrette (1969)

Fortin, Claude: 100% Bio (Hundred Percent Biography) (2003), Autobiography of an Amateur Filmmaker, The (L'autobiographe amateur) (1999), Camera Thief, The (1993)

Fortin, Gaspard: Autobiography of an Amateur Filmmaker, The (L'autobiographe amateur) (1999)

Fortin, Gélinas: Bar Salon (1974)

Fortin, Jean-Guy: Aventures d'un agent très spécial, Les (1985)

Fortin, Kathleen: Three Madeleines, The (Les fantômes des trois Madeleines) (1999)

Fortin, Reynaud: Elvis Gratton (1985)

Fortin, Simon: Pays dans la gorge, Le (The Country on Your Chest) (1999)

Fortineau, Thierry: Hiver de tourmente, Un (A Winter of Torment) (1999), Homme de ma vie, L' (The Man in My Life) (1993)

Fossy, Brigitte: For Those I Loved (1983)

Foster, Barry: Quiet Day in Belfast, A (1973)

Foster, Christine: Shadow Dancing (1988)

Foster, Doreen: Christopher's Movie Matinée (1969)

Foster, Jodie: Blood of Others, The (Le sang des autres) (1984), Echoes of a Summer (1976), Hotel New Hampshire (1984), Little Girl Who Lives Down the Lane, The (1977)

Foster, Meg: Back Stab (1990), Ticket to Heaven (1981), To Catch a Killer (1991)

Foster, Patricia: Heads or Tails (Pile ou face) (1971)

Foster, Thomas: Watchers II (1990)

Foster, Tony: Alexander Bell: The Sound and the Silence (1991)

Foucault, Andreanne: Oranges of Israel, The (Valse à trois) (1974)

Foucault, Guy: Dream Life (La vie revée) (1972)

Founev, Ivaylo: Burnt Eden (1997)

Fourier, Guy: Trois femmes, un amour (Three Women in Love) (1994)

Fournier, Christian: Boys, Les (The Boys) (1997), Incompris, L' (1997)

Fournier, Claude: Alien Thunder (Dan Candy's Law) (1973), Apple, the Stem and the Seeds, The (La pomme, la queue et les pépins) (1974), Book of Eve (Histoires d'Eve) (2002), Far From You Sweetheart (Juis suis loin de toi mignonne) (1976), Giornata particolare, Una (A Special Day) (1977), Golden Fiddles (1991), Hot Dogs (Clean Up Squad, The) (1980), Je n'aime que toi (2003), J'en suis (1997), Master Cats, The (1971), Night of the High Tide, The (La notte dell'alta marea) (1976), Two Women of Gold (Deux femmes en or) (1970), Tin Flute, The (Bonheur d'occasion) (1983), Tisserands du pouvoir, Les (The Mills of Power) (1988)

Fournier, Guy: Maria Chapdelaine (1983)

Fournier, Jacques: Ange gardien, L' (The Guardian Angel) (1978)

Fournier, Marcel: Death of a Lumberjack (1973), Moonshine (1982), Pyx, The (1973)

Fournier, Roger: Aventures d'une jeune veuve, Les (1974), Awakening, The (L'amour humain) (1970), Day in a Taxi, A (Une journée en taxi) (1982), Goodbye, See You Monday (Au revoir, à lundi) (1979), Heads or Tails (1971)

Fowler, Almeda: Damaged Lives (1933)

Fox, Colin: Beautiful Dreamers (1990), Butterbox Babies (1995), Canada's Sweetheart: The Saga of Hal C. Banks (1985), Chocolate Eclair (Éclair au chocolat) (1979), Christmas Story, A (1983), Deadbolt (1984), Food of the Gods II (1989), Inside Out (1979), Man Called Intrepid, A (1979), Murder by Phone (1982), My Pleasure Is My Business (1975), Noncensus (1964), Reincarnate, The (1971), On My Own (1992), Partners 'n Love (1992), Samuel Lount (1985), Scanners III: The Takeover (1992), Seeds of Doubt (1997), Silence of the North (1981)

Fox, David: Circle Game, The (1994), Clutch (1998), Conquest (1998), Ganesh (Ordinary Magic) (1993), Grey Owl (1999), Parallels (1980), Rats (1999), When Night Is Falling (1995)

Fox, Edward: Galileo (1973), I Was a Rat (Cinderella and Me) (When I Was a Rat) (2001)

Fox, Fred: Wendy (1966)

Fox, Joan: Cannibal Girls (1973), Foxy Lady (1971)

Fox, Kelly: For Those Who Hunt the Wounded Down (1996)

Fox, Kerry: Hanging Garden, The (1997), To Walk with Lions (1999)

Fox, Michael J.: Class of 1984 (1982)

Fox, Norman: Intruder, The (1981), Something's Rotten (1978)

Fox, Stacie: In the Dead of Space (2000)

Fox, Stanley: Plastic Mile, The (1969)

Frag, Pierre: Ruffian, The (1983)

Frame, Frederick: Home Movie (1992)

France, Reine: Jacques and November (1984)

France, Ronald: *Amanita pestilens* (1963), *Corde au cou, La* (1966), Wings in the Wilderness (1975)

Franciosa, Anthony: Julie Darling (1982)

Francis, Carol Ann: Champagne for Two (1987)

Franciscus, James: City on Fire (1979), Man Inside, The (1975)

Franck, Vanya: Noncensus (1964)

Francks, Don: Diviners, The (1993), Drying Up the Streets (1978), Drylanders (1963), Fallen Knight (The Minion) (1998), Fast Company (1979), Fish Hawk (1979), Honourable Member, An (1982), Hostile Advances: The Kerry Ellison Story (1996), Ivy League Killers (The Fast Ones) (1959), Johnny Mnemonic (1995), Love Come Down (2000), My Bloody Valentine (1981), *Riel* (1979), One Heart Broken Into Song (1998), Paint Cans (1994), Planet of Junior Brown, The (1997) Summer of the Monkeys (1998), Summer's Children (1979), Terminal Choice (Deathbed) (1985)

Francks, Rainbow Sun: see Francks, Don

Francoeur, Louise: You Are Warm, You Are Warm (*Tu brûles, tu brûles*) (1973)

François, Jacques: Myth That Wouldn't Die (*Dan Seurs du Mozambique, Les*) (1991)

Frandsen, Jano: Xtro II: The Second Encounter (1991)

Franis Lane, John: Dear Father (*Caro Papa*) (1979)

Frank, Astrid: All About Women (*À propos de la femme*) (1969)

Frank, Brian: Battle Queen 2020 (Millennium Queen 2000) (2000), Love Letters: A Romantic Trilogy (2001)

Frank, David: Homecoming, The (Good Luck, Jennifer Gagnon) (1978)

Frank, Robert: Candy Mountain (1987)

Frankel, Mark: Young Catherine (1990)

Franklin, Barbara: Oedipus Rex (1956)

Franklin, Jan: Echoes in Crimson (1987)

Chloé, Franks: Uncanny, The (1977)

Franz, Allan: Vigil, The (1998)

Frappier, Jill: Night in America, A (*Une Nuit en Amérique*) (1975), Strange Brew (1983)

Frappier, Roger: Cosmos (1997), Great Ordinary Movie, The (Joan of Arc Is Alive and Well and Living in Québec) (*Le grand film ordinaire*) (1971), Last Glacier, The (1984), *Réjeanne Padovani* (1973)

Fraser, Angus: Girl Is a Girl, A (1999), Kissed (1996)

Fraser, Brad: Leaving Metropolis (2002), Love and Human Remains (Unidentified Human Remains and the True Nature of Love) (1994), Symposium (1996)

Fraser, David: Airborne (1998)

Fraser, Duncan: Kingsgate (1989), Not Just a Dirty Little Movie (1985), Overnight (1985), Trust in Me (1995), Watchers (1988)

Fraser, Fiona: King Solomon's Treasure (1979)

Fraser, Kathryn: City of Champions (1990)

Fraser, Will: Dying Fall (2002)

Frazzi, Andrea: Almost America (2001)

Frazzi, Antonio: Almost America (2001)

Fréchette, Carole: Jacques and November (1984), *Sept Jours de Simon Labrosse, Les* (The September Days of Simon) (2003)

Fréchette, José: Chili's Blues (*C'était le 12 du 12 et Chili avait les Blues*) (1994), Soho (1994)

Fréchette, Richard: Confessional, The (*Le confessionnal*) (1995), No (1998)

Frédérique, Ariane: *Équinoxe* (1986), Woman of Colours, A (1985), Ruth (1994)

Fredrick, Tara: Lotus Eaters, The (1993)

Freed, Josh: Ticket to Heaven (1981)

Freed, William: Watchers (1988)

Freedman, Danny: Fortune and Men's Eyes (1971), One Man (1977)

Freedman, Gilles: One Man (1977)

Freedman, Harry: Storm (1985)

Freedman, Robert L.: Me and My Shadows (2000)

Freeman, Gillian: That Cold Day in the Park (1969)

Freeman, Jon: Ascent, The (1994)

Freeman, Morgan: Execution of Raymond Graham, The (1985)

Freeman, Paul: Eminent Domain (1990)

Freiss, Stephane: Wanted (Crime Spree) (2003)

Frémont, Thierry: *Arthur Rimbaud: L'homme aux semelles de vent* (1995)

French, David: Of the Fields, Lately (1975)

French, Michael: Powder Heads (1980)

French, Myra: Connecting Lines (1990)

French, Robert: Noroc (1999)

Frénette, Rosa Hugues: *Jeune fille à la fenêtre, Une* (2001)

Fresh Wes, Maestro: Harmoney (1999)

Freundlich, Bart: World Traveler (2001)

Frewer, Matthew: Case of the Whitechapel Vampire, The (2001), Hound of the Baskervilles, The

Frewer, Matthew continued:
(2000), Jailbait! (2000), Kissinger and Nixon (1994), Royal Scandal, The (2001), Sign of Four, The (2001)

Frey, Sami: Sweet Movie (1974)

Frichot, Nicholas: *Frontières* (Border Line) (2003)

Fricker, Brenda: Alexander Bell: The Sound and the Silence (1991), I Was a Rat (Cinderella and Me) (When I Was a Rat) (2001), Painted Angels (1998), Swann (1996), Torso: The Evelyn Dick Story (2000), War Bride, The (2001)

Frid, Jonathan: Seizure (Tango Macabre) (1974)

Fried, Jiri: Flying Sneaker, The (1992)

Friedland, Dalia: Seven Times a Day (1971)

Friedlander, Howard: Deadly Portrayal (2003)

Friedman, Danny: Slipstream (1973)

Friedman, Elyse: Suddenly Naked (2001)

Friel, Anna: War Bride, The (2001)

Friend, Philip: Vulture, The (1967)

Friend, Rachel: Golden Fiddles (1991)

Friesen, John: Adolescence of P-I, The (Hide and Seek) (1983), Nest of Shadows (1976) Tools of the Devil (1985), Why Shoot the Teacher (1977)

Frissell, Varick: Viking, The (1931)

Fritz-Nemeth, Paul: *Deux amis silencieux* (1969)

Frizzell, John: Dance Me Outside (1994), Getting Married in Buffalo Jump (1990), I Love a Man in Uniform (1984), Life With Billy (1993), *Mémoire tronquée* (1990), On My Own (1992), Winter Tan, A (1988)

Frohman, Mel: Execution of Raymond Graham, The (1985)

Frolick, Lari: Christopher's Movie Matinée (1969)

Fromager, Alain: *Ou le roman de Charles Pathé* (1995)

Frost, Harvey: Something's Rotten (1978)

Frost, Helen: Another Day (2001)

Fruet, William: Bedroom Eyes (1984), Brothers by Choice (1985), Chasing Rainbows (1988), Chatwill's Verdict (Killer Instinct) (Baker County, U.S.A) (Trapped) (1982), Death Bite (Spasms) (1983), Death Weekend (House by the Lake) (1976), Drylanders (1963), Funeral Home (Cries in the Night) (1982), Goin' Down the Road (1970), Rip-Off (1971), Wedding in White (1972), Slipstream (1973), One of Our Own (1977), Search and Destroy (1979)

Fruitier, Edgar: Don Quichotte (2001)

Fryer, Eric: Terry Fox Story, The (1983)

Fuerstenberg, Anna: Eva Guerrilla (1987)

Fugère, Jean-Paul: December (1978)

Fulford, Wendii: Warriors (1994)

Fuller, Edwin: Roger and Elvis (1993)

Fuller, Nancy Belle: Hard Part Begins, The (1973)

Fullerton, Grant: Vacant Lot, The (1989)

Fullerton, Richard: Melting Pot, The (1975)

Fulsco, Amy: Cry in the Night, A (1996)

Furey, Lewis: Angel and the Woman, The (1977), Champagne for Two (1987), Fantastica (1980), Goodbye, See You Monday (*Au revoir, à lundi*) (1979), Night Magic (1985), Rats and Rabbits (2000), Shadow Dancing (1988)

Furie, Sidney J.: Circle, The (2001), Collectors, The (1999), Cool Sound From Hell, A (1959), Cord (2000), Dangerous Age, A (1958), Global Heresy (2002), Going Back (2002), Hollow Point (1997), In Her Defense (1998), Iron Eagle (1986), My Five Wives (2000)

Furrow, Murray: Too Much Sex (1999)

Furtado, Janou: *Mon oeil* (My Eye) (1971)

Fusco, Angela: Catsplay (1977), Undergrads, The (1985)

Fyfe, Mak: Excalibur Kid, The (1998)

Fylan, Nicky: Dream on the Run (1977), Pleasure Palace (Angela) (1973), Point of No Return (1976), Stone Cold Dead (1979)

Gabay, Eli: Watchtower, The (2001)

Gabereau, Vicki: Pleasure Palace (Angela) (1973)

Gaboriau, Linda: J'me Marie, J'me Marie (1974), Lilies (1996)

Gabourie, Mitchell: Buying Time (1988)

Gabourie, Richard: Buying Time (1988), Final Assignment (1980), Three-Card Monte (1978), Title Shot (1980)

Gada, Michiko: Rowing Through (1996)

Gadouas, Daniel: Not Me! (*Sous-sol*) (1996), Waiting for Caroline (1967)

Gadsden, Terry: Mutagen (1987)

Gadzala, Heidi: *Frontières* (Border Line) (2003)

Gaël, Anna: House of Lovers (*La maison des amants*) (1972), *Lit, Le* (1974)

Gage, Patricia: Hostile Advances: The Kerry Ellison Story (1996), Keep It in the Family (1973), Little Kidnappers, The (1990), Looking for Miracles (1989), Rabid (Rage) (1977), Silence of Adultery, The (1995), When Tomorrow Dies (1965), Why Rock the Boat? (1974)

Gagliani, Ely: Born for Hell (*Né pour l'enfer*) (1976)

Gagliardi, Laurent: *Demoiselle sauvage, La* (The Wild Girl) (Wild Damsel) (1991)

Gagné, Jacques: Death of a Lumberjack (*La mort d'un boucheron*) (1973)

Gagné, Jean: Barbaloune (2002), Crinoline Madness (*La folie des crinolines*) (1995), Encircled Colour, The (*La couleur encerclée*) (1986), Kingdom or the Asylum, The (1989)

Gagné, Jeannine: Au fil de l'eau (By the Riverside) (2002)

DIRECTORS, SCRIPTWRITERS & ACTORS

Gagné, Serge: *Barbaloune* (2002), Crinoline Madness (*La folie des crinolines*) (1995), Encircled Colour, The (*La couleur encerclée*) (1986), Kingdom or the Asylum, The (1989), One Who Sees the Hours, The (*Celui qui voit les heures*) (1985)

Gagné, Théo: Thetford in the Middle of Our Life (*Thetford au milieu de notre vie*) (1980)

Gagné, William: Ti-Ken (*Les plans mystèrieux*) (1965)

Gagné, Yves: *Homme renversé, L'* (1987)

Gagnier, Holly: Undertaker's Wedding, The (1996)

Gagnon, André: Gina (1975), Merry World of Léopold Z, The (1965), Rape of a Sweet Young Girl, The (*Le viol d'une jeune fille douce*) (1968)

Gagnon, Bernard: Exile, The (*L'exil*) (1971)

Gagnon, Bertrand: Beat (1976), Lies My Father Told Me (1975), Rebels 1837, The (*Quelques arpents de neige*) (1972)

Gagnon, Blaise: At the Autumn of Life (The Human Misery) (*À l'automne de la vie*) (*La misère humaine*) (1987)

Gagnon, Claude: Chili's Blues (*C'était le 12 du 12 et Chili avait les Blues*) (1994), Keiko (1979), Kid Brother, The (1987), Larose, Pierrot and Luce (1982), Pianist, The (1991), *Visage pâle* (Pale Face) (1986)

Gagnon, Gérald: Between the Moon and Montevideo (2000)

Gagnon, Gloria: Dream on the Run (1977)

Gagnon, Hélène: Red Bells, Blue Tears (*Grelots rouges, sanglots bleus*) (1987)

Gagnon, J.-Léo: Amanita pestilens (1963), Angel and the Woman, The (*L'ange et la femme*) (1977), *Aventures d'une jeune veuve, Les* (1974), Before the Time Comes (*Le temps de l'avant*) (1975), Bernie and the Gang (*Ti-mine Bernie pis la gang*) (1977), Death of a Lumberjack (*La mort d'un bûcheron*) (1973), Dollar, The (The Other Side of the River) (*La piastre*) (*L'autre bord du fleuve*) (1976), Fantastica (1980), Goodbye, See You Monday (*Au revoir, à lundi*) (1979), Head of Normande St. Onge, The (*La tête de Normande St-Onge*) (1975), Last Betrothal, The (1973), Little Aurore's Tragedy (*La petite Aurore, l'enfant martyre*) (1952), Men, The (1971), Moonshine (1982), *Noël et Juliette* (1973), On Est Loin Du Soleil (*One is Far From the Sun*) (*The Brother Andre and the Sun*) (1971), Orders, The (*Les ordres*) (1974), Pacemaker and a Sidecar, A (*L'eau chaude, l'eau frette*) (1997), Panic (*Panique*) (1977), Pigs Are Seldom Clean (*On n'engraisse pas les cochons a l'eau claire*) (1973), *Père Chopin* (1945), Promised Land,

The (*Les brûlés*) (1958), *Séraphin* (1950), Star Is Lost, A (1974), That Darned Loot (*La maudite galette*) (1972), Ordinary Tenderness (*Tendresse ordinaire*) (1973), There Once Was a War (*Il était une guerre*) (1958), We Are Far From the Sun (*On est loin du soleil*) (1971), Why Rock the Boat? (1974)

Gagnon, Jacques: Conquête, La (1973), My Uncle Antoine (1971)

Gagnon, Jacques-Henri: Femmes savantes, Les (The Wise Women) (2001)

Gagnon, Louise: Pacemaker and a Sidecar, A (*L'eau chaude, l'eau frette*) (1997)

Gagnon, Marie-Hélène: *Emporte-moi* (Set Me Free) (1998)

Gagnon, Michel: Beautiful Facade, A (*La belle apparence*) (1979), Memoirs (1984), Mother's Meat, Freud's Flesh (1984)

Gagnon, Pat: Big Rock, the Big Man, The (*Le Grand Rock*) (1969), Jacques and November (1984), Sensations (1973)

Gagnon, René: Blanche and the Night (*Blanche et la nuit*) (1989), Desjardins, His Life and Times (*La vie d'un homme*) (1991), *Enfant sur le lac, L'* (A Child on the Lake) (1993), *Siamoises, Les* (The Siamese Twins) (1999)

Gagnon, Stéphane: *Môtel Hélène* (1999)

Gagnon, Sylvie-Marie: *Fabuleux voyage de l'ange, Le* (The Fabulous Voyage of the Angel) (1991)

Gai, Claude: *Grands enfants, Les* (Day by Day) (1980), *Lac de la lune, Le* (1994), Once Upon a Time in the East (*Il était une fois dans l'est*) (1974), Sun Rises Late, The (1977)

Gai, Djeinaba Diop: Karmen Gel (2001)

Gaik, Claude: Jacob Two-Two Meets the Hooded Fang (1977)

Gail, Max: Sodbusters (1995)

Gainsbourg, Charlotte: Nuremberg (2000)

Galabru, Michel: Grand Recess, The (*La grande récré*) (1976), *Lit, Le* (1977)

Galani, Jane: Sex and the Single Sailor (1967)

Galati, Tony: Darkside, The (1986)

Gale, David: Brain, The (1988)

Gale, Vincent: Dirty (1998), Last Wedding, The (2001)

Galianos, Melissa: Going to Kansas City (1998)

Galipeau, Annie: Grey Owl (1999), Map of the Human Heart (1993)

Galipeau, Jacques: It Can't Be Winter, We Haven't Had Summer Yet (1981)

Gallacher, William: Morning! (1992)

Gallagher, Bronagh: Painted Angels (1998)

Gallagher, Christopher: Undivided Attention (1987)

Gallagher, David: Kart Racer (2002)

Gallagher, Don: Freakshow (1988)

Gallagher, Sean: Revenge of the Land (2000), Royal Scandal, The (2001)

Gallanders, James: Babyface (1998), Reluctant Angel (1997)

Gallant, Patsy: Yellowknife (2002)

Galligan, Patrick: At the End of the Day: The Sue Rodriguez Story (1998)

Galligan, Zach: Prodigious Hickey, The (1987), Psychic (1991)

Gallo, Max: For Those I Loved (Au nom de tous les miens) (1983)

Gallo, Vincent: Cord (Hide and Seek) (2000)

Galloway, Lindsay: Don't Forget to Wipe the Blood Off (1966)

Gallus, Agi: Psycho Girls (1986)

Galmont, Alexis: Thousand Wonders of the Universe, The (1997)

Galwey, Isadora: Three Madeleines, The (Les fantômes des trois Madeleines) (1999)

Galwey, James: Katryn's Place (2002)

Gamache, Marcel: Push but Push Reasonably (Scarlatina) (Pousse mais pousse égal) (1975)

Gamache, René: Sacrifice, The (La sacrifiée) (1955)

Gamalsetter, Maureen: Downtime (1985)

Gambon, Michael: Bullet to Beijing (Len Deighton's Bullet to Beijing) (1995)

Gamer, Henry: Agency (1980), Hey Babe! (1984), Honeymoon (1985), Isla the Tigress of Siberia (1977), Let's Talk About Love (1976), Mourning Suit, The (1976), Prologue (1970)

Gammell, Robin: Circle of Two (1980), Haunting of Julia, The (Full Circle) (1976), Highpoint (1980), King's Gambit (1985), Klondike Fever (1979), Man Called Intrepid, A (1979), Murder by Phone (1982), Net Worth (1997), Pyx, The (1973), Rituals (The Creeper) (1977), Striker's Mountain (1985)

Gampu, Ken: King Solomon's Treasure (1979)

Ganatra, Nisha: Fast Food High (2003)

Gander, Mogeus: Lyon's Den (1983)

Gang, Pierre: Incompris, L' (1997), Legend of Sleepy Hollow, The (1999), Not Me! (Sous-sol) (1996), Society's Child (2001)

Gann, Angela: Sweet Substitute (Caressed) (1964)

Gann, Merrilyn: Heart of the Sun (1998)

Garand, Roger: For Better, for Worse (1975), My Uncle Antoine (1971)

Garant, Annette: Craque la vie (Life Blossoms) (1994), Desjardins, His Life and Times (1991)

Garber, Evan: Truckin' (1972)

Garber, Victor: Colder Kind of Death, A (2000), Deadly Appearances (1999), Exotica (1994), External Affairs (1999), First Circle, The (1991), Grand Larceny (1991), Hostile Advances: The Kerry Ellison Story (1996), Love and Murder (1999), Me and My Shadows (2000), Monkeys in the Attic (1974), Torso: The Evelyn Dick Story (2000), Wandering Soul Murders, The (2000)

Garceau, Raymond: Big Rock, the Big Man, The (Le Grand Rock) (1969), In the Name of the Son (1972), Long Live France (1970)

Garceau, Roger: Esprit du mal, L' (Spirit of Evil, The) (1954), Those Damned Savages (Les maudits sauvages) (1971)

Garceau, Suzanne: Great Ordinary Movie, The (Joan of Arc Is Alive and Well and Living in Québec) (Le grand film ordinaire) (1971), Little Tougas (1976), Two Actresses (Deux actrices) (1993)

Garcia, Andy: Unsaid, The (2001)

Garcia, Eugene: Burnt Eden (1997)

Garcia, Nicole: Betty Fisher and Other Stories (Betty Fisher et autres histoires) (2001)

Gardiner, Faith: Room for a Stranger (1968)

Gardner, Ava: City on Fire (1979), Kidnapping of the President, The (1980)

Gardner, David: Artichoke (1978), Bethune (1977), Certain Practices (1979), Class of 1984 (1982), Double Negative (1979), If You Could See What I Hear (1982), Insurance Man From Ingersoll, The (1976), Oedipus Rex (1956), One of Our Own (1977), Paper People, The (1967), Perfect Pie (2002), Prom Night (1980), Trial and Error (1993), Who Has Seen the Wind (1977)

Gardner, Katya: Women Without Wings (2002)

Gardner, Layce: Hostile Advances: The Kerry Ellison Story (1996)

Gardner, Rita: One Plus One (The Kinsey Report) (Exploring the Kinsey Report) (1961)

Gariépy, Jean-Pierre: Si belles (So Pretty) (1994), Sous les draps, les étoiles (Stargazing and Other Passions) (1989)

Garneau, Amulette: Angelo, Fredo and Roméo (1996), Aventures d'une jeune veuve, Les (1974), Grands enfants, Les (Day by Day) (1980), Maria Chapdelaine (1983), Once Upon a Time in the East (Il était une fois dans l'est) (1974), Orders, The (Les ordres) (1974), Paths of the World, The (Les allées de la terre) (1973), Vultures, The (Les vautours) (1975), Years of Dreams and Revolt (Les années de rêves) (1984)

Garneau, Constance: Company of Strangers, The (Strangers in Good Company) (1990)

Garneau, Kathy: Tokyo Cowboy (1994)

Garneau, Michel: Celebrations, The (1979), Song for Julie, A (Chanson pour Julie) (1976)

Garner, James: Dead Silence (1997)

Garnett, Gale: Journey (1972), Not Just a Dirty Little Movie (1985), Tribute (1980), Overnight (1985), Park Is Mine, The (1986)

Garofalo, Janeane: Dog Park (1998)

Garon, Pauline: Critical Age, The (1923), Man from Glengarry, The (1920)

Garrard, James: Cold Comfort (1989)

Garreaud, Jean-François: *Violette Nozière* (1978)

Garret, Susan: Pleasure Palace (Angela) (1973)

Garrett, Amos: Christopher's Movie Matinée (1969)

Garrick, Timothy: Jailbait! (2000)

Garrity, Sean: Inertia (2001)

Garrow, Patrick: Dying Fall (2002)

Garson, Edward: Possible Worlds (2000), Silencing the Guns (*Le silence des fusils*) (1996), *Sucre amer* (1997), Young Magician, The (*Le jeune magicien*) (1987)

Gascon, Gabriel: *Au fil de l'eau* (By the Riverside) (2002), Immortal Scoundrel, The (*Étienne Brûlé, gibier de potence*) (1952), Looking for Leonard (2002), *Marais, Le* (2002), *Maîtres anciens* (1998), Possible Worlds (2000), *Sucre amer* (1997)

Gascon, Jean: Absence, The (*L'absence*) (1976), Lucky Star, The (1980), Silencing the Guns (Le silence des fusils) (1996)

Gascon, Louis: Ford: The Man and the Machine (1987)

Gascon, Nathalie: *Amoureux fou* (Madly in Love) (1991), Passing Through the Pine Trees (*M'en revenant par les épinettes*) (1977)

Gasoi, Lowell: Women Without Wings (2002)

Gass, Ken: Squamish Five, The (1988)

Gassman, Vittorio: Dear Father (*Caro Papa*) (1979)

Gates, Leonard-John: City Girl, The (1984)

Gatto, James: Stolen Heart (1998)

Gaudette, Maxim: Three Madeleines, The (*Les fantômes des trois Madeleines*) (1999)

Gaudette, Maxime: Bilan (2003)

Gaudette-Loiseau, Roxanne: *Forteresse suspendue, La* (The Hidden Fortress) (2001), *Station nord* (North Station) (2002)

Gaudreault, Émile: *Louis XIX, le roi des ondes* (1994), *Nuit de noces* (Night of the Wedding) (2001)

Gaudreault, Magdalena: Red Bells, Blue Tears (*Grelots rouges, sanglots bleus*) (1987)

Gaudreault, Peter Kelly: Dream Storm: A North of 60 Mystery (2001), In the Blue Ground (1999)

Gaudry, Éric: J.A. Martin, Photographer (1977)

Gaudry, Marie-Stéfane: Case of the Witch Who Wasn't, The (*Pas de répit pour Mélanie*) (1990)

Gault, Connie: Solitude (2001)

Gault, Judith: Breaking All the Rules (1985), Ernie Game, The (1967), Journey (1972), Lies My

Father Told Me (1975), Merry Wives of Tobias Rouke, The (1972), Partners (1976), Running Time (1978), Turnabout (1987)

Gaup, Nils: Misery Harbour (1999)

Gauthier, Claude: Between Sweet and Salt Water (Drifting Downstream) (*Entre la mer et l'eau douce*) (1967), *Dernier havre, Le* (1986), Dollar, The (The Other Side of the River) (*La piastre*) (*L'autre bord du fleuve*) (1976), *Homme de rêve, L'* (The Dream Man) (1991), Orders, The (*Les ordres*) (1974)

Gauthier, Gilles: Mustang (1975)

Gauthier, Louis: *Valérie* (1969)

Gauthier, Marie-Josée: *Automne sauvage, L'* (The Savage Autumn) (1992), *Sous les draps, les étoiles* (Stargazing and Other Passions) (Stars Under the Sheets) (1989)

Gauthier, Michel: Revolutionaries, The (*Le révolutionnaire*) (1965)

Gauthier, Paul: Between Sweet and Salt Water (Drifting Downstream) (*Entre la mer et l'eau douce*) (1967), Men, The (1971), Red (1969), Sacrifice, The (1955), True Nature of Bernadette, The (1972)

Gauthier, Régis: One Who Sees the Hours, The (*Celui qui voit les heures*) (1985)

Gauthier, Robert: Mayday (1996)

Gauthier, Sandy: Ups and Downs (1983)

Gautier, Blanch: Forbidden Journey (1950), Village Priest, The (*Le curé de village*) (1949)

Gautier, Philippe: Hathi (1998)

Gauvin, Maurice: Butler's Night Off, The (1948), Grand Bill, The (1949), Lights of My City (1950), That Darned Loot (*La maudite galette*) (1972)

Gava, Casandra: Amityville Curse, The (1990)

Gavin, John: Keep It in the Family (1973)

Gavine, Graham: Dragonwheel (2002)

Gavon, Igors: Ivy League Killers (1959)

Gay, Mary: It's Not Jacques Cartier's Fault (1968)

Gayet, Julie: *Turbulence des fluides, La* (Chaos and Desire) (2002)

Gazelle, Wendy: Understudy, The: Graveyard Shift II (1988)

Gazzara, Ben: Believe (2000), List, The (2000), Neptune Factor, The (The Neptune Disaster) (An Undersea Odyssey) (1973), Stag (1997)

Gazzo, Michael V.: Nothing to Lose (1994)

Geary, Cynthia: Awakening, The (1995), Hostile Force (The Heist) (1996)

Geddis, Jeff: Daydream Believers: The Monkees' Story (2000)

Gedrick, Jason: Still Life (Still Life: The Fine Art of Murder) (1990)

Geer, Will: Rowdyman, The (1972)

Geeson, Judy: Duke, The (1999)

Gei, Angela: Expecting (2002)

Geirhardsdottir, Halldora: Regina (2002)

Geiss, Louisette: Wishmaster 3: Beyond the Gates of Hell (2001)

Gelbart, Arnie: Gun Runner, The (1984), Rape of a Sweet Young Girl, The (1968)

Gélinas, Gratien: Agnes of God (1985), Red (1969), *Tisserands du pouvoir, Les* (The Mills of Power, Parts 1 and 2) (1988), *Tit-Coq* (1953)

Gélinas, Hugo: *Valérie* (1969)

Gélinas, Marc: *Histoire inventée, Une* (An Imaginary Tale) (1990), Men, The (1971)

Gélinas, Mitsou: Coyote (1993)

Gélinas, Pascal: *Montréal Blues* (1972)

Gélinas, Yves: Mustang (1975), True Nature of Bernadette, The (1972)

Gellman, Yani: Children of my Heart (2000)

Gendel, Morgan: Tek War: Tek Justice (1994)

Gendreau, Alain: Man from the Movies, The (1976)

Gendron, François-Éric: Blood of the Hunter (*Sang du chasseur, Le*) (Lone Eagle) (1995)

Gendron, Steve: *Matusalem* (1993), *Matusalem II, le dernier des Beauchesne* (1996), *Postière, La* (The Postmistress) (1992)

Genesse, Bryan: Guardian, The (1999), Screwballs II: Loose Screws (1985)

Genest, Claude: Rowing Through (1996)

Genest, Émile: Incredible Journey, The (1963), Nikki, Wild Dog of the North (1961), *Nous deux, À* (1979), *Plouffe, Les* (1981), Separation (1978)

Genet, Jean: Black Mirror (1981)

Geoffrion, Robert: Blue Man, The (1985), Frame-Up Blues (*La danse du scorpion*) (1991), *Frontière du crime* (Double Identity) (1990), Joy (1983), Hollow Point (1997), Honeymoon (*Lune de miel*) (1985), Legends of the North (1996), Peacekeeper, The (1997), Sally Marshall Is Not An Alien (1999), Scandale (1982), Scream of Stone (*Cerro Torra*) (1991), Surrogate (1984), Tracker, The (1999), *Vents contraires* (Crosswinds) (1995), Watchtower, The (2001)

George, Chief Dan: Alien Thunder (Dan Candy's Law) (1973), Cold Journey (1976), Nothing Personal (1980), Shadow of the Hawk (1976)

George, Christopher: Inbreaker, The (1974)

George, Leonard: Inbreaker, The (1974)

George, Susan: Tomorrow Never Comes (1978)

Georgeson, Thomas: No Surrender (1985), Lyddie (1995)

Georgiades, Evan: Vivid (1996), Two or Three Words (1999)

Géral, Hubert: *Dur-Dur* (1981)

Gerber, Fred: Closer and Closer (1996), Due South (1994)

Germain, Nicole: *Homme et son pêché, Un* (*Séraphin*) (A Man and His Sin) (1949), Nightingales and the Bells (*Le rossignol et les cloches*) (1952), Whispering City (1947)

Gernon, Edward: Adrift (1993)

Gerretsen, Peter: Kidnapping of Baby John Doe, The (1985), Night Friend (A Cry From the Heart) (1987), Three More Days (1995)

Gerretsen, Terry: Adrift (1993)

Gershon, Gina: Flinch (1994), Picture Claire (2001)

Gerussi, Bruno: Oedipus Rex (1956)

Gervais, Lisette: It's Not Jacques Cartier's Fault (1968)

Gervais, Monique: *Dernier havre, Le* (1986)

Gessner, Nicolas: Little Girl Who Lives Down the Lane, The (1977)

Getty, Balthazar: Habitat (1995), Red Hot (1993)

Getz, John: Fly, The (1986)

Ghini, Massimo: Almost America (*Come l'America*) (2001), Lucille: The Lucille Teasdale Story (1999)

Ghorayeb, Michel: When I Will Be Gone (*L'âge de braise*) (1998)

Ghris, Abderranhmane: Life, A (1988)

Giannini, Giancarlo: Brown Bread Sandwiches (1990), Heaven Before I Die (1997), Whole Shebang, The (2001)

Giannotti, Anna Maria: Absent One, The (1997)

Gibb, Cynthia: Death Warrant (1990), Wandering Soul Murders, The (2000)

Gibb, Robert: Naked Flame, The (1964)

Gibbon, Mark: Things to Do on a Saturday Night (1998)

Gibbon, Sharon: War Between Us, The (1995)

Gibbons, Rodney: Artificial Lies (*Le manipulateur*) (2000), Case of the Whitechapel Vampire, The (2001), Digger (1993), Hound of the Baskervilles, The (2000), Louisa May Alcott's Little Men (1998), Neighbour, The (1993), Royal Scandal, The (2001), Sign of Four, The (2001)

Gibbs, Fabian: Sitting in Limbo (1985)

Gibbs, Lesley: Melting Pot, The (1975)

Gibbs, Timothy: Witchboard II (1993)

Gibson, Alan: Martin's Day (1984)

Gibson, Dan: Wings in the Wilderness (*Les voyageurs d'été*) (1975)

Gibson, Henry: Tulips (1981)

Gibson, Jane: Turnabout (1987)

Gibson, Luke: Journey (1972)

Gibson, Martha: Family of Strangers (1993), Marriage Bed, The (1986), Outrageous! (1977), Sanity Clause (1990), Terminal Choice (Deathbed) (1985)

Gibson, Michael: Defy Gravity (1990)

Gibson, Scott: Jack and Jill (1998)

Gibson, Thomas: Love and Human Remains (Unidentified Human Remains and the True Nature of Love) (1994), Stardom (15 Minutes) (Fandom) (2000)

Gibson, William: Johnny Mnemonic (1995)

Gideon, Raynold: Man, a Woman and a Bank, A (1979)

Gidwani, Kitu: Earth (1998)

Gielgud, John: Galileo (1973), Murder by Decree (1979)

Gifford, Thomas: Dirty Tricks (1980)

Gignac, Madeleine: Gobital (1975)

Gignac, Marie: Confessional, The (*Le confessionnal*) (1995), No (1998), Tectonic Plates (1992)

Gignac, Monique: *Peau et les os, La* (Skin and Bones) (1988)

Giguère, Marcel: *Deux pieds dans la même bottine, Les* (Two Feet in the Same Ankle Boot) (The Clumsy Klutz) (1974)

Giguère, Réal: Cain (1965)

Gilbert, Gaston: Adventures of Ti-ken, The (1961)

Gilbert, John: Art of Woo, The (2001), Eclipse (1994), Rats (1999)

Gilbert, Melissa: Family of Strangers (1993)

Gilbert, Sky: Bubbles Galore (1996), My Summer Vacation (1996)

Gilchrist, Jane: Rainbow (1995)

Gill, Akesh: Burning Season, The (1993)

Gill, Nancy Lou: Now That April's Here (1958)

Gillan, Heather: Gladiator Cop (1994)

Gillard, Stuart: Draw! (1984), Kart Racer (2002), If You Could See What I Hear (1982), Indigo Autumn (1987), Midnight Magic (1988), Neptune Factor, The (The Neptune Disaster) (An Undersea Odyssey) (1973), Paradise (1982), Reincarnate, The (1971), Rowdyman, The (1972), Sneakers (Spring Fever) (1982), Threshold (1981), Why Rock the Boat? (1974)

Gilles, Frédéric: *15 février 1839* (2001)

Gilliam, Katy: Secondary High (2003)

Gilliere, Jolynine: White Road, The (1929)

Gillies, Andrew: Big Meat Eater (1982)

Gilman, Kenneth: Bedroom Eyes (1984)

Gilmour, Danny: *Crème glacée, chocolat et autres consolations* (Ice Cream, Chocolate and other Consolations) (2001), Marie's Sons (*Les fils de Marie*) (2002), Winter Lily (1998)

Gilmour, Dawn: Morning! (1992)

Gilmore, Julia: Memoirs (1984)

Gilsenan, Marion: Coming of Age (1983), Getting Married in Buffalo Jump (1990)

Gima, Gheorghe: *Deux amis silencieux* (Dogs to the Rescue) (Two Silent Friends) (1969)

Gingras, René: *Homme renversé, L'* (1987)

Giovanni, Jose: Ruffian, The (1983)

Girard, Benoît: *Quarantaine, La* (Beyond Forty) (1982), *Duo pour une soliste* (Duet for a Soloiste) (Duet for One) (1998), House of Lovers (*La maison des amants*) (1972), Let's Talk About Love (1976)

Girard, François: Cargo (1990), Thirty-two Short Films About Glenn Gould (1994), Red Violin, The (*Le violon rouge*) (1998)

Girard, Jean: *Dur-Dur* (1981)

Girard, Louis-Georges: Black List (*Liste noire*) (1995)

Girard, Martin: Cuervo, the Private Detective (1990)

Girard, Pierre: Angel and the Woman, The (*L'ange et la femme*) (1977)

Girard, Rémy: *Amoureux fou* (Madly in Love) (1991), Barbarian Invasions, The (*Invasions Barbares, Les*) (2003), Blizzard, The (*Rafales*) (1990), *Boys III, Les* (The Boys III) (2001), *Boys, Les* (The Boys) (1997), Crime of Ovide Plouffe, The (*Le crime d'Ovide Plouffe*) (*Les Plouffe, II*) (1984), Damascus Road, The (*Le chemin de Damas*) (1988), Decline of the American Empire, The (*Le declin de l'empire Américain*) (1986), *Dernier cri* (The Last Cry) (1996), Don Quichotte (2001), Fish Tale Soup (1997), Florida, La (1993), Happy Memories (Old Memories) (*Les beaux souvenirs*) (1981), Ideal Man, The (*L'homme idéal*) (1996), In the Belly of a Dragon (1989), *Jésus de Montréal* (1989), Kalamazoo (1988), Million Dollar Babies (1995), Red Eyes (Accidental Truths) (*Les yeux rouges*) (*Les verités accidentelles*) (1983), Seat of the Soul, The (Crisis of Conscience, A) (*Le siege de l'âme*) (1997), Secret of Jerome, The (*Le secret de Jérôme*) (1994), Varian's War (2001), *Séraphin* (Heart of Stone) (A Man and His Sin) (2002)

Girard, Renée: Head of Normande St. Onge, The (*La tête de Normande St-Onge*) (1975)

Girardi, Robert: *Automne sauvage, L'* (The Savage Autumn) (1992)

Girardot, Annie: When I Will Be Gone (*L'âge de braise*) (1998)

Giraudeau, Bernard: Ruffian, The (1983)

Girling, Cindy: I Miss You, Hugs and Kisses (1978), Julie Darling (1982), Kidnapping of the President, The (1980), Meatballs (1979)

Girolami, Bob: One Man (1977)

Girolami, Budd: One Man (1977)

Girolami, Jacques: One Man (1977)

Girolami, Larry: One Man (1977)

Giroux, Antoinette: *Séraphin* (1950)

Giroux, Carmen: Head of Normande St. Onge, The (*La tête de Normande St-Onge*) (1975)

Giroux, Chantal: *Crabe dans la tête, Un* (A Crab in My Head) (2001)

Giroux, Fernande: Red (1969)

Giroux, Germaine: Awakening, The (*L'amour humain*) (1970)

Giroux, Marcel: List, The (2000)

Gish, Sheila: Mansfield Park (1998)

Gissing, Matt: Drawing Flies (1996), Tail Lights Fade (1999)

Giverin, Daniel: So Faraway and Blue (2001)

Glaser, Paul Michael: Phobia (1980)

Glass, Gaston: Cameron of the Royal Mounted (1921), God's Crucible (1921)

Glass, Joanna McClelland: Artichoke (1978), Woman Wanted (1999)

Glatzer, Richard: Fubar (2002)

Gleason, Paul: Nothing to Lose (1994)

Glenen, Brent: Roller Coaster (1999)

Glenn, Scott: Shipping News, The (2001)

Glickman, Cindy: Christopher's Movie Matinée (1969)

Glogovac, Nebojsa: Boomerang (2002)

Glover, Bruce: Chain Dance (1991)

Glover, Julian: Book of Eve (*Histoires d'Eve*) (2002), Luther (1973)

Glover, Kara: Caribe (1988)

Glover, Susan: Rainbow (1995)

Glowacz, Stefan: Scream of Stone (1991)

Glyn-Jones, David: Air Bud: World Pup (2000)

Gobeil, Pierre: Before the Time Comes (*Le temps de l'avant*) (1975), *Quarantaine, La* (Beyond Forty) (1982), *Cordélia* (1980), Swindle, The (*La gammick*) (1974),

Godbout, Claude: Cat in the Bag, The (*Le chat dans le sac*) (1964)

Godbout, Ghislaine: Kid Sentiment (1967)

Godbout, Jacques: Alias Will James (1988), IXE-13 (1972), Kid Sentiment (1967), Swindle, The (*La gammick*) (1974), YUL 871 (Montréal Flight 871) (1966)

Godden, Mark: Dracula: Pages From a Virgin's Diary (2003)

Godin, Gérald: Between Sweet and Salt Water (Drifting Downstream) (1967)

Godin, Guy: *Corde au cou, La* (1966), *Délivrez-nous du mal* (1967), Heartbreak (*L'arrache-coeur*) (1979), *Valérie* (1969)

Godin, Jacques: *Alisée* (1991), Amateur, The (1981), Being at Home With Claude (1992), *Quarantaine, La* (Beyond Forty) (1982), By the Blood of Others (*Par le sang des autres*) (1974), *Corde au cou, La* (1966), December (1978), *Délivrez-nous du mal* (Deliver Us From Evil) (1967), *Équinoxe* (1986), *Gaspard et fils* (1988), Luck of Ginger Coffey, The (1964), Heartbreak (*L'arrache-coeur*) (1979), Henri (1986), Man Inside, The (1975), Mario (1984),

Mission of Fear (1965), In the Name of the Son (*Et du fils*) (1972), Intimate Power (Blind Trust) (*Pouvoir intime*) (1985), Man Inside, The (1975), Night of the Flood (*La nuit du déluge*) (1996), No Holiday for Idols (*Pas de vacances pour les idoles*) (1965), OK Liberty (1973), One Man (1977), Pyx, The (1973), *Salut, Victor!* (1988), *Valérie* (1969)

Godin, Maurice: Awakening, The (1995), Double Take (1998), White Room (1989)

Godin, Patrice: Full Blast (*L'ennemi*) (1999), Not Me! (*Sous-sol*) (1996)

Godin-Vigneau, Noemie: *Je n'aime que toi* (I Don't Love You) (2003)

Godsman, Carroll: Beefcake (1999)

Godson, Tobias: Waydowntown (2000)

Godson, Clayton: Hey, Happy! (2000)

Goff, Carolyn: Ride, The (2000)

Going, Joanna: Lola (2001)

Gold, Benjamin: Warriors (1994)

Gold, Dave: Wow (1970)

Gold, L. Harvey: Various Postions (2002)

Goldberg, Dan: Meatballs (1979)

Goldblum, Jeff: Fly, The (1986), Threshold (1981)

Goldhar, Marvin: Deadline (Anatomy of a Horror) (1980), Offering, The (1966), Never Trust an Honest Thief (1979), Scoop (1978)

Goldman, Mel: Ryan's Babe (2000)

Goldrick, Daphne: Harry Tracy, Desperado (1981)

Goldsmith, George: Nowhere to Hide (1987)

Goldsmith, John: Armen and Bullik (1993)

Goldstein, Allan A.: 2001: A Space Travesty (2001), Chain Dance (Common Bonds) (1991), Cold Front (1989), Death Wish V: The Face of Death (1994), Home Team (1999), Memory Run (1995), Outside Chance of Maximillian Glick, The (1988), Phone Call, The (*Ligne interdite*) (1989), *Vents contraires* (Crosswinds) (1995)

Goldstein, Carl Alexander: Shadow Lake (2000)

Goldstein, Josh: Partners 'n Love (1992)

Gonella, David: Little Boy Blues (2000)

Gonick, Noam: Hey, Happy! (2000)

Gonzalez, Simon: Heat Line, The (*La ligne de chaleur*) (1987)

Gomes, Mary Jane: Angel in a Cage (1998)

Gomes, Maurina: Angel in a Cage (1998)

Good, Janet: Eat Anything (1971)

Goodall, Caroline: Love and Murder (1999), Secret Laughter of Women, The (1999)

Goodger, Michele: Strange and Rich (1994)

Goodhand, Donna: Waiting for the Parade (1984)

Goodhew, Philip: Intimate Relations (1995)

Goodhue, Clarence: Luck of Ginger Coffey, The (1964)

Goodier, Robert: Apprenticeship of Duddy Kravitz,

The (1974), Fortune and Men's Eyes (1971), My Pleasure Is My Business (1975), Oedipus Rex (1956), To Kill the King (1974), Power Play (*Coup d'état*) (State of Shock) (Operation Overthrow) (1978), Second Wind (1976), Sins of the Fathers (1948)

Goodsell, Heather: Return of Tommy Tricker, The (1994)

Goodspeed, Donald: Powder Heads (1980)

Goorjian, Michael: Dukes, The (1998), Something More (1999)

Gorardot, Annie: Cry in the Night, A (1996)

Goranson, Linda: American Christmas Carol, An (1979), Execution of Raymond Graham, The (1985), Fan's Notes, A (1972), Gross Misconduct (1992), Inside Out (1979), More Joy in Heaven (1975), Rowdyman, The (1972)

Gorch, Lyle: Park Is Mine, The (1986)

Gorden, Bruce: Slow Run (1969)

Gordon, Alan: Foxy Lady (1971)

Gordon, Barbara: Chatwill's Verdict (Killer Instinct) (Baker County, U.S.A) (Trapped) (1982), Children of my Heart (2000), Christina (1974), Coming Out Alive (1980), Dead Ringers (Alter Ego) (Twins) (1988), Kate Morris, Vice President (1984), Kidnapping of Baby John Doe, The (1985), Plague, The (1979), Running Man (1980), Special Delivery (1982), Three and a Half (2002), White Room (1989)

Gordon, Bernard: Surfacing (1981)

Gordon, Donald: Out of the Blue (1980)

Gordon, Eve: Almost Grown (1987)

Gordon, Graham: Roses in December (1965)

Gordon, Joyce: Deadly Appearances (1999), Improper Channels (1981), Man in 5A, The (1982)

Gordon, Kenneth: Music of the Spheres, The (1984)

Gordon, Lewis: Chasing Rainbows (1988)

Gordon, Russell: Make Mine Chartreuse (1987)

Gordon, Sarah: Fast Food High (2003)

Gordon-Sinclair, John: A.K.A. Albert Walker (2002)

Gorling, Wendy: Overcoat, The (*Le manteau*) (2002)

Gorman, Lynne: Nobody Waved Goodbye (1964), Videodrome (1983)

Gorman, Patrick: Trouble (1996)

Gorodsky, Alexandre Shar: *Miss Moscou* (1992)

Gorodsky, Lev Shar: *Miss Moscou* (1992)

Gorshin, Frank: Twilight of the Ice Nymphs (1997)

Gorski, Tamara: Lost World, The (1992), Striking Poses (1999)

Gosling, Andrew: King of Friday Night, The (1985)

Gosselin, Bernard: Big Sabotage, The (*Le grand sabordage*) (1973), Christmas Martian, The (*Le martien de Noël*) (1971), *Réjeanne Padovani* (1973)

Gosselin, François: Christmas Martian, The (*Le martien de Noël*) (1971)

Gosselin, Pierrette: Sacrifice, The (*La sacrifiée*) (1955)

Gosselin, Roger: Taureau (1972)

Gossett Jr., Louis: Captive Heart: The James Mink Story (1996), Dr. Lucille: The Lucille Teasdale Story (1999), Highwayman, The (1999)

Gotell, Walter: KGB: The Secret War (1984)

Gottli, Michael: Archangel (1990), Tales From the Gimli Hospital (1988)

Gottlieb, David: Memory Run (1995)

Gottlieb, Paul: In Praise of Older Women (1978)

Gottraud, Serge: To Kill to Live (*Mourir pour vivre*) (1973)

Goudreau, Richard: Believe (2000), Frankenstein and Me (1995), *Boys, Les* (The Boys) (1997)

Gough, William: Accident at Memorial Stadium, The (1983), Dying Hard (1978), Family of Strangers (1993), Far Cry From Home, A (1980), High Card (1982)

Gough, Michael: Galileo (1973)

Gould, Elliott: Dirty Tricks (1980), Silent Partner, The (1978)

Gould, Kenneth: Night of the Flood (1996)

Gould, L. Harvey: Various Positions (2002)

Goulem, Alain: Drive, The (1996)

Goulem, Eric: Katryn's Place (2002)

Goulem, Romy: Drive, The (1996)

Goulet, Charles: Nightmare, The (*Cauchemar*) (1979)

Goulet, Johanne: Camera Thief, The (*Le voleur de caméra*) (1993)

Goulet, Mireille: Precious Hours, The (*Les heures précieuses*) (1989)

Goulet, René: Revolutionaries, The (*Le révolutionaire*) (1965)

Goulet, Robert: Atlantic City, U.S.A (1980)

Goulet, Stella: Case of the Witch Who Wasn't, The (*Pas de répit pour Mélanie*) (1990)

Goulet, Teddy-Burns: Clean Hands (*Les mains nettes*) (1958)

Goulet-Robitaille, Anaïs: Friends for Life (*Des amis pour la vie*) (1988), Keep an Eye on the Trombone (1992), *Vengeance de la femme en noir, La* (1996)

Goulin, Benoît: Seven Streams of the River Ota, The (1998)

Goupil, Pierre: Autobiography of an Amateur Filmmaker, The (*L'autobiographe amateur*) (1999), One Who Sees the Hours, The (*Celui qui voit les heures*) (1985)

Gowan, Lee: Paris or Somewhere (1995)

Goy, Luba: Improper Channels (1981), Murder by Phone (1982)

Goyer, David: Death Warrant (1990)

Goyer, Jean-Pierre: Story of the Three, A (1989)

Goyette, Jocelyne: Night in America, A (1975)

Goyette, Michel: Dead End (1999)

Goyette, Patrick: Confessional, The (Le confessionnal) (1995), Four Days (1999), Polygraph, Le (1996), Seven Streams of the River Ota, The (1998), Three Madeleines, The (Les fantômes des trois Madeleines) (1999), Task Force (2000)

Graham, Carrie: Trust in Me (1995)

Graham, Currie: Cowboys and Indians (2003), Deadly Arrangement (1998), Edge of Madness (Station Sauvage) (Wilderness Station) (2003)

Graham, Gerald: Royal Journey (1952)

Graham, Holter: Fly Away Home (1996)

Graham, Hugh: Palais Royale (1988)

Graham, Nancy: Bush Pilot (1946)

Graham, Ron: Dead Wrong (1983)

Graham, Rose: Psycho Girls (1986)

Graham, Sheenan: Slavers, The (1984)

Graham, Stuart: Misery Harbour (1999)

Graham, William A.: Harry Tracy, Desperado (1981)

Grahay, Christian: Family Pack (Que faisaient les femmes, pendant que l'homme marchait sur la lune?) (2000)

Graie, Madison: Zacharia Farted (1998)

Grammer, Kelsey: Real Howard Spitz, The (1998)

Grana, Felice: Masculine Mystique, The (1984)

Grana, Sam: 90 Days (1985), Boys of St. Vincent, The (1992), Last Straw, The (1987), Welcome to Canada (1989)

Grana, Stefanie: Masculine Mystique, The (1984)

Granbery, Don: Blackout (Blackout in New York) (1978), Homecoming, The (Good Luck, Jennifer Gagnon) (1978), Supreme Kid, The (1976)

Grandbois, Geneviève: Fabuleux voyage de l'ange, Le (The Fabulous Voyage of the Angel) (1991)

Grandison, Pippa: Golden Fiddles (1991)

Grandnetti, Dario: Dark Side of the Heart, The (El lado oscuro del corazon) (1993)

Grandpré, Elizabeth: Jeunes Québécoises, Les (The Younger Generation) (1980)

Grandpré, Frederick de: Piege d'Issoudun, Le (Trapped in Issoudun) (2002)

Granger, Luc: Straight to the Heart (1969)

Granger, Philip: Lunch with Charles (2001)

Granik, Jon: Final Assignment (1980), Fortune and Men's Eyes (1971), Heatwave Lasted Four Days, The (1973), In Praise of Older Women (1978), Last Act of Martin Weston, The (1971), Megantic Outlaw, The (1971), Never Trust an Honest Thief (Going for Broke) (1979), Power Play (Coup d'état) (State of Shock) (Operation Overthrow) (1978), Ragtime Summer (Age of Innocence) (1977)

Granik, Lise: Sweeter Song, A (1976)

Granofsky, Anaïs: Invitation (2000), Have Mercy (1999), On Their Knees (2001)

Grant, Allan: Sylvan Lake Summer (1991)

Grant, Catherine: Understanding Bliss (1990)

Grant, David Marshall: Happy Birthday Gemini (1980), Jenifer Estess Story, The (2001)

Grant, Debbie: Sitting in Limbo (1985)

Grant, Eddy: Mustard Bath (1993)

Grant, George: Little Canadian, The (1955)

Grant, Glen: Touch and Go (2002)

Grant, Julian: Airborne (1998), Bust a Move (1993)

Grant, Lee: Visiting Hours (Fright) (1982)

Grant, Michael: Head On (Fatal Attraction) (1980)

Grant, Ronald: Little Canadian, The (1955)

Grant, Schuyler: Anne of Green Gables (1985), Anne of Green Gables: The Continuing Story (Series) (1985-1999)

Graton, Françoise: Crinoline Madness (La folie des crinolines) (1995)

Graton, Thomas: Pin-Pon, The Film (1999)

Gratton, Vincent: Années, Les (The Years) (1997)

Grauer, Ona: House of the Dead (2003)

Gravel, Robert: Erreur sur la personne (The Wrong Person) (1995), Grands enfants, Les (Day by Day) (1980), Head of Normande St. Onge, The (La tête de Normande St-Onge) (1975), Intimate Power (1985), Last Glacier, The (1984), Pudding chômeur (Bread Pudding) (1996), Vultures, The (Les vautours) (1975)

Graves, Ernest: One Plus One (The Kinsey Report) (Exploring the Kinsey Report) (1961)

Graves, Rupert: Intimate Relations (1995)

Gray, Adele: Return of Tommy Tricker, The (Le retour des aventuriers du timbre perdu) (1994)

Gray, Bruce: Room for a Stranger (1968)

Gray, Erin: Myth That Wouldn't Die (Dan Seurs du Mozambique, Les) (1991)

Gray, Jack: Quiet Day in Belfast, A (1973)

Gray, John: Haven (2001), Legend of Kootenai Brown, The (1990), Secret Life of Algernon, The (1996), Showdown at Williams Creek (Kootenai Brown) (1991)

Gray, Marguerite: Ten Girls Ago (1962)

Gray, Martin: For Those I Loved (Au nom de tous les miens) (1983)

Gray, McKenzie: 2103: The Deadly Wake (1996)

Gray, Sally: Keeper, The (1975)

Gray, William: Blood and Guts (1978), Changeling, The (1980), Cross Country (1983), Humongous (1982), Prom Night (1980)

Grayhm, Steven: Tribe of Joseph (2001)

Grazioli, Irene: Red Violin, The (1998)

Grdevich, Sabrina: Lola (2001), Mile Zero (2001), Washed Up (2002)

Greco, Jessica: Treed Murray (2001)

Gréco, Pierre: *Petit vent de panique, Un* (A Gust of Panic) (2000)

Green, Bob: Sex and the Single Sailor (1967)

Green, Calvin: Exotica (1994)

Green, Christopher: Going Home (1987)

Green, Faith: Cameron of the Royal Mounted (1921), Critical Age, The (1923), God's Crucible (1921), Man from Glengarry, The (1920)

Green, Guy: Luther (1973)

Green, Janet-Laine: Bullies (1986), Chautauqua Girl (1984), Circle Game, The (1994), Cowboys Don't Cry (1987), Diamond Fleece, The (1992), Harry's Case (2000), Haven (2001), Julia (see Acts of the Heart) (1980), Kidnapping of Baby John Doe, The (1985), Medicine River (1993), Murder Sees the Light (1987), Primo Baby (1989), Shower, The (1992), Striking Poses (1999), Vita Cane (1994) Tagged: The Jonathan Wamback Story (2002)

Green, Lewis: Never Talk to Strangers (1995)

Green, Liz: Screwballs II: Loose Screws (1985)

Green, Lynda Mason: Isaac Littlefeathers (1984), Kidnapping of the President, The (1980), Return of Ben Casey, The (1988), Shape of Things to Come, The (1979), Silence of the North (1981), Vindicator, The (Frankenstein '88) (1986)

Green, Martin: Footsteps in the Snow (*Des pas sur la neige*) (1966)

Green, Melvyn: Slow Run (1969)

Green, Rick: All in Good Taste (1983)

Green, Tom: Clutch (1998), Super Star (1999)

Greenall, Douglas: Reasonable Force (1983), Sister Blue (2001)

Greenberg, Daniel: Guardian, The (1999)

Greenberg, Harold: Draw! (1984)

Greenblatt, Natasha: This Matter of Marriage (1998)

Greene, Candy: Love in a Four Letter World (1970)

Greene, David: Breach of Faith: A Family of Cops II (1996), Frostfire (1995)

Greene, Gael: Love on Your Birthday(see Acts of Love Series) (1980)

Greene, Graham: Bad Money (1999), Camilla (1994), Clear Cut (1991), Dead Innocent (1996), Desire (2000), Grey Owl (1999), Heart of the Sun (1998), Herd, The (1998), Lost and Delirious (2000), Lost in the Barrens (1990), Medicine River (1993), Misery Harbour (1999), Murder Sees the Light (1987), Out of Sight, Out of Mind (The Seventh Circle) (1983), Running Brave (1983), Pathfinder, The (1996), Red Green's Duct Tape Forever (2002), Shadow Lake (2000), Song of Hiawatha, The (1996), Spirit Rider (1993), Stranger in Town (1998),

Where the Heart Is (1985), Wounded (1996)

Greene, Lorna: Klondike Fever (1979),Wings in the Wilderness (*Les voyageurs d'été*) (1975)

Greene, Peter: Coyote Run (1996)

Greenhalgh, Dawn: Circle Game, The (1994), Conspiracy of Silence (1991), Deadly Harvest (1980), Fish Tale Soup (1997), Journey Into Darkness: The Bruce Curtis Story (1990), Rowdyman, The (1972), Tell Me My Name (1977), Undergrads, The (1985), Wrong Woman, The (1995)

Greenhouse, Kate: Assistant, The (1996), Fools Die Fast (1995)

Greenspan, Larry: Winter Kept Us Warm (1965)

Greenwald, Barry: I, Maureen (1980)

Greenwalt, David: Utilities (1981)

Greenwood, Bruce: Adrift (1993), Ararat (2002), Bear Island (1979), Climb, The (1987), Cord (Hide and Seek) (2000), Exotica (1994), Haven (2001), Little Kidnappers, The (1990), Paint Cans (1994), Striker's Mountain (1985), Sweet Hereafter, The (1996), Treacherous Beauties (1994)

Greenwood, Joan: Uncanny, The (1977)

Greenwood, Kathryn: Wind at My Back (2001)

Greenwood, Rochelle: Water Game, The (2002)

Greer, James: This Is a Film (That Was a Film) (1989)

Greer, Michael: Fortune and Men's Eyes (1971)

Gregg, Clark: Lana in Love (1991), Ride Me (Ego Trip) (1995)

Greggio, Ezio: 2001: A Space Travesty (2001)

Grégoire, Hélène: Duplessis' Orphans (1999)

Grégoire, Lise: Medium Blues (1985)

Grégoire, Pierre: King of Fire (1985)

Grégori, Jacques: French Love (*Un amour comme le nôtre*) (1974)

Gregory, Karen: Proud Rider, The (The Last Run) (1972), Neptune Factor, The (The Neptune Disaster) (An Undersea Odyssey) (1973)

Gregory, Shelby: Freeloading (1986)

Gregson, Joan: Neptune Factor, The (The Neptune Disaster) (An Undersea Odyssey) (1973), Sea People (1999)

Gren, Roman: Julie Walking Home (2002)

Grenfell, Sir Wilfred: Viking, The (1931)

Grenier, Jennifer: Just a Game (1983)

Grenier, Zack: Kid Brother, The (1987)

Grenon, Macha: *Concièrgerie, La* (The Caretaker's Lodge) (The Prison) (1997), Coyote Run (1996), *Erreur sur la personne* (The Wrong Person) (1995), Ideal Man, The (*L'homme idéal*) (1996), Family Pack (*Que faisaient les femmes, pendant que l'homme marchait sur la lune?*) (2000), Legends of the North (1996),

Grenon, Macha continued:
Mayday (1996), Pianist, The (1991), Power Games (*Jeux de pouvoir*) (1990), You Can Thank Me Later (1998)

Grey, Bruce: Nobody Makes Me Cry (Between Friends) (1983)

Grey, Tony: Now That April's Here (1958)

Greyeyes, Carol: Girl Who Married a Ghost, The (2003)

Greyeyes, Michael: Big Bear (1988), Dance Me Outside (1994), Fallen Knight (1998)

Greyson, John: Law of Enclosures, The (2000), Lilies (1996), Uncut (1997), Urinal (1988), Zero Patience (1993)

Grice, Dermot: Noncensus (1964)

Grieco, Richard: Blackheart (1997)

Grier, Pam: Vindicator, The (Frankenstein '88) (1986), Night of the High Tide, The (*La notte dell'alta marea*) (1976)

Gries, Jon: Snow Walker, The (2002)

Grieve, Neil: Stuart Bliss (1998)

Griffin, Joseph: Men With Guns (1996), Striking Poses (1999)

Griffin, Lynne: Black Christmas (Silent Night, Evil Nights) (Stranger in the House) (1974), Curtains (1983), Every Person Is Guilty (1979), Hitting Home (Obsessed) (1989), Man Inside, The (1975), Strange Brew (1983)

Griffin, Nonnie: If You Could See What I Hear (1982)

Griffith, Diane: Bitter Ash, The (1963)

Griffith, Hugh: Luther (1973)

Griffith, Kenneth: Why Shoot the Teacher (1977)

Griffith, Thomas Ian: Hollow Point (1997)

Griffiths, Alison: Net Worth (1997)

Griffiths, Linda: Darling Family, The (1994), Execution of Raymond Graham, The (1985), Mama's Going to Buy You a Mockingbird (1987), Marriage Bed, The (1986), Passion and Paradise (1989), Reno and the Doc (1984), Samuel Lount (1985)

Grigg, Daniel: Tragic Diary of Zero, the Fool, The (1970)

Grignon, Claude-Henri: *Homme et son péché, Un (Séraphin)* (A Man and His Sin) (1949)

Grigsby, Wayne: And Then You Die (1987), Task Force (2000)

Grimaldi, Francine: Pacemaker and a Sidecar, A (1997), Sex in the Snow (*Après-ski*) (1971)

Grismer, Christopher: Clutch (1998)

Groom, Sam: Deadly Eyes (The Rats) (1982)

Gross, Mary: Jailbait! (2000)

Gross, Marty: Lover's Exile, The (1981)

Gross, Paul: Buried on Sunday (1993), Chasing Rainbows (1988), Cold Comfort (1989), Due South (1994), Getting Married in Buffalo Jump (1990), Gross Misconduct (1992), In This Corner (1986), Men With Brooms (2002), Murder Most Likely (1999), Whale Music (1994)

Gross, Peter: Rip-Off (1971)

Grossen, Susanna: Sex and the Lonely Woman (1966)

Grosser, Arthur: Lilac Dream (1987)

Grossman, Suzanne: Don't Let It Kill You (*Il ne faut pas mourir pour ça*) (1968)

Grou, Daniel: *Exils* (2002)

Groulx, Gilles: Cat in the Bag, The (*Le chat dans le sac*) (1964), So Where Are You? (*Où étes-vous donc?*) (1969), *Entre tu et vous* (Between "tu" and "you") (1970), In the Land of Zom (1983), Now Where Are You? (*Où étes-vous, donc?*) (1969), *Trop c'est Assez (Too Much is Enough)* (1996) (111mins) (b&w&col) d&s: Richard Brouillette With: Gilles Groulx, Jean-Paul Mousseau, Denis Vanier, Josee Yvon, Barbara Ulrich, Raphaelle Groulx. Gilles Groulx (1931-1994) is considered by many film people and audiences in Quebec to be one of Canada's most important and original filmmakers. Richard Brouillette knew him well, and in this heart-felt record of Groulx's life and work we hear interviews by friends and see scenes from his films.

Groulx, Raphaelle: *Trop c'est assez* (Too Much Is Enough) (1996)

Groulx, Sylvie: *J'aime, j'aime pas* (1995)

Grove, Bill: Ghostkeeper (1981)

Grove, Richard: Scanner Cop (1994)

Grover, Deborah: Mark of Cain, The (1984)

Gruault, Jean: *Ou le roman de Charles Pathé* (The Life of Charles Pathé) (1995)

Gruben, Patricia: Low Visibility (1984)

Grunberg, Andreas: Poison (Tease) (1999)

Gruselle, Pascal: Dark Harbour (1997)

Guadagni, Nicky: Cube (1997), Squamish Five, The (1988), Turning to Stone (1986)

Guang, Qi: Small Pleasures (1993)

Guardagni, Nicky: Turning to Stone (1986)

Guare, John: Atlantic City, U.S.A (1980)

Guay, Marie-Ginette: *Femmes savantes, Les* (The Wise Women) (2001), Large Abode, A (1978), *Shift de nuit, Le* (The Night Shift) (1979)

Guay, Philippe le: *Mémoire tronquée* (1990)

Guenette, Réjean: Bingo (1974)

Guenette, Serge: Mis-Works, The (1959)

Guérard, Sandra: Stuff (1999)

Guérin, Luc: Angelo, Fredo and Roméo (1996), *Boys III, Les* (The Boys III) (2001), *Boys, Les* (The Boys) (1997), Winter Stories (*Histoires d'hiver*) (1999)

Guérin, Maude: *La beauté de Pandore* (2000), *Collectionneur, Le* (The Collector) (2001), Matroni and Me (1999), *Môtel Hélène* (1999)

Guerra, Blanca: Falcon's Gold (1982), Separate Vacations (1986)

Guertin, Lisette: *Dernière condition, La* (1982)

Guevara, Nacha: Dark Side of the Heart, The (*El lado oscuro del corazon*) (1993)

Guèvremont, Paul: Dust from Underground (*Poussière sur la ville*) (1965), Grand Bill, The (*Le gros Bill*) (1949), Luck of Ginger Coffey, The (1964), Mother's Heart, A (1953), My Childhood in Montréal (1971), *Père Chopin* (1945), Village Priest, The (*Le curé de village*) (1949), Waiting for Caroline (1967), Where Two Roads Cross (Between Two Loves) (*À la croisée des chemins*) (*Entre deux amours*) (1943)

Guèvremont, Richard: Gaia (1994)

Gugino, Carla: Red Hot (1993)

Guichard, Benoît: *Bouteille, La* (The Bottle) (2000)

Guiguet, Jean-Claude: *Mirage, Le* (1992)

Guilbault, Élise: *Albertine, en cinq temps* (Albertine in Five Times) (1999), *Cap Tourmente* (Cape Torment) (1993), *Dernières fougères, Les* (The Last Ferns) (1991), *Femme qui boit, La* (The Woman Who Drinks) (2001), OK Liberty (*Ok...Laliberté*) (1973), Ordinary Tenderness (*Tendresse ordinaire*) (1973), *Réjeanne Padovani* (1973), That Darned Loot (*La maudite galette*) (1972), Time of the Hunt, The (*Le temps d'une chasse*) (1972), *Secret de banlieue, Un* (The Secret of a Suburb) (2002)

Guilbeault, Luce: Angela (1978), Beautiful Sundays (*Les beaux dimanches*) (1974), Before the Time Comes (*Le temps de l'avant*) (1975), *Quarantaine, La* (Beyond Forty) (1982), Big Sabotage, The (*Le grand sabordage*) (1973), IXE-13 (1972), J.A. Martin, Photographer (1977), Mustang (1975), Ordinary Tenderness (Tendresse ordinaire) (1973), Time of the Hunt, The (Le temps d'une chasse) (1972)

Guilhe, Albane: *Anne Trister* (1986)

Guillaume, Robert: Death Warrant (1990)

Guillermin, John: Mr. Patman (1981)

Guillier, François: Mission of Fear (1965)

Guimond, Ernest: Big Rock, the Big Man, The (*Le Grand Rock*) (1969), Christmas Martian, The (*Le martien de Noël*) (1971), *Corde au cou, La* (1966), Death of a Lumberjack (*La mort d'un boucheron*) (1973), True Nature of Bernadette, The (*La vraie nature de Bernadette*) (1972)

Guimond, Gaétan: Head of Normande St. Onge, The (*La tête de Normande St-Onge*) (1975)

Guiomar, Julien: *Léolo* (1992)

Guit, Graham: *Ciel est à nous, Le* (Shooting Stars) (1997)

Guite, Jean-François: Dream Life (*La vie revée*) (1972)

Gumbert, Thea: Sally Marshall Is Not An Alien (1999)

Gunn, Moses: Certain Fury (1985)

Gunnarsson, Sturla: 100 Days in the Jungle (2002), Diana Kilmury: Teamster (1996), Diplomatic Immunity (1991), We the Jury (1996), Scorn (2000), Sturla: Rare Birds (2001), Such a Long Journey (1998)

Gunston, Maggie: Montréal Main (1974)

Gunton, Robert: When Billie Beat Bobby (2001)

Gurik, Robert: Vultures, The (*Les vautours*) (1975), Woman in Transit, A (*La femme de l'hôtel*) (1984), Years of Dreams and Revolt (*Les années de rêves*) (1984)

Gurney, Scott: Fubar (2002)

Gury, Paul: *Homme et son pêché, Un* (*Séraphin*) (A Man and His Sin) (1949)

Gustafsson, Jon Einarsson: Kanadiana (2000)

Guthrie, Tyrone: Oedipus Rex (1956)

Guttenberg, Steve: Airborne (1998), Home Team (1999)

Guttman, Richard: Highpoint (1980), Nasty Burgers (1994)

Guttman, Ronald: Frame-Up Blues (*La danse du scorpion*) (1991), *Ou le roman de Charles Pathé* (The Life of Charles Pathé) (1995)

Guy, François: Kid Sentiment (1967)

Guy, Sylvain: Black List (*Liste noire*) (1995), List, The (2000)

Guza Jr., Robert: Curtains (1983), Melanie (1982)

Guzman, Janet: Max (2001)

Gwynne, Michael: Harry Tracy, Desperado (1981)

Gyles, Anna Benson: Swann (1996)

Gyllenhaal, Stephen: Certain Fury (1985)

John, Dr.: Candy Mountain (1987)

Ha, Benita: Exiles in Paradise (2001)

Haas, Charles: Reckless Disregard (1985)

Haas, Derek: Invincible (2001)

Haas, Lukas: Lathe of Heaven (2002), Warrior Spirit (1994)

Haas, Philip: Lathe of Heaven (2002)

Habashi, Youssef: Secret Ballot (*Raye Makhfi*) (2001)

Habich, Mathias: *Corps perdu, À* (Straight to the Heart) (1988), *Demoiselle sauvage, La* (The Wild Girl) (Wild Damsel) (1991)

Hackett, Buddy: Hey Babe! (1984)

Haddon, Dayle: Bedroom Eyes (1984), Paperback Hero (1973), *Paroles et musique* (Love Songs) (1985)

Hadjithomas, Joana: *Autour de la maison rose* (Around the Pink House) (1999)

Hadrava, Vratislav: Absent One, The (1997)

Haentjens, Brigitte: *Révolutions, d'ébats amoureux, éperdus, douloureux* (Revolutions...Forever and Ever) (1984)

Hagan, Anna: Lydia (1964)

Haggard, Piers: Conquest (1998)

Haggerty, Dan: Abducted (1985)

Haggis, Paul: Due South (1994), Red Hot (1993)

Hagon, Garrick: Rough Justice (1984)

Haig, Terry: Blackout (Blackout in New York) (1978), Champagne for Two (1987), One Man (1977), Pyx, The (1973), Strange Blues of Cowboy Red, The (1995)

Haim, Corey: Anything For Love (1992)National Lampoon's Last Resort (1994), Never Too Late (1996), Oh, What a Night (1992), Watchers (1988), Without Malice (2000)

Hainsworth, Myles: Hatley High (2003), Summer (2002)

Haje, Khrystyne: Scanners: The Showdown (Scanner Cop II: Volkin's Revenge) (1994)

Halberstam, David: Rowing Through (1996)

Haldane, Donald: Drylanders (1963), Dying Hard (1978), Hank (1977), Nikki, Wild Dog of the North (1961), Reincarnate, The (1971), Someday Soon (1977)

Hale, Georgia: Butley (1974)

Hale, Jeremy: Last Train Home, The (1990)

Haley, Jackie Earle: Losin' It (1983)

Haley, Robert: Adolescence of P-l, The (Hide and Seek) (1983)

Halfon, Emily: Secondary High (2003)

Hall, Amelia: Coming Out Alive (1980)

Hall, Bradley: Spider (2002)

Hall, Donald: Great Shadow, The (1920)

Hall, Jarvis: Cheerful Tearful (1998)

Hall, Peter: Never Talk to Strangers (1995)

Hall, Zooey: Fortune and Men's Eyes (1971)

Hallam, John: Haunting Harmony, A (1993), Incredible Adventures of Marco Polo, The (1998)

Haller, Ty: Deserters (1983)

Hallier, Lori: Blindside (1986), My Bloody Valentine (1981)

Hallis, Ronald: Rainy Day Woman (1970)

Halloran, Gordon: Singing the Bones (2001)

Hallstrom, Lasse: Shipping News, The (2001)

Hallyday, Johnny: Wanted (Crime Spree) (2003)

Halsey, Brett: Back Stab (1990), Searching for Diana (1992)

Hamann, Susan: No Angel (1992)

Hamel, Annik: *Erreur sur la personne* (The Wrong Person) (1995)

Hamill, Mark: Raffle, The (1994)

Hamilton, Barbara: Change of Heart (1993), Dangerous Age, A (1958), Johnny Belinda (1977)

Hamilton, Colin: Naked Flame, The (1964)

Hamilton, John: Kid, The (1997), Myth of the Male Orgasm, The (1993), Perpetrators of the Crime (1999)

Hamilton, Josh: Drive, She Said (1997)

Hamilton, Leigh: Man, a Woman and a Bank, A (1979)

Hamilton, Murray: Mazes and Monsters (1982)

Hamilton, Patricia: Anne of Green Gables (1985), Anne of Green Gables: The Continuing Story (Series) (1985-1999), Change of Heart (1984), Chasing Rainbows (1988), Honourable Member, An (1982), Who Has Seen the Wind (1977), Why Rock the Boat? (1974)

Hamilton, Richard: August 32nd on Earth (1998)

Hamilton, Robert: Ford: The Man and the Machine (1987)

Hamilton, Victoria: Mansfield Park (1998)

Hamlin, Harry: Stranger in Town (1998)

Hamm, Sam: Never Cry Wolf (1983)

Hammond, Corrina: Low Self-Esteem Girl (2000)

Hampshire, Emily: Boy Meets Girl (1998), Chasing Cain (2001), Dead Innocent (1996), Posers (2002)

Hampton, Danielle: Ginger Snaps (2000)

Hampton, Demetra: National Lampoon's Last Resort (1994)

Hanalis, Blanche: Fish Hawk (1979)

Hanchar, Yves: *En vacances* (Summer Holidays) (2000)

Hancock, Sheila: Love and Death on Long Island (1997)

Handford, Roscoe: Dory (1965)

Hands, Marina: Barbarian Invasions, The (*Invasions Barbares, Les*) (2003)

Hanec, Greg: Downtime (1985), Tunes a Plenty (1989)

Haney, Darel: Siege (1983)

Haney, Mary: Nest of Shadows (1976)

Hanin, Roger: Erotic Love Games (1971), *Trilogie Marsellaise, La* (2001)

Hanks, Tom: Mazes and Monsters (1982)

Hanley, Jim: Junior (1985)

Hanna, Willie John: Zacharia Farted (1998)

Hannah, Brian: Circle, The (The Fraternity) (2001)

Hannah, Daryl: Cord (Hide and Seek) (2000)

Hann-Byrd, Adam: Digger (1993)

Hannigan, Michael: Morning! (1992)

Hannon, Gerald: Symposium (1996)

Hans, Marie-Françoise: Joy (1983)

Hansen, David: Shot in the Face (2002)

Hansen, Gale: Double Vision (1992)

Directors, Scriptwriters & Actors

Hansen, Jaymie: Shot in the Face (2002)

Hanson, Curtis Lee: Losin' It (1983), Never Cry Wolf (1983), Silent Partner, The (1978)

Hanson, Hart: Guitarman (1994), Trust in Me (1995)

Hanzlik, Jaromir: Flying Sneaker, The (1992)

Harada, Masato: Rowing Through (1996)

Haraldsson, Rurik: Regina (2002)

Harbour, Matthew: Two Summers (2002)

Harbury, Martin: Hockey Night (1984)

Harding, Paul: Man Called Intrepid, A (1979)

Hardt, Arnie: Freeloading (1986)

Hardwicke, Edward: Haunting of Julia, The (Full Circle) (1976)

Hardy, Jacques: Short Change (Une fille impossible) (1989)

Harel, Pierre: Angel Life (Vie d'ange) (1979), Bulldozer (1974), Entre tu et vous (Between "tu" and "you") (1970), Red Bells, Blue Tears (Grelots rouges, sanglots bleus) (1987)

Hargreaves, Nancy Ann: Carry on Sergeant (1927–1928)

Harker, Rebecca: Little Boy Blues (2000)

Harkness, Percy: Golden Apples of the Sun (Ever After All) (1973)

Harlow, Robert: When Tomorrow Dies (1965)

Harms, Kelly: Art of Woo, The (2001), Fairy Tales & Pornography (2003), Picture Claire (2001), Uncles, The (2000)

Harnois, Elizabeth: One Magic Christmas (1985)

Harper, Gary: Nasty Burgers (1994)

Harper, Tess: Reckless Disregard (1985)

Harrington, Adam: Without Malice (2000)

Harrington, Kenneth: Parsley Days (2000)

Harrington, Laura: City Girl, The (1984)

Harris, Barbara Eve: Justice (1998), Night Magic (1985), Remembering Mel (1986), Return of Ben Casey, The (1988), Tek War: Tek Justice (1994)

Harris, Daniel: Ghost Mom (1993)

Harris, Douglas: Remembering Mel (1986)

Harris, George: Soul Survivor (1995)

Harris, Jackie: Kids in the Hall: Brain Candy (1996)

Harris, Laura: Come Together (2001), Come Together (2001), Habitat (1995), Highwayman, The (1999), Kitchen Party (1997)

Harris, Matthew: Dragonwheel (2002)

Harris, Melvin: Broken Lullaby (1994)

Harris, Neil Patrick: Joan of Arc (1999), Man in the Attic, The (1994)

Harris, Nettie: Shirley Pimple in the John Wayne Temple (1999)

Harris, Richard: Echoes of a Summer (1976), Grizzly Falls (2000), Highpoint (1980), Martin's Day (1984), To Walk with Lions (1999), Your Ticket Is no Longer Valid (1982)

Harris, Rosemary: Sunshine (1999)

Harris, Sydney: My Uncle Antoine (1971)

Harrison, Gregory: Cadillac Girls (1993)

Harrison, James: Critical Age, The (1923)

Harrison, John Kent: Alexander Bell: The Sound and the Silence (1991), Beautiful Dreamers (1990), Coming Out Alive (1980), Murder by Phone (1982), One Night Only (1986), Whose Child Is This? The War for Baby Jessica (1993)

Harrison, Matthew: Sister Blue (2001)

Harrison, Mike: Passion (2001)

Harrison, Richard: Explosion, L' (The Hideout) (1971)

Harron, Donald: Once (1981), Peep (1984), Riel (1979)

Harron, Mary: American Psycho (2000)

Harry, Deborah: My Life Without Me (Mi Vida Sin Mí) (2003), Videodrome (1983)

Hart, Celia: Battle Queen 2020 (2000)

Hart, Derrick: War Boy, The (Point of Escape) (1985)

Hart, Harvey: Fortune and Men's Eyes (1971), Goldenrod (1976), High Country, The (The First Hello) (1981), Mahoney's Last Stand (1976), Murder Sees the Light (1987), Reckless Disregard (1985), Passion and Paradise (1989), Pyx, The (1973), Shoot (1976), Utilities (1981)

Hart, Jeremy: I'm Going to Get You...Elliot Boy (1971)

Hart, John: Disappearance, The (1977)

Hart, Susan: Freeloading (1986)

Hartford, David: Back to God's Country (1919)

Harth, Erndt: Zacharia Farted (1998)

Hartley, Bill: Sweet Substitute (Caressed) (1964)

Hartley, Mariette: Improper Channels (1981), Passion and Paradise (1989)

Hartley, Nina: Bubbles Galore (1996)

Hartman, Ron: Hostile Advances: The Kerry Ellison Story (1996)

Hartmann, Ron: Bloody Brood, The (1959), Double Negative (Deadly Companion) (1979), Heatwave Lasted Four Days, The (1973)

Harvey, Abel: So That the World Goes On (Pour la suite du monde) (1963)

Harvey, Delphine: Great Coups of History (1969)

Harvey, Gail: Cold Sweat (1993), Shower, The (1992), Striking Poses (1999)

Harvey, Gary: Another Country: A North of 60 Mystery (2003)

Harvey, Grant: American Beer (1996)

Harvey, Jean: Silencing the Guns (1996)

Harvey, Joachim: So That the World Goes On (Pour la suite du monde) (1963), Water Cars (Les voitures d'eau) (1970)

Harvey, Jordan: Divine Ryans, The (1998)

Harvey, Louis: So That the World Goes On (*Pour la suite du monde*) (1963), Water Cars (*Les voitures d'eau*) (1970)

Harvey, Nerée: Water Cars (*Les voitures d'eau*) (1970)

Harvey, Thea: Dying Fall (2002)

Harvey, Tom: Cool Sound From Hell, A (The Young and the Beat) (1959), Crowd Inside, The (1971), Fortune and Men's Eyes (1971), Homer (1970), Luck of Ginger Coffey, The (1964), Never Trust an Honest Thief (Going for Broke) (1979), Park Is Mine, The (1986), Second Wind (1976), Silence of the North (1981), Strange Brew (1983), Star Is Lost, A (1974), Terminal Choice (Deathbed) (1985), Threshold (1981)

Harvie, Ellie: Croon Maury and Mrs. B. (2003)

Harvie, John: Three by Paizs (1984)

Harz, Claude: Between Friends (Get Back) (1973), Homer (1970)

Hashigucki, Shinji: Absent One, The (1997)

Haskell, Charles: Fearless (1999)

Haskell, Peter: Christina (1974)

Hass, Amelia: Champagne for Two (1987)

Hassett, Marilyn: Shadow of the Hawk (1976)

Hastings, Matthew: Decoys (2003)

Hatte, T.H.: Anchor Zone (1994)

Hauer, Rutger: Dark Harbour (1997)

Hauff, Thomas: Brethren (1976), Christina (1974), Climb, The (1987), Cop (Heller) (1981), Silence of the North (1981), Summer's Children (1979), Who Has Seen the Wind (1977)

Hauka, David: Impolite (1992)

Hauka, Don: Jinnah on Crime (2002), Jinnah On Crime – White Knight, Black Widow (2003)

Hauser, Wings: Carpenter, The (1987), Watchers III (1994)

Havers, Nigel: Haunting of Julia, The (Full Circle) (1976)

Hawkes, Terri: Book of Eve (*Histoires d'Eve*) (2002), Foreign Nights (1990), Prom Night II: Hello Mary Lou (1987)

Hawkins, Madonna: Welcome to Canada (1989)

Hawkins, Robert: Hard Part Begins, The (1973)

Hawkins, Ronnie: SnakeEater (1990)

Hawkins, William: Christopher's Movie Matinée (1969)

Hawthorne, Christopher: Whiskers (1997), Sea People (1999)

Hawtrey, Kay: Ada (1981), Face Off (1971), Fish Hawk (1979), Funeral Home (Cries in the Night) (1982), Hank Williams: The Show He Never Gave (1982), High-Ballin' (1978), Intruder, The (1981), One of Our Own (1977), Perfect Pie (2002), Secret Life of Algernon, The (1996), Summer's Children (1979), Silence of the North (1981), Tyler (1977), Videodrome (1983)

Hayden, Stirling: Gas (1981)

Hayes, Allison: Wolf Dog (1958)

Hayes, Andrew: Hayseed (1997)

Hayes, Dennis: Running Man (1980)

Hayes, Elton: Isabel (1968), Journey (1972)

Hayes, Isaac: It Seemed Like a Good Idea at the Time (1975)

Hayes, Philip Maurice: Middlemen (2000)

Hayes, Rob: Isabel (1968)

Hayeur, Isabelle: Angel in a Cage (The Woman in the Cage) (*La bête de foire*) (1993), *Siamoises, Les* (The Siamese Twins) (1999)

Hayman, David: Wild Dogs, The (2002)

Haynes, Peter: Birds of Prey (1985), Sentimental Reasons (Death Target) (1984)

Hays, Robert: Deadly Appearances (1999), Utilities (1981)

Hayward, Rachel: Breaking All the Rules (1985), Watchtower, The (2001)

Hayworth, Peter: Sweet and the Bitter, The (1962)

Hayworth, Rita: Convicted (1938)

Haywood, Rachel: Watchtower, The (2001)

Hazlett, John: Bad Money (1999)

Head, James: Excalibur Kid, The (1998)

Head, Murray: *Grand serpent du monde, Le* (The Great World Serpent) (1999)

Headey, Lena: Twice Upon a Yesterday (1998)

Headly, Glenne: Ganesh (Ordinary Magic) (1993)

Healey, Christopher: Stolen Heart (1998)

Heard, John: Best Revenge (Misdeal) (1981), Silent Cradle (1998)

Heath, Colin: Overcoat, The (*Le manteau*) (2002)

Heatherington, Dianne: Zero Patience (1993)

Hébert, Anne: Kamouraska (1973)

Hébert, Bernard: Favourite Game, The (2003), Night of the Flood (*La nuit du déluge*) (1996)

Hébert, Charles: Enchanted Village, The (*Le village enchanté*) (1956)

Hébert, Jean-Louis: Tramp at the Door (1985)

Hébert, Marc: My Childhood in Montréal (1971)

Hébert, Paul: Christmas Martian, The (*Le martien de Noël*) (1971), Dernier havre, Le (1986), Few Days More, A (*De jour en jour*) (1981), Friends for Life (*Des amis pour la vie*) (1988), Happy Memories (Old Memories) (*Les beaux souvenirs*) (1981), It's Not Jacques Cartier's Fault (1968), Luck of Ginger Coffey, The (1964), Merry World of Léopold Z, The (1965), Oreille d'un sourd, L' (The Deaf Man's Ear) (1996)

Hébert, Pierre: Revolutionaries, The (1965)

Hecht, Paul: Only God Knows (1974), Scar Tissue (2002)

Heck, Angela: Tales From the Gimli Hospital (1988)

Hedley, Thomas: Circle of Two (1980), Double Negative (Deadly Companion) (1979), Mr. Patman (1981)

Hedley-James, Brian: Room for a Stranger (1968)

Heffernan, Terence: Bananas From Sunny Québec (1993), Change of Heart (1993), Great Big Thing, A (1968), Heartaches (1981), Mahoney's Last Stand (1976)

Heffron, Richard T.: French Revolution, The (1989)

Hegedos, Georgina: Big Meat Eater (1982)

Heikin-Pépin, Nancy: Vents contraires (1995)

Heinrihsone, Anna: Morning in the Pine Forest (1998)

Heitmeyer, Jayne: Dead End (False Pretense) (1998), Hawk's Vengeance (1997), Suspicious Minds (1996)

Helin, Mats: Misery Harbour (1999)

Helliker, John: Reluctant Angel (1997)

Helm, Levon: Best Revenge (Misdeal) (1981)

Helms, Norman: Cabaret neiges noires (1997), Life After Love (2000)

Hemblen, David: Adjuster, The (1991), Breach of Faith: A Family of Cops II (1996), Family Viewing (1988), Firing Squad (1990), Herd, The (1998), Homecoming, The (Good Luck, Jennifer Gagnon) (1978), I Love a Man in Uniform (1993), Inside Out (1979), Mesmer (1994), Rats (1999), Replikator (1994), Sarabande (1997), Seer Was Here (1978), Song Spinner, The (1996), Speaking Parts (1989), Switch in Time, A (1987), We the Jury (1996)

Hemingway, Mariel: Louisa May Alcott's Little Men (1998)

Hemmings, David: Blood Relatives (Les liens de sang) (1978), Disappearance, The (1977), Murder by Decree (1979), Power Play (Coup d'état) (State of Shock) (Operation Overthrow) (1978)

Hemphill, John: Sodbusters (1995), Partners 'n Love (1992)

Henderson, Marcia: Back to God's Country (1953)

Henderson, Meredith: Kayla (1998), Song Spinner, The (1996)

Hendrix, Elaine: Super Star (1999)

Hendryx, Shirley: Running Brave (1983)

Heney, Joan: Sincerely Violet (1987), Tangerine Taxi (1988)

Henley, Ted: Rowdyman, The (1972)

Hennelly, Dermot: Deserters (1983), Regeneration (1988)

Hennessey, Bryan: Bingo Robbers, The (2000), Dance Goes On, The (1991), Extraordinary Visitor (1998), No Apologies (1990), Understanding Bliss (1990), Violet (2000)

Hennessy, Dan: Sudden Fury (1975)

Hennessy, Ellen Ray: Clutch (1998), Shoemaker (1997)

Hennessy, Jill: Nuremberg (2000)

Hennessy, Mary Lou: Butler's Night Off, The (1948)

Hennig, Kate: Lives of Girls and Women, The (1996)

Henriksen, Lance: Profile for Murder (The Fifth Season) (1997), To Kill the King (1974)

Henry, Anna: Fishing Trip, The (1998)

Henry, Buck: Kurt Vonnegut's Harrison Bergeron (2000)

Henry, David Lee: Harry Tracy, Desperado (1981)

Henry, Donald: Haunting of Lisa, The (1995)

Henry, Joan: Emerald Tear, The (1988), Too Much Sex (1999)

Henry, Justin: Martin's Day (1984)

Henry, Laura: Heavenly Bodies (1985)

Henry, Linda: Rainy Day Woman (1970)

Henry, Martha: Back to Beulah (1974), Dancing in the Dark (1986), Glory Enough for All (1988), Long Day's Journey Into Night (1996), Mustard Bath (1993), Québec-Canada 1995 (1983), Wars, The (1983), Waiting for the Parade (1984), White Light (1991)

Henry, Tim: 125 Rooms of Comfort (1974), Dawson Patrol, The (1985), Homer (1970), Sunday in the Country (1975)

Henry, Yves: Grand Bill, The (Le gros Bill) (1949)

Henshall, Carole: Cyberteens in Love (1994)

Henshall, Douglas: Twice Upon a Yesterday (1998)

Henshaw, Jim: Another Woman (1994), Broken Lullaby (1994), Change of Place, A (1994), Deadly Harvest (1980), Lions for Breakfast (1975), Monkeys in the Attic (1974), Supreme Kid, The (1976), Sweeter Song, A (1976), Treacherous Beauties (1994)

Henstridge, Natasha: Dog Park (1998), Kevin of the North (2001), Second Skin (2000), Steal (Riders) (2002)

Heppel, Sylvie: Lies My Father Told Me (1975)

Hepton, Bernard: Baroness and the Pig, The (2002), Eminent Domain (1990)

Herbert, Eric: Where the Heart Is (1985)

Herbert, Henri: Isis From the 8th Rang (1972)

Herbert, John: Fortune and Men's Eyes (1971)

Herelle, Johanne: Tout prendre, À (Take It All) (The Way It Goes) (1963)

Herkema, Reginald: Girl Is a Girl, A (1999)

Herle, Marsha: 24 Store, The (1990)

Herman, Jimmy: Warrior Spirit (1994)

Héron, Frank: Red (1969), Sins of the Fathers (1948)

Héroux, Denis: Awakening, The (*L'amour humain*) (1970), Born for Hell (*Né pour l'enfer*) (1976), Enuff is Enuff (*J'ai mon voyage!*) (1973), Initiation, The (1970), Jacques Brel Is Alive and Well and Living in Paris (1975), No Holiday for Idols (1965), Over My Head (*Jusqu'au cou*) (1964), Push but Push Reasonably (1975), Rebels 1837, The (*Quelques arpents de neige*) (1972), Seven Times a Day (*Sept fois par jour*) (1971), There's Always a Way to Get There (*Y a toujours moyen de moyenner!*) (1973), *Valérie* (1969), Uncanny, The (1977)

Héroux, Pierre: Body and Soul (1971)

Herrier, Mark: Porky's (*Chez Porky*) (1981), Porky's II: The Next Day (*Chez Porky 2*) (1983), Porky's Revenge (*Revanche de Porky, La*) (1985)

Hershey, Barbara: Man Called Intrepid, A (1979)

Herzfeld, John: Hard Feelings (1981)

Herzog, Werner: Scream of Stone (1991)

Hess, Heather: Where the Spirit Lives (1989)

Hess, Jon: Watchers (1988)

Heston, Charlton: Little Kidnappers, The (1990)

Hetherington, Penny: Haro (1994)

Hewgill, Roland: Oedipus Rex (1956)

Hewitt, Rod: Coyote Run (1996)

Hewitt, Sean: Hank Williams: The Show He Never Gave (1982), Swann (1996)

Hewlett, David: Century Hotel (2001), Clutch (1998), Cube (1997), Ice Men, The (2001), Joe's Wedding (1996), Pin (1988), Scanners II: The New Order (1991), Nothing (2002) Treed Murray (2001)

Heyerdahl, Christopher: Nowhere in Sight (2000)

Hibbert, Guy: Shot Through the Heart (1998)

Hibler, Winston: Nikki, Wild Dog of the North (1961)

Hickey, John Benjamin: Me and My Shadows (2000)

Hicks, Caitlin: Singing the Bones (2001)

Hicks, Kevin: Deadly Appearances (1999), Higher Education (1986)

Hidalgo, Federico: Silent Love, A (2003)

Higgins, Anthony: Sweet Killing (1993)

Higgins, Charley: Brothers by Choice (1985)

Higgins, David: Wrong Guy, The (1998)

Higgins, Jack: Midnight Man (1995)

Higgins, Jonathan: House on Turk Street, The (2002), Life in the Balance (2001), Woman Hunted, A (2003)

Higginson, Torri: Airborne (1998), Balls Up (1998), Jungleground (1995), Memory Run (1995), Tek War: Tek Justice (1994), Rats (1999), Turning Paige (Shepherd Park) (2002)

Highsmith, Ripley: Fallen Knight (1998)

Highway, Tomson: Symposium (1996)

Hill, Arthur: Amateur, The (1981), Dirty Tricks (1980), Don't Let the Angels Fall (1969), One Magic Christmas (1985), *Riel* (1979), Tell Me My Name (1977)

Hill, Bernard: Nobody Waved Goodbye (1964), No Surrender (1985)

Hill, Jack: City on Fire (1979)

Hill, Karen: Expecting (2002)

Hill, Samantha: Nature of Nicholas, The (2002)

Hilliard, Stern Steven: Silence of Adultery, The (1995)

Hill-Tout, Wendy: Perfect Man, The (1993)

Hillyer, Steven: Event, The (2003)

Hilmarsson, Bjorn Ingi: Regina (2002)

Hilton, David: My Little Eye (2002)

Hiltz, Jonathan: Harmoney (1999)

Hiltz, Naomi: Harmoney (1999)

Himelstein, Howard: Power of Attorney (1995)

Hindle, Art: Black Christmas (Silent Night, Evil Nights) (Stranger in the House) (1974), Brood, The (1979), Covert Action (1986), Face Off (1971), Foxy Lady (1971), Into the Fire (1987), Legend of Wolf Lodge, The (1988), Nest of Shadows (1976), Porky's (*Chez Porky*) (1981), Porky's II: The Next Day (*Chez Porky 2*) (1983), Proud Rider, The (The Last Run) (1972), Silence of Adultery, The (1995), Sleeping Dogs Lie (1999), Surrogate (1984), Tom Stone: For the Money (2002), Waiting Game, The (1998)

Hinds, Cindy: Brood, The (1979)

Hines, Alan: Built By Association (2002), Interrogation of Michael Crowe, The (2002)

Hines, Karen: Married Life: The Movie (2000)

Hingle, Pat: Going Berserk (1983), Running Brave (1983)

Hirsh, Michael: Do You Want to Sleep With God? (*Voulez-vous coucher avec Dieu?*) (1972)

Hirt, Christianne: First Season, The (1988), For the Moment (1994), Heart of the Sun (1998), Lyddie (1995), Skate (1987), Rookies (1990), Sylvan Lake Summer (1991), Wozeck: Out of the Fire (1992), Tokyo Cowboy (1994)

Hitchcock, Peter: Truckin' (1972)

Hitching, Alix: Ryan's Babe (2000)

Hivon, Julie: *Crême glacée, chocolat et autres consolations* (2001)

Hizkyau, Avner: Seven Times a Day (*Sept fois par jour*) (1971)

Hladecek, Joel: Cord (Hide and Seek) (2000)

Hlady, Gregory: *Marais, Le* (2002)

Hoa, Nguyen: Eleventh Child, The (*Nguol Thua*) (1998)

Nguyen, Kim: Marais, Le (2002)

Hodges, Mike: Lifeforce Experiment (1994)

Hoe, Hunt: Deaf and Mute (1986), Foreign Ghosts

(*Fantômes étrangers*) (1997), I Won't Dance (1992), Seducing Maarya (1999)

Hoffman, Gaby: Strike! (1998)

Hoffman, Guy: Agnes of God (1985), Immortal Scoundrel, The (*Étienne Brûlé, gibier de potence*) (1952), *Misanthrope, Le* (1966), Oh, If Only My Monk Would Want (*Ah! Si mon moine voulait*) (1973), Odyssey of the Pacific (*L'Empereur du Pérou*) (1982), Twelfth Hour, The (*La douzième heure*) (1966), *Tout prendre, À* (Take It All) (The Way It Goes) (1963)

Hoffman, Philip Seymour: Owning Mahowny (2001)

Hoffman, Roseline: I Love You (*Je t'aime*) (1974)

Hoffman, Sherry: Becoming Laura (1982)

Hoffmeyer, Stig: Misery Harbour (1999)

Hofschneider, Marco: *Mirage, Le* (1992)

Hofsess, John: Columbus of Sex, The: My Secret Life (1969)

Hogan, Dominic: Sudden Fury (1975)

Hogan, Gabriel: Halfback of Notre Dame, The (1994), Peacekeepers (1997), Pit Pony (1998), Shadow Lake (2000), Stolen Miracle (2001)

Hogan, Irene: Something's Rotten (1978)

Hogan, Kim: Heart of the Sun (1998), Two Brothers, a Girl and a Gun (1993)

Hogan, Michael: Accident at Memorial Stadium, The (1983), Ambush at Iroquois Pass (1979), Betrayed (2003), Boy Next Door, The (1984), Clear Cut (1991), Deadly Eyes (The Rats) (1982), Diplomatic Immunity (1991), Final Edition (1982), For Those Who Hunt the Wounded Down (1996), Gas (1981), High-Ballin' (1978), Klondike Fever (1979), Lost! (1986), Maintain the Right (1982), Marine Life (2000), Nights Below Station Street (1997), Road to Saddle River (1994), Pathfinder, The (1996), *Palais Royale* (1988), Suicide Murders, The (1986), Solitaire (1991), Takeover (1981), Title Shot (1980), Wozeck: Out of the Fire (1992)

Hogan, Susan: American Christmas Carol, An (1979), Bordertown Café (1991), Brood, The (1979), Certain Practices (1979), Cop (Heller) (1981), Golden Will: The Silken Laumann Story (1997), I Miss You, Hugs and Kisses (1978), One Night Stand (1978), Phobia (1980), Title Shot (1980), Rupert's Land (1998), Sweeter Song, A (1976)

Hogarth, Meg: Cop (Heller) (1981)

Hohmeyer, Michael: Post Concussion (1999)

Holbrook, Hal: Haven (2001), Rituals (The Creeper) (1977), Kidnapping of the President, The (1980)

Holcomb, Sarah: Happy Birthday Gemini (1980)

Holden, Arthur: Remembering Mel (1986)

Holden, Jackie: Montréal Main (1974)

Holden, Katrina: Uncanny, The (1977)

Holden, Laurie: Expect No Mercy (1995), Pathfinder, The (1996)

Holden, Winifred: Company of Strangers, The (Strangers in Good Company) (1990)

Holder, Geoffrey: *Hasards ou coïncidences* (1998)

Hole, Jeremy: Betrayed (2003), External Affairs (1999), Firing Squad (1990), Killing Spring, A (2001), Tom Alone (1989), Verdict in Blood (2001)

Holec, Jeff: Borrower, The (1985)

Holender, Jacques: Rats (1999)

Holland, Nelson: Plastic Mile, The (1969)

Holland, Tom: Class of 1984 (1982)

Hollander, Xaviera: My Pleasure Is My Business (1975)

Holloway, Ann: My Summer Vacation (1996)

Holloway, Stanley: Journey Into Fear (1975)

Hollyman, Ryan: Seducing Maarya (1999)

Holm, Ian: Sweet Hereafter, The (1996), Naked Lunch (1992)

Holmes, Ed: Hired Gun (The Devil's Spawn) (The Last Gunfighter) (1959), Oedipus Rex (1956)

Holmes, Emily: Jinnah on Crime (2002)

Holmes-Robert, Pam: Rubber Gun, The (1977)

Holt, Sandrine: Black Robe (1991), Century Hotel (2001), Legends of the North (1996), John Woo's Once a Thief (1997)

Holzwarth, Eric: Noncensus (1964)

Hombert, Madeleine: Personal Exemptions (1988)

Hong, James: Art of War, The (2000), Bethune (1977), G-2 (1998)

Hong, Wan Chi: Dreamtrips (2000)

Honigman, Heddy: Hersenschimmen (Mind Shadows) (1987)

Honor, Andrew: Shrew in the Park, The (2000)

Hood, Alan: Now That April's Here (1958)

Hood, Kit: Dancing on the Moon (*Viens danser sur la lune*) (1997), School's Out! The Degrassi Feature (1992), X-Rated (1994)

Hood, Melissa: Fishing Trip, The (1998)

Hook, Harry: A.K.A. Albert Walker (2002)

Hoolboom, Mike: House of Pain (1995), Kanada (1993), Valentine's Day (1994), Panic Bodies (1998)

Hoover, Darcy: Dinner's on the Table (1994)

Hoover, Elva Mai: Hayseed (1997), Terry Fox Story, The (1983)

Hope, Leslie: Big Slice, The (1991), Boozecan (1995), Dance Goes On, The (1991), Dead Aviators (1998), Deadly Friends: The Nancy Eaton Story (2003), Double Frame (1999), Fun (1993), Incredible Mrs Ritchie, The (2003), Paris, France (1993), Rowing Through (1996), Summer of the Monkeys (1998), Spreading

Hope, Leslie continued:
Ground, The (2000), Stolen Miracle (2001), Sweet Killing (1993), Sword of Gideon (1986), This Matter of Marriage (1998), True Confections (1991), Ups and Downs (1983), Water Damage (1999)

Hopkins, John: Hiroshima (1996), Murder by Decree (1979), Stranger in Town (1998)

Hopkins, Bernard: Elizabeth Rex (2003)

Hopley, Jason: War Boy, The (Point of Escape) (1985)

Hopper, Dennis: LAPD: To Protect and Serve (2001), Out of the Blue (No Looking Back) (1980), Spreading Ground, The (2000)

Hopper-Ransen, Joan: Touched (1999)

Horn, Rebecca: Buster's Bedroom (1991)

Hornecker, William: Two Brothers, a Girl and a Gun (1993)

Horner, Kathy: Seductio (1987)

Horon, James: Scanner Cop (1994)

Horowitz, Israel: Today I Am a Fountain Pen (A Good Place to Come From) (1980)

Horovitz, Israel: Sunshine (1999)

Horsfall, Marjorie: White Road, The (1929)

Horswill, Adrienne: Neon Palace, The: A '50s and '60s Trip (1971)

Horton, John: Day My Grandad Died, The (1976), Man Inside, The (1975)

Horton, Lennette: Tangerine Taxi (1988)

Horton, Susan: Psychic (1991)

Hosea, Bobby: Going Back (2002)

Hoskins, Bob: Felicia's Journey (1999), Rainbow (1995)

Hosmalin, Catherine: En vacances (Summer Holidays) (2000)

Hossack, Alison: Anthrax (2001), White Light (1991)

Hotz, Jeremy: Married Life: The Movie (2000)

Houchen, Claudette: Paper People, The (1967)

Houde, Germain: Craque la vie (Life Blossoms) (1994), Good Riddance (Les bons débarras) (1980), Keep an Eye on the Trombone (1992), Love Me (1991), Scream for Silence, A (Mourir à tue-tête) (1979), Secret of Jerome, The (Le secret de Jérôme) (1994), Shellgame (1986), Terminal City Ricochet (1990), Vengeance de la femme en noir, La (The Revenge of the Lady in Black) (1996), Zoo la nuit, Un (1987)

Houde, Louis-Jose: Je n'aime que toi (I Don't Love You) (2003)

Houde, Paul: Boys, Les (The Boys) (1997), Boys III, Les (The Boys III) (2001)

Houde, Serge: Dancing on the Moon (Viens danser sur la lune) (1997), Dead End (Le dernier souffle) (1999), Portrait, The (1992), October (Octobre) (1994)

Houde, Serge: Justice (1998), Legends of the North (1996), Wrong Woman, The (1995)

Houdet, Vincent: Angel in a Cage (The Woman in the Cage) (La bête de fiore) (1993)

Hough, John: Incubus (1981)

Houle, Camil: Revolutionaries, The (1965)

Houle, Ronald: Seat of the Soul, The (Crisis of Conscience, A) (Le siege de l'âme) (1997), Hochelaga (2000), Lac de la lune, Le (1994)

House, Dakota: Another Country: A North of 60 Mystery (2003), Dream Storm: A North of 60 Mystery (2001)

House, Eric: Act of the Heart (1970), Highpoint (1980), Honourable Member, An (1982), Oedipus Rex (1956), Star Is Lost, A (1974), Strange Brew (1983)

House, Rosemary: Understanding Bliss (1990), Violet (2000)

Houseman, John: Murder by Phone (1982)

Housni, Youssef: Adolescente sucré d'amour, L' (1985)

Howard, Adam Coleman: Ride Me (Ego Trip) (1995)

Howard, Clint: House of the Dead (2003)

Howard, Elisabeth: Heart of America: Homeroom (2003)

Howard, Fred: Life, A (1988)

Howard, Leslie: 49th Parallel (The Invaders) (1941)

Howard, Lisa: Bounty Hunters (1996)

Howard, Mrs. Fred: Life, A (1988)

Howard, Richard: Oedipus Rex (1956)

Howard, Clint: Heart of America: Homeroom (2003)

Howay, Robert: Naked Flame, The (1964), Sweet Substitute (Caressed) (1964), Waiting for Caroline (1967)

Howco, Allan: Making Love in St. Pierre (2003)

Howe, John: Star Is Lost, A (1974), Why Rock the Boat? (1974)

Howe, Reginald: Double Frame (1999)

Howell, Hoke: Stuart Bliss (1998)

Howes, Sally Ann: Death Ship (1980)

Hoziel, Eric: Sphinx, The (1995)

Hreno, Jason: Deadly Portrayal (2003), Wicked Minds (2002)

Huang, George: Live Through This (2000)

Huard, Patrick: Boys, Les (The Boys) (1997), Boys III, Les ((2001), Comment ma mere accoucha de moi durant sa ménopause (How My Mother Was Giving Birth to Me During Menopause) (2001), J'en suis (1997), Life After Love (2000), Nez rouge (2003), Sur le seuil (2003)

Huart, Gérard-Antoine: Joy (1983)

Huband, David: Diamond Fleece, The (1992)

Hubbard, Paul: Julie Darling (1982)

Huberdeau, Sébastien: Île de Sable, L' (1999), Yellowknife (2002)

Hubert, Cam: Matter of Choice, A (1978)

Hubert, Jacques: Dream-Speaker (1976), Drying Up the Streets (1978), Harry Tracy, Desperado (1981), Shadow of the Hawk (1976)

Hucalak, Robert: Nature of Nicholas, The (2002)

Huculak, Maggie: Desire (2000), For Those Who Hunt the Wounded Down (1996)

Hudson, Ernest: Spacehunters: Adventures in the Forbidden Zone (1983)

Hudson, Kirk: Dinner's on the Table (1994)

Hudson, Larry: Roadkill (1989)

Hudson, Rochelle: Bush Pilot (1946)

Hudson, Rock: Back to God's Country (1953)

Huffman, Kim: Looking for Leonard (2002), Murder Most Likely (1999), Recipe for Revenge (1998), Three and a Half (*Trois et demi*) (2002)

Huffman, Linda: Only Thing You Know, The (1971)

Hughes, Barnard: Tell Me My Name (1977)

Hughes, Bob: *Ménace, La* (1977)

Hughes, David: Brethren (1976), Megantic Outlaw, The (1971), Wedding in White (1972), Sunday in the Country (1975)

Hughes, Douglas: Gross Misconduct (1992)

Hughes, Helen: Amityville Curse, The (1990), Falling Over Backwards (1990), For Those I Loved (*Au nom de tous les miens*) (1983), High Card (1982), Incubus (1981), Kidnapping of Baby John Doe, The (1985), Lucky Star, The (1980), Off Your Rocker (1982), Outrageous! (1977), Peanut Butter Solution, The (*Opération beurre de pinottes*) (1985), Suicide Murders, The (1986), Suzanne (1980), Till Death Do Us Part (1982), Visiting Hours (Fright) (1982), Wild Horse Hank (1979)

Hughes, Richard: Eternal Husband, The (1997)

Hughes, Stuart: Skate (Blades of Courage) (1987)

Hughson, Randy: Shoemaker (1997), Stolen Heart (1998), Washed Up (2002)

Hugli, William: Solitude (2001)

Huire, Kimberley: Wishmaster 4: The Prophecy Fulfilled (2002)

Hulme, Lachy: Men With Guns (1996)

Hulme, Ron: Obstruction of Justice (1995)

Hume, Edward: Terry Fox Story, The (1983)

Humes, Mary-Margaret: Stalking of Laurie Show, The (2000)

Humphrey, Mark: Iron Eagle (1986)

Humphrey, Renée: Drawing Flies (1996), Fun (1993)

Humphries, David: Haunting of Julia, The (Full Circle) (1976)

Humphries, Peter: Flaming Frontier (1958)

Hunnicut, Gayle: Man Called Intrepid, A (1979), Special Magnum (1977)

Hunt, Ed: Brain, The (1988), Plague, The (1979), Pleasure Palace (Angela) (1973), Point of No Return (1976), Starship Invasions (1977)

Hunt, Rel: Stalking of Laurie Show, The (2000)

Hunter, Holly: Burning, The (1981), Crash (1996), When Billie Beat Bobby (2001), Woman Wanted (1999)

Hunter, Ian McLellan: Your Ticket Is no Longer Valid (Finishing Touch) (1982)

Hunter, John: Blood and Guts (1978), Boy Next Door, The (1984), Cross Country (1983), Fast Company (1979), Grey Fox, The (1982), Hard Part Begins, The (1973), Prom Night (1980)

Hunter, Kaki: Porky's (*Chez Porky*) (1981), Porky's II: The Next Day (*Chez Porky 2*) (1983), Porky's Revenge (*Revanche de Porky, La*) (1985)

Hunter, Kim: Here's To Life (The Old Hats) (2000)

Hunter, Stephen: Bullies (1986)

Huntington, Lawrence: Vulture, The (1967)

Huntington, Louise: Viking, The (1931)

Huot, Juliette: Crime of Ovide Plouffe, The (*Le crime d'Ovide Plouffe*) (*Les Plouffe, II*) (1984), *Dis-moi le si j'dérange* (Tell Me if I Bother or Disturb You) (1989), Far From You Sweetheart (*Juis suis loin de toi mignonne*) (1976), Little One Is Coming Soon, The (1972), Luck of Ginger Coffey, The (1964), Nightingales and the Bells (*Le rossignol et les cloches*) (1952), *Plouffe, Les* (The Plouffe Family) (1981), Village Priest, The (*Le curé de village*) (1949)

Huppert, Isabelle: *Violette Nozière* (1978)

Hurd, Mitzi: Sweet Substitute (Caressed) (1964)

Hurdle, James: Climb, The (1987)

Hurley, Elizabeth: Weight of Water, The (2000)

Hurley, Joan: Sunday in the Country (1975), Parallels (1980)

Hurman, Kate: Juiced (1999)

Hurnik, Veronica: Uncles, The (2000)

Hurst, Michael: New Blood (1999)

Hurt, John: Krapp's Last Tape (2000), Love and Death on Long Island (1997), *Mémoire tronquée* (1990), New Blood (1999), Owning Mahowny (2001)

Hurt, William: Blue Butterfly, The (*Papillon Bleu, Le*) (2003), Nearest to Heaven (*Au plus pres du paradis*) (2002), Rare Birds (2001), Sunshine (1999), Varian's War (2001)

Hurtubise, Troy James: Project Grizzly (1996)

Hushes, David: Sweet and the Bitter, The (1962)

Hussain, Shaf: Wheat Soup (1987)

Hussenot, Olivier: Final Blow, The (The Finishing Stroke) (*Le coup de grâce*) (1965)

Hussey, Olivia: Black Christmas (Silent Night, Evil Nights) (Stranger in the House) (1974)

Hustak, Allen: Wendy (1966)

Huston, John: Angela (1978), Head On (Fatal Attraction) (1980), Phobia (1980)

Huston, Nancy: *Emporte-moi* (Set Me Free) (1998)

Hutchings, Edward: Proxyhawks (1970)

Hutchison, Douglas: House on Turk Street, The (2002)

Hutson, James: Middlemen (2000), Red Deer (2000)

Hutt, Peter: Elizabeth Rex (2003)

Hutt, William: Covergirl (1984), Long Day's Journey Into Night (1996), Oedipus Rex (1956), Wars, The (1983)

Hutton, Joan: I, Maureen (1980)

Hutton, Lauren: We the Jury (1996)

Hutton, Robert: Vulture, The (1967)

Hwang, David Henry: M. Butterfly (1993)

Hyatt, Pam: Circle of Two (1980), Only God Knows (1974), Trial and Error (1993)

Hyde, Jonathon: Eisenstein (2000)

Hyde-White, Wilfred: King Solomon's Treasure (1979)

Hyem, Jill: Leopard in the Snow (1978)

Hyland, Frances: Another Smith for Paradise (1972), Catsplay (1977), Changeling, The (1980), Drylanders (1963), Happy Birthday to Me (1981), Home to Stay (1978), Hounds of Notre Dame, The (1981), Lotus Eaters, The (1993), Pathfinder, The (1996), Pygmalion (1983)

Hylands, Scott: Coming Out Alive (1980), Halfback of Notre Dame, The (1994), Isaac Littlefeathers (1984), Kate Morris, Vice President (1984), Passengers (1981), Scoop (1978), Slipstream (1973), Visitor, The (1974)

Hynd, Noel: Agency (1980)

Hyndman, James: Caboose (1996), Eldorado (1995), Memories Unlocked (1999), Rowing Through (1996), Thousand Wonders of the Universe, The (1997)

Hynes, Ron: Bingo Robbers, The (2000), Secret Nation (1991)

Hynes, Tyler: Home Team (1999), Tagged: The Jonathan Wamback Story (2002)

Hype, Chris: Chained Heat II (1993)

Hyslop, Jeff: Wars, The (1983)

Ice-T: Johnny Mnemonic (1995)

Ida, Hiromoto: Tokyo Cowboy (1994)

Ifans, Rhys: Formula 51 (The 51st State) (2002), Shipping News, The (2001)

Iger, Brian: Outcast (1991)

Ikeuchi, Takuma: Keiko (1979)

Ilial, Léo: Crazy Manette and Cardboard Gods (*Manette: la folle et les dieux de carton*) (1964)

Illidge, Paul: Head On (Fatal Attraction) (1980)

Illienko, Pylyp: Swan Lake: The Zone (*Lebedyne ozero-zona*) (1996)

Illienko, Yuri: Swan Lake: The Zone (*Lebedyne ozero-zona*) (1996)

Imani, Besa: Women Without Wings (2002)

Imbeault, Laurent: Encircled Colour, The (*La couleur encerclée*) (1986)

Impey, Ray: Downtime (1985), Tunes a Plenty (1989)

Inch, Jennifer: State Park (1987)

Ingall, Mark: Ascent, The (1994)

Inglis, Raul Sanchez: CrashCrash (Breach of Trust) (1995) (1995), Falling, The (2000)

Ingolfsdottir, Sigurbjorg Alma: Regina (2002)

Ingram, Malcolm: Drawing Flies (1996), Tail Lights Fade (1999)

Inha, Pamela S: Jinnah On Crime – White Knight, Black Widow (2003)

Inkol, Sheldon: Carver's Gate (1996)

Innocent, Numa: Little Man Abroad, A (1989)

Inuit elders: Atanarjuat: The Fast Runner (*L'homme nu*) (2000)

Inukpuk, Adamie: Kabloonak (1994)

Ireland, Galen: More to Love (2000)

Ireland, Ian: Big Rock, the Big Man, The (1969), Don't Let the Angels Fall (1969), *Naufragés du Labrador, Les* (Stranded in Labrador) (1991), Oranges of Israel, The (1974)

Ireland, John: Courage of Kavik the Wolf Dog, The (1980), Crossbar (1979), Graveyard Story (1989), Incubus (1981), Martin's Day (1984), Seasons in the Sun (1986), Shape of Things to Come, The (1979), Takeover (1981), Tomorrow Never Comes (1978), Salut! J.W. (1981)

Irons, Jeremy: Dead Ringers ((Twins) (1988), Fourth Angel, The (2001), M. Butterfly (1993)

Ironside, Michael: Arrow, The (1997), Best Revenge (Misdeal) (1981), Borderline Normal (2000), Café Romeo (1992), Chain Dance (Common Bonds) (1991), Coming Out Alive (1980), Cross Country (1983), Deadly Arrangement (1998), Destiny to Order (1989), Double Negative (Deadly Companion) (1979), Fairy Tales & Pornography (2003), Ford: The Man and the Machine (1987), Going to Kansas City (1998), I, Maureen (1980), Kids of the Round Table (1995), Killer Image (1992), Last Chapter (Biker Wars) (2002), Matter of Choice, A (1978), Mind Field (1989), Mindstorm (2001), Nowhere to Hide (1987), Nuremberg (2000), Office Party (1988), Off Your Rocker (1982), Outrageous! (1977), Probable Cause (1994), Prom Night II: Hello Mary Lou (1987), Question of Privilege, A (1998), Scanners (1981), Spacehunters:

Adventures in the Forbidden Zone (1983), Stone Cold Dead (1979), Summer's Children (1979), Surfacing (1981), Surrogate (1984), Suzanne (1980), Sweet Killing (1993), Visiting Hours (1982), Watchers (1988)

Irvin, John: Eminent Domain (1990), Fourth Angel, The (2001)

Irving, George: Damaged Lives (1933)

Isabel, Richard: Guitar (*Guitare*) (1974)

Isabelle, Jean: *Jean-François-Xavier de...* (1971)

Isabelle, Katharine: Ginger Snaps (2000), Ginger Snaps: The Sequel (2003), Shot in the Face (2002), Turning Paige (Shepherd Park) (2002)

Isbell, Tammy: Joe's Wedding (1996), Rendering, The (Portrait for Murder) (2002)

Iscove, Rob: Chautauqua Girl (1984), Love and Larceny (1985), Prodigious Hickey, The (1987)

Ishido, Toshira: Hiroshima (1996)

Ishimoto, Dale: Sweet and the Bitter, The (1962)

Isobel, Katharine: Salt Water Moose (1996)

Israël, Charles: Angela (1978), Jigsaw (Angry Man, An) (*L'homme en colère*) (1979), Klondike Fever (1979), Louisiana (1993)

Istrate, Vasilica: Reach for the Sky (*La championne*) (1991)

Ito, Robert: Best Bad Thing, The (1997), Trial at Fortitude Bay (1994), War Between Us, The (1995)

Itso, Tyron Le: House of the Dead (2003)

Ittimangnaq, Zachary: Never Cry Wolf (1983)

Ivalu, Sylvia: Atanarjuat: The Fast Runner (*L'homme nu*) (2000)

Jaaferi, Jaaved: Fire (1996)

Jabon, Luc: Babylone (Halfway House) (1991)

Jacks, Terry: Seasons in the Sun (1986)

Jackson, Andrew: Deadly Portrayal (2003), Nowhere in Sight (2000), Paperboy, The (1994), Whispers (1990), Wind at My Back (2001), Wrong Woman, The (1995)

Jackson, Avrum: Malarek: A Street Kid Who Made It (1988)

Jackson, Boyd: Ivy League Killers (1959)

Jackson, Dory: Autumn Born (1979)

Jackson, Douglas: Dead End (False Pretense) (1998), Deadbolt (1984), Front Line, The (1985), Heatwave Lasted Four Days, The (1973), Paperboy, The (1994), Whispers (1990), Wrong Woman, The (1995)

Jackson, Glenda: Maids, The (1975)

Jackson, Joshua: Digger (1993)

Jackson, Kate: Adrift (1993), Dirty Tricks (1980), Silence of Adultery, The (1995)

Jackson, Philip: 2103: The Deadly Wake (1996), Music of the Spheres, The (1984), Replikator (1994), Strange Horizons (1992)

Jackson, Samuel L.: Formula 51 (The 51ST State) (2002), House on Turk Street, The (2002), Red Violin, The (*Le violon rouge*) (1998)

Jackson, Sydney: Bonjour, Timothy (1995)

Jackson, Tom: Diviners, The (1993), Dream Storm: A North of 60 Mystery (2001), Grizzly Falls (2000), Medicine River (1993), Spirit Rider (1993) Trial by Fire: A North of 60 Mystery

Jackson, Wren: Undivided Attention (1987)

Jacob, Jacques: Henri (1986), *Marguerite Volant* (1996), Vultures, The (*Les vautours*) (1975)

Jacob, Peter: Melting Pot, The (1975)

Jacob, Suzanne: Beauty of Pandora, The (*La beauté de Pandore*) (2000)

Jacobi, Lou: Isaac Littlefeathers (1984), Lucky Star, The (1980), Off Your Rocker (1982)

Jacobs, André: Second Skin (2000)

Jacobs, Joke: Secret Laughter of Women, The (1999)

Jacobs, Michael: Certain Fury (1985)

Jacobs, Tanya: Suicide Murders, The (1986)

Jacobson, Avrum: Family Reunion (1987)

Jacoby, Scott: Little Girl Who Lives Down the Lane, The (1977)

Jacot, Christopher: Bay of Love and Sorrows, The (2002), Tagged: The Jonathan Wamback Story (2002)

Jacot, Michael: Last Act of Martin Weston, The (1971)

Jacquemont, Maurice: Story of Dr. Louise, The (Docteur Louise) (1949)

Jacques, Céline: Larose, Pierrot and Luce (1982)

Jacques, Denis: Gobital (1975)

Jacques, Stéphane: *Temps d'une vie, Le* (1998)

Jacques, Sylvie: *Quiconque meurt, meurt à douleur* (Whoever Dies, Dies in Pain) (1998)

Jacques, William: Desire in Motion (*Mouvements du désire*) (1994)

Jacques, Yves: Barbarian Invasions, The (*Invasions Barbares, Les*) (2003), *Bob Million: Le jackpot de la planète* (Bob Million and His World Jackpot) (1997), Decline of the American Empire, The (*Le declin de l'empire Américain*) (1986), *Jésus de Montréal* (1989), Life After Love (2000), *Louis XIX, le roi des ondes* (1994), Memories Unlocked (1999), *Meurtre en musique* (1994), *Nuit de noces* (Night of the Wedding) (2001), *Ou le roman de Charles Pathé* (The Life of Charles Pathé) (1995)

Jaeckin, Just: Girls (*Les femmes-enfant*) (1980)

Jaenicke, Hannes: Hostile Force (The Heist) (1996), Midnight Man (1995)

Jaffe, Chapelle: Boy Next Door, The (1984), Confidential (1985), Defy Gravity (1990), Me (1974), July Group, The (1981), One Night

Jaffe, Chapelle continued
  Stand (1978), Silence of the North (1981), Terminal Choice (Deathbed) (1985), Winnings of Frankie Walls, The (1980), Who Has Seen the Wind (1977)

Jaffrey, Saeed: Lulu (1995), Masala (1992)

Jaffrey, Sakina: Masala (1992)

Jafri, Javed: Sam and Me (1991)

Jakub, Lisa: Painted Angels (1998)

Jalil, David: Justice Express (1990)

Jamaan, Natja: Ms. Bear (1999)

Jamain, Patrick: Honeymoon (*Lune de miel*) (1985)

James, Anthony: Slow Burn (1989)

James, Blake: *Amanita pestilens* (1963)

James, Brenda: LAPD: To Protect and Serve (2001)

James, Brion: Cyberjack (1995)

James, John: Partners 'n Love (1992) ,

James, Ken: Blood and Guts (1978), Breaking Point (1976), Cementhead (1979), Change of Heart (1984), City on Fire (1979), Cop (Heller) (1981), Crowd Inside, The (1971), Double Negative (Deadly Companion) (1979), Fan's Notes, A (1972), Fish Hawk (1979), Heatwave Lasted Four Days, The (1973), Highpoint (1980), Hired Gun (The Devil's Spawn) (The Last Gunfighter) (1959), Kidnapping of Baby John Doe, The (1985), Man Called Intrepid, A (1979), Man Inside, The (1975), Never Trust an Honest Thief (Going for Broke) (1979), One Night Only (1986), Psychic (1991), Question of the Sixth, A (1981), Riel (1979), Rituals (The Creeper) (1977), Running Time (1978), Star Is Lost, A (1974), Summer's Children (1979), Switching Channels (1988), Threshold (1981), To Kill the King (1974), Utilities (1981), Welcome to Blood City (1977), Why Rock the Boat? (1974)

James, Ronald: Undergrads, The (1985)

James, Simon: Lyddie (1995)

James, Brenda: Incredible Mrs Ritchie, The (2003)

Jamila, Begum: Hathi (1998)

Jan, Pyare: Hathi (1998)

Janghali, Gholbahar: Secret Ballot (2001)

Jannot, Véronique: Crime of Ovide Plouffe, The (*Le crime d'Ovide Plouffe*) (*Les Plouffe, II*) (1984)

January, Michael: Hostile Force (The Heist) (1996)

Janver, Richard: One Plus One (The Kinsey Report) (Exploring the Kinsey Report) (1961)

Janvier, Michel: It's a Wonderful Love (*C'est bien beau l'amour*) (1971)

Jao, Radmar: Shopping for Fangs (1996)

Jarda, Judes-Antoine: Snail's Point of View, A (*La position de l'escargot*) (1998)

Jardine, Paully: Summer's Children (1979)

Jarosiewicz, Larry: Mothers and Daughters (1992)

Jarosiewicz, Linda: Mothers and Daughters (1992)

Jarrett, Paul: For Those Who Hunt the Wounded Down (1996), Road to Saddle River (1994)

Jarrett, Phillip: Pilgrim (Inferno) (1999)

Jarrott, Charles: Amateur, The (1981), At the Midnight Hour (1995), Boy in Blue, The (1986), Secret Life of Algernon, The (1996), Treacherous Beauties (1994)

Jarry, Daniaile: Ideal Man, The (1996)

Jarsky, Joris: Fool Proof (2003)

Jarvis, Graham: Amateur, The (1981), Draw! (1984), Middle-Age Crazy (1980)

Jarvis, John: Fish Tale Soup (1997)

Jarvis, Leon: Columbus of Sex, The: My Secret Life (1969)

Jarvis, Richard: Forbidden Journey (1950), Village Priest, The (*Le curé de village*) (1949)

Jasmin, Claude: *Corde au cou, La* (1966)

Jasmin, François: Kid Sentiment (1967), Wow (1970)

Jasmin, Michel: *Dis-moi le si j'dérange* (Tell Me if I Bother or Disturb You) (1989)

Jasny, Vojtech: Great Land of Small, The (*C'est pas parce qu'on est petit qu'on peut pas être grand!*) (1987)

Jean, Fayolle: Little Man Abroad, A (1989)

Jean, Vadim: Real Howard Spitz, The (1998)

Jeanneret, Valerie: Apartment Hunting (1999)

Jeannin, Marcel: Sign of Four, The (2001)

Jedman, Rusty: Young Magician, The (1987)

Jefford, Jacqueline: *Ange gardien, L'* (The Guardian Angel) (1978)

Jendly, Roger: *Demoiselle sauvage, La* (The Wild Girl) (Wild Damsel) (1991)

Jenkins, Noam: Century Hotel (2001), Luck (2003), Two or Three Words (1999)

Jenkins, Rebecca: Bye Bye Blues (1989), Clear Cut (1991), Cowboys Don't Cry (1987), Family Reunion (1987), Harvest (1993), Marion Bridge (2002), Past Perfect (2002), Recommendation for Mercy (1975), South of Wawa (1991), Stranger in Town (1998)

Jenkins, Timothy: Happy Birthday Gemini (1980)

Jenkins, Veronique: Danny in the Sky (2002)

Jennings, Claudia: Fast Company (1979)

Jennings, Fabian: Recommendation for Mercy (1975)

Jennings, Peter: Immortal Scoundrel, The (1952)

Jenoff, Art: Hired Gun (The Devil's Spawn) (The Last Gunfighter) (1959), Ivy League Killers (The Fast Ones) (1959), Now That April's Here (1958)

Jephcott, Samuel: Merry Wives of Tobias Rouke, The (1972)

Jetté, Michel: *Lac de la lune, Le* (1994), *Histoire de Pen* (Inside) (2002), Hochelaga (2000)

DIRECTORS, SCRIPTWRITERS & ACTORS

Jewison, Jennifer: Becoming Laura (1982)

Jewison, Norman: Agnes of God (1985)

Jezek, Robert: Formula 51 (The 51ST State) (2002)

Jiayue, Zhu: Cry Woman (*Ku qi de nu ren*) (2002)

Joachim, Suzy: Barbeque: A Love Story (1997), Guitarman (1994)

Joamie, Robert: Map of the Human Heart (1993)

Jobin, Peter: Divided Loyalties (1989), Don't Forget (1979), Till Death Do Us Part (1982)

Joe, Yvon: Finding Mary March (1989)

Johanasson, Paul: Incredible Mrs Ritchie, The (2003)

Johanna, Mary: Three More Days (1995)

Johanson, David: Candy Mountain (1987)

Johansson, Paul: Darkness Falling (2002), Edge of Madness (*Station Sauvage*) (Wilderness Station) (2003), Midnight Witness (1992)

Johns, Glynis: 49th Parallel (The Invaders) (1941), Super Star (1999)

Johnson, Ben: Terror Train (1980)

Johnson, Brooke: Circle Game, The (1994), Dead Aviators (1998), For Those Who Hunt the Wounded Down (1996)

Johnson, Cindy Lou: *Années, Les* (The Years) (1997)

Johnson, Clark: Have Mercy (1999), Lulu (1995), Man in 5A, The (1982), Silent Witness: What a Child Saw (1994), Soul Survivor (1995), Rude (1995), Planet of Junior Brown, The (1997), Task Force (2000)

Johnson, Damon: Vigil, The (1998)

Johnson, Don: Melanie (1982)

Johnson, Eric: Bear With Me (2000), Ginger Snaps: The Sequel (2003), Scorn (2000)

Johnson, Geordie: Circle Game, The (1994), Change of Place, A (1994)

Johnson, Georgann: Fatal Memories (The Eileen Franklin Story) (1992)

Johnson, Gray: Summerlust (1973)

Johnson, Ivar: Hustler White (1996)

Johnson, Kirsten: Jack of Hearts (1993)

Johnson, Lamont: Escape from Iran: The Canadian Caper (Desert Blades) (1981), Spacehunters: Adventures in the Forbidden Zone (1983)

Johnson, Lynn: Silence (1997)

Johnson, Mike: Nashville Bound (1996)

Johnson, Richard: Happy Days (Beckett on Film series) (2000)

Johnson, Sean C.W.: My Little Eye (2002)

Johnson, Shaun: Tribe of Joseph (2001)

Johnson, Taborah: One Night Only (1986)

Johnson, Tara: Jack and Jill (1998)

Johnson, Tim: Passion (2001)

Johnson, Toni Ann: Courage to Love, The (Quadroon Ball) (1999)

Johnson, Van: Kidnapping of the President, The (1980)

Johnson, Victoria: Starship Invasions (1977)

Johnston, Aaron Kim: For the Moment (1994), Last Winter, The (1989)

Johnston, Andrew: Capture of Karna Small, The (1987)

Johnston, Justine: Duke, The (1999)

Johnston, Shaun: Agent of Influence (2002), Dinosaur Hunter, The (2000), Heart of the Sun (1998), Ms. Bear (1999), Two Brothers, a Girl and a Gun (1993), Stranger in Town (1998)

Johnston, Tony: Airborne (1998), All the Fine Lines (Full Disclosure) (1999), Joe's Wedding (1996), Killing Moon (1998), Triggermen (2000), Tunnel (2000), Water Damage (1999)

Johnston, Wayne: Divine Ryans, The (1998)

Johnston, William: Long Road Home, The (1988)

Johson, Ed: Panic Bodies (1998)

Jolicoeur, Clermont: *Crème glacée, chocolat et autres consolations* (Ice Cream, Chocolate and other Consolations) (2001)

Joliffe, Charles: Covergirl (1984), Harvest (1981), Parting (see Acts of Love Series) (1980), Something's Rotten (1978)

Jolin, Carmen: House That Hides the Town, The (*La maison qui empêche de voir la ville*) (1975)

Jolivet, Pierre Alain: Black Mirror (*Haute surveillance*) (1981)

Joly, Dominique: My Uncle Antoine (1971)

Joly, Monique: Merry World of Léopold Z, The (1965), *Tout prendre, À* (Take It All) (The Way It Goes) (1963), Three Madeleines, The (*Les fantômes des trois Madeleines*) (1999)

Joly, Thierry: Big Sabotage, The (1973)

Jonasz, Michel: Babel (1999)

Jones, Andrew: Extraordinary Visitor (1998)

Jones, Andy: Adventures of Faustus Bidgood, The (1986), Bingo Robbers, The (2000), Stations (1983), Paint Cans (1994), Random Passage (2001), Rare Birds (2001)

Jones, Barbara: Sincerely Violet (1987)

Jones, Barry: Proxyhawks (1970), Undivided Attention (1987)

Jones, Beth: Ten Girls Ago (1962)

Jones, Cathy: Secret Nation (1991)

Jones, Daryn: Doulike2Watch.Com (2002)

Jones, David: Cold Journey (1976)

Jones, Eva: Agaguk (Shadow of the Wolf) (1993)

Jones, Grace: Welcome to the Freakshow (2001), Wolf Girl (2001)

Jones, Jason: Public Domain (2003)

Jones, Kevin: Cheerful Tearful (1998)

Jones, Lloyd: Dangerous Age, A (1958)

Jones, Marianne: Shadow of the Hawk (1976)

Jones, Michael: Adventures of Faustus Bidgood, The (1986), Stations (1983), Secret Nation (1991), Pasta King of the Caribbean, The (1999)

Jones, Norma Jean: Love Letters: A Romantic Trilogy (2001)

Jones, Pat: Slow Run (1969)

Jones, Rebecca: Separate Vacations (1986)

Jones, Rian: Whispering City (*La forteresse*) (1947)

Jones, Ronalda: Alligator Shoes (1981)

Jones, Tommy Lee: Eliza's Horoscope (1975), Park Is Mine, The (1986)

Jorah, Samson: Never Cry Wolf (1983)

Jordan, Derwin: Expecting (2002)

Jordan, Gerard: Intruder, The (1981)

Jordan, Richard: Kamouraska (1973)

Joreige, Khalil: *Autour de la maison rose* (Around the Pink House) (1999)

Joseph, Robert: Echoes of a Summer (1976)

Joshua, Larry: Burning, The (1981)

Josue, Erol: Royal Bonbon (2002)

Joubert, Roger: *Alisée* (1991), Friends for Life (*Des amis pour la vie*) (1988)

Jourdan, Danielle: Now Where Are You? (*Où êtes-vous, donc?*) (1969)

Jourde, Cédric: Dog Who Stopped the War, The (*La guerre des tuques*) (1984)

Jovanovic, Dragan: Boomerang (2002)

Jovovich, Milla: Claim, The (2000), House on Turk Street, The (2002)

Joy, Robert: Adventures of Faustus Bidgood, The (1986), Atlantic City, U.S.A (1980), Death Wish V: The Face of Death (1994), Divine Ryans, The (1998), Escape from Iran: The Canadian Caper (Desert Blades) (1981), Grand Larceny (1991), Haven (2001), Henry and Verlin (1994), Joshua Then and Now (1985), Nuremberg (2000), Terminal Choice (Deathbed) (1985), Ticket to Heaven (1981), Threshold (1981), Out of Sight, Out of Mind (The Seventh Circle) (1983), Prodigious Hickey, The (1987), Shipping News, The (2001), Sword of Gideon (1986)

Joyce, Stephen: Affair with a Killer (1967

Joyeux, Odette: Notre-Dame of the Mouise (*Notre-Dame de la Mouise*) (1941)

Jubarbal, Camilo: Melting Pot, The (1975)

Jubenvill, Kenneth: Promise the Moon (1997)

Judd, Ashley: Eye of the Beholder (1999)

Judd, Robb: Recommendation for Mercy (1975)

Judes-Antoine: Snail's Point of View, A (*La position de l'escargot*) (1998)

Judson, Deanne: Lilly (1993)

Juhnevica, Eva: Morning in the Pine Forest (1998)

Julian, Janet: Humongous (1982)

Juliani, John: Dirty Tricks (1980), Inside Out (1979), Madeleine Is... (1971), Latitude 55 (1982), Marie-Anne (1978), Under the Piano (1998)

Julien, Pauline: Between Sweet and Salt Water (Drifting Downstream) (*Entre la mer et l'eau douce*) (1967), Bulldozer (1974), Death of a Lumberjack (*La mort d'un boucheron*) (1973), Earth to Drink, The (*La terre à boire*) (1964)

Jung, Clint: Shopping for Fangs (1996)

Junor, Douglas: Who Has Seen the Wind (1977)

Jurshevski, Sven: Rainy Day Woman (1970)

Jutra, Claude: Act of the Heart (1970), Ada (1981), Between Sweet and Salt Water (Drifting Downstream) (*Entre la mer et l'eau douce*) (1967), By Design (1981), Clean Hands (*Les mains nettes*) (1958), Dream-Speaker (1976), Flower Between the Teeth, The (*La fleur aux dents*) (1976), For Better, for Worse (*Pour le meilleur et pour le pire*) (1975), Kamouraska (1973), *Mains nettes, Les* (1957), Knowing to Learn (1965), My Uncle Antoine (1971), *Tout prendre, À* (Take It All) (The Way It Goes) (1963), Rape of a Sweet Young Girl, The (*Le viol d'une jeune fille douce*) (1968), Seer Was Here (1978), *Riel* (1979), Surfacing (1981), Till Death Do Us Part (1982), Two Solitudes (*Deux solitudes*) (1978), We Are Far From the Sun (*On est loin du soleil*) (1971), Woman of Colours, A (*La dame en couleurs*) (1985), Wow (1970), *Claude Jutra, Portrait Sur Film* (Claude Jutra, An Unfinished Story) (2002) (85mins) Director and narrator: Paule Baillargeon. Producer: Anne Frank. Scriptwriter: Jefferson Lewis. An intimate portrait of Claude Jutra celebrating his extraordinary passion and talent as a filmmaker. This portrait traces his personal and creative journey during the extraordinary years of his film career, up until his tragic and untimely death. Excerpts from his interviews, films, writings, drawings, paintings, and works in the theatre, provide us with a detailed film-bio of one of our outstanding screen artists.

Jutras, Richard: Nowhere in Sight (2000), Summer With the Ghosts (*Un été avec les fantômes*) (2002), Wrong Woman, The (1995)

Kably, Amine: Casablancais, Les (The Casablancans) (1998)

Kaczender, George: Agency (1980), Don't Let the Angels Fall (1969), In Praise of Older Women (1978), U-Turn (The Girl in Blue) (1973), Your Ticket Is no Longer Valid (1982)

Kaczmarck, Jane: Jenifer Estess Story, The (2001)

Kadar, Jan: Lies My Father Told Me (1975)

Kadar, Roland: Absent One, The (1997)

Kaden, Henri-Mathieu: Patricia and Jean-Baptiste (1966)

Kaden-Lacroix, Patricia: Patricia and Jean-Baptiste (1966)

Kae-Kazim, Hakim: Secret Laughter of Women, The (1999)

Kaese, Jacqui: M.V.P. 2: Most Valuable Primate (2001), Passion (2001)

Kahn, Jan Jaffe: Prodigious Hickey, The (1987)

Kahn, Madeline: Happy Birthday Gemini (1980)

Kaier, Suki: Home Movie (1992)

Kalangis, John: Jack and Jill (1998), Two or Three Words (1999)

Kalejs, Guntis Vindulis: Morning in the Pine Forest (1998)

Kalem, Toni: For Life (see Acts of Love Series) (1980)

Kalfon, Jean-Pierre: *Répétition, La* (2001)

Kam, Kahil: Malarek: A Street Kid Who Made It (1988)

Kamp-Groeneveld, Alexandra: 2001: A Space Travesty (2001)

Kanagawa, Hiro: Protection (2000)

Kane, Alden: Prom Night IV: Deliver Us From Evil (1992)

Kane, Carol: Baby on Board (1992), Wedding in White (1972)

Kane, Kerrie: Spasms (Snake Bite) (1983)

Kane, Margo: Running Brave (1983), Where the Heart Is (1985)

Kane, Michael: Cross Country (1983), Love in a Four Letter World (1970), Your Ticket Is no Longer Valid (Finishing Touch) (1982)

Kane, Sam: Storm (1985)

Kanev, Michael: Khaled (2002)

Kanner, Alexis: Ernie Game, The (1967), Kings and Desperate Men (1981), Mahoney's Last Stand (1976)

Kapelos, John: Bad Faith (Cold Blooded) (1999), Croon Maury and Mrs. B. (International Title) (2003)

Kaplan, Gable: Tulips (1981)

Kapoor, Pankaj: Burning Season, The (1993)

Kaprisky, Valérie: Desire in Motion (*Mouvements du désire*) (1994)

Karasevich, Joan: Day My Grandad Died, The (1976), Question of the Sixth, A (1981)

Kardish, Larry: Slow Run (1969)

Karlzen, Gunilla: Scream of Stone (1991)

Karn, Denyse: Timing (1985)

Karn, Richard: M.V.P. 2: Most Valuable Primate (2001)

Karpov, Anatoly: Great Chess Movie, The (1982)

Karras, Alex: Jacob Two-Two Meets the Hooded Fang (1977), Porky's (*Chez Porky*) (1981)

Karsenti, Sabine: Bonjour, Timothy (1995), Favourite Game, The (2003)

Kartheiser, Vincent: Unsaid, The (2001)

Karyo, Tcheky: Babel (1999), Habitat (1995), Thousand Wonders of the Universe, The (1997), Vincent and Me (*Vincent et moi*) (1990)

Karystinos, Dimitri: Sex and the Single Sailor (1967)

Kasborf-Stinson, Dawn: 24 Store, The (1990)

Kasemets, Udo: Crimes of the Future (1970)

Kash, Daniel: Gross Misconduct (1992), Haven (2001), Hurt Penguins (1992), Killing Moon (1998), Me and My Shadows (2000), Michelle Apartments, The (1995), Pilgrim (Inferno) (1999), Sleeproom, The (1998), Wounded (1996)

Kash, Linda: Bookfair Murders, The (1999), Partners 'n Love (1992), Urban Safari (1995)

Kasma, Jacques: Mission of Fear (1965)

Kastner, Daphna: Crack Me Up (1993), Eviction (*Evixion) (1986),* Julia Has Two Lovers (1990), Lana in Love (1991)

Kastner, John: Don't Let the Angels Fall (1969)

Kastner, Peter: Footsteps in the Snow (*Des pas sur la neige*) (1966), Nobody Waved Goodbye (1964), Unfinished Business (1984)

Kata, Edmond: War Between Us, The (1995)

Kates, Kimberley: Chained Heat II (1993)

Katrapani, Atanas: Home (2002)

Katrapani, Phyllis: Home (2002)

Katsumi, Mark: Spreading Ground, The (2000)

Katt, William: Paperboy, The (1994)

Katz, Allan: Hard Feelings (1981), Way to Meet Single Women, The (1985)

Katz, Judah: True Confections (1991)

Katz, Stephen: Catsplay (1977)

Katzman, Ion: *Ménace, La* (1977)

Kaufman, James: Back Stab (1990), Make Mine Chartreuse (1987), Nightwaves (2002), Sincerely Violet (1987), Whiskers (1997)

Kaufman, Robert: Nothing Personal (1980), Separate Vacations (1986)

Kawchuk, Brent: American Beer (1996)

Kawchuk, Harvey: American Beer (1996)

Kawchuk, Jordan: American Beer (1996)

Kay, Barnaby: Eisenstein (2000)

Kay, Hadley: Blood and Donuts (1995)

Kay, Jonathon: Starlight (1995)

Kay, Susan: *Entre tu et vous* (Between "tu" and "you") (1970), IXE-13 (1972), Rape of a Sweet Young Girl, The (1968)

Keach, James: Dance Goes On, The (1991), Till Death Do Us Part (1982)

Keach, Stacy: Luther (1973), Pathfinder, The (1996), Trust in Me (1995), Two Solitudes (*Deux solitudes*) (1978)

Keanan, Staci: Haunting of Lisa, The (1995)
Keane, Kerrie: Death Bite (Spasms) (1983), Distant Thunder (1988), Hitting Home (Obsessed) (1989), Incubus (1981), Malarek: A Street Kid Who Made It (1988), Morning Man, The (*Un matin, une vie*) (1986)
Keane, Laurence: Big Meat Eater (1982), Samuel Lount (1985)
Keating, Lulu: Midday Sun, The (1989)
Keatley, Philip: Ma Murray (1983)
Keaton, Buster: Ten Girls Ago (1962)
Keaton, Diane: Crossed Over (2001)
Keaton, Tom: Killing Spring, A (2001)
Kedrova, Lila: Eliza's Horoscope (1975)
Kee, James: Shadow Dancing (1988)
Keefe, Peter: Christopher's Movie Matinée (1969)
Keeler, Amanda: French Without Dressing (1964)
Keen, Patricia: Lyddie (1995)
Keena, Monica: Strike! (1998)
Keenan, Helen: Rainy Day Woman (1970)
Keene, Jennifer: Birds of Prey (1985)
Keenleyside, Eric: Blue City Slammers (1987)
Keens-Douglas, Richardo: Zero Patience (1993)
Keeper, Tina: Another Country: A North of 60 Mystery (2003), Dream Storm: A North of 60 Mystery (2001), Heater (1999), In the Blue Ground (1999), Trial by Fire: A North of 60 Mystery
Keitel, Harvey: Blindside (1986), Wanted (Crime Spree) (2003)
Keith, David: Anthrax (2001), Liar's Edge (1992), Red Blooded 2 (1996), Question of Privilege, A (1998), Whose Child Is This? The War for Baby Jessica (1993), World Traveler (2001)
Keklikian, Selma: Family Viewing (1988)
Keleghan, Peter: Screwballs (1983), Water Damage (1999)
Kell, Joseph: White Lies (1998)
Kelleher, Tim: Understudy, The: Graveyard Shift II (1988)
Keller, Joel: Art of Woo, The (2001), Sleeping Dogs Lie (1999)
Keller, Marthe: Amateur, The (1981), *Mémoire tronquée* (1990), *Mon amie Max* (1993), Young Catherine (1990)
Keller, Susan: Clown Murders, The (1976)
Kellerman, Sally: Drop Dead Gorgeous (Victim of Beauty) (1991), Head On (1980), KGB: The Secret War (1984), Meatballs, Part III: The Climax (1987), Verdict in Blood (2001)
Kellet, Robert: Spanish Fly (1975)
Kelly, Daniel Hugh: Nowhere to Hide (1987)
Kelly, Edward J: Noncensus (1964)
Kelly, Joanne: Bay of Love and Sorrows, The (2002), Wanted (Crime Spree) (2003)

Kelly, Lesley: Understudy, The: Graveyard Shift II (1988)
Kelly, Moira: Drive, She Said (1997)
Kelly, Morgan: Hatley High (2003)
Kelly, Peter: Dawson Patrol, The (1985)
Kelly, Ron: Megantic Outlaw, The (1971), Waiting for Caroline (1967)
Kelly, Terence: Accident at Memorial Stadium, The (1983), Chautauqua Girl (1984), Other Kingdom, The (1985), Silence (1997), Silencer, The (1999) Tom Stone: For the Money (2002)
Kelly-Gaudreault, Peter: Trial by Fire: A North of 60 Mystery
Kelman, Paul: My Bloody Valentine (1981), Slim Obsession (1984)
Kelsey, Tamsin: Bad Money (1999)
Kemble, Alison: Ups and Downs (1983)
Kemeny, John: Apprenticeship of Duddy Kravitz, The (1974), see Bethune (1977)
Kemp, Bill: More Joy in Heaven (1975)
Kemp, Jeremy: Leopard in the Snow (1978)
Kendall, Nicholas: Cadillac Girls (1993), Great Goose Caper, The (2003), Kayla (1998), Mr. Rice's Secret (2000)
Kendall, Simon: Lunch with Charles (2001)
Kennedy, Burt: Canadians, The (1961)
Kennedy, Caroline: When Tomorrow Dies (1965)
Kennedy, Florence: Bush Pilot (1946)
Kennedy, George: Death Ship (1980), Search and Destroy (1979)
Kennedy, Karen: Life and Times of Alonzo Boyd, The (1982)
Kennedy, Michael: Broken Lullaby (1994), Caribe (1988), Hostile Force (The Heist) (1996), Joe's Wedding (1996), One Man Out (*Erik*) (1989), Swordsman, The (1993)
Kensit, Patsy: At the Midnight Hour (1995), Darkness Falling (2002)
Kent, Larry: Apprentice, The (*Fleur bleue*) (1971), Bitter Ash, The (1963), Facade (1970), High (1968), High Stakes (1986), Keep It in the Family (1973), Mothers and Daughters (1992), One Man (1977), Q-bec My Love (A Commercial Success) (1970), Rape of a Sweet Young Girl, The (*Le viol d'une jeune fille douce*) (1968), Running Time (1978), Slavers, The (1984), Sweet Substitute (Caressed) (1964), When Tomorrow Dies (1965), Yesterday (1981)
Kent, Susan: Violet (2000)
Kenzie, Leila: Dogmatic (1996)
Kerigan, John: Deadly Arrangement (1998)
Kermoyan, Mathieu: Bananas From Sunny Québec (1993)
Kernochan, Sarah: Strike! (1998)
Kerns, Todd: Horsey (1997)

Kerr, Edie: Isabel (1968)

Kerr, John: Amateur, The (1981)

Kerr, Nancy: Pygmalion (1983)

Kerr, Richard: Willing Voyeur, The (1996)

Kershner, Irvin: Luck of Ginger Coffey, The (1964)

Kerwin, William: Playgirl Killer (Decoy for Terror) (1965)

Kesden, Bradley: Meatballs, Part III: The Climax (1987)

Keti, Chloe: Sex and the Single Sailor (1967)

Keusch, Michael: Anything For Love (1992)

Keyloun, Mark: Separate Vacations (1986)

Kezin, Michael: Haro (1994)

Khaja, Jameel: Passage to Ottawa, A (2002)

Khan, Aamir: Earth (1998)

Khandia, Carlos: Dangerous Dreams (1986)

Khaner, Julie: Friends at Last (1995), Justice (1998)

Khanjian, Arsinée: Adjuster, The (1991), Ararat (2002), *Boîte à soleil, La* (The Box of the Sun) (1988), Calendar (1993), Exotica (1994), Family Viewing (1988), Felicia's Journey (1999), Next of Kin (1984), Sarabande (1997), Speaking Parts (1989), Sweet Hereafter, The (1996)

Khanna, Rahul: Bollywood/Hollywood (2002), Earth (1998)

Kharbanda, Kulbushan: Fire (1996), Sam and Me (1991)

Kiberlain, Sandrine: Betty Fisher and Other Stories (*Betty Fisher et autres histoires*) (2001)

Kidawa-Blonski, Jan: *Journal d'un bossu, Le* (1993)

Kidder, Janet: Darkness Falling (2002), Ginger Snaps: The Sequel (2003), Tom Stone: For the Money (2002), Too Much Sex (1999), Xchange (2000)

Kidder, Margot: Best Damn Fiddler From Calabogie to Kaladar, The (1968), Black Christmas (Silent Night, Evil Nights) (Stranger in the House) (1974), *Florida, La* (1993), Heartaches (1981), Henry and Verlin (1994), Keeping Track (1987), Louisiana (1993), Mob Story (1987), Pygmalion (1983), Planet of Junior Brown, The (1997), Quiet Day in Belfast, A (1973), Silent Cradle (1998), Society's Child (2001), White Room (1989)

Kienner, Hans-Ulrich: Scream of Stone (*Cerro Torra*) (1991)

Kier, Udo: Johnny Mnemonic (1995)

Kiki, Kirin: Best Bad Thing, The (1997)

Kilbertus, Nicholas: Kiss, The (1988), Touch of Murder, A (1990)

Kilbourn, Joanne: Deadly Appearances (1999)

Kilpatrick, Patrick: Scanners: The Showdown (Scanner Cop II: Volkin's Revenge) (1994)

Kim, Laura: Goldirocks (2003)

Kinberg, Jud: To Catch a Killer (1991)

King, Alan Winton: Last Season, The (1987), One Night Stand (1978), Termini Station (1990)

King, Allan: Maria (1977), Ready for Slaughter (1983), Silence of the North (1981), Sunday in the Country (1975), Warrendale (1967), Who Has Seen the Wind (1977)

King, Charmion: Anne of Green Gables (1985), Anne of Green Gables: The Continuing Story (Series) (1985-1999), Don't Forget to Wipe the Blood Off (1966), Don't Let the Angels Fall (1969), Nobody Waved Goodbye (1964), Who Has Seen the Wind (1977), Once (1981)

King, David: Harmony Cats (1993)

King, George: Hurt Penguins (1992)

King, Kevin: Defcon 4 (1984)

King, Morgana: Brooklyn State of Mind, A (1997)

King, Perry: Class of 1984 (1982), Cry in the Night, A (1996), Search and Destroy (1979)

King, Robert: Dukes, The (1998), Murder Seen (2000)Something More (1999), Without Malice (2000)

King, Stephen: More to Love (2000), see Dead Zone, The

King, Thomas: Medicine River (1993)

King, Vanessa: My Father's Angel (West of Sarajevo) (1999)

Kingsley, Jean-Paul: Mother's Heart, A (1953)

Kinney, Jim: City of Dark (1997), Fishing Trip, The (1998)

Kinney, Terry: Fly Away Home (1996)

Kinsey, Nicholas: Short Change (*Une fille impossible*) (1989), Women Without Wings (2002)

Kinski, Nastassja: Blind Terror (2000), Claim, The (2000), Say Nothing (2001)

Kinsolving, William: Fan's Notes, A (1972)

Kipling, Madeleine: Horsey (1997)

Kipp, Deborah: Becoming Laura (1982), Someday Soon (1977)

Kipping, Patricia: Stations (1983)

Kirby, Luke: Lost and Delirious (2000), Luck (2003)

Kirby, Michael: Between Friends (Get Back) (1973), By Reason of Insanity (1982), In Praise of Older Women (1978), Keep It in the Family (1973), Meatballs (1979), Mr. Patman (1981), My Pleasure Is My Business (1975), Silent Partner, The (1978), U-Turn (The Girl in Blue) (1973)

Kiritake, Kanjuro: Lover's Exile, The (1981)

Kirk, Stacy: Barbeque: A Love Story (1997)

Kiroual, Mariette: Barbara James (2001)

Kirshner, Mia: Cadillac Girls (1993), Century Hotel (2001), Exotica (1994), Love and Human Remains (1994), Now and Forever (2001)

Kirsner, Jacques: Run for it, Lola! (*Sauve-toi, Lola*) (1986)

Kirwan, Jo-Anne: All in Good Taste (1983)

Kish, Colin: Horses in Winter (*Chevaux en hiver*) (1988)

Kisseliov, Oleg: Two Thousand and None (2000)

Kistabish, Richard: Windigo (1994)

Kitamura, Akiko: Keiko (1989)

Kittles, Tory: Invincible (2001)

Kjollesdal, Heather: Night Friend (A Cry From the Heart) (1987)

Klein, Ramona: Shelley (Turned Out) (1987)

Klein, Robert Dean: Heart of America: Homeroom (2003)

Kleinschmit, Carl: Middle-Age Crazy (1980)

Klenman, Norman:Ivy League Killers (The Fast Ones) (1959)), Now That April's Here (1958)

Klerk, Paul: Vincent and Me (*Vincent et moi*) (1990)

Kletter, Richard: Never Cry Wolf (1983)

Kligman, Paul: Off Your Rocker (1982)

Klimbo: Requiem for a Handsome Bastard (*Requiem pour un beau sans-coeur*) (1992)

Klymkiw, Greg: Smoked Lizard Lips (1991)

Knapp, Budd: Child Under a Leaf (1974), Hank (1977), In Praise of Older Women (1978), Kings and Desperate Men (1981), More Joy in Heaven (1975), One Man (1977), *Riel* (1979), Snowbirds (1981), Two Solitudes (*Deux solitudes*) (1978), Why Rock the Boat? (1974)

Knaup, Herbert: Nuremberg (2000)

Kneebone, Tom: Counterstrike (1993), Housekeeper, The (Judgement in Stone) (1986), Luck of Ginger Coffey, The (1964)

Knight, Angele: Mystery of the Million Dollar Hockey Puck (1975)

Knight, Jordan: Harmoney (1999)

Knight, Keith: Mr. Nice Guy (1986), Siege (1983), Whodunit (1986)

Knight, Victor: Because Why (*Parce que Pourquoi*) (1993), Ford: The Man and the Machine (1987), Happy Birthday to Me (1981), Lies My Father Told Me (1975), One Man (1977), Terror Train (1980), Prologue (1970), Scanners (1981), Summer (2002), Visiting Hours (Fright) (1982)

Knight, Wyatt: Porky's (*Chez Porky*) (1981), Porky's II: The Next Day (*Chez Porky 2*) (1983), Porky's Revenge (*Revanche de Porky, La*) (1985)

Kniveton, Audrey: Sweet and the Bitter, The (1962)

Knoles, Harley: Great Shadow, The (1920)

Knop, Patricia: Silence of the North (1981)

Knowles, Paul: Home Team (1999)

Knox, Alexander: Joshua Then and Now (1985)

Knox, Ann: Only Thing You Know, The (1971)

Kobrin, Tannis: Ballerina and the Blues, The (1987)

Koenig, Laird: Little Girl Who Lives Down the Lane, The (1977)

Kogen, Jay: Wrong Guy, The (1998)

Kohanyi, Julius: War Boy, The (Point of Escape) (1985), Summer's Children (1979)

Kok, Marja: Hersenschimmen (1987)

Kolber, Sandra: Tell Me That You Love Me (1983)

Kolk, Jaan: Shoemaker (1997)

Koll, Claudia: Red River (*Rivière Rouge*) (1996)

Kollek, Amos: Sue Lost in Manhattan (Sue) (1997)

Kolomeir, Robert: Remembering Mel (1986)

Komack, James: Porky's Revenge (1985)

Komorowska, Liliana: Art of War, The (2000), Royal Scandal, The (2001), Scanners III: The Takeover (1992), Screamers (1995), Suspicious Minds (1996)

Koncz, Christoph: Red Violin, The (*Le violon rouge*) (1998)

Kondracki, Jacek: *Journal d'un bossu, Le* (1993)

Konner, Lawrence: Almost Grown (1987)

Kopsa, Michael: Timing (1985)

Korbin, Tannis: Midnight Magic (1988)

Korbut, William: Isaac Little feathers (1984)

Korchnoi, Viktor: Great Chess Movie, The (1982)

Koren, Steve: Super Star (1999)

Korican, Michael: Recorded Live (1982)

Kormakur, Baltasar: Regina (2002)

Koslo, Paul: Chained Heat II (1993), Xtro II: The Second Encounter (1991)

Kotcheff, Ted: Apprenticeship of Duddy Kravitz, The (1974), Joshua Then and Now (1985), Switching Channels (1988)

Koteas, Elias: Adjuster, The (1991), Ararat (2002) (126mins), Camilla (1994), Crash (1996), Crazy Horse (She Drives Me Crazy) (Friends, Lovers & Lunatics) (1989), Exotica (1994), Malarek: A Street Kid Who Made It (1988), One Magic Christmas (1985), Power of Attorney (1995)

Kotto, Maka: How to Make Love to a Negro Without Getting Tired (*Comment faire l'amour avec un nègre sans se fatiguer*) (1989), Silent Love, A (2003), *Sucre amer* (1997)

Kotto, Yaphet: Park Is Mine, The (1986), Ride, The (2000), Whisper to a Scream (1988)

Kouf, James: Utilities (1981)

Kourouma, Lansana: *Station nord* (2002)

Kovach, Edward: Xtro II: The Second Encounter (1991)

Kovacs, Eva: Crime Wave (1985)

Kovacs, Tom: Pinball Summer (1980)

Koval, Paul: Back Stab (1990), Life in the Balance (2001), Psychic (1991)

Kovacs, Geza: Baby on Board (1992)

Kowalchuk, Jean: Summerlust (Goodbye Neighbours and Wives) (1973)

Kowalchuk, William: Summerlust (Goodbye Neighbours and Wives) (1973)

Kowalewich, Len: Dead Wrong (1983)

Kowarsky, Ori: Various Positions (2002)

Koyamo, Alex: Skin Deep (Sadness of the Moon) (1995)

Kozak, John: Dory (1965), Hell Bent (1994)

Kozlova, Helene: Morning in the Pine Forest (1998)

Kozlowski, Linda: Neighbour, The (1993)

Krakowski, Andzej: Eminent Domain (1990)

Kramer, Stephanie: Beyond Suspicion (1993)

Kramreither, Anthony: Thrillkill (1984), All in Good Taste (1983), *Deux amis silencieux* (Dogs to the Rescue) (Two Silent Friends) (1969)

Krancer, Burton: Lift, The (1965), Lydia (1964)

Kranz, Janet: Slim Obsession (1984)

Krasny, Paul: Christina (1974)

Kraulis, Andrew: On Hostile Ground (2000)

Krayker, Naomi: Three More Days (1995)

Kretschmann, Thomas: Poison (Tease) (1999)

Krige, Alice: Deadly Friends: The Nancy Eaton Story (2003), Habitat (1995), Twilight of the Ice Nymphs (1997)

Krishna, Srinivas: Lulu (1995), Masala (1992)

Kristen, Ilene: Vivid (1996)

Kristofferson, Kris: Millennium (1988), Sodbusters (1995)

Krizanc, John: Men With Brooms (2002)

Kroeker, Allan: Heaven on Earth (1987), Hostile Advances: The Kerry Ellison Story (1996), Legend of Kootenai Brown, The (1990), Showdown at Williams Creek (Kootenai Brown) (1991), Tramp at the Door (1985)

Krome, Konnie: Odd Balls (1984)

Kronby, Madeleine: Cool Sound From Hell, A (The Young and the Beat) (1959)

Kronold, Richard: Forbidden Journey (1950)

Krueger, Jacob: Matthew Shepard Story, The (2001)

Kruger, Michael: Amityville Curse, The

Krushen, Francesca: August and July (1973)

Krystyn, Vieslav: Year of the Sheep (1997)

Kuhn, Catherine: Pictures at the Beach (1990)

Kukulewich, Mike: Rip-Off (1971)

Kunuk, Zacharias: Atanarjuat: The Fast Runner (*L'homme nu*) (2000)

Kupferberg, Tuli: Do You Want to Sleep With God? (*Voulez-vous coucher avec Dieu?*) (1972)

Kurahara, Koreyoshi: Hiroshima (1996)

Kurtzman, Robert: Wishmaster 1 (1997)

Kuzk, Mimi: Fairy Tales & Pornography (2003)

Kuzmyn, Natalia: Recorded Live (1982)

Kuzyk, Mimi: Fairy Tales & Pornography (2003), Kiss, The (1988), Lifeforce Experiment (1994), Lost and Delirious (2000), Malicious (1995), Striker's Mountain (1985), Water Damage (1999)

Kwietniowski, Richard: Love and Death on Long Island (1997), Owning Mahowny (2001)

Kwok, Wayne: Dreamtrips (2000)

Kwouk, Burt: Bullet to Beijing (Len Deighton's Bullet to Beijing) (1995)

Kyle, Christopher: Weight of Water, The (2000)

Kynaston, Nigel: Ascent, The (1994)

L'Allier-Matteau, Geneviève: *Si belles* (So Pretty) (1994)

L'Allier-Matteau, Jolianne: Desire in Motion (*Mouvements du désire*) (1994)

L'Écuyer, Gérard: Eternal Husband, The (1997)

L'Écuyer, Guy: *90 jours, Les* (90 Days) (1959), Apparition, The (The Unexpected Phantom*)* (1972), Bar Salon (1974), Bernie and the Gang (*Ti-mine Bernie pis la gang*) (1977), Christmas Martian, The (*Le martien de Noël*) (1971), Cold Journey (1976), *Corde au cou, La* (1966), Fantastica (1980), Flower Between the Teeth, The (*La fleur aux dents*) (1976), Hot Dogs (Clean Up Squad, The) (1980), Jacob Two-Two Meets the Hooded Fang (1977), J.A. Martin, Photographer (1977), Let's Talk About Love (1976), Lies My Father Told Me (1975), Little Tougas (1976), Lucky Star, The (1980), *Mains nettes, Les* (1957), *Maria Chapdelaine* (1983), Men, The (1971), Merry World of Léopold Z, The (1965), Moonshine (1982), Night in America, A (*Une nuit en Amérique*) (1975), Pacemaker and a Sidecar, A (*L'eau chaude, l'eau frette*) (1997), Time of the Hunt, The (*Le temps d'une chasse*) (1972), Vultures, The (*Les vautours*) (1975), Woman Inflamed, A (*Tout feu, tout femme*) (1975), You Are Warm, You Are Warm (*Tu brûles, tu brûles*) (1973)

L'Écuyer, John: Curtis's Charm (1995), Live Through This (2000), Saint Jude (2000), Tagged: The Jonathan Wamback Story (2002)

L'Écuyer, Patrice: Ideal Man, The (*L'homme idéal*) (1996), *Présence des ombres, La* (The Presence of Shadows) (1996)

L'Heureux, Gaston: 100% Bio (Hundred Percent Biography) (2003)

L'Heureux, Lise: To Be Sixteen (*Avoir 16 ans*) (1979)

L'Italien, Jean: Blanche and the Night (*Blanche et la nuit*) (1989), *Louis XIX, le roi des ondes* (1994), *Naufragés du Labrador, Les* (Stranded in Labrador) (1991), *Nez rouge* (Red Nose) (2003)

L'Italien, Serge: Gone to Glory (1975)

La Haye, David: *Ange noir, L'* (The Black Angel) (Nelligan) (1991), Angel in a Cage (The Woman in the Cage)(*La bête de foire*) (1993), *Concièrgerie, La* (The Caretaker's Lodge) (The Prison) (1997), Cosmos (1997), Courage to Love, The (Quadroon Ball) (1999), *Crabe dans la tête, Un* (A Crab in My Head) (2001), Full Blast (*L'ennemi*) (1999), *Hasards ou coïnci-*

La Haye, David continued:
  dences (1998), In the Belly of a Dragon (1989), Invention of Love, The (2000), *Méchant party* (2000), Water Child (*L'enfant d'eau*) (1995)

La Rue, Jack: Bush Pilot (1946)

La Russa, Adrienne: Keep It in the Family (1973)

Labarthe, Samuel: *Arthur Rimbaud: L'homme aux semelles de vent* (1995)

Labbé, Patrick: Coyote (1993), *Forteresse suspendue, La* (The Hidden Fortress) (2001), J'aime, j'aime pas (1995), Stone Woman, The (*Femme de pierre*) (1990), *Ne dis rien* (Don't Say Anything) (2001)

Labeau, Pierre: *Dangereux, Les* (2003)

Labelle, Pierre: Apparition, The (The Unexpected Phantom) (1972)

LaBelle, Rob: Burial Society, The (2002)

Laberge, Marie: Part des choses, La (*Un léger vertige*) (A Part of Things) (A Light Vertigo) (1991), Precious Hours, The (*Les heures précieuses*) (1989), Years of Dreams and Revolt (*Les années de rêves*) (1984)

Lablanc, Mireille: Night of the Flood (*La nuit du déluge*) (1996)

Lablanc, Yole: Little Man Abroad, A (1989)

Labonté, François: Bombardier (1992), Castle of Cards, The (1980), *Gaspard et fils* (1988), Henri (1986), Manuel: A Son by Choice (1990), *Marchands du silence, Les* (1994)

Labourier, Dominique: Run for it, Lola! (*Sauve-toi, Lola*) (1986)

Labow, Hilary: City on Fire (1979)

Labow, John: Winter Kept Us Warm (1965)

Labrèche, Gaétan: *Corde au cou, La* (1966), Don't Let It Kill You (*Il ne faut pas mourir pour ça*) (1968), Straight to the Heart (*Jusqu'au coeur*) (1969), Those Damned Savages (1971)

Labrèche, Marc: *Grand zélé, Le* (The Great Zeal) (1993), Odyssée d'Alice Tremblay, L' (2002), Matusalem (1993), *Matusalem II, le dernier des Beauchesne* (1996)

Labrecque, Jacques: *Amanita pestilens* (1963)

Labrecque, Jean-Claude: *André Mathieu, Musicien* (1994), *Bonjour, monsieur Gauguin* (Good Day, Mr. Gauguin) (1989), Brother André (*Le frère André*) (1987), Coffin Affair, The (*L'affaire Coffin*) (1980), Court-Circuit (1983), No Holiday for Idols (*Pas de vacances pour les idoles*) (1965), Two Wise Men, The (*Les smattes*) (1972), Story of the Three, A (*L'histoire des trois*) (1989), Vultures, The (*Les vautours*) (1975), Years of Dreams and Revolt (*Les années de rêves*) (1984)

Labrie, France: Tanzi (1987)

Labrosse, Sarah-Jeanne: Summer With the Ghosts (*Un été avec les fantômes*) (2002)

LaBruce, Bruce: Hayseed (1997), Hustler White (1996), Super 8 (1994)

Labyorteaux, Patrick: National Lampoon's Last Resort (1994)

Lacasse, Brigitte: 100% Bio (Hundred Percent Biography) (2003), Autobiography of an Amateur Filmmaker, The (1999)

Lacelle, Hélène: Cowboyz (1988)

Lachance, Bertrand: Danny in the Sky (2002)

Lachance, Beth: With Friends Like These (*Avec des amis*) (1990)

Lachance, Catherine: Angel in a Cage (The Woman in the Cage) (*La bête de fiore*) (1993)

Lachance, Gilbert: *Louis XIX, le roi des ondes* (1994)

Lachance, Pierrette: *Esprit du mal, L'* (1954)

Lachapelle, Andrée: *Albertine, en cinq temps* (Albertine in Five Times) (1999), Beautiful Sundays (*Les beaux dimanches*) (1974), Cap Tourmente (Cape Torment) (1993), *Comme un voleur* (Like a Thief) (1991), *Corde au cou, La* (1966), Dear Father (*Caro Papa*) (1979), *Dernières fougères, Les* (The Last Ferns) (1991), Don't Let the Angels Fall (1969), *Même sang, Un* (The Same Blood) (1994), *Misanthrope, Le* (1966), Moody Beach (1990), YUL 871 (Montréal Flight 871) (1966), *Pays dans la gorge, Le* (The Country on Your Chest) (1999), *Trois femmes, un amour* (Three Women in Love) (1994)

Lachapelle, Julie: Facade (1970), Rape of a Sweet Young Girl, The (*Le viol d'une jeune fille douce*) (1968), *Retour de l'Immaculée Conception, Le* (The Return of the Immaculate Conception) (1970)

Lack, Stephen: 20th Century Chocolate Cake, A (1983), Dead Ringers (1988), Head On (Fatal Attraction) (1980), Maintain the Right (1982), Montréal Main (1974), Rubber Gun, The (1977), Scanners (1981)

Lackaye, Wilton: God's Crucible (1921)

Lacombe, Simon: *Ne dis rien* (Don't Say Anything) (2001)

Lacombe, Sylvie: *Révolutions, d'ébats amoureux, éperdus, douloureux* (Revolutions...Forever and Ever) (1984)

Lacomblez, Antoine: *Des chiens dans la neige* (Dogs in the Snow) (2001)

Lacoste, André: Homme renversé, L' (1987), *Lac de la lune, Le* (1994), *Laura Laur* (1988)

Lacoste, Céline: *Strass Café* (1980), Woman in Transit, A (*La femme de l'hôtel*) (1984)

Lacroix, Denis: Running Brave (1983), *Visage pâle* (Pale Face) (1986)

Lacroix, Fanny: Book of Eve (2002)

LaCroix, Peter: Bounty Hunters (1996), Noroc (1999), Silencer, The (1999)

Lacroix, Richard: Revolutionaries, The (1965), Patricia and Jean-Baptiste (1966)

Ladd, Cheryl: Haunting of Lisa, The (1995), Millennium (1988)

Ladd, Diane: Breach of Faith: A Family of Cops II (1996), Hush Little Baby (Mother of Pearl) (1993), Law of Enclosures, The (2000)

Lade, Bernd Michael: Bookfair Murders, The (1999)

Ladouceur, Louise: *Strass Café* (1980)

Ladouceur, Robert: Tragic Diary of Zero, the Fool, The (1970)

Lafebvre, Jean-Pierre: Q-bec My Love (A Commercial Success) (1970)

Laferrie, Kimberly: Winter Lily (1998)

Laferrière, Dany: How to Make Love to a Negro Without Getting Tired (*Comment faire l'amour avec un nègre sans se fatiguer*) (1989)

Lafferrere, André: When Wolves Howl (*Quand hurlent les loups*) (1973)

Laflame, Yvonne: Little Aurore's Tragedy (*La petite Aurore, l'enfant martyre*) (1952), Mother's Heart, A (1953)

Laflamme, Michel: *Dernière condition, La* (1982)

Lafléche, Alice: Timing (1985)

Lafleur, Denise: *Entre tu et vous* (Between "tu" and "you") (1970), Men, The (1971)

Lafleur, Gilles: Moonshine (1982)

Lafleur, Jean: Isla the Tigress of Siberia (1977), Mystery of the Million Dollar Hockey Puck (1975)

LaFleur, Joy: Whispering City (*La forteresse*) (1947), Sins of the Fathers (1948)

Lafont, Bernadette: *Bob Million: Le jackpot de la planète* (Bob Million and His World Jackpot) (1997), *Violette Nozière* (1978)

Lafontaine, Pierre-Luc: *Piege d'Issoudun, Le* (Trapped in Issoudun) (2002)

Lafontaine, Rita: And I Love You Dearly (*La maîtresse*) (1973), Bernie and the Gang (*Ti-mine Bernie pis la gang*) (1977), *Grands enfants, Les* (Day by Day) (1980), *Grande Séduction, La* (2003), *Homme de rêve, L'* (The Dream Man) (1991), Ideal Man, The (*L'homme idéal*) (1996), *Mon amie Max* (1993), Once Upon a Time in the East (*Il était une fois dans l'est*) (1974), Oh, If Only My Monk Would Want (*Ah! Si mon moine voulait*) (1973), Soho (1994), Sun Rises Late, The (*Le soleil se leve en retard*) (1977), Swindle, The (*La gammick*) (1974), Vultures, The (*Les vautours*) (1975), Woman of Colours, A (*La dame en couleurs*) (1985)

Laforce, Jean-Yves: Big Day, The (*Le grand day*) (1988), Heart Exposed, The (*Le coeur découvert*) (1986), Madame B (1986), Paspébiac: The Games Country (*Paspébiac: Terre des Jeux*) (1985)

Laforet, Amanda: Grand Bill, The (*Le gros Bill*) (1949)

Lafortune, Roc: Believe (2000), Boys, Les (The Boys) (1997), Fallen Knight (The Minion) (1998), Kids of the Round Table (1995), List, The (2000), *Méchant party* (2000)

Laganière, Carole: *Aline et Michel* (Aline) (1992)

Lager, Martin: Deadly Harvest (1980), Ivy League Killers (The Fast Ones) (1959), Klondike Fever (1979), Lions for Breakfast (1975), Offering, The (1966), Out of Sight, Out of Mind (The Seventh Circle) (1983), Shape of Things to Come, The (1979), Slim Obsession (1984)

Lago, Betty: *Marchands du silence, Les* (1994)

Lagtaa, Abdelkader: *Casablancais, Les* (The Casablancans) (1998)

Lague, Jacinte: Home (2002)

Lahr, Bert: Ten Girls Ago (1962)

Laidlaw, Ralph: Back to God's Country (1919)

Laing, John: Rubber Gun, The (1977)

Lajeunesse, Isabelle: *Ou le roman de Charles Pathé* (The Life of Charles Pathé) (1995)

Lajeunesse, Jean: Little Aurore's Tragedy (*La petite Aurore, l'enfant martyre*) (1952), Promised Land, The (*Les brûlés*) (1958), *Réjeanne Padovani* (1973), Tadpole and the Whale (*La grenouille et la baleine*) (1988)

Lajeunesse-Guy, Felix: Marie's Sons (*Les fils de Marie*) (2002)

Lakatos, Istvan: Absent One, The (1997)

Lakatos, Rozsika: Absent One, The (1997)

Lake, Donald: Murder Sees the Light (1987)

Lake, Stanley: Dear John (1988)

Lake, Suzy: Montréal Main (1974)

Lake, Veronica: Footsteps in the Snow (*Des pas sur la neige*) (1966)

Lakeman, Elaine: Honeymoon (1996)

Lala: Watchers (1988)

Lalande, Dan: House of Luk (2000)

LaLanne, Jack: Beefcake (1999)

Laliberté, Roger: Adventures of Ti-ken, The (1961), Ti-Ken (*Les plans mystèrieux*) (1965)

Laliberté, Bruno: *Gratien* (1989)

Laliberté, Hélène: *Gratien* (1989)

Lalka, Tina: Rubber Carpet (1995)

Lalonde, Andrée: Master Cats, The (1971), That Darned Loot (*La maudite galette*) (1972)

Lalonde, Bernard: Crinoline Madness (1995)

Lalonde, Claude: *Grand zélé, Le* (1993)

Lalonde, Jack: Dream on the Run (1977)

Lalonde, Larry: Top of the Food Chain (1999)

Lalonde, Michèle: *Conquête, La* (1973)

Lalonde, Pierre: And I Love You Dearly (*La maîtresse*) (1973)

Lalonde, Robert: Fighting Men, *Séraphin* (Heart of Stone) (A Man and His Sin) (2002)

LaMaistre, Philip: Winter Lily (1998)

Lamarre, Margot: Paperback Hero (1973)

Lamas, Lorenzo: Gladiator Cop (1994), SnakeEater (1990), SnakeEater II: The Drug Buster (1990), SnakeEater III: The Revenge (1992), Swordsman, The (1993)

Lamb, Derek: Golden Apples of the Sun (1973)

Lambert, Christopher: *Paroles et musique* (Love Songs) (1985), *Vercingétorix* (2001)

Lambert, Locky: Witchboard III: The Possession (1995)

Lambert, Marie-France: Cosmos (1997)

Lambert, Philippe: Pin-Pon, The Film (*Pin-Pon, Le film*) (1999)

Lambert, Roger: Traces (1978)

Lambert, Rollande: Luke or the Part of Things (1982)

Lambert, Vincent: Babel (1999)

Lamberts, Heath: Blind Faith (1982), Change of Heart (1993), Ganesh (Ordinary Magic) (1993), Great Big Thing, A (1968), Noncensus (1964), Nothing Personal (1980), Partners (1976), Sam and Me (1991), Tools of the Devil (1985), Utilities (1981), What We Have Here Is a People Problem (1976)

LaMond, Bill: Yesterday (1981)

LaMonica, Liza: Super 8 (1994)

Lamothe, Arthur: Dust from Underground (*Poussière sur la ville*) (1965), *Équinoxe* (1986), Heavenly Bodies (*Les corps célestes*) (1973), *Mémoire battante* (1983), Silencing the Guns (*Le silence des fusils*) (1996), Snow Has Melted on the Manicouagan, The (*La neige a fondu sur la Manicouagan*) (1965)

Lamothe, Claude: Eldorado (1995)

Lamothe, Pierre: *Grand zélé, Le* (1993)

Lamothe, Raymond: Frost Bite (*La gélure*) (1968)

Lamothe, Willie: Death of a Lumberjack (*La mort d'un boucheron*) (1973), Doves, The (*Les colombes*) (1972), I Love You (*Je t'aime*) (1974), *Lit, Le* (1974), Mustang (1975), On Est Loin Du Soleil (*One is Far From the Sun*) (*The Brother Andre and the Sun*) (1971), There's Always a Way to Get There (*Y a toujours moyen de moyenner!*) (1973), True Nature of Bernadette, The (*La vraie nature de Bernadette*) (1972)

Lamy, Dominique: *Ne dis rien* (Don't Say Anything)

(2001), *Trois femmes, un amour* (Three Women in Love) (1994),

Lanaud, Pierre: Enchanted Village, The (*Le village enchanté*) (1956)

Lancaster, Erica: Death Wish V: The Face of Death (1994)

Lancaster, Burt: Atlantic City, U.S.A (1980), Jeweller's Shop, The (1988)

Lanctôt, Micheline: Apprenticeship of Duddy Kravitz, The (1974), Blood and Guts (1978), Blood Relatives (*Les liens de sang*) (1978), Child Under a Leaf (1974), Coffin Affair, The (*L'affaire Coffin*) (1980), Comment ma mere accoucha de moi durant sa ménopause (How My Mother Was Giving Birth to Me During Menopause) (2001), Eleventh Special, The (*Onzième spéciale*) (1988), Handyman, The (*L'homme à tout faire*) (1980), Heat Line, The (*La ligne de chaleur*) (1987), Heavenly Bodies (*Les corps célestes*) (1973), Life of a Hero, The (*La vie d'un héros*) (1994), Little Tougas (1976), *Noël et Juliette* (1973), Oreille d'un sourd, L' (The Deaf Man's Ear) (1996), *Piege d'Issoudun, Le* (Trapped in Issoudun) (2002), Ruth (1994), Scream for Silence, A (*Mourir à tue-tête*) (1979), *Sonatine* (1984), Today or Never (Aujourd'hui ou jamais) (1998), True Nature of Bernadette, The (*La vraie nature de Bernadette*) (1972), Two Actresses (*Deux actrices*) (1993), When I'm Gone You'll Still Be Alive (When I'll Be Gone) (*Quand je serai parti vous vivrez encore*) (1999), Women Without Wings (2002)

Landau, Martin: Haven (2001), Special Magnum (Strange Shadows in an Empty Room) (1977)

Landers, Audrey: Freakshow (1988)

Landers, Harry: Return of Ben Casey, The (1988)

Lando, Joseph: Seeds of Doubt (1997)

Landry, Aude: Blood Relatives (1978)

Landry, Bernard: Over My Head (*Jusqu'au cou*) (1964)

Landry, Diane: Nightmare, The (*Cauchemar*) (1979)

Landry, Francine: YUL 871 (Montréal Flight 871) (1966)

Landry, Samuel: It's Your Turn, Laura Cadieux (1998), *Laura Cadieux, la Suite* (2000)

Landsdell, Elizabeth: Not Another Love Story (1979)

Lane, Lori: French Without Dressing (1964), Proud Rider, The (The Last Run) (1972)

Lane, Robyn: Draghoula (1998)

Lang, k.d.: Eye of the Beholder (1999)

Lang, Pierre: Gaia (1994)

Lange, Hope: Ford: The Man and the Machine (1987)

Langedijk, Jack: Blind Terror (2000), Divided Loyalties (1989), Evil Judgement (1984), Dead

End (False Pretense) (1998)

Langella, Frank: *Alégria* (1998), Stardom (15 Minutes) (Fandom) (2000)

Langevin, André: Dust from Underground (*Poussière sur la ville*) (1965)

Langevin, Christopher: High-Ballin' (1978), Lyon's Den (1983), Three-Card Monte (1978)

Langevin, Jacques: Unknown From Montréal, The (*Son copain*) (1950)

Langevin, Samantha: Winnings of Frankie Walls, The (1980)

Langfelder, Dulcinée: *Part des choses, La* (*Un léger vertige*) (A Part of Things) (A Light Vertigo) (1991)

Langhorn, Jack: Life and Times of Alonzo Boyd, The (1982)

Langley, Lee: Another Woman (1994)

Langlois, Denis: Danny in the Sky (2002), Escort, The (*L'escorte*) (1996)

Langlois, Lisa: Blood Relatives (*Les liens de sang*) (1978), Class of 1984 (1982), Deadly Eyes (The Rats) (1982), Happy Birthday to Me (1981), Hard Feelings (1981), Klondike Fever (1979), Mind Field (1989), Phobia (1980), *Violette Nozière* (1978)

Langlois, Madeleine: Case of the Witch Who Wasn't, The (*Pas de répit pour Mélanie*) (1990)

Langlois, Michel: *Cap Tourmente* (Cape Torment) (1993), Cargo (1990), Close to Falling Asleep (*Trois pommes à côté du sommeil*) (1988), *Comme un voleur* (Like a Thief) (1991), *Corps perdu, À* (Straight to the Heart) (1988), *Demoiselle sauvage, La* (The Wild Girl) (Wild Damsel) (1991), *Même sang, Un* (The Same Blood) (1994), *Part des choses, La* (*Un léger vertige*) (A Part of Things) (A Light Vertigo) (1991), Woman in Transit, A (1984),

Langlois, Suzanne: Act of the Heart (1970), Sensations (1973), There's Nothing Wrong With Being Good to Yourself (*Y a pas d'mal à se faire du bien*) (She's So Young and Knows All!) (*C'est jeune et ça sait tout!*) (1974), True Nature of Bernadette, The (*La vraie nature de Bernadette*) (1972), Woman Inflamed, A (*Tout feu, tout femme*) (1975)

Langlois, Yves: Ford: The Man and the Machine (1987), Rape of a Sweet Young Girl, The (*Le viol d'une jeune fille douce*) (1968)

Langrick, Margaret: American Boyfriends (1989), My American Cousin (1985), Cold Comfort (1989), Martha, Ruth and Edie (1987), Sweet Angel Mine (1996)

Languirand, Jacques: *Grand serpent du monde, Le* (The Great World Serpent) (1999), Kid Sentiment (1967)

Lanies, Diane: To Kill to Live (*Mourir pour vivre*) (1973)

Lanning, Frank: Cameron of the Royal Mounted (1921)

Lanoux, Victor: Louisiana (1993), Snail's Point of View, A (*La position de l'escargot*) (1998)

Lanselle, Corinne: Until the Heart (*Jusqu'au coeur*) (1980), South of Wawa (1991)

Lansens, Lori: Marine Life (2000), South of Wawa (1991), Welcome to the Freakshow (2001), Wolf Girl (2001)

LaPaglia, Anthony: Killer (1994)

Lapalme, Denis: Secret of Jerome, The (*Le secret de Jérôme*) (1994)

Laparé, Louise: Crime of Ovide Plouffe, The (*Le crime d'Ovide Plouffe*) (*Les Plouffe, II*) (1984), Two Wise Men, The (*Les smattes*) (1972), Salut! J.W. (1981)

Laperrière, Michel: *Si belles* (So Pretty) (1994), Windigo (1994)

Lapersonne, Franck: *Arthur Rimbaud: L'homme aux semelles de vent* (1995)

Lapierre, Laurier: Oranges of Israel, The (*Valse à trois*) (1974)

Lapinskie, Clare: Sister Blue (2001)

Laplante, Fleur-Ange: Don't Let It Kill You (*Il ne faut pas mourir pour ça*) (1968)

Laplante, Sonia: *Meurtre en musique* (1994)

Lapointe, Bruce: Two Summers (2002)

Lapointe, Jean: Apple, the Stem and the Seeds, The (*La pomme, la queue et les pépins*) (1974), Bernie and the Gang (*Ti-mine Bernie pis la gang*) (1977), *Bouteille, La* (The Bottle) (2000), Évangéline the Second (*Évangéline Deusse*) (1985), *Histoire inventée, Une* (An Imaginary Tale) (1990), *Immortels, Les* (The Immortals) (2003), J.A. Martin, Photographer (1977), Never Too Late (1996), OK Liberty (*Ok...Laliberté*) (1973), One Man (1977), Orders, The (*Les ordres*) (1974), Pacemaker and a Sidecar, A (*L'eau chaude, l'eau frette*) (1997), Saracen, The (*La Sarrasine*) (1991), *Ti-mine, Bernie pis la gang* (1977), Two Women of Gold (*Deux femmes en or*) (1970), Woman Inflamed, A (*Tout feu, tout femme*) (1975)

Lapointe, Jean-Marie: Ideal Man, The (1996)

Lapointe, Pauline: Childhood Friend, A (*Une amie d'enfance*) (1978), Day in a Taxi, A (*Une journée en taxi*) (1982), Florida, La (1993)

Lapointe, Priscella: Angel Life (*Vie d'ange*) (1979)

Laprade, Guy: Remembering Mel (1986)

Laprade, Louise: *Femme de Pablo Ruiz, La* (*Pablo qui court*) (On the Run) (1991), Last Glacier, The (1984), On the Run (*Pablo qui court*) (1993)

Laprade, Serge: 100% Bio (Hundred Percent Biography) (2003)

Laprise, Michel: Time Zero (No Game Without Sun) (*Le temps zéro*) (*Pas de jeu sans soleil*) (1972)

Lara, Christian: *Sucre amer* (1997)

Larivée, Francine: *J'me Marie, J'me Marie* (1974)

Larivière, Claude: Mule and the Emeralds, The (1995)

Larivière, Jean-Marc: *Révolutions, d'ébats amoureux, éperdus, douloureux* (Revolutions...Forever and Ever) (1984)

Larkin, Ryan: Running Time (1978)

Larkin, Sheena: Make Mine Chartreuse (1987), Two Summers (2002)

Laroche, Armand: Deaf and Mute (1986)

Laroche, Claude: *Au fil de l'eau* (2002), Great Ordinary Movie, The (Joan of Arc Is Alive and Well and Living in Québec) (*Le grand film ordinaire*) (1971), *Montréal Blues* (1972)

Laroche, Gil: Head of Normande St. Onge, The (*La tête de Normande St-Onge*) (1975)

Laroche, Martin: *Petit vent de panique, Un* (A Gust of Panic) (2000)

LaRoche, Pierre: Goin' Down the Road (1970)

Larochelle, Annie: *Exils* (2002)

Larochelle, France: *Exils* (2002)

Larochelle, Julie: Savage Messiah (2001)

Larouche, Caroline: Like the Six Fingers of a Hand (1978)

Larry, Sheldon: At the End of the Day: The Sue Rodriguez Story (1998), Family of Strangers (1993), First Circle, The (1991), Keeping the Promise (1997)Terminal Choice (Deathbed) (1985)

Larson, Donna: Trip to Serendipity, A (1992)

Larson, Wolf: Avalanche Alley (2001), Expect No Mercy (1995), Hostile Force (The Heist) (1996)

Larue, Roger: King of Fire (1985)

Lasalle, Lise: Flower Between the Teeth, The (*La fleur aux dents*) (1976)

LaSalle, Martin: Pilgrim (Inferno) (1999)

Laser, Martin: Wings in the Wilderness (*Les voyageurs d'été*) (1975)

Lasker, Jeannine: 20th Century Chocolate Cake, A (1983)

Laskey, Kathleen: Fish Tale Soup (1997), Kathleen: Love and Murder (1988)

Laskin, Larissa: Peacekeepers (1997)

Laskos, Andrew: Passion and Paradise (1989)

Laskowski, Marcia: X-Rated (1994), Punch (2002)

Lasnier, Hélène: Medium Blues (1985)

Lassez, Sarah: Malicious (1995)

Latour, Clément: Nightingales and the Bells (*Le rossignol et les cloches*) (1952), *Tit-Coq* (1953)

Latour, Jean-Guy: Isla the Tigress of Siberia (1977)

Latraverse, Louise: *Autre homme, Un* (Another Man) (1991), Beauty of Women, The (*La beauté des femmes*) (1994), Between Sweet and Salt Water (Drifting Downstream) (*Entre la mer et l'eau douce*) (1967), Great Big Thing, A (1968), Orders, The (*Les ordres*) (1974), Two Actresses (*Deux actrices*) (1993)

Latraverse, Michèle: Men, The (1971)

Latulippe, Gilles: Oh, If Only My Monk Would Want (*Ah! Si mon moine voulait*) (1973), Push but Push Reasonably (Scarlatina) (*Pousse mais pousse égal*) (1975)

Lau, Charmaine: Iron Road (2002)

Lau, Jamie: Dreamtrips (2000)

Lau, John: Second Skin (2000)

Lau, Sean: Lunch with Charles (2001)

Lauer, Andrew: Screamers (1995)

Laurance, Matthew: Eddie and the Cruisers Part II: Eddie Lives! (1989)

Laure, Carole: Angel and the Woman, The (*L'ange et la femme*) (1977), Apprentice, The (*Fleur bleue*) (1971), Born for Hell (*Né pour l'enfer*) (1976), Death of a Lumberjack (*La mort d'un boucheron*) (1973), Fantastica (1980), Goodbye, See You Monday (*Au revoir, à lundi*) (1979), Head of Normande St. Onge, The (*La tête de Normande St-Onge*) (1975), Heavenly Bodies (*Les corps célestes*) (1973), Inside Out (1979), IXE-13 (1972), *Maria Chapdelaine* (1983), Marie's Sons (*Les fils de Marie*) (2002), *Ménace, La* (1977), My Childhood in Montréal (1971), Night Magic (1985), Night with Hortense, The (*La nuit avec Hortense*) (1987), Pacemaker and a Sidecar, A (*L'eau chaude, l'eau frette*) (1997), Rats and Rabbits (2000), Run for it, Lola! (*Sauve-toi, Lola*) (1986), Special Magnum (Strange Shadows in an Empty Room) (1977), Surrogate (1984), Sweet Movie (1974), Thousand Moons, A (1977)

Lauren, Tammy: Wishmaster 1 (1997)

Laurence, André: Love in a Four Letter World (1970)

Laurendeau, Daniel: Beat (1976)

Laurendeau, Francine: Story of the Three, A (*L'histoire des trois*) (1989)

Laurent, Catherine: French Love (*Un amour comme le nôtre*) (1974)

Laurent, Jacqueline: Final Blow, The (The Finishing Stroke) (*Le coup de grâce*) (1965)

Lauriault, Anne: Q-bec My Love (A Commercial Success) (1970)

Laurie, Hugh: Me and My Shadows (2000)

Laurier, Charlotte: Aurora Borealis (*Une aurore boréale*) (1981), Babylon (Halfway House) (1991), Big Day, The (*Le grand day*) (1988),

Good Riddance (*Les bons débarras*) (1980), *Histoire inventée, Une* (An Imaginary Tale) (1990), *J'en suis* (1997), Party, The (*Party, Le*) (1990), Something Organic (*Quelque chose d'organique*) (1998), Tin Flute, The (*Bonheur d'occasion*) (1983), Two Seconds (*2 secondes*) (1998), Woman of Colours, A (*La dame en couleurs*) (1985), *Vent de galerne* (The Wind From Galerne) (1991)

Laurier, Lucie: *Anne Trister* (1986), Chili's Blues (*C'était le 12 du 12 et Chili avait les Blues*) (1994), *Comment ma mere accoucha de moi durant sa ménopause* (How My Mother Was Giving Birth to Me During Menopause) (2001), Devil at Four, The (*Le diàble à quatre*) (1988), Henri (1986), *J'aime, j'aime pas* (1995), Stiletto Dance (2000)

Laurin, Audrey: *Hiver de tourmente, Un* (A Winter of Torment) (1999)

Laurin, William: John Woo's Once a Thief (1997)

Laurin-Ouellette, Rémi: *J'aime, j'aime pas* (1995)

Laurion, Adrien: Little Aurore's Tragedy (*La petite Aurore, l'enfant martyre*) (1952)

Lauteman, Peter: Another Country: A North of 60 Mystery (2003)

Lauter, Edward: Crash (Breach of Trust) (1995)

Lauterman, Peter: Harry's Case (2000), Recipe for Revenge (1998), This Matter of Marriage (1998), Stolen Miracle (2001)

Lautrec, Donald: Apple, the Stem and the Seeds, The (*La pomme, la queue et les pépins*) (1974), *Diable aime les bijoux, Le* (The Devil Likes Jewels) (The Devil's Jewellery) (*Las joyas del diablo*) (1969), *Maria Chapdelaine* (1983), Master Cats, The (1971), Two Women of Gold (*Deux femmes en or*) (1970)

Lauzier, Fanny: Bye Bye Red Riding Hood (*Bye bye, chaperon rouge*) (1989), Tadpole and the Whale (*La grenouille et la baleine*) (1988)

Lauzon, Jean-Claude: *Léolo* (1992), Zoo la nuit, Un (A Zoo, by Night) (1987), *Lauzon Lauzone* (2001) (90mins) Documentary by Isabelle Hebert providing a personal look at the late Jean-Claude Lauzon with scenes from his controversial films.

Lavallee, Diane: *Karmina 2: L'enfer de Chabot* (K2 2001) (2001), *Nuit de noces* (Night of the Wedding) (2001), Winter Stories (*Histoires d'hiver*) (1999)

Lavasseur, William: Ryan's Babe (2000)

Lavendahl, Willie: Rainbow (1995)

Lavender, Barry: Ivy League Killers (The Fast Ones) (1959)

Laverdière, Alexandra: Clean Machine, The (*Tirelire, combines & cie*) (1992)

Lavigne, Dominique: Day Without Evidence, A (*Ainsi soient-ils*) (1970)

Lavigueur, Pierrette: Straight to the Heart (*Jusqu'au coeur*) (1969)

Lavoie, Daniel: Book of Eve (*Histoires d'Eve*) (2002), *Fabuleux voyage de l'ange, Le* (The Fabulous Voyage of the Angel) (1991)

Lavoie, Denis: *Aventures d'un agent très spécial, Les* (The Adventures of a Very Special Agent) (1985)

Lavoie, Richard: Guitar (*Guitare*) (1974)

Lavoie, Robert: *Riel* (1979)

Lavut, Martin: Becoming Laura (1982), Certain Practices (1979), Charlie Grant's War (1985), Marriage Bed, The (1986), *Palais Royale* (1988), Mask, The (1961), War Brides (1980), Winnings of Frankie Walls, The (1980)

Lawrence, André: Loving and Laughing (1971)

Lawrence, Burke: Myth of the Male Orgasm, The (1993)

Lawrence, Cary: *Canvas, artiste et voleur* (Canvas) (1993), Case of the Whitechapel Vampire, The (2001), Favourite Game, The (2003)

Lawrence, David: Fubar (2002)

Lawrence, Dea: Stuart Bliss (1998)

Lawrence, James: High Country, The (The First Hello) (1981)

Lawrence, Marc: Convicted (1938)

Lawrence, Peter: Burning, The (1981)

Lawrence, Shawn: Case of the Whitechapel Vampire, The (2001)

Lawrenchuck, Michael: Girl Who Married a Ghost, The (2003)

Lawson, Shannon: Butterbox Babies (1995), Sleeping Dogs Lie (1999), War Between Us, The (1995), Short Change (*Une fille impossible*) (1989)

Lawther, Chas: Ford: The Man and the Machine (1987), Terminal Choice (Deathbed) (1985), Paint Cans (1994), Where the Heart Is (1985)

Layton, Peter: Without Malice (2000)

Lazare, Carole: Lies My Father Told Me (1975), Megantic Outlaw, The (1971), One Man (1977)

Lazarus, John: Skip Tracer (1977)

Lazarus, Tom: Mazes and Monsters (1982)

Lazer, Charles: Diamond Girl (1998), Loving Evangeline (1998), Nothing Too Good for a Cowboy (1998)

Lazure, Gabrielle: French Revolution, The (1989), *Tisserands du pouvoir, Les* (The Mills of Power, Parts 1 and 2) (1988)

Lazure, Jacques: Sleep Walkers, The (*Les somnambules*) (1986)

Lazure, Gabrielle: Joshua Then and Now (1985)

Le Bel, Roger: *Zoo la nuit, Un* (1987)

Le Blanc, Mike: Parsley Days (2000)

Le Breton, Julie: Québec-Montréal (2002)

Le Coq, Bernard: Nearest to Heaven ((2002)

Le Devehat, Gaela: *Trilogie Marsellaise, La* (2001)

Le Flaguais, Véronique: Dream Life (*La vie revée*) (1972), Life of a Hero, The (1994)

Le Sieur, Elizabeth: *Misanthrope, Le* (1966)

Lea, Nicholas: Impossible Elephant, The (2001), Investigation (2002), John Woo's Once a Thief (1997), Lunch with Charles (2001), Shot in the Face (2002)

Lea, Ronald: Clear Cut (1991), Cursed (1990), Diamond Fleece, The (1992), Emerald Tear, The (1988), Gun Runner, The (1984), Live Through This (2000), Neighbour, The (1993), Phone Call, The (*Ligne interdite*) (1989), Replikator (1994), Spike of Love (1994), Summer With the Ghosts (*Un été avec les fantômes*) (2002), Touch of Murder, A (1990)

Leachman, Cloris: Yesterday (1981), Never Too Late (1996)

Lean, David: Desire in Motion (*Mouvements du désire*) (1994)

Leandro, Natalina Di: Ladies Room (1999)

Leano, Yvette: Lolo's Child (2002)

Léaud, Jean-Pierre: *Folle Embellie* (Out of this World) (2003), *Pornographe, Le* (The Pornographer) (2001)

Leavens, Chris: Hanging Garden, The (1997)

Lebeau, Pierre: *Maelström* (2000), *Maîtres anciens* (1998), Matroni and Me (1999), *Nez rouge* (Red Nose) (2003), *Père et Fils* (Father and Son) (2003), *Séraphin* (Heart of Stone) (A Man and His Sin) (2002), When I'm Gone You'll Still Be Alive (When I'll Be Gone) (*Quand je serai parti vous vivrez encore*) (1999)

Lebel, Janine: You Are Warm, You Are Warm (1973)

Lebel, Pauline: Song Spinner, The (1996)

Lebel, Roger: Crime of Ovide Plouffe, The (*Le crime d'Ovide Plouffe*) (*Les Plouffe, II*) (1984), Death of a Lumberjack (*La mort d'un boucheron*) (1973), *Réjeanne Padovani* (1973), Vultures, The (*Les vautours*) (1975)

Leblanc, André: Cat in the Bag, The (*Le chat dans le sac*) (1964)

Leblanc, Diana: Lies My Father Told Me (1975), Mahoney's Last Stand (1976)

Leblanc, Nicole: Claire: Tonight and Tomorrow (*Claire: cette nuit et demain*) (1985)

Leblanc, Sadie: Doulike2Watch.Com (2002)

Leboeuf, Marcel: Aurora Borealis (*Une aurore boréale*) (1981), Blizzard, The (*Rafales*) (1990), Bombardier (1992), Crime of Ovide Plouffe, The (*Le crime d'Ovide Plouffe*) (1984)

Lebrero, Derek: Home Team (1999)

Lebreton, Julie: *Peau Blanche, La* (2003)

Lebrun, Michel: There's Nothing Wrong With Being Good to Yourself (*Y a pas d'mal à se faire du bien*) (She's So Young and Knows All!) (*C'est jeune et ça sait tout!*) (1974)

Lechowick, Bernard: Live Through This (2000)

Leckie, Keith Ross: Arrow, The (1997), Children of my Heart (2000), Crossbar (1979), Journey Into Darkness: The Bruce Curtis Story (1990), Lost in the Barrens (1990), Milgaard (1998), Morrison Murders, The (1997), Special Delivery (1982), Trial at Fortitude Bay (1994), To Walk with Lions (1999), Where the Spirit Lives (1989)

Leckie, Keith: I, Maureen (1980)

Leclair, Elisabeth: French Love (*Un amour comme le nôtre*) (1974), I Have the Right to Pleasure (*J'ai droit au plaisir*) (1975), Stallion (1988)

Leclerc, Francis: *Jeune fille à la fenêtre, Une* (2001), Seven Streams of the River Ota, The (1998), Whispers (1990)

Leclerc, Jean: Garnet Princess, The (1987), What the Hell Are They Complaining About?) (Hold on, Papa!) (*Tiens-toi bien après les oreilles à Papa*) (1971), House of Lovers (*La maison des amants*) (1972), Ideal Man, The (*L'homme idéal*) (1996), Justice Express (1990), Special Magnum (1977), Uncanny, The (1977), Wars, The (1983), Whispers (1990)

Leclerc-Couture, Jérôme: *Forteresse suspendue, La* (2001), *Incompris, L'* (1997)

Leclercq, Éric: Letter From New France, A (1979)

Leclos, Grégoire: Notre-Dame of the Mouise (*Notre-Dame de la Mouise*) (1941)

Lecroix, Lisa: Dance Me Outside (1994)

Lécuyer, Olivier: Time of the Hunt, The (*Le temps d'une chasse*) (1972)

Ledbetter, Gary: Henry and Verlin (1994)

Ledford, Brandy: Ice Men, The (2001), Zebra Lounge (2001)

Ledoux, José: Jacques and November (1984), Trouble Makers (*Trouble-fête*) (1964)

Ledoux, Laura: Enchanted Village, The (*Le village enchanté*) (1956)

Leduc, Catherine: Christmas Martian, The (*Le martien de Noël*) (1971)

Leduc, Dominique: *Aline et Michel* (Aline) (1992), *Ange noir, L'* (The Black Angel) (Nelligan) (1991), *Revoir Julie* (See Julie Again) (Julie and Me) (1998)

Leduc, Jacques: Close to Falling Asleep (*Trois pommes à côté du sommeil*) (1988), *Enfant sur le lac, L'* (A Child on the Lake) (1993), Last Glacier, The (1984), Montréal Sextet (1991), Ordinary Tenderness (*Tendresse ordinaire*)

Legault, Marc: Brother André (*Le frère André*) (1987), Christmas of Madame Beauchamp, The (*Le revanche noël de Madame Beauchamp*) (1981), Swindle, The (*La gammick*) (1974), One Man (1977)

Legault, Raymond: Bach and Broccoli (*Bach et bottine*) (1986), *Part des choses, La* (*Un léger vertige*) (A Part of Things) (A Light Vertigo) (1991)

Legault, Sylvie: Crinoline Madness (*La folie des crinolines*) (1995), Devil at Four, The (*Le diable à quatre*) (1988), Winter Stories (1999)

Legendre, Pierre-Francois: Québec-Montréal (2002)

Legendre, Vallon: Trouble Makers (1964)

Léger, Roger: 24 Poses (2002), *Jardin d'Anna, Le* (1994), Kingdom or the Asylum, The (1989)

Léger, Viola: Évangéline the Second (*Évangéline Deusse*) (1985), Secret of Jerome, The (*Le secret de Jérôme*) (1994)

Legros, Greg: Goldirocks (2003)

Leguet, Armand: Unknown From Montréal, The (*Son copain*) (1950)

Lehman, Kristen: Dog Park (1998), Dark Harbour (1997)

Lehman, Lewis: Phobia (1980), Teddy (The Pit) (1980)

Lehmann, Dan: Rat Tales (1987)

Leigh, Adam: American Beer (1996)

Leigh, Jennifer Jason: Crossed Over (2001)

Leigh, Trevor: Trouble (1996)

Leighton, Lilian: Grub-Stake, The (1922)

Leighton, Margaret: Galileo (1973)

Leighton, Roberta: Covergirl (1984)

Leitch, Donovan: Size of Watermelons, The (1996)

Leitch, Megan: Day Drift (1999)

Leiterman, Douglas: Maintain the Right (1982)

Lejeune, André: Red (1969)

Lelièvre, Jean-Marie: Paspébiac: The Games Country (*Paspébiac: Terre des Jeux*) (1985)

Lelouch, Claude: *Hasards ou coïncidences* (1998), *Nous deux, À* (An Adventure for Two) (1979)

Lemaire, Carole: Danger to Society, A (1970)

Lemaire, Francis: *Ange gardien, L'* (1978)

Lemaire, Ken: Music of the Spheres, The (1984)

Lemaître-Auger, Liliane: Dream Life (1972)

Lemarchand, Louis: Duration of the Day (*Le règne du jour*) (1967)

Lemay, Anick: *Île de Sable, L'* (1999)

Lemay, Germain: Luke or the Part of Things (1982)

Lemay, Jean: Luke or the Part of Things (1982)

Lemay, Joannie: *Secret de banlieue, Un* (The Secret of a Suburb) (2002)

Lemay-Thivierge, Guillaume: Deaf to the City (*Le sourd dans la ville*) (1987), *Immortels, Les* (The Immortals) (2003), Nylon Heart, A (*Coeur de nylon*) (1989), Woman of Colours, A (*La dame en couleurs*) (1985)

Lemche, Kris: Ginger Snaps (2000), Johnny (1999), My Little Eye (2002)

Lemelin, Paul: Legend of Sleepy Hollow, The (1999)

Lemelin, Roger: Crime of Ovide Plouffe, The (*Le crime d'Ovide Plouffe*) (*Les Plouffe, II*) (1984), *Plouffe, Les* (The Plouffe Family) (1981), Odyssey of the Pacific (1982)

Lemesieur, Glen: Strange Blues of Cowboy Red, The (1995)

Lemieux, Claude: House That Hides the Town, The (*La maison qui empêche de voir la ville*) (1975)

Lemieux, Eve: *Mystérieuse Mademoiselle C, La* (2001)

Lemieux, Françoise: There's Nothing Wrong With Being Good to Yourself (*Y a pas d'mal à se faire du bien*) (She's So Young and Knows All!) (*C'est jeune et ça sait tout!*) (1974)

Lemieux, Jean-Marie: Coffin Affair, The (*L'affaire Coffin*) (1980), Gone to Glory (*Partis pour la gloire*) (1975), Red Eyes (Accidental Truths) (*Les yeux rouges*) (1983)

Lemieux, Karyne: *Histoire de Pen* (Inside) (2002)

Lemieux, Réal: Immortal Scoundrel, The (*Étienne Brûlé, gibier de potence*) (1952)

Lemir, Marguerite: Taureau (1972)

Lemme, Isabelle: *Immortels, Les* (2003)

Lemmo, James: Nowhere in Sight (2000)

Lemmon, Jack: Tribute (1980)

Lemoine, Jacques: *Lit, Le* (1974)

Lemoine, Suzanne: *Cabaret neiges noires* (1997) *Neg', Le* (2002)

Lemoyne, Jean: Knowing to Learn (1965)

Lenkov, Peter: Dr. Jekyll and Mr. Hyde (1999)

Lennick, Ben: Flaming Frontier (1958)

Lennick, Sylvia: Visiting Hours (Fright) (1982)

Lennox, Douglas: Herd, The (1998), Kelly (Touch the Wind) (1981), Last Chase, The (1980), Siege (1983)

Lenoir, Geneviève: Marie in the City (1987)

Lenoir, Pierre: Carpenter, The (1987)

Lente, Miklos: Odd Balls (1984)

Léonard, Sylvie: *Karmina 2: L'enfer de Chabot* (K2 2001) (2001), Life After Love (2000)

Leonetti, Irene: Stuff (1999)

Léotard, Philippe: Kamouraska (1973)

Lepage, Gaston: Being at Home With Claude (1992), *Cordélia* (1980), Countess of Baton Rouge, The (*La Comtesse de Baton Rouge*) (1997), *Gaspard et fils* (1988), *Joyeux calvaire* (1997), *Marchands du silence, Les* (1994), Moonshine (1982)

LePage, Gerard: Parallels (1980)

Lepage, Jocelyne: *J'me Marie, J'me Marie* (1974)

Levine, Ted: You Can Thank Me Later (1998)

Levitin, Jacqueline: Eva Guerrilla (1987)

Levson, Allan: Second Wind (1976), Today I Am a Fountain Pen (1980)

Levy, Dani: *Répétition, La* (The Repetition) (2001)

Levy, Eugene: Cannibal Girls (1973), Dogmatic (1996), Double Negative (Deadly Companion) (1979), Going Berserk (1983), Kurt Vonnegut's Harrison Bergeron (2000), Running (1979), Partners 'n Love (1992), Sodbusters (1995), Nothing Personal (1980),

Levy, Jefery: Invincible (2001)

Levy, Josh: Doulike2Watch.Com (2002), Hayseed (1997)

Lévy, Raphaël: Christmas of Madame Beauchamp, The (*Le revanche noël de Madame Beauchamp*) (1981)

Levy, Shuky: Exception to the Rule (1996)

Lewis, Dawn: Race for Freedom: The Underground Railroad (1993), Trial by Vengeance (1989)

Lewis, Dierdre: Jesus' Son (1999)

Lewis, Donna: Dory (1965)

Lewis, Gary: Many Trials of One Jane Doe, The (2002)

Lewis, Gordon: Anomaly (*Anomie*) (1973)

Lewis, Jefferson: Ganesh (Ordinary Magic) (1993), *Mon amie Max* (1993), Paper Wedding (*Les noces de papier*) (1989)

Lewis, Juliette: Picture Claire (2001)

Lewis, Larry: Gun Runner, The (1984)

Lewis, Mary: No Apologies (1990)

Lewis, Michael: 125 Rooms of Comfort (1974)

Lewis, Richard: Justice (1998), Whale Music (1994)

Lewis, Robert: Misbegotten (1997)

Lewis, Sharon: Rude (1995)

Leyden, Leo: Circle of Two (1980), Deadly Harvest (1980), Far Shore, The (1976), Luck of Ginger Coffey, The (1964), Quiet Day in Belfast, A (1973), Wars, The (1983)

Leyrac, Monique: Act of the Heart (1970), Lights of My City (1950)

Liconti, Carlo: Brown Bread Sandwiches (1990), Concrete Angels (1987), Vita Cane (1994)

Lidolt, Jon: Crimes of the Future (1970)

Lieu, Kim: Lulu (1995)

Light, Beverley: Rainy Day Woman (1970)

Lightfoot, Gordon: Harry Tracy, Desperado (1981)

Lightfoot: Song of Hiawatha, The (1996)

Lightning, Georgina: Johnny Greyeyes (2001)

Lightstone, Marilyn: Anne of Green Gables (1985), Anne of Green Gables: The Continuing Story (Series) (1985-1999), Death Bite (Spasms) (1983), Foxy Lady (1971), In Praise of Older Women (1978), Lies My Father Told Me (1975), Little White Lies (1988), Love on Your Birthday

(see Acts of Love Series) (1980), Mary and Joseph: A Story of Faith (1979), Surrogate (1984), Tin Flute, The (1983)

Liimatainen, Arvi: Sentimental Reasons (Death Target) (1984), Strange and Rich (1994)

Liitoja, Hillar: Last Supper, The (1994)

Liliefeldt, Louise: Wasaga (1994)

Lillo, Larry: Low Visibility (1984)

Limonchik, Macha: *Albertine, en cinq temps* (Albertine in Five Times) (1999), Angelo, Fredo and Roméo (1996), *Cap Tourmente* (Cape Torment) (1993), Eldorado (1995)

Lin, Justin: Shopping for Fangs (1996)

Linch, Serge: *Aventures d'un agent très spécial, Les* (1985)

Linde, Betty: Zacharia Farted (1998)

Linder, Cec: American Christmas Carol, An (1979), Atlantic City, U.S.A (1980), City on Fire (1979), Clown Murders, The (1976), Courage of Kavik the Wolf Dog, The (1980)

Linder, Cec: Deadly Eyes (The Rats) (1982), Deadly Harvest (1980), Explosion (1980), Flaming Frontier (1958), For Those I Loved (*Au nom de tous les miens*) (1983), Foxy Lady (1971), Heavenly Bodies (1985), High-Ballin' (1978), Honeymoon (*Lune de miel*) (1985), I Miss You, Hugs and Kisses (1978), Only God Knows (1974), To Kill the King (1974), Point of No Return (1976), Ragtime Summer (Age of Innocence) (1977), Second Wind (1976), Something's Rotten (1978), Sunday in the Country (1975), Tomorrow Never Comes (1978), Why Rock the Boat? (1974)

Lindfors, Viveca: North of Pittsburgh (1992)

Lindo, Eleanore: Touching Wild Horses (2002)

Lindton, John: Watchers III (1994)

Lineham, Hardee T.: Shoemaker (1997), Top of the Food Chain (1999), Out of Sight, Out of Mind (The Seventh Circle) (1983), Wars, The (1983), Wild Horse Hank (1979)

Linehan, Brian: Crimes of the Future (1970)

Linehan, Rosaleen: Happy Days (Beckett on Film series) (2000)

Link, André: Possession of Virginia, The (1972)

Linka, Emil: Escape Velocity (1999)

Linnell, Robert: Terra X (The Curse of Oak Island) (1997)

Liotta, Ray: Pilgrim (Inferno) (1999)

Lipinski, Eugene: Boozecan (1995), Borderline Normal (2000), Century Hotel (2001), Conquest (1998), Dead Aviators (1998), Never Talk to Strangers (1995), Perfectly Normal (1990), Risen, The (2003), Strange and Rich (1994), Water Damage (1999), Solitude (2001)

Lipinski, Stanley: French Without Dressing (1964),

Room for a Stranger (1968)

Lipman, Nicola: Madeleine Is... (1971)

Lipp, Rudy: Kathy Karuks Is a Grizzly Bear (1976)

Lippe, Anneke von der: Misery Harbour (1999)

Lippe, Julien: That Darned Loot (*La maudite galette*) (1972), True Nature of Bernadette, The (*La vraie nature de Bernadette*) (1972)

Lipper, David: Wrong Number (2001)

Lishman, Anne: Juiced (1999)

Lishman, Eda: Primo Baby (1989)/

List, Shelley: Nobody Makes Me Cry (Between Friends) (1983)

Lister, Steven: Slow Burn (1989), Xtro II: The Second Encounter (1991)

Lithgow, John: Distant Thunder (1988), Hollow Point (1997)

Littel, Robert: Amateur, The (1981)

Littin, Miguel: *Los Naufragos* (1994)

Little, Chris: Summerlust (1973)

Little, Dwight: KGB: The Secret War (1984)

Little, Michelle: Blood Clan (1991), Perfect Man, The (1993)

Little, Rich: Dirty Tricks (1980)

Litvack, Jack: Eat Anything (1971)

Litz, Nadia: After the Harvest (Wild Geese) (2000), Love That Boy (2002), Public Domain (2003)

Liu, Harrison: Bethune: *The Making of a Hero* (1990) see Bethune (1977)

Lively, Gerry: Guardian, The (1999)

Lively, Roger: Dog Who Stopped the War, The (1984)

Livingston, David: Eat Anything (1971)

Lloyd, Christopher: Dinner at Fred's (1997)

Lloyd, Sue: Bullet to Beijing (Len Deighton's Bullet to Beijing) (1995), Spanish Fly (1975)

Lo Bianco, Tony: Ascent, The (1994)

Lochner, Hannah: Interrogation of Michael Crowe, The (2002), Torso: The Evelyn Dick Story (2000)

Lock, Keith: Small Pleasures (1993)

Lock, Tom: Live Through This (2000)

Locke, Jeannine: All the Days of My Life (1982), Chautauqua Girl (1984), Greening of Ian Elliot, The (1991), Island Love Song (1987), You've Come a Long Way, Katie (1981), Other Kingdom, The (1985), Private Capital, The (1988)

Lockhart, Araby: Insurance Man From Ingersoll, The (1976)

Locklear, Heather: Big Slice, The (1991)

Loder, Anne Marie: Reluctant Angel (1997)

Loewi, Fiona: Blackheart (1997), Love and Death on Long Island (1997), Top of the Food Chain (1999)

Logan, Bob: Kelly (Touch the Wind) (1981), Meatballs, Part IV (1992)

Logan, Lyn: Columbus of Sex, The: My Secret Life (1969)

Logue, Donal: Men With Guns (1996)

Lohr, Aaron: Daydream Believers: The Monkees' Story (2000)

Loiseau, Roxanne: *Secret de banlieue, Un* (The Secret of a Suburb) (2002)

Loiselle, Hélène: *Bouteille, La* (The Bottle) (2000), *Dernières fougères, Les* (The Last Ferns) (1991), What the Hell Are They Complaining About?) (Hold on, Papa!) (*Tiens-toi bien après les oreilles à Papa*) (1971), Little One Is Coming Soon, The (1972), *Mariages* (2001), Montréal Sextet (1991), Post Mortem (1999), Orders, The (*Les ordres*) (1974), There Once Was a War (*Il était une guerre*) (1958), Sweet Lies and Tender Oaths (*Les doux aveux*) (1982), Uncle Antoine (1971)

Loiselle, Hubert: Mission of Fear (1965)

Lom, Herbert: Dead Zone, The (1983), Incredible Adventures of Marco Polo, The (1998)

Lomas, Daniel: Connecting Lines (1990)

Lomez, Céline: Apparition, The (The Unexpected Phantom) (1972). Far Shore, The (1976), Gina (1975), High Card (1982), Initiation, The (1970), It Can't Be Winter, We Haven't Had Summer Yet (1981), Loving and Laughing (1971), Plague, The (1979), Push but Push Reasonably (Scarlatina) (*Pousse mais pousse égal*) (1975), *Réjeanne Padovani* (1973), Sex in the Snow (*Après-ski*) (1971), Silent Partner, The (1978)

Loncraine, Richard: Haunting of Julia, The (Full Circle) (1976)

London, Jason: Hound of the Baskervilles, The (2000)

London (dog): *Deux amis silencieux* (Dogs to the Rescue) (Two Silent Friends) (1969)

London-Thompson, Alexandra: Summer of the Colt (*Fierro ou l'été des secrets*) (1989)

Lone, John: M. Butterfly (1993)

Long, Barrie Wexler: Hide and Seek (1984)

Long, Francesca: When Tomorrow Dies (1965)

Long, Jason: Turning Paige (Shepherd Park) (2002)

Long, Mary: Only God Knows (1974), Special Delivery (1982)

Long, Nia: Secret Laughter of Women, The (1999)

Long, Shelley: Fatal Memories (The Eileen Franklin Story) (1992), Lilly (1993), Losin' It (1983)

Longboat, Jerry: Girl Who Married a Ghost, The (2003)

Longchamps, Marie-Josée: Sensations (1973)

Longfellow, Brenda: Gerda (1992)

Longjun, Li: Cry Woman (*Ku qi de nu ren*) (2002)

Longo, Robert: Johnny Mnemonic (1995)

A CENTURY OF CANADIAN CINEMA

Longstreet, Harry: Wounded (1996)

Longtin, Jean-Louis: Body and Soul (1971)

Lonsdale, Michel: Galileo (1973)

Lonsdale-Smith, Michelle: What's Your Verdict? (1995)

Loogue, Donal: Size of Watermelons, The (1996)

Lopes-Curval, Philippe: Red River (*Rivière Rouge*) (1996)

Lorain, Sophie: Home Team (1999), In Her Defense (1998), *Odyssée d'Alice Tremblay, L'* (2002), *Scandale* (1982), Sign of Four, The (2001)

Lord, Barbara: Bloody Brood, The (1959)

Lord, Jean-Claude: Bingo (1974), Chocolate Eclair (*Éclair au chocolat*) (1979), Covergirl (1984), *Délivrez-nous du mal* (Deliver Us From Evil) (1967), Doves, The (*Les colombes*) (1972), Eddie and the Cruisers Part II: Eddie Lives! (1989), Let's Talk About Love (1976), Mind Field (1989), Panic (*Panique*) (1977), Tadpole and the Whale (*La grenouille et la baleine*) (1988), Station nord (North Station) (2002), Toby McTeague (1986), Trouble Makers (*Trouble-fête*) (1964), Vindicator, The (Frankenstein '88) (1986), Visiting Hours (Fright) (1982)

Loren, Sophia: Angela (1978), Between Strangers (2002), *Giornata particolare, Una* (A Special Day) (1977)

Loreys, Margaret: Next of Kin (1984)

Loriot, Charles: Darkside, The (1986)

Lorte, Daniel: Danny in the Sky (2002)

Losey, Joseph: Galileo (1973)

Loubert, Patrick: 125 Rooms of Comfort (1974), Do You Want to Sleep With God? (*Voulez-vous coucher avec Dieu?*) (1972)

Louis, Justin: Blood and Donuts (1995), Prom Night II: Hello Mary Lou (1987)

Louise, Lynette: South Pacific, 1942 (1981)

Louretta, M.A.: Fishing Trip, The (1998)

Loussine, Gérard: *Ou le roman de Charles Pathé* (The Life of Charles Pathé) (1995)

Louzier, Fanny: Chili's Blues (1994)

Love, Lucretia: *Donnez-nous notre amour quotidien* (In Love With Sex) (1974), French Love (*Un amour comme le nôtre*) (1974)

Lovgren, David: Dukes, The (1998), Live Bait (1995), Roller Coaster (1999), Something More (1999)

Lowe, Rob: Hotel New Hampshire (1984), Midnight Man (1995), Wendy (1966)

Lowe, Wesley: Exiles in Paradise (2001)

Lower, Peter: Reasonable Force (1983)

Lowery, Andrew: Nothing (2003)

Lowry, Otto: Another Smith for Paradise (1972)

Lubaszenko, Edward Linde: *Journal d'un bossu, Le* (1993)

Lubaszenko, Olaf: *Journal d'un bossu, Le* (1993)

Luca, Stephen: Diplomatic Immunity (1991)

Lucas, Byron: Middlemen (2000)

Lucas, Donny: Vigil, The (1998)

Lucas, Jim: Dinner's on the Table (1994)

Lucas, Josh: American Psycho (2000), Weight of Water, The (2000)

Lucas, Laurent: Something Organic (*Quelque chose d'organique*) (1998), Tiresia (2003)

Lucas, Steve: Major Crime (1998)

Lucente, Francesco: 2001: A Space Travesty (2001)

Lucie, Laurier: *Grande Séduction, La* (2003)

Lucien, Didier: *Cabaret neiges noires* (1997)

Luckham, Claire: Tanzi (1987)

Lucot, René: Aurora Borealis (1981)

Ludwig, Adam: Paper People, The (1967)

Luft, Uriel: Nikki, Wild Dog of the North (1961)

Luke, Michael: Anchor Zone (1994)

Lukeman, Elaine: Sentimental Reasons (Death Target) (1984)

Lumsden, Sue: Silent Partner, The (1978)

Lund, Kevin: Blacktop (2000)

Lungdren, Dolph: Fallen Knight (The Minion) (1998), Peacekeeper, The (1997)

LuPone, Patti: Bad Faith (Cold Blooded) (1999), Song Spinner, The (1996)

Luret, Jean: *Dur-Dur* (1981)

Lussier, Jacques: Intimate Power (1985), Switch in Time, A (1987)

Lussier, Judith-Emmanuelle: *Trois femmes, un amour* (Three Women in Love) (1994)

Lussier, Sylvie: *Odyssée d'Alice Tremblay, L'* (2002)

Lutz, Mark: Harry's Case (2000)

Lutz, Pam: Black Swan (2002)

Lyman, Laura: Évangéline (1913)

Lymposs, Richard: Whole of the Moon, The (1996)

Lynas, Jeffrey: Breaking Point (1976), Lies My Father Told Me (1975)

Lynch, Kate: Cementhead (1979), Curtains (1983), Defcon 4 (1984), Double Negative (Deadly Companion) (1979), Haunting of Lisa, The (1995), Improper Channels (1981), Meatballs (1979), Population of One, A (1980), Reckless Disregard (1985), Shower, The (1992), Summer's Children (1979), Taking Care (Prescription for Murder) (1987)

Lynch, Paul: Blindside (1986), Blood and Guts (1978), Bullies (1986), Cross Country (1983), Drop Dead Gorgeous (Victim of Beauty) (1991), Flying (1986), Hard Part Begins, The (1973), Herd, The (1998), Humongous (1982), Magician's House, The (1999), More to Love (2000), Prom Night (1980)

Lynch, Peter: Project Grizzly (1996)

Lynch, Richard: Scanner Cop (1994)

Lynch, Thomas W.: Pathfinder, The (1996)

Lynd, Laurie: House (1995), I Was a Rat (Cinderella and Me) (When I Was a Rat) (2001)

Lynley, Carol: Shape of Things to Come, The (1979)

Lynn, Marc: In Her Defense (1998)

Lynn, Sharon: French Without Dressing (1964)

Lyon, Wendy: Prom Night II: Hello Mary Lou (1987)

Lyu, Soo: Rub & Tug (2002)

Ma, Yo Yo: Sarabande (1997)

Mabe, Ricky: Louisa May Alcott's Little Men (1998)

Mabey, Judith: Parallels (1980)

MacCabe, Christopher: Life of a Hero, The (*La vie d'un héros*) (1994)

Maccari, Ruggero: *Una giornata particolare* (A Special Day) (1977)

Macchio, Ralph: Distant Thunder (1988)

MacCorkindale, Simon: Counterstrike (1993), Dinosaur Hunter, The (2000), Falcon's Gold (1982), Sincerely Violet (1987)

MacDonald, Ann: In Praise of Older Women (1978)

MacDonald, Anne-Marie: Better Than Chocolate (1999), Island Love Song (1987), I've Heard the Mermaids Singing (1987), Paint Cans (1994), Wars, The (1983), Where the Spirit Lives (1989)

MacDonald, Barbara: Crime Wave (1985)

Macdonald, Bruce: Master of Images, The (1972)

MacDonald, Cassie: Touch and Go (2002)

MacDonald, Dan: Butterbox Babies (1995), Conquest (1998), Nothing Too Good for a Cowboy (1998), Rowdyman, The (1972)

MacDonald, Gerard: Lifeforce Experiment (1994)

MacDonald, Jean: Fade to Black (2001)

MacDonald, Jo-Ann: Girl Is a Girl, A (1999)

Macdonald, John: Saturday,s Passage (1969)

MacDonald, Kelly: Regeneration (1996)

MacDonald, Kevin: Dinner at Fred's (1997)

MacDonald, Krista: Dragonwheel (2002)

MacDonald, Mary Anne: Far Cry From Home, A (1980), Murder Sees the Light (1987)

MacDonald, Michael: Mr. Nice Guy (1986), Mystery of the Million Dollar Hockey Puck (1975), Odd Balls (1984)

MacDonald, Mike: Once in a Blue Moon (1995)

MacDonald, Monique: Another Planet (2000)

MacDonald, Shauna: Jack and Jill (1998)

MacDonald, Tom: Freeloading (1986)

MacDonald, Wendy: Dinner's on the Table (1994)

MacDonald, William: Barnone (1997), Blackheart (1997), Men With Guns (1996), Rupert's Land (1998), Protection (2000), Rhino Brothers, The (2002), Vigil, The (1998)

MacEachern, Robin: Nowhere to Hide (1987)

MacFadyen, Angus: Second Skin (2000)

MacFadyen, Christie: Knock! Knock! (1985), Top of His Head, The (1989)

MacGillivray, Alan: South Pacific, 1942 (1981)

MacGillivray, William: Life Classes (1987), Stations (1983), Understanding Bliss (1990), Vacant Lot, The (1989)

MacGinnis, Niall: 49th Parallel (The Invaders) (1941)

MacGregor, Doreen: Convicted (1938)

MacGregor, Justin: Vigil, The (1998)

MacGregor, Roy: Cementhead (1979), Honourable Member, An (1982), Last Season, The (1987), Tyler (1977), Ready for Slaughter (1983)

Machackova, Katerina: Flying Sneaker, The (1992)

Macht, Stephen: No Blame (*L'incroyable vérité*) (1988)

MacInnes, Angus: Strange Brew (1983)

MacInnis, Christine: Strange and Rich (1994)

MacIntosh, Keegan: At the Midnight Hour (1995), Henry and Verlin (1994)

MacIvor, Daniel: Beefcake (1999), Bubbles Galore (1996), Eclipse (1994), Five Senses, The (1999), Hayseed (1997), House (1995), Justice Denied (1989), Last Supper, The (1994), Marion Bridge (2002), Past Perfect (2002), My Summer Vacation (1996), Uncut (1997), Wasaga (1994)

Mack, Gene: Diamond Fleece, The (1992), Reno and the Doc (1984), Trial and Error (1993)

Mack, James: Tek War: Tek Justice (1994)

MacKay, Danette: Witchboard III: The Possession (1995)

MacKay, David: Bob's Garage (2001)

MacKay, Don: Dead Wrong (1983)

MacKay, Eleanor: Only Thing You Know, The (1971)

MacKay, Frank: King of Friday Night, The (1985)

MacKay, Matthew: *Mémoire tronquée* (1990), Peanut Butter Solution, The (*Opération beurre de pinottes*) (1985)

MacKay, Tanya: *J'me Marie, J'me Marie* (1974)

MacKenzie, Alex: New Shoes (1990)

MacKenzie, Catherine: Warriors (1994)

MacKenzie, George: Montréal Main (1974)

MacKenzie, Gwyn: Don't Let the Angels Fall (1969)

MacKenzie, Jessica: Two Seconds (1998)

MacKenzie, Karina: M.V.P. 3 (2003)

Mackenzie, Michael: Baroness and the Pig, The (2002)

Mackenzie, Phillip: Small Pleasures (1993)

Mackey, Clarke: Eat Anything (1971), Only Thing You Know, The (1971), Taking Care (Prescription for Murder) (1987)

Mackey, Douglas: Only Thing You Know, The (1971)

MacKinnon, Derek: Terror Train (1980)

MacKinnon, Eleanor: Masculine Mystique, The (1984)

MacKinnon, Gilles: Regeneration (1996)

MacKinnon, Margo: *Réjeanne Padovani* (1973)

Mackintosh, Steven: Many Trials of One Jane Doe, The (2002), Many Trials of One Jane Doe, The (2003)

MacLachlan, Kyle: Xchange (2000)

MacLaine, Shirley: Joan of Arc (1999), Salem Witch Trials (2001)

Maclean, Alison: Jesus' Son (1999)

Maclean, Iain: Big Bear (1988), Willing Voyeur, The (1996)

MacLean, Janet: Killing Spring, A (2001), Martha, Ruth and Edie (1987), Verdict in Blood (2001)

MacLean, Maria: Parsley Days (2000)

MacLean, Rhonda: Terra X (1997)

MacLennan, Michael: Ice Men, The (2001)

MacLeod, Alison: Brethren (1976)

MacLeod, Donald: Another Country: A North of 60 Mystery (2003), Another Day (2001)

MacLeod, Douglas: Ghostkeeper (1981)

MacLeod, Margaret Anne: Smoked Lizard Lips (1991)

MacLeod, Matthew: Trust in Me (1995)

MacLiam, Eanna: On the Nose (2001)

MacMillan, Diane: Little Canadian, The (1955)

MacMillan, Janet: South Pacific, 1942 (1981)

MacMillan, Ross: Barbara James (2001)

MacNaughton, Ann: Medicine River (1993)

MacNee, Patrick: Hot Touch (*Coup de maître*) (1982), King Solomon's Treasure (1979)

MacNeil, Marguerite: Divine Ryans, The (1998)

MacNeill, Peter: Butterbox Babies (1995), Closer and Closer (1996), Events Leading up to My Death, The (1991), Gross Misconduct (1992), Hanging Garden, The (1997), Justice Denied (1989), Rookies (1990), Violet (2000), Whispers (1990)

Macomber, Debbie: This Matter of Marriage (1998)

MacPherson, Jeff: Come Together (2001)

MacRae, Henry: Cameron of the Royal Mounted (1921), Critical Age, The (1923), God's Crucible (1921), Man from Glengarry, The (1920)

MacRae, Liz: Warriors (1994)

MacRae, Meredith: Footsteps in the Snow (*Des pas sur la neige*) (1966)

Macri, Arthur: Noncensus (1964)

MacRury, Malcolm: Curse of the Viking Grave (1990), Harvest (1993), Hemingway vs Callaghan (2003), Wozeck: Out of the Fire (1992)

MacWilliam, Keenan: Must Be Santa (1999)

Macy, William: Jerry and Tom (1998)

Madden, Nwamiko: Hatley High (2003)

Madden, Jeffery Owen: Crime Wave (1985)

Madden, Peter: One Man (1977)

Maddin, Guy: Archangel (1990), Careful (1992), Dracula: Pages From a Virgin's Diary (2003), Twilight of the Ice Nymphs (1997), Tales From the Gimli Hospital (1988)

Maddox, Diana: Amateur, The (1981), Changeling, The (1980)

Madia, Stefano: Dear Father (*Caro Papa*) (1979)

Madigan, Amy: Nowhere to Hide (1987)

Madsen, Michael: LAPD: To Protect and Serve (2001)

Madsen, Virginia: All the Fine Lines (1999)

Madson, Michael: Pressure Point (2000)

Maeder, Pascal: *Môtel St-Laurent* (1998)

Magana, Simon: Smoked Lizard Lips (1991)

Magda, Cass: Hawk's Vengeance (1997)

Magder, Daniel: Zebra Lounge (2001)

Magder, Zale: Never Trust an Honest Thief (Going for Broke) (1979)

Magee, Allan: Darkside, The (1986)

Magee, Michael: Brood, The (1979), Clown Murders, The (1976), Insurance Man From Ingersoll, The (1976)

Magee, Patrick: Galileo (1973), Luther (1973)

Magicovsky, Allan: Man, a Woman and a Bank, A (1979)

Magnatta, Constantino: Darkside, The (1986), Freakshow (1988), Ghost Mom (1993)

Magnier, Thierry: Coyote (1993)

Magny, Michèle: Dollar, The (The Other Side of the River) (*La piastre*) (*L'autre bord du fleuve*) (1976), Don't Let the Angels Fall (1969), House of Light, The (*La chambre blanche*) (1969), O or the Invisible Infant (*O ou l'invisible enfant*) (1971), Taureau (1972), Wild Flowers, The (*Les fleurs sauvages*) (1982)

Magny, Nicole: *Giornata particolare, Una* (A Special Day) (1977)

Magwood, Robbie: One Magic Christmas (1985)

Mahaffey, Valerie: Tell Me My Name (1977)

Maher, Claude: Little Tougas (1976)

Maher, Joseph: Killer (1994)

Maher, Olivier: *Immortels, Les* (The Immortals) (2003)

Maheu, Arianne: *Ciel sur la tête, Le* (On Your Head) (2001)

Maheu, Gilles: *Zoo la nuit, Un* (A Zoo, by Night) (1987)

Maheu, Sophie: Letter From New France, A (1979)

Maheu, Sue: Sweet Angel Mine (1996)

Mahonen, Michael: Giant Steps (1992)

Mahoney, Mary Ellen: Blue City Slammers (1987)

Maiden, Cecil: Forbidden Journey (1950)

Maiden, Rita: *Ils sont nus* (1966)

Maillet, Antonine: Gapi (1982)

Maillot, Michel: Isla the Tigress of Siberia (1977)

Mailloux, Pierre: *Morte amoureuse, La* (1997)

Main, David: Cop (Heller) (1981), Find the Lady (1976), It Seemed Like a Good Idea at the Time (1975), Sweeter Song, A (1976), Takeover (1981)

Majic, Meeka: Love Letters: A Romantic Trilogy (2001)

Major, Aimé: There Once Was a War (*Il était une guerre*) (1958)

Major, Hélène: Story of the Hunt, The (*Histoire de chasse*) (1990)

Majoros, George: Airport In (1996)

Majors, Lee: Agency (1980), Last Chase, The (1980)

Mak, Bonnie: Foreign Ghosts (*Fantômes étrangers*) (1997)

Makavejev, Dusan: Sweet Movie (1974)

Makay, Margit: Bye Bye Red Riding Hood (*Bye bye, chaperon rouge*) (1989)

Makbul, Kawadi: Hathi (1998)

Makepeace, Chris: Last Chase, The (1980), Mazes and Monsters (1982), Meatballs (1979), Memory Run (1995), Terry Fox Story, The (1983), Undergrads, The (1985)

Makhmalbaf, Moshen: Return to Kandahar (2002)

Makichuk, James: Ghostkeeper (1981)

Makin, Kelly: Kids in the Hall: Brain Candy (1996)

Makkena, Wendy: Air Bud (1997)

Mako: *Alégria* (1998)

Malavoy, Christophe: Red River (*Rivière Rouge*) (1996)

Malazorewicz, Christopher: With Friends Like These (*Avec des amis*) (1990)

Malenfant, Robert: Desjardins, His Life and Times (*La vie d'un homme*) (1991)

Malet, Laurent: *Arthur Rimbaud: L'homme aux semelles de vent* (1995), Jigsaw (Angry Man, An) (*L'homme en colère*) (1979), Sword of Gideon (1986)

Malet, Pierre: *Incompris, L'* (1997)

Malette, Yvon: *Mon oeil* (My Eye) (1971)

Malicki-Sanchez, Keram: Skin Deep (Sadness of the Moon) (1995)

Malka, Jessica: *Peau Blanche, La* (White Skin) (2003)

Malkin, Sam: Caribe (1988), Still Life (Still Life: The Fine Art of Murder) (1990)

Malko, George: Alien Thunder (Dan Candy's Law) (1973), Courage of Kavik the Wolf Dog, The (1980)

Malkovich, John: Ladies Room (1999)

Malle, Louis: Atlantic City, U.S.A (1980)

Mallett, Jane: Love at First Sight (1974), Megantic Outlaw, The (1971), Nothing Personal (1980),

Sweet and the Bitter, The (1962), Sweet Movie (1974), Utilities (1981)

Mallette, Fanny: *Femme qui boit, La* (The Woman Who Drinks) (2001), *Jeune fille à la fenêtre, Une* (2001), Orphan Muses, The (*Les muses orphelines*) (2000)

Malone, Jena: Hitler: The Rise of Evil (2003)

Malone, Dorothy: Off Your Rocker (1982)

Malone, Greg: Adventures of Faustus Bidgood, The (1986), Extraordinary Visitor (1998)

Malone, Marisa: Burnt Eden (1997)

Malone, Mark: Killer (1994), Last Stop, The (1999)

Maltais, Robert: Beautiful Sundays (*Les beaux dimanches*) (1974)

Maltais-Borris, Rose: Alligator Shoes (1981)

Malus, Elaine: Prologue (1970)

Malus, Michael: Prologue (1970)

Mamet, David: Lakeboat (2000)

Manatis, Janine: I, Maureen (1980)

Manchild, Israel: Sentimental Reasons (Death Target) (1984)

Mancini-Gagner, Suzanne: *Si belles* (So Pretty) (1994)

Mancuso, Nick: Avalanche Alley (2001), Death Ship (1980), Flinch (1994), *Frontière du crime* (Double Identity) (1990), Last Train Home, The (1990), Loving Evangeline (1998), *Maria Chapdelaine* (1983), Misbegotten (1997), Night Magic (1985), *Paroles et musique* (Love Songs) (1985), Question of Privilege, A (1998), Red River (*Rivière Rouge*) (1996), Sweeter Song, A (1976), Tell Me That You Love Me (1983), Thousand Moons, A (1977), Ticket to Heaven (1981), Tom Alone (1989)

Mandan, Robert: National Lampoon's Last Resort (1994)

Mandel, Howard: Kurt Vonnegut's Harrison Bergeron (2000)

Mandel, Howie: Gas (1981)

Mandert, Pekka: Going to Kansas City (1998)

Mandlsohn, Sol: Winter Kept Us Warm (1965)

Mandylor, Costas: Double Take (1998)

Manga, Roger: *Ribo ou 'le soleil sauvage'* (1978)

Mangaard, Annette: Fish Tale Soup (1997)

Mankiewicz, Francis: And Then You Die (1987), Childhood Friend, A (*Une amie d'enfance*) (1978), Conspiracy of Silence (1991), Good Riddance (*Les bons débarras*) (1980), Happy Memories (Old Memories) (*Les beaux souvenirs*) (1981), Love and Hate (1989), Matter of Choice, A (1978), Time of the Hunt, The (*Le temps d'une chasse*) (1972), What We Have Here Is a People Problem (1976), *Portes tournantes, Les* (The Revolving Doors) (1988)

Mankuma, Blu: Blacktop (2000), Middlemen (2000)

Mann, Byron: Invincible (2001)

Mann, Daniel: Journey Into Fear (1975)

Mann, Delbert: Home to Stay (1978), Tell Me My Name (1977)

Mann, Edward: Seizure (Tango Macabre) (1974)

Mann, Frederick: White Road, The (1929)

Mann, Larry: Flaming Frontier (1958)

Mann, Michael: Now That April's Here (1958)

Mann, Ron: Listen to the City (1984)

Mann, Stanley: Breaking Point (1976), Butler's Night Off, The (1948), Draw! (1984)

Manners, Yvonne: Leopard in the Snow (1978)

Manninen, Sarah: A.K.A. Albert Walker (2002), Live Through This (2000)

Manning, Carl: Utilities (1981)

Manning, Preston: Tom Stone: For the Money (2002)

Manning-Albert, Jacqueline: Dancing on the Moon (Viens danser sur la lune) (1997)

Manon, Gloria: Woman Inside, The (1981)

Manov, Paulina: Boomerang (2002)

Manser, James: Oedipus Rex (1956)

Manson, Graeme: Lucky Girl (2000), Rupert's Land (1998)

Mantegna, Joseph: Boy Meets Girl (1998), Jerry and Tom (1998), Lakeboat (2000)

Mantel, Browen: Rose Cafe, The (1987)

Mantel, Cynthia: Night of the Dribbler (1990)

Manual, Richard: Eliza's Horoscope (1975)

Manual, Tara: Finding Mary March (1989)

Manuel, Tata Maria: Carver's Gate (1996)

Manz, Linda: Out of the Blue (1980)

Manzano, Jorge Manuel: Johnny Greyeyes (2001)

Manzor, René: Legends of the North (1996), Warrior Spirit (1994)

Mappin, Jefferson: July Group, The (1981)

Marano, Nancy: Trip to Serendipity, A (1992)

Maraviglia, Susila: Mule and the Emeralds, The (1995)

Marback, Tim: Event, The (2003)

Marceau, Jacinthe: Camera Thief, The (Le voleur de caméra) (1993)

Marcel, Sylvain: Loi du cochon, La (The Pig's Law) (2001), Nez rouge (Red Nose) (2003)

Marcenay, Guy: Rape of a Sweet Young Girl, The (Le viol d'une jeune fille douce) (1968)

March, Barbara: Deserters (1983), Portrait, The (1992)

Marchand, Andrée: French Love (Un amour comme le nôtre) (1974)

Marchand, Corinne: Louisiana (1993)

Marchand, Guy: Hold-Up (1985)

Marchand, Jean: Special Magnum (1977), Trudeau (2002)

Marchand, Nicole: Femmes savantes, Les (2001)

Marchand, Yves: My Friend Pierrette (1969)

Marchant, Pam: Montréal Main (1974)

Marchildon, Michel: Solitude (2001)

Marchildon, Micheline: Inertia (2001)

Marciano, David: Due South (1994)

Marciano, Harry: Bach and Broccoli (Bach et bottine) (1986)

Marcotte, Ginette: Gobital (1975)

Marcotte, Jacques: Bar Salon (1974), Histoire inventée, Une (An Imaginary Tale) (1990), J'aime, j'aime pas (1995), Kalamazoo (1988), Pacemaker and a Sidecar, A (L'eau chaude, l'eau frette) (1997), Retour de l'Immaculée Conception, Le (The Return of the Immaculate Conception) (1970), When I Will Be Gone (L'âge de braise) (1998)

Marcotte, Marie-France: Ne dis rien (Don't Say Anything) (2001)

Marcoux, Benoît: My Uncle Antoine (1971)

Marcoux, David: Lilly (1993)

Marcoux, Jean-Raymond: Devil at Four, The (Le diable à quatre) (1988)

Marcovicci, Andrea: Kings and Desperate Men (1981), Spacehunters: Adventures in the Forbidden Zone (1983)

Margaret, Ann: Middle-Age Crazy (1980)

Margolese, E.M.: Lies My Father Told Me (1975), Partners 'n Love (1992)

Margolin, Janet: Distant Thunder (1988)

Margolin, Stuart: Diana Kilmury: Teamster (1996), Impolite (1992), Iron Eagle (1986), Man, a Woman and a Bank, A (1979), Medicine River (1993), Salt Water Moose (1996), Stranger in Town (1998), Tom Stone: For the Money (2002)

Margotta, Michael: Partners (1976)

Margulies, Julianna: Hitler: The Rise of Evil (2003)

Marie, Lisa: Tail Lights Fade (1999)

Marie, Venetia: Bust a Move (1993)

Marielle, Jean-Pierre: Hold-Up (1985)

Marier, Nicholas: Laure Gaudreault: A Remarkable Woman (1983)

Marier, Paule: Close to Falling Asleep (Trois pommes à côté du sommeil) (1988), Pin-Pon, The Film (Pin-Pon, Le film) (1999)

Marin, Andrew Peter: Hog Wild (Les fous de la moto) (1980), Trial and Error (1993)

Marinaro, Edward: Avalanche Alley (2001), Emerald Tear, The (1988)

Marinier, Robert: Juiced (1999)

Marinkovic, Dragan: Boomerang (2002)

Marinne, Morgan: Folle Embellie (Out of this World) (2003)

Marino, Vincent: Noncensus (1964)

Marjanovic, Davor: My Father's Angel (1999)

Mark, Emmanuel: Johnny Shortwave (1995)

Mark, Gene: Offering, The (1966)

Markiew, Gabriel: Mob Story (1987)

Markiew, Jancarlo: Mob Story (1987)

Markiewicz, Andrzej: Dreams Beyond Memory (1987)

Markinson, Brian: 100 Days in the Jungle (2002), Harry's Case (2000)

Markle, Fletcher: Incredible Journey, The (1963)

Markle, Peter: Virginia's Run (2003)

Markle, Stephen: Ambush at Iroquois Pass (1979), Me (1974), Ticket to Heaven (1981), Perfect Timing (1984)

Markowitz, Murray: August and July (1973), I Miss You, Hugs and Kisses (1978), Recommendation for Mercy (1975)

Marks, Michael: My Kind of Town (1984)

Markson, Morley: Monkeys in the Attic (1974), Tragic Diary of Zero, the Fool, The (1970), Off Your Rocker (1982)

Marleau, Denis: *Maîtres anciens* (1998)

Marleau, Louise: *Anne Trister* (1986), *Autre homme, Un* (Another Man) (1991), Awakening, The (*L'amour humain*) (1970), Baroness and the Pig, The (2002), Black Mirror (*Haute surveillance*) (1981), Cruising Bar (*Meat Market*) (1989), Dance Goes On, The (1991), Don't Forget (*Je me souviens*) (1979), *Duo pour une soliste* (Duet for a Soloiste) (Duet for One) (1998), Exit (1986), External Affairs (1999), Flower of Youth (That Tender Age, The Adolescents) (*La fleur de l'âge*) (*Les adolescentes*) (1967), Girls (*Les femmes-enfant*) (1980), Good Riddance (*Les bons débarras*) (1980), Heartbreak (*L'arrache-coeur*) (1979), *Histoire inventée, Une* (An Imaginary Tale) (1990), In Praise of Older Women (1978), Madame B (1986), *Mirage, Le* (1992), *Pays dans la gorge, Le* (The Country on Your Chest) (1999), Possession of Virginia, The (*Le diable est parmi nous*) (1972), Stone Woman, The (*Femme de pierre*) (1990), YUL 871 (Montréal Flight 871) (1966), Woman in Transit, A (*La femme de l'hôtel*) (1984)

Marley, John: Dead of Night (Deathdream) (1974), Falcon's Gold (1982), Honourable Member, An (1982), Threshold (1981), Tribute (1980), Utilities (1981)

Marlowe, Scott: Journey Into Fear (1975)

Marotte, Carl: At the End of the Day: The Sue Rodriguez Story (1998), Breaking All the Rules (1985), Conspiracy of Silence (1991), Hard Feelings (1981), Kayla (1998), Mayday (1996), Net Worth (1997), Shoemaker (1997), Pinball Summer (1980), *Vents contraires* (1995)

Marquis, Marguerite: Évangéline (1913)

Marquis, Nicole: Nightmare, The (*Cauchemar*) (1979)

Marquis, Normand Canac: *Années, Les* (The Years) (1997)

Marr, Leon: Dancing in the Dark (1986)

Marriott, Gordon: Powder Heads (1980)

Marsac, Laure: In the Shadow of the Wind (1986)

Marsh, Jean: Changeling, The (1980)

Marshall, Ruth: Love and Human Remains (Unidentified Human Remains and the True Nature of Love) (1994), Myth of the Male Orgasm, The (1993), Waiting for Michelangelo (1995)

Marshall, Steven: Tangerine Taxi (1988)

Marshall, Tonie: Nearest to Heaven (*Au plus pres du paradis*) (2002)

Marshall, William: Curtains (1983), Flick (Dr. Frankenstein on Campus) (1970)

Martel, Marcel: Two Wise Men, The (*Les smattes*) (1972)

Martial, Jean-Michel: Man on the Shore, The (1993), *Sucre amer* (1997)

Martimbeau, Jean: Danger to Society, A (*Danger pour la société*) (1970), Twelfth Hour, The (*La douzième heure*) (1966)

Martin, Roger: Roger and Elvis (1993)

Martin, Smith Charles: Snow Walker, The (2002)

Martin, Alexis: August 32nd on Earth (*Un 32 août sur terre*) (1998), Cosmos (1997), *Maîtres anciens* (1998), Matroni and Me (1999), No (1998)

Martin, Andrea: Believe (2000), Black Christmas (Silent Night, Evil Nights) (Stranger in the House) (1974), Cannibal Girls (1973), Foxy Lady (1971), Guitarman (1994), Kurt Vonnegut's Harrison Bergeron (2000), Martha, Ruth and Edie (1987)

Martin, Andrew: Man in 5A, The (1982)

Martin, Bruce: Crimes of the Future (1970)

Martin, Caitlin: When Billie Beat Bobby (2001)

Martin, Catherine: *Mariages* (2001)

Martin, Chris William: Tom Stone: For the Money (2002)

Martin, Chris: Johnny (1999)

Martin, Dick: Air Bud: Golden Receiver (1998)

Martin, Donald: Coming of Age (1983), Myth That Wouldn't Die (*Dan Seurs du Mozambique, Les*) (1991), Never Too Late (1996), Phone Call, The (*Ligne interdite*) (1989), Secret of Nandy, The (1991), Symposium (1996)

Lhermitte, Thierry: Myth That Wouldn't Die (*Dan Seurs du Mozambique, Les*) (1991)

Martin, Glenn: Roger and Elvis (1993)

Martin, James: Waydowntown (2000)

A Century of Canadian Cinema

Martin, John Benjamin: Wishmaster 4: The Prophecy Fulfilled (2002)

Martin, Karen: Recommendation for Mercy (1975)

Martin, Laurie: Columbus of Sex, The: My Secret Life (1969)

Martin, Megan: Ginger Snaps: The Sequel (2003)

Martin, Mitch: Gun Runner, The (1984)

Martin, Pauline: Childhood Friend, A (*Une amie d'enfance*) (1978), *Grands enfants, Les* (Day by Day) (1980)

Martin, Pheilm: Anchor Zone (1994)

Martin, Richard: Air Bud: Golden Receiver (1998), Beautiful Sundays (*Les beaux dimanches*) (1974), *Corde au cou, La* (1966), Desjardins, His Life and Times (*La vie d'un homme*) (1991), *Finalemente* (In the End) (1971), Justice Express (1990), Matinée (1989), North of Pittsburgh (1992), Roger and Elvis (1993), White Tiger (1995), Wounded (1996)

Martin, Robert: Adolescence of P-I, The (Hide and Seek) (1983), Duration of the Day (*Le règne du jour*) (1967)

Martin, Ron: Goin' Down the Road (1970)

Martin, Susan: Little White Lies (1988)

Martin, Tantoo: Marie-Anne (1978), Where the Heart Is (1985)

Martin, Vera: Loyalties (1985)

Martin, Walter: Last Straw, The (1987)

Martines, Alessandra: Hasards ou coïncidences (1998)

Martinez, Camille: Foreign Ghosts (*Fantômes étrangers*) (1997), I Won't Dance (1992)

Martinez, Vanessa: Solitude (2001)

Martini, Max: Another Day (2001), Bear Walker (Backroads) (2000)

Martiniak, Liz: Truckin' (1972)

Marull, Laia: Café Olé (2000)

Marut, Marc: Bananas From Sunny Québec (1993), Paperboy, The (1994)

Marx, Brett: Lucky Star, The (1980)

Maryk, Michael: Death Bite (Spasms) (1983)

Marykuca, Kathy: Archangel (1990)

Marzena, Trybala: Journal d'un bossu, Le (1993)

Masiell, Joe: Jacques Brel Is Alive and Well and Living in Paris (1975)

Maslany, Tatiana: Ginger Snaps: The Sequel (2003)

Masmith, Cathy: Christopher's Movie Matinée (1969)

Mason, Cyndi: Overcoat, The (*Le manteau*) (2002)

Mason, Damon: Dreamtrips (2000)

Mason, James: Murder by Decree (1979)

Mason, Kenneth: Ascent, The (1994)

Mason, Lynda: Shape of Things to Come, The (1979)

Mason, Marlyn: Christina (1974)

Mason, Marsha: Dead Aviators (1998), Me and My Shadows (2000)

Masse, Jean-Pierre: House That Hides the Town, The (*La maison qui empêche de voir la ville*) (1975)

Massey, Anna: Sweet Angel Mine (1996)

Massey, Daniel: Risen, The (2003)

Massey, Gina: Thrillkill (1984)

Massey, Raymond: 49th Parallel (The Invaders) (1941), Now That April's Here (1958)

Massey, Val: Killing Spring, A (2001)

Massey, Walter: Agency (1980), Blood Relatives (*Les liens de sang*) (1978), Boy in Blue, The (1986), Breaking All the Rules (1985), Cool Sound From Hell, A (The Young and the Beat) (1959), Don't Let the Angels Fall (1969), Evil Judgement (1984), Gas (1981), Happy Birthday to Me (1981), Hard Feelings (1981), Heatwave Lasted Four Days, The (1973), Jacob Two-Two Meets the Hooded Fang (1977), What the Hell Are They Complaining About?) (Hold on, Papa!) (*Tiens-toi bien après les oreilles à Papa*) (1971), J.A. Martin, Photographer (1977), Jigsaw (Angry Man, An) (*L'homme en colère*) (1979), Lilac Dream (1987), Loving and Laughing (1971), Now That April's Here (1958), Tomorrow Never Comes (1978), Morning Man, The (*Un matin, une vie*) (1986), Two Solitudes (*Deux solitudes*) (1978), Varian's War (2001)

Massicotte, François: Coyote (1993)

Massicotte, Yves: Head of Normande St. Onge, The (*La tête de Normande St-Onge*) (1975)

Massombagi, Asghar: Khaled (2002)

Masson, Han: Apple, the Stem and the Seeds, The (*La pomme, la queue et les pépins*) (1974), *Cuisine rouge, La* (The Red Food) (1980), Jos Carbone (1975)

Massot, Claude: Kabloonak (1994)

Mastai, Elan: M.V.P. 2: Most Valuable Primate (2001)

Masters, Sharon: Deadline (Anatomy of a Horror) (1980)

Mastroianni, Joe: City Girl, The (1984)

Mastroianni, Marcello: Giornata particolare, Una (A Special Day) (1977)

Mastroianni, Pat: School's Out! The Degrassi Feature (1992)

Matalon, Eddy: Blackout (1978), Cathy's Curse (1977), Sweet Killing (1993)

Matanski, Lawrence: Naked Flame, The (1964)

Matchett, Kari: 19 Months (2002), Apartment Hunting (1999), Betrayed (2003), Great Goose Caper, The (2003)

Mather, Ann: Leopard in the Snow (1978)

Mather, Jack: High Card (1982), To Kill the King (1974)

Mathers, Joshawa: Return of Tommy Tricker, The (Le retour des aventuriers du timbre perdu) (1994)

Matheson, Hans: Regeneration (1996)

Matheson, Murray: Mary and Joseph: A Story of Faith (1979)

Matheson, Neil: Dragonwheel (2002)

Matheson, Tim: Trial and Error (1993)

Mathieson, Heather: Because Why (Parce que Pourquoi) (1993)

Mathieson, Shawn: After the Harvest (Wild Geese) (2000)

Mathieu, Francine: My Friend Pierrette (1969)

Mathieu, Jean: Friends for Life (Des amis pour la vie) (1988), Grands enfants, Les (Day by Day) (1980), Jacques and November (1984), Montréal Sextet (1991), Paper Wedding (Les noces de papier) (1989)

Mathieu, René: 90 jours, Les (90 Days) (1959)

Mathis, Samantha: American Psycho (2000)

Mathison, Cameron: Washed Up (2002)

Mathy, Mimie: Family Pack (Que faisaient les femmes, pendant que l'homme marchait sur la lune?) (2000)

Matiko, Marie: Art of War, The (2000)

Matlin, Marlee: Dead Silence (1997), In Her Defense (1998)

Matson, Robert: Life and Times of Chester-Angus Ramsgood, The (1971)

Matsumura, Tatsuo: Hiroshima (1996)

Matsurra, Bryan: Best Bad Thing, The (1997)

Matte, Jean-Pierre: Ballerina and the Blues, The (1987)

Matte, Lou: Larose, Pierrot and Luce (1982)

Matte, Luc: Claire: Tonight and Tomorrow (Claire: cette nuit et demain) (1985), Red Bells, Blue Tears (Grelots rouges, sanglots bleus) (1987), Visage pâle (Pale Face) (1986)

Matteau, Louise: Magnificent Blue, The (1990)

Matteo, Mona: Johnny Shortwave (1995)

Mattes, Eva: Born for Hell (Né pour l'enfer) (1976)

Matthews, Brian: Burning, The (1981)

Mauffette, Guy: Lights of My City (1950), Village Priest, The (Le curé de village) (1949), Unknown From Montréal, The (Son copain) (1950)

Maunder, Roger: Bingo Robbers, The (2000), Extraordinary Visitor (1998)

Maunder, Stephen: Expect No Mercy (1995)

Maunsell, Micki: Live Bait (1995)

Maurer, Michael: Red Hot (1993)

Maurice, Gail: Johnny Greyeyes (2001)

Mauro, Rebecca: Three More Days (1995)

Max, Jean: By the Blood of Others (Par le sang des autres) (1974)

Maxie, Judith: What's Your Verdict? (1995)

Maxwell, Carolyn: Black Mirror (Haute surveillance) (1981)

Maxwell, Jeremy: Duke, The (1999)

Maxwell, John: Junior (1985)

Maxwell, Lois: Hard to Forget (So Hard to Forget) (1998), Mr. Patman (1981), Ragtime Summer (Age of Innocence) (1977), Peep (1984)

Maxwell, Paisley: Flaming Frontier (1958), Now That April's Here (1958)

Maxwell, Robert: Sunday in the Country (1975)

Maxwell, Roberta: All the Fine Lines (Full Disclosure) (1999), Changeling, The (1980), Dinosaur Hunter, The (2000), Great Big Thing, A (1968), Kingsgate (1989), Matter of Choice, A (1978), Scar Tissue (2002), We the Jury (1996), Water Damage (1999)

May, Alice: Critical Age, The (1923)

May, Derek: Ernie Game, The (1967)

May, Jackie: Fast Food High (2003)

May, Jodhi: Eminent Domain (1990)

May, John: Rubber Carpet (1995)

May, Mathilda: Scream of Stone (Cerro Torra) (1991)

Mayall, Rik: Kevin of the North (2001)

Maydelle, Sabina: Ada (1981), Child Under a Leaf (1974), Double Negative (Deadly Companion) (1979), Paper People, The (1967), Rowdyman, The (1972), Scoop (1978)

Mayer, Charles: Golden Fiddles (1991), Stallion (1988)

Mayer, Clara: Kill (1969), Stereo (1969)

Mayer, Gerald: Man Inside, The (1975)

Mayerovitch, Harry: Lies My Father Told Me (1975)

Mayersberg, Paul: Disappearance, The (1977)

Mayeska, Irena: Amateur, The (1981), Courage of Kavik the Wolf Dog, The (1980), Drylanders (1963), Just Jessie (1981), Partners (1976)

Maylam, Tony: Burning, The (1981)

Mayne, Ferdy: Man Called Intrepid, A (1979)

Mayr, Friedich: Stone Coats (1997)

Mazeika, Jack Griffen: Beefcake (1999)

Mazouz, A.: Fille du Maquignon, La (1990)

Mazurik, Judy: Wendy (1966)

Mazursky, Paul: Man, a Woman and a Bank, A (1979)

Mazzone, Dora: Passage des hommes libres (Passage of Free Men) (1996)

McAdams, Rachel: Perfect Pie (2002)

McAleesa, Jim: More to Love (2000)

McAnally, Ray: No Surrender (1985)

McAuley, Annie: Screwballs II: Loose Screws (1985)

McBeath, Tom: Quarantine (1989)

McBeth, Rob: Low Self-Esteem Girl (2000)

McBrearty, Donald: Arrow, The (1997), Butterbox Babies (1995), Coming Out Alive (1980), Haunting of Lisa, The (1995),I Love a Man in Uniform (1984), Interrogation of Michael Crowe, The (2002), Private Capital, The (1988), Race for Freedom: The Underground Railroad (1993)

McBride, Joseph: Blood and Guts (1978)

McBurney, Simon: Eisenstein (2000)

McCabe, Chris: Winter Lily (1998)

McCallum, David: King Solomon's Treasure (1979), Terminal Choice (Deathbed) (1985)

McCamus, Tom: Century Hotel (2001), Circle Game, The (1994), I Love a Man in Uniform (1993), Long Day's Journey Into Night (1996), Nature of Nicholas, The (2002), Possible Worlds (2000), Perfect Pie (2002), Spreading Ground, The (2000), Switch in Time, A (1987), Sweet Hereafter, The (1996) Trinity (2002)

McCann, Sean: Atlantic City, U.S.A (1980), Bordertown Café (1991), Canada's Sweetheart: The Saga of Hal C. Banks (1985), Courage of Kavik the Wolf Dog, The (1980), Far Shore, The (1976), Flying (1986), Gerda (1992), Hank Williams: The Show He Never Gave (1982), Hog Wild (Les fous de la moto) (1980), Hostile Advances: The Kerry Ellison Story (1996), Justice (1998), Kate Morris, Vice President (1984), King Chronicle, The: Parts 1, 2 and 3 (1988), In This Corner (1986), Law of Enclosures, The (2000), Million Dollar Babies (1995), Neighbour, The (1993), Nothing Personal (1980), Possible Worlds (2000), Reckless Disregard (1985), Quiet Day in Belfast, A (1973), Terry Fox Story, The (1983), Trial and Error (1993), Three-Card Monte (1978), Title Shot (1980), Off Your Rocker (1982), Tulips (1981), Starship Invasions (1977), Sudden Fury (1975), Swann (1996), Uncanny, The (1977), Woman Wanted (1999)

McCann, Shirley: More to Love (2000)

McCarthy, Andrew: Dragonwheel (2002), Hostile Force (The Heist) (1996), New Waterford Girl (1999), Nowhere in Sight (2000), Stag (1997)

McCarthy, Heather: Rhino Brothers, The (2002) Nowhere in Sight (2000)

McCarthy, Kevin: Alien Thunder (Dan Candy's Law) (1973), Passion and Paradise (1989)

McCarthy, Sheila: Awakening, The (1995), Beautiful Dreamers (1990), Crazy Horse (She Drives Me Crazy) (Friends, Lovers & Lunatics) (1989), George's Island (1989), Haven (2001), I've Heard the Mermaids Singing (1987), I Was a Rat (Cinderella and Me) (When I Was a Rat) (2001), Lathe of Heaven (2002), Lotus Eaters, The (1993), Marriage Bed, The (1986), Montréal Sextet (1991), Waiting for the Parade (1984), Red Green's Duct Tape Forever (2002), White Room (1989)

McCarthy, Steven: Steal (Riders) (2002)

McCauley, Glenn: Stereo (1969)

McClary, Michael: Halfback of Notre Dame, The (1994)

McClemens, Julie: Night of the Flood (La nuit du déluge) (1996), Pays dans la gorge, Le (1999)

McClintock, Libby: Luck of Ginger Coffey, The (1964)

McCloud, Don: Tanya's Island (1980)

McClure, Doug: Firebird 2015 AD (1980)

McConnachie, Brian: Strange Brew (1983)

McCord, Scott: Two or Three Words (1999)

McCormack, Peter: Blue Butterfly, The (2003)

McCormack, Catherine: Weight of Water, The (2000)

McCormack, Eric: Exception to the Rule (1996), Family of Strangers (1993), Here's To Life (The Old Hats) (2000), Lost World, The (1992)

McCowan, George: Inbreaker, The (1974), July Group, The (1981), Never Trust an Honest Thief (1979), To Kill the King (1974), Shadow of the Hawk (1976), Shape of Things to Come, The (1979), Sanity Clause (1990)

McCoy, Matt: Memory Run (1995)

McCracken, Jeff: Running Brave (1983)

McCracken, Melinda: High (1968)

McCreath, Muerdine: Wendy (1966)

McCubbin, Peter: Borrower, The (1985)

McCulloch, Bruce: Dog Park (1998), Kids in the Hall: Brain Candy (1996), Super Star (1999)

McCulloch, Kyle: Archangel (1990), Careful (1992), Tales From the Gimli Hospital (1988), True Confections (1991), Smoked Lizard Lips (1991)

McDermott, Dean: Lives of Girls and Women, The (1996), Stolen Miracle (2001)

McDermott, Kathleen: Morvern Callar (2002)

McDonald, Bruce: Dance Me Outside (1994), Hard Core Logo (1996), Highway 61 (1992), Knock! Knock! (1985), Platinum (1997), Picture Claire (2001), Roadkill (1989)

McDonald, Judi: Heavenly Bodies (Les corps célestes) (1973)

McDonald, Kevin: Boy Meets Girl (1998), Kids in the Hall: Brain Candy (1996)

McDonald, Mary Ann: Life and Times of Alonzo Boyd, The (1982)

McDonald, Mary Anne: Love at First Sight (1974)

McDonald, Peter: Felicia's Journey (1999)

McDonald, Storma: Barbara James (2001)

McDonell, Arch: Homer (1970), Luck of Ginger Coffey, The (1964)

McDonnell, Mary: You Can Thank Me Later (1998)

McDougall, Ken: Last Supper, The (1994)

McDow, Val: Dying Fall (2002)

McDowall, Roddy: Class of 1984 (1982)

McDowell, Malcolm: 2103: The Deadly Wake (1996), Between Strangers (2002), Kids of the Round Table (1995)

McEachin, James: Christina (1974)

McEachren, Dale: Passion (2001)

McEwan, Tom: Silence of the North (1981)

McFadden, Christie: Too Much Sex (1999)

McFadden, Sheri: Ghostkeeper (1981)

McFarlane, David: One of Our Own (1977)

McFarlen, Susinn: Grocer's Wife, The (1991)

McFee, Dwight: Iron Road (2002)

McGara, Marven: Isla the Tigress of Siberia (1977)

McGavin, Darren: Christmas Story, A (1983), Firebird 2015 AD (1980)

McGaw, Patrick: Malicious (1995)

McGeachie, Meredith: Punch (2002)

McGee, Ronald: Daydream Believers: The Monkees' Story (2000)

McGibbon, Ed: Paper People, The (1967)

McGill, Carole: City Girl, The (1984)

McGill, Don: Paper People, The (1967), Partners (1976)

McGill, Donald: Immortal Scoundrel, The (Étienne Brûlé, gibier de potence) (1952)

McGill, Everett: Quest for Fire (La guerre du feu) (1981)

McGill, Maureen: I'm Going to Get You...Elliot Boy (1971)

McGillis, Kelly: We the Jury (1996), Painted Angels (1998)

McGinley, Sean: Claim, The (2000)

McGoohan, Patrick: Kings and Desperate Men (1981), Scanners (1981)

McGovern, Elizabeth: Handmaid's Tale, The (1990), Twice Upon a Yesterday (1998)

McGowan, David: Class Warfare 2001 (2000)

McGowan, George: Don't Forget to Wipe the Blood Off (1966), Separation (1978)

McGowan, Michael: My Dog Vincent (1997)

McGowan, Rose: Last Stop, The (1999)

McGowan, Sharon: Better Than Chocolate (1999)

McGrath, Debra: Expecting (2002), Partners 'n Love (1992), Termini Station (1990)

McGrath, Derek: Draw! (1984), That's My Baby (1984), Stuart Bliss (1998)

McGrath, Doug: Black Christmas (Silent Night, Evil Nights) (Stranger in the House) (1974), Cold Front (1989), Coming Out Alive (1980), Goin' Down the Road (1970), Hard Part Begins, The (1973), Nest of Shadows (1976), Porky's (Chez Porky) (1981), Rowdyman, The (1972), Wedding in White (1972)

McGrath, Kevin: Slavers, The (1984)

McGrath, Patrick: Spider (2002)

McGrath, Stephen: Bayo (1985)

McGreevy, John: Captains Courageous (1996), Québec-Canada 1995 (1983)

McGreggor, Kaya: Willing Voyeur, The (1996)

McGregor, Ewan: Eye of the Beholder (1999)

McGregor, Jane: Flower & Garnet (2002), Live Through This (2000)

McGregor, Ken: Bob's Garage (2001), Prom Night IV: Deliver Us From Evil (1992)

McGregor, Roy: Every Person Is Guilty (1979)

McGuffin, Mary Beth: Life and Times of Chester-Angus Ramsgood, The (1971)

McGuire, Michael: Home to Stay (1978)

McHattie, Stephen: Caribe (1988), Highwayman, The (1999), Life With Billy (1993), Mary and Joseph: A Story of Faith (1979), One Man Out (Erik) (1989), Tomorrow Never Comes (1978)

McHugh, Fiona: Haunting Harmony, A (1993), Lantern Hill (1990)

McIlwraith, David: Harvest (1981), Moving Targets (1983), Special Delivery (1982), Vindicator, The (Frankenstein '88) (1986), On My Own (1992), Trudeau (2002)

McInnis, Christine: Sylvan Lake Summer (1991)

McIntosh, Duncan: Incubus (1981)

McIntyre, Andrew: Girl Is a Girl, A (1999), Walk Backwards (2001)

McIntyre, Eileen: Only Thing You Know, The (1971)

McIntyre, Hugh: Only Thing You Know, The (1971)

McIntyre, Stephen: Fear X (2003)

McIsaac, Chelsea: Shirley Pimple in the John Wayne Temple (1999)

McIsaac, Marianne: Suzanne (1980)

McKay, Amanda: Sally Marshall Is Not An Alien (1999)

McKay, Bruce: Solitude (2001)

McKay, Caryl: Famous Dead People (1999)

McKay, George: Convicted (1938)

McKay, Willie: Truckin' (1972)

McKeeghan, Gary: Megantic Outlaw, The (1971)

McKeehan, Luke: Concrete Angels (1987), Point of No Return (1976)

McKeever, Michael: Junior (1985)

McKellar, Don: Adjuster, The (1991), Art of Woo, The (2001), Dance Me Outside (1994), Event, The (2003), Exotica (1994), Giant Steps (1992), Highway 61 (1992), Herd, The (1998), I Was a Rat (Cinderella and Me) (When I Was a Rat) (2001), Joe's So Mean to Josephine (1997),

McKellar, Don continued
Last Night (1998), Preludes (2000), Public Domain (2003), Red Violin, The (Le violon rouge) (1998), Roadkill (1989), Rub & Tug (2002), Sarabande (1997), Sea People (1999), Thirty-two Short Films About Glenn Gould (1994), Trudeau (2002), Waydowntown (2000), When Night Is Falling (1995)

McKenna, Brian: Pierre Elliott Trudeau: Memoirs (1993)

McKenna, Patrick: Real Howard Spitz, The (1998), Red Green's Duct Tape Forever (2002), Trudeau (2002)

McKenna, Seana: Hanging Garden, The (1997)

McKenna, Terence: Pierre Elliott Trudeau: Memoirs (1993)

McKenna, Virginia: Disappearance, The (1977)

Mckenzie, Jacqueline: Eisenstein (2000), When Billie Beat Bobby (2001)

McKeon, Lindsay: Class Warfare 2001 (2000)

McKeon, Nancy: Wrong Woman, The (1995)

McKewin, Vince: Fly Away Home (1996)

McKinley, Michael: Impolite (1992)

McKinney, Mark: Hayseed (1997), Herd, The (1998), Jacob Two Two Meets the Hooded Fang (1999), Kids in the Hall: Brain Candy (1996)

McKinney, Nicholas: Herd, The (1998)

McKinnon, Jane: Bay Boy, The (1984)

McKinstry, Curt: Cheerful Tearful (1998)

McKissack, Lana: Best Bad Thing, The (1997)

McLane, Janet: Wendy (1966)

McLaren, David: By Reason of Insanity (1982)

McLaren, Hollis: Atlantic City, U.S.A (1980), Jigsaw (Angry Man, An) (L'homme en colère) (1979), Just Jessie (1981), Outrageous! (1977), Partners (1976), Sudden Fury (1975), Sunday in the Country (1975), Today I Am a Fountain Pen (1980), Too Outrageous (1987), Welcome to Blood City (1977)

McLaughlin, Maya: Morrison Murders, The (1997)

McLean, Aloka: Lotus Eaters, The (1993)

McLean, Barrie Angus: Golden Apples of the Sun (Ever After All) (1973)

McLean, Grant: Royal Journey (1952)

McLean, Stuart: Looking for Miracles (1989)

McLeod, Brian Kit: Reasonable Force (1983)

McLeod, David: Squamish Five, The (1988)

McLeod, Douglas: Cheerful Tearful (1998)

McLoughlin, Aurora: Bob's Garage (2001)

McLoughlin, Tom: Unsaid, The (2001)

McLuhan, Marshall: Third Walker, The (1980)

McLuhan, Teri: Third Walker, The (1980)

McMahon, Aoife: Random Passage (2001)

McMahon, Julian: Another Day (2001)

McManus, Barney: Luck of Ginger Coffey, The (1964)

McManus, Donald: Johnny Belinda (1977)

McManus, Michael: Speaking Parts (1989), Squamish Five, The (1988)

McMillan, Andrew Ian: Goldenrod (1976)

McMillan, Glenn: Sally Marshall Is Not An Alien (1999)

McMillan, Ian: Courage of Kavik the Wolf Dog, The (1980)

McMillan, Sara: For the Moment (1994)

McMurty, Michael: Too Much Sex (1999)

McNally, Dave: Rat Tales (1987), Probable Cause (Sleepless) (1994), Things to Do on a Saturday Night (1998)

McNamara, Ed: Bayo (1985), Death Weekend (House by the Lake) (1976), Find the Lady (1976), Gentle Sinners (1984), Goldenrod (1976), Mahoney's Last Stand (1976), Riel (1979), Shoot (1976), Tramp at the Door (1985), Who Has Seen the Wind (1977)

McNamara, Martin: Dirty Tricks (1980)

McNamara, Michael: Cockroach That Ate Cincinnati, The (1996), Dirty Tricks (1980)

McNeail, Marguerite: Marion Bridge (2002)

McNeil, Kathy: Now That April's Here (1958)

McNeil, Peter: Gross Misconduct (1992)

McNichol, Joel: Suburbanators, The (1995)

McNulty, Kevin: Kitchen Party (1997), Live Bait (1995)

McPetrie, Tori: Silence of Adultery, The (1995)

McPhaden, Michael: Nights Below Station Street (1997)

McPhail, Marnie: Circle Game, The (1994), Nights Below Station Street (1997), Stolen Miracle (2001), Tagged: The Jonathan Wamback Story (2002)

McPherson, Scott: Things to Do on a Saturday Night (1998)

McQuade, Mark: Psychic (1991)

McQueen, Shirley: Stolen Heart (1998)

McRae, Allan: Keep It in the Family (1973), Peep (1984)

McRae, Maureen: Question of the Sixth, A (1981)

McRae, Murray: Touching Wild Horses (2002)

McReynolds, Reg: Sweet and the Bitter, The (1962), Waiting for Caroline (1967)

McRoberts, Anna: M.V.P. 3 (2003)

McShane, Ian: Journey Into Fear (1975)

McSorley, Gerard: Felicia's Journey (1999)

Meacock, Heather-Lynne: Timing (1985)

Mead, Taylor: Buster's Bedroom (1991)

Meadowfield, J.W.: Diana Kilmury: Teamster (1996)

Meaney, Colm: Four Days (1999), Random Passage (2001)

Means, Russell: Pathfinder, The (1996)

Meatloaf: Blacktop (2000), Formula 51 (The 51st State) (2002)

Medak, Peter: Changeling, The (1980)

Meddings, Cissy: Company of Strangers, The (Strangers in Good Company) (1990)

Medina, Ofelia: Diplomatic Immunity (1991)

Meehan, Thomas: One Magic Christmas (1985)

Meek, Kerrie: Little Canadian, The (1955)

Meeks, Edward: Blood of the Hunter (*Sang du chasseur, Le*) (Lone Eagle) (1995)

Mehler, Tobias: Wishmaster 3: Beyond the Gates of Hell (2001)

Mehra, Vinod: Love in Canada (1979)

Mehta Saltzman, Deepa: Martha, Ruth and Edie (1987)

Mehta, Deepa: Bollywood/Hollywood (2002), Camilla (1994), Earth (1998), Fire (1996), Martha, Ruth and Edie (1987), Reasonable Force (1983), Sam and Me (1991)

Mehta, Nabil: Passage to Ottawa, A (2002)

Mehta, Vijay: Seducing Maarya (1999)

Meideiros, Maria de: *Homme de ma vie, L'* (1993)

Meier, Shane: Matthew Shepard Story, The (2001)

Meigs, Mary: Company of Strangers, The (Strangers in Good Company) (1990)

Meilen, Bill: Burial Society, The (2002)

Meilleur, Carole: *Jeunes Québécoises, Les* (The Younger Generation) (1980)

Mejias, Isabelle: Bay Boy, The (1984), Girls (*Les femmes-enfant*) (1980), Higher Education (1986), Lucky Star, The (1980), Meatballs, Part III: The Climax (1987), Midday Sun, The (1989), State Park (1987), Scanners II: The New Order (1991), Unfinished Business (1984)

Mejias, Isabelle: Julie Darling (1982)

Melançon, André: *Albertine, en cinq temps* (Albertine in Five Times) (1999), Bach and Broccoli (*Bach et bottine*) (1986), Big Sabotage, The (*Le grand sabordage*) (1973), Blizzard, The (*Rafales*) (1990), *Ciel sur la tête, Le* (On Your Head) (2001), Dark Side of the Heart, The (*El lado oscuro del corazon*) (1993), Dog Who Stopped the War, The (*La guerre des tuques*) (1984), *Équinoxe* (1986), Gone to Glory (*Partis pour la gloire*) (1975), *Joyeux calvaire* (1997), Like the Six Fingers of a Hand (1978), *Nenette* (The Young Girl) (1991), Odyssey of the Pacific (*L'Empereur du Pérou*) (1982), Paths of the World, The (*Les allées de la terre*) (1973), *Petite fille particulière, Une* (The Lottery Ticket) (1995), *Réjeanne Padovani* (1973), Summer of the Colt (*Fierro ou l'été des secrets*) (1989), Sweet Lies and Tender Oaths (*Les doux aveux*) (1982), Taureau (1972)

Melbourne, Gordon: Killer (1994), White Tiger (1995)

Meldrum, Wendel: Beautiful Dreamers (1990), Diplomatic Immunity (1991), Divine Ryans, The (1998), Due South (1994), Hush Little Baby (Mother of Pearl) (1993), Song Spinner, The (1996), Sodbusters (1995)

Melega, Michele: On My Own (1992)

Melford, George: Viking, The (1931)

Melisis, Tom: Expecting (2002), Harry's Case (2000), Timing (1985)

Mellot, Greg: Going Back (2002)

Meloche, Bruno: Story of the Three, A (*L'histoire des trois*) (1989)

Meloche, Nadine: *Femmes savantes, Les* (The Wise Women) (2001)

Melski, Michael: Mile Zero (2001), Touch and Go (2002)

Melymick, Mel: Big Bear (1988)

Memmon, Chris: Wishmaster 1 (1997)

Menard, Brenda: Singing the Bones (2001)

Ménard, Julie: *Collectionneur, Le* (The Collector) (2001), So Faraway and Blue (2001), Today or Never (*Aujourd'hui ou jamais*) (1998)

Ménard, Robert: *Amoureux fou* (Madly in Love) (1991), Beauty of Women, The (*La beauté des femmes*) (1994), *Cruising Bar* (Meat Market) (1989), Day in a Taxi, A (*Une journée en taxi*) (1982), Exit (1986), *Homme de rêve, L'* (The Dream Man) (1991), Water Child (*L'enfant d'eau*) (1995), You Are Beautiful Jeanne (*T'es belle, Jeanne*) (1988)

Menatti, John: Meatballs, Part II (1984)

Mendel, Stephen: Scanners: The Showdown (Scanner Cop II: Volkin's Revenge) (1994)

Mendelson, Ben: Map of the Human Heart (1993)

Mendeluk, George: Kidnapping of the President, The (1980), Meatballs, Part III: The Climax (1987), Men of Means (1999), Merry Wives of Tobias Rouke, The (1972), Stone Cold Dead (1979)

Mendez, Catherine: Foreign Body, A (*Sinon, oui*) (1997)

Mendez, Malika: Best of Both Worlds (1983)

Mendoza, Natalie: Fearless (1999)

Mennell, Nick: My Little Eye (2002)

Merali, Abdul: Reasonable Force (1983)

Merasty, Billy: Justice Denied (1989), X-Rated (1994):

Mercer, Darren Peter: Lost World, The (1992)

Mercer, Kenneth: No Apologies (1990)

Mercer, Michael: What We Have Here Is a People Problem (1976)

Mercer, Rick: Secret Nation (1991)

Merchant, Vivien: Maids, The (1975)

Mercier, Denis: Life After Love (2000), *Présence des ombres, La* (The Presence of Shadows) (1996), Sex Among the Stars (*Le sexe des étoiles*) (1993),

Mercier, Denise: Elvis Gratton (1985)

Mercier, Hélène: And When the CWAC's Go Marching On (*Du poil aux pattes*) (1985)

Mercier, Jean: Day in a Life, A (1999)

Mercier, Marianne-Coquellcot: Sex Among the Stars (*Le sexe des étoiles*) (1993)

Mercure, Marthe: *Équinoxe* (1986), Taureau (1972)

Mercure, Michèle: *Cuisine rouge, La* (The Red Food) (1980), Don't Forget (*Je me souviens*) (1979), In the Land of Zom (1983), Kid Sentiment (1967), Loving and Laughing (1971), Lucky Star, The (1980), Wow (1970)

Mercure, Monique: Absence, The (*L'absence*) (1976), *Albertine' en cinq temps* (Albertine in Five Times) (1999), *Quarantaine, La* (Beyond Forty) (1982), Blood of Others, The (*Le sang des autres*) (1984), Confidences of the Night (*L'amour blessé*) (1975), Conquest (1998), *Contrecoeur* (1983), *Cuisine rouge, La* (The Red Food) (1980), Day in a Taxi, A (*Une journée en taxi*) (1982), *Dernières fougères, Les* (The Last Ferns) (1991), Don't Let the Angels Fall (1969), *Emporte-moi* (Set Me Free) (1998), *Finalemente* (In the End) (1971), For Better, for Worse (*Pour le meilleur et pour le pire*) (1975), In the Belly of a Dragon (1989), J.A. Martin, Photographer (1977), Let's Talk About Love (1976), Front Line, The (1985), Love in a Four Letter World (1970), Mission of Fear (1965), Story of the Hunt, The (*Histoire de chasse*) (1990), My Uncle Antoine (1971), Naked Lunch (1992), Odyssey of the Pacific (*L'Empereur du Pérou*) (1982), Question of Loving, A (*Qui à tiré sur les histoires d'amour?*) (1986), Red Violin, The (*Le violon rouge*) (1998), Stone Cold Dead (1979), Third Walker, The (1980), Time of the Hunt, The (*Le temps d'une chasse*) (1972), Tramp at the Door (1985), *Tout prendre, À* (Take It All) (The Way It Goes) (1963), Two Women of Gold (*Deux femmes en or*) (1970), Vultures, The (*Les vautours*) (1975), Waiting for Caroline (1967), Whiskers (1997), Window, The (*La fenêtre*) (1992), Woman of Colours, A (*La dame en couleurs*) (1985), Years of Dreams and Revolt (*Les années de rêves*) (1984)

Meredith, Burgess: Fan's Notes, A (1972), Final Assignment (1980), Last Chase, The (1980)

Merhi, Jalal: Expect No Mercy (1995)

Meril, Macha: Double Vision (1992), For Those I Loved (*Au nom de tous les miens*) (1983)

Mérineau, Alexandre: Hiver de tourmente, Un. (A Winter of Torment) (1999)

Merkatz, Karl: Summer With the Ghosts (*Un été avec les fantômes*) (2002)

Merlin, Claude: Foreign Body, A (*Sinon' oui*) (1997)

Merrick, Gregory: Haro (1994)

Merril, Judith: Do You Want to Sleep With God? (*Voulez-vous coucher avec Dieu?*) (1972)

Merrithew, Lindsay: At the Midnight Hour (1995), Drop Dead Gorgeous (Victim of Beauty) (1991)

Mervil, Luck: Betty Fisher and Other Stories (*Betty Fisher et autres histoires*) (2001)

Mesadieu, Anne-Louise: Royal Bonbon (2002)

Messier, Marc: *Boys III, Les* (The Boys III) (2001), *Boys, Les* (The Boys) (1997), *Ciel sur la tête, Le* (On Your Head) (2001), *Dangereux, Les* (2003), Dream Life (*La vie revée*) (1972), Few Days More, A (*De jour en jour*) (1981), Looking for Eternity (1989), *Pots cassés, Les* (Broken Dishes) (1994), Sonia (1986), Sphinx, The (1995), Wind From Wyoming, A (*Le vent du Wyoming*) (1994)

Messier, Monique: *Craque la vie* (Life Blossoms) (1994), Exit (1986), Just a Game (1983), *Marguerite Volant* (1996)

Messinger, Jack: Crimes of the Future (1970), Winter Kept Us Warm (1965), Stereo (1969)

Meszaros, Marta: Bye Bye Red Riding Hood (*Bye bye, chaperon rouge*) (1989)

Metcalf, Laurie: Execution of Raymond Graham, The (1985)

Metcalfe, Robert: Deserters (1983), Low Visibility (1984)

Metchie, Anthony: What's Your Verdict? (1995)

Metellus, Mirielle: Man on the Shore, The (1993)

Methe, François: Woman of Colours, A (*La dame en couleurs*) (1985), *Portes tournantes, Les* (The Revolving Doors) (1988)

Mettler, Peter: Top of His Head, The (1989), Tectonic Plates (1992)

Meunier, Claude: Ding and Dong, The Film (1990)

Mewes, Jason: Drawing Flies (1996)

Meyer, Breckin: Tail Lights Fade (1999)

Meyer, Dina: Johnny Mnemonic (1995)

Meyer, Turi: Wicked Minds (2002)

Meyjes, Menno: Max (2001)

Meyrink, Michelle: One Magic Christmas (1985)

Mezzogiorno, Vittorio: Scream of Stone (*Cerro Torra*) (1991)

Miano, Clipper: *Alégria* (1998)

Michael, Champion: One Man Out (*Erik*) (1989)

Michael, Janet: Extraordinary Visitor (1998)

Michael, Robert: Jesus' Son (1999)

Michael, Ryan: Lighthouse (1989)

Michael, Thomas: Juiced (1999)

Michaelson, Jonathan: Don't Let the Angels Fall (1969)

Michaud, Claude: Aventures d'une jeune veuve, Les (1974), Bingo (1974), Deux pieds dans la même bottine, Les (Two Feet in the Same Ankle Boot) (The Clumsy Klutz) (1974), What the Hell Are They Complaining About?) (Hold on, Papa!) (Tiens-toi bien après les oreilles à Papa) (1971), Let's Talk About Love (1976), Red (1969)

Michaud, Marie: Laure Gaudreault: A Remarkable Woman (1983), Maîtres anciens (1998)

Michaud, Michel: Caboose (1996), Coyote (1993), Louis XIX, le roi des ondes (1994)

Michaud, Sophie: Counterstrike (1993)

Michel, Dominique: Barbarian Invasions, The (Invasions Barbares, Les) (2003), Aventures d'une jeune veuve, Les (1974), Crime of Ovide Plouffe, The (Le crime d'Ovide Plouffe) (Les Plouffe, II) (1984), Decline of the American Empire, The (Le declin de l'empire Américain) (1986), Enuff is Enuff (J'ai mon voyage!) (1973), Far From You Sweetheart (Juis suis loin de toi mignonne) (1976), Laura Cadieux, la Suite (2000), Louis XIX, le roi des ondes (1994), There's Always a Way to Get There (Y a toujours moyen de moyenner!) (1973)

Michie, John: To Walk with Lions (1999)

Middlemass, Frank: Haunting Harmony, A (1993)

Middleton, Lane: Burnt Eden (1997)

Middleton, Max: Hitting Home (Obsessed) (1989)

Middleton, Robert: Wrong Number (2001)

Midkiff, Dale: Air Bud: World Pup (2000)

Mifune, Toshiro: Agaguk (Shadow of the Wolf) (1993)

Mighton, John: Possible Worlds (2000)

Mignacco, Darlene: Psycho Girls (1986)

Mignot, Pierre: Magnificent Blue, The (1990)

Mihalka, George: Blue Man, The (1985), Bullet to Beijing (Len Deighton's Bullet to Beijing) (1995), Child, The (1994), Damascus Road, The (Le chemin de Damas) (1988), Dr. Lucille: The Lucille Teasdale Story (1999), Florida, La (1993), Ideal Man, The (L'homme idéal) (1996), Midnight Magic (1988), My Bloody Valentine (1981), Office Party (1988), Pinball Summer (1980), Psychic (1991), Relative Fear (1994), Scandale (1982), Watchtower, The (2001)

Mike, Mikey: Super 8 (1994)

Milani, Alexander: Whole Shebang, The (2001)

Milburn, Oliver: Sweet Angel Mine (1996)

Miles, Christopher: Maids, The (1975)

Miles, Deke: Melting Pot, The (1975)

Milhand, David: Agaguk (1993)

Millaire, Albert: Exile, The (L'exil) (1971), Misanthrope, Le (1966), Mission of Fear (1965), Mustang (1975), No Holiday for Idols (Pas de vacances pour les idoles) (1965), Sur Le Seuil (Under the Sky) (2003), Window, The (La fenêtre) (1992)

Melinand, Monique: Nous deux, À (1979)

Milland, Ray: Blackout (Blackout in New York) (1978), Uncanny, The (1977)

Millard, James: I Was a Rat (Cinderella and Me) (When I Was a Rat) (2001)

Millenbach, George: Kidnapping of Baby John Doe, The (1985)

Miller, "Big" Clarence: Big Meat Eater (1982)

Miller, Andrew: Cube (1997), Nothing (2003), Oh, What a Night (1992), South of Wawa (1991)

Miller, Beverlee: Plastic Mile, The (1969)

Miller, Charles: Little Kidnappers, The (1990)

Miller, Christine: Marchands du silence, Les (1994)

Miller, Claude: Betty Fisher and Other Stories (Betty Fisher et autres histoires) (2001), see Eye of the Beholder

Miller, Dennis: Never Talk to Strangers (1995)

Miller, Gabrielle: Marine Life (2000), Rupert's Land (1998), Silencer, The (1999)

Miller, Joel: Case of the Whitechapel Vampire, The (2001)

Miller, Jonny Lee: Regeneration (1996)

Miller, Maxine: Rip-Off (1971)

Miller, Michael Alexander: Joan of Arc (1999)

Miller, Monique: Court-Circuit (1983), For Better, for Worse (Pour le meilleur et pour le pire) (1975), Gaspard et fils (1988), Tit-Coq (1953), Scream for Silence, A (Mourir à tue-tête) (1979), Snow Has Melted on the Manicouagan, The (La neige a fondu sur la Manicouagan) (1965)

Miller, Peggy: House in Order, A (La maison en ordre) (1936)

Miller, Penelope Ann: All the Fine Lines (Full Disclosure) (1999), Killing Moon (1998)

Miller, Rick: Possible Worlds (2000)

Miller, Rudy: Pilgrim (Inferno) (1999)

Miller, Sherry: Harry's Case (2000), Lucky Girl (2000), This Matter of Marriage (1998)

Miller, Stephen E.: Legend of Kootenai Brown, The (1990)

Millette, Jean-Louis: Confessional, The (Le confessionnal) (1995), Corde au cou, La (1966), Intimate Power (1985), Mission of Fear (1965), Mystery of the Million Dollar Hockey Puck (1975), Why Is the Strange Mr. Zolock So Interested in Comic Strips? (Pourquoi l'étrange Monsieur Zolock s'intéressait-il tant à la bande dessinée)

Milligan, Deanna: Barbeque: A Love Story (1997), Justice (1998), Must Be Santa (1999), Once in a Blue Moon (1995), Rhino Brothers, The (2002), Suspicious River (2000)

Milligan, Helen: When Tomorrow Dies (1965)

Milligan, John: Ma Murray (1983)

Milligan, Mike: Once in a Blue Moon (1995)

Millman, Edythe: Little Canadian, The (1955)

Mills, Alan: Unknown From Montréal, The(1950)

Mills, Alley: Going Berserk (1983)

Mills, Mark: Global Heresy (Rock My World) (2002)

Mills, Pat: Secondary High (2003)

Mills, Richard: Milk and Honey (1988)

Mills, Robert: Recorded Live (1982)

Mills, Walter: High Country, The (1981)

Milord, François: Nightmare, The (Cauchemar) (1979)

Mimieux, Yvette: Journey Into Fear (1975), Neptune Factor, The (The Neptune Disaster) (An Undersea Odyssey) (1973)

Mina, Mina E.: Hank (1977), Seer Was Here (1978), One Night Stand (1978)

Minas, Susan: Dream on the Run (1977), Point of No Return (1976)

Miner, Jan: Ten Girls Ago (1962)

Miou-Miou: Folle Embellie (Out of this World) (2003), Goodbye, See You Monday (Au revoir, à lundi) (1979), Portes tournantes, Les (The Revolving Doors) (1988)

Miquet, Anne: Life, A (1988)

Miranda, Robert Guy: Virginia's Run (2003)

Mirman, Brad: Wanted (Crime Spree) (2003)

Mirren, Helen: Bethune: The Making of a Hero (1990), see Bethune (1977)

Mirvish, Dan: Peacekeeper, The (1997)

Mistysyn, Stacie: Princes in Exile (1990), Prom, The (1991), School's Out! The Degrassi Feature (1992), X-Rated (1994)

Mitchell, Adrienne: Knock! Knock! (1985)

Mitchell, Bill: Act of the Heart (1970)

Mitchell, Caroline: Trois femmes, un amour (Three Women in Love) (1994)

Mitchell, David: Screwball Academy (Divine Light) (Loose Ends) (1986)

Mitchell, James: Pathfinder, The (1996)

Mitchell, Joni: The Black Cat in the Black Mouse Socks (see Acts of Love) (1980)

Mitchell, Ken: Hounds of Notre Dame, The (1981), Front Line, The (1985)

Mitchell, Lucie: Little Aurore's Tragedy (La petite Aurore, l'enfant martyre) (1952), True Nature of Bernadette, The (La vraie nature de Bernadette) (1972)

Mitchell, Mildred: House in Order, A (La maison en ordre) (1936)

Mitchell, Sherry: Explosion (1969)

Mitchell, Thomas: Giant Mine (1996)

Mitchum, Jim: Blackout (Blackout in New York) (1978)

Mitchum, Robert: Agency (1980)

Mitsou: Odyssée d'Alice Tremblay, L' (2002)

Miville, Lucie: Moonshine (1982)

Mlodzik, Arlene: Stereo (1969)

Mlodzik, Ronald: Crimes of the Future (1970), Stereo (1969)

Mochrie, Colin: Expecting (2002)

Modine, Matthew: Hitler: The Rise of Evil (2003)

Modugno, Enrica Maria: Saracen, The (La Sarrasine) (1991)

Mofatt, Richard: Not Me! (Sous-sol) (1996)

Moffat-Lynch, Tony: Flick (Dr. Frankenstein on Campus) (1970)

Moffit, Jimmy: Jesus' Son (1999)

Mohan, Peter: Race for Freedom: The Underground Railroad (1993)

Mojsovski, Boris: Three and a Half (2002)

Moldovan, Izabela: Reach for the Sky (1991)

Molina, Alfred: My Life Without Me (2003)

Molina, Kena: Between the Moon and Montevideo (2000)

Molina, Vidal: Diable aime les bijoux, Le (1969)

Mollin, Larry: Borderline Normal (2000), Fearless (1999)

Monahan, Dan: Porky's (Chez Porky) (1981), Porky's II: The Next Day (Chez Porky 2), (1983), Porky's Revenge (Revanche de Porky' La) (1985)

Monahana, Brent: Death Bite (Spasms) (1983)

Monday, Dick: Love and Greed (1992)

Mondie, Michel: Heartbreak (L'arrache-coeur) (1979)

Monette, Francine: Rape of a Sweet Young Girl, The (Le viol d'une jeune fille douce) (1968)

Monette, Jacques: Revolutionaries, The (Le révolutionnaire) (1965)

Monette, Marie-France: Hiver de tourmente, Un (1999), Matusalem II, le dernier des Beauchesne (1996), Water Child (1995)

Monette, Richard: Certain Practices (1979), Dancing in the Dark (1986), Far Cry From Home, A (1980), Find the Lady (1976), Prom Night II: Hello Mary Lou (1987)

Monfette, Claudine: Bulldozer (1974), Don't Let It Kill You (Il ne faut pas mourir pour ça) (1968), Straight to the Heart (Jusqu'au coeur) (1969)

Monfette, Dolores: Entre tu et vous (Between "tu" and "you") (1970)

Monfils, Chantal: Fabrication d'un meurtrier, La (The Making of a Murderer) (1996)

Mongeau, Julie: Just a Game (1983)

Mongeau, Michel: 100% Bio (Hundred Percent Biography) (2003)

Mongrieff, Karen: Midnight Witness (1992)

Monpetit, Marie-Hélène: Cosmos (1997)

Monpetit, Pascale: *Marguerite Volant* (1996)

Montand, Yves: *Ménace, La* (1977)

Montayne, Loreya: Red Deer (2000)

Montesano, Vittorio: Evil Judgement (1984), *Jeunes Québécoises, Les* (Younger Generation, The) (1980)

Montesi, Jorge: Birds of Prey (1985), Hush Little Baby (Mother of Pearl) (1993), Sentimental Reasons (Death Target) (1984)

Montgomery, Belinda: Blackout (Blackout in New York) (1978), Breaking Point (1976), Stone Cold Dead (19790, Tell Me That You Love Me (1983)

Montgomery, Claire: Zebra Lounge (2001)

Montgomery, Lee: Legend of Wolf Lodge, The (1988)

Montgomery, Lucy Maud: Anne of Green Gables (1985)

Montgomery, Monte: Zebra Lounge (2001)

Montgomery, Peter: *Vida, La* (The Document of Michael da Vida) (1965)

Montmolin, Gabrielle de: Music of the Spheres, The (1984)

Montmorency, André: *Alisée* (1991), Once Upon a Time in the East (*Il était une fois dans l'est*) (1974)

Monton, Vincent: In the Dead of Space (2000)

Montperrin, Antoine: *Folle Embellie* (Out of this World) (2003)

Montpetit, Alain: Night of the High Tide, The (*La notte dell'alta marea*) (1976)

Montpetit, Pascale: Eclipse (1994), Eldorado (1995), *Folle Embellie* (Out of this World) (2003), H (Heroin and Hell) (1990), *Incompris, L'* (1997), Invention of Love, The (2000), Katryn's Place (2002), Savage Messiah (2001), Snail's Point of View, A (*La position de l'escargot*) (1998), Soho (1994), Stork Derby, The (2001), Streetheart (*Le coeur au poing*) (1998)

Monty, Michel: Cyberjack (2003)

Mood, Ron: Dogpound Shuffle (1975)

Moodie, Andrea: Morning! (1992)

Moody, Ron: Dogpound Shuffle (1975)

Moore, Barry: To Kill the King (1974)

Moore, Brian: Black Robe (1991), Blood of Others, The (*Le sang des autres*) (1984), Luck of Ginger Coffey, The (1964)

Moore, Carmen: Tom Stone: For the Money (2002)

Moore, Christopher Michael: Witchboard II (1993)

Moore, Deborah: Midnight Man (1995)

Moore, Frank: Ambush at Iroquois Pass (1979), Blood and Donuts (1995), Drying Up the Streets (1978), Face Off (1971), Far Shore, The (1976), Food of the Gods II (1989), Goodbye, See You Monday (*Au revoir, à lundi*) (1979), Kings and Desperate Men (1981), Lions for Breakfast (1975), Rabid (Rage) (1977), Seeds of Doubt (1997), Stone Cold Dead (1979), Supreme Kid, The (1976), That's My Baby (1984), Thrillkill (1984), Third Walker, The (1980)

Moore, Jenny: Day in a Life, A (1999)

Moore, Joyce: Christopher's Movie Matinée (1969)

Moore, Julianne: Shipping News, The (2001), World Traveler (2001)

Moore, Lisa Bronwyn: Courage to Love, The (Quadroon Ball) (1999)

Moore, Lisa: Rainbow (1995)

Moore, Mavor: City on Fire (1979), Dirty Tricks (1980), Fighting Men, The (1977), Fish Hawk (1979), Honourable Member, An (1982), Insurance Man From Ingersoll, The (1976), Never Trust an Honest Thief (Going for Broke) (1979), Ready for Slaughter (1983), Scanners (1981), Tar Sands, The (1977), Threshold (1981)

Moore, Michael: Bowling for Columbine (2002)

Moore, Micki: Heavenly Bodies (1985)

Moore, Roy: Black Christmas (Silent Night, Evil Nights) (Stranger in the House) (1974), *Riel* (1979)

Moore, Sheila: Bye Bye Blues (1989), By Reason of Insanity (1982)

Moore, Tedde: Amateur, The (1981), Christmas Story, A (1983), Lyon's Den (1983), Man in the Attic, The (1994), Murder by Decree (1979), Overnight (1985), Rip-Off (1971), Second Wind (1976)

Moore, Terry: My American Cousin (1985)

Moore, Tracey: Defy Gravity (1990)

Moore, Yan: School's Out! The Degrassi Feature (1992)

Moore-Ede, Carol: King's Gambit (1985), Where the Heart Is (1985)

Moores, Margaret: Recorded Live (1982)

Moorman, Elizabeth: Eliza's Horoscope (1975)

Moran, Jim: Mask, The (1961)

Moran, Nick: New Blood (1999)

Morand, Francine: Pyx, The (1973), Ultimatum (1975), Yellow Island, The (*L'île jaune*) (1975)

Morange, Thérèse: Apple, the Stem and the Seeds, The (*La pomme' la queue et les pépins*) (1974)

Moranis, Rick: Hockey Night (1984), Strange Brew (1983)

Morasse, Louis-David: *Jeune fille à la fenêtre, Une* (2001)

Morcelli, Robert: Back Stab (1990)

More, Kenneth: Leopard in the Snow (1978)

Moreau, Jean-Guy: Angel Life (*Vie d'ange*) (1979), Confidences of the Night (*L'amour blessé*) (1975), IXE-13 (1972), Mama's Going to Buy You a Mockingbird (1987), There's Always a Way to Get There (*Y a toujours moyen de moyenner!*) (1973)

Moreau, Jeanne: I Love You (*Je t'aime*) (1974), Map of the Human Race (1993), Run for it, Lola! (*Sauve-toi, Lola*) (1986), Your Ticket Is no Longer Valid (Finishing Touch) (1982)

Moreau, Marsha: Mama's Going to Buy You a Mockingbird (1987)

Moreau, Nathaniel: George's Island (1989), Haunting Harmony, A (1993)

Moreau, Sylvie: Bouteille, La (The Bottle) (2000), Comment ma mere accoucha de moi durant sa ménopause (How My Mother Was Giving Birth to Me During Menopause) (2001), *Manuscrit erotique, Le* (2002), Post Mortem (1999)

Moreau, Véronique: Hasards ou coïncidences (1998)

Morehouse, Jennifer: *Marais, Le* (2002)

Morelle, Denis: Confidences of the Night (*L'amour blessé*) (1975), Don't Let It Kill You (*Il ne faut pas mourir pour ça*) (1968), Those Damned Savages (*Les maudits sauvages*) (1971), Yellow Island, The (*L'île jaune*) (1975)

Morelli, Robert: Fools Die Fast (1995)

Morello, Dedena: It Happened in Canada (1961)

Morency, Alain: Day Without Evidence, A (*Ainsi soient-ils*) (1970)

Morency, François: *Nuit de noces* (Night of the Wedding) (2001)

Morency, Joanne: Deux super-dingues (Heaven Help Us) (1982)

Moreno, Rita: Happy Birthday Gemini (1980)

Moreno, Ruben: Why Rock the Boat? (1974)

Morenzie, Leon: Golden Apples of the Sun (Ever After All) (1973)

Morey, Ronald: Thousand Moons, A (1977)

Morganstern, Stephanie: Believe (2000), Café Olé (2000), Forbidden Love: The Unashamed Stories of Lesbian Lives (1992), *Revoir Julie* (See Julie Again) (Julie and Me) (1998), Toby McTeague (1986), *Maelström* (2000)

Moriarty, Cathy: New Waterford Girl (1999)

Moriarty, Michael: Arrow, The (1997), Art of Murder, The (1999), Bad Faith (Cold Blooded) (1999), Children of my Heart (2000), House of Luk (2000), Major Crime (1998), Mindstorm (2001), Woman Wanted (1999)

Moricz, Barna: My Mother's Ghost (1996)

Morin, Ginette: Bilan (2003)

Morin, Charlotte: Sky's the Limit, The (1986)

Morin, Daniel: *Station nord* (North Station) (2002)

Morin, Donald: Windigo (1994)

Morin, Ginette: Bernie and the Gang (*Ti-mine Bernie pis la gang*) (1977)

Morin, Jean: OK Liberty (*Ok… Laliberté*) (1973), Sacrifice, The (*La sacrifiée*) (1955), Bernie and the Gang (1977)

Morin, Joëlle: Chili's Blues (*C'était le 12 du 12 et Chili avait les Blues*) (1994)

Morin, Michel: Isla the Tigress of Siberia (1977)

Morin, Nicole: Foxy Lady (1971), Goin' Down the Road (1970), Hot Dogs (1980)

Morin, Robert: *Neg', Le* (2002), *Réception, La* (1989), Requiem for a Handsome Bastard (*Requiem pour un beau sans-coeur*) (1992), Sadness, Reduced to Go (*Tristesse modèle réduit*) (1987), *Quiconque meurt, meurt à douleur* (1998), Windigo (1994)

Morin, Xavier: Duplessis' Orphans (1999)

Morina, Johnny: Salt Water Moose (1996), Kids of the Round Table (1995)

Morin-Dupont, Geneviève: *Petite fille particulière, Une* (The Lottery Ticket) (1995)

Morin-Lefort, Xavier: Station nord (North Station) (2002)

Morissette, Luc: *Ange noir, L'* (Nelligan) (1991)

Morita, Pat: House of Luk (2000

Morley, Natasha: Kissed (1996)

Morris, Andrea: Margaret's Museum (1995)

Morris, James: Home to Stay (1978)

Morris, Maggie: Circle of Two (1980)

Morris, Mary: Haunting of Julia, The (Full Circle) (1976)

Morriseau, Renae: Bear Walker (Backroads) (2000)

Morrisey, Neil: Triggermen (2000)

Morrison, Arthur: Évangéline (1913)

Morrison, Lewis: Traveller, The (1989)

Morrison, Paige: Girl Is a Girl, A (1999)

Morrow, Rob: Jenifer Estess Story, The (2001)

Morrow, Max: Great Goose Caper, The (2003)

Morse, Barry: Changeling, The (1980), Funeral Home (Cries in the Night) (1982), Hounds of Notre Dame, The (1981), Klondike Fever (1979), Love at First Sight (1974), Memory Run (1995), Murder by Phone (1982), One Man (1977), Power Play (*Coup d'état*) (State of Shock) (Operation Overthrow) (1978), *Riel* (1979), Shape of Things to Come, The (1979), Welcome to Blood City (1977)

Morsely, Christopher: Turning April (1996)

Mortensen, Elisabeth: Joy (1983)

Morter, Mary: Cathy's Curse (1977)

Mortil, Janne: Tokyo Cowboy (1994)

Mortimer, Emily: Formula 51 (The 51st State) (2002)

Morton, Samantha: Jesus' Son (1999), Morvern Callar (2002)

Mosca, Angelo: Balls Up (1998)

Mosebach, Martin: Buster's Bedroom (1991)

Moses, William: Fun (1993)

Moskowitz, Julie: Hush Little Baby (Mother of Pearl) (1993)

Fresh Wes, Maestro: Harmoney (1999)

Moss, Bradley: So Faraway and Blue (2001)

Moss, Carrie-Anne: New Blood (1999), Secret Life of Algernon, The (1996)

Moss, Jesse: Ginger Snaps (2000)

Moss, Peter: External Affairs (1999), Scar Tissue (2002)

Moss, Tegan: Sea People (1999)

Mossley, Robin: Deserters (1983)

Mostel, Zero: Journey Into Fear (1975)

Mostovoy, Michelle: Final Assignment (1980)

Motluk, James: Nasty Burgers (1994)

Mottram, Anna: Painted Angels (1998)

Mouawad, Wajdi: Don Quichotte (2001)

Moufette, Guy: Père Chopin (1945)

Moushimi: Love in Canada (1979)

Mousseau, Jean-Paul: Trop c,est assez (1996)

Mousseau, Katerine: Apparition, The (The Unexpected Phantom) (1972), Jos Carbone (1975), Master Cats, The (1971), Men, The (1971), Rape of a Sweet Young Girl, The (Le viol d'une jeune fille douce) (1968)

Moustaki, Georges: C'est bien beau l'amour (1971)

Moverman, Oren: Jesus' Son (1999)

Moxan, Winston Washington: Barbara James (2001)

Moyer, Stephen: Trinity (2002)

Moyle, Allan: East End Hustle (1976), Jailbait! (2000), Montréal Main (1974), Mourning Suit, The (1976), New Waterford Girl (1999), Outrageous! (1977), Rabid (Rage) (1977), Rubber Gun, The (1977), Say Nothing (2001), Xchange (2000)

Mucci, David: Net Worth (1997)

Mueller-Stahl, Armin: Assistant, The (1996), Red Hot (1993), Pilgrim (Inferno) (1999)

Muirhead, Oliver: M.V.P.: Most Valuable Primate (2000)

Mulcahy, Sean: Quiet Day in Belfast, A (1973)

Mulholland, Mark: No Surrender (1985)

Mulholland, Paul: Crimes of the Future (1970), Stereo (1969)

Mulkey, Chris: Deadbolt (1984)

Mullally, Guy: Broken Lullaby (1994), Myth That Wouldn't Die (Dan Seurs du Mozambique, Les) (1991)

Mullan, Peter: Claim, The (2000)

Mulligan, Richard: Meatballs, Part II (1984)

Mulot, Claude: There's Nothing Wrong With Being Good to Yourself (Y a pas d'mal à se faire du bien) (She's So Young and Knows All!) (C'est jeune et ça sait tout!) (1974)

Munch, Tony: Ride, The (2000), Spike of Love (1994)

Mundle, Troy: Doulike2Watch.Com (2002)

Mundley, Craig: Disappearance, The (1977)

Mundy, Kevin: Better Than Chocolate (1999), Jailbait! (2000)

Mune, Ian: Whole of the Moon, The (1996)

Munger, Léo: Celebrations, The (1979)

Muni, Roger: Ménace, La (1977)

Munro, Grant: Star Is Lost, A (1974)

Munro, Lochlyn: Blacktop (2000), Global Heresy (Rock My World) (2002), Investigation (2002), Kevin of the North (2001), Sylvan Lake Summer (1991)

Munro, Neil: By Reason of Insanity (1982), Confidential (1985), Dancing in the Dark (1986), Dying Hard (1978), Final Edition (1982), Freedom of the City, The (1976), Murder by Phone (1982)

Munroe, Christine: Waiting Game, The (1998)

Murnik, Peter: Rowing Through (1996)

Murphy, Colleen: Desire (2000), Shoemaker (1997), Termini Station (1990)

Murphy, Gerry: Violet (2000)

Murphy, Michael: Never Trust an Honest Thief (Going for Broke) (1979), Sleeping Dogs Lie (1999)

Murphy, Patricia: Columbus of Sex, The: My Secret Life (1969)

Murphy, Renée: Flying (1986)

Murphy, Richard: Kidnapping of the President, The (1980)

Murphy, Rosemary: Fan's Notes, A (1972)

Murray, Ashley: Rainy Day Woman (1970)

Murray, Beverley: Cathy's Curse (1977), East End Hustle (1976), Last Straw, The (1987), Still Life (Still Life: The Fine Art of Murder) (1990)

Murray, Bill: Meatballs (1979)

Murray, Daniel: Like the Six Fingers of a Hand (1978)

Murray, George: Love at First Sight (1974)

Murray, James: Three More Days (1995)

Murray, Joshua: Last Winter, The (1989)

Murrell, John: Waiting for the Parade (1984)

Musallam, Izadore K.: Foreign Nights (1990), Heaven Before I Die (1997), Nothing to Lose (1994)

Musser, Larry: Strange and Rich (1994)

Mustain, Minor: SnakeEater III: The Revenge (1992)

Musy, Allan: Warrior Spirit (1994)

Muszynski, Jan: By Design (1981). Crossbar (1979), Threshold (1981)

Muzzi, Michele: Fish Tale Soup (1997), Hurt Penguins (1992)

Myers, Kim: State Park (1987)

Myers, Mike: Wayne's World 2 (1993)

Mykytiuk, Lubomir: Tools of the Devil (1985)

N'Doua-Legare, Iannicko: *Neg', Le* (2002)

Nadeau, Marthe: Crazy Manette and Cardboard Gods (Manette: la folle et les dieux de carton) (1964), Last Betrothal, The (1973), Pigs Are Seldom Clean (*On n'engraisse pas les cochons à l'eau claire*) (1973), We Are Far From the Sun (*On est loin du soleil*) (1971), Wild Flowers, The (*Les fleurs sauvages*) (1982)

Nadiuska: Spanish Fly (1975)

Nadon, Branden: Jet Boy (2001)

Nadon, Claire: Eviction (*Evixion*) (1986), Memoirs (1984), Mother's Meat, Freud's Flesh (1984)

Nadon, Guy: Close to Falling Asleep (*Trois pommes à côté du sommeil*) (1988), *Craque la vie* (Life Blossoms) (1994), *Dangereux, Les* (2003), Streetheart (*Le coeur au poing*) (1998), Thousand Wonders of the Universe, The (1997), Windigo (1994)

Nagy, Bruce: Bob's Garage (2001)

Naha, Edward: Odd Balls (1984)

Nahoum, Jacques: *Trilogie Marsellaise, La* (2001)

Naimer, Douglas: Here Am I (1999)

Najman, Charles: Royal Bonbon (2002)

Nakamura: Spreading Ground, The (2000)

Naked, Bif: Lunch with Charles (2001)

Nalee, Elaine: Kelly (Touch the Wind) (1981)

Nama, Joseph Henri: *Ribo ou 'le soleil sauvage'* (1978)

Nance, Jack: Meatballs, Part IV (1992)

Nankin, Michael: Gate, The (1987)

Nantais, Aude: *Ange noir, L'* (The Black Angel) (Nelligan) (1991)

Nappo, Tonny: Better Than Chocolate (1999)

Narayana, P.L.: Seetha and Carole (1997)

Nardi, Tony: Almost America (*Come l'America*) (2001), *Amoureuses, Les* (Women in Love) (1993), Angel in a Cage (1998), Bad Faith (Cold Blooded) (1999), Brown Bread Sandwiches (1990), *Embrasse-moi, c'est pour la vie* (Embrace Me, This Is for Life) (1994), Kalamazoo (1988), Mr. Aiello (1998), My Father's Angel (West of Sarajevo) (1999), Saracen, The (*La Sarrasine*) (1991), Speaking Parts (1989), *Vita Cane* (1994)

Nardini, Tom: Siege (1983)

Narizzano, Silvio: Why Shoot the Teacher (1977)

Narr, Ralph Ellis: Wings in the Wilderness (*Les voyageurs d'été*) (1975)

Nash, Jason: Profile for Murder (The Fifth Season) (1997)

Natali, Vincenzo: Cube (1997), Nothing (2003)

Nathanson, Daniel: Higher Education (1986)

Nation, Maria: Awakening, The (1995), Salem Witch Trials (2001)

Naubert, Nathalie: Heads or Tails (*Pile ou face*) (1971), *Salut! J.W.* (1981)

Naud, Danielle: Stop (1971)

Nauffts, Geoffrey: Jenifer Estess Story, The (2001)

Naughton, David: Boy in Blue, The (1986), Separate Vacations (1986), Urban Safari (1995)

Naughton, James: Second Wind (1976)

Navin, John: Losin' It (1983)

Navratil, Ludek: Flying Sneaker, The (1992)

Naylor, Geoff: Airport In (1996), Legal Memory (1992)

Ndiaye, El Hadji: Karmen Gel (2001)

Ndo, Daniel: *Ribo ou 'le soleil sauvage'* (1978)

Neal, Dylan: Golden Will: The Silken Laumann Story (1997), Prom Night III: The Last Kiss (1989)

Neale, David: Probable Cause (Sleepless) (1994)

Nearing, Daniel: Fortune's Sweet Kiss (2002)

Nebout, Claire: Moody Beach (1990)

Necakov, Eli: In the Dead of Space (2000), Mutagen (1987)

Nedjar, Claude: *Vent de galerne* (The Wind From Galerne) (1991)

Needles, William: Spasms (Snake Bite) (1983), Waiting for Caroline (1967)

Neff, Kesnamelly: Case of the Witch Who Wasn't, The (*Pas de répit pour Mélanie*) (1990)

Negin, Louis: Ernie Game, The (1967), Oedipus Rex (1956)

Negri, Paul: Take Her by Surprise (1967)

Neighbors, Rob: LAPD: To Protect and Serve (2001)

Neil, Christopher: Train of Dreams (1987)

Neill, Sam: Blood of Others, The (*Le sang des autres*) (1984), French Revolution, The (1989)

Neilsen, Richard: Labour of Love (1985)

Neilson, Bonnie: Cannibal Girls (1973)

Neilson, Caroline: Eternal Husband, The (1997)

Nelligan, Kate: Bethune (1977), Blessed Stranger: After Flight 111 (2001), Boy Meets Girl (1998), Captive Heart: The James Mink Story (1996), Diamond Fleece, The (1992), Golden Fiddles (1991), Love and Hate (1989), Margaret's Museum (1995), Million Dollar Babies (1995), Mr. Patman (1981), White Room (1989)

Nelson, B.J.: Scanners II: The New Order (1991), Scanners III: The Takeover (1992), Scanners: The Showdown (Scanner Cop II: Volkin's Revenge) (1994)

Nelson, Francis: Little Man Abroad, A (1989)

Nelson, Ida: Funeral Home (1982)

Nelson, Judd: Flinch (1994)

Nelson, Rebecca: Mothers and Daughters (1992)

Nelson, Sandra: Halfback of Notre Dame, The (1994), Trust in Me (1995)

Nelson, Willie: Starlight (1995)

Nelson-Jacobs, Robert: Shipping News, The (2001)

Nemec, Corin: Lifeforce Experiment (1994)

Nemeth, Andrea: Urban Safari (1995)

Nercer, Richard: No Apologies (1990)

Nerman, David: Live Through This (2000), Nightwaves (2002), Witchboard III: The Possession (1995)

Nero, Franco: Young Catherine (1990)

Néron, Caroline: J'aime, j'aime pas (1995)

Nesbit, Cathleen: Haunting of Julia, The (1976)

Nesbit, Margo: Ups and Downs (1983)

Nesterenko, Eric: Cementhead (1979)

Nettleton, Lois: Echoes of a Summer (1976)

Neuberger, Bernd: Summer With the Ghosts (Un été avec les fantômes) (2002)

Neufeld, Martin: H (Heroin and Hell) (1990), Tin Flute, The (Bonheur d'occasion) (1983)

Neumann, Kurt: Fly, The (1986)

Névé, Éric: Ciel est à nous, Le (1997)

Neville, Helen: Sally Marshall Is Not An Alien (1999)

Neville, John: By Reason of Insanity (1982), Dinner at Fred's (1997), Duke, The (1999), Québec-Canada 1995 (1983), Riel (1979), Song Spinner, The (1996), Spider (2002), Stork Derby, The (2001), Swann (1996),Trudeau (2002), Water Damage (1999)

Neville, Sarah: Archangel (1990)

Nevins, Claudette: Mask, The (1961)

Newell, Mike: Of the Fields, Lately (1975)

Newfield, Sam: Flaming Frontier (1958), Wolf Dog (1958)

Newhook, Barry: Bingo Robbers, The (2000), Violet (2000)

Newley, Anthony: It Seemed Like a Good Idea at the Time (1975)

Newman, Barry: City on Fire (1979)

Newman, Brenda: Strange Blues of Cowboy Red, The (1995), Suspicious Minds (1996)

Newman, Carl: Low Self-Esteem Girl (2000)

Newman, Laraine: Witchboard II (1993)

Newmarch, Johanna: Sylvan Lake Summer (1991)

Newson, Bridget: Century Hotel (2001)

Newton, Christopher: Covergirl (1984), Samuel Lount (1985)

Ng, Alice: Soul Investigator, The (Stories of Chide the Wind) (1994)

Ng, John: House of Luk (2000)

Ng, Kal: Dreamtrips (2000), Soul Investigator, The (Stories of Chide the Wind) (1994)

Nguyen, Kim: Eleventh Child, The (Nguol Thua) (1998), Marais, Le (2002)

Niang, Magaye Adama: Karmen Gel (2001)

Niang, Rokhaya: Madame Brouette (2002)

Nichol, Cecil: House in Order, A (La maison en ordre) (1936)

Nichol, James: Turning April (1996)

Nicholas, James: Silence (1997)

Nicholls-King, Melanie: Rude (1995), Society's Child (2001)

Nichols, Nick: Whodunit (1986)

Nichols, Paul: Return of Tommy Tricker, The (1994)

Nicholsen, Jack: Last Supper, The (1994)

Nicholson, William: Grey Owl (1999)

Nickel, Jochen: Mayday (1996)

Nickle, Frances: No Apologies (1990)

Nicol, Alex: Homer (1970)

Nicol, Eric: Ma Murray (1983)

Nicolas, Paul: Julie Darling (1982)

Nicoll, Kristina: Giant Steps (1992)

Nicolle, Victor: First Season, The (1988)

Nielsen, Brigitte: Chained Heat II (1993)

Nielsen, Leslie: 2001: A Space Travesty (2001), City on Fire (1979), Digger (1993), Kevin of the North (2001), Men With Brooms (2002), Prom Night (1980), Reckless Disregard (1985), Riel (1979), Striker's Mountain (1985)

Nielsen, Susin: X-Rated (1994)

Nielson, Brenda: Out of the Blue (No Looking Back) (1980)

Nielson, Richard: Balls Up (1998), Oh, What a Night (1992)

Nightingale, Caron: Battle Queen 2020 (2000)

Nights, Robert: Double Vision (1992)

Nijboer, Donald: Knock! Knock! (1985)

Niklas, Ian: Red Hot (1993)

Nikolaidis, Stephanie: Hurt (2002)

Nilska, Beata: Dernier cri (The Last Cry) (1996)

Nimchuk, Michael John: Day My Grandad Died, The (1976)

Niquette, Richard: Dangerous Dreams (1986), East Coast (Côte est) (1986), Larose, Pierrot and Luce (1982)

Nirenberg, Les: Lies My Father Told Me (1975), Star Is Lost, A (1974)

Nishida, Akihiro: Eleventh Child, The (1998)

Niven, David: Man Called Intrepid, A (1979)

Nixon, Lester: Drylanders (1963)

Noble, Neal: State Park (1987)

Noël, Gilles: Contrecoeur (1983), Erreur sur la personne (The Wrong Person) (1995), Pays dans la gorge, Le (The Country on Your Chest) (1999)

Noël, Jean-Guy: Contrecoeur (1983), Embrasse-moi, c'est pour la vie (Embrace Me, This Is for

Noël, Jean-Guy continued
  Life) (1994), Tinamer (1987), Little Tougas (1976), You Are Warm, You Are Warm (1973)
Noel, Louise: Québec Operation Lambda (1985)
Noël, Magali: Little One Is Coming Soon, The (1972)
Noël, Paolo: Danger to Society, A (*Danger pour la société*) (1970)
Noiles, Paul: Seetha and Carole (1997)
Noiret, Philippe: *Père et Fils* (Father and Son) (2003)
Nolan, Karyn: Stork Derby, The (2001)
Nolan, Louis: *Révolutions, d'ébats amoureux, éperdus, douloureux* (1984)
Nolan, Marie-Claire: Battle of St. Denis... Yesterday, Today, The (*St-Denis dans le temps*) (1969)
Nolan, Patricia: *Quarantaine, La* (Beyond Forty) (1982), Looking for Eternity (1989), Earth to Drink, The (*La terre à boire*) (1964)
Noorullah: Hathi (1998)
Norbert, Henri: Dust from Underground (*Poussière sur la ville*) (1965), Mother's Heart, A (1953), Possession of Virginia, The (*Le diable est parmi nous*) (1972), Twelfth Hour, The (*La douzième heure*) (1966), Valérie (1969)
Norell, Michael: Diamond Fleece, The (1992)
Normand, Jacques: *Ils sont nus* (1966), YUL 871 (Montréal Flight 871) (1966)
Normandin, Guylaine: Question of Loving, A (*Qui à tiré sur les histoires d'amour?*) (1986)
Normandin, Pierre: Luke or the Part of Things (1982)
Normandin, Roger: *Aventures d'un agent très spécial, Les* (The Adventures of a Very Special Agent) (1985)
Normil, Widemir: When I Will Be Gone (*L'âge de braise*) (1998)
Noro, Line: Story of Dr. Louise, The (1949)
Norry, Marilyn: Flinch (1994)
Northcott, Alison: Hell Bent (1994)
Northrop, Wayne: Haunting of Lisa, The (1995)
Norton, B.W.L.: Losin' It (1983)
Norvell, Rose: Amityville Curse, The (1990)
Notz, Thierry: Watchers II (1990)
Nouri, Michael: Psychic (1991)
Nousiainen, Mikko: Going to Kansas City (1998)
Novara, Maria: *El jardin del Eden* (1994)
Novara, Beatriz: *El jardin del Eden* (1994)
Nowak, Jerzy: Julie Walking Home (2002)
Nowicki, Jan: Bye Bye Red Riding Hood (*Bye bye, chaperon rouge*) (1989)
Noyes, Joanna: Between Friends (Get Back) (1973)
Nozawa, Kinshi: Lover's Exile, The (1981)
Nunes, Maxine: Seasons in the Sun (1986)
Nunn, William: Bullies (1986), Megantic Outlaw, The (1971)

O'Bannon, Dan: Screamers (1995)
O'Beirn, Tadriac: Downtime (1985)
O'Brien, Edna: Julia (see Acts of Love) (1980)
O'Brien, Michael: Solitude (2001)
O'Brien, Terry: Stolen Heart (1998)
O'Byrne, Sean: 100 Days in the Jungle (2002), Burn: The Robert Wraight Story (2003)
O'Callaghan, Richard: Butley (1974)
O'Connell, Maura: George's Island (1989), Siege (1983)
O'Conner, Candace: Brethren (1976), Till Death Do Us Part (1982)
O'Conner, Dennis: Ballerina and the Blues, The (1987), Slavers, The (1984)
O'Conner, Frances: Mansfield Park (1998)
O'Conner, Glynnis: Melanie (1982)
O'Conor, Hugh: Red Hot (1993)
O'Conner, Kevin: Candy Mountain (1987)
O'Dwyer, Heather: Life, A (1988)
O'Dwyer, Linda: Indigo Autumn (1987)
O'Flaherty, Frank: No Apologies (1990)
O'Gorman, Dean: Bonjour, Timothy (1995), Fearless (1999)
O'Grady, Gail: Lip Service (2001)
O'Hara, Catherine: Double Negative (Deadly Companion) (1979), Life Before This, The (1999), Nothing Personal (1980)
O'Hara, Gerry: Leopard in the Snow (1978)
O'Hara, Kenneth: Critical Age, The (1923), Man from Glengarry, The (1920)
O'Hearn, Mona: Homer (1970)
O'Keefe, Dennis: Naked Flame, The (1964), Miles: Silent Hunter (1993)
O'Keefe, Miles: Silent Hunter (1993)
O'Kelly, Barbara: Martha, Ruth and Edie (1987), Skin Deep (Sadness of the Moon) (1995), Waiting Game, The (1998)
O'Leary, Véronique: *Futur intérieur, Le* (1982)
O'Malley, Martin: Giant Mine (1996), see Gross Misconduct
O'Neal, Patrick: To Kill the King (1974)
O'Neal, Ryan: List, The (2000)
O'Neal, Tatum: Certain Fury (1985), Circle of Two (1980)
O'Neil, Heather: Saint Jude (2000)
O'Neill, Jennifer: Scanners (1981)
O'Neill, Sally: Echo Lake (2000)
O'Reilly, Stephen: My Little Eye (2002)
O'Rourke, Denise: Reluctant Angel (1997)
O'Toole, Annette: Keeping the Promise (1997)
O'Toole, Peter: Global Heresy (Rock My World) (2002), Hitler: The Rise of Evil (2003), Joan of Arc (1999), Power Play (*Coup d,état*) (State of Shock) (Operation Overthrow) (1978), Pygmalion (1983)

Oakman, Wheeler: Back to God's Country (1919)

Oatman, Patti: Slipstream (1973)

Obadia, Ron: Dinner's on the Table (1994)

Obodiac, Hadley: Willing Voyeur, The (1996)

Oboler, Arch: One Plus One (The Kinsey Report) (Exploring the Kinsey Report) (1961)

Obomsawin, Alanis: Eliza's Horoscope (1975)

Obonsawin, Annick: Silence (1997)

Odell, Deborah: Fancy Dancing (2002)

Odette, Terence: Heater (1999), Saint Monica (2002)

Odjig, Allison: *Visage pâle* (Pale Face) (1986)

Ogier, Bulle: Candy Mountain (1987)

Oh, Sandra: Double Happiness (1994), Last Night (1998), Long Life, Happiness & Prosperity (2002), Red Violin, The (*Le violon rouge*) (1998)

Ohama, Linda: Obachan's Garden (2001)

Ohama, Natsuka: Skin Deep (1995)

Okuda, Eiji: Pianist, The (1991)

Okuma, Enuka: Day Drift (1999), Dinosaur Hunter, The (2000)

Olbryscki, Daniel: Jeweller's Shop, The (1988)

Olejniczak, Zenon: *Journal d'un bossu, Le* (1993)

Olek, Henry: Tulips (1981)

Oleksiak, Richard: Deadline (Anatomy of a Horror) (1980), Myth That Wouldn't Die (*Dan Seurs du Mozambique, Les*) (1991)

Oliffe, Jack: Proud Rider, The (The Last Run) (1972)

Oligny, Huguette: *Amanita pestilens* (1963), Lights of My City (1950), Push but Push Reasonably (Scarlatina) (*Pousse mais pousse égal*) (1975), Sun Rises Late, The (*Le soleil se leve en retard*) (1977)

Oliver, Michael: Butler's Night Off, The (1948)

Oliver, Nicole: Falling, The (2000)

Oliver, Pita: Intruder, The (1981)

Oliver, Ron: Liar's Edge (1992), Prom Night II: Hello Mary Lou (1987), Prom Night III: The Last Kiss (1989)

Oliver, Russell: Stuff (1999)

Olivier, Christine: Rebels 1837, The (*Quelques arpents de neige*) (1972)

Olivier, Laurence: 49th Parallel (The Invaders) (1941)

Oliviero, Silvio: Graveyard Shift (1987), Psycho Girls (1986), Understudy, The: Graveyard Shift II (1988)

Olsen, Arne: Here's To Life (The Old Hats) (2000)

Olsen, Dana: Going Berserk (1983)

Olson, Stanley: Artichoke (1978)

Olteanu, Draga: *Deux amis silencieux* (Dogs to the Rescue) (Two Silent Friends) (1969)

Ond, Dieudonné Ond: *Ribo ou 'le soleil sauvage'* (1978)

Ong, Alannah: Double Happiness (1994)

Onodera, Midi: Skin Deep (Sadness of the Moon) (1995)

Ontkean, Michael: Bear With Me (2000), Blood of Others, The (*Le sang des autres*) (1984), Bye Bye Blues (1989), Cold Front (1989), Summer of the Monkeys (1998), Swann (1996), Whose Child Is This? The War for Baby Jessica (1993)

Ooms, Amanda: Buster's Bedroom (1991), Mesmer (1994)

Opez, Rosy: To Kill to Live (*Mourir pour vivre*) (1973)

Orbach, Jerry: Fan's Notes, A (1972)

Ord, Catherine: Dear John (1988)

Ord, Murray: Ghostkeeper (1981)

Ord, Wendy: Black Swan (2002)

Orenstein, Joan: Henry and Verlin (1994), Sees the Light (1987)

Oringer, Barry: Return of Ben Casey, The (1988)

Ormond, Julia: Varian's War (2001), Young Catherine (1990)

Ormond, Sasha: Goldirocks (2003)

Ormsby, Alan: Dead of Night (Deathdream) (1974)

Ormsby, Anya: Dead of Night (Deathdream) (1974)

Ornolfsdottirsjon, Margret: Regina (2002)

Orofino, Jean-Luc: *Clandestins* (1997)

Orr, James: Breaking All the Rules (1985)

Orsini, Marina: Agent of Influence (2002), Dr. Lucille: The Lucille Teasdale Story (1999), Eddie and the Cruisers Part II: Eddie Lives! (1989), Last Chapter (Biker Wars) (2002), Orphan Muses, The (*Les muses orphelines*) (2000), Tadpole and the Whale (La grenouille et la baleine) (1988)

Orwin, Josh: One of Our Own (1977)

Ory, Meghan: Decoys (2003)

Orzari, Romano: Burnt Eden (1997), *Des chiens dans la neige* (Dogs in the Snow) (2001), List, The (2000), Stiletto Dance (2000)

Osborne, Jim: Summer's Children (1979), Risen, The (2003)

Osborne, John: Tomorrow Never Comes (1978)

Osborne, Sammy Jay: Black Swan (2002)

Osborne, Vivienne: Cameron of the Royal Mounted (1921)

Osborne, William: Kevin of the North (2001)

Osler, William: Clown Murders, The (1976), Lions for Breakfast (1975), U-Turn (1973)

Osmond, Stephen: Recruits (1987)

Otero, Rodolfo: Summer of the Colt (*Fierro ou l'été des secrets*) (1989)

Otis, Carre: Going Back (2002)

Otto, Kevin: Diamond Girl (1998)

Otto, Miranda: Julie Walking Home (2002)

Ouchi, Mieko: War Between Us, The (1995)

Ouellet, Cherie: Making Love in St. Pierre (2003)

Ouellet, Jean-René: I Love You (*Je t'aime*) (1974), Pigs Are Seldom Clean (*On n'engraisse pas les cochons à l'eau claire*) (1973), Story of the Hunt, The (*Histoire de chasse*) (1990), Ultimatum (1975), *Même sang, Un* (1994)

Ouellet, Marie: Cuisine rouge, La (The Red Food) (1980)

Ouellette, Andre: *Immortels, Les* (The Immortals) (2003)

Ouellette, Antonio: Long Live France (1970)

Ouellette, Rose: Mother's Heart, A (1953)

Ouimet, Danielle: Apple, the Stem and the Seeds, The (*La pomme, la queue et les pépins*) (1974), Initiation, The (1970), Possession of Virginia, The (*Le diable est parmi nous*) (1972), There's Always a Way to Get There (*Y a toujours moyen de moyenner!*) (1973), There's Nothing Wrong With Being Good to Yourself (*Y a pas d'mal à se faire du bien*) (She's So Young and Knows All!) (1974), Valérie (1969)

Ouimette, Stephen: Destiny to Order (1989), Firing Squad (1990), Heater (1999), House (1995),I Was a Rat (Cinderella and Me) (When I Was a Rat) (2001), Top of His Head, The (1989)

Oury, Gérard: *La-haut* (2002)

Outerbridge, Peter: Another Woman (1994), Bay of Love and Sorrows, The (2002), Better Than Chocolate (1999), Captive Heart: The James Mink Story (1996), Chasing Cain (2001), Closer and Closer (1996), Drop Dead Gorgeous (Victim of Beauty) (1991), Escape Velocity (1999), Fools Die Fast (1995), For the Moment (1994), Giant Mine (1996), Killing Moon (1998), Kissed (1996), Lip Service (2001), Marine Life (2000), Men With Brooms (2002), Michelle Apartments, The (1995), Paris, France (1993), Rendering, The (Portrait for Murder) (2002), Trudeau (2002)

Ouyahia, Rabah Ait: *Ange de goudron, L'* (2001)

Oversier, Stacy: Invincible (2001)

Owen, Bill: In Celebration (1975)

Owen, Donald: Crimes of the Future (1970), Ernie Game, The (1967), Nobody Waved Goodbye (1964), Partners (1976), Turnabout (1987), Unfinished Business (1984), Waiting for Caroline (1967)

Owen, Elizabeth: Facade (1970)

Owen, Lisa: Pilgrim (Inferno) (1999)

Owen, Rex: When Tomorrow Dies (1965)

Owens, Christopher: Boy Next Door, The (1984), Paris or Somewhere (1995), Uncles, The (2000)

Oxenberg, Catherine: Collectors, The (1999), Treacherous Beauties (1994)

Ozep, Fedor: *Père Chopin* (1945), Whispering City (*La forteresse*) (1947)

Ozeray, Madeleine: Père Chopin (1945)

Pacheco, Bruno Lázaro: City of Dark (1997), Traveller, The (1989)

Pachter, Charles: Symposium (1996)

Pacula, Joanna: Art of Murder, The (1999), Heaven Before I Die (1997), Kiss, The (1988)

Padamsee, Pearl: Such a Long Journey (1998)

Paetz, Laurel: Whiskers (1997)

Pagé, André: Don't Let It Kill You (*Il ne faut pas mourir pour ça*) (1968)

Page, Ellen: Marion Bridge (2002), Touch and Go (2002)

Paguette, Brigette: Requiem for a Handsome Bastard (1992)

Paiement, Mahee: Bach and Broccoli (*Bach et bottine*) (1986)

Painchaud, Brian: Who Has Seen the Wind (1977)

Paizs, John: Crime Wave (1985), Three by Paizs (1984), Top of the Food Chain (1999)

Paje, Michel: *Valérie* (1969)

Pak, Christine: 90 Days (1985), Last Straw, The (1987)

Pal, Alexandre: Woman Hunted, A (2003)

Palance, Jack: Incredible Adventures of Marco Polo, The (1998), Shape of Things to Come, The (1979), Treasure Island (2001), Welcome to Blood City (1977)

Palardy, Jean: Grand Bill, The (*Le gros Bill*) (1949)

Palfy, David: Storm (1985)

Palk, Nancy: Mary Silliman's War (1994)

Pall, Larry: Off Your Rocker (1982)

Pallascio, Aubert: *Quarantaine, La* (Beyond Forty) (1982), Chocolate Eclair (*Éclair au chocolat*) (1979), To Be Sixteen (*Avoir 16 ans*) (1979)

Pallascio, Marcelle: Head of Normande St. Onge, The (La tête de Normande St-Onge) (1975)

Palleske, Heidi von: 2103: The Deadly Wake (1996), Dead Ringers (Alter Ego) (Twins) (1988), Impolite (1992), Shadows of the Past (*Mortelle Amnesie*) (1991)

Palmer, John: Me (1974), Monkeys in the Attic (1974)

Palmer, Michael: Watchers III (1994)

Palmer, Philip: A.K.A. Albert Walker (2002)

Palmisano, Conrad: Busted Up (1986)

Paluck, Richard: Melanie (1982)

Pannaccio, Valerie: Song for Julie, A (*Chanson pour Julie*) (1976)

Panneton, André: *Jean-François-Xavier de...* (1971)

Panneton, Danièle: Body and Soul (*Corps et âme*) (1971), Frost Bite (*La gélure*) (1968), Chocolate Eclair (*Éclair au chocolat*) (1979), Gaia (1994), *Jean-François-Xavier de...* (1971)

Pantoliano, Joe: Life Before This, The (1999)

Panych, Morris: Overcoat, The (*Le manteau*) (2002)

Panzer, Wolfgang: Bookfair Murders, The (1999)

Papadakos, Anna: *Môtel St-Laurent* (1998)

Papanika, Keti: Sex and the Single Sailor (1967)

Papas, Helen: Graveyard Shift (1987)

Papatie, Brenda: *Attache ta tuque* (2003)

Papineau, François: Bean Pole Man, The (*Homme perché*) (1996), *Bouteille, La* (The Bottle) (2000), Clandestins (1997), Confessional, The (Le confessionnal) (1995), Home (2002), *Manuscrit érotique, Le* (2002), *Môtel Hélène* (1999)

Papineau, Lucille: Crazy Manette and Cardboard Gods (*Manette: la folle et les dieux de carton*) (1964), OK Liberty (Ok...Laliberté) (1973)

Papps, Bill: South Pacific, 1942 (1981)

Paquet, Marc: *Peau Blanche, La* (White Skin) (2003)

Paquette, Brigitte: Bean Pole Man, The (*Homme perché*) (1996)

Paquette, Pierre: *Valérie* (1969)

Paquin, Anna: Fly Away Home (1996)

Paradis, Bianca: I Won't Dance (1992)

Paradis, Danièle: Christmas of Madame Beauchamp, The (*Le revanche noël de Madame Beauchamp*) (1981)

Paradjanov, Serge: Swan Lake: The Zone (*Lebedyne ozero-zona*) (1996)

Paragamian, Arto: Because Why (*Parce que Pourquoi*) (1993), Cosmos (1997), Two Thousand and None (2000)

Pjaras, Dean: X-Rated (1994)

Paré, Jessica: Bollywood/Hollywood (2002), Deadly Friends: The Nancy Eaton Story (2003), Downtime (2001), Lost and Delirious (2000), Posers (2002), Random Passage (2001), Stardom (2000)

Paré, Judith: Q-bec My Love (1970)

Paré, Michael: 2103: The Deadly Wake (1996), Carver's Gate (1996), Coyote Run (1996), Eddie and the Cruisers Part II: Eddie Lives! (1989), In the Dead of Space (2000), Men of Means (1999), Warriors (1994)

Paré, Nicolas: Angel in a Cage (The Woman in the Cage) (*La bête de foire*) (1993),

Parent, Daniel: *Jeune fille à la fenêtre, Une* (2001), *Sept Jours de Simon Labrosse, Les* (2003)

Parent, Guy: Enchanted Village, The (*Le village enchanté*) (1956)

Parent, Jean-Marc: *Pots cassés, Les* (Broken Dishes) (1994)

Parent, Manda: Bingo (1974), Once Upon a Time in the East (*Il était une fois dans l'est*) (1974)

Parent, Pascal: *Immortels, Les* (The Immortals) (2003)

Parenti, Mauro: *Donnez-nous notre amour quotidien* (In Love With Sex) (1974), French Love (*Un amour comme le nôtre*) (1974), Justine (1972)

Parfitt, Judy: Falling Through (2000), Galileo (1973)

Parillaud, Anne: Girls (*Les femmes-enfant*) (1980), Map of the Human Heart (1993)

Paris, Jacques: Mario (1984)

Paris, Jean-Louis: Trouble Makers (*Trouble-fête*) (1964)

Paris, John: Ivy League Killers (The Fast Ones) (1959)

Parisot, Dean: Still Life (1990)

Parizeau, Louis: Kid Sentiment (1967)

Parker, G. Ross: Hitler: The Rise of Evil (2003)

Parker, Dave: House of the Dead (2003)

Parker, Graham: Inside Out (1979), Lyon's Den (1983), Question of the Sixth, A (1981), Suicide Murders, The (1986)

Parker, Kelly: Someday Soon (1977)

Parker, Leni: Deadly Portrayal (2003), Strange Blues of Cowboy Red, The (1995)

Parker, Mary-Louise: Five Senses, The (1999)

Parker, Michael: Lunch with Charles (2001)

Parker, Molly: Five Senses, The (1999), Kissed (1996), Ladies Room (1999), Last Wedding, The (2001), Looking for Leonard (2002), Marion Bridge (2002), Max (2001), Men With Brooms (2002), Paris or Somewhere (1995), Rare Birds (2001), Sunshine (1999), Suspicious River (2000), War Bride, The (2001)

Parker, Monica: Coming Out Alive (1980), Improper Channels (1981), Switching Channels (1988)

Parker, Nicole: Halfback of Notre Dame, The (1994)

Parker, Ronald: Joan of Arc (1999)

Parkes, Gerard: American Christmas Carol, An (1979), Apprentice, The (1971), Draw! (1984), Every Person Is Guilty (1979), Fan's Notes, A (1972), Great Big Thing, A (1968), Gun Runner, The (1984), Honourable Member, An (1982), Isabel (1968), Last Winter, The (1989), Must Be Santa (1999), Of the Fields, Lately (1975), Pyx, The (1973), Running Time (1978), Second Wind (1976), Speaking Parts (1989), Suicide Murders, The (1986), Who Has Seen the Wind (1977), Yesterday (1981)

Parkins, Barbara: Bear Island (1979), Christina (1974)

Parks, Michael: Between Friends (Get Back) (1973), Death Wish V: The Face of Death (1994)

Paroissien, Pascale: Two Actresse (1993)

Parr, Anthony: Mark of Cain, The (1984)

Parrish, Steve: Scanners III: The Takeover (1992)

Parro, Andrea: *Fille du Maquignon, La* (The Girl of Maquignon) (1990), Secret of Jerome, The (*Le secret de Jérôme*) (1994)

Parry, Michel: Uncanny, The (1977)

Parsons, Nancy: Porky's II: The Next Day (Chez Porky 2) (1983), Porky's Revenge (Revanche de Porky, La) (1985)

Partington, Richard: King's Gambit (1985)

Pasco, Nicholas: Red Blooded 2 (1996), Swordsman, The (1993)

Pascoe, Isabelle: Not Me! (Sous-sol) (1996)

Pascornek, Michael: Meatballs, Part III: The Climax (1987)

Pasdar, Adrian: Wounded (1996)

Paseornek, Michael: Screwball Academy (Divine Light) (Loose Ends) (1986), SnakeEater (1990), SnakeEater II: The Drug Buster (1990)

Pass, Cyndi: Deadbolt (1984)

Pasternak, Reagan: Jailbait! (2000)

Pastinsky, Carol: Sweet Substitute (1964)

Pastko, Earl: Barbeque: A Love Story (1997), Century Hotel (2001), Eclipse (1994), Highway 61 (1992), Rats (1999)

Pataki, Eva: Bye Bye Red Riding Hood (Bye bye, chaperon rouge) (1989)

Patenaude, Danyèle: Dog Who Stopped the War, The (La guerre des tuques) (1984)

Paterson, Andrew: Wasaga (1994)'

Paterson, Florence: Freedom of the City, The (1976), Hank (1977), Of the Fields, Lately (1975)

Paterson, Jayne: Drive, The (1996)

Pathak, Dina: Bollywood/Hollywood (2002)

Patni: My Little Devil (2000)

Paton, Laurie: Switch in Time, A (1987)

Patrick, David: Adolescence of P-I, The (Hide and Seek) (1983), Crunch (1981), Kings and Desperate Men (1981)

Patrick, Joseph: Birds of Prey (1985)

Patry, Ivan: Day Without Evidence, A (Ainsi soient-ils) (1970)

Patry, Pierre: Cain (1965), Corde au cou, La (1966), Trouble Makers (Trouble-fête) (1964)

Patry, Yves: Day Without Evidence, A (1970)

Patterson, Marnette: Stalking of Laurie Show, The (2000)

Patterson, Pat: Highway of Heartaches (1994)

Paul, Adrian: Graveyard Story (1989)

Paul, Alexandra: Nothing to Lose (1994), Paperboy, The (1994)

Paul, Andrée: Mon oeil (My Eye) (1971)

Paul, Francine: Bust a Move (1993)

Paul, Martin: My Kind of Town (1984)

Paul, Oscar: Fantastica (1980)

Paul, Richard Joseph: Wounded (1996)

Paulson, Sarah: Friends at Last (1995)

Pauzé, Anne: Exile, The (L'exil) (1971)

Pavlou, Stel: Formula 51 (The 51st State) (2002)

Pavlovic, Asja: Echo Lake (2000), My Father's Angel (West of Sarajevo) (1999)

Pax, James: Bethune: The Making of a Hero (1990), see Bethune (1977)

Payami, Babak: Secret Ballot (Raye Makhfi) (2001)

Paymer, David: Burial Society, The (2002)

Payne, Bruce: Ripper: Letter from Hell (2001), Steal (Riders) (2002)

Payne, Daniel: Random Passage (2001)

Payne, Denis: Q-bec My Love (A Commercial Success) (1970)

Payne, Dolores: Dead Innocent (1996)

Payne, Louise: When Tomorrow Dies (1965)

Payne, Sam: Sweet and the Bitter, The (1962)

Peace, Joshua: Beefcake (1999)

Peace, Warren: Wasp, The (La guêpe) (1986)

Peach, Mary: Mothers and Daughters (1992)

Peacocke, Thomas: Bay Boy, The (1984), Chasing Rainbows (1988), Justice Denied (1989), Hounds of Notre Dame, The (1981), Running Brave (1983), Striker's Mountain (1985)

Pearce, Richard: Threshold (1981)

Pearl, Aaron: Little Boy Blues (2000)

Pearson, Anne: Dangerous Age, A (1958)

Pearson, Barry: Ambush at Iroquois Pass (1979), Brain, The (1988), Covert Action (1986), Firebird 2015 AD (1980), Iron Road (2002), Isaac Littlefeathers (1984), Me (1974), Paperback Hero (1973), Plague, The (1979), Sally Fieldgood and Co. (1975), Someday Soon (1977)

Pearson, Gerry: Whodunit (1986)

Pearson, Jean-Philippe: Québec-Montréal (2002)

Pearson, Neil: Magician's House, The (1999)

Pearson, Peter: Bananas From Sunny Québec (1993), Best Damn Fiddler From Calabogie to Kaladar, The (1968), Heaven on Earth (1987), Insurance Man From Ingersoll, The (1976), Kathy Karuks Is a Grizzly Bear (1976), One Man (1977), Only God Knows (1974), Paperback Hero (1973), Snowbirds (1981), Tar Sands, The (1977)

Pearson, Valerie: Solitaire (1991)

Peck, Raoul: Man on the Shore, The (1993)

Peck, Raymond: Critical Age, The (1923)

Peckinpah, David: Paperboy, The (1994)

Peddie, Jim: Hired Gun (The Devil's Spawn) (The Last Gunfighter) (1959)

Pedersen, Jon: Tuesday, Wednesday (1987)

Peguy, Robert: Notre-Dame of the Mouise (1941)

Pelham, Christopher: Xchange (2000)

Pell, Vic: Wendy (1966)

Pelland, Louis: Esprit du mal, L' (1954)

Pelland, Michel: Mis-Works, The (1959)

Pellegrin, Raymond: Louisiana (1993)

Pellegrino, Frank: Short Change (*Une fille impossible*) (1989)

Pellerin, Michael: Dying Fall (2002)

Pelletier, Alec: Flower of Youth (That Tender Age, The Adolescents) (*La fleur de l'âge*) (*Les adolescentes*) (1967), Mission of Fear (1965),

Pelletier, Andrée: Anchor Zone (1994), Bach and Broccoli (*Bach et bottine*) (1986), Born for Hell (*Né pour l'enfer*) (1976), East End Hustle (1976), Finding Mary March (1989), Handyman, The (*L'homme à tout faire*) (1980), Ladies Room (1999), Latitude 55 (1982), Marie-Anne (1978), Men, The (1971), Mustang (1975), *Nenette* (The Young Girl) (1991), Outrageous! (1977), Smoked Lizard Lips (1991), Tell Me That You Love Me (1983), Third Walker, The (1980), Until the Heart (*Jusqu'au coeur*) (1980), Vincent and Me (1990), Walls (1984)

Pelletier, Denise: *Corde au cou, La* (1966), *Tit-Coq* (1953), Where Two Roads Cross (Between Two Loves) (*À la croisée des chemins*) (*Entre deux amours*) (1943)

Pelletier, Gabriel: *Automne sauvage, L'* (The Savage Autumn) (1992), Karmina (1998), *Karmina 2: L'enfer de Chabot* (K2 2001) (2001), Life After Love (2000), *Meurtre en musique* (1994), Shadows of the Past (1991)

Pelletier, Gérard: *90 jours, Les* (90 Days) (1959)

Pelletier, Gilles: Bingo (1974), Coyote Run (1996), Dust from Underground (*Poussière sur la ville*) (1965), Earth to Drink, The (*La terre à boire*) (1964), Gapi (1982), *Jésus de Montréal* (1989), Vultures, The (*Les vautours*) (1975)

Pelletier, Louise: Nenette (The Young Girl) (1991)

Pelletier, Maryse: And When the CWAC's Go Marching On (*Du poil aux pattes*) (1985), Claire: Tonight and Tomorrow (*Claire: cette nuit et demain*) (1985)

Pelletier, Melissa J.: Nightwaves (2002)

Pelletier, Michèle-Barbara: *Embrasse-moi, c'est pour la vie* (1994), Favourite Game, The (2003), Lotus Eaters, The (1993), Mr. Aiello (1998), *Nez rouge* (Red Nose) (2003)

Pelletier, Tobie: *Du pic au coeur* (From Spades to Hearts) (2000), Sex Among the Stars (*Le sexe des étoiles*) (1993), Phantom Life, A (1992

Pelletier, Yves: Karmina (1998), *Karmina 2: L'enfer de Chabot* (K2 2001) (2001), Two Seconds (*2 secondes*) (1998)

Pendleton, Austin: Men of Means (1999)

Peng, Diana: Chinese Chocolate (1995)

Peng, Jin Xiao: Yellow Wedding (1998)

Penhaligon, Susan: Leopard in the Snow (1978), Uncanny, The (1977)

Penn, Christopher: Boys' Club, The (1996)

Penn, Sean: Weight of Water, The (2000)

Pennington, Earl: Jacob Two-Two Meets the Hooded Fang (1977)

Penot, Jacques: For Those I Loved (*Au nom de tous les miens*) (1983)

Penotti, David: Collectors, The (1999)

Pépin, Pierre-Yves: *Équinoxe* (1986), *Fille du Maquignon, La* (The Girl of Maquignon) (1990)

Pepin, Richard: Mindstorm (2001)

Pepin, Thierry: Danny in the Sky (2002)

Peppard, George: Your Ticket Is no Longer Valid (Finishing Touch) (1982)

Pepper, Barry: Snow Walker, The (2002), We All Fall Down (2000)

Perabo, Piper: Lost and Delirious (2000)

Perez, Mary: Anomaly (Anomie) (1973)

Perez, Shane: Men of Means (1999)

Perez, Vincent: Shot Through the Heart (1998)

Périard, Jean-Roger: Heatwave Lasted Four Days, The (1973)

Perier, Étienne: Louisiana (1993)

Perisson, Alain: Big Sabotage, The (*Le grand sabordage*) (1973)

Perkins, Anthony: Double Negative (Deadly Companion) (1979)

Perkins, Dawn: Water Game, The (2002)

Perkins, Emily: Ginger Snaps (2000), Ginger Snaps: The Sequel (2003)

Perlich, Max: Men With Guns (1996)

Perlman, Ron: Quest for Fire (1981)

Perlmutter, Dara: Zebra Lounge (2001)

Perlmutter, David: Draw! (1984), Personal (1980)

Pernel, Florence: *Arthur Rimbaud: L'homme aux semelles de vent* (1995)

Pernie, Steve: Face Off (1971)

Perraud, Jean: Mission of Fear (1965)

Perrault, Pierre: Duration of the Day (*Le règne du jour*) (1967), So That the World Goes On (*Pour la suite du monde*) (1963), Water Cars (*Les voitures d'eau*) (1970)

Perreault, Marie: Eleventh Special, The (1988)

Perret, Jean-Marc: Haunting Harmony, A (1993)

Perrin, Jacques: *La-haut* (2002), *Paroles et musique* (Love Songs) (1985), Silencing the Guns (*Le silence des fusils*) (1996), *Petite fille particulière, Une* (The Lottery Ticket) (1995)

Perrin, Jean: All About Women (1969)

Perrine, Valerie: Agency (1980)

Perris, Anthony: Scoop (1978)

Perron, Clément: Gone to Glory (*Partis pour la gloire*) (1975), It's Not Jacques Cartier's Fault (1968), My Uncle Antoine (1971), Stop (1971), Taureau (1972), Two Wise Men, The (1972)

Perron, Éloi: Water Cars (*Les voitures d'eau*) (1970)

Perron, Marie-Chantal: *Mystérieuse Mademoiselle C, La* (2001)

Perron, Michael: Home Team (1999), Case of the Whitechapel Vampire, The (2001), Legend of Sleepy Hollow, The (1999), Sign of Four, The (2001)

Perrot, François: Lola Zipper (1991), Old Country Where Rimbaud Died, The (*Le vieux pays où Rimbaud est mort*) (1977)

Perrotta, Michael: *Bob Million: Le jackpot de la planète* (1997)

Perry, Frank: Accident at Memorial Stadium, The (1983), Bush Pilot (1946), Heatwave Lasted Four Days, The (1973), Neptune Factor, The (The Neptune Disaster) (An Undersea Odyssey) (1973)

Perry, Len: Alligator Shoes (1981)

Perry, Mark: Plastic Mile, The (1969)

Persky, Stan: Symposium (1996)

Persoff, Nehemiah: Deadly Harvest (1980)

Persson, Lars Goran: Misery Harbour (1999)

Pertwee, Sean: Formula 51 (The 51st State) (2002)

Pérusse, Roméo: Apple, the Stem and the Seeds, The (*La pomme, la queue et les pépins*) (1974)

Petawabano, Buckley: Cold Journey (1976)

Petermann, Xavier Norman: Mario (1984)

Peters, Bernadette: Tulips (1981)

Peters, Richard: This Matter of Marriage (1998)

Petersen, David: Grey Fox, The (1982), Low Visibility (1984), Skip Tracer (1977)

Peterson, Alan: Noroc (1999)

Peterson, Craig: Life and Times of Chester-Angus Ramsgood, The (1971)

Peterson, Eric: Captive Heart: The James Mink Story (1996), Earth (1998), Fairy Tales & Pornography (2003), Henry and Verlin (1994), Kid Who Couldn't Miss, The (1982), King of Friday Night, The (1985), Last Season, The (1987), Many Trials of One Jane Doe, The (2002), Park Is Mine, The (1986), Seer Was Here (1978), Sleeping Dogs Lie (1999), Sleeproom, The (1998), Stork Derby, The (2001), Tramp at the Door (1985), Trudeau (2002), Visitor, The (1974), Win, Again! (1998)

Peterson, Katherine: Lyddie (1995)

Peterson, Marion: *Mémoire tronquée* (1990)

Peterson, Shelley: Housekeeper, The (Judgement in Stone) (1986), Welcome to Blood City (1977)

Peterson, Trudi: Vacant Lot, The (1989)

Petitclerc, Jean: *Cabaret neiges noires* (1997), King of Fire (1985)

Petraglia, Sandro: 90 jours, Les (90 Days) (1959), Almost America (*Come l'America*) (2001)

Petrella, Ian: Christmas Story, A (1983)

Petrie, Anne: Close to Home (1986)

Petrie, Daniel: Assistant, The (1996), Bay Boy, The (1984), Dead Silence (1997), Execution of Raymond Graham, The (1985), Kissinger and Nixon (1994), Neptune Factor, The (The Neptune Disaster) (1973)

Petrie, Doris: Catsplay (1977), Funeral Home (Cries in the Night) (1982), Home to Stay (1978), Never Trust an Honest Thief (Going for Broke) (1979), Snowbirds (1981), Ticket to Heaven (1981), Wedding in White (1972)

Petrie, Juliette: Paspébiac: The Games Country (*Paspébiac: Terre des Jeux*) (1985)

Petrie, Susan: Far Shore, The (1976), Lions for Breakfast (1975), Parasite Murders (Shivers) (They Came from Within) (1975), Point of No Return (1976), Rip-Off (1971), Sunday in the Country (1975), Sweeter Song, A (1976), Takeover (1981)

Petries, Daniel: Dead Silence (1997)

Petronzio, Nina: Vincent and Me (1990)

Petrovic, Nenad: In the Dead of Space (2000)

Petrovicz, Robert: Middlemen (2000)

Petrucci, Luigi: It Happened in Canada (1961)

Petty, Dini: Kathy Karuks Is a Grizzly Bear (1976)

Petty, Lori: Deadly Arrangement (1998)

Petty, Ross: Housekeeper, The (1986)

Pevney, Joseph: Back to God's Country (1953)

Phattigo, Mort: Dead Innocent (1996)

Philippe, Marie: Shabbat Shalom (1994)

Phillips, Leo: Wedding in White (1972)

Phillips, Leslie: Spanish Fly (1975)

Phillips, Lou Diamond: Agaguk (Shadow of the Wolf) (1993), Boulevard (1994)

Phillips, Patricia: Bayo (1985), Lantern Hill (1990), Last Straw, The (1987), Sincerely Violet (1987)

Phillips, Robin: Waiting for the Parade (1984), Wars, The (1983)

Phillips, Sian: Magician's House, The (1999)

Phillips, William: Fool Proof (2003), Treed Murray (2001)

Philpott, Chris: Eternal Husband, The (1997), Fairy Tales & Pornography (2003)

Philpott, Tony: On the Nose (2001)

Phipps, Jennifer: Coming of Age (1983)

Pia, Conrad: Rendering, The (Portrait for Murder) (2002)

Piazza, Ben: Dangerous Age, A (1958)

Picard, Béatrice: 90 jours, Les (90 Days) (1959), Deaf to the City (*Le sourd dans la ville*) (1987)

Picard, Bernard: Tanzi (1987)

Picard, Luc: *15 février 1839* (February 15, 1839) (2001), Dead End (*Le dernier souffle*) (1999), En vacances (Summer Holidays) (2000), *Erreur sur la personne* (The Wrong Person) (1995),

DIRECTORS, SCRIPTWRITERS & ACTORS

Femme qui boit, La (The Woman Who Drinks) (2001), *Collectionneur, Le* (The Collector) (2001), October (Octobre) (1994), Savage Messiah (2001), Sex Among the Stars (*Le sexe des étoiles*) (1993)

Picard, Marie-Josée: Si belles (So Pretty) (1994)

Picazo, Angel: *Diable aime les bijoux, Le* (The Devil Likes Jewels) (The Devil's Jewellery) (Las joyas del diablo) (1969)

Piccoli, Michel: Atlantic City, U.S.A (1980), Final Blow, The (The Finishing Stroke) (*Le coup de grâce*) (1965)

Piché, Jean-Marc: Fallen Knight (The Minion) (1998)

Piché, Paul: Guitar (Guitare) (1974)

Pichette, Jean-François: Being at Home With Claude (1992), Desire in Motion (*Mouvements du désire*) (1994), Femme de Pablo Ruiz, La (*Pablo qui court*) (On the Run) (1991), On the Run (*Pablo qui court*) (1993), *Secret de banlieue, Un* (The Secret of a Suburb) (2002), *Temps d'une vie, Le* (The Times of Our Life) (1998)

Pichette, Lise: Blue Winter (*L'hiver bleu*) (1980)

Pickett, Tom: What's Your Verdict? (1995)

Pickles, Christina: Seizure (*Tango Macabre*) (1974)

Pickup, Ronald: Bethune: The Making of a Hero (1990) see Bethune (1977)

Pidal, Nachal: *Diable aime les bijoux, Le* (The Devil Likes Jewels) (The Devil's Jewellery) (1969)

Pidgeon, Walter: Neptune Factor, The (The Neptune Disaster) (An Undersea Odyssey) (1973)

Piedalue, Bob: Man Who Guards the Greenhouse, The (1988)

Pielmeier, John: Agnes of God (1985), Hitler: The Rise of Evil (2003)

Pierard, Annie: *Secret de banlieue, Un* (The Secret of a Suburb) (2002)

Pierce, Eric Gregor: Eviction (*Evixion*) (1986)

Pierce, John: Someday Soon (1977)

Pierce, Justin: Looking for Leonard (2002)

Pierre, Frederic: *Peau Blanche, La* (White Skin) (2003)

Pierson, Claude: All About Women (*À propos de la femme*) (1969), *Donnez-nous notre amour quotidien* (In Love With Sex) (1974), Erotic Love Games (1971), Grand Recess, The (*La grande récré*) (1976), I Have the Right to Pleasure (*J'ai droit au plaisir*) (1975), *Ils sont nus* (1966), Justine (1972), Oh, If Only My Monk Would Want (*Ah! Si mon moine voulait*) (1973)

Pierson, Isabelle: *Ils sont nus* (1966)

Pietrobruno, Ilena: Girl King (2002)

Pigeon, Maryse: Crinoline Madness (*La folie des crinolines*) (1995)

Pill, Alison: Dinosaur Hunter, The (2000), Fast Food High (2003), Perfect Pie (2002), Stranger in Town (1998)

Pilon, Daniel: By the Blood of Others (Par le sang des autres) (1974), Collectors, The (1999), Death of a Lumberjack (La mort d'un boucheron) (1973), Hitting Home (Obsessed) (1989), Hot Dogs (Clean Up Squad, The) (1980), Plague, The (1979), Possession of Virginia, The (Le diable est parmi nous) (1972), In Her Defense (1998), List, The (2000), Rape of a Sweet Young Girl, The (*Le viol d'une jeune fille douce*) (1968), Rebels 1837, The (*Quelques arpents de neige*) (1972), Red (1969), Scanners III: The Takeover (1992), Sex in the Snow (Après-ski) (1971), Starship Invasions (1977), Suspicious Minds (1996), Vents contraires (Crosswinds) (1995), Two Wise Men, The (Les smattes) (1972)

Pilon, Donald: *Ababouinée* (1994), Bulldozer (1974), Child Under a Leaf (1974), City on Fire (1979), Crime of Ovide Plouffe, The (*Le crime d'Ovide Plouffe*) (*Les Plouffe, II*) (1984), Fantastica (1980), Gerda (1992), Gina (1975), Heavenly Bodies (Les corps célestes) (1973), I Miss You, Hugs and Kisses (1978), Keeping Track (1987), Man Called Intrepid, A (1979), Master Cats, The (1971), Men, The (1971), Pyx, The (1973), Rape of a Sweet Young Girl, The (*Le viol d'une jeune fille douce*) (1968), Red (1969), True Nature of Bernadette, The (*La vraie nature de Bernadette*) (1972), Two Wise Men, The (*Les smattes*) (1972), Two Women of Gold (*Deux femmes en or*) (1970), Uncanny, The (1977), Wasp, The (*La guêpe*) (1986)

Pilon, Luc: *Morte amoureuse, La* (1997)

Pilon, Sylvia: Ideal Man, The (*L'homme idéal*) (1996), *Nez rouge* (Red Nose) (2003)

Pilote, Marcia: Sadness, Reduced to Go (*Tristesse modèle réduit*) (1987), Sonatine (1984)

Pilote, Marie-Lise: Ideal Man, The (1996)

Pimparé, Claire: *Salut! J.W.* (1981), Yesterday (1981)

Pineo, Audley: Nashville Bound (1996)

Pinheiro, Christopher: Angel in a Cage (1998)

Pinnock, Arnold: Apartment Hunting (1999), Must Be Santa (1999)

Pinnock, Rob: In Her Defense (1998)

Pinoteau, Claude: Jigsaw (Angry Man, An) (*L'homme en colère*) (1979)

Pinsent, Gordon: And Miles to Go (1985), Blind Terror (2000), Blood Clan (1991), Case of Libel, A (1985), Don't Forget to Wipe the Blood Off (1966), Due South (1994), Escape from Iran: The Canadian Caper (Desert Blades) (1981),

Pinsent, Gordon continued
Far Cry From Home, A (1980), Heatwave Lasted Four Days, The (1973), Life and Times of Alonzo Boyd, The (1982), Hemingway vs Callaghan (2003), John and the Missus (1986), Klondike Fever (1979), Life and Times of Alonzo Boyd, The (1982), Lydia (1964), Nothing (2002), Once (1981), Only God Knows (1974), Pale Saints (1997), Ready for Slaughter (1983), Red River (*Rivière rouge*) (1996), Rowdyman, The (1972), Shipping News, The (2001), Silence of the North (1981), Termini Station (1990), Two Men (1988), Win, Again! (1998), Who Has Seen the Wind (1977) *The Life and Times of Gordon Pinsent* (2001) (60mins) Documentary about fifty years in the life and work of this highly accomplished actor, writer and filmmaker, whose witty, dramatic and astonishing range of achievement has brought him to the top of Canada's English-speaking community of the arts. By Cythnia Banks and Paul McGrath.

Pinsent, Leah: Bay Boy, The (1984), Emerald Tear, The (1988), *Frontière du crime* (1990), Little Kidnappers, The (1990), Win, Again! (1998)

Pintal, Lorraine: *Ange noir, L'* (The Black Angel) (Nelligan) (1991), Bilan (2003)

Pinter, Harold: Butley (1974), Handmaid's Tale, The (1990), Mansfield Park (1998)

Piper, Roddy: Jungleground (1995)

Piperni, Delphine: Clean Machine, The (1992)

Piquet, Robert: All About Women (1969)

Pires, Gerard S.: Steal (Riders) (2002)

Pirie, Mary: Fish Hawk (1979), Lyon's Den (1983)

Pisana, Jennifer: Perfect Pie (2002)

Pisier, Marie-France: Hot Touch (1982)

Pittman, Bruce: Captive Heart: The James Mink Story (1996), Confidential (1985), Kurt Vonnegut's Harrison Bergeron (2000), Mark of Cain, The (1984), No Alibi (2000), Prom Night II: Hello Mary Lou (1987), Silent Witness: What a Child Saw (1994), Where the Spirit Lives (1989)

Pittman, Ken: Finding Mary March (1989), Making Love in St. Pierre (2003), No Apologies (1990)

Pitts, Charles Kristian: Edge of Madness (*Station Sauvage*) (Wilderness Station) (2003), Lives of Girls and Women, The (1996)

Pitts, Charlott: Ladies Room (1999)

Pitts, Jonathan: Torso: The Evelyn Dick Story (2000)

Piugattuk, Annabella: Snow Walker, The (2002)

Pizano, Beatriz: City of Dark (1997)

Plant, Jean-Pierre: Night in America, A (*Une nuit en Amérique*) (1975), *Noël et Juliette* (1973)

Plante, André: Thetford in the Middle of Our Life (*Thetford au milieu de notre vie*) (1980)

Plante, Pierre: Angelo, Fredo and Roméo (1996)

Platt, Deborah: Spacehunters: Adventures in the Forbidden Zone (1983)

Plaxton, Gary: Footsteps in the Snow (*Des pas sur la neige*) (1966)

Playter, Wellington: Back to God's Country (1919)

Pleasence, Donald: Blood Relatives (*Les liens de sang*) (1978), Goldenrod (1976), Jigsaw (Angry Man, An) (*L'homme en colère*) (1979), Journey Into Fear (1975), Power Play (*Coup d'état*) (State of Shock) (Operation Overthrow) (1978), Rainbow Boys, The (1973), Uncanny, The (1977), Wedding in White (1972)

Pleszczyhski, Stefan: Bean Pole Man, The (1996)

Plitz, Adrianna: Ladies Room (1999)

Plotnick, Marcy: Great Big Thing, A (1968)

Plowright, Joan: Assistant, The (1996), Global Heresy(2002), Great Goose Caper, The (2003)

Plummer, Amanda: Hotel New Hampshire (1984), My Life Without Me (Mi Vida Sin Mi) (2003), Triggermen (2000), Under the Piano (1998), Whose Child Is This? The War for Baby Jessica (1993), You Can Thank Me Later (1998), Christopher Plummer: A Man for all Stages (2003) (58mins) By Ron Allen. Scriptwriters: Susan Stranks, Lois Siegel, Ron Allen, Hoda Elatawi. Narrator: Henry Ramer. An engaging documentary showing the stages, theatrical, cinematic, and personal, in this talented actor's extraordinary life in Montreal, Los Angeles, New York and London.

Plummer, Christopher: Agent of Influence (2002), All the Fine Lines (Full Disclosure) (1999), Amateur, The (1981), Ararat (2002), Arrow, The (1997), Blackheart (1997), Boy in Blue, The (1986), Counterstrike (1993), Dinosaur Hunter, The (2000), Disappearance, The (1977), First Circle, The (1991), Highpoint (1980), Impolite (1992), Kingsgate (1989), Kurt Vonnegut's Harrison Bergeron (2000), Liar's Edge (1992), Mind Field (1989), Murder by Decree (1979), Nuremberg (2000), Pyx, The (1973), Riel (1979), Shadow Dancing (1988), Silent Partner, The (1978), We the Jury (1996), Young Catherine (1990)

Podbrey, Maurice: Last Straw, The (1987)

Podemski, Jennifer: Dance Me Outside (1994), Diviners, The (1993)

Podeswa, Jeremy: After the Harvest (Wild Geese) (2000), Eclipse (1994), Five Senses, The (1999), Preludes (2000)

Pogue, Charles Edward: Fly, The (1986)

Pogue, Kenneth: Ambush at Iroquois Pass (1979), American Christmas Carol, An (1979), Climb,

The (1987), Due South (1994), Every Person Is Guilty (1979), Execution of Raymond Graham, The (1985), Ford: The Man and the Machine (1987), Gentle Sinners (1984), Grey Fox, The (1982), Harvest (1993), July Group, The (1981), Louisiana (1993), Murder by Phone (1982), Neptune Factor, The (The Neptune Disaster) (An Undersea Odyssey) (1973), Never Trust an Honest Thief (Going for Broke) (1979), Second Wind (1976), Silence of the North (1981), Silent Partner, The (1978), Suzanne (1980), Tar Sands, The (1977), What We Have Here Is a People Problem (1976)

Poindexter, Buster: Candy Mountain (1987)

Poire, Normand: Shift de nuit, Le (The Night Shift) (1979)

Poirier, Anne-Claire: Before the Time Comes (Le temps de l'avant) (1975), Quarantaine, La (Beyond Forty) (1982), J'me marie, J'me marie (1974), Salut, Victor! (1988), Scream for Silence, A (Mourir à tue-tête) (1979), Tu as crié (Let Me Go) (1997)

Poirier, Gérard: Beautiful Sundays (Les beaux dimanches) (1974), Bonjour, monsieur Gauguin (Good Day, Mr. Gauguin) (1989), Grand zélé, Le (The Great Zeal) (1993), Soleil des autres, Le (The Sun of the Others) (Give Us Our Daily Love) (1979)

Poirier, Jean-Marie: Lights of My City (1950)

Poirier, Kim: Decoys (2003)

Poirier, Michel: Big Day, The (Le grand day) (1988), Heart Exposed, The (Le coeur découvert) (1986)

Poissant, Isabelle: Fabrication d'un meurtrier, La (The Making of a Murderer) (1996)

Poirier, Pierre: Odyssée d'Alice Tremblay, L' (2002)

Poitevin, Jean-Marie: Where Two Roads Cross (Between Two Loves) (À la croisée des chemins) (Entre deux amours) (1943)

Poitras, Andrée: Little Aurore's Tragedy (La petite Aurore, l'enfant martyre) (1952)

Poitras, Diane: Part des choses, La (Un léger vertige) (A Part of Things) (A Light Vertigo) (1991)

Poitras, Henri: Story of Dr. Louise, The (Docteur Louise) (1949)Séraphin (1950), Tit-Coq (1953), Homme et son péché, Un (Séraphin) (A Man and His Sin) (1949), Whispering City (La forteresse) (1947)

Poitras, Lucie: Little Aurore's Tragedy (La petite Aurore, l'enfant martyre) (1952) There Once Was a War (Il était une guerre) (1958), Trouble Makers (Trouble-fête) (1964), Waiting for Caroline (1967), Whispering City (La forteresse) (1947)

Poitras, Marc: Passing Through the Pine Trees (M'en revenant par les épinettes) (1977)

Pojar, Bretislav: Flying Sneaker, The (1992)

Pokorna, Katka: Flying Sneaker, The (1992)

Poliquin, Odile: Caboose (1996)

Pollack, Janet: Life and Times of Chester-Angus Ramsgood, The (1971)

Pollard, Michael J.: Sunday in the Country (1975)

Polley, Sarah: Claim, The (2000), Event, The (2003), Exotica (1994), Hanging Garden, The (1997), Joe's So Mean to Josephine (1997), Last Night (1998), Law of Enclosures, The (2000), Life Before This, The (1999), Love Come Down (2000), Luck (2003), My Life Without Me (Mi vida sin mí) (2003), One Magic Christmas (1985), Planet of Junior Brown, The (1997), Sweet Hereafter, The (1996), Weight of Water, The (2000), White Lies (1998)

Pollitt, Deborah: Random Passage (2001), Washed Up (2002)

Polly, Diane: Never Trust an Honest Thief (Going for Broke) (1979)

Polly, Shannon: Hard to Forget (So Hard to Forget) (1998), Trudeau (2002)

Polo, Teri: Unsaid, The (2001)

Pomerantz, Earl: Cannibal Girls (1973), Merry Wives of Tobias Rouke, The (1972)

Pomerleau, Alice: Blue Winter (L'hiver bleu) (1980)

Ponti, Edoardo: Between Strangers (2002)

Ponton, Yvan: Boys III, Les (The Boys III) (2001), Boys, Les (The Boys) (1997), Fighting Men, The (1977), Scanners II: The New Order (1991)

Pool, Léa: Anne Trister (1986), Blue Butterfly, The (Papillon Bleu, Le) (2003), Corps perdu, À (Straight to the Heart) (1988), Demoiselle sauvage, La (The Wild Girl) (Wild Damsel) (1991), Desire in Motion (Mouvements du désire) (1994), Emporte-moi (Set Me Free) (1998), Lost and Delirious (2000), Montréal Sextet (1991), Strass Café (1980), Woman in Transit, A (La femme de l'hôtel) (1984)

Poole, Duane: Man in the Attic, The (1994)

Pooley, Olaf: Falcon's Gold (1982)

Poolman, Willem: Crimes of the Future (1970)

Pope, Carly: Various Positions (2002)

Portal, Louise: Amoureuses, Les (Women in Love) (1993), Angel Life (Vie d'ange) (1979), Barbarian Invasions, The (Invasions Barbares, Les) (2003), Beautiful Sundays (Les beaux dimanches) (1974), Cordélia (1980), Dangereux, Les (2003), Decline of the American Empire, The (Le declin de l'empire Américain) (1986), Deux pieds dans la même bottine, Les (Two Feet in the Same Ankle Boot)

et la nuit) (1989), Duplessis' Orphans (1999), Île de Sable, L' (1999), Peau et les os, La (Skin and Bones) (1988)

Presle, Micheline: Blood of Others, The (Le sang des autres) (1984)

Pressburger, Emeric: 49th Parallel (The Invaders) (1941)

Preston, Cyndy: Brain, The (1988), Darkside, The (1986), Pin (1988), Prom Night III: The Last Kiss (1989), Whale Music (1994)

Preston, David: Best Bad Thing, The (1997), Bonjour, Timothy (1995), Shadows of the Past (1991), Spacehunters: Adventures in the Forbidden Zone (1983), Twin Sisters (1993), Vindicator, The (Frankenstein '88) (1986)

Preuss, Ruben: Art of Murder, The (1999)

Prevost, Jean-Pierre: Petite fille particulière, Une (The Lottery Ticket) (1995)

Price, Allan: Piano Man's Daughter, The (2000)

Price, Phil: Hatley High (2003), Summer (2002)

Price, Vincent: Journey Into Fear (1975)

Priestley, Jason: Darkness Falling (2002), Eye of the Beholder (1999), Fancy Dancing (2002), Fourth Angel, The (2001), Highwayman, The (1999), Lion of Oz (2000), Love and Death on Long Island (1997)

Priestly, Justine: Cyberteens in Love (1994)

Prieto, Paco Christian: Street Law (Law of the Jungle) (1995)

Prince, Jonathan: Partners 'n Love (1992)

Principal, Victoria: Dancing in the Dark (1995)

Procak, Ihor: Autumn Born (1979)

Prochnow, Jurgen: Heart of America: Homeroom (2003), House of the Dead (2003), Last Stop, The (1999), Other Side of the Law (Outside the Law) (1994), Poison (Tease) (1999), Ripper: Letter from Hell (2001)

Procopio, Frank: Café Romeo (1992)

Procyk, Joseph: Red Deer (2000)

Prokhorova, Olga: Strange Horizons (1992)

Proslier, Jean-Marie: Oh, If Only My Monk Would Want (Ah! Si mon moine voulait) (1973)

Proteau, Rodrigue: Aline et Michel (Aline) (1992)

Proulx, Danielle: Amoureux fou (Madly in Love) (1991), Jardin d'Anna, Le (1994), Looking for Eternity (1989), Water Child (L'enfant d'eau) (1995)

Proulx, Denise: Hey Babe! (1984), OK Liberty (Ok...Laliberté) (1973), Red Eyes (Accidental Truths) (Les yeux rouges) (Les verités acciden-telles) (1983), Vultures, The (1975)

Proulx, Denyse: Lights of My City (1950)

Proulx, Georges: Vultures, The (Les vautours) (1975)

Proulx, Gilles: Confidences of the Night (L'amour blessé) (1975)

Proulx, Jacques: Cain (1965)

Proulx, Luc: Équinoxe (1986), Kingdom or the Asylum, The (1989), Oreille d'un sourd, L' (The Deaf Man's Ear) (1996), Temps d'une vie, Le (The Times of Our Life) (1998), Three Madeleines, The (Les fantômes des trois Madeleines) (1999), Trudeau (2002)

Proulx, Monique: Gaspard et fils (1988), Grand ser-pent du monde, Le (The Great World Serpent) (1999), Memories Unlocked (1999), Sex Among the Stars (Le sexe des étoiles) (1993), Streetheart (Le coeur au poing) (1998)

Proulx-Cloutier, Émile: Matusalem (1993), Matusalem II, le dernier des Beauchesne (1996)

Provencher, Anne-Marie: Bingo (1974), Dernières fougères, Les (The Last Ferns) (1991), East End Hustle (1976), Vultures, The (Les vautours) (1975), Years of Dreams and Revolt (Les années de rêves) (1984)

Provencher, Dylan: Wind at My Back (2001)

Provencher, Guy: Lac de la lune, Le (1994), Twelfth Hour, The (La douzième heure) (1966)

Provost, Denise: Clean Hands (Les mains nettes) (1958), Mains nettes, Les (1957), Misanthrope, Le (1966)

Provost, Guy: Deux pieds dans la même bottine, Les (Two Feet in the Same Ankle Boot) (The Clumsy Klutz) (1974), Évangéline the Second (Évangéline Deusse) (1985), Gapi (1982), Homme et son pêché, Un (Séraphin) (A Man and His Sin) (1949), Misanthrope, Le (1966), Orders, The (Les ordres) (1974)

Provost, Jacques: Ti-Ken (1965)

Prucnal, Anna: Sweet Movie (1974)

Pruner, Karl: Expecting (2002), Thick As Thieves (1990), Trudeau (2002)

Pryce, Craig: Revenge of the Radioactive Reporter (1992)

Pryce, Jonathan: Regeneration (1996)

Pryce-Jones, Ellis: Great Coups of History (1969)

Pryor, Allan: King Solomon's Treasure (1979)

Pryor, Hilary: Croon Maury and Mrs. B. (International Title) (2003)

Pugliano, Victor: Jeunes Québécoises, Les (1980)

Puley, Ken: My Script Doctor (1997)

Pullicino, Gerard: Babel (1999)

Pullman, William: Guilty, The (2000)

Purcell, Dominic: Invincible (2001)

Purcell, James: Another Woman (1994), Chinese Chocolate (1995), Counterstrike (1993), Fools Die Fast (1995)

Purdy, Jim: Concrete Angels (1987), Destiny to Order (1989)

Purefoy, James: Mansfield Park (1998), Great Goose Caper, The (2003)

Puri, Om: Burning Season, The (1993), My Little Devil (2000), Such a Long Journey (1998)

Purl, Linda: High Country, The (The First Hello) (1981), Visiting Hours (Fright) (1982)

Pursall, David: Tomorrow Never Comes (1978)

Purves-Smith, Esther: Primo Baby (1989)

Purvis, Alexandra: Marine Life (2000)

Purvis, Peter: Eternal Husband, The (1997)

Purvs, Inta: Kathy Karuks Is a Grizzly Bear (1976)

Pustil, Jeff: Siege (1983)

Putzulu, Bruno: *Père et Fils* (Father and Son) (2003)

Pyper-Ferguson, John: Hard Core Logo (1996), Home Movie (1992), Killer Image (1992), Legend of Kootenai Brown, The (1990), Waiting Game, The (1998)

Qin, Liao: Cry Woman (*Ku qi de nu ren*) (2002)

Qing, Wen: Cry Woman (*Ku qi de nu ren*) (2002)

Quade, John: Seasons in the Sun (1986)

Quaid, Randy: Apprenticeship of Duddy Kravitz, The (1974), Kart Racer (2002), Legends of the North (1996)

Qualles, Paris: Silent Witness: What a Child Saw (1994)

Quamaniq, David: Frostfire (1995)

Quantrill, Harper: Bob's Garage (2001)

Quarrington, Paul: Perfectly Normal (1990), Camilla (1994), Giant Steps (1992), Men With Brooms (2002), Whale Music (1994)

Quarshie, Hugh: To Walk with Lions (1999)

Quatermain, Philip: Reasonable Force (1983)

Quayle, Anthony: Murder by Decree (1979)

Quentin, John: King Solomon's Treasure (1979)

Quesnel, Dominique: Don Quichotte (2001)

Quester, Hughes: Anne Trister (1986)

Quigley, Charles: Convicted (1938)

Quigley, David: Thick As Thieves (1990)

Quigley, Gary: Roadkill (1989)

Quigley, Gerry: Spike of Love (1994)

Quinn, Aidan: Handmaid's Tale, The (1990), This Is My Father (1998)

Quinn, Daniel: Scanner Cop (1994), Scanners: The Showdown (Scanner Cop II: Volkin's Revenge) (1994)

Quinn, Elizabeth: Alexander Bell: The Sound and the Silence (1991)

Quinn, Kathy: French Without Dressing (1964)

Quinn, Paul: This Is My Father (1998)

Quinn, Tony: No Apologies (1990)

Quintal, Jeanne: Village Priest, The (*Le curé de village*) (1949)

Quirk, Jackson: Battle of St. Denis... Yesterday, Today, The (*St-Denis dans le temps*) (1969)

Qulitalika, Paul: Atanarjuat: The Fast Runner (*L'homme nu*) (2000)

Rabal, Francisco: Manuel: A Son by Choice (1990)

Rabman, Hanane: Clandestins (1997)

Raboy, David: Lies My Father Told Me (1975)

Racette, Francine: Alien Thunder (Dan Candy's Law) (1973), Big Rock, the Big Man, The (1969), Disappearance, The (1977)

Rachuk, Lesley: Proxyhawks (1970)

Racicot, Karen: Hold-Up (1985)

Racicot, Marcel: Enchanted Village, The (*Le village enchanté*) (1956)

Racicot, Réal: Enchanted Village, The (*Le village enchanté*) (1956)

Racine, Lionel: Passing Through the Pine Trees (*M'en revenant par les épinettes*) (1977)

Racine, René: In the Land of Zom (1983)

Racine, Roger: Butler's Night Off, The (1948), *Ribo ou 'le soleil sauvage'* (1978)

Rack, Tom: Blue Man, The (1985), Case of the Whitechapel Vampire, The (2001), Cursed (1990), Lola Zipper (1991)

Racz, Nicholas: Burial Society, The (2002)

Radcliffe, Rosemary: Anne of Green Gables (1985), Anne of Green Gables: The Continuing Story (Series) (1985-1999), Events Leading up to My Death, The (1991), Married Life: The Movie (2000)

Radclyffe, Curtis: Sweet Angel Mine (1996)

Radecki, Barbara: Expecting (2002)

Rader, Gary: Prologue (1970)

Radick, Jeremy: Angel Square (Angel Street) (1990)

Radzan, Soni: Such a Long Journey (1998)

Rae, Claude: Busted Up (1986), Dangerous Age, A (1958), Nobody Waved Goodbye (1964)

Rae, James: Echoes in Crimson (1987), Paperboy, The (1994)

Rafelson, Bob: House on Turk Street, The (2002)

Rafferty, Frances: Wings of Chance (Kirby's Gander) (1961)

Raffill, Stewart: Grizzly Falls (2000)

Raffin, Deborah: Scanners II: The New Order (1991)

Rai Berzins, Andrew: Cowboys and Indians (2003)

Railsback, Steve: Angela (1978)

Rain, Douglas: Love and Larceny (1985), Oedipus Rex (1956), One Plus One (The Kinsey Report) (Exploring the Kinsey Report) (1961)

Rainone, Frank: Brooklyn State of Mind, A (1997)

Rainville, Jacques: Encircled Colour, The (*La couleur encerclée*) (1986)

Rainville, Paul: Juiced (1999)

Rakoff, Alvin: City on Fire (1979), Death Ship (1980), Dirty Tricks (1980), Haunting Harmony, A (1993), King Solomon's Treasure (1979)

Ramaka, Joseph Gai: Karmen Gei (2001)

Ramanathan, S.: Love in Canada (1979)

Ramayya, Ray: Ryan's Babe (2000), Seetha and Carole (1997)

Rambo, Dack: Lilac Dream (1987)

Rameau, Patrick: Man on the Shore, The (1993)

Ramer, Henry: Another Smith for Paradise (1972), Apprenticeship of Duddy Kravitz, The (1974), Butler's Night Off, The (1948), Cop (Heller) (1981), Covergirl (1984), Forbidden Journey (1950), In Praise of Older Women (1978), It Seemed Like a Good Idea at the Time (1975), J.A. Martin, Photographer (1977), Lies My Father Told Me (1975), My Pleasure Is My Business (1975), Never Trust an Honest Thief (Going for Broke) (1979), Nobody Makes Me Cry (Between Friends) (1983), Pyx, The (1973), Réjeanne Padovani (1973), Reno and the Doc (1984), Screwball Academy (Divine Light) (Loose Ends) (1986), Starship Invasions (1977), Welcome to Blood City (1977), Why Rock the Boat? (1974)

Ramey, Kathryn: Panic Bodies (1998)

Ramirez, Bruno: Mr. Aiello (1998), Saracen, The (La Sarrasine) (1991)

Rampling, Charlotte: Fourth Angel, The (2001)

Ramsay, Bruce: Shot in the Face (2002)

Ramsay, Lynne: Morvern Callar (2002)

Randall, Mark: Touching Wild Horses (2002)

Randolph, Anders: Man from Glengarry, The (1920)

Rands, Sylvia: Bonjour, Timothy (1995)

Ranger, Benoît: Barbaloune (2002)

Ranger, Bernard: Gaia (1994)

Ranger, Christianne: Esprit du mal, L' (Spirit of Evil, The) (1954)

Rankin, Andrea: Grocer's Wife, The (1991)

Ransen, Mort: Bastards (2003), Bayo (1985), Christopher's Movie Matinée (1969), Emerald Tear, The (1988), Falling Over Backwards (1990), Margaret's Museum (1995), Masculine Mystique, The (1984), My Father's Angel (1999), Running Time (1978), Sincerely Violet (1987), Tangerine Taxi (1988), Touched (1999)

Raoul, Philippe: Wow (1970)

Rappaport, Michael: Triggermen (2000)

Rascheff, Julius: Lydia (1964)

Raskin, Laurence: Remembering Mel (1986)

Rasselet, Louise: Revolutionaries, The (Le révolutionnaire) (1965)

Ratchford, Jeremy: Change of Heart (1993), Fly Away Home (1996), Junior (1985), Peacekeepers (1997)

Ratib, Jamil: Échec et mat (Checkmate) (1994)

Ratner, Benjamin: 19 Months (2002), Crash (Breach of Trust) (1995), Dirty (1998), Last Wedding, The (2001), Looking for Leonard (2002), Question of Privilege, A (1998), Shot in the Face (2002), Zacharia Farted (1998)

Ratte, Sylvain: Dangereux, Les (2003)

Raven, Nicole: Deadend.com (2002)

Ravina, Dax: Love That Boy (2002)

Ravins-Janis, Mara: Morning in the Pine Forest (1998)

Rawi, Ousama: Housekeeper, The (Judgement in Stone) (1986)

Raxlen, Rick: Horses in Winter (Chevaux en hiver) (1988), Running Time (1978), Strange Blues of Cowboy Red, The (1995)

Raxlen, Susan: Strange Blues of Cowboy Red, The (1995)

Ray, Andrew: Passion and Paradise (1989)

Ray, Anthony: Cool Sound From Hell, A (The Young and the Beat) (1959)

Rae, Claude: To Kill the King (1974)

Ray, Lisa: Bollywood/Hollywood (2002)

Ray, Tim: Julia Has Two Lovers (1990)

Ray, Wallace: Critical Age, The (1923)

Raymond, Jacques: Deux super-dingues (1982)

Raymond, Katherine Lee: Nature of Nicholas, The (2002)

Raymond, Jennie: Pit Pony (1998)

Raymond, Marie-José: Apple, the Stem and the Seeds, The (La pomme, la queue et les pépins) (1974), Hot Dogs (Clean Up Squad, The) (1980), J'en suis (1997), Master Cats, The (1971), Seul ou avec d'autres (Alone or With Others) (1962), Two Women of Gold (Deux femmes en or) (1970)

Rea, Stephen: This Is My Father (1998)

Rea, Steven: Life Before This, The (1999)

Read, Peter: Freakshow (1988), Outcast (1991)

Rebar, Alex: Nowhere to Hide (1987)

Rebar, Kelly: Bordertown Café (1991), Lives of Girls and Women, The (1996)

Rebiere, Richard: Heavenly Bodies (1985)

Reckziegel, David: Myth of the Male Orgasm, The (1993)

Redbone, Leon: Candy Mountain (1987)

Reddick, Grant: Oedipus Rex (1956)

Reddy, Francis: Mario (1984), Vent de galerne (The Wind From Galerne) (1991), When I'm Gone You'll Still Be Alive (When I'll Be Gone) (Quand je serai parti vous vivrez encore) (1999)

Redford, Ryan: Three and a Half (2002)

Redgrave, Lynn: Deeply (2000), Lion of Oz (2000), Spider (2002), Strike! (1998), Touched (1999), Varian's War (2001), White Lies (1998)

Redgrave, Vanessa: Bear Island (1979), Young Catherine (1990)

Redmond, Liam: Luck of Ginger Coffey, The (1964)

Redmond, Sheila: Bingo Robbers, The (2000)

Rednikova, Yekaterina: Falling Through (2000)

Reed, Jerry: High-Ballin' (1978)

Reed, Oliver: Bite (Spasms) (1983), Brood, The (1979), Incredible Adventures of Marco Polo, The (1998), Tomorrow Never Comes (1978)

Reed, Tom: Back to God's Country (1953)

Reems, Harry: Hot Dogs (1980)

Rees, Jed: Day Drift (1999), Luck (2003), Men With Brooms (2002)

Reese, Lawrence: Hounds of Notre Dame, The (1981)

Reeve, Christopher: Switching Channels (1988)

Reeves, Christopher: Sea Wolf, The (1993)

Reeves, Keanu: Flying (1986), Johnny Mnemonic (1995)

Refn, Nicolas Winding: Fear X (2003)

Regan, Laura: My Little Eye (2002)

Regehr, Duncan: Haunting of Lisa, The (1995), Little White Lies (1988), Primo Baby (1989)

Reggiani, Serge: Fantastica (1980)

Regolo, Agnès: Foreign Body, A (Sinon, oui) (1997)

Regules, Sergio: Sex and the Lonely Woman (1966)

Rehum, Samir: Invitation (2000)

Rehwaldt, Frank: Deadbolt (1984)

Reid, David: Passion and Paradise (1989)

Reid, Douglas: Bitter Ash, The (1963)

Reid, Ernest: Sex and the Single Sailor (1967)

Reid, Fiona: Accident at Memorial Stadium, The (1983), Blood and Donuts (1995), Honourable Member, An (1982), Hot Dogs (Clean Up Squad, The) (1980), Matter of Choice, A (1978), Red Green's Duct Tape Forever (2002)

Reid, Howard: Low Self-Esteem Girl (2000)

Reid, Kate: Ada (1981), Atlantic City, U.S.A (1980), Best Damn Fiddler From Calabogie to Kaladar, The (1968), Blood of Others, The (Le sang des autres) (1984), Boy Next Door, The (1984), Bye Bye Blues (1989), Circle of Two (1980), Crossbar (1979), Dangerous Age, A (1958), Death Ship (1980), Double Negative (Deadly Companion) (1979), Execution of Raymond Graham, The (1985), Highpoint (1980), One Plus One (The Kinsey Report) (1961), Paper People, The (1967), Plague, The (1979), Rainbow Boys, The (1973), Shoot (1976)

Reidstra, Maria: Uncut (1997)

Reilly, Luke: Bye Bye Blues (1989)

Reineke, Gary: Agency (1980), Canada's Sweetheart: The Saga of Hal C. Banks (1985), Clown Murders, The (1976), Day My Grandad Died, The (1976), George's Island (1989), Greening of Ian Elliot, The (1991), Grey Fox, The (1982), If You Could See What I Hear (1982), Kidnapping of the President, The (1980), Matter of Choice, A (1978), Murder by Phone (1982), Murder Sees the Light (1987), Nothing Personal (1980), Power Play (Coup d'état) (State of Shock) (1978), Riel (1979), Rituals (The Creeper) (1977), Spider (2002), Sunday in the Country (1975), Surrogate (1984), Top of His Head, The (1989), Welcome to Blood City (1977), Why Shoot the Teacher (1977), Wild Horse Hank (1979)

Reiner, Jeffrey: Another Day (2001)

Reinhardt, Adèle: It's Your Turn, Laura Cadieux (1998), Laura Cadieux, la Suite (2000)

Reinhold, Judge: Baby on Board (1992)

Reis, Diana: Kurt Vonnegut's Harrison Bergeron (2000), Thrillkill (1984)

Reis, Vivian: Face Off (1971)

Reitman, Ivan: Cannibal Girls (1973), Foxy Lady (1971), Meatballs (1979) The Making of Ivan Reitman (2002) (45mins) Shows us how the former Czech refugee in Vamada managed to make his way to Hollywood and there worked his way into the big money by making popular comedies.

Reizes, Stephen: Eviction (Evixion) (1986)

Rekert, Winston: Agnes of God (1985), (The Black Cat in the Black Mouse Socks) (see Acts of Love) (1980), Blue Man, The (1985), Captive Heart: The James Mink Story (1996), Coming Out Alive (1980), Dead Wrong (1983), Heartaches (1981), Loving Evangeline (1998), Suzanne (1980), Toby McTeague (1986), Walls (1984), Wicked Minds (2002), Your Ticket Is no Longer Valid (Finishing Touch) (1982)

Rekhi, Kushal: Fire (1996)

Remar, James: Double Frame (1999)

Remick, Lee: Tribute (1980)

Rémy, Louise: Quarantaine, La (Beyond Forty) (1982)

Renaud, Andre: Wanted (Crime Spree) (1974)

Renaud, Bernadette: Renaud, Chantal: Finalemente (In the End) (1971), Initiation, The (1970)

Renaud, Gilles: Conquête, La (1973), Day in a Taxi, A (Une journée en taxi) (1982), Don't Forget (Je me souviens) (1979), Fantastica (1980), Far From You Sweetheart (Je suis loin de toi mignonne) (1976), Femme qui boit, La (The Woman Who Drinks) (2001), Handyman, The (L'homme à tout faire) (1980), Heart Exposed, The (Le coeur découvert) (1986), One Man (1977), Once Upon a Time in the East (Il était une fois dans l'est) (1974), O or the Invisible Infant (O ou l'invisible enfant) (1971), Sous les draps, les étoiles (Stargazing and Other Passions) (Stars Under the Sheets) (1989), Stone Woman, The (Femme de pierre) (1990)

Renaud, Isabelle: Présence des ombres, La (The Presence of Shadows) (1996)

Renaud: Wanted (Crime Spree) (2003)

Renault, Norma: Back to Beulah (1974)

Rendak, Mark: Impossible Elephant, The (2001)

Rendall, Mark: Interrogation of Michael Crowe, The (2002)

Renderer, Scott: South of Wawa (1991)

René, Jacinthe: Crème glacée, chocolat et autres consolations (Ice Cream, Chocolate and other Consolations) (2001)

Renfret, Louise: Nest of Shadows (1976)

Renier, Jérémie: Pornographe, Le (The Pornographer) (2001)

Renier, Yves: Other Side of the Law (Outside the Law) (1994)

Rennhofer, Linda: All in Good Taste (1983), Love on Your Birthday (see Acts of Love Series) (1980)

Rennie, Callum Keith: Curtis's Charm (1995), Double Happiness (1994), Flower & Garnet (2002), For Those Who Hunt the Wounded Down (1996), Hard Core Logo (1996), Last Night (1998), Men With Guns (1996), Paris or Somewhere (1995), Picture Claire (2001), Raffle, The (1994), Suspicious River (2000), Torso: The Evelyn Dick Story (2000)

Reno, Ginette: Dis-moi le si j'dérange (Tell Me if I Bother or Disturb You) (1989), Million Dollar Babies (1995)

Reno, Ginette: It's Your Turn, Laura Cadieux (1998), Laura Cadieux, la suite (2000), Léolo (1992)

Renton, David: Terra X (The Curse of Oak Island) (1997)

Renucci, Robin: Dames galantes (Romantic Ladies) (1990), Firing Squad (1990), Weep No More My Lady (1992)

Repo-Martell, Liisa: American Boyfriends (1989), Bastards (2003), Lives of Girls and Women, The (1996), Nights Below Station Street (1997), Washed Up (2002)

Resnick, Patricia: Jenifer Estess Story, The (2001)

Retaileau, Marc: Noroc (1999)

Retes, Gabriel: Coup at Daybreak, A (Coup d'état au petit matin) (1998)

Rettino, Jose: Orders, The (Les ordres) (1974)

Reuben, Gloria: Bad Faith (Cold Blooded) (1999), Pilgrim (Inferno) (1999), Salem Witch Trials (2001)

Reval, Judith: Lola Zipper (1991)

Revelin, Pierre: In the Belly of a Dragon (1989)

Revere, Roy: French Without Dressing (1964)

Revill, Clive: Galileo (1973), Sea Wolf, The (1993)

Rey, Edith: Breaking All the Rules (1985), Hey Babe! (1984), Vindicator, The (Frankenstein '88) (1986)

Rey-Duzil, Rose: Cain (1965), Dust from Underground (Poussière sur la ville) (1965), I Love You (Je t'aime) (1974), Possession of Virginia, The (Le diable est parmi nous) (1972), Where Two Roads Cross (Between Two Loves) (À la croisée des chemins) (Entre deux amours) (1943)

Reynolds, Burt: Frankenstein and Me (1995), Switching Channels (1988)

Reynolds, Jonathan: Switching Channels (1988)

Reynolds, Larry: Brethren (1976), Man Called Intrepid, A (1979), Question of the Sixth, A (1981), Silence of the North (1981), Welcome to Blood City (1977)

Reynolds, Michael: Fighting Men, The (1977), Final Edition (1982), Net Worth (1997), Plague, The (1979), Trial and Error (1993), Vicky (1973), Why Shoot the Teacher (1977)

Reynolds, Ryan: Fool Proof (2003), Ganesh (Ordinary Magic) (1993)

Reynolds, Simon: Defy Gravity (1990), Journey Into Darkness: The Bruce Curtis Story (1990), Lifeline to Victory (1993)

Reynolds, Stephen: Divine Ryans, The (1998)

Rhineheart, Susan: Silence of Adultery, The (1995)

Rhoades, Michael: Eddie and the Cruisers Part II: Eddie Lives! (1989), Lulu (1995)

Rhodes, Andrew: Sylvan Lake Summer (1991)

Rhodes, Donnelly: Goldenrod (1976), Guitarman (1994), Hard Part Begins, The (1973), Kathy Karuks Is a Grizzly Bear (1976), Legend of Kootenai Brown, The (1990), Neptune Factor, The (The Neptune Disaster) (An Undersea Odyssey) (1973), Showdown at Williams Creek (Kootenai Brown) (1991), Tom Stone: For the Money (2002), Urban Safari (1995)

Rhone, Trevor: Milk and Honey (1988)

Rhys-Davies, John: Best Revenge (Misdeal) (1981), Canvas, artiste et voleur (Canvas) (1993), Lost World, The (1992)

Ribeiro, Catherine: Ils sont nus (1966)

Riberolles, Jacques: Awakening, The (L'amour humain) (1970), Finalemente (In the End) (1971), Initiation, The (1970)

Ribisi, Marissa: Size of Watermelons, The (1996)

Ribowski, Nicholas: Trilogie Marsellaise, La (2001)

Ricard, Pierre: Morte amoureuse, La (1997)

Rich, Allan: Burial Society, The (2002)

Rich, Claude: La-haut (2002), Maria Chapdelaine (1983)

Richard, Claire: *Joyeux calvaire* (1997)

Richard, Michèle: *Explosion, L'* (The Hideout) (1971), *Postière, La* (The Postmistress) (1992)

Richards, Alyson: Secondary High (2003)

Richards, David Adams: Bay of Love and Sorrows, The (2002), For Those Who Hunt the Wounded Down (1996), Nights Below Station Street (1997), Tuesday, Wednesday (1987)

Richards, Dean: Foreign Nights (1990)

Richards, Denise: Tail Lights Fade (1999)

Richards, John: Obstruction of Justice (1995)

Richards, Kim: Meatballs, Part II (1984)

Richards, Paul: Sweet and the Bitter, The (1962)

Richards, Simon: Mutagen (1987), My Script Doctor (1997)

Richardson, Elizabeth: War Brides (1980)

Richardson, Ian: M. Butterfly (1993), Magician's House, The (1999)

Richardson, Jackie: Turning to Stone (1986)

Richardson, Janet: Searching for Diana (1992)

Richardson, Jody: Bingo Robbers, The (2000), Violet (2000)

Richardson, Miranda: Jacob Two Two Meets the Hooded Fang (1999), Spider (2002), Swann (1996)

Richardson, Natasha: Handmaid's Tale, The (1990), Haven (2001)

Richardson, Robina: Here I Will Nest (1941)

Richardson, Tony: Hotel New Hampshire (1984)

Riche, Edward: Secret Nation (1991)

Richer, Gilles: What the Hell Are They Complaining About?) (Hold on, Papa!) (*Tiens-toi bien après les oreilles à Papa*) (1971), Enuff is Enuff (*J'ai mon voyage!*) (1973), Woman Inflamed, A (1975)

Richer, Guy: Trudeau (2002)

Richer, Isabel: Countess of Baton Rouge, The (La Comtesse de Baton Rouge) (1997), Eldorado (1995), *Loi du cochon, La* (2001)

Richer, Louise: Cry in the Night, A (Le cri de la nuit) (1996), Jacques and November (1984), Unfaithful Mornings (1988)

Richie, Edward: Rare Birds (2001)

Richings, Julian: Claim, The (2000), Cube (1997), Hard Core Logo (1996), On Their Knees (2001), Two Thousand and None (2000)

Richler, Mordecai: Apprenticeship of Duddy Kravitz, The (1974), Joshua Then and Now (1985)

Richmond, Warner: Man from Glengarry, The (1920)

Richter, W.D.: Hard Feelings (1981)

Rickman, Alan: Mesmer (1994)

Rickman, Thomas: Bethune (1977)

Ricossa, Maria: Hostile Advances: The Kerry Ellison Story (1996)

Ridler, Vicki: George's Island (1989)

Ridley, Phil: Hounds of Notre Dame, The (1981)

Riegert, Peter: City Girl, The (1984)

Riel, Lyne: *Manuscrit érotique, Le* (2002)

Riemann, Katja: Desire (2000)

Rigert, Peter: Jerry and Tom (1998)

Riis, Sharon: Change of Heart (1984), Latitude 55 (1982), Loyalties (1985), Revenge of the Land (2000), Savage Messiah (2001)

Riley, Jill: True Confections (1991)

Riley, Michael: 100 Days in the Jungle (2002), Because Why (*Parce que Pourquoi*) (1993), Black Swan (2002), Butterbox Babies (1995), Chasing Rainbows (1988), Diplomatic Immunity (1991), Dogmatic (1996), Heart of the Sun (1998), Interrogation of Michael Crowe, The (2002), Lifeline to Victory (1993), Mile Zero (2001), Mustard Bath (1993), Pale Saints (1997), Perfectly Normal (1990), Punch (2002), Race for Freedom: The Underground Railroad (1993), To Catch a Killer (1991), Win, Again! (1998)

Rill, Eli: Point of No Return (1976), Slipstream (1973)

Rillie, Maisie: Adventures of Faustus Bidgood, The (1986), Extraordinary Visitor (1998), No Apologies (1990)

Rilwan, Joy Elias: Secret Laughter of Women, The (1999)

Rimmer, Shane: Dangerous Age, A (1958), Flaming Frontier (1958)

Rinfret, Louise: Woman of Colours, A (*La dame en couleurs*) (1985)

Ringham, Jon: Ivy League Killers (The Fast Ones) (1959)

Ringwald, Molly: Malicious (1995), Spacehunters: Adventures in the Forbidden Zone (1983)

Rintels, David W.: Nuremberg (2000), Execution of Raymond Graham, The (1985)

Riopelle, Jacques: Adventures of Ti-ken, The (1961)

Rioux, Geneviève: Cargo (1990), Cruising Bar (Meat Market) (1989), Decline of the American Empire, The (*Le declin de l'empire Américain*) (1986), Kingdom or the Asylum, The (1989), Magnificent Blue, The (1990), *Hiver de tourmente, Un* (A Winter of Torment) (1999)

Ripoll, Maria: Twice Upon a Yesterday (1998)

Risacher, Paul: Platinum (1997)

Risi, Dino: Dear Father (*Caro Papa*) (1979)

Ristic, Suzanne: Regeneration (1988)

Ristovski, Lazar: Boomerang (2002)

Ritschel, Derek: Men With Guns (1996)

Rittenhouse, Charles: Butler's Night Off, The (1948)

Ritzmann, Margit: Waiting for Michelangelo (1995)

Riva, Emmanuele: Final Blow, The (The Finishing

Stroke) (*Le coup de grâce*) (1965)

Rivard, Claude: Frost Bite (La gélure) (1968)

Rivard, Michel: Last Glacier, The (1984), Why Is the Strange Mr. Zolock So Interested in Comic Strips? (*Pourquoi l'étrange Monsieur Zolock s'intéressait-il tant à la bande dessinée*)

Rivard, Pierre: *15 février 1839* (February 15, 1839) (2001), October (Octobre) (1994), And I Love You Dearly (*La maîtresse*) (1973), *Dernier havre, Le* (1986), *Esprit du mal, L'* (Spirit of Evil, The) (1954), Night in America, A (*Une nuit en Amérique*) (1975), True Nature of Bernadette, The (*La vraie nature de Bernadette*) (1972)

Rivard, Robert: And I Love You Dearly (1973), *Dernier havre, Le* (1986), *Esprit du mal, L'* (Spirit of Evil, The) (1954), Night in America, A (*Une nuit en Amérique*) (1975), My Childhood in Montréal (1971), Nikki, Wild Dog of the North (Nomades Du Nord) (1961),True Nature of Bernadette, The (*La vraie nature de Bernadette*) (1972)

Rivard, Yvon: Blanche and the Night (*Blanche et la nuit*) (1989), Enfant sur le lac, L' (A Child on the Lake) (1993), Phantom Life, A (1992)

Rives, Nicolas-François: *Postière, La* (The Postmistress) (1992)

Rivière, Marc: Arthur Rimbaud: *L'homme aux semelles de vent* (1995)

Rizacos, Angelo: Hog Wild (*Les fous de la moto*) (1980)

Rizzardo, Mariliese: Nothing to Lose (1994)

Roa, Angela: Eva Guerrilla (1987)

Roach, Catherine: Company of Strangers, The (Strangers in Good Company) (1990)

Roach, Daryl: Watchers III (1994)

Roache, Linus: Shot Through the Heart (1998)

Robarts, Jason: Damaged Lives (1933)

Robb, Airlie: Little Canadian, The (1955)

Robb, David: Treasure Island (2001)

Robb, John: Prologue (1970)

Robb, Wallace Havelock: Little Canadian, The (1955)

Robbins, Paul: Matthew Shepard Story, The (2001)

Robbins, Ryan: Horsey (1997)

Robek, Kirsten: Avalanche Alley (2001), Middlemen (2000)

Robert, Francine: When Wolves Howl (*Quand hurlent les loups*) (1973)

Robert, Jacques: *Jeunes Québécoises, Les* (The Younger Generation) (1980)

Robert, Kevin: Little Canadian, The (1955)

Robert, Patrick: Barbaloune (2002)

Robert, Pierre: Rubber Gun, The (1977)

Roberts, Amanda: Ladies Room (1999)

Roberts, Art: Pleasure Palace (Angela) (1973)

Roberts, Colin: Flower & Garnet (2002)

Roberts, Cynthia: Bubbles Galore (1996), Jack of Hearts (1993), Last Supper, The (1994)

Roberts, Eliza: Dead End (False Pretense) (1998)

Roberts, Eric: Dead End (False Pretense) (1998)), Mindstorm (2001), No Alibi (2000), Stiletto Dance (2000), Wrong Number (2001)

Roberts, Fissy: Secret Laughter of Women, The (1999)

Roberts, Jake: Sparkle (1998), Willing Voyeur, The (1996)

Roberts, Ken: Honeymoon (*Lune de miel*) (1985), Junior (1985), Power Games (*Jeux de pouvoir*) (1990)

Roberts, Madge: New Shoes (1990)

Roberts, Margot: Carnival in Free Fall (*Carnaval en chute libre*) (1966)

Roberts, Rick: Love and Human Remains (Unidentified Human Remains and the True Nature of Love) (1994), Waiting for Michelangelo (1995)

Roberts, Sean: Prom, The (1991)

Roberts, Shawn: Sea People (1999)

Robertson, Alan: Visitor, The (1974)

Robertson, Cliff: Ford: The Man and the Machine (1987), Shoot (1976)

Robertson, David: Firebird 2015 AD (1980)

Robertson, Françoise: Fallen Knight (The Minion) (1998), Shabbat Shalom (1994), Tracker, The (1999), We All Fall Down (2000)

Robertson, George: Dawson Patrol, The (1985), Sunset Court (1988)

Robertson, George C.: Waiting for Caroline (1967)

Robertson, Gordon: Madeleine Is... (1971), Saturday's Passage (1969)

Robertson, Kathleen: Dog Park (1998), *Mémoire tronquée* (1990), Prom, The (1991), Torso: The Evelyn Dick Story (2000)

Robertson, William: Apartment Hunting (1999), Events Leading up to My Death, The (1991)

Robillard, Jean-Claude: Grand Bill, The (Le gros Bill) (1949)

Robins, Brenda: Low Visibility (1984), Shellgame (1986)

Robins, John: Death Ship (1980)

Robinson, Amilia: Haunting of Lisa, The (1995)

Robinson, Christopher: Suburban Legend (1995)

Robinson, Elizabeth: Savage Messiah (2001)

Robinson, John: Zero Patience (1993)

Robinson, Julia Anne: Fan's Notes, A (1972)

Robinson, Laura: Thrillkill (1984)

Robinson, Linette: One Heart Broken Into Song (1998)

Robinson, Madeleine: Story of Dr. Louise, The (1949), *Tisserands du pouvoir, Les* (1988)

Robitaille, Claudette: Straight to the Heart (1969)

Robitaille, Marc: *Petit vent de panique, Un* (A Gust of Panic) (2000), Winter Stories (1999)

Robitaille, Patrice: Québec-Montréal (2002)

Robitaille, Pierrette: It's Your Turn, Laura Cadieux (1998), *Laura Cadieux, la suite* (2000), *Odyssée d'Alice Tremblay, L'* (2002), Nuit de noces (Night of the Wedding) (2001)

Robitaille, Richard: Task Force (2000)

Robles, Paulina: Silent Love, A (2003)

Robson, Flora: Man Called Intrepid, A (1979)

Robson, Wayne: Another Smith for Paradise (1972), Bye Bye Blues (1989), Cube (1997), Diviners, The (1993), Grey Fox, The (1982), Justice Denied (1989), Madeleine Is... (1971), One Magic Christmas (1985), Red Green's Duct Tape Forever (2002), Wolfpen Principle (1974)

Roby, Daniel: *Peau Blanche, La* (White Skin) (2003)

Roc, Patricia: Unknown From Montréal, The (*Son copain*) (1950)

Roche, Luis Armando: *Passage des hommes libres* (Passage of Free Men) (1996)

Rochefort, Jean: *Amoureux fou* (1991)

Rocher, Miche: Until the Heart(1980)

Rochette, Geneviève: Gaia (1994), Night of the Flood (*La nuit du déluge*) (1996)

Rochfort, Spencer: Sylvan Lake Summer (1991)

Rochon, Martine: Because Why (*Parce que Pourquoi*) (1993)

Rockwell, Sam: Jerry and Tom (1998)

Rodat, Robert: Fly Away Home (1996)

Roderick, B.: Recruits (1987)

Rodrigue, Jean: Full Blast (*L'ennemi*) (1999), Traces (1978), Yellowknife (2002)

Rodriguez, Percy: Trouble Makers (1964)

Rodriguez, Ruddy: Coup at Daybreak, A (*Coup d'état au petit matin*) (1998)

Roe, Matt: Fallen Knight (The Minion) (1998)

Roel, Gabriela: *El jardin del Eden* (1994)

Roffman, Julian: Ballerina and the Blues, The (1987), Bloody Brood, The (1959), Champagne for Two (1987), Echoes in Crimson (1987), Garnet Princess, The (1987), Lilac Dream (1987), Mask, The (1961), Rose Cafe, The (1987), Sincerely Violet (1987)

Roger, Claire: Garnet Princess, The (1987)

Rogers, Adrian: Deadend.com (2002)

Rogers, Anthony: Tommy Tricker and the Stamp Traveller (*Les aventuriers du timbre perdu*) (1988)

Rogers, Arthur: This Is a Film (That Was a Film) (1989)

Rogers, Ivan: Slow Burn (1989)

Rogers, Kasey: Naked Flame, The (1964)

Rogers, Mimi: Ginger Snaps (2000), Killer (1994)

Rogers, Richard: Midwife's Tale, A: The Discovery of Martha Ballad (1996)

Rogers, Shirley: Lift, The (1965)

Rogers, Wayne: Hot Touch (*Coup de maître*) (1982), Passion and Paradise (1989)

Rogers, William: This Is a Film (That Was a Film) (1989)

Rogosian, Eric: Ararat (2002)

Rohl, Michael: Zacharia Farted (1998)

Roland, Ruth: From Nine to Nine (1936)

Rolland, Louis: *Père Chopin* (1945)

Rollin, Georges: Notre-Dame of the Mouise (*Notre-Dame de la Mouise*) (1941)

Rollin, Pascal: Court-Circuit (1983)

Rolston, Mark: Scanner Cop (1994)

Roman, Susan: Sanity Clause (1990)

Romano, Andy: Midnight Witness (1992)

Romo, Marcelo: *Los Naufragos* (1994)

Rompré, Evelyn: *Jeune fille à la fenêtre, Une* (2001)

Ronalds, Lolita: Watchers III (1994)

Rondeau, Pierre: Immortal Scoundrel, The (*Étienne Brûlé, gibier de potence*) (1952)

Ronfard, Jean-Pierre: Today or Never (Aujourd'hui ou jamais) (1998)

Roodt, Darrell: Second Skin (2000)

Rooney, Mickey: Find the Lady (1976), Odyssey of the Pacific (*L'Empereur du Pérou*) (1982)

Rosata, Toni: Haunting of Lisa, The (1995), Busted Up (1986), Shellgame (1986)

Rose, Chloé: Strange Blues of Cowboy Red, The (1995)

Rose, Clyde: Dying Hard (1978)

Rose, Gabrielle: Adjuster, The (1991), Family Viewing (1988), Five Senses, The (1999), Kanada (1993), Milgaard (1998), My Mother's Ghost (1996), Portrait, The (1992), Rhino Brothers, The (2002), Sleeproom, The (1998), Speaking Parts (1989), Valentine's Day (1994), Win, Again! (1998)

Rose, Hubert-Yves: Heat Line, The (*La ligne de chaleur*) (1987)

Rose, Jane: One Plus One (The Kinsey Report) (Exploring the Kinsey Report) (1961)

Rose, Les: Covert Action (1986), Gas (1981), Hog Wild (*Les fous de la moto*) (1980), Isaac Littlefeathers (1984), Life and Times of Alonzo Boyd, The (1982), Maintain the Right (1982), Paperback Hero (1973), Title Shot (1980), Three-Card Monte (1978)

Rose, Pierre: *Deux pieds dans la même bottine, Les* (The Clumsy Klutz) (1974)

Rose, Richard: Giant Steps (1992)

Rose, Sebastien: *Comment ma mere accoucha de moi durant sa ménopause* (How My Mother Was Giving Birth to Me During Menopause) (2001)

Rose, Sheile: When I Will Be Gone (*L'âge de braise*) (1998)

Rose, Vanya: Two Thousand and None (2000)

Rose-Davis, Ben: Pit Pony (1998)

Rosen, Abigail: Do You Want to Sleep With God? (*Voulez-vous coucher avec Dieu?*) (1972)

Rosen, Elisabeth: Babyface (1998), Heart of America: Homeroom (2003), My Mother's Ghost (1996)

Rosen, Jason: Do You Want to Sleep With God? (*Voulez-vous coucher avec Dieu?*) (1972)

Rosen, Mark: Final Assignment (1980)

Rosen, Phil: Sins of the Fathers (1948)

Rosenbaun, Jeffrey: In Her Defense (1998)

Rosenberg, Alan: Happy Birthday Gemini (1980)

Rosenberg, Philip: We the Jury (1996)

Rosenberg, Stephen: Jacob Two-Two Meets the Hooded Fang (1977)

Rosenburg, Ellen: Only Thing You Know, The (1971)

Rosenfeld, Robyn: Ride Me (Ego Trip) (1995)

Rosenthal, Jack: Lucky Star, The (1980)

Rosenthal, Rick: Distant Thunder (1988)

Rosling, Tara: Uncles, The (2000)

Ross, Brian: First Season, The (1988), On Hostile Ground (2000)

Ross, Tracee Ellis: Sue Lost in Manhattan (1997)

Ross, Jennifer: Dying Fall (2002)

Ross, Merrie Lynn: Class of 1984 (1982)

Ross, Neil: Sanity Clause (1990)

Rossellini, Isabella: *Dames galantes* (Romantic Ladies) (1990)

Rossi, Vittorio: *Canvas, artiste et voleur* (Canvas) (1993), Sphinx, The (1995), Suspicious Minds (1996)

Rossignol,Michèle: Angela (1978), *Au fil de l'eau* (By the Riverside) (2002), *Quarantaine, La* (Beyond Forty)(1982), *Conquête, La* (1973), Dust from Underground (*Poussière sur la ville*) (1965),Laure Gaudreault: A Remarkable Woman (*Rencontre avec une femme remarquable: Laure Gaudreault*) (1983), Once Upon a Time in the East (*Il était une fois dans l'est*) (1974), Suzanne (1980)

Rossini, Bianca: Ride Me (Ego Trip) (1995)

Rossini, Katherine: Ryan's Babe (2000)

Roston, John: Rainy Day Woman (1970)

Rota, Carlo: City of Dark (1997), Clutch (1998)

Roth, Andrea: Change of Place, A (1994), Psychic (1991)

Roth, Bobby: Crossed Over (2001)

Roth, Ivan E.: Lana in Love (1991)

Rothberg, David: Best Revenge (Misdeal) (1981)

Rothberg, Jeff: Whole Shebang, The (2001)

Rothery, Teryl: Mr. Rice's Secret (2000), Urban Safari (1995)

Rothhaar, Will: Kart Racer (2002)

Rothpan, Mitchell David: Babel (1999)

Rothwell, Amber: Red Deer (2000)

Rothwell, Gloria: Master of Images, The (1972)

Rotundo, Nick: G-2 (1998), Gladiator Cop (1994)

Roubanis, Theodorous: Sex and the Single Sailor (1967)

Rouch, Jean: Flower of Youth (That Tender Age, The Adolescents) (*La fleur de l'âge*) (*Les adolescentes*) (1967)

Roudier, Gilbert: Ordinary People (*Ti-peuple*) (1971)

Roudier, Joanne: Ordinary People (*Ti-peuple*) (1971)

Rouffio, Jacques: *Ou le roman de Charles Pathé* (The Life of Charles Pathé) (1995)

Rouleau, Joseph: In the Land of Zom (1983)

Rouleau, Mario: Don Quichotte (2001)

Rouleau, Yolaine: *Futur intérieur, Le* (1982)

Roulet, Dominique: Sweet Killing (1993)

Rourke, Mickey: Picture Claire (2001)

Rousseau, Chantal: Trouble Makers (*Trouble-fête*) (1964)

Rousseau, Pierre: Jacques and November (1984)

Rousseau, Stéphane: Barbarian Invasions, The (*Invasions Barbares, Les*) (2003), *Dangereux, Les* (2003)

Rousseau, Sylvie: *Shift de nuit, Le* (The Night Shift) (1979)

Roussel, Daniel: And When the CWAC's Go Marching On (*Du poil aux pattes*) (1985), *Dernières fougères, Les* (The Last Ferns) (1991), *Dis-moi le si j'dérange* (Tell Me if I Bother or Disturb You) (1989)

Rousset, Anne: *Des chiens dans la neige* (Dogs in the Snow) (2001)

Routhier, Lucie: And When the CWAC's Go Marching On (*Du poil aux pattes*) (1985)

Roux, Jean-Louis: Beauty of Women, The (*La beauté des femmes*) (1994), Chocolate Eclair (*Éclair au chocolat*) (1979), *Cordélia* (1980), Courage to Love, The (Quadroon Ball) (1999), Odyssey of the Pacific (*L'Empereur du Pérou*) (1982), Pyx, The (1973), Riel (1979), *Salut, Victor!* (1988), Story of Dr. Louise, The (1949)

Roux, Jean-Michel: Thousand Wonders of the Universe, The (1997)

Rowan, Gay: Sudden Fury (1975), U-Turn (The Girl in Blue) (1973)

Rowan, Gerald: Sins of the Fathers (1948), Forbidden Journey (1950)

Rowan, Kelly: Adrift (1993), Jet Boy (2001), Long Road Home, The (1988), Loving Evangeline (1998)

Rowe, Misty: Meatballs, Part II (1984)

Rowe, Peter: Best Bad Thing, The (1997), Final Edition (1982), Lost! (1986), Neon Palace, The: A '50s and '60s Trip (1971), Personal Exemptions (1988), Reasonable Force (1983), Takeover (1981), Tar Sands, The (1977), Treasure Island (2001)

Rowlands, Gena: Incredible Mrs Ritchie, The (2003)

Rowsome, Andrew: Recorded Live (1982)

Roy, Danielle: Song for Julie, A (*Chanson pour Julie*) (1976)

Roy, Fernand: *Retour de l'Immaculée Conception, Le* (1970)

Roy, Gildor: *Autre homme, Un* (Another Man) (1991), Caboose (1996), *Comme un voleur* (Like a Thief) (1991), Florida, La (1993), Karmina (1998), *Karmina 2: L'enfer de Chabot* (K2 2001) (2001), *Mystérieuse Mademoiselle C, La* (2001), Requiem for a Handsome Bastard (*Requiem pour un beau sans-coeur*) (1992)

Roy, Linda: Angel in a Cage (The Woman in the Cage) (*La bête de fiore*) (1993)

Roy, Lise: Bean Pole Man, The (*Homme perché*) (1996), *Comme un voleur* (Like a Thief) (1991), Village Priest, The (*Le curé de village*) (1949)

Roy, Lise: *Peau Blanche, La* (White Skin) (2003)

Roy, Louise: Childhood Friend, A (*Une amie d'enfance*) (1978), Eleventh Special, The (*Onzième spéciale*) (1988)

Roy, Marcel: Québec Operation Lambda (1985)

Roy, Maxim: Blind Terror (2000), Woman Hunted, A (2003)

Roy, Richard: Caboose (1996), *Café Olé* (2000), Last Chapter (Biker Wars) (2002), Moody Beach (1990)

Roy, Yolande: Gone to Glory (Partis pour la gloire) (1975)

Roy, Yvan: *Morte amoureuse, La* (1997), Nightmare, The (*Cauchemar*) (1979), Gaia (1994)

Royal, Allan: Blind Faith (1982), Chatwill's Verdict (Killer Instinct) (Baker County, U.S.A) (Trapped) (1982), Fighting Men, The (1977), Fish Hawk (1979), Man Inside, The (1975), Moving Targets (1983), Only Thing You Know, The (1971), Takeover (1981), Title Shot (1980), Welcome to Blood City (1977)

Royce, Lee: *Solitaire* (1991)

Royer, Raymond: *Lac de la lune, Le* (1994)

Rozema, Patricia: Happy Days (Beckett on Film series) (2000), I've Heard the Mermaids Singing (1987), Mansfield Park (1998), Montréal Sextet (1991), Preludes (2000), Symposium (1996),

When Night Is Falling (1995), White Room (1989)

Rozet, François: Notre-Dame of the Mouise (*Notre-Dame de la Mouise*) (1941), *Père Chopin* (1945)

Rozon, Madeleine: Don't Let the Angels Fall (1969)

Rubbo, Michael: Peanut Butter Solution, The (*Opération beurre de pinottes*) (1985), Return of Tommy Tricker, The (*Le retour des aventuriers du timbre perdu*) (1994), Tommy Tricker and the Stamp Traveller (*Les aventuriers du timbre perdu*) (1988), Vincent and Me (1990)

Rubenfeld, Michael: Summer (2002)

Rubens, Mary Beth: Firebird 2015 AD (1980), Michelle Apartments, The (1995), Perfect Timing (1984)

Rubes, Jan: Amateur, The (1981), Amityville Curse, The (1990), Anthrax (2001), Believe (2000), Boozecan (1995), Burial Society, The (2002), Catsplay (1977), Charlie Grant's War (1985), Coming of Age (1983), Day My Grandad Died, The (1976), Deadly Harvest (1980), Forbidden Journey (1950), Garden, The (1991), Harvest (1981), Kiss, The (1988), Lions for Breakfast (1975), Marriage Bed, The (1986), Mesmer (1994), Mr. Patman (1981), Never Too Late (1996), On My Own (1992), One Magic Christmas (1985), Outside Chance of Maximillian Glick, The (1988), Sarabande (1997), Something About Love (1988), Two Men (1988), Utilities (1981), Your Ticket Is no Longer Valid (Finishing Touch) (1982)

Rubin, Jennifer: Drop Dead Gorgeous (Victim of Beauty) (1991), Screamers (1995)

Rubinek, Saul: Agency (1980), Bookfair Murders, The (1999), By Design (1981), Death Ship (1980), Death Wish V: The Face of Death (1994), Falling Over Backwards (1990), Highpoint (1980), Hitting Home (Obsessed) (1989), Jerry and Tom (1998), Lakeboat (2000), Love on the Nose (1978), Memory Run (1995), Murder Sees the Light (1987), Outside Chance of Maximillian Glick, The (1988), Pale Saints (1997), Quarrel, The (1990), Seer Was Here (1978), Suicide Murders, The (1986), Taking Care (Prescription for Murder) (1987), Terry Fox Story, The (1983), Ticket to Heaven (1981), Triggermen (2000)

Rudd, Paul: Size of Watermelons, The (1996)

Ruddell, Juno: War Between Us, The (1995)

Rudder, Michael: Blindside (1986), Perfect Timing (1984)

Ruehl, Mercedes: Guilt By Association (2002)

Ruel, Francine: Ideal Man, The (*L'homme idéal*) (1996)

Ruel, Marc: Power Games (*Jeux de pouvoir*) (1990), With Friends Like These (*Avec des amis*) (1990)

Ruffalo, Mark: My Life Without Me (Mi Vida Sin Mi) (2003)

Ruffman, Mag: Happy Christmas, Miss King (1999)

Ruffolo, Pasquale: Dangerous Dreams (1986)

Ruggiero, Alfonse: Stiletto Dance (2000)

Rugoff, Edward: Double Take (1998)

Rugoff, Ralph: Double Take (1998)

Ruhi, Michel: Ménace, La (1977)

Rulli, Stefano: Almost America (Come l'America) (2001)

Runte, Kurt Max: Day Drift (1999)

Runyan, Tygh: Bastards (2003), Come Together (2001), Kitchen Party (1997), My Father's Angel (West of Sarajevo) (1999), Touched (1999), Various Positions (2002), Watchtower, The (2001)

Ruptash, Troy: Leaving Metropolis (2002)

Ruscio, Al: Naked Flame, The (1964)

Rush, Jordan: Never Talk to Strangers (1995)

Rushabh: My Little Devil (2000)

Rusich, Stellina: Guardian, The (1999)

Russell, Christy: Highway of Heartaches (1994)

Russell, Clive: Margaret's Museum (1995)

Russell, Craig: Outrageous! (1977), Too Outrageous (1987)

Russell, Franz: Paperback Hero (1973), Sunday in the Country (1975)

Russell, Keri: Mad About Mambo (2000)

Russell, Scott: Jailbait! (2000)

Russell, Theresa: Now and Forever (2001)

Russo, Rafa: Twice Upon a Yesterday (1998)

Rutherford, Camille: Stardom (Fandom) (2000)

Rutherford, John: Great Shadow, The (1920), Picture Claire (2001)

Rutten, Joseph: Real Howard Spitz, The (1998)

Rutter, John: Three-Card Monte (1978)

Ruvinsky, Morrie: Going to Kansas City (1998), Improper Channels (1981), Plastic Mile, The (1969)

Ruvinsky, Morris: Woman Hunted, A (2003)

Ryan, Helen: Lift, The (1965)

Ryan, Kate: Things to Do on a Saturday Night (1998)

Ryan, Kris: Morning! (1992)

Ryan, Robert: Canadians, The (1961), Wings in the Wilderness (Les voyageurs d'été) (1975)

Ryan, Terry: Going Home (1987)

Ryane, Dusty: Highway of Heartaches (1994)

Ryder, Lisa: Blackheart (1997), City of Dark (1997), Stolen Heart (1998)

Ryder, Robert: Kanadiana (2000)

Ryerson, Robert: Spanish Fly (1975)

Ryre, Janieta: Panic Bodies (1998)

Ryshpan, Howard: Apprentice, The (*Fleur bleue*) (1971), Lies My Father Told Me (1975)

Saab, Jamedar Sabu: Hathi (1998)

Saab, Jocelyn: *Adolescente sucré d'amour, L'* (1985)

Saadallah, Aziz: *Casablancais, Les* (The Casablancans) (1998)

Saal, Michka: Snail's Point of View, A (*La position de l'escargot*) (1998)

Sabas, Christelle: Clandestins (1997)

Sabato Jr., Antonio: Mindstorm (2001)

Sabba, Evan: Lucky Girl (2000)

Sabiston, Andrew: Ups and Downs (1983)

Sabourin, Gabriel: *Incompris, L'* (1997)

Sabourin, Jean-Guy: Mission of Fear (1965)

Sabourin, Jeanne: Family Viewing (1988)

Sabourin, Marcel: Bean Pole Man, The (*Homme perché*) (1996), Bernie and the Gang (*Ti-mine Bernie pis la gang*) (1977), Castle of Cards, The (*Le château de cartes*) (1980), Christmas Martian, The (*Le martien de Noël*) (1971), *Cordélia* (1980), Death of a Lumberjack (*La mort d'un bucheron*) (1973), Don't Let It Kill You (*Il ne faut pas mourir pour ça*) (1968), Eliza's Horoscope (1975), *Équinoxe* (1986), *Fabuleux voyage de l'ange, Le* (The Fabulous Voyage of the Angel) (1991), *Fille du Maquignon, La* (The Girl of Maquignon) (1990), Gina (1975), Handyman, The (*L'homme à tout faire*) (1980), House of Light, The (*La chambre blanche*) (1969), J.A. Martin, Photographer (1977), Last Betrothal, The (1973), Mario (1984), Memories Unlocked (1999), *Meurtre en musique* (1994), Million Dollar Babies (1995), Mission of Fear (1965), Mustang (1975), *Ne dis rien* (Don't Say Anything) (2001), Night with Hortense, The (*La nuit avec Hortense*) (1987), Oh, If Only My Monk Would Want (*Ah! Si mon moine voulait*) (1973), Old Country Where Rimbaud Died, The (*Le vieux pays où Rimbaud est mort*) (1977), Oreille d'un sourd, L' (The Deaf Man's Ear) (1996), *Revoir Julie* (See Julie Again) (Julie and Me) (1998), Riel (1979), *Salut! J.W.* (1981), S Day (*Le jour S*) (1984), *Sous les draps, les étoiles* (Stargazing and Other Passions) (Stars Under the Sheets) (1989), Sweet Lies and Tender Oaths (*Les doux aveux*) (1982), Taureau (1972), That Darned Loot (*La maudite galette*) (1972), Those Damned Savages (*Les maudits sauvages*) (1971), Time of the Hunt, The (*Le temps d'une chasse*) (1972), Today or

Sabourin, Marcel continued:
Never (*Aujourd'hui ou jamais*) (1998), Trial at Fortitude Bay (1994), Two Wise Men, The (*Les smattes*) (1972), Two Women of Gold (*Deux femmes en or*) (1970), We Are Far From the Sun (*On est loin du soleil*) (1971)

Sachs, Shelly: Plastic Mile, The (1969)

Sachs, Susan: Summerlust (Goodbye Neighbours and Wives) (1973)

Sadikh, Aoubacar: *Madame Brouette* (2002)

Sadiq, Laara: Live Bait (1995)

Sadler, Laura: Intimate Relations (1995)

Sadler, Richard: Coyote (1993), How to Make Love to a Negro Without Getting Tired (1989)

Safa, Mireilla: *Autour de la maison rose* (1999)

Safdie, Oren: You Can Thank Me Later (1998)

Sagal, Boris: Angela (1978)

Sagay, O.O.: Secret Laughter of Women, The (1999)

Sage, Willard: Butler's Night Off, The (1948)

Sagrav, Rosario: *El jardin del Eden* (The Garden of Eden) (1994)

Sahay, Vik: Ride, The (2000)

Sahr, Sara: Eternal Husband, The (1997)

Saia, Louis: *Boys, Les* (The Boys) (1997), *Boys II, Les* (The Boys II) (1998), Boys III, Les (The Boys III) (2001), Childhood Friend, A (*Une amie d'enfance*) (1978), *Dangereux, Les* (2003), Sphinx, The (1995)

Saint-Amant, Marcella: Power Play (*Coup d'état*) (State of Shock) (Operation Overthrow) (1978)

Saint-Amant, Mario: *Même sang, Un* (The Same Blood) (1994)

Saint-Denis, Stéphane: *Dangereux, Les* (2003)

Saint-Pierre, Nathalie: *Silence nous guette, Le* (2002)

Sakovich, Nancy Anne: Golden Will: The Silken Laumann Story (1997)

Salazar, Suzanna: Silent Love, A (2003)

Salenger, Meredith: Kiss, The (1988)

Sales, Sammy: Bloody Brood, The (1959)

Sali, Richard: Rubber Carpet (1995)

Salimbeni, Reto: Urban Safari (1995)

Salin, Kari: Red Blooded 2 (1996), Vivid (1996)

Salinas, Carmen: Silent Love, A (2003)

Sallows, Roy: Strange and Rich (1994)

Salmerone, Gustavo: Twice Upon a Yesterday (1998)

Salt, Jennifer: Stalking of Laurie Show, The (2000)

Salt, Jim: *Vida, La* (The Document of Michael da Vida) (1965)

Salter, James: Threshold (1981)

Salutin, Rick: Maria (1977)

Salvatore, Diana: Killing Moon (1998)

Salvatore, René: My Uncle Antoine (1971)

Salverson, George: Marie-Anne (1978)

Salvin, Pedro: Waiting Game, The (1998)

Salvy, Jean: Chocolate Eclair (*Éclair au chocolat*) (1979), Panic (Pa*nique*) (1977), Stone Woman, The (*Femme de pierre*) (1990)

Salvy, Sarah-Jeanne: *Ababouinée* (1994), Tinamer (1987), Wind From Wyoming, A (*Le vent du Wyoming*) (1994)

Salwen, Hal: Probable Cause (Sleepless) (1994)

Salzman, Bert: Just Jessie (1981)

Salzman, Glen: Milk and Honey (1988)

Samms, Emma: Treacherous Beauties (1994)

Samples, William: Powder Heads (1980)

Sampson, Will: Fish Hawk (1979)

Samuda, Jackie: Mutagen (1987)

Samuels, Arthur: Black Mirror (1981)

Samuels, Maxine: Affair with a Killer (1967)

San Giacomo, Laura: Jenifer Estess Story, The (2001)

Sanche, Guy: Dust from Underground (*Poussière sur la ville*) (1965)

Sanchez, Elizabeth: Avalanche Alley (2001)

Sanchez, Kiele: Class Warfare 2001 (2000)

Sanchez, Victoria: Perpetrators of the Crime (1999), Saint Jude (2000), Welcome to the Freakshow (2001), Wolf Girl (2001)

Sand, Anne: I Have the Right to Pleasure (1975)

Sand, Paul: Great Big Thing, A (1968)

Sander, Anna: Family of Strangers (1993)

Sanders, Alvin: What's Your Verdict? (1995)

Sanders, Harry: Another Smith for Paradise (1972)

Sanders, Jay: Salem Witch Trials (2001)

Sanders, Jon: Painted Angels (1998)

Sanders, Kenny: Misery Harbour (1999)

Sanders, Norma-Jean: Memoirs (1984)

Sanderson, Derek: Face Off (1971)

Sanderson, James: Head On (1980)

Sandler, Robert: Cannibal Girls (1973), Foxy Lady (1971)

Sandler, Susan: Friends at Last (1995)

Sandomirsky, Kerry: Home Movie (1992)

Sandor, Anna: Charlie Grant's War (1985), High Card (1982), Mama's Going to Buy You a Mockingbird (1987), Marriage Bed, The (1986), Martha, Ruth and Edie (1987), Population of One, A (1980), Running Man (1980), Two Men (1988)

Sands, Julian: Naked Lunch (1992)

Sanford, Garwin: Max (1994), Mr. Rice's Secret (2000), Perfect Man, The (1993), Quarantine (1989)

Sangster, Jimmy: Phobia (1980)

Sanguedolce, Steve: Panic Bodies (1998)

Santa Maria, Marcella: Train of Dreams (1987)

Santamaria, Erick: Playgirl Killer (Decoy for Terror) (1965)

Sandheim, Kurtis: Agent of Influence (2002)

Santi, Jacques: Flag (1987)

Santini, Pierre: *Dernier cri* (The Last Cry) (1996)

Santoni, Reni: Great Big Thing, A (1968)

Sanvido, Guy: Merry Wives of Tobias Rouke, The (1972)

Sapieha, Michael: Marguerite Volant (1996), Random Passage (2001)

Sapritch, Alice: *Lit, Le* (1974)

Sara, Mia: Bullet to Beijing (Len Deighton's Bullet to Beijing) (1995), Impossible Elephant, The (2001)

Saraiva, Luiz: Manuel: A Son by Choice (1990)

Sarakola, Patrushka: Year of the Sheep (1997)

Sarandon, Chris: Louisa May Alcott's Little Men (1998), Whispers (1990)

Sarandon, Susan: Apprentice, The (*Fleur bleue*) (1971), Atlantic City, U.S.A (1980)

Sardana, Sushma: Reasonable Force (1983)

Sargent, Joseph: Salem Witch Trials (2001)

Sargent, Richard: Tanya's Island (1980)

Sarin, Vic: Bye Bye Blues (1989), Cold Comfort (1989), Family Reunion (1987), Hard to Forget (So Hard to Forget) (1998), Island Love Song (1987), Other Kingdom, The (1985), Passengers (1981), Sea People (1999), Trial at Fortitude Bay (1994), Waiting Game, The (1998), You've Come a Long Way, Katie (1981)

Sarner, Arlene: Julie Walking Home (2002)

Sarrasin, Donna: Witchboard III: The Possession (1995)

Sarrazin, Jean-Alexandre: *André Mathieu, Musicien* (1994)

Sarrazin, Marisol: Before the Time Comes (*Le temps de l'avant*) (1975)

Sarrazin, Michael: Bullet to Beijing (Len Deighton's Bullet to Beijing) (1995), Double Negative (Deadly Companion) (1979), Keeping Track (Double Impasse) (1987), Joshua Then and Now (1985), Malarek: A Street Kid Who Made It (1988), Midnight Man (1995), Passion and Paradise (1989), Peacekeeper, The (1997), Phone Call, The (*Ligne interdite*) (1989), Secret of Nandy, The (1991)

Sartor, Max: Perpetrators of the Crime (1999)

Sarvil, René: Notre-Dame of the Mouise (*Notre-Dame de la Mouise*) (1941)

Sasdy, Peter: Welcome to Blood City (1977)

Sasseville, Christian: It's a Wonderful Love (*C'est bien beau l'amour*)(1971)

Sassy, Jean-Paul: House of Lovers (*La maison des amants*) (1972)

Sastre, Ines: *Vercingétorix* (2001)

Sastri, Lina: Brown Bread Sandwiches (1990)

Sather, Joe: Stuff (1999)

Sauer, Richard: Crunch (1981)

Saulnier, Jean-Pierre: Jos Carbone (1975), Pigs Are Seldom Clean (*On n'engraisse pas les cochons à l'eau claire*) (1973), Réjeanne Padovani (1973), That Darned Loot (*La maudite galette*) (1972), Vultures, The (*Les vautours*) (1975), When Wolves Howl (Quand hurlent les loups) (1973), Yellow Island, The (*L'île jaune*) (1975)

Saumier, Jeff: Kid, The (1997)

Saunders, George: Malicious (1995), Scanner Cop (1994)

Saunders, Karen: Defy Gravity (1990)

Saunders, Jennifer: Magician's House, The (1999)

Saunders, Rod: Nashville Bound (1996)

Saunders, Shannon: Lunch with Charles (2001)

Sauriol, Brigitte: Absence, The (L'absence) (1976), Just a Game (1983), *Laura Laur* (1988)

Saury, Alain: I Have the Right to Pleasure (*J'ai droit au plaisir*) (1975), *Ils sont nus* (1966)

Sauvageau, Jean: Body and Soul (1971)

Sauvageau, Lina: It's a Wonderful Love (*C'est bien beau l'amour*) (1971)

Sauvé, Gilbert: Only Thing You Know, The (1971)

Savage, Booth: Chasing Rainbows (1988), Curtains (1983), Every Person Is Guilty (1979), Last Season, The (1987), Ready for Slaughter (1983), Samuel Lount (1985), Sanity Clause (1990), Silence of the North (1981), Striker's Mountain (1985)

Savage, Brad: Echoes of a Summer (1976)

Savage, John: Amateur, The (1981), Caribe (1988)

Savage, Mary: Drylanders (1963)

Savage, Tyrone: Wind at My Back (2001)

Savard, Gilles: Make Mine Chartreuse (1987)

Savath, Phil: Big Meat Eater (1982), Fast Company (1979), Net Worth (1997), Outside Chance of Maximillian Glick, The (1988), Samuel Lount (1985), Terminal City Ricochet (1990)

Savenkoff, Elizabeth Carol: Watchtower, The (2001)

Saviakjuk-Jaw, Matthew: Kabloonak (1994)

Savo, Jimmy: Carry on Sergeant (1927–1928)

Savoie, Jacques: *Bombardier* (1992), *Bonjour, monsieur Gauguin* (Good Day, Mr. Gauguin) (1989), Duplessis' Orphans (1999), *Portes tournantes, Les* (The Revolving Doors) (1988)

Savoie, Paul: For Better, for Worse (*Pour le meilleur et pour le pire*) (1975), Looking for Eternity (1989), *Lucien Brouillard* (1983*)*, *Part des choses, La* (*Un léger vertige*) (A Part of Things) (A Light Vertigo) (1991), Scream for Silence, A (*Mourir à tue-tête*) (1979)

Sawa, Devon: Boys' Club, The (1996), Guilty, The (2000)

Sawatzky, Sandra: Girl Who Married a Ghost, The (2003)

Sawyer, Denis: In the Land of Zom (1983)

Sawyer, Kathleen: Flick (Dr. Frankenstein on Campus) (1970)

Saxer, Walter: Scream of Stone (Cerro Torra) (1991)

Saxon, John: Black Christmas (Silent Night, Evil Nights) (Stranger in the House) (1974), Fast Company (1979), Saxon John Special Magnum (Strange Shadows in an Empty Room) (1977). Special Magnum (1977)

Saxton, John C.W.: Blackout (Blackout in New York) (1978), Class of 1984 (1982)

Saxton, John: Happy Birthday to Me (1981), Kate Morris, Vice President (1984), Title Shot (1980)

Saxton, Juliana: Final Edition (1982)

Scacchi, Greta: Ladies Room (1999), Red Violin, The (Le violon rouge) (1998)

Scaini, Stefan: Anne of Green Gables: The Continuing Story (Series) (1985-1999), Burn: The Robert Wraight Story (2003), Double Frame (1999), Happy Christmas, Miss King (1999), Lyddie (1995), Sleeping Dogs Lie (1999), Under the Piano (1998), Wind at My Back (2001)

Scalia, Jack: Beyond Suspicion (1993)

Scammell, David: Revenge of the Radioactive Reporter (1992)

Scani, Stefan: Wind at My Back (2001)

Scanlan, Donald: Running Man (1980)

Scanlan, Joseph L.: Return of Ben Casey, The (1988), Sneakers (Spring Fever) (1982)

Scant, Nicole: Beat (1976), Blue Winter (L'hiver bleu) (1980)

Scarabelli, Michèle: Deadbolt (1984), Labour of Love (1985), Perfect Timing (1984), SnakeEater II: The Drug Buster (1990), Wrong Woman, The (1995)

Scarbeck, Christopher: Mirage, Le (1992)

Scarborough, Matt: Eve (2002)

Scardino, Don: Homer (1970), Rip-Off (1971)

Scarfe, Alan: A.K.A. Albert Walker (2002), Adolescence of P-I, The (1983), Bay Boy, The (1984), Bitter Ash, The (1963), Burn: The Robert Wraight Story (2003), Cathy's Curse (1977), Certain Practices (1979), Deserters (1983), Execution of Raymond Graham, The (1985), Final Edition (1982), Iron Eagle (1986), Joshua Then and Now (1985), Keeping Track (1987), Kingsgate (1989), Murder by Phone (1982), Not Just a Dirty Little Movie (1985), Overnight (1985), Portrait, The (1992), Silence (1997), Walls (1984), Wars, The (1983)

Scarfe, Jonathan: 100 Days in the Jungle (2002), Bay of Love and Sorrows, The (2002), Burn: The Robert Wraight Story (2003), Dead Innocent (1996), Morrison Murders, The (1997), Sheldon Kennedy Story, The (1999), White Lies (1998)

Scattini, Luigi: Night of the High Tide, The (La notte dell'alta marea) (1976)

Scaville, Diane: Ten Girls Ago (1962)

Schaarwachter, Lutz: Julie Darling (1982)

Schachte, Hank: Silence (1997)

Schaeffer, Francis: Baby on Board (1992)

Schechter, Jeff: Tracker, The (1999)

Schechter, Rebecca: Taking Care (1987)

Schechter, Steven: Mary Silliman's War (1994)

Scheider, Roy: Falling Through (2000), Naked Lunch (1992), Peacekeeper, The (1997)

Scheindel, Max: Melting Pot, The (1975)

Schell, Maximilian: Joan of Arc (1999), Young Catherine (1990)

Schellenberg, August: Bear Island (1979), Best Revenge (Misdeal) (1981), Between Friends (Get Back) (1973), Black Robe (1991), Coffin Affair, The (L'affaire Coffin) (1980), Confidential (1985), Covergirl (1984), Cross Country (1983), Day My Grandad Died, The (1976), Drying Up the Streets (1978), Fan's Notes, A (1972), Homecoming, The (Good Luck, Jennifer Gagnon) (1978), Kings and Desperate Men (1981), Latitude 55 (1982), Mark of Cain, The (1984), One Man (1977), Power Play (Coup d'état) (State of Shock)(1978), Riel (1979), Rip-Off (1971), Ruffian, The (1983), Running Brave (1983), Silence (1997), Striker's Mountain (1985), Tramp at the Door (1985)

Schellenberg, Joanna: Tramp at the Door (1985)

Scherberger, Aiken: Whodunit (1986)

Schetagne, Gilles: Passing Through the Pine Trees (M'en revenant par les épinettes) (1977)

Scheunhage, Janna Jo: Girl Who Married a Ghost, The (2003)

Schiaffino, Rosanna: Seven Times a Day (Sept fois par jour) (1971)

Schiegl, Kurt: Mystery of the Million Dollar Hockey Puck (1975)

Schiffler, Carrie: Stone Coats (1997)

Schiffman, Karl: Dead End (False Pretense) (1998)

Schioler, Tom: Kanadiana (2000), Storm (1985)

Schiro, Meeka: G-2 (1998)

Schlaht, Robin: Solitude (2001)

Schliessler, Martina: My Kind of Town (1984)

Schlitt, Robert: Pyx, The (1973)

Schlondorff, Volker: Handmaid's Tale, The (1990)

Schmid, Kyle: Fast Food High (2003)

Schmidt, Gisèle: Nenette (The Young Girl) (1991)

Schmidt, William: Alexander Bell: The Sound and the Silence (1991)

Schmolzer, August: Frostfire (1995)

Schnarre, Monika: Killer (1994), Peacekeeper, The (1997)

Schneck, Stephen: Welcome to Blood City (1977)

Schneider, Danielle: Christmas of Madame Beauchamp, The (Le revanche noël de Madame Beauchamp) (1981), Vents contraires (Crosswinds) (1995)

Schneiderman, Perry: Tangerine Taxi (1988)

Schoenberg, Mark: Parallels (1980)

Schoendoerffer, Ludovic: La-haut (2002)

Schoendoerffer, Pierre: La-haut (2002)

Scholte, Tom: Dirty (1998), Last Wedding, The (2001), Live Bait (1995), Lunch with Charles (2001), No More Monkeys Jumpin' on the Bed (2000)

Schorpion, Franck: I Won't Dance (1992), Wicked Minds (2002)

Schrader, Rolf: Stone Coats (1997)

Schrage, Lisa: Dreams Beyond Memory (1987), Food of the Gods II (1989), Indigo Autumn (1987), Prom Night II: Hello Mary Lou (1987)

Schraner, Kim: Harry's Case (2000)

Schreiber, Liev: Hitler: The Rise of Evil (2003)

Schreiber, Tell: Keeper, The (1975)

Schreier, Jessica: Class Warfare 2001 (2000)

Schubert, Karin: Oranges of Israel, The (Valse à trois) (1974)

Schull, Joseph: Nightingales and the Bells (Le rossignol et les cloches) (1952)

Schultz, Albert: Balls Up (1998), Circle Game, The (1994), Squamish Five, The (1988), White Lies (1998)

Schultz, Carl: To Walk with Lions (1999)

Schultz, David: Anthrax (2001), Jet Boy (2001), Question of Privilege, A (1998), Silent Cradle (1998)

Schultz, Jeff: Buying Time (1988), Matinée (1989), North of Pittsburgh (1992)

Schultz, Leroy: Grocer's Wife, The (1991)

Schulz, Bob: Falcon's Gold (1982)

Schwabach, Peter: Secret Laughter of Women, The (1999)

Schwartz, Larry: Surfacing (1981)

Schwartz, Lisa: Crunch (1981)

Schwartz, Mark Evan: Louisa May Alcott's Little Men (1998)

Schweig, Eric: Cowboys and Indians (2003), Red River (Rivière Rouge) (1996)

Sciorra, Annabella: Jenifer Estess Story, The (2001)

Scoffie, Lenie: Trilogie Marsellaise, La (2001)

Scoggins, Tracy: Watchers II (1990)

Scola, Ettore: Giornata particolare, Una (1977)

Scooler, Zvee: Apprenticeship of Duddy Kravitz, The (1974)

Scopp, Alfie: Flick (Dr. Frankenstein on Campus) (1970), Never Trust an Honest Thief (Going for Broke) (1979), Undergrads, The (1985)

Scorer, Andrew: Bubbles Galore (1996), Jack of Hearts (1993)

Scorsone, Caterina: Borderline Normal (2000)

Scott, Allan: Fourth Angel, The (2001), Regeneration (1996)

Scott, Campbell: Top of the Food Chain (1999)

Scott, Carolyn: Falling Over Backwards (1990)

Scott, Cynthia: Company of Strangers, The (Strangers in Good Company) (1990)

Scott, Daniel: Letter From New France, A (1979)

Scott, Frank: Three More Days (1995)

Scott, George C.: Changeling, The (1980)

Scott, John: Caribe (1988)

Scott, Judith: Soul Survivor (1995)

Scott, Ken: Grande Séduction, La (2003)

Scott, Kenneth: Life After Love (2000)

Scott, Kevin: Hustler White (1996)

Scott, Larry: SnakeEater II: The Drug Buster (1990)

Scott, Michael: Curse of the Viking Grave (1990), Harvest (1993), Lost in the Barrens (1990), Spirit Rider (1993)

Scott, Munro: Inside Out (1979)

Scott, Robert: SnakeEater (1990)

Scott, Sandra: Brethren (1976), Head On (Fatal Attraction) (1980), Home to Stay (1978), Incredible Journey, The (1963), Power Play (Coup d'état) (State of Shock) (Operation Overthrow) (1978)

Scott, T.J.: Blacktop (2000)

Scott, Tom Everett: Top of the Food Chain (1999)

Scott-Cummins, Gregory: Watchers III (1994)

Scott-Thomas, Kristin: Confessional, The (1995), Weep No More My Lady (1992)

Seaborn, Rosanna: Esprit du mal, L' (Spirit of Evil, The) (1954), Mother's Heart, A (1953)

Sealy-Smith, Alison: Ride, The (2000)

Sears, Djanet: Milk and Honey (1988), One Heart Broken Into Song (1998)

Sears, Janet: April One (1994)

Seatle, Dixie: Hank Williams: The Show He Never Gave (1982), Joe's So Mean to Josephine (1997), I Love a Man in Uniform (1984), Kathy Karuks Is a Grizzly Bear (1976), Piano Man's Daughter, The (2000), Population of One, A (1980), Stranger in Town (1998), The Black Cat in the Black Mouse Socks (see Acts of Love) (1980), Ticket to Heaven (1981)

Seaton, Aileen: Dangerous Age, A (1958), Waiting for Caroline (1967)

Sébastien, Michel: Yellow Island, The (L'île jaune) (1975), Secret de banlieue, Un (The Secret of a Suburb) (2002)

Secter, David: Offering, The (1966), Winter Kept Us Warm (1965)

Sedaka, Neil: Playgirl Killer (Decoy for Terror) (1965)

Seddon, Jack: Tomorrow Never Comes (1978)

Seelinger, Robert: Deadly Portrayal (2003)

Segal, George: Man in 5A, The (1982)

Segal, Ivan: Harmoney (1999)

Segal, Mathew: Fortune and Men's Eyes (1971), Foxy Lady (1971), Dulcima (1970)

Segal, Zohra: Masala (1992)

Séguin, Robert: Sensations (1973)

Seidle, Stephanie: Draghoula (1994)

Seidler, David: Dancing in the Dark (1995)

Seigner, Mathilde: Betty Fisher and Other Stories (*Betty Fisher et autres histoires*) (2001)

Selby, David: U-Turn (The Girl in Blue) (1973)

Selby, Hubert Jr.: Fear X (2003)

Selich, Nadja: Summer With the Ghosts (*Un été avec les fantômes*) (2002)

Selignac, Arnaud: Baree, Son of Kazan (1994), Kazan (1994)

Sen, Nandana: Seducing Maarya (1999)

Sénart, Catherine: Angel in a Cage (The Woman in the Cage) (*La bête de foire*) (1993), Marguerite Volant (1996), *Méchant party* (2000), *Pays dans la gorge, Le* (The Country on Your Chest) (1999), Angel in a Cage (1993)

Senatore, Paola: *Donnez-nous notre amour quotidien* (In Love With Sex) (1974), French Love (Un amour comme le nôtre) (1974)

Senecal, Patrick: *Sur le seuil* (2003)

Sens-Cazenave, Alain: Cathy's Curse (1977)

Septien, Al: Wicked Minds (2002)

Serafian, Deran: Death Warrant (1990)

Seremba, George: Midday Sun, The (1989)

Sergei, Ivan: John Woo's Once a Thief (1997)

Sergichiev, Josef: Here Am I (1999)

Serkis, Andy: Regeneration (1996)

Serpa, Cody: Once in a Blue Moon (1995)

Serra, Raymond: Men of Means (1999)

Servien, Gilbert: Dur-Dur (1981)

Setbon, Philippe: Honeymoon (1985)

Seth, Gaurav: Passage to Ottawa, A (2002)

Seth, Roshan: Such a Long Journey (1998)

Sethna, Maia: Earth (1998)

Sevier, Corey: Decoys (2003), Edge of Madness (*Station Sauvage*) (Wilderness Station) (2003)

Sevigny, Chloe: American Psycho (2000)

Seweryn, Andrzey: French Revolution, The (1989)

Sexton, Shauny: Bubbles Galore (1996)

Sexton, Tommy: Buried on Sunday (1993)

Seymour, Cara: American Psycho (2000)

Seymour, Jane: French Revolution, The (1989), Touching Wild Horses (2002)

Seymour, Johanne: *Homme renversé, L'* (1987)

Shackelford, Ted: Harvest (1993)

Shaffer, Mandy: Poison (Tease) (1999)

Shah, Naseeruddinn: Such a Long Journey (1998)

Shallows, Roy: White Tiger (1995)

Shamata, Chuck: 19 Months (2002), Between Friends (Get Back) (1973), Canada's Sweetheart: The Saga of Hal C. Banks (1985), Death Weekend (House by the Lake) (1976), Death Wish V: The Face of Death (1994), Due South (1994), Dulcima (1970), Family of Strangers (1993), Hank (1977), High Card (1982), I Miss You, Hugs and Kisses (1978), Joshua Then and Now (1985), Kidnapping of Baby John Doe, The (1985), Night Friend (A Cry From the Heart) (1987), Nobody Makes Me Cry (Between Friends) (1983), Power Play (*Coup d'état*) (State of Shock) (Operation Overthrow) (1978), Princes in Exile (1990), Running (1979), Running Man (1980), Scanners (1981), Spreading Ground, The (2000), Stone Cold Dead (1979), Terry Fox Story, The (1983), Touch of Murder, A (1990), Unfinished Business (1984), Welcome to Blood City (1977)

Shandel, Pia: Another Smith for Paradise (1972), Plastic Mile, The (1969), Shadow of the Hawk (1976), Visitor, The (1974)

Shandel, Tom: Another Smith for Paradise (1972), Walls (1984)

Shane, Myles: Famous Dead People (1999)

Shannon, Jamie: Hayseed (1997)

Shannon, Jay: Hired Gun (The Devil's Spawn) (The Last Gunfighter) (1959)

Shannon, Molly: My Five Wives (2000), Super Star (1999)

Shannon, Polly: Men With Brooms (2002), Sheldon Kennedy Story, The (1999)

Shapiro, Paul: Choices of the Heart: The Margaret Sanger Story (1994), Hockey Night (1984), Jewel (2000), Lotus Eaters, The (1993), Rookies (1990), Undergrads, The (1985)

Shara, Mike: Iron Road (2002)

Sharif, Omar: Heaven Before I Die (1997)

Sharkey, Stephen: Touch and Go (2002)

Sharma, Satyajit: My Little Devil (2000)

Sharp, Alan: Lathe of Heaven (2002)

Sharp, Donald: Bear Island (1979)

Shart, Raffy: Armen and Bullik (1993)

Shatalow, Peter: Blue City Slammers (1987)

Shatner, William: Butler's Night Off, The (1948), Family of Strangers (1993), Kidnapping of the President, The (1980), Oedipus Rex (1956), Riel (1979), Tek War: Tek Justice (1994), Third Walker, The (1980), Visiting Hours (1982)

Shaver, Helen: Bear With Me (2000), Bethune: The Making of a Hero (1990) see Bethune (1977), Christina (1974), Coming Out Alive (1980), Fatal Memories (The Eileen Franklin Story) (1992), Gas (1981), Harry Tracy, Desperado (1981), High-Ballin' (1978), Lost! (1986), In Praise of Older Women (1978), No Blame (L'incroyable vérité) (1988), Nowhere in Sight (2000), Off Your Rocker (1982), Outrageous! (1977), Park Is Mine, The (1986), Risen, The (2003), Rowing Through (1996), Shoot (1976), Starship Invasions (1977), Supreme Kid, The (1976), Trial and Error (1993), War Boy, The (Point of Escape) (1985), We All Fall Down (2000), Who Has Seen the Wind (1977), Wolfpen Principle (1974)

Shaver, Vanessa: Johnny (1999)

Shavick, James: Baby on Board (1992)

Shaw, Robert: Luck of Ginger Coffey, The (1964)

Shaw, Stan: Busted Up (1986)

Shawn, Sylvia: Noncensus (1964)

Shayne, Linda: Screwballs (1983)

Shbib, Bashar: Clear-Dark (Clair obscur) (1988), Crack Me Up (1993), Draghoula (1994), Eviction (Evixion) (1986), Julia Has Two Lovers (1990), Lana in Love (1991), Love and Greed (1992), Memoirs (1984), Mule and the Emeralds, The (1995), Ride Me (Ego Trip) (1995), Seductio (1987), Senses, The (1996)

Shea, John: Honeymoon (Lune de miel) (1985)

Shearman, Alan: 2001: A Space Travesty (2001)

Shebib, Donald: Ascent, The (1994), Between Friends (Get Back) (1973), By Reason of Insanity (1982), Change of Heart (1993), Climb, The (1987), Fighting Men, The (1977), Fish Hawk (1979), Goin' Down the Road (1970), Heartaches (1981), Little Kidnappers, The (1990), Pathfinder, The (1996), Rip-Off (1971), Running Brave (1983), Second Wind (1976), Slim Obsession (1984)

Shebib, Noah: Deadly Appearances (1999)

Shechter, Becky: Only Thing You Know, The (1971)

Sheedy, Ally: Interrogation of Michael Crowe, The (2002)

Sheehan, Nik: Symposium (1996)

Sheehy, Jocelyn: Guitar (Guitare) (1974)

Sheen, Martin: Cold Front (1989), Dead Zone, The (1983), Little Girl Who Lives Down the Lane, The (1977)

Sheer, Tony: Fighting Men, The (1977), Final Edition (1982), For Those I Loved (1983), Lifeline to Victory (1993), Lyon's Den (1983), Maintain the Right (1982), Man Inside, The (1975)

Sheffer, Craig: Double Take (1998), Without Malice (2000)

Sheilds, Nick: Liar's Edge (1992)

Sheldon, Larry: Family of Strangers (1993)

Sheldon, Rod: To Kill the King (1974)

Shellen, Stephen: April One (1994), Drop Dead Gorgeous (Victim of Beauty) (1991), Honeymoon (1996), Rude (1995), Still Life (Still Life: The Fine Art of Murder) (1990), Vivid (1996)

Shelley, Carole: Waiting for the Parade (1984)

Sheng, Reimonna: Small Pleasures (1993)

Shengli, Wu: Cry Woman (Ku qi de nu ren) (2002)

Shepard, Hilary: Scanner Cop (1994)

Shepard, Sam: After the Harvest (Wild Geese) (2000)

Shephard, Richard: Class Warfare 2001 (2000)

Shepherd, Cybill: Marine Life (2000)

Shepherd, Elizabeth: Desire (2000), Double Negative (Deadly Companion) (1979), Julia (see Acts of Love) (1980), Kidnapping of the President, The (1980), Spreading Ground, The (2000)

Shepherd, Jean: Christmas Story, A (1983)

Sheppard, Gordon: Eliza's Horoscope (1975)

Sheppard, John: Bullies (1986), Flying (1986), Higher Education (1986), Mark of Cain, The (1984)

Sher, Emil: Café Olé (2000)

Sheridan, James: Slavers, The (1984)

Sheridan, Nicolette: Deadly Portrayal (2003)

Sherman, David: Frankenstein and Me (1995), Kids of the Round Table (1995)

Sherriff, Steven: Neon Palace, The: A '50s and '60s Trip (1971)

Sherrin, Robert: Population of One, A (1980), Today I Am a Fountain Pen (1980)

Sherwood, Anthony: Closer and Closer (1996), Eddie and the Cruisers Part II: Eddie Lives! (1989)

Shiach, Dominic: Blackheart (1997), Darkness Falling (2002)

Shields, Nicholas: Curse of the Viking Grave (1990), Lost in the Barrens (1990), Princes in Exile (1990)

Shimada, Teru: Sweet and the Bitter, The (1962)

Shipman, Nell: Back to God's Country (1919), Grub-Stake, The (1922)

Shire, Talia: Whole Shebang, The (2001)

Shirinian, Benjamin: Neighbour, The (1993)

Shirriff, Cathie: Covergirl (1984)

Shojail, Farrokh: Secret Ballot (Raye Makhfi) (2001)

Shonteff, Lindsay: Hired Gun (The Devil's Spawn) (The Last Gunfighter) (1959)

Shore, Harold: Christopher's Movie Matinée (1969)

Shore, Jeffrey: Song of Hiawatha, The (1996)

Short, Martin: Cementhead (1979), Seer Was Here (1978)

Shortliffe, Margaret: Little Canadian, The (1955)

Shoub, Max: Forbidden Journey (1950)

Show, Jane: Dreamtrips (2000)

Shower, Kathy: Love Letters: A Romantic Trilogy (2001)

Shulman, Dr. Morton: Tar Sands, The (1977)

Shum, Mina: Double Happiness (1994), Drive, She Said (1997), Long Life, Happiness & Prosperity (2002)

Shuman, Mort: Jacques Brel Is Alive and Well and Living in Paris (1975), Little Girl Who Lives Down the Lane, The (1977)

Shuman, Sandra: I, Maureen (1980)

Shuster, Aaron: Pictures at the Beach (1990)

Shyer, Christopher: Falling, The (2000), Little Boy Blues (2000)

Si'Ulepa, Nikki: Whole of the Moon, The (1996)

Sibley, Sheila: Golden Fiddles (1991)

Sicotte, Gilbert: Bombardier (1992), *Cap Tourmente* (Cape Torment) (1993), Castle of Cards, The (Le château de cartes) (1980), *Comme un voleur* (Like a Thief) (1991), *Contrecoeur* (1983), Cordélia (1980), Day in a Taxi, A (*Une journée en taxi*) (1982), Every Person Is Guilty (1979), Fantastica (1980), Far From You Sweetheart (*Je suis loin de toi migonne*) (1976), Goodbye, See You Monday (*Au revoir, à lundi*) (1979), *Grands enfants, Les* (Day by Day) (1980), Life of a Hero, The (*La vie d'un héros*) (1994), *Marguerite Volant* (1996), Little Tougas (1976), Maria Chapdelaine (1983), Paths of the World, The (*Les allées de la terre*) (1973), *Pots cassés, Les* (Broken Dishes) (1994), Saracen, The (*La Sarrasine*) (1991), Shabbat Shalom (1994), Visage pâle (Pale Face) (1986), Vultures, The (*Les vautours*) (1975), Water Child (*L'enfant d'eau*) (1995), Years of Dreams and Revolt (*Les années de rêves*) (1984)

Sidaway, Ashley: Rainbow (1995)

Sidaway, Robert: Rainbow (1995)

Sidney, Ernest: White Road, The (1929)

Siegel, Lois: 20th Century Chocolate Cake, A (1983)

Siemasko, Nina: Power of Attorney (1995)

Siemaszko, Casey: Big Slice, The (1991)

Sigaloff, Eugene: From Nine to Nine (1936)

Sigurdardottir, Maria: Regina (2002)

Sigurgierson, W.: Inbreaker, The (1974)

Sillas, Karen: Bad Money (1999)

Silva, Henry: Chatwill's Verdict (Killer Instinct) (Baker County, U.S.A) (1982), Shoot (1976)

Silver, Joe: Apprenticeship of Duddy Kravitz, The (1974), Love on the Nose (1978), Mr. Nice Guy (1986), Rabid (Rage) (1977)

Silver, Ron: Kissinger and Nixon (1994), When Billie Beat Bobby (2001)

Silver, Véronique: Mirage, Le (1992)

Silverman, Robert: 125 Rooms of Comfort (1974), Brood, The (1979), Head On (Fatal Attraction) (1980), It Seemed Like a Good Idea at the Time (1975), One Night Stand (1978), Partners (1976), Prom Night (1980), Rabid (Rage) (1977), Scanners (1981), Sweet Substitute (Caressed) (1964), Thousand Moons, A (1977)

Silverstone, Alicia: Global Heresy (2002)

Sim, Heather: Slow Run (1969)

Simaga, Tiemoko: Another Planet (2000)

Simandl, Lloyd: Autumn Born (1979), Chained Heat II (1993), Escape Velocity (1999)

Simard, Anouk: Beautiful Facade, A (*La belle apparence*) (1979), *Contrecoeur* (1983), Salut! J.W. (1981)

Simard, Liane: *Manuscrit érotique, Le* (2002)

Simard, Marcel: Lost Words (1993), Love Me (1991)

Simard, Monique: Wow (1970)

Simard, Régis: Enuff is Enuff (*J'ai mon voyage!*) (1973)

Simard, René: Enuff is Enuff (*J'ai mon voyage!*) (1973)

Simard, Renée: Kids of the Round Table (1995)

Simenon, Marc: By the Blood of Others (*Par le sang des autres*) (1974), Explosion, L' (The Hideout) (1971)

Simmonds, Alan: In the Blue Ground (1999), Striker's Mountain (1985)

Simon, Claire: Foreign Body, A (Sinon, oui) (1997)

Simon, Jean: André Mathieu, Musicien (1994)

Simon, Josette: Milk and Honey (1988)

Simon, Marie-Loup: Why Is the Strange Mr. Zolock So Interested in Comic Strips? (*Pourquoi l'étrange Monsieur Zolock s'intéressait-il tant à la bande dessinée*)

Simon, Marie-Nicole: Clear-Dark (Clair obscur) (1988)

Simon, Zoe Kelli: Midnight Witness (1992)

Simone, Johnny: Hey, Happy! (2000)

Simoneau, Yves: Celebrations, The (1979), In the Belly of a Dragon (1989), In the Shadow of the Wind (1986), Intimate Power (1985), Nuremberg (2000), Perfectly Normal (1990), Red Eyes (Accidental Truths) (Les yeux rouges) (*Les verités accidentelles*) (1983), Why Is the Strange Mr. Zolock So Interested in Comic Strips? (*Pourquoi l'étrange Monsieur Zolock s'intéressait-il tant à la bande dessinée*)

Simpson, Brad: Blackheart (1997), Darkness Falling (2002)

Simpson, Brock: Blackheart (1997), Fancy Dancing (2002), First Offender (1987), Grizzly Falls (2000), Prom Night IV: Deliver Us From Evil (1992)

Simpson, Colin D.: Darkness Falling (2002)

Simpson, George: Here I Will Nest (1941)

Simpson, Peter: Curtains (1983)

Simpson, Scott: Touch and Go (2002)

Simpson, Terry: Stork Derby, The (2001)

Sims, Clair: Mothers and Daughters (1992)

Sims, Elliot: Cold Comfort (1989)

Sims, George: High Country, The (The First Hello) (1981)

Sinclair, Carol: Greening of Ian Elliot, The (1991)

Sinclair, Diane: Damaged Lives (1933)

Sinclair, Lister: July Group, The (1981)

Singer, Bruce: Meatballs, Part II (1984)

Singer, Daniel: Vida, La (The Document of Michael da Vida) (1965)

Singer, Gail: True Confections (1991)

Singer, Linda: Dead End (Le dernier souffle) (1999), Junior (1985), Trial by Vengeance (1989)

Singer, Lori: Sarabande (1997)

Singer, Marc: If You Could See What I Hear (1982), Indigo Autumn (1987), LAPD: To Protect and Serve (2001), Watchers II (1990)

Singh, Sheora: Love in Canada (1979)

Sinha, Pamela: Jinnah on Crime (2002)

Sirois, Monique: Corde au cou, La (1966)

Sirola, Joseph: Seizure (Tango Macabre) (1974)

Sisk, Stephen J.M.: Recipe for Revenge (1998)

Sisson, Rosemary Anne: Change of Place, A (1994)

Sivak, Nancy: Last Wedding, The (2001), No More Monkeys Jumpin' on the Bed (2000), Protection (2000)

Sivertsen, David: Change of Heart (1984)

Skarsgard, Stellan: House on Turk Street, The (2002)

Skarsten, Rachel: Virginia's Run (2003)

Skerritt, Tom: Dead Zone, The (1983), Silence of the North (1981)

Skidd, Andrew: Recommendation for Mercy (1975)

Skinner, Colin: Ups and Downs (1983)

Skogland, Kari: Courage to Love, The (Quadroon Ball) (1999), Men With Guns (1996), Nothing Too Good for a Cowboy (1998), Size of Watermelons, The (1996), White Lies (1998), Zebra Lounge (2001)

Sky, Jennifer: My Little Eye (2002)

Skye, Ione: Size of Watermelons, The (1996)

Slabotsky, Arthur: Merry Wives of Tobias Rouke, The (1972)

Slack, Lyle: Another Woman (1994)

Slade, Bernard: Tribute (1980)

Slade, Gloria: Touching Wild Horses (2002)

Slater, Vanessa: Suburban Legend (1995)

Sloan, Amy: Heart: The Marilyn Bell Story (2000), Summer (2002), Wicked Minds (2002)

Slobodin, Katharine: Columbus of Sex, The: My Secret Life (1969)

Smart, Jane: Day Breaks Once More (1995)

Smegal, Brian: Day My Grandad Died, The (1976)

Smiley, Desmond: When Tomorrow Dies (1965)

Smith, Alexis: Little Girl Who Lives Down the Lane, The (1977)

Smith, Andrea: Day Breaks Once More (1995)

Smith, Andrew Martin: Hurt (2002)

Smith, Bruce: Investigation (2002), Sleeproom, The (1998)

Smith, Cedric: Butterbox Babies (1995), Curse of the Viking Grave (1990), Fast Company (1979), Firing Squad (1990), Golden Will: The Silken Laumann Story (1997), Happy Christmas, Miss King (1999), In This Corner (1986), Iron Road (2002), Samuel Lount (1985), Sleeping Dogs Lie (1999), Who Has Seen the Wind (1977), Witchboard III: The Possession (1995)

Smith, Charles Martin: Air Bud (1997), Dead Silence (1997), Never Cry Wolf (1983), Snow Walker, The (2002), Touching Wild Horses (2002)

Smith, Charles: Facade (1970)

Smith, David: Soul Survivor (1995)

Smith, Garfield: Eat Anything (1971)

Smith, Hank: Sex and the Single Sailor (1967)

Smith, Hilda Hooke: Here I Will Nest (1941)

Smith, Ivan: Passage to Ottawa, A (2002)

Smith, Jamie Renee: M.V.P.: Most Valuable Primate (2000)

Smith, John D.: Boys of St. Vincent, The (1992)

Smith, John N.: Random Passage (2001), Revenge of the Land (2000)

Smith, John: Day in a Life, A (1999), Love on the Nose (1978), Masculine Mystique, The (1984), Sitting in Limbo (1985), Train of Dreams (1987), Welcome to Canada (1989)

Smith, Kavan: Fearless (1999)

Smith, Kim: Cool Sound From Hell, A (The Young and the Beat) (1959), Melting Pot, The (1975)

Smith, Linda: Joshua Then and Now (1985), Little White Lies (1988), Rose Cafe, The (1987)

Smith, Lois: Execution of Raymond Graham, The (1985)

Smith, Murray: Bear Island (1979)

Smith, Paula J.: Shadow Lake (2000)

Smith, Peter: My Kind of Town (1984), No Surrender (1985)

Smith, Rex: Ballerina and the Blues, The (1987)

Smith, Robert: Xtro II: The Second Encounter (1991)

Smith, Roland: Eviction (*Evixion*) (1986), *Femme de Pablo Ruiz, La* (*Pablo qui court*) (1991)

Smith, Ryan: Julie Walking Home (2002)

Smith, Sally: This Is a Film (That Was a Film) (1989)

Smith, Scott: Roller Coaster (1999)

Smith, Sean: Art of Murder, The (1999)

Smith, Sharon: August and July (1973)

Smith, Stacy: Marion Bridge (2002)

Smith, Steve: Red Green's Duct Tape Forever (2002)

Smith, Tom: Trouble (1996)

Smith, Truman: One Plus One (The Kinsey Report) (Exploring the Kinsey Report) (1961)

Smith, William: Blood and Guts (1978), Fast Company (1979), Slow Burn (1989)

Smithee, Alan: Woman Wanted (1999)

Smithers, Jan: Mr. Nice Guy (1986)

Smits, Sonja: Ambush at Iroquois Pass (1979), Diviners, The (1993), Me and My Shadows (2000), Screwball Academy (Loose Ends) (1986), Teddy (The Pit) (1980), That's My Baby (1984), Videodrome (1983), War Brides (1980)

Smolinski, Aaron: Wishmaster 3: Beyond the Gates of Hell (2001)

Smythe, Alan: Another Woman (1994)

Snell, Jerry: Môtel St-Laurent (1998)

Snider, Norman: Dead Ringers (Alter Ego) (Twins) (1988), Partners (1976)

Snipes, Wesley: Art of War, The (2000)

Snow, Victoria: Blind Terror (2000), Destiny to Order (1989), Getting Married in Buffalo Jump (1990), Millennium (1988), Yellow Wedding (1998)

Snyder, Ari: Buster's Bedroom (1991)

Snyders, Sammy: Teddy (The Pit) (1980)

Snytar, Nancy: Foreign Ghosts (*Fantômes étrangers*) (1997)

Sobel, Mark: Trial and Error (1993)

Sobieski, Leelee: Joan of Arc (1999), Max (2001)

Sobol, Amy: Passage to Ottawa, A (2002)

Soesbe, Douglas: Blind Terror (2000), Wrong Woman, The (1995)

Sofer, Rena: Hostile Advances: The Kerry Ellison Story (1996)

Sokolov, Harvey: Something's Rotten (1978)

Soldevila, Philippe: Exils (2002)

Sole, Alfred: Tanya's Island (1980)

Soles, Paul: Falling Over Backwards (1990), Gun Runner, The (1984), Hush Little Baby (Mother of Pearl) (1993), Lotus Eaters, The (1993), Ticket to Heaven (1981)

Solomon, Aubrey: *Deux pieds dans la même bottine, Les* (Two Feet in the Same Ankle Boot) (The Clumsy Klutz) (1974)

Solomon, Geneviève: Large Abode, A (1978)

Solovyow, Victor: Swan Lake: The Zone (Lebedyne ozero-zona) (1996)

Solway, Larry: Brood, The (1979), Flaming Frontier (1958), I Miss You, Hugs and Kisses (1978), Meatballs (1979), Title Shot (1980), Utilities (1981)

Sommer, Joseph: Execution of Raymond Graham, The (1985)

Somers, Brett: Paper People, The (1967)

Somers, Suzanne: Nothing Personal (1980)

Somerset, John: Take Her by Surprise (1967)

Somme, Judi: Life and Times of Chester-Angus Ramsgood, The (1971)

Sommer, Elke: I Miss You, Hugs and Kisses (1978)

Sommer, Judi: Life and Times of Chester-Angus Ramsgood, The (1971)

Sone, John: Love in a Four Letter World (1970), Loving and Laughing (1971)

Sonmor, Gordon: Big Bear (1988)

Soo, Park Jong: Search and Destroy (1979)

Sooder, Ain: Seasons in the Sun (1986)

Soper, Mark: Understudy, The: Graveyard Shift II (1988)

Sorenson, Linda: Another Smith for Paradise (1972), Breaking Point (1976), Class of 1984 (1982), Courage of Kavik the Wolf Dog, The (1980), Draw! (1984), Hard Part Begins, The (1973), Heavenly Bodies (1985), I Miss You, Hugs and Kisses (1978), Joshua Then and Now (1985), Merry Wives of Tobias Rouke, The (1972), Paperback Hero (1973), Running Man (1980), Stone Cold Dead (1979), Whispers (1990)

Sorgini, Linda: *Craque la vie* (Life Blossoms) (1994), Tin Flute, The (*Bonheur d'occasion*) (1983)

Soroka, Judy: Neon Palace, The: A '50s and '60s Trip (1971)

Soroka, Liza: Recorded Live (1982)

Sorvino, Mira: Between Strangers (2002)

Sorvino, Paul: Melanie (1982), Men With Guns (1996)

Soualem, Zinedine: *Ange de goudron, L'* (Tar Angel) (2001)

Soucy, Martin: *100% Bio* (Hundred Percent Biography) (2003)

Soul, David: Dogpound Shuffle (1975), Vents contraires (Crosswinds) (1995)

Souriol, Jean-Pierre: Trouble Makers (Trouble-fête) (1964)

Southam, Tim: Bay of Love and Sorrows, The (2002), Tale of Teeka, The (1999)

Soutière, Yves: Pin-Pon, The Film (*Pin-Pon, Le film*) (1999)

Sowerby, Jane: Welcome to the Parade (1986)

DIRECTORS, SCRIPTWRITERS & ACTORS

Spacey, Kevin: Shipping News, The (2001)

Spader, James: Crash (1996)

Spangler, Bruce: Protection (2000)

Spano, Joe: Terminal Choice (Deathbed) (1985)

Spano, Vincent: Ascent, The (1994), Brooklyn State of Mind, A (1997)

Sparks, Jeremiah: One Heart Broken Into Song (1998)

Sparling, Gordon: House in Order, A (La maison en ordre) (1936)

Sparrow, Walter: Treasure Island (2001)

Sparrow, Wendy: Inbreaker, The (1974)

Spaziani, Giola: Almost America (Come l'America) (2001)

Spaziani, Monique: Alley Cat, The (Le matou) (1985), Beauty of Women, The (La beauté des femmes) (1994), Blizzard, The (Rafales) (1990), Happy Memories (Old Memories) (Les beaux souvenirs) (1981), Million Dollar Babies (1995), Portes tournantes, Les (The Revolving Doors) (1988), Petite fille particulière, Une (The Lottery Ticket) (1995), Water Child (L'enfant d'eau) (1995)

Spear, Winston: Stuff (1999)

Speciale, Linda: Screwballs (1983)

Speckmaier, Kevin: Middlemen (2000)

Speedman, Scott: Harmoney (1999), Kitchen Party (1997), My Life Without Me (Mi Vida Sin Mi) (2003)

Spelling, Tori: Perpetrators of the Crime (1999)

Spenard, Mario: Woman of Colours, A (La dame en couleurs) (1985)

Spence, Jane: Vigil, The (1998)

Spence, Janis: Bingo Robbers, The (2000)

Spence, Paul: Fubar (2002)

Spence, Peter: Bay Boy, The (1984), Clutch (1998), Undergrads, The (1985), Unfinished Business (1984)

Spencer-Nairn, Tara: New Waterford Girl (1999), Rub & Tug (2002), Wishmaster 4: The Prophecy Fulfilled (2002)

Sebastian, Spence: Boys of St. Vincent, The (1992), Breach of Faith: A Family of Cops II (1996), Drive, She Said (1997)

Spencer, David: Slavers, The (1984)

Spencer, Susan: Proxyhawks (1970)

Spender, Stephen: Bad Money (1999), Suburbanators, The (1995)

Spensley, Philip: Moody Beach (1990)

Sperdakos, George: Cross Country (1983), Insurance Man From Ingersoll, The (1976), Journey (1972), My Pleasure Is My Business (1975), Sarabande (1997)

Spevlin, George: Urinal (1988)

Spier, Riva: Deux super-dingues (Heaven Help Us) (1982), Ghostkeeper (1981)

Spiers, Bob: Kevin of the North (2001)

Spink, Philip: Duke, The (1999), Once in a Blue Moon (1995)

Spinney, Frank: Nashville Bound (1996)

Spivak, Nancy: Dirty (1998)

Sporleder, Gregory: Men With Guns (1996)

Spottiswood, Gregory: Ice Men, The (2001), Looking for Miracles (1989)

Spottiswoode, Roger: Hiroshima (1996), Matthew Shepard Story, The (2001), Mesmer (1994), Terror Train (1980)

Spring, Sylvia: Madeleine Is... (1971), Plastic Mile, The (1969)

Springbett, Winnifred: Sunday in the Country (1975)

Springfield, Richard: Change of Place, A (1994)

Springford, Ruth: American Christmas Carol, An (1979), Changeling, The (1980), Improper Channels (1981), Sunday in the Country (1975)

Sprinkle, Annie: Bubbles Galore (1996)

Sprintz, Danial: Hell Bent (1994)

Spry, Robin: Action: The October Crisis of 1970 (1974), Cry in the Night, A (1996), Don't Forget (Je me souviens) (1979), Drying Up the Streets (1978), Flowers on a One-Way Street (1968), Hiroshima (1996), Hitting Home (Obsessed) (1989), Keeping Track (1987), Kings and Desperate Men (1981), One Man (1977), Prologue (1970), Suzanne (1980)

St. Amour, Jason: Train of Dreams (1987)

St. Clair, Neil: Eve (2002)

St. Goddard, Lyle: Stone Coats (1997)

St. John, Michelle: Conspiracy of Silence (1991), Spirit Rider (1993), Where the Spirit Lives (1989)

St. Laurent, Peter: Rats (1999)

St. Pierre, Leopold: Platinum (1997)

St. Gerard, Michael: Replikator (1994) (96mins), Starlight (1995)

Stackhouse, Susan: Change of Heart (1984)

Staehli, Anne-Dominique: Lost Words (1993)

Stait, Brent: For Those Who Hunt the Wounded Down (1996), Nights Below Station Street (1997)

St-Amand, Mario: Love Me (1991), Power Play (Coup d'état) (State of Shock) (Operation Overthrow) (1978)

Stambaugh, David: Home to Stay (1978)

Stamford, Jeremy: Watchers III (1994)

Stamou, Irene: Invention of Love, The (2000)

Stanchev, George: Daydream Believers: The Monkees' Story (2000)

Standing, John: Pygmalion (1983)

393

Stanek, Patrik: Escape Velocity (1999)

Stanford, Nathania: Lost World, The (1992)

Stankova, Maruska: Hey Babe! (1984)

Stanley, Jill: Tommy Tricker and the Stamp Traveller (*Les aventuriers du timbre perdu*) (1988)

Stanley, Paul: Where the Heart Is (1985)

Stansfield, Claire: Swordsman, The (1993)

Stanton, Harry Dean: Never Talk to Strangers (1995), One Magic Christmas (1985)

Stanulis, Edward: Rub & Tug (2002)

Stapleton, Bernard: Pasta King of the Caribbean, The (1999), Violet (2000)

Stapleton, Jean: Ghost Mom (1993)

Stapleton, Kevin: Carver's Gate (1996)

Stapley, Alex: Baby on Board (1992)

Stapley, Holly: Baby on Board (1992)

Starblanket, Noel: Cold Journey (1976)

Stark, Anthony: Art of Murder, The (1999)

Stark, Wendy: Wendy (1966)

Starkman, Card: Bloody Brood, The (1959)

St-Arneault, Lynda: East Coast (*Côte est*) (1986)

Starr, Anick: Odyssey of the Pacific (*L'Empereur du Pérou*) (1982)

Starr, Beau: Murder Most Likely (1999), Never Talk to Strangers (1995)

Starr, Jonathan: Odyssey of the Pacific (*L'Empereur du Pérou*) (1982)

Starrett, Charles: Viking, The (1931)

St-Denis, André: Bulldozer (1974)

St-Denis, Ginette: Traveller, The (1989)

Stebbings, Peter: Drive, She Said (1997), On Hostile Ground (2000)

Steed, Emily: Eat Anything (1971)

Steed, Judy: Eat Anything (1971)

Steel, Anthony: Night of the High Tide, The (*La notte dell,alta marea*) (1976)

Steele, Lisa: Legal Memory (1992)

Steen, Jessica: Flying (1986), On Hostile Ground (2000), Question of Privilege, A (1998), Society's Child (2001), Still Life (1990), Striker's Mountain (1985)

Steenburgen, Mary: One Magic Christmas (1985)

Stefan, Fred: Sneakers (Spring Fever) (1982)

Stefaniuk, Rob: Law of Enclosures, The (2000), Size of Watermelons, The (1996), Super Star (1999)

Steiger, Rod: Choices of the Heart: The Margaret Sanger Story (1994), Kid, The (1997), Klondike Fever (1979), Lucky Star, The (1980), Neighbour, The (1993), Passion and Paradise (1989), Sword of Gideon (1986)

Stein, David: Amityville Curse (1990), The, Scoop (1978)

Stein, Rita: Slow Run (1969)

Steinberg, David: Going Berserk (1983), Wrong Guy, The (1998)

Steinberg, Harriet: Drop Dead Gorgeous (Victim of Beauty) (1991)

Steinberg, Ziggy: Porky's Revenge (*Revanche de Porky, La*) (1985)

Steiner, Elsa: *Alisée* (1991)

Steinhouse, Don: Goin' Down the Road (1970)

Stella, Penelope: Low Visibility (1984)

Ste-Marie, Chlöé: Miss Moscou (1992), *Postière, La* (The Postmistress) (1992), Pudding chômeur (Bread Pudding) (1996), Wasp, The (*La guêpe*) (1986)

Stephanson, Ross: I'm Going to Get You...Elliot Boy (1971)

Stephen, Karen: Pinball Summer (1980)

Stephen, Mary: Until the Heart (*Jusqu'au coeur*) (1980)

Stephen, Rosenberg: Jacob Two-Two Meets the Hooded Fang (1977)

Stephens, Gary: Hush Little Baby (Mother of Pearl) (1993)

Stephens, Robert: Luther (1973)

Stephens, Russel: Regeneration (1988)

Sterling, Philip: Execution of Raymond Graham, The (1985)

Stern, Daniel: Crazy Horse (She Drives Me Crazy) (Friends, Lovers & Lunatics) (1989)

Stern, Jessica: Housekeeper, The (Judgement in Stone) (1986)

Stern, Sandor: Incubus (1981), Pin (1988), Separation (1978)

Stern, Steven Hilliard: Draw! (1984), Love and Murder (1988), Mazes and Monsters (1982), Park Is Mine, The (1986), Running (1979), Undergrads, The (1985)

Stevan, Robyn: Bye Bye Blues (1989), Giant Steps (1992), Paint Cans (1994), Shelley (Turned Out) (1987), Squamish Five, The (1988), Sylvan Lake Summer (1991)

Stevens, Barry: Rubber Carpet (1995)

Stevens, Casey: Prom Night (1980)

Stevens, Garry: Tools of the Devil (1985)

Stevens, Laird: Trial by Vengeance (1989)

Stevens, Louis: Flaming Frontier (1958), Wolf Dog (1958)

Stevens, Margot: Sex and the Lonely Woman (1966)

Stevens, Michael: Return of Tommy Tricker, The (*Le retour des aventuriers du timbre perdu*) (1994)

Stevens, Paul: Mask, The (1961)

Stevens, Sarah: Improper Channels (1981)

Stevenson, Colette: Promise the Moon (1997), Rats (1999)

Stevenson, Cynthia: Air Bud: Golden Receiver (1998)

Stevenson, Parker: Rose Cafe, The (1987)

Stevenson, Patrick: Little Boy Blues (2000)

Stevenson, Rick: Anthrax (2001), Dinosaur Hunter, The (2000), Question of Privilege, A (1998)

Stewart, Alexandra: Agency (1980), Bingo (1974), Blood of Others, The (Le sang des autres) (1984), Croon Maury and Mrs. B. (International Title) (2003), Final Assignment (1980), Heatwave Lasted Four Days, The (1973), In Praise of Older Women (1978), Last Chase, The (1980), Phobia (1980), Uncanny, The (1977), Waiting for Caroline (1967), Your Ticket Is no Longer Valid (Finishing Touch) (1982)

Stewart, Barry: Luck of Ginger Coffey, The (1964)

Stewart, Catherine Mary: Café Romeo (1992), Passion and Paradise (1989), Powder Heads (1980), Psychic (1991), Sea Wolf, The (1993)

Stewart, Donald: Dead Silence (1997)

Stewart, Edward: Apprentice, The (Fleur bleue) (1971), Keep It in the Family (1973)

Stewart, Elizabeth: Tagged: The Jonathan Wamback Story (2002)

Stewart, Ewan: Regeneration (1996)

Stewart, James H.: Hollow Point (1997), Peacekeeper, The (1997)

Stewart, Job: Lift, The (1965)

Stewart, Julie: Chasing Rainbows (1988)

Stewart, Lynn: Bitter Ash, The (1963)

Stewart, Mark David: Maxwell's Dream (1999)

Stewart, Nan: Who Has Seen the Wind (1977)

Stewart, Robert: Broken Lullaby (1994)

St-Gelais, Jean-Guy: Adventures of Ti-ken, The (1961)

St-Hamont, Daniel: Hold-Up (1985)

Stiklin, Marie: Various Postions (2002)

Stiladis, Nicolas: Gladiator Cop (1994), Red Blooded 2 (1996)

Stiller, Jerry: My Five Wives (2000)

Stillin, Marie: Various Positions (2002)

Stitzel, Robert: Distant Thunder (1988)

St-Jean, Raymond: Cabaret neiges noires (1997)

Stock, Nigel: Man Called Intrepid, A (1979)

Stocker, Margarita: Capture of Karna Small, The (1987), Claire: Tonight and Tomorrow (Claire: cette nuit et demain) (1985)

Stocker, Veronica: Capture of Karna Small, The (1987)

Stocki, Chester: Proud Rider, The (The Last Run) (1972)

Stockton, Brian: 24 Store, The (1990), Wheat Soup (1987)

Stockwell, Dean: Buying Time (1988), Fatal Memories (The Eileen Franklin Story) (1992), Palais Royale (1988), Water Damage (1999)

Stockwell, John: Losin' It (1983), Stag (1997)

Stoddard, Gordon: No Blame (1988)

Stoffels, Royston: Diamond Girl (1998)

Stoffman, Nicole: Anchor Zone (1994)

Stoker, Cliff: Graveyard Shift (1987)

Stokes, Michael: Jungleground (1995), Striking Poses (1999)

Stone, Cindy: Expecting (2002)

Stone, Elly: Jacques Brel Is Alive and Well and Living in Paris (1975)

Stone, Oliver: Seizure (Tango Macabre) (1974)

Stone, Stuart: Boys' Club, The (1996), Heavenly Bodies (1985)

Stoneham, John: Teddy (The Pit) (1980)

St-Onge, Guylaine: Montréal Sextet (1991)

St-Onge, Marie: Last Glacier, The (1984)

Stopkewich, Lynne: Kissed (1996), Suspicious River (2000)

Stoppel, Frederick: Brooklyn State of Mind, A (1997)

Storeoff, Michael: Life and Times of Chester-Angus Ramsgood, The (1971)

Storey, David: Question of the Sixth, A (1981)

Storey, Raymond: Butterbox Babies (1995), Happy Christmas, Miss King (1999), Sleeping Dogs Lie (1999)

Storm, Gregory: Fearless (1999)

Stormare, Peter: Hitler: The Rise of Evil (2003)

Storms, Waneta: Joe's So Mean to Josephine (1997)

Story, Richard: Echo Lake (2000)

St-Pierre, Denyse: Esprit du mal, L' (Spirit of Evil, The) (1954), Mother's Heart, A (1953)

St-Pierre, Julie: Falling Over Backwards (1990), Vengeance de la femme en noir, La (The Revenge of the Lady in Black) (1996)

St-Pierre, Louis: Revolutionaries, The (1965)

St-Pierre, Marc: Ange noir, L' (1991)

St-Pierre, Nicole: Large Abode, A (1978)

Strain, Jim: Summer of the Monkeys (1998)

Strain, Julie: Battle Queen 2020 (Millennium Queen 2000) (2000)

Strange, Derrick: Revenge of the Radioactive Reporter (1992)

Strange, Marc: Blindside (1986), Isabel (1968), Kate Morris, Vice President (1984), Morning Man, The (1986), Frostfire (1995), Paper People, The (1967), Tools of the Devil (1985)

Strange, Sarah: Kitchen Party (1997)

Straram, Patrick: Earth to Drink, The (La terre à boire) (1964)

Strasberg, Susan: In Praise of Older Women (1978), Mazes and Monsters (1982)

Stratas, Teresa: Canadians, The (1961), Under the Piano (1998)

Strathairn, David: April One (1994), Lathe of Heaven (2002), Song of Hiawatha, The (1996)

Stratten, Dorothy: Autumn Born (1979)

Stratton, David: Prom Night III: The Last Kiss (1989)

Strauss, Peter: Joan of Arc (1999), Spacehunters: Adventures in the Forbidden Zone (1983)

Stromberg, Paula: House of Lovers (*La maison des amants*) (1972)

Strong, Danny: Perpetrators of the Crime (1999)

Strong, Mark: Twice Upon a Yesterday (1998)

Stroud, Donald: Explosion (1969), Search and Destroy (1979), Death Weekend (House by the Lake) (1976)

Strube, Cordelia: Tools of the Devil (1985)

Strummer, Joe: Candy Mountain (1987)

Stryker, Jonathan: Curtains (1983)

Stuart, Eleanor: Forbidden Journey (1950), Oedipus Rex (1956)

Stuart, Ian: Teddy (The Pit) (1980)

Stuart, Katie: Summer of the Monkeys (1998), Magician's House, The (1999)

Stuck, Herman: Bookfair Murders, The (1999)

Study, Lomax: M.V.P.: Most Valuable Primate (2000

Sturgess, Peter: Butler's Night Off, The (1948), Funeral Home (Cries in the Night) (1982), Nothing Personal (1980), Off Your Rocker (1982), Only God Knows (1974), Power Play (*Coup d'état*) (State of Shock) (1978)

Subiela, Elisso: Dark Side of the Heart, The (*El lado oscuro del corazon*) (1993)

Suchanek, Michael: Various Positions (2002)

Suchet, David: Fool Proof (2003), Iron Eagle (1986)

Sudana, Tapa: Eleventh Child, The (1998)

Sugar, Ted: Goin' Down the Road (1970)

Suissa, Danièle: Évangéline the Second (*Évangéline Deusse*) (1985), Garnet Princess, The (1987), Kate Morris, Vice President (1984), Martha, Ruth and Edie (1987), Morning Man, The (1986), No Blame (*L'incroyable vérité*) (1988), Rose Cafe, The (1987), Secret of Nandy, The (1991)

Sukowa, Barbara: Johnny Mnemonic (1995)

Suli, Ania: Stuart Bliss (1998)

Sullivan, Brett: Ginger Snaps: The Sequel (2003)

Sullivan, Charlotte: Tagged: The Jonathan Wamback Story (2002)

Sullivan, E.P.: *Évangéline* (1913)

Sullivan, Kevin: Anne of Green Gables (1985), Anne of Green Gables: The Continuing Story (Series) (1985-1999), Lantern Hill (1990), Looking for Miracles (1989), Piano Man's Daughter, The (2000), Promise the Moon (1997)

Sullivan, Sean: 125 Rooms of Comfort (1974), Atlantic City, U.S.A (1980), Best Revenge (Misdeal) (1981), Boy in Blue, The (1986), Crossbar (1979), Dangerous Age, A (1958), Face Off (1971), Flick (Dr. Frankenstein on Campus) (1970), Grey Fox, The (1982), Hard

Part Begins, The (1973), Heavenly Bodies (1985), High Card (1982), Nobody Waved Goodbye (1964), Nothing Personal (1980), Of the Fields, Lately (1975), One Man (1977), Room for a Stranger (1968), Silence of the North (1981), Silent Partner, The (1978), Vicky (1973), Why Rock the Boat? (1974)

Summer, Bart: Last Stop, The (1999)

Summers, Jaron: Killer Image (1992), Parallels (1980)

Sunshine, Madeline: Say Nothing (2001)

Surguy, Philip: Plastic Mile, The (1969)

Surjik, Stephen: Grand Larceny (1991), Wayne's World 2 (1993), Little Criminals (1996), Mary Silliman's War (1994)

Sutcliffe, David: Two or Three Words (1999)

Sutherland, Ann: God's Crucible (1921)

Sutherland, Anne: Montréal Main (1974)

Sutherland, Dave: Montréal Main (1974)

Sutherland, Donald: Act of the Heart (1970), Agaguk (Shadow of the Wolf) (1993), Alien Thunder (Dan Candy's Law) (1973), Art of War, The (2000), Bear Island (1979), Bethune: The Making of a Hero (1990) see Bethune (1977), Blood Relatives (Les liens de sang) (1978), Buster's Bedroom (1991), Disappearance, The (1977), Eminent Domain (1990), Gas (1981), Hollow Point (1997), Lifeforce Experiment (1994), Man, a Woman and a Bank, A (1979), Murder by Decree (1979), Nothing Personal (1980), Red Hot (1993), Scream of Stone (*Cerro Torra*) (1991), Threshold (1981)

Sutherland, Doug: In Her Defense (1998)

Sutherland, Ian: Blind Faith (1982), Certain Practices (1979), Highpoint (1980), Improper Channels (1981), Moving Targets (1983), Rituals (The Creeper) (1977)

Sutherland, Joe: Freeloading (1986)

Sutherland, John: Montréal Main (1974)

Sutherland, Kiefer: Bay Boy, The (1984), Crazy Moon (1986), Woman Wanted (1999)

Sutherland, Ronald: Suzanne (1980)

Suto, Janine: Apple, the Stem and the Seeds, The (*La pomme, la queue et les pépins*) (1974), Dernier cri (The Last Cry) (1996), Little One Is Coming Soon, The (1972), Mission of Fear (1965), Père Chopin (1945), Push but Push Reasonably (Scarlatina) (*Pousse mais pousse égal*) (1975), Two Women of Gold (*Deux femmes en or*) (1970)

Sutton, Jeff: Nature of Nicholas, The (2002)

Sutton, John: Canadians, The (1961)

Sutton, Richard: Bob's Garage (2001)

Sutton, Ted: Great Coups of History (1969)

Suttor, Carmel: Croon Maury and Mrs. B.

(International Title) (2003)

Suzanne, Natalie: Traces (1978)

Suzuki, Elizabeth: Golden Apples of the Sun (Ever After All) (1973)

Svandova, Jana: Chained Heat II (1993)

Svatek, Peter: Dark Harbour (1997), Mystery of the Million Dollar Hockey Puck (1975), Rendering, The (Portrait for Murder) (2002), Witchboard III: The Possession (1995)

Svendsen, Linda: At the End of the Day: The Sue Rodriguez Story (1998), Diviners, The (1993)

Svenson, Bo: Breaking Point (1976)

Swale, Tom: Man in the Attic, The (1994)

Swan, James: Nine B (1986)

Swanson, Brenda: Scanners: The Showdown (Scanner Cop II: Volkin's Revenge) (1994)

Swanson, Kristy: Zebra Lounge (2001)

Swayne, Marion: Man from Glengarry, The (1920)

Sweeney, Bruce: Dirty (1998), Last Wedding, The (2001), Live Bait (1995)

Sweeney, Michelle: Company of Strangers, The (Strangers in Good Company) (1990)

Sweete, Barbara Willis: Perfect Pie (2002), Elizabeth Rex (2003)

Swerdfager, Bruce: Oedipus Rex (1956), Out of Sight, Out of Mind (The Seventh Circle) (1983)

Swerhone, Elise: My Mother's Ghost (1996)

Swinton, Tilda: Possible Worlds (2000)

Switzer, Bill: Scorn (2000), Dinosaur Hunter, The (2000), Mr. Rice's Secret (2000)

Sydow, Max Von: Nuremberg (2000)

Sylvain, Gabbi: Cain (1965), Corde au cou, La (1966), Don't Let It Kill You (Il ne faut pas mourir pour ça) (1968)

Sylvain, Marcel: Séraphin (1950)

Symons, Scott: Symposium (1996)

Szabo, Istvan: Sunshine (1999)

Szabo, Rudy: Skip Tracer (1977)

Szanosi, Annie: Yellow Wedding (1998)

Sze, Gary: Dreamtrips (2000)

Ta, Siu: Art of Woo, The (2001), Iron Road (2002)

Taav, Michael: Crazy Horse (She Drives Me Crazy) (Friends, Lovers & Lunatics) (1989), Still Life (Still Life: The Fine Art of Murder) (1990)

Tabra, Roger: Gaia (1994)

Tacchella, Jean Charles: Dames galantes (Romantic Ladies) (1990), Homme de ma vie, L' (The Man in My Life) (1993)

Tagawa, Cary-Hiroyuki: Art of War, The (2000), White Tiger (1995)

Tager, Aaron: Curtis's Charm (1995), Mothers and Daughters (1992)

Taggert, Brian: Of Unknown Origin (1983), Visiting Hours (Fright) (1982)

Taghmaoui, Said: Wanted (Crime Spree) (2003)

Taillefer, Paul-Antoine: Escort, The (L'escorte) (1996)

Takacs, Tibor: Gate, The (1987)

Takahashi, Kohji: Hiroshima (1996)

Takata, Yas: Cord (Hide and Seek) (2000)

Takei, George: Best Bad Thing, The (1997), Kissinger and Nixon (1994)

Takemoto, Koshijidayu: Lover's Exile, The (1981)

Takemoto, Mojidayu: Lover's Exile, The (1981)

Takemoto, Oritayu: Lover's Exile, The (1981)

Takeshi: Johnny Mnemonic (1995)

Talbot, Lise: My Uncle Antoine (1971)

Talbot, Michel: My Uncle Antoine (1971)

Talbot, Patricia: Blue Man, The (1985), Echoes in Crimson (1987)

Talebi, Niloufar: Post Concussion (1999)

Tallo, Katie: Juiced (1999), Posers (2002)

Talve, Merika: Undivided Attention (1987)

Tamasy, Paul: Air Bud (1997), Air Bud: Golden Receiver (1998), Air Bud: World Pup (2000)

Tamiroff, Akim: Vulture, The (1967)

Tammuz, Jonathan: Rupert's Land (1998)

Tana, Paul: Grands enfants, Les (Day by Day) (1980), Mr. Aiello (Le Deroute) (1998), Saracen, The (La Sarrasine) (1991) Les Artisans du Cinema (1990) (60mins) The documentary by Serge Giquere about the making of Paul Tanna's Le Deroute.

Tandy, Jessica: Butley (1974), Camilla (1994)

Tang, Dai Sijie: Eleventh Child, The (1998)

Tani, Yoko: Sweet and the Bitter, The (1962)

Tanner, Gordon: Inertia (2001), Vulture, The (1967)

Tanner, Joy: Prom Night IV: Deliver Us From Evil (1992), Shadow Lake (2000)

Tanvir, Habib: Burning Season, The (1993)

Tapp, Gordon: Wild Horse Hank (1979)

Tapp, Jimmy: What the Hell Are They Complaining About?) (Hold on, Papa!) (Tiens-toi bien après les oreilles à Papa) (1971), Loving and Laughing (1971)

Taraporevala, Sooni: Such a Long Journey (1998)

Tarbes, Jean-Jacques: Blackout (Blackout in New York) (1978)

Tarbes, Monique: Grand Recess, The (1976)

Tarbet, Andrew: Apartment Hunting (1999), Café Olé (2000), Rowing Through (1996), Touching Wild Horses (2002)

Tarmoush, Michael: Louisa May Alcott's Little Men (1998)

Tarnow, Toby: Nobody Waved Goodbye (1964), Only God Knows (1974), Till Death Do Us Part (1982), Utilities (1981)

Tarvainen, Henry: Winter Kept Us Warm (1965)

Tassé, François: Act of the Heart (1970), Conquête, La (1973), Madame B (1986), Waiting for Caroline (1967)

Tassé, Gérald: Heads or Tails (Pile ou face) (1971)
Tate, Larenz: Love Come Down (2000)
Tate, Michael: Certain Practices (1979)
Tate, Scott: Airport In (1996)
Taubes, Frank: Mask, The (1961)
Tavares, Fernanda: 90 Days (1985)
Tavarone, Dino: *Café Olé* (2000), Snail's Point of View, A (*La position de l'escargot*) (1998), Two Seconds (*2 secondes*) (1998), Uncles, The (2000)
Tavi, Tuvia: Paradise (1982)
Taviss, Norman: Lies My Father Told Me (1975), Mourning Suit, The (1976)
Taylor, Carole: Inside Out (1979)
Taylor, Carolyn: 19 Months (2002)
Taylor, Cherilee: Leaving Metropolis (2002)
Taylor, Courtney: Prom Night III: The Last Kiss (1989)
Taylor, Don: Echoes of a Summer (1976)
Taylor, Douglas: Carpenter, The (1987)
Taylor, Elizabeth: Nobody Makes Me Cry (Between Friends) (1983)
Taylor, Emily:Three and a Half (*Trois et demi*) (2002)
Taylor, Gilbert: Flick (Dr. Frankenstein on Campus) (1970)
Taylor, Gladys: Homecoming, The (Good Luck, Jennifer Gagnon) (1978), Riel (1979)
Taylor, Greg: Summer of the Monkeys (1998)
Taylor, Jan: Borrower, The (1985)
Taylor, Judy: My Five Wives (2000)
Taylor, Ian: Meatballs, Part III: The Climax (1987)
Taylor, Lee: Reasonable Force (1983)
Taylor, Noah: Max (2001)
Taylor, Ronald: Bloody Brood, The (1959), Cool Sound From Hell, A (The Young and the Beat) (1959), Nobody Waved Goodbye (1964)
Taylor, Scott: Going Back (2002)
Taylor, Tammy: Meatballs, Part II (1984)
Taylor, William: One Plus One (The Kinsey Report) (Exploring the Kinsey Report) (1961)
Taylor, Willie: Highway of Heartaches (1994)
Teasdale, Jeannette: *Séraphin* (1950), Village Priest, The (*Le curé de village*) (1949)
Tejada-Flores, Miguel: Unsaid, The (2001)
Teles, Thiago: Tiresia (2003)
Telfer, Jay: You've Come a Long Way, Katie (1981)
Telford, Zoe: Hitler: The Rise of Evil (2003)
Temblay, Johanne Marie: Barbarian Invasions, The (*Invasions Barbares, Les*) (2003)
Templeton, Charles: Boy Next Door, The (1984)
Templeton, Deborah: Scoop (1978)
Templeton, Jean: Ivy League Killers (The Fast Ones) (1959)
Tenault, Norma: All the Days of My Life (1982)

Tench, John: Bear Walker (Backroads) (2000), Darkside, The (1986), Johnny Shortwave (1995)
Tennant, Victoria: Handmaid's Tale, The (1990), Whispers (1990)
Tenny, Kevin: Witchboard I (1985), Witchboard II (1993), Witchboard III: The Possession (1995)
Tepperman, Joy: Winter Kept Us Warm (1965)
Terrazzano, Maurizio: Saint Monica (2002)
Terry, Donald: Roger and Elvis (1993)
Terzo, Venus: Home Movie (1992)
Teshigahara, Hiroshi: Flower of Youth (That Tender Age, The Adolescents) (*La fleur de l'âge*) (*Les adolescentes*) (1967)
Tessier, Eric: Sur Le Seuil (Under the Sky) (2003)
Tessier, Geneviève: Divine Ryans, The (1998), Real Howard Spitz, The (1998)
Tessler, Howard: Deaf and Mute (1986)
Tétreault, Emmanuelle: *Part des choses, La* (*Un léger vertige*) (A Part of Things) (A Light Vertigo) (1991)
Teyssier, Frédéric: Ruth (1994)
Thal, Eric: Joe's So Mean to Josephine (1997)
Thatcher, Torin: Canadians, The (1961), Sweet and the Bitter, The (1962)
Thauberger, Rudy: Rhino Brothers, The (2002)
Thauvette, Guy: Absence, The (*L'absence*) (1976), Anne Trister (1986), *Au fil de l'eau* (By the Riverside) (2002), Big Rock, the Big Man, The (Le Grand Rock) (1969), Blizzard, The (Rafales) (1990), Cargo (1990), Confidences of the Night (*L'amour blessé*) (1975), Crinoline Madness (*La folie des crinolines*) (1995), Great Ordinary Movie, The (Joan of Arc Is Alive and Well and Living in Québec) (1971), *Sous les draps, les étoiles* (Stars Under the Sheets) (1989), *Visage pâle* (Pale Face) (1986)
Théberge, André: Matter of Life, A (1971), Paths of the World, The (*Les allées de la terre*) (1973)
Theriault, Eric: In Her Defense (1998)
Thériault, Janine: Murder Most Likely (1999), Stork Derby, The (2001)
Thériault, Pierre: Quarantaine, La (Beyond Forty) (1982), Deaf to the City (Le sourd dans la ville) (1987), Dollar, The (The Other Side of the River) (*La piastre*) (*L'autre bord du fleuve*) (1976), Panic (*Panique*) (1977), Réjeanne Padovani (1973)
Thériault, Serge: *Boys III, Les* (2001), *Boys, Les* (The Boys) (1997), Ding and Dong, The Film (1990), Gina (1975), Sphinx, The (1995)
Thériault, Yves: Initiation, The (1970)
Thérien, André: Summer of the Monkeys (1998)

Thério, Marie-Jo: Book of Eve (*Histoires d'Eve*) (2002), Full Blast (*L'ennemi*) (1999)

Theroux, Justin: American Psycho (2000)

Thevenet, Maurice: Night of the Dribbler (1990)

Thibault, Benoît: Taureau (1972)

Thibault, Mireille: It Can't Be Winter, We Haven't Had Summer Yet (1981)

Thibault, Madeleine: My Friend Pierrette (*Mon amie Pierrette*) (1969)

Thibault, Olivette: *Délivrez-nous du mal* (Deliver Us From Evil) (1967), My Uncle Antoine (1971)

Thicke, Alan: Bear With Me (2000), Hitting Home (Obsessed) (1989)

Thiéry, Marthe: *Esprit du mal, L'* (Spirit of Evil, The) (1954))

Thiffault, Alain: Luke or the Part of Things (1982)

Thinel, Paul: Pin-Pon, The Film (*Pin-Pon, Le film*) (1999)

Thisdale, Jacques: Gone to Glory (*Partis pour la gloire*) (1975), Panic (*Panique*) (1977), Song for Julie, A (*Chanson pour Julie*) (1976), Those Damned Savages (1971)

Thom, James: Cyberjack (1995)

Thom, Robert: Third Walker, The (1980)

Thomas, Christine: Wedding in White (1972)

Thomas, Dave: Cold Sweat (1993), Double Negative (Deadly Companion) (1979), Fancy Dancing (2002), Ghost Mom (1993), Riel (1979), Strange Brew (1983)

Thomas, Ian: Hurt Penguins (1992)

Thomas, James: Ice Men, The (2001)

Thomas, Jerry: I'm Going to Get You...Elliot Boy (1971)

Thomas, Les: Wendy (1966)

Thomas, Powys: Luck of Ginger Coffey, The (1964)

Thomas, Ralph: Ambush at Iroquois Pass (1979), Cementhead (1979), Every Person Is Guilty (1979), First Season, The (1988), Hank (1977), Kathy Karuks Is a Grizzly Bear (1976), Tar Sands, The (1977), Terry Fox Story, The (1983), Ticket to Heaven (1981), Tyler (1977)

Thomas, Ruth: Lies My Father Told Me (1975)

Thomas, Terry: Spanish Fly (1975)

Thomason, Edward: All the Days of My Life (1982), Gentle Sinners (1984)

Thomey, Gregory: Boys of St. Vincent, The (1992), Ladies Room (1999)

Thompson, Ambroise: Royal Bonbon (2002)

Thompson, Gordon: Suzanne (1980)

Thompson, Hugh: 100 Days in the Jungle (2002), Another Country: A North of 60 Mystery (2003), Blessed Stranger: After Flight 111 (2001), Net Worth (1997), Recipe for Revenge (1998), Society's Child (2001), Stolen Miracle (2001)

Thompson, J. Lee: Happy Birthday to Me (1981)

Thompson, Jane: Coming of Age (1983)

Thompson, Jason: American Beer (1996), Wishmaster 4: The Prophecy Fulfilled (2002)

Thompson, Joy: Chatwill's Verdict (Killer Instinct) (Baker County, U.S.A) (Trapped) (1982), Prom Night (1980)

Thompson, Judith: City Girl, The (1984), Life With Billy (1993), Lost and Delirious (2000), Perfect Pie (2002), Turning to Stone (1986)

Thompson, Neil: Secret of Jerome, The ((1994)

Thompson, Patricia: Peanut Butter Solution, The (Opération beurre de pinottes) (1985)

Thompson, Peggy: Lotus Eaters, The (1993)

Thompson, Perry: Face Off (1971)

Thompson, Scott: Hayseed (1997), Kids in the Hall: Brain Candy (1996), Super 8 (1994)

Thompson, Shawn Alex: Dinner at Fred's (1997)

Thompson-Allen, John: Change of Heart (1984)

Thomsen, Ulrich: Max (2001)

Thomson, Christopher: Morrison Murders, The (1997)

Thomson, Cicely: Snowbirds (1981)

Thomson, Gordon: Explosion (1969), Intruder, The (1981), Leopard in the Snow (1978), Love From the Market Place (see Acts of Love) (1980), Starship Invasions (1977)

Thomson, Kristen: Flower & Garnet (2002), Law of Enclosures, The (2000)

Thomson, Melissa: Summer of the Monkeys (1998)

Thomson, R.H.: Ambush at Iroquois Pass (1979), American Christmas Carol, An (1979), And Then You Die (1987), Canada's Sweetheart: The Saga of Hal C. Banks (1985), Case of the Whitechapel Vampire, The (2001), Charlie Grant's War (1985), Defy Gravity (1990), Dinosaur Hunter, The (2000), Escape from Iran: The Canadian Caper (Desert Blades) (1981), Every Person Is Guilty (1979), First Season, The (1988), Ford: The Man and the Machine (1987), Glory Enough for All (1988), Happy Memories (Old Memories) (*Les beaux souvenirs*) (1981), Heaven on Earth (1987), If You Could See What I Hear (1982), Jigsaw (Angry Man, An) (*L'homme en colère*) (1979), Lotus Eaters, The (1993), Marriage Bed, The (1986), Max (1994), Net Worth (1997), Of the Fields, Lately (1975), Piano Man's Daughter, The (2000), Population of One, A (1980), Quarrel, The (1990), Royal Scandal, The (2001), Samuel Lount (1985), Stork Derby, The (2001), Surfacing (1981), Terry Fox Story, The (1983), Ticket to Heaven (1981), Trudeau (2002), Twilight of the Ice Nymphs (1997), Tyler (1977)

Thor, Jon-Mikl: Rock 'n Roll Nightmare (The Edge of Hell) (1987)

Thorn, Mike: Three and a Half (Trois et demi) (2002)

Thorne, Dyanne: Isla the Tigress of Siberia (1977)

Thorne, Kika: House of Pain (1995)

Thornton, Frank: Spanish Fly (1975)

Thornton-Sherwood, Madeleine: Changeling, The (1980)

Thorson, Linda: Curtains (1983)

Thorvik, Astri: High (1968)

Thouin, Lise: Chocolate Eclair (Éclair au chocolat) (1979), Doves, The (Les colombes) (1972), Tadpole and the Whale (1988)

Thout, Yvette: Christmas of Madame Beauchamp, The (1981)

Thrush, Michelle: Isaac Littlefeathers (1984), Legend of Kootenai Brown, The (1990), Showdown at Williams Creek (Kootenai Brown) (1991)

Thurier, Blaine: Low Self-Esteem Girl (2000)

Thuy, Hoa: Eleventh Child, The (Nguol Thua) (1998)

Tian, Valerie: Long Life, Happiness & Prosperity (2002)

Tibaldi, Antonio: On My Own (1992)

Tiberius, Paula: Goldirocks (2003)

Ticotin, Rachel: All the Fine Lines (Full Disclosure) (1999)

Tiefenbach, Dov: Flower & Garnet (2002), Welcome to the Freakshow (2001), Public Domain (2003)

Tierney, Aidan: Family Viewing (1988)

Tierney, Brigid: Paperboy, The (1994)

Tierney, Jacob: Dead End (False Pretense) (1998), This Is My Father (1998), Ford: The Man and the Machine (1987), Horses in Winter (1988), Many Trials of One Jane Doe, The (2002), Rainbow (1995), Tek War: Tek Justice (1994), This Is My Father (1998), Whiskers (1997), You Can Thank Me Later (1998)

Tierney, Kevin: Dancing on the Moon (Viens danser sur la lune) (1997), 20th Century Chocolate Cake, A (1983)

Tierney, Patrick: In This Corner (1986), Next of Kin (1984)

Tifo, Marie: Babylone (Halfway House) (1991), Conquête, La (1973), Day in a Taxi, A (Une journée en taxi) (1982), Good Riddance (Les bons débarras) (1980), Île de Sable, L' (1999), In the Belly of a Dragon (1989), Intimate Power (1985), Jour "S," Le (1984), Just a Game (1983), Kalamazoo (1988), Lucien Brouillard (1983), Marguerite Volant (1996), Maria Chapdelaine (1983), Pots cassés, Les (Broken Dishes) (1994), Père et Fils (Father and Son) (2003), Red Eyes (Accidental Truths) (Les yeux rouges) (Les verités accidentelles) (1983), S

Day (Le jour S) (1984), Séraphin (Heart of Stone) (A Man and His Sin) (2002), Stop (1971), You Are Beautiful Jeanne (1988)

Tighe, Kevin: Fast Food High (2003), I Love a Man in Uniform (1993)

Tijeriha, Cecilia: One Man Out (Erik) (1989)

Till, Eric: American Christmas Carol, An (1979), Back to Beulah (1974), Bethune (1977), Case of Libel, A (1985), Challengers, The (1990), Fan's Notes, A (1972), Freedom of the City, The (1976), Gentle Sinners (1984), Getting Married in Buffalo Jump (1990), Glory Enough for All (1988), Golden Will: The Silken Laumann Story (1997), Great Big Thing, A (1968), If You Could See What I Hear (1982), Improper Channels (1981), Lifeline to Victory (1993), Mary and Joseph: A Story of Faith (1979), Oh, What a Night (1992), Pit Pony (1998), Red Green's Duct Tape Forever (2002), Terra X (1997), To Catch a Killer (1991), Turning to Stone (1986), Wild Horse Hank (1979), Win, Again! (1998)

Tilly, Jennifer: Cord (Hide and Seek) (2000), Agaguk (Shadow of the Wolf) (1993), Wrong Guy, The (1998)

Tilly, Meg: Agnes of God (1985)

Tilson, Amanda Jane: Deadly Portrayal (2003)

Timmins, Cali: Hostile Force (The Heist) (1996)

Timoschuk, Natalie: Remembering Mel (1986)

Tinen, Paul: Immortels, Les (The Immortals) (2003)

Tinkler, Robert: M.V.P. 3 (2003)

Tinnell, Robert: Believe (2000), Frankenstein and Me (1995), Kids of the Round Table (1995)

Tobias, Oliver: Broken Lullaby (1994), Grizzly Falls (2000)

Tognetti, Anne: Duo pour une soliste (1998)

Toles, George: Archangel (1990), Careful (1992), Three by Paizs (1984), Twilight of the Ice Nymphs (1997)

Toll, Meghan: Stolen Heart (1998)

Tomassini, Mirella: Snail's Point of View, A (La position de l'escargot) (1998)

Tomczak, Kim: Legal Memory (1992)

Tompson, Paul: Jean-François-Xavier de... (1971)

Tonisso, Karina: And I Love You Dearly (La maîtresse) (1973)

Tootoosis, Gordon: Alien Thunder (Dan Candy's Law) (1973), Bear With Me (2000), Big Bear (1988), Curse of the Viking Grave (1990), Dream Storm: A North of 60 Mystery (2001), Keeping the Promise (1997), Marie-Anne (1978), My Mother's Ghost (1996), Now and Forever (2001), Song of Hiawatha, The (1996), Spirit Rider (1993), Tom Alone (1989) Stage, Screen and Reserve: The Life and Times of Gordon Tootoosis (2003) (60mins) Director:

Guo Fangfang. Producer: Gerald B. Sperling. Scriptwriter: Maggie Siggins. A documentary tracing 'the winding path' of Gordon Tootoosis, from his childhood on Saskatchewan's Poundmaker Reserve, to success in Hollywood and Canadian films. An example of determination and identity.

Topol, Frank: Barnone (1997)

Topol: Galileo (1973)

Torens, Jonathan: Beefcake (1999)

Torens, Pip: Eminent Domain (1990)

Torgov, Sarah: Drying Up the Streets (1978), If You Could See What I Hear (1982), July Group, The (1981)

Torn, Rip: Beautiful Dreamers (1990)

Toro (dog): *Deux amis silencieux* (1969)

Torr, Michèle: *Diable aime les bijoux, Le* (1969)

Torrent, Agnès: Joy (1983)

Tory, Tess: Hired Gun (The Devil's Spawn) (The Last Gunfighter) (1959)

Tosato, Tony: Hog Wild (*Les fous de la moto*) (1980)

Toth, Leslie: Buying Time (1988), Once (1981)

Toth, Terri: Summerlust (1973)

Tougas, Sébastien: Devil at Four, The (1988)

Touliatos, George: Agency (1980), Dreams Beyond Memory (1987), Falcon's Gold (1982), Firebird 2015 AD (1980), Gladiator Cop (1994), Heartaches (1981), I Miss You, Hugs and Kisses (1978), Last Chase, The (1980), Only God Knows (1974), Power Play (*Coup d'état*) (State of Shock) (Operation Overthrow) (1978), Prom Night (1980), Short Change (Une fille impossible) (1989), Tar Sands, The (1977), Utilities (1981), We the Jury (1996)

Toupin, Georges: Now That April's Here (1958), Promised Land, The (*Les brûlés*) (1958)

Tourell, Wayne: Bonjour, Timothy (1995)

Tousey, Sheila: Bear Walker (Backroads) (2000), Medicine River (1993)

Touzet, Corinne: First Circle, The (1991)

Towers, Harry Alan: Lost World, The (1992)

Townsend, Bud: High Country, The (1981)

Toy, Maxim: Artificial Lies (*Le manipulateur*) (2000)

Tracey, Ian: Change of Heart (1984), Dream-Speaker (1976), Home Movie (1992), Ice Men, The (2001), Lola (2001), Milgaard (1998), Rookies (1990), Rupert's Land (1998), Touched (1999), Trust in Me (1995), Shelley (Turned Out) (1987), War Between Us, The (1995)

Tracy, Arthur: This Is a Film (1989)

Tracy, Marlene: Woman Inside, The (1981)

Trade, Rough: One Night Stand (1978)

Trafficante, Mara: Deadbolt (1984), Halfback of Notre Dame, The (1994)

Trapp, Markle: Virginia's Run (2003)

Trapp, Valarie: Virginia's Run (2003)

Trash, Ryan: Truckin' (1972)

Travalena, Fred: Night of the Dribbler (1990)

Travanti, Daniel J.: Case of Libel, A (1985), Millennium (1988), Weep No More My Lady (1992)

Travassos, Almerinda: Recorded Live (1982)

Travers, Gail: Pianist, The (1991)

Traverse, Zoé: *Grand serpent du monde, Le* (The Great World Serpent) (1999)

Traviss, Norman: Sins of the Fathers (1948)

Traya, Jihad: Suburbanators, The (1995)

Tremblay, Alexis: Duration of the Day (*Le règne du jour*) (1967), So That the World Goes On (*Pour la suite du monde*) (1963), Water Cars (*Les voitures d'eau*) (1970)

Tremblay, Anthony: Ti-Ken (1965)

Aurèle Tremblay: Water Cars ((1970)

Tremblay, Carmen: Vultures, The (*Les vautours*) (1975), Years of Dreams and Revolt (1984)

Tremblay, Eddy: *Séraphin* (1950)

Tremblay, Ghislain: *Piege d'Issoudun, Le* (2002)

Tremblay, Guy: Carnival in Free Fall (1966)

Tremblay, Guylaine: 24 Poses (2002), *Albertine, en cinq temps* (Albertine in Five Times) (1999), Life After Love (2000), Mariages (2001), Matroni and Me (1999), Streetheart(1998)

Tremblay, Henri: Trouble Makers (1964)

Tremblay, Hugues: *Jos Carbone* (1975)

Tremblay, Jean-Joseph: *Ange noir' L'* (1991), Deaf to the City (1987)

Tremblay, Johanne-Marie: *Corps perdu, À* (Straight to the Heart) (1988), *Jésus de Montréal* (1989), Phantom Life, A (1992)

Tremblay, Kay: Real Howard Spitz, The (1998)

Tremblay, Laurent: Water Cars (1970)

Tremblay, Léopold: Duration of the Day (1967), So That the World Goes On (*Pour la suite du monde*) (1963), Water Cars ((1970)

Tremblay, Marie-Paule: Duration of the Day (*Le règne du jour*) (1967)

Tremblay, Maurice: Mission of Fear (1965)

Tremblay, Michel: *Albertine, en cinq temps* (1999), Big Day, The (Le grand day) (1988), Heart Exposed, The (*Le coeur découvert*) (1986), Let's Talk About Love (1976), Once Upon a Time in the East (*Il était une fois dans l'est*) (1974), Sun Rises Late, The (1977), *Backyard Theatre* (1972) (28mins) Documentary by Jean-Pierre Lefebvre. On another important Quebec personality of film and theatre, Michel Tremblay, who is seen working with his players for *Les Belles Soeurs* and *St. Carmen de la Main*, in, of all places, a Montreal backyard, with much heat and passion.

Tremblay, Régent: Mis-Works, The (1959)

Tremblay, Régis: Traces (1978)

Tremblay, Robert: Ordinary Tenderness (1973), We Are Far From the Sun (1971)

Tremblay, Roger: Mis-Works, The (1959)

Tremblay, Yvan: Water Cars (1970)

Trembles, Rick: Shirley Pimple in the John Wayne Temple (1999)

Tremblett, Ken: Guilty, The (2000)

Trench, John: Outcast (1991)

Trent, John: Best Revenge (Misdeal) (1981), Blind Faith (1982), Crossbar (1979), Find the Lady (1976), Homer (1970), It Seemed Like a Good Idea at the Time (1975), Middle-Age Crazy (1980), Moving Targets (1983), Sunday in the Country (1975)

Trépanier, Gisèle: For Better, for Worse (1975)

Tretter, Richard: Wings of Chance (1961)

Trevor, Clifford: Paper People, The (1967)

Trier, Michael: Air Bud (1997)

Trinque, Jean-Guy: C'est bien beau l'amour (1971)

Triolo, Lori: Drive, She Said (1997)

Tripp, Louis: Gate, The (1987), Mama's Going to Buy You a Mockingbird (1987)

Triton, John: Rock 'n Roll Nightmare (1987)

Trividic, Anne Louise: Nearest to Heaven (Au plus près du paradis) (2002)

Trnka, Jiri: Joan of Arc (1999)

Trogi, Ricardo: Québec-Montréal (2002)

Trope, Tzipi: Tell Me That You Love Me (1983)

Trotter, Kate: First Season, The (1988), Golden Will: The Silken Laumann Story (1997), Joshua Then and Now (1985), Kate Morris, Vice President (1984), Running Man (1980), That's My Baby (1984), Threshold (1981)

Trotter, Richard: Wings of Chance (1961)

Trottier, François: Scandale (1982)

Trotz, Alissa: Mustard Bath (1993)

Trucco, Michael: Wishmaster 4: The Prophecy Fulfilled (2002)

Truchon, Natalie: Traces (1978)

Truchon, Normand: Carnival in Free Fall (1966)

Truckey, Donald: Net Worth (1997), Rough Justice (1984), Sylvan Lake Summer (1991), Tools of the Devil (1985)

Trudeau, Catherine: Loi du cochon, La (The Pig's Law) (2001), Ange de goudron, L'(2001)

Trudeau, Charles: In the Land of Zom (1983)

Trudeau, Margaret: Ange gardien, L' (1978), Kings and Desperate Men (1981)

Trudeau, Pierre Elliot: Pierre Elliott Trudeau: Memoirs (1993), Two Solitudes (1978)

Trudel, Denis: 15 février 1839 (February 15, 1839) (2001), October (1994), Two Seconds (1998)

Trudel, Louise: Gobital (1975)

Trudel, Yves: Miracle in Memphis (1999)

True, Monica: Day Breaks Once More (1995)

Trujillo, Raoul: Automne sauvage, L' (1992), Betrayed (2003), Paris, France (1993), Scanners II: The New Order (1991), Swordsman, The (1993), Trial at Fortitude Bay (1994)

Truninger, Curt: Waiting for Michelangelo (1995)

Tseng, Chang: Dr. Jekyll and Mr. Hyde (1999), Long Life, Happiness & Prosperity (2002)

Tsuruzawa, Enza: Lover's Exile, The (1981)

Tsuruzawa, Seiji: Lover's Exile, The (1981)

Tsvetkov, Ivailo: Here Am I (1999)

Tucci, Stanley: Whole Shebang, The (2001)

Tuck, Mel: Freedom of the City, The (1976), Quiet Day in Belfast, A (1973)

Tucker, Paul: Lighthouse (1989)

Tucker, Tami: Artichoke (1978)

Tuckett, Rita: Parting (see Acts of Love) (1980)

Tuit, Mark: Barnone (1997)

Tulasne, Patricia: Demoiselle sauvage, La (The Wild Girl) (Wild Damsel) (1991), Enfant sur le lac, L' (1993), Louis XIX, le roi des ondes (1994), Présence des ombres, La (1996)

Tulkweemult: Silence (1997)

Tulugarjuk, Lucy: Atanarjuat: The Fast Runner (L'homme nu) (2000)

Turbide, Yves: In Her Defense (1998)

Turcot, Louise: Apple, the Stem and the Seeds, The (1974), Few Days More, A (1981), Initiation, The (1970), Master Cats, The (1971), Oh, If Only My Monk Would Want (Ah! Si mon moine voulait) (1973), Peau et les os, La (Skin and Bones) (1988), Two Women of Gold (Deux femmes en or) (1970)

Turcotte, Isabelle: Femmes savantes, Les (2001)

Turcotte, Roger: Grands enfants, Les (1980)

Turcotte, Rose: Moonshine (1982)

Turenne, Jou: Peau Blanche, La (White Skin) (2003)

Turgeon, Jacques: Frontières (Border Line) (2003)

Turgeon, Marthe: Katryn's Place (2002), Medium Blues (1985), Woman in Transit, A (La femme de l'hôtel) (1984)

Turgeon, Pierre: Flower Between the Teeth, The (La fleur aux dents) (1976), Swindle, The (1974)

Turmel, Gilles: Gratien (1989)

Turnbull, David: Nature of Nicholas, The (2002)

Turner, Bonnie: Wayne's World 2 (1993)

Turner, Bradford: Colder Kind of Death, A (2000), Jinnah on Crime (2002), Jinnah On Crime –White Knight, Black Widow (2003), Major Crime (1998), Must Be Santa (1999), Paris or Somewhere (1995), Peacekeepers (1997), Prom, The (1991), This Matter of Marriage (1998), Wandering Soul Murders, The (2000)

Turner, Colin: King Solomon's Treasure (1979)

Turner, Guinevere: American Psycho (2000)

Turner, Kathleen: Friends at Last (1995), Switching Channels (1988)

Turner, Melburn: Here I Will Nest (1941), Immortal Scoundrel, The (*Étienne Brûlé, gibier de potence*) (1952), Little Canadian, The (1955)

Turner, Robert: Digger (1993)

Turner, Terry: Wayne's World 2 (1993)

Turner, Zara: On the Nose (2001)

Turp, Gilbert: Sweet Lies and Tender Oaths (*Les doux aveux*) (1982)

Turpin, André: Cosmos (1997), *Crabe dans la tête, Un* (A Crab in My Head) (2001)

Turpin, Armand: Zigrail (1995) Zigrail (1995)

Turton, Bradley: Sparkle (1998)

Turton, Kett: Roller Coaster (1999)

Turturro, Aida: Hemingway vs Callaghan (2003)

Turturro, John: Fear X (2003), Two Thousand and None (2000)

Turvey, Joe: Bad Money (1999)

Tushingham, Rita: Flying (1986), Housekeeper, The (Judgement in Stone) (1986)

Tutangata, Tommy Pierre: Return of Tommy Tricker, The (1994)

Tweed, Jill: Impolite (1992)

Tweed, Shannon: Cold Sweat (1993), Liar's Edge (1992), Meatballs, Part III: The Climax (1987), Of Unknown Origin (1983), Surrogate (1984)

Tweed, Tommy: Incredible Journey, The (1963)

Twidle, Aeryn: Girl Is a Girl, A (1999)

Tyas, Gertrude: Oedipus Rex (1956)

Tyler, Victor: Blackout (Blackout in New York) (1978)

Tylor, Evan: Stag (1997)

Tylor, Judy: My Five Wives (2000)

Tyrrell, Susan: To Kill the King (1974)

Tyson, Cicely: Jewel (2000)

Tyson, Tan: Alias Will James (1988)

Tyzack, Margaret: Wars, The (1983)

Ubaldo, Pino: It Happened in Canada (1961)

Udy, Claudia: Deux super-dingues (Heaven Help Us) (1982), Joy (1983)

Udy, Helene: One Night Only (1986), Pinball Summer (1980)

Ulc, Anthony: Honeymoon (1996)

Ullman, Elwood: Bloody Brood, The (1959)

Ullmann, Liv: Bay Boy, The (1984), Parting (see Acts of Love Series) (1980)

Ulmer, Edgar G.: Damaged Lives (1933), From Nine to Nine (1936)

Ulrich, Barbara: Cat in the Bag, The (*Le chat dans le sac*) (1964), *Trop c'est assez* (1996)

Ulrich, Laurel: Midwife's Tale, A: The Discovery of Martha Ballad (1996)

Ulrich, Skeet: Kevin of the North (2001)

Underhay, Nicole: Making Love in St. Pierre (2003)

Ungalaaq, Natar: Atanarjuat: The Fast Runner (*L'homme nu*) (2000), Kabloonak (1994)

Ungalaaq, Seporah Q.: Kabloonak (1994)

Unger, Deborah Kara: Between Strangers (2002), Crash (1996), Fear X (2003), Sunshine (1999)

Ungurianu, Marcel: Wild Dogs, The (2002)

Unsell, Eve: Great Shadow, The (1920)

Upmalis, Mike: Recommendation for Mercy (1975)

Ure, Mary: Luck of Ginger Coffey, The (1964)

Urich, Robert: Captains Courageous (1996)

Urquart, Scott: American Beer (1996)

Urquhart, Caird: Sunset Court (1988)

Urrutia, David: Jesus' Son (1999)

Ustinov, Peter: French Revolution, The (1989), Salem Witch Trials (2001)

Vaccaro, Brenda: Death Weekend (1976)

Vachet, Aloysius: Story of Dr. Louise, The (1949)

Vachon, Roger: Gobital (1975)

Vacratsis, Maria: Hayseed (1997)

Vadas, Kenny: Captains Courageous (1996)

Vadim, Christian: *Passage des hommes libres* (Passage of Free Men) (1996)

Vadim, Roger: Hot Touch (*Coup de maître*) (1982)

Vaillancourt, Christiane: Timing (1985)

Vajda, Sophie: *Sept Jours de Simon Labrosse, Les* (The September Days of Simon) (2003)

Valadez, Joe: Ascent, The (1994)

Valandrey, Charlotte: In the Shadow of the Wind (1986)

Valcour, Pierre: *Esprit du mal, L'* (1954)

Vale, Michael: Seasons in the Sun (1986)

Valenta, Vladimir: Sunday in the Country (1975), Wolfpen Principle (1974)

Valéry, Suzanne: Awakening, The (*L'amour humain*) (1970), Between Sweet and Salt Water (Drifting Downstream) (*Entre la mer et l'eau douce*) (1967), Merry World of Léopold Z, The (1965), Seven Times a Day (*Sept fois par jour*) (1971), That Darned Loot (*La maudite galette*) (1972)

Vallance, Louise: Falcon's Gold (1982), Man Who Guards the Greenhouse, The (1988)

Vallée, Jacques: Song for Julie, A (*Chanson pour Julie*) (1976)

Vallée, Jean-Marc: Black List (*Liste noire*) (1995)

Vallerand, Noël: No Holiday for Idols (1965)

Valois, Valerie: Scanners III: The Takeover (1992)

Vamos, Thomas: Exile, The (1971), Flower Between the Teeth, The (*La fleur aux dents*) (1976)

Van Bridge, Tony: Back to Beulah (1974), Chasing Rainbows (1988), If You Could See What I Hear (1982), Oedipus Rex (1956), Population of One, A (1980), Prodigious Hickey, The (1987), Riel (1979)

Van Damme, Jean-Claude: Death Warrant (1990)

Van de Water, Anton: And I Love You Dearly (La maîtresse) (1973)

Van der Kolk, Lance: Screwballs II: Loose Screws (1985)

Van der Velde, Nadine: Shadow Dancing (1988)

Van der Walter, Anton: Butler's Night Off, The (1948)

Van Devere, Trish: Changeling, The (1980)

Van Dine, Aline: Gun Runner, The (1984)

Van Dien, Casper: Collectors, The (1999), Going Back (2002), Tracker, The (1999)

Van Dyck, Paul: Hatley High (2003)

Van Hecke, Ivan: Secret Life of Algernon, The (1996)

Van Hool, Roger; Bob Million: Le jackpot de la planète (1997)

Van Patten, Timothy: Class of 1984 (1982)

Van Patten, Vincent: When Billie Beat Bobby (2001), Yesterday (1981)

Van Peebles, Mario: Stag (1997)

Van Riel, Gregory: 20th Century Chocolate Cake, A (1983)

Van Slet, Deborah: Sheep Calls and Shoplifters (1995)

Van Til, Beatrix: Ruffian, The (1983)

Van Valkenburgh, Deborah: One Man Out (Erik) (1989)

Van Winkle, Joseph: Woman Inside, The (1981)

Van, Victoria: Dur-Dur (1981)

Vanasse, Karine: Du pic au coeur (From Spades to Hearts) (2000), Emporte-moi (Set Me Free) (1998), Séraphin (Heart of Stone) (2002)

Vance, Courtney B.: Race for Freedom: The Underground Railroad (1993)

Vandenberghe, Paul: Story of Dr. Louise, The (Docteur Louise) (1949)

Vanden Hurek, Rico: Ascent, The (1994)

Vander Stappen, Christine: Family Pack (Que faisaient les femmes, pendant que l'homme marchait sur la lune?) (2000)

Vandernoot, Alexandra: Blood of the Hunter (1995), Petite fille particulière, Une (1995)

Vane, Norman Thaddeus: Shadow of the Hawk (1976)

Vanherweghem, Robert: Dernier havre, Le (1986)

Vanier, Denis: Trop c'est assez (Too Much Is Enough) (1996)

Vanlint, Derek: Spreading Ground, The (2000)

Vannicola, Joanna: Love and Human Remains (1994)

Vansier, Nathalie: Dancing on the Moon (Viens danser sur la lune) (1997), Sally Marshall Is Not An Alien (1999)

Vargas, Esther: Mother's Meat, Freud's Flesh (1984)

Vargas, Valentina: Los Naufragos (1994)

Varley, John: Millennium (1988)

Varley, Mike: Suburban Legend (1995)

Varughese, Sugith: Best of Both Worlds (1983), Colder Kind of Death, A (2000)

Vasconcelos, Paula de: Laura Laur (1988)

Vasil, Nadia: Until the Heart (Jusqu'au coeur) (1980)

Vatcher, John: Making Love in St. Pierre (2003)

Vaughan, Vanessa: Alexander Bell: The Sound and the Silence (1991), Crazy Moon (1986)

Vaughn, Robert: Dancing in the Dark (1995), Starship Invasions (1977)

Vaugier, Emmanuelle: Halfback of Notre Dame, The (1994), Mindstorm (2001), Wishmaster 3: Beyond the Gates of Hell (2001)

Vauthier, Guy: Medium Blues (1985)

Veber, Francis: Hold-Up (1985)

Vecchio, Giuditta del: Léolo (1992)

Vanderveen, Jace: Plastic Mile, The (1969)

Veinotte, Troy: Hanging Garden, The (1997)

Velasquez Jr., Andy: Heaven Before I Die (1997)

Veninger, Ingrid: Adolescence of P-I, The (Hide and Seek) (1983), On Their Knees (2001)

Venne, Stéphane: Now Where Are You? (Où êtesvous, donc?) (1969), Seul ou avec d'autres (Alone or With Others) (1962)

Venninger, Ingrid: War Boy, The (1985)

Venora, Diane: Terminal Choice (Deathbed) (1985)

Ventura, Gianpaolo: Circle, The (2001)

Ventura, Lino: Jigsaw (Angry Man, An) (L'homme en colère) (1979), Ruffian, The (1983), Sword of Gideon (1986)

Verdant, Claudie: Heavenly Bodies (Les corps célestes) (1973)

Verdi, Marie: Sucre amer (1997)

Verdier, France: Justine (1972)

Verley, Bernard: Erotic Love Games (1971)

Vermette, Gérard: Deux pieds dans la même bottine, Les (Two Feet in the Same Ankle Boot) (The Clumsy Klutz) (1974)

Vernac, Francine: Time Zero (No Game Without Sun) (Le temps zéro) (1972)

Vernon, Hilary: Paper People, The (1967)

Vernon, John: Angela (1978), Blood of Others, The (Le sang des autres) (1984), Crunch (1981), Curtains (1983), Face Off (1971), Fantastica (1980), Journey (1972), Malicious (1995), Mob Story (1987), More Joy in Heaven (1975), Nobody Waved Goodbye (1964), Paris or Somewhere (1995), Rat Tales (1987), Sodbusters (1995), Someday Soon (1977), Sweet Movie (1974), Two Men (1988), Giornata particolare, Una (A Special Day) (1977), Uncanny, The (1977), Wozeck: Out of the Fire (1992)

Vernon, Kate: Joe's Wedding (1996), Mob Story (1987), Office Party (1988), Probable Cause

(Sleepless) (1994)

Verreault, Jean-Nicolas: Hochelaga (2000), *Je n'aime que toi* (I Don't Love You) (2003), *Loi du cochon, La* (The Pig's Law) (2001), *Maelström* (2000), *Turbulence des fluides, La* (Chaos and Desire) (2002)

Vetrino, Ricky: Brooklyn State of Mind, A (1997)

Vette, Richard: *Bonjour, Timothy* (1995)

Vezerian, Ross: Keeper, The (1975)

Vézina, Alain: Morte amoureuse, La (1997)

Vézina, Francine: Gerda (1992)

Vian, Bobo: Clear-Dark (*Clair obscur*) (1988), Draghoula (1994)

Viau, Jean-Guy: Childhood Friend, A (*Une amie d'enfance*) (1978)

Vickers, Patricia: Visitor, The (1974)

Viens, Ivanhoe: Man from the Movies, The (1976)

Viergever, Dru: Goldirocks (2003)

Vigard, Kristen: Home to Stay (1978)

Vigliante, Franco: To Kill to Live (1973)

Vigneault, Gilles: Act of the Heart (1970), Snow Has Melted on the Manicouagan, The (*La neige a fondu sur la Manicouagan*) (1965), Tinamer (1987)

Vigneault, Richard: When Wolves Howl (*Quand hurlent les loups*) (1973)

Vigneault, Sonia: Zigrail (1995)

Vigoda, Abe: Brooklyn State of Mind, A (1997), Wanted (Crime Spree) (2003)

Viguier, Alain: Big Sabotage, The (*Le grand sabordage*) (1973)

Viharo, Robert: Happy Birthday Gemini (1980)

Vilbert, Véronique: Cat in the Bag, The (1964), My Childhood in Montréal (1971)

Villafana, Martin: Planet of Junior Brown, The (1997), Reluctant Angel (1997)

Villagra, Nelson: Cuervo, the Private Detective (1990)

Villard, Juliette: Erotic Love Games (1971)

Villechaize, Hervé: Seizure (Tango Macabre) (1974)

Villemaire, James: Dead Silence (1997)

Villeneuve, Denis: August 32nd on Earth (*Un 32 août sur terre*) (1998), Cosmos (1997), Maelström (2000)

Villeneuve, Lionel: I Love You (*Je t'aime*) (1974), My Uncle Antoine (1971)

Villeneuve, Lise: Grand Bill, The (*Le gros Bill*) (1949)

Villeret, Jacques: Hold-Up (1985), *Nous deux, À* (An Adventure for Two) (1979)

Villiers, Nick: Falling Through (2000)

Vince, Ann: M.V.P.: Most Valuable Primate (2000), Air Bud: Seventh Inning Fetch (2002), Duke, The (1999), M.V.P. 3 (2003)

Vince, Robert: Air Bud: Seventh Inning Fetch (2002), Duke, The (1999), M.V.P. 2: Most Valuable Primate (2001), M.V.P. 3 (2003), M.V.P.: Most Valuable Primate (2000)

Vincent, Hélène: Family Pack (2000)

Vincent, Jan-Michael: Midnight Witness (1992), Shadow of the Hawk (1976), Xtro II: The Second Encounter (1991)

Vincent, Josée: *Esprit du mal, L'* (1954)

Vincent, Julie: *Grands enfants, Les* (Day by Day) (1980), Happy Memories (Old Memories) (*Les beaux souvenirs*) (1981), *Marchands du silence, Les* (1994), Salut, Victor! (1988), Scream for Silence, A (*Mourir à tue-tête*) (1979)

Vincid, Bob: Find the Lady (1976)

Vinell, Joan: Columbus of Sex, The: My Secret Life (1969)

Vint, Angela: 19 Months (2002)

Vinton, Arthur: Viking, The (1931)

Vipond, Neil: Hard Part Begins, The (1973), Kings and Desperate Men (1981), Oedipus Rex (1956), Paradise (1982), Phobia (1980)

Virgo, Clement: Love Come Down (2000), One Heart Broken Into Song (1998), Planet of Junior Brown, The (1997), Rude (1995)

Virieux, Denise: Buried on Sunday (1993)

Visden, Robert: Glory Enough for All (1988)

Vismeg, Joseph: City of Champions (1990)

Vitale, Frank: East End Hustle (1976), Montréal Main (1974)

Vittorio, Montesano: *Jeunes Québécoises, Les* (The Younger Generation) (1980)

Vnese, Terra: Hurt (2002)

Voisine, Roch: Armen and Bullik (1993)

Voita, Michel: *Corps perdu, À* (Straight to the Heart) (1988), *Demoiselle sauvage, La* (1991)

Voizard, Marc F.: Hawk's Vengeance (1997), Lilac Dream (1987), Man Who Guards the Greenhouse, The (1988), *Présence des ombres, La* (The Presence of Shadows) (1996), Sunset Court (1988)

Vokins, Twyla-Dawn: Kelly (Touch the Wind) (1981)

Voletti, Michel: Until the Heart (1980)

Volk, Stephen: Kiss, The (1988)

Volka, Ioulia: *Attache ta tuque* (2003)

Volter, Philippe: *Aline et Michel* (Aline) (1992)

Von Brucker, Klaus: Super 8 (1994)

Von Glatz, Ilse: Understudy, The: Graveyard Shift II (1988)

Von Palleske, Heidi: 2103: The Deadly Wake (1996), Shadows of the Past (1991)

Von Pfetten, Stefanie: Decoys (2003), Posers (2002)

Von Radvanyi, Geza: Born for Hell (1976)

Von Sydow, Max: Strange Brew (1983), *Vercingétorix* (2001)

Voronka, Arthur: Love in a Four Letter World (1970)

Vouchard, Michael Marc: Tale of Teeka, The (1999)

Voulfow, Jean-Luc: Girls (1980)

Vrana, Vlasta: Grey Owl (1999)

Wachs, Caitin: Air Bud: World Pup (2000)

Wacko, Wendy: Striker's Mountain (1985)

Waddell, Justine: Mansfield Park (1998)

Wadden, Brad: Siege (1983)

Wade, Michael: Boys of St. Vincent, The (1992), Secret Nation (1991)

Wadek, Maggie: Lyddie (1995)

Wadimoff, Nicolas: Clandéstins (1997)

Wagner, Jack: Artificial Lies (2000)

Wagner, Lindsay: Martin's Day (1984), Second Wind (1976)

Wagner, Robert: Dancing in the Dark (1995)

Wagner, Sara: Connecting Lines (1990)

Wahlberg, Donnie: Triggermen (2000)

Waight, George: Someday Soon (1977), What We Have Here Is a People Problem (1976)

Waisglass, Elaine: Housekeeper, The (1986)

Waite, Liam: Second Skin (2000)

Waits, Tom: Candy Mountain (1987)

Wakashiba, Junko: Keiko (1979)

Wakeham, Deborah: Covergirl (1984), Lighthouse (1989), Middle-Age Crazy (1980), Starlight (1995)

Walbrook, Anton: 49th Parallel (1941)

Walczewski, Janet: Montréal Main (1974)

Waldau, Coster: Misery Harbour (1999)

Walden, Monty: Fortune's Sweet Kiss (2002)

Waldman, Marian: Black Christmas (Silent Night, Evil Nights) (Stranger in the House) (1974)

Walior, Charlotte: Girls (Les femmes-enfant) (1980)

Walken, Christopher: Dead Zone, The (1983), Wayne's World 2 (1993)

Walker, Andrew: Wicked Minds (2002)

Walker, Bill: Mask, The (1961)

Walker, Clint: Deadly Harvest (1980)

Walker, Clinton: Johnny (1999), My Summer Vacation (1996)

Walker, David: Amanita pestilens (1963)

Walker, Giles: 90 Days (1985), Blind Terror (2000), Ganesh (1993), Harvest (1981), Last Straw, The (1987), Masculine Mystique, The (1984), Never Too Late (1996), Princes in Exile (1990)

Walker, Jean: Crunch (1981)

Walker, John: Winter Tan, A (1988)

Walker, Mark: Sunday in the Country (1975)

Walker, Matthew: Intimate Relations (1995), Misbegotten (1997)

Walker, Polly: Savage Messiah (2001)

Walker, Wendy: Girl Who Married a Ghost, The (2003)

Wall, Estelle: Dying Hard (1978), Rowdyman, The (1972)

Wallace, David: Humongous (1982), Mazes and Monsters (1982)

Wallace, Earl: Song of Hiawatha, The (1996)

Wallace, Ratch: Act of the Heart (1970), Inside Out (1979), Isabel (1968), Journey (1972), Megantic Outlaw, The (1971), Merry Wives of Tobias Rouke, The (1972), Offering, The (1966), Ragtime Summer (Age of Innocence) (1977), Sunday in the Country (1975)

Wallace, Trevor: Christina (1974), Journey Into Fear (1975)

Wallach, Eli: Bookfair Murders, The (1999)

Wallack, June: Grand serpent du monde, Le (The Great World Serpent) (1999)

Waller, Anthony: Guilty, The (2000)

Waller, Russ: Saturday's Passage (1969)

Walling, Elyzebeth: Grand serpent du monde, Le (1999)

Walmsley, Tom: Paris, France (1993)

Walsh, Bill: Flaming Frontier (1958)

Walsh, Desmond: Boys of St. Vincent, The (1992), Random Passage (2001)

Walsh, Dylan: Jet Boy (2001)

Walsh, Gwyneth: Portrait, The (1992), 2103: The Deadly Wake (1996), Challengers, The (1990), Return of Ben Casey, The (1988)

Walsh, M. Emmet: Child, The (1994), Killer Image (1992), Relative Fear (1994)

Walsh, Mary: Adventures of Faustus Bidgood, The (1986), Divine Ryans, The (1998), Extraordinary Visitor (1998), New Waterford Girl (1999), Random Passage (2001), Secret Nation (1991), Stations (1983), Violet (2000)

Walsh, Vincent: Hemingway vs Callaghan (2003)

Walter, Jessica: Sneakers (Spring Fever) (1982)

Walters, Julie: Intimate Relations (1995)

Walters, Martin: Marie-Anne (1978)

Walton, Jess: Monkeys in the Attic (1974)

Walton, Karen: Ginger Snaps (2000), Heart: The Marilyn Bell Story (2000), Many Trials of One Jane Doe, The (2002), Many Trials of One Jane Doe, The (2003)

Wang, Henry: Chinese Chocolate (1995)

Warburton, Valerie: Three-Card Monte (1978)

Ward, David Oren: Yellow Wedding (1998)

Ward, Edmund: Kings and Desperate Men (1981)

Ward, Fred: All the Fine Lines (Full Disclosure) (1999), Train of Dreams (1987)

Ward, George: Do You Want to Sleep With God? (Voulez-vous coucher avec Dieu?) (1972)

Ward, Lyman: Milk and Honey (1988)

Ward, Rachel: Ascent, The (1994)

Ward, Robin: Explosion (1969), Flick (Dr. Frankenstein on Campus) (1970), Mark of Cain, The (1984), Paper People, The (1967), Sudden Fury (1975), Thrillkill (1984)

Ward, Tony: Hustler White (1996)

Ward, Vincent: Map of the Human Heart (1993)

Warden, Jack: Apprenticeship of Duddy Kravitz, The (1974)

Waring, Todd: Love and Murder (1988)

Warnat, Kimberley: Bear With Me (2000), Ms. Bear (1999)

Warner, David: Disappearance, The (1977), Investigation (2002), Lost World, The (1992), Office Party (1988), Ragtime Summer (Age of Innocence) (1977)

Warner, Lucy: Paper People, The (1967)

Warner, Robert: Hank (1977), Partners (1976)

Warren, Lesley Ann: Welcome to the Freakshow (2001), Wolf Girl (2001)

Warren, Mark: Crunch (1981)

Warren, Kiersten: Snow Walker, The (2002)

Warren-Joseph, Samuel: Off Your Rocker (1982)

Warrilow, David: Buster's Bedroom (1991)

Warton, Leigh: Roses in December (1965)

Washington, Jackie: Hank Williams: The Show He Never Gave (1982)

Wass, Ted: Sunset Court (1988)

Wasserman, Jerry: Low Visibility (1984), Quarantine (1989)

Wasson, Craig: Yellow Wedding (1998)

Wasyk, Darrell: H (Heroin and Hell) (1990), Mustard Bath (1993)

Waterman, Daisy: Kill (1969)

Waters, Sneezy: Hank Williams: The Show He Never Gave (1982)

Waterston, Sam: Journey Into Fear (1975), Lantern Hill (1990), Matthew Shepard Story, The (2001), Mahoney's Last Stand (1976)

Watkins, James: My Little Eye (2002)

Watson, Alberta: After the Harvest (Wild Geese) (2000), Art of Woo, The (2001), Best Revenge (Misdeal) (1981), Black Mirror (Haute surveillance) (1981), Built By Association (2002), Chasing Cain (2001), Deeply (2000), Desire (2000), Destiny to Order (1989), Dirty Tricks (1980), Giant Mine (1996), In Praise of Older Women (1978), Passengers (1981), Power Play (Coup d'état) (State of Shock) (Operation Overthrow) (1978), Risen, The (2003), Seeds of Doubt (1997), Shoemaker (1997), Stone Cold Dead (1979), Sweet Angel Mine (1996), Wild Dogs, The (2002)

Watson, Glenn: Love and Oysters (1995)

Watson, Hugh: Mahoney's Last Stand (1976)

Watson, Julie: More to Love (2000)

Watson, Miako: Barbara James (2001)

Watson, Neil: Carry on Sergeant (1927–1928)

Watson, Patricia: Who Has Seen the Wind (1977), Terry Fox Story, The (1983)

Watt, Len: And I Love You Dearly (La maîtresse) (1973), Don't Let the Angels Fall (1969)

Waxman, Al: At the End of the Day: The Sue Rodriguez Story (1998), Atlantic City, U.S.A (1980), Child Under a Leaf (1974), Class of 1984 (1982), Clown Murders, The (1976), Cop (Heller) (1981), Crowd Inside, The (1971), Death Bite (Spasms) (1983), Diamond Fleece, The (1992), Double Negative (Deadly Companion) (1979), Heatwave Lasted Four Days, The (1973), Hired Gun (The Devil's Spawn) (The Last Gunfighter) (1959), Isabel (1968), Last Act of Martin Weston, The (1971), Love on the Nose (1978), Malarek: A Street Kid Who Made It (1988), Me and My Shadows (2000), Meatballs, Part III: The Climax (1987), My Pleasure Is My Business (1975), Net Worth (1997), Return of Ben Casey, The (1988), Ride, The (2000), Scream of Stone (Cerro Torra) (1991), Spasms (Snake Bite) (1983), Star Is Lost, A (1974), Sunday in the Country (1975), Switching Channels (1988), Tulips (1981), White Light (1991), Wild Horse Hank (1979), Winnings of Frankie Walls, The (1980)

Waxman, Keoni: Highwayman, The (1999)

Way, Rick: Trial and Error (1993)

Waymouth, Belinda: Fearless (1999)

Wayne, David: American Christmas Carol, An (1979)

Wayne, Paul: Only God Knows (1974)

Weaver, David: Century Hotel (2001)

Webb, Jessica: Platinum (1997)

Webb, Simon: Grocer's Wife, The (1991)

Webber, Beth: I Love a Man in Uniform (1984), Company of Strangers, The (1990)

Webber, Marilyn: Murder Seen (2000)

Webber, Timothy: Grey Fox, The (1982), My Father's Angel (West of Sarajevo) (1999), That's My Baby (1984), Ticket to Heaven (1981), Tom Stone: For the Money (2002)

Weber, Jacques: Adolescente sucré d'amour, L' (1985)

Weber, Ross: Michelle Apartments, The (1995), No More Monkeys Jumpin' on the Bed (2000)

Webster, Beverly: Tragic Diary of Zero, the Fool, The (1970)

Webster, Hugh: Agency (1980), Bayo (1985), Between Friends (Get Back) (1973), Certain Practices (1979), Dirty Tricks (1980), Drying Up the Streets (1978), Fortune and Men's Eyes (1971), Freedom of the City, The (1976), Honourable Member, An (1982), If You Could See What I Hear (1982), Last Chase, The (1980), Mr. Patman (1981), Nothing Personal (1980), Reincarnate, The (1971), Rip-Off (1971), Who Has Seen the Wind (1977)

Webster, Sandy: Nothing Personal (1980), Partners (1976), Running Time (1978), What We Have Here Is a People Problem (1976)

Webster, Victor: Wishmaster 4: The Prophecy Fulfilled (2002)

Webster, William: Me (1974)

Wehrftitz, Curtis: Four Days (1999)

Weiger, Alisa: Have Mercy (1999)

Weils, Helen: Far Cry From Home, A (1980)

Weiner, Debra: Strange Blues of Cowboy Red, The (1995)

Weingartner, Kristin: Golden Apples of the Sun (Ever After All) (1973)

Weinstein, Bob: Burning, The (1981)

Weinthal, Eric: Timing (1985)

Weintraub, William: Drylanders (1963), Why Rock the Boat? (1974)

Weiss, Roberta: Abducted (1985), Cross Country (1983), High Stakes (1986), Tangerine Taxi (1988)

Weiss, Trudy: Something's Rotten (1978)

Weissman, Adam: Life in the Balance (2001)

Weissman, Aerlyn: Forbidden Love: The Unashamed Stories of Lesbian Lives (1992), Winter Tan, A (1988)

Weisz, Rachel: Sunshine (1999)

Welbeck, Peter: Bullet to Beijing (1995)

Welch, Jennifer: Post Concussion (1999)

Welch, Jessica: Live Through This (2000), Warrior Spirit (1994)

Welch, Judy: Now That April's Here (1958)

Welch, Nils: Carry on Sergeant (1927–1928)

Welch, Tahnee: Sue Lost in Manhattan (Sue) (1997)

Weller, Peter: Falling Through (2000), Naked Lunch (1992), Of Unknown Origin (1983), Screamers (1995)

Welles, Orson: Never Trust an Honest Thief (1979)

Wellington, David: Blessed Stranger: After Flight 111 (2001), Carpenter, The (1987), Dead Aviators (1998), I Love a Man in Uniform (1993), Long Day's Journey Into Night (1996), Touch of Murder, A (1990)

Wellington, Peter: Boys' Club, The (1996), Joe's So Mean to Josephine (1997), Luck (2003)

Wells, Dara: Take Her by Surprise (1967)

Wells, Vernon: Circle Man (1987)

Welsh, Jonathan: All in Good Taste (1983), Canada's Sweetheart: The Saga of Hal C. Banks (1985), Population of One, A (1980), Second Wind (1976), Special Delivery (1982)

Welsh, Justin: Boozecan (1995)

Welsh, Kenneth: Adrift (1993), Amoureuses, Les (Women in Love) (1993), And Then You Die (1987), Another Woman (1994), Bad Faith (Cold Blooded) (1999), Brethren (1976), Case of the Whitechapel Vampire, The (2001), Cementhead (1979), Climb, The (1987), Covergirl (1984), Dancing in the Dark (1995), Dead Silence (1997), Death Wish V: The Face of Death (1994), Double Negative (Deadly Companion) (1979), External Affairs (1999), Grand Larceny (1991), Habitat (1995), Haven (2001), Hiroshima (1996), Hound of the Baskervilles, The (2000), I Love a Man in Uniform (1984), Journey Into Darkness: The Bruce Curtis Story (1990), Joy (1983), Kissinger and Nixon (1994), Lost! (1986), Love and Hate (1989), Love Come Down (2000), Loyalties (1985), Margaret's Museum (1995), Murder Sees the Light (1987), Never Trust an Honest Thief (Going for Broke) (1979), Of Unknown Origin (1983), Perfectly Normal (1990), Phobia (1980), Québec-Canada 1995 (1983), Reno and the Doc (1984), Revenge of the Land (2000), Riel (1979), Rowing Through (1996),

Royal Scandal, The (2001), Screwball Academy (Divine Light) (Loose Ends) (1986), Sign of Four, The (2001), Tar Sands, The (1977), Tell Me That You Love Me (1983), Turning April (1996), War Boy, The (Point of Escape) (1985), Whale Music (1994)

Welterlin, Michel: Des chiens dans la neige (2001)

Wendt, George: Rupert's Land (1998)

Werner, Louise: More to Love (2000)

West, Adam: Size of Watermelons, The (1996)

West, Chandra: Dukes, The (1998), Perfect Son, The (2000), Revenge of the Land (2000), Something More (1999), True Confections (1991), Waiting Game, The (1998), Lost World, The (1992)

West, James: Falling Through (2000)

West, Samuel: Rupert's Land (1998)

West, Wash: Fubar (2002)

Westgate, Murray: Cool Sound From Hell, A (The Young and the Beat) (1959), Courage of Kavik the Wolf Dog, The (1980), Crossbar (1979), Far Shore, The (1976), Fish Hawk (1979), Goodbye, See You Monday (Au revoir, à lundi) (1979), Happy Birthday to Me (1981), Heavenly Bodies (1985), Homer (1970), Jigsaw (Angry Man, An) (L'homme en colère) (1979), Rituals (The Creeper) (1977), Rowdyman, The (1972), Running (1979), Silence of the North (1981), Sunday in the Country (1975), Tell Me My Name (1977), Threshold (1981), To Kill the King (1974), Two Solitudes (Deux solitudes) (1978), Tyler (1977)

Weston, Amber-Lea: Thick As Thieves (1990)

Weston, Eric: Pressure Point (2000)

Wever, Merritt: Strike! (1998)

Wexler, Barrie: Adolescence of P-I, The (1983)

Wexler, Gerald: Hard to Forget (So Hard to Forget) (1998), Manuel: A Son by Choice (1990), Margaret's Museum (1995)

Weyman, Ronald: More Joy in Heaven (1975)

Whalen, Eric: Famous Dead People (1999)

Whalley, Joanne: Guilty, The (2000), No Surrender (1985), Virginia's Run (2003)

Wheatly, Leo: Little Kidnappers, The (1990)

Wheaton, Martha: Révolutions, d'ébats amoureux, éperdus, douloureux (1984)

Wheeler, Anne: Angel Square (Angel Street) (1990), Betrayed (2003), Better Than Chocolate (1999), Bye Bye Blues (1989), Change of Heart (1984), Cowboys Don't Cry (1987), Diana Kilmury: Teamster (1996), Diviners, The (1993), Investigation (2002), Edge of Madness (Station sauvage) (A Wilderness Station) (2003), Loyalties (1985), Marine Life (2000), Sleeproom, The (1998), Suddenly Naked (2001), War Between Us, The (1995), War Story, A (1981)

Wheeler, Jane: Kid, The (1997), Neighbour, The (1993)

Whitaker, Forest: Fourth Angel, The (2001)

White, Bryon: Captive Heart: The James Mink Story (1996)

DIRECTORS, SCRIPTWRITERS & ACTORS

White, Doris: Day in a Life, A (1999)

White, Edward: Singing the Bones (2001)

White, Helen: Love in a Four Letter World (1970)

White, Ian: Not Just a Dirty Little Movie (1985), Overnight (1985)

White, John: Fast Food High (2003)

White, Jonathan: Rowdyman, The (1972), Sunday in the Country (1975)

White, Kevin: Another Planet (2000)

White, Melissa: Love and Greed (1992)

White, Peter: Peacekeepers (1997), Striker's Mountain (1985)

White, Robert: This Is a Film (That Was a Film) (1989)

White, Robin: Face Off (1971)

White, Ron: Another Country: A North of 60 Mystery (2003), Arrow, The (1997), Cowboys Don't Cry (1987), Harvest (1993), Heart: The Marilyn Bell Story (2000), Kissinger and Nixon (1994), Joan of Arc (1999), Last Train Home, The (1990), Matinée (1989), Pygmalion (1983), Race for Freedom: The Underground Railroad (1993), Ride, The (2000), Screamers (1995), Strange and Rich (1994), Tagged: The Jonathan Wamback Story (2002), Treacherous Beauties (1994), Trudeau (2002), Where the Spirit Lives (1989)

White, Tony: Master of Images, The (1972)

White, Trevor: Vigil, The (1998)

Whitehead, Andrew: Tommy Tricker and the Stamp Traveller (1988)

Whitehead, Paxton: Riel (1979)

Whitelaw, Billie: Leopard in the Snow (1978)

Whiteley, Chris: Christopher's Movie Matinée (1969)

Whiteley, Jenny: Suburban Legend (1995)

Whiteley, Ken: Christopher's Movie Matinée (1969)

Whitfield, Lynn: Planet of Junior Brown, The (1997)

Whiting, Glynis: Blood Clan (1991)

Whitman, Kari: Chained Heat II (1993)

Whitman, Stuart: Special Magnum (1977)

Whitman, Walt: Grub-Stake, The (1922)

Whitmey, Nigel: Formula 51 (The 51st State) (2002)

Whitmore, James: Here's To Life (The Old Hats) (2000)

Whittaker, Erik: Airport In (1996), No More Monkeys Jumpin' on the Bed (2000)

Whittaker, Erin: Horses in Winter (1988)

Whittal, Peter: Neon Palace, The: A '50s and '60s Trip (1971)

Whittall, Ted: Agent of Influence (2002)

Whyte, Patrick: Wings of Chance (Kirby's Gander) (1961)

Wickes, Kenneth: Bloody Brood, The (1959), Mr. Patman (1981)

Wickman, Caryl: Echoes in Crimson (1987)

Wicks, Ben: Kathy Karuks Is a Grizzly Bear (1976)

Widdows, Conner: Mile Zero (2001)

Widmark, Richard: Bear Island (1979)

Wiebe, Rudy: Big Bear (1988), Someday Soon (1977)

Wiechorek, David: Artificial Lies (Le manipulateur) (2000), Seeds of Doubt (1997)

Wiederhorn, Ken: Meatballs, Part II (1984)

Wieland, Joyce: Far Shore, The (1976)

Wiele, Catherine: Fortune and Men's Eyes (1971)

Wiener, Charles: Recruits (1987)

Wierick, John: Captive Heart: The James Mink Story (1996), Crossed Over (2001), Matthew Shepard Story, The (2001)

Wiesenfeld, Joe: At the Midnight Hour (1995), Case of the Whitechapel Vampire, The (2001), By Design (1981), Hound of the Baskervilles, The (2000), Legend of Sleepy Hollow, The (1999), Mourning Suit, The (1976), Princes in Exile (1990), Recommendation for Mercy (1975), Royal Scandal, The (2001), Sign of Four, The (2001)

Wiggins, Chris: American Christmas Carol, An (1979), Bay Boy, The (1984), Best Damn Fiddler From Calabogie to Kaladar, The (1968), Courage of Kavik the Wolf Dog, The (1980), Divided Loyalties (1989), Escape from Iran: The Canadian Caper (Desert Blades) (1981), Fish Hawk (1979), Ford: The Man and the Machine (1987), High-Ballin' (1978), Jigsaw (Angry Man, An) (L'homme en colère) (1979), Man Called Intrepid, A (1979), Murder by Decree (1979), Neptune Factor, The (The Neptune Disaster) (An Undersea Odyssey) (1973), Noncensus (1964), Riel (1979), Two Solitudes (Deux solitudes) (1978), Welcome to Blood City (1977), Why Shoot the Teacher (1977)

Wiggins, Trudi: Noncensus (1964)

Wightman, Dawna: Amityville Curse, The (1990)

Wilbrod, Jacques: Devil at Four, The (1988)

Wilby, James: Regeneration (1996)

Wilcox, Amanda: Johnny Belinda (1977)

Wilcox, Kim: Valérie (1969)

Wilcox, Robin: Royal Scandal, The (2001)

Wild, Gregory: Highway of Heartaches (1994)

Wilder, James: Midnight Magic (1988)

Wilder, Marlyse: Clear-Dark (Clair obscur) (1988)

Wilding, Gavin: Raffle, The (1994), Stag (1997)

Wildman, John: American Boyfriends (1989), By Reason of Insanity (1982), Exit (1986), Humongous (1982), Jacob Two-Two Meets the Hooded Fang (1977), Jigsaw (Angry Man, An) (1979), My American Cousin (1985)

Wildman, Julie: Facade (1970), House of Lovers (1972), In Praise of Older Women (1978), Keep It in the Family (1973), Little Girl Who Lives Down the Lane, The (1977), Loving and Laughing (1971), Special Magnum (1977), Parasite Murders (Shivers) (1975), Pyx, The (1973), Rainy Day Woman (1970)

Wildman, Peter: Giant Steps (1992)

Wilds, Peter: Lunch with Charles (2001)

Wilkening, Catherine: Jésus de Montréal (1989)

Wilkes, Christie: Kanadiana (2000)

Wilkey, Susan: Honeymoon (1996)

Wilkins, Glen: Freeloading (1986)

Wilkinson, Charles: Blood Clan (1991), Crash (Breach of Trust) (1995), Max (1994), My Kind of Town (1984), Quarantine (1989)

Wilkinson, Fabio: Max (1994)

Willett, Chad: Nothing Too Good for a Cowboy (1998)

William, Scoular: Deadly Friends: The Nancy Eaton Story (2003)

William, David: Little Canadian, The (1955)

Williams III, Clarence: Mindstorm (2001)

Williams, Alan: Cockroach That Ate Cincinnati, The (1996), Darling Family, The (1994)

Williams, Amir Jamal: Silent Witness: What a Child Saw (1994)

Williams, Barbara: Breach of Faith: A Family of Cops II (1996), By Reason of Insanity (1982), Diana Kilmury: Teamster (1996), Digger (1993), Firebird 2015 AD (1980), Lyon's Den (1983), Oh, What a Night (1992), Perfect Pie (2002), Tell Me That You Love Me (1983), Watchers (1988)

Williams, Bill: Hired Gun (The Devil's Spawn) (The Last Gunfighter) (1959)

Williams, Billy Dee: Giant Steps (1992)

Williams, Cynda: Courage to Love, The (1999)

Williams, Douglas: Best of Both Worlds (1983)

Williams, Fred: Silent Hunter (1993)

Williams, Heathcote: Alégria (1998)

Williams, Karen: Courage to Love, The (1999)

Williams, Lia: Shot Through the Heart (1998)

Williams, Lyman: Damaged Lives (1933)

Williams, Montel: Peacekeeper, The (1997)

Williams, Paul: Stone Cold Dead (1979)

Williams, Peter: Jungleground (1995), Love Come Down (2000), Soul Survivor (1995)

Williams, Scott: Unsaid, The (2001)

Williams, Stephen: Harry's Case (2000), Killing Spring, A (2001), Milgaard (1998), Soul Survivor (1995), Verdict in Blood (2001)

Williams, Treat: Circle, The (The Fraternity) (2001)

Williams, Vanessa: Courage to Love, The (1999)

Williamson, Alistair: Lift, The (1965)

Williamson, Christofer: My Summer Vacation (1996)

Williamson, Debbie: Downtime (1985)

Williamson, Fred: Silent Hunter (1993)

Willis, Austin: Affair with a Killer (1967), Boy in Blue, The (1986), Bush Pilot (1946), Dangerous Age, A (1958), Don't Forget to Wipe the Blood Off (1966), Face Off (1971), Flick (Dr. Frankenstein on Campus) (1970), One Plus One (The Kinsey Report) (1961), Sins of the Fathers (1948), Ten Girls Ago (1962), Wolf Dog (1958)

Willocks, Tim: Sweet Angel Mine (1996)

Willoughby, Leueen: Other Kingdom, The (1985)

Willows, Alec: Kelly (Touch the Wind) (1981), Tokyo Cowboy (1994)

Wilson, Andrew: House of Pain (1995)

Wilson, Cheryl: Once in a Blue Moon (1995)

Wilson, Dale: Dead Wrong (1983), Partners (1976), Watchers (1988)

Wilson, David: Masculine Mystique, The (1984), Sitting in Limbo (1985)

Wilson, Jonathan: Rubber Carpet (1995)

Wilson, Lambert: Blood of Others, The (1984)

Wilson, Luke: Dog Park (1998)

Wilson, Patricia: When Tomorrow Dies (1965)

Wilson, Rachel: Jungleground (1995)

Wilson, Roger: Porky's (Chez Porky) (1981), Porky's II: The Next Day (Chez Porky 2) (1983), Power of Attorney (1995)

Wilson, Ronald: Lives of Girls and Women, The (1996), Swindle, The (La gammick) (1974)

Wilson, Sandy: American Boyfriends (1989), Harmony Cats (1993), Mama's Going to Buy You a Mockingbird (1987), My American Cousin (1985)

Wilson, Thick: Strange Brew (1983)

Wilson, Valentina: Barbara James (2001)

Wiltse, David: Ascent, The (1994)

Wimbles, Juliana: Dead Aviators (1998)

Wimbs, John Beckett: Memoirs (1984)

Wimmer, Kurt: Child, The (1994), Neighbour, The (1993), Relative Fear (1994)

Wincott, Jeff: Battle Queen 2020 (Millennium Queen 2000) (2000), Pressure Point (2000), Profile for Murder (The Fifth Season) (1997), Street Law (1995), Undertaker's Wedding, The (1996)

Wincott, Michael: Wild Horse Hank (1979)

Winder, Michael: Welcome to Blood City (1977)

Windom, William: Echoes of a Summer (1976)

Windsor, Chris: Big Meat Eater (1982)

Wing, Anna: Haunting of Julia, The (Full Circle) (1976)

Wingfield, Peter: Edge of Madness (2003)

Winkler, Henry: American Christmas Carol, An (1979)

Winning, David: Exception to the Rule (1996), Killer Image (1992), Profile for Murder (The Fifth Season) (1997), Storm (1985)

Winningham, Mare: Threshold (1981)

Winston, Helene: Utilities (1981)

Wint, Maurice Dean: Cube (1997), Curtis's Charm (1995), Downtime (2001), Rude (1995), Trial and Error (1993)

Winter, Ophelie: 2001: A Space Travesty (2001)

Winterbottom, Michael: Claim, The (2000)

Winters, Dede: Tanya's Island (1980)

Winters, Kristoffer Ryan: Red Blooded 2 (1996)

Winters, Shelley: City on Fire (1979), Journey Into Fear (1975), Weep No More My Lady (1992)

Wirth, Billy: Starlight (1995)

Wisden, Robert: Blood Clan (1991), Diana Kilmury: Teamster (1996), Firebird 2015 AD (1980), Impolite (1992), In This Corner (1986), Nine B (1986), Sheldon Kennedy Story, The (1999), War Between Us, The (1995)

Wise, Stevie: Paper People, The (1967)

Wiseman, Joseph: Apprenticeship of Duddy Kravitz, The (1974), Journey Into Fear (1975)

Witham, Roy: Cathy's Curse (1977), Guitar (1974)

Witham, Todd: Echo Lake (2000)

Witherspoon, Reese: American Psycho (2000)

Withrow, Steve: Crazy Horse (She Drives Me Crazy) (Friends, Lovers & Lunatics) (1989)

Witt, Alicia: Fun (1993)

Witt, Kathryn: Seasons in the Sun (1986)

Wodchis, Walter: Odd Balls (1984)

Wodoslawsky, Stefan: 90 Days (1985), Crazy Moon (1986), Last Straw, The (1987), Masculine Mystique, The (1984), Mind Field (1989), Something About Love (1988)

Wojas, Claire: *Amoureux fou* (Madly in Love) (1991), Beauty of Women, The (*La beauté des femmes*) (1994), Cruising Bar (Meat Market) (1989), *Homme de rêve, L'* (The Dream Man) (1991), Magnificent Blue, The (1990), Water Child (*L'enfant d'eau*) (1995), You Are Beautiful Jeanne (*T'es belle, Jeanne*) (1988)

Wolde, Cindy: Low Self-Esteem Girl (2000)

Wolf, Richard: Gas (1981)

Wolfe, Ashley: Jewel (2000)

Wolfe, Maurice: Running Brave (1983)

Wolff, Jurgen: Midnight Man (1995), Real Howard Spitz, The (1998)

Wolfond, Henry: Mr. Nice Guy (1986)

Wolkowitch, Bruno: Mayday (1996)

Woloshyn, Illya: Hush Little Baby (1993)

Wolowick, Jack: Neon Palace, The: A '50s and '60s Trip (1971)

Wong, Edmond: Water Game, The (2002)

Wong, Russell: Tracker, The (1999)

Woo, John: John Woo's Once a Thief (1997)

Wood, Jan: Strange and Rich (1994)

Wood, Karen: Screwballs II: Loose Screws (1985)

Wood, Martin: Impossible Elephant, The (2001)

Wood, Paul: Change of Heart (1984)

Woodbine, John: Glory Enough for All (1988)

Woodman, Don: White Tiger (1995)

Woods, Grahame: Cop (Heller) (1981), Glory Enough for All (1988), Nine B (1986), Question of the Sixth, A (1981), Vicky (1973), War Brides (1980)

Woods, James: Hatley High (2003), Joshua Then and Now (1985), Videodrome (1983)

Woodward, Charlaine: Hard Feelings (1981)

Wooldridge, Susan: Loyalties (1985)

Wooley, Édouard: *Esprit du mal, L'* (1954)

Woolf, Henry: Revenge of the Land (2000)

Woolvet, Gordon: Joshua Then and Now (1985)

Woolvett, Gordon Michael: Bordertown Café (1991), Clutch (1998), Highwayman, The (1999), X-Rated (1994)

Woolvett, Jaimz: Global Heresy (Rock My World) (2002), Going Back (2002), Guilty, The (2000), Joan of Arc (1999), Journey Into Darkness: The Bruce Curtis Story (1990), Pathfinder, The (1996), Prom, The (1991), Reluctant Angel (1997), Tail Lights Fade (1999)

Wordsworth, Roy: Bedroom Eyes (1984), It Seemed Like a Good Idea at the Time (1975)

Workman, Angela: War Bride, The (2001)

Workman, Eric: Butler's Night Off, The (1948)

Workman, Nanette: Evil Judgement (1984), Ladies Room (1999), Scandale (1982)

Workman, Tata: Deaf and Mute (1986)

Woronov, Mary: Seizure (Tango Macabre) (1974), Watchers II (1990)

Worthy, Calum: I Was a Rat (Cinderella and Me) (When I Was a Rat) (2001)

Wreggitt, Andrew: Another Country: A North of 60 Mystery (2003), Colder Kind of Death, A (2000), Dream Storm: A North of 60 Mystery (2001), In the Blue Ground (1999), Tom Stone: For the Money (2002), Trial by Fire: A North of 60 Mystery (NA), Wandering Soul Murders, The (2000)

Wright, Alex: Wishmaster 3: Beyond the Gates of Hell (2001)

Wright, Herbert: Shadow of the Hawk (1976)

Wright, Janet: Betrayed (2003), Bordertown Café (1991), Jinnah On Crime –White Knight, Black Widow (2003), Lola (2001), My Mother's Ghost (1996)

Wright, John: Visitor, The (1974), Walls (1984)

Wright, Nicolas: Hatley High (2003)

Wright, Ralph: Nikki, Wild Dog of the North (1961)

Wright, Susan: Slim Obsession (1984), Waiting for the Parade (1984)

Wright, Tracy: Apartment Hunting (1999), Bubbles Galore (1996), Highway 61 (1992), Wasaga (1994), When Night Is Falling (1995)

Wright, Trevor: M.V.P. 3 (2003)

Wright, William: Dragonwheel (2002)

Wuhrer, Kari: Boulevard (1994), Undertaker's Wedding, The (1996)

Wurlitzer, Rudy: Agaguk (Shadow of the Wolf) (1993), Candy Mountain (1987)

Wyman, J.H.: Mr. Rice's Secret (2000)

Wyn Davies, Geraint: Dancing in the Dark (1995), Hush Little Baby (Mother of Pearl) (1993)

Wyner, Joel: Pale Saints (1997)

Wynorski, Jim: Screwballs (1983)

Xin, Liu: Yellow Wedding (1998)

Xingkun, Wei: Cry Woman (Ku qi de nu ren) (2002)

Xu, Andy X.: Small Pleasures (1993)

Yadin, Yossi: Lies My Father Told Me (1975)

Yakir, Leonard: Mourning Suit, The (1976), Out of the Blue (No Looking Back) (1980)

Yalden-Thomson, Peter: Rough Justice (1984), Shellgame (1986), Tools of the Devil (1985)

Yamasaki, Ellen: Offering, The (1966)

Yankie, Edward: Sign of Four, The (2001)

Yanne, Jean: Day in a Taxi, A (1982)

Yarmush, Michael: Dancing on the Moon (*Viens danser sur la lune*) (1997)

Yaroshevskaya, Kim: Castle of Cards, The (1980), Cuervo, the Private Detective (1990), Manuel: A Son by Choice (1990), Sonia (1986)

Yates, Rebecca: Milk and Honey (1988)

Ye, Deng: Cry Woman (*Ku qi de nu ren*) (2002)

Ye, Liu: Cry Woman (*Ku qi de nu ren*) (2002)

Yearwood, Richard: Street Law (1995)

Yefymenko, Liudmyla: Swan Lake: The Zone (*Lebedyne ozero-zona*) (1996)

Yeo, Leslie: *Automne sauvage, L'* (1992), Improper

Yeo, Leslie Continued:
Channels (1981), Luck of Ginger Coffey, The (1964), Sleeping Dogs Lie (1999)

Yesno, Johnny: Cold Journey (1976), Courage of Kavik the Wolf Dog, The (1980), Inbreaker, The (1974)

Yip, Francoise: Lunch with Charles (2001)

Yolles, Edie: That's My Baby (1984)

Yoon, C.B.: Post Concussion (1999)

Yoon, Daniel: Post Concussion (1999)

York, John J.: Closer and Closer (1996)

York, Michael: Final Assignment (1980), For Those I Loved (Au nom de tous les miens) (1983), Man Called Intrepid, A (1979), Sword of Gideon (1986)

York, Susannah: Book of Eve (2002), Maids, The (1975), Silent Partner, The (1978)

Yorston, David: Sudden Fury (1975)

Yoshida, Minnosuke: Lover's Exile, The (1981)

Yoshida, Tamao: Lover's Exile, The (1981)

You, Frances: Double Happiness (1994)

Young, Aden: Black Robe (1991), War Bride, The (2001)

Young, Burt: Red Blooded 2 (1996), Undertaker's Wedding, The (1996)

Young, David: Swann (1996)

Young, Donny: King's Gambit (1985)

Young, Gail: Hockey Night (1984)

Young, Karen: Execution of Raymond Graham, The (1985)

Young, Ric: Long Life, Happiness & Prosperity (2002)

Young, Sean: Exception to the Rule (1996)

Young, Stephen: Breaking Point (1976), Clown Murders, The (1976), Deadline (Anatomy of a Horror) (1980), Don't Forget to Wipe the Blood Off (1966), Nobody Makes Me Cry (1983)

Young, Trudy: Face Off (1971), Home to Stay (1978), Homer (1970), Melanie (1982), Ragtime Summer (Age of Innocence) (1977), Reincarnate, The (1971), Running (1979)

Young, Willam Allen: Fear X (2003)

Young, Trudy: Last Chase, The (1980)

Younghusband, Andrew: Violet (2000)

Yu, Ronny: Formula 51 (The 51st State) (2002)

Yuen, Jeremie: Hey, Happy! (2000)

Yulin, Harris: Candy Mountain (1987)

Yusa, Reine: Seven Streams of the River Ota, The (1998)

Yvon, Josée: Trop c'est assez (1996)

Zabriskie, Grace: House on Turk Street, The (2002)

Zacharie, Rosa: Jeune fille à la fenêtre, Une (2001)

Zack, Lawrence: Palais Royale (1988)

Zagarino, Frank: Guardian, The (1999)

Zahoruk, Dennis: Brethren (1976)

Zak: Dogmatic (1996)

Zaloum, Alain: Canvas, artiste et voleur (Canvas), Suspicious Minds (1996)

Zaloom, George: Whole Shebang, The (2001)

Zamprogna, Dominic: Almost America (Come l'America) (2001), Boys' Club, The (1996), Wozeck: Out of the Fire (1992)

Zamprogna, Gema: Challengers, The (1990), Johnny (1999)

Zane, Billy: Invincible (2001)

Zann, Lenore: Babyface (1998), Black Mirror (Haute surveillance) (1981), Change of Heart (1993), Cold Sweat (1993), Defcon 4 (1984), Gross Misconduct (1992), Happy Birthday to Me (1981), Hounds of Notre Dame, The (1981), Murder by Phone (1982), One Night Only (1986), That's My Baby (1984), Visiting Hours (Fright) (1982)

Zapponi, Bernardino: Dear Father (1979)

Zarzour, Antoine: Réception, La (1989)

Zdunek, Gisela: It Happened in Canada (1961)

Zeg, Kevin: Silence of Adultery, The (1995)

Zegart, Kevin: Incredible Mrs Ritchie, The (2003)

Zegers, Kevin: Air Bud (1997), Air Bud: Golden Receiver (1998), Air Bud: World Pup (2000), Four Days (1999), M.V.P.: Most Valuable Primate (2000), Treasure Island (2001), Virginia's Run (2003)

Zeilinski, Rafal: National Lampoon's Last Resort (1994)

Zeiniker, Michael: Glory Enough for All (1988)

Zellinger, Beatrice: Better Than Chocolate (1999)

Zelnicker, Michael: Ticket to Heaven (1981), Pinball Summer (1980), Stuart Bliss (1998), Terry Fox Story, The (1983)

Zelniker, Richard: Pinball Summer (1980), Obstruction of Justice (1995), Power Games (1990)

Zelniker, Michael: Pinball Summer (1980), Stuart Bliss (1998)

Zeman, Richard: Obstruction of Justice (1995), Power Games (Jeux de pouvoir) (1990)

Zenna, Kathryn: Jack and Jill (1998)

Zenon, Michael: Bloody Brood, The (1959), Hired Gun (The Last Gunfighter) (1959), Rituals (1977)

Zentilli, Patricia: Touch and Go (2002)

Zerbe, Anthony: Dead Zone, The (1983)

Zetterling, Mai: see Acts of Love (love) (1980) for: Julia, Love From the Market Place, The Black Cat in the Black Mouse Socks

Zhang, Lily: Small Pleasures (1993)

Ziegler, Joseph: Greening of Ian Elliot, The (1991)

Zielinski, Rafal: Breaking All the Rules (1985), Fun (1993), Hey Babe! (1984), Recruits (1987), Screwballs (1983), Screwballs II: Loose Screws (1985), State Park (1987)

Ziernicki, Edward: Absent One, The (1997)

Zilber, Jacob: Inbreaker, The (1974)

Ziller, Paul: Avalanche Alley (2001), Bear With Me (2000), Beyond Suspicion (1993), Ms. Bear (1999), Probable Cause (Sleepless) (1994), Silent Cradle (1998)

Zimbalist, Stephanie: Borderline Normal (2000)

Zimmer, Sonia: By Design (1981)

Znaimer, Moses: Love on Your Birthday (see Acts of Love Series) (1980), Best Revenge (Misdeal) (1981), Last Chase, The (1980), Scoop (1978)

DIRECTORS, SCRIPTWRITERS & ACTORS

Zoler, Stephen: Office Party (1988)
Zordan, Nello: It Happened in Canada (1961)
Zorich, Louis: Sunday in the Country (1975)
Zorrilla, China: Summer of the Colt (*Fierro ou l'été des secrets*) (1989)
Zsigovics, Gabor: Absent One, The (1997)
Zubar, Jennifer: Man on the Shore, The (1993)
Zuniga, Daphne: Artificial Lies (2000)
Zweig, Alan: Darling Family, The (1994), Foreign Nights (1990)
Zylberman, Noam: Last Train Home, The (1990), Outside Chance of Maximillian Glick, The (1988), Tom Alone (1989)
Zylberstein, Elsa: Alisée (1991)
Zyp, Philip: City of Champions (1990)

Gordon Pinsent and Will Geer in *The Rowdyman*, (d: Peter Carter, 1972)

Little Aurore's Tragedy (*La petite Aurore, l'enfant martyre*) (d: Jean-Yves Bigras, 1952)

Geneviève Bujold in *Isabel* (d: Paul Almond, 1968)

Jackie Burroughs and Richard Farnsworth in *The Grey Fox* (d: Phillip Borsos, 1982)

Jacques Gagnon, and Jean Duceppe in *My Uncle Antoine* (*Mon oncle Antoine*) (d: Claude Jutra, 1971)

Jennifer Dale and Winston Rekert in *Suzanne* (d: Robin Spry, 1980)

Peter Kastner and Julie Biggs in *Nobody Waved Goodbye* (d: Donald Owen, 1964)

Monique Mercure and Marcel Sabourin in *J.A. Martin, Photographer* (*J.A. Martin, photographe*) (d: Jean Beaudin, 1977)

Raymond Cloutier and Roger Blay in *Riel* (d: George Bloomfield, 1979)

Guy L'Écuyer and Paul Hébert in *The Merry World of Léopold Z* (*La vie heureuse de Léopold Z*) (d: Gilles Carle, 1965)

Micheline Lanctôt and Richard Dreyfuss in *The Apprenticeship of Duddy Kravitz* (1974) (d: Ted Kotcheff, 1974)

Looking Back: A Prequel in Tribute

Following are the titles of CBC Television Films, shot on film, some on tape, in studios and on locations, between 1950 and 1989, and in which a new generation of writers, directors, producers and players became prominent and were much admired. Many are named here in tribute to their creativity and contribution to our pleasure and knowledge with thoughtful, artistic, imaginative works in the classic tradition. Sadly, many have passed away, but those still with us continue to appear on tv, on the stage and in cinemas to this day. Mostof these are complete works. Space does not permit full descriptions, and we hope that future tv histories will bring us the Kensington Kings, Home Fires and Beachcombers. All the titles listed here, however, remind us of the CBC's glorious years, the greatness of which is not to be found in the programming of today. To all the talent artists who worked with and around them, my hearfelt thanks.

The Films:

And Then Mr. Jones
The Apprenticeship of Duddy Kravitz (tv)
Ashes in the Wind
Baptizing
The Baron of Brewery Bay
Bells of Hell The
Bespoke Overcoat
Betrayal The
Big League Goalie
The Blood is Strong
The Bottle Imp
The Brass Pounder From Illinois
Brothers in the Black Art
A Business of His Own
Canadian Mirror The
Captain of Kopenick
The Case of Posterity vs. Joseph
    Howe
Clearing in the Woods
The Concert
A Country Fable
The Crucible
Death
The Devil's Instrument
The Discoverers
A Distinguished Gathering
Explorations
The Eye of the Beholder
The Eye Opener Man
Father and Son
A Feast of Stephen
Festering Forefathers and Running
    Sons
Flight Into Danger
Freedom of the City
Get Volopchi
Going Down Slow
The Golden Age
The Good and Faithful Servant
The Grass Harp
The Grown Ones
The Hand and the Mirror
The Haven

Head Guts and Sound Bone Dance
Hedda Gabler
His Mother
Home Is Where the Heart Ain't
ThImportance of Being Earnest e
Ivan
John A and the Double Wedding
Kim
The Last of the Four Letter Words
The Man in the Tin Canoe
The Man Who Ran Away
Mandelstam's Witness
A Matter of Some Importance
The Megantic Outlaw
Microdramas
The Mission of the Vega
The National Dream
The New Men
Now I Met My Husband
Of the Fields Lately
The Offshore Island
One Night Stand
Other People's Children
Pale Horse Pale Rider
Panic at Parth Bay
The Paper People
The Prophet
The Quare Fellow
Queen After Dark
Raisins and Almonds
Raku Fire
Red Emma
Riel, Parts 1 and 2
Rigmarole
The Ronarelli Affair
The Sand Castle
Sarah
Saturday, Sunday, Monday
Seeds of Power The
Servant Girl
Silent Night, Lonely Night
Small Rain The
Some Are So Lucky
Stagecoach Bride

Teach Me How to Cry
Temperance
Ten Lost Years
Tiger at the Gates
To Set Our House in Order
Token Gesture A
The Trial of James Whelan
The Trial of Lady Chatterley
A Trip to the Coast
Troubled Heart The
Tulip Garden
Unburied Dead The
Under Milk Wood
Veteran and the Lady
Ward Number Six
When Greek Meets Greek
White Oaks of Jalna
Wife and Man
A Woman's Point of View
You're Alright Jamie Boy
Zone

Those Who Made Them:

Sharon Acker
Robert Allen
Paul Almond
Janet Amos
Jacqueline Barnett
Josephine Barrington
Bernard Behrens
Katherine Blake
George Bloomfield
Lloyd Bochner
Peter Boretski
William Brydon
Geneviève Bujold
Alan Burke
Helen Burns
Jackie Burroughs
Lally Cadeau
Zoe Caldwell
Anna Cameron
Douglas Campbell

A CENTURY OF CANADIAN CINEMA

Nicholas Campbell
Norman Campbell
Len Cariou
Brent Carver
Christopher Champman
Marigold Charlesworth
Barbara Chilcott
Dinah Christie
Margot Christie
Robert Christie
Leo Ciceri
Susan Clark
Eric Clavering
Robert Clothier
Joy Coghill
John Colicos
Patricia Collins
Corinne Conley
Lee Cosette
Jack Creley
Neil Dainard
Cynthia Dale
Jennifer Dale
Geraint Wyn Davies
Donald Davis
Dawn Greenhalgh
Louis Del Grande
Sutherland Donald
Peter Donat
Len Doncheff
James Doohan
Claire Drainie
John Drainie
Daryl Duke
Rosemary Dunsmore
Peter Dvorsky
Jayne Eastwood
Ralph Endersby
Gillie Fenwick
Anne Fielding
Timothy Findley
Nuala Fitzgerald
Sharry Flett
Ted Follows
Sidney J. Furie
Anne Frank
Pat Galloway
David Gardner
Jean Gascon
Gratien Gélinas
Bruno Gerussi
Martha Gibson
Sylvia Gillespie
Linda Goranson
Barbara Gordon

Lynne Gorman
William Gough
Janet-Laine Green
David Greene
Lynne Griffin
Linda Griffiths
Don Haig
Amelia Hall
Barbara Hamilton
Paul Harding
Rosemary Harris
Donald Harron
Harvey Hart
Ronald Hartmann
Kay Hawtrey
Max Helpman
Martha Henry
Michael Hogan
Susan Hogan
Eric House
William Hutt
Frances Hyland
Anne Jackson
Robert Jackson
Chapelle Jaffe
Douglas James
Kenneth James
Charles Jarrott
George Jonas
Robert Joy
Claude Jutra
Henry Kaplan
Philip Keatley
Ron Kelly
Margot Kidder
Alan King
Charmion King
Paul Kligman
Jack Klugman
Budd Knapp
Tom Kneebone
Ted Kotcheff
Franz Kraemer
Heath Lamberts
Betty Leighton
Samuel Levene
Leo Leyden
Cec Linder
Esse Ljungh
Jeannine Locke
Terence Macartney-
Filgate
Dan MacDonald
Patrick MacNee
Diana Maddox

Jane Mallett
Larry Mann
Ron Mann
Paul Massie
Murray Matheson
Roberta Maxwell
Sean McCann
Sheila McCarthy
George McCowan
Maryke McEwen
Grant McLean
Norman McLevel
Ed McNamara
Richard Monette
Frank Moore
Mavor Moore
Ann Morrish
Barry Morse
Neil Munro
James Murray
Silvio Narizzano
William Needles
Kate Nelligan
John Neville
Christopher Newton
Leslie Nielsen
Leo Orenstein
Donald Owen
Gerard Parkes
David Peddie
Frank Peddie
Frank Perry
Gordon Pinsent
Kenneth Pogue
Mario Prizek
Douglas Rain
Thomas Ralph
Henry Ramer
Harry Rasky
Fiona Reid
Janet Reid
Kate Reid
Gary Reineke
Michael Riley
George Robertson
Toby Robins
Allan Royal
Saul Rubinek
Michael Sarrazin
Mary Savidge
Alan Scarfe
Alfie Scopp
Dixie Seatle
Aileen Seaton
William Shatner

Donald Shebib
Patricia Sheppard
Muriel Sherrin
Robert Sherrin
Bernard Slade
Sonja Smits
Linda Sorensen
Ruth Springford
Robin Spry
Marc Strange
Sean Sullivan
Donald Sutherland
Toby Tarnow
Henry Tarvainen
Powys Thomas
Gordon Thomson
R.H. Thomson
Kevin Tierney
Eric Till
John Trent
Deborah Turnbull
Tony Van Bridge
John Vernon
Bill Walker
Al Waxman
Hugh Webster
Anne Wedgeworth
Kenneth Welsh
Norman Welsh
Murray Westgate
Ronald Weyman
Paxton Whitehead
Nancy Wickwire
Christopher Wiggins
Peter Wildeblood
Austin Willis
Helene Winston
Irene Worth
Leslie Yeo
Bernard Zuckerman